Social Work, Social Welfare, and American Society

SIXTH EDITION

Philip R. Popple
The University of North Carolina at Charlotte

Leslie Leighninger
Arizona State University

Boston ■ New York ■ San Francisco
Mexico City ■ Montreal ■ Toronto ■ London ■ Madrid ■ Munich ■ Paris
Hong Kong ■ Singapore ■ Tokyo ■ Cape Town ■ Sydney

Series Editor: *Patricia Quinlin*
Editorial Assistant: *Sara Holliday*
Marketing Manager: *Kris Ellis-Levy*
Editorial-Production Service: *Omegatype Typography, Inc.*
Manufacturing Buyer: *JoAnne Sweeney*
Composition and Prepress Buyer: *Linda Cox*
Cover Administrator: *Kristina Mose-Libon*
Electronic Composition: *Omegatype Typography, Inc.*

For related titles and support materials, visit our online catalog at www.ablongman.com.

Copyright © 2005, 2002, 1999, 1996, 1993, 1990 Pearson Education, Inc.

All rights reserved. No part of the material protected by this copyright notice may be reproduced or utilized in any form or by any means, electronic or mechanical, including photocopying, recording, or by any information storage and retrieval system, without written permission from the copyright owner.

To obtain permission(s) to use material from this work, please submit a written request to Allyn and Bacon, Permissions Department, 75 Arlington Street, Boston, MA 02116 or fax your request to 617-848-7320.

Between the time Website information is gathered and then published, it is not unusual for some sites to have closed. Also, the transcription of URLs can result in typographical errors. The publisher would appreciate notification where these errors occur so that they may be corrected in subsequent editions.

Library of Congress Cataloging-in-Publication Data

Popple, Philip R.
Social work, social welfare, and American society / Philip R. Popple, Leslie Leighninger.—6th ed.
p. cm.
Includes bibliographical references and index.
ISBN 0-205-40181-3
1. Public welfare—United States. 2. Social welfare—United States. I. Leighninger, Leslie. II. Title.

HV91.P68 2005
361.973—dc22

2004057265

Printed in the United States of America

10 9 8 7 6 5 4 3 RRD-VA 09 08 07 06 05

Photo credits appear on page 664, which constitutes an extension of the copyright page.

Welcome to

Social Work, Social Welfare, and American Society

with Research Navigator™

This text contains some special features designed to aid you in the research process and in writing research papers. At the end of each chapter you will find key terms that you can use for further research using Research Navigator™.

To gain access to Research Navigator™, go to **www.researchnavigator.com** and login using the passcode you'll find on the inside front cover of your text.

Research Navigator™ includes three databases of dependable source material to get your research process started.

- **EBSCO's ContentSelect Academic Journal Database** EBSCO's ContentSelect Academic Journal Database contains scholarly, peer-reviewed journals. These published articles provide you with specialized knowledge and information about your research topic. Academic journal articles adhere to strict scientific guidelines for methodology and theoretical grounding. The information obtained in these individual articles is more scientific than information you would find in a popular magazine, in a newspaper article, or on a Web page.

- **The *New York Times* Search by Subject Archive™** Newspapers are considered periodicals because they are issued in regular installments (e.g., daily, weekly, or monthly), and provide contemporary information. Information in periodicals—journals, magazines, and newspapers—may be useful, or even critical, for finding up-to-date material or information to support specific aspects of your topic. Research Navigator™ gives you access to a one-year, "search by subject" archive of articles from one of the world's leading newspapers—the *New York Times.*

- **"Best of the Web" Link Library** Link Library, the third database included on Research Navigator™, is a collection of Web links, organized by academic subject and key terms. Searching on your key terms will provide you a list of five to seven editorially reviewed Web sites that offer educationally relevant and reliable content. The Web links in Link Library are monitored and updated each week, reducing your incidence of finding "dead" links.

In addition, Research Navigator™ includes extensive online content detailing the steps in the research process, including:

- Starting the Research Process
- Finding and Evaluating Sources
- Citing Sources
- Internet Research
- Using Your Library
- Starting to Write

For more information on how to use Research Navigator™ go to **www.ablongman.com/aboutrn.com.**

to Linda
to rachel elaine morris, 1971–1994

Brief Contents

Contents

Preface

Political events in the 1980s played a major part in the inspiration of the first edition of this book. Before Ronald Reagan's two terms in office, most social workers assumed that many of the basic elements of a liberal welfare state were firmly entrenched in U.S. society. True, the country had not yet achieved a nationalized health system, and programs such as Aid to Families of Dependent Children did not seem to adequately address the problems of poor families. True, the 1970s had brought reductions in social welfare spending. Despite such setbacks, most social workers anticipated continued progress toward the liberal goals of ensuring a minimum standard of living as well as adequate job opportunities, health care, and housing for all citizens. Government, especially the federal government, was to play a major role in the achievement of these goals.

Beginning in the 1980s, however, liberal ideas of progress toward a more complete social welfare system were severely shaken. Economic difficulties and growing federal budget deficits helped pave the way for a major reconsideration of the goals and shape of social welfare programs in our society. A revived conservative agenda emerged, forcefully articulated by Ronald Reagan. Many of his ideas and programs were continued under the presidency of George Bush.

Most social workers, including the writers of social work textbooks, were slow to respond to the new social welfare era ushered in by the Reagan presidency. They failed at first to grasp that Reagan was acting not as a social renegade, but as a politician mirroring a wide growth of conservatism in the United States. This conservatism included resentment about the rise of "big government" and the expansion of the welfare state. Despite the political shift, many social work faculty continued to teach Introduction to Social Welfare courses with the liberal perspective and faith in continued progress as unexamined assumptions. Social welfare text writers failed to openly acknowledge and examine their liberal approach. Equally important, they neglected to describe and analyze the conservative critique and its alternative proposals.

Social work teachers, the authors included, gradually became aware that some students did not share the liberal assumptions and were unconvinced by the standard liberal arguments. We found discussions of liberal and conservative approaches to problems creeping into our classes with increasing frequency. This led to another realization. Although students had self-images of being liberal or conservative (or even radical), few had any real idea what these labels meant. Not only were many students unprepared to clearly articulate their points of view, but also most were unable to either respond effectively to or appreciate the arguments of alternative political perspectives.

Because we ourselves identify most clearly with a liberal approach, we were particularly concerned about our students' inability to evaluate and respond to the increasingly popular conservative critique of social welfare.

Thus we felt the need to help students grasp the meaning of different political perspectives and understand social welfare developments in light of those perspectives. Accordingly, we revised our outlines to begin the course with an analysis of the political context of social welfare. When we tried to find course material for this endeavor, we discovered that little was available. We realized that in order to achieve our goals, we would have to write the material ourselves. That realization was the beginning of this book.

When the second edition of this text was published, the election of President Bill Clinton seemed to promise a political shift back toward liberal policies. Health care reform was on the horizon, and interest in such issues as lesbian and gay rights and a woman's right to an abortion was renewed. Yet, within a brief two-year period, the country took another political about-face, electing a Republican majority in the Senate and the first Republican-dominated House of Representatives in forty years. Clinton's national health care reform proposal was declared "dead," and fears of "domination by big government," which were so common during the Reagan years, returned in full strength. With Clinton preempting many Republican issues in his successful campaign for a second term, the stage was set for sweeping changes in public welfare, intense scrutiny of the Social Security system, and reductions in Medicaid and Medicare. Yet, although public welfare was "reformed" and some incremental changes were made in health care, problems with Social Security and with health coverage and delivery were left largely to the succeeding Republican administration of George W. Bush.

Supported by Republican majorities in both the House and the Senate, Bush has reinstated a conservative agenda. This agenda stresses incorporation of elements of privatization into social welfare programs such as the Social Security system and Medicare. This approach is at odds with a liberal conviction that government should continue to play an important role in the social welfare system.

Thus it is clear that social policies and social welfare issues will continue to be central to political debate in the United States. In this sixth edition, therefore, the original purpose of this text—increasing an understanding of political perspectives on social welfare—has become even more relevant for people preparing to become social workers.

This is not a book about politics per se. It is a book about social welfare, but social welfare within a political context. It does not assume that the liberal perspective is the only relevant perspective in discussions of how we have chosen, continue to choose, and ought to choose the structure of our welfare programs and goals. We have written this book out of a conviction that social work students and practitioners need to deal intelligently with all approaches to social welfare in order to be effective advocates for their clients.

Plan of the Book

The book begins with a chapter outlining the major ideologies in a liberal to conservative matrix. We examine each ideology in terms of the following dimensions: attitude toward change, view of human nature, explanation of individual behavior, view of the social system, view of government and the economic system, and general value systems. In each of the remaining chapters, this material is integrated in analyses of the major concepts and areas of social welfare in terms of political perspectives.

Chapter 2 examines the concept of social welfare. It focuses on the important question: What is the function of social welfare in modern society? We argue that social welfare exists to manage issues of dependency and interdependency among and between individuals, communities, and social institutions. Our definition of dependency includes both a lack of concrete resources and a lack of skills, knowledge, and power necessary to cope with a particular set of circumstances. We recognize that no one is truly independent in our society and that promotion of healthy interdependence can be a goal of social welfare programs. The chapter concludes with an examination of conservative, liberal, and radical approaches to the management of dependency and interdependency.

Chapter 3 discusses the social work profession. It looks at the concept of professionalism and what the pursuit of professional status has meant for social work. The history of the profession is examined in light of that pursuit. The chapter also describes the effects of different political perspectives on the development of social work as well as the important topic of values, ethics, and ethical dilemmas in social work practice. This is followed by an overview of social work methods, a presentation of a model of social work practice, a description of the broad range of practice settings, and an identification and analysis of current professional issues. The chapter concludes by relating political perspectives to contemporary social work.

Chapter 4 expands the material on baccalaureate social work practice by giving students an understanding of basic generalist methodologies, the role of a case manager, and ways to deal with common ethical dilemmas. The goals of this chapter are to offer students a better basis on which to choose social work as a profession and to help prepare them for their first practice course.

Chapter 5 develops an understanding of issues of diversity and discrimination within the social welfare system. It discusses the development of the United States as a country of many different racial and ethnic groups, and it describes the ways in which social welfare programs and policies have responded to these groups. The chapter analyzes the phenomena of discrimination and prejudice as they relate to women, minorities of color, homosexual and lesbian individuals, and other frequently oppressed groups. As in the chapter on religion, this chapter encourages students to look at their own attitudes and biases in working with people.

Chapter 6 covers new ground for a social welfare text in its presentation of a comprehensive analysis of the interaction among religion, social work, and social welfare. Political changes in the 1980s brought renewed attention to the relationship between religion and public life. Increasing numbers of students now seem to be drawn to social work out of religious impulses. This has been a topic of lively discussion among social work educators. The main source of concern has not been religion as a motive for social work per se because, as the historical discussion in the chapter explains, religious impulses have inspired social welfare efforts from their very beginnings. The current concern has been with the type of religious orientation of some students—a fundamentalist, often socially and politically conservative, and sometimes evangelical approach. Questions about the appropriateness of this particular religious orientation in social work practice have led to broader discussions of the general relationship between religion and social work. In Chapter 6 we look at the issue in both its specific and its broader forms. In doing so, we have been careful not to preach and not to advocate our own motives and brand of religion. We try to affirm the appropriateness of social work as a career choice for people wishing to operationalize their faith. However, we attempt to sensitize students to the importance of a nonjudgmental attitude, the inappropriateness of evangelizing among clients, and the need to examine the various issues that a social worker with a strong religious orientation is likely to face.

Chapters 7, 8, and 9 deal with the topic of poverty. We devote three chapters to this subject, compared with one chapter for each of the other problems discussed, because we believe that poverty is *the* central social welfare problem. Virtually every other social problem has poverty as one of its causative factors. Chapter 7 examines the complex topic of measuring and defining poverty. Chapter 8 describes the poverty population in the United States and examines the major theories of the causes of poverty. Chapter 9 focuses on a historical presentation of the development of antipoverty programs in this country. All three chapters detail ideological perspectives on the definition and causes of poverty and the most effective ways of dealing with it.

The remainder of the book is devoted to a comprehensive discussion of major areas in social welfare. These include child welfare, crime and delinquency, health care, mental health and developmental disability, and aging. The book also explores a crucial aspect of social welfare that has received far too little attention in courses aimed at preparing knowledgeable and effective social work practitioners. Chapter 14 not only discusses the causes and effects of homelessness but also places this discussion in the larger context of the relationships among housing, community life, and individual well-being. Each of these special topic chapters relates varying political perspectives to theory and practice in that particular area. In addition, each chapter details the role of social workers in that specific field. The book concludes with a chapter urging students to develop and articulate their own perspectives on social welfare and social work practice.

This updated edition includes new or expanded material on welfare reform; increasing diversity in the United States; managed care in health and mental health; the continuing rise in the prison population; proposals for changes in Social Security; revitalization of community life; and new developments in child welfare, including court orders for massive system reform. "A Closer Look" features give more concentrated emphasis to case histories and examples. The "Focus on Diversity" selections help students recognize the important effects of cultural diversity, discrimination, and oppression in our society. New boxes on "What Americans Believe" use data from National Opinion Research Corporation (NORC) interviews to demonstrate the range of ideological identifications among Americans and to describe the corresponding range of positions on particular social welfare issues. The book also features lists of relevant web sites at the end of each chapter and "Social Work Destinations" boxes that suggest the kinds of places students can visit to learn more about social welfare issues and the development of institutions to deal with them. We believe that this sixth edition will do an even better job of preparing students to understand social welfare issues in the real world.

Acknowledgments

We would like to acknowledge the following reviewers who have offered valuable guidance to us in writing this edition: Richard Holody, Lehman College; Maureen T. Lagana, Salisbury University; and Jeff Schrenzel, Western New England College.

We would like to give a special acknowledgment to Alice Lieberman for her suggestion that became the "Social Work Destinations" feature.

Many students helped us by reviewing various drafts of this material and offering a "client's-eye view." Hope Haslam Straughn, Wheelock College, reviewed and offered insightful suggestions for revision of Chapter 6, Religion and Social Work. In addition, many colleagues read specific chapters and made useful suggestions: Linda Reeser, Gary Mathews, Marion Wijnberg, Danny Thompson, Frederick MacDonald, Linda Petersen, Leslie Decker, William R. Barnes, William Archambeault, Taryn Lindhorst, Maggie Leighninger, Matt Leighninger, and Aneesah Nadir. Todd Atkins consulted on web sites, and Drayton Vincent advised us regarding social work ethics. Deborah Abston provided invaluable assistance in navigating data from the National Opinion Research Corporation (NORC). Unfortunately, Edith Pope and William Burian, who contributed thoughtful critiques, did not live to see the final result.

David Popple, Tesha Hensley, and Reece Manceaux helped the production of the manuscript go more smoothly. We appreciate the enthusiasm of Karen Hanson and Bill Barke in the initial stages of this project. We also want to acknowledge the support of Pat Quinlin and Annemarie Kennedy.

Finally, we honor the memory of rachel morris. The article "The world is a box of crayons" on pages 181–182 is one of her many legacies.

PART ONE

Research Navigator™

What Is Research Navigator™?

Research Navigator™ is the easiest way for you to start a research assignment or research paper. Complete with extensive help on the research process and three exclusive databases of credible and reliable source material (including EBSCO's ContentSelect™ Academic Journal and Abstract Database, *New York Times* Search by Subject Archive, and Link Library), Research Navigator™ helps you quickly and efficiently make the most of your research time.

Research Navigator™ includes three databases of dependable source material to get your research process started:

1. EBSCO's ContentSelect™ Academic Journal and Abstract Database, organized by subject, contains fifty to one hundred of the leading academic journals per discipline. Instructors and students can search the online journals by keyword, topic, or multiple topics. Articles include abstract and citation information and can be cut, pasted, e-mailed, or saved for later use.
2. The *New York Times* Search by Subject Archive is organized by academic subject and searchable by keyword, or multiple keywords. Instructors and students can view full-text articles from the world's leading journalists from the *New York Times*. The *New York Times* Search by Subject Archive is available exclusively to instructors and students through Research Navigator™.
3. Link Library, organized by subject, offers editorially selected "Best of the Web" sites. Link libraries are continually scanned and kept up to date, providing the most relevant and accurate links for research assignments.

In addition, Research Navigator™ includes extensive online content detailing the steps in the research process, including:

- Starting the Research Process
- Finding and Evaluating Sources
- Citing Sources
- Internet Research
- Using Your Library
- Starting to Write

Registering with Research Navigator™

www.researchnavigator.com

Research Navigator™ is simple to use and easy to navigate. The goal of Research Navigator™ is to help you complete research assignments or research papers quickly and efficiently. The site is organized around the following tabs:

- Home
- Research Process
- Finding Sources
- Using Your Library

In order to begin using Research Navigator™, you must first register using the personal access code that appears in the front cover of this book.

To Register:

1. Go to **www.researchnavigator.com**
2. Click "Register" under "New Users" on the left side of the screen.
3. Enter the access code exactly as it appears on the inside front cover of this book. (Note: Access codes can be used only once to complete one registration. If you purchased a used guide, the access code may not work. Please go to **www.researchnavigator.com** for information on how to obtain a new access code.)
4. Follow the instructions on screen to complete your registration—you may click the Help button at any time if you are unsure how to respond.
5. Once you have successfully completed registration, write down the Login Name and Password you just created and keep them in a safe place. You will need to enter them each time you want to revisit Research Navigator™.
6. Once you register, you have access to all the resources in Research Navigator™ for twelve months.

Getting Started

From the Research Navigator™ homepage, you have easy access to all of the site's main features, including a quick route to the three exclusive databases of source content that will be discussed in greater detail on the following pages. If you are new to the research process, you may want to start by clicking the Research Process tab, located in the upper right-hand section of the page. Here you will find extensive help on all aspects of the research process, including:

- Introduction to the Research Paper
- Gathering Data
- Searching the Internet
- Evaluating Sources
- Organizing Ideas
- Writing Notes

- Drafting the Paper
- Academic Citation Styles (MLA, APA, CME, and more)
- Blending Reference Material into Your Writing
- Practicing Academic Integrity
- Revising
- Proofreading
- Editing the Final Draft

For those of you who are already familiar with the research process, you already know that the first step in completing a research assignment or research paper is to select a topic. (In some cases, your instructor may assign you a topic.) According to James D. Lester in *Writing Research Papers,* choosing a topic for the research paper can be easy (any topic will serve) yet very complicated (an informed choice is critical). He suggests selecting a person, a person's work, or a specific issue to study—President George W. Bush, John Steinbeck's *Of Mice and Men,* or learned dexterity with Nintendo games. Try to select a topic that will meet three demands.

1. It must examine a significant issue.
2. It must address a knowledgeable reader and carry that reader to another level of knowledge.
3. It must have a serious purpose, one that demands analysis of the issues, argues from a position, and explains complex details.

You can find more tips from Lester in the Research Process section of Research Navigator™.

Research Navigator™ simplifies your research efforts by giving you a convenient launching pad for gathering data on your topic. The site has aggregated three distinct types of source material commonly used in research assignments: academic journals (ContentSelect™); newspaper articles (*New York Times*); and World Wide Web sites (Link Library).

EBSCO's ContentSelect Academic Journal and Abstract Database

EBSCO's ContentSelect Academic Journal and Abstract Database contains scholarly, peer-reviewed journals (such as the *Journal of Clinical Psychology* or the *Journal of Social Work Education*). A scholarly journal is an edited collection of articles written by various authors and is published several times a year. All the issues published in one calendar year comprise a volume of that journal. For example, the *American Sociological Review* published volume 65 in the year 2000. This official journal of the American Sociological Association is published six times a year, so issues 1–6 in volume 65 are the individual issues for that year. Each issue contains between four and eight articles written by a variety of authors. Additionally, journal issues may contain letters from the editor, book reviews, and comments from authors. Each issue of a journal does not necessarily revolve around a common theme. In fact, most issues contain articles on many different topics.

Scholarly journals are similar to magazines in that they are published several times a year and contain a variety of articles in each issue; however, they are *not* magazines. What sets them apart from popular magazines like *Newsweek* or *Science News* is that the content of each issue is peer reviewed. This means that each journal has, in addition to an editor and editorial staff, a pool of reviewers. Rather than employing a staff of writers who write something on assignment, journals accept submissions from academic researchers all over the world. The editor relies on these peer reviewers both to evaluate the articles, which are submitted, and to decide if they should be accepted for publication. These published articles provide you with specialized knowledge and information about your research topic. Academic journal articles adhere to strict scientific guidelines for methodology and theoretical grounding. The information obtained in these individual articles is more scientific than information you would find in a popular magazine, in a newspaper article, or on a web page.

Using ContentSelect

Searching for articles in ContentSelect is easy! Here are some instructions and search tips to help you find articles for your research paper.

Step 1: **Select an academic subject and topic area.** When you first enter the ContentSelect Research Database, you will see a list of disciplines. To search within a single academic subject, click the name of that subject. In order to search in more than one academic subject, hold down the Alt or Command key. In the space below where all the subjects are listed, you must enter a topic area. For example if you choose Psychology as an academic subject, you might enter "Freud" as a topic area.

Step 2: Click the **GO** button to start your search.

Step 3: **Basic Search.** By clicking **GO,** you will be brought to the Basic Search tab. Basic Search lets you search for articles using a variety of methods. You can select from Standard Search, All Words, Any Words, or Exact Phrase. For more information on these options, click the **Search Tips** link at any time!

Step 4: After you have selected your method, Click **Search.**

Some ways to improve your search:

Tip 1: **Using AND, OR, and NOT** to help you search. In Standard Search, you can use AND, OR, and NOT to create a very broad or very narrow search:

- **AND** searches for articles containing all of the words. For example, typing **education AND technology** will search for articles that contain **both** education AND technology.
- **OR** searches for articles that contain at least one of the terms. For example, searching for **education OR technology** will find articles that contain either education OR technology.
- **NOT** excludes words so that the articles will not include the word that follows "NOT." For example, searching for **education NOT technology** will find articles that contain the term *education* but NOT the term *technology.*

Tip 2: **Using All Words.** When you select the "All Words" option, you do not need to use the word AND—you will automatically search for articles that contain all of the words. The order of the search words entered in does not matter. For example, typing **education technology** will search for articles that contain **both** education AND technology.

Tip 3: **Using Any Words.** After selecting the "Any Words" option, type words, a phrase, or a sentence in the window. ContentSelect will search for articles that contain any of the terms you typed (but will not search for words such as **in** and **the**). For example, type **rising medical costs in the United States** to find articles that contain *rising, medical, costs, United,* or *States.* To limit your search to find articles that contain exact terms, use quotation marks—for example, typing "United States" will search only for articles containing "United States."

Tip 4: **Using Exact Phrase.** Select this option to find articles containing an exact phrase. ContentSelect will search for articles that include all the words you entered, exactly as you entered them. For example, type **rising medical costs in the United States** to find articles that contain the exact phrase "rising medical costs in the United States."

Search by Article Number

Each and every article in EBSCO's ContentSelect Academic Journal and Abstract Database is assigned its own unique article number. In some instances, you may know the exact article number for the journal article you want to retrieve. Perhaps you noted it during a prior research session on Research Navigator™. Such article numbers might also be found on the companion web site for your text, or in the text itself.

To retrieve a specific article, simply type that article number in the "Search by Article Number" field and click the **GO** button.

Advanced Search

The following tips will help you with an Advanced Search.

Step 1: To switch to an **Advanced Search,** from the Basic Search click the AdvancedSearch tab on the navigation bar, just under the EBSCO Host logo. The AdvancedSearch tab helps you focus your search using keyword searching, search history, and limiters.

Step 2: Type the words you want to search for in the **Find** field.

Step 3: Click on **Field Codes** to see a list of available field codes for limiting your search. For example, AU-Author will limit your search to an author. Enter one of these two-letter field codes before your search term. For example, if you enter AU-Smith, this will limit your results to SMITH in the Author field. For more information on field codes, click **Search Tips.**

Step 4: After you have added the appropriate field code to your topic, click **Search.**

Some ways to improve your search:

Tip 1: You can enter additional search terms in the **Find** field, and remember to use *and, or,* and *not* to connect multiple search terms (see Tip 1 under Basic Search for information on *and, or,* and *not*).

Tip 2: With Advanced Searches you can also use **Limiters** and **Expanders** to refine your search. For more information on Limiters and Expanders, click **Search Tips**.

The *New York Times* Search-by-Subject Archive

Newspapers, also known as periodicals because they are issued in periodic installments (e.g., daily, weekly, or monthly), provide contemporary information. Information in periodicals—journals, magazines, and newspapers—may be useful, or even critical, when you are ready to focus in on specific aspects of your topic, or to find more up-to-date information.

There are some significant differences between newspaper articles and journal articles, and you should consider the level of scholarship that is most appropriate for your research. Popular or controversial topics may not be well covered in journals, even though coverage in newspapers and "general interest" magazines such as *Newsweek* and *Science* for that same topic may be extensive.

Research Navigator™ gives you access to a one-year, "search by subject" archive of articles from one of the world's leading newspapers—the *New York Times.* To learn more about the *New York Times,* visit them on the web at **www.nytimes.com.**

Using the search-by-subject archive is easy. Simply type a word, or multiple words separated by commas, into the search box and click "go." You will see a list of articles that have appeared in the *New York Times* over the last year, sorted by most recent article first. You can further refine your search as needed. Articles can be printed or saved for later use in your research assignment. Be sure to review the citation rules for how to cite a newspaper article in endnotes or a bibliography.

"Best of the Web" Link Library

The third database included on Research Navigator™, Link Library, is a collection of web links, organized by academic subject and key terms. To use this database, simply select an academic subject from the dropdown list, and then find the key term for the topic you are searching. Click on the key term and see a list of five to seven editorially reviewed web sites that offer educationally relevant and reliable content. For example, if your research topic is "Allergies," you may want to select the academic subject Biology and then click on "Allergies" for links to web sites that explore this topic. Simply click on the alphabet bar to view other key terms in Biology and their corresponding links. The web links in Link Library are monitored and updated each week, reducing your incidence of finding "dead" links.

Using Your Library

After you have selected your topic and gathered source material from the three databases of content on Research Navigator™, you may need to complete your research by going to your school library. Research Navigator™ does not try to replace the library, but rather helps you understand how to use library resources effectively and efficiently.

You may put off going to the library to complete research assignments or research papers because the library can seem overwhelming. Research Navigator™ provides a bridge to the library by taking you through a simple step-by-step overview of how to make the most of your library time. Written by a library scientist, the Using Your Library tab explains:

- Major types of libraries
- What the library has to offer
- How to choose the right library tools for a project
- The research process
- How to make the most of research time in the library

In addition, when you are ready to use the library to complete a research assignment or research paper, Research Navigator™ includes thirty-one discipline-specific "library guides" for you to use as a road map. Each guide includes an overview of the discipline's major subject databases, online journals, and key associations and newsgroups.

For more information and detailed walk-throughs, please visit
www.ablongman.com/aboutRN

PART TWO

Conducting Online Research

Finding Sources: Search Engines and Subject Directories

Your professor has just given you an assignment to give a five-minute speech on the topic "gun control." After a (hopefully brief) panic attack, you begin to think of what type of information you need before you can write the speech. To provide an interesting introduction, you decide to involve your class by taking a straw poll of their views for and against gun control, and to follow this up by giving some statistics on how many Americans favor (and oppose) gun control legislation and then by outlining the arguments on both sides of the issue. If you already know the correct URL for an authoritative web site such as Gallup Opinion Polls (www.gallup.com) or other sites, you are in great shape! However, what do you do when you don't have a clue as to which web site would have information on your topic? In these cases, many, many people routinely (and mistakenly) go to Yahoo! and type in a single term (e.g., guns). This approach is sure to bring first a smile to your face when the results offer you 200,874 hits on your topic, but just as quickly make you grind your teeth in frustration when you start scrolling down the hit list and find sites that range from gun dealerships, to reviews of the video *Young Guns*, to aging fan sites for the rock group Guns 'n Roses.

Finding information on a specific topic on the Web is a challenge. The more intricate your research need, the more difficult it is to find the one or two web sites among the billions that feature the information you want. This section is designed to help you avoid frustration and focus in on the right site for your research by using search engines, subject directories, and meta-sites.

Search Engines

Search engines (sometimes called search services) are becoming more numerous on the web. Originally, they were designed to help users search the web by topic. More recently, search engines have added features that enhance their usefulness, such as searching a particular part of the web (e.g., only sites of educational institutions—dot.edu), retrieving just one site that the search engine touts as most relevant (such as Ask Jeeves, www.ask.com), or retrieving up to ten sites that the search engine ranks as most relevant (such as Google {www.google.com}).

Search Engine Defined

According to Cohen (1999):

> A search engine service provides a searchable database of Internet files collected by a computer program called a wanderer, crawler, robot, worm, or spider. Indexing is created from the collected files, and the results are presented in a schematic order. There are no selection criteria for the collection of files.
>
> A search service therefore consists of three components: (1) a spider, a program that traverses the Web from link to link, identifying and reading pages; (2) an index, a database containing a copy of each Web page gathered by the spider; and (3) a search engine mechanism, software that enables users to query the index and then returns results in a schematic order. (p. 31)

One problem students often have in their use of search engines is that they are deceptively easy to use. Like our example of "guns," no matter what is typed into the handy box at the top, links to numerous web sites appear instantaneously, lulling students into a false sense of security. Because so much was retrieved, surely SOME of it must be useful. WRONG! Many web sites retrieved will be very light on substantive content, which is not what you need for most academic endeavors. Finding just the right web site has been likened to finding diamonds in the desert.

As you can see by the preceding definition, one reason for this is that most search engines use indexes developed by machines. Therefore they are indexing terms, not concepts. The search engine cannot tell the difference between the keyword *crack* meaning a split in the sidewalk, and *crack,* referring to crack cocaine. Using search engines properly takes some skill, and this chapter will provide tips to help you use search engines more effectively. First, however, let's look at the different types of search engines with examples:

Types of Search Engines

Type	Description	Examples
1st Generation	■ Nonevaluative, do not evaluate results in terms of content or authority. ■ Return results ranked by relevancy alone (number of times the term[s] entered appear, usually on the first paragraph or page of the site).	AltaVista (www.altavista.com) Excite (www.excite.com) HotBot (www.HotBot.com) Infoseek (guide.infoseek.com) Ixquick Metasearch (ixquick.com) Lycos (www.lycos.com)
2nd Generation	■ More creative in displaying results. ■ Results are ordered by characteristics such as concept, document type, web site, popularity, etc., rather than relevancy.	Ask Jeeves (www.ask.com) Direct Hit (www.directhit.com) Google! (www.google.com) HotLinks (www.hotlinks.com)

Types of Search Engines *(continued)*

Type	Description	Examples
2nd Generation *(continued)*		Simplifind (www.simpli.com) SurfWax (www.surfwax.com) Also see Meta-Search engines below. EVALUATIVE SEARCH ENGINES About.Com (www.about.com) WebCrawler (www.webcrawler.com)
Commercial Portals	■ Provide additional features such as customized news, stock quotations, weather reports, shopping, etc. ■ They want to be used as a "one stop" web guide. ■ They profit from prominent advertisements and fees charged to featured sites.	GONetwork (www.go.com) Google Web Directory (directory.google.com) LookSmart (www.looksmart.com) My Starting Point (www.stpt.com) Open Directory Project (dmoz.org) NetNow (www.inetnow.com) Yahoo! (www.yahoo.com)
Meta-Search Engines	Run searches on multiple search engines.	There are different types of meta-search engines. See the next 2 boxes.
Meta-Search Engines *Integrated Result*	■ Display results for search engines in one list. ■ Duplicates are removed. ■ Only portions of results from each engine are returned.	Beaucoup.com (www.beaucoup.com) Highway 61 (www.highway61.com) Cyber411(www.cyber411. com) Mamma (www.mamma.com) MetaCrawler (www.metacrawler.com) Visisimo (www.vivisimo.com) Northern Light (www.nlsearch.com) SurfWax (www.surfwax.com)
Meta-Search Engines *Nonintegrated Results*	■ Comprehensive search. ■ Displays results from each search engine in separate results sets. ■ Duplicates remain. ■ You must sift through all the sites.	Dogpile (www.dogpile.com) Global Federated Search (jin.dis.vt.edu/fedsearch) GoHip (www.gohip.com) Searchalot (www.searchalot.com) 1Blink (www.1blink.com) ProFusion (www.profusion.com)

Quick Tips for More Effective Use of Search Engines

1. Use a search engine:
   - When you have a narrow idea to search
   - When you want to search the full text of countless web pages
   - When you want to retrieve a large number of sites
   - When the features of the search engine (such as searching particular parts of the web) help with your search
2. Always use Boolean operators to combine terms. Searching on a single term is a sure way to retrieve a very large number of web pages, few, if any, of which are on target.
   - Always check search engine's HELP feature to see what symbols are used for the operators as these vary (e.g., some engines use the & or + symbol for AND).
   - Boolean operators include:

     AND to narrow search and to make sure that **both** terms are included

     e.g., children AND violence

     OR to broaden search and to make sure that **either** term is included

     e.g., child OR children OR juveniles

     NOT to **exclude** one term

     e.g., eclipse NOT lunar
3. Use appropriate symbols to indicate important terms and to indicate phrases (Best Bet for Constructing a Search According to Cohen [1999]: Use a plus sign (+) in front of terms you want to retrieve: +solar +eclipse. Place a phrase in double quotation marks: "solar eclipse." Put together: "+solar eclipse" "+South America").
4. Use word stemming (a.k.a. truncation) to find all variations of a word (check search engine HELP for symbols).
   - If you want to retrieve child, child's, or children use child* (some engines use other symbols such as !, #, or $)
   - Some engines automatically search singular and plural terms; check HELP to see if yours does.
5. Since search engines only search a portion of the web, use several search engines or a meta-search engine to extend your reach.
6. Remember, search engines are generally mindless drones that do not evaluate. Do not rely on them to find the best web sites on your topic; use subject directories or meta-sites to enhance value (see below).

Finding Those Diamonds in the Desert: Using Subject Directories and Meta-sites

Although some search engines, such as WebCrawler (www.webcrawler.com), do evaluate the web sites they index, most search engines do not make any judgment on the worth of the content. They just return a long—sometimes very long—list of sites that contained your keyword. However, subject directories exist that are developed by human indexers, usually librarians or subject experts, and are defined by Cohen (1999) as follows:

> A subject directory is a service that offers a collection of links to Internet resources submitted by site creators or evaluators and organized into subject categories. Directory services use selection criteria for choosing links to include, though the selectivity varies among services. (p. 27)

World Wide Web subject directories are useful when you want to see sites on your topic that have been reviewed, evaluated, and selected for their authority, accuracy, and value. They can be real time savers for students, because subject directories weed out the commercial, lightweight, or biased web sites.

Meta-sites are similar to subject directories but are more specific in nature, usually dealing with one scholarly field or discipline. Some examples of subject directories and meta-sites are found in the table on the next page.

Choose subject directories to ensure that you are searching the highest quality web pages. As an added bonus, subject directories periodically check web links to make sure that there are fewer dead ends and out-dated links.

Smart Searching—Subject Directories and Meta-Sites

Types—Subject Directories	Examples
General, covers many topics	Access to Internet and Subject Resources (www2.lib.udel.edu/subj/)
	Best Information on the Net (BIOTN) (http://library.sau.edu/bestinfo/)
	Federal Web Locator (www.infoctr.edu/fwl/)
	Galaxy (galaxy.einet.net)
	INFOMINE: Scholarly Internet Resource Collections (infomine.ucr.edu/)
	InfoSurf: Resources by Subject (www.library.ucsb.edu/subj/)
	Librarian's Index to the Internet (www.lii.org/)
	Martindale's "The Reference Desk" (www-sci.lib.uci.edu/HSG/ref.html)
	PINAKES: A Subject Launchpad (www.hw.ac.uk/libWWW/irn/pinakes/pinakes.html)
	Refdesk.com (www.refdesk.com)
	Search Engines and Subject Directories (College of New Jersey) (www.tcnj.edu/~library/research/internet_search.html)
	Scout Report Archives (www.scout.cs.wisc.edu/archives)
	Selected Reference Sites (www.mnsfld.edu/depts/lib/mu~ref.html)
	WWW Virtual Library (http://vlib.org)

Smart Searching—Subject Directories and Meta-Sites *(continued)*

Types—Subject Directories	Examples
Subject Oriented	
■ Communication Studies	The Media and Communication Studies Site (www.aber.ac.uk/media)
	University of Iowa Department of Communication Studies (www.uiowa.edu/~commstud/resources)
■ Cultural Studies	Sara Zupko's Cultural Studies Center (www.popcultures.com)
■ Education	Educational Virtual Library (www.csu.edu.au/education/library.html)
	ERIC [Education ResourcesInformation Center] (ericir.sunsite.syr.edu/)
	Kathy Schrock's Guide for Educators (kathyschrock.net/abceval/index.htm)
■ Journalism	Journalism Resources (bailiwick.lib.uiowa.edu/journalism/)
	Journalism and Media Criticism page (www.chss.montclair.edu/english/furr/media.html)
■ Literature	Norton Web Source to American Literature (www.wwnorton.com/naal)
	Project Gutenberg [Over 3,000 full text titles] (www.gutenberg.net)
■ Medicine & Health	PubMed [National Library of Medicine's index to Medical journals, 1966 to present] (www.ncbi.nlm.nih.gov/PubMed/)
	RxList: The Internet Drug Index (rxlist.com)
	Go Ask Alice (www.goaskalice.columbia.edu) [Health and sexuality]
■ Technology	CNET.com (www.cnet.com)

Another closely related group of sites are the virtual library sites, also referred to as digital library sites. Hopefully, your campus library has an outstanding web site for both on-campus and off-campus access to resources. If not, there are several virtual library sites you can use, although you should realize that some of the resources would be subscription based and not accessible unless you are a student of that particular university or college. These are useful because, like the subject directories and meta-sites, experts have organized web sites by topic and selected only those of highest quality.

You now know how to search for information and use search engines more effectively. In the next section, you will learn more tips for evaluating the information that you found.

Virtual Library Sites

Public Libraries

■ Internet Public Library	www.ipl.org
■ Library of Congress	lcweb.loc.gov/homepage/lchp.html
■ New York Public Library	www.nypl.org
University/College Libraries	
■ Bucknell	jade.bucknell.edu/
■ Case Western	www.cwru.edu/uclibraries.html
■ Dartmouth	www.dartmouth.edu/~library
■ Duke	www.lib.duke.edu/
■ Franklin & Marshall	www.library.fandm.edu
■ Harvard	www.harvard.edu/museums/
■ Penn State	www.libraries.psu.edu
■ Princeton	infoshare1.princeton.edu
■ Stanford	www.slac.stanford.edu/FIND/spires.html
■ ULCA	www.library.ucla.edu
Other	
■ Perseus Project [subject specific—classics, supported by grants from corporations and educational institutions]	www.perseus.tufts.edu

Evaluating Sources on the Web

Congratulations! You've found a great web site. Now what? The web site you found seems like the perfect web site for your research. But are you sure? Why is it perfect? What criteria are you using to determine whether this web site suits your purpose?

Think about it. Where else on earth can anyone "publish" information regardless of the accuracy, currency, or reliability of the information? The Internet has opened up a world of opportunity for posting and distributing information and ideas to virtually everyone, even those who might post misinformation for fun, or those with ulterior motives for promoting their point of view. Armed with the information provided in this guide, you can dig through the vast amount of useless information and misinformation on the World Wide Web to uncover the valuable information. Because practically anyone can post and distribute their ideas on the web, you need to develop a new set of critical thinking skills that focus on the evaluation of the quality of information, rather than be influenced and manipulated by slick graphics and flashy moving java script.

Before the existence of online sources, the validity and accuracy of a source was more easily determined. For example, in order for a book to get to the publishing stage, it must go through many critiques, validation of facts, reviews, editorial changes, and the like. Ownership of the information in the book is clear because the author's name is attached to it. The publisher's reputation is on the line too. If the book turns out to have incorrect information, reputations and money can be lost. In addition, books available in a university library are further reviewed by professional librarians and selected for library purchase because of their accuracy and value to students. Journal articles downloaded or printed from online subscription services, such as Infotrac, ProQuest, EbscoHost, or other full-text databases, are put through the same scrutiny as the paper versions of the journals.

On the World Wide Web, however, Internet service providers (ISPs) simply give web site authors a place to store information. The web site author can post information that may not be validated or tested for accuracy. One mistake students typically make is to assume that all information on the web is of equal value. Also, in the rush to get assignments in on time, students may not take the extra time to make sure that the information they are citing is accurate. It is easy just to cut and paste without really thinking about the content in a critical way. However, to make sure you are gathering accurate information and to get the best grade on your assignments, it is vital that you develop your critical ability to sift through the dirt to find the diamonds.

Web Evaluation Criteria

So, here you are, at this potentially great site. Let's go though some ways you can determine if this site is one you can cite with confidence in your research. Keep in mind, ease of use of a web site is an issue, but more important is learning how to determine the validity of data, facts, and statements for your use. The five traditional ways to verify a paper source can also be applied to your web source: *accuracy, authority, objectivity, coverage,* and *currency.*

Evaluating Web Sites Using Five Criteria to Judge Web Site Content

Accuracy—How reliable is the information?

Authority—Who is the author and what are his or her credentials?

Objectivity—Does the web site present a balanced or biased point of view?

Coverage—Is the information comprehensive enough for your needs?

Currency—Is the web site up to date?

Use additional criteria to judge web site content, including

- **Publisher, documentation, relevance, scope, audience, appropriateness of format,** and **navigation**
- Judging whether the site is made up of **primary (original)** or **secondary (interpretive) sources**
- Determining whether the information is **relevant** to your research

Content Evaluation

Accuracy. Internet searches are not the same as searches of library databases because much of the information on the web has not been edited, whereas information in databases has. It is your responsibility to make sure that the information you use in a school project is accurate. When you examine the content on a web site or web page, you can ask yourself a number of questions to determine whether the information is accurate.

1. Is the information reliable?
2. Do the facts from your other research contradict the facts you find on this web page?
3. Do any misspellings and/or grammar mistakes indicate a hastily put together web site that has not been checked for accuracy?
4. Is the content on the page verifiable through some other source? Can you find similar facts elsewhere (journals, books, or other online sources) to support the facts you see on this web page?
5. Do you find links to other web sites on a similar topic? If so, check those links to ascertain whether they back up the information you see on the web page you are interested in using.
6. Is a bibliography of additional sources for research provided? Lack of a bibliography doesn't mean the page isn't accurate, but having one allows you further investigation points to check the information.
7. Does the site of a research document or study explain how the data were collected and the type of research method used to interpret the data?

If you've found a site with information that seems too good to be true, it may be. You need to verify information that you read on the web by cross-checking against other sources.

Authority. An important question to ask when you are evaluating a web site is, "Who is the author of the information?" Do you know whether the author is a recognized authority in his or her field? Biographical information and references to publications, degrees, qualifications, and organizational affiliations can help to indicate an author's authority. For example, if you are researching the topic of laser surgery, citing a medical doctor would be better than citing a college student who has had laser surgery.

The organization sponsoring the site can also provide clues about whether the information is fact or opinion. Examine how the information was gathered and the research method used to prepare the study or report. Other questions to ask include:

1. Who is responsible for the content of the page? Although a webmaster's name is often listed, this person is not necessarily responsible for the content.
2. Is the author recognized in the subject area? Does this person cite any other publications he or she has authored?
3. Does the author list his or her background or credentials (e.g., Ph.D. degree, title such as professor, or other honorary or social distinction)?
4. Is there a way to contact the author? Does the author provide a phone number or e-mail address?
5. If the page is mounted by an organization, is it a known, reputable one?
6. How long has the organization been in existence?

7. Does the URL for the web page end in the extension .edu or .org? Such extensions indicate authority compared to dotcoms (.com), which are commercial enterprises. (For example, www.cancer.com takes you to an online drugstore that has a cancer information page; www.cancer.org is the American Cancer Society web site.)

A good idea is to ask yourself whether the author or organization presenting the information on the Web is an authority on the subject. If the answer is no, this may not be a good source of information.

Objectivity. Every author has a point of view, and some views are more controversial than others. Journalists try to be objective by providing both sides of a story. Academics attempt to persuade readers by presenting a logical argument, which cites other scholars' work. You need to look for two-sided arguments in news and information sites. For academic papers, you need to determine how the paper fits within its discipline and whether the author is using controversial methods for reporting a conclusion.

Authoritative authors situate their work within a larger discipline. This background helps readers evaluate the author's knowledge on a particular subject. You should ascertain whether the author's approach is controversial and whether he or she acknowledges this. More important, is the information being presented as fact or opinion? Authors who argue for their position provide readers with other sources that support their arguments. If no sources are cited, the material may be an opinion piece rather than an objective presentation of information. The following questions can help you determine objectivity:

1. Is the purpose of the site clearly stated, either by the author or the organization authoring the site?
2. Does the site give a balanced viewpoint or present only one side?
3. Is the information directed toward a specific group of viewers?
4. Does the site contain advertising?
5. Does the copyright belong to a person or an organization?
6. Do you see anything to indicate who is funding the site?

Everyone has a point of view. This is important to remember when you are using web resources. A question to keep asking yourself is, What is the bias or point of view being expressed here?

Coverage. Coverage deals with the breadth and depth of information presented on a web site. Stated another way, it is about how much information is presented and how detailed the information is. Looking at the site map or index can give you an idea about how much information is contained on a site. This isn't necessarily bad. Coverage is a criteria that is tied closely to *your* research requirement. For one assignment, a given web site may be too general for your needs. For another assignment, that same site might be perfect. Some sites contain very little actual information because pages are filled with links to other sites. Coverage also relates to objectivity. You should ask the following questions about coverage:

1. Does the author present both sides of the story or is a piece of the story missing?
2. Is the information comprehensive enough for your needs?

3. Does the site cover too much too generally?
4. Do you need more specific information than the site can provide?
5. Does the site have an objective approach?

In addition to examining what is covered on a web site, equally revealing is what is not covered. Missing information can reveal a bias in the material. Keep in mind that you are evaluating the information on a web site for your research requirements.

Currency. Currency questions deal with the timeliness of information. However, currency is more important for some topics than for others. For example, currency is essential when you are looking for technology-related topics and current events. In contrast, currency may not be relevant when you are doing research on Plato or Ancient Greece. In terms of web sites, currency also pertains to whether the site is being kept up to date and links are being maintained. Sites on the web are sometimes abandoned by their owners. When people move or change jobs, they may neglect to remove the site from the company or university server. To test currency, ask the following questions:

1. Does the site indicate when the content was created?
2. Does the site contain a last revised date? How old is the date? (In the early part of 2001, a university updated its web site with a "last updated" date of 1901! This obviously was a Y2K problem, but it does point out the need to be observant of such things!)
3. Does the author state how often he or she revises the information? Some sites are on a monthly update cycle (e.g., a government statistics page).
4. Can you tell specifically what content was revised?
5. Is the information still useful for your topic? Even if the last update is old, the site might still be worthy of use *if* the content is still valid for your research.

Relevancy to Your Research: Primary versus Secondary Sources

Some research assignments require the use of primary (original) sources. Materials such as raw data, diaries, letters, manuscripts, and original accounts of events can be considered primary material. In most cases, these historical documents are no longer copyrighted. The web is a great source for this type of resource.

Information that has been analyzed and previously interpreted is considered a secondary source. Sometimes secondary sources are more appropriate than primary sources. If, for example, you are asked to analyze a topic or to find an analysis of a topic, a secondary source of an analysis would be most appropriate. Ask yourself the following questions to determine whether the web site is relevant to your research:

1. Is it a primary or secondary source?
2. Do you need a primary source?
3. Does the assignment require you to cite different types of sources? For example, are you supposed to use at least one book, one journal article, and one web page?

You need to think critically, both visually and verbally, when evaluating web sites. Because web sites are designed as multimedia hypertexts, nonlinear texts, visual elements, and navigational tools are added to the evaluation process.

Help in Evaluating Web Sites. One shortcut to finding high-quality web sites is using subject directories and meta-sites, which select the web sites they index by similar evaluation criteria to those just described. If you want to learn more about evaluating web sites, many colleges and universities provide sites that help you evaluate web resources. The following list contains some excellent examples of these evaluation sites:

- Evaluating Quality on the Net—Hope Tillman, Babson College
  www.hopetillman.com/findqual.html
- Critical Web Evaluation—Kurt W. Wagner, William Paterson University of New Jersey
  euphrates.wpunj.edu/faculty/wagnerk/
- Evaluation Criteria—Susan Beck, New Mexico State University
  lib.nmsu.edu/instruction/evalcrit.html
- A Student's Guide to Research with the WWW
  www.slu.edu/departments/english/research/
- Evaluating Web Pages: Questions to Ask & Strategies for Getting the Answers
  www.lib.berkeley.edu/TeachingLib/Guides/Internet/EvalQuestions.html

Critical Evaluation Web Sites

Web site and URL	Source
Critical Thinking in an Online World **www.library.ucsb.edu/untangle/jones.html**	*Paper from "Untangling the Web" 1996*
Educom Review: Information **www.educause.edu/pub/er/review/reviewArticles/31231.html**	*EDUCAUSE Literacy as a Liberal Art (1996 article)*
Evaluating Information Found on the Internet **MiltonsWeb.mse.jhu.edu/research/education/net.html**	*University of Utah Library*
Evaluating Web Sites **www.lib.purdue.edu/InternetEval**	*Purdue University Library*
Evaluating Web Sites **www.lehigh.edu/~inref/guides/evaluating.web.html**	*Lehigh University*
ICONnect: Curriculum Connections Overview **www.ala.org/ICONN/evaluate.html**	*American Library Association's technology education initiative*
Kathy Schrock's ABC's of Web Site Evaluation **www.kathyschrock.net/abceval/**	*Author's web site*
Kids Pick the Best of the Web "Top 10: Announced" **www.ala.org/news/topkidpicks.html**	*American Library Association initiative underwritten by Microsoft (1998)*

Resource Selection and Information Evaluation **_alexia.lis.uiuc.edu/~janicke/InfoAge.html_**	*Univ of Illinois, Urbana–Champaign (Librarian)*
Testing the Surf: Criteria for Evaluating Internet Information Sources **info.lib.uh.edu/pr/v8/n3/smit8n3.html**	*University of Houston Libraries*
Evaluating Web Resources **www2.widener.edu/Wolfgram-Memorial-Library/webevaluation/webeval.htm**	*Widener University Library*
UCLA College Library Instruction: Thinking Critically about World Wide Web Resources **www.library.ucla.edu/libraries/college/help/critical/**	*UCLA Library*
UG OOL: Judging Quality on the Internet **www.open.uoguelph.ca/resources/skills/judging.html**	*University of Guelph*
Web Evaluation Criteria **lib.nmsu.edu/instruction/evalcrit.html**	*New Mexico State University Library*
Web Page Credibility Checklist **www.park.pvt.k12.md.us/academics/research/credcheck.htm**	*Park School of Baltimore*
Evaluating Web Sites for Educational Uses: Bibliography and Checklist **www.unc.edu/cit/guides/irg-49.html**	*University of North Carolina*
Evaluating Web Sites **www.lesley.edu/library/guides/research/evaluating_web.html**	*Lesley University*

Tip

Can't seem to get a URL to work? If the URL doesn't begin with www, you may need to put the http:// in front of the URL. Usually, browsers can handle URLs that begin with www without the need to type in the "http://" but if you find you're having trouble, add the http://.

Documentation Guidelines for Online Sources

Your Citation for Exemplary Research

There's another detail left for us to handle—the formal citing of electronic sources in academic papers. The very factor that makes research on the Internet exciting is the same factor that makes referencing these sources challenging: their dynamic nature. A journal article exists, either in print or on microfilm, virtually forever. A document on the Internet can come, go, and change without warning. Because the purpose of citing sources is to allow another scholar to retrace your argument, a good citation allows a reader to obtain information from your primary sources, to the extent possible. This means you need to include not only information on when a source was posted on the Internet (if available) but also when you obtained the information.

The two arbiters of form for academic and scholarly writing are the Modern Language Association (MLA) and the American Psychological Association (APA); both organizations have established styles for citing electronic publications.

MLA Style

In the fifth edition of the *MLA Handbook for Writers of Research Papers,* the MLA recommends the following formats:

- **URLs:** URLs are enclosed in angle brackets (<>) and contain the access mode identifier, the formal name for such indicators as "http" or "ftp." If a URL must be split across two lines, break it only after a slash (/). Never introduce a hyphen at the end of the first line. The URL should include all the parts necessary to identify uniquely the file/document being cited.

```
<http://www.csun.edu/~rtvfdept/home/index.html>
```

- **An online scholarly project or reference database:** A complete online reference contains the title of the project or database (underlined); the name of the editor of the project or database (if given); electronic publication information, including version number (if relevant and if not part of the title), date of electronic publication or latest update, and name of any sponsoring institution or organization; date of access; and electronic address.

```
The Perseus Project. Ed. Gregory R. Crane. Mar.1997.
  Department of Classics, Tufts University. 15 June 1998
  <http://www.perseus.tufts.edu/>.
```

If you cannot find some of the information, then include the information that is available. The MLA also recommends that you print or download electronic documents, freezing them in time for future reference.

- **A document within a scholarly project or reference database:** It is much more common to use only a portion of a scholarly project or database. To cite an essay, poem, or other short work, begin this citation with the name of the author and the title of the work (in quotation marks). Then include all the information used when citing a complete online scholarly project or reference database; however, make sure you use the URL of the specific work and not the address of the general site.

Cuthberg, Lori. "Moonwalk: Earthlings' Finest Hour." *Discovery Channel Online.* 1999. Discovery Channel. 25 Nov. 1999 <http://www.discovery.com/indep/newsfeatures/moonwalk/challenge.html>.

- **A professional or personal site:** Include the name of the person creating the site (reversed), followed by a period, the title of the site (underlined), or, if there is no title, a description such as homepage (such a description is neither placed in quotes nor underlined). Then specify the name of any school, organization, or other institution affiliated with the site and follow it with your date of access and the URL of the page.

Packer, Andy. Homepage. 1Apr. 1998 <http://www.suu.edu/~students/Packer.htm>.

Some electronic references are truly unique to the online domain. These include e-mail, newsgroup postings, MUDs (multiuser domains) or MOOs (multiuser domains, object-oriented), and IRCs (Internet relay chats).

E-mail. In citing e-mail messages, begin with the writer's name (reversed) followed by a period, then the title of the message (if any) in quotations as it appears in the subject line. Next comes a description of the message, typically "E-mail to," and the recipient (e.g., "the author"), and finally the date of the message.

Davis, Jeffrey. "Web Writing Resources." E-mail to Nora Davis. 3 Jan. 2000.

Sommers, Laurice. "Re: College Admissions Practices." E-mail to the author. 12 Aug. 1998.

Listservers and Newsgroups. In citing these references, begin with the author's name (reversed) followed by a period. Next include the title of the document (in quotes) from the subject line, followed by the words "Online posting" (not in quotes). Follow this with the date of posting. For listservers, include the date of access, the name of the list (if known), and the online address of the list's moderator or administrator. For newsgroups, follow "Online posting" with the date of posting, the date of access, and the name of the newsgroup, prefixed with "news:" and enclosed in angle brackets.

Applebaum, Dale. "Educational Variables." Online posting. 29 Jan. 1998. Higher Education Discussion Group. 30 Jan. 1993 <jlucidoj@unc.edu>.

Gostl, Jack. "Re: Mr. Levitan." Online posting. 13 June 1997. 20 June 1997 <news:alt.edu.bronxscience>.

MUDs, MOOs, and IRCs. Begin with the name of the speaker(s) followed by a period. Follow with the description and date of the event, the forum in which the communication took place, the date of access, and the online address. If you accessed the MOO or MUD through telnet, your citation might appear as follows:

```
Guest. Personal interview. 13 Aug. 1998.
  <telnet://du.edu:8888>.
```

For more information on MLA documentation style for online sources, check out their web site at www.mla.org/style/sources.htm.

APA Style

The newly revised *Publication Manual of the American Psychological Association* (5th ed.) now includes guidelines for Internet resources. The manual recommends that, at a minimum, a reference of an Internet source should provide a document title or description, a date (either the date of publication or update or the date of retrieval), and an address (in Internet terms, a uniform resource locator, or URL). Whenever possible, identify the authors of a document as well. It's important to remember that, unlike the MLA, the APA does not include temporary or transient sources (e.g., letters, phone calls, etc.) in its "References" page, preferring to handle them in the text. The general suggested format is as follows:

Online periodical:

Author, A. A., Author, B. B., & Author, C. C. (2000). Title of article. *Title of Periodical,* xx, xxxxx. Retrieved month, day, year, from source.

Online document:

Author, A. A. (2000). *Title of work.* Retrieved month, day, year, from source.

Some more specific examples are as follows:

FTP (File Transfer Protocol) Sites. To cite files available for downloading via FTP, give the author's name (if known), the publication date (if available and if different from the date accessed), the full title of the paper (capitalizing only the first word and proper nouns), the date of access, and the address of the FTP site along with the full path necessary to access the file.

Deutsch, P. (1991) Archie: An electronic directory service for the Internet. Retrieved January 25, 2000 from File Transfer Protocol: ftp://ftp.sura.net/pub/archie/docs/whatis.archie

WWW Sites (World Wide Web). To cite files available for viewing or downloading via the World Wide Web, give the author's name (if known), the year of publication (if known and if different from the date accessed), the full title of the article, and the title of the complete work (if applicable) in italics. Include any additional information (such as versions, editions, or revisions) in parentheses immediately following the title. Include the date of retrieval and full URL (the http address).

Burka, L. P. (1993). A hypertext history of multi-user dungeons. *MUDdex*. Retrieved January 13, 1997 from the World Wide Web: http://www.utopia.com/talent/lpb/muddex/essay/

Tilton, J. (1995). Composing good HTML (Vers. 2.0.6). Retrieved December 1, 1996 from the World Wide Web: http://www.cs.cmu.edu/~tilt/cgh/

Synchronous Communications (MOOs, MUDs, IRC, etc.). Give the name of the speaker(s), the complete date of the conversation being referenced in parentheses, and the title of the session (if applicable). Next, list the title of the site in italics, the protocol and address (if applicable), and any directions necessary to access the work. Last, list the date of access, followed by the retrieval information. Personal interviews do not need to be listed in the References, but do need to be included in parenthetic references in the text (see the APA *Publication Manual*).

Cross, J. (1996, February 27). Netoric's Tuesday cafe: Why use MUDs in the writing classroom? *MediaMoo*. Retrieved March 1, 1996 from File Transfer Protocol: ftp://daedalus.com/pub/ACW/NETORIC/catalog

Gopher Sites. List the author's name (if applicable), the year of publication, the title of the file or paper, and the title of the complete work (if applicable). Include any print publication information (if available) followed by the protocol (i.e., gopher://). List the date that the file was accessed and the path necessary to access the file.

Massachusetts Higher Education Coordinating Council. (1994). Using coordination and collaboration to address change. Retrieved July 16, 1999 from the World Wide Web: gopher://gopher.mass.edu:170/00gopher_root%3A%5B_hecc%5D_plan

E-mail, Listservs, and Newsgroups. Do not include personal e-mail in the list of References. Although unretrievable communication such as e-mail is not included in APA References, somewhat more public or accessible Internet postings from newsgroups or listservs may be included. See the APA *Publication Manual* for information on in-text citations.

Heilke, J. (1996, May 3). Webfolios. Alliance for Computers and Writing Discussion List. Retrieved December 31, 1996 from the World Wide Web: http://www.ttu.edu/lists/acw-l/9605/0040.html

Other authors and educators have proposed similar extensions to the APA style. You can find links to these pages at:

```
www.psychwww.com/resource/apacrib.htm
```

Remember, "frequently referenced" does not equate to "correct" or even "desirable." Check with your professor to see if your course or school has a preference for an extended APA style.

PART THREE

Web Activities

Web Activities for the Helping Professions

Using Usenet Newsgroups

Until a couple of years ago, Usenet newsgroups represented one of the best ways to learn about a subject area. Because of the increase in Internet traffic over the past two years, and also because of inappropriate use of Usenet to advertise commercial and often shady enterprises, it has become somewhat less useful. Still, social work and counseling students may find Usenet to be a relatively easy way to learn information about a given subject area.

Surfing the Web for Social Work and Counseling Information

Surfing the Web can be one of the most rewarding strategies for finding information, but you have to remain disciplined and try not to get lost. To beat the metaphor almost to a pulp, it's easy to find yourself bobbing in the waves with the baby sea lions and the sharks if you don't keep your information objectives in mind while you are surfing.

Using Social Work Academic Sites

Exercise

Go to the Columbia University site at **www.cc.columbia.edu/cu/ssw/.** Point your mouse cursor over **Students** on the left, and then over **Library** on the drop-down list. Click on the Online Social Work Journals link, and then examine the list of journals with full-text articles. Imagine being able to do some of your suggested reading without leaving the comfort of your computer! Now, select one of the listed journals to read.

- What happened when you tried to read from this journal? Why do you think this happened? Does your library provide such a service?

Using Government Resources

Exercise

Go to the National Library of Medicine at **www.nlm.nih.gov/** and click on Health Information and then scroll down the page to CancerNet. Click on Cancer Literature.

This will take you to the latest information the U.S. government has published on the topic of cancer.

- How authoritative is the information presented on this site?
- How might you use information from the National Library of Medicine for your professional practice?

Using Professional Association Sites

Exercise

Visit the National Association of Social Workers (NASW) site at **www.socialworkers.org** and click on the **Chapters** link under **ABOUT NASW** on the left side of the page. Does your state chapter of NASW have e-mail? Do they have a web site of their own? Visit the California Chapter of NASW at **http://naswca.org.**

- How do you think this site will be used by the chapter membership?
- What aspects of the site do you think will be most helpful to social workers?

Using Electronic Journals and Newsletters

Exercise

Go to Alcohol Alerts at **www.niaaa.nih.gov/publications/alalerts.htm.** This is a quarterly bulletin of the National Institute on Alcohol Abuse and Alcoholism that disseminates important research findings on a single aspect of alcohol abuse and alcoholism. Notice that you can get free copies of these bulletins by filling out the form on the page. Select a topic of interest to you and click on the link.

- How authoritative is this information?
- How useful would this information be for writing a paper on a related topic?

Using Social Work Areas of Practice Sites

Exercise

Go to Neighborhoods Online at **www.neighborhoodsonline.net/** and click on the **Community** button near the top of the page. Click on the **Neighbornets Networks** button under Community Networking. Now, go to **www.moveon.org** (Move On). We're just beginning to see the potential of the Internet as an organizing tool.

- What, if anything, was interesting about these sites? Is there anything that can be used for social work? If so, what and how?

Exercise

Go to the Detroit Community AIDS Library at **www.libraries.wayne.edu/dcal/aids.html.** Click on the PubMed link under Searchable Databases. This takes you to a free Medline search page, which is a wonderful resource for finding any health-related resource.

- How useful might this resource be for you in your practice?

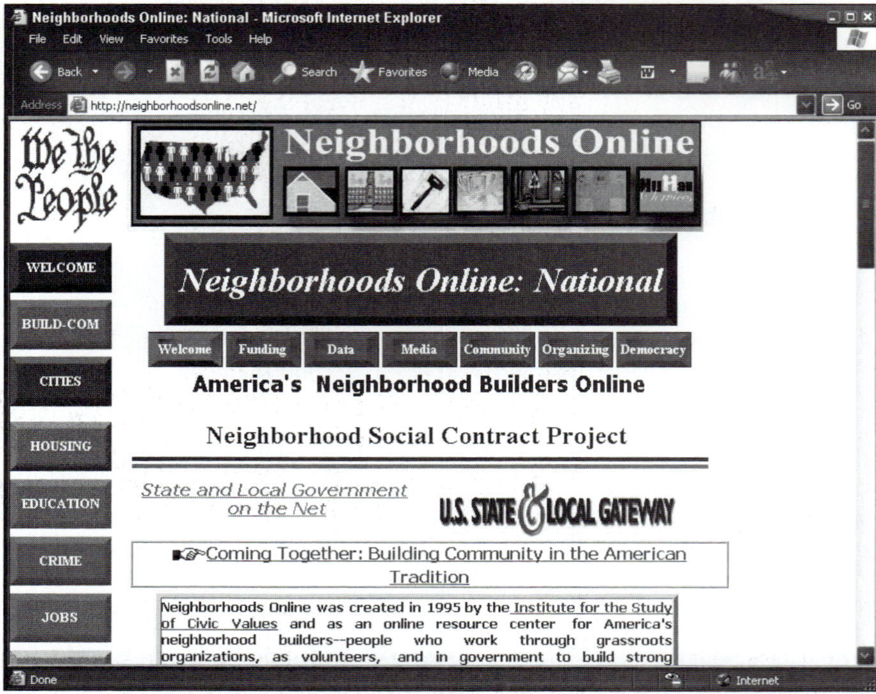

Exercise

Go to NetPsych.com at **http://netpsych.com/.** This site explores the new uses of the Internet to deliver psychological and health care services. NetPsych is the first site to focus exclusively on online resources. Click the HUH? button.

- What do you think of the sites you find linked here?
- What are your impressions of online psychotherapy? Should the social work profession consider an amendment to the Code of Ethics to cover practice in such circumstances?

Exercise

Go to the Domestic Violence Handbook at **www.domesticviolence.org.** This online resource is designed to assist women who are experiencing domestic abuse. Click on Index at the bottom of the page and follow the link to Personalized Safety Plan.

- Would you be comfortable knowing that some victims of domestic violence have no other resources to help them? Why or why not?

CHAPTER

1

Competing Perspectives on Social Welfare

In Dallas, Texas, the manager of a twenty-four-hour convenience store called the police at about 11:00 one morning to report that there was a small child wandering around the store by himself. When the police arrived, they found the little boy contentedly munching on a bag of potato chips and drinking a Coke. They asked him where he lived and where his parents were. He pointed down the street to several apartment complexes and said, "Mama's asleep." The officers took the child to the apartments and asked if anyone recognized him. The manager of the third complex knew the child. He told the officers, "This is Bobby Patrick. I think he turned three about two weeks ago. With his parents, I wouldn't be surprised if he never turns four. The father travels all the time for his job and returns home only long enough to scream at his wife and knock her around a little bit. The police have come out several times, but Ms. Patrick won't press charges. She just stays in the apartment with the drapes drawn, watches soap operas on TV, and drinks. I don't think she ever wakes up before noon, and Bobby has learned not to disturb her. If he can't find anything to eat in the apartment, he goes outside to see if a neighbor will feed him. Lately he has started to wander off to the shopping center, which means he has to cross a very busy street." The manager looked at the officers, sighed, and said, "Something should be done about situations like this."

Five months into the fiscal year, the emergency welfare fund at First Church was out of money. Because of cuts in welfare programs, the church had been deluged with requests for emergency assistance. The minister appealed to the congregation for more money, explaining that people just couldn't live on the amount available from existing welfare programs. Everyone agreed that "something should be done about situations like this."

In Detroit a woman called the police one February to report that for some time she had seen no activity from the residence of the elderly woman next door, and she feared that something might be wrong. When the police entered the house, they found the elderly woman's body. An investigation revealed that she had been dead for several weeks, having frozen to death after the power company shut off the electricity because she was behind on her payments. The woman had a son in town, but their relationship had not been good. He was just as happy when he did not hear from her. Likewise, she had alienated her neighbors over the years, so no one visited her. The result was an impoverished elderly person who was completely at the mercy of her environment. When things began to go wrong, she had no personal or financial resources to draw on. The neighbor said, "Something should be done about situations like this."

In a small college town in the South, it was revealed one year that out of 246 girls in the junior high school, 6 were pregnant. Of the 6, 4 were in the seventh grade. The school board had a meeting, the PTA had a meeting, and the teachers' organization had a meeting. Everyone said, "Something should be done about situations like this."

Something should be done about situations like this. That is the subject of this book. How do we as a society deal with social issues that we collectively recognize as problems? Although it is easy to agree on the general principle that we should do something, it is not so easy to agree on what should be done, who should do it, how much should be done, and how efforts should be financed. Inside each of us is a fairly consistent set of principles that we use to judge the world. We refer to this set of principles as a personal ideology or a political perspective. Many schemes have been developed to classify and explain these ideologies or perspectives, but we prefer the old commonsense classification of liberal and conservative. Although liberals and conservatives agree that something should be done about problems like those described here, their analysis of the problems and their proposed solutions are usually very different.

Political Perspectives and Social Welfare Issues

An aspect of being a social worker that we have found to be one of the most attractive or one of the most irritating, depending on our moods at the time, is that nearly everyone has strong opinions about social welfare issues. And they are generally more than willing to share these opinions with us and with anyone else who will listen. As we have listened to people voice their opinions about social welfare policies and programs, we have noticed that different people can take exactly the same issue, event, and data and come to very different conclusions, sometimes completely opposite conclusions. The really interesting thing is that in many instances the different analyses all make perfectly good sense.

Take, for example, a conversation we were part of a while back regarding the topic of whether the government, through expansion of the Medicare program, should cover a significant portion of the cost of prescription drugs for senior citizens. A friend, who happens to be an elementary school teacher, vigorously expressed the view that health care is a right, that it should not be denied to a person due to cost, that many elderly people are on limited incomes through no fault of their own, and that government should guarantee access to health care, including prescription drugs, even

People with liberal and conservative worldviews often have strong, sometimes emotional, differences of opinion regarding many social welfare issues, including welfare reform.

if a tax increase is necessary to finance this. This argument made good sense. Then another friend, an accountant, weighed in. She agreed that everyone should have access to quality health care, but argued that if people would plan for their retirement they would have sufficient income and insurance to provide health care for themselves. If people had not made sufficient preparations, their families should help them out. We should all contribute to our churches and private charities so that these institutions, rather than government, can assist those people still in need. Her final point was that charity is a virtue, that people should assist others out of the goodness of their hearts, and that if government relieves us of this responsibility by legislating all forms of assistance we will be denied the opportunity to practice this virtue. Hmmm, this argument also seems to make some sense.

Another conversation we overheard concerned the major welfare reform bill passed in 1996. An investment banker opined that, while the reform plan has its strengths, it misses the point. The point, according to our friend, is that welfare is not the problem—poverty is the problem. The only real long-term solution lies in reforming the economic system in our country so that everyone has a shot at the American dream. This would involve reforming education, day care, health care, and transportation and greatly increasing the minimum wage. His conclusion was, "Who would live on welfare if people could get affordable day care for their kids, had safe and convenient public transportation available, accessible job training and retraining nearby, and jobs available that paid twelve to fifteen dollars an hour and included benefits such as vacations, health insurance, and retirement programs? The answer is no one except those too sick or handicapped to work. If we would end poverty, we wouldn't have to worry about reforming welfare." This sounded so good to us that we began humming the old John Lennon song "Imagine." Then a computer programmer friend weighed in with her opinion and ruined the mood. She argued that there are already numerous jobs available and that the current minimum wage of $5.15 an hour is all that many workers are worth to a business. She argued that you can't hire a person at twelve dollars an hour if the person's employment is only going to result in approximately six dollars an hour of additional revenue to the firm. People start out at the minimum wage, but those who work hard and strive for excellence will quickly increase their earnings. If they start out at an artificially high level, what will motivate them to work harder?

Finally, we watched a panel discussion on television regarding child abuse and neglect. One panelist pointed out that the majority of parents who maltreat their children suffer from numerous social problems such as poverty, poor housing, unemployment, living in high crime areas, and so forth. He attributed child maltreatment to the stress resulting from these factors and argued that to end child abuse and neglect we need to alter the environment of parents in order to free them up to pay better attention to the needs of their children. This sounded persuasive. Then another panelist stated that caring for one's children is the most basic instinct in the animal kingdom. He argued that when a person sinks so low that he or she fails to heed this instinct, that person is too far gone to benefit from help. Although it is true that poverty, poor housing, unemployment, and living in a high crime area are factors correlated with child maltreatment, they do not cause the problem. Rather, the personal limitations of the parents lead to both the child abuse and having to live under these conditions. He concluded that child maltreatment is a crime and should be treated as any other crime. The parents should be tried and sent to jail and the children placed in alternative settings that can meet their needs. This man's argument also seemed to make some sense.

These are just a few of many conversations we have heard illustrating widely varying views on social welfare issues. Why are these views so different? Is one position right and the others wrong? One informed and the others ignorant? One progressive and the others old-fashioned? The answer is "none of the above." Like the old fable about the blind people trying to describe the elephant, these people represent different political perspectives; stated another way, they represent different social attitudes or ideologies. These terms, *political perspective, ideology,* and *social attitude,* are, as we are using them, essentially interchangeable.

Ideology, social attitudes, and political perspectives describe what we might call a collective mind-set. They refer to the beliefs and values of a group of people that are systematized enough to have a semblance of universality, or "worldview."[1] Attitudes are expressed by evaluating a particular situation or thing with some degree of favor or disfavor.[2] These are filters through which we screen our experiences and impose some sense on them. Social attitudes express the psychological orientation of people to their social environment; they enable us to make sense of our incredibly complex world. As Kerlinger has said, "Whether directed toward social issues, ethnic groups, or abstract ideas, attitudes are efficient psychological mechanisms that strongly influence social behavior—they represent emotional, motivational, and cognitive reactions of people to the social 'objects' of the environment and their predisposition to act toward those social objects."[3]

We generally classify political perspectives into two big groups, which we label *liberal* and *conservative.* Although these are rather crude categories, most people in the United States would describe themselves as belonging to one or the other of these classifications. There are, in addition, three other groups. One consists of people holding a radical perspective, a view described by one writer as a "small but frequently refreshing stream" of thought in U.S. life.[4] The radical perspective is sometimes referred to as the "far left." Then there is the perspective generally referred to as *reactionary,* or "far right." In most cases this is an extreme version of the conservative perspective, and we will discuss it only when it differs from that perspective. Finally, there is the perspective referred to as *moderate,* which could perhaps be thought of as a nonperspective. Moderates deny that they have any set worldview and contend that they judge each issue on its unique merits. Because the perceived reality of social welfare issues changes based on the political perspective within which they are viewed, we will present these issues in the light of the various perspectives. We will devote the most time to the liberal and the conservative perspectives because these are dominant in U.S. society. But we will devote some space to the radical perspective because people with this point of view have presented some influential critiques.

In the United States, the Republican Party is considered to be conservative and the Democratic Party is considered to be liberal. Although there are such things as conservative Democrats and liberal Republicans, the Democrats are generally to the left of the political spectrum and the Republicans are to the right. Kerlinger has noted that "[a]lthough it has been said that there is no real difference between the policies and behaviors of Republicans and Democrats in the United States, there are actual and deep differences, especially in policies that affect the conduct of business and social welfare of people. Such differences spring, at least in part, from ideological concerns that are reflected in liberal and conservative attitudes."[5] At the same time, both liberals and conservatives reflect traditional American beliefs in property rights and in individualism, although the value they place on these beliefs differs. There is no mainstream political party expressing the beliefs of either radicals or reactionaries, although occasionally the Socialist Party or the reactionary Libertarian Party is successful in getting a member elected to some minor political post.

The Worldview of Conservatives, Liberals, and Radicals

Liberals and conservatives share a basic belief in maintaining our society as it is currently structured. Radicals and reactionaries have major reservations about the existing social arrangements. All four perspectives differ in important areas, the most important being their attitudes toward change; their views of human nature, individual behavior, the family, the social system, the government and the economic system; and their basic values. These views have important implications for their positions on social welfare.

Attitudes toward Change

Perhaps the most fundamental difference among liberals, conservatives, radicals, and reactionaries is their attitude toward change. Conservatives (the word is derived from the

Electoral politics have great implications for social welfare programs. Democratic candidates are generally considered to be more sympathetic to the expansion of these programs than Republicans, although this does not always turn out to be true.

verb "to conserve") tend to resist change. They believe that change usually produces more negative than positive consequences; thus, they generally favor keeping things as they are. Conservatives strongly emphasize tradition. Liberals are generally in favor of change; they believe that the world can be changed for the better. Liberals view history as progress, and they believe that continuing change will bring continuing progress. They usually view change as the reform, rather than the radical restructuring, of existing institutions. Radicals are also in favor of change but think that liberal proposals for change do not get to the core of problems. They doubt that moderate change can deal with the pervasive inequities in society. Therefore, radicals stress the need for more fundamental alterations in the social system. Reactionaries, on the other hand, believe that change has already gone too far and that things should be changed back to the way they used to be.

These attitudes toward change go a long way toward explaining the general attitudes toward social welfare among people holding the different political ideologies. Social welfare programs generally represent nontraditional means of dealing with problems. Public assistance substitutes a government subsidy of some kind for labor market participation; child protective services involve public agencies' participating in matters traditionally considered to be "family business"; health care reform substitutes some form of publicly managed medical care for that provided by the free market. Liberals, with their faith that change can make things better, advocate for more and better social welfare programs. Conservatives are suspicious of almost all social welfare programs, believing that problems should be handled in time-tested, traditional ways to the greatest extent possible. Radicals believe that social welfare efforts do not go nearly far enough and that in all probability fundamental changes will need to be made in the basic structure of society to alleviate most of the problems being targeted by welfare programs. Radicals, in fact, suspect that the real purpose of social welfare programs is to distract attention from the real, deep-seated problems of society and thereby to obstruct meaningful change. Reactionaries believe that many, if not all, social welfare programs should never have been implemented to begin with, and that completely eliminating them would be a good thing.

Views of Human Nature

Our views of human nature undergird and color our attitudes toward nearly everything else. The meaning and purpose of human life, what we ought to do, and what we can hope to achieve—all of these issues are fundamentally affected by our beliefs about the real or true nature of people. There are some basic differences between conservative and liberal views on this subject.

Conservatives tend to take a basically pessimistic view of human nature. People are perceived as being corrupt, self-centered, lazy, and incapable of true charity. They need to be encouraged to work. Conservative commentator Thomas Sowell says that those "who look everywhere for the mysterious causes of poverty, ignorance, crime, and war need look no further than their own mirrors. We are born into this world poor and ignorant, and with thoroughly selfish and barbaric impulses."[6] People need to be controlled because of their fundamentally negative nature, and they should be swiftly and sternly punished when they get out of line. This is the only way they can live harmoniously with one another. Because of this view, conservatives have a basic distrust of democracy, doubting the ability of the masses to make decisions for the common good. They support democracy, however, because they believe it is better than the available alternatives.

Liberals take a much more optimistic view of human nature. They accept the "blank slate" view of John Locke that people are born with infinite possibilities for being shaped for the good, or the view of Jean-Jacques Rousseau or more recently Abraham Maslow that people are born good and, if not corrupted, are naturally social, curious, and loving. People do not need to be controlled; they simply need to be protected from corrupting influences and given the freedom to follow their natural inclinations, which will lead to the good.

Like liberals, radicals believe that people are basically good. Moreover, they believe that people are inherently industrious and creative. Like conservatives, radicals regard hard work as a virtue. Unlike conservatives, who follow the Puritan assumption that people are naturally lazy and must be forced to work, radicals believe that if people have control over their working conditions, they will take pleasure in working hard.

These different views of human nature have tremendous consequences for views of social welfare. If you regard people as being basically bad, you will design social welfare systems to control people. You will suspect that people will take advantage of the system whenever possible, and thus you will make the prevention of cheating a major focus. You will view crime, drug dependency, child abuse, and similar problems as expressions of the basically negative nature of people and of the failure of external forces to control this nature. You will probably see punishment as the logical solution. On the other hand, if you regard people as being basically good, you will design social welfare systems to free people from problems that are preventing them from realizing their natural potential. You will be less concerned with control because of your conviction that people, if given the chance, will naturally do what is right.

Views of Individual Behavior

Our explanations of why people behave as they do are closely related to our views of human nature. Our ideas about the importance of heredity, the environment, and individual free will are all important components of our concept of individual behavior.

Conservatives generally view individuals as autonomous; that is, self-governing. Regardless of what a person's situation is or what problems he or she has had in the past, each person is responsible for his or her own current behavior. People choose to do whatever they are doing, and they are responsible for whatever gains or losses result from these choices. The conservative theorist Irving Kristol, for example, asserts that individual behavior is a result of motivation, which he views as an innate (inborn) characteristic present in all people in varying degrees. People possess free will and thus can choose to engage in behaviors such as hard work that help them get ahead, or activities such as excessive leisure that contribute to failure.[7] Thus, poverty is often caused by individuals' lack of responsibility.

Although liberals and radicals do not completely deny free will and motivation, they put much more emphasis on the environment as a factor in individual behavior. An early expression of this view comes from Sigmund Freud, who said that individuals are programmed by early experiences, primarily with their parents, and that an individual's behavior in later life results from this programming. More recent theorists, such as Erikson, Glaser and Strauss, and Levinson,[8] assert that the programming takes place throughout life, resulting in a series of developmental crises. If people successfully resolve the crises, they will experience happiness and fulfillment; if they do not, they will experience failure and discontent. Another view is based on the work of behavioral psychologists, notably Watson and Skinner.[9] According to this perspective, behavior is the result not of programming but of the immediate consequences of behavior. If an individual perceives the consequences of a behavior as positive, the behavior will increase; behavior in which the consequences are perceived as negative will decrease.

Our explanations of human behavior have important implications for our approach to social welfare. If we assume that people are autonomous and guided completely by free will, poverty and other social welfare problems will be seen as a result of laziness, irresponsibility, or lack of self-control. Conservative scholar Thomas Sowell asserts that welfare recipients "are people who didn't bother to learn when they were in school, didn't bother to get work experience or job skills afterwards, and often don't bother to obey the law either. There are consequences to that kind of behavior. What the welfare state does is to force others to pay the consequences."[10] In other words, poor people would not be poor if they really wanted to be otherwise. Social welfare programs simply need to make sure that nothing interferes with people's efforts to better themselves and to solve their own problems.

If, on the other hand, we assume that people's behavior is strongly influenced by the environment, we will see changing the environment as the proper response to social welfare problems. For example, liberals support prison programs that provide counseling and education for convicted criminals, or that even divert them from prison altogether and place them in community-based alternatives. Their argument is that criminal behavior is learned and therefore can be unlearned.

Views of the Family

Social welfare programs generally perform some function traditionally handled by the family. For this reason, attitudes toward the family have a significant influence on social welfare policy. This influence, however, is often confusing. In this area more than others, it seems, theory and practice are further apart for all groups. Conservatives and radicals have particular difficulty reconciling their ideals to the world in which they live.

Conservatives revere the "traditional" family and try to devise policies to preserve it. They see the family as a source of strength for individuals and as the primary unit of society. They oppose abortion, public funding of day care centers, sex education in schools, birth-control counseling for minors, legal recognition of gay marriage, and other developments that might undermine parental authority or make family breakups easier by giving too much independence to women and children. Conservatives believe that governmental welfare programs have weakened the family and thus contributed to poverty. Conservative theorist George Gilder asserts that

> The key to the intractable poverty of the hardcore American poor is the dominance of single and separated men in poor communities. . . . Once a family is headed by a woman, it is almost impossible for it to greatly raise its income even if the woman is highly educated and

> trained. . . . Her family responsibilities and distractions tend to prevent her from the kind of all-out commitment that is necessary for the full use of earning power. Few women with children make earning money the top priority in their lives. . . . The first priority of any serious program against poverty is to strengthen the male role in poor families.[11]

The difficulty with this position is that the "traditional" model—father as sole wage earner outside the home and mother as full-time homemaker and caregiver—was the majority situation for a relatively brief period of U.S. history, and it is now obtainable by only a minority. A majority of women now work outside the home; many work because they have to. The argument against government intrusion in family life, which conservatives use to resist sex education or birth-control counseling for minors, must be put aside when conservatives advocate the outlawing of abortion. Divorce, long opposed by conservatives, has now been accepted by many of them. Thus, conservatives find themselves on a fairly small and uncomfortable base from which to defend their narrow definition of the family.

Radicals regard the conservatives' traditional family perspective as oppressive and as a distortion of both male and female talents. It denies women a choice of careers and men an opportunity to participate in family life. However, radicals share with conservatives the recognition that strong families are essential to a healthy society. Accordingly, they favor ways of supporting "new" families—those consisting of two working parents, single parents, communal groups, or homosexual parents. Radicals, along with most liberals, favor equal rights and equal pay, day care centers, maternity *and* paternity leaves, flextime, and job sharing.

Yet radicals also have difficulty harmonizing theory and practice. Civil rights advocates, antiwar activists, and other political groups supported by radicals have often been as oppressive to and patronizing of their women members as any conservative organization. In his own family, Karl Marx was a conventional authoritarian father; the home lives of modern radicals do not always reflect the equal division of labor and power called for by their ideals.

Liberals may have the easiest time in this difficult area. They view the family as an evolving institution, and they can be more flexible and pragmatic in the ways in which they support it.

Views of the Social System

Is our social system fair? Do people really get rewards in proportion to their contributions to society? Do people have equal opportunities? How important is change to the ideal of the good society? Is conflict inevitable and, indeed, desirable? These are some of the questions related to our view of the social system.

Conservatives view society in a manner that is close to what sociologists call the *functional perspective.* The basic assumption of this perspective is that society is a system composed of interrelated and interdependent parts. Each part makes a contribution to the operation of the system, and thus the entire system works. Each part fulfills a different function but contributes to the overall well-being of society. In this way, society is seen as analogous to a biological organism.

For our purposes, the most crucial aspect of this conservative perspective is the view that all parts of society, *as they are,* are beneficial to both society and the individuals within it. Society would not work as well without any of its existing arrangements or with major changes in any of its arrangements. Thus, the average salary of physicians is over $100,000 a year and the average salary of preschool teachers is under $23,000 a year because this is the arrangement that is most socially effective. Conservatives would argue that the large discrepancy in earnings is the result of the greater effort and ability necessary to become a physician, the greater workload and responsibility of a physician, and the greater importance to the general well-being of society of a physician's work. If the salary gap were narrowed, fewer highly qualified people would choose the rigors of becoming a physician, and society would suffer. In this view, social inequality is a device by which societies ensure that the most important positions are filled by the most capable people.[12]

Liberals, like conservatives, tend to view society as an organic system, but they have less faith that the system will regulate itself without intervention. They point out, for example, that nature is notoriously inefficient; the average tree sends out thousands of seedlings, but only a few will grow into mature trees. With the intervention of human horticulture, those seedlings can be replanted, watered, fertilized, protected from insects, and allowed to grow to maturity. Liberals believe that the social system needs nurturing and regulating as well.

Liberals also see (and value) more diversity and friction in the social system than do conservatives. Different groups have different interests—things that are beneficial to them—and what is in the interest of one group may be to the disadvantage of another. Each group will struggle to promote its own interests, but it will usually have to compromise with and accommodate other groups in order to attain its goals. If there are

Senator Barbara Mikulski (Democrat, Maryland) is a social worker who has championed the liberal policies favored by her profession.

enough interest groups, and if none are powerful enough to dominate the others, the system will embody the "checks and balances" of the Constitution. Government provides the rules and limits that keep the contest fair and open. Liberal economists such as Paul Krugman and political scientists such as Robert Dahl describe the virtues of this pluralistic system.[13]

Radicals, who usually follow the analysis of Karl Marx, see the social system as a class hierarchy in which one class has predominant power and uses it to control the others. This view is sometimes called the *conflict perspective.* To radicals, the interest-group politics that preoccupies liberals is only a sideshow. Behind the scenes, the important decisions are being made by an elite of wealthy and powerful people.[14]

Radicals believe that inequality is the result of the group with greater power using this power to perpetuate its position of advantage. Thus, the physician has six times the income of the preschool teacher not because physicians are six times more valuable to the social system but because they have wealth and power and use these resources to increase, or at least to maintain, their affluence. The facts that the medical profession is predominantly male and that early childhood education is predominantly female are viewed as being significant. Also viewed as significant is the fact that as the proportion of physicians who are female has increased, the average salary has declined.

The conservative perspective sees the social system as inherently fair. If some groups are poorer than others and have less power and lower status, it is because this situation is necessary for the well-being of society. Thus, conservatives view change with a great deal of suspicion. What exists is useful and necessary. Rapid and major changes may benefit particular groups, but they will usually result in a net loss to society. Change is sometimes necessary, but it must be slow and incremental.

The liberal perspective regards the social system as potentially fair but frequently unfair. Some interest groups are more powerful than others and, if unchecked by government regulation, will use their power to take advantage of less powerful groups. Change takes place, sometimes rapidly and sometimes slowly, through the competition and compromise of interest groups.

Radicals believe that fairness is unattainable in the present system. Fairness can be achieved only if society restructures its existing institutions to redistribute wealth and power.

It is not difficult to deduce the implications of these different perspectives for social welfare. Conservatives believe that everything in society has a function, and they are skeptical of proposals for change. If poverty were eliminated by, for example, the creation of millions of jobs and an increase in the minimum wage, conservatives would argue that:

1. The new jobs would compete with private business.
2. A tax increase would be necessary and would hurt the economy.
3. The increased minimum wage would force businesses to pay more, which would cause them either to go broke or to raise their prices. This would cause inflation, which would reduce the value of the minimum wage to the same level it was before the increase.

The result would be a net loss to the U.S. economy. Thus, conservatives argue that kind-hearted efforts to help the poor would only result in harm to society. Conservatives tend to support social welfare programs that help people adjust to society as it currently exists and that help people improve their living standard within the current social and economic structure; they generally oppose programs that seek to change society.

Liberals do not view the existing society as the best one possible. They believe in changes that will reduce inequality and increase social justice. With regard to the previous example, many liberals would assert that the wealthiest members of society are putting forth these arguments in a predictable effort to retain their power, resources, and positions. Liberals reject social welfare programs that simply help people adjust to society as it is. They see these programs as means for the powerful to keep the powerless "in their place" rather than as efforts to help them. Liberals view programs that change society more favorably than they do those that change individuals.

For radicals, the only way to prevent inequality is to change society completely. When power and wealth are distributed equitably and everyone is guaranteed the necessities of life, cooperation, rather than competition and conflict, will predominate. The struggle of oppressed groups to liberate themselves produces change in society. Some radicals believe that society can be restructured gradually and democratically; others see only revolutionary change as sufficient.

Views of the Government and the Economic System

Perhaps the area of the strongest and most emotional disagreement between liberal and conservative perspectives is the view of the proper role of government in the economy and in the lives of people. Conservatives embrace the old adage "that government governs best which governs least." They think that most government activities constitute grave threats to individual liberty and to the smooth functioning of the free market. Ginsberg observes that "the classic, conservative belief was that the federal government should provide defense, operate a money system, and maintain relations with other nations." He quotes the political satirist P. J. O'Rourke who said of conservatives, "opposition is where we belong. Being opposed to government is what defines true conservatism."[15]

Reactionaries become vocal about government and the economic system. Reactionaries, currently represented by the Libertarian Party, believe that government, beyond a bare minimum, is inherently evil. They support government activity only in areas such as national defense, criminal justice, and the maintenance of certain public utilities such as roads and sewers. Libertarians consider most taxation to be legal thievery. They advocate for the abolition of public welfare, public education, public social services, and almost every other tax-supported activity. Harry Browne, the Libertarian Party candidate for president in 2000, summarizes the party's platform: "For each problem America faces today, my solution is *less* government, rather than new government programs, new regulations, new taxes, and new powers for the politicians. I want you to live your life as you think best—not as the politicians claim is best for America." The platform calls for abolishing the income tax, dismantling the Social Security system, ending the war on drugs, repealing all gun laws, and bringing all U.S. troops home.[16]

Liberals believe that our social and economic systems contain imperfections that can be corrected only by governmental intervention. Such intervention is therefore justifiable and desirable.

Radicals see liberal tinkering with government as inadequate; they feel that complete restructuring is necessary. The Socialist Party USA summarizes its basic philosophy in this regard as:

> In contrast to the Democratic and Republican parties, the Socialist Party has an underlying philosophy that is both coherent and radical. It is coherent in the sense that members of the Socialist Party differ on details, but are united on certain fundamental principles. It is radical in the sense that all members of the Socialist Party recognize the need for fundamental change in our society. Socialists believe that the problems facing America and the world, such as environmental despoliation, the systematic waste of public resources for private profit, persistent unemployment concentrated among women and racial minorities, and the maldistribution of wealth, power, and income, are not mere aberrations of the capitalist system—they are the capitalist system.[17]

The government is involved in the economy in two main areas, both of which grew tremendously during the twentieth century, particularly during the past sixty years. The first area is taxation and government expenditure. Before 1913 there was no federal income tax; the spending by all levels of government (federal, state, and local) amounted to only $3 billion, less than 9 percent of national income. Government spending in 2001 was $1,858 billion, more than 40 percent of national income. A special bone of contention between liberals and conservatives is the government redistribution of income: government's taking income from one group by means of taxes and giving it to another group in the form of cash grants (such as Social Security and public welfare) or some other form of benefit (such as food stamps and public housing). Before the onset of the Great Depression in 1929, the federal government spent almost nothing on income redistribution programs. The Office of Management and Budget reports that in 2002 federal spending on Medicare, Social Security, and other income security programs was $980 billion, 48 percent of the federal budget.

The second area of government involvement in the economy includes laws, regulations, and executive orders governing economic affairs. For most of the nineteenth century there was virtually no governmental regulation of the economy. Economists Paul Samuelson and William Nordhaus have noted that

> This philosophy permitted people great personal freedom to pursue their economic ambitions and produced a century of rapid material progress. But critics saw many flaws in this laissez-faire idyll. Historians record periodic business crises, extremes of poverty and inequality, deep-seated racial discrimination, and poisoning of water, land, and air by pollution. Muckrakers and progressives called for a bridle on capitalism so that people could steer this wayward beast in more humane directions.[18]

Government regulation began to grow as a result of the problems Samuelson and Nordhaus list. In 1887 the Interstate Commerce Commission was established; in 1890 the Sherman Antitrust Act was passed; in 1913 the Federal Reserve System was established; and later the Federal Deposit Insurance Corporation, the Federal Power Commission, the Federal Communications Commission, the Pure Food and Drug Acts, the Securities and Exchange Commission, and numerous other commissions and laws were established and enacted. Of major importance were the Social Security Act of 1935, which made an "economic safety net" for all citizens a responsibility of the government, and the Employment Act of 1946, which established as a governmental responsibility the maintenance of "maximum employment, production and purchasing power."

With Adam Smith's *Wealth of Nations* as their bible,[19] conservatives fear and resist this growth of governmental involvement in the economy. They believe that for the economy to function efficiently, economic exchanges must be, to the greatest degree possible, unregulated. As stated by Friedman and Friedman:

> Adam Smith's key insight was that both parties to an exchange can benefit and that, *so long as cooperation is strictly voluntary,* no exchange will take place unless both parties do benefit. No external force, no coercion, no violation of freedom is necessary to produce cooperation among individuals all of whom can benefit. That is why, as Adam Smith put it, an individual who "intends only his own gain" is "led by an invisible hand to promote an end which was not part of his intention. Nor is it always the worse for the society that it was no part of it. By pursuing his own interest he frequently promotes that of the society more effectually than when he really intends to promote it. I have never known much good done by those who affected to trade for the public good."[20]

In other words, a free-market economy is the best way to ensure that the country prospers and individual needs are met.

Conservatives feel that government regulations substitute the "dead hand of bureaucracy" for the invisible hand of the free market. The result will be, they feel, that "sooner or later—and perhaps sooner than many of us expect—an even bigger government will destroy both the prosperity that we owe to the free market and the human freedom proclaimed so eloquently in the Declaration of Independence."[21] We should note again, however, that government involvement constitutes a conservative paradox; government interventions that benefit business, such as the periodic "bailouts" of large corporations, are often viewed as necessary and desirable.[22] The earliest examples of government involvement in the market were at the urging of conservative businesspeople. In the early 1900s, for example, employers reacted to the spread of lawsuits against them from injured workers by pressing the government to establish workers' compensation laws.[23] Government intervention to support the free-market process is, therefore, considered legitimate. Intervention that subverts the market process is not.

The liberal perspective, based on the economic theories of John Maynard Keynes, is that the government must be involved in all areas of the economy in order to ensure its optimal functioning.[24] Liberals believe that if the economy is left totally alone, people with power will take unfair advantage of those with less power; people with more resources than they need will not necessarily share with those with fewer resources than they need; and, with totally free choice, people will not always make the right decisions (for example, a person may choose to buy drugs rather than food). They assert that certain goods, such as roads and national defense, must be provided by the government because such goods cannot be divided up and paid for as used by consumers. Liberals accept the capitalist system but believe it needs regulation to avoid wild swings from prosperity to depression and back again. They contend that the government, through regulating the money supply (monetary policy) and expanding or decreasing government spending and taxation (fiscal policy), can stabilize the economy and prevent depressions.

What **Americans** Believe

This book is organized around a specific argument: Understanding social welfare is less a matter of understanding facts than it is of understanding the ideological lenses through which people filter these facts. In this chapter, we describe major ideologies of the American people within a liberal to conservative matrix. This brings up the obvious question—a question that can be addressed with data—of how many Americans subscribe to different belief systems within this matrix.

The National Opinion Research Corporation (NORC) has, since 1972, conducted over 40,000 interviews with a scientifically selected sample of Americans. The interviews have been conducted almost every year, most recently with 2,765 people in 2002. The questionnaire used in these interviews is called the General Social Survey (GSS). The GSS collects an immense amount of data from the respondents, including demographic data (age, race, gender, income, job, and much more), a few pieces of behavioral data (Who did you vote for in the 2000 presidential election? How often do you attend religious services?), and opinion data on a large number of social, political, and personal issues.

One of the questions asked of respondents to the GSS is to identify where they would place themselves on a seven-point scale ranging from "very liberal" on one end to "very conservative" on the other. For our analysis of these data, we have collapsed the categories into three levels: liberal, moderate, and conservative. An argument could be made that we should have designated the "very liberal" position as radical and the "very conservative" position as reactionary, but the GSS does not use these terms, so neither do we. Throughout this book, we will use these data to identify how Americans with different self-identified ideological positions feel about the various social welfare issues we discuss.

For this chapter, we have prepared three tables from the GSS data. Table 1.1 summarizes all of the responses people have given since 1972 to the question regarding how they would identify their political perspective, cross-tabulated by a number of demographic characteristics. Table 1.2 summarizes the data for 1998 to 2002 regarding political perspective cross-tabulated with income level. Table 1.3 shows how people identified their political perspective at three points in time: 1974, 1988, and 2002.

We would like to be able to tell you that we spent hours running appropriate tests on all of the differences between the groups represented in these tables to determine statistical significance. But, actually, the Statistical Products and Service Solutions (SPSS) data analysis software ran the tests; all we did was sit in our chairs, click a mouse, and report the results to you. The tests indicated that all of the differences shown in these tables are statistically significant, although some (gender, for example) are small. "Statistically significant" means that the differences are real, that they did not occur as a function of chance.

These tables provide a lot of information that will be useful as we study the American approach to social welfare. What is this information? First, Americans in general are more conservative than liberal, but the largest group of all is people who identify themselves as moderate. This means, we presume, that they will swing toward either end of the conservative–liberal scale depending on the issue. In the chapters that follow, we will see how the various groups align themselves within the liberal to conservative matrix regarding various social welfare issues. Second, more men consider themselves to be conservative than do women, but the difference is small. Third, blacks are considerably more liberal and less conservative than whites. Next, older people tend to be more conservative and less liberal than younger people. Finally, higher-income people are considerably less liberal and more conservative than less affluent people. If you've been staying awake and paying attention as you have been reading this, you are probably thinking, "Well, that's pretty much what I thought." In this observation, you would be correct—these data support conventional wisdom regarding the kind of people who are liberal and the kind who are conservative.

TABLE 1.1

Political Leanings, Cumulative

"We hear a lot of talk these days about liberals and conservatives. On a seven-point scale from extremely liberal to extremely conservative, where would you place yourself?"

(percent responding by sex, race, age, and education: 1976–1996)

	Liberal (slightly to extremely)	Moderate	Conservative (slightly to extremely)
Total	27.3	38.7	33.9
Men	27.6	35.5	36.9
Women	27.1	41.3	31.6
Black	36.5	37.8	25.6
White	25.7	38.8	35.5
Age 18 to 29	33.9	38.7	27.3
Age 30 to 39	30.7	36.6	32.6
Age 40 to 49	27.0	37.0	35.9
Age 50 to 59	23.2	39.1	37.6
Age 60 to 69	20.7	41.7	37.5
Age 70 or older	19.9	41.8	38.2
Not high school graduate	25.9	43.0	31.1
High school graduate	24.9	41.9	33.2
Associate's degree	28.5	36.3	35.1
Bachelor's degree	32.8	26.8	40.3
Graduate degree	40.2	24.3	35.4

Note: Numbers may not total 100 because "don't know" and no answer are not included.

Source: James Allan Davis and Tom W. Smith, *General Social Surveys,* 1972–2002 [machine-readable data file]: Principal Investigator, James A. Davis; Director and Co-Principal Investigator, Tom W. Smith; Co-Principal Investigator, Peter V. Marsden, NORC ed. (Chicago: National Opinion Research Center, producer 2002; Storrs, CT: The Roper Center for Public Opinion Research, University of Connecticut, distributor). 1 data file (43,698 logical records) and 1 codebook (1,769 pp.).

(continued)

The relationship between education and political perspective is interesting. There is a relationship between increased education and increased liberalism/decreased conservatism. The really interesting thing, however, is that as education increases, so does the tendency to identify with one of the consistent ideologies, liberal or conservative. As the level of education increases, the number of people identifying themselves as moderate decreases at a fairly steep rate. Less than one person out of every four with a graduate degree identifies as moderate. This is consistent with the findings of political scientists, that most people do not hold consistent (or coherent) political positions, but the number increases as a function of increased education.*

The most important (at least in our opinion) point shown by these data is the trend. Another part of conventional wisdom says that political ideology is like a pendulum that swings from liberal to conservative and back again. We, and all of our liberal friends, have been waiting thirty years for the pendulum to begin its swing back to the left. The GSS data give no reason to think this is going to happen soon. The population has been moving more and more to the right for the entire thirty years of the survey. This means that conservative values and accompanying positions will continue to have a major influence on social welfare policies and programs for the foreseeable future. This underscores the point that for those of us (and maybe some of you) who hold to liberal values and positions, understanding conservative values and positions is immensely important.

*Linda J. Skitka and Elizabeth Mullan, "Psychological Determinants of Public Opinion," in Victor C. Ottati, R. Scott Tindale, John Edwards, Fred B. Bryant, Linda Heath, Daniel C. O'Connell, Yolanda Suarez-Balcazar, and Emil J. Posavac, eds., *The Social Psychology of Politics* (Chicago: Loyola University Press, 2002), 107–134.

TABLE 1.2

Political Perspectives and Family Income, 1998–2002

	Liberal	Moderate	Conservative
Total Family Income:			
Under $14,999	32.0%	38.0%	30.0%
$15,000–$29,999	27.9%	41.4%	30.7%
$30,000–$59,999	27.4%	37.9%	34.8%
$60,000–$89,999	25.8%	36.8%	37.4%
Over $90,000	26.7%	30.8%	42.5%

TABLE 1.3

Political Perspectives: 1974, 1988, 2002

	Liberal	Moderate	Conservative
1974	30.6	40.0	29.5
1988	28.1	36.3	35.6
2002	26.1	39.2	34.6

Like conservatives and liberals, radicals have come to accept a "mixed" economy that contains both public and private elements. In terms of government involvement, they may prefer more public ownership of industry and services than do the other two groups, but they have seen in the experience of European socialist governments that public ownership does not guarantee either an equal distribution of power or a higher standard of living for workers. Some argue that ownership is irrelevant; what matters is who is in control. For example, U.S. corporations are "owned" by stockholders, many of whom are elderly women, but are controlled by a small group of mostly male managers.

Radicals would prefer an economic system in which workers have control over the conditions of their work; in which goods are produced for genuine need and not to satisfy whims created by advertising; in which money is not the measure of worth; and in which basic rights, such as medical care and housing, are not reduced to commodity status and sold in the marketplace to the highest bidder. Some radicals support the development of a welfare state in which government organizes the provision of medical care, housing, and other social welfare benefits to all citizens.

The conservative economic perspective is profoundly suspicious of, but not entirely unsympathetic to, social welfare programs. Reid observes that "the 'new conservatives' do not deny that government has responsibility for society, they simply want that responsibility carried out in a particular way."[25] That conservatives are not insensitive to social welfare is what George W. Bush meant when, as a 2000 presidential candidate, he used the term *compassionate conservatism.* Harris has written that "it is a major failing of [conservatives] that more thought has not been given to the problem of public welfare and benevolence." Harris summarizes the basic principles of the conservative economic perspective on social welfare this way:

1. The needy do not have a "right" to assistance, but those who are able have a moral duty to be benevolent, "which, within certain limits, can be enforced by the state."
2. Social welfare programs should be designed to make use of the power of incentive: "It has been an assumption of capitalism since the time of Adam Smith that self-interest is a powerful motivating factor in human behavior. . . . In other words, we should use the natural motivating factors in human beings for moral ends."
3. "Finally, the advocate of the conservative welfare state will be suspicious of government programs to create jobs, remedy social ills, and care for the sick and the old. . . . The creation of new wealth and new jobs is the best way to alleviate poverty. Furthermore, governmental make-work programs can never be an adequate foundation for human dignity."[26]

Based on these principles, Harris argues that private retirement programs that invest contributions are preferable to government programs that immediately pay out contributions as benefits; a negative income tax would be preferable to the current welfare system; welfare benefits should be designed to increase incentive to work; and small, regional, private health programs such as health maintenance organizations (HMOs) are preferable to a large, centralized national health insurance program.

Many of today's conservatives find the voucher system a particularly appealing way to deal with poverty. Such a system works within the existing market economy. Vouchers are government certificates issued to people to use instead of money to pay for specific goods and services such as housing and education. (Food stamps are a good example.) Government plays a role in financing the vouchers and in making them available to people with low incomes, but essentially the vouchers turn their recipients into "powerful consumers," able to exercise free choice in the open market. Rather than having the government provide public housing or education to the needy, vouchers enable low-income individuals to purchase such goods and services directly from private organizations or businesses.[27]

The liberal economic perspective generally prefers governmental welfare programs to private programs. One reason is that although private welfare programs may be preferable to government programs, as the conservatives argue, history has demonstrated that private charity is simply unable to deal with the massive problems of a modern industrial society. When the Great Depression began in 1929, the private relief organizations were overwhelmed within a few months. The government took over welfare programs not because it wanted to but because it had to. A second argument is that welfare programs are good for the economy. The taxes that are taken from the wealthy come from idle funds (such as bank accounts, real estate, and jewelry), which are not being spent and are therefore not contributing to national income. When they are given out in the form of welfare benefits, they are immediately spent and thus contribute to national income. Finally, liberals argue that governmental welfare programs have grown in response to increasing societal standards of health, nutrition, and security. Samuelson writes:

> Society now rules that children shall not have rickets and bowed legs for life because of the bad luck or weakness of their parents. That poor people shall not die young because of insufficient money for operations and needed care. That the old shall be able to live out their years with some minimum of income.[28]

These increasing standards require programs beyond the capacity of private charity. They can be met only by the government.

A study by Sirgo and Eisenman examined the perceptions of governmental fairness by liberals and conservatives. It is interesting that both groups perceived government as basically unfair. However, the ways in which the groups perceived the unfairness were surprisingly predictable. The authors found that "liberals see government as favoring economic elites (including business, corporations, and the wealthy), whereas conservatives see government as favoring minorities such as black people and the poor."[29]

Table 1.4 summarizes various conservative, liberal, and radical perspectives.

Value Systems

Underlying all of the differences among liberals, radicals, and conservatives that we have discussed are basically different, although occasionally overlapping, value systems. Values are based on what we find desirable; they are stated in terms of right or wrong, good or bad, beautiful or ugly, pleasant or unpleasant, appropriate or inappropriate. The analysis of American value systems we draw on here was developed by Alan Keith-Lucas.[30] It is a bit old, dating from 1972, but we think it remains the best discussion of values in relation to social welfare that has been written.

TABLE 1.4

Comparison of Conservative, Liberal, and Radical Perspectives

Attitudes Toward	Conservative	Liberal	Radical
Change	Change is generally not desirable; it is better to keep things as they are.	Change is generally good; it brings progress. Moderate change is best.	Change is a good thing, especially if it means a fundamental change in the system.
Human Nature	People are essentially selfish; they need to be controlled.	People are basically good; they need structure to reinforce good impulses.	People are basically good; they can be corrupted by institutions.
Individual Behavior	Individuals have free will; they are responsible for their own lives and problems.	Individuals are not entirely autonomous or self-governing; environment plays a part in problems people face.	Individual behavior is strongly influenced by social and economic structures.
Family	The traditional family is the basic unit of society; it should not face government interference.	The family is changing; it needs social and government supports.	The traditional family is oppressive; the changing family needs government supports.
Society	Society is inherently fair, it functions well on its own, and it is a system of interrelated parts.	Society needs regulation to ensure fair competition between various interests.	Society contains inequalities, conflict between those with power and those without, and thus it needs changing.
Roles of the Government and the Economic System	A free-market economy is the best way to ensure prosperity and fulfillment of individual needs; the government role is to support, not regulate, the market.	A free-market economy needs regulation by government to ensure fairness; government programs are necessary to help meet basic human needs.	A market economy is exploitative and inherently unfair; alternatives include mixed public/private economy and a socialist system.

The value system that is the basis of conservative thinking in the United States is referred to by Keith-Lucas as the *capitalist–puritan value system,* or CP for short. He summarizes the basic assumptions of the CP value system as follows:

1. People are responsible for their own success or failure.
2. Human nature is basically evil but can be overcome by an act of will.
3. A person's primary purpose is the acquisition of material prosperity, which is achieved through hard work.

4. The primary purpose of society is to maintain law and order so that this acquisition is possible.
5. The unsuccessful or deviant person is not deserving of help, although efforts should be made, up to a point, to rehabilitate or spur the person to greater efforts on his or her own behalf.
6. The primary incentives to change are to be found in economic or physical rewards and punishments.

Keith-Lucas refers to the value system that is generally characteristic of liberals in America as the *humanist–positivist–utopian value system,* or HPU for short. He summarizes the HPU value system as follows:

1. The primary purpose of society is to fulfill people's material and emotional needs.
2. If people's needs were fulfilled, then they would attain a state that is variously described, according to the vocabulary used by the specific HPU system, as that of goodness, maturity, adjustment, or productivity, in which most individual and social problems would be solved.
3. What hampers people from attaining this state is the impact of external circumstances that are not generally under people's individual control. Various HPU systems cite lack of education, economic circumstance, childhood relationships, and social environment.

Franklin Roosevelt, a liberal Democrat, was responsible for the Social Security Act, which created the framework for the social welfare system in the United States.

4. These circumstances are subject to manipulation by those who possess sufficient technical and scientific knowledge and who use, in general, what is known as the "scientific method."
5. Consequently, individuals and society are ultimately perfectible.

Keith-Lucas identifies a third value system that he says is "behind, and yet parallel with these two systems." He calls this the *Judeo-Christian* tradition. Both liberals and conservatives accept parts of this value system, although they may interpret their meanings in very different ways. Keith-Lucas summarizes the basic assumptions of the Judeo-Christian tradition as follows:

1. People are created beings; one of their major problems is the fact that they act as if they were not and try to be autonomous.
2. People are fallible, but at the same time capable of acts of great courage or unselfishness.
3. The difference between individuals in terms of good and bad is insignificant compared with the standard demanded by their creator; as a consequence, a person cannot judge others in such terms.
4. People's greatest good lies in terms of their relationships with others and with their creator.
5. People are capable of choice, in the "active and willing" sense, but may need help in making this choice.
6. Love is always the ultimate victor over force.

It is apparent that the conservative, capitalist–puritan value system will not lead to enthusiastic support of social welfare efforts. As Keith-Lucas has said, "If man is totally responsible for his own actions, if he can better his condition by an act of will, if he can be induced to change by punishment or reward, then helping becomes a simple matter of us arranging the appropriate rewards and punishments. There is no room for relationship, or concern for another, except in a highly condescending and judgmental way."[31] It is this value system that is behind work requirements for the receipt of welfare, even if the work is meaningless; prosecution and jailing of parents who neglect their children; jail as the solution to all crime, regardless of the age or circumstance of the offender; and the general attitude of making the receipt of aid as unpleasant as possible to ensure that "only those who really need it will be willing to apply."

The liberal, humanist–positivist–utopian value system is far more conducive to the support of social welfare efforts. Under this way of thinking, people are not perceived as being totally responsible for their problems, so they are not totally responsible for the solutions. People are responsible for helping each other, and, given enough time and resources, all problems are solvable. Therefore, society can and should help inadequate parents become good parents, provide poor people with the means necessary for a comfortable life, and help criminals become productive citizens.

It should be noted that Keith-Lucas does not think that the CP value system is all bad or the HPU all good, as might easily be inferred from the brief descriptions given earlier. In their extreme form, both can have negative consequences, which can be mitigated by the Judeo-Christian value system that undergirds them. The CP system can lead to a harsh and callous approach to social welfare needs that should be softened by the Judeo-Christian tenet that all people fall short of the standard expected of them, as well as by its emphasis on love as a virtue. Keith-Lucas criticizes the HPU system as failing to recognize that in the final analysis, it is the person in trouble who must bear the major responsibility for his or her own betterment.

Political Perspectives in the Real World

Like many academic constructs, political perspectives are "ideal types"—pure forms—that rarely, if ever, match the realities of the day-to-day world. People's perspectives generally tend to lean toward conservatism, liberalism, radicalism, or ultraconservatism, but generally contain any number of inconsistent elements. Ginsberg gives as examples:

> Robert Dole (the 1996 Republican candidate for president) considers himself a political conservative, even though he has long been an ardent supporter of the food stamp program, a program some conservatives would call "liberal." Now retired from the Senate, Dole represented Kansas, which is one of the largest grain and other food producing states. Therefore, many of Dole's constituents benefitted from the food stamp program. Dole may consider food stamps an exception to his conservatism or he may rationalize the program as fitting with his particular approach to conservatism. . . . Another example is Pat Buchanan, who is considered a "conservative" political commentator and ran as a conservative candidate during the 1996 Republican primaries. But Buchanan told a group of people in New Hampshire in early 1996 that he wanted to eliminate the earnings test so social security recipients could earn and retain more of their social security benefits, even though conservatives have tended to be less than enthusiastic supporters of social security. Although he said that as president he would examine the social security system, he pledged he would not cut any money from the benefits of people who were currently retired.[32]

In recent years there have been attempts to develop categories of political perspectives that reflect reality more closely than do the old categories of liberal, conservative, and so on. Some people have revived the nineteenth-century categories of populist and progressive. According to journalist Michael Lind, the new progressives, a group he labels the "moderate middle,"

> tend to be old-fashioned Eisenhower and Rockefeller Republicans alienated by the supply-siders and religious right activists who, since the 1970s, have taken over the G.O.P. The moderate middle also includes neoliberal New Democrats based in the suburbs and successful in the private sector. The ranks of the moderate middle are heavy with managers and professionals with advanced degrees. They tend to combine liberal views on social issues like abortion and gay rights with concern about excess government spending on welfare and middle-class entitlements."

In other words, the progressives take a liberal stance on social issues and a conservative stance on economic issues. The new populists, a group Lind calls the "radical center,"

> consist largely of alienated Democrats, who broke away from the New Deal coalition to vote for George Wallace in 1968, Nixon in 1972, and then, in 1980, for Ronald Reagan. These former Wallace–Reagan Democrats tend to be white, blue-collar, high-school educated, and concentrated in the industrial Middle West, the South and the West. They are liberal, even radical in matters of economics, but conservative in morals and mores."[33]

An ambitious attempt to describe the modern political landscape is a large survey research project titled the Post-Modernity Project run by sociologists James Davison Hunter and Carl Bowman. These researchers conducted lengthy face-to-face interviews with a random sample of more than 2,000 people and did a cluster analysis of the results. This analysis identified six significantly different political groups, which Hunter and Bowman label traditionalists, neotraditionalists, conventionalists, communitarians, pragmatists, and permissivists. Although these groups were found to differ along several dimensions (age, race, political involvement, religion, etc.), they appear to reflect pretty well the characteristics we have identified as conservative and liberal political ideology. The traditionalists, neotraditionalists, and conventionalists reflect a conservative to moderate stance. Communitarians, pragmatists, and permissivists tend toward the liberal end of the spectrum.[34]

Although we recognize that the reality of the political landscape is more complicated than our conservative/liberal/radical typology, we believe that the typology is still a useful analytic tool. Even if *people* cannot be classified as purely liberal, conservative, and so forth, their ideas can be. Most people have a relatively consistent ideology toward social welfare issues, and this ideology generally follows fairly closely the attributes we have outlined.

The Authors' Perspective

At one time it was thought that social scientists could be value-free and therefore could write completely objective papers and texts. It is now generally agreed that this is not possible; no matter how hard authors try, their own social attitudes are bound to color their work. Therefore, we feel it is important that the reader know the authors' perspective before proceeding with this text.

We are both social workers and reflect the generally liberal bias of our profession. One of us finds merit in many tenets of radicalism as well. We both vote Democratic, favor most welfare legislation, believe in social and racial equality for all men and women, and favor social action to further these ends. However, we recognize that there is also value in many conservative ideas. We believe that individuals, when possible, should take primary responsibility for the solution of their own problems; we believe that there is fulfillment in meaningful work; we believe that the family, in both its traditional and newer forms, is a strong source of support for individuals; and we recognize that the economic consequences of welfare programs need to be carefully thought out before the programs are enacted.

It is not accidental that most social workers proceed from a liberal perspective. It is partly a matter of pragmatism—in other words, of what works. The conservative perspective leads to a pessimistic view of both social welfare problems and the potential for their solution. If people are viewed as autonomous, if they are totally in control of their own fate and can change it by a simple act of will, if society is fair and change will most likely make it worse, if government is to be feared and governmental programs viewed as harmful to the economy, what is the use of trying to solve social welfare problems? Many conservatives agree with Thomas Sowell that there are no solutions, only trade-offs.[35] On the other hand, if we view people as being basically good and their problems as at least partially the result of factors they cannot control, and if we believe that there are ways of structuring society that will make it more just and that government can be a force for good, then the opportunities for constructive social intervention are immense.

Social attitudes are neither right nor wrong; they just are. As a matter of practicality, however, the liberal perspective simply works better for those of us who are concerned with helping individuals and society solve problems.

Visit **www.researchnavigator.com** to research these important concepts from the chapter:

Conservatism
Liberalism
Minimum wage
Poverty
Public assistance
Radicalism

Web Sites on Political Perspectives

Alphabetical List of Political Links <www1.mhv.net/~btuchman/links.html>: This is an alphabetized listing of over 700 web sites devoted to political topics. The list tends to be slanted toward the Democratic Party and includes the web sites of numerous local Democratic organizations while including very few Republican organizations.

The CATO Institute <www.cato.org>: This web page includes news updates, copies of articles, speeches, and so on, all from the perspective of this conservative group.

Democratic Party Online <www.democrats.org/index.html>: The official web page of the Democratic Party. Includes news releases, speeches, information on becoming involved in the political process, and information on numerous other partisan matters.

Libertarian Party <www.lp.org>: News and views from the conservative Libertarian Party. Includes philosophy and practice, membership information, current activities, information by state, directories and lists, official documents, history, news, and announcements.

The Republican National Committee—Mainstreet <www.rnc.org>: The official web page of the Republican Party, including similar information as the Democrats' site.

Presidential Libraries

There are a number of presidential libraries, and all have web sites. These sites give complete descriptions of the libraries, including their collections, public displays, researcher information, directions, and so on. These libraries are great places to find primary data on social welfare activities of liberal and conservative presidential administrations. Some of the major libraries are the following:

Franklin D. Roosevelt Library and Museum <www. fdrlibrary.marist.edu>

John F. Kennedy Library and Museum <www.jfklibrary.org>

Dwight D. Eisenhower Library and Museum <eisenhower.archives.gov>

Richard Nixon Library and Birthplace <www.NixonFoundation.org>

Lyndon B. Johnson Library and Museum <www. lbjlib.utexas.edu>

Herbert Hoover Presidential Library and Museum <hoover.archives.gov>

Gerald R. Ford Library and Museum <www.ford.utexas.edu>

Endnotes

1. Frank Beasley, Richard A. Chapman, and Michael Sheehan, *Elements in Political Science* (Edinburgh, Scotland: Edinburgh University Press, 1999), 149.
2. Alice H. Eagly and Shelly Chaiken, "Attitude Structure and Function," in Daniel T. Gilbert, Susan T. Fiske, and Gardner Lindzey, eds., *The Handbook of Social Psychology,* 4th ed., vol. 2 (Boston: McGraw-Hill, 1998), 269.
3. Fred N. Kerlinger, *Liberalism and Conservatism: The Nature and Structure of Social Attitudes* (Hillsdale, NJ: Lawrence Erlbaum, 1984), 1.
4. Kenneth Dolbeare, *American Political Thought,* 3rd ed. (Chatham, NJ: Chatham House, 1996), 7.
5. Kerlinger, *Liberalism and Conservatism,* 11.
6. Thomas Sowell, *Compassion versus Guilt and Other Essays* (New York: William Morrow, 1987), 17.
7. Irving Kristol, "Human Nature and Social Reform," in Mark Gerson, ed., *The Essential Neoconservative Reader* (Reading, MA: Addison-Wesley, 1996), 209–212.
8. Erik Erikson, *Childhood and Society* (New York: Norton, 1963); Barney Glaser and Anselm Strauss, *Status Passage* (Chicago: Aldine, 1971); Daniel Levinson, *The Seasons of a Man's Life* (New York: Alfred A. Knopf, 1978).
9. John B. Watson, *Psychology from the Standpoint of the Behaviorist* (Philadelphia: J. B. Lippincott, 1919); B. F. Skinner, *The Behavior of Organisms* (New York: Appleton Century Crofts, 1938).
10. Sowell, *Compassion versus Guilt,* 35–36.
11. George Gilder, "The Nature of Poverty," in A. Serow, W. Shannon, and E. Ladd, eds., *The American Policy Reader* (New York: Norton, 1990), 662–663.
12. Kingsley Davis and Wilbert Moore, "Some Principles of Stratification," *American Sociological Review 10* (April 1945), 242–249.
13. Paul Krugman, *The Great Unraveling: Losing Our Way in the New Century* (New York: W. W. Norton, 2003); Robert Dahl, *Who Governs?* (New Haven, CT: Yale University Press, 1961).
14. This analysis is advanced by sociologists such as Robert Lynd and Helen Lynd, in *Middletown in Transition* (New York: Harcourt Brace, 1937); Floyd Hunter, in *Community Power Structure* (Chapel Hill: University of North Carolina Press, 1953); and C. Wright Mills, in *The Power Elite* (New York: Oxford University Press, 1956); and by psychologists such as G. William Domhoff, in *Who Rules America?* (Englewood Cliffs, NJ: Prentice Hall, 1967).
15. Leon Ginsberg, *Conservative Social Welfare Policy: A Description and Analysis* (Chicago: Nelson-Hall, 1998), 93–94.
16. Harry Browne, "I Want You to Be Free," Photocopy, n.p., n.d.
17. Socialist Party USA, "Who We Are," http://sp-usa.org.
18. Paul A. Samuelson and William D. Nordhaus, *Microeconomics,* 15th ed. (New York: McGraw-Hill, 1995), 279.
19. Adam Smith, *The Wealth of Nations,* 5th ed., Edwin Connan, ed. (London: Methuen, 1930).
20. Milton Friedman and Rose Friedman, *Free to Choose: A Personal Statement* (New York: Harcourt Brace Jovanovich, 1980), 1–2.
21. Friedman and Friedman, *Free to Choose,* 1–2.
22. Ronald M. Glassman, *Caring Capitalism: A New Middle-Class Base for the Welfare State* (New York: St. Martins Press, 2000), pp. 79–81.
23. Edward Berkowitz and Kim McQuaid, *Creating the Welfare State* (New York: Praeger, 1980), 33–36.
24. John Maynard Keynes, "General Theory of Employment, Interest, and Money," in Charles W. Needy, ed., *Classics of Economics* (Oak Park, IL: Moore, 1980), 324–338.
25. P. Nelson Reid, "Four Conservative Ideas," *Arete 8* (Summer 1983), 40.
26. Charles E. Harris Jr., "Capitalism and Social Justice," *The Intercollegiate Review 20* (Spring/Summer 1984), 35–49.
27. Stuart M. Butler and Anna Kondratas, *Out of the Poverty Trap* (New York: Free Press, 1987), 77–79.
28. Paul A. Samuelson, *Economics,* 11th ed. (New York: McGraw-Hill, 1980), 147.
29. Henry B. Sirgo and Russell Eisenman, "Perceptions of Government Fairness by Liberals and Conservatives," *Psychological Reports 67* (December 1990), 1331–1334.

30. From Alan Keith-Lucas, *Giving and Taking Help* (Chapel Hill: University of North Carolina Press, 1972), 138–142. Reprinted with permission.
31. From Alan Keith-Lucas, *Giving and Taking Help* (Chapel Hill: University of North Carolina Press, 1972), 142. Reprinted with permission.
32. Leon Ginsberg, *Conservative Social Welfare Policy,* 42.
33. Michael Lind, "The Radical Center or the Moderate Middle?," *New York Times Magazine* (3 December 1995), 72.
34. James Davison Hunter and Carl Bowman, *The State of Disunion: 1996 Survey of American Political Culture* (Ivy, VA: In Medias Res Educational Foundation, 1996).
35. Sowell, *Compassion versus Guilt,* 21–24.

CHAPTER

2

Social Welfare: Basic Concepts

The four friends were having lunch together at the Rotary Club, and the conversation turned to the previous week's guest speaker, a United Way official who had spoken on the subject of social welfare. "He had some good things to say," said Ron, an energetic retired banker. "But, you know, I really resented his saying that Social Security and Medicare are social welfare benefits. They're insurance, not welfare, and after all the money deducted from my paychecks over the years for them, I sure don't want anyone saying I'm on welfare." "Yeah," said William, the local Ford dealer, "and what did he mean when he referred to the Family Guidance Clinic as a social welfare agency? My wife used to work there, and they don't give away money or food, and most people who go there pay for counseling. One of my salespeople went there for marriage counseling, and they charged her seventy-five dollars an hour." "I'll tell you what social welfare is," said Hank, a retired Marine lieutenant colonel. "Welfare is freebies given to people who are too lazy to work and to people who have so many illegitimate kids that they can't afford to work." "Garbage!" said Hal, the youngest member of the group, whose generally disagreeable nature was widely suspected to be the result of his having taken too many drugs while in college. "I'll tell you what welfare is. Welfare is government handouts to people who are already rich, like the phone company or big farmers."

The preceding discussion illustrates various popular conceptions about what is meant by the term *social welfare*. The first is the belief that social welfare involves a stigma; in other words, that it is shameful and involves only low-status people. Thus, Hank believes that social welfare involves only the able-bodied unemployed and mothers of illegitimate children (two very low-status groups); and Ron was offended by the reference to benefits he receives as being social welfare, because as a retired banker he is not a low-status person. The second conception is that social welfare involves only the provision of material goods (such as money or food) or perhaps counseling to help people obtain these goods on their own. Thus, William took issue with the speaker's characterization of a family guidance agency as a social welfare service. The third conception is that social welfare is anything given away (generally by the government) for free or below market value. Thus, Ron does not feel that his Social Security benefits are social welfare, because he believes he has paid for them. William does not view a family guidance clinic as a social welfare agency, because many clients pay for the service they receive. Hal argues that rich people are the major recipients of social welfare benefits.

The main idea with which we begin this chapter is that social welfare is a difficult concept to define. It is difficult and confusing, and it is debated not only among laypeople like our group of Rotarians but also among social welfare professionals. As Gilbert and Terrell observe, "Students entering the field of social welfare policy quickly come to feel somewhat like Alice at the Queen's croquet party. They confront a puzzling and complex landscape, with changing features and hazy boundaries."[1] We believe this haziness in our understanding of the concept of social welfare is the result of two major factors. The first is that social welfare does carry a stigma. Therefore, people do not want to include in their definition of social welfare benefits and services that they or people they care about receive. The second problem is that most definitions are descriptive. They try to capture what social welfare "looks like"; that is, to delineate types of agencies, methods of finance, and types and numbers of people served. These definitions generally ignore the *function* of social welfare; in other words, why we provide the services described. In our attempt to define the concept of social welfare, we begin with a discussion of stigma and then present a brief review of descriptive definitions. Next we move to what we consider to be the critical element in the concept of social welfare—its function in society. We then present a categorization of major social welfare services; and finally we discuss perspectives on the function of, and motivation for, social welfare.

Stigma and Social Welfare

The term *stigma* as used by sociologists refers to an aspect of a person's life that ruins his or her identity. The stigmatized individual is a person whose social identity, or membership in some social category, calls into question his or her full humanity—the person is devalued, spoiled, or flawed in the eyes of others and, as a consequence, is denied full social acceptance.[2] There is no doubt that in U.S. society considerable stigma attaches to the receipt of social welfare services. The British sociologist Paul Spicker asserts that "a stigma marks the recipient of welfare, damages his reputation, and undermines his dignity."[3] Some sociologists have argued that stigma is such an important concept that it is the central issue in the study of social welfare.[4] Blau contends that welfare policy consciously "includes shaming recipients by referring to them as lazy and irresponsible, stigmatizing benefits as charity, a handout, or the dole . . . and in general denying the poor any dignified treatment."[5] Mills asserts that *welfare* is a stigmatized term because it has been associated by conservatives with concepts of dependence, addiction, illegitimacy, and promiscuity.[6]

Why is social welfare a "moral category," and why are recipients stigmatized in our society? The first thing to note is that most people who have written about this subject tend to view social welfare as synonymous with poverty and the receipt of financial or material assistance, as we noted earlier. Matza asserts that poverty itself is considered disreputable, but that to be poor and to receive financial assistance is even more disreputable.[7] Sociologists relate this attitude to two factors—the value placed on work in our society and the norm of reciprocity. Spicker argues that the amount of stigma attached to welfare benefits is directly related to how closely the benefits can be connected to contributions from work: "Contribution is measured largely by work status. Pensioners are respectable; they have paid their dues by working most of their lives. Student [aid recipients] are accepted, perhaps with some reservations, because they are going to contribute in the future."[8] Recipients of benefits under the old Aid to Families with Dependent Children (AFDC) program were viewed as unacceptable because the benefits were not tied to work. The program that replaced AFDC, Temporary Assistance to Needy Families (TANF), closely ties benefits to work and/or job training, theoretically reducing the stigma of receiving benefits under the program.

A related but more general explanation of the stigma attached to social welfare benefits involves the norm of reciprocity: It is considered in our society to be a general obligation to make some return for the things received. Exchange, the anthropologist Claude Lévi-Strauss writes, "provides the means of binding men together."[9] Because the recipient of welfare benefits is seen as unable to offer anything in return for those benefits, he or she violates this reciprocity norm and is stigmatized as a result.

Economists Timothy Beasley and Stephen Coates propose two theories to explain welfare stigma. The first they label (for some reason known only to economists) as statistical discrimination. This theory observes that society values certain individual characteristics such as self-reliance and a willingness to work hard. Welfare recipients are regarded negatively because they are perceived as possessing fewer of these desirable characteristics. Beasley and Coates label the other theory the taxpayer resentment theory of welfare stigma. This theory is based on the propositional statement that taxpayers view many welfare recipients as undeserving. Welfare costs money, which must be paid by taxpayers; taxpayers don't like paying taxes; therefore, taxpayers resent welfare recipients, and this resentment results in the stigmatization of recipients.[10]

These explanations may be adequate to explain why there is a stigma attached to the receipt of financial and material assistance, but what of other types of social welfare services? As we discuss later in this chapter, many social welfare services do not involve material assistance, such as child welfare services, child guidance, marriage and family counseling, drug and alcohol services, employee assistance programs, and others. Do these services also involve a stigma? We argue that they do, although not to as great an extent as material assistance. The explanation for the stigma attached to these services is related to what Wilensky and Lebeaux identify as one of the primary components of American culture, the concept of individualism.[11]

Wilensky and Lebeaux argue that of central importance to U.S. society, which they characterize as the "culture of capitalism," is its great emphasis on the rational, acquisitive, self-interested individual. They explain individualism as two sets of beliefs, one set about what *should be* and another set about what *is.*

> Large and influential segments of the American people (not just businessmen) believe strongly that
>
> 1. The individual should strive to be successful in competition with others, under the rules of the game.
> 2. These rules involve "fair play": (a) everyone should start with equal opportunity, and (b) no one should take unfair advantage through force, fraud, or "pull."
> 3. The test of reward should be ability (especially ability to contribute to the productive and other purposes of the enterprise). There should be unequal reward for unequal talents and unequal contributions.
>
> Americans also believe strongly that
>
> 1. Those who work hard and have the ability will be rewarded with success. (Success is a tangible package that mainly includes income and wealth, possessions, occupational prestige, and power—along with the style of life those permit.)
> 2. Success is the reward also of virtue; virtue will bring success. Failure (if it is not a temporary way-station to success) is sin and shows lack of virtue.
> 3. When the lazy, incompetent, and unvirtuous attain success it is purely a matter of luck; it could happen to anybody. Besides, it does not happen too often.[12]

The upshot of the idea of individualism is that success and failure are directly attributable to the individual. He or she gets all the credit as well as all the blame. Individualism has strong moral overtones. Those who achieve at high levels are, by definition, virtuous; those who do not are at least incompetent and perhaps even lazy and immoral. Although Wilensky and Lebeaux are speaking mainly of economic success, the idea is generalizable to noneconomic areas of life as well. Individuals are considered to be totally responsible for the success or failure of their children, their career, their marriage, and their mental health. When something goes wrong with one of these, such as when a couple's marriage begins to crumble, society and the individuals affected tend to feel it is a personal failure and perhaps an indication of some moral defect. Social workers in family guidance settings often hear statements such as the following:

> Ever since Bill and I separated, I feel like such a failure. I need to look for a better job, but every time I hear about an opening I'm overwhelmed by the feeling that no one would want to hire a woman who can't even keep a marriage together. I guess I'm just not worth very much.

The fact that stigma is attached to social welfare complicates any discussion of the concept. People do not want to be associated with a stigmatized entity and therefore tend to define benefits and programs with which they are personally involved as outside the boundaries of social welfare. Therefore, Grandma's Supplemental Security Income grant is not social welfare, it is a "pension"; Uncle Ed's vocational rehabilitation program is not social welfare, it is "career guidance"; Cousin Bob's family, who are receiving help with family problems that affect Bob's school performance, are not receiving social welfare services from the school social worker but are being helped by a "visiting teacher." This is the main reason that descriptive definitions of social welfare rarely are satisfactory. In the following section we discuss two descriptive definitions and the problems with each one.

Descriptive Definitions of Social Welfare

Numerous authors have attempted to develop clear and adequate descriptive definitions of social welfare. All have fallen short of their goal because of the problem of arriving at a definition of *social welfare* that is both exclusive (fitting no other activity) and inclusive (encompassing every social welfare activity). As Macarov notes, "Definitional problems arise both because social welfare actually overlaps with the activities of many other institutions and because the activities of social welfare itself are so varied."[13]

The descriptive definitions that have been developed fall into two categories:

1. Social welfare defined as economic transfers outside the market system.
2. Social welfare defined as benefits and services to help people meet basic needs. Some restrict the definition to economic needs, and some include other areas of well-being such as physical and mental health.

Social Welfare as Nonmarket Economic Transfers

In a market economy such as the United States', the primary mode of economic activity is that when a person desires a good or a service, he or she pays for it at market value—the amount it is worth. An obvious feature of social welfare services is that many do not operate this way. People receiving Medicare get medical services for free, food stamp recipients do not pay cash for their groceries, and couples going to a United Way family guidance agency frequently pay much less than full cost for the services they receive. Some analysts have seized on this aspect of social welfare and use it as a basis of their definition. For example, Burns says,

> To an economist the most significant fact about social welfare as an institution is that it is a set of organizational arrangements which results in the production and distribution to consumers of economic output by methods, or on the basis of principles, which differ from those of the free economic market or prevailing under the family system.[14]

In a similar manner, Gilbert and Terrell speak of social welfare as "a benefit-allocation mechanism functioning outside the economic marketplace."[15]

This method of describing social welfare has two distinct advantages. The first is that it is conceptually clear and unambiguous. It is easy to separate social welfare services from other services. If someone pays full price for something, such as a shopping cart full of groceries, they are not involved with the social welfare system. If someone pays less than full value and buys some of the groceries with food stamps, that person is receiving social welfare.

The second advantage of this description of social welfare, one much touted by social workers (who are often political liberals), is that it includes many services to nonpoor, nonstigmatized people; thus it is viewed as reducing the stigma of welfare. Walz and Askerooth use this definition in an entertaining little book titled *The Upside Down Welfare State,* in which they say, "Somebody is getting something for nothing, but as usual, it's not the folks who had nothing in the beginning."[16] On the same theme, Abramovitz says,

> The social welfare system—direct public provision of cash and in-kind benefits to individuals and families, free or at below market cost—is popularly regarded as serving only poor people. However, the record shows that social welfare programs serving the middle and upper classes receive more government funding, pay higher benefits, and face fewer budget cuts than programs serving only poor people. . . . In 2000 the federal government spent $1,093 billion on the social welfare components of federal entitlement (mandatory) and discretionary outlays. . . . The overwhelming majority of these dollars, however, do not go to people who are poor. In 2000 the federal government spent $235.9 billion for means-tested public assistance programs that serve the poor but a much larger $793.9 billion on non-means-tested programs that do not use poverty or need as a criterion for receiving aid.[17]

This means of defining social welfare is extremely appealing because it emphasizes that the stigmatization of welfare recipients as people who get "something for nothing" is irrational; *many* people get "something for nothing," and in fact the nonpoor get much more than the poor. Conceptually, however, this approach is of limited value. Many social welfare programs do not involve economic transfers; or, if they do, the transfers are within the market system. For example, the recipients of services at a mental health clinic do not obtain anything of direct economic value and often pay market rates for the services they receive. Residents in a retirement home are generally considered to be recipients of social welfare services. However, not only do many residents pay the full cost of their care, but also many homes are run as for-profit businesses. Hence, this definition is not inclusive, because it does not cover all social welfare services. The second problem is that this definition is not exclusive; it includes many things that most people would not define as social welfare. Most people do not consider agricultural subsidies, loans to Chrysler Corporation, or FHA home loans to be social welfare programs. The second major class of definitions, to which we now turn, addresses this problem.

Social Welfare as Services to Meet Basic Needs

The philosopher Nicholas Rescher points out that the word *welfare* as currently used is derived from the original root meaning of "having a good trip or journey," thus conveying the idea of traveling smoothly on the road of life. However, Rescher argues, on reflection it becomes clear that welfare does not relate to all aspects of a smooth journey, but only to the basic requisites of a person's well-being in general, and it deals most prominently with health and economic adequacy. "This characterization—with its explicit reference to the basic—makes transparently clear one critical negative feature of welfare in its relationship to human well-being in general, namely, that welfare is a matter of 'well-being' not in its global totality but in its 'basic requisites,' its indispensable foundations."[18]

This approach to social welfare, which defines it as services designed to bring people's well-being up to some minimum level, is popular. Reid, writing in the *Encyclopedia of Social Work,* the standard reference source in the field, gives the following definition: "Social welfare [is] most often . . . defined in terms of organized activities, interventions, or some other element that suggests policy and programs to respond to recognized social problems or to improve the well-being of those at risk."[19] In his classic text on social welfare, Walter Friedlander gave the following definition:

> *Social welfare* is the organized system of social services and institutions, designed to aid individuals and groups to attain satisfying standards of life and health. It aims at personal and social relationships which permit individuals the development of their full capacities and the promotion of their well-being in harmony with the needs of the community.[20]

Martin and Zald say, "Our definition of social welfare is relatively exclusive: Social welfare attempts to enable people in need to attain a minimum level of social and personal functioning."[21] Finally, Wickenden defines social welfare as "including those laws, programs, benefits, and services which assure or strengthen provisions for meeting social needs recognized as basic to the well-being of the population and the better functioning of the social order."[22]

Rescher notes that social welfare is broader than physical and material welfare. It also deals with people's relations with one another and their personal and close-range interactions (family contacts, professional interactions, friendships, and other human relationships), which are key aspects of well-being. Therefore, this means of defining social welfare includes services such as recreation and socialization facilities and counseling. "Yet," Rescher cautions, "it is important to recognize that despite its diversified and multifaceted character, the issue of a man's welfare has a certain *minimality* about it. Welfare—in all its dimensions—deals only with the basic essentials."[23]

We agree that this definition—social welfare as laws, services, and programs designed to bring people's level of well-being up to some minimum—offers a fairly adequate description. By and large, it meets the tests of being inclusive and exclusive.

However, it offers no explanation of what we consider to be the most interesting part of the definition of social welfare—namely, what is the function of social welfare in society? We now turn to this question.

A Functional Definition of Social Welfare

Our preliminary functional definition of social welfare is as follows:

> For society to survive, individuals must function as interdependent units, each carrying out the full range of his or her roles and responsibilities. A society cannot survive if it contains too many individuals who cannot function in an interdependent manner (i.e., who are dependent). On the other hand, the social system cannot endure if it contains too many dysfunctional culture patterns and inefficient structures that inhibit people's ability to function in an interdependent manner.
>
> Up until the late nineteenth century, the basic institutions of family, economy, religion, and politics were able to handle the problem of dependency. When we say that these institutions handled the problem of dependency, we do not mean to imply that they handled it well. People were poor, sick, mentally ill, and starving to death. But dependent people were relatively few in number and were spread out, and the basic institutions were able to do enough so that the needs of dependent people did not constitute a threat to the stability of society. As society evolved from rural agricultural to urban industrial, these institutions lost the ability to handle dependency. When society recognized dependency as a threatening state of affairs, *social welfare as an institution began to emerge to handle dependence and to facilitate interdependence.*

At this point it is likely that this definition does not mean much to you because it contains a number of terms with which you are probably not familiar—terms such as *role* and *institution,* which are two concepts sociologists use to explain *social structure,* or how society works. The terms *dependence* and *interdependence* also may be unfamiliar. The following subsections explain all these terms.

Social Structure

When sociologists speak of *social structure,* they are referring to how individuals achieve identity (status and role) and fit into groups and organizations, and how these in turn fit into institutions, communities, and finally society. In order to understand our functional definition of social welfare, you need to understand some basic concepts of social structure, including status, role, and institution.

Status and Role. A *status* is simply a socially defined position in a group or society. Statuses include things such as being black, male, a social worker, a father, or a student. The most familiar statuses are related to gender, marital status, age, education, ethnic background, religion, and occupation. Obviously, any one person will occupy a large number of statuses, and many will change and evolve throughout a person's life span.

Each status, or set of statuses, has connected with it a *role,* which is a set of expectations and behaviors. Most statuses have multiple roles associated with them, and the

Most people associate social welfare with poor people. The popular stereotype is a single mother who is a member of a minority group. In reality most social welfare expenditures go for programs such as Social Security or Medicaid that mainly serve non-poor white people.

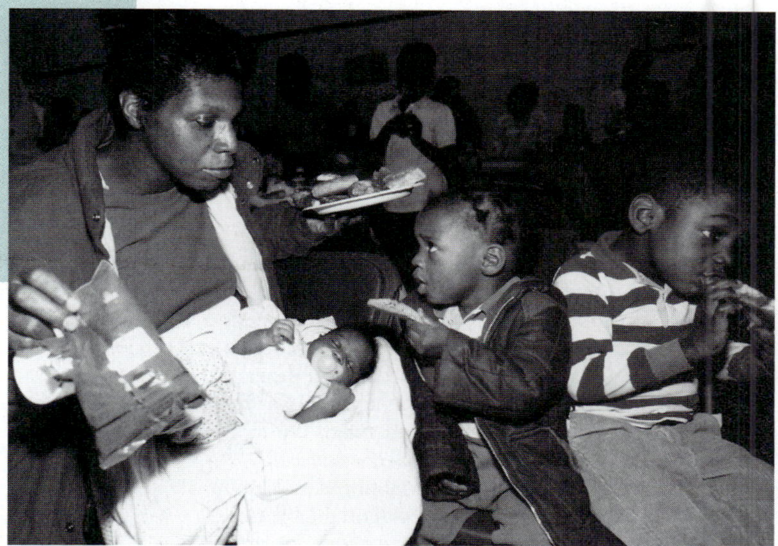

term for all the roles associated with a particular status is a *role set.* Roles associated with the status of parent, for example, generally include those of breadwinner, disciplinarian, household maintenance and repair person, and family business representative. The role set for a social worker teaching in a university includes, among other things, teaching classes, arranging for field placements, advising students, doing research, participating on university committees, and volunteering in community social agencies.

Social Work **Destinations**

Presidential Libraries

The progress of the social work profession and of social welfare policy is greatly influenced by the person occupying the presidency. During the administrations of liberal, progressive presidents such as Franklin Roosevelt, John F. Kennedy, and Lyndon Johnson, bold experiments in social policy have been implemented. During conservative administrations of presidents such as Herbert Hoover, Richard Nixon, and Ronald Reagan, social welfare policy has either been ignored or reversed. Social work students will find much material for study and reflection in presidential libraries.

There are currently ten presidential libraries. These are administered by the Office of Presidential Libraries, which is part of the National Archives and Records Administration (NARA), located in College Park, Maryland. These are not traditional lending libraries, but rather repositories for preserving and making available the papers, records, and other historical materials of U.S. presidents since Herbert Hoover. Each presidential library contains a museum and provides an active series of public programs. Also included in the presidential library system is the Nixon Presidential Materials Staff, which administers the Nixon presidential materials under the terms of the Presidential Recording and Materials Preservation Act. When a president leaves office, NARA establishes a presidential project until a new presidential library is built.

The current presidential libraries are:

George Bush Presidential Library and Museum
http://bushlibrary.tamu.edu
1000 George Bush Drive West
College Station, TX 77845

Jimmy Carter Library and Museum
http://jimmycarterlibrary.org
441 Freedom Parkway
Atlanta, GA 30307-1498

Dwight D. Eisenhower Library
www.eisenhower.utexas.edu
200 SE 4th Street
Abilene, KS 67410-2900

Gerald R. Ford Library and Museum
www.ford.utexas.edu
1000 Beal Avenue
Ann Arbor, MI 48109-2114

Herbert Hoover Presidential Library-Museum
http://hoover.archives.gov/
210 Parkside Drive
P.O. Box 488
West Branch, IA 52358-1488

Lyndon B. Johnson Library and Museum
www.lbjlib.utexas.edu
2313 Red River Street
Austin, TX 78705-5702

John F. Kennedy Library and Museum
www.jfklibrary.org
Columbia Point
Boston, MA 02125-3398

Nixon Presidential Materials Staff
www.archives.gov/nixon
National Archives at College Park
8601 Adelphi Road
College Park, MD 20740-6001

Ronald Reagan Presidential Library
www.reagan.utexas.edu
40 Presidential Drive
Simi Valley, CA 93065-0600

Franklin D. Roosevelt Presidential Library
www.fdrlibrary.marist.edu
4079 Albany Post Road
Hyde Park, New York 12538-1999

Harry S. Truman Presidential Library
www.trumanlibrary.org
500 West U.S. Highway 24
Independence, MO 64050-1798

People do not always fulfill roles in ways that meet with everyone's approval. The *role expectation* is the generally accepted way a role should be played, whereas *role performance* is the way a person actually plays a role. Role expectation of the status of mother generally includes being married and financially supporting the children in some way. When a woman gives birth out of wedlock and supports the child through a public welfare grant, people often perceive a gap between role expectation and role performance.

This description of the concept of role is highly simplified. There is a large area of sociology called *role theory* that studies roles in society. Sociologists in this area are interested in the roles that make up groups and organizations; how people assume roles and learn the roles associated with various statuses; and special problems such as role strain, role conflict, and roles and self-identity, as well as numerous other questions. For our purposes, however, it is sufficient to understand that a basic component of social structure (how society works) is the concept of status and role. People occupying various statuses have to appropriately carry out the roles associated with those statuses in order for society to function smoothly. For example, the status of parent has associated with it roles of providing financial support for children, providing nurturance and supervision, and providing appropriate discipline. If parents are unable to fulfill one or more of these roles (for example, if they do not support their children), they create a problem for society. We will return to this later. Now we need to deal with another component of social structure related to our functional definition of social welfare: social institutions.

Social Institutions. Sociologists and anthropologists have developed a list (actually several similar lists) of essential functions that must be performed if a society is to survive. To illustrate these functions, we ask you to imagine that you are a member of a group of the last two hundred surviving people on earth. Everyone else in the world has died of some strange disease, and you and your companions survived because you were on a cruise ship far out at sea. You have landed on a tropical island, and on taking inventory you discover you have all the basic resources necessary for survival (such as tools, books, and seeds) and all the basic skills needed (doctors, dentists, engineers, teachers, and farmers). The only thing you do not have is a society. You have no rules, laws, family structure (you are all single), or anything. Think about this—what functions will have to be accomplished in order for your group of two hundred individuals to remake and continue society? Your answer will probably, in some form, include the following:

- *Production–Distribution–Consumption.* How will you produce the many things needed for your group to survive? Will people grow their own food, or will certain people be given the status of farmer and its associated roles? If the tasks are divided up (sociologists call this "division of labor"), with some people being farmers, some builders, and so on, how will the fruits of their labor be divided up? Will the physicians be entitled to a larger share of what your society produces than the farmers, for example?
- *Population and Socialization.* What arrangements will be made for having children? And, once the children arrive, some provisions must be made to induct them into the knowledge systems, social values, roles, and behavior patterns of the group.

- *Social Integration.* Processes will have to be established by which individuals will come to value their membership in your society and to feel a responsibility for abiding by its rules. These processes are aimed at developing a level of solidarity and morale necessary for the ongoing life of the group.
- *Mutual Support.* It will be necessary for members of your group to feel some obligation to help one another out. Mutual support is necessary among members of any social group if individuals within the group are to grow, develop, and function comfortably and effectively as human beings.
- *Social Control and Social Order.* Arrangements will need to be made by which your society will attempt to ensure that its members behave in conformity with its generally accepted norms of social behavior.
- *Social Change.* Finally, if your group, like any group, is to survive, it must develop means to provide for orderly, lawful change in the ways in which the institutions of your society function and interrelate.

All societies, whether simple, as in the preceding example, or highly differentiated and complex, such as the United States, must perform these basic functions. How is this done? Sociologists explain that societies organize life into enduring patterns of statuses and roles that ensure that these functions are carried out. These patterns are called *social institutions.* Sociologist David Popenoe says that "institution" is one of "the most abstract concepts sociologists use." He goes on to define an *institution* as "a stable cluster of social structures that is organized to meet the basic needs of societies."[24] Lenski and Lenski say that "a social institution is essentially a system of social relationships and cultural elements that has developed in a society in response to some set of basic and persistent needs. These cultural elements are such things as rules, laws, customs, role definitions, and values that serve to regulate people's behavior and organize their activities in certain basic areas of life."[25] The basic needs of society referred to by these sociologists are, of course, the functions we listed above.

What are these vague and abstract things called social institutions? You may be surprised to learn that they are familiar and everyday things. One basic social institution is present in every society, no matter how simple—the family. There are three other institutions in all but the most primitive societies: government, the economy, and religion. As societies modernize, two other institutions develop. Education is one, and it is accepted by nearly all social theorists as a basic social institution in modern societies. Finally, many people, including the authors, now consider social welfare to be a basic institution in modern societies. Let's look at each of these institutions in more detail, with special emphasis on the social welfare institution.

Family and Kinship. The family is the most basic institution, and in simple societies it fulfills all necessary functions. In modern societies the family's main functions are population, socialization, and mutual support; its secondary functions include social integration and social order—social control. One of the decisions you will need to make in your island society is what kind of family you want to have. Will you want to establish the institution as it presently exists in the United States, with a nuclear family in which the husband and wife are almost entirely responsible for each other's emotional needs and for the care and upbringing of their children? Or will you want to establish something else, perhaps resembling an Israeli kibbutz, in which there is more shared responsibility for child rearing?

Government and Politics. Two of the earliest questions you will deal with in your island society are how decisions are going to be made and how the power to enforce these decisions is going to be exercised. These are the central questions of the political institution. The primary functions of the political institution are social control/social order and social change. Secondary functions are mutual support, social integration, and production–distribution–consumption.

Economics. A central principle in the study of economics is that of scarcity. That is, there are never enough goods and services available to satisfy 100 percent of everyone's needs and desires. Therefore, the economic institution develops to regulate the production, distribution, and consumption of goods and services. As Compton says, "a society must organize a system to [ensure] the production of enough goods and services for its own survival and must arrange for the distribution of the fruits of its production so that more production can take place."[26] In our island example, will each person be expected to produce as much as he or she is capable of and be entitled to receive an equal share of the total production (basically a socialist system)? Or will each person sell as much as he or she can produce for as much money as possible (basically a capitalist system)? If you choose the latter, you will then need to decide how to deal with people who, because of illness, injury, old age, or whatever, produce less than they need to survive.

Religion. The religious institution seeks to answer our questions about the meaning and purposes of life. The major functions of religious institutions are social integration and mutual support. Secondary but still very important functions are socialization, social control/social order, and social change.

Education. The primary function of the educational institution, that of passing along formal knowledge systems, is one part of socialization. Until the nineteenth century, the family generally carried out this function, with some help from the church. However, as knowledge rapidly expanded and there was a corresponding increase in the amount individuals had to master to function adequately in society, the ability of the family to fulfill this function deteriorated. At the beginning of the nineteenth century, the family was held responsible for passing along knowledge; by the end of the century, education was assigned to the schools—it had become institutionalized. As the twentieth century progressed, we saw an ever increasing number of functions assigned (often with considerable controversy) to the educational institution. In addition to traditional education, schools are often asked to pass along values and provide career counseling, vocational training, sex education, and general life skills training. And not only are schools expected to provide sex education, but also in some cases they are now under pressure to provide medical family planning services. Many people, mainly but not exclusively conservatives, think this is a bad trend and that the schools are serving functions that are the proper territory of the family and religion.

Dependence, Interdependence, and the Social Welfare Institution

You may already have observed that statuses and roles nearly always come in groups. The status and role of physician assumes that of patients, teacher assumes students, husband assumes wife, and parent assumes child. You may also have observed that roles occur within (and in fact they are one of the defining characteristics of) social institutions. The statuses and roles of parent and children occur within the institution of the family; citizen, voter, and taxpayer occur within government. Therefore, although we often speak of people as being independent, no one really is. It is common to hear statements such as, "My grandfather is eighty-six years old, but he is still completely independent." In actuality, unless he is a hermit, he is not independent. He depends on his wife and children and grandchildren, on the dentist, neighbors, police, and grocer—the list goes on and on. These people, in turn, depend on him. The proper term is *interdependent*, which, according to Atherton, means "carrying one's own load in a social situation in which other actors do the same."[27] In other words, an interdependent person adequately performs all the roles connected with a given status and has role partners who do the same.

Adequate societal functioning has two levels. One is that of individual role performance. For example, for society to function well, parents must fully discharge their roles. If they do not feed and supervise their children and the kids wander the streets searching for food or begging, we have a social problem. The other level is that of institutional performance: Social institutions must function well enough so that people are able to perform their individual roles. One role of parents is to financially support their children. However, if the economic institution does not function well enough for everyone to be employed (and it in fact does not), many people are not going to be able to fulfill this role. Another role of parents is to supervise, or arrange for the supervision of, their young children. If the economic and governmental institutions do not provide affordable, accessible day care for everyone who needs it (and in fact they do not), many people are not going to be able to fulfill this role. Individuals are interdependent with institutions as well as with one another for role performance.

When a person is unable to perform his or her roles in an interdependent manner, whether the problem is on the individual or the institutional level, we speak of the person as being *dependent*. To quote Atherton again,

> Dependent is intended to connote a state of being in which one is not able to participate as a social being in rewarding ways and, thus, is the proper opposite for interdependent. . . . The point is that, in all human societies and in all human actors, situations come about in which people are unable to perform their roles in ways that satisfy both themselves and the society. Quite obviously, dependency is only one of a whole series of problematical conditions which societies and actors face. It is, however, a very basic problem to the continued existence of the social system and the individual actor.
>
> Since dependency, deviant behavior, and social dysfunction constitute threats to society, such conditions must be kept in bounds if society is to survive. Some way must exist either to repair or to change the social system so that it is organized as well as it can be to fulfill the needs and requirements of its actors. There also must be some way of focusing on the problematical aspects of actors' behavior and life situations, assuring the actor satisfying role performance within the limits of social norms and offering corrective experiences for harmful forms of deviance and dependency.[28]

Social welfare is the institution in modern industrial society that functions to promote interdependence and to deal with the problem of dependence. Before industrialization this function was performed by the other basic social institutions, mainly by the family and religion. If a person was sick, elderly, out of work, or whatever, that person was generally cared for by his or her family (often extended) or was aided by the church. As industrialization progressed, two things happened that impaired the ability of these institutions to deal with dependency. The first was that the combination of urbanization, industrialization, immigration, and mobility caused some deterioration in these institutions. Fewer and fewer people lived close to their extended family, had lifelong ties to one church, or lived in an area with a strong sense of community and neighborly obligation. People came to be pretty much on their own. Many people who were sick, elderly, or out of work found themselves with no one to help them. The second factor was that along with industrialization, urbanization, and immigration came a massive increase in the risk of becoming dependent. A family living in the country in a house they built and owned themselves, with land for a garden, a few animals, and opportunities to hunt, fish, and gather, could weather a temporary period of misfortune. A family living in a city, working in a factory, buying food at a grocery store, and living in a tenement where rent was due weekly was only one paycheck away from destitution.

Radical theorists argue that the changes brought about by rapid industrialization were not accidental. They see a deliberate attempt on the part of employers and other members of the power structure to reorganize working-class life in order to ensure the survival of capitalism in the United States. As Ehrenreich notes,

> the reorganization of the working class involved the fragmentation of the labor process at the workplace and the radical isolation of worklife from home life and of workplace from home. In the process, indigenous networks of support and mutual aid were disrupted, and central aspects of working-class and immigrant cultures were destroyed and replaced by "mass culture," as defined by the individual, privatized consumption of commodities.[29]

This meant not only an increase in levels of dependency, but also a weakened working class—a working-class population that was unable to promote the kind of changes in the system that might have helped protect them against unemployment, industrial accidents, and other factors leading to dependency.

In a process similar to what occurred with education, social welfare began to emerge as an institution when it became apparent that the family and the church were unable to deal with the problem of dependency. For example, when the number of people needing food, shelter, and financial assistance because of unemployment became too great for churches to deal with, first private and then public welfare programs developed; when the number of orphans became so great as to be seen as a threat to social order, child welfare services evolved; and when more and more elderly were left with no family to care for them, services for the aged developed. The list could go on and on. Specific details of the emergence of various welfare services are provided in later chapters.

Dependency and Opportunity. As unmanaged dependency reaches a level at which social stability is threatened, one obvious social response to the problem is repression. This, in fact, is how societies have initially reacted to increasing dependency. The first responses to poverty were prison and the poorhouse; the first response to juvenile delinquency was to stiffen penalties for juvenile crime and to jail offenders; the first response to child abuse and neglect was to prosecute the parents and remove the children from the home and place them more or less permanently in orphanages. Charles Dickens eloquently illustrated this approach in *A Christmas Carol*, in the brief conversation between Ebenezer Scrooge and a man soliciting a charitable donation:

> "At this festive season of the year, Mr. Scrooge," said the gentleman, taking up a pen, "It is more than usually desirable that we should make some slight provision for the poor and destitute, who suffer greatly at the present time. Many thousands are in want of common necessaries; hundreds of thousands are in want of common comforts, sir."
>
> "Are there no prisons?" asked Scrooge.
>
> "Plenty of prisons," said the gentleman, laying down the pen again.
>
> "And the Union workhouses?" demanded Scrooge. "Are they still in operation?"
>
> "They are. Still," returned the gentleman, " I wish I could say they were not."
>
> "The Treadmill and the Poor Law are in full vigour, then?" said Scrooge.
>
> "Both very busy, sir."
>
> "Oh! I was afraid, from what you said at first, that something had occurred to stop them in their useful course," said Scrooge. "I'm very glad to hear it." [30]

When repressive measures are used as a response to dependency, it quickly becomes apparent that they do not work. As the Ghost of Christmas Present warns Scrooge:

> "This boy is Ignorance. This girl is Want. Beware them both and all of their degree, but most of all beware this boy, for on his brow I see that written which is Doom, unless the writing be erased. Deny it!" cried the Spirit, stretching out its hand towards the city. "Slander those who tell ye! Admit it for your factious purposes, and make it worse! And bide the end!"
>
> "Have they no refuge or resource?" cried Scrooge.
>
> "Are there no prisons?" said the Spirit, turning on him for the last time with his own words. "Are there no workhouses?"[31]

The repressive approach assumes that people become dependent due to bad decisions they have made, decisions that were under their conscious control. Experience quickly indicates, however, that the majority of dependent people are in their situation because of factors over which they have little or no control. Generally these factors are due to a lack of opportunity for education, for medical care, for job advancement, and for a legitimate means of attaining social status. A social welfare approach to social problems emerges when people begin to realize that the provision of opportunity, not the exercise of repression, is the only way to effectively manage dependency. Therefore, it is important to extend and clarify our definition of social welfare by expanding it to include the notion that social welfare is the institution in society that manages dependency *through the provision of opportunity.*

Institutional and Residual Conceptions of Social Welfare. In this chapter we have identified social welfare as the sixth major social institution, an institution that emerged in the nineteenth and twentieth centuries to deal with the problem of dependency when the other major institutions, mainly family and the church, were no longer able to deal with this problem. At this point we need to note that although most social workers and social scientists accept this conception of social welfare, it is not shared by everyone in our society.

Writing in the late 1950s, Wilensky and Lebeaux identified in U.S. society two opposing conceptions of social welfare, which they labeled *institutional* and *residual.* The description of social welfare in the preceding section represents a straight institutional view, which Wilensky and Lebeaux say

> implies no stigma, no emergency, no "abnormalcy" [on the part of those receiving services]: Social welfare becomes accepted as a proper, legitimate function of modern industrial society in helping individuals achieve self-fulfillment. The complexity of modern life is recognized. The inability of the individual to provide for himself, or to meet all his needs in family and work settings, is considered a "normal" condition; and the helping agencies achieve "regular" institutional status.[32]

In other words, the *institutional conception* recognizes that life in modern society is so complex that nearly everyone will need help achieving and maintaining interdependence and that the level of this help needs to be greater than the forms the basic institutions can provide. Families cannot provide 100 percent of the care needed by their children; the economy cannot provide 100 percent employment for the entire population at all times; and families and churches cannot care for all the elderly now that people are living many years past retirement and an ever increasing proportion of the population is elderly. Social welfare is viewed as a first-line, permanent social institution.

Wilensky and Lebeaux call the other view of social welfare present in American society the *residual conception.* This is

> based on the premise that there are two "natural" channels [institutions] through which an individual's needs are properly met: the family and the market economy. These are the preferred structures of supply. However, sometimes these institutions do not function adequately: family life is disrupted, depressions occur. Or sometimes the individual cannot make use of the normal channels because of old age or illness. In such cases, according to this idea, a third mechanism of need fulfillment is brought into play—the social welfare structure. This is conceived as a residual agency, attending primarily to emergency functions, and is expected to withdraw when the regular social structure—the family and the economic system—is again working properly. Because of its residual, temporary, substitute characteristic, social welfare thus conceived often carries the stigma of "dole" or "charity."[33]

In this conception, social welfare is not an institution but an emergency backup system. If the other institutions of society could be made to perform properly—the family to take responsibility for its elderly members, the church to care for the less fortunate, and the economy to provide enough jobs for everyone—social welfare would not be necessary.

Throughout the twentieth century, until about the last twenty years, we saw a steady movement away from a residual approach toward an institutional approach to social welfare. Unemployment insurance recognizes that everyone is at risk of periods of unemployment and that a provision must be made to help people deal with this "normal" problem of modern industrial life. Old Age, Survivors, and Disability Insurance (Social Security) recognizes three major hazards of living in an urban society and depending on a paycheck and, once again, treats these hazards as "normal." Medicare recognizes that the cost of medical care for the elderly is likely to be beyond the reach of all but the very wealthy. In other words, "normal" people will need help. In recent years, however, we have seen a reversal of this trend. The social philosophy of the Reagan and

George Bush Republican administrations was that the family should care for children (that is, mothers should stay home), and thus they opposed increased provision of day care; that work should be required of welfare recipients because the solution to financial dependency resides in the economic institution (that is, welfare mothers should not stay home, even though there is no day care); and that social welfare is really the proper role of the church. This is a traditional conservative approach, emphasizing individual responsibility, minimum government, tradition, and fiscal restraint.

The Clinton administration's attempt to move health care from a residual to an institutional approach failed. The movement of social welfare to a more institutional approach appears to have lost momentum. Conservative social theorists are now openly advocating a return to a residual approach to social welfare. Marsland, for example, substitutes the term *community care* for residual and argues that we should be suspicious of demands for assistance as a right. He envisions community care as a temporary, market-oriented system of mutual aid with a "mission of providing help for those in real and unusual need." At the heart of Marsland's approach is the belief that "neglect of family responsibilities should be stigmatized and heroic service should be honored; but self-care by families should be regarded as normal."[34]

But the authors believe that this is a temporary phenomenon. Society continues to become larger, more technological, more urbanized, and more fragmented, and these developments continue to erode the ability of the basic institutions to deal with dependency in society.

Is the United States a Welfare State? A term often used in the press and in political dialogue to refer to a society that has thoroughly accepted the institutional conception of social welfare, one that makes the well-being of people the responsibility of government, is a *welfare state.*[35] From the passage of the Social Security Act in 1935 until the early 1970s, a period Blau refers to as "the ideological consensus," liberals and conservatives alike generally accepted that the United States either was, or was well on its way to becoming, a European-style welfare state.[36] Since the 1970s there has been a spirited debate on whether we are a welfare state and whether it is even desirable to be one.

Conservatives, believing that a welfare state exists in the United States as well as in Europe, are riding the current political mood to attack the concept. Marsland, referring specifically to Britain but stating an argument that has found favor with U.S. conservatives, contends that the deficiencies in the welfare state concept are becoming obvious to everyone. He argues that, first, the concept of the welfare state is philosophically incoherent. "It means all things to all people, and arguably nothing rationally justifiable in any of them. This inevitably produces confusions in practice." Second, Marsland believes, economic progress has produced such wealth that it "renders the existing extensive system of universal state welfare provision unnecessary. Some people need help, but most don't." Third, the welfare state has become so costly that it poses a threat to the health of the whole economy. Fourth, the system is ineffective, squandering "the billions of pounds which it costs every year on third-rate services delivered to mostly the wrong people, in inappropriate ways, to little useful effect." Finally, Marsland argues, the welfare state harms those it seeks to help by making them dependent. In a bit of overblown prose eerily reminiscent of the report of the 1832 Royal Poor Law Commission, he asserts that the welfare state constitutes "a lethal threat to our freedom" and has "made the British people a nation of greedy wastrels . . . an ungovernable mob, bereft of values and scornful of rules."[37]

The economist John Kenneth Galbraith believes that arguments for the death of the welfare state made by conservatives such as Marsland are nonsense based on a flawed understanding of history. Galbraith argues that liberals, like himself, "have allowed conservatives and the public at large to credit us with social action that was not our initiative. We were merely accommodating to the great thrust of history. History compelled the changes for which we [liberals] took, and were given, credit—and for which we are now being blamed. And history cannot be reversed." Galbraith explains that before the passage of the Social Security Act in 1935, old age assistance was not needed, because in a rural, agricultural society "the young on a farm took care of the old." Before twentieth-century technological advances in health care, Medicaid, Medicare, and other forms of medical insurance and assistance were not needed, because "the problem of paying the local doctor was on a par with paying the grocer." With the development of costly medical technology, "the poor or even the modestly affluent could not decently be consigned to illness or death merely because of inability to pay. Again, government changed in response to changed circumstance." Galbraith's point is that the evolution from a residual approach to an institutional welfare state

The majority of people who receive financial assistance would rather be working. The major concern of this welfare-to-work program participant is whether her job will actually lead to opportunities that will enable her to permanently escape the welfare roles.

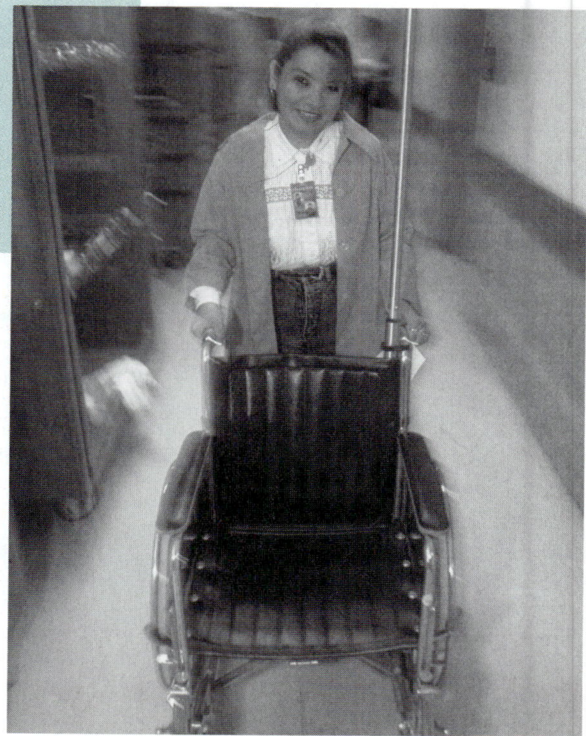

What Americans Believe

The General Social Survey (GSS) includes two items that bear on the question of the degree to which Americans support the idea of a welfare state. The first question asked respondents to indicate which of two statements they agreed with the most. The first statement was, "Our system of social services goes much too far. It takes too much care of people and deprives them of too much individual responsibility." The second statement was, "Our system of social services is on the right track. It provides security for the elderly, the sick, and other people in distress without depriving people of individual responsibility." The responses to this item, cross-tabulated with political perspective, are summarized in Table 2.1.

The second item of interest focuses on people's feelings about income redistribution by the government. The item reads, "Some people think that the government in Washington ought to reduce the income differences between the rich and the poor, perhaps by raising the taxes of wealthy families or by giving income assistance to the poor. Others think that the government should not concern itself with reducing this income difference." Respondents were asked to indicate their feelings about this issue on a scale of one to seven, with one indicating a strong belief that "Government should do something to reduce income differences between rich and poor," and seven indicating a strong belief that "Government should not concern itself with income differences." We collapsed the categories of this item from seven into three, with one and two indicating a belief that government should reduce income inequality, three to five indicating maybe/maybe not, and six and seven indicating that the respondent believes that the government should not concern itself with income

TABLE 2.1

Government Concern for Social Welfare

	Liberal	Moderate	Conservative	Total
Our System of Social Services Goes Much Too Far	22.2%	20.9%	36.5%	28.8%
Our System of Social Services Is on the Right Track	77.8%	79.1%	63.5%	73.2%

Note: Numbers may not add to 100 because "don't know" and no answer are not included.

Source: Based on James Allan Davis and Tom W. Smith, *General Social Surveys*, 1972–2002 [machine-readable data file]: Principal Investigator, James A. Davis; Director and Co-Principal Investigator, Tom W. Smith; Co-Principal Investigator, Peter V. Marsden, NORC ed. (Chicago: National Opinion Research Center, producer 2002; Storrs, CT: The Roper Center for Public Opinion Research, University of Connecticut, distributor), 1 data file (43,698).

approach to social problems was not a product of liberal social design efforts but an inevitable adjustment made by society to the social problems of modernization. He concludes that conservatives "are now persuaded that they can reverse the tide. Were [liberals] responsible for the change, they could. . . . History is something else; it has its differences. The data from this item, once again cross-tabulated with political perspective, are summarized in Table 2.2.

The results of these questions are interesting, and to an extent counterintuitive (meaning different from what one would expect based only on intuition or common sense). Popular wisdom says that people in the United States are generally skeptical about social welfare in general, and downright hostile to the idea of income redistribution. In the body of this text, we cite Charles Atherton, who posits that Americans may be accepting of a welfare state, but not if it is a redistributive welfare state. These two items from the GSS indicate that this may not be true. On the item asking if the government is exhibiting an appropriate level of concern for social services, three-quarters of the respondents indicated a belief that it is. Even among people identifying themselves as conservatives, nearly two-thirds expressed support for government social service efforts. Even more surprising are the data on the item asking opinions on income redistribution. Over three-quarters of the respondents indicated that they either strongly support income redistribution (26.2 percent) or they thought that it might be okay (51.1 percent). Less than one-quarter indicated a strong opposition to government income redistribution. Only about one-half of people identifying themselves as conservatives indicated a strong opposition to income redistribution.

As social workers, we sometimes tend to despair about what we perceive as a low level of support for social welfare and perhaps even meanness among the general population. These two items cannot be seen as proof of much of anything, but they do at least provide us with a glimmer of hope.

TABLE 2.2

Should the Government Reduce Income Differences between the Rich and the Poor?

	Liberal	Moderate	Conservative	Total
Yes	36.6%	40.4%	24.0%	26.2%
Maybe	25.9%	41.3%	32.7%	51.1%
No	17.6%	30.1%	52.3%	22.7%

Note: Numbers may not add to 100 because "don't know" and no answer are not included.

Source: Based on James Allan Davis and Tom W. Smith, *General Social Surveys,* 1972–2002 [machine-readable data file]: Principal Investigator, James A. Davis; Director and Co-Principal Investigator, Tom W. Smith; Co-Principal Investigator, Peter V. Marsden, NORC ed. (Chicago: National Opinion Research Center, producer 2002; Storrs, CT: The Roper Center for Public Opinion Research, University of Connecticut, distributor), 1 data file (43,698).

own dynamic. And as those engaged in politics pass from general rhetoric . . . to the specifics of particular programs, they increasingly will discover this."[38]

Atherton has pointed out that it is important to recognize that there are at least two views of the welfare state. The first, which he refers to as the *programmatic welfare state,* is "a capitalist state that devotes a portion of its gross national product, through taxation, to the solution of certain social problems without changing the basic nature of the economy." The programmatic welfare state is closely tied to the labor market; its intended beneficiaries are workers who are experiencing temporary problems. Atherton calls the other view the *redistributive welfare state.* According to this perspective, the primary aim of the welfare state is the redistribution of wealth and resources.[39] The popular press sometimes refers to this as *welfare socialism.*[40]

Atherton says that if you are referring to the programmatic view of the welfare state, the United States certainly is one, and that even conservatives will not forcefully argue against this as a desirable social goal. However, if you are referring to a redistributive welfare state, there is little evidence that much support for this exists in the United States. This argument is supported by a recent analysis of welfare state theories by Myles and Quadagno that found a dramatic shift in the patterns of spending in the United States, with more aid going to those who work, or those who clearly cannot work such as the elderly and the disabled (programmatic social welfare), and much less going for direct assistance to families and adults who do not work for reasons that are less clear (redistributive social welfare).[41] Putting this together with the work of Wilensky and Lebeaux on conceptions of social welfare, it is probably accurate to say that the United States is a *residual welfare state.* In other words, there is strong support for the belief that the government should provide a safety net of services and benefits for all citizens and that no one should have to go without food, clothing, and medical care, but that our economic system is basically sound and that the institutions of family, economy, and religion, with a little help from government, should be able to meet the needs of all citizens.

A Classification of Social Welfare Services

For two chapters we have been discussing social welfare based on the presumption that the reader has a pretty good idea about what social welfare services are. This is probably an accurate presumption; nearly everyone is familiar with at least the major service categories such as financial assistance and child welfare. However, social welfare covers a wide spectrum of services, and few people are familiar with the entire picture. We will now present a fairly complete, although perhaps not exhaustive, description of the social welfare system.

There are several possible ways to classify social welfare services. Compton identifies four major schemes; the first is classification by the type of client served.[42] Under this scheme, thirteen types of programs are listed: programs serving the aged, dependent children, neglected and abused children, delinquent offenders, the unemployed, the emotionally disturbed, the physically disabled, the mentally disabled, the mentally ill, veterans, railroad workers, the disabled, and various special interest groups. These groups can be combined to form fewer groups or further subdivided to form more groups. They are not mutually exclusive; one client can be classified under several categories. The second method of classification is by source of funding. Using this method we get two large groups of services: those that are financed by public (tax) monies and those that are private or voluntary. A third classification method is by level of administration. This method classifies only public programs, and it divides them into federally administered programs, federal–state programs, and state, state–local, and local programs. A fourth method, which is widely disseminated in the work of Kamerman and Kahn, is classification by nature of service. Kamerman and Kahn list six categories: income maintenance, health care, housing, education, employment, and personal social services.[43]

The preceding classification methods are all useful and valid ways of describing the social welfare system. However, we are going to use a different method. In keeping with our functional definition of social welfare, we are going to classify services according to broad societal function. To do this we first need to expand on our definition of *dependency.* You will recall that dependency connotes a state of being in which a person, because of either individual or institutional dysfunction, is unable to adequately carry out essential social roles. For the purpose of our definition, we will divide dependency into three broad types. The first type of dependency is *economic dependency,* in which the fundamental problem is a lack of sufficient resources to meet basic needs. If social welfare services make enough resources available, the person will resume his or her position as an interdependent member of society. An example of this type of service is food stamps, which are given to people who lack sufficient resources to adequately feed themselves and their families. The second type of dependency is *role dependency as defined by self,* in which the person defines himself or herself as needing help fulfilling some social role. Examples of this kind of help are parent effectiveness training classes for people who feel they are having difficulty fulfilling their parental roles, and job counseling services for women who want to enter or reenter the workforce but are having difficulty with the role change. The third type of dependency is *role dependency as defined by others,* in which the person is defined by others as needing help fulfilling some essential social role. Examples of this are child welfare services that protect children from harm by helping parents fulfill their roles, and probation services that offer supervision and counseling instead of prison to people convicted of crimes. In this third type of service the clients are referred to as "involuntary" because, at least initially, they do not want to receive help. The following is a description of the major social welfare services in each of the three categories.

I. *Services for People Who Are Economically Dependent*

A. Cash Support Programs. These are programs that seek to mitigate or to alleviate economic dependence by the direct provision of money.

1. Old Age, Survivors, and Disability Insurance (OASDI). This is the program that is usually called "Social Security." It is an insurance-type program in which in order to receive benefits you generally must have paid into the program. As the name implies, OASDI provides a cash income to retired or permanently disabled workers that is related to worker age and income at the time benefits commence. Dependents and survivors can receive set proportions of this benefit, subject to a family maximum. Coverage under this program is vast and extensive—nearly 96 percent of the workforce is covered. In 1999, 44.6 million retirees were receiving an average individual OASDI benefit of $731 a month.[44]

2. Public Assistance Programs. These programs assist people who are needy (economically dependent) but who are not eligible for OASDI or whose OASDI benefits are below a minimum level. These are not insurance programs, because recipients of benefits have not directly paid into the system. (However, it can be argued that everyone who has ever worked has paid into public assistance because it is funded by tax revenues.) When people speak of "welfare," they are usually referring to public assistance. Major categories of public assistance are as follows:
   a. Temporary Assistance to Needy Families (TANF). This is a relatively new program enacted on August 22, 1996, when President Clinton signed H.R. 3734, the Personal Responsibility and Work Opportunity Reconciliation Act. This program replaces the fifty-year-old Aid to Families with Dependent Children (AFDC) program, the costliest and most controversial public assistance program. From October 1996 to September 1999, the number of families receiving TANF declined from 4.3 to 2.5 million. Benefit levels from TANF are very low; the maximum for a family of four ranges from a high of $924 a month in Alaska to a low of $164 a month in Alabama.[45] These benefit levels have declined precipitously since 1994, in both actual and inflation-adjusted dollars. The main beneficiaries of TANF, and previously of AFDC, payments are children in fatherless families in which the mother is either unemployed or employed with an income greatly below the poverty level.
   b. Supplemental Security Income (SSI). This really includes three programs: SSI for the aged, SSI for the blind, and SSI for the disabled. It provides benefits for people in these three groups who are without adequate support. Benefits are considerably more generous than those of TANF because these groups are less stigmatized. The SSI federal benefit rate is currently $512 a month for an individual with no other income and $769 for a couple. Many states with a high cost of living further supplement this amount.
   c. General Assistance. TANF (formerly AFDC) and SSI are largely federally financed. For the needy who do not qualify for these programs, most states provide some general assistance benefits. Some states provide cash assistance for a limited period; others limit the benefits to health care or burial expenses. Benefits under this program are generally meager.
3. Veterans Compensation and Pensions. Veterans as a group have received preferential treatment in the United States since the Revolutionary War. Compensation is paid to veterans (or their dependents) for injury, disability, or death incurred while in the armed forces. Pensions are paid to war veterans (or their dependents) whose annual income is below a specified level and who are permanently and totally disabled. In 1999 expenditures on veterans compensation and pensions were over $23 billion.
4. Unemployment Insurance. This is an insurance program to protect workers against need during temporary periods of unemployment. Benefits are related to past earnings and work experience and are not based on level of need. Therefore, the poor are often excluded or receive meager benefits.

5. Workers' Compensation. This program is administered by private insurance companies under state regulation. It is designed to protect workers and their families from financial need during periods when wages are interrupted because of work-related injuries. It provides cash benefits, medical care, and rehabilitation services for injured workers. The program also compensates workers' survivors in the event of fatal injuries.
6. Private Pensions. A growing proportion of the elderly are protected from economic dependency by private pensions that generally supplement their OASDI benefits. There are no accurate statistics available, but it is estimated that in 1999 56 percent of full-time workers and 21 percent of part-time workers were protected by pension plans. This adds up to 99.5 million workers, an increase of almost 23 million since 1990.[46]

B. In-Kind Programs. These programs seek to mitigate or alleviate economic dependency by the direct provision of various goods and services to needy people as supplements to, or instead of, cash benefits.

1. Medical Services
   a. Medicaid and Medicare. These programs were added to the Social Security Act in 1965. Medicare covers most hospital and medical costs for people age sixty-five or older, as well as for disabled Social Security recipients. Medicaid, funded by state and federal governments under a matching formula, provides health care coverage to persons receiving federally supported public assistance in all states except Arizona. The majority of the states extend this coverage to persons not actually receiving public assistance but whose incomes are low enough to qualify them as "medically needy."
   b. Community, Maternal, and Child Health. With funding primarily from federal block grants, states provide certain services to supplement Medicare and Medicaid. Among these are community health centers, programs to reduce infant mortality, rehabilitative services for blind and disabled children, and prenatal health services.
   c. Veterans Health Services. The Veterans Administration health care system provides free medical services to low-income veterans regardless of whether their problems are connected to their term of service. The system is currently composed of 173 medical centers, 133 nursing homes, 40 domiciliaries, 398 ambulatory clinics and 206 readjustment counseling centers.[47]
   d. Indian Health Service. Because of poverty and geographic isolation, Native Americans fare poorly on almost any measure of health. To deal with this, the Indian Health Service has been established within the U.S. Department of Health and Human Services. This service directly operates 37 hospitals, 59 health centers, 4 school health centers, and 44 smaller health stations and satellite clinics. The service contracts with tribes for the operation of an additional 12 hospitals, 116 health centers, 3 school health centers, 56 health stations, and 167 Alaskan village clinics. In addition, 36 urban American Indian health projects provide a variety of health and referral services.[48]

2. Shelter
   a. Public Housing. This federally sponsored program nominally provides apartments for families whose incomes are less than 80 percent of the median income in their area; however, in most areas eligibility is restricted to those below 50 percent of the median income. Federal public housing, as well as subsidized housing, is not an entitlement program. This means that people who qualify may receive assistance only if a housing unit is available. The apartments are rented at well below market value, with the rent being set at 30 percent of the tenant's income.
   b. Subsidized Housing. In this program the federal government does not provide an actual apartment but subsidizes the rent for a privately owned house or apartment. The largest rent supplement program was established by Section 8 of the Housing and Community Development Act of 1974. Section 8 has overtaken public housing as the largest federal housing assistance program and currently serves approximately 2.8 million families.[49]
   c. Direct Home Ownership Assistance. The federal government assists some low- and moderate-income households in becoming homeowners. There are two major programs, one run by the Rural Housing Service (RHS) and one by the Department of Housing and Urban Development (HUD). Both programs reduce mortgage payments, property taxes, and insurance costs to a fixed percentage of income, 20 percent for the RHS program and 28 percent for the latest commitments made under the HUD program. Between 1977 and 2000, 108,000 commitments were funded under the HUD program.[50]
   d. The federal government, in partnership with the states, funds a number of programs related to homelessness under the Stewart B. McKinney Homeless Assistance Act of 1987. These programs include the Emergency Shelter Grants Program, the Supportive Housing Program, and the Moderate Rehabilitation for Single Room Occupancy Dwelling Program. Under these programs, HUD funds housing assistance indirectly in the form of block grants to state and local governments.[51]
   e. Energy Assistance. Because of the drastic increase in fuel costs in the 1970s and 1980s, fuel and weatherization assistance programs became a part of the social welfare system. The Low-Income Home Energy Assistance Program (LIHEAP) was begun in 1978 by the Department of Health and Human Services. The program distributes block grants to states to use to cover residential heating and cooling costs for the poor and very poor. States may use the block grant to provide three types of energy assistance. States can (1) help eligible households pay their home heating or cooling bills; (2) use up to 15 percent for weatherization assistance; or (3) provide assistance to households during weather-related emergencies. LIHEAP funding has decreased, from a high of $2.1 billion in 1985 to $1.25 billion in 1999.[52] In addition to public programs, many private programs have been established, often as cooperative efforts between utility companies and social agencies such as the Red Cross.

3. Nutrition
   a. Food Stamps. This is by far the largest nutrition program, providing $21.2 billion in benefits to a monthly average of 19.8 million people in 1999. The benefits are in the form of coupons that can be used just like money to purchase any food for human consumption. All recipients of public assistance are eligible for food stamps, as are households not eligible for public assistance that have incomes at or below the poverty level. Currently the maximum monthly food stamp allotment for a family of four living in the forty-eight continental states and the District of Columbia is $426.[53]
   b. Child Nutrition. In addition to food stamps, there are several nutrition programs focused on children. A number of programs now provide breakfast, lunch, and milk to more than 34 million children in private and public schools and day care centers at a federal cost of $7.4 billion. The largest of these programs is the school lunch program, which provides subsidized lunches to about 27 million children, more than half of the entire population of school-age children. Children receive free meals if their family income is below 130 percent of the federal poverty level, and reduced-price meals if it is between 130 percent and 185 percent of this level.[54]
   c. Special Supplemental Nutrition Program for Women, Infants, and Children (WIC). The WIC program provides food assistance, nutrition risk screening, and related services to low-income pregnant and postpartum women and their infants, as well as low-income children up to age five. Participants in the program must have a family income below 185 percent of the poverty level, and must be judged nutritionally at risk. In 1999, 1.74 million women, 1.9 million infants, and 3.67 million children were receiving WIC benefits, at a cost of $3.9 billion.[55]

II. *Services for People Who Are Dependent Because They Are Unable to Fulfill Roles, as Defined by Themselves*

A. Mental Health Services. A wide variety of services, both public and private, are available to people with mental health problems. Public services are provided in most areas by community mental health centers. These centers offer individual and group counseling and drug and alcohol treatment, as well as other services. They are staffed by psychiatrists, psychologists, social workers, nurses, and other specialists. These services are also available in the private sector through United Way and church-affiliated agencies, as well as from providers in private practice.

B. Family and Relationship Counseling. Family counseling is offered in most larger communities either through the community mental health center or from a private family service agency. These agencies are generally sponsored by the United Way or by one of the major religious denominations. The Catholic, Jewish, and Lutheran religions all have extensive networks of family service agencies. The counselors in these agencies are mostly master's-level social workers.

C. Employment Services. Many services assist people having problems with employment-related roles. The largest provider is the State Employment Service, with nearly 1,700 offices throughout the country. This is primarily a placement service, and about 18 million individuals apply for placement help annually. The federally sponsored vocational rehabilitation programs provide job training and medical, educational, and other services to the physically and mentally disabled in order to help them become employable.

D. Recreation and Socialization Services. A wide variety of services provides recreation and socialization for children and youth. There are numerous government recreation services (such as swimming pools and soccer leagues), but those that combine recreation with socialization are generally private. Notable among these are Young Men's and Young Women's Christian Associations (YMCA and YWCA), Jewish Community Centers Association (JCCA), Boy Scouts and Girl Scouts, and Boys and Girls Clubs. In recent years an increasing number of such services have been made available to the elderly through senior citizens' centers.

E. Advocacy, Liaison, and Access. With the growing complexity of the social service system, mechanisms have been developed to help people find the services they need and to make sure they are provided the services to which they are entitled. Examples are the information and referral services provided by most United Way organizations and ombudsman services provided by some government agencies.

III. *Services for People Who Are Dependent Because They Are Unable to Fulfill Roles, as Defined by Others*

A. Probation and Parole. Often a person convicted of a crime will be placed on probation rather than actually sent to prison. People released from prison are generally not released unconditionally but are placed on parole, which means that they are released before their sentence is completed on the condition that they submit to supervision and a stringent set of rules. Parolees are defined by society as needing help in fulfilling all the roles of citizenship, and they are required to accept this help as a condition for being out of jail.

B. Child Protective Services. Parents having difficulty adequately caring for their children may be required by court action, or by threat of court action, to accept help in better fulfilling their roles as parents. Common reasons for intervention are abuse, neglect, and exploitation. In severe cases it may be determined that the parents will never be able to adequately fulfill their roles, and the children will be permanently removed.

C. Adult Protective Services. Elderly and disabled people who are heavily dependent on others for care face some of the same problems of abuse, neglect, and exploitation as children. Our society has only recently begun to recognize this problem and to provide services to protect this vulnerable group.

D. Mandatory Employment and Training Programs. The previously discussed services for the economically dependent also could be described as helping people who are having difficulty with various roles associated with being a breadwinner. Assistance is given to many of these people on the condition that they accept help in becoming able to fulfill these roles. The original mandatory employment program was the WIN program, which reached nearly one million people a year. However, because only one-fifth ever actually left employed, the WIN program was not considered to be effective. The new Temporary Assistance to Needy

Families program requires that all the recipients of aid either be employed or be in employment training within two years of entering the program.

E. Involuntary Mental Health Services. We classified mental health services under section II above as services for people who define themselves as being unable to fulfill roles. We need to note that there are also mental health services for people who are defined by others as being unable to fulfill their roles to such an extent that they are judged to be a danger to themselves or to others. The most obvious situation is a person who is involuntarily committed to a mental hospital. Community mental health centers also provide outpatient services to people who have been ordered by a court to receive treatment for problems such as alcoholism, drug addiction, suicidal behavior, and various compulsions such as stealing.[56]

Perspectives on Social Welfare

In this chapter, we have developed the definition of social welfare as the institution that serves the function of managing the problem of dependency in society. We have said that liberals argue that social welfare has become a major social institution and that conservatives argue that it is (or should be) a residual function of other institutions. Two targets for social welfare intervention have been identified: individual role performance and the functioning of social institutions. We noted that conservatives think that the target of services should be almost exclusively the individual but that liberals are much more willing to support strategies for institutional change. We now turn to questions that indicate another area of major difference among conservative, liberal, and radical perspectives on social welfare—that is, what are the major motivations behind social welfare activities, and what are the major goals?

The Conservative Perspective

Basically, conservatives view the purpose of social welfare as the maintenance of the status quo. Social welfare is perceived as fulfilling an integrative social function; it sustains morale and cohesiveness in society and thereby contributes to efficiency, stability, and order. As Room observes, conservatives advocate social welfare that would "reinforce and uphold the capitalist market system and that would therefore not hinder but multiply the benefits of a market civilization."[57] Conservatives believe that dependency should be addressed on a case-by-case basis and that economic growth will, without redistribution of income, eliminate poverty and thus the need for most social welfare services. There are two central ideas behind the conservative definition of social welfare: *noblesse oblige* and *enlightened self-interest.*

Noblesse Oblige. This term is French for "nobility obligates." It refers to the obligation of honorable, generous, and responsible behavior associated with high rank or birth. The idea is that those who are fortunate, originally because of birth, but now also because of achievement, have a moral obligation to assist those who are less fortunate.

Thus, the motivation to help the dependent in society stems not from any right of these people to demand help, but rather from a moral obligation of the more fortunate to provide it. This approach is paternalistic: It views welfare as charity to the unfortunate, and it leads to clear distinctions between givers and receivers and between the worthy and the unworthy poor.

Enlightened Self-Interest. Conservatives believe that in order for the status quo to be maintained, dependency must be managed in a humanitarian way that prevents it from disrupting society while hopefully not costing too much. As Rescher remarks, "Under current conditions in technologically advanced societies, we are brought back with a vengeance to the doctrine of the Stoics of antiquity that due care for this interest of others with whom one coexists in a social context is, in the final analysis, a matter not just of altruism but of enlightened self-interest."[58] In other words, conservatives realize that helping others is simply a cost of living in modern society and that it ultimately benefits the helpers themselves.

The Liberal Perspective

The liberal position on social welfare is known in Europe as *social democracy* or *citizenship*[59] and in the United States is sometimes referred to as the *mass society thesis.*[60] This position views social welfare as more humanitarian and less utilitarian than the conservative position. Liberals see social welfare programs as basically humanitarian responses by the state to social problems endemic to industrialized society. The central feature of the liberal perspective on social welfare is a conception of individual rights.

The liberal position views the history of Western society as characterized by an ever expanding conception of individual rights. First, people were accorded civil rights, such as the right to vote, the right to move freely about the country, and the right to accumulate wealth. More recently society has evolved, according to this perspective, to a point at which people are accorded social rights. The concept of social rights means that people are guaranteed, by virtue of being citizens, a certain (generally minimum) standard of living as well as other life-sustaining, life-enhancing services. Schram and Turbett explain that under the liberal definition,

> all persons are seen by the state as having legitimate entitlements as citizens. The movement toward a "mass society" constitutes an expansion in the concept of citizenship beyond basic political rights to include social and economic rights. In a "mass society," poor people as citizens are vested with the right to receive government assistance when their basic social and economic rights cannot legitimately be fulfilled through private means.[61]

Under the conservative approach, people who are dependent are assisted by those who are able because helping is considered a moral obligation. Under the liberal approach, people are assisted because they have a right to assistance.

Conservatives agree with liberals that there has been a tremendous expansion of individual rights, but, unlike liberals, they believe that it has gone too far. Donahue argues,

> Rights mania began once liberty was seen as rights alone and freedom from responsibility became respectable. The behavior of government had a lot to do with both. The creation of new rights for the individual, many of them long overdue, had the unanticipated effect of

> raising the expectations for yet more rights, rights without a grounding in justice and the common good. This occurred at the same time government was redistributing responsibilities from the individual to institutions. It was the interaction between the two—more individual rights and less individual responsibilities—that proved to be decisive.[62]

The Radical Perspective

Radicals view social welfare as a deliberate effort by the power elite in society to control the masses and to prevent any meaningful social change. By "meaningful social change" they mean radical change in the distribution of resources and power. Room, for example, says that

> [Radicals] deny that attempts at non-revolutionary reform are other than misconceived or that the social policies developed over the past century introduce fundamental changes in the dominant mode of social integration. On the contrary, welfare state institutions have served as relatively successful agencies for the perpetuation of a "false consciousness" among members of the working class. Through its social policies, the state is able to mitigate the most glaring deprivations wrought by the capitalist system and to pretend to a concern with social welfare.[63]

An extremely influential book promoting a radical perspective on social welfare, *Regulating the Poor: The Functions of Public Welfare* by Frances Fox Piven and Richard A. Cloward, has sparked a lively debate. Piven and Cloward argue, and support their argument with historical data, that the social welfare system is a servant of the economic system and that its chief function is to regulate labor. The system regulates labor in two ways. "First, when mass unemployment leads to outbreaks of turmoil, relief programs are ordinarily initiated or expanded to absorb and control enough of the unemployed to restore order; thus, as turbulence subsides, the relief system contracts, expelling those who are needed to populate the labor market." In addition, the welfare system serves as a motivator for the labor force because the treatment of the dependent "is so degrading and punitive as to instill in the laboring masses a fear of the fate that awaits them should they relax into beggary and pauperism. To demean and punish those who do not work is to exalt by contrast even the meanest labor at the meanest wage."[64] Fellin observes that one of the demands by radicals is that the government not only recognize people's rights to more benefits, but also that it "back away from some of the political and economic functions of the welfare state, such as regulating the poor."[65]

Summary

All three perspectives would agree with our functional definition of social welfare as being concerned with managing the problem of dependency in society. They strongly disagree on whether this function is residual or institutional; whether the major target for services is the individual with role difficulties or social institutions failing to support role performance; and whether the function of social welfare, as currently carried out, is good or bad.

Conservatives believe that:

1. Social welfare should be a residual social function. The family, church, and economy should be the front line of defense against dependency, and social welfare

should be a temporary function that comes into play only when these institutions are overwhelmed.

Liberals believe that:

1. Social welfare has become, or is fast becoming, a first-line social institution. Society, they argue, has become so fragmented and so complex, and the traditional institutions have deteriorated to such a point, that very few individuals can function in a totally interdependent manner without some help. Employment services, family counseling, mental health services, and day care are all necessary supports for life in modern society.
2. Individual problems in role performance result from an interaction between individual and institutional causes. Thus, social welfare has two targets: (1) individual change through counseling, therapy, education, and training, and (2) social change through environmental manipulation, social planning, and political action. This is the traditional position of the social work profession, and it is referred to as viewing problems from the perspective of person-in-environment.
3. The motivation for social welfare is primarily humanitarian. People help one another out of a true caring for one another and out of the gradually evolving recognition that everyone has a right to a share of society's resources.

Radicals believe that:

1. Social welfare has become institutional, but it is an institution set up by, controlled by, and serving the interests of the elite in society.
2. Problems of dependency are almost entirely the result of repressive social institutions. The goal of the social welfare institution *is* to keep the masses in line by promoting the idea that individuals are to blame for their own problems and by helping people adjust to a repressive society. The goal of social welfare *should be* to promote radical social change that results in a more humane, equalitarian social order.
3. The motivation for social welfare is social control. Social welfare institutions keep the masses in their place and head off any genuinely meaningful social change.

Conclusion

Most likely, after reading this chapter you are a little confused. This is typical and is not something to be concerned about. Social welfare is an extremely confusing concept. When you take a geology course, you learn exact properties of various types of rocks. All rocks of any one type share the same properties, and all geologists agree on what they are. Those of us who study social welfare are not so fortunate. Two concepts we have been discussing make social welfare extremely difficult to understand. The first is ideology. Social welfare is an extremely ideological thing. Liberals, conservatives, radicals, reactionaries, and people with perspectives in between will define and discuss social welfare on entirely different terms. The second concept is stigma. Because social welfare tends to be highly stigmatized in our society, people tend to define social welfare as not including services they themselves, or the people they care for, are involved in.

One thing, however, is very clear. The social welfare institution has grown steadily for more than four centuries, and the growth in the twentieth century, especially since World War II, was explosive. In 1900, government expenditure for social welfare was virtually nothing; in 1929, state and federal expenditures were a little less than $4 billion; by 1950, this had grown sixfold to nearly $24 billion; and by 1995, federal, state, and local governments spent more than $1,505 billion on social welfare programs. The total cost of social welfare expenditures in the United States, public and private, was 13.5 percent of the gross national product in 1968; it had risen to 33 percent by 1993.[66] Although much has been made of the retreat from the welfare state and of the "devolution" of social services, data indicate that total spending continues to increase, although perhaps at a slower rate than in the past. Measured in constant 1998 dollars, combined federal and state spending on programs for the poor rose 419 percent from 1968 to 1998. With the exception of the years 1981, 1982, and 1996, spending has increased every year.[67]

During recent years, very conservative federal Congresses, supported by a public reacting to the tremendous increase in expenditures, have succeeded in slowing the growth of many social welfare programs and have actually reduced the size of some others. However, most agree that this is a temporary phenomenon and that over the long haul the growth will continue, probably at a slower rate than during earlier eras. The politicians have not succeeded in reversing any of the social forces that have created the need for social welfare services. We continue to see an increase in births out of wedlock, divorces, desertion, illiteracy, school dropout rates, and drug abuse. The recent economic recovery has been referred to as a jobless recovery because the unemployment rate has not declined. The underemployment rate is even higher. New problems are being recognized that call for social welfare services, including eating disorders, agoraphobia, spouse abuse, and new sexually transmitted diseases, to name a few. In addition, our society continues to become more complex and in many ways less secure. Unions do not provide the security they once did; an increasing proportion of new jobs are high-tech but low in pay and in job security; and vocational experts predict that soon it will be common for a person to have to train for and enter completely new careers two or three times during his or her working life. Fewer and fewer employers are providing health benefits to their employees, and an increasing number of elderly people cannot afford to fill their prescriptions. All of these factors create or reflect individual and societal stresses and tensions that will require new responses, and many of them will involve the expansion of the social welfare institution.

Visit **www.researchnavigator.com** to research these important concepts from the chapter:

Capitalism
Food stamps
Medicare
Social welfare
Social Security Act
TANF
Welfare state

Web Sites on General Social Welfare Concepts

Center for Law and Social Policy <www.clasp.org>: CLASP is a national nonprofit organization with expertise in both law and social policy affecting the poor. Through education, policy research, and advocacy, CLASP seeks to improve the economic conditions of low-income families and children and to secure access for the poor to the U.S. civil justice system. Site provides documents related to current social welfare issues.

Idea Central Welfare and Families Link <www.movingideas.org>: Links to sources on social policy, welfare reform, children's issues, and numerous other social welfare sources.

Social Work History Online Time Line <www.gnofn.org/~jill/swhistory>: A good time line featuring the major events in the development of social work and social welfare in the United States. Includes links to detailed histories of many of the featured dates and events.

Social Work Online <geocities.com/athens/9050/socwork.html>: This site includes information on Internet resources, social services and community action, associations and organizations, social work schools and universities, social work journals, articles, chatrooms, and other features related to social work and social welfare.

SWAN—Social Work Access Network <www.sc.edu/swan-news.html>: Run by the University of South Carolina College of Social Work, this site includes information about numerous areas of social work and social welfare, as well as links to other resources.

University of California Data <ucdata.berkeley.edu>: University of California–Berkeley's principal archive of computerized social science and health statistics information. It is a bit more difficult to use than most web sites, but it contains a wealth of information on issues related to social welfare.

Endnotes

1. Neil Gilbert and Paul Terrell, *Dimensions of Social Welfare Policy,* 5th ed. (Boston: Allyn and Bacon, 2002), 1.
2. Erving Goffman, *Stigma: Notes on the Management of Spoiled Identity* (Englewood Cliffs, NJ: Prentice Hall, 1963), Preface, 1; Jennifer Crocker, Brenda Major, and Claude Steele, "Social Stigma," in Daniel T. Gilbert, Susan T. Fiske, and Gardner Lindzey, *The Handbook of Social Psychology,* 4th ed., vol. 2 (Boston: McGraw-Hill, 1998), 504.
3. Paul Spicker, *Stigma and Social Welfare* (New York: St. Martin's, 1984), 175.
4. Robert Pinker, *Social Theory and Social Policy* (London: Heinemann, 1971), 139.
5. Joel Blau, with Mimi Abramovitz, *The Dynamics of Social Welfare Policy* (New York: Oxford University Press, 2004), 137.
6. Frederick B. Mills, "The Ideology of Welfare Reform: Deconstructing Stigma," *Social Work 41* (July 1996), 391.
7. David Matza, "Poverty and Disrepute," in Robert K. Merton and Robert Nisbet, eds., *Contemporary Social Problems,* 3rd ed. (New York: Harcourt Brace Jovanovich, 1971), 601–616.
8. Spicker, *Stigma and Social Welfare,* 96.
9. Claude Lévi-Strauss, *The Elementary Structures of Kinship* (Andover, Great Britain: Eyre & Spottiswoode, 1949), 480.
10. Timothy Beasley and Stephen Coates, "Understanding Welfare Stigma: Taxpayer Resentment and Statistical Discrimination," *Journal of Public Economics 48* (Fall 1992), 165–183.
11. Harold L. Wilensky and Charles N. Lebeaux, *Industrial Society and Social Welfare,* enlarged pbk. ed. (New York: Russell Sage Foundation, 1958), 34–35.
12. From Harold L. Wilensky and Charles N. Lebeaux, *Industrial Society and Social Welfare,* enlarged pbk. ed. (New York: Russell Sage Foundation, 1958), 34–35. Reprinted with permission of the Russell Sage Foundation.

13. David Macarov, *The Design of Social Welfare* (New York: Holt, Rinehart & Winston, 1978), 22–23.
14. Eveline M. Burns, "Some Economic Aspects of Welfare as an Institution," in John M. Romanyshan, ed., *Social Science and Social Welfare* (New York: Council on Social Work Education, 1974), 89.
15. Neil Gilbert and Paul Terrell, *Dimensions of Social Welfare Policy,* 5th ed., 56.
16. Thomas H. Walz and Gary Askerooth, *The Upside Down Welfare State* (Minneapolis, MN: Elwood Printing, 1973), 2.
17. Mimi Abramovitz, "Everyone Is Still on Welfare: The Role of Redistribution in Social Policy," *Social Work 46* (October 2001), 299.
18. Nicholas Rescher, *Welfare: The Social Issues in Philosophical Perspective* (Pittsburgh, PA: The University of Pittsburgh Press, 1972), 4–5.
19. P. Nelson Reid, "Social Welfare History," in Richard L. Edwards, ed., *Encyclopedia of Social Work,* 19th ed. (Washington, DC: NASW Press, 1996), 2206.
20. Walter A. Friedlander, *Introduction to Social Welfare* (New York: Prentice Hall, 1955), 4.
21. George T. Martin Jr. and Mayer N. Zald, eds., *Social Welfare in Society* (New York: Columbia University Press, 1981), 4.
22. Elizabeth Wickenden, *Social Welfare in a Changing World* (Washington, DC: Department of Health, Education and Welfare, 1965), vii.
23. Rescher, *Welfare,* 8.
24. David Popenoe, *Sociology,* 4th ed. (Englewood Cliffs, NJ: Prentice Hall, 1980), 85.
25. Gerhard Lenski and Jean Lenski, *Human Societies: An Introduction to Macro-Sociology,* 3rd ed. (New York: McGraw-Hill, 1978), 74.
26. Beulah R. Compton, *Introduction to Social Welfare and Social Work: Structure, Function, and Process* (Homewood, IL: Dorsey, 1980), 41.
27. From Charles Atherton, "The Social Assignment of Social Work," *Social Service Review 43* (May 1969), 421–429. Reprinted with permission.
28. From Charles Atherton, "The Social Assignment of Social Work," *Social Service Review 43* (May 1969), 423. Reprinted with permission.
29. John H. Ehrenreich, *The Altruistic Imagination: A History of Social Work and Social Policy in the United States* (Ithaca, NY: Cornell University Press, 1985), 30–33.
30. Charles Dickens, *A Christmas Carol: In Prose: Being a Ghost Story of Christmas* (New York: Garden City, 1938), 11–12.
31. Dickens, *A Christmas Carol,* 94–95.
32. From Harold L. Wilensky and Charles N. Lebeaux, *Industrial Society and Social Welfare,* enlarged pbk. ed. (New York: Russell Sage Foundation, 1958), 140. Reprinted with permission of the Russell Sage Foundation.
33. From Harold L. Wilensky and Charles N. Lebeaux, *Industrial Society and Social Welfare,* enlarged pbk. ed. (New York: Russell Sage Foundation, 1958), 139. Reprinted with permission of the Russell Sage Foundation.
34. David Marsland, "Community Care as an Alternative to State Welfare," *Social Policy and Administration 30* (September 1996), 186–187.
35. Mimi Abramovitz, "Definitions and Functions of Social Welfare Policy: Setting the Stage for Social Change," in Joel Blau, with Mimi Abramovitz, *The Dynamics of Social Welfare Policy,* 21.
36. Joel Blau, "Theories of the Welfare State," *Social Service Review 63* (March 1989), 22–29.
37. David Marsland, *Welfare or Welfare State? Contradictions and Dilemmas in Social Policy* (Hampshire and London: Macmillan, 1996), 21.
38. John Kenneth Galbraith, "Blame History, Not the Liberals," *New York Times* (19 Sept. 1995), A21; Galbraith, "Newt Notwithstanding, the Welfare State Is Here to Stay," *New Perspectives Quarterly 13* (Winter 1996), 66–70.
39. Charles R. Atherton, "The Welfare State: Still on Solid Ground," *Social Service Review 63* (June 1989), 169.
40. See, for example, David Moller, "The Nation That Tried to Buy Happiness," *Reader's Digest* (September 1991), 100–104.
41. Atherton, "The Welfare State," 177–178; Myles and Quadango, as discussed by Michael R. Sosin, "Editor's Introduction: The Seventy-Fifth Anniversary Issue of *Social Service Review,*" *Social Service Review 75* (March 2001), 2.
42. Compton, *Introduction to Social Welfare and Social Work,* 60.
43. Sheila Kamerman and Alfred J. Kahn, *Social Services in the United States* (Philadelphia: Temple University Press, 1976), 4.
44. House Committee on Ways and Means, "Background Material and Data on Programs within the Jurisdiction of the Committee on Ways and Means," *2000 Green Book* (106th Congress, 2nd Session, 2000), 1–96.
45. House Committee on Ways and Means, *2000 Green Book,* 377, 381.

46. U.S. Department of Labor, Pension and Welfare Benefits Administration, *Private Pension Plan Bulletin 10* (Winter 2001); U.S. Bureau of Labor Statistics, *News*, 01–473 (19 Dec. 2001), 75.
47. House Committee on Ways and Means, *2000 Green Book*, 982.
48. "Indian Health Service Fact Sheet" at www.ihs.gov/AboutIHS/ThisFacts.asp.
49. *Statistical Abstract of the United States* (2000, Vol. 61, No. 4), 380.
50. House Committee on Ways and Means, *2000 Green Book*, 945.
51. House Committee on Ways and Means, *2000 Green Book*, 945.
52. House Committee on Ways and Means, *2000 Green Book*, 976.
53. House Committee on Ways and Means, *2000 Green Book*, 878, 884.
54. House Committee on Ways and Means, *2000 Green Book*, 957–958.
55. House Committee on Ways and Means, *2000 Green Book*, 959–961.
56. For an interesting discussion of involuntary commitment, see Thomas Szasz, "Psychiatry and the Control of Dangerousness: On the Apotropaic Function of the Term 'Mental Illness,'" *Journal of Social Work Education 39* (Fall 2003), 375–381.
57. Graham Room, *The Sociology of Welfare: Social Policy, Stratification and Political Order* (New York: St. Martin's, 1979), 51.
58. Rescher, *Welfare*, 35.
59. Richard M. Titmuss, *Essays on the Welfare State* (London: Allen & Unwin, 1963); T. H. Marshall, *Class, Citizenship and Social Development* (Garden City, NY: Doubleday, 1964).
60. Kirsten A. Gronbjerg, *Mass Society and the Extension of Welfare, 1960–1970* (Chicago: University of Chicago Press, 1977).
61. Sanford F. Schram and Patrick Turbett, "The Welfare Explosion: Mass Society versus Social Control," *Social Service Review 57* (December 1983), 616.
62. William A. Donahue, "The Social Consequences of the Rights Revolution," *Intercollegiate Review 22* (Spring 1987), 41–46.
63. Room, *The Sociology of Welfare*, 46.
64. Frances Fox Piven and Richard A. Cloward, *Regulating the Poor: The Functions of Public Welfare*, updated ed. (New York: Vintage, 1993), 3–4.
65. Phillip Fellin, *The Community and the Social Worker*, 3rd ed. (Itasca, IL: F. E. Peacock, 2001), 41.
66. Ann K. Bixby, "Public Social Welfare Expenditures, Fiscal Year 1995," *Social Security Bulletin 62* (February 1999), 86; Wilmer Kerns, "Private Social Welfare Expenditures, 1972–94," *Social Security Bulletin 60* (March 1997), 54.
67. House Committee on Ways and Means, *2000 Green Book*, 1393–1396.

CHAPTER

3

Social Work as a Profession

What happens when you tell family friends, your spouse, or Great-Uncle Jerome that you would like to major in social work? A gasp, then, "Oh, but you know you won't make any money," or "Do you *really* want to work with people on welfare?" Or "You'll never get a job—unless maybe you decide to get a master's degree." Then, after a moment's reflection, "But on the other hand, since you're so patient and self-denying, maybe it is the best career for you after all. . . ." These responses give you a good idea of the confused, sometimes negative image of social work in our society. It is an image reflecting several factors, including ambivalence about the degree of responsibility society should take in dealing with dependence, negative feelings about the "typical" clients of social workers, and questions about the status of a "woman's profession" in our society. Consider, for example, the most popular TV shows involving working people and professions. Rarely is a series based on the job of a social worker. Instead we are caught up in the glamour and excitement of police detectives, lawyers, doctors, and even sportswriters at work. Sometimes these actors are portrayed performing tasks that are really those of a social worker. When social workers do appear directly on these shows or on soap operas, they are often depicted as grim but well-meaning child welfare workers who are determined to remove children from their homes, or as well-meaning but naive young women. One exception is the positive portrayal of child welfare work by actress Tyne Daly, the mother of the main character in *Judging Amy.* But by and large, public ambivalence and confusion about the role of social workers continues in our society.

This chapter explores the reality behind the various images of social work. It examines some of the reasons for society's stereotypes and ambivalence about the profession. An introduction to the broad outlines of the history of social work in the United States will help you understand both the bases for stereotypes as well as the sources of social work's strengths. An analysis of varying political perspectives on the functions of social work offers further insight into the conflicting expectations of the field. In addition, the chapter provides an overview of social work's practice settings and methods, philosophical foundations, values and value dilemmas, professional issues, education and knowledge base, and relation to the broader field of social welfare. The intent of this chapter is to increase your understanding of the current shape and scope of social work. The next chapter presents a closer look at two areas of social work practice, generalist practice and case management, and expands on the application of social work values and ethics in these two areas.

Social Work and Professionalism

The frequent confusion about social work is reflected in the question, "Is social work a 'real' profession?" In order to attempt an answer, we should recognize that there are several models for describing what "profession" and the process of becoming a profession mean. One model looks to the traditional professions—medicine, the clergy, and law—and sees these as possessing a specific group of attributes.[1] Although lists of attributes differ somewhat from theorist to theorist, most include (1) possession of a unique skill valued by society; (2) expectation of lengthy, specialized training for practitioners; (3) possession of systematic theory on which such training is based; (4) existence of a code of ethics to guide practice; and (5) organization of members of the profession into associations that protect their interests. Occupational groups claiming professional status can be measured against these specific attributes. If they possess them, they have earned the label of profession.

Some observers of occupations are critical of this way of thinking about professionalism.[2] They argue that the attributes model is a static approach. A more realistic perspective, they contend, would be to concentrate on the process groups go through in trying to establish a cohesive professional identity (and to worry less about finding a universal definition of that identity). What is most interesting and important about professions, according to proponents of the process model, are the ways in which they try to build internal unity, to win public acceptance of their functions, and to compete with other groups to establish their exclusive expertise and right to practice in a particular area. For example, physicians and midwives can be viewed as two groups vying for control over delivering babies in our society. The winner of the conflict will be labeled the professional group in that area of practice. In the United States, physicians, the stronger group, have won out so far; they have been able to establish themselves as the major profession handling childbirth. As you can see, this way of thinking about professions often stresses power—for example, the ability of one group to "control the market" for a particular social function, or the authority gained by an occupation that convinces the public that its definitions of social or health problems and its solutions to them are the correct ones. The process model stresses conflict and diversity, not only among occupations, but also among segments within them. These internal segments struggle over defining the profession's goals and functions and deciding just who will be a member. The conflict within social work about whether professionals can be trained at the baccalaureate level is an example of such a debate. As you will see in our discussion of social work history, we view the process model as a fruitful way of understanding social work's development and search for professional identity.[3]

So far, this discussion has not answered the question, "Is social work a profession?" Those who study professions have given a variety of responses. A widely read article by sociologist Ernest Greenwood uses the attributes approach to defining professionalism. Measuring social work against a list of professional characteristics, Greenwood asserts that the field has "passed the test" and that it is a true profession. Others are less sure. Using Greenwood's own list of professional attributes, Toren defines social work as a "semi-profession" because not all of its attributes are fully developed. She argues that social work's theory base, for example, is not yet well articulated. In a similar vein, Gilbert, Miller, and Specht define social work as a "developing profession," which has, at this point, a relatively low degree of professional authority and community sanction. (Requirements for social work licensing, for example, are less stringent than those for the practice of medicine.)[4] Using the process model of professionalism, one might argue that social work is not yet powerful enough to lay claim to an exclusive area of practice. Social work shares some of its methods and goals with members of other occupational groups, including counselors, public health nurses, and psychologists, and so faces a challenge in trying to establish its own autonomy and legitimacy as a profession.

Rather than prolonging the debate about social work's professional status, we would prefer to examine some different issues. These include (1) the effects the process of seeking a professional identity has had on the development of social work and (2) the social functions social work might stress in its attempt to define its particular role in society.

The first issue is examined in some detail in the section on social work history. The second issue involves a different way of looking at the concept of profession. One might say that the professions exist to deal with particular problems faced by society. The occupational group that seems most effective in handling a specific problem is "assigned" this social function by society. In other words, this is the problem that officials and the public expect the occupational group to handle. That problem then becomes the occupation's professional domain. Does social work possess such a professional domain? We suggest that the field does indeed have a legitimate social assignment or professional task: that of managing dependency and promoting productive interdependence in our society. As we discussed in Chapter 2, dependency can be defined as the inability to adequately fulfill one's social roles. This inability can stem from a lack of resources, skills, knowledge, or power. Institutional failings contribute to inadequate role functioning. Therefore, social work deals with dependency both by changing the behavior and life situations of individuals and by changing dysfunctional elements in society itself.[5]

This discussion of social work and the concept of profession should help you gain perspective on the goals, functions, and identity-seeking activities of the field. Yet it may seem less helpful in terms of your developing a personal sense of professional identity. In other words, the discussion has focused on the meaning of "profession" for an occupational group, rather than on the significance to an individual of being a "professional." When we discuss the latter with our classes, we find that although students may be critical of professions and the way some professionals behave, they tend to have a strong personal sense of what it means to act in a professional manner. They speak of having a commitment to clients, being honest and reliable, and becoming as knowledgeable and skilled as possible in dealing with social problems. We urge you to think about professionalism on this level as well, and to draw on your experience and education to develop your own definition of "being professional."

Social Work's Historical Development

A description of social work's history illustrates how a search for professional identity has shaped social work's growth. It also sheds light on current stereotypes and on the conflicting expectations of the field. In keeping with the major focus of this book, the following history is in part a political history of social work. That is, it discusses how a number of ideological perspectives have been used by social workers and others to define the desired goals and practice of the profession.

A conservative approach to social work's task reflects two major tenets of conservative ideology: a belief in individual and family responsibility and a preference for private rather than public action. Conservatives view individual factors as the dominant force in social problems and see individual strengths and weaknesses as being rooted in family and community structures and traditions. Social work's major function, in this view, is that of helping individuals and families resolve their own difficulties. This sometimes involves dealing with environmental conditions but most often stresses personal adjustment or change. Often some personal "defect," such as inadequate education or a lack of willingness to work, needs to be attended to. In the conservative view, the job of social work should be carried out under private auspices whenever possible. A minimum "safety net" of government services may be necessary to support the elderly and the "truly needy." But beyond this, government involvement in social welfare only furthers individual or family dependency.

The liberal perspective does not deny individual autonomy and responsibility. Yet it emphasizes the ways in which existing economic and social institutions contribute to problems and inequities in our society. Social workers should therefore attend to both individual and institutional change. A legitimate role for the profession is the promotion of government involvement in the social welfare system. Government policies can safeguard against the hazards of modern industrial life both through regulation (such as laws forbidding child labor) and through the provision of social welfare benefits to ensure that all citizens have adequate food, shelter, and health care. Social workers can play the role of advocates in the system, ensuring that existing public welfare programs do their jobs effectively. Private agencies are seen as supplementing the work of government programs. Thus, liberals often envision social services as being carried out through a partnership of public and private services.[6]

A very liberal, or radical, approach to social work stresses the need for a broad restructuring of existing political, social, and economic institutions. Such restructuring is necessary in order to redistribute income in our society, increase democratic control over economic and other institutions, and provide comprehensive social welfare benefits for all. Radicals, both within and outside the field, criticize social workers for seeking to adjust individuals to society and for pursuing only minimal social change. Some see the profession's major function as helping to manage the workforce so as to produce a docile labor supply for the capitalist system. Others portray social workers more generally as pawns in a social welfare industry whose main aim is to control the poor and powerless and to keep them from causing trouble. One book on welfare, edited by Betty Reid Mandell, even uses this idea in its title: *Welfare in America: Controlling the Dangerous Classes.*[7]

Radicals are often critical of social work's pursuit of professionalism. They argue, as Malcolm Payne notes, that "professionalization of social work leads to social workers being rewarded by society with status, income, and other advantages of the profession, thus promoting their acceptance of the status quo and rejection of critical analyses of the problems they are dealing with." Radical thinkers urge social workers to reject this stance and to join clients in working for meaningful change in the system. Michael Reisch, for example, encourages social workers to identify openly with groups lacking resources and power. "This role," he adds, "challenges some of our tacit assumptions about professionalism, particularly those that compel social workers to seek the approval of elite sponsors for economic, political, and ideological support."[8]

Proponents of all these perspectives can be found throughout social work's history. Various social work programs and approaches to practice can be categorized as very conservative, conservative, liberal, or radical, or even as combining elements of several perspectives. These categories thus become broad lenses through which to view social work's development.

These broad ideological outlines do not present the entire picture, however. Social work's history is also the story of internal professional conflicts and debate. These issues often relate to various political perspectives, but they also have a life of their own. Chief among social work's internal conflicts have been the following: (1) Should social workers put major stress on building a profession or on delivering a service? (2) How should social work relate to a national system of public welfare? and (3) What is the appropriate role of a profession in political activity and social change?[9]

The following history looks at both the internal struggles and the effects of larger ideological perspectives in shaping social work. This discussion focuses specifically on the development of the profession. A fuller history of the United States' social welfare programs will be presented in Chapter 9.

State Charitable Institutions

Although one could trace the antecedents of social work in the United States back to early Judeo-Christian practices of almsgiving to the poor, the more relevant place to begin is with the rise of state charitable institutions in the mid-1800s. Before such institutions, communities in the United States dealt with the dependent poor by "auctioning out" their care to the lowest bidder or, more commonly, by distributing public outdoor relief—small amounts of money or goods provided directly to the poor by local governments. Another alternative was the dreaded poorhouse, where orphans, the elderly, the unemployed, and those with physical problems or mental illness were crowded together in often unpleasant surroundings. The state institutions, in their inception, represented a progressive experiment in a more scientific, state-supported response to the needs of dependent groups. Social reformers such as Dorothea Dix led the way by campaigning for special state institutions for the mentally ill. Shocked at the conditions in which many people with mental problems were forced to live, such as unheated jail cells or dismal attics, Dix successfully lobbied state legislatures to create mental hospitals that could provide more humane treatment. Similar movements grew up around the needs of delinquents, poor children, people with developmental disabilities, and those with physical disabilities. At the same time, the earlier system of poorhouses expanded. The result was what one historian has called "the discovery of the asylum"—the creation of large, specialized, often state-financed institutions that attempted to deal more adequately with dependent populations.[10]

By the late 1800s, although public outdoor relief remained in use, these large institutions dominated the care and treatment of dependent people. Eighteen state governments had set up boards of charities to monitor and coordinate the growing system of poorhouses, mental asylums, state schools for the blind, and reformatories. The growth and regulation of these institutions led to increased occupational identity among administrators and a cohesiveness among the philanthropists appointed to state boards. Annual conferences, such as the National Conference of Charities and Correction, drew these people together to discuss common problems, staff training procedures, and other administrative issues. Their growing professional identity was one contribution to the development of social work.[11]

By the end of the 1800s, however, state institutions had greatly deteriorated. Their initial aim—to offer rational, humane care to various groups of dependent people—had been subverted by high numbers, high costs, and a recurring tendency on the part of public officials and others to use such institutions to isolate certain groups from society and to maintain social control. Although state institutions persisted well into the twentieth century, it became increasingly clear that large, overcrowded asylums and reformatories could not solve the problems of dependency.

The Charity Organization Society

As state institutions began their decline, two new social welfare movements held promise for dealing with dependency. Each was to have significant impact on the creation of social work as a profession. The first, the Charity Organization Society (COS), was initially established in England and was transplanted to the United States in 1877. The COS stressed individual factors in the development of poverty. The second movement, the rise of the social settlement, also had its roots in England and began its growth in the United States in the 1880s. The settlement house movement proposed a different approach to dependency, focusing on the environmental and social aspects of human problems.

Early charity workers and people concerned with social reform often focused on the plight of orphans and poor children.

The charity organization movement developed in part as a reaction to the proliferation of small private charities in the United States and England during the nineteenth century. Some of these organizations, notably the New York Association for Improving the Condition of the Poor, used systematic home visiting by volunteers to ensure that the "moral deficits" of poor families would be attended to as well as their economic needs. Yet by the 1870s the private charity scene consisted mostly of perfunctory almsgiving with little organized investigation of the recipients. There was also a lack of coordination among the various charitable groups. In both England and the United States, charity reformers began to call for a more systematic, "scientific" approach. In the United States particularly, the ill effects of industrialization—overcrowded cities; an exploited, low-paid working class; periodic economic depressions; and structural unemployment—led to great increases in the numbers of people asking for relief. These same social phenomena fanned the fears of middle- and upper-class people that the lower classes would revolt. At the same time, faith in progress and in the visible signs of prosperity around them allowed most Americans to view poverty as individual deviation, rather than as the fault of economic and social institutions.

This mixture of concerns—awareness of increasing demands for relief made on a poorly organized system, fear of militancy among the poor and working classes, and a belief in individual responsibility for dependency—led to the rise of the COS movement in the United States. The main premise of the movement held that private, carefully orchestrated relief efforts offered the greatest promise for the eradication of poverty. Charity organization societies proposed to coordinate the work of all private charities in a given locality in order to prevent recipients from receiving aid from several sources. Each family's application was to be thoroughly investigated. Then, in a revival of the earlier system of home visiting, volunteer "friendly visitors" would be assigned to needy families. Visitors were urged to be friendly but firm; their primary functions were to correct the character flaws of the poor and to inspire them to strive for independence and the moral life.[12]

The goals and values of the movement reflected a conservative interpretation of the causes of poverty. As espoused by leaders such as Josephine Shaw Lowell, a reformer from a well-to-do Boston family, this interpretation viewed individual dependency as one of the greatest evils of modern industrial life. The poor were in need largely because of their own shortcomings, including drunkenness and idleness; haphazard charity furthered their dependency. Government-sponsored outdoor relief was an even greater obstacle to rehabilitation. Only patient, skilled visiting by dedicated volunteers could guide families to economic independence. In Lowell's words, well-to-do visitors, generally women, brought not alms but "kind action" and served as good moral examples for the poor.[13] Direct cash help was to be avoided if at all possible. Loans and assistance in finding jobs were the preferred type of aid to "deserving" families.

Charity organization societies spread rapidly among American cities in the late 1800s. However, the initial goals of COS leaders were difficult to sustain. Individual approaches to the problems of poverty failed to stem its growth. The continuing demand for relief led many charitable societies to rely on direct cash payments to the poor. In addition, there was an insufficient pool of volunteers to maintain effective friendly visiting. For this reason, and because of a growing sense of the need for a permanent, trained staff, charities turned increasingly to the use of paid staff, called "agents," to investigate applications and to visit the poor.

These agents were a major forerunner of professional social workers. Like the volunteers before them, they were chiefly women; and they were usually Protestant, white, and middle class. This job offered an outlet for college-educated women at a time when nurturance of a family took center stage and career possibilities for women were few and far between. Charity work was a reasonably acceptable endeavor for women, as it made use of traditional feminine roles such as caring for others.

Gradually, agencies began to train their visitors. They offered informal lectures and short courses on working with poor families. The realization that friendly visiting demanded specific skills that could be generalized and taught was particularly well articulated by Mary Richmond, head of first the Baltimore and then the Philadelphia COS. Richmond had risen from the position of clerk to administrator, an unusual role for a woman at a time when most charity societies were headed by men. A

A CLOSER Look

Josephine Shaw Lowell: Leader in the Charity Organization Society

Josephine Shaw Lowell was born into a wealthy Boston family in 1843. Her parents had strong social reform commitments, and from them Lowell inherited a belief in the importance of public service. Her life was greatly affected by the Civil War. Her parents were abolitionists, and she herself joined a women's relief organization that provided aid to Union soldiers. In 1864 Lowell's husband of one year was wounded in combat; when he died, she was pregnant with their only child. This loss seemed to spur Lowell to even greater involvement in social reform. She became a major figure in the organized charity movement of the late nineteenth century. In 1872, as chair of a committee of the New York State Charities Aid Association, she conducted a statewide investigation of pauperism. Impressed by this study, the governor appointed her the first woman Commissioner of the State Board of Charities. This board dealt with both public and private charitable organizations. However, Lowell was particularly drawn to the field of private charity. She helped organize the New York Charity Organization Society in 1882 and guided its activities over the next two decades.

Lowell dressed in black and seemed to be the symbol of a self-sacrificing reformer; but she was also tough, sharp, and pragmatic. She held strong views about the causes of poverty and the appropriate remedies for it. Many of these opinions are expressed in her book *Private Charity and Public Relief* (1884). Although she is sometimes portrayed as exhibiting a moralistic and punitive attitude toward the poor, Lowell displayed a mixture of values and beliefs about dependency. On the one hand, she saw idleness as a major defect of the poor and believed that government aid to paupers made matters worse by decreasing the incentive to work. Only private charity, through its program of friendly visiting, could elevate the moral nature of the poor. Lowell also had little sympathy for "drunkards" and felt that aid to their families would simply encourage such men to count on charity to feed their wives and children. Similarly, she had little use for vagrant women and mothers of illegitimate children, and she recommended that they be committed to long terms in reformatories.

On the other hand, Lowell believed that certain people, such as orphans, widows, and the sick, were poor through no fault of their own. In these cases she regarded public responses, such as institutions or widows' pensions, as appropriate forms of relief. She viewed low wages as one cause of poverty, and she fought to improve job conditions for working women. In these situations Lowell appreciated the importance of environmental factors in poverty. Yet she tended to apply these insights and responses only to the situation of the "deserving" poor (those showing a desire to work, for example). In essence, then, she believed that personal character was the most significant element determining one's position in life.

Sources: Barbara R. Beatty, "Josephine Shaw Lowell," in Walter I. Trattner, ed., *Biographical Dictionary of Social Welfare in America* (Westport, CT: Greenwood Press, 1986), 511–515; Michael Katz, *In the Shadow of the Poorhouse* (New York: Basic Books, 1986), 68–72.

dynamic administrator and a fervent believer in charity organization, Richmond worked hard to define and to publicize the particular tasks performed by charity workers, especially the job of careful investigation into the causes of a family's dependency. In a famous speech at the National Conference of Charities and Corrections in 1897, she called for the creation of training schools in charitable work. The following year the New York Charity Organization Society responded by founding the New York Summer School of Applied Philanthropy. This series of courses for charity workers soon expanded to become a full-fledged school of social work (now

A CLOSER Look

Mary Richmond: Pioneer in Social Casework

Unlike many early charity organization and settlement leaders, Mary Richmond did not come from a well-to-do family. She was born in 1861, the daughter of a carriage blacksmith. Her mother died when Richmond was three, and she was brought up by a widowed grandmother and two maiden aunts. Her grandmother operated a boardinghouse in a lower-middle-class neighborhood in Baltimore. Richmond graduated from a highly academic girls' high school but did not go on to college. Instead, she held a series of clerical and bookkeeping jobs. In 1889 she became assistant treasurer of the Baltimore Charity Organization Society, thus beginning her career in social work.

Growing up in a household in which discussions of women's rights, race relations, education, and political reform were commonplace, Richmond inherited a concern for the weak and the oppressed. This was strengthened by involvement in church activities and volunteer work with working-women's clubs. In addition, prominent women reformers in Baltimore served as mentors and friends. The support of one of these women helped Richmond to secure the position of director of the Baltimore COS in 1891; this post had formerly been held by men with graduate training. Richmond soon rose to prominence in the charity movement. As an administrator, author, and promoter of research and training, Richmond was instrumental in establishing "scientific" casework as a foundation of social work practice. Her search for the common skills and approaches within a broad profession anticipated the development of today's generalist social work.

Sources: Muriel W. Pumphrey, "Mary Ellen Richmond," in Walter I. Trattner, ed., *Biographical Dictionary of Social Welfare in America* (Westport, CT: Greenwood Press, 1986), 622–625; Peggy Pittman-Munke, "Sisterhood Is Powerful: The Role of Women's Clubs in the Early Career of Mary Richmond," Social Welfare History Symposium, Council on Social Work Education Meetings, March 1986; Leslie Leighninger, *Creating a New Profession: The Beginnings of Social Work Education in the United States* (Alexandria, VA: Council on Social Work Education, 2000), 53–54.

Columbia University School of Social Work). Other schools began to develop in the same period.[14] And of course, formal training called for textbooks; Richmond wrote the first one, *Social Diagnosis,* in 1917.

The Social Settlement

While the charity movement was beginning to become professionalized, another approach to poverty was taking shape. The social settlement, again an idea imported from England, added a different dimension to the development of social work. Unlike the charity movement, with its stress on individual defects, social settlements focused on environmental factors in poverty.

During the 1880s and 1890s, a number of reformers from the United States visited Toynbee Hall in a slum area of London; this was a large house that served as a sort of live-in laboratory for the study of poverty by young university students. Toynbee Hall brought students in close contact with the poor and encouraged efforts at social reform. One visitor who found the idea appealing was Jane Addams. Together with her friend Ellen Gates Starr, Addams founded Hull House in a poor immigrant neighborhood in

Chicago in 1889. Although it was not the first American settlement, Hull House came to exemplify the particular brand of research, service, and reform that was to characterize much of the U.S. settlement movement.

Jane Addams grew up in a comfortable home in a small town in Illinois. Like a growing number of young, well-to-do women of her generation, she received a college education. Yet, like her peers, she faced constraints on the uses to which this education could be put. Hull House offered a way to put her education and commitment to service into action. When she and Starr first moved into the settlement, they had vague notions of being "good neighbors" to the poor around them and studying the conditions in which they lived. As they observed the structural elements of poverty, however, the two began to create a specific agenda of services and reform. Exploitation of immigrants from southern and eastern Europe, poor employment conditions and inadequate wages, lack of educational opportunities, substandard housing, and inefficient city government were the factors that contributed greatly to the poverty of the area and called for specific responses. Hull House soon offered a day nursery for children, a club for working girls, lectures and cultural programs, and meeting space for neighborhood political groups. Along with a remarkable group of reformers who came to live at the settlement, Addams supported labor union activity, lobbied city officials for sanitary and housing reforms, and established the Immigrants' Protective League to fight discrimination in employment and other exploitation of newcomers. In addition, Hull House members carried on an active program of research. Residents surveyed conditions in tenements and workplaces. They publicized their results widely, attempting to create an atmosphere conducive to governmental and legislative reform.[15]

As with the Charity Organization Society movement, the settlement experiment spread to cities across the country. Although reformers' approaches varied and some settlement workers spoke disapprovingly of the "city wilderness" around them, most held a liberal interpretation of the causes of poverty.[16] Living alongside the poor, they saw firsthand the role of environmental factors in dependence. They did not subscribe to the belief that poverty was a matter of individual defect; they felt it stemmed largely from social and economic conditions, which they worked to change. Although settlements were supported by private donations, they often looked to government as the source of reforms, both on a local level (as in city sanitation regulations) and on a national scale (as in child labor laws). In their attempts to empower the poor through support of the labor movement and democratization of political institutions, settlements like Hull House verged on a radical view of the need for fundamental social change.[17]

Those who worked in the settlements resembled the charity workers in many respects. Residents were generally middle to upper class, white, and Protestant (although settlements were also founded by black and Jewish groups). Interestingly, however, the fields differed in terms of the roles played by women and men. Male administrators dominated the leadership of the COS, with women making up the vast majority of the societies' friendly visitors. The settlement movement, on the other hand, included a fair proportion of men (about a third) among its frontline workers. Women took on a more visible leadership role, constituting about two-thirds of all settlement directors. A powerful network of women social reformers emerged from the Hull House setting,

Social Work Destinations

Hull House

Many facets of modern social work, especially its interest in the social environment and its concern with social justice, can be traced to the settlement movement. The best-known settlement of them all was Jane Addams's Hull House, located on Chicago's West Side. Although the surrounding neighborhood of Italian, Polish, German, Russian, and Bohemian residents has been largely displaced by the buildings of the University of Illinois at Chicago, two of the original Hull House buildings have been converted into a museum. A visit to the Jane Addams Hull-House Museum* offers a valuable glimpse into a pioneering period in social work's history.

The Hull-House Museum is owned and operated by the University of Illinois at Chicago. The two-building complex (the other eleven buildings of the settlement project are now gone) includes the original Hull Mansion that Addams and her friend Ellen Gates Starr first occupied in 1889 as they set out to create a center of neighborliness in a poor immigrant community. The interior, restored to look as it did in the early days of the settlement, houses rotating exhibits on the history of the settlement and the work of its residents.

The second building in the complex is the Residents' Dining Hall (1905). It contains an exhibit on the history of the surrounding neighborhood as it appeared at the turn of the century. *Address:* 800 South Halsted Street, Chicago, on the campus of the University of Illinois at Chicago. *Days and Hours:* Open Tuesday through Friday 10 A.M. to 4 P.M., Sunday noon to 4 P.M. *Admission:* Free. www.uic.edu/jaddams/hull/hull_house.

*In Addams's time, the settlement's name was hyphenated.

Source: Reprinted by permission of the Jane Addams Hull-House Museum at the University of Illinois at Chicago.

A CLOSER Look

Lillian Wald, Graham Taylor, and Lugenia Burns Hope: Three Settlement Leaders

Lillian Wald, Graham Taylor, and Lugenia Burns Hope founded settlements in New York, Chicago, and Atlanta, respectively. Coming from different backgrounds, all three leaders found in the settlement house movement a means for promoting community development and individual and social change.

Lillian Wald came to settlement work from nursing. Following graduation from nursing school in 1891, she practiced for a year and then decided to go on to medical school. As a student at the Women's Medical College in New York City, she was asked to teach a mothers' class on hygiene in a Lower East Side immigrant neighborhood. Wald was appalled by the poverty she found there and decided to leave medical school to live among those who needed her nursing skills. She and several other nurses established the Nurses' Settlement, and there they served their Russian and Romanian neighbors. By 1900 the organization, now called the Henry Street Settlement, offered a visiting nurse service staffed by fifteen resident nurses. This was the first independent public health nursing system in the United States. Wald's social reform impulse spread beyond her immediate neighborhood. In 1904 she learned of the federal government's plan to carry out a large-scale campaign against the boll weevil, a threat to the southern cotton crop. Angry that the government took no notice of the "decimation of the nation's crop of young children," she came up with a plan for a federal bureau to carry out research and exchange information on the welfare of children. Wald's idea was the seed for the U.S. Children's Bureau, which was established in 1912.

Graham Taylor was born in upstate New York in 1851. The son of a Dutch Reformed Church minister, he himself was ordained in 1873. A ministry in an inner-city parish in Hartford, Connecticut, involved Taylor in missionary work with the poor and led to a post as a professor of "practical theology" in a Hartford seminary. His work in Hartford convinced him that the church must play an active role in social reform. In 1892 Taylor moved to Chicago to organize a department of Christian sociology at the Chicago Theological Seminary. Committed to extending Christianity to an urban–industrial society, he founded the Chicago Commons settlement house in 1894. Patterned after Hull House, the Commons was set in an Irish–German–Scandinavian neighborhood. Taylor and his wife and four children became the first family to live in an American settlement house.

Lugenia Burns Hope, the youngest of seven children, was born in St. Louis in 1871. Both of her parents came from racially mixed marriages. Her father was a prosperous carpenter and farmer who died fairly young. After his death, her mother moved the family to Chicago, hoping to provide Lugenia, still in school, with better educational facilities. However, financial difficulties necessitated that Lugenia drop out of high school to become the family's principal breadwinner. She worked as a bookkeeper and dressmaker before taking a position as secretary to a charity organization, the Board of Directors of Kings Daughters. She was the first African American to do so. The organization helped the sick and needy and provided services to working teenage girls. Hope later credited this experience with giving her the idea of community organizing to prevent crime and poverty.

In 1897 she married John Hope, a college classics teacher. The couple moved to Atlanta, where John would become the president of Atlanta Baptist (later Morehouse) College. In 1908 Lugenia Burns Hope led a group of women in founding the Neighborhood Union, the first female social welfare organization for blacks in Atlanta. The Union's goal was to improve "the standard of living in the community and to make the West Side of Atlanta a better place to raise our children." As part of a plan to build a network of settlements for community development, the Union had established branches throughout the city by 1914.

Sources: Robyn Muncy, *The Female Dominion of Reform: 1890–1935* (New York: Free Press, 1991), 19, 38–39; Walter I. Trattner, *From Poor Law to Welfare State,* 6th ed. (New York: Free Press, 1999), 215–217; Louise C. Wade, "Graham Taylor," and Robenia B. Gary, "Lugenia Burns Hope," in Walter I. Trattner, ed., *Biographical Dictionary of Social Welfare in America* (Westport, CT: Greenwood Press, 1986), 707–710, 396–399; Jacqueline Anne Rouse, *Lugenia Burns Hope: Black Southern Reformer* (Athens: University of Georgia Press, 1989).

including Julia Lathrop and Grace Abbott, prominent figures in the U.S. Children's Bureau; Florence Kelley, labor and consumer advocate; Alice Hamilton, physician and social activist; and Edith Abbott and Sophonisba Breckinridge, social researchers and key leaders in the development of social work education.[18]

A CLOSER Look

Grace Abbott, Edith Abbott, and Sophonisba Breckinridge: Partners in Social Change and Development of a Profession

The Abbott sisters and their colleague, Sophonisba Breckinridge, represent a formidable trio in the development of public welfare and professional social work in the United States. Grace Abbott is perhaps the best known of the three because of her position as head of the U.S. Children's Bureau from 1921 to 1933. Yet as educators, researchers, and active members of social work and social welfare organizations, Edith Abbott and Sophonisba Breckinridge also made a major impact on the profession and its practice.

The three had excellent backgrounds for their work. Breckinridge came from a distinguished Kentucky family that had a long history of political and philanthropic service. Her father was a lawyer and member of the U.S. House of Representatives. Several women relatives had been involved in charitable work. Breckinridge herself studied law and became the first woman to pass the Kentucky bar exam. Failing to be accepted as a "woman lawyer," however, she completed a doctorate in political science at the University of Chicago in 1901 and remained there to teach. She met the Abbott sisters as students in her series of lectures on social welfare.

Grace and Edith Abbott came from a small town in Nebraska. Their lawyer father held a state political office; their mother had been a school principal. Both parents imbued their children with a strong commitment to education, women's rights, and progressive ideas. Edith Abbott studied at the London School of Economics and received a Ph.D. in economics at the University of Chicago in 1905. Her sister, more an activist than a scholar, received a master's degree in political science several years later.

All three women had important connections to Jane Addams's Hull House. The Abbott sisters lived there during their early years in Chicago; Breckinridge joined them every summer. The settlement and its immigrant neighborhood served as the setting for Breckinridge and Edith Abbott's research on housing conditions of the poor, the employment situation of working women, and child labor. Grace Abbott, with her more activist bent, headed the Immigrants' Protective League, an organization established by Addams and others as an advocacy group for newcomers to the United States. This division of labor was typical of their activities in later years. Grace Abbott went to Washington to administer the Children's Bureau; there she played an active role in developing policy and creating programs serving women and young children. She helped draft the legislation that established the Aid to Dependent Children's program (later AFDC) in 1935. Edith Abbott and Breckinridge chose to make their contribution to society as educators, scholars, and analysts of public policy. The two helped establish the School of Social Service Administration at the University of Chicago, a social work school with a primary focus on public welfare. Both were active in social work organizations and used them as forums for several major concerns: the development of a fair and comprehensive government-sponsored welfare system, the promotion of public welfare as a legitimate concern of social work, and the creation of a social work profession based on scientific knowledge gained in graduate education. The three women's major legacy was thus a wedding of professionalism with a concern for social reform.

Sources: Lela B. Costin, *Two Sisters for Social Justice* (Chicago: University of Illinois Press, 1983); Judith Sealander, "Sophonisba Breckinridge," in Walter I. Trattner, ed., *Biographical Dictionary of Social Welfare* (Westport, CT: Greenwood Press, 1986), 126–129.

In contrast to many charity workers, settlement residents were wedded to a cause rather than to a set of skills. Although less conscious of building an occupation, they developed a sense of shared purpose and cooperated with one another in campaigns for women's suffrage, protective legislation for working women and children, and municipal reform. Because they often worked with groups, they contributed to the development of group work as a social work method.

At first, charity workers and settlement residents regarded each other with suspicion. As one friendly visitor put it, the settlement house worker was like "a man who found a drunkard lying in the gutter and said to him, 'I can't help you, my friend, but I will sit down in the gutter beside you.' "[19] Gradually, however, both types of workers began to mingle in settings such as the annual meetings of the National Conference of Charities and Correction. Broadened since the days of state institutions, this group now served as a national forum for ideas about social welfare and social reform. Rapprochement between settlement and charity folk was made possible by a shift in philosophy on the part of charity organization leaders, influenced to a large extent by the devastating effects of a national depression in 1893. Key figures such as Mary Richmond and Edward Devine began to recognize that work with individual poor people needed to be coupled with broader social change. Devine headed the New York Charity Organization Society and edited the journal *Charities.* Believing that social work should move beyond charitable relief to social reform, he played an important role in campaigns for child labor laws and tenement house improvements. A growing awareness of the need to deal with economic and social causes of poverty allowed charity workers like Devine to develop a greater sense of common cause with their settlement colleagues.

Growth of a Profession

The notion of a distinct occupation—social work—was beginning to take shape. Settlement and charity work were soon joined by two new specialties, social work in medical settings and in school settings. In 1915 organizers of the National Conference of Charities and Correction invited Abraham Flexner, an educator nationally known for his expertise in evaluating professional standards, to discuss the question, "Is Social Work a Profession?" In a frequently quoted reply, Flexner answered *no.* He described social workers as mediators between clients and other professionals, such as lawyers and doctors, rather than as practitioners with their own specific competency and set of skills. Social workers appear to have taken Flexner's words as a challenge. As they pursued professional standing, they heeded the observations of Flexner and others that professions need systematic technique and specialized education based on scientific knowledge; this seemed to many of them to justify further development of individualized charity work, or, as it was coming to be called, *social casework,* and a turn away from social reform. The climate of the country in the years following World War I supported such a shift. The public was becoming suspicious of social activists, including some social workers, who seemed to promote radical change. The United States was moving away from interest in broad social reform and toward a concern with rationality and scientific expertise in government and industry. The move to build a scientific and professional social work, which came particularly from caseworkers out of the charity tradition, fit nicely with this new approach.[20]

The 1920s witnessed an expansion of the kinds of settings in which social work was carried out. Many social workers practiced in private family welfare agencies, as most charity organization societies were now called. Others worked in schools, hospitals, and children's aid societies. A new method, social work with groups, was developing within settlement houses and the YMCA/YWCA. Social workers also staffed the Home Service Program set up by the American National Red Cross soon after World War I. This program marked the beginnings of rural social work, providing casework services to the families of servicemen and disaster victims in small towns and rural areas as well as in larger communities. Child guidance clinics and other mental health facilities offered a prestigious new area for practice. These settings, which were the products of a mental hygiene movement that stressed treatment and prevention rather than custodial care, spurred social workers' interest in the use of psychological theory in their practice. One school of social work, founded by Smith College in 1918, chose to focus specifically on the new area of psychiatric social work. Settlement work and legislative reform activity continued as well, although these had lost strength since the early 1900s.[21]

The 1920s saw the establishment of the private social agency as the prototypical setting for social work practice. Although social workers were also employed in public welfare establishments, hospitals, and clinics, the social agency set the tone for much of professional development. As Roy Lubove has noted, the fact that the private agencies of the 1920s focused increasingly on administrative hierarchy, order, rational procedures, and the use of specialized skills made these agencies a compatible home for an occupation moving from volunteerism to a "scientific" professionalism.[22]

There has been a tendency among historians to think in terms of a strict division between private agencies and the various levels of government that was bridged beginning in the 1960s, and more so from the 1980s on. Yet government support for nonprofit social service organizations has been extensive for a long time. In the late 1800s, many large cities paid private institutions to care for the dependent. A study of private organizations for orphans and elderly people in New York State, for example, showed that twice as much of their support came from public as from private sources. In Chicago, many private children's institutions received public subsidies. A national survey in 1901 concluded that in almost all of the states some financial aid was given to private charities by the state, counties, or cities. Today's private agency social workers will find this a familiar theme, as they note the importance in their own organizations' budgets of government grants and contracts with public agencies.[23]

Diversity and Unification

Although the field of social work was predominantly white and Protestant, the profession also included Catholic, Jewish, and African American practitioners. Catholicism has had a long history of benevolence and the provision of assistance to people in need. The Catholic Church established hospitals and orphanages in North America as early as the 1600s. Later, in response to the Protestant focus of the COS, Catholics developed their own services for Catholic immigrants to help maintain their religious faith. A national Catholic social welfare organization, Catholic Charities, was founded in 1910. The group gave Catholic social workers a sense of purpose and identity, and helped lead to the establishment of social work programs in Catholic universities. Similarly, Jewish groups often formed their own agencies and professional schools of social work.[24]

African Americans had little choice but to follow a similar path. Several prominent African American social workers were influential in the National Conference of Social Work and similar forums, yet by and large the black social work community found it difficult to win acceptance in the field. Because of segregation laws and customs, African Americans were often unable to enroll in white graduate schools or to intern and practice in white agencies. Atlanta University School of Social Work and the National Urban League were two institutions created by African Americans partly in response to this exclusion from mainstream social work. In addition to professional development, there was a strong tradition of self-help in many black communities, with members of African American women's clubs and churches being particularly involved in social welfare activities.[25]

A CLOSER Look

George Haynes: Social Work Education and the National Urban League

George Haynes was the first executive director of the National Urban League, which he helped to found in 1910. He was born in a small Arkansas community in 1880; his mother worked as a domestic servant and his father was an occasional laborer. Haynes's mother instilled in her children strong religious and moral ideas and a belief in the importance of education. A visit to the Chicago World's Fair brought exposure to a philosophical and political ferment within urban black communities and helped Haynes develop his view that the problems of blacks in America would be solved not by emigration to Africa but rather through interracial cooperation to create equity and justice in the United States. Improved education for African Americans would help in achieving such equity.

Haynes attended Agricultural and Mechanical College in Alabama for one year and then transferred to Fisk University, where he completed his degree in 1903. Building on an excellent academic record, he received a master's degree from Yale. In his first job as Secretary of the Colored Men's Department of the International Committee of the YMCA, Haynes traveled through the South working with African American college students and encouraging high academic standards. Continuing his interest in bettering conditions for blacks, Haynes attended the New York School of Philanthropy and became its first black graduate in 1910. He completed a Ph.D. in economics at Columbia University two years later. While pursuing these degrees, the energetic Haynes maintained his involvement in the community. He worked with several organizations aimed at dealing with the problems of the large numbers of African Americans moving into New York City in the early 1900s. With Haynes's help, the activities of these groups led to the formation of the National Urban League. The new organization had a social work orientation and a commitment to interracial efforts to help African Americans achieve better employment and living conditions in urban areas. In Detroit, for example, the league helped African Americans, newly arrived from rural areas in the South, find jobs in the city's automobile plants. In a creative effort to provide training for black social workers who could then staff the league, Haynes assumed a teaching position at Fisk University. In consultation with his New York School mentor Edward Devine, Haynes set up a program in which Fisk social science students engaged in field work at the league offices. At a time when little social work training was available to minority members, Haynes's efforts were an important impetus to the entry of African Americans into the profession.

Sources: Rayford Logan and Michael Winston, *Dictionary of American Negro Biography* (New York: W. W. Norton, 1982), 297–301; Guichard Parris and Lester Books, *Blacks in the City: A History of the National Urban League* (Boston: Little, Brown, 1971), 23–28; John C. Dancy, *Sand against the Wind* (Detroit, MI: Wayne State University Press, 1966), 138.

As social work diversified and expanded, it also created unifying mechanisms. The growing number of schools of social work joined together in the American Association of Schools of Social Work in 1919. These schools varied in their structure; some were undergraduate programs, some were graduate programs, some were affiliated with universities, and others were freestanding schools closely tied to social work agencies. However, by the 1920s a movement was growing to standardize schools and to promote a master's degree as the only qualifying degree for professional practice. Although some social work educators and practitioners argued for a broader, more flexible approach to training, others successfully convinced association members that the symbol of professionalism in the United States was a graduate degree. By the mid-1930s, member schools had to offer at least one year of graduate training and to follow prescribed guidelines on course content.[26]

Similar standardization and emphasis on professionalism was beginning to be seen in the practice organizations. By the 1920s, several specialist organizations existed—one for school social workers, another for hospital social workers, and so on. In addition to these organizations, the American Association of Social Workers (AASW) developed; this was a broader group that offered membership to caseworkers across fields. The AASW tended to exclude settlement and group workers, however, as they often lacked the formal specialized training required for membership. In the late 1920s, a move within the AASW to legislate even stiffer membership requirements caused much controversy. At stake was the concept of how broad a profession social work should be. Should it, as some members argued, include a diverse group of people with different levels of professional training? Or should it, as others contended, concentrate on developing itself as a select professional group with high educational standards? The latter group won out, convincing the membership that selective professionalism was a good thing. From the early 1930s until the end of the 1960s, the major social work professional association mandated graduate training as a requirement for membership.[27]

Social work at the end of the 1920s had become rather complacent. Professional development was proceeding, and services concentrating on an individual approach to people's problems were expanding. In a famous series of meetings, the Milford Conference, caseworkers produced a report affirming that a core of casework skills existed, uniting the various fields of practice. These changes were summed up in a famous speech by Porter Lee, the Director of the New York School of Social Work. As Lee explained, social work had changed from a "cause" to a "function," from social reform to the organized provision of casework and other help to individuals with problems.[28]

The Depression and the Development of Federal Social Welfare Programs

The Great Depression that followed the stock market crash of 1929 brought a severe jolt to social work practice. As the depression spread, social workers were often the first to view its effects. In family welfare agencies, settlements, and elsewhere, social workers encountered increasing numbers of the unemployed. Their caseloads included not just the traditional poor—the elderly, minorities, and those with disabilities—but also growing numbers of working- and middle-class families. Slowly, as they looked at clients often much like themselves, social workers began to shift their ideological perspective from a focus on individual defects back to an appreciation of the social and economic factors causing dependency. As they did so, they embraced the liberal view that government should help to ensure an adequate standard of living for all citizens.

Social workers joined other groups in demanding a federal response to the problems of unemployment. They testified in congressional committee hearings on relief and helped to draft welfare legislation. Most supported President Franklin Roosevelt's creation of federally funded relief and the subsequent development of unemployment insurance and a Social Security system that dealt with the financial needs of the elderly, dependent children, and individuals with physical disabilities. It was no coincidence that Roosevelt's emergency relief program was headed by social worker Harry Hopkins and that the public assistance part of the Social Security program was directed by another member of the profession, Jane Hoey.[29]

A CLOSER Look

Jane Hoey

As head of the federal Bureau of Public Assistance from 1936 to 1954, Jane Hoey sought to build a professional public welfare service in the United States. The bureau was a part of the new Social Security program developed by Franklin Delano Roosevelt during the depression years. Hoey came to the position as a trained social worker. The youngest of nine children in an Irish immigrant family, she had attended college with the financial help of her brothers and sisters. After earning a master's degree in political science and a diploma from the New York School of Philanthropy in 1916, Hoey worked in a variety of health and public welfare jobs in New York City. She was a good friend of Harry Hopkins, the social worker who would later head Roosevelt's federal emergency relief operation. Hoey was Hopkins's assistant when he was secretary of the New York Board of Child Welfare. Hoey's brother served two terms in the state legislature, and through him she met Roosevelt and New York's governor, Al Smith. Smith appointed her as the first woman member of the State Crime Commission.

Hoey brought to her position in the Roosevelt administration a sound knowledge of state and local government and a commitment to social work in the public arena. The new Bureau of Public Assistance was in charge of developing the congressionally mandated programs of federal aid for the poor elderly, the blind, and dependent children. Hoey began with a staff of three; all were filled with excitement and enthusiasm for the new ideas being generated in New Deal Washington. Her task was to guide states in developing their own systems for administering these jointly funded programs. She promoted the use of professionally trained social workers on both the state and federal levels, against the objection that any educated person of goodwill could be a social worker. She fought vigorously against the attempts of several states to discriminate against African Americans, American Indians, and Mexicans or Latinos in providing welfare grants. One state official angrily complained to the head of the Social Security Board, "That red-headed devil of yours is in my office. She's telling me certain things that I need to do. Do I have to ?" "Yes, sir," was the unwelcome reply. Hoey was not always successful in her attempts to improve public welfare, however. Lack of state funds and trained personnel, as well as a continued aversion to the idea of government welfare programs on the part of many people, prevented the United States from developing the type of comprehensive social welfare system that was common in Europe. However, Hoey left her mark by bringing professionalism to most state welfare departments.

Sources: The Reminiscences of Jane Hoey, Social Security Project, 1965, Oral History Research Office Collection of Columbia University, The Trustees of Columbia in the City of New York; Blanche D. Coll, "Jane Margueretta Hoey," in Barbara Sicherman and Carol Hurd Green, eds., *Notable American Women: The Modern Period* (Cambridge, MA: Belknap Press, 1980), 341–343.

This was the first time the federal government had entered the realm of social welfare on a major scale. The Freedmen's Bureau, set up after the Civil War to offer aid to freed slaves, and the Children's Bureau, established by social workers in 1912, were significant but limited early endeavors. A system of veterans' pensions and services, beginning as early as 1818 with the Revolutionary War Pension Act, provided a broader precedent for federal involvement.[30] Now, during the depression, state and local public relief departments, dispensing a combination of local and federal funds, expanded at a rapid rate and provided countless jobs for social workers. As new young workers, often without professional training, swelled social work's ranks, they helped found a movement with a more radical perspective on social welfare problems. The Rank and File movement was a loose coalition of social work unions and other activist groups that grew up in the depression era. Many of the unions were formed by the new public welfare workers in an attempt to deal with demanding working conditions: huge caseloads, crowded workplaces, little job security, and salary cutbacks. Although the unions stressed improvements in job conditions, they also joined groups of established social work professionals in calling for far-reaching changes in American economic and political life. Believing that only radical changes could eradicate poverty, many Rank and File members called for such measures as a planned national economy and redistribution of income. They stressed working through the organized labor movement in their attempt to create a better society. Although it represented a minority faction within social work, the Rank and File movement provided a useful challenge to more traditional social work professional organizations and attracted prominent social workers to its cause. Harry Lurie, a well-respected Jewish charities executive, was one example; Bertha Reynolds, associate dean of the Smith College School of Social Work, was another. A leading psychiatric social worker, Reynolds sought to reconcile the ideas of Marx and Freud in a holistic view of human problems.[31]

The Rank and File movement and social work's involvement in New Deal reforms brought a new political activism to the field. Yet social workers debated the degree to which political action conflicted with professional development. Whereas some argued that politics and union activity were compatible with professionalism, particularly in a field concerned with bettering social conditions, others embraced a more traditional view of professions as objective, nonpolitical bodies. This debate remains an ongoing dilemma in social work.[32] In the depression era, mainstream social work chose to resolve the dilemma by endorsing the role of the expert witness and the consultant to the policymakers rather than that of the more direct political activist.

A growing national backlash against New Deal reforms, along with the escalation of war in Europe and Asia, contributed not only to the demise of the Rank and File movement in the early 1940s but also to social work's renewed interest in individual treatment. At the same time, social workers felt that government welfare programs were well on their way to solving the most pressing problems of poverty. Providing relief was now almost entirely the responsibility of public, rather than private, agencies. This meant that social workers could concern themselves with the more personal aspects of family and individual difficulties. They could deal with these issues in private family and children's agencies and expand their services to a middle-class clientele. The psychology of Sigmund Freud took on a tremendous appeal, and social work educators incorporated his theories in their teaching. Practitioners were even urged to undergo psychoanalysis to improve their therapeutic skills.

The commitment to an involvement in public welfare and the social policy arena did not completely disappear, however. While many schools of social work trained students primarily for casework practice in private agencies, the School of Social Service Administration at the University of Chicago, under the guidance of Edith Abbott and Sophonisba Breckinridge, carried on a tradition of educating students for leadership positions in public welfare. Jane Hoey in the Social Security Administration worked tirelessly to raise professional standards among workers in the federal public assistance programs. This was a difficult job, partly because many local communities, especially in rural areas, lacked trained social workers. These communities did not always welcome what they viewed as the intrusion of the outside expert. State and federal politicians, who wanted to grant favors by employing local residents, sometimes railed against those "damned social workers [who] are going to . . . tell our people whom they shall hire."[33]

During this time, undergraduate social work programs were established in a number of state universities and land grant colleges, with the primary goal of preparing personnel for the expanding public welfare arena. These programs, often growing out of sociology departments, formed their own organization, the National Association of Schools of Social Service Administration, in 1942. The organization grew to number more than thirty members, with a nucleus of southern and southwestern institutions, but including schools from all over the United States. The group argued that social work's stress on graduate education as the only way into the profession was both elitist and impractical in a time of growing staffing needs. By and large, however, the field of social work resisted wide-scale involvement in the developing public welfare system, perhaps because it seemed less glamorous and less professional than psychologically oriented casework in a private agency. Undergraduate social work programs were among the major victims in the debate between a public service commitment and the maintenance of high professional standards. By not allowing undergraduate programs to become members, the American Association of Schools of Social Work successfully blocked their attempt to offer accredited social work professional training on the undergraduate level. Although this would have been a practical way to staff public welfare programs, the association continued to argue that social work needed graduate training to build its public image.[34]

Continued Professional Growth

New, broader social work organizations emerged in the 1950s. These embraced a number of factions of social work, although they maintained a stress on graduate education as the symbol of professional status. The National Association of Social Workers (NASW), formed in 1955, brought together all the existing specialist organizations, including psychiatric social workers, medical social workers, group workers, and practitioners in the emerging fields of community organization and social work research. In 1952 the Council on Social Work Education (CSWE) encompassed graduate schools and undergraduate programs, although the latter were restricted to a preprofessional curriculum.

By the 1950s, social work had matured and solidified. The NASW adopted a Code of Ethics for practice and began to explore the possibility of state licensing for social workers. Schools of social work experimented with a "generic" curriculum that exposed students to a variety of practice methods and stressed the similarities among them. The idea was that whether social workers dealt with groups, communities, or individuals, they used certain common skills that should be taught to all students. The field was no longer strictly a women's profession; during the preceding several decades, men had been entering its ranks. Ironically, they tended to replace women in leadership roles in the professional organizations and schools.[35]

Once again, however, national events placed new demands on the field. The 1960s were a time of great social change. The civil rights movement, spearheaded by leaders such as Martin Luther King Jr., forced people to recognize the extent of prejudice and discrimination in a supposedly open society. A renewed concern about poverty emerged at the same time. One factor in this rediscovery of the poor was the publication of Michael Harrington's *The Other America,* a book that called attention to pockets of poverty in the midst of plenty and influenced the thinking of President John F. Kennedy and other national leaders. This revived interest in poverty led to a variety of new social welfare initiatives, such as Head Start and community-based antipoverty programs.

In the ferment of the 1960s, social work was challenged to respond effectively to the needs of African Americans, Latinos, and other minorities and to facilitate the entry of minorities into the profession. In addition, the renewed focus on poverty revived a call for political activism. Critics within and outside the field denounced social work's emphasis on individual treatment and its narrow, "objective" professionalism. Some social workers became community workers in President Lyndon Johnson's War on Poverty programs. Others, remaining in the casework field, began to stress advocacy for clients' rights within the various social welfare systems. The traditional emphasis on individual change was again augmented by attention to social and economic problems.

Other shifts took place in social work education and practice. The expansion of social services brought renewed interest in undergraduate social work training. Baccalaureate-level workers were needed to fill the increasing demand for personnel, and this time the undergraduate movement achieved legitimacy within the field. The federal government began to provide funding for undergraduate as well as graduate education. In the early 1970s, both the NASW and the CSWE accepted the BSW as an entry-level professional degree in social work. In addition to federal funding for public social services, support for social work training and activities in the field of mental health came from the National Institute of Mental Health (NIMH). NIMH was developing a new approach called "community mental health" and gave substantial assistance to social work and other disciplines, including generous fellowships for MSW students.[36]

Since the 1970s, social work has broadened its membership base to include baccalaureate-level workers and a more diverse group of practitioners. Currently, people of color make up about 10 percent of NASW membership. In the larger social service workforce, 25 percent of workers are African American and over 7 percent are Latino. Ethnic minorities constitute about 30 percent of the students enrolled in graduate schools of social work and 34 percent of those enrolled in undergraduate social work programs. There is a National Association of Black Social Workers, founded in

A CLOSER Look

Important Dates in Social Work History

1843 Dorothea Dix begins her campaign for state sponsorship of special institutions for the mentally ill.

Establishment of New York Association for Improving the Condition of the Poor.

1874 Formation of National Conference of Charities and Correction.

1877 Foundation of first American Charity Organization Society in Buffalo, New York.

1889 Jane Addams and Ellen Gates Starr found Hull House.

1904 Beginnings of formal social work education: establishment of the New York School of Philanthropy (now the Columbia University School of Social Work), the University of Chicago–affiliated Institute of Social Science (a precursor of the University of Chicago School of Social Service Administration), and the Boston School for Social Workers (later Simmons College School of Social Work).

1908 Establishment of Chicago School of Civics and Philanthropy (now the School of Social Service Administration at the University of Chicago).

1912 Formation of U.S. Children's Bureau.

1915 Abraham Flexner invited to National Conference of Charities and Correction to discuss "Is Social Work a Profession?"

1917 Mary Richmond publishes first social work textbook, *Social Diagnosis*.

1919 Organization of American Association of Schools of Social Work.

1920 Establishment of Atlanta School of Social Work to train African American social workers.

1921 Formation of American Association of Social Workers (professional organization preceding National Association of Social Workers).

1933 Franklin Roosevelt initiates Federal Emergency Relief Administration under Harry Hopkins.

1935 Passage of Social Security Act.

First national conference of Rank and File movement in social work (collection of social work unions).

1942 Rise of undergraduate social work education movement with formation of National Association of Schools of Social Administration.

1952 Establishment of single social work education association, the Council on Social Work Education (CSWE).

1955 Formation of National Association of Social Workers (NASW).

1964 Passage of Economic Opportunity Act, heralding War on Poverty.

1970 NASW grants full membership to baccalaureate social workers graduating from CSWE-approved undergraduate programs. CSWE establishes Commission on Minority Groups.

1974 CSWE begins accreditation of undergraduate social work programs. NASW reports that six states license social work practice.

1975 CSWE establishes Commission on Role and Status of Women in Social Work Education.

1982 CSWE establishes Task Force on Gay/Lesbian Issues.

1996 NASW Delegate Assembly adopts new Code of Ethics, the first major revision since 1979.

1968. African American, Latino, American Indian, and Asian American social workers are represented on committees and in the leadership of NASW and CSWE. About a third of all social workers are men; the membership of NASW is 20 percent male; and men represent about 16 percent of all students enrolled in MSW programs and about 14 percent of those in BSW programs.[37]

Working at the state and national levels, social work lobbyists promote legislation in such areas as mental health insurance parity, patients' rights, protection of victims of domestic violence, and improved staffing in the child welfare system.

The social work practice base maintains a healthy diversity. A number of social workers are active as lobbyists, chiefly within the NASW, and as advocates for client rights in areas such as developmental disability and domestic violence. Schools of social work offer training in administration, planning, and policy analysis. However, clinical social work remains the preferred area of practice for many, and an increasing number of social workers have been attracted to the private practice arena.

During the 1980s and early 1990s, a politically conservative national climate, coupled with cutbacks and underfunding of public social welfare programs, reinforced an emphasis on individual problems as opposed to systems reform. Private agency practice and entrepreneurial practice were in the ascendant. Shortly after President Bill Clinton took office, the new administration's ambitious efforts at reform in health care and other areas refocused attention on systems change. Social workers once again had access to the White House and to the federal policymaking process. NASW leaders, for example, consulted on health care and other policy issues.[38] However, the failure of Clinton's health care initiative and increased concern about the continuation of the federal deficit, among other factors, led to a resurgence of conservative ideology and the election of a Republican House and Senate in 1994. As the Clinton administration moved to the political center, endorsing budget cuts in Medicaid and Medicare and signing a restrictive welfare reform measure, social workers had to double their efforts to advocate for their clients. These efforts have continued under the presidency of George W. Bush, who has further tightened welfare policies and promoted privatization in Medicare and Social Security.

The profession's history of swings between an individual and an environmental focus may suggest a dichotomy between these emphases, yet it can be interpreted in another way. That is, social work can be viewed as having developed a unique dual perspective—an awareness of the interplay between individual behavior and larger social, economic, and political structures. Social work practice can, in fact, be rather schizophrenic, as workers try to deal both with individual and family issues and with the impact of the larger environment. But it is this dual perspective that gives social work its greatest strength.

Social Work Values and Philosophical Base

Although the work of all professions is based on certain values and assumptions—either explicit or implicit—social work is probably the most self-consciously values-based profession of all, with the possible exception of the clergy. That is, social workers pride themselves on bringing values into their practice. These values are part of a larger philosophical foundation of social work, which includes ideological and political ideas such as those discussed in Chapter 1. What are these philosophical underpinnings of social work? Do all practitioners adhere to a common set of values and ideologies? Is there consensus about the profession's principal obligations and commitments to clients and society?

Frederic Reamer is a social worker who has written extensively on these questions. He argues that social work is built on certain general philosophical assumptions, but that there is a range of possible positions related to each assumption. Social workers should therefore learn how to "think philosophically" and to analyze the various facets of these assumptions.[39]

For example, as Barbara Simon notes, the original twin missions of social work were "relieving the misery of the most desperate among us" and "building a humane and just social order." Most social workers believe that government can help achieve these goals, particularly through a fair allocation of resources. Yet social workers differ on what constitutes a right to receive resources: Is this right based on one's contribution to society, or is it based on need? Social workers also believe in the concept of equality. However, in the case of distribution of resources, some believe in absolute equality, which means that resources should be divided equally; others believe in equality of opportunity, which calls for equal *access* to resources.[40]

Social workers also believe in the *common good;* that is, in Reamer's words, in a society "whose members join in a shared pursuit of values and goals . . . and . . . understand that the good of individuals is dependent on the good of the broader community." For many, but not all, social workers, notions of the common good include a commitment to joining with others in an active attempt to improve life in the broader community.[41]

At the same time, social workers also stress individual rights and freedom, sometimes expressed as *the public interest.* This phrase refers to what Reamer calls the "assumption that society is a rational alliance of primarily self-interested individuals" in which the collective good, or public interest, consists of the sum of all private interests. Reamer sees the conflict between the concepts of the public interest and the common good as the most central philosophical debate in social work today. Which is more important—individual freedom (which in the United States often means the right to be left alone, free of the demands of others) or cooperation with other people in maintaining a strong community (a community that may not always take into account the needs and preferences of particular individuals)? Similar questions emerge in discussions of independence and interdependence (see Chapter 2) and of client self-determination and community interests. The client's right to self-determination is a cardinal principle in social work. Yet the right of clients to be autonomous persons pursuing "their own distinctive visions of their lives" may intrude on another social work value—the importance of people working together for common goals.[42]

The current social work stress on *empowerment* can be seen as yet another version of the same debate between the public interest and the common good. Empowerment has been described as "a process of increasing personal, interpersonal, and political power so that individuals can take action to improve their life situations." Again the issue is raised—should the emphasis be primarily on empowering individuals to take more control over their lives, or on empowering individuals, groups, and communities to work together to maintain, develop, and change institutions to create the good society?[43] Read in a broad way, the definition encompasses both goals, a dual commitment that is particularly characteristic of social work. Yet sometimes the goals conflict. For example, how does a social worker respond when a twenty-one-year-old client, who has grown up in an economically disadvantaged yet close-knit community and has recently received a degree in nursing, asks for feedback on his decision to move out of the area in order to work in a more affluent community? The social worker's belief in individual empowerment (and in the American dream of upward mobility) may lead to immediate positive feedback; yet further reflection might suggest the important contribution the client could make by staying in the community and working with others to maintain and strengthen community life. In another instance, a social worker in a mental hospital may help empower an individual patient by building her confidence to challenge a psychiatrist who is overmedicating her. Yet until patients (and their families and advocates) work collectively to confront the general problem of overmedication, many patients will continue to suffer.

Social workers share general goals of helping to improve individual lives and to bring about a better, more humane society. Yet as we have seen here, the profession's philosophical foundation is complex and carries certain built-in tensions and contradictions. Careful analysis and awareness of these tensions and contradictions will not resolve them but will enable us to make more informed decisions and to better understand the implications of particular philosophical approaches.

Social Work Ethics and Ethical Dilemmas

Many of social work's goals and values are embodied in the NASW Code of Ethics. The code affirms social workers' responsibilities to clients, colleagues, agencies, the profession, and the broader society. Although a code can provide general guidelines for behavior and practice, the attempt to fulfill so many responsibilities to so many groups often leads to ethical dilemmas. For example, suppose you are a social worker employed by a community center. The center is in a poor neighborhood, and many of the residents are trying to improve their surroundings by fixing up buildings, planting flowers, and asking the city to repair streets and sidewalks. One community resident, a seemingly eccentric man, persists in filling his yard with carefully hoarded trash. If residents complain to you, what do you do? How do you, as the community worker, choose between the principle of client self-determination and the concept of promoting the general welfare of the community?

The principle of client self-determination poses some of the thorniest ethical dilemmas for social workers. Philosopher Raymond Plant has noted the problems that arise for a profession so committed to caring for people and to developing effective responses to problems of dependency.[44] After all, social workers believe that they have developed an expertise in diagnosing individual and institutional problems and working toward solutions. It often seems much more effective and humane to guide clients to these solutions rather than to leave them "floundering" on their own. And yet, when a social worker counters an elderly woman's decision to live on the city streets rather than to accept the regimentation of a downtown mission, on the grounds that the woman is "too confused to know what's best for her," the worker denies the woman's right to self-determination. A similar situation arises when social workers confront the issue of whether people involuntarily committed to a psychiatric facility have the right to refuse all treatment. In a survey of clinical social workers, more than 60 percent opposed this right.[45] Respect for individual autonomy can clash not only with the social worker's sense of expertise but also with his or her desire to protect and help clients.

The client's right to confidentiality also presents problems in practice. Often the issue becomes the safety and well-being of others—as when a man confides in a social worker that he has thoughts of killing his estranged wife, or when a teen describes a drunk driving incident. Sharing information with colleagues can also involve ethical questions. For example, a field internship director may deem it necessary to confide personal information about a prospective social work intern to a field instructor. Should he or she be able to do this, and in what circumstances?[46]

"Whistle-blowing," or calling attention to illegal or harmful practices within an organization, is an important responsibility for social workers, in keeping with our commitments to the broader community. But whistle-blowing can also be difficult to carry out because of the threat of reprisals. What steps should a student intern take, for example, on learning that an agency is fraudulently billing Medicaid by misrepresenting the intern's credentials? What does a social worker do when an agency discriminates against clients based on race, sexual orientation, or other attributes?

The following description of the development of a revised code of ethics for social workers demonstrates the challenges of helping social workers deal with ethical dilemmas and value conflicts, and illustrates the complicated process of creating guidelines for ethical practice.

Updating a Professional Code of Ethics: Interview with a Key Player

Where does the NASW Code of Ethics come from? Who produces it and decides what's ethical and what isn't? How is it changed? The answers are not particularly mysterious; like many things in the world of organizations, a professional code of ethics is generally developed by a committee and adopted, after a series of consultations and revisions, by the organization's governing body. Although not mysterious, the process is complex, reflecting as it does the attempt to create an ethical code to cover a broad range of people in a wide variety of practice situations.

The latest version of the NASW Code was adopted in 1996. As Drayton Vincent, a member of the Code of Ethics Revision Committee, explains, the first code was established in 1960 (shortly after the formation of NASW). This brief code was enlarged and extensively revised in 1979. Several changes were subsequently added, but by 1995 it was clear that developments in social work practice, including the expansion of mental health managed care, necessitated a major overhaul of the standards.[47]

The president of NASW appointed a committee to review the existing code and propose revisions. The group was chaired by Frederic Reamer, who has written extensively on social work ethics, and consisted of other social workers, like Vincent, with expertise in the area, as well as a professional ethicist who headed an ethics committee in a large children's hospital.

The committee sought to create a code that would cover all fields of social work practice. In creating this set of ethical principles, the group took care not to give the impression that ethical decision making was easy or that the code was a cookbook that could "prescribe how social workers should act in all situations." Instead, the committee recognized that value conflicts and ethical dilemmas frequently arise in day-to-day practice, and that practitioners need guidelines for thinking through such situations.[48]

In revising the code, the committee consulted with state NASW chapters and licensing boards and with the major social work and social welfare organizations, such as the Council on Social Work Education, the National Association of Black Social Workers, and the Child Welfare League of America. The group periodically submitted drafts to NASW chapters and to the Delegate Assembly, which votes on all of the association's public policy positions. Development of the code was thus a highly interactive process.

The committee rewrote the code to respond to important changes in the practice environment, including the rise of computerized record keeping and the growth of managed care in health and mental health services. Such changes necessitated greater attention to issues such as protecting client confidentiality. The social worker who works in a mental health managed care setting, for example, often must supply detailed information on a client's problem to a representative of the managed care organization in order to be authorized to offer treatment. In such a situation, as the revised code points out, the social worker should inform the client about the need to disclose confidential information to the managed care company representative and should be careful that the client fully understands the nature of the disclosure before giving his or her consent. Similarly, social workers are mandated to "take precautions to ensure and maintain the confidentiality of information transmitted to other parties through the use of computers, electronic mail, facsimile machines . . . and other electronic or computer technology."[49]

The mission statement of the 1996 code emphasizes social justice as a central canon of the profession. This mission is reflected in strengthened standards on social and political action. For example, "Social workers should be aware of the impact of the political arena on practice and should advocate for changes in policy and legislation to improve social conditions in order to meet basic human needs and promote social justice." The mission also speaks of sensitivity to cultural and ethnic diversity and of the need to fight discrimination and oppression. The code states that "social workers should act to prevent and eliminate . . . discrimination against any person, group, or class on

A CLOSER Look

Excerpts from the 1996 Code of Ethics of the National Association of Social Workers

Purpose of the NASW Code of Ethics

Professional ethics are at the core of social work. The profession has an obligation to articulate its basic values, ethical principles, and ethical standards. The NASW Code of Ethics sets forth these values, principles, and standards to guide social workers' conduct. The Code is relevant to all social workers and social work students, regardless of their professional functions, the settings in which they work, or the populations they serve.

The NASW Code of Ethics serves six purposes:

1. The Code identifies core values on which social work's mission is based.
2. The Code summarizes broad ethical principles that reflect the profession's core values and establishes a set of specific ethical standards that should be used to guide social work practice.
3. The Code is designed to help social workers identify relevant considerations when professional obligations conflict or ethical uncertainties arise.
4. The Code provides ethical standards to which the general public can hold the social work profession accountable.
5. The Code socializes practitioners new to the field to social work's mission, values, ethical principles, and ethical standards.
6. The Code articulates standards that the social work profession itself can use to assess whether social workers have engaged in unethical conduct. NASW has formal procedures to adjudicate ethics complaints filed against its members. . . . In subscribing to this Code, social workers are required to cooperate in its implementation, participate in NASW adjudication proceedings, and abide by any NASW disciplinary rulings or sanctions based on it.

The Code offers a set of values, principles, and standards to guide decision making and conduct when ethical issues arise. It does not provide a set of rules that prescribe how social workers should act in all situations. Specific applications of the Code must take into account the context in which it is being considered and the possibility of conflicts among the Code's values, principles, and standards. . . .

In addition to this Code, there are many other sources of information about ethical thinking that may be useful. Social workers should consider ethical theory and principles generally, social work theory and research, laws, regulations, agency policies, and other relevant codes of ethics, recognizing that among codes of ethics social workers should consider the NASW Code of Ethics as their primary source. . . . For additional guidance social workers should consult the relevant literature on professional ethics and ethical decision making and seek appropriate consultation when faced with ethical dilemmas. This may involve consultation with an agency-based or social work organization's ethics committee, a regulatory body, knowledgeable colleagues, supervisors, or legal counsel.

Source: National Association of Social Workers, *Code of Ethics* (Washington, DC: NASW, 1996), 2–3. Copyright © 1996, National Association of Social Workers, Inc. To obtain a copy of the NASW Code of Ethics, contact your state NASW chapter.

the basis of race, ethnicity, national origin, color, sex, sexual orientation, age, marital status, political belief, religion, or mental or physical disability."[50]

One of the major issues addressed by the revised code is that of "dual relationships." These occur when social workers interact with current or former clients, colleagues, field students, or supervisees in more than one relationship. This relationship can be a professional, social, or business interaction. For example, a social worker might belong to the same golf club as a client or frequent a client-owned business. Of the ethics violations cases filed with NASW from 1986 to 1997, the most frequent violation was a dual relationship based on sexual activity. The majority of complaints were filed by women. Over one-third of the cases filed against men resulted in findings of violations; about one-quarter of cases filed against women resulted in such findings. Cases against private practitioners tended to yield a higher rate of violations than those against social workers in agency settings. As one researcher notes, "it may be that practitioners in agency settings, with institutionally created policies, procedures, and supervision, are better protected when complaints are raised," and that employees and clients may use internal grievance procedures to deal with the situation.[51]

Various debates developed in setting standards for dual relationships, including the concern of rural practitioners that in small communities relationships such as a social worker patronizing the only dry cleaning store in town, which happens to be owned by her client, could not be avoided. For this type of situation, the group agreed on a standard that states that in cases in which dual relationships are unavoidable, "social workers should take steps to protect clients and are responsible for setting clear, appropriate, and culturally sensitive boundaries."

By far the most controversial topic was that of developing standards related to sexual relationships. Neither the ethics committee nor the Delegate Assembly objected to the existing restriction on sexual contact with current clients. Conflicts arose, however, over the proposed prohibition of sexual activity with former clients. Some members of the committee argued that social workers play a variety of roles in their practice, ranging from short-term referral work to longer and more intensive counseling. Should the rule prohibiting future sexual activity apply in all cases? For example, should future sexual relationships be prohibited when the worker–client interaction consists of a one-visit consultation between a hospital employee and the social worker in the hospital's Employee Assistance Office over the availability of community resources for an aging parent? In this case, Drayton Vincent notes, the committee recognized that a ban on future personal relationships would seem unreasonable.

However, some delegates objected to the committee's addition of a statement that an exception to the restriction might be warranted in extraordinary circumstances if the social worker had clearly thought through all the ramifications of his or her actions. The final standard retained the possibility of an exception but noted that social workers, not their clients, bore the "full burden of demonstrating that the former client has not been exploited, coerced, or manipulated, intentionally or unintentionally."[52]

Such debates, and resulting revisions, led to a final version of the Code of Ethics that was acceptable to the great majority of delegates. The new code was formally adopted by the Delegate Assembly in August 1996.

Social Work Methods

Social work methods, or interventions, are the specific ways in which practitioners work with clients and communities. These interventions are influenced by the profession's value system and particularly by its dual commitment to individual and environment. One succinct definition of social work describes it as work with a person-in-situation; that is, as an effort to help individuals interact effectively with their environments.[53] This dual perspective has given rise to a broad range of social work methods, which include interventions with individuals, families, groups, organizations, and communities.

Describing and categorizing methods has not been an easy task for social work. At first, practitioners saw the field as consisting of two methods: casework and group work. The term *casework* was used to encompass a variety of interactions with individuals and families, including helping people get financial resources, providing counseling about personal and family problems, and serving as a link between clients and community services such as health care and vocational programs. *Group work*, with its roots in the social settlement and recreation work, meant providing recreational and socializing

A CLOSER Look

Social Work Roles

Outreach Worker—identifies individuals, groups, or communities that are experiencing difficulty (in crises) or that are in danger of becoming vulnerable (at risk). Outreach workers also try to detect and identify conditions in the environment that are contributing to the problems.

Broker—steers people toward existing services that may be useful to them. A goal is to enable people to use the system and to negotiate its pathways.

Mediator—intervenes between two individuals, an individual and a group, or two groups to assist people in resolving differences and working productively together.

Advocate—fights for the rights and dignity of people in need of help. This includes fighting for services on behalf of a single person, group, or community (case advocacy) and fighting for changes in laws or practices on behalf of an entire class of persons or a segment of society (class advocacy).

Evaluator—gathers information; assesses individual, group, or community problems; and helps make decisions for action.

Mobilizer—assembles, energizes, and organizes existing groups or new groups to deal with problems. Mobilization can also be carried out on the individual level.

Teacher—conveys information and knowledge and helps people develop skills.

Behavior Change Agent—works to bring about changes in behavioral patterns, habits, and perceptions of individuals or groups.

Consultant—works with other workers or agencies to help them increase their skills and solve clients' problems.

Community Planner—assists neighborhood planning groups, agencies, community agents, or governments in the development of community programs.

Data Manager—collects, classifies, and analyzes data generated within the social welfare environment.

Administrator—manages an agency, an institution, or a program or service unit.

Caregiver—provides concrete, ongoing care (physical, custodial, financial) in either an institutional or a community setting.

Sources: Adapted with permission of the Southern Regional Education Board from Harold L. McPheeters and Robert M. Ryan, *A Core of Competencies for Baccalaureate Social Welfare* (Atlanta, GA: Southern Regional Board of Ethics, 1971), 18–20; also from Betty J. Piccard, *Introduction to Social Work,* 4th ed. (Chicago: Dorsey Press, 1988), 27–28. Reprinted by permission of Brooks/Cole Publishing Company.

experiences to groups of clients. By the 1930s, *community organization* was accepted as a third method; it generally meant community planning activities such as those carried out by the Community Chest, which helps coordinate and raise funds for private social agencies. In the 1950s, administration and social work research were added to the list. More recently, many schools of social work have collapsed this array of methods into two categories, or tracks, often labeled "direct practice" or "clinical social work" and "planning, administration, and community organization." Planning and community organization are now listed separately because the latter has come to mean work with neighborhood groups and individual residents to strengthen communities and to help the people within them achieve greater power over their lives.

Conceptualizing social work methods as a division between the direct practice and planning/organization tracks creates some problems. First, it encourages the idea that practitioners must choose a single area in which to work. Second, it can lead to the assumption that all social change activity belongs on the community organizing and social planning side of the dividing line and that the direct practice approach is concerned only with adjusting clients to the status quo. Finally, this rather arbitrary separation fails to take into account skills and roles that cut across the categories.

One way to deal with these problems is to add to the picture an understanding of the various roles social workers play. These include behavior changer, advocate for client rights, consultant, mediator, and evaluator. Most of these roles apply to the whole range of methods described previously. For example, advocacy for the right of an individual with a developmental disability to receive a public education can be a part of the job of the clinical social worker working with individuals and families, the group worker, or the community organizer. The interchangeability of such a role indicates that certain commonalities exist among the various methods and that social change activity is not limited to one side of the dichotomy.

Social work methods and roles have evolved over the years. Group work, for example, now includes group therapy, self-help groups, and problem-specific groups such as those focusing on adult children of alcoholics. Community organizers concentrate more on economic development than on organizing people around issues of power. Clinical social work with individuals and families draws on a wide variety of therapeutic approaches, including behavior modification, short-term counseling models, and cognitive therapy. An increasingly important social work role within social treatment is that of case manager, which we describe in detail in Chapter 4. Finally, social workers in the area of planning and administration use a range of skills, including budgeting, evaluation of social agency programs, and personnel administration.

A Model of Social Work Practice

Social work methods are a part of the larger phenomenon of social work practice. This larger picture includes additional elements: fields of practice, social problems, and the different sizes and types of social groupings with which practitioners are concerned. Fields of practice are the broad areas in which social work takes place, including the medical, juvenile justice, and mental health systems. A social problem is anything that either the majority of people in society or the people in power decide needs special attention. Social problems include mental illness, substance abuse, and poverty. Finally, the social groupings that social workers relate to range from individuals to entire communities.

A social worker might choose, for example, to practice in school social work. In this job, the worker would be concerned with a variety of social problems such as juvenile delinquency, substance abuse, and racial discrimination. He or she might work with individual students, families, and groups of staff, including teachers. Finally, the school social worker would engage in whatever methods were appropriate to the particular situation, including individual counseling, group work, and social planning.

Nancy K. Carroll developed a three-dimensional model to illustrate the interaction of these variables in social work practice.[54] We have adapted the model here by adding the element of fields of practice, making it a four-dimensional model; see Figure 3.1. We find this model a useful way to envision the many facets of social work.

FIGURE 3.1 **A Four-Dimensional Model of Social Work Practice**

Source: Adapted from Nancy K. Carroll, "Three-Dimensional Model of Social Work Practice," *Social Work 22* (September 1977), 431.

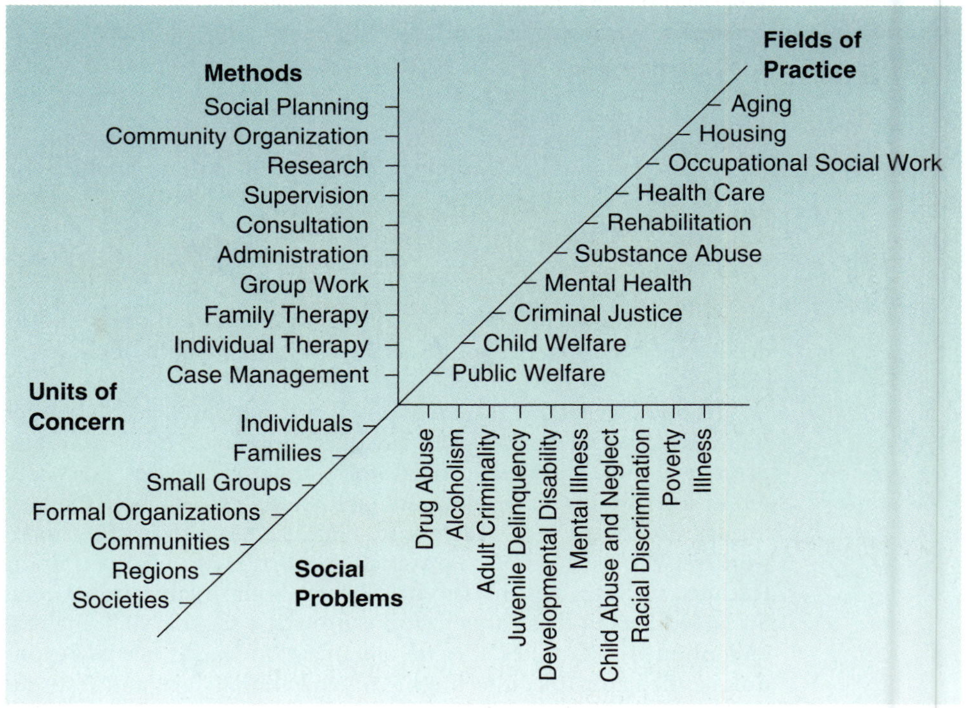

The various dimensions of practice offer numerous opportunities for specializations in social work. One can opt to be a medical social worker, a community organizer, or a psychiatric social worker with a particular expertise in treating substance abuse. Whereas some social workers view specialization as an effective and indeed necessary division of labor within an unusually broad field, others argue that practitioners should be generalists who are familiar with a variety of methods, settings, and social problems. The advantage of the specialist approach lies in the depth of expertise a worker can offer in a particular area. The merit of a generalist stance is its flexibility. The worker can view the client situation in a holistic manner, and can either use a variety of methods or refer clients to other resources for these different approaches. The specialist–generalist debate has a long history in social work.[55] The debate raises several important issues: How can clients best be served? How can specialization be reconciled with a need for coherence within the profession? And how can social work best gain public recognition for its expertise—through developing specializations or through promoting an integrated set of skills? The tension between specialization and generalist practice may never be completely resolved, and the profession may continue to combine both approaches. One way this division has been formalized since the mid-1970s is the Council on Social Work Education's designation of baccalaureate training as education for generalist practice and MSW programs as the arena for specialization. However, even this tidy division can break down as graduates pursue subsequent careers.

Practice Settings

Beyond the diversity of methods, fields of practice, and social problems, social workers encounter additional variety in the range of settings in which their work is carried out. Social workers practice in nursing homes, hospitals, county social service departments, mental health clinics, family and children's services agencies, centers for independent living for clients with disabilities, homes for delinquent youth, substance abuse programs, crisis phone line programs, private counseling practice, schools, community centers, social research and planning organizations—and the list goes on. Indeed, one of the advantages of social work is the breadth of choice it offers in places to practice.

As one surveys this vast array of settings, it helps to keep a few general categories in mind. First, social work is generally divided between practice in host institutions and practice in more specifically social work–oriented agencies. Host organizations include public schools, hospitals, and nursing homes—places where the dominant goal of the organization is not social service but education, health maintenance, or the like. Social workers, who usually make up a small proportion of the organization's staff, work with teachers, nurses, and others to help bring about organizational goals (see Figure 3.2). Social workers in these organizations provide a specific skill, such as counseling or intervention with families, that the organization feels it needs. Beyond this, they play a unique mediator role, interpreting organizational aims and restrictions to clients and conveying client needs to the organization. Thus, a hospital social worker may explain the importance of the physician's prescribed medications to a patient and at the same

FIGURE 3.2 **Organizational Chart for the Patient Services Division of Hanley Falls Hospital**

Note: The social work staff are located in the Social Services Department.

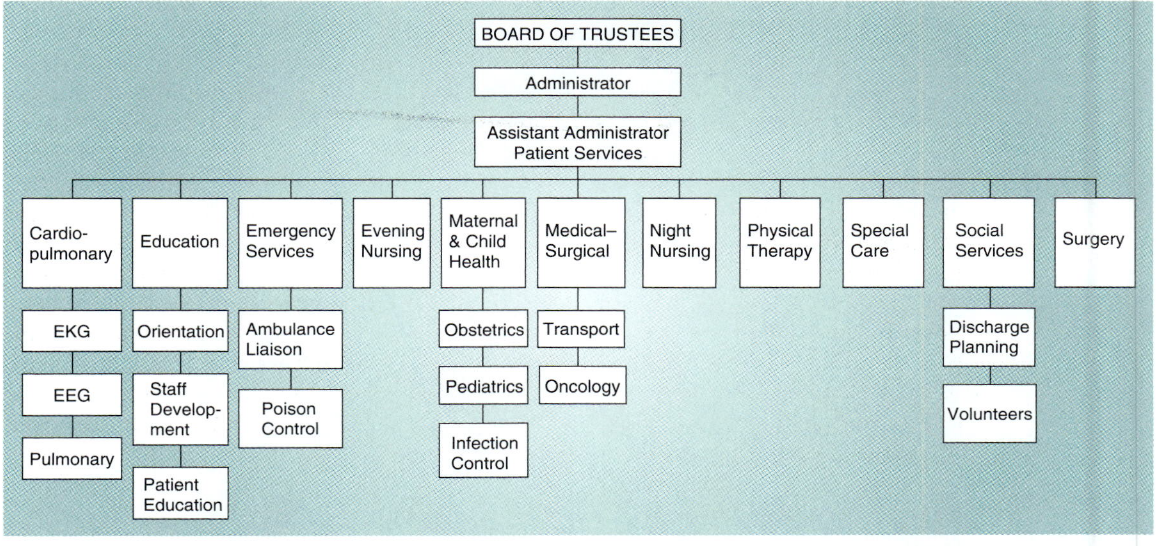

time convey to the nursing staff that the patient's "troublesome behavior" regarding medication stems from a fear of dependence on drugs.

An alternate kind of setting is the one staffed primarily by social workers. Family and children's services agencies, which provide individual and family counseling, referral services, and parent education, are a good example (see Figure 3.3). One advantage of these settings is the sense of professional cohesion and common identity they can offer. Finally, there exists a middle ground between the host institution and the social work setting. A number of human services organizations, such as outpatient mental health centers and educational programs for teenage parents, use staff from a variety of disciplines. In those settings, professionals can work together to provide a broad set of services for clients.

Another traditional distinction between social work settings has been the division between public and private sponsorship. The growth of public social services increased dramatically during and after the Great Depression. Federal involvement in mental health and veterans' programs has also expanded. And, of course, state and local governments continue to play an important role in providing health and human services. Alongside these exists the long-standing network of privately funded social agencies, including those sponsored by religious denominations. However, the distinction between public and private institutions obscures the great degree of interdependence between the two.

FIGURE 3.3 **Organizational Chart for Utopian Family Organization, Inc.**

Source: Courtesy of Danny Thompson and John Flynn, School of Social Work, Western Michigan University.

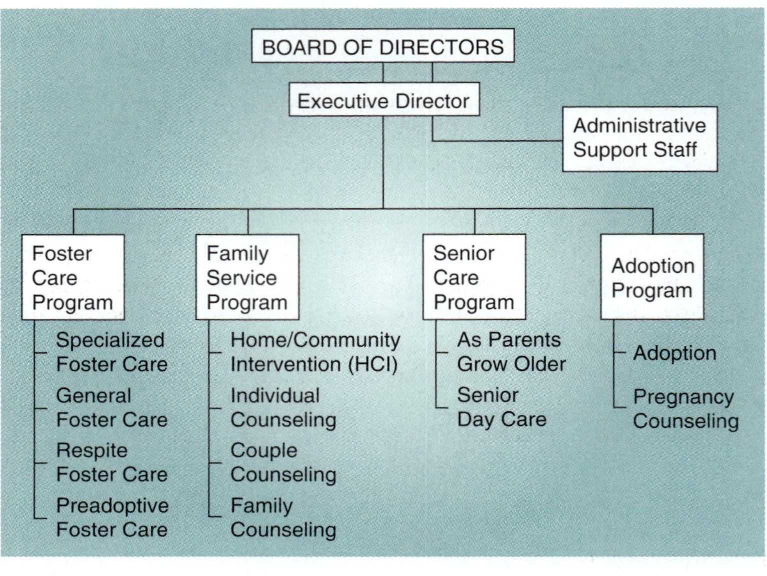

Today, many public agencies contract out their services to private organizations; for example, a county social services department may delegate its job training program to a private agency. As managed care has grown as a technology for delivering health and social services, state health and welfare departments have increasingly turned to private, often for-profit managed care companies to manage services to Medicaid and public assistance clients. (See Chapters 12 and 13 for more detail on managed care.) A growing area for social work practice is in private, for-profit organizations, including mental health managed care companies (such as those that contract to serve a Medicaid population), for-profit nursing homes, and private psychiatric facilities for children and adolescents. According to a recent NASW survey, about 36 percent of NASW members worked in such organizations in 2002. For-profit organizational work also includes social workers in private practice, in which social workers "deliver [their] services autonomously to clients in exchange for mutually agreed payment." Most private practice involves clinical services. In 2002, 20 percent of NASW members were engaged in full-time, solo private practice, while another 5 percent worked in a private practice group. About 35 percent of the association's membership worked in private nonprofit organizations, and about one-fourth worked in public settings such as state child welfare departments.[56]

Finally, practice settings differ in terms of whether their programs are mandatory or voluntary for clients. Although social work students are sometimes led to believe that all services are freely chosen by clients, many settings are required by law to constrain clients and to mandate their involvement in particular programs. These are the "involuntary services" referred to in Chapter 2 for people whose dependency stems from an inability to fulfill roles as defined by others. Obvious examples are incarceration in correctional institutions and involuntary commitment to mental hospitals. However, clients are also ordered by courts to attend therapy sessions in marital counseling programs and are required to work with social workers in child abuse cases. Even "voluntary" clients may be attending a substance abuse treatment group, for example, under pressure from family and employers. Greater attention to this voluntary–involuntary continuum within practice settings would help social workers grapple with issues surrounding authority and develop skill in intervening effectively with involuntary clients.

No matter what the setting, the majority of social workers practice in a complex organization. The importance of the organizational context for practice cannot be overstated. Although not all settings are as highly bureaucratic as, for example, a Veterans Administration hospital or a large county department of social services, most agencies (even small ones) contain some bureaucratic features. These include specialization of tasks, a hierarchy of authority, formal rules and guidelines, and documentation of activities and procedures—the infamous "paperwork." Some practitioners view organizational rules and structure as obstructions to practice, and, in fact, the desire to escape such perceived constraints has been one motivation for entering private practice. Other practitioners concentrate on realizing the organization's potential for providing equitable and effective services to clients and on developing their own ability to shape organizational goals.[57]

Salaries and Job Opportunities

There are two major sources of data on social work jobs and salaries, the U.S. Bureau of Labor Statistics (BLS) and NASW. NASW membership surveys offer the most precise information on practice areas and salaries, but because only a small proportion of BSW practitioners belong to the organization, the information focuses largely on MSW practice. The BLS covers all persons in the occupational category of social work, including those without social work professional degrees. The U.S. Current Population Survey lists 782,000 people who identify themselves as social workers. The majority of these hold bachelor's degrees (although not necessarily BSWs). Overall, only a quarter of those with bachelor's and master's degrees belong to NASW.[58]

A recent NASW survey offers detailed information on salaries and job placement. In 2001 the median salary for full-time MSWs was $49,500, a $4,000 increase from 1999. About 40 percent of MSWs made between $50,000 and $80,000. Eleven percent of MSW social workers made $80,000 or more, and 6 percent made less than $30,000. Although the MSW survey had too few BSW respondents to yield reliable salary information, it is estimated that BSWs, on average, make about $10,000 to $12,000 less than MSWs (prompting NASW to lower its dues to two-thirds of MSW member rates). According to the BLS, the average wage for all social workers (bachelor's and master's levels, professional and nonprofessional degrees) was almost $33,000 in 1998. The highest salaries were for medical and public health social workers.[59]

The field of mental health employs the largest number of social workers, and, in fact, social workers represent the greatest single group of mental health professionals. Currently, 50 percent of NASW members identify mental health as their major area of practice. The next largest practice areas are child welfare and family services (16 percent of NASW members), followed by health, school social work, and aging.[60]

Baccalaureate social workers are more likely than MSWs to work in the public sector, which is in keeping with the original goal of undergraduate education for professional social work. The primary areas in which BSWs work are children and family services, mental health, health, and aging.[61]

Social work has recently become a high-growth area. The BLS predicts that the number of mental health and substance abuse social workers with master's degrees will increase by 39 percent between 2000 and 2010. Social work education has also expanded, with 149 accredited MSW programs and 431 accredited BSW programs in 2002. Social work's image may also be improving. Of the many newspaper and magazine stories sent monthly to NASW by a clipping service, the vast majority are positive portrayals of social workers. Sixty percent of respondents to a phone survey on social workers conducted by Dr. Craig LeCroy of the Arizona State University School of Social Work reported that social workers were "very valuable" to the community.[62]

As we noted at the beginning of this chapter, you will encounter a certain amount of skepticism regarding the ability of BSW graduates to find a "real" social work position. However, although a few areas in the field, such as school social work and intensive individual counseling, are normally closed to BSWs, most other types of social work have opportunities and challenges for practitioners at both the baccalaureate and master's levels.

Social Work Education and Knowledge for Practice

Social work's breadth and diversity present a particular challenge to professional education. How can practitioners be trained in all the diverse aspects of the field? How can they develop an effective grounding in the dual perspectives of individual behavior and environmental influence? A part of the solution is to use knowledge from many disciplines in educating social workers. Sociology, anthropology, psychology, political science, and economics are among the fields from which social work draws. This is why many social work undergraduate programs require students to take courses in the social sciences. Yet this use of knowledge from other areas can be problematic. A familiar complaint of social work students is, "That sociology [or psychology or economics] course has too much theory in it and doesn't have anything to do with social work!" Application of theoretical material to practice is a difficult task, especially if the material has been developed by another discipline. In addition, profession building seems to some social workers to call for an independent knowledge base. This might imply less use of other disciplines.

The desire for autonomy, in addition to conflicting goals of different fields, has led to tensions between social work and other disciplines, especially sociology.[63] Over the years, social work has struggled to deal with these dilemmas by adapting knowledge borrowed from other fields as well as developing its own body of theory and research. The discovery of unifying intellectual frameworks, such as social systems theory, has helped social work bring some coherence to this diversity of facts and theories.

Social work research has been emphasized particularly in the field's doctoral programs, which have expanded greatly since the 1950s. Sixty-four schools now offer doctoral degrees in social work. These schools prepare students primarily for positions as teachers and researchers, although a few programs specialize in advanced clinical work. The BSW and MSW degrees equip individuals for beginning- and advanced-level professional practice. A final piece of the social work educational continuum is the two-year college degree in social work or human services, which prepares students for work as social work aides or technicians in mental health, social services, or similar settings.

Current Professional Issues

The several levels of social work education are often seen as relating to a continuum of practice. Defining the steps in this continuum has been a difficult task, yet it seems a necessary response to the need to staff a large number and variety of social work positions. Numerous studies have been conducted to differentiate between MSW and BSW social workers in terms of skills and job functions. The results have been conflicting and often inconclusive. So far, we know little about variations in types or levels of skills between the two groups, although according to one study BSWs perform better in the social broker role of obtaining resources for clients. Another study concluded that MSWs working in public social services settings are more effective in intake and counseling than are BSWs in those settings. Although reports on actual job functions of the two levels of social workers have often found few differences, a comprehensive task analysis by Robert Teare and Bradford Sheafor revealed that although both BSWs and MSWs function primarily as providers of direct services, within that area BSWs focus more on case management and MSWs on therapeutic interventions. BSWs, Teare and Sheafor noted, tend to have a stronger orientation toward change in the client's situation, whereas MSWs generally display a more specialized clinical approach to practice.[64]

Further effort is needed to clarify the abilities and skills of BSWs and MSWs and to create a workable practice continuum that spells out appropriate job functions and/or skill levels for each group. Social work education faces a similar challenge in its attempt to define and to differentiate between the foundation and the advanced curriculum. A particular flashpoint for this attempt is the development of Advanced Standing programs, in which graduates of accredited BSW programs receive some degree of credit toward an MSW degree. The fact that Advanced Standing arrangements vary greatly across the country stems in part from the profession's continued difficulty in seeing how the foundation or generalist part of social work education and the advanced curriculum fit together.

The continuum issue also plays a role in discussions of social work licensing. All fifty states now have laws regulating social work practice. Yet these vary from state to state. Many states license the practice of social work, whereas some simply protect the title (i.e., people without the license can't call themselves social workers). In addition, states differ on which levels of practice are regulated. Some states license at only one level, generally that of "advanced clinician." Achievement of this designation typically requires a licensee to undergo two years in supervised clinical practice after receiving the MSW and to pass a standardized clinical licensing exam. Thirty-four states have "multiple-level licensing" that includes the BSW and/or the MSW without post-master's practice experience. Social workers in several of the states with one level are debating among themselves whether to develop multilevel licensing. These debates reawaken all the questions about "Who can do what?" and "Who is trained for what?" and the uncertainties about how the different portions of the field fit together.[65]

A major rationale given for social work licensing is the necessity of protecting the public by ensuring the competence of social work professionals. (Complaints against incompetent or unethical practitioners can be brought before a licensing board, which investigates the case and can enact sanctions.) A less publicized goal is that shared by many professions: the maintenance of a gatekeeping function, which restricts entry to a field. One group that appears to be particularly invested in social work licensing is the growing body of private practitioners who offer clinical services. These social workers compete with psychologists, counselors, and other mental health workers for recognition by the organizations, including managed care companies, that reimburse for treatment. A clinical social work license becomes an important credential for social workers in private practice, who may fear that the introduction of licensing for BSWs and just-graduated MSWs will water down the strength of their own credential. In Louisiana, for example, when several social work groups proposed moving from a single advanced clinical license to a multilevel structure, the loudest protests came from private practitioners.

The latest development in social work credentialing is the creation of a model licensing act by the Association of Social Work Boards (ASWB), which represents all state social work licensing organizations. The model act seeks to improve public protection by establishing basic standards regarding (1) minimal social work competence, (2) fair methods for addressing consumer complaints, and (3) objective processes for recognizing incompetent and/or unethical practitioners and removing them from practice. Under the model act, states have some leeway in adapting the law to their particular circumstances. At the same time, by accepting basic national standards, the states will contribute to a greater consistency in social work practice. The ASWB hopes that such consistency will lead to increased public understanding and acceptance of social work.[66]

The model act calls for licensing of all three levels of social work practice: BSW, MSW, and advanced clinical work. It increases the status of BSW practice by recognizing that all social workers, not just those with a master's degree, can practice independently (i.e., outside of a supervised agency setting) after two years of supervised experience. The developers of the act report that the most difficult part of their job was differentiating between the definition of BSW and MSW entry-level practice. They concluded that although both degrees provided a generalist social work education, the MSW degree offered preparation for specialized practice. Thus, the act describes baccalaureate social work as "basic generalist practice that includes assessment, planning, intervention, evaluation, case management, information and referral, counseling, supervision, consultation, education, advocacy, community organization, and the development, implementation, and administration of policies, programs, and activities." The act defines MSW practice as the "application of specialized knowledge and advanced practice skills" in the exact same areas. Although an improvement over past definitions, these distinctions still lack the precision that many social workers hoped for.[67]

Some social workers have also expressed concerns about what they see as a shift of focus within the profession toward private, clinically based practice. In a widely read book, *Unfaithful Angels: How Social Work Has Abandoned Its Mission,* Harry Specht and Mark Courtney criticize this change. They argue that by leaving public and private agency social services to enter private practice, social workers have turned to a middle-class, mostly white clientele, and away from the poor and oppressed. Specht and Courtney, along with others in the field, ask whether social work will maintain its ideal of building a stronger society through social action and a commitment to the public social services, or whether it will become yet another profession of therapists.[68] All these debates—controversies about the nature of the social work continuum, the structure of social work licensing, and the major mission of the profession—can be difficult and uncomfortable. Yet, in keeping with the model of professionalization described at the beginning of this chapter, they are part of a dynamic process of shaping a cohesive professional identity.

Two other developments in social work bear mentioning, as they will have great influence on the future of social work education and practice. The first is the growing importance of an international perspective on social work and social welfare, and an appreciation of the interconnectedness of all regions of the globe. The breakup of the Soviet Union has led to the struggle of former communist states to create new economic and social welfare structures. At the same time, developing countries have been expanding their social welfare systems. U.S. social workers have consulted in both situations to help with welfare planning and the expansion of social work education. In the process they have gained new perspectives that have value for social work in this country, particularly in the area of community development. The increasing immigration of Latino and Asian groups to the United States creates another impetus for global awareness. Effective social work with immigrant groups calls for knowledge of the international economic forces that lead to migration and of the social, cultural, and political systems that immigrants come from. The emergence of a global women's movement brings worldwide issues of social services and supports for women and children to the fore. Finally, a small but growing number of U.S. social workers attend international conferences where they share ideas and experiences with social work educators and practitioners from around the world.[69]

Social workers are also becoming increasingly involved in electoral politics, either as members of the staff of elected officials or as politicians in their own right. Becky Fast is an example of the former group. She directs constituent services for Rep. Dennis Moore, a member of the U.S. House of Representatives from Kansas. These services include help with small business loan applications; immigration, naturalization, and citizenship matters; and questions about Social Security, Medicare, student loans, and veterans' benefits. There are also over 170 social workers currently serving in national, state, and local elected positions. The U.S. House of Representatives includes Ciro Rodriguez (Texas), Barbara Lee and Susan Davis (California), and Ed Towns (New York). Barbara Mikulski (Maryland) and Debbie Stabenow (Michigan) serve in the U.S. Senate. Social workers also hold office in state and local governments. Look around you—chances are you'll discover political social workers in your own community.[70]

Social workers are often seen by the public as politically and socially liberal. This assumption seems reasonably accurate. In a study of first-year MSW students at a large midwestern state university, 46 percent of respondents identified themselves as liberal, 31 percent as "middle of the road," and 23 percent as conservative.[71] Other research indicates that, on social issues such as abortion and divorce, social workers as a group are more liberal than people affiliated with conservative religious denominations (see Table 3.1).

Perhaps the greatest changes in social work in the coming years will arise from the second development: the extraordinary growth of information technology. Computers

TABLE 3.1 Opinions on Abortion and Divorce: Social Workers as a Group and People Affiliated with Conservative and Liberal Religious Denominations

	Total Population of Social Workers		People Belonging to Conservative Religious Denominations	People Belonging to Liberal Religious Denominations
Legal abortion should be available if	%[1]	n	%[1]	%[1]
Health endangered	95	(109)	87	96
Raped	90	(103)	75	94
Unable to afford child	91	(91)	35	69
Wanted for any reason	65	(60)	28	60
Divorce laws should	%[1]	n	%	%
Be easier	30	(29)	26	31
Be more difficult	37	(35)	54	40
Stay the same	29	(28)	16	24
Don't know	4	(4)	5	6

Source: David R. Hodge, "Differences in World Views between Social Workers and People of Faith," *Families in Society 84* (April/June 2003), 285–295. Reprinted by permission from Families in Society (www.familiesinsociety.org), published by the Alliance for Children and Families. Data based on General Social Surveys, conducted by National Opinion Research Center (NORC).

[1]Percentages in tables may not add up due to rounding.

already assist in client assessment and in decisions about appropriate services; for example, there are computer programs that help practitioners determine the existence of child abuse and neglect and give guidance in child placements. The Internet provides numerous sources of information regarding direct practice, research, and policy, such as web sites on health care policy, social welfare legislation, and psychiatric diagnosis. Compressed video systems and online courses make distance education viable for colleges and universities. Listservs and e-mail bind us together, allowing for discussion of issues, consultations with other practitioners on problem cases, and descriptions of grant opportunities. Because of the potential of these electronic resources to improve social work education and practice, we have provided representative samples at the end of most chapters.

Yet the new technology raises various ethical, legal, and political issues for social workers. Confidentiality of client records must be protected in the electronic age just as it was in the age of paper files and intake forms. The "information highway" has reached the upper and middle classes, but it has not been extended to many poorer individuals and families. Social workers will need to advocate for equal access to these resources. Used fairly and wisely, computer technology can be a powerful tool to build community and improve social work practice.[72]

Social Work in the Larger Field of Social Welfare

Social work's interest in continuum, licensing, technology, and practice issues reflects the profession's need to define itself and its role within a larger social welfare system. Many occupations have some relationship to this system, and each struggles to maintain a professional identity and control over a particular realm of practice. Tendencies toward competition are countered by the desire to help clients, which often means cooperation with members of other disciplines. Thus, social workers are challenged to develop positive working relations with nurses, psychologists, planners, and others. Much of current practice is multidisciplinary and ranges from interdisciplinary treatment teams in mental health facilities to ongoing consultation between teachers and social workers in school settings. Social workers bring unique skills and perspectives to these joint endeavors: an expertise in helping clients use a broad network of social welfare services; an appreciation of the individual's right to self-determination; and, most significantly, an ability to focus on both individual and social change in dealing with issues of dependency.

Perspectives on Practice

Present-day social work continues to encompass several ideological perspectives on practice. The conservative approach holds that individuals, families, and communities, rather than the federal government, should bear the major responsibility for dealing with social problems. These problems, including poverty, hunger, teenage pregnancy, and substance abuse, are defined primarily in individual terms. That is, poverty stems from a person's unwillingness to work, and hunger arises from a lack of knowledge of community programs that provide food. Although few social workers adopt this position in its entirety, some have embraced another tenet of recent conservatism: a focus on the private marketplace as the provider of social services.

Social workers who see themselves as liberals generally argue against both the individualization of social problems and the growth of a "privatized" social welfare system. They view individual problems as being related both to personal factors and to larger structural difficulties in our country. Such structural problems include unemployment and the lack of opportunities for women and minority group members to advance into meaningful roles in society. Although liberal social workers support individual and local community involvement in problem solving, they tend to stress the necessity for broader governmental intervention, particularly on the federal level.

Finally, radicals within social work continue to push for greater client involvement in the planning and provision of services, more attention to the social control function of social welfare, and fundamental changes in social and economic structures. For example, radical social workers working with the homeless might argue that homeless families should be given a chance to develop and run cooperative low-income housing units. Such social workers would be publicly critical of what they would term city merchants' efforts at social control, such as "sweeping the homeless off of downtown streets" and relegating them to large shelters. Finally, radical practitioners would draw connections between homelessness and the market economy's stress on the development of profitable luxury housing rather than on the provision of decent accommodations for people with modest incomes.

Conclusion

Social work, like other professions, contains conflict and diversity—although social work is probably broader and more diverse than most. One internal debate centers on whether dependency is caused by individual or broad social factors. Out of this debate has arisen a dual focus on individual and social change, and on the personal and the environmental factors in social problems. The liberal and radical perspectives express this duality most clearly. Even at the conservative end of the continuum, however, social workers acknowledge some degree of external influence on individual difficulties.

This consciousness of an interrelatedness between what C. Wright Mills terms "private troubles" and "public issues" is one of social work's greatest strengths. As *Judging Amy* star Tyne Daly proclaimed in a speech at NASW's Social Work 2000 Conference, "I [learn] from you because you are the ones dealing with all the bad institutions of our society: institutionalized poverty, institutionalized racism, institutionalized cynicism. . . . If I can represent you in some way, I find it a huge responsibility because you're the real deal and I'm the reflection."[73]

Visit **www.researchnavigator.com** to research these important concepts from the chapter:

Community organizing
Jane Addams
National Association of Social Workers
Social work education
Social work practice
Social work profession

Web Sites of Use to Social Workers

Allyn and Bacon <www.ablongman.com>: The latest information on textbooks, including social work and social welfare textbooks, published by Allyn and Bacon.

American Public Human Services Association <www.aphsa.org>: Information on organization and on welfare reform legislation, publications, conferences, and events. Links with state, federal, and other web sites on related subjects.

Association of Baccalaureate Social Work Program Directors <www.bpdonline.org>: Description of organization, association's online newsletter, list of accredited MSW and BSW programs. Information on Internet resources for social work education, information technology resources, social service databases, curriculum resources, social issues, and more.

Association of Social Work [licensing] Boards <www.aswb.org>: Information on social work licensing and certification in all fifty states, District of Columbia, Puerto Rico, and Virgin Islands. Descriptions of ASWB licensing exams, study materials, applications.

Clinical Social Work Federation <www.cswf.org>: Information on clinical issues.

Council on Social Work Education <www.cswe.org>: Information on structure and purpose of CSWE, accreditation, Annual Program Meeting, publications. Directory of accredited MSW and BSW programs.

Handsnet on the Web <www.handsnet.org>: Web site of Handsnet, a national nonprofit organization promoting information sharing, collaboration, and advocacy among individuals and human service/public interest organizations working on broad range of public interest issues. Forums, policy alerts, and research on health issues, child welfare, housing, welfare reform, and juvenile justice.

In Motion <www.inmotionmagazine.com>: Multicultural online magazine promoting grassroots organizing and providing information for community organizers on issues such as affirmative action, civil rights, health care, and needs of rural communities.

Latino Social Work Organization <www.lswo.org>: Web site of organization open to all social work students, social work professionals, educators, psychologists, counselors, and community activists serving the Latino community. Advocacy, workplace issues, conference information, links to other web sites.

National Association of Social Workers <www.naswdc. org>: Information on structure and purpose of NASW, current policies, lobbying, and other activities. Legislative alerts, documents such as the revised Code of Ethics, links to NASW chapter sites.

The New Social Worker <www.socialworker.com>: Online magazine for social work students and recent graduates. Covers social work practice specialities, social work ethics, people in the profession, job search/career guidance, and news from campuses.

World Wide Web Resources for Social Workers <www.nyu.edu/socialwork/wwwrsw>: Links to journals, newsletters, policy reports, professional associations, government agencies, and more.

Endnotes

1. Ernest Greenwood, "Attributes of a Profession," *Social Work 2* (July 1957), 45–55; William J. Goode, "The Theoretical Limits of Professionalization," in *The Semi-Professions and Their Organization,* Amitai Etzioni, ed., (New York: Free Press, 1969), 266–313; Wilbert E. Moore, *The Professions: Roles and Rules* (New York: Russell Sage, 1970).
2. Harold Wilensky, "The Professionalization of Everyone?" *American Journal of Sociology 70* (September 1964), 137–158; Jeffrey Berlant, *Professions and Monopoly* (Berkeley: University of California Press, 1975); Eliot Freidson, *The Professions and Their Prospects* (Beverly Hills, CA: Sage, 1973); Rue Bucher and Anselm Straus, "Professions in Process," *American Journal of Sociology 66* (January 1961), 325–334.
3. Leslie Leighninger, *Social Work: Search for Identity* (Westport, CT: Greenwood Press, 1987), a history of social work based on the process model of professionalism. See also Gary Lowe, "Social Work's Professional Mistake: Confusing Status for Control and Losing Both," *Journal of Sociology and Social Welfare 14* (June 1987), 187–206.
4. Greenwood, "Attributes of a Profession," 54; Nina Toren, *Social Work: The Case of a Semi-Profession* (Beverly Hills, CA: Sage, 1972), 37–42; Neil Gilbert, Henry Miller, and Harry Specht, *An Introduction to Social Work Practice* (Englewood Cliffs, NJ: Prentice Hall, 1980), 14–16.
5. The use of professional domain as a more satisfactory model for understanding professionalism than the process or trait models is further detailed in Philip Popple, "The Social Work Profession: A Reconceptualization," *Social Service Review 59* (December 1985), 560–574.
6. James Leiby, *A History of Social Welfare and Social Work in the United States* (New York: Columbia University Press, 1978), 340–358; Willard C. Richan and Allan R. Mendelsohn, *Social Work: The Unloved Profession* (New York: New Viewpoints, 1973), 126–162.
7. Peter Leonard, "Towards a Paradigm for Radical Practice," in Ron Bailey and Mike Brake, eds., *Radical Social Work* (New York: Pantheon Books, 1975), 46–61; Michael B. Katz, *In the Shadow of the Poorhouse* (New York: Basic Books, 1986), 164–167; Mimi Abramovitz, *Regulating the Lives of Women* (Boston: South End Press, 1989); Linda Gordon, *Pitied but Not Entitled: Single Mothers and the History of Welfare* (New York: Free Press, 1994), 102–108; Betty Reid Mandell, ed., *Welfare in America: Controlling the Dangerous Classes* (Englewood Cliffs, NJ: Prentice Hall, 1975).
8. Malcolm Payne, *Modern Social Work Theory: A Critical Introduction* (Chicago: Lyceum Books, 1991), 201–217; Michael Reisch, "The Political Context of Social Work," in Michael Reisch and Eileen Gambrill, eds., *Social Work in the 21st Century* (Thousand Oaks, CA: Pine Forge Press, 1997), 88–89; Linda Reeser, "The Future of Professionalism and Activism in Social Work," in Paul R. Raffoul and C. Aaron McNeece, eds., *Future Issues for Social Work Practice* (Boston: Allyn and Bacon, 1996), 240–253.
9. For a more complete discussion of these debates as they affected social work between 1930 and 1960, see Leighninger, *Social Work: Search for Identity.*
10. David Rothman, *The Discovery of the Asylum: Social Order and Disorder in the New Republic* (Boston: Little, Brown, 1971).
11. Leiby, *A History of Social Welfare and Social Work in the United States,* 344; Katz, *In the Shadow of the Poorhouse,* 27–28.
12. Blanche D. Coll, *Perspectives in Public Welfare* (Washington, DC: U.S. Department of Health, Education, and Welfare, 1969), 40–62; Roy Lubove, *The Professional Altruist* (New York: Atheneum, 1969), 22–54; Katz, *In the Shadow of the Poorhouse,* 66–84.
13. Katz, *In the Shadow of the Poorhouse,* 71.
14. "The Need for a Training School in Applied Philanthropy," National Conference of Charities and Correction, *Proceedings* (1897), 181–188; Linda M. Shoemaker, "Early Conflicts in Social Work Education," *Social Service Review 72* (June 1998), 182–191; Carol Coohey, Letter to the Editor, "Notes on the Origins of Social Work Education," *Social Service Review 73* (September 1999), 418–422; Leslie Leighninger, *Creating a New Profession: The Beginnings of Social Work Education in*

the United States (Alexandria, VA: CSWE, 2000), 3–12, 16–18.

15. An excellent discussion of Addams and the settlement movement can be found in Allen F. Davis, *American Heroine: The Life and Legend of Jane Addams* (New York: Oxford University Press, 1973).
16. William I. Cole, Introduction, in *The City Wilderness,* Robert A. Woods, ed., (Boston: Houghton Mifflin, 1898), 1–9; Barbara Solomon, *Ancestors and Immigrants* (New York: John Wiley, 1956), 14–143; Allen F. Davis, *Spearheads for Reform: The Social Settlements and the Progressive Movement, 1890–1914* (New York: Oxford University Press, 1967), 3–25.
17. Christopher Lasch, *The New Radicalism in America* (New York: Alfred A. Knopf, 1965), xiv–xv, 141–180.
18. Clarke Chambers, "Women in the Creation of the Profession of Social Work," *Social Service Review 60* (March 1986), 8–12; Robyn Muncy, *Creating a Female Dominion in American Reform: 1890–1935* (New York: Oxford University Press, 1991).
19. Walter I. Trattner, *From Poor Law to Welfare State,* 6th ed. (New York: Free Press, 1999), 171.
20. Abraham Flexner, "Is Social Work a Profession?" National Conference of Charities and Correction, *Proceedings* (1915), 576–590; Lubove, *The Professional Altruist,* 118–156.
21. Leighninger, *Social Work: Search for Identity,* 7–26.
22. Lubove, *The Professional Altruist,* 157–167.
23. Lester A. Salamon, "Of Market Failure, Voluntary Failure, and a Third-Party Government: Toward a Theory of Government—Nonprofit Relations in the Modern Welfare State," in Susan A. Ostrander and Stuart Langton, eds., *Shifting the Debate: Public/Private Sector Relations in the Modern Welfare State* (New Brunswick, NJ: Transaction Books, 1987), 31–32; Katz, *In the Shadow of the Poorhouse,* 42–46.
24. Charles Edmund Degeneffe, "What Is Catholic about Catholic Charities?" *Social Work 48* (July 2003), 2–5.
25. Wilma Peebles Wilkins, "Black Women and American Social Welfare: The Life of Fredericka Douglass Sprague Perry," *Affilia 4* (Spring 1989), 33–44; Anne Firor Scott, *Natural Allies: Women's Associations in American History* (Urbana: University of Illinois Press, 1993), 118–119, 127, 140–141; Leslie Leighninger, *Creating a New Profession,* 19–36.
26. Leighninger, *Social Work: Search for Identity,* 15–16; David M. Austin, *A History of Social Work Education* (Austin: School of Social Work, University of Texas at Austin, Social Work Education Monograph Series, 1986), 1–9; Gary Lowe, "The Graduate-Only Debate in Social Work Education, 1937–1959, and Its Consequences for the Profession," *Journal of Social Work Education 21* (Fall 1985), 52–62; Leighninger, *Creating a New Profession,* 37–61.
27. Leighninger, *Social Work: Search for Identity,* 27–36.
28. Porter Lee, "Social Work as Cause and Function," National Conference of Social Work, *Proceedings* (1929), 2–20.
29. William Bremer, *Depression Winters: New York Social Workers and the New Deal* (Philadelphia: Temple University Press, 1984), 63–75, 88–113; Leighninger, *Social Work: Search for Identity,* 52–68.
30. Trattner, *From Poor Law to Welfare State,* 63, 83–84, 216–218; Theda Skocpol, *Protecting Soldiers and Mothers: The Political Origins of Social Policy in the United States* (Cambridge, MA: Belknap Press of Harvard University Press, 1992), 7, 102–151.
31. Bertha Reynolds, *An Uncharted Journey* (New York: Citadel Press, 1963), 135–187; Jacob Fisher's *The Response of Social Work to the Depression* (Cambridge, MA: Schenkman, 1980) is a detailed description of the movement by one of its leaders.
32. Marian Mahaffey, "Political Action in Social Work," in Ann Minahan et al., eds., *Encyclopedia of Social Work,* 18th ed., vol. 2 (New York: NASW, 1987), 283–293; Karen S. Haynes, "The Future of Political Social Work," in Raffoul and McNeece, eds., *Future Issues for Social Work Practice,* 266–270.
33. Quoted in George Martin, *Madame Secretary: Frances Perkins* (Boston: Houghton Mifflin, 1986), 354–355.
34. Leighninger, *Social Work: Search for Identity,* 86, 92–94, 125–143.
35. Chambers, "Women in the Creation of the Profession of Social Work," 1–4, 22–24.
36. Paul H. Stuart, Leslie Leighninger, and Jana Newton Donahoe, *A History of the Association of Baccalaureate Social Work Program Directors* (Eau Claire, WI: Association of Baccalaureate Social Work Program Directors, 1993), 1–17; Michael Austin, Jude Mary Antonyappan, and Leslie Leighninger, "Federal Support for Social Work

Education: Section 707 of the 1967 Social Security Act Amendments," *Social Service Review 70* (March 1996), 83–97.

37. John V. O'Neill, "Profile Sees Little Change," *NASW News 48* (February 2003), 9; *Statistical Abstract of the United States: 2002,* 122nd ed. (Washington, DC: 2002), 381; Todd Lennon, *Statistics on Social Work Education in the United States: 2003,* in press (Alexandria, VA: Council on Social Work Education, 2004), Tables 26 and 27.
38. Sheldon R. Goldstein, "As I See It: If Past Is Prologue, Future Is Bright," *NASW News 39* (July 1994), 2.
39. Frederic Reamer, *The Philosophical Foundations of Social Work* (New York: Columbia University Press, 1993), xiii, 1–37.
40. Barbara Levy Simon, *The Empowerment Tradition in American Social Work: A History* (New York: Columbia University Press, 1994), 23; Reamer, *Philosophical Foundations,* 1–27.
41. Reamer, *Philosophical Foundations,* 34–35.
42. Reamer, *Philosophical Foundations,* 34–36; Robert N. Bellah, Richard Madsen, William M. Sullivan, Ann Swidler, and Steven M. Tipton, *Habits of the Heart: Individualism and Commitment in American Life* (New York: Harper & Row, 1985), 23–24; Jerome Carl Wakefield, "Psychotherapy, Distributive Justice, and Social Work, Part I," *Social Service Review 62* (June 1988), 208.
43. Lorraine M. Gutierrez, "Working with Women of Color: An Empowerment Perspective," *Social Work 35* (March 1990), 149–150; see also Simon, *The Empowerment Tradition in American Social Work,* for an excellent discussion of the nature of the profession's conception of empowerment.
44. Raymond Plant, *Social and Moral Theory in Casework* (London: Routledge and Kegan Paul, 1970), 6–34.
45. Ruta J. Wilk, "Are the Rights of People with Mental Illness Still Important?" *Social Work 39* (March 1994), 167–175.
46. Frederic G. Reamer, *Ethical Dilemmas in Social Service,* 2nd ed. (New York: Columbia University Press, 1990), 105–110; Theresa J. Zakutansky and Elizabeth A. Sirles, "Ethical and Legal Issues in Field Education: Shared Responsibility and Risk," *Journal of Social Work Education 29* (Fall 1993), 338–347.
47. The material in this section is based on an interview with Drayton Vincent, MSW, clinical social worker, Mental Health Service, Student Health Center, Louisiana State University, 14 April 1997.
48. *Code of Ethics* (Washington, DC: National Association of Social Workers, 1996), 2–3; Frederic G. Reamer's *Ethical Standards in Social Work: A Critical Review of the NASW Code of Ethics* (Washington, DC: NASW Press, 1998) gives a detailed overview of the new code, including a historical context and a full discussion of ethical issues in the profession.
49. *Code of Ethics,* 7–8, 10–12; Jeanette Kim Strom-Gottfried, "Is 'Ethical Managed Care' an Oxymoron?" *Families in Society 79* (May–June 1998), 4; Jeanette R. Davidson and Tim Davidson, "Confidentiality and Managed Care: Ethical and Legal Concerns," in Gerald Schamess and Anita Lightburn, eds., *Humane Managed Care?* (Washington, DC: NASW Press, 1998), 281–292; Sheldon R. Gelman, Daniel Pollack, and Adele Weiner, "Confidentiality of Social Work Records in the Computer Age," *Social Work 44* (May 1999), 243–252.
50. Jay J. Cayner, "Code Commits Us to Social Justice," *NASW News 41* (November 1996), 2; *Code of Ethics,* 1, 27.
51. Frederic Reamer, "Boundary Issues in Social Work: Managing Dual Relationships," *Social Work 48* (January 2003), 122–131; Kimberly Strom-Gottfried, "Understanding Adjudication: Origins, Targets, and Outcomes of Ethics Complaints," *Social Work 48* (January 2003), 85–94.
52. *Code of Ethics,* 13.
53. Florence Hollis, *Casework: A Psychosocial Therapy,* 2nd ed. (New York: Random House, 1972), 10.
54. Nancy K. Carroll, "Three-Dimensional Model of Social Work Practice," *Social Work 22* (September 1977), 428–432.
55. Leslie Leighninger, "The Generalist-Specialist Debate in Social Work," *Social Service Review 54* (March 1980), 267–273.
56. John O'Neill, "Private Sector Employs Most Members," *NASW News 48* (February 2003), 8; quoted in Margaret Gibelman and Philip H. Schervish, "The Private Practice of Social Work: Current Trends and Projected Scenarios in a Managed Care Environment," *Clinical Social Work Journal 24* (Fall 1996), 324.
57. Robert L. Barker, "Private Practice," in Edwards and Hopps, *Encyclopedia of Social Work,* 19th ed., vol. 3, 1908; Robert Pruger, "The Good Bureaucrat," *Social Work 18* (July 1973), 26–32; Rino J.

Patti and Herman Resnick, "Changing the Agency from Within," *Social Work 17* (July 1972), 48–57; Edward J. Pawlak, "Organizational Tinkering," *Social Work 21* (September 1976), 376–380.

58. *Statistical Abstract of the United States: 2002,* 381.
59. John V. O'Neill, "Practitioners Surveyed; Incomes Increase," *NASW News 48* (February 2003), 1, 8.
60. O'Neill, "Private Sector Employs Most Members."
61. Margaret Gibelman and Philip H. Schervish, *Who We Are: A Second Look* (Washington, DC: NASW, 1997), 71, 103.
62. *Statistical Abstract of the United States: 2002,* 400; John V. O'Neill, "Educating Media on the 'Social Worker,'" *NASW News 47* (November 2002), 3; John V. O'Neill, "Profession Perceived Favorably by Public," *NASW News 48* (March 2003), 1, 14.
63. Leighninger, *Social Work: Search for Identity,* 151–170.
64. John Rogers, Marshall L. Smith, Grafton H. Hull Jr., and JoAnn Ray, "How Do BSWs and MSWs Differ?" *Journal of Baccalaureate Social Work 1* (1995), 97–110; Lenore Olsen and William M. Holmes, "Educating Child Welfare Workers: The Effects of Professional Training on Service Delivery," *Journal of Education for Social Work 18* (Winter 1982), 94–102; *The Maryland Social Work Services Job Analysis and Personnel Qualifications Study* (State of Maryland Department of Human Resources, 1987), III–12; Robert J. Teare and Bradford W. Sheafor, *Practice-Sensitive Social Work Education: An Empirical Analysis of Social Work Practice and Practitioners* (Alexandria, VA: Council on Social Work Education, 1995).
65. Corinna Vallianatos, "State Requirements Vary Widely: Licensure's Hurdles Hinder Easy Moves," *NASW News 45* (July 2000), 3; Gibelman and Schervish, "The Private Practice of Social Work," 329, 334.
66. Association of Social Work Boards, Model Social Work Practice Act, online at www.aswb.org, 1–2, 8; Marilyn Biggerstaff, "A Critique of the Model State Social Work Practice Act," *Social Work 45* (March 2000), 105–115.
67. Model Social Work Practice Act, 4–5, 8–9, 12–13, 26–28. The ASWB web site has the entire model licensing law at www.aswb.org.
68. Harry Specht and Mark Courtney, *Unfaithful Angels: How Social Work Has Abandoned Its Mission* (New York: Free Press, 1994).
69. Jim Midgley, "International and Comparative Social Welfare," in Edwards and Hopps, *Encyclopedia of Social Work,* 1490–1499; Lynn M. Healy, *International Social Work* (New York: Oxford University Press, 2001).
70. John V. O'Neill, "Politics School Goes West," *NASW News 47* (May 2002), 9; Congressman Dennis Moore, *Guide to Constituent Services,* 2002; www.naswdc.org/pressroom/features/general/profession.asp; Lynn Stoesen, "Colleagues Enter a Range of Public Offices," *NASW News 48* (May 2003), 4.
71. Lisa Raiz, Carla Curtis, and Keith Kilty, "Responsibility for Social Welfare and Advocacy: The Graduate Student Perspective," Council on Social Work Education Annual Program Meeting (28 February 2004), 6.
72. Paula Allen-Meares and Yosikazu DeRoos, "The Future of the Social Work Profession," in Reisch and Gambrill, *Social Work in the 21st Century,* 381–385; Wallace Gingrich and Ronald Green, "Information Technology: How Social Work Is Going Digital," in Raffoul and McNeece, *Future Issues for Social Work Practice,* 19–28; John McNutt, "National Information Infrastructure Policy and the Future of the American Welfare State: Implications for the Social Welfare Policy Curriculum," *Journal of Social Work Education 32* (Fall 1996), 375–388.
73. C. Wright Mills, *The Sociological Imagination* (New York: Oxford University Press, 1959), 8–11; "Tyne Daly Wows 'Social Work 2000,'" *NASW News 46* (January 2001), 14.

CHAPTER

4

Generalist Social Work Practice

Tom Watson is in the last year of his BSW program and has just started his field placement at Friendship House, a multipurpose social agency in a city in Arizona. Friendship House began in the 1920s as a settlement house serving a Mexican American community; the neighborhood still has a large Chicano population. Many of the residents are recent arrivals from Mexico, but the area also includes a small African American population. From its settlement house beginnings, the agency has expanded to include job training, legal services for immigrants, a day care center, English-language classes, support groups for pregnant teens, a job center for undocumented immigrants, a magnet school, and a program that hires and helps pay neighborhood residents to provide services to the elderly and disabled in the community. The agency also advocates for fair treatment of immigrants in the schools and the health and public welfare systems.

As he goes through his orientation to the agency, Tom is excited about all the services Friendship House provides, but he's also beginning to feel overwhelmed. "How am I going to work with all of this?" he wonders. "They do counseling, group work, and I guess the people visiting the elderly must do case management. They even testify at the state capitol. What's the social work niche?"

When Tom sits down with his new supervisor at Friendship House, he confides his sense of confusion. His supervisor smiles and says gently, "Do you remember what you learned about generalist social work? Here's your chance to put this to work."

Baccalaureate social work education focuses on preparing students for generalist social work practice. There are several definitions of generalist practice, which this chapter explores. Some definitions present a generalist social worker as a jack-of-all-trades, able to use a variety of specific methodologies with different types of client groups. Others specify the ability to work in all three levels of social work practice: direct practice with individuals, groups, and families; administration; and social planning/community development.[1] A major role within generalist practice is that of the case manager; this too has a variety of definitions. Our aim in this chapter is not to teach you all the skills of generalist practice; this will be the focus of your internship and practice courses. We intend instead to provide a basic understanding of that practice and its methodologies and roles in order to help prepare you for more in-depth course work and skills training. We provide a history of the development of the generalist approach within the context of a broader history of social work practice, define the concepts and describe the skills of generalist practice and case management, and present types of ethical dilemmas you may encounter as a generalist social work practitioner.

History and Development of Social Work Practice

As we say again and again in this book, social work's uniqueness lies in its focus on the individual-in-environment. This two-sided approach was laid out in Chapter 3, in which we explained that social work methods were initially divided between the social casework approach of the Charity Organization Societies and the community and group work approaches of the settlement movement. The casework approach focused on the problems of individuals and families. The settlement approach focused on groups, communities, and the larger society.

We now let you in on a secret—this unique dual focus is both social work's blessing and its curse. This holistic focus is a blessing because it allows social workers to view and deal with problems in a much more realistic manner than is possible if a helper views a problem from only one angle. It is an old truism that if you give a child a hammer, everything he or she comes in contact with will need to be hammered. Similarly, if you train a person in one technique, individual therapy, for example, every person the social worker comes in contact with will appear to be in need of therapy. And if you train a person only in social action/advocacy, every problem will appear to call for this approach. Modern social workers, who are trained to view both the individual and the social environment aspects of problems, will not (or at least should not) make this mistake. This dual perspective is, in large part, the richness of social work.

For those responsible for developing theory, knowledge, techniques, and frameworks, however, this dual focus has always posed a difficult, although challenging, problem. The approaches and skills necessary for engaging in some form of individual treatment are often different from those necessary for social action. Let's look at a simple, and common, situation confronting a social worker within a state department of social services. The social worker has been assigned the case of a woman who has been on public assistance, off and on, for ten years. Under the new TANF program, she can remain on assistance for a maximum of two years for any one period, and five years total. So she and her social worker are now under the gun. The woman has a limited amount of time in which to become totally self-sufficient. Following the woman's assessment, the social worker finds two categories of factors related to this client's inability to maintain self-support. The first group of factors is individual. The client has a problem with substance abuse and often misses work due to a hangover and even has been known to show up to work while under the influence. She also has a problem with her attitude toward work. She will, for example, frequently show up fifteen to thirty minutes late and then react angrily when her boss fusses at her because "It's only a few minutes, chill out." She has a bad temper, which occasionally manifests itself in screaming fits directed at her coworkers, customers, or employer. As a result of these individual factors, she has never managed to keep a job for more than six weeks. Looking only at the individual factors in this situation, the approach appears obvious—this woman is in need of intensive individual therapy/counseling to remedy these problems so she will be able to keep a job. But there is another set of factors related to this client's employability. Previous social workers have attempted to get her into a substance abuse program, and she remains on several waiting lists. Her social worker suspects that her chronic tardiness to work may be less a result of bad work habits than of bad day care and poor public transportation. Similarly, her bad temper may well be the result of being expected to care for several children while becoming self-sufficient without the support of a mate or of adequate housing, day care, transportation, medical insurance, and an entire range of other supportive programs.

The history of social work practice is a history of attempts to figure out a way to address both sides of the person-in-environment equation. For much of our history we have attempted to deal with this dualism by developing different practice specializations. A person went to social work school and learned to be either a caseworker/therapist/micropractice specialist, or a community organizer/administrator/planner/policy advocate/macropractice specialist. In recent years, social work has attempted to merge both types of practice into one unified theory and method—generalist practice.

The Evolution of Social Work Practice

Before the Civil War, very little existed in the United States that could be considered social work as we think of it today. The few social welfare programs that did exist were based on the 1601 Elizabethan Poor Law, which firmly established family responsibility for dependent persons and assigned responsibility for those with no family to the smallest unit of government. Generally, dependent children were apprenticed or were boarded at the cheapest place; able-bodied persons were put to work; and the old or incapacitated who did not have families were either given a small grant (outdoor relief) or were placed in an institution (indoor relief).

Before the middle of the nineteenth century, there was actually little need for a profession such as social work. The United States was what the historian James Leiby refers to as the "rural democracy."[2] The country was large and underdeveloped; the population was small, prosperous (by nineteenth-century standards), and homogeneous (except for African Americans and American Indians, whose social welfare concerned few other people); and the economy was relatively simple. The traditional institutions of the family, the marketplace, and the church were seen as well able to handle any social welfare problems that arose.

In the second half of the century, American society changed drastically, and a number of interacting forces created a situation in which social work developed. The country witnessed tremendous economic growth, an increase in population (much of it due to immigration), the massive and chaotic growth of cities, the stratification of society (a small group of wealthy businessmen at the top and a large group of poorly paid laborers on the bottom), and a business cycle characterized by periods of depression and unemployment alternating with periods of growth. Added to all this was the development of a faith in the seemingly unlimited potential of science, technology, and rationality to solve the problems of modern life, and a belief that problems should be dealt with by specialized professions.[3]

During the last half of the nineteenth century, people began to perceive that the growing problems in the relationship between people and their social environment demanded new solutions. Two new types of organizations (discussed in detail in Chapter 3), the settlements and the charity organization societies, emerged in the 1870s and 1880s as attempts to resolve these problems. Together, these two types of organizations formed the roots of the social work profession in the United States. Their differing perspectives on the solution to social problems have continued to pose problems in conceptualizing a unified social work practice. The idea of generalist practice is the latest attempt to resolve this dilemma.

Settlement Houses and the Origins of Macropractice. The general history of the settlement house movement is discussed in Chapter 3. What is important here is the approach to social work practice first formulated in the settlements. The settlements stressed the social and economic causes of poverty and other urban problems rather than the individual causes. They promoted the neighborhood ideal and were less interested in changing individuals than they were in changing social conditions. Their reform activities generally began in the immediate neighborhood of the settlement and addressed issues such as trash collection, housing conditions, and the like. Settlement workers and neighborhood residents engaged in political action directed at these issues.[4]

In addition to neighborhood programs, settlement workers engaged in broader social reform activities. Hull House residents spearheaded the fight against child labor during the early years of the twentieth century. Settlement workers were key participants in the labor movement and in the push to enact public welfare statutes and civil rights laws for blacks and immigrants. One important contribution the settlements made to the cause of civil rights for blacks was their aid in founding several self-help organizations. In 1909 settlement workers helped create the National Association for the Advancement of Colored People (NAACP). Its first meeting was held at the Henry Street settlement in New York. Of the thirty-five members on the NAACP executive committee, eight were settlement workers.[5]

It is important to note that the settlements were not only advocates of macropractice but that they also, to a fair extent, rejected the very notion of the development of expert technique. The settlements emphasized democracy, group process, and neighborliness, all phenomena that, they claimed, did not involve specific techniques. As we will see, it was not until somewhat later in the history of social work practice that people interested in macropractice realized the importance of using specific methods in that practice.

At the same time the settlements were developing, another group of social workers, known as charity workers, was working on the other side of the person-in-environment equation. They sought to solve social problems by changing the individual. By the end of the Progressive Era, this type of social work was known as social casework. Although the social work techniques of administration, community organization, and group work can be traced to the settlements, workers there did not intentionally foster the development of technique. The settlement workers prided themselves instead on being pragmatists. It was the caseworkers who began to chase the elusive status of "profession" and who consciously sought to meet its criteria, mainly that a profession have an expert technique that is uniquely its own.

Charity Organization Societies and the Development of Micropractice. The conditions leading to the settlement house movement also spurred the development of the charity organization society (COS) movement, which we described in Chapter 3. As we noted, the COS held that destitution could be reduced, hardship ameliorated, and mendicancy prevented by instituting a system of scientific charity and replacing the existing chaos in almsgiving with systematically coordinated private philanthropy. The primary technique was "friendly visiting" by a wealthy volunteer, who befriended a needy family and through his or her (usually her) example and guidance showed the family the way out of poverty. Effective friendly visiting was thought to require moral insight rather than technical training or scientific understanding of human behavior.

Although the COS volunteers possessed a nineteenth-century outlook on the world, which from our perspective appears quaint and naive, it cannot be said that they were dumb. In only a very short time, the volunteer friendly visitors and the volunteer agency boards realized they were dealing with something much more complex than simple moral shortcomings. In the years between 1877 and 1900, the role of the volunteer friendly visitor gradually diminished, and the role of the paid agent was upgraded, until at the turn of the century Mary Richmond was promoting education for "the profession of applied philanthropy."[6]

The main reason for the decline in friendly visiting and the turn to paid charity workers was the contact of theory with reality. Through extensive contacts with poor people, the COS movement was forced to drop its cherished belief that poverty was the result of personal moral shortcomings. By the turn of the century, COS representatives were beginning to realize that the causes of poverty were social, economic, and psychological rather than the result of personal moral failure. If moral failure was not the cause of poverty, then friendly visiting was not the solution. Although volunteers continued to play an important role in charity organizations after the 1890s, they were gradually replaced in client contact positions by staff trained in methods of investigation and in the social sciences and, eventually, in the new methods of social casework.

The Expansion of Social Casework. A special skill applied to a special function is a basic criterion of any profession. After 1900, in keeping with the general social trend toward professionalization, caseworkers made a concerted effort to limit, define, and clarify their particular knowledge and technique and to delineate a special function. They began to explore investigative techniques and methods of diagnosis and treatment that would result in an understanding of the unique problems of each client.

Prior to the early 1900s, what is now known as social casework had been limited to children's aid and charity organization societies. However, along with new techniques and reforms that recognized the significant effects of the environment on different aspects of people's well-being, social work began to spread into new areas, such as medical, psychiatric, and school social work.

In 1905, Dr. Richard C. Cabot introduced medical social work at Massachusetts General Hospital. He had wondered how much illness could be traced to social conditions such as "vice, ignorance, overcrowding, sweatshops, and poverty."[7] Cabot felt that the hospital did not really treat the sick, but only isolated physical symptoms. Often it failed to cure patients who returned to the environment that had produced the illness in the first place. He believed that social services would overcome the hospital's separation from the social roots of disease and contribute to the development of preventive medicine. The emergence of medical social work added an entirely new institutional setting in which to develop the casework approach.

Shortly after Cabot introduced the first medical social work program, a second casework specialty emerged—school social work. Like the hospitals, schools felt they had lost contact with the students' environment, and reformers began to stress establishing such contact. The school social worker's contact with the child in his or her own environment was the "logical place to detect symptoms of future inefficiency, whether they be departures from the mental, social, or physical standards."[8] Like medical social work, school social work helped shape the social caseworker's image as a skilled professional representing a social institution.

Just as Cabot, a physician, had taken the initiative in promoting medical social work, psychiatrists in rebellion against the prevailing institutional methods of care for the mentally ill worked to integrate therapy with environment. They substituted a clinical, empirical approach to mental illness for the institutionalization and custodianship of the nineteenth century. Prominent in this movement was Dr. Adolph Meyer, who envisioned the development of community mental health programs. The mental hospital would be the nucleus of the system, but it had to be "socialized" like Cabot's general hospital. Meyer felt that the cornerstone of success in the socialized mental hospital was the "organization of social work and home visitation."[9]

The development of specialists in medical, school, and psychiatric aspects of social work left no one responsible for the most important social institution—the family. It gradually dawned on charity workers that specialization had made them experts on family adjustment, and they began to see their task as the discovery of internal and external pressures that interfered with normal family life. Thus, family casework emerged from the friendly visiting of the charity organization societies.

By the end of the Progressive Era, four social work specializations had emerged related to what is now referred to as micro social work practice. Medical, school, psychiatric, and family social work all shared a common core: They all were based on micropractice, they all emphasized changing the individual as the solution to social problems, and they all held the opinion that this could be done by developing an expert technique. Despite these commonalities, however, the development of specializations could be seen, in hindsight, as undercutting a more general approach to people's problems.

Social Work Practice and the Quest for Professionalization, 1915–1930. Although social workers in the settlements never developed a great interest in achieving professional status, persons working in the casework field became interested in it at a very early date. As early as 1897, Mary Richmond said of persons entering charity work: "Surely, they have a right to demand from the profession of applied philanthropy that which they have a right to demand from any other profession—further opportunities for education and development, and incidentally the opportunity to earn a living."[10] From the time Richmond's paper was written until 1915, the move to professionalize social work slowly built momentum. Social casework began to be practiced in a variety of settings, and schools of social work began to emerge. The professionalization movement did not achieve critical mass until 1915, however, when Abraham Flexner presented his paper analyzing social work as a profession at the National Conference of Charities and Corrections.

Flexner's paper, as we described in Chapter 3, concluded that social work could not legitimately be considered a profession. In an important impetus to the development of social work practice techniques, however, in that same program several leading social workers presented papers outlining their own ideas about how social work could correct the deficiencies outlined by Flexner. All of these reports emphasized the individual treatment aspects of social work, and, although recognizing social work's involvement with social problems, relegated this aspect to a position of secondary importance.

In the fifteen years between the Flexner report and the onset of the Great Depression, social work rapidly professionalized and narrowed to a casework, micropractice focus. This concentration on an individual treatment approach reflected the fact that caseworkers were interested in improving their professional status, and social reformers and settlement workers were not. In addition, fears of "radicalism" following the Russian Revolution, along with growing prosperity for many Americans, contributed to a backlash against social reform efforts. Thus the methodology of the caseworker, with its individual focus, came to dominate professional social work in the 1920s. Only a few settlement workers had formal professional training or qualified for membership in the American Association of Social Workers (AASW). The settlement movement continued to place more emphasis on social issues than on professionalization.[11]

Two important events accelerated social work's shift toward individual treatment: (1) the concurrent opportunity to provide services to people other than the poor and (2) the application of psychoanalytic theory to social work practice. As we noted earlier, the World War I Home Service Division of the American Red Cross provided casework services to soldiers and their families. Social workers in this setting quickly found themselves dealing with problems, such as war-induced neurosis, for which their experiences provided no help. In a search for solutions they joined up with psychologists and psychiatrists. At the same time, Freud's theory of psychoanalysis was beginning to gain popularity in the United States. The conceptual attractiveness of psychoanalytic theory, the opportunity to work with physicians in a clinical setting, and the fact that psychoanalysis provided the theoretical base Flexner had criticized social work for lacking, all furthered the dominance of the individual treatment approach in social work during the 1920s. Social work had become "professionalized," and many within the field no longer felt responsible for social reform.

The growth of specializations within this nascent profession did, however, raise some concern. Was social casework in fact one profession practiced in a variety of settings, or a group of loosely related professions? The Milford Conference, a series of meetings between social work leaders to discuss this question in the 1920s, concluded that there was indeed such a thing as a "generic social casework" that cut across practice in all settings.[12]

The Great Depression and the Broadening of Social Work Practice. As we noted earlier in this book, the direction of social work practice in the 1920s put the profession in a poor position for responding to the crisis of the depression. Social workers in private charitable and family agencies were soon overwhelmed by the mass of people needing economic relief and the scarcity of resources to provide it. Many in the field rediscovered the importance of social and economic reform to improve the environment in which clients—and indeed a large number of the American people—found themselves.

Although many social workers and their organizations lobbied for and supported federal and state responses to the crisis, thus honing their skills in social reform, others continued to pursue issues related to direct practice. They did so within the context of rapid change. As the federal and state governments developed a system of public relief agencies, private family agencies were stripped of their traditional function, that of providing a range of services to families in financial difficulty. At the same time, many social workers were drawn into the new public social services, where they discovered the challenge of working within a more bureaucratic setting to meet the basic needs of large numbers of clients, for whom individually focused casework was neither practical nor, in most cases, appropriate.

By the end of the 1930s, family agencies had begun to deal with their new situation by embracing the growing interest in psychotherapy and developing highly skilled "casework treatment to assist individuals in removing their own handicaps."[13] Edith Abbott and Sophonisba Breckenridge of the Chicago School of Social Service Administration were well on their way to developing social work administration as a recognized method of practice.[14] Group workers and community organizers had begun to clarify their methods and objectives, and to identify more strongly with the social work profession. Throughout the thirties there was lively debate about the definition of group work. Most social workers eventually came to accept the definition identified by Grace Coyle, who wrote,

> Social group work is an educational process carried on usually in voluntary groups during leisure time with the assistance of a group leader. It aims at the development of persons through the interplay of personalities in group situations, and at the creation of such group situations as provide for integrated, cooperative group action for common ends. Group workers believe that such group experience provides a medium for the social adjustment of individuals.[15]

As Goldstein notes, the work on developing a definition of group work introduced a new way of perceiving social work practice. Group workers defined their practice as an educational process, as opposed to the medical definition used by caseworkers.[16]

Community workers also began to develop methods and to seek to identify themselves as members of the social work profession, but members with their own distinct techniques and contributions. A 1939 report defined community organization as a method of social work on the same level as casework and group work. Prior analyses of community organization had tended to define it as a distinct field but had identified its methods as the same as those employed by caseworkers and group workers. The new report defined community organization as both a field and a distinct method. In 1941, community organization appeared for the first time as a separate entry in the *Social Work Yearbook*, which noted, "There is general agreement among most social workers that there is used within the field of social work a process distinct from social case work and social group work, which does not concern itself primarily with individual relationships within a single group, but with inter-group or community relationships." The techniques of the community organization social worker were those related to the tasks of social welfare planning, organization, and coordination.[17] With the recognition of group work and community organization, the profession was now moving to a specialization by method, as well as by setting.

Expansion and Elaboration, 1940–1960. The huge demand for goods and services caused by World War II brought an end to the Great Depression, which the Roosevelt administration's New Deal programs had succeeded in ameliorating but not ending. The war and postwar era was one of prosperity and optimism but unfortunately was accompanied by attitudes of complacency and conservatism. The prevailing attitude in the country was that the problem of poverty was rapidly disappearing in the "affluent society," so termed by economist Galbraith.[18] To the extent that poverty still existed, most people, including many social workers, believed that it was being dealt with by the public welfare system and therefore was little cause for concern. In this atmosphere, social work was free to return to a focus on the individual side of the person-in-environment equation.

Social workers once again felt free to concentrate on the individual causes of distress and on developing knowledge and techniques to deal with them. Several developments tended to push social work even further in this direction. The testing of millions of military recruits during the war had revealed a greater prevalence of mental health problems than anyone could have imagined. The result of these findings was a push for mental health services, which resulted in the National Mental Health Act of 1946. The National Mental Health Act stressed community treatment and prevention and provided new opportunities for social workers who were interested in psychopathology.

The psychotherapeutic orientation that had begun in the 1920s and been de-emphasized in the 1930s found wide acceptance in the 1940s and 1950s. This approach made sense not only to social workers but also to persons who supported social agencies. The general feeling of the era could be summed up as a belief that the social system works; therefore, problems are due to some defect of the individual, and the appropriate approach is to find and cure the defect. During the 1950s, 85 percent of the students in schools of social work chose casework as their major. This interest in individual counseling was reinforced by the fact that more and more persons with

Social workers in hospital settings in the 1940s found many different problems to deal with.

incomes above the poverty line were turning to social workers for help. A 1960 study of family service agencies revealed that 9 percent of the clients were upper class and 48 percent were middle class.[19]

Although casework clearly remained the dominant method during the 1940s and 1950s, group work and community organization continued to develop and to refine their techniques and specializations. In 1946, Grace Coyle established a group work specialty at the Western Reserve University School of Social Work, the first time that group workers could be trained at the graduate level. Coyle argued that casework, group work, and community organization were all social work methods based on a common understanding of human relationships. The acceptance of group work as a legitimate method by social workers was also furthered by the demonstration of the usefulness of group techniques in mental health therapy settings. Thus, group work, to a certain extent, bought its acceptance into the social work profession at the cost of giving up much of its normal human development focus and replacing this with an individual treatment mental health approach.

Although community organization made inroads into the profession during this era, it had a more difficult time than group work. In 1942, Helen Witmer wrote that while social workers carried out some types of community organization activities, the field itself was broader and involved other professions as well. Arlien Johnson responded in 1945 that the community organizer was a professional social worker because he or she helps people in a community discover the common problems that may interfere with the desirable norms of living and assists them in doing something about these problems. Johnson thus identified community organization as sharing a goal with casework—the well-being of individuals.[20] As Goldstein has observed, these early efforts to define community organization were not directed toward changing the existing structures or institutions of society, but rather viewed the method as a means for sustaining the existing processes for dealing with problems of social relationship and adjustment.

1960–1975, Years of Contradictory Trends. What are generally thought of as the sixties, the years of flower power, student radicals, anti-Vietnam War protest, and the like, actually did not end, in the sociological sense, until 1975. These were years of great changes in the social welfare institution, changes that are discussed elsewhere in this book. Obviously, the Social Service Amendments, the Economic Opportunity Act, and all the other massive social programs tended to give legitimacy to, and to encourage the development of, the social action side of the profession. However, although social action loomed large in the minds, training, and activities of social workers, it did not have a major effect on actual practice techniques.

Practice techniques during this era tended to develop at polar ends of the micro–macro continuum. On the macro end, motivated in part by the development and growth of public welfare programs, schools of social work began to develop specializations in administration and planning. Social workers trained in these methods followed curriculums that more closely resembled those of business or public administration students than the curriculum studied by caseworkers. These students learned theories and skills in areas such as budgeting, planning, program evaluation, human resource management, and organizational design. They would finish school, be issued a briefcase and a three-piece suit, and take a job as a middle manager with the welfare department or as an executive with a United Way agency.

In addition, community organization methods took on a new life in the 1960s. Earlier community organization work had focused on "bringing about . . . an effective adjustment between social welfare resources and social welfare needs" in a particular locale by ensuring that social service agencies met the needs of their communities.[21] This work took place primarily in Community Chests, which helped fund and coordinate the activities of private social agencies. In the 1960s a new type of grassroots community organizing had emerged, in which organizers helped residents of poor and minority neighborhoods identify community problems and develop ways to get these resolved. The tactics used to do so—questioning public officials; publicizing inadequate public services, such as inefficient street lighting or poor public schools; and picketing City Hall—were often seen as radical by the general public and by many members of the social work profession. Yet a number of schools of social work added community organization tracks for those wanting to focus on this work.

On the micro side, the sixties witnessed a continued increase in definitions of social work as a psychotherapeutic profession. A bewildering assortment of therapy techniques was now being taught at schools of social work. A partial, and by no means exhaustive, list would include behavioral therapy, client-centered therapy, crisis intervention treatment, ego psychology, gestalt therapy, the problem-solving method, psychoanalytic therapy, psychosocial treatment, task-centered practice, and transactional analysis.[22]

At the same time that social work was becoming increasingly specialized at the ends of the continuum, a slow momentum was growing to once again look for a more common basis for all practice. In 1965, Francis Purcell and Harry Specht wrote a seminal article in *Social Work* titled "The House on Sixth Street." The article was a case study of work by a Mobilization For Youth agency that began with a client with housing problems. The study documented the various methods and system levels that had to be used in working on this case. The authors concluded:

> Social work helping methods as currently classified are so inextricably interwoven in practice that it no longer seems valid to think of a generic practice as consisting of the application of casework, group work, or community organization skills as the nature of the problem demands. . . . This paper has presented a new approach to social work practice. The knowledge, values, attitudes, and skills were derived from a generalist approach to social work. Agencies that direct their energies to social problems by affecting institutional change will need professional workers whose skills cut across the broad spectrum of social work knowledge.[23]

Based on the thinking and observations of people such as Purcell and Specht, social work began to look for theories that would unify the various types and levels of practice. One that was adapted for social work during the sixties was systems theory, which stressed the similarities of all systems, both natural and social, and pointed out the folly of studying and treating any one part of a system without attention to the rest of the system. Social workers also began to develop ecological theory and the problem-solving method as unified ways of viewing practice. In the early 1970s, these theories were used to combine casework, group work, and community organization approaches to practice into a single model called integrated methods.

As this history indicates, there have been a variety of attempts to bring the different social work methods and the dual perspective on the individual in society into a coherent whole. Although specializations have their place in social work practice, there has been an ongoing search for the common threads that underlie both different practice approaches (e.g., individual, group, and community work) and the dual focus on the person-in-environment. The integrated methods approach deals with one part of this search by focusing on commonalities between the various methodologies used by social workers. Yet it does not do as well in integrating the emphases on person and environment in a way that is useful for practitioners. Probably the most successful approach that has emerged so far is the concept of generalist social work, which provides a model of a social worker who is not only skilled in a variety of methods, but who also can work in the various systems—individual, family, group, organization, and community—that represent the different elements in the person-in-environment picture. The concept of generalist social work has the added advantage of providing a way to differentiate between undergraduate and graduate social work education and practice.

Development of the Concept of Generalist Social Work

The concept of generalist social work developed concurrently with some of the other attempts at integration described above. As early as the 1940s and 1950s, the formation of undergraduate social work education programs put pressure on the field to differentiate between preparation for first-level and advanced practice. This refocused attention on a foundation or basic level of social work practice.

This generalist social worker draws from a broad core of skills and knowledge to help a young mother use her own strengths and outside resources to cope with daily problems.

Social work educators had earlier identified a group of core areas in social work—such as human behavior in the social environment, group work, casework, and social work research—that all social work educational programs should cover. But a basic concept to undergird this notion of a foundation of social work practice was needed if the field was to create a sensible division between basic (baccalaureate) and advanced or specialized (graduate) social work practice. The concept of generalist social work fit this need.

Generalist social work probably arose from a number of sources, but the most specific development of the concept grew out of the work of the Southern Regional Education Board (SREB) in the late 1960s and early 1970s. SREB was an educational organization that included a focus on the expansion of social work education in the South through consultation with schools, faculty-development workshops, and other projects. The board received funding from the National Institute of Mental Health and the U.S. Department of Health and Human Services to carry out its work. Although SREB was active in the graduate and undergraduate social work arenas, it was particularly successful in promoting baccalaureate social work education.

In 1967, SREB received funding from the Department of Health, Education, and Welfare (HEW) for a several-year program to meet critical shortages of trained social workers in the South by helping colleges in southern states develop undergraduate training programs in social work and social welfare. The project director, Harold McPheeters (a psychiatrist), put together a consultant group made up of social work program directors and faculty from existing undergraduate social work specializations or majors in southern colleges and universities. These consultants conducted curriculum workshops and visited programs to help them plan courses. Out of their work, and in discussion with the SREB staff, the concept of generalist practice developed. The consultants and SREB staff were particularly interested in educating undergraduate social workers for positions in the public welfare system. To do this, they saw the need to develop a core of competence for such workers, who would need to deal with a wide variety of problems. Early in the project it had become apparent that there was no consensus in the profession regarding what was expected of an undergraduate social worker. Some undergraduate programs were preparing students for graduate school "with virtually no specific competence in skills of social intervention," some programs were preparing graduates for a single method such as casework, and others were educating students to work in a single agency. Clearly a broad core of skills and knowledge was needed. In conjunction with undergraduate social work educators and practitioners, SREB project leaders developed the set of twelve basic practice roles described in Chapter 3, which included outreach worker, advocate, behavior changer, caregiver, and community planner. Generalist practitioners would be able to carry out all twelve roles, and they would use whatever roles and activities were necessary to help a person, family, group, or community in need. Their major focus would be the individual or group, not "specific tasks or techniques or professional prerogatives," or even the requirements of the social work agency. The term *generalist social work* was coined to describe this process of meeting all the needs of an individual, family, or community.[24]

The notion of a broad base of beginning social work practice made sense as the underpinning of all undergraduate social work education, and in 1984 the Council on Social Work Education identified the knowledge, values, and skills of generalist practice as the primary focus of undergraduate education. (At the same time, generalist practice was established as the focus of the foundation year of graduate education, which enabled Advanced Standing programs to continue and also ensured that students entering a master's degree program without undergraduate preparation would receive the basics they needed before moving to the advanced curriculum.) Thus the concept of generalist practice helped define and legitimize undergraduate social work practice and provided a useful way of thinking about the relationship between BSW and MSW education.

Generalist Practice

Definition

As we have noted, there are a variety of definitions of generalist practice. It can be seen as the ability of a practitioner to work with all levels of social work clients: individuals, couples, families, groups, organizations, neighborhoods, and communities. Generalist social workers can also be viewed as having the ability to employ a variety of social work methods. We find it most useful to combine the multilevel and multimethod definitions into a broader concept of generalist practice in which social workers use a broad range of methods to intervene with "various systems sizes, including individuals, groups, organizations, and communities." Another way to put this is that generalist practice "entails direct work [such as counseling and referral work] with client systems of all sizes as well as indirect work [such as advocacy and policymaking] on behalf of client systems."[25]

The generalist practitioner can also be seen as a person who can make a broad assessment of individual, group, or organizational needs and then make the connection to resources that will meet these needs. This role is often one of the functions of a case manager. Dean Hepworth and Jo Ann Larson explain that generalist practitioners "should be able to view problems holistically and be prepared to plan interventions that address all systems implicated in clients' [or client systems'] problems."[26] In planning these interventions, generalist social workers will sometimes refer clients to social workers who specialize in particular techniques or approaches, such as marriage counseling, helping people cope with the death of a family member, or assisting a community group in writing a grant proposal.

Other elements are sometimes added to the definition of generalist practice. A common one is the idea that generalist practitioners see human behavior in the context of a broader social, political, economic, and physical environment. This leads to the notion that the environment might be as much (or more) in need of change as the individual, group, family, or organization defined as the client. Therefore, work toward social and economic justice and political equality would be an integral part of a generalist approach.[27]

Two other, interrelated concepts are often described as part of a generalist approach. One is the "strengths perspective," a concept developed in the last several decades by Dennis Saleeby, Ann Weick, Charles Rapp, and others. The strengths perspective holds that it makes far more sense to focus on the strengths and abilities a client brings to working on a particular life difficulty than to stress the client's deficiencies. Thus a homeless adolescent might be seen in terms of his ingenuity in surviving on his own, and an elderly widow with Parkinson's disease could be viewed as a person with a good sense of humor and an ability to reach out to neighbors for help. Those working from a strengths perspective assume that "people have untapped, undetermined reservoirs of mental, physical, emotional, social, and spiritual abilities" that can be called on at times of emotional, physical, and environmental challenges. Groups, organizations, and communities have similar strengths. Generalist social workers who proceed from a strengths perspective recognize and respect these abilities and capacities for change.[28]

The notion of "empowerment" can be seen as a natural corollary of a strengths perspective. An empowerment orientation means that generalist practitioners stress clients' "unique coping and adaptive patterns, mobilizing their actual or potential strengths, emphasizing the role of natural helping networks, and using environmental resources."[29] For example, a school social worker assigned to work with a third-grade girl who stuttered and had few friends in school found several strengths to build on in empowering the girl to cope with her stuttering and to build relationships with her peers. First, the girl herself was bright, worked hard, made good grades in school, and was eager to make friends with the social worker. Her mother was a lonely and rather isolated person (the girl's father was a truck driver who was away from home much of the time) who did not seem at first to have much sympathy for her daughter's difficulties, criticizing her when she stuttered. Yet, despite the criticism, it was clear that she loved her daughter and also that she had ambitions of working outside the home but lacked the confidence to carry this out.

The worker took an empowerment approach with both the third grader and her mother. She developed a close relationship with the girl, praising her mastery of schoolwork and encouraging her to talk about her conviction that other children wouldn't like her because she stuttered (a conviction that kept her from approaching them to make friends). Understanding that this fear undermined her chance to make friends was an important discovery for the girl. At the same time, the social worker encouraged the mother to explore her interest in working and to think about her skills and areas of work that appealed to her. Because the mother expressed curiosity about what it might be like to work in an elementary school classroom, she and the worker visited a first-grade class and watched the activities of the teacher's aide in that classroom. Within several months, with the social worker's support, the mother was hired as a teacher's aide in a Head Start program in her daughter's school; her hours allowed her to be home with her daughter after school.

As the mother became more involved in her own activities and received good feedback on her role in the classroom, she spent less and less time criticizing her daughter. The lack of pressure seemed to work wonders on the girl, who stuttered less in class and began a friendship with another girl who was also shy. By the end of the school year, the worker was able to terminate her involvement with the family, knowing that the mother had built on her own interests and resources to find a fulfilling job and that the girl had been empowered to reach out to other children.

Well, this sounds great, you might think—here are all the key elements of generalist practice. They make sense and they get results. But, you may wonder, what's the difference between generalist practice and specialized or advanced practice? This is a good question, because the previous definitions might lead you to believe that all of social work practice is really generalist. Those extolling the virtues of the generalist approach may in fact have overreached a bit in their definitions of that approach. The themes of empowering clients, building on a strengths perspective, basing interventions on an awareness of the larger societal context of client systems' problems, and pursuing social justice are not limited to generalist practice—in fact, these have become the very basics of all social work practice. What does seem unique to generalist practice is the ability to work with all levels of client systems; to use a broad range of methodologies or interventions, at least at a basic level; and perhaps a greater tendency to take a broad view, including social, economic, and political factors, in defining client situations.

The discussion about the differences between generalist and specialized practice is not just an academic exercise. After all, as a BSW social worker, you will want to know when to call on the services and insights of a specialist practitioner in a particular case, either an MSW or a person in another profession. In addition, you may be contemplating completing the MSW degree yourself and wonder how that might change the way you would work. The following definition may be helpful: "Specialists . . . are prepared to help with more defined, time-limited problems or issues that can be addressed and managed with specific approaches and technologies. Specialists have expertise to work with specific populations and problems, while generalists . . . work more comprehensively in client situations."[30]

To flesh out this definition of specialist practice, consider the following examples. An MSW social worker specializing in work with the elderly would be a good choice to help a family determine what type of long-term care facility would best meet the needs of their seventy-five-year-old father with Alzheimer's disease. The worker would bring to this situation a knowledge of the causes and effects of Alzheimer's and ways of dealing with these effects; an appreciation of the caregiver burdens that families experience in this situation; and an understanding of the local options for long-term care and the types of financial support that might be available. As another example, an MSW worker who specializes in substance abuse would have skills in specific interventions with those who abuse drugs or alcohol, and would be knowledgeable about the specific ways, both positive and negative, in which families interact with the family member who is involved in abuse.

There is one more thing to add about the definition of generalist practice and its differentiation from advanced practice. We have already noted that the term *generalist practice* is related to the existence of two levels of social work: baccalaureate- and master's-level practice. As undergraduate social work education began to develop and gain more acceptance within the field, questions arose about how best to define the practice of a BA-level social worker in order to differentiate it from that of a person with an MSW. The first distinctions tended to be based on fields of practice: BSW workers were expected to work in public welfare settings, for example, and areas such as school social work and individual and family therapy were to be restricted to master's-level practitioners. But this did not recognize the fact that there were various levels of practice within such areas as public welfare and school social work. It gradually became apparent that a broader and more useful distinction could be drawn between a broad, general practice and more specialized approaches. Therefore, in order to clarify the issue within the profession of social work, as well as to help other professions and the public understand the difference between the BSW and MSW levels, the Council on Social Work Education designated undergraduate-level practice as "generalist practice" and graduate-level practice as "advanced, specialized practice."

Skills

The skills of generalist practice include assessment, referral work, brokering between clients and agencies and other sources of help, and evaluation of services in terms of usefulness to clients. Generalist practitioners must also possess communication skills including empathy and an understanding of the needs and strengths of clients within all the levels of client systems, from micro to macro systems.

Assessment is the core of generalist practice. It entails a thorough exploration and analysis of the client's situation, whether the client/client system is an individual, a family, a group, an organization, or a community. For example, suppose you are doing a field placement at an after-school recreation program for kids in a predominantly African American working-class community in a large city. You notice that one of the kids in the program is a withdrawn fourth-grade girl, Tamara, who hangs at the edge of the group and is clearly hesitant about joining in any of the sports or crafts activities. However, she comes regularly to the program and seems reluctant to leave at closing time. You realize that part of your job is to assess, with Tamara's help, her current situation—her feelings about the after-school program, the reasons behind her withdrawn behavior, her expectations of the program, and the source of her reluctance to leave each day. A conversation with Tamara may bring out various pieces of information. You might learn, for example, that she is new to the neighborhood and is simply finding it hard to make friends. She may instead have a low self-image and find it difficult to believe that any of the other children would like her. She might have a "hidden" disability such as impaired hearing, which makes it harder for her to interact with other kids. She might view the program as a sanctuary and be afraid to go home to a situation in which her father abuses her mother. Or it could be that she's from a single-parent family in which her mother works, and going home means several hours by herself. In each instance, a different intervention on your part might be called for. Interventions might range from your engaging in counseling with Tamara, to her involvement in a small socialization group run by one of the staff social workers, to a visit to her family to assess the situation there, to an appointment at a clinic to check her hearing. The ability to assess the variety of possible problems and to connect Tamara with an appropriate intervention is an important skill of generalist social work.

Assessment, then, involves exploring and analyzing the client's situation, in collaboration with the client. In the assessment process, you would help an individual, family, or group identify and clarify problem areas and look at possible sources of these problems within themselves or the larger environment. From here, you would go on to formulate plans to address these problems or concerns.[31]

A second basic skill in generalist work is the ability to refer clients to various sources of help. This often calls for referrals to other professionals; in Tamara's case, it might mean referral to a psychiatrist if your assessment leads you to believe that she has a serious clinical depression. However, referrals can often entail providing clients with sources of information. Perhaps Tamara's mother, new to the community, needs to find sources of care for Tamara after the after-school program ends. You might be able to direct her to a child care information service.

Assessment and referral work calls for communication skills and the ability to build on client strengths. Simple as this sounds, the ability to listen to clients often needs to be practiced. Particularly when you are starting out, there can be a tendency to want to "get right down to helping the client" before you have really heard all that he or she has to say. Your practice classes and field placement will give you a chance to work at listening to another's story and to draw out pertinent details and feelings. This is sometimes called empathic listening, in which you try to hear responses nonjudgmentally and to put yourself in the client's place, whether you are listening to an individual or to a group of people. You will also come to rely on approaches such as asking open-ended questions ("How did you feel about that?") and avoiding asking "why" (such as asking a young child why he or she played with matches and accidentally set the couch on fire), as in many cases the person may not readily understand the reason behind his or her behavior. As mentioned earlier, an approach with growing acceptance across all types of social work practice is that of stressing client skills rather than deficits. A recent social work practice text emphasizes "strengths-based generalist practice," in which generalist practitioners work "to discover and embellish, explore and exploit clients' strengths and resources."[32] In Tamara's case, you might discover that she has a fondness for drawing; this could lead you to involving her in arts projects with other kids at the after-school center.

Ending a relationship with a client is also a specific skill, called termination. As Zastrow notes, a final evaluation is usually part of the termination process. This involves not only an assessment of what occurred during the client–worker relationship, but also an evaluation of the entire change process.[33] It includes an assessment of where the client is at this point in time and what further steps the client might pursue on his or her own, or with the help of family, friends, and other supports, to continue to resolve problems.

A final set of skills involves brokering between clients and agencies and other sources of help, as well as evaluation of services. We describe these in the sections on case management.

Relationship between Generalist and Specialized Practice

Generalist and specialized social work practitioners need to work together to enhance client functioning and support client resiliency. Generalist practitioners often refer clients to practitioners or agencies with specialized skills. For example, in the situation described in the beginning of this chapter, Tom Watson may call on a psychiatric social worker at the mental health counseling center at Friendship House to help with people he identifies as having trouble with depression. He might also refer a neighborhood resident to a psychologist to do testing for a youngster who appears to have attention deficit hyperactivity disorder (ADHD).

Sometimes, friction between generalist and specialist practitioners calls for special interpretive skills on the part of both groups. Baccalaureate social workers, for example, may find it important to give a clear explanation to other professionals of the scope and purpose of their work. For their part, specialists may need to clarify those situations in which they may be needed to extend the work done by the generalist practitioner.

Case Management: A Major Skill for Generalist Practitioners

Definition

The term *case management* has been broadly applied to describe a method or process of service delivery and a set of roles assumed by various providers of health and social services, including social workers. Nurses and other professionals and paraprofessionals also engage in case management activities. In general, the term connotes "a way of helping people identify the areas where they need help and connecting them to the personnel and community resources that will help them." In addition, case managers ensure that these resources are provided effectively. According to the National Association of Social Workers, case management is "a mechanism for ensuring a comprehensive program that will meet an individual's need for care by coordinating and linking components of a service delivery system."[34]

History

As Arthur J. Frankel and Sheldon R. Gelman point out, case management has a rich and lengthy history in social work. Both the settlement houses and the charity organization workers of the late 1800s and early 1900s pioneered in connecting residents of poor neighborhoods and the clients of charitable agencies to resources such as day care, public health and other medical services, English-language classes, church-based charities, public relief programs in the larger cities, and help from family members. Despite Abraham Flexner's assertion in 1915 that social workers' use of the expertise and services of others in helping clients led to the field's lack of professional status, social workers continued to develop their referral skills as the field progressed.[35]

The concept of case management has been further honed in the last twenty-five years, in part as the result of a proliferation of private agencies, both for-profit and nonprofit, in the social welfare arena. As county, state, and federal agencies have both cut back direct services due to loss in funding since the 1980s and contracted out much of their services, the need has grown to develop coordination of such services at the client level. In addition, as deinstitutionalization has moved those with mental illness from hospitals to communities, clients with multiple challenges have faced the need to locate resources and services that would help them live more independently. Consequently, case management has become pervasive in the field of human services and is used particularly in the areas of mental health, services for people with HIV and AIDS, developmental disability, long-term care, immigrant services, child welfare, and programs for elderly people.[36]

As case management has grown, a number of other professions have begun to develop this skill. Nurses have become particularly active in this area, but occupational therapists, medical assistants, and other groups have also become involved. Managing the relations between the various professions that include case management as an area of practice is beginning to emerge as a significant challenge.

Skills

At first glance, the work of case management appears to be the same as that of generalist social work practice. As Frankel and Gelman note, "the major differences between generalist practice, the specialized methods of social work practice, and case management are those of degree." All of these realms of practice involve in-depth assessments, development of goals and intervention plans, and assessment of these plans when completed. Case management work, however, tends to emphasize the broad use of community resources to help clients build on their own strengths and meet their needs.[37]

As Stephen Rose and Vernon Moore explain, case managers need a wide variety of skills. They are typically "assigned responsibility for identifying and engaging clients, assessing their needs, locating appropriate services and planning for their use, linking clients to resources, and monitoring the process for targeted or desired outcomes."[38] How might this look in practice? Suppose you are working with an African American man, Mr. Marshall, who is seventy-six years old and beginning to have difficulty managing his diabetes. Mr. Marshall lost his wife five years ago and has since been living on his own in their small house in a city neighborhood. The couple was never able to have children; he does have several siblings and cousins, but none live near by. Mr. Marshall has been referred to your place of work, a local nonprofit agency working with families and the elderly, for help with his health problems and current living situation.

Your immediate concern, after establishing rapport with Mr. Marshall, is to assess his situation. Following a strengths perspective, this will be a joint assessment in which together you examine his needs, his concerns, and the resources he has to draw on. You quickly establish that a major resource is Mr. Marshall's spirit of independence coupled with a sense of practicality: "Young woman," he tells you, "I want to stay here in my house, but I also want to find out how best I can find help to do that." Your assessment turns out to be far ranging, including information on his health situation, the physical state of his house (which is in need of some major repairs), his financial situation (a small pension from work at a local printing business, plus a modest amount of Social Security), the proximity of his relatives, his daily activities, his ability to continue to cook and clean for himself, and his goals for the future (would he like to stay in his house as long as possible, would he rather begin to think about moving into an apartment or an assisted living situation, etc.).

Out of this joint assessment of his situation you and Mr. Marshall begin to develop a plan. Because his goal is to remain in his house as long as possible, together you explore the resources he might need to achieve this goal. These include continued medical support; sources for home upkeep, particularly the repairs, which he is no longer able to do; help with financial planning; and the like. Having identified the areas in which resources are needed, you begin to apply your expert knowledge of community programs, health facilities, and sources for financial planning. Mr. Marshall assesses the ability of neighbors and relatives to help out. You and he both begin the process of contacting these various resources, developing a "package" of supports that will enable him to stay at home. Along the way, you hit some obstacles—for example, a particularly motherly and concerned neighbor has just decided to move away to be closer to her daughter and grandchild. On the other hand, you discover some unexpected help; a nearby branch of a large do-it-yourself home repair chain has decided to become involved in community service. Mr. Marshall can apply to their "we fix it for you" program for elderly and low-income people to have his leaky roof fixed.

At the completion of your work together, you and Mr. Marshall evaluate the resources you have located. Do they cover all his current needs? Will they continue to be available, or are they time limited? Are the services efficient? You decide that at this point in time, his needs are being met. But you plan to stay in touch so that if Mr. Marshall's health situation deteriorates, you will be able to go through the same process to see that he can get to the resources he needs.

As this practice vignette shows, case management involves a series of steps in which the social worker, in consultation with the client, "organizes, coordinates, and [helps maintain] a network of formal and informal supports and activities designed to maximize the functioning and well-being of people with multiple needs."[39] As in any type of generalist practice, good communication skills and the ability to empathize are essential; these help establish rapport and set the stage for working together. Assessment, the next step, is a complex process, about which large chapters in social work practice texts are written. In this case, assessment included jointly surveying Mr. Marshall's strengths, needs, and challenges; his physical surroundings; the resources in his environment that might be helpful to him; and his desires and goals for the future. Had Mr. Marshall displayed signs of confusion, forgetfulness, or anxiety, it might have been helpful to bring in another professional, such as a psychiatrist or a clinical social worker, to help gauge his emotional state and his ability to maintain the independence he desires. Such a professional might even have become part of the case management plan, working with Mr. Marshall to help him deal with emotional difficulties.

Developing a plan with Mr. Marshall would also involve another type of assessment: locating and evaluating the usefulness of the resources available to him. As Table 4.1 shows, the existence of a resource doesn't guarantee its relevance to each client's situation, its availability when needed, or its practicality. Gathering this information helps the social worker and the client develop a practical plan for a resource network. The plan includes deciding who will do what to build the network; in this case, for example, Mr. Marshall took the responsibility for approaching his relatives and neighbors about helping him out.

Finally, ongoing evaluation of the services and resources you and Mr. Marshall have established is essential. Without such an evaluation, you will not know whether the resource network is meeting Mr. Marshall's present situation and goals, and you will not know when the two of you should modify it to meet new needs. As in the case of assessment, there are a variety of ways to carry out evaluations. A simple, informal way is to simply check in with Mr. Marshall regularly to ask if he feels his specific goals are being met. Depending on the particular aims and resources in his plan, you might also ask the staff in agencies that are working with him to evaluate his current situation and

TABLE 4.1 Schema for Assessing Resources

Criteria	Description
Relevance	Does the resource offer services that are congruent with the client system's identified needs? Will the resource meet the client system's goals?
Availability	Will the resource be available when the client system requires it? Is there a waiting list? Do certain circumstances qualify for a quick response?
Accessibility	Is the office located on convenient travel routes? Does the resource offer services in the client's language? Sign language? Are the facilities accessible to those with disabilities?
Eligibility	What are the guidelines for receiving this service? Are there income, location, age, or other qualifiers?
Applications	Is there a formal application process? Who needs to fill out what form? What time frame is imposed on the application process? Are supporting documents required?
Fee	Is there a sliding fee scale? If fees are involved, has the client system been informed of the fee schedule? Will the client realistically be able to pay for the service? Under what circumstances can the fee be waived?
Feasibility	Considering all of the aforementioned factors, is this a viable resource?

Source: Karla Krogsrud Miley, Michael O'Melia, and Brenda DuBois, *Generalist Social Work Practice: An Empowering Approach*, 3rd ed. Published by Allyn and Bacon, Boston, MA. Copyright © 2001 by Pearson Education.

his progress towards meeting his goals. Evaluation in case management can include not only a focus on whether the client's goals were met, but also an assessment of the case management services themselves. This involves questions about whether the client, Mr. Marshall in this case, was satisfied with the services, whether they were helpful to him, and in what ways.[40]

Institutional Framework

Social workers carry out case management activities in a variety of settings. They may be employed by hospitals, nursing homes, psychiatric facilities, community centers, schools, and broad-purpose social agencies such as Friendship House. In other words, they can be found in any setting where clients need a variety of resources to help them make changes in their lives. Case management may be one facet of a social worker's job, or the entire purpose of that position.

Case managers work in public and private organizations. Those working in private, for-profit settings sometimes face difficulty, as some of these organizations can limit the types of resources case managers can utilize for clients. This is one of the situations that calls for client advocacy.

Advocacy

Case managers are essentially client advocates; they exist to help people, groups, and communities find appropriate resources for their needs. These resources do not always exist, or if they do, they can be too expensive or difficult to access. Sometimes access is blocked for clients who are women or people of color, who are homeless, or who live in rural areas or the inner city. Case managers will often need to publicize the lack of certain resources and make sure that existing resources can in fact be used by clients.

In addition, case managers in for-profit organizations need to be vigilant to ensure that these organizations do not limit the scope of services available to clients. Managed care companies may also interfere with access to resources (e.g., by limiting the number of therapy sessions a person with depression can receive). Social work case managers should consider joining with NASW, the National Mental Health Association, the National Association for the Mentally Ill, and other advocacy groups in protecting the ability of people with difficulties to receive necessary health and mental health services.

Practice Ethics and Ethical Dilemmas

Generalist social workers, like all social work and human services professionals, face ethical dilemmas in their practice. A major dilemma is that described earlier: How does a case manager work within agency restrictions to make sure that clients receive the necessary resources? As Woodside and McClam note, "Effective human service delivery often requires a delicate balance of commitment to the client, the agency for which the case manager works, laws and regulations, court rulings, and professional codes of ethics." These conflicting commitments often require the case manager to make difficult choices.[41] For example, a case manager for a managed health care company might face a situation in which the child of a couple enrolled in a managed care plan has a rare form of cancer. The physician recommends a new treatment, which she feels has a good chance of success. The managed care company does not cover that particular treatment. To make matters more complicated, the child's parents are uneasy about trying a new approach, despite the physician's explanation of its positive clinical trials. The physician relays to the case manager her frustration at not being able to carry out her professional obligation to heal. Who does the case manager advocate for in this situation—the child or the parents? Should he or she help the parents come to a decision about what is best for the child? Should he or she support the decision of the managed care company, or promote the doctor's recommendation?

Similarly, generalist practitioners involved with several systems at once can face ethical dilemmas when the needs and goals of these systems conflict. For example, a woman in an assisted living facility is very withdrawn and tells her social worker she prefers "keeping myself to myself." The nursing and activities staff feel, however, that it's important to "draw her out" and involve her in outings and group recreation. They look to the social worker for help in doing this. Here, the principles of an individual client's right to self-determination conflict with a staff's concern for her well-being and their interest in maintaining a supportive and interactive community.

Workers in these situations can do more than just take a stab at the right decision and hope for the best. Social work and other professions have developed guidelines and processes for dealing with the many ethical dilemmas they encounter in their practice. As we discussed in Chapter 3, the NASW has worked hard to develop a meaningful Code of Ethics and suggestions for putting it to use. We close this chapter with descriptions of ethical dilemmas encountered by social work practitioners that have been gathered, with suggestions on how to resolve these dilemmas, in an excellent handbook put out by NASW.[42]

> A social worker employed in a county social services department as an eligibility worker has learned that local welfare reforms direct that she report any new children born to current welfare recipients. She fears that this new reporting requirement could prevent children born into welfare families from receiving income supports later in their lives. The worker is aware of the requirements that social workers should comply with the law. However, she is convinced that reporting newborns might preclude future essential services. [She] also believes that the new regulations will create a new class of citizens (children born to welfare mothers) that might be discriminated against in various ways. She feels caught between complying with the law and ignoring the law to prevent what she views as likely injustice.[43]

The NASW commentary on this dilemma is as follows:

> An addition to the 1996 *Code of Ethics* includes a statement on how to think about situations in which social workers feel their ethical obligations conflict with agency policies or relevant laws or regulations. The Code . . . leaves open the possibility that a social worker may decide that the ethical course of action is not to enforce agency policy or a law or regulation. The Code . . . states that the social worker must make a responsible effort to resolve the conflict and should seek proper consultation before making a decision. . . . The Code . . . also speaks to social workers' responsibility to not allow their employing agencies to interfere with their ethical practice.[44]

Another dilemma is as follows: "Many of a clinical case manager's clients with serious and persistent mental illness are members of a local advocacy group for individuals with mental illness. One of these clients asked the case manager to join them in a letter-writing effort and demonstration to oppose recently proposed budget cuts for mental health services."[45]

The NASW comments that

> the dilemma posed in this situation is the social worker's mandate to advocate for resources for clients as opposed to the problem of entering into a dual relationship with clients, which generally should be avoided. Even dual relationships that seem to be in the client's best interests can become complicated and negatively affect the professional relationship. Social workers do have an ethical mandate to facilitate informed participation by the public in shaping public policies. Appropriate encouragement of clients who wish to engage in letter-writing and demonstration efforts around social policy issues fits into this mandate. This can, of course, be done in other ways besides joining clients as a comrade, such as researching information, helping with strategy, and otherwise facilitating the clients' endeavor, thus fulfilling the social worker's responsibility to engage in social and political action on behalf of social justice issues.[46]

In another case of an ethical dilemma,

> A social worker in a private case management agency received a request from a national news program to document the life of a family receiving services. The social worker's supervisor

is encouraging the social worker to pursue the opportunity, seeing it as a chance to shed positive light on the profession and as a marketing opportunity. The news program staff have asked that they meet and interview a consenting family just starting services and to have access to them over a period of months for videotaped interviews to be edited and later presented on national television.[47]

The NASW's response to this situation is that

the ethics dilemma this social worker faces is a desire to enhance the public understanding of the social work profession and the reputation of the agency in conflict with breaching the privacy of the client and the confidentiality of the professional relationship. The importance of respecting clients' right to privacy and the need to protect the confidentiality of clients when responding to the requests of the media must be considered. The issue of whether consent could be truly informed should be examined because even if the clients gave consent for the videotaping, they could not really know the impact of this videotaping of their interviews on their families. The Code of Ethics makes clear that because of the vulnerability of clients, social workers should not engage in solicitation of testimonial endorsements. The potential conflict with the social worker's supervisor, who is in favor of pursuing this opportunity, is also dealt with in the Code of Ethics, which addresses the importance of not allowing the interests of the employing organization to interfere with the ethical practice of social work.[48]

In a final description of an ethical dilemma,

a school social worker provides clinical services to a number of children with disabilities in the school setting. In light of budget constraints and aware that some services performed by school social workers could be billed to Medicaid, the principal has asked the social worker to bill Medicaid for her work with students with disabilities. The social worker feels caught among wanting to serve students; helping the school stretch its tight budget; and her concern that she is being asked to "double bill," because funds authorized by federal legislation pay for social work done with students with disabilities.[49]

NASW experts explain that in this situation

the Code of Ethics can be helpful to the social worker in dealing with the competing demands in her agency. The first ethical standard to consider is that social workers should not solicit remuneration for providing services to clients who are entitled to the same services through the social worker's agency. Further, if the social worker educates the principal about the ethical standards of the profession, she can join with the principal by ensuring that she is a diligent steward of the resources of the agency.[50]

Conclusion

As you have now learned, generalist practice and case management are wide-ranging approaches in social work. Each has a long history in the profession, although the concepts appeared earlier under different names. Each is an essential method of practice for the BSW social worker. The generalist approach has been particularly useful in differentiating between the roles of the BSW and the MSW practitioner.

Generalist social workers, and the case managers among them, have developed a specific set of skills and approaches for working with clients (individuals, families, groups, organizations, and communities) across systems. They have identified, and worked to resolve, a variety of ethical dilemmas that they encounter in their practice. They make an important contribution to the profession and the people they serve.

Visit **www.researchnavigator.com** to research these important concepts from the chapter:

- Case management
- Case worker
- National Association for the Advancement of Colored People
- New Deal
- Settlement house
- Social work AND generalist strengths perspective

Endnotes

1. D. H. Hepworth and J. A. Larson, *Direct Social Work Practice: Theory and Skills,* 14th ed. (Pacific Grove, CA: Brooks/Cole, 1993), 20–22.
2. James Leiby, *A History of Social Welfare and Social Work in the United States* (New York: Columbia University Press, 1978).
3. Walter I. Trattner, *From Poor Law to Welfare State,* 6th ed. (New York: Free Press, 1999), 77–103.
4. Allen F. Davis, *Spearheads for Reform* (New York: Oxford University Press, 1967), 60–83.
5. Trattner, *From Poor Law to Welfare State,* 179; Davis, *Spearheads for Reform,* 99–102.
6. Mary E. Richmond, "The Need of a Training School in Applied Philanthropy," in *Proceedings of the National Conference of Charities and Correction* (Chicago: The Conference, 1897), 186.
7. Richard C. Cabot, *Social Service and the Art of Healing* (New York: Moffett, Yard, 1909), 33.
8. Lydia H. Hodge, "Why a Visiting Teacher?" in *Addresses and Proceedings of the National Education Association* (New York: Fitchfarnsworth, 1917), 225.
9. Roy Lubove, *The Professional Altruist: The Emergence of Social Work as a Career* (Cambridge, MA: Harvard University Press, 1965), 60.
10. Mary E. Richmond, "The Need for a Training School in Applied Philanthropy," 182.
11. Judith A. Trolander, *Settlement Houses and the Great Depression* (Detroit, MI: Wayne State University Press, 1975), 47.
12. American Association of Social Workers, *Social Casework Generic and Specific: A Report of the Milford Conference* (New York: American Association of Social Workers, 1929), 3.
13. June Axinn and Mark Stern, *Social Welfare: A History of the American Response to Need* (Boston: Allyn and Bacon, 2001), 198–199.
14. Leslie Leighninger, *Social Work: Search for Identity* (Westport, CT: Greenwood Press, 1987), 77–101.
15. Grace Coyle, "Social Group Work," in Russell H. Kurtz, ed., *Social Work Yearbook, 1937* (New York: Russell Sage Foundation, 1937), 461–462.
16. Howard Goldstein, *Social Work Practice: A Unitary Approach* (Columbia, SC: University of South Carolina Press, 1973), 36.
17. Clarence King, "Community Organization for Social Work," in Russell H. Kurtz, ed., *Social Work Yearbook, 1941* (New York: Russell Sage Foundation, 1941), 128–133.
18. John K. Galbraith, *The Affluent Society* (Boston: Houghton Mifflin, 1958).
19. Leiby, *A History of Social Welfare and Social Work in the United States,* 282.
20. Helen Leland Witmer, *Social Work: An Analysis of a Social Institution* (New York: Farrar & Rinehart, 1942), 35–39; Arlien Johnson, "Community Organization in Social Work," in Russell H. Kurtz, ed., *Social Work Yearbook, 1945* (New York: Russell Sage Foundation, 1945), 92–98.
21. Leighninger, *Social Work: Search for Identity,* 189.

22. Francis J. Turner, ed., *Social Work Treatment: Interlocking Theoretical Approaches,* 4th ed. (New York: Free Press, 1996).
23. Francis P. Purcell and Harry Specht, "The House on Sixth Street," *Social Work 10* (October 1965), 69–76.
24. Paul H. Stuart, Leslie Leighninger, and Jana Newton Donahoe, *A History of the Association of Baccalaureate Program Directors* (Eau Claire, WI: Association of Baccalaureate Program Directors, 1993), 5; Harold L. McPheeters and Robert M. Ryan, Southern Regional Education Board, *A Core of Competence for Baccalaureate Social Welfare* (Atlanta, GA: Undergraduate Social Welfare Manpower Project, December, 1971), 5, 18–22.
25. G. H. Hull, *Social Work Internship Manual* (Eau Claire, WI: University of Wisconsin–Eau Claire, Department of Social Work, 1990), 17, quoted in Charles Zastrow, *Social Work and Social Welfare,* 7th ed. (Belmont, CA: Wadsworth, 2000), 70; Karla Krogsrud Miley, Michael O'Melia, and Brenda DuBois, *Generalist Social Work Practice: An Empowering Approach,* 3rd ed. (Boston: Allyn and Bacon, 2001), 9–10.
26. John Poulin et al., *Collaborative Social Work: Strengths-Based Generalist Practice* (Itasca, IL: F. E. Peacock, 2000), 4; Hepworth and Larson, *Direct Social Work Practice,* 20–22.
27. Miley, O'Melia, and DuBois, *Generalist Social Work Practice,* 10, 82–94; Barry Locke, Rebecca Garrison, and James Winship, *Generalist Social Work Practice* (Pacific Groves, CA: Brooks/Cole, 1998), 23–28
28. Locke, Garrison, and Winship, *Generalist Social Work Practice,* 9–11, 17, 109–110; Dennis Saleeby, "Introduction: Beginnings of a Strengths Approach to Practice," in Dennis Saleeby, ed., *The Strengths Perspective in Social Work Practice* (New York: Longman Press, 1992), 41–58; Ann Weick, Charles Rapp, W. Patrick Sullivan, and Walter Kisthardt, "A Strengths Perspective for Social Work Practice," *Social Work 34* (July 1989), 350–354.
29. A. N. Maluccio and M. F. Libassi, "Competence Clarification in Social Work Practice," *Social Thought 10* (1984), 52.
30. Robert L. Jackson, *The Clubhouse Model: Empowering Applications of Theory to Generalist Practice* (Pacific Groves, CA: Brooks/Cole, 2001), 8.
31. Poulin, *Collaborative Social Work,* 55–56.
32. Dennis Saleeby, quoted in Poulin, *Collaborative Social Work,* 6.
33. Zastrow, *Introduction to Social Work and Social Welfare,* 74.
34. Arthur J. Frankel and Sheldon R. Gelman, *Case Management: An Introduction to Concepts and Skills* (Chicago: Lyceum Books, 1998), 3–4; National Association of Social Workers, *NASW Standards and Guidelines for Social Work Case Management for the Functionally Impaired* (Silver Spring, MD: NASW Press, 1984); Karen K. Kirst-Ashman and Grafton H. Hull Jr., *Understanding Generalist Practice,* 2nd ed. (Chicago: Nelson-Hall, 1999), 579–580.
35. Frankel and Gelman, *Case Management,* 3; Stephen M. Rose and Vernon L. Moore, "Case Management," in Richard L. Edwards and June Gary Hopps, eds., *Encyclopedia of Social Work,* 19th ed., vol. 1 (Washington, DC: National Association of Social Workers Press, 1995), 335; Marianne Woodside and Tricia McClam, *Generalist Case Management: A Method of Human Service Delivery* (Pacific Grove, CA: Brooks/Cole, 1998), 41–51.
36. Frankel and Gelman, *Case Management,* 6-7; Miley, O'Melia, and Du Bois, *Generalist Social Work Practice,* 339; Jackson, *The Clubhouse Model,* 122; Joseph Walsh, *Clinical Case Management with Persons Having Mental Illness* (Belmont, CA: Brooks/Cole, 2000), 26–28.
37. Frankel and Gelman, *Case Management,* 16.
38. Rose and Moore, "Case Management," 335.
39. D. P. Moxley, quoted in Miley, O'Melia, and Du Bois, *Generalist Social Work Practice,* 338.
40. Nancy Summers, *Fundamentals of Case Management Practice* (Belmont, CA: Brooks/Cole, 2001), 279–282; Frankel and Gelman, *Case Management,* 24–26, 49–50; Kirst-Ashman and Hull, *Understanding Generalist Practice,* 592.
41. Woodside and McClam, *Generalist Case Management,* 280.
42. NASW, *Current Controversies in Social Work Ethics: Case Examples* (Washington, DC: NASW, 1998). Copyright © 1998, National Association of Social Workers, Inc.
43. NASW, *Current Controversies,* 7.
44. NASW, *Current Controversies,* 7.
45. NASW, *Current Controversies,* 33.
46. NASW, *Current Controversies,* 33.
47. NASW, *Current Controversies,* 38.
48. NASW, *Current Controversies,* 38.
49. NASW, *Current Controversies,* 57.
50. NASW, *Current Controversies,* 57.

CHAPTER

5

Responses to Human Diversity

For over twenty years, a Georgia businessman named David Morris has been hiring people with disabilities to work in his business, Habitat International, Inc., which supplies home products to retailers like Lowe's and Home Depot. Three of every four of his employees has a physical or mental disability, or both. His workers include recovering alcoholics; people with schizophrenia; and workers who have suffered severe head injuries, strokes, or loss of an arm or leg. He also employs those with Down syndrome, autism, and cerebral palsy. All his workers are cross-trained to cover every task in the plant.

Working closely with workers and encouraging employees to help one another, Morris has created a positive as well as productive work environment. His business has tripled its sales since 2001, despite the economic downturn. When asked the secret of his company's success, Morris says simply: "I hire the people no one else wants to hire."[1]

Carlos Ortiz is out on the street early this morning, waiting with six other Mexican immigrants for employers to come by to hire them for day jobs—landscaping, tree trimming, roofing, ditch digging, and the like. The pay is OK—$6 or $7 an hour—although sometimes the employer shortchanges him, and the work conditions can be hard. He once had to spend two days with several other men unloading heavy office furniture in 115-degree heat, with a boss who hardly let them stop for water. What gets to Carlos most, however, is the stares and angry looks from many of the people who walk or drive by. He overhears comments about how the day laborers are fugitives or wetbacks who harass people and "spoil the neighborhood for everyone else." He dreams of the day when he'll have a full-time job and can save enough money to go back to Mexico and buy a nice house.

In 1964, fifteen women were admitted to Harvard Law School. The dean of the school invited them to dinner at his home, where he proceeded to ask them, "Why are you at Harvard Law School, taking the place of a man?" He spoke of the concern that female law students would waste their valuable legal education because they would inevitably get married, have children, and quit their legal careers. Among the women was Judith Richards Hope, who went on to become a domestic policy advisor for President Gerald Ford and the first woman on the Governing Board of Harvard University. Another member of the class is a judge on the U.S. Court of Appeals for the D.C. Circuit. Pat Scott Schroeder, a third member of the group, served in the U.S. House of Representatives for twelve terms. Women entering Harvard Law School during the mid 1960s became corporate lawyers, professors, entrepreneurs, and authors. One of them was Janet Reno, the first woman to serve as U.S. Attorney General. While they were law students, they encountered various types of discrimination, including a class in which they were never called on to speak, except on a designated day, when they were placed on stage and drilled. They survived in part by helping one another. These women were part of an early wave in a national change in attitude toward women. In those times, only 3 percent of law students were women; now almost half of them are.[2]

Marie Donaldson is making chocolate chip cookies to take to the potluck at her ten-year-old son Kurt's school. She smiles to herself when she thinks that her contribution—such an American staple—may seem unusual to many of the kids and their parents.

The Donaldsons live in northern Virginia, near Washington, D.C., and Kurt's classmates are from El Salvador, Korea, Somalia, Bangladesh, Pakistan, and over twenty other countries. About a fifth of the students are African American. The hallways ring with different languages; classrooms are a swirl of different skin tones. "I guess maybe sometimes it seems confusing to the kids," Marie muses, "but what a chance to learn from each other before someone starts to tell them they should stick to their own kind."

Marianne, Josh, and Emily are having lunch in the student union after their Introduction to Social Policy course. The topic of discussion that day had been racism, sexism, and homophobia, and the ways in which these relate to the power and privilege of dominant groups. All three students are feeling a bit unsettled. Josh complains to the others, "Boy, if that wasn't an exercise in political correctness, I don't know what is. Dr. Thomas obviously wanted us to say the 'right' thing—I'm going to have to be careful about what I put on my exam if I want a good grade from her!" "Oh, I don't worry so much about her," Marianne responds. "It's the minority students in the room—I'm afraid if I say something the wrong way they'll think I'm racist." Emily doesn't respond but thinks about how uncomfortable these classroom discussions are; the topics of diversity and discrimination are too personal for her, as a lesbian woman, to talk about in class.[3]

The United States is a country of diversity. Its population is composed of members of a variety of races, religions, and ethnic groups, some recently arrived and others longtime residents. For most of our history, African Americans have constituted the country's largest minority group. In recent years, however, Hispanic and Asian populations have grown tremendously. In 2001, to the surprise of most population analysts, the size of the Hispanic population surpassed the size of the African American population in the United States. Currently, minorities constitute about a third of the country's population; by 2030 that figure will have risen to 40 percent. California and several other western states are the harbingers of the diversity to come. In 1999 minorities became the majority in California, led by Latinos (almost a third of the population) and Asians (over 11 percent). Other groups add to the vibrancy of our country's mix, including American Indians and Eskimos and immigrants from India, Africa, and the Arab countries. In addition, Americans had the chance to identify themselves as belonging to more than one race in the 2000 census. Nearly 7 million people (2.4 percent of the population) described themselves as multiracial. Relations between majority and minority groups, as well as between and even within minority groups, present extraordinary challenges, but also the potential of a new energy in American life.[4]

In the United States, like any other country, other groups are also singled out as different or "special": those with physical and mental disabilities; the elderly; gays, lesbians, bisexual, and transgendered persons; and even the group that makes up half the population—women. All this diversity can bring great strength to a society by providing a wide variety of values, talents, and points of view. Yet all too often difference has been accompanied by prejudice and discrimination and has been used to justify oppression. In the past decade we have witnessed a heightened sensitivity to issues related to race, ethnicity, gender, and sexual orientation. Numerous policies have emerged regarding immigration, affirmative action, gay rights, and bilingual education in the public schools. Questions are raised by the white majority about the effects of growing diversity on our "American way of life." Minority groups vie uneasily with one another for resources and recognition.

National, regional, and community reactions to diversity—either acceptance of difference or discrimination—are reflected in our social welfare policies and services. In addition, the variables of ethnicity, race, gender, sexual orientation, age, and physical and mental capabilities often have a profound impact on people's lives. These variables can determine income level, job and educational opportunities, access to housing and health care, and degree of participation in various political and social institutions. Finally, the existence of diversity raises questions about the type of society we want to foster. Should that society be pluralistic, allowing a certain autonomy for different groups and cultures? Should it go further and support separatism—a situation in which groups that wish to can maintain their own very separate and distinct lifestyles? Or should it instead strive for a more homogenized whole—perhaps even endeavoring to fit all people into a white, Anglo-Saxon model?

All three areas related to diversity—social policy, individual development, and the relationship within or between groups and the larger community—are of vital importance to social workers. This chapter looks at the impact and meaning of "difference" for individuals, groups, and society and explores the ways in which the social welfare system has responded to diversity. Its ultimate aim is to encourage you to think about how these issues affect your own life and the ways in which you judge and interact with others.

Definition of the Problem

There is no single problem related to human diversity. Rather, there are a variety of issues and consequences, some negative and some positive, related to belonging to a group that is seen as somehow different from the "majority." (We discuss the concepts of majority and minority in the next section of this chapter.) Before proceeding further, however, it is important to note the issue of minority group names and how they are chosen. Sometimes this choice is clearly negative or demeaning, as in the pejorative terms that have been developed to refer to African Americans, Italians, Jews, Mexicans, and other groups. The names chosen may also reflect the attempt of a dominant culture to subordinate minority groups and cultures. The title *American Indian* can be seen as one example. The term *Indian* stems from Columbus's confusion regarding which continent he was on. The addition of the adjective *American* ignores the fact that indigenous peoples lived in this part of the world long before European explorers decided to call it America. While some of the descendants of these peoples are comfortable retaining the titles of *American Indian* or *Native American,* others see names such as *indigenous* or *First Nations* peoples as more accurate and respectful. Similarly, the titles *Hispanic* and *Latino* have political and cultural differences in meaning. The term *Hispanic,* denoting a person from a Spanish-speaking country or his or her descendants, is seen by some as a catchall label imposed by members of the majority on groups of people representing many different cultures. In contrast, the titles *Latino* and *Latina,* which encompass people of all colors from Latin America, have originated from within the groups themselves, in part as an attempt to build a common identity. The terms *Chicano* and *Chicana* have more specific meanings referring to Mexican Americans. In this book, we have chosen to use a variety of titles in referring to particular minority groups.

Although it is important to appreciate the strengths of being part of a minority group, it is the negative aspects that often draw our attention and mobilize us to seek change. Racism, for example, remains a prominent feature of U.S. society. Despite the gains of the civil rights movement of the 1950s and 1960s and the various social policies and programs aimed at eradicating discrimination and its effects, for many, being African American still means being disadvantaged. This disadvantage extends to other minorities, including Latinos and indigenous peoples. As Figure 5.1 shows, African Americans and Latinos are far more likely than non-Latino whites to live in poverty. About a third of all African American children and 27 percent of all Latino children are poor, compared with less than 9 percent of white children (see Figure 5.2). Close to a third of Native American people on reservations live below the poverty line, and reservation unemployment rates from 45 to 90 percent are not uncommon.[5]

Upcoming chapters describe in detail the effects of race and minority status on health, housing, and other areas of social welfare. To summarize here: Minorities of color face disparities in disease and mortality rates and access to adequate health care. An African American man between the ages of forty-five and sixty-four is more than three times as likely as his white counterpart to die of a stroke. Hispanic children are over thirteen times more likely than non-Hispanic white children to be infected with tuberculosis. Indigenous peoples, African Americans, and Latinos have higher rates of type 2 diabetes than whites. Type 2 diabetes generally begins after age forty-five, but it

FIGURE 5.1 **All People in Each Racial Group below the Poverty Level Each Year**

Note: Persons of Hispanic origin may be of any race. The 2001 poverty rate for non-Hispanic whites is only 7.8 percent.

Source: U.S. Census Bureau, Current Population Survey, 1960–2002, Figure 3, *Poverty Rates by Race and Hispanic Origin: 1959–2001,* online at www.census.gov/hhs/poverty/poverty01/povrac01cht.gif.

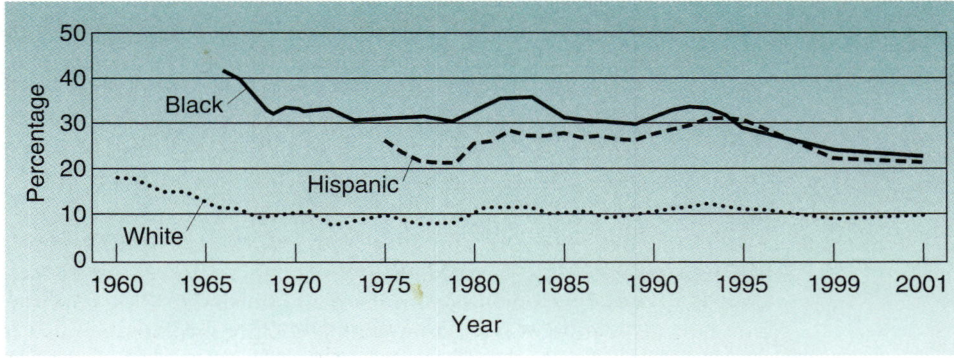

FIGURE 5.2 **Percentages of Children in Poverty**

Source: U.S. Bureau of the Census, "Poverty Status of People, by Family Relationship, Race, and Hispanic Origin: 1959 to 2001," [Table 3], online at www.census.gov/income/histpov/histpov03.1st.

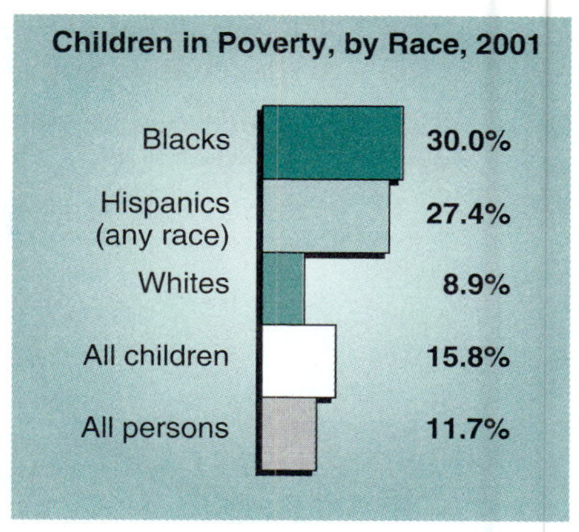

is becoming more common among younger people. The rise in incidence and earlier onset is particularly acute for American Indians, who have a 12.2 percent rate of type 2 diabetes for those over the age of nineteen, compared to a national average of 4 percent. The death rate for diabetes among American Indians has tripled from 1980 to 2001. Minority status can also mean less access to health services, such as children's vaccinations. In 2002, 80 percent of white children, 76 percent of Hispanic children, and 71 percent of African American children under three received a combined series of vaccinations. Housing is still a major arena for discrimination, with housing segregation rates remaining high in many cities, particularly in the Northeast and Midwest. Detroit, Chicago, and New York City are among the most segregated cities in the United States.[6]

Education and employment are also affected by discrimination. Although the use of busing led to greater integration in U.S. schools from the 1960s through the 1980s, recent figures show an ominous trend back toward segregation. African American children are now increasingly likely to sit in classes with few, if any, non-minority faces. Attainment of high school and college degrees varies by race and ethnicity (see Figure 5.3). Although the proportion of African Americans completing college has increased greatly since 1940, in 2000 the rate was still only 63 percent that of whites. Latinos continue to lag behind whites and African Americans in the percentage graduating from high school. Finally, as states such as California and Texas have jettisoned their programs of affirmative action in higher education (often over the protests of college and university officials), educational institutions have struggled to find ways to maintain minority enrollments.[7]

Lower education levels can limit employment for African Americans and Hispanics. In the 1940s, African American men migrating from the rural South found good employment opportunities in northern factories and steel mills. When these industries drastically reduced jobs in the 1970s and early 1980s, seniority rules disproportionately pushed African Americans out. The new service sector positions that replaced the factory jobs favored those with education, and there were more educated white men than African Americans and Latinos. Even with relatively low national jobless rates, unemployment can remain high for minorities. In 2003, for example, the unemployment rate

FIGURE 5.3 **Educational Attainment by Race and Hispanic Origin, 1960–2000 (Persons Twenty-Five Years Old and Over)**

Note: Persons of Hispanic origin may be of any race. Data for 1960 and 1965 not available for persons of Hispanic origin.

Source: U.S. Census Bureau, *Statistical Abstract of the United States, 2002,* No. 208, online at www.census.gov/prod/2003pubs/02statab/edu.pdf.

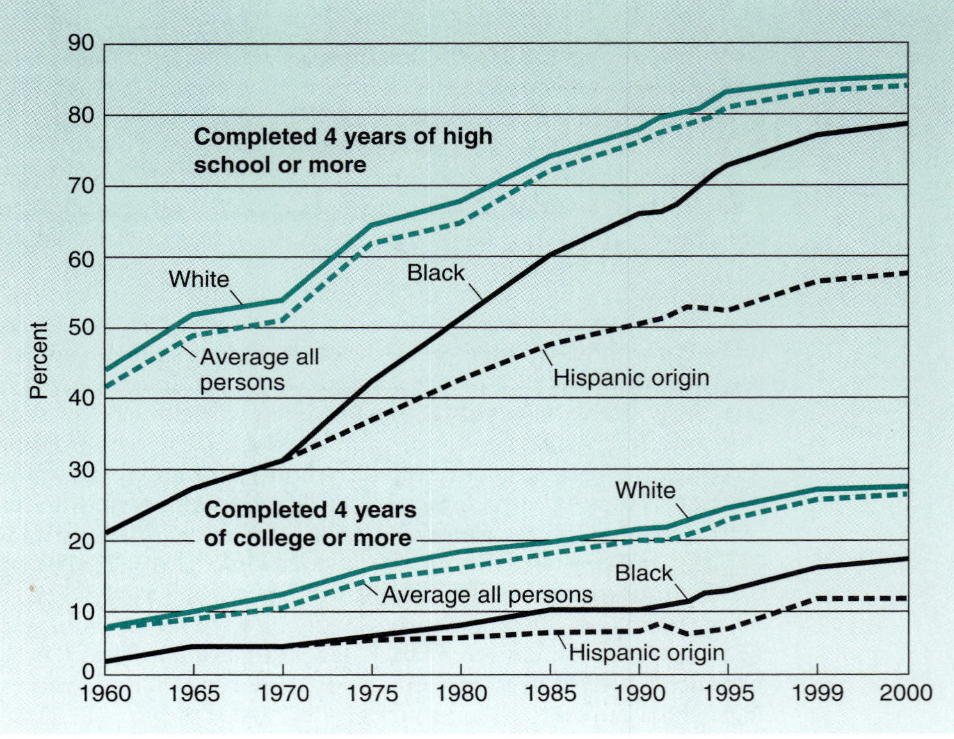

was 4.9 percent for whites, 7.3 percent for Hispanics, and 10 percent for African Americans. About 15 percent of all teenagers were unemployed in 2001, but the percentage was 29 percent for African American teens.[8]

Education levels do not fully account for these employment discrepancies; various forms of discrimination are also at work. African American teens who look for jobs often can't find them. Many recount incidents of discrimination, such as a prospective employer's saying the job is filled but later handing out an application to a white teenager. Studies using teenagers of different races but with similar resumes, clothing, and scripts for speaking to employers have found that white applicants are still chosen disproportionately over African American ones. Similarly, discrimination helps explain why the average salary of college-educated whites over a lifetime is $13,640 more than that of college-educated African Americans.[9]

Being a minority member has ramifications in the crucial areas of employment, income, health, housing, and education. Vast new waves of immigration further complicate the picture and lead to questions about whether the United States can "absorb the newcomers," both culturally and economically. About 10 million immigrants entered the United States in the 1980s, even more than the influx of immigrants from southern and eastern Europe at the turn of the century. (See Figures 5.4 and 5.5.)

Between 1991 and 1999, about 1.3 million immigrants came to the United States from Europe and Canada. In the same period, almost 7 million entered from other countries. The rate of immigration continues to rise. In 2001 alone, 2.4 million people arrived in the United States. The country's foreign-born population hit a record high in 2002, with 32.5 million foreign-born residents.[10]

In addition to legal immigrants, at least 300,000 illegal immigrants enter the United States each year. The foreign-born are more geographically concentrated than the native population. The largest proportion live in the West and Northeast, the

FIGURE 5.4 **Immigration to the United States by Decade, 1881–1990**

Source: Adapted from Michael E. Fix and Jeffery S. Passel, "Setting the Record Straight: What Are the Costs to the Public?" *Public Welfare 52* (Spring 1994), 8.

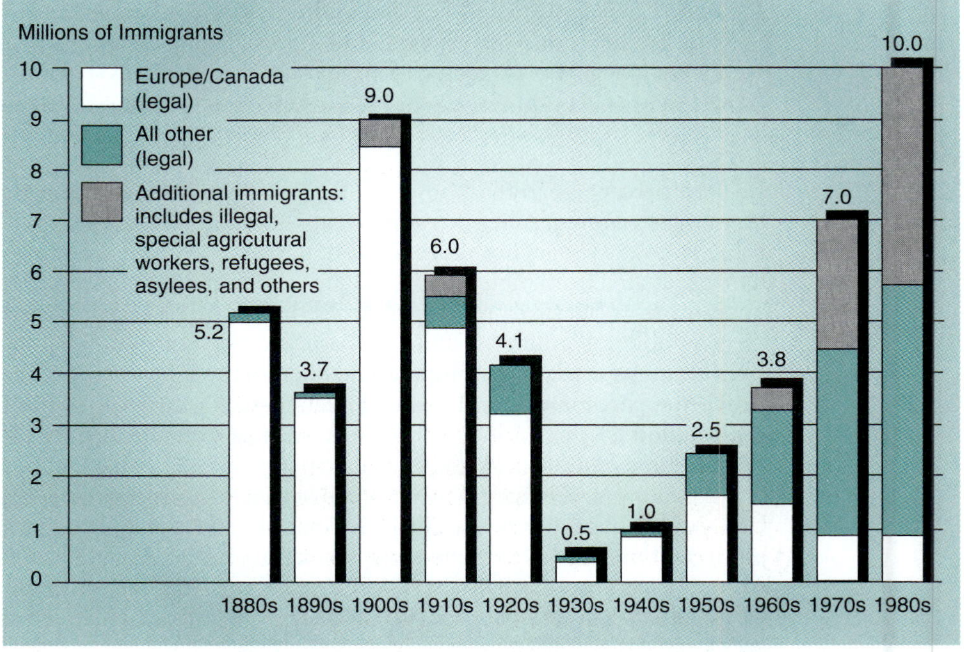

FIGURE 5.5 **Percentages of U.S Population Who Were Foreign-Born, 1900–2000**

Sources: U.S. Bureau of the Census, Current Population Reports, P20–494, *The Foreign-Born Population: 1996* (Washington, DC: U.S. Government Printing Office, March 1997), 1; Genaro C. Armas, "U.S. Foreign-Born Grow to 28.3 Mil.," *Arizona Republic* (3 January 2000) 1, 14.

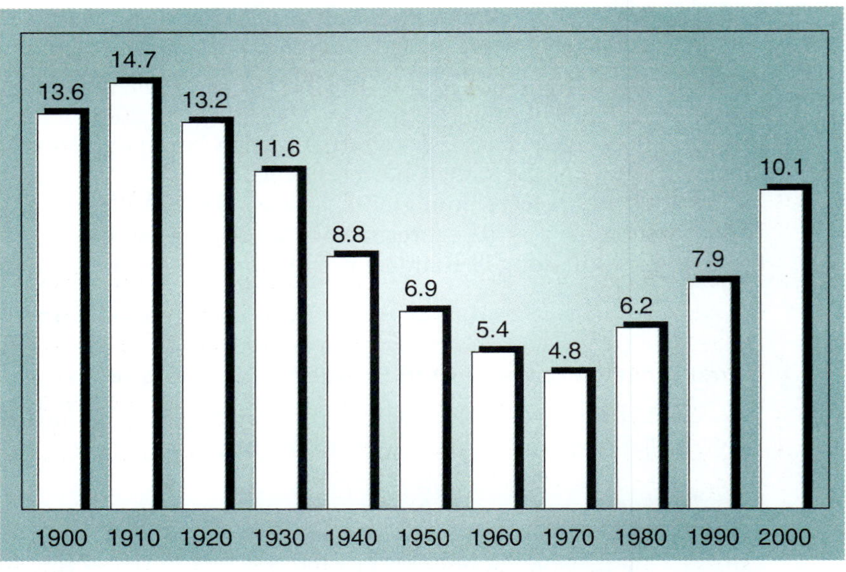

smallest percentage in the Midwest. Like European immigrants at the turn of the century, today's immigrants generally live in a small number of large cities and their suburbs. The newcomers are more likely than natives to have large families, less likely to have graduated from high school, and more likely to live in poverty. Sixty percent of immigrants from Mexico and Central American countries earn less than $20,000 a year.[11]

As Table 5.1 indicates, most of the new arrivals are of Asian and Latino descent. This is an important factor in projected demographic changes in the United States, in which the percentage of whites will decline, that of African Americans will increase slightly, and that of Latinos and Asians will rise dramatically. By 2050, almost half of the residents of the United States will be people of color (see Figure 5.6, p. 152).

Immigration brings an energizing diversity of cultures and ethnic backgrounds to U.S. society. Immigrants also fill jobs, especially in a tight labor market. Yet many people argue that the new arrivals strain education, health, social services, and housing resources. Headlines such as "Mexican Immigrants Sap Citizens, Report Says" capture such ambivalence and concerns. In the last ten years or so, reactions against immigrants have been embodied in new and restrictive state and federal policies, which we discuss in the Current Issues section of this chapter. A particularly strong reaction against a mi-

TABLE 5.1 Countries of Origin for the Foreign-Born in the United States, 1980, 1990, and 2000

	1980	1990	2000
Europe	36.6%	22.0%	15.3%
Asia	18.0%	25.2%	25.5%
Mexico	15.6%	21.7%	*
Caribbean	8.9%	9.8%	9.9%
Central America	2.5%	5.7%	34.5%*
South America	4.0%	5.2%	6.6%
Other Countries	14.4%	10.4%	8.1%
Total Number of Foreign-Born	14.1 million	19.8 million	28.4 million

*In the 2000 report, Mexico is included in the figures for Central America. The vast majority of foreign-born from Central America are Mexican.

Sources: U.S. Bureau of the Census, Current Population Reports, P23–185, *Population Profile of the United States: 1993* (Washington, DC: U.S. Government Printing Office, 1993), 40; U.S. Bureau of the Census, Current Population Reports, P20–534, *The Foreign-Born Population in the United States* (Washington, DC: U.S. Government Printing Office, January 2001), 1.

nority group made up of both immigrants and U.S. citizens came after the September 11, 2001, attacks. Muslims of various national origins were targeted for profiling by the U.S. government and became the subjects of hate crimes.[12]

Women, the elderly, those with disabilities, and people with different sexual orientations also face inequities and discrimination in our society. Statistics on economic inequities are all too familiar: Women earn only 77 percent of men's salaries; female-headed families, regardless of race, represent the largest group of poor people in the United States; the elderly, currently almost 13 percent of the population, constitute 10 percent of the country's poor; and Social Security benefits for people with physical and mental disabilities remain at low levels.[13]

Beyond the statistics lie issues of prejudice and discrimination. Many women, for example, still encounter a glass ceiling when they attempt to rise to the higher ranks of business management. Only a handful of women head Fortune 500 companies. When a Massachusetts court ruled in November 2003 that gay and lesbian couples had the right to marry, responses were quick and intense. Gay couples and their friends and advocates rejoiced in the decision; opponents saw the move as a dangerous threat to the sanctity of marriage. Finally, self-styled vigilantes, angry about illegal immigration, roam the borders of southwestern states, beating or shooting those who cross over.[14]

People with physical and mental disabilities constitute another minority group in our society. It is often a disadvantaged minority. Although a Harris Poll reports that 71 percent of those with disabilities feel that life has improved for them over the last

FIGURE 5.6 **A Head Count by Race, 1999 and 2050**

Note: All categories except Hispanic exclude people of Hispanic origin, who can be people of any race.

Sources: Newsweek—Tom Morganthau, "The Face of the Future" (27 January 1997), 58. Copyright © 1997, Newsweek, Inc. All rights reserved. Reprinted by permission; U.S. Census Bureau, *Statistical Abstract of the United States: 2002,* 18.

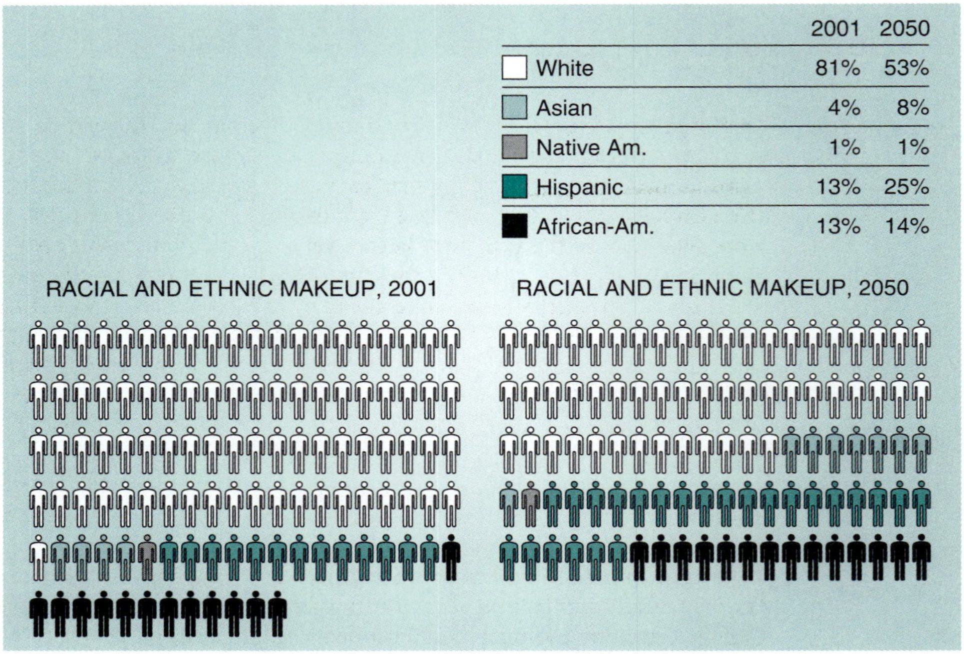

	2001	2050
White	81%	53%
Asian	4%	8%
Native Am.	1%	1%
Hispanic	13%	25%
African-Am.	13%	14%

RACIAL AND ETHNIC MAKEUP, 2001

RACIAL AND ETHNIC MAKEUP, 2050

decade, only 32 percent of working-age people with disabilities hold full- or part-time jobs, almost half feel isolated from the communities in which they live, and a disproportionate number live in poverty. Although the Americans with Disabilities Act (1990) and other legislation aim to protect employment rights, educational opportunities, and access to buildings and public transportation for those with disabilities, such legislation is not consistently enforced. Instances of denial of field placements or jobs to social workers who are blind are just one example of society's continued failure to see the person behind the disability. Even though laws exist to prohibit such discrimination, legal action may prove too costly or too risky for an individual to pursue.[15]

In sum, diversity can bring discrimination and exploitation. We have even invented terms to capture this phenomenon: *sexism, racism, ageism,* and *homophobia* (the fear of homosexuals and homosexual lifestyles). On the other hand, diversity has great advantages, both for the nation as a whole and for members of groups viewed as "different." The social and kinship ties within ethnic communities; the cultural traditions of

Latino, Asian American, and African American families; the coping skills of the "physically challenged" (a new term for people with physical disabilities) and of working mothers; the wisdom of older persons—all can enrich individual and communal life. An understanding of both the positive and the negative effects of diversity is a vital part of social work practice.

Definition of Terms

Terminology is important in discussions of diversity and difference. *Minority group* and *majority* are common labels, for example. Their use suggests that exploitation or discrimination focuses on a group smaller in number than the exploiters. Further, *minority* often implies nonwhite. Lately, the term *minority* has been expanded. Women constitute more than half of the U.S. population, yet they are often considered a minority group. Black South Africans, although they are numerically the majority in their country, have been seen as a minority group in terms of their historic subjugation in a white-controlled society. More useful terms for analyzing exploitation and discrimination might be *dominant* and *subordinate* groups. A subordinate group is one that is singled out for differential or unequal treatment by a dominant group that has higher rights and privileges.[16]

The concepts of "race" and "ethnic group" are also used in varying and sometimes overlapping ways. Traditionally, the word *race* has meant "a distinct category of human beings with physical characteristics transmitted by descent."[17] In other words, people throughout the ages have found it reasonable to divide one another into groups based on obvious external criteria, such as skin color or eye shape, even though over time these characteristics have blurred because of intermarriage. The concept of race also carries social connotations that are particularly attached to differences in skin color. That is, from the early days of European colonization, dominant white groups have viewed color as a symbol of status and cultural difference. They have defined dark-skinned people as backward or less evolved. This outlook underlies *racism*, or the idea that physical differences between groups of people signify meaningful differences in intelligence and ability. The racist belief that one group is inherently inferior and another is inherently superior allows one group to justify its oppression of another. Richard Herrnstein and Charles Murray's book *The Bell Curve,* which argues that differences between IQ scores of African Americans and whites are due to genetic factors, has been criticized for its potential to legitimize such oppression. The basic argument of the book also runs counter to twin studies suggesting that only about 60 percent of general cognitive ability is inherited and that environmental factors, including maternal nutrition, contribute to intelligence levels.[18]

The term *ethnic group* is an even broader concept than race. Ethnic groups can be defined as those "whose members share a unique social and cultural heritage passed on from one generation to the next." Such groups often have distinctive patterns of language, family life, religion, and other customs.[19] Race and nationality might be subsumed under the term *ethnic group,* and some writers use *ethnicity* to talk not only of Jews and Polish Americans but also of African Americans. This book, however, limits the term to groups distinguished primarily by cultural or national characteristics, rather than by race.

These Nazi symbols on a trash can are chilling symbols of prejudice.

Ethnic and racial relations are all too often marred by prejudice and discrimination. The term *prejudice* applies to attitudes, and the term *discrimination* applies to behaviors. To be prejudiced is to have unfavorable feelings about a group and its individual members; these feelings are based on stereotypes rather than on comprehensive knowledge. Discrimination is differential (usually negative) treatment of individuals from certain groups or social categories. To say that Jews are only interested in making money is prejudice; to prohibit Jews from living in certain suburban neighborhoods is discrimination.

Racism, sexism, ageism, and similar phenomena are forms of prejudice. It is important to note that these attitudes take both an individual and an institutional form. As an example of *individual racism,* a college professor might routinely ignore the comments and questions of minority students, even though university regulations prohibit such differential treatment. *Institutional racism,* on the other hand, refers to beliefs and actions of large numbers of people that are supported by organizational or community norms. Institutional racism occurs when a belief in white supremacy becomes deeply ingrained in the dominant culture, becomes embodied in customs and laws, and leads to discriminatory patterns that many take for granted. These patterns are so deeply and subtly ingrained that it is possible to act in a racist way without being conscious of doing so. At a high school dance, for example, the security staff may turn away African American students who say they have forgotten their tickets while letting in white students with a similar story. To the extent that white students ignore this discriminatory action, they are a part of a racist response.

The presence of diverse racial, ethnic, and other distinct groups in society gives rise to various notions about the proper relationship between individual groups and "the whole." Such notions emerge particularly in discussions of immigration, although they have relevance also to the situations of longtime residents (African Americans and American Indians) and of those belonging to categories such as the elderly or people with disabilities. A traditional version of "ideal group relations" in the United States is the idea of a melting pot, in which the cultures of all groups join to produce a new, distinctly American culture. In real life, this early twentieth-century idea of a "blended American" proved unrealistic. Newcomers were unwilling to give up all of their traditions and customs; and, perhaps more significantly, the dominant society had a stake in maintaining its own identity.

A more common and attainable goal for intergroup relations has been that of *assimilation*, in which new and subordinate groups are expected to adapt to American ways and to pattern themselves on a white, Protestant, Anglo-Saxon model. Theorist Milton Gordon has divided the concept of assimilation into a variety of categories. *Structural assimilation*, for example, means the entrance of the new group into "the cliques and associations of the core society at the primary-group level" of family, club, and social relations. Acceptability of intermarriage between dominant and subordinate groups and acceptability of minority membership in the local country club are the signs of structural assimilation. *Cultural assimilation* occurs when the new group changes its cultural patterns and beliefs as well as its behaviors to match those of the core society. For example, cultural assimilation was at work when European immigrants of the early 1900s adopted the American preoccupation with material success. Gordon and others note that assimilation of ethnic groups in America has most frequently been of the cultural rather than the structural type.[20] The lack of structural assimilation may stem from ethnic or racial group reluctance to interact with the dominant group on the level of family and social networks; or, more likely, it may indicate mainstream society's intention of keeping them out.

A final image of intergroup relations is that of *cultural pluralism*. This occurs when people of different cultures retain their own unique individual character and traits, but at the same time interact with other groups, taking on additional traits, such as a common language. In the United States these common traits have tended to supplant individual group practices and attitudes, so full-scale cultural pluralism cannot be said to exist. However, social scientists such as Andrew Greeley, Nathan Glazer, and others have documented various types of ethnic group persistence in our country. Looking at the continuing presence of ethnic ties among third- and fourth-generation European immigrants (seen, for example, in tight-knit Italian or Polish communities), Greeley and Glazer conclude that ethnicity is still alive and well in the United States.[21] Furthermore, the prospect of a pluralistic society that draws on the unique contributions of a variety of groups remains an attractive ideal for many, including the authors of this text.

Different possibilities for intergroup relations, then, include (1) assimilation (taking on the characteristics of the dominant group); (2) blending (joining together to create a new type of dominant group); and (3) pluralism (maintaining a degree of group distinctiveness). As we see in succeeding sections of this chapter, the element of power plays a role in all of these alternatives. In addition, these models have been more available to some groups than to others. In some cases, two final models of intergroup relations have relevance: colonialism and separatism. *Colonialism*, or control by a nation or a dominant group over a dependent territory, can be used to describe the relations between Americans of European descent and First Nations peoples, or even perhaps the subjugation of regions such as Appalachia. The notion of colonialism is sometimes extended to describe the continued oppression of African Americans, whose ancestors were brought into this country as slaves.[22] Another concept, *separatism,* characterizes situations in which groups attempt to divorce themselves as much as possible from mainstream society, as in the case of Amish communities.

Dynamics of Intergroup Relations

What lies behind the prejudice and discrimination that are often part of relationships between different groups? Social and behavioral scientists have come up with a variety of theories to explain negative feelings and actions toward groups and individuals perceived as *different.* One set of theories focuses on internal personality traits. Prejudice may spring from inner frustrations and aggressive urges, which are converted into hatred or suspicion of a convenient scapegoat. Sexual feelings may also play a part. Homophobia, fears of sexual aggression by African American men toward white women, beliefs that Jewish (or Italian, or Mexican) women are sexually promiscuous—all seem to express an uncomfortableness with sexuality and a fascination with the "forbidden fruit" represented by other groups with whom close interaction is forbidden. Still another psychological interpretation has been offered by social psychologist T. W. Adorno. Adorno's work on the concept of an authoritarian personality holds that some people are more likely than others to be prejudiced. These individuals have the following traits: They glorify power, they tend to view people as good or bad, they repress their sexual feelings, they are concerned about status and toughness, and they generally "blame others rather than themselves for misdeeds and troubles." Subsequent studies of Adorno's theories, however, find that prejudice is not confined to the authoritarian personality.[23] In sum, although prejudice cannot be explained solely by psychological traits, these traits no doubt play a part in the larger picture of bias against others.

Prejudice often relates to social and economic factors. The sociologist Max Weber contended that groups compete for access to society's resources based in part on the idea that these resources are scarce. He theorized that any "identifiable characteristic" could be used to determine which were the privileged groups and which the nonprivileged. Skin color was one easy characteristic to use. The more resources the privileged groups (e.g., whites) obtained, the more these groups gained in stature over nonprivileged groups (e.g., blacks).[24] One example of the struggle over resources can be found in Chapter 14, which describes how competition over affordable living space can lead to discriminatory housing policies and even race riots.

Sometimes, groups who already feel discriminated against may try to characterize other groups as being even lower in the social pecking order. For example, African Americans may at times express prejudice against Latinos, or vice versa. Also, a group may seek to maintain solidarity and to define its values by contrasting itself to "outsiders." This may help explain the existence for most of our history of men's groups that prohibit membership by women.

Many observers argue that the element of power is the most important component of prejudice and discrimination. This power may be used to maintain a particular social status. In other words, certain elements in the United States have assumed positions of social superiority, and they have attempted to keep these positions by setting up psychological and physical barriers against other groups. White Americans, for example, have bolstered their status through beliefs about the inferiority of African Americans and other people of color. They have constructed discriminatory policies leading to segregated education, housing covenants, and lack of access to the ballot box. Diane J. Goodman calls this the "privileging of the dominant group," through which people in privileged groups gain "greater access to power, resources, and opportunities that are denied to others and usually gained at their expense."[25]

As one example of gaining wealth and power at the expense of others, American employers have frequently used a cheap labor force, such as African slaves in the early years of this country, Chinese railroad workers in the mid-1800s, unskilled immigrants from Europe at the turn of the century, or Mexican farmworkers in the present day. Discriminatory practices have helped to control this labor force. For example, if access to better-paying jobs is denied to them, members of subordinate groups have no choice but to remain in menial labor. Feminist scholars point out that white males have similarly exploited women in this country. In *Regulating the Lives of Women,* Abramovitz describes male domination of women both at work and at home. Discrimination has channeled women into low-paying jobs, thus sustaining the market supply of low-cost labor. Stereotypes about women's inferior intelligence and lack of drive have also helped keep women "in their place" at home, where they do unpaid work to support the family.[26]

These examples lend credence to the idea that the roots of racial, ethnic, and gender inequities, as well as prejudices, are grounded in the U.S. economic system. Race, ethnicity, and gender help dictate the economic class to which one will belong. African American scholar William Julius Wilson has taken this argument in a somewhat different direction, contending that in the present day, class differences are more important than race in explaining the plight of African Americans in U.S. society. In *The Declining Significance of Race* and *The Truly Disadvantaged,* Wilson contended that racism is not the major cause of current problems in the inner-city ghetto. Instead, the exodus of "more stable working- and middle-class" African Americans from the ghetto has left behind an underclass, a grouping of families and individuals who remain outside the occupational mainstream. African American dependency, Wilson suggests, stems more from factors such as the lack of skills among the men and the growth of female-headed families than from racial discrimination. If discrimination were still widespread, he asks, how does one explain the recent economic rise of the African American middle class?[27]

Critics of Wilson's arguments have pointed out that even the more privileged African American middle class is not as well off or as well treated as the white middle class. Racism has affected the lives of even these "successful" African Americans. In addition, Wilson has been taken to task for failing to acknowledge that poverty in female-headed families occurs largely because discrimination based on race and gender keeps women's salaries low. Finally, as sociologist Charles Willie notes, discrimination and segregation created the African American urban ghetto. This residential segregation leads to fewer economic opportunities because businesses and industrial plants tend not to locate in or near these areas.[28]

In another study, *When Work Disappears: The World of the New Urban Poor,* Wilson acknowledges the role of racial discrimination in perpetuating poverty among African Americans, although he continues to favor universal remedies, such as more school funding, rather than those focused on racial issues. Wilson's work, and reactions to it, contribute to an ongoing debate about the relationship of economic factors and discrimination in shaping the lives of those in subordinate groups.[29]

Economic and social factors may in fact be the major factors behind racial categorizations. Although the concept of race seems simple and straightforward, there is growing evidence that it is no such thing. Biological research indicates that there is more genetic difference between people *within* one race than there is between people of one race and people of another. As one writer notes, "the differences that divide one race from another add up to a drop in the genetic ocean." With the decreased emphasis on the biology of race, scientists are increasingly coming to view race as a social, political, and cultural concept based largely on superficial appearances. Race, seen in this light, has really been a way for people to distinguish among various social groups, often to justify discrimination and oppression.[30]

Historically, mainstream America has defined race relations as bipolar, or between black and white. Yet where do Latinos—who are neither a race nor an ethnic group, but rather people of a collection of nationalities descended from Europeans, African slaves, and Indian people—fit into this picture? Or, as the author of a history of Asian Americans ponders, "Is Yellow White or Black?"[31]

Perspectives

Conservatives, liberals, and radicals take different ideological positions on how best to deal with the discrimination and disadvantages faced by subordinate groups.

The Conservative Perspective

Consistent with their approach to other social problems, conservatives warn against relying on government regulation to deal with discriminatory practices; they are particularly critical of affirmative action policies. Sometimes conservatives question whether significant discrimination even exists in the United States today. Those who take this position argue that individual defects—in the form of lack of skills, low motivation for work, or no commitment to independence—are the real factors behind the problems of groups such as African Americans, American Indians, and Hispanics. Similarly, the low salaries of women are attributed to such factors as their having less education and a tendency to leave work "to have children."

The conservative response to the situation of minorities stems from the presumption that "the United States is an open society with no systemic barriers to success." As one Republican senator noted in a discussion of immigrant eligibility provisions, "the kind of immigrants we want are people who will take responsibility for themselves and not rely on the federal government." Because there are no major external barriers to success, what immigrants and minorities need is an extension of opportunity. The chance for upward mobility should be offered through freedom of choice in the marketplace; for example, in the form of educational or housing vouchers that would allow poor African Americans, Hispanics, and others to move into "better" neighborhoods and to equip their children for occupational success.[32]

The Liberal Perspective

Liberals generally relate the problems of subordinate groups to social structural causes rather than to individual causes. They see discrimination as an important factor in the difficulties faced by women, African Americans, and others. Some liberals believe in a modified version of the "individual defect" argument, stressing inadequate education, poor health, and lack of role models who could point the way to success. Yet this view differs from the conservative interpretation of defect because it emphasizes that these individual problems are caused by larger socioeconomic forces.

Liberals stress the necessity of government intervention to counteract discrimination in our society. They question the ability of the market to enforce equality in jobs and living arrangements. They back legislation and regulation to guarantee equal employment, education, and housing opportunities. In the case of persons with physical disabilities, for example, liberals support laws that mandate accessibility in both public and private buildings. Conservatives would have preferred that such accessibility be provided on a voluntary basis, particularly in buildings within the private sector.

In addition to their emphasis on regulation, liberals look to government to provide welfare benefits and compensatory programs to deal with those problems caused in part by discrimination: poverty, unemployment, and the lack of adequate education and skills. The War on Poverty in the 1960s constituted one such attempt to "break the cycle of poverty," particularly minority group poverty, by increasing welfare benefits and services and committing large amounts of public monies to job training programs and early childhood education.

The Radical Perspective

Radicals agree with liberals that social structural factors are the basis for difficulties faced by African Americans, Hispanics, women, and other oppressed groups. However, the radical viewpoint places major emphasis on the role of power in dominant–subordinate group relations. Many radicals argue, for example, that a capitalist society creates oppressed groups in order to ensure a supply of cheap labor. Radical feminists contend that men have historically discriminated against women in order to control their work. In general, the radical perspective depicts prejudice as a mask for privilege, or as a rationale through which dominant groups maintain their own status quo.[33]

Radicals note that those in power often encourage competition between subordinate groups in order to maintain control. In the years following the Civil War, Southern planters fanned antiblack feelings among poor Southern whites; in some areas they brought in Chinese laborers to supplant newly freed African American laborers. In the 1980s and 1990s, radicals contend, some conservative politicians exploited white fears that their taxes were being used to subsidize an African American underclass, in order to divert their attention from the massive transfer of wealth to the white upper class. In reports on the riots following the Rodney King verdict in Los Angeles, the mainstream media often portrayed the disturbances as a "Black–Korean" conflict between African Americans and local Korean American merchants. Sagely observing the role of power in intergroup relations, a member of the Watergate Crips gang responded, "It's not a Korean/Black thing; the merchants were there, there were problems, but it's a diversion to get us not to think about the real problem, which is the oppressor, which is the main majority which are Whites."[34]

To combat discrimination, radicals support the same sorts of government regulation that liberals stress. But they also point out the importance of equalizing income and wealth so that oppressed people can gain more power in the system. In order to overcome powerlessness among subordinate groups, radicals seek ways to increase people's control over resources and over the major decisions that will affect their lives. Strategies of empowerment include raising consciousness (that is, helping people see that they are oppressed); teaching people how to analyze the existing power structure; and fostering the use of groups—advocacy groups, unions, and protest groups—to counter that power structure.[35] Finally, radicals look to the restructuring of social institutions to eradicate discrimination and oppression.

History of Intergroup Relations in the United States

A comprehensive history of intergroup relations in the United States is too large a task for the present book. In this section, we instead take a brief look at society's treatment of European ethnic groups, African Americans, and women, with a primary stress on these groups' relationships with the social welfare system.

Social Workers, Social Welfare Institutions, and the "New Immigration"

At the end of the nineteenth century and the beginning of the twentieth century, the United States witnessed the greatest influx of European immigration in its history. A large proportion of today's U.S. citizens can trace their roots to a relative who immigrated during this period. Between 1901 and 1910, 8.7 million people, largely from southern and eastern Europe, landed on American shores. These were called the "new immigrants" because they appeared fundamentally different from those groups—the British, Germans, French, Scandinavians, and other northern Europeans—that had come before. Only the Irish, largely poor folk escaping poverty and famine, had some characteristics in common with the newer arrivals. Often uprooted peasants, at least half of the new immigrants were classified as unskilled laborers. One-third were illiterate. Many of them had little or no experience in the process of representative government. Most joined friends and families in the slum neighborhoods of large cities. This influx strained the facilities of existing health and welfare services and posed a potential job market threat to native-born workers (even though the coming of the new immigrants had in part been fostered by industrialists in search of cheap labor).[36]

Most obvious, the newcomers looked different. Often they wore "peasant clothes" such as the *babushka* (the Russian woman's head scarf). Some, like many Italians, had dark complexions. They ate unusual foods and spoke a variety of languages: Yiddish, Russian, Polish, Greek, and many more. Unlike the Protestant Anglo-Saxon mainstream, they attended Catholic and Greek Orthodox churches and Jewish synagogues.

Because of these differences, and because of their potential as competitors for jobs, the new immigrants encountered fear and prejudice on the part of many people in the United States. Large numbers of the public felt that the newcomers represented an inferior stock, lacking the intelligence and physical attributes of northern Europeans. Interestingly, some of the newcomers were seen as "black," especially those from Italy and the Balkan countries, although this distinction disappeared as they began to be Americanized. Discrimination in jobs, education, and housing soon developed. In addition, businesses exploited this cheap and powerless labor force, paying low wages, demanding long hours, and failing to provide safe and healthy working conditions.

Social welfare institutions—in particular, the social settlement—developed a variety of responses to the new immigrants. The newcomers were, after all, the major "clients" of most settlement houses. Jewish neighborhoods in New York, Polish enclaves in Cleveland, and Italian communities in Boston each had their own neighborhood settlements. In some cases, settlement workers' philosophies and actions regarding the immigrant community mirrored reactions in the larger public. In others, settlements led the way in thinking about the possibilities of a pluralistic society.

One segment of the settlement movement stressed assimilation as the appropriate path for immigrants to take. This emphasis stemmed from a belief in the importance of social harmony in U.S. communities, and in some cases from negative stereotypes about the newcomers. A particularly blatant example of prejudice against immigrant groups appears in the 1911 Annual Report of Boston's Peabody House:

> This district is virtually transplanted from another order of civilization. Our foreign neighbors bring with them habits which cannot be followed in this country without danger to our own standards. . . . [T]he constituents of our district [must] sink individuality in common neighborhood purposes.

Sinking individuality in common purposes often meant assimilation into a "coherent and distinctively American nationality." For some settlement workers, "American" meant "Anglo-Saxon." Fearful of the lowering of Anglo-Saxon standards, and concerned about building close-knit, harmonious communities, these workers strove to Americanize their foreign neighbors. They promoted English and "good citizenship" classes and stressed such behaviors as responsible voting, obedience to the law, hard work, and thrift.[37]

Other settlement workers saw things differently. In cities such as New York, Cleveland, and particularly Chicago, a philosophy of cultural pluralism characterized many settlements' work with immigrants. Jane Addams was a particularly articulate champion of the pluralist ideal. Unlike those who looked to a past Anglo-Saxon harmony in America, Addams applauded newness and change. Society's new unity would be based on synthesis rather than standardization. Addams envisioned a cosmopolitanism that allowed for the appreciation of cultural differences along with the recognition of commonalities among all human beings.[38]

As director of Hull House in Chicago, Addams stressed the strengths and "immigrant gifts" of her Greek and Bohemian neighbors. "One thing seemed clear in regard to . . . immigrants," she noted: that it was important "to preserve and keep whatever of value their past life contained." To this end, Hull House developed a Labor Museum, where people exhibited the tools and processes used in their countries of origin. The settlement sponsored foreign-language plays and provided a meeting place for nationality groups. Through such activities, Hull House strove to publicize the immigrants' contributions to the larger community and to encourage immigrant children to respect their parents' culture. Above all, Addams hoped "to have made a genuine effort to find the basic experience upon which a cosmopolitan community may unite."[39]

In another response to the immigrant situation, Hull House also pioneered immigrant protection work, or what we might now describe as advocacy for the newcomers' rights. This activity led to new governmental structures designed to deal with immigrants' problems. Recognizing the varieties of exploitation and fraud perpetrated on immigrants by employment agencies, banks serving the newcomers, and employers, Hull House resident Grace Abbott helped found the League for Protection of Immigrants. The league acted as an advocacy group; it helped bring about state legislation protecting immigrants from fraudulent practices by employment agencies, and it was instrumental in the creation of an Illinois Immigration Commission. In promoting government regulation to counteract discrimination and exploitation of European immigrants, the league's work reflected a liberal approach to the problems of subordinate groups.[40]

The influx of southern and eastern Europeans was ended abruptly by immigration restriction legislation passed in 1924. Fears of job competition, uneasiness about "foreign radicalism" after the Russian Revolution and World War I, and outright prejudice against the newcomers helped create an atmosphere conducive to exclusion. Rejecting notions of cultural pluralism and skeptical of the ability of immigrants to assimilate, many people saw restriction as the only reasonable solution to the "immigrant problem." This reaction has resurfaced in discussions of today's immigration, particularly that from Latin America.

Social Workers, Social Welfare Institutions, and African Americans

Settlement house work with the new immigrants constituted an early arena for testing out the relationship between subordinate groups and social welfare programs and goals. Social workers were slower to identify African Americans as a specific client group, in part because a large proportion lived in southern rural areas, where few social work organizations existed. Also, inattention to the problems faced by African Americans reflected either overt prejudice or an unthinking involvement in institutional racism on the part of some social workers and social reformers.

African Americans came to the United States under circumstances different from other immigrant groups. Brought over by force, they began their experience as an enslaved and colonized people. Prejudices used to justify such oppression persisted even after the Civil War ended the institution of slavery. Biases against African Americans were kept alive partly by white laborers fearing competition from freed slaves in the Southern job market and partly by a white Southern elite wishing to retain the traditional system of agricultural production and to keep African Americans in subordinate positions.[41]

Prejudice against African Americans and the desire to "keep them in their place" played a role in the difficulties faced by the Freedmen's Bureau, a social welfare program established by the national government in 1865 to foster the economic rehabilitation of freed slaves. The first federal social welfare program other than veterans' pensions, the bureau promoted education for African Americans and public relief for both freedmen and displaced whites. It also proposed to furnish land and tools to former slaves. Although accomplishing a good deal in the area of education, the bureau was unable to fulfill its economic objectives. Inadequate funds, lack of support by President Andrew Johnson, and opposition from the Southern gentry contributed to the abolishment of the Freedmen's Bureau in 1872.[42] Soon after, in the 1880s, Southern states and cities began enacting statutes (the infamous Jim Crow laws) to legalize segregation and deny African Americans access to good jobs, public services, and equal education.

In increasing numbers after the turn of the century, African Americans moved to northern cities in search of jobs and greater equality. More often than not, they encountered the same racism and discriminatory practices they had left behind. The growth of segregated communities in the North gave rise to new issues in intergroup relations. Were African Americans simply another group, like the Italian or the Polish immigrants, in a pluralistic society? Or did they constitute "a people apart"? These questions were particularly relevant for settlement workers.

Reactions of Chicago settlement personnel, as examined by historian Steven Diner, indicate a range of responses probably typical of settlement and charity workers across the country. Chicago settlement workers, Diner reports, developed different perspectives regarding African Americans. One response, perhaps that of the majority, was to recognize their poverty and difficult living situations but at the same time to believe that these difficulties were best overcome by hard work and initiative. African Americans did not face any greater hardships than the immigrants, although they were probably so "inherently different" from whites that they would never really assimilate into American society.[43]

A smaller group of settlement leaders, including Jane Addams, argued that African Americans faced distinctive difficulties that made their situation even worse than that of the immigrants. In particular, they encountered greater economic and political discrimination—and almost total residential segregation. In attempts to help them deal with these problems, Addams and other settlement leaders helped found the NAACP and the Chicago Urban League. They researched the specific problems of African American residents of Chicago, and they publicized their findings to the larger community.[44]

Yet despite greater understanding of the problems faced by African Americans, these leaders joined the rest of the Chicago settlement movement in maintaining the color line. None of the white settlements worked directly with residents of the ghetto. Perhaps because it seemed to them the only possibility in the context of the times, Addams and her colleagues did not push for integration. Instead, they promoted exclusive settlements founded and run by African Americans. These centers were poorly funded and sometimes lasted only a few years. On the national level, the majority of settlements either excluded African Americans, conducted segregated activities, or followed former white neighbors out of African American neighborhoods.[45]

Social service agencies in Chicago (and no doubt in other northern cities) followed similar patterns of separation. In addition, most lacked the special concern for African Americans expressed by reformers like Addams. Public agencies were required by state law to serve both races, but wherever possible they kept the two groups separate. For example, clinics and other facilities were located in areas where African Americans and whites were unlikely to mingle. Private welfare agencies could, and did, discriminate. Some refused to serve African Americans at all. Others offered separate services at different times or in different offices. Goodwill Industries, for example, would help all people with disabilities except African Americans. The United Charities, a relief organization, maintained separate branches in the ghetto.[46] As late as the 1960s, YMCAs had separate hours for African American youngsters to use their swimming pools.

In response to the needs of their communities and the failure of the larger society to meet those needs, African Americans developed their own network of charitable organizations. African American churches and voluntary associations were major sources of social welfare activity, with the women members playing a prominent role. In 1809 free African American women in Newport, Rhode Island, set up an organization to care for one another and for the poor in their community. Other, similar female mutual aid societies soon sprang up in the Northeast. After the Civil War, these organizations were joined by women's clubs, whose membership was made up largely of educated middle-class African American women. These clubs were similar to the philanthropic white women's groups from which African Americans were barred. The clubs supported a host of social welfare organizations, including children's nurseries, homes for young working women, settlements, and homes for the aged. Lugenia Burns Hope's Neighborhood Union in Atlanta, local African American branches of the YWCA, and the southern rural school settlements inspired by the Tuskegee Institute were among the more successful of these organizations. Yet many of them lacked the financial resources available to most white charitable endeavors. In the city of Chicago, for example, only the Urban League, which concentrated on employment services and became the city's dominant African American social welfare organization after World War I, was able to obtain substantial support from white philanthropists.[47]

Discrimination and lack of financial support continued to characterize the treatment of African Americans in the social service system during and after the 1930s. Although some moves were made toward integration and improvement of services, elements of racism found their way into the new federal public welfare programs developed during the New Deal. The state of Mississippi, for example, instructed its county relief offices to put a 10 percent quota on the number of African American citizens receiving assistance, even in locations where African Americans were the majority. (In a similar vein, Texas excluded Mexican American applicants from its programs, and Nevada had no Aid to Families with Dependent Children program for twenty years in order to avoid giving benefits to American Indian families.)[48] On the other hand, New Deal social welfare programs, with their greater resources and introduction of some national standards, provided improved levels of benefits and services for large numbers of African Americans.

The relationship between the social welfare system and African Americans remains a highly complex one, characterized both by institutional racism and by provision of appropriate aid (see Table 5.2). To the extent that it has been effective, the system owes a good degree of credit to the efforts of African American churches, women's clubs, and

A CLOSER Look

The Destruction of a Black Community in Tulsa, Oklahoma

In the years following the Civil War, some African Americans left the Southern states to settle in southwestern communities such as Tulsa. An oil boom had led to the city's explosive growth between 1910 and 1920. Because African Americans were forbidden by law to own businesses or live in the white city, a black community called Greenwood developed on its outskirts. In its heyday, Greenwood "included as many as 15,000 people and supported 191 businesses, including 15 doctors, 2 dentists, . . . and 3 law offices," and had its own newspaper. Many white Tulsans felt threatened by the presence of independent black businesspeople and professionals who fought discrimination and Jim Crow laws. Hemmed in by a river and by Greenwood, a growing Tulsa also looked hungrily at the community's land.

In 1921 an incident in which an African American man allegedly grabbed a white woman elevator operator in a downtown Tulsa building led to a threatened lynching, which in turn provided the spark for a fight between a white mob and a group of armed black men. The Tulsa police deputized many white men from the lynch mob, who proceeded to invade the Greenwood community. Although Greenwood residents attempted to fight back, as many as 100,000 whites joined the attack, killing residents and looting and burning homes and buildings. At the same time, airplanes strafed the black city with machine gun fire. Survivor Kinney Booker, a child at the time, remembers white men invading his home and his father saying, "Please don't set the house on fire." "Soon as he left, they set our house on fire and we were up in the attic." He and his five siblings managed to get out to the street without injury. As bullets "zinged" around them, his sister, two years younger than he, asked, "Kinney, is the world on fire?"

In less than twenty-four hours, "virtually all of black Tulsa had gone up in smoke and ash." An estimated three hundred people were killed, 90 percent of them black. The city paid no reparations; insurance companies denied all damage claims. As time went on, most black Tulsans banned the riot from conversation for fear of a recurrence. Only recently has the story been revived, yet another example of the early twentieth-century race wars, like those in Chicago and the all-black community of Rosewood, Florida. An Oklahoma legislator, justifying a recent request for payment of reparations to survivors and their descendants, argued, "We told these people to lift themselves up by their bootstraps, and they did, by forming the most successful black community in America. And once they had lifted themselves up by their bootstraps, we destroyed them for it."

Sources: Brent Staples, "Unearthing a Riot," *New York Times Magazine* (19 December 1999), 64–69; Ross E. Milloy, "Panel Calls for Reparations in Tulsa Race Riot," *New York Times* (1 March 2001), A12.

social welfare workers. African American scholars and social work educators such as E. Franklin Frazier, George E. Haynes of Fisk University, and Forrester B. Washington of the Atlanta School of Social Work contributed by helping to train social work practitioners. Together, these individuals and organizations struggled to provide benefits to the African American population and to publicize inadequate and unequal treatment in the American social welfare institution.

The United States recently marked the fiftieth anniversary of the 1954 Supreme Court decision *Brown* v. *Board of Education.* Social workers in the 1950s and earlier, like all Americans, had felt the direct and indirect effects of segregation. At the time of the court decision, fifteen southern states mandated segregation and four others (Arizona, Kansas, New Mexico, and Wyoming) allowed the practice. While sixteen states prohibited

TABLE 5.2 **How Americans Feel about Improving the Conditions of African Americans: Are We Spending Too Little, Too Much, or the Right Amount?**

	1993	1994	1996	1998	2000	2002
Too Little	35%	31%	31%	34%	33%	31%
About Right	39%	40%	39%	40%	40%	46%
Too Much	15%	20%	19%	16%	15%	17%
Don't Know	9%	8%	10%	9%	12%	6%
Total	n = 793	1,502	1,437	1,375	1,399	1,346

Source: James A. Davis, Tom W. Smith, and Peter V. Marsden, *General Social Surveys, 1972–2002* (Chicago: National Opinion Research Center, 2003), 101. Reprinted by permission.

the practice, many states had de facto segregation in neighborhoods, schools, and the workplace. The anniversary brought back painful memories for those who had attended segregated schools, including those of African American social workers:

> The terrible feeling that somehow my classmates and I were not good enough, along with the . . . notion that we would never become anyone of value to society, often resulted in reduced expectations, lowered self-esteem, and a preoccupation with the unsatisfying details of being second class. (John Oliver, Director, Department of Social Work, California State University/Long Beach)

It also stirred joyful memories, such as those of an African American woman who was ten years old at the time:

> Jubilation, optimism, and hope filled my home. Through a child's eyes, I could see the veil of oppression lift from my parents' shoulders. It seemed they were standing taller. And for the first time in my life I saw tears in my father's eyes.[49]

Although a great milestone, the *Brown* v. *Board of Education* decision did not end racial segregation or other forms of discrimination in our society. Neither did the *Mendez* v. *Westminster, Orange County, California School District* decision that prohibited the segregation of Mexican schoolchildren. Today, Latino students "are the most segregated minority group in U.S. schools."[50]

Social Workers, Social Welfare Institutions, and Women

One unique aspect of the relationship of women and social welfare is the fact that women constitute both the majority of clients and the majority of workers in the system. Women, for example, make up a large percentage of Social Security recipients and mental health clients. The biggest program within the federal public welfare system, Temporary Assistance to Needy Families (TANF), serves primarily women and their children. The social welfare system, built on the need to deal with dependency, has traditionally included widows, deserted wives, and young unmarried women (potential "wayward girls") among its concerns.

How well has the system served women? What have been its major goals in dealing with a female clientele? To a certain degree, one can argue that these goals have been humanitarian and supportive ones. This seems most true of the programs developed and advocated in large part by women themselves. For example, women's organizations and female settlement and charity leaders played an important role in the creation of a system of state pensions for destitute mothers between 1910 and 1920. These pensions marked a move away from temporary charity and toward a more lasting form of assistance for female-headed families. They constituted a precedent for the Aid to Dependent Children program established in 1935.[51]

Similarly, a powerful lobby of feminist groups and individual women leaders, many of them connected with Hull House and the U.S. Children's Bureau, was instrumental in the passage of the Sheppard–Towner Act in 1921. This act provided federal matching grants to states for maternal and child health services. The American Medical Association, anti–women's suffrage groups, and self-styled patriotic organizations attacked the program for its "encroachment" into the medical domain, its involvement of the federal government in social welfare activities, and its undermining of men's capacity to care for their families. This opposition helped bring about the program's demise in 1929. Yet the Sheppard–Towner Act was significant in establishing official attention to the needs of women and children, and it led the way for subsequent government programs protecting infant and maternal health.[52]

Women also set up private organizations and agencies that provided social welfare services specifically for women. These included the YWCA, boardinghouses for single working women, mothers' clubs in settlement houses, and county cooperative extension services.

Of course, it would be a mistake to assume that programs and services developed or administered by women were automatically free of bias, nonjudgmental, and helpful to their clients. Well-to-do women charity workers, for example, generally felt little compunction about applying their moralistic standards to the lives of poor women. Even mothers' pensions laws often restricted benefits to those women deemed "fit and deserving."[53] By the same token, services developed and supported by men could be appropriate and sympathetic to the needs of women.

On the other hand, some scholars argue that the social welfare institution has been used by the male patriarchy, or authority system, as a means of controlling the lives and labor of women. In an analysis of social welfare policy in relation to women, Abramovitz contends that historically, welfare programs have supported certain roles for women and discouraged others. The system has tended to reward women whose lives combined the traditional roles of wife, mother, and homemaker. It has often penalized those, such as working wives or unmarried women, who either by choice or by necessity followed different paths. In addition to reinforcing a certain view of women's roles, the welfare system has "helped to meet the economy's need for women's unpaid labor in the home."[54]

As evidence of the system's aim of regulating women's lives, Abramovitz and others point to the practices of the Charity Organization Societies (COSs) in the late nineteenth and early twentieth centuries. COS workers were urged to "dissuade restless wives from seeking outside employment" and to deny aid to immoral, vagrant, or degraded women. The majority of clients accepted for assistance were "deserving" married couples or widows.[55] A goal of controlling women can be seen in public welfare policies as early as the 1820s. It was not unusual for local public relief authorities to remove children from poor families and to place them in almshouses or children's institutions. The rationale was that such families offered harmful home conditions and that many poor mothers were unfit to raise their children.[56]

Those who see welfare as a mechanism for social control also argue that welfare policies have been used to maintain a low-paid female labor force. Although AFDC began as a program to allow poor women to stay home with their children, since the late 1950s pressure has been put on "welfare mothers" to "get off the welfare rolls" and seek employment. President Nixon's WIN program and the 1996 welfare reform act are examples of attempts to put women on welfare to work (see Chapter 9). Because many women on welfare either lack the proper skills or are denied access to decent-paying jobs, they are forced by these measures to join a convenient pool of low-wage labor. A particularly blatant example of this manipulation of women's labor in the past was the refusal of many states to grant assistance to African American women if their eligibility for AFDC conflicted with the local demand for domestic workers.[57]

Although the social control interpretation has been useful in bringing the variables of economics and power into the discussion of women and welfare, some historians contend that we have gone too far in picturing women as helpless victims of charity workers and the welfare system. Beverly Stadum writes of the ways in which women charity recipients of the early 1900s resisted agency attempts to change their behavior. In a history of family violence, Linda Gordon points out that victims of such violence have often welcomed professional intervention and have attempted both to influence agency policy and to shape the approaches used by professional "helpers."[58]

The concepts of domination and independence can also be applied to descriptions of women's roles as professionals in the social welfare system. Some have argued that women were channeled into social work jobs by men who saw this occupation as appropriate to women's nurturing and "emotional" natures. At the same time, men maintained control over the powerful supervisory positions in the field. It is true that women filled most of the frontline jobs in charity work, as well as many of the jobs in the settlements in the late 1800s and early 1900s. Yet, at the same time, women assumed leadership roles in these fields. This was particularly true in the settlement movement, which boasted such prominent figures as Jane Addams, Grace Abbott, Lillian Wald of New York's Henry Street Settlement, and many others. In 1910, women constituted about two-thirds of all settlement directors.[59] Charity work was more likely to be under the direction of a man, although the movement produced important figures such as Josephine Shaw Lowell and Mary Richmond, who occupied leadership positions in the field. In social work education, up through the 1930s and 1940s, women shared leadership roles with men. Most of the early developers of methodologies in social work—casework, group work, and Freudian and other therapies—were women.

Many of these early leaders saw in social work the chance to build a new career for women. Edith Abbott and Sophonisba Breckinridge were instrumental in founding and developing the social work graduate school at the University of Chicago. Although they had degrees in other fields—Abbott in economics and Breckinridge in law—they faced discrimination in these disciplines. In their development of graduate education for social work, they consciously molded a new occupation for women.[60]

Although women held prominent leadership positions in social work's earlier years and the number of women administrators increased when men left for war in the 1940s, by the 1950s men were increasingly taking over administrative roles in social welfare organizations. Between 1957 and 1976, for example, the percentage of women heading member agencies of the Family Service Association of America fell from 60 to 20 percent. In 1999, only 17 percent of all female NASW members were administrators. Men have also come to play a major role in the social work education hierarchy. Women served as deans in two-thirds of all graduate schools of social work in 1925. More than seventy-five years later, despite the fact that the vast majority of students are women, less than 50 percent of the schools have women deans.[61]

Varied explanations have been put forth for these changes. Some feminist scholars argue that the increase in male leadership is evidence of the ability of the male patriarchy to continue to control the lives of women. Others prefer gender role socialization explanations, pointing out that women may gravitate toward direct practice because this is an area of activity commonly expected of them. Clarke Chambers suggests that since the 1950s, women's new freedom to combine both career and marriage may have, paradoxically, undercut their chances to rise within the profession. Unlike the earlier, unmarried leaders, women who now took some time out for family involvement or who worked part time found themselves unable to stay on the promotion track in a university or agency. In addition, the expansion of welfare bureaucracies following the New Deal opened up career positions in public administration that tended to favor men. After World War II, women social work leaders actively recruited men into the profession, partly in an attempt to increase the field's prestige. On a similar ironic note, the expansion of women's job opportunities has drawn a number of bright and ambitious women away from the more traditional "women's fields" and into the challenging areas of the sciences, medicine, engineering, and law. One thing that has not changed is the ratio between male and female social workers' salaries. Women social workers have consistently been paid less than men from the profession's beginnings to the present.[62]

Increasingly, many women social workers (as well as men) have become conscious of what they see as the power imbalance within the profession as well as the need to address the needs of women clients more appropriately. Groups fostering attention to women's concerns have emerged within the National Association of Social Workers and the Council on Social Work Education. A growing body of scholarship addresses women's issues within the social welfare system. These developments have taken place within the context of a national women's movement, which began in the 1960s and which in many ways represents the attempts of a subordinate group to gain greater control over its position in society.

Current Issues Regarding Social Welfare and Human Diversity

Many groups in today's society—women, immigrants, African Americans, ethnic groups, people with disabilities, and homosexuals—have their own specific concerns and needs. Rather than focus specifically on each group, however, we find it more useful to explore the broad phenomenon of multiculturalism in the United States today, and to analyze several broad policy debates concerning diversity and how best to deal with patterns of discrimination and inequality.

Multiculturalism

The United States is in the midst of an unprecedented experiment in the interaction and coexistence of many different racial and ethnic groups—among them Mexicans, African Americans, Vietnamese, Americans of European descent, Salvadorans, Koreans, Puerto Ricans, Indian or indigenous peoples, Lebanese, Italians, Russians, Nigerians, Cubans, Hmong people from Laos, and Saudi Arabians. According to one observer, increased immigration, and the expanding variety of immigrant backgrounds, has meant that "race in this country is no longer just an issue of color. It is also one of ethnicity."[63]

Almost one in every five Americans now speaks a language other than English at home. About a fifth of these people live in homes where no one age fourteen or older knows English "very well." Some analysts worry that the latter group will have difficulty assimilating into American society. On the other hand, the country is witnessing a phenomenon among young Americans in which the old ethnic identities no longer apply. As Rumulo Cisneros, an architect in Houston, explains, "my daughter listens to hip-hop, belongs to the Asian engineering society and has a crush on a black guy. . . . There's no identification with any group or race." Currently, 40 percent of Americans under age twenty-five belong to a race or category other than non-Hispanic white. Young Latinos and Asian Americans both have a strong tendency to intermarry. Mixed-race and mixed-ethnicity births are on the rise. All of these phenomena point to an increasingly blended culture in the United States.[64]

The concept of "race" is itself being challenged. Sonia Perez of the National Council of La Raza notes that "categories of race just don't have a lot of meaning for Latino Americans. Those concepts of black and white are just not at all how people are used to defining themselves." There is a historic context to this issue in that during America's Jim Crow period, Mexican Americans often resented being lumped with African Americans. Mexican American organizations emphasized that their members and constituents were white, "and therefore not subject to racial segregation."[65] This is not an unusual phenomenon; in the era of European immigration at the turn of the last century, the discrimination and control carried out by members of the dominant society helped fuel competition between immigrants of different nationalities.

Movement toward a new society that abandons its traditional racism and accommodates and even celebrates difference will be a complicated endeavor, however. In many U.S. cities, competition for unskilled jobs has increased tensions between African Americans and Latinos. A national survey found that Latinos were almost three times as likely as whites to agree that African Americans "aren't capable of getting ahead." Cleavages also exist between the various immigrant groups. In Orange County, California, for example, tensions run deep between Filipino and Vietnamese teenagers; a teacher reports "a lot of talk of who's survived the most and who . . . has the most visible success." The group we call "Asians" is made up of a variety of nationalities who may have little in common with one another, other than the continent from which they come and the inability of some other Americans to tell them apart.[66]

A CLOSER Look

The Experience of Having a Mixed Heritage

Corinne was born in Miami, Arizona, to a Mexican American father and a Spanish American mother. The family later moved to Phoenix. As a Spanish Mexican girl in the 1940s, Corinne learned to be proud of both sides of her heritage. But having a mixed heritage was not always easy. Corinne recalls the day she entered public school in Phoenix:

> My first day of school I was eager and happy to go. I recall two school buildings standing in direct contrast to each other; one looked nice and the other looked ignored [and] in disrepair. My mother filled out papers, and we were led out the door toward the sad-looking building. Mother came to a stop, looking angry. We returned to the office. I remember the sinking feeling that we weren't going to get to go to school after all. Mother spoke quietly to a man, and then to my relief we were led out the door again. This time we were going toward the nice building. But I felt a little less confident and a little less enthusiastic about going to school. I kept thinking that maybe I was supposed to be in the sad building and that I didn't belong in the nice one at all.
>
> Maybe it was the fact that we had dark hair and eyes or that my mother had to repeat our last name several times. . . . Later I learned it was all those things rolled into one word called prejudice. The sad-looking building was for Mexican children. Our Spanish heritage had gotten us into the better school.

Source: "Strong Heritage Staves Off Prejudice," *The Arizona Republic* (4 February 2001), F5.

What will the United States look like in another fifty years? Will black/white distinctions cease to matter? Will most of today's immigrant groups be assimilated into the existing culture, or will we create a new culture of intermarried, "blended" Americans? Or will our country instead be a mosaic of many different groups that maintain their heritage but also identify with basic American values such as freedom and equality? We are clearly undergoing many movements at once, movements "whose impact on the course of American history," one observer notes, "will be as profound as the great migrations of the mid-19th and early-20th centuries and will alter our public life in a way not seen since the civil rights movement."[67]

Immigration

Immigration brings strengths and challenges to the maintenance of a diverse society. As we discussed earlier, the current immigration of Latinos and Asians, like the "new" European immigration at the turn of the century, could threaten the position of African Americans through competition for jobs and the revival of the ill-informed question, "If immigrants can make it, why can't blacks?" The latest immigration also contributes to the shift, feared by some whites, from a white to a nonwhite majority by the middle of the century. In addition, the fact that many immigrants come to the United States with few resources leads to the concern that newcomers will strain state and local economies through their use of health, education, and other public services.

Of course, the presence of Asians and Latinos in the United States is not a new phenomenon. Chinese laborers were brought to the southern and western states as contract laborers in the mid-1800s; they were not allowed to become citizens, and the conditions they lived in were close to slavery. In 1925 the Pullman Company hired Filipinos to serve on its trains as attendants, cooks, and busboys; African Americans, newly unionized by A. Philip Randolph, lost these jobs and were relegated to work as porters. Japanese settlers arrived in California in the 1860s; prejudice against them led to laws in the early 1900s forbidding them to own land. Their long presence in this country did not prevent internment of Japanese Americans in U.S. concentration camps during World War II.[68]

Latino immigrants faced similar discrimination and were also used as a source of cheap labor. Mexicans have lived in what is now the United States for the past three centuries. Early arrivals included descendants of Spanish colonists; these were later joined by Mexican farm laborers leaving their country to avoid economic hardship and political turmoil. After the Mexican Revolution of 1910, the numbers of Mexican Americans grew dramatically, reaching two million in 1930. Mexican immigrants became the primary labor force for southwestern and Californian farms and food-processing plants. As Bruce Jansson notes, the Mexicans "were subject to the punitive labor policies of large landowners, who paid low wages and brutally suppressed protest." When large numbers of unemployed Mexican immigrants sought welfare relief during the Great Depression, local officials responded with forced evacuation to Mexico. Mexicans who settled in urban areas did not fare much better. In Los Angeles, they were confined to a well-defined adobe enclave, forbidden from living and working in more prosperous areas.[69]

The 1950s saw a large influx of Puerto Ricans to East Coast cities. Displaced by the expansion of large U.S. sugar and coffee corporations in Puerto Rico, Puerto Ricans responded to the need for cheap labor in New York and other cities. In addition, many Cubans settled in Florida following the Cuban Revolution of 1959.[70]

It was not until the Immigration Act of 1965, however, that Asian and Latino immigration began its dramatic climb. By eliminating discriminatory quotas that had favored Europeans, the new law opened the doors to huge numbers of immigrants from

Hispanic day laborers negotiate with an employer for work.

Mexico and Central America, and from Asian nations such as Vietnam, South Korea, China, Laos, and the Philippines. Often fleeing political troubles and economic hardship, the newcomers were also welcomed by manufacturing and farming interests seeking cheap and compliant labor. As we saw in the previous section, these groups now dominate the immigration scene. Their presence has sparked anti-immigrant sentiments and restrictive legislation.

The first alarmed response emanated from California, which has borne the brunt of increased immigration. In 1994, responding to the rise of undocumented Mexicans in the state, a large majority of voters approved an anti–illegal immigration initiative. Proposition 187 barred illegal immigrants from attending public schools and from receiving nonemergency and preventive public health services. The initiative was eventually declared unconstitutional by a federal court. In 1996, however, national legislation was passed aimed at controlling both legal and illegal immigration and limiting immigrants' access to the health and social service safety net. The Illegal Immigration Reform and Immigrant Responsibility Act of 1996 strengthened the U.S.–Mexico border by doubling the number of border patrol agents, attempted to stop employers from hiring illegal workers by imposing fines, and put new limits on public benefits for legal immigrants (the welfare reform legislation of the same year also cut back on health and social services for newcomers). The law also made it easier to deport immigrants by expanding the list of previous crimes (including possession of small amounts of marijuana) that could lead to deportation. Most important, the immigration law established that all legal immigrants must have sponsors who agree to support them if necessary or to reimburse the government for any public benefits they might use.[71]

Difficulty in finding sponsors has left many Mexicans seeking work in the United States with only one alternative—illegal entry. And even though some Americans deplore the practice, employers have been eager to hire illegal immigrants. An article on the United States' love/hate relationship with immigrants reports that "were the nation's estimated six million illegal immigrants to leave tomorrow, thousands of hotels, restaurants, meat-packing plants, landscaping companies and garment factories would likely close." Yet, despite this reliance on immigrant labor, opposition to illegal immigration is alive and well. The U.S. Border Patrol has been so effective at patrolling the easier crossing areas that undocumented immigrants now take much more difficult routes through the desert. Newspapers in southwestern cities continually report stories about immigrants dying in the desert or in tractor trailers packed so tightly that those inside die of heat and asphyxiation. Self-appointed vigilantes—including members of white supremacist and anti-immigrant groups—have taken the law into their own hands, detaining migrants at gunpoint or even shooting them. Anti-immigrant sentiment has bred responses such as "Protect Arizona Now," a proposed state initiative requiring immigrants to produce proof of citizenship or legal residency in order to receive any public services, and mandating that state and local officials enforce immigration law (which is now done by the federal government).[72]

Immigrants from Mexico also face hardships once they arrive in the United States. Many live in ramshackle shacks in *colonias* along the Texas border and scratch out a bare living as migrant farmworkers. Migrant workers and those in other jobs receive few health benefits or other social services. They are often unable to get drivers' licenses. The jobs that are open to them have poor working conditions and provide salaries below the minimum wage. As a report by the National Council of La Raza, a leading voice for the Hispanic community, concludes, "Undocumented workers live in the shadows . . . unable to become full members of the U.S. economy and society."[73]

At the same time, many Americans remain critical about the influx of immigrants, arguing that they generate heavy costs in education and in health and social services. How accurate is this argument? A study by the Urban Institute found that while welfare use in the overall foreign-born population is slightly higher than in the native population, it is unequally distributed among immigrant groups. Refugees, who represent only about 10 percent of new immigrants each year, report high rates of welfare receipt, as do elderly nonrefugee immigrants. However, working-age immigrants have a lower rate of welfare use than working-age natives. Overall, immigrants tend to have a positive impact on the U.S. economy. They work, pay taxes, and buy the goods and services produced by other workers. They help to create jobs and to revitalize poor neighborhoods. Although they often begin work in low-paying jobs, many immigrants experience relatively fast growth in earnings during their working lives. Finally, there is little evidence that immigrants are drawn to the United States to gain access to education, health care, and social services. The key motives for most newcomers are the availability of jobs, higher wages, and the chance to reunite with relatives.[74]

In January 2004, after three years in office and ten months from the next presidential election, President George W. Bush proposed a sweeping overhaul of the country's immigration laws. Under his plan, an undocumented worker could apply for temporary worker status for a three-year period. Congress could potentially approve the possibility of additional three-year periods. In this status, the worker would receive all the employee benefits given to those legally employed. A U.S. employer would have to sponsor the worker. In outlining the new program, the president spoke of allowing "willing workers to . . . fill jobs that Americans are not filling." Those approved could travel freely between the United States and their home countries and could apply for a green card guaranteeing permanent residency in this country. However, the Bush administration did not say how many green cards would be issued, and the president noted that those who did not get green cards would be expected to return permanently to their home countries.[75]

Bush's plan met with mixed reactions. Some analysts called it a tentative but important first step. Generally, the business sector was pleased. However, immigration advocates were skeptical, noting that the plan would favor business "by forcing workers to tie their fates to employer 'sponsors' who could ship them back home for complaining about job conditions." Immigrants themselves were conflicted about the proposal; some were pleased at the chance for more permanent status, while others worried that they could be deported after their three years expired. One Hispanic columnist called it "a boon to businesses in search of cheap labor in perpetuity." Finally, members of the far right of the Republican party raised an outcry against what they saw as rewarding illegal immigration "with amnesty." Clearly, immigration, and particularly illegal immigration, remains a complex and heated topic in the United States.[76]

Affirmative Action

Like immigration policies, affirmative action programs involve issues of access to opportunity and power in American society. And, as in the history of immigration, these programs have faced restriction and even abolishment. The dismantling of the affirmative action programs of the 1960s has been occurring on a small scale at least since the Bakke case of 1978, in which a white man in California gained entry to medical school after having been denied admission under a quota system that saved spaces for minorities. The Bakke decision did confirm that race could be considered one element among many in admissions decisions.[77]

The attack on affirmative action broadened and accelerated in the 1990s, with California and Texas leading the way. In 1996, California voters approved Proposition 209, a comprehensive measure that required the state to refrain from granting preferential treatment in public employment, public education, or public contracting to any individual or group on the basis of race, sex, color, ethnicity, or national origin. That same year a federal appeals court in Texas ruled that race could not be used as a factor in student admissions, recruitment, or financial aid at the University of Texas at Austin. These policies have had a chilling effect on minority enrollments in institutions of higher education in both states. Colleges and universities in both states have begun to fight back, however. With the encouragement of educators, Texas passed a law guaranteeing the top 10 percent of graduates from the state's high schools admission to the public university of their choice. California schools began a concerted and expensive minority recruitment effort. In both states, minority enrollments have been restored to their affirmative action levels.[78]

A new approach to protecting affirmative action policies in higher education has recently emerged in the state of Michigan. There, a federal judge rejected two class action suits against the University of Michigan's admissions policies, ruling that "diversity is a critical component of higher education and that colleges and universities can continue to consider race and ethnicity in admissions decisions." The new element in this case was the marshaling of social scientific data on the benefits of racial diversity in higher education. The university produced studies indicating that whites exposed to a diverse student body while in college were more likely to expand their reasoning skills, to live and work in integrated settings, and to be involved in their communities. The use of this type of research to support affirmative action policies was bolstered by the 1998 publication of a new book on the topic by Derek Bok, former president of Harvard University, and William Bowen, former president of Princeton University. In *The Shape of the River: Long Term Consequences of Considering Race in College and University Admissions,* these two prominent educators mustered a wealth of data on twenty-eight educational institutions to demonstrate the positive effects of affirmative action policies on both white and minority students.[79]

Affirmative action policies such as those recently challenged in higher education were initially developed to compensate for past discrimination against minorities and women and to eliminate existing barriers in education and employment. Most affirmative action programs stem from the 1964 Civil Rights Act, which declared it illegal for employers of twenty-five or more people "to discriminate against any individual . . . because of race, color, religion, sex, or national origin." In the 1970s, federal regulations and court decisions strenghtened the act by specifying that employers and educational institutions had to take "affirmative actions" to end discrimination and to ensure equal opportunity in education and employment. Organizations were to do this by working under guidelines and setting specific goals and timetables.[80] Similarly, a court might rule that a school system must have a certain proportion of members of each race in each school by a certain date. These guidelines have since been extended to older people and to people with disabilities, although generally not to gay men and lesbians.

Although affirmative action policies have improved opportunities for many people, they have been criticized for some time. Critics have objected to the use of formal and informal quotas in some affirmative action systems, and have argued that practices such as allowing lower merit test scores for minorities can lead to a concomitant lowering of standards and the selection of "unqualified" students and employees. (Defenders of affirmative action counter that standardized test–type measures of merit may be biased and do not correlate well with actual job or scholastic performance.) Affirmative action's detractors have generally proceeded from an assumption that discrimination is no longer a problem in U.S. society. They reject the notion of the need to compensate groups for discriminatory practices of the past, often labeling affirmative action "reverse discrimination"—the denial of opportunities to members of the dominant group.[81]

In the face of opposition to affirmative action programs, many liberals and members of subordinate groups continue to argue that such programs are necessary. They point out that there is little hard data to support charges of "reverse discrimination." They contend that affirmative action is needed to combat entrenched, ongoing discrimination. As Barbara Bergman cogently writes, the goal is not to redress past crimes: "Our need for affirmative action depends not on what happened 100 years ago but on the situation in the labor market today." As we noted earlier in this chapter, that situation remains problematic for women and minorities of color.[82]

In addition to what appear to be institutionalized discrepancies in salaries and opportunities, women and minorities continue to face blatant racism and sexism in the work world and elsewhere. In a slaughterhouse in North Carolina, for example, African Americans and Mexicans get the hard and dirty job of carving up carcasses on the conveyor belt while white men supervise. A few American Indians also supervise; most get menial jobs like warehouse work. Several years ago, African American farmers won a lawsuit based on twenty years of discrimination by the U.S. Department of Agriculture, which admits it consistently denied government loans, crop subsidies, and other assistance to African American farmers because of their race. Coca-Cola has reached a settlement with African American employees whose lawsuit contended that the company denied them promotions, raises, and other opportunities based on the color of their skin. College women's sports have had to fight for equal footing with men's sports. Situations like these suggest the wisdom of Bergman's assertion that affirmative action policies are best justified by the great staying power of discrimination in our society.[83]

Separatism or Integration?

A third debate related to diversity revolves around issues of separatism versus integration. Although the "separate but equal" principle in education was long ago discarded by the Supreme Court, separatism is still practiced, and debated, in other realms. In the area of housing, for example, questions have been posed about whether it is more desirable for the elderly to live in separate housing complexes or to be in age-integrated housing and communities. Similarly, one might ask whether American Indians should remain on reservations, where their unique culture can best be preserved. The federal government recognizes the inherent sovereignty of Indian nations, which makes it possible, for example, for tribes to run their own TANF and child welfare programs. Some reservations have their own colleges and radio stations. Tribal culture includes traditions of healing and helping tribal members in need. Moving away from the reservation can mean leaving these traditions behind.[84]

Finally, a major debate has developed over whether states in the South should preserve and enhance their historically black colleges and universities. These institutions continue to play a vital role in educating students within a setting that reinforces their African American heritage. For many African Americans the issue has now become whether it is more important to pursue the elusive goal of integration in higher education or to push state governments to share their resources equally among all publicly funded educational institutions.[85]

Gay men, and more recently, lesbian women tend also to see themselves as representing separate communities of interest. At an earlier point in history, homosexuals were often integrated into society and not viewed as "different." Since the 1700s, however, homosexuality has been illegal in most European countries, with the notable exception of Scandinavian countries and the Netherlands. In reaction, a male homosexual underground had become well established in Europe and the United States by the nineteenth century. Because women were tied to the private world of the home until relatively recently, the practice of lesbianism remained hidden for a longer period. Following the development of social networks, political movements promoting gay and lesbian rights emerged first in Europe and then spread to the United States in the 1900s. Many lesbians and gay men have seen the creation of these separate social groups and advocacy organizations as crucial to their emotional and physical survival in an insensitive, frequently hostile world. On the other hand, the more visible presence of gays in state and local political offices, the legalization of civil unions in the state of Vermont, the recent Massachusetts Supreme Court ruling sanctioning gay marriage, and increasing public support for gay rights in the workplace suggest the growing possibility of integration into mainstream society. At the same time, however, these changes have contributed to a backlash, producing, for example, significant public support for a constitutional ban on gay marriage.[86]

In the social welfare arena, issues of separate treatment arise in discussions of special agencies for special groups, mainstreaming, and the matching of workers and clients. Many of those concerned about women's issues, for example, have argued the need for alternative social services for women. Thus, we have witnessed the emergence of women's health clinics, women's counseling centers, and programs for female victims of sexual abuse. Although less prevalent today, African Americans and European ethnic groups have a history of group-specific services, such as the black settlement or the Jewish charitable organization. The presence of new immigrant groups, including people from Asia and Central America, has led to the development of agencies attending specifically to these groups' needs, with workers who speak their languages.

The alternative to separate services and treatment is integration of diverse groups into a common social welfare system. Mainstreaming of those with disabilities, a policy applied initially to the education arena, has relevance for social welfare programs as well. During the 1970s, state and federal legislation developed that guaranteed the right

Disabilities don't preclude happiness.

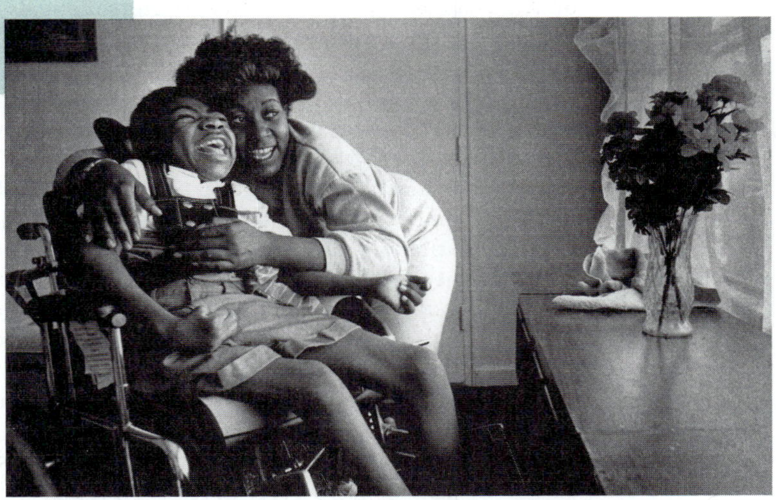

of youngsters with disabilities to receive a public education. Whenever possible such education is to take place in regular classrooms in the public schools. This notion of mainstreaming has most recently been expanded to job training and job placement. "Supported employment" programs place those with physical, mental, or emotional disabilities in normal job situations rather than in the traditional separate sheltered workshop.

In addition, the 1990 Americans with Disabilities Act helps bring those with physical, cognitive, and mental disabilities into the mainstream by protecting their rights in areas such as employment, transportation, and public accommodations. Under the employment section, for example, the act requires employers to provide "reasonable accommodation" to employees with disabilities: accommodations such as modifying office furniture and equipment to allow a person using a wheelchair to work as a dental hygienist, or providing room dividers for employees with disability-related difficulties in concentrating. The 1999 Supreme Court decision in *Olmstead* v. *L. C.* furthered the integration of people with disabilities into the mainstream by ruling that two women with mental disabilities who were found capable of living in the community and who wanted to leave their institution had the right to appropriate community placements.[87]

The debate between separatism and integration also emerges in discussions of client–worker matching, or the selection of a social worker who has the same background as the client. For example, one might argue that only a counselor who is herself lesbian can understand the specific issues faced by a lesbian client. An African American teenager might identify best with an African American guidance counselor.

The idea of matching plays an important role in policies regarding adoption and foster care placement. There the issue centers on the importance of placing children in settings that duplicate their own racial, religious, or ethnic backgrounds. The National Association of Black Social Workers, for example, has successfully argued that African

American children should be placed in African American families that will help maintain an awareness of their cultural heritage. Many states include this approach in their adoption policies. Critics of the system argue that the offer of a loving home outweighs the need to match the child's own background. Many minority groups counter that the maintenance of ethnic or racial identity is an important goal for all children. They also question how well someone from a different, particularly a nonminority, background can empathize with the personal experience of prejudice and teach children how to deal with it. Recent court cases have challenged "race matching" in adoptions, and in 1997 Congress passed legislation that could deny states a percentage of foster care funds if race is used to delay or deny adoptions.[88]

American Indians living on reservations have had particular concerns about matching children in foster and institutional care and adoptive homes. For many years they witnessed an excessive rate of placement of American Indian children in white-run boarding schools or homes away from the reservation. The problem stemmed in part from the tendency of state welfare departments to see American Indian families as unfit and to ignore the usefulness of extended families in caring for children. A long period of opposition to these practices by American Indian groups and civil liberties advocates led to passage of the Indian Child Welfare Act of 1978. This legislation establishes minimum federal standards for the removal of American Indian children from their families, and states that placement of such children should reflect the unique values of American Indian culture. The act has helped Indian tribes achieve substantial control over the foster care and adoptive placement of American Indian children.[89]

Questions relating to separate services, mainstreaming, and matching are thorny ones for social workers. On the one hand, separatism can mean more empathetic attention to client needs and to the experience of subordinate group membership. The women's counseling center might provide babysitting services to clients during their appointments and a more sensitive understanding of women's issues, such as the difficulties in leaving an abusive marital situation. The school social worker who is himself Chinese might best understand the conflict of a first-generation Chinese student who feels the pull between a family structure that stresses obedience to authority and a school setting that encourages assertive behavior.

On the other hand, matching may not always be helpful or appropriate. An African American middle-class social worker in the Department of Social Services might unfairly expect greater self-initiative from her African American clients than from her white ones. A homosexual man would not necessarily choose a gay therapist if the areas he wanted to deal with were phobic behaviors or substance abuse. In such a situation, the therapist's ability to deal with those areas might well be the client's primary criterion, rather than personal experience of what it means to be gay.

Perhaps the best approach to these issues is to ensure choice within social welfare settings. Clients could then decide for themselves whether in some situations they would be more comfortable with a worker who shared a similar background, and if they would prefer services delivered within special settings. On the other hand, they should always be assured fair and sensitive treatment within "mainstream" agencies and programs.

Social Work Roles Related to Diversity

Social workers have a long history of dealing with diversity. Their concerns with the needs and problems of specific groups can be traced through the social work literature and through changing curricula in social work educational programs. The charity worker or settlement worker in the early 1900s heard conference papers or read articles on the plight of the new immigrants. Social workers of the 1930s and 1940s were exposed to discussions of "Cultural Factors and Family Case Work" or "The Case Worker's Need for Orientation to the Culture of the Client." The 1940s also brought national attention to race relations. Social workers joined social scientists and others in their concern for the problems of African Americans in a country that had just fought "to make the world safe for democracy."[90] The development of the civil rights and women's movements in the 1960s and 1970s furthered pressure on the social work curriculum to provide meaningful material on the concerns and lifestyles of subordinate groups.

All this is not to say that the social work profession has a perfect record of attention to issues of discrimination and diversity. Individual social workers are not immune from prejudices such as homophobia. All too often, curriculum or practice changes have been a belated response to outside pressure (or to internal pressure from diverse groups within the profession). Yet at the same time, social work's traditions of valuing client self-determination, stressing the importance of environmental factors in people's lives, and working with a broad range of populations should make the profession particularly sensitive to the problems and strengths of subordinate groups.

How might this sensitivity be translated into social work practice? First, as one hears in numerous social work courses, it is important "to recognize one's own biases and assumptions about others." Yet even for well-intentioned students (and practitioners), such advice is easier to give than to carry out. For example, social work students in a field work seminar were asked to go around the room and provide social/psychological information on one of their clients. Each student spoke in turn. Each provided all conceivable kinds of information except for his or her client's race—even when this fact might have been particularly pertinent to an understanding of that individual's life situation. When asked about this omission by the instructor, class members responded that it would be "impolite" to speak openly of someone's racial background. This answer suggests that we are often uncomfortable about openly acknowledging race, ethnicity, and subordinate group membership as significant factors in people's lives. Then, too, it is difficult to perceive the subtle power of institutional racism, sexism, and other forms of discrimination over our own beliefs and behaviors.

There is no easy answer to this problem. One starting point is the simple determination to try to be sensitive to issues of discrimination and difference. We can cultivate this sensitivity through learning foreign languages; traveling to various parts of the country; and reading feminist novels and books about members of different ethnic or racial groups (such as Kay Mills's biography of the African American civil rights activist Fannie Lou Hamer or James P. Comer's story of his family in *Maggie's American Dream: The Life and Times of a Black Family*). One can also live in a racially integrated neighborhood; learn about gay and lesbian issues; visit agencies with a large proportion of minority clients or those with disabilities; and most important, work with people of different backgrounds on common projects.[91]

The next step is to translate awareness of the needs and strengths of people of diverse groups into practice, both in building relationships with individual clients and families and in developing agency services. On the individual level, this means such things as understanding the importance of extended family support for an African American teenage mother, appreciating the devastating effects of unemployment on the self-image of a Latino father, and acknowledging the frustration of a woman trapped in the "pink-collar ghetto" of a low-paying clerical job. On the agency level, awareness means thinking about whether agency services are appropriate to the needs of specific client groups and developing policies to combat discriminatory practices. On a broader level, it means advocating for policies that combat discrimination, such as the NASW policy on affirmative action.[92] The NASW *Standards for Cultural Competence in Social Work Practice* is another useful resource. Finally, sensitivity to issues of diversity should include an understanding of power differentials between dominant and subordinate groups in our society. This can lead to a goal of empowering clients on individual, group, and community levels and assisting them in their attempts to bring about structural change.

In addition, attention to diversity ought to include a sense of the type of society in which we would like to live. Is greater homogeneity a desirable goal? Is cultural pluralism our ideal? These are important questions for social workers, as well as for all citizens. One version of an answer is contained in the following article written for a high school newspaper:

"The world is a box of crayons" by rachel morris, 1988*

10:06 A.M. The buzz of an artificially lit classroom swarms around its third hour occupants. Slouched in my chair at the back of the room, I try to ignore the sweat running into the collar of my t-shirt, the incessant tapping of my foot. I chew anxiously on my pen top, and the words on the paper before me swim around in a mocking blur.

No, I'm not struggling over a physics test, or an essay question in College English. This is simply a survey on student–teacher relationships given to the whole school and I haven't made it past the first section.

Name _____. Okay, got that one. Age _____. Grade _____. Sex _____.

Yeah, these are easy. Race _______. What? RACE. 1. White. 2. Black. 3. Oriental. 4. Hispanic. 5. American Indian. This is where my panic begins. I read my choices again, and my brow furrows. Basically, the problem is this: I'm racially mixed, and there is no option for me.

Now, this is not the first time this has happened. All my life, I've had to decide what race I am, which half of me to deny. I remember asking my sister one day in third grade which one I was. "We're mixed, Rach," she told me. Mixed. And for every survey, every technical form I received in every grade after, I looked for that word. The closest I ever found was "other." That always kind of amused me, but I tried it. Other: mixed. But my teachers came to me. "Mixed what, honey?" And they looked at me. "You're black. Next time, just put black, okay?" And I would go home to my mother, my single, cream-colored mother, who wanted nothing but to raise us well. Even as an intelligent 8-year-old, I was a bit confused.

My next practice, starting about seventh grade, was to circle both white and black. It made the most sense, really, but even here in high school I got trouble. Again, the tender pressure: "Hon, you can't be *both*." So I ended up selecting "Caucasian" for the day. Recently,

*Reprinted by permission of the family of rachel morris (sic) and Jack Sizer.

I went to my counselor and had that changed. See, I'm a junior, and considering colleges, and I know that as a "minority student" I'll be eligible for certain scholarships. Also, it will give me an edge at schools that are looking for a diverse student body. So I figure I'll be black for the next 5 years or so, and then go back to being myself.

But can I really go back? Can I really be comfortable with who I am if society ignores that people like me exist? Well, I can—but you must realize that I'm lucky. I grew up in Hyde Park (in Chicago), one of the most liberal integrated neighborhoods in America. My 14 years there taught me that I could exist as a mixed person, with both black and white friends. That I could be proud of my brown skin, even have fun with it. It's always great to see the look on people's faces when my mom and sister and I go out, especially with my white stepfather.

But for some kids, there is no joke. Only confusion, and the total lack of a sense of identity. These children are pressured to choose a group of friends, and in effect to choose a parent, a race, a way of life, a heritage—and to completely deny the other. But do black people really want a friend who's only half black, and vice-versa?

Social Work **Destinations**

Destinations to Enhance an Appreciation of Diversity

Many destinations can help you appreciate diversity. We've listed some here, but we encourage you to look around in your own town, city, or region—many communities have small museums dedicated to presenting the local history of African Americans or ethnic groups.

Martin Luther King, Jr., National Historic Site, Atlanta, Georgia

Most people know about this one, and it's well worth seeing. The site not only includes the house in which Dr. King was born, his grave site, and the Ebenezer Baptist Church where he and his father preached, but also gives you a sense of the African American neighborhood in which he grew up. King's grave site is part of the Center for Non-Violent Social Change, which houses a museum of Dr. King's life and work. It is a place for reverence and reflection. *For further information:* 404-524-1956.

Museum of African American History, Detroit, Michigan

The largest of its kind in the world, this museum is a monument to African American history and culture in the United States. Its permanent exhibit includes eight "historical stations," one of which features a slave ship replica. Detroit public school students served as models for the ship's life-size figures. Highlighting the achievements of African Americans are one hundred artifacts, among them the dress worn by Carlotta Walls on the first day she faced angry mobs to integrate Central High School in Little Rock, Arkansas. *For further information:* 313-494-5800.

The Lower East Side Tenement Museum, New York City

The museum is lodged in an actual tenement house built in the 1870s; its goal is to depict the variety of the urban immigrant experience on Manhattan's Lower East Side. Because the tenement is still in the process of restoration, the museum's curators rely on a unique six-foot-high "dollhouse" to convey that experience. This replica of the building is filled with immigrant apartments from different time periods. In an 1870 front apartment, for example, a German couple nurse a sick baby. By 1915 the change in ethnicity of new arrivals is evident; in the second-floor rear apartment, Abraham and Fannie Rogarshevsky and their six children prepare to celebrate Passover. *For further information:* 212-431-0233.

That was the problem facing the first mixed kids—the children born of slaves and their owners. It should not exist now. In this age, the so-called "modern civilization" we're supposed to have reached, being racially mixed shouldn't be a dilemma, it should be considered a blessing. We are graced with the best of both worlds, exposure to two entirely different walks of life. In fact, our parents should be congratulated for creating a higher, enlightened race with such a large sphere of influences and possibilities. Instead, they have been scolded. God forbid we should pollute one race by adding another to it.

The world is a box of crayons. Though they're all different colors, they're all made of the same thing. And even though yellow and blue are combined to make green, once the wax has set, it's a green crayon, and that's all. It's never asked to make a choice between blue and yellow. One of the things my sister and I did together is draw pictures of the family, coloring them from our big box of Crayolas. And I always thought it was neat that a drawing of four people could use up three crayons—peach, light brown, and dark brown, when the other kids only got to use one.[93]

The Ellis Island Immigration Museum, New York

In the shadow of the Statue of Liberty is this memorial to the vast migration of European immigrants to the United States in the late 1880s and early 1900s. The museum is located in the main building of the federal immigration facility through which millions passed. You can stand in the great hall and imagine yourself a new arrival—waiting to be inspected and processed, fearful of being turned down for health reasons, and struggling to understand and be understood. Exhibits include taped reminiscences of immigrants, historical artifacts, and many photographs. *For further information:* 212-363-3200.

Mexican Fine Arts Center, Chicago

This is the first Mexican cultural center in the Midwest. A large and busy place, it has regularly changing exhibitions and live multilingual shows. *For further information:* 312-738-1503.

Japanese American National Museum, Los Angeles

This museum is located in Little Tokyo, the largest Japanese American community in the United States. It houses changing exhibits from the museum's large collection of artifacts, films, paintings, and other objects. Together, these trace the Japanese experience in the United States from the earliest immigration to the present, including the traumatic experience of war and internment on Japanese Americans. One exhibit conveys that experience through a reconstructed tar-paper barracks from the relocation camp at Heart Mountain, Wyoming. *For further information:* 213-625-0414.

Cherokee, North Carolina

The Cherokee Indians lived in this area before their forced relocation to Oklahoma along the Trail of Tears. Some were able to stay behind, and others have since returned to what is now the center of the Cherokee people. You can visit the Oconaluftee Indian Village, a replica showing life in an eighteenth-century Cherokee community. There is also a Museum of the Cherokee Indian, owned by the Eastern Band of Cherokee. *For further information:* 828-497-2911 (village); 828-497-3481 (museum). Note that there are American Indian sites and reservations all over the United States. A good travel guide is Eagle/Walking Turtle, *Indian America: A Travelers' Companion,* 4th ed. (Sante Fe, NM: John Muir Publications, 1995).

Visit **www.researchnavigator.com** to research these important concepts from the chapter:

Affirmative action
Americans with Disabilities Act
Bilingual education
Cultural pluralism
Homophobia
Racism
Sexism

Web Sites on Diversity

The African-American Mosaic <www.loc.gov/exhibits/african/intro.html>: A Library of Congress resource guide for the study of black history and culture. Covers the library's extensive African American collections, including books, photographs, music, and film.

InMotion Magazine <www.inmotionmagazine.com>: An online magazine that includes material on affirmative action and human rights.

Latino Social Workers Organization <www.whittier.cps.k12.il.us/Community/PrOrg/LSWO.html>: An organization dedicated to promoting the professional development of Latino social workers and to addressing concerns and issues that affect the Latino community.

NAACP <www.naacp.org>: The NAACP web site has up-to-date material on issues, policies, and legislation relating to African Americans and other minority groups of color.

NOW <www.now.org>: The National Organization of Women's site has material on key issues and policies related to women, including affirmative action, economic equity, violence against women, and racial and ethnic diversity.

The Urban Institute <www.urban.org>: Material on immigration and civil rights (see the "Hot Topics" page).

Endnotes

1. Nancy Beard Henderson, "Doing the Right Thing," *Southwest Airlines Spirit* (May 2003), 38.
2. Susan Page, "Class of '64: 15 Harvard Women Who Blazed a Legal Trail," *USA Today* (10 February 2003), E1, 8.
3. Cheryl A. Hyde and Betty J. Ruth, "Multicultural Content and Class Participation: Do Students Self-Censor?" *Journal of Social Work Education 38* (Spring/Summer 2002), 241–256.
4. Eric Schmitt, "New Census Shows Hispanics Now Even with Blacks in U.S." *New York Times* (8 March 2001), 1; Jon Meacham, "The New Face of Race," *Newsweek* (18 September 2000), 40; D'Vera Cohn and Darryl Fears, "In 10 Years, We've Changed," *Washington Post National Weekly Edition* (19–25 March 2001), 30; William Booth, "California, the Majority Minority State," *Washington Post National Weekly Edition* (4 September 2000), 31; Eric Schmitt, "U.S. Now More Diverse, Ethnically and Racially," *New York Times* (1 April 2001), 18.
5. Stephanie Brzuzy, Layne Stromwall, Polly Sharpe, Regina Wilson, and Elizabeth Segal, "The Vulnerability of American Indian Women in the New Welfare State," *Affilia 15* (Summer 2000), 193.
6. National Center for Health Statistics, *Health, United States, 2002,* Table 38, online at www.cdc.gov/nchs/products/pubs/pubd/hus/2010/2010.htm; Lindsey Tanner, "More Health Woes, Less Care for Hispanic Kids, Report Says," *Arizona Republic* (3 July 2002), A4; Jerry Adler and Claudia Kalb, "An

American Epidemic: Diabetes," *Newsweek* (4 September 2000), 40–47; *Health, United States,* 2003, Tables 31 and 71, online at www.cdc.gov/hchs/hus.htm; Sarah Cohen and D'Vera Cohn, "Continental Shift," *Washington Post National Weekly Edition* (9–15 August 2001), 6.

7. Ellis Close, "Brown v. Board: A Dream Deferred." *Newsweek* (17 May 2004), 53–59.
8. National Conference of La Raza, "State of Hispanic America 2004: Latino Perspectives on the American Agenda" (February 2004), 28, online at www.nclr.org; U.S. Bureau of the Census, *Statistical Abstract, 2002,* Unemployed Workers—Summary, 1980–2001, online at www.census.gov/prod/2003pubs/02statab/labor.pdf.
9. U.S. Census Bureau, *Current Population Reports* (July 2002), "The Big Payoff: Educational Attainment and Synthetic Estimates of Work-Life Earnings," Table 3, 12–13.
10. U.S. Census Bureau, *Statistical Abstract of the United States: 2002,* 11; Genaro C. Armas, "U.S. Foreign-Born Population Hits Record High in Past Year, *Arizona Republic* (10 March 2002), 2.
11. Eric Schmitt, "Americans (a) Love (b) Hate Immigrants," *New York Times* (4 January 2001), sec. 4, 1, 3; Brad Edmondson, "Immigration Nation," *Historic Preservation* (January/February 2000), 31–33.
12. Jerry Kammer, "Mexican Immigrants Sap Citizens, Report Says," *Arizona Republic* (13 July 2001), 8; Dianne Cardwell, "Muslims Face Deportation, but Say U.S. Is Their Home," *New York Times* (13 June 2003), 20; Michael Janofsky, "War Brings New Surge of Anxiety for Followers of Islam," *New York Times* (29 March 2003), B15.
13. Shannon Henry, "The Widening Pay Gap," *Washington Post Weekly Edition* (28–23 January 2002), 34; U.S. Bureau of the Census, Current Population Survey, online at www.census.gov/income/histpov/histpov3.1st, Table 3; Jeff Madriek, "Economic Scene," *New York Times* (10 June 2004), C2.
14. Del Jones, "Few Women Hold Top Executive Jobs," *Arizona Republic* (10 February 2003), D4; "Women Still Confined to Pink-Collar Jobs," *Arizona Republic* (5 May 2003), 1; Lynn Stoesen, "Gay Marriage Rights Upheld," *NASW News 49* (January 2004), 6; Elisabeth Bumiller and Richard W. Stevenson, "Speech to Nation, Strongest Denunciation of Gay Marriage Is among Themes," *New York Times* (21 January 2004), 1.
15. "Harris Poll Reflects the Status of People with Disabilities," *Monday Morning,* [Newsletter of New Jersey Development Disabilities Council] (August 2000), 3; Sybil Walker Barnes, "Inside Story," *Policy and Practice 61* (March 2002), 2.
16. Joe R. Feagin, *Racial and Ethnic Relations,* 2nd ed. (Englewood Cliffs, NJ: Prentice Hall, 1984), 10; Peter I. Rose, *They and We: Racial and Ethnic Relations in the United States,* 3rd ed. (New York: Random House, 1981), 8–9.
17. Feagin, *Racial and Ethnic Relations,* 5.
18. R. A. Schermerhorn, *Comparative Ethnic Relations* (New York: Random House, 1970), 73–74, 102–103; Richard J. Herrnstein and Charles Murray, *The Bell Curve: Intelligence and Class Structure in American Life* (New York: Free Press, 1994); E. J. Dionne Jr., "Race and IQ: Stale Notions," *Washington Post National Weekly Edition* (24–30 October 1994), 29; Gerald E. McClearn et al., "Substantial Genetic Influence on Cognitive Abilities in Twins 80 or More Years Old," *Science 276* (6 June 1997), 1560–1563; Steve Blinkhorn, "Symmetry as Destiny: Taking a Balanced View of I.Q.," *Nature 387* (26 June 1997), 849–850.
19. Rose, *They and We,* 7.
20. Milton M. Gordon, *Human Nature, Class, and Ethnicity* (New York: Oxford University Press, 1978), 166–180.
21. Gerard A. Postiglione, *Ethnicity and American Social Theory* (Lanham, MD: Universal Press of America, 1983), 18–21, 125–148; Leonard Dinnerstein, Roger L. Nichols, and David M. Reimers, *Natives and Strangers: Blacks, Indians, and Immigrants in America,* 2nd ed. (New York: Oxford University Press, 1990), 285–292, 328–332.
22. Denise Giardina, "America's Exploited Colony of West Virginia," *Manchester Guardian Weekly* (15 September 1985), 17; Hermon George, *American Race Relations Theory: A Review of Four Models* (Lanham, MD: University Press of America, 1984), 85–120.
23. Rose, *They and We,* 105–106.
24. King Davis, "Expanding the Theoretical Understanding of Oppression," Carl A. Scott Memorial Lecture, February 2002 (printed by Council on Social Work Education), 20.
25. Rose, *They and We,* 115–138; Feagin, *Racial and Ethnic Relations,* 15; Diane J. Goodman, *Promoting Diversity and Social Justice* (Berkeley, CA: Sage, 2001), 20–21.

26. Mimi Abramovitz, *Regulating the Lives of Women: Social Welfare Policy from Colonial Times to the Present* (Boston: South End Press, 1988).
27. William Julius Wilson, *The Truly Disadvantaged* (Chicago: University of Chicago Press, 1987); William Julius Wilson, *The Declining Significance of Race* (Chicago: University of Chicago Press, 1980).
28. Andrew Billingsly, "The Sociology of Knowledge of William J. Wilson: Placing 'The Truly Disadvantaged' in Its Sociohistorical Context," *Journal of Sociology and Social Welfare 16* (December 1989), 7–41; Charles Vert Willie, *The Caste and Class Controversy* (Bayside, NY: General Hall, 1979), 145–158.
29. Douglas S. Massey, review of William Julius Wilson, *When Work Disappears: The World of the New Urban Poor* (New York: Alfred A. Knopf, 1996), in *Contemporary Society: A Journal of Reviews 26* (July 1997), 416–418.
30. Sharon Begley, "Three Is Not Enough: Surprising New Lessons from the Controversial Science of Race," *Newsweek* (13 February 1995), 67; Tom Morganthau, "What Color Is Black?" *Newsweek* (13 February 1995), 63–65; Robert S. Byrd, "Discoveries Contradict Notion of Separate Races," *New Orleans Times-Picayune* (13 October 1996), A4; Ellis Cose, "What's White Anyway?" *Newsweek* (18 September 2000), 64; Jacqueline Jones, "The Color of Blood," review of Scott L. Malcomson, "One Drop of Blood: The American Misadventure of Race," *Washington Post National Weekly Edition* (18 December 2000), 33.
31. Gary Y. Okihiro, *Margins and Mainstreams: Asians in American History and Culture* (Seattle: University of Washington Press, 1994), 31–34; Peter Skerry, *Mexican Americans: The Ambivalent Minority* (New York: Free Press, 1993), 7–10.
32. Nancy Abelmann and John Lie, *Blue Dreams: Korean Americans and the Los Angeles Riots* (Cambridge, MA: Harvard University Press, 1995), 149; Roberto Suro, "Huddled Masses Need Not Apply," *Washington Post National Weekly Edition* (2–8 January 1995), 16.
33. Paula Dressel, "Patriarchy and Social Welfare Work," *Social Problems 34* (June 1987).
34. Okihiro, *Margins and Mainstream,* 44–48; Abelmann and Lie, *Blue Dreams,* 148–162; Sharin Elkholy and Ahmed Nassef, "Crips and Bloods Speak for Themselves," *Against the Current 39* (July–August 1992), 7–10.
35. Barbara Bryant Solomon, *Black Empowerment: Social Work in Oppressed Communities* (New York: Columbia University Press, 1976); Ann Bookman and Sandra Morgen, eds., *Women and the Politics of Empowerment* (Philadelphia: Temple University Press, 1988).
36. Begley, "America's Changing Face," 49; Leslie Leighninger, "Social Workers, Immigrants, and Historians: A Re-examination," *Journal of Sociology and Social Welfare 2* (Spring 1975), 327.
37. Elizabeth Peabody House, *Fifteenth Annual Report* (Boston, 1911), 10–13; Leighninger, "Social Workers, Immigrants, and Historians," 331–334; Ruth Hutchinson Crocker, *Social Work and Social Order: The Settlement Movement in Two Industrial Cities, 1889–1930* (Urbana: University of Illinois Press, 1992), 41–67.
38. Jane Addams, *Newer Ideals of Peace* (New York: Macmillan, 1911).
39. Addams, *Newer Ideals,* 69–75, 204.
40. Leighninger, "Social Workers, Immigrants, and Historians," 337–338.
41. Charles Marden and Gladys Meyer, *Minorities in American Society,* 4th ed. (New York: D. Van Nostrand, 1973), 162; Feagin, *Racial and Ethnic Relations,* 227.
42. Marden and Meyer, *Minorities in American Society,* 162–165; Eric Foner, *Reconstruction: America's Unfinished Revolution* (New York: Harper & Row, 1988), 68–69, 144, 159–161, 170.
43. Steven J. Diner, "Chicago Social Workers and Blacks in the Progressive Era," *Social Service Review 44* (December 1970), 393–410; Thomas Lee Philpott, *The Slum and the Ghetto: Neighborhood Deterioration and Middle-Class Reform, Chicago 1880–1930* (New York: Oxford University Press, 1978), 295–299.
44. Diner, "Chicago Social Workers and Blacks in the Progressive Era," 396–408.
45. Philpott, *The Slum and the Ghetto,* 301, 314–342; Iris Carlton-LaNey, "The Career of Birdye Henrietta Haynes, a Pioneer Settlement House Worker," *Social Service Review 68* (June 1994), 254–271; Elisabeth Lasch-Quinn, *Black Neighbors: Race and the Limits of Reform in the American Settlement House Movement, 1890–1945* (Chapel Hill: University of North Carolina Press, 1993), 3.
46. Philpott, *The Slum and the Ghetto,* 301–308; Philip Johnson, "Black Charity in Progressive Era Chicago," *Social Service Review 52* (September 1978), 400–415.

47. Anne Firor Scott, "Most Invisible of All: Black Women's Voluntary Associations," *Journal of Southern History 56* (February 1990), 3–22; Gerda Lerner, "Community Work of Black Club Women," *Journal of Negro History 59* (April 1974), 158–167; Iris Carlton LaNey, "African American Social Work Pioneers' Response to Need," *Social Work* (July 1999), 311–321; Lasch-Quinn, *Black Neighbors,* 75–115; "The Legacy of African-American Leadership in Social Welfare," Special Issue, *Journal of Sociology and Social Welfare 21* (March 1994); Philpott, *The Slum and the Ghetto,* 320–342; Johnson, "Black Charity in Progressive Chicago."
48. Leslie Leighninger, *Social Work: Search for Identity* (Westport, CT: Greenwood Press, 1987), 90–91; Jacqueline Jones, *Labor of Love, Labor of Sorrow: Black Women, Work, and the Family from Slavery to the Present* (New York: Vintage Books, 1985), 223–224, 263.
49. Brian Willoughby, "An American Legacy," *Teaching Tolerance* (Spring 2004), Southern Poverty Law Center, 40–56; John Oliver, "We're Going to School with White People," *Reflections 10* (Winter 2004), 12.
50. Rebecca A. Lopez, "Mendez v. Westminster: The Latino Brown v. Board of Education," *Reflections 10* (Winter 2004), 39–48; Gary Orfield and Erica Frankenberg, "Where Are We Now?" *Teaching Tolerance* (Spring 2004), Southern Poverty Law Center, 57–59.
51. Michael B. Katz, *In the Shadow of the Poorhouse: A Social History of Welfare in America* (New York: Basic Books, 1986), 128–129.
52. Lela Costin, *Two Sisters for Social Justice: A Biography of Grace and Edith Abbott* (Urbana: University of Illinois Press, 1983), 132–150.
53. Beverly Stadum, *Poor Women and Their Families: Hard Working Charity Cases* (Albany: State University of New York Press, 1992); Linda Gordon, *Pitied but Not Entitled: Single Mothers and the History of Welfare* (New York: Free Press, 1994), 45–49.
54. Abramovitz, *Regulating the Lives of Women,* 4; Paula Dressel, "Patriarchy and Social Welfare Work," 294–309.
55. Abramovitz, *Regulating the Lives of Women,* 152–154.
56. Ruth Sidel, *Women and Children Last* (New York: Penguin Books, 1986), 80–81.
57. Abramovitz, *Regulating the Lives of Women,* 333.
58. Stadum, *Poor Women and Their Families,* 133–155; Linda Gordon, *Heroes of Their Own Lives: The Politics and History of Family Violence* (New York: Penguin Books, 1989), 293–299.
59. Dressel, "Patriarchy and Social Welfare Work," 294–295; Clarke Chambers, "Women in the Creation of the Profession of Social Work," *Social Service Review 60* (March 1986), 12.
60. Leighninger, *Social Work: Search for Identity,* 10–11; Costin, *Two Sisters for Social Justice,* 21–25, 44.
61. Dressel, "Patriarchy and Social Welfare Work," 298; "72 Percent Work for Private Organizations," *NASW News* (January 2001), 8.
62. Leslie Leighninger, "Social Work: The Status of Women in a 'Female' Profession," in Joyce Tang and Earl Smith, eds., *Women and Minorities in American Professions* (Albany: State University of New York Press, 1996), 123–124, 127–129; Chambers, "Women in the Creation of the Profession of Social Work," 22–24.
63. Paul M. Ong, quoted in Michael A. Fletcher, "The Challenge of Success: The Achievements of Asian Americans Are a Blessing and a Curse," *Washington Post National Weekly Edition* (13 March 2000), 30.
64. Genero C. Armas, "20% Don't Speak English at Home, Census Shows," *Arizona Republic* (9 October 2003), 7; Joel Kotkin and Thomas Tseng, "All Mixed Up," *Washington Post National Weekly Edition* (16–22 June 2003), 22–23; "Biracial Relationships More Accepted," *Arizona Republic* (6 July 2001), A7.
65. Cohn and Fears, "In 10 Years We've Changed"; Craig A. Kaplowitz, "A Distinct Minority: LULAC, Mexican American Identity, and Presidential Policymaking, 1965–1972," *The Journal of Policy History 15* (2) (2003), 192–199.
66. Blaine Harden, "In N. Y., Anger Is No Longer Defined in Black and White," *Washington Post* (9 June 1998), A3; Michael A. Fletcher, "In Rapidly Changing L. A., a Sense of Future Conflicts," *Washington Post* (17 April 1998), 1, 4; Meacham, "The New Face of Race," 41; Jonathan Tilove, "Professor Works to Unify Asian-American Voters, *New Orleans Times-Picayune* (18 June 2000), 16; Arian Campo-Flores, "Brown against Brown," *Newsweek* (18 September 2000), 49–51; Mireya Navarro, "Latinos Gain Visibility in Cultural Life of U.S.," *New York Times* (19 September 1999), 18.
67. Ruben Martinez, "The Next Chapter," *New York Times Magazine* (16 July 2000), 11.

68. Okihiro, *Margins and Mainstreams,* 39–59; Abelmann and Lie, *Blue Dreams,* 91–92.
69. Skerry, *Mexican Americans,* 22, 26; Bruce S. Jansson, *The Reluctant Welfare State* (Pacific Grove, CA: Brooks/Cole, 1997), 133, 189; Abelmann and Lie, *Blue Dreams,* 90.
70. Jansson, *The Reluctant Welfare State,* 229–230.
71. Kenneth B. Noble, "California Immigration Measure Faces Rocky Legal Path," *New York Times* (11 November 1994), A17; B. Drummond Ayres Jr., "Anti-Alien Movement Spreading in Wake of California's Measure," *New York Times* (4 December 1994), 1; Katherine Hutt, "Legal Immigrants in U.S. Face Grim Prospects without Welfare," *Baton Rouge Advocate* (10 August 1996), 12A.
72. Schmitt, "Americans (a) Love (b) Hate Immigrants"; Louis Freedberg, "Labor's Catch-22: We Need Those 'Illegal' Immigrants to Do Our Work," *Washington Post National Weekly Edition* (14 February 2000), 21; "Vigilante Watch: A Newly Elected Congressman Discusses Anti-Immigrant Vigilantism and Racism in His Southern Arizona District," *Intelligence Report,* Southern Poverty Law Center (Spring 2003), 20–23; Tom Zeller, "Migrants Take Their Chances on a Harsh Path of Hope," *New York Times* (18 March 2001), 14; Juan A. Lozano, "Smuggling Deaths Hit 19," *Arizona Republic* (17 May 2003), 4.
73. Lee Hockstader, "Dreams among the Poorest of the Poor," *Washington Post National Weekly Edition* (2–8 September 2002), 29; Sergio Bustos, "Day Laborers Prone to Abuse, GAO Says," *Arizona Republic* (27 September 2002), 5; Robert Jablon, "California Hispanics, Riled by License Repeal, Boycott," *Arizona Republic* (13 December 2003), 36; Walter A. Ewing, "Not Getting What They Paid For: Limiting Immigrants' Access to Benefits Hurts Families," *Immigration Policy Report* (2003), online at www.ailf.org/ipc/policy_reports_2003_benefits.asp; National Council of La Raza, *Latino Perspectives on the American Agenda,* online at www.hclr.org/special/harpt, 2004.
74. Michael Fix and Jeffrey S. Passel, "Who's on the Dole? It's Not Illegal Immigrants," *Los Angeles Times* (3 August 1994), B7; Amy Waldman, "In Harlem's Ravaged Heart, Revival," *New York Times* (18 February 2001), 14; Daniel Gonzalez, "Illegal Workers Fueled New Economy, Study Says," *Arizona Republic* (19 February 2001), 1.
75. Elizabeth Bumiller, "Bush Would Like to Give Illegal Workers Broad New Rights," *New York Times* (7 January 2004), 1, 17; "Excerpts from Bush's Address on Allowing Immigrants to Fill Some Jobs," *New York Times* (8 January 2004), 20.
76. Jeff Madrick, "Economic Scene: The Bush Proposal on Illegal Immigrants Is a Tentative but Important First Step," *New York Times* (22 January 2004), C2; George Schneider and Kirsten Downey, "Bush Proposal Stirs Debate," *New York Times* (9 January 2004), 1; Nina Bernstein, "Immigrants Are Divided on Bush Proposal," *New York Times* (8 January 2004), 21; O. Ricardo Pimentel, "Bush is Re-Frying Old Bracero Policy," *Arizona Republic* (8 January 2004); Rachel L. Swarns, "Outcry on Right Over Bush Plan on Immigration," *New York Times* (21 February 2004), 1, 10.
77. "Affirmative Action in University Admissions Is Challenged in Michigan," *NASW News 45* (June 2000), 1.
78. James Traub, "The Class of Prop. 209," *New York Times Magazine* (21 May 1999), 44; Sue Anne Pressley, "Texas Campus Attracts Fewer Minorities," *Washington Post* (27 August 1997), 1, 14; Jodi Wilgoren, "Rights Panel Criticizes Shift in College Admissions Plans," *New York Times* (9 April 2000), 14; Jodi Wilgoren, "Texas Experiment Brings Minority Members to Flagship University," *Minneapolis Star Tribune* (26 November 1999), 6; Kevin Peranino, "Berkeley's New Colors," *Newsweek* (18 September 2000), 61; Traub, "The Class of Prop. 209," 44–51, 76–79; "University of California Points to Rebound in Admissions of Minority Undergraduates," *New York Times* (4 April 1999), 16.
79. Jodi Wilgoren, "Affirmative Action Plan Is Upheld at Michigan," *New York Times* (14 December 2000), 32; Steven A. Holmes, "A Most Diverse University's New Legal Tack," *New York Times* (11 May 1999), 1, 20; Ben Gose, "A Sweeping New Defense of Affirmative Action," *Chronicle of Higher Education 45* (18 September 1998); Jacques Steinberg, "Defending Affirmative Action with Social Science," *New York Times* (17 December 2000), 29.
80. Elizabeth D. Huttman, *Introduction to Social Policy* (New York: McGraw-Hill, 1981), 124, 321–346.
81. Peter T. Kilborn, " 'Race Norming' Tests Becomes a Fiery Issue," *New York Times* (19 May 1991), 5; Richard Morin, "Feelings That Aren't Set in Con-

crete," *Washington Post National Weekly Edition* (13–19 March 1995), 37.

82. Quoted in David Greenberg, "A Hand Up or a Handout?," review of Barbara R. Bergman, *In Defense of Affirmative Action* (New York: New Republic/Basic Books, 1996) in *The Washington Post Book World* (23 June 1996), 3.
83. Charlie LeDuff, "At a Slaughterhouse, Some Things Never Die: Who Kills, Who Cuts, Who Bosses Can Depend on Race," *New York Times* (16 June 2000), 1, 22; Michael A. Fletcher, "For Black Farmers, a Hollow Victory," *Washington Post National Weekly Edition* (18 January 1999), 29; Constance L. Hays, "Coca-Cola Reaches a Settlement with Some Workers in Bias Suit," *New York Times* (15 June 2000), G1.
84. Catherine C. Robbins, "Indian Country Sends a Stronger Signal," *New York Times* (4 February 2001), 33; Rene Sanchez, "Education's Last Stand?" *Washington Post National Weekly Edition* (28 July 1997), 34; Richard W. Voss, Victor Couville, Alex Little Soldier, and Gayla Twiss, "Tribal and Shamanic-Based Social Work Practice: A Lakota Perspective," *Social Work 44* (May 1999), 228–239.
85. Julie Oxford, "Are Black Colleges Worth Saving?" *Time* (11 November 1991), 81–83; "Where Brown Didn't Reach: America's Colleges," *Washington Post National Weekly Edition* (23–29 May 1994), 24.
86. Barry D. Adam, *The Rise of a Gay and Lesbian Movement* (Boston: Twayne, 1987); John D'Emilio, *Sexual Politics, Sexual Communities* (Chicago: University of Chicago Press, 1983); Sandra J. Potter and Trudy E. Darty, "Social Work and the Invisible Minority: An Exploration of Lesbianism," *Social Work 26* (May 1981), 187–192; Bruce Bawer, "More Respect, but Too Few Rights," *New York Times* (26 January 2001), 23; "Most Americans Oppose Gay Marriage, Poll Indicates," *The Arizona Republic* (11 April 2004), A7; Elizabeth Bumiller, "Bush Backs Ban in Constitution on Gay Marriage," *New York Times* (11 April 2004), 7.
87. John T. Pardeck, *Social Work after the Americans with Disabilities Act* (Westport, CT: Auburn House, 1998); Sara Rosenbaum, "The Olmstead Decision: Implications for State Health Policy," *Health Affairs 19* (September/October 2000), 228–232.
88. Sue Anne Pressley, "The Colors of Adoption: Black vs. White: A Texas Case Reflects a National Debate," *Washington Post Weekly Edition* (13 January 1997), 30–31.
89. Feagin, *Racial and Ethnic Relations,* 178–205; Ann E. MacEachron, Nora S. Gustavsson, Suzanne Cross, and Allison Lewis, "The Effectiveness of the Indian Child Welfare Act of 1978," *Social Service Review* (September 1996), 458. For firsthand reports of life in federally founded Indian boarding schools, see Margaret L. Archuleta, Brenda J. Child, and K. Tsianina Lomawaima, eds., *Away from Home: American Indian Boarding School Experiences* (Phoenix, AZ: Heard Museum, 2000); and Zitkala-Sa, "This Semblance of Civilization," in Linda K. Kerber and Jane Sherron De Hart, eds., *Women's America: Refocusing the Past* (New York: Oxford University Press, 1995), 265–267.
90. Mary A. Young, "Cultural Factors and Family Case Work," *The Family 19* (May 1938), 76–79; Maurine Boie, "The Case Worker's Need for Orientation to the Culture of the Client," *National Conference of Social Work, Proceedings* (1937); Leighninger, *Social Work: Search for Identity,* 162–163.
91. Kay Mills, *This Little Light of Mine: The Life of Fannie Lou Hamer* (New York: Dutton, 1993); James P. Comer, *Maggie's American Dream: The Life and Times of a Black Family* (New York: New American Library, 1988). Another useful book is Diane de Anda, ed., *Controversial Issues in Multiculturalism* (Boston: Allyn and Bacon, 1997), which features debates on various issues regarding multiculturalism.
92. National Association of Social Workers, *NASW Priorities for Civil Rights: Affirmative Action* (Washington, DC: NASW, September 2000).
93. rachel morris, "The world is a box of crayons," *KnightLife* (30 March 1988), Loy Norrix High School, Kalamazoo, MI. Reprinted by permission of the family of rachel morris and Loy Norrix High School.

CHAPTER

6

Religion and Social Work

An interesting and little researched question is, "Why do people choose social work as a career?" Although, as discussed in Chapter 3, the career prospects are nowhere near as bleak as popularly believed, there is little doubt that few people choose social work for the money. People whose main career objective is to make a lot of money generally choose business, law, or perhaps engineering. Social work, we presume, is chosen for other reasons.

Historically, one of the major reasons for choosing social work as a career has been personal religious belief. There is speculation among social work educators, although it is not yet supported by formal data, that the number of students choosing to major in social work because of religious commitment is increasing. At the school of one of the authors, an essay is required of students entering the social work program; in the essay students are asked to explain their reasons for choosing social work as a major. From a steadily increasing number of students we are receiving statements such as the following:

> I believe my main qualification as a social work candidate has been my life because I've been where a lot of people needing services are today, and with God's grace and a lot of help, I hope to become what I dreamed of being . . . a social worker.

Another student wrote

> As I sit back and look over the last few years, I can honestly say there is only one major reason why I am in social work. I have been called into the field because of my love for people and their needs, along with my wholehearted desire to serve God.

The fact that a person chooses social work out of a desire to live his or her faith is commendable and in most cases desirable. However, the relationship between social work and religion is not without problems. Although social work grew out of organized religion, during the profession's development it has become increasingly secularized. People with strong religious values sometimes find it difficult to subscribe to certain social work values. For example, one of the students cited earlier also said in her essay, "One issue that I have difficulty in is being accepting of all people, especially homosexuals. I believe this lifestyle is against the will of God and therefore have difficulty condoning it." As a professional social worker, this person will be expected to work with all kinds of people, homosexuals included, and to do so in a nonjudgmental and accepting manner, although there is no requirement that she personally approve of the lifestyle. This potential conflict between the values currently dominant in social work and the religious values of some individual social workers can be problematical for both the individual and the profession. Individual workers in a secular agency are often worried that they will be required to compromise their own values, and the agency is concerned that religiously oriented workers will use their position within the agency to attempt to convert clients to their belief system.

In this chapter we discuss the relationship between social work and religion, as well as some of the problems inherent in this relationship. We conclude that these problems are by no means unsolvable. The student cited earlier was well on the way to solving her own problem in this area. She concluded her essay with the following statement:

> This area I am still working on. Besides acceptance being important to social work, it is even more important as a Christian to love everyone: even those different than myself. I John 4:20 is why I see such a need to love all people, "If anyone says, 'I love God' yet hates his brother,

he is a liar. For anyone who does not love his brother whom he has seen, cannot love God, whom he has not seen."

The Religious Roots of Social Welfare

One of the leading scholars in the area of social work and religion, Alan Keith-Lucas, points out that the desire to help someone is not, as far as we know, instinctive.[1] The very desire to help others, and therefore the beginning of social welfare, seems to have developed as a part of religion. Almost all religions have obligated their followers to engage in acts of charity, sometimes only to members of their sect and sometimes to anyone in need.[2] All major religions have to some extent stressed responsibility for one's fellows, kindness or justice to the needy, and self-fulfillment through service.

Early Egyptian Roots

Egyptian civilization is the oldest culture to have left a substantial written record. It is therefore used here to illustrate the early development of religious injunctions regarding social welfare. Morris points out that a similar evolution was taking place in Assyrian, Mesopotamian, and Chinese societies.[3] The early Egyptian holy book, called the "Book of the Dead," was a group of writings collected around 3500 B.C. In the book is a list of seven acts of mercy, including relief of hunger, thirst, and nakedness; care of prisoners; help for the stranger; and care for the sick and the dead.[4] The book also contains an early version of what we now call the Golden Rule, "Do to the doer in order to cause him to do [for thee]."[5] The "Book of the Dead" contains mainly negative injunctions; that is, it focuses more on not doing harm than on actively doing good. It suggests behaviors that should be avoided because such avoidance will ensure a good life after death. Writings buried with the dead for the apparent purpose of providing evidence that the person had lived a correct life contain statements such as "I have not done violence to a poor man"; "I have not made anyone sick or weak"; and "I have not taken milk from the mouths of children." There is also some evidence of positive injunctions such as "I gave bread to the hungry, I clothed the naked, I ferried him who had no boat."[6]

Jewish Roots

In Jewish thought there is no concept of salvation or damnation, so thoughts of a good afterlife did not provide any motive for charitable behavior. However, it was believed that once a year there should be a Day of Atonement in which people would be afflicted with earthly torments—flood, fire, plague, death, and the like—in punishment for their misdeeds. Repentance, prayer, and charity were ways a person could avoid these sufferings. Thus, although charitable behavior was not believed to ensure a good afterlife as the Egyptians thought, it could at least help one escape some earthly torments.

Probably the most significant advance of Jewish charitable thought over Egyptian thought was the assertion that individuals have a positive obligation to perform acts of helping and doing good for others. For example:

> If there is among you a poor man, one of your brethren, in any of your towns within your land which the Lord your God gives you, you shall not harden your heart or shut your hand

> against your poor brother, but you shall open your hand to him, and lend him sufficient for his need, whatever it may be. Take heed lest there be a base thought in your heart, and you say, "The seventh year, the year of release is near," and your eye be hostile to your poor brother, and you give him nothing, and he cry to the Lord against you, and it be sin in you. You shall give to him freely, and your heart shall not be grudging when you give to him because for this the Lord your God will bless you in all your work and in all that you undertake. [Deuteronomy 15:7–10]

The Egyptian concept of charity mainly meant the avoidance of doing harm to others. The Jewish concept added the obligation to do positive acts of good.

Interestingly, the Hebrew word *tsedakah*, which has generally been translated as "charity," actually could more accurately be translated as "justice."[7] From this can be inferred that not only did people have an obligation to help those in need but also the needy had a right to help. Charitable acts were to be done simply because they were the right thing to do, and the giver should expect no repayment from the recipient. The Jewish philosopher Maimonides outlined eight degrees of charity, from lowest to highest:

> Give, but with reluctance and regret. This is the gift of the hand but not of the heart.
>
> The second is to give cheerfully, but not proportionately to the distress of the sufferer.
>
> The third is to give cheerfully and proportionately, but not until we are solicited.
>
> The fourth is to give cheerfully and proportionately, and even unsolicited; but to put it in the poor man's hand, thereby exciting in him the painful emotion of shame.
>
> The fifth is to give charity in such a way that the distressed may receive the bounty and know their benefactor, without being known to him.
>
> The sixth, which rises still higher, is to know the objects of our bounty, but remain unknown to them.
>
> The seventh is still more meritorious, namely, to bestow charity in such a way that the benefactor may not know the relieved persons, nor they the name of their benefactor.
>
> Lastly, the eighth and most meritorious of all, is to anticipate charity by preventing poverty; i.e., to assist a reduced person so that he may earn an honest livelihood and not be forced to the dreadful alternative of holding up his hand for charity.[8]

From these ideas, along with the Ten Commandments, prophetic exhortations, the Proverbs, and general moral teachings, the Jews developed a number of social welfare practices. Among them were hospitable reception of strangers; education of orphans; redemption of lawbreakers; endowment of marriages; visitation of the ill and infirm; burial of the dead; consolation of the bereaved; and care of widows, slaves, divorcees, and the aged. Provision for the poor was mainly through various agricultural practices such as "corners," whereby farmers were commanded to leave a small portion of every field unharvested; "gleanings," the practice of leaving grain dropped during harvest to be picked up by the poor; "forgotten sheaves," leaving any corn missed by harvesters for the poor; and "grape droppings," leaving dropped grapes and small clusters so they may be picked by the poor.[9]

Christian Roots

To the moral teachings and concept of justice from the Old Testament, the early Christians added an emphasis on love and compassion. The "theological virtues" were set forth as faith, hope, and charity, the greatest of these being charity.[10] The basis of the Christian approach to social welfare is generally considered to be in Jesus' depiction of the welcome to the righteous as blessed inheritors of the Kingdom.

> "For I was hungry and you gave me food, I was thirsty and you gave me drink, I was a stranger and you welcomed me, I was naked and you clothed me, I was sick and you visited me, I was in prison and you came to me." Then the righteous will answer him, "Lord, when did we see thee hungry and feed thee, or thirsty and give thee drink? And when did we see thee a stranger and welcome thee, or naked and clothe thee? And when did we see thee sick or in prison and visit thee?" And the King will answer them, "Truly, I say to you, as you did it to one of the least of these my brethren, you did it to me." [Matthew 25:35–40]

In Christian doctrine, Jesus is seen as the revelation of God and as the model that believers are to follow and emulate. The teachings of Jesus centered on the law of obedient love, which takes its cue from the nature of God rather than from the worthiness of any other object. Miller contends that the Good Samaritan parable, which emphasizes this love response, has probably done more to encourage humanitarian social welfare than any other single influence in all of history.[11]

A somewhat different, although not conflicting, rationale for charity is found in the writings of St. Paul. As discussed by Douglas,

> St. Paul, in his famous description of the virtue of charity, implies an almost total merging of the interests of the individual with those of the collectivity of which he or she is a member. In the Church of Corinth, he was faced with the fairly typical problem of a collectivity riven by doubts, jealousies, and schisms. His principal response was to elaborate the analogy between a collectivity, the church, and a human body. "A man's body is all one although it has a number of different organs and all this multitude of organs goes to make up one body. . . . The eye cannot say to the hand, I have no need of thee." [I Corinthians 12:15–21] The diversity is to be prized. After all, "if the whole were one single organ, what would become of the body?" Charity is the unifying force: "God has established a harmony in the body . . . all the different parts of it were to make each other's welfare their common care" [I Corinthians 12:19, 24–25]. He follows the analogy immediately with the famous description and praise of charity of Chapter Thirteen. The same point, also in relation to the analogy of the body, is made more succinctly in the Letter to the Ephesians: "Thus each limb receiving the active power it needs; it [the body] achieves its natural growth building itself up through charity." [Ephesians 4:16][12]

Thus, charity was not only viewed as a theological virtue but also as a practical necessity to maintain the organic unity of the church and community.

The early Christian church, and the generations that followed, took seriously the command of Jesus to carry out the expression of love that occurs so frequently in the New Testament. Since its earliest days, the church has engaged in at least twelve areas of social ministry: the care of widows, orphans, the sick, the poor, the disabled, prisoners, captives, slaves, and victims of calamity; burial of the poor; provision of employment services; and meals for the needy.[13] Because Christianity and traditional Judaism both sprang from the same source, the lists of charitable activities of the two groups are very similar.

Muslim Roots

Of the major religions in the United States, Islam is the youngest, beginning in Mecca, Saudi Arabia, in the 7th century. There are currently about 1.3 billion Muslims, making this the second largest religion in the world, surpassed only by Christianity. It is estimated that 22 percent of the world's population are Muslim and 33 percent are Christian, with the growth rate of Islam exceeding that of Christianity. In the United States,

Muslims constitute only about 1 percent of the population, although it is estimated that the population of Muslims in the public school system may exceed 5 percent. Like the worldwide situation, the growth rate of the Muslim population in the United States exceeds that of the general population. For these reasons, understanding the Islamic roots of and traditions regarding social welfare will become increasingly important.[14]

Islamic thought differentiates between social justice and charity. The faith, based on the Prophet Muhammad's advocacy on behalf of women, children, and the disadvantaged, has a strong tradition of social reform. This tradition is operationalized through the requirement that every Muslim who is financially able contribute 2.5 percent of his or her net wealth each year for support of the needy, a practice called *zakah*. This is not considered to be charity, but rather an act of social justice through the redistribution of wealth.[15]

Contributions over and above the *zakah,* called *sadaqa,* a word borrowed from Hebrew, are considered to be charity. The importance of charity in the Muslim faith is illustrated by the fact that of the five pillars of Islam, the third pillar is charity.[16] The Koran specifies eight categories of uses for which the *sadaqa* (charitable contributions) may be spent:

> The alms are for the poor, the needy, those who collect them, and those whose hearts must be reconciled, to redeem the captives, the debtors, for God's cause, and the wayfarer. It is a duty imposed by God. God is all-knowing and all-wise.

The aim of this charity is not social reform but individual perfection of the giver, with the expectation of eternal reward from God.[17]

It can be seen that Islamic belief, through the combination of the *zakah,* the annual contribution toward achieving a more just society, and the *sadaqa,* which emphasizes charity in addition to the *zakah,* provides a strong foundation for social welfare.

The Religious Roots of Organized Social Work

The philosophical basis for social welfare is largely found in religious teachings, so it is not surprising that the earliest forms of organized social work all had religious progenitors. Even before the rise of modern European states, the church was providing social services of a primitive sort. The early church provided alms to the poor, shelter for the homeless, and care and comfort for the sick; monasteries often served as all-purpose social service agencies, acting as hospitals, homes for the aged, orphanages, and travelers' aid stations. As discussed in Chapter 2, however, it was not until the onset of industrialization and urbanization, when the informal helping systems of the church and family began to break down, that organized social welfare services began to emerge. The natural first step was for the church to begin to formalize what it had previously done on an informal basis.

As we noted in Chapter 3, the profession of social work is generally considered to have emerged from three general movements: the charity organization society (COS) movement; the settlement house movement; and a third, less clearly defined movement, the development of institutions to deal with an entire range of social problems. All of these had their period of most rapid growth during the nineteenth century, and all grew out of the church.

Churches and the Charity Organization Society Movement

The earliest development of the COS has been traced to Thomas Chalmers, a minister of the Church of Scotland. Chalmers was called to Glasgow in 1814 to be the minister of one of its most important churches. Appalled by the poverty he witnessed in the parish of St. John's, and detesting the Poor Law, he set out to do something about the situation. What he did was to divide the parish into twenty-five units and to assign the direction of each unit to a deacon of his church. Each unit was composed of approximately fifty families who had requested aid from the church. The deacon in charge was to get to know each of the families, thoroughly investigate their situations, and help them solve the problems that had led to their state of dependency.[18] Chalmers is credited with conceiving the individualized approach and the person-centered philosophy that have become the central tenets of social work practice.

In 1819, five years after Chalmers began his work in Glasgow, a Unitarian clergyman, Joseph Tuckerman, was beginning similar work in Boston. Until failing health caused his retirement in 1833, Tuckerman pursued many projects in his efforts to better the condition of the poor. Bremner wrote that "housing, wages, education, delinquency, and relief all occupied his attention. From his 'Poor's Purse,' derived from contributions from wealthy supporters of his ministry, he gave charitable assistance to the needy. . . ."[19] In 1834, one year after his official retirement, Tuckerman began an association of more than twenty benevolent societies operating in Boston for the purpose of cooperation and coordination of services to the poor.

The COS movement, widely recognized as the parent of organized social work, began in England in 1869 and in the United States in 1877, building on the work of Chalmers and Tuckerman. In the United States a cleric was once again credited with the development of the COS—this time an Episcopalian, the Reverend S. Humphries Gurteen of Buffalo, New York. Gurteen was alarmed by what he perceived as the chaotic and indiscriminate approach to poor relief in Buffalo. He traveled to London and observed the work of the Charity Organization Society there; then he returned to the United States to implement a similar system. His basic goal was to set up a rational, objective system of poor relief, emphasizing the investigation of each individual case and the coordination of the activities of all charitable agencies to avoid duplication of services. In 1882, Gurteen stated the basic philosophy of the charity organization societies:

> If left to themselves . . . [the poor] will inevitably sink lower and lower, till perchance they end their course in suicide or felony. If . . . our charity is not tempered by judgment, they will inevitably learn to be *dependent*. . . . To avoid these two extremes, both of which are fatal, is the grand object of the Charity Organization Society. It views man as God has made him, with capabilities of manliness and self-respect and holy ambition. . . . Its axiom, accordingly, is, "HELP THE POOR TO HELP THEMSELVES."[20]

Unlike the work of Chalmers and Tuckerman, the COS movement was an immediate success. Within twenty years virtually every city of any size in the United States had a Charity Organization Society or an Associated Charities, as they were sometimes called. Interestingly, although begun by a minister and often directed and staffed by clergy, the charity organization societies always viewed themselves as secular and put their faith in science and professionalism, rather than in religion, as the solution to social problems.

Churches and the Settlement House Movement

The settlement house movement began in Victorian England as part of a broad attempt to preserve human and spiritual values in an age of urbanization and industrialization. The first settlement was Toynbee Hall, founded in 1884 by Canon Samuel A. Barnett. Barnett's idea was to have university graduates move into the worst area of London and get to know the people living there. He felt that university men were cut off from the real work of the world and that they were restless and needed to do something useful. On the other hand, he felt that working men were cut off from culture and civilization. Toynbee Hall was strongly Protestant in nature, and Barnett hoped that it would result in a spiritual reawakening in both the laborer and the university man.

Although it was founded in England by a clergyman and was strongly religious in nature, the settlement movement was imported to the United States by laypeople who had little interest in its religious aspects. Stanton Coit, a young American who had just finished a Ph.D. at the University of Berlin, visited Toynbee Hall in 1886, was greatly impressed with the concept, and returned to New York to found the Neighborhood Guild, the first settlement in the United States. Jane Addams visited Toynbee Hall in 1888 and returned to Chicago to found Hull House, the most famous settlement in the world.

The Neighborhood Guild and Hull House, like many settlements in the United States, were secular from the very beginning, and their focus was on social change rather than on spiritual goals.

Many other settlements, however, grew from religious roots. Probably the best known is Chicago Commons, founded by the Reverend Graham Taylor, who was the first professor of Christian sociology at Chicago Theological Seminary. He founded the settlement in 1894, partially as a social laboratory for his students. Although historians almost always characterize Taylor's work in the most positive light, the religious roots of the settlements are not always regarded so kindly. Mohl and Betten, for example, have written that

> most settlements were religious missions that reflected, acted upon, and transmitted the values and attitudes of the larger society; beyond their proselytizing activities, they adopted a derogatory view of ethnic traditions and assumed that their proper role was that of Americanizing the immigrant with all possible speed.[21]

The Church and the Institutional Roots of Social Work

Probably the most popular way of dealing with dependency during the early years of social welfare was the establishment of institutions such as orphanages, poorhouses, and

The provision of social welfare services is one of the main ways that churches express their concern for worldly problems.

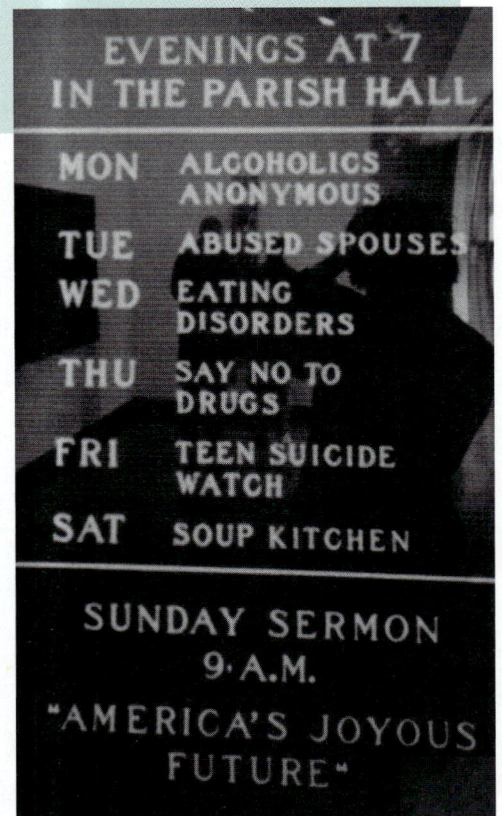

asylums. The church had a leading role in fostering this approach to social problems; it also had a leading role in seeking alternatives once the shortcomings of institutions became known.

Residential institutions for children and the aged in America were initially established by Catholic orders; the first was an orphanage opened by the Ursuline Sisters in New Orleans in 1727. "These early Catholic institutions were American transplants from established institutional networks maintained by Catholic sisterhoods in Europe. The European sisterhoods continued to be a source of the development of specialized residential institutions in this country, including such innovations as institutions providing protective care for girls," Reid writes.[22]

Many institutions were established by Lutherans, a group not often associated with early developments in social welfare. The person associated with the beginning of these activities was a German pastor, Johann Hinrich Wichern. Wichern worked in Hamburg's poorest area and became concerned about the great problems he was seeing that were related to industrialization and immigration. His first project was the opening of a home for delinquent boys, Das Rauhe Haus (The Rescue Home). Within a short time, people trained by Wichern had established "rescue homes" for alcoholics, the poor, seamen, and inner-city dwellers. Wichern's work, which came to be known as the "inner mission" of the church, was carried over into American Lutheranism by William Alfred Passavant, a pastor called to Pittsburgh in 1844. Shortly after coming to Pittsburgh, he visited Europe and observed the work of Wichern's followers. He returned to the United States and established a large number of orphanages, hospitals, homes for the aged, and other "rescue home"–type services.[23]

But it was not long before the shortcomings of institutions, especially those for children, were recognized. These institutions tended to be overcrowded, understaffed, impersonal, and generally ineffective in meeting the developmental needs of the residents. Thus, people began to look for alternatives almost as soon as the institutions were built. One of the earliest and best-known alternatives came from a churchman, the Reverend Charles Loring Brace, who established the Children's Aid Society in New York City in 1853. Brace's main idea was to remove orphan children from the streets of the city and, instead of sending them to an institution, to send them to the Midwest to be cared for by families. As discussed in greater detail in Chapter 10, Brace's program was subjected to harsh criticism both from his contemporaries and from historians. However, he should at least be credited with an idea that led to some real advances in child welfare.

As the preceding brief review indicates, the interest of social workers in religion, and the interest of religious people in social work, is hardly a new one. F. Ernest Johnson has gone so far as to say that the church is the "mother of social work." Reid argues that virtually all social work in the voluntary sector originated from religion. He states that today's voluntary social services either operate under religious auspices (sectarian services) or began under religious auspices and over time have become secularized.[24] It is to this secularization of social work that we now turn.

The Secularization of Social Work

Although religion has provided the philosophical basis for most social welfare activities, and although most modern social work agencies can trace their origins to religion, social work has always had a strong secular leaning. There is no evidence that S. Humphries Gurteen or Charles Loring Brace ever intended their agencies to be anything but secular. Graham Taylor envisioned his Christian sociology as rooted more firmly in science than in theology. Social work has evolved so far from its religious roots that Spencer has observed that "social work literature [is] almost totally lacking in any treatment of the subject of man's spiritual needs and practices and their interrelatedness with his other needs and adjustment."[25] Marty observed, "Secularization has many meanings, but at least it includes [among social workers] the notion that religion in both ideological and institutional senses has little part in informing the world of social work. . . . [M]ost of the time the literature of the profession genially and serenely ignores religion."[26] In a recent study, Cnaan investigated the coverage of religious issues by social work institutions and social service agencies. His methodology consisted of a content analysis of the abstracts of papers presented at social work meetings, abstracts of articles published in social work journals, textbooks used in social work education, course outlines used in schools of social work, and social work yearbooks and encyclopedias. He concluded "that all five methods and the evidence from the field of practice produced strikingly similar results: little or no mention of religious-based social services."[27]

Why did social work, with its clear and strong religious parentage, become so secular so quickly? There appear to be several factors that worked simultaneously over the twentieth century to accomplish this end. The most important factors are the general secularization of society, the growth of government within the field of social welfare, and (more speculatively) the development of the New Left and student movements of the 1960s and early 1970s.

The Secularization of Society. When we discuss the secularization of social work, we have to look at it within the context of a more general secularization of society. Scholars working in the area of the sociology of religion identify two general understandings of this phenomenon. The first is the assertion that (in Johnstone's words) beginning in the nineteenth century and continuing until the present time,

> there has been a displacement of religious interpretations of reality and religious orientations toward life by an orientation that seeks explanations for and justifications of human behavior and other phenomena in scientific and rational terms. One has undergone a secularization process if, for example, instead of asserting that marriages are made in heaven and

for eternity, he or she says that marriages are made by human beings, in time, on the basis of propinquity, and in response to biological and psychological needs.[28]

Because of the trend of secularization, people see fewer things as being explained in terms of "God's will," and they seek scientific, rational explanations for more of life's events.

The secularization process can be seen clearly in the history of social work. In the early years the causes of many types of dependency were believed to be related to moral factors. The charity organization societies, for example, felt that poverty was a result of a lack of abstinence, diligence, and thrift among the poor—all moral failings. After thousands of contacts with families of "exemplary piety" and diligence who were overwhelmed by circumstances beyond their control—abominable housing, illness, low wages, and unemployment—the COS people were forced to conclude that in many, and perhaps most, cases of dependency, morals had little to do with the problem. The failure of the moral explanation of problems made the problems, and hence social work, less religious and more secular. COS workers, as well as other social workers, quickly began to search for scientific explanations to replace the moral explanations of problems.

The second general understanding of secularization is that "it is a process of increasing differentiation between the religious and the secular (nonreligious) spheres of life—a process, moreover, coinciding with and perhaps in part resulting from increasing specialization within society as it grows and becomes more urbanized and industrialized."[29] This trend relates to the process of professionalization discussed in Chapter 3. During the twentieth century the ministry, like many other professions, has come to be considered a specialized profession. The specialty of ministers is now considered to be limited to worship and spiritual matters. Ministers who wish to engage in counseling, for example, are no longer considered to be qualified for this role simply by virtue of being ordained. They are expected to have training beyond the seminary level in either pastoral counseling or social work. At one time a person wanting to enter social work could do so by attending seminary. This is no longer true. If a person wants to enter social work, he or she must now attend a specialized social work school or program, which is generally located in a secular college or university.

The Growth of Government Services. When social work first began during the nineteenth century, virtually all services were privately funded, and the source of the great majority of funds was religious groups. Thus, most of social work occurred under religious auspices. During the twentieth century, government rapidly assumed responsibility for more and more social services. The biggest development in this process was the Social Security Act of 1935, which firmly established the federal government as the major source of social welfare funding. Currently more than 90 percent of social welfare funding in the United States comes from governmental sources. With the long-standing tradition of separation of church and state in the United States, the fact that most social workers work for government-funded programs virtually mandates the secularization of social work.

The New Left and the Student Movement of the 1960s and 1970s. The final reason for the secularization of social work is, admittedly, more speculative on the part of the authors, but we think it is valid. Although social work was considered to be a secular profession, for most of the twentieth century a large number of people who entered social work continued to do so out of religious motives. During the 1960s and 1970s, however, the social work profession grew at a tremendous rate, more than doubling in size. And among the reasons for this rapid growth was the fact that many young people of that generation viewed it as a "relevant" profession. That is, they saw it as related to the liberal, social change–oriented ethos that was characteristic of college-age people at that time. Thus a large, perhaps dominant, proportion of the huge cohort of new social workers was entering the profession out of political or ideological rather than religious motives. We speculate that this cohort brought fundamental changes to the nature of the social work profession. Among these changes was the completion of the process of secularization that had been evolving for most of the profession's history.

The Reversal of Secularization?

Although it is a difficult speculation to prove, there are indicators that the trend toward secularization in society in general, and in social welfare and social work in particular, is slowing and perhaps even reversing. In society in general, the clearest indicator seems to be the large amount of growth that conservative churches have been experiencing.[30] At the same time that conservative churches have been growing, mainline churches have experienced a decline in membership. This decline appears to be related to these churches' growing attention to secular social issues and decreasing concern with basic questions of faith and evangelism.[31] Another indicator is found in data collected on a regular basis by the Gallup organization for the Princeton Religious Research Center. The responses to two questions that Gallup polls have asked periodically since the early 1950s are summarized in Figure 6.1. Figure 6.1 shows the percentages of respondents who believe that religious influence is increasing or decreasing in U.S. life. The number who felt that the influence of religion was increasing declined from 69 percent in 1957 to 27 percent in 1991. Table 6.1 reports people's assessment of the importance of religion in their own lives. The number of people who stated that religion was very important declined from 75 percent in 1952 to 55 percent in 1991. However, beginning in 1991 there seems to have been a reversal of this trend. Between 1991 and 2002 the number of people reporting a belief that religious influence was increasing grew from 27 percent to 43 percent. Similarly, the number reporting that religion is very important in their lives grew from 55 percent in 1991 to 61 percent in 1997, dropping back slightly to 60 percent in 1998.

In social welfare in general, the reversal of secularization has been forced by the trend in government in recent years—beginning first with the Reagan administration; continuing under George Bush; to the surprise of many social workers, unvarying under Bill Clinton; and accelerating under George W. Bush—to abdicate responsibility for social welfare. The argument that social welfare is "the historic mission of the churches" has been used as the justification for cutting government programs. Since early in the Reagan administration, the stance of government has been that it should do less and the churches should do more, because social welfare is really the proper role of the

FIGURE 6.1 Is Religion Increasing or Losing Its Influence on American Life?

*This brief discontinuity in the trend is attributed to a reaction to the 9/11 terrorist attacks.

Source: The Gallup Poll Tuesday Briefings (24 December 2002), 12.

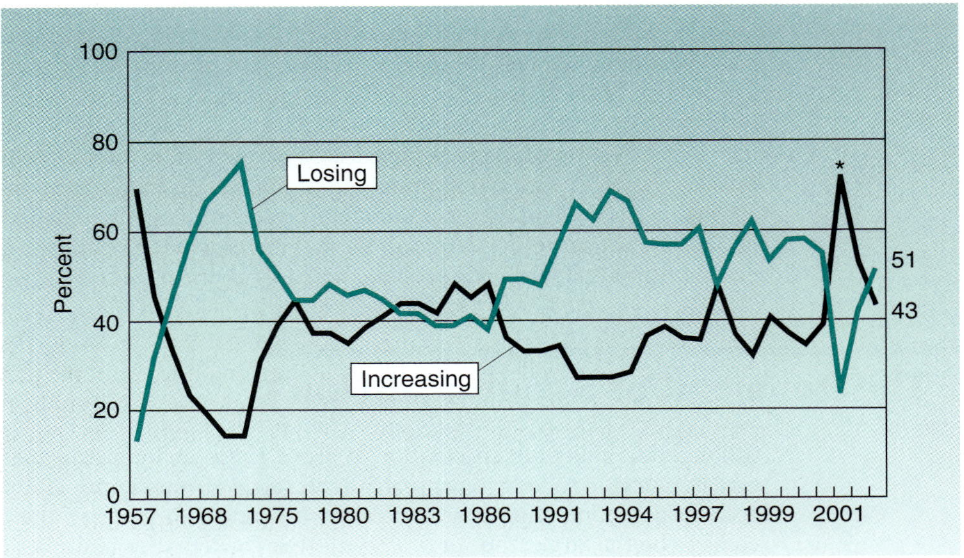

TABLE 6.1 Importance of Religion in People's Own Lives

	Very	Fairly	Not Very	No Opinion		Very	Fairly	Not Very	No Opinion
1998	60%	27%	12%	1%	*1987*	53%	32%	14%	1%
1997	61	27	11	1	*1986*	55	30	14	1
1996	55	31	13	1	*1985*	55	31	13	1
1995	58	30	11	1	*1984*	56	30	13	1
1994	59	29	11	1	*1983*	56	30	13	1
1993	59	32	9	•	*1982*	56	30	13	1
1992	59	28	12	1	*1981*	56	29	14	1
1991	55	29	15	1	*1980*	55	31	13	1
1990	58	29	13	•	*1978*	52	32	14	2
1989	55	30	14	1	*1965*	70	22	7	1
1988	54	31	14	1	*1952*	75	20	5	•

•Less than 0.5%.

Source: The Gallup Poll Monthly, online at www.gallup.com/poll/news/970329.html. Used by permission.

church rather than of government.[32] Unfortunately, although churches are aware of the challenge, it is plain that they are not up to meeting it. A survey by the Council on Foundations reported that churches felt "inundated since the federal budget cuts, in 1983 receiving the largest volume of requests for aid in their history. Several warned that no methods could come close to replacing government funds and that religious organizations would never be able to take over the role of government in meeting human needs."[33] A recent Gallup poll included the interesting finding that the majority of Americans do not agree that social welfare is the responsibility of the churches; most consider it to be the responsibility of government (see Figure 6.2).

The government moved from rhetoric to action in 1996 with the passage of the Personal Responsibility and Work Opportunity Reconciliation Act. Section 104 of this act, known as Charitable Choice, makes it possible for religion-based organizations and congregations to receive public funds for the provision of social services. It has always been possible for religious organizations to receive public funds, but in the past they were required to strictly separate their religious activities from the publicly funded program. Under Section 104 a religious organization can receive public funding for a program even if that program has explicitly religious content. For example, a church can now receive public funding for a job placement program that requires prayer and Scripture reading as part of the job search strategy, or a church can provide problem pregnancy services that include instruction on biblical injunctions against abortion. In the seven years since the passage of this law, very few congregations or religious organizations have taken advantage of it. It appears that many religious leaders fear that if congregations become government-funded service providers this may have the unintended effect of stamping out the voluntary spirit that distinguishes American congregations and will result in rigid bureaucratic programs replacing flexible voluntary ones. There also seems to be a fear on the part of many leaders that, in spite of the spirit of Section 104, there is a high risk of arbitrary, unfair treatment by the government. Although Charitable Choice is off to a slow start, there is little doubt that it will grow and gain in influence in the future.[34]

In the social work profession there is also evidence of a reversal of the trend toward secularization. One indicator is the establishment and growth of a professional organization specifically devoted to the interests of Christians in social work, the North American Association of Christians in Social Work. This organization currently has more than a thousand members, holds a well-attended annual convention, and publishes a journal, *Social Work and Christianity.* There is also a journal devoted to the interests of Catholics in social work, *Social Thought,* and one devoted to the interests of Jews, the *Journal of Jewish Communal Service.* Another indicator of the renewed interest of social workers in religion is the topics chosen for journal articles and doctoral dissertations. In the 1960s and early 1970s, one rarely encountered an article or dissertation dealing with a topic related to religion. In recent years this too has changed, and we find, often in mainline journals, articles dealing with topics such as religious content in social work education, the relationship of clients' spirituality to various practice issues, and liberation theology, as well as many others.[35] Social work educators have begun to demonstrate a renewed interest in the subject of religion, with articles being published on religion in social work education, religion as a component of both micro- and macropractice courses, and spirituality as an important component in human behavior courses.[36] Several recently published books are apparently designed as supplementary

FIGURE 6.2 **Survey Results on the Issue of Responsibility for Social Welfare in the United States**

Source: George Gallup and D. Michael Lindsey, *Surveying the Religious Landscape: Trends in U.S. Beliefs* (Harrisburg, PA: Morehouse, 1999), 135. Reprinted by permission.

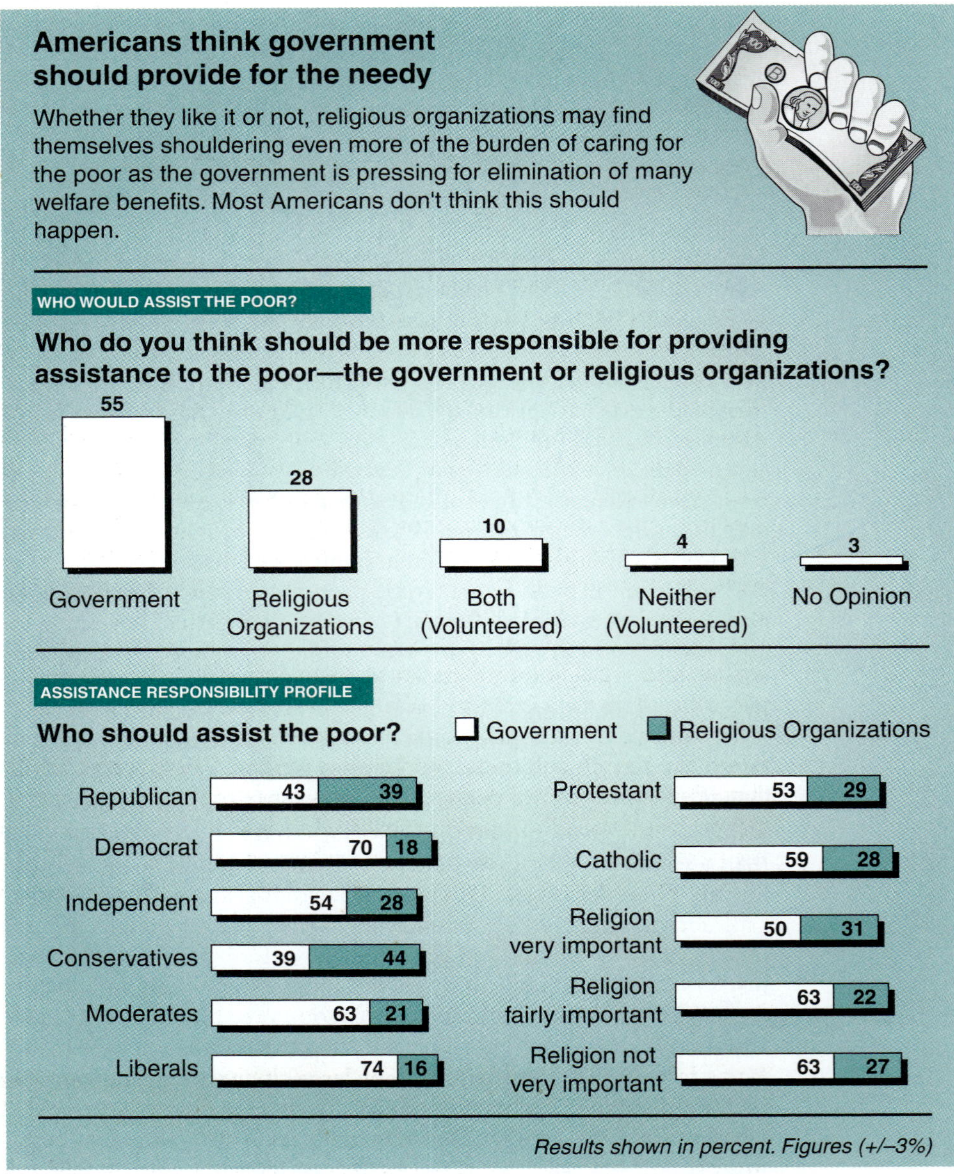

texts for the purpose of introducing religion and spirituality content into social work practice courses.[37] We are also witnessing doctoral degrees being granted by major graduate schools of social work for dissertations on topics such as the development of social responsibility among Lutherans, evangelical Christianity and social work, a Christian interpretation of humanity for social work, a conceptualization of spirituality for social work, the relationship of social work to religion and the church, and a quantitative analysis of social workers' clinical decisions regarding religious and spiritual issues in direct practice.[38]

Another indicator has been the development of social work education programs with a religious focus. On the undergraduate level, programs in "Bible social work" have been developed and accredited by the Council on Social Work Education at schools such as Eastern College and the Philadelphia College of the Bible. On the graduate level, schools of social work and theological seminaries are cooperating in offering joint degree programs. The University of Texas at Arlington and Southwestern Baptist Theological Seminary have such a program; it enables a student to earn both a Master of Social Work degree and a Master of Arts in Ministry-Based Evangelism degree at the same time. At least one conservative religious university, Andrews University (which is affiliated with the Seventh-Day Adventist Church), has developed an accredited MSW program. Baylor University, affiliated with the Southern Baptist Convention, has established an MSW program with church social work as one specialization.

Finally, data now indicate an awareness of the importance of religion/spirituality in social work practice. Practicing social workers surveyed by Furman and Chandy in 1994 reported that they were encountering religious and spiritual issues in 33 percent of their caseloads. Of licensed practicing social workers, 52 percent felt it was important to deal with the religious/spiritual issues of their clients, and 50 percent felt that religious and spiritual issues should be part of the social work curriculum.[39]

It would be a mistake to interpret these developments as an indication that social welfare and social work will return to being primarily religious endeavors. If for no reason other than their immense size, social welfare and social work in the United States will continue to be largely secular enterprises. However, there is a natural alliance between the church and social work/social welfare. These recent trends seem to indicate that after some years of neglect, the importance of this alliance is once again being recognized; and the alliance will probably continue to develop in a productive manner. In the next section, we turn to a brief examination of services provided by agencies with a connection to organized religion, generally known as *sectarian agencies.*

Current Sectarian Services

If you look in the yellow pages of any large city under the heading "Social Services," the enduring religious connection of social welfare is clearly illustrated. Take, for example, Charlotte, North Carolina. Out of 84 agencies listed, 16 have names that clearly indicate some formal religious ties. Listed are the Jewish Federation, Bethlehem Center, Crisis Assistance Ministry, Second Harvest Food Bank, and 12 other sectarian agencies. Or look at agencies funded by the United Way, a clearly secular organization. A 1996 report by that body states:

> The secular United Way funds the following sectarian services in local communities nationwide: 717 religious Family Service Agencies such as Catholic Family Services, Lutheran Family Services and Jewish Family Services in communities around the country receive United Way allocations for "non-religious" service provision; 1,273 Salvation Army agencies with community-based secular programs are allocated funds and the funds comprise 14% of their budgets. It should be pointed out that the Salvation Army is a church. A combined 1,902 YMCAs and YWCAs receive United Way funding, and the funds comprise 6 percent and 14 percent of their budgets, respectively.[40]

It is not possible to give accurate figures on the number of sectarian agencies in the United States. As Reid has noted, "Data on numbers and types of sectarian organizations are, at best, fragmentary, and at worst, misleading.[41] One thing that is clear, however, is that sectarian agencies provide an immense amount of services. An example of the size and scope of these organizations is Catholic Charities, a network of services comprising more than 1,400 organizations, using nearly 283,000 staff and volunteers, serving more than 12 million people annually, and with a budget of $2.1 billion. These agencies provide nearly every type of social work service.[42] The best figures currently available on the number of sectarian agencies come from a now somewhat dated study conducted by Netting, who surveyed the national headquarters of religious groups in the United States to obtain the number of social service agencies affiliated with each group. Approximately 14,000 agencies were reported to be affiliated with national religious groups. Netting explains that this is an underestimate of the total number of sectarian agencies because it does not include those that are not affiliated with a national body.[43]

We should also note that sectarian agencies have differing degrees of relatedness to the religious groups with which they are affiliated. Reid posits a sectarian–secular continuum,[44] varying on criteria such as degree of control exercised by the parent religious body, the amount of financial support derived from sectarian sources, the proportion of board members who are of the faith, the extent to which decisions of the board and administration are guided by religious considerations, the amount of religious content in agency programs, and the religious identification of the agency's clientele. At the sectarian end of the continuum might be a Catholic adoption program that is funded entirely by Catholic sources; has a board consisting only of church members; provides services mainly to pregnant, unmarried, church-affiliated women; and will place children only in Catholic homes. At the secular end of the continuum might be a United Methodist community center that began as a settlement house with strong church ties but over the years has evolved to the point where the board is only nominally United Methodist; the staff is hired on the basis of professional credentials with no consideration of church affiliation; funding comes mainly from the United Way and government sources with only a very small percentage coming from the Methodist church; and the clients reflect the changing character of the neighborhood in which the center is located, which is currently not very Methodist.

For the reasons discussed earlier, the data on the services provided by churches are sketchy and fragmentary, at best. Two recent surveys of social services provided by religious congregations give some indication of the size and scope of these activities. Table 6.2 summarizes the results of a survey of congregations in a midsize U.S. city conducted

TABLE 6.2

Services Provided by 128 Congregations in a Midsize American City

	Program Characteristics					
Service	**Formal**	**Informal**	**For Members of Congregation Only**	**Fee Charged**	**Open to the Community**	**Fee Charged**
Emergency food	18	56	5	1	39	2
Clothing	20	40	7	2	30	2
Congregate meals	8	6	9	2	6	2
Soup kitchen	7	4	4	1	1	1
Emergency shelter	3	11	2	2	2	2
Cash	30	31	12	0	27	0
Mobile meals	22	8	1	0	9	0
Personal counseling	27	37	17	0	25	0
Family counseling	19	31	16	0	19	0
Phone reassurance	11	21	12	0	11	0
Transportation	3	15	11	1	8	0
Housework for disabled	2	8	7	0	1	0
Housework for elderly	2	9	7	0	1	0
Home health care	4	3	2	0	2	1
Food preparation	6	11	6	1	3	0
Legal help	3	7	5	0	2	0
Help find service	12	23	7	0	11	0
Child care	16	4	4	2	8	6
After-school care	12	4	3	2	7	5
Adult day care	1	1	1	0	1	0
Tutoring	6	4	1	0	6	0
Employment help	5	12	4	0	4	0
Pregnancy counseling	7	8	4	0	5	0
Foster care	3	1	0	0	2	0
Alcoholics Anonymous	23	3	2	0	10	2
Alateen	6	0	2	0	1	1
Narcotics Anonymous	8	0	0	0	3	0
Overeaters Anonymous	4	1	0	0	3	0
Mental health	4	0	0	0	1	0

Source: Robert V. Winburg, "Local Human Services Provision by Religious Congregations: A Community Analysis," *Nonprofit and Voluntary Sector Quarterly 21* (Summer 1992), 112. Used by permission.

TABLE 6.3

Monthly Replacement Value of an Average Program and Congregational Social and Community Programs (N = 3,316)

Source	Percentage of Programs Reporting Cost	Average Cost per Program ($)		Average Cost per Congregation ($)
Financial support by the congregation	53.8	610.34	(1,914.3)	1,470.92
Value of in-kind support	58.1	235.27	(897.7)	567.00
Value of utilities for program	59.7	258.91	(774.3)	623.97
Estimated value of space used for the program	68.1	814.42	(1,747.8)	1,962.75
Number of clergy hours (@ $20)	59.5	317.67	(1,395.1)	765.58
Number of staff hours (@ $10)	29.7	449.17	(391.7)	1,082.50
Number of volunteer hours (@ $11.58)	78.8	1,512.38	(2,341.8)	3,644.84
Total		4,198.16		10,117.76
Income to the congregation	9.6	123.11	(221.2)	296.70
Total net replacement value		4,075.05		9,821.06

Source: Ram A. Cnaan and Stephanie Boddie, "Philadelphia Census of Congregations and Their Involvement in Social Services Delivery," *Social Service Review 75* (December 2001). Reprinted by permission of the University of Chicago Press.

by Robert Winburg in 1992. Table 6.3 summarizes the results of a 2001 survey, conducted by Cnaan and Boddie, of social services provided by religious congregations in Philadelphia. In contrast to an earlier Council on Foundations survey, which concluded that congregations prefer "hard" services such as soup kitchens and clothing closets to "soft" services such as mental health counseling and support groups, the surveys by Winburg and Cnaan and Boddie found both types of services to be fairly equally represented. Regardless of the type of services provided, one thing is made abundantly clear by these studies: Religious congregations are major players in the provision of social services. Cnaan and Boddie's estimation of the cash value of the services provided by congregations in Philadelphia, summarized in Table 6.4, is that the annual replacement value of these services would be $246,901,440.[45]

Social Work and Religion—Uneasy Bedfellows

The discussion so far has demonstrated that there is a definite and complex relationship between social work and religion. In addition, the relationship, which weakened for many years, is showing signs of intensifying. The reader is justified at this point in ask-

TABLE 6.4

Thirty Examples of 215 Services Provided by Congregations in Philadelphia (Percentage of Congregations Providing Service)

Type of Service	Total (%)	Type of Service	Total (%)
Drug and alcohol prevention	14.1	Community bazaars and fairs	19.2
Neighborhood cleanup	14.1	Neighborhood associations	20.3
Blood drives	14.2	After-school care	20.4
Job counseling and placement	14.3	Programs for gang members	20.9
Street outreach to the homeless	14.3	Choral groups	20.9
Mentoring/rites of passage	14.8	Prison ministry	21.2
Computer training (for youth)	15.4	Visitation/buddy program	21.8
Health screening	15.4	International relief	22.3
Crime watch	15.4	Educational tutoring	24.0
Parenting skills	15.8	Soup kitchens	24.1
Scout troops	16.5	Music performances	26.2
Health education	16.9	Summer programs for teens	27.4
Interfaith collaboration	17.0	Clothing closets	33.8
Premarriage counseling	17.5	Recreational programs for teens	35.0
Day care (preschool)	17.6	Recreational programs for children	35.5
Shelter for homeless people	17.9	Summer day camp	38.2
Marriage encounters (retreats)	17.9	Food pantries	46.8
Recreational programs for seniors	18.3		

Sources: Ram A. Cnaan and Stephanie Boddie, "Philadelphia Census of Congregations and Their Involvement in Social Services Delivery," *Social Service Review 75* (December 2001). Reprinted by permission of the University of Chicago Press.

ing, "So what's the big deal? For this you spend a whole chapter?" The "big deal" is that the relationship between social work and religion is by no means problem free, as the following situation illustrates.

> In an earlier time Penny might have become a nun. She had been reared in a conservative and devout Catholic family and had grown up with the idea that her role in life was to serve the church and her fellow human beings. When she took a social work class during her first year of college, she felt she had found her calling. She did her senior field placement at Catholic Social Services and hoped to be offered a job on graduation. However, no positions were available at CSS and so she went to work for the local public health clinic as a social worker. She loved her job and felt she was doing what she was meant to do. That is, until this morning.

Penny stared numbly at the doctor's referral before her. The doctor had written: "I am referring for counseling Monica Freeman, white female, age thirteen years five months. Patient is pregnant, still in the first trimester. Please explore options with patient and her parents. Medically, the obvious choice is abortion. This child is not mature enough physically or emotionally to go through a pregnancy and birth."

Penny went to her supervisor for help. Pointing to a framed document on the wall, her supervisor said, "Well, Penny. You're aware that this clinic subscribes to the NASW Code of Ethics." She turned to the document, reading out loud the sections that state, "The social worker should provide clients with accurate and complete information regarding the extent and nature of the services available to them" and "The social worker should make every effort to foster maximum self-determination on the part of clients." After reading the items from the code, Penny's supervisor added some clarification, saying, "This means that you don't need to actually advocate for an abortion as the physician apparently wants you to, but it does mean that you need to make the family aware that it is an option, and do all you can to help them reach their own decision, not yours."

Penny replied, "I understand that, but you must realize that my religion teaches that abortion is murder, regardless of the fact that it is legal. I could no more help those people obtain an abortion than I could help them go upstairs to the nursery and murder one of the babies." The supervisor ended the discussion by saying, "OK, Penny, I'll assign this case to one of the other social workers. However, working in a public clinic you'll run into situations like this fairly often, and I'll not always be able to get you off the hook. You need to resolve this within yourself, and if you can't, you'll need to look for work in a setting where you won't face this dilemma."

In this section we discuss the major areas of potential conflict between social work and religion. To be more precise, we talk about the relationship between social work and Christianity. The other major religion active in social work in the United States, Judaism, has always had a more comfortable relationship with social work than has Christianity. There are two reasons for this. The first is that "as far as Judaism is concerned, there [is] little competition between religious and secular understandings of social work." Also, "from the first, American Jewish social service was relatively independent of the synagogue, while Christian effort grew from the churches."[46] The second reason is that Jews have no equivalent of the Great Commission. Thus, they are under no obligation to seek converts to their faith. As the number of people in the United States identifying themselves as Muslim has rapidly increased, the profession has begun to consider its relation to Islamic theology.[47] However, at the present time only a little work has been done on this increasingly important subject.

We now consider several broad issues. The first is whether the church has any business being involved in social welfare in the first place. Next, we consider the problems resulting from conservative religion and the social change mission of social work. We conclude with a discussion of the general question of the fit between religious values and social work values.

Should the Church Be Involved in Social Work and Social Welfare?

There are those both in the church and in the social work profession who do not feel that the church should be involved in social welfare. From the perspective of the church, this is an issue that assumed more importance in the past than it does now. The major argument is that the church should be concerned with saving souls, not with redeeming society. The colorful nineteenth-century evangelist Billy Sunday is quoted by Marty as having said, "The road to the kingdom of God is not by the bathtub or the gymnasium [two common services provided by social welfare agencies of the time], nor the university, but by the blood red hand of the cross of Christ." Sunday criticized Christian social welfare agencies of the time, such as the YMCA, because "they have taken up sociology and settlement work but are not winning souls to Christ." He was overheard by a reporter to say, "We've had enough of this godless social service nonsense. I'll go with you in eugenics, in social service, oyster soup, and institutional churches, but when you leave Jesus Christ out of it, good night."[48] Very few people in the church are concerned with this today, but it does still occasionally pop up. For example, an essay in *Evangelical Missions Quarterly* suggested that social service directed toward community development "probably is the greatest foe of Christianity." Sanzanbach speculates that "it is probable that a fundamentalist review of leading social work textbooks, journals, or proceedings of national conferences and meetings would conclude that, despite the profession's good intentions, social work is hopelessly infused with the atheistic doctrines of secular humanism."[49] Loewenberg observes that "some ministers view social workers as competitors. They are especially concerned that nonreligious social workers provide help that they believe to be incompatible with the teachings of their church."[50] Finally, on becoming president of Southern Baptist Theological Seminary, the Reverend Al Mohler, in a statement reminiscent of Billy Sunday, said that "he did not see how a school based on the New Testament teachings of Jesus could stand or support a school of social work." Three years later the seminary's well-regarded Carver School of Social Work was shut down.[51]

Few people on the social work side of the relationship feel that, as a general principle, social work and religion are not compatible. The only general concern is that many persons, probably a majority of the profession, feel that the mission of social work is to become an empirically based, scientific profession, and they fear that religion, which they often associate with dogma, will retard this development. Imre observes:

> The tendency to equate dogmatism with religion . . . can be seen to be rooted in the history of science. The development of logical positivism is intertwined with this history. Academic social work, where much of the current literature originates, is still very much committed to the positivistic definition of science. [The social work profession's] hidden assumptions, such as that all religion is dogmatic and ideological, continue to operate, even while recognition is given to the roots of [social work] values in religious and moral tradition.[52]

Conservative Religion and Social Change

Many within social work are uncomfortable with what we discussed earlier as the reversal of secularization. This discomfort is a result not of disapproval of religion, but of disapproval of a particular kind of religion. Social workers are generally very comfortable with mainline liberal Protestant, Catholic, and Jewish faith. However, many people now entering social work out of religious motivation are coming from somewhere else. They are generally perceived as being "conservative," "fundamentalist," or "evangelical." Mike Elliott, a social worker on the staff of a Baptist church in Kentucky, relates the following:

> [C]hurch related social workers are often considered "unclean" by secular social workers. It seems as if I was regarded as an evangelist who had the ulterior motive of conversion in mind for my clients. I was pegged a social work evangelist who, with or without hair spray or wing-tipped shoes, only used social work to rack up conversions.[53]

However, the concern of secular social workers goes deeper than a fear that social workers with conservative religious orientations will use their profession to evangelize. The major concern is that conservative religion goes hand in hand with conservative politics and will tend to blunt, or even thwart, the social change mission of social work.

Social workers are not the only people who fear that conservative religion will hamper efforts at achieving a just society. Magnuson writes:

> When Ernest Fremont Tittle, the noted liberal preacher, wrote more than three decades ago that "Evangelical religion" could never hope to produce a humane social order, he gave voice to what has been the opinion of many throughout the present century. Tittle thought that evangelicals had since the reformation era habitually sanctioned the social order and refused "to cry out against social injustice," thus clearly demonstrating the social impotence of a gospel of individual salvation.[54]

Is this the case? Is conservative Christianity incompatible with the social change aspect of social work? The answer, found mainly in the writings of Christian social workers, is interesting. It is that yes, this is often the case; but no, it should not and need not be.

The criticism of conservative Christianity as being opposed to social change has some justification, and Christian social workers are the first to admit this. Keith-Lucas says that the Christian is "looked on with suspicion by social work educators, and most rightly, too." The reason for this suspicion is "the noninvolvement in human problems that can all too easily accompany a religion that has metaphysical or otherworldly interests."[55] Speaking of the renewed interest in social change that emerged in social work in the 1960s, Kuhlmann observes, "Christians, particularly those holding an evangelical viewpoint, have tended to resist these trends, both in social work as well as in the larger society."[56] Van Hook observes that "despite biblical mandates to support a social justice agenda, the church and Christian community have frequently supported and legitimized a status quo that created and supported inequalities."[57] Speaking specifically of social work's interest in gender equity for the sexes, Faver and Hunter report that some students "have reacted with indifference or hostility to curriculum content on women's issues. And, alarmingly, some of those most strongly opposed to this material openly assert incompatibility of the material with their Christian beliefs. . . . They counter the notions of freedom and equality by maintaining that the Bible teaches women to be subordinate to men, and to confine their activity primarily to homemaking, childrearing, and volunteer work."[58]

Why have conservative Christians tended to resist social change? Eckardt traces the problem to the development of "higher criticism" of the Bible, which developed in Europe during the first half of the nineteenth century, and to the growth of the ideologies of communism and socialism during the late nineteenth and early twentieth centuries.

Basically, higher criticism refers to the intellectual analysis of the Scriptures, which includes interpreting them in relation to the social and historical context in which they were written, as well as to the motivations of their authors. The bottom line is that the Scriptures are viewed as God-inspired but written by humans and, therefore, fallible. The hallmark of conservative, or evangelical, Christians is their belief that the Scriptures represent the actual word of God and are thus infallible and therefore not open to interpretation by mere humans. A popular bumper sticker reflecting this attitude reads: "God said it; I believe it; That settles it!" As a result of higher criticism, fundamentalist Christians became preoccupied with defending their faith, and this has tended to cause them to withdraw from worldly concerns such as social justice and equality. The great theological debates among conservative Christians during the late nineteenth and early twentieth centuries centered on the "fundamentals" of faith rather than on any social issues. Social issues became the territory of the liberal sects; this made them even less attractive to the fundamentalists, who rejected "anything associated with liberal theology [because they] feared that if part of it was bad all the rest would soon be contaminated."[59]

The second reason for the rejection of social change by conservative Christians is the development of the ideologies of communism and socialism. These ideologies, particularly communism, are often militant in their rejection of religion in general and Christianity in particular. This led to "an alignment of evangelical Christianity with conservative politics and economics. There developed an unquestioned acceptance of capitalism as the Christian's economy and of democracy as God's political preference."[60] This acceptance of the political status quo as being ordained by God has resulted in evangelical Christians viewing any effort to change the social system as being, by definition, against the will of God.

Numerous writers have pointed out that the identification of conservative Christians with a reactionary position on social change is strange because, historically, evangelicals have been heavily involved in social change, with their activities often exceeding those of their liberal counterparts. Magnuson did an in-depth study of evangelical social work from 1865 to 1920. He found that although liberals talked about social change and conservative Christians tended to avoid such rhetoric, when actual behaviors were studied, it was the evangelicals who had the greater record of social change activities. He observes,

> No matter how troublesome the persons they helped—former prisoners, prostitutes, unwed mothers, vagrants, or the unemployed—revivalists accepted them with openness and warmth. Placing the blame largely on environmental pressures, rescue workers argued that given a proper chance even the most difficult persons would perform creditably. Frederick Booth-Tucker, commander of the Salvation Army in the United States from 1896 to 1903, estimated that 90 percent or more of the unemployed would gladly work if they had the opportunity. That kind of optimistic acceptance generally characterized these organizations.[61]

Magnuson contrasts this attitude with that of many liberal religious reformers, such as Washington Gladden, whose attitude was often somewhat harsh, advocating that applicants for assistance should be treated with "prison-like restraint."[62]

The attitude of Christian social workers writing today is clearly that the identification of conservative Christianity with conservative politics, although often a fact, has been a sort of historical accident and is really based on a misinterpretation of faith. Keith-Lucas says, "these are not actually beliefs in the Judeo-Christian or Biblical tradition. They are

What **Americans** Believe

In the 2002 General Social Survey (GSS), the researchers included a module that asked questions that were then converted into scales measuring altruism and empathy. The altruism scale was based on questions in the module asking respondents about fifteen different acts of altruism they may have performed, such as talking with someone who is depressed, helping with housework, giving up a seat to a stranger, giving money to charity, volunteering, helping someone find a job, or helping in other ways such as lending money. The empathy scale was developed by asking respondents seven self-assessment questions such as "I often have tender, concerned feelings for people less fortunate than me," and "When I see someone being taken advantage of, I feel kind of protective toward them."

This module revealed that the most significant relationship of both the empathy and the altruism scale was with religion. Those who reported themselves to be religious tended to have higher scores on both the altruism and the empathy scales. There was also a strong relationship between these variables and the frequency of church attendance, with scores on the scales increasing with increased attendance.

Before he began the study, Tom W. Smith, director of the General Social Survey, said that he expected to find that people who are more socially involved, and people who support spending on social welfare programs, would be found to be the most empathic and altruistic groups. He found that these attitudes, however, were only weakly associated with altruism and empathy, of much less importance than religiousness and church

FIGURE 6.3 **Church Attendance**

Source: University of Chicago News Office Press Release, "Americans Practice What They Hear Preached: Going to Services Leads to More Charity, University of Chicago Study Shows," July 2003. Reprinted by permission of the National Opinion Research Center, University of Chicago.

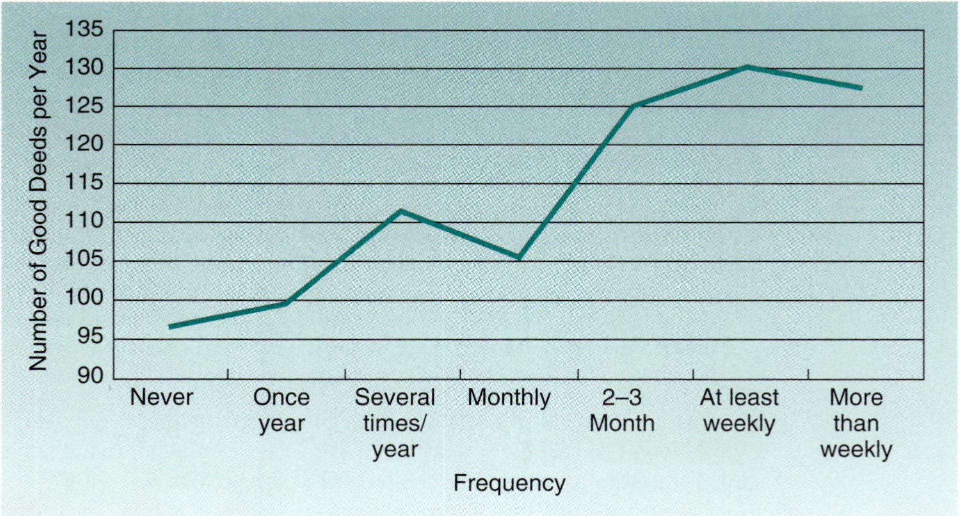

attendance. "The connection between good deeds and religion probably indicates that people are reflecting the religious teachings of charity that are central beliefs of most major religions," Smith said. "For most religions, an important part of the belief system is an admonition to love other people and to do good deeds. The people who attend weekly services hear that quite a lot. . . . Also, people in a religious congregation are nested in a community that provides them with opportunities to do good deeds and reach out to others."

The relationships between altruism and church attendance and altruism and religiousness are illustrated in Figures 6.3 and 6.4.

In this chapter we make the argument that religion and social work are natural allies. This module of the GSS provides strong support for this argument.

Source: Tom W. Smith, "Altruism in Contemporary America: A Report from the National Altruism Study," report prepared for the Fetzer Institute by the National Opinion Research Center/University of Chicago (25 July 2003); "Americans Practice What They Hear Preached: Going to Services Leads to More Charity, University of Chicago Study Shows," press release, The University of Chicago News Office (25 July 2003).

FIGURE 6.4 **Religiousness**

Source: University of Chicago News Office Press Release, "Americans Practice What They Hear Preached: Going to Services Leads to More Charity, University of Chicago Study Shows," July 2003. Reprinted by permission of the National Opinion Research Center, University of Chicago.

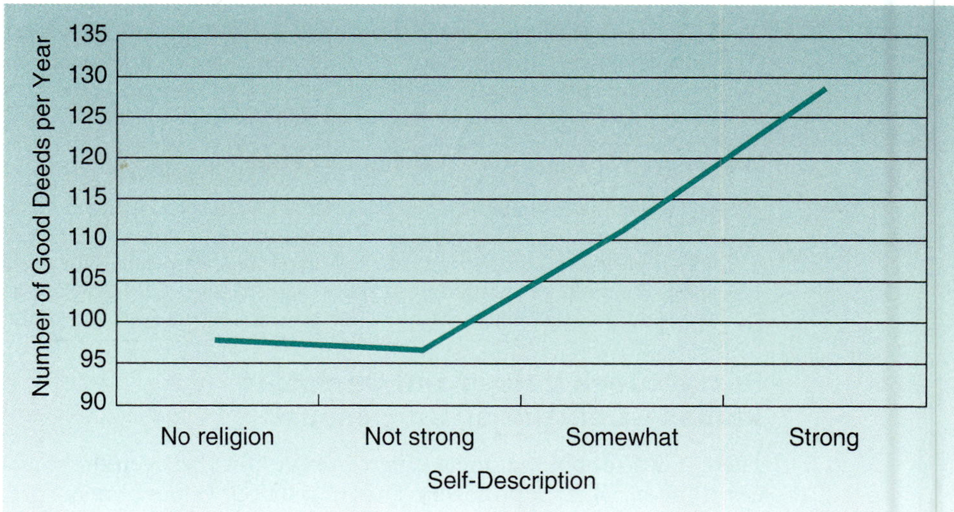

perversions of these beliefs in the capitalist–puritan set of assumptions."[63] Kuhlmann says, "such a view [that social action is not good], although it is quite prevalent in the contemporary evangelical community, and also reflects much that is consistent with Biblical Christianity, is not fully Christian, in the sense that it does not reflect the whole of Biblical truth on the subject."[64] Moberg asserts that concern among Christians for individual salvation at the expense of social change "leaves out significant aspects of the teaching of the Bible. It easily results in loving only 'our own brethren,' avoiding needy neighbors in our own community and other parts of the world, . . . and it reflects paying greater attention to cultural values than to biblical norms."[65]

In an interesting article, theologian Richard F. Lovelace argues that revival movements have historically begun with concentration on individual salvation and have then moved into a period of emphasis on social change. He argues that the United States is in the early stages of a great religious awakening and predicts that it will eventually move into an era of social change based on this awakening.[66] The foundation for this has been identified as a 1973 meeting that took place among evangelical leaders during which they wrote "A Declaration of Evangelical Social Concern."[67] The survey of philanthropic activities by organized religion conducted by the Council on Foundations found that groups who identified themselves as conservative were funding social justice activities "just like [their] non-conservative brethren."[68]

To sum up this section, we refer to Ralph Eckardt, a well-known figure among Christian social workers. Eckardt makes two general points regarding Christianity and social action. The first is that political involvement is a legitimate activity for Christian social workers. The second is that conservative Christianity is not synonymous with conservative politics. Eckardt says,

> I am a patriotic American and support the democratic way of life, but it is not God breathed. I also assert my allegiance to Jesus Christ. The two are very important to me but they are not synonymous. In this regard my allegiance to Jesus Christ stands above any other and I must serve Him primarily and I assert my obligation to criticize this or any government, when what it does is not in consonance with the revealed will of God.[69]

In a similar vein, the British social worker Robert Holman says,

> So I argue that Christians in general and Christian social workers in particular should have a collective voice to address society. Its support for the poor might seem to lean towards the left, its views on the sanctity of life and marriage towards the right. It belongs to no political party. It should be an attempt to show that a distinct Christian opinion can be expressed about those social issues which confront social workers every day of the week.[70]

Social Work Values and Christian Values—Conflict or Consensus?

There is little doubt that there is perceived conflict between the secular, humanistic values of the social work profession and the religious values of many practitioners. Eckardt describes

> the preconceived notion on behalf of many in the profession that social work and religion do not mix. More specifically, this attitude suggests that if a person is a committed evangelical Christian his values are so different from those of the social work profession as to render

> him an unacceptable, or at least second rate, practitioner in the field. Most professionals would deny this discrimination and bias; but as an evangelical I have felt it when I have applied for positions in the profession, sought further education, or attended gatherings of professionals discussing professional issues.[71]

In a study of social work in church-related agencies, Netting found that church representatives feared that "spiritual values will be sacrificed on the altar of professional know-how," while social workers felt that religion interfered with maintaining a nonjudgmental attitude.[72] Buckner observes concerns in the profession that emerging issues such as abortion, gay and lesbian rights, and increasing numbers of non-Christian immigrants "may threaten the beginning social worker's ability to recognize the professional values of self-determination and unconditional positive regard in their dealings with clients whose religious beliefs differ from their own."[73] Pellebon studied members of three nondenominational evangelical churches and found that "statistically significant findings indicate that this sample both perceives a high degree of conflict with social work and disagrees with humanistic interpretations of social work values."[74]

This conflict of values has grown out of the process of secularization of the profession. Siporin, in an article that is sharply critical of the profession, asserts that social work was once based on a normative philosophy. That is, social work was seen as being a moral agent of society, charged with enforcing religiously based social norms. As such, social workers actively sought to prevent, in their clients, behavior that was generally considered by society to be undesirable or immoral, such as divorce, premarital sex, homosexuality, and the use of alcohol or drugs. Siporin asserts that "in recent years, however, this social work value system and its moral vision have been fragmented and weakened. Many social workers now believe that people should be free to choose their own life-styles, values, and moral norms." He calls this the *libertarian philosophy* and

Same-sex marriage is one of a number of issues with a strong religious component that affect social welfare and social work practice.

observes that it rejects the labeling of behaviors such as those listed earlier as deviant, and that it instead labels them as "variant" or "normal." "It is further argued that the social work profession should advocate and support the social redefinition of such conduct as 'normal,' and should actively support or approve these behavior patterns as rightful, viable options for people in our society." Siporin believes that this trend has been harmful to the profession and that it has led to the perception by much of the public of social work as an immoral, or at least amoral, profession. He thinks that "social work as a profession needs to regain its moral vision and idealism and even the moral passion that the old-time social workers had. Social work also needs to be able to present itself again as a representative moral agent of society."[75]

Keith-Lucas takes a much less extreme view than Siporin with regard to both social work's current moral state and what its position should be. Rather than viewing social work as having abandoned a normative position and adopted a libertarian position, Keith-Lucas believes that social work has simply abandoned the concept of sin, and with good reason. The concept of sin has often been used to justify harshness toward people with problems, and it has been interpreted legalistically and simplistically. This often led to punitive attitudes toward clients, attitudes that Keith-Lucas believes are both "bad social work and questionable Christianity."[76] Keith-Lucas also believes that Christian values have sometimes been perverted by our society.

> To the extent that Christian doctrine has been identified with capitalism, to the extent that it ensures, even implicitly, that worldly success and grace have anything to do with each other, to the extent that there is any room in it for judgmentalism, or distinction between people on the basis of their supposed goodness or badness, to the extent that it rejects the sinner rather than his sin, the church . . . deserves all that the humanists have said about it.[77]

Whatever the reasons, it is clear there is the potential for conflict between the values of the social work profession and those of religion, particularly conservative Christianity. The basis for the conflict lies in the principles considered almost sacred by social work, and referred to earlier in the case of Penny: principles of the client's right to self-determination, the worker's obligation to provide information on all options, and the worker's need to maintain a nonjudgmental attitude. In practice terms, this means that a social worker, at least when working in a secular agency, is obligated to consider all legal options for clients. These options sometimes involve practices that certain religions consider to be sinful. Common examples are homosexuality, abortion, premarital sex, and contraceptives and sexual information for teenagers, among many others. We should note that the problem of helping clients find solutions that are at variance with the personal values of the social worker is by no means confined to social workers with strong religious convictions. For example, many social workers with strong feminist convictions find themselves in the position of helping women strengthen traditional marriages in which the husband is the "boss" and the wife is the "helpmate." The social worker may find this type of relationship personally distasteful; but if it is the kind of marriage the client desires, the social worker has no right to impose his or her own values of equalitarian relationships on the client.

Problems stemming from the relationship of social work and religion have two sides; they present difficulties for both the agency and the individual social worker. From the standpoint of the agency, religion presents several problems. The first has to do with a problem noted by Keith-Lucas, that social workers with strong religious beliefs tend to be less concerned than social workers in general about the material needs of clients "and more concerned that their clients should behave in a generally acceptable way."[78] The policy of most social work agencies is that the client's material needs should be taken care of before the social worker deals with behavioral change. The second problem has to do with agency administrators' concern that agency policies regarding client self-determination and worker nonjudgmentalism be followed. They are generally concerned, and rightly so, that social workers with strong religious beliefs may have difficulty following these policies. The third problem for agencies has to do with witnessing. It is not uncommon for social workers with strong Christian beliefs to feel that the root of many clients' problems is that they are out of alignment with God, and that finding and accepting Jesus Christ is the only solution to their problems. Be that as it may, in secular agencies the practice of witnessing is almost always against policy. Mark MacDonald, a graduate student at the University of Chicago, recalled that at the end of his first week of field placement, "the executive director and another staff member confronted me with the policy of not overtly expressing my personal faith in the agency (they knew of my strong Christian background). I began to realize that the agency desired to approach only the physical and emotional/mental needs of an individual, not the spiritual. I knew that as a Christian I could not agree with this kind of incomplete therapy."[79] Whether a social worker agrees with a nonspiritual approach to client problems is not a concern of the agency; however, ensuring that workers follow policy and refrain from using their positions to witness to clients is very much a concern.

From the standpoint of the social worker with strong religious beliefs, the issue is one of balancing the sometimes conflicting values of profession and religion without unacceptably compromising either. Social workers writing in this area have developed guidelines that may be of help. The following list is based on writings of Sherwood and Keith-Lucas.[80]

1. Integrating faith and practice involves difficult judgments and *compromise*, because every choice will advance certain values at the expense of other values.
2. Religion will provide a fundamental value base from which to practice but will not give prescriptive, mechanical guidance.
3. It is possible to work with clients whose values and goals are at variance with your own. Sherwood recalls: "In doing marriage counseling in a secular setting this author often found clients choosing goals counter to his own. One consequence was that he often found himself doing divorce counseling. It was neither his right nor in his power to prevent such a choice on the part of his clients. And once the choice was made, he believes he served them better by helping to minimize the damage of the divorce."
4. It is acceptable to express one's own values, when appropriate, as long as they are clearly labeled and with emphasis on the client's right to and responsibility for his or her own choices and their consequences.
5. The agency setting and the social worker's position should never be used in a manipulative or coercive way, even "for the client's own good." This means, among other things, that a social agency, particularly a secular one, is not an appropriate setting for witnessing.

A CLOSER **Look**

Guidelines from the North American Association of Christians in Social Work

As a member of NACSW I practice, learn, and teach social work within the following philosophical frame:

1. Human beings are of infinite worth, irrespective of gender, race, age, or behavior.
2. At the same time human beings, including myself, are fallible, limited creatures. They are not capable, and never will be, of solving all their problems or of creating the perfect society. Nevertheless they are sometimes capable, with appropriate help, of transcending their nature in acts of courage and compassion.
3. As a fallible being myself I have no right to pass moral judgments on others, to assume authority over them except as mandated by law, or to imagine that I know everything about them.
4. Human beings have been endowed with the faculty of choice, which must not be denied them except by due process of law, or where their actions or threatened actions are demonstrably gravely harmful to others or self-destructive, or where they voluntarily surrender this right for a prescribed purpose.
5. They are, however, responsible for the consequences of their choices, and may need help in perceiving what these are likely to be.
6. No person is beyond help, although at this time we may not have the knowledge or skill to help.
7. All programs and policies that depreciate people, treat them as objects rather than as subjects, seek to impose on them behavior not mandated by law, manipulate them without their knowledge and consent, or deny them choices permitted others in our society, are to be avoided or resisted.
8. Our society is far from perfect, and it is not my business to act as a representative, but rather to help people determine their relationship to it.
9. Love, understanding, and compassion are the source of well-being and acceptable behavior, rather than the reward for them.
10. While force is sometimes the quickest way of obtaining an immediate result, in the long run it is self-defeating. Compassion, understanding, and concern are the eventual victors.
11. The social sciences provide much useful knowledge for practice, but they cannot explain all phenomena and their pronouncements need constantly to be evaluated in terms of the values they subsume.
12. There are outcomes to human helping that cannot be measured statistically as well as those which can.
13. All human institutions, ideals, and commitments are liable to subtle perversion of their values, unless these are constantly examined. The new is not necessarily the best, nor does new knowledge always invalidate the old.
14. Professional education and training in self-discipline are indispensable to good social work.
15. As a Christian committed to the dissemination of what I believe to be the truth, my task as a social worker is not so much to convince others of this truth, as to provide them with the experience of being loved, forgiven, and cared for so that the Good News I believe in may be a credible option for them.

Source: Alan Keith-Lucas, *So You Want to Be a Social Worker: A Primer for the Christian Student* (St. Davids, PA: North American Association of Christians in Social Work, 1985), 34–35. Used with permission.

6. When working in a social agency, the social worker has an obligation to carry out the policy of the agency. A social worker in a public health clinic must discuss abortion as an alternative to a problem pregnancy, must discuss the use of condoms with homosexuals and unmarried clients as a means of AIDS prevention, must furnish birth-control information to teenagers, and must discuss with drug addicts ways to get clean needles. About this, Keith-Lucas says, "One has no right to ignore policies or give them subtly some other meaning than that which the agency intends. Clients have a right to rely on an agency's consistency and Government or a Board of Trustees that its money be spent as it directs."[81]

What if a social worker is asked to do something that he or she cannot in good conscience do? Keith-Lucas says the worker has two choices. One is to resign, and the other is to refuse openly to carry out the policy, in which case the worker will probably be fired.

Incidentally, these guidelines can be turned around. Many religiously affiliated agencies employ social workers who are themselves not particularly religious. It is entirely possible for a social worker who believes in abortion as a viable alternative to pregnancy to be employed by a Catholic agency that has a strict policy against offering abortion to clients as an option. The worker in such a setting is also under an obligation to follow agency policy and not to discuss abortion. It is perfectly ethical for an agency to have such a policy as long as clients know about it ahead of time. It is not ethical, however, for an agency to call itself something like "Pregnancy Counseling Center" and imply that it offers all options when in fact preventing abortions is its major goal.

The North American Association of Christians in Social Work has developed a useful set of guidelines for Christians in social work. These are presented in "A Closer Look" on page 220.

Conclusion

Religion and social work have a long and closely intertwined history. They are natural allies and collaborators, both being concerned with the well-being of people, justice, and problems of the oppressed, as well as many other mutual interests. But as social work has become more secularized and more tolerant of "atypical" behavior, and as conservative religion has become a more powerful force in society, the potential for problems between these old allies has increased.

How great have these problems actually proved to be? Because it has been only in the past few years that many people have even perceived the potential for conflict, we really do not have much data on which to base a firm conclusion. However, the data that are beginning to come in indicate that the relationship between religion and social work is not presenting as great a problem as feared. A study by Eckardt compared the practice of graduates of the social work program at Temple University, who identified themselves as secular in orientation, with graduates of the social work program at the Philadelphia College of the Bible, who identified themselves as evangelical Christians. Eckardt concluded that

> The overwhelming difference in religious beliefs was matched by an equally overwhelming similarity in practice. There was not always a positive affirmation of the values of the profession through the practice decisions, but the nature of the responses was similar. A generalization which can be made from this study is that although the groups tested were diverse in religious beliefs, they were similar in professional practice.[82]

A similar finding was reported by Epstein and Buckner, who surveyed practicing social workers in Georgia, in the heart of the Bible Belt. Of the 214 social workers surveyed, only 4.4 percent identified themselves as fundamentalist Christians, but 35.5 percent identified their religion as "central to my life and philosophy." Epstein and Buckner found that "those social work professionals participating in the study have not experienced significant conflicts or pressures related to Fundamentalism or to differences in religious beliefs."[83]

By way of conclusion, the authors agree with Cnaan who, in a recent study of the relation of social work and religion, states

> The separation of social work from its religious roots not only jeopardizes its moral foundation and public support but also makes it difficult for the profession to chart its future course—one that will undoubtably find strong connections between secular and religious-based social services at many levels. Post-1980 social policy is focusing on service development at the local level, where agencies, both public and private, sectarian and secular, are using the resources of religious organizations. This, in turn, is forcing social work to reconnect with its religious roots.[84]

Visit **www.researchnavigator.com** to research these important concepts from the chapter:

- Altruism
- Christianity AND charity
- Faith-based initiative
- Religion AND charity
- Religion AND social work
- Social justice AND religion

Web Sites Related to Social Work and Religion

American Friends Service Committee Archives <www. afsc.org/archives.htm>: A description of the services and holdings of the archives of the American Friends Service Committee. This group, affiliated with the Quaker religion, has a long history of social action related to social welfare issues.

Christian Coalition <www.cc.org>: Web site of the conservative Christian Coalition. Includes general information about the group, membership information, news of state affiliates, news releases, information on contacting Congress, religious rights watch, and links to other sites.

Joseph and Matthew Payton Philanthropic Studies Library <www.lib.iupui.edu/special/ppsl.html>: Holdings of a library at the Indiana University–Purdue University Indianapolis Center on Philanthropy that includes extensive material related to the religious context of philanthropy.

North American Association of Christians in Social Work <www.nacsw.org>: Includes general information on the organization including its mission, news releases, calendar of upcoming events, online bookstore, membership information and application material, local chapter information and news, and a list of board members.

Swarthmore College Peace Collection <www.swarthmore.edu/Library/peace/index.html>: A large collection of papers and photographs related to peace activities. Includes holdings on activities of social workers involved in the peace movement, including Jane Addams.

Endnotes

1. Alan Keith-Lucas, *Giving and Taking Help* (Chapel Hill: University of North Carolina Press, 1972), 200.
2. David Macarov, *The Design of Social Welfare* (New York: Holt, Rinehart & Winston, 1978), 76.
3. Robert Morris, *Rethinking Social Welfare: Why Care for the Stranger?* (New York: Longman, 1986), 66.
4. Bob Brackney and Derrel Watkins, "An Analysis of Christian Values and Social Work Practice," *Social Work and Christianity 10* (Spring 1983), 6.
5. Morris, *Rethinking Social Welfare,* 66.
6. Morris, *Rethinking Social Welfare,* 67.
7. Morris, *Rethinking Social Welfare,* 72.
8. As cited in Macarov, *The Design of Social Welfare,* 78–79.
9. Frank M. Lowenberg, *From Charity to Social Justice: The Emergence of Communal Institutions for the Support of the Poor in Ancient Judaism* (New Brunswick, NJ: Transaction, 2001), 91–93.
10. Macarov, *The Design of Social Welfare,* 79.
11. Cited in Brackney and Watkins, "An Analysis of Christian Values and Social Work Practice," 7.
12. James Douglas, *Why Charity?* (Beverly Hills, CA: Sage, 1983), 78.
13. Brackney and Watkins, "An Analysis of Christian Values and Social Work Practice," 7.
14. David R. Hodge, "Working with Muslim Youths: Understanding the Values and Beliefs of Islamic Discourse," *Children and Schools 24* (January 2002), 6–8; Shireen S. Rajaram and Anahita Rashidi, "African-American Muslim Women and Health Care," *Women and Health 37* (2003), 82–84.
15. Scianna Elizabeth Bowman Augustine, "Islam and the Peoples of the Book: A Social Work Perspective," *The New Social Worker* (Spring 2002), 18–20.
16. Edward Canda and Leola Furman, *Spiritual Diversity in Social Work Practice—The Heart of Helping* (New York: Free Press, 1999), 137–138; A. Al-Krenawi and J. R. Graham, "Islamic Theology and Prayer: Relevance for Social Work Practice," *International Social Work 43*(3) (July 2000), 289–304.
17. Norman A. Stillman, "Charity and Social Service in Medieval Islam," *Societas—A Review of Social History 5* (1975), 105–115.
18. Arthur E. Fink, Everett E. Wilson, and Merrill B. Conover, *The Field of Social Work,* 4th ed. (New York: Holt, Rinehart & Winston, 1964), 29–30.
19. Robert H. Bremner, *From the Depths: The Discovery of Poverty in the United States* (New York: New York University Press, 1956), 33.
20. S. Humphries Gurteen, *A Handbook of Charity Organization* (Buffalo, NY: Author, 1882), 129.
21. Raymond Mohl and Neil Betten, "Paternalism and Pluralism: Immigrants and Social Welfare in Gary, Indiana, 1906–1940," *American Studies 15* (Spring 1974), 6.
22. William J. Reid, "Sectarian Agencies," in John Turner, ed., *Encyclopedia of Social Work 17* (New York: National Association of Social Workers, 1977), 1245.
23. Robert R. Hildebrandt, "The History of Developing Responsibility among Lutherans through Cooperative Efforts of the Church Bodies and the Place of Social Welfare in the Mission of the Lutheran Church Today" (DSW dissertation, Tulane University, 1978), 32–35.
24. F. Ernest Johnson, "Protestant Social Work," in *Social Work Yearbook 6,* Russell H. Kurtz, ed. (New York: Russell Sage Foundation, 1941), 404; Reid, "Sectarian Agencies," 1247.
25. Sue Spencer, "What Place Has Religion in Social Work Education?" *Social Service Review 35* (April 1961), 161.
26. Martin E. Marty, "Social Service: Godly and Godless," *Social Service Review 54* (December 1980), 465.
27. Ram A. Cnaan, with Robert J. Wineburg and Stephanie C. Boddie, *The Newer Deal—Social Work and Religion in Partnership* (New York: Columbia University Press, 1999), 47.
28. Ronald R. Johnstone, *Religion in Society: A Sociology of Religion,* 2nd ed. (Englewood Cliffs, NJ: Prentice Hall, 1983), 270.
29. Johnstone, *Religion in Society,* 271.
30. Tom W. Smith, "Counting Flocks and Lost Sheep: Trends in Religious Preference since World War II," *GSS Social Change Report No. 26* (January 1991).
31. George H. Gallup Jr., "Factors in the Slide of Mainline Churches," *The Gallup Poll Tuesday Briefing* (4 February 2003), 1–2.

32. F. Ellen Netting, "The Religiously Affiliated Agency: Implications for Social Work Administration," *Social Work and Christianity 13* (Fall 1986), 50.
33. Council on Foundations, *The Philanthropy of Organized Religion* (Washington, DC: Council on Foundations, 1985), 63; The Gallup Organization, "Though Very Religious, Americans Most Likely to Say Government Is Responsible for the Poor," *The Gallup Poll Tuesday Briefing* (30 January 2001), 1.
34. Ram A. Cnaan and Stephanie Broddie, "Charitable Choice and Faith-Based Welfare: A Call for Social Work," *Social Work 47* (July 2002), 224–235; Ram A. Cnaan and Stephanie Broddie, "Philadelphia Census of Congregations and Their Involvement in Social Service Delivery," *Social Service Review 75* (December 2001), 559–589; David R. Hodge, "Welfare Reform and Religious Providers: An Examination of the New Paradigm," *Social Work and Christianity 25* (Spring 1998), 24–48.
35. Larry P. A. Ortiz, "Religious Issues: The Missing Link in Social Work Education," paper presented at the 37th Annual Program Meeting of the Council on Social Work Education, New Orleans, LA, March 14–17, 1991; Edward R. Canda, "Religious Content in Social Work Education: A Comparative Approach," *Journal of Social Work Education 25* (Winter 1989), 36–45; F. Ellen Netting, Jane M. Thibault, and James W. Ellor, "Integrating Content on Organized Religion into Macropractice Courses," *Journal of Social Work Education 26* (Winter 1990), 15–24; M. Vincentia Joseph, "Religion and Social Work Practice," *Social Casework 69* (September 1988), 443–452; James R. Dudley and Chava Helfgott, "Exploring a Place for Spirituality in the Social Work Curriculum," *Journal of Social Work Education 26* (Fall 1990), 287–294.
36. Julie Sahlein, "When Religion Enters the Dialogue: A Guide for Practitioners," *Clinical Social Work Journal 30* (Winter 2002), 381–401; David R. Hodge, "Spiritual Assessment: A Review of Major Qualitative Methods and a New Framework for Assessing Spirituality," *Social Work 46* (July 2001), 203–214; David R. Hodge, "Equipping Social Workers to Address Spirituality in Practice Settings: A Model Curriculum," *Advances in Social Work Practice 3* (Fall 2002), 85–103; Frederick A. DiBlasio, "The Role of Social Workers' Religious Beliefs in Helping Family Members Forgive," *Families in Society* (March 1993), 163–170; Estella Norwood Evans, "Liberation Theology, Empowerment Theory and Social Work Practice with the Oppressed," *International Social Work 35* (1992), 135–147; Patricia Sermabeikian, "Our Clients, Ourselves: The Spiritual Perspective and Social Work Practice," *Social Work 39* (March 1994), 178–183.
37. Ronald K. Bullis, *Spirituality in Social Work Practice* (Washington, DC: Taylor & Francis, 1996); Canda and Furman, *Spiritual Diversity in Social Work Practice—The Heart of Helping;* James W. Ellor, F. Ellen Netting, and Jane M. Thibault, *Religious and Spiritual Aspects of Human Service Practice* (Columbia: University of South Carolina Press, 1999).
38. Hildebrandt, "The History of Developing Social Responsibility among Lutherans through Cooperative Efforts of the Church Bodies and the Place of Social Welfare in the Mission of the Lutheran Church Today"; Ralph William Eckardt, "Evangelical Christianity and Social Work: A Study of the Beliefs and Practices of Graduates of the Social Work Majors" (University of Pennsylvania, DSW, 1986); D. J. Pezzulo, "Social Workers' Clinical Decisions Regarding Religious and Spiritual Issues in Direct Practice: A Quantitative Analysis" (University of Pittsburgh, Ph.D., April 1997).
39. Leola D. Furman and Joseph M. Chandy, "Religion and Spirituality in Social Work Education: Preparing the Culturally Sensitive Practitioner for the Future," paper presented at the 1994 Biennial Social Work Education Conference, St. Paul, MN (29 April 1994), 11.
40. Cited in Cnaan, *The Newer Deal—Social Work and Religion in Partnership,* 2.
41. Reid, "Sectarian Agencies," 1247.
42. Charles Edmund Degeneffe, "What Is Catholic about Catholic Charities?" *Social Work 48* (July 2003), 375.
43. Netting, "The Religiously Affiliated Agency," 55.
44. Reid, "Sectarian Agencies," 1251.
45. Council on Foundations, *The Philanthropy of Organized Religion;* Cnaan and Boddie, "Philadelphia Census of Congregations and Their Involvement in Social Services Delivery," *Social Service Review 75* (December 2001), 585.
46. Marty, "Social Service: Godly and Godless," 467–468.
47. See, for example, Al-Krenewi and Graham, "Islamic Theology and Prayer."

48. Marty, "Social Service: Godly and Godless," 463–481.
49. Paul Sanzanbach, "Religion and Social Work: It's Not That Simple!" *Social Casework 70* (November 1989), 572.
50. Frank M. Loewenberg, *Religion and Social Work Practice in Contemporary American Society* (New York: Columbia University Press, 1988), 12.
51. Hope Haslam Straughn, personal communication, 6 September 2003.
52. Roberta Wells Imre, *Knowing and Caring* (Lanham, MD: University Press of America, 1982), 57.
53. Michael Elliott, "The Church Related Social Worker," *Social Work and Christianity 11* (Fall 1984), 41.
54. Norris Magnuson, *Salvation in the Slums: Evangelical Social Work, 1865–1920* (Metuchen, NJ: Scarecrow Press, 1977), ix.
55. Alan Keith-Lucas, "Christianity and the Church in Today's Social Scene," *The Paraclete 1* (Spring 1974), 4–5.
56. Edward G. Kuhlmann, "A Christian View of Man for Social Action," *The Paraclete 1* (Spring 1974), 4–5.
57. Mary P. Van Hook, "Christian Social Work," in Richard L. Edwards, ed., *Encyclopedia of Social Work,* 19th ed. (Washington, DC: NASW Press, 1997), 71.
58. Catherine A. Faver and Mary "Ski" Hunter, "Feminism, Christianity, and Social Work Education," *Social Work and Christianity 9* (Spring–Fall 1981), 57.
59. Eckardt, "Evangelical Christianity and Social Work," 54–57.
60. Eckardt, "Evangelical Christianity and Social Work," 55–56.
61. Magnuson, *Salvation in the Slums,* xii–xiv.
62. Magnuson, *Salvation in the Slums,* xii.
63. From *Giving and Taking Help* by Alan Keith-Lucas (pp. 201–202). © 1972 The University of North Carolina Press. Reprinted by permission.
64. Kuhlmann, "A Christian View of Man for Social Action," 23.
65. David O. Moberg, "The Christian and Social Change," *The Paraclete 4* (Summer 1977), 17.
66. Richard F. Lovelace, "Completing an Awakening," *Christian Century* (18 March 1981), 296–300.
67. John D. Bower, "Social Action: A Christian Mandate," *The Paraclete 2* (Summer 1975), 40–50.
68. Council on Foundations, *The Philanthropy of Organized Religion,* 22.
69. Ralph W. Eckardt, "Christianity and Government: A Plea for Sane Social Action," *The Paraclete 1* (Spring 1974), 45.
70. Robert Holman, "The Christian Social Worker: A British View," *The British Journal of Social Work 15* (1985), 59.
71. Eckardt, "Evangelical Christianity and Social Work," iv.
72. F. Ellen Netting, "Social Work and Religious Values in Church Related Social Agencies," *Social Work and Christianity 9* (Spring–Fall 1982), 10–11.
73. Rebecca R. Buckner, "Teaching Acceptance of Religious Diversity to Undergraduate Social Work Students," paper presented at the Alabama–Mississippi Conference on Social Work Education, Cleveland, MS, 7 October 1993.
74. Dwain A. Pellebon, "Perceptions of Conflict between Christianity and Social Work: A Preliminary Study," *Social Work and Christianity, 27*(1) (Spring 2000), 29–39.
75. Max Siporin, "Moral Philosophy in Social Work Today," *Social Service Review 56* (1982), 519–520.
76. Alan Keith-Lucas, *So You Want to Be a Social Worker: A Primer for the Christian Student* (St. Davids, PA: North American Association of Christians in Social Work, 1985), 20–22.
77. From *Giving and Taking Help* by Alan Keith-Lucas (Chapel Hill: University of North Carolina Press, 1972), 201.
78. Keith-Lucas, *So You Want to Be a Social Worker,* 30.
79. Mark MacDonald, "The Christian Social Worker in a Secular Drop-In Center Setting," *Social Work and Christianity 10* (Spring 1983), 68–69.
80. David A. Sherwood, "Add to Your Faith Virtue: The Integration of Christian Values and Social Work Practice," *Social Work and Christianity 8* (Spring–Fall 1981), 41–54; Keith-Lucas, *So You Want to Be a Social Worker,* 31–33. Used with permission.
81. Keith–Lucas, *So You Want to Be a Social Worker,* 32.
82. Eckardt, "Evangelical Christianity and Social Work," 32.
83. Howard Epstein and Ed Buckner, "Social Work and Fundamental Religious and Political Values" (Unpublished paper, Social Work Department, Georgia State University, Atlanta, GA, 1987), 9.
84. Cnaan, *The Newer Deal—Social Work and Religion in Partnership,* 3.

CHAPTER

7

Poverty: The Central Concept

The alarm wakes Patty with its obnoxious buzz. She groans as she slaps the bedside table in an attempt to shut it off before it wakes the kids. Lying in bed, trying to wake up but wishing she did not have to, Patty thinks about her day—it is going to be a killer. Whoever said life on welfare is easy has never been there.

Patty Sanchez is a twenty-three-year-old divorced mother of two children, four-year-old Tina and two-year-old Ray. She has been receiving welfare—Temporary Assistance to Needy Families (TANF)—for fourteen months, ever since her husband Ernesto deserted her. Ernie lost his job as a truck driver just about the time Patty discovered that she was pregnant with Ray. For a while, they lived on unemployment benefits; then they scraped by on what Patty's mother could spare (not much) and on what Ernie made from the few odd jobs he could get (also not much). After Ernie overcame his pride, they applied for and received food stamps. After he lost his job as a trucker, Ernie never did get another "real job." It was a horrible time. Patty was pregnant and sick, Tina was demanding and whiny, and they were evicted from their apartment. They were able to move into the dump where Patty still lives only because a local church helped them out. Finally Ernie became depressed and began to abuse Tina; then he moved out.

After Ernie left, Patty and the kids began receiving TANF and Medicaid in addition to their food stamps. Their name is at the top of the waiting list for a rent-subsidized apartment, and Patty has calculated that with low-cost housing she will finally be able to balance her budget. The prospect of going through a day without fear of the power being turned off or of creditors at the door seems almost too good to be true.

Patty and Ernie's relationship had been unstable since before Tina's birth. Ernie's unemployment was the last straw. After Ernie left, Patty saw him around the neighborhood occasionally for a few months, but then he dropped out of sight. One of his friends told Patty that Ernie had gone to California because he had heard they were hiring truckers, but Patty felt that he had left because he couldn't stand the embarrassment of seeing his family supported by welfare while he just sat around and did nothing.

Before waking the kids, Patty sits down with a cup of coffee and thinks about her day. At 9:00 in the morning Chuck Patterson, a social worker with the child welfare office, will be coming by for the last time. In the months before Ernie left, he had begun to drink and to take out his frustration on his family, mainly on Tina. After one particularly bad incident, Patty took Tina to the emergency room to see if she had any broken bones. Tina did not, but the physician called the hospital social worker, who in turn called the child welfare office. Chuck Patterson was the social worker assigned to the case. At first Patty was scared, thinking that her children would be taken away from her. It turned out that Mr. Patterson was helpful, and he spent a lot of time with Ernie helping him to develop better ways of dealing with anger and frustration. But now that Ernie is gone there is really no reason for the child welfare people to be involved, so this will be the last visit. Patty feels both happy and sad that she will no longer be seeing Chuck—happy because she feels that there are too many people involved in her life, but sad because with all of her responsibilities she can use all the friends she can get.

After Chuck Patterson leaves, Patty plans to bundle up baby Ray and take him to the public health clinic for an evaluation. He has not been developing as quickly as he should, and the doctors are afraid there may be something wrong with him. Patty is afraid that Ray's problems may be the result of the fact that she did not eat right and did not get any medical care during her pregnancy. Because they had so little money, her diet consisted mainly of bread, rice, potatoes, and other cheap, starchy food. She had heard of a program called WIC (Women, Infants, and Children) that would have given her coupons to buy supplementary food during her pregnancy and Ray's infancy, but Ernie was in his macho proud phase and refused even to consider it. Now it looks as though little Ray is going to pay the price for his father's pride. At two, he is not yet walking, talking, or even responding well when someone plays with him.

At noon Patty has a group meeting at the community mental health center. After Ernie left she felt so bad that she spent most of each day in bed crying. Chuck Patterson helped her join a support group at the center. The group is composed of eight other women who are undergoing life crises of various sorts, and they spend an hour each week just talking and comparing notes on how they cope. The group is led by a clinical social worker named Carol Crenshaw who gets the group going, occasionally makes a suggestion or interpretation of what is being said, and sums up at the end of the meeting. Patty thinks about how much better she is doing now than when she first joined the group, and the thought of quitting enters her mind, as it has frequently in the past few weeks. She decides that she will continue to go for a little longer because she enjoys the fellowship of the group and feels that the other women need her.

After the meeting at the community mental health center, Patty will rush home, feed the kids, and put them down for a short nap while she does her laundry and housework. At 2:30 she will wake up the kids and walk two blocks to the Learning Center, a local child care facility. At the Learning Center, Patty drives the van that picks up kids after school; then she supervises their play group until 6:00, when the last parents will pick up their children. Patty is paid only minimum wage for this job, but it includes child care for her own children as a benefit. She looked at other jobs, including full-time ones, after Ernie left, but when she deducted child care expenses, she would be left with almost nothing. Patty's TANF grant allows her to make a small amount of income with no reduction in her grant or other benefits, so this job improves her life a little bit and strengthens her self-image a whole lot.

After work at the child care center Patty will rush home, feed her kids, and take them to her mother's house for the evening. While her mother cares for the kids, Patty will go to the local high school where she is enrolled in night classes. Patty quit school when she was sixteen, shortly after she met Ernesto. She thought she had it made. He had a good job and seemed to have lots of money, and Patty was sure he would take care of her forever. With a setup like that, why did she need an education? "Well," she thinks, "once again I learn the hard way." The course she is pursuing at the high school will not only lead to a high school diploma but will also get her a certificate in drafting with emphasis on computer-assisted design (CAD). Patty has always been good in art, and the counselor at the school told her the salary and job prospects of drafters with computer skills are very good. She likes school and plans to continue after she gets a job. Her dream is to eventually become a civil engineer.

With her coffee finished, Patty gets the kids up. Ray, who is sluggish at the best of times, is positively inert in the morning, and it will take the better part of an hour to feed him. Tina will want some attention, and the apartment needs to be straightened up before Chuck Patterson arrives. Facing two cranky kids, a messy apartment, and a schedule that is full until 10:00 P.M., Patty thinks, "Boy, being a welfare mother sure isn't all it's cracked up to be!"

The case of Patty Sanchez illustrates a number of key points discussed in this chapter and the two that follow. The first point, and probably the most important, is that nearly all of the social welfare problems discussed in this book are closely related to poverty. The Sanchez family has experienced unemployment and underemployment, marital breakdown, health problems, alcohol abuse, mental health problems, educational deficits, and child abuse. Some of these have contributed to their poverty and some have resulted from it; in most cases the relation has been circular—lack of education has led to poverty and poverty in turn has led to a lack of educational opportunity. That is why we are devoting three chapters to poverty and only one chapter to each of the other major social welfare problems. Scratch any social welfare problem and underneath it you will find poverty.

The Sanchez family, following Ernesto's abandonment, consists of a woman and her children. This is typical and is becoming even more common. As discussed later in this chapter, two out of three poor adults are women, 50 percent of poor families are headed by females, and one-half of the children in female-headed families are poor. This trend has come to be identified by a phrase coined by Diana Pearce in 1978: "the feminization of poverty."

The next notable fact about the Sanchez family is that they belong to a minority group, in this case Hispanic. This fact may seem to fit a popular stereotype about poor people in the United States—that they are mainly members of minority groups. This stereotype is not true—more than half of the poor people in this country are white. However, it is true that minority groups are greatly overrepresented among the poor. One out of three African Americans in the United States lives in poverty, one out of four Hispanic people is poor, but only one out of ten non-Hispanic whites falls below the poverty line. It is only because whites make up such a large majority of the population that they are numerically the largest group in poverty.

Another popular stereotype about poor people and welfare recipients is that they remain in this condition for an extended time, and that most likely their kids will inherit their poverty. Social workers and social scientists have been as guilty as laypeople of perpetuating this belief. Recent data provide a strong basis for refuting this idea and indicate that the case of Patty Sanchez may be fairly typical. A study discussed in this chapter, the Michigan Panel Study of Income Dynamics, has found that only about one-half of people who are classified as poor during one year will be so classified the next, and only one-tenth of poor people will remain so for an extended period. Far more common are people like Patty Sanchez, who use welfare for a short time while they deal with problems in their lives and then go on to more prosperous futures.

In this chapter we discuss basic factors about poverty—what it is, how we define it, how we measure it, and whom it affects. In Chapter 8 we look at characteristics of the poor and at theories and data about the causes and potential solutions to poverty. Finally, in Chapter 9, we look at social responses to the problem of poverty—how we have historically dealt with it and how we deal with it now.

Poverty: Major Issues and Common Terms

The question and the answer are familiar. You will hear them during almost any political campaign.

Reporter: "Ms. Porkbarrel, the figures recently released by the Census Bureau indicate that over the past ten years, the share of income of the richest people in this country has gotten significantly larger while the share of the poorest has become smaller. In fact, there are still more than 34 million Americans living below the poverty line. So what we have is a situation with a small number of people spending money on second homes, European vacations, jewelry, and the like, while an increasingly larger number can't afford even the necessities of life. My question is, do you consider this to be a problem? And, if so, what will you do about it if you are elected?"

Candidate Porkbarrel: "Well, John, I'm glad you asked that question. Let me say this. First, I want to say that I firmly believe that the problem is the size of the pie, not how we cut it. I have an economic development program that will increase the size of the pie, and thereby deal with the people below the poverty level without cutting into the good life earned by hardworking people. Second, I'm not sure that I agree with the figures released by the Census Bureau. I think that our poverty line is set at an unrealistically high level. Do you realize that a middle-income person in England has an income that would place him or her below our poverty line? Also, our poverty figures do not include all of the in-kind benefits we give poor people. We may have more people below the poverty line than we had in the 1960s, but these people have many benefits their 1960s counterparts did not have—benefits like food stamps and Medicaid, to name just two."

When listening to an exchange like this, we say, "Wait a minute. What does she mean that she would make the pie bigger rather than cutting it differently? What does she mean

Poverty in the United States is different from poverty in developing nations. We refer to our poverty as relative poverty because people in the United States are poor relative to other people in this country, but would not be considered poor in relation to the people pictured here.

that the poverty line is too high? And what's all this business about in-kind benefits?" These are some of the major issues and common terms that come up in discussions of the problem of poverty. The size-of-the-pie question refers to the distribution of income in our country. Some people believe that the rich are too rich, and they propose a kind of Robin Hood solution to poverty—you simply take from the rich and give to the poor. Others feel this is not a good idea and that to reduce poverty, we must have economic growth. The other questions have to do with defining and measuring poverty. Discussion of these issues can, we realize, be somewhat tedious. To discuss poverty intelligently, however, you must understand them. Even though on the surface the issues may seem rather dry, we hope that by the end of this chapter you will realize they have a very human face.

Rich Country, Poor Country

Poverty in developing nations such as Haiti or Bangladesh is explainable in terms of the total wealth of the nation. If you were to take the total income of these nations and divide it up evenly among the population, everyone in the country would be poor. This is not the case in the United States. In 2002 the total personal income of the United States was $8,922.2 billion and the number of household units was 109,297,000.[1] By dividing the number of households into the total personal income, you can see that if income were distributed evenly, every household would have received $81,633 in 2002, an adequate amount of money by almost anyone's standards. However, income in the United States is not divided evenly. A few people have incomes greatly in excess of $81,633, and a larger number of people have incomes below this figure, with many far, far below it. Columnist Molly Ivins has given a particularly graphic description of the income distribution in the United States: "If we visualize the class structure at all in this country, we tend to think it looks like a fat jar with a small base (poor folks). Actually, what it looks like is the profile of a fireplace with an immensely tall chimney. There's this big huddle of folks at the bottom and along the ledge of the fireplace; then it slopes back into this chimney that goes up, up, up, so that as a chart on your wall, the chimney hits your ceiling long before it even gets near the truly rich."[2]

To understand poverty in the United States, first we must understand economic inequality. In this section we look at how inequality is measured, how income is distributed in this country, whether the income distribution is becoming more or less equal, and how the distribution of income is viewed from liberal and conservative perspectives.

The Measurement of Economic Inequality

The U.S. Bureau of the Census is one of the most highly regarded data collection agencies in the world. On a regular basis, the Census Bureau collects a wide range of information regarding the population in the United States. Among this data is information on income and wealth. For purposes of summary and comparison, the Census Bureau aggregates the data on income and wealth into quintiles (fifths) of the population. In this form we can see how much income and wealth is earned or held by the poorest fifth of the population, the next poorest fifth, and so on up to the wealthiest fifth. In addition, the bureau also figures the income of the richest 5 percent and the wealth held by the top 1 percent and one-half percent of the population. These data are also broken down by racial and ethnic group and geographic region, and they are gathered and reported in a consistent manner so comparisons over time can be made. An example of Census Bureau data on income is presented in Table 7.1. The data in this table are discussed later in this section.

Data such as that presented in Table 7.1 are useful, and they tell us a few things; but the information is not really clear, particularly for the purposes of comparison. Imagine, for example, trying to compare two or three such tables that presented data for several points in time or for different geographic regions. To make better sense of this type of data, economists have developed two techniques, the Lorenz curve and the Gini coefficient. The *Lorenz curve* is a curve that "shows the percentage of total household incomes received by successively larger fractions of the population, starting with the poorest group."[3] It traces out the share of total income held by different subgroups in the population. In the case of Census Bureau figures, it shows the income held by the lowest 20, 40, 60, 80, and 100 percent of the population. If income were distributed

TABLE 7.1 Money Income of Families: Income of Selected Positions and Percentage of Income Received by Each Fifth and Top 5 Percent of Families, 2001

Item	All Families
Income at Selected Positions (dollars)	
Upper Limit of Each Fifth:	
Lowest	17,970
Second	33,313
Third	53,000
Fourth	83,500
Highest	No limit
Lower Limit of Top 5 Percent	150,499
Percent Distribution of Aggregate Income:	
Lowest Fifth	3.5
Second Fifth	8.7
Third Fifth	14.6
Fourth Fifth	23.0
Highest Fifth	50.1
Top 5 Percent	22.4

Source: U.S. Bureau of the Census, Current Population Survey (Washington, DC: U.S. Government Printing Office, 2003). Available online at www.census.gov

evenly—that is, if 20 percent of the population had 20 percent of the income, 40 percent of the population had 40 percent of the income, and so on—the Lorenz curve would be a straight line, as shown in Figure 7.1. If, on the other hand, one person held all the income, the Lorenz curve would form a right angle, as shown in Figure 7.2. It is obvious that neither situation actually occurs; the curve always falls somewhere between the 45° slope representing perfect equality and the vertical line representing perfect inequality. Examples of two Lorenz curves, one for a very equal distribution of income and one for a very unequal distribution, are presented in Figure 7.3.

The Lorenz curve gives a nice graphic depiction of income structure, but it is still difficult to make comparisons over time and between countries. For these purposes, a summary statistic called the *Gini coefficient* is necessary. Using the situations depicted in Figure 7.3 as examples, the Gini coefficient is the area between the Lorenz curve and line OE, divided by the area of OEZ. As you can see, as the Lorenz curve approaches equality (curve a), the Gini coefficient approaches zero. As the Lorenz curve approaches inequality (curve b), the Gini coefficient approaches one. Thus, the Gini coefficient has possible values ranging from zero (perfect equality) to one (perfect inequality). The Gini coefficient makes comparisons clear and easy. If country A has a Gini coefficient of .423 and country B has a Gini coefficient of .297, we can clearly see that country B has a more equal income distribution. Likewise, if the Gini coefficient for country A was .324 in 1960 and .423 in 1998, we can conclude that the distribution of income is becoming even more unequal.

Now that you are familiar with some of the major sources of data and some of the tools used to study income and wealth, let's look at the situation in the United States.

FIGURE 7.1

Lorenz Curve for Absolute Income Equality

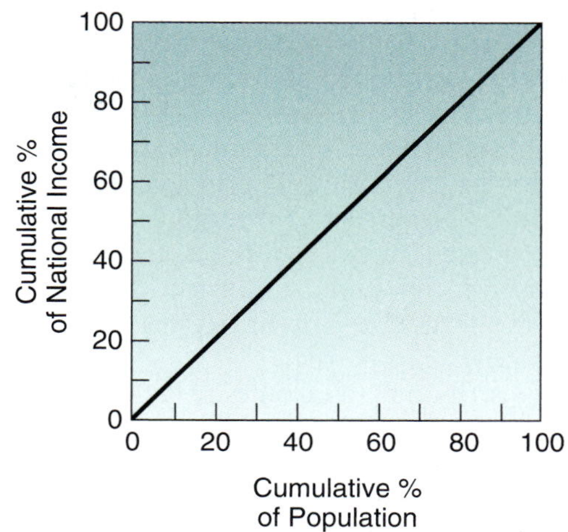

FIGURE 7.2

Lorenz Curve for Absolute Income Inequality

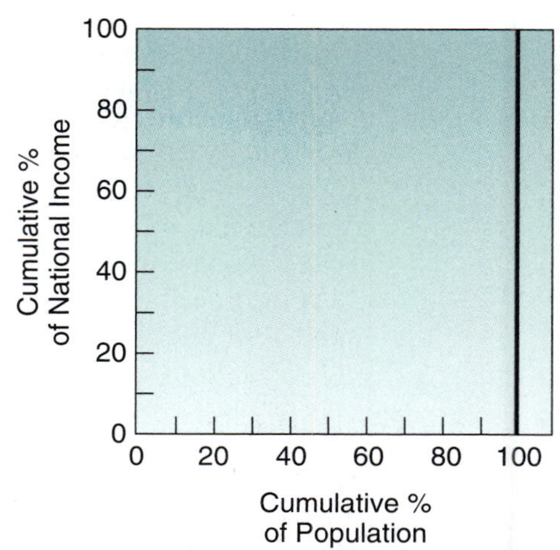

FIGURE 7.3 **Extreme Cases of the Lorenz Curve**

Source: John Craven, *Introduction to Economics: An Integrated Approach to Fundamental Principles* (Oxford, England: Blackwell Publishers Ltd., 1984), 100. Reprinted by permission.

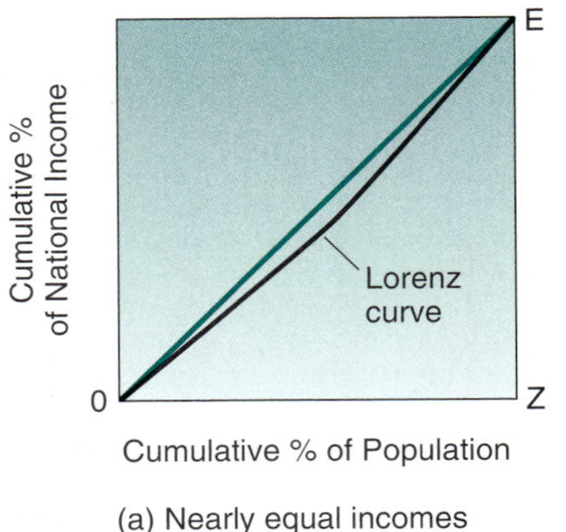

(a) Nearly equal incomes

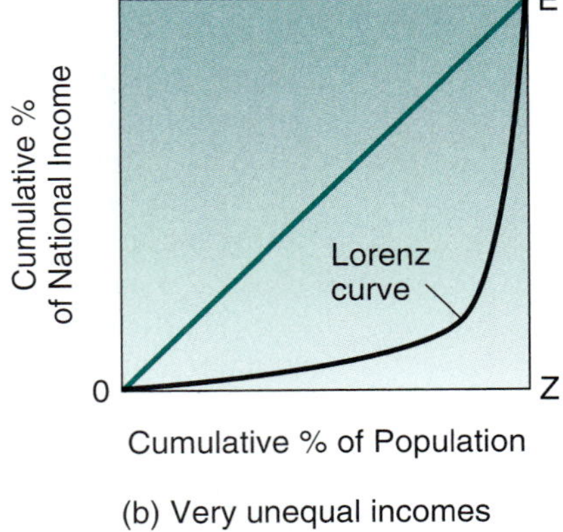

(b) Very unequal incomes

The Distribution of Income and Wealth in the United States

If you spend an hour driving around any city in the United States, it will be readily apparent that income and wealth are unequally divided. Within the space of a few miles you can see neighborhoods with houses valued at half a million dollars or more and neighborhoods with houses that most people would judge to be unfit for human habitation. You will see BMW dealerships next to Fast Freddie's Used Cars ("no credit, no problem—we tote the note"). You will see an Ethan Allen Furniture Gallery and a Salvation Army Thrift Store. We could go on and on, but there is no point in belaboring the obvious. What is not obvious, however, is just how unequal the distribution of income and wealth is.

In 2002 the Census Bureau reported the data presented in Table 7.1. In 1990, when we wrote the first edition of this book, we suggested that a convenient and illustrative way to summarize this type of data was what we called the 20/5 principle. This principle stated that in the United States the bottom 20 percent of the population received about 5 percent of the income, and the top 5 percent received a little less than 20 percent of the income. But we can no longer use this principle because inequality has grown so rapidly over the life of this book that now the bottom 20 percent receives only 3.5 percent of the income and the top 5 percent receives 22.4 percent.

The most precise ways to illustrate the distribution of income are the Lorenz curve and Gini coefficient. The data in Table 7.1, summarized in a form from which a Lorenz curve can be drawn, are presented in Table 7.2. The Lorenz curve derived from these data is presented in Figure 7.4. The Gini coefficient derived from the data is .466. We will return to this coefficient later when we look at trends in inequality in the United States over time and as compared with other countries.

TABLE 7.2

Income Data from Table 7.1 Prepared for Presentation on a Lorenz Curve

Point	Group	Percentage of Population	Cumulative Percentage of Population	Upper Limit of Group Income	Percentage of National Income	Cumulative Percentage of National Income
A	Poorest	20	20	17,970	3.5	3.5
B	Next Poorest	20	40	33,314	8.7	12.3
C	Next	20	60	53,000	14.5	26.8
D	Next	20	80	83,500	23.0	49.9
E	Richest	20	100	no limit	50.1	100

We can see from the preceding data that the distribution of income in this country is very unequal. This is not the entire story, however. Annual income refers only to the amount of money coming in during a one-year period; it does not say much about wealth. Income is the flow of money into a household; wealth consists of accumulated assets and includes things such as houses, real estate, cars, jewelry, savings accounts, stocks, and bonds. Wealth is much harder to measure than income. Income must be reported each year on federal income tax returns; and although it is acknowledged that tax reporting is not precise, it is at least a fairly close estimate. The only required reporting of wealth occurs when estates must be reported to the federal government on the death of their owners. Only a small proportion of estates are large enough to be affected by this requirement.

FIGURE 7.4

Lorenz Curve Showing Income Distribution for the United States in 2001

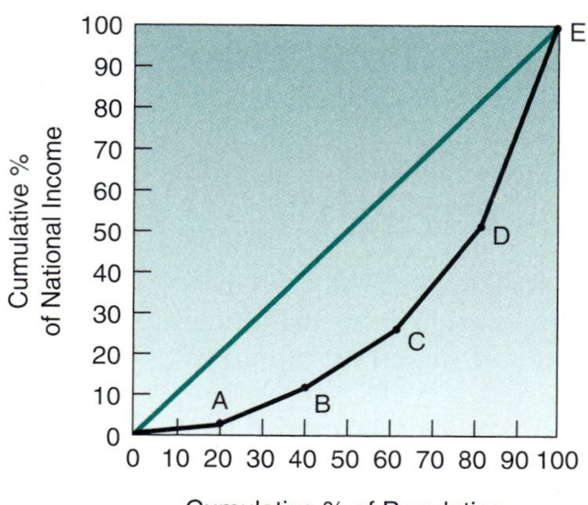

The distribution of wealth is even more unequal than the distribution of income. Data gathered from several governmental surveys by Keister, summarized in Table 7.3, indicate that the vast majority of the total wealth in the United States, 83.9 percent, is owned by one-fifth of the families. Even more astounding is the finding that as of 1995 the top 1 percent of families owned 38.5 percent of all privately held wealth. Think about that—one one-hundredth of the population owns nearly two-fifths of everything in the country.[4]

The fact that some people are very rich is not in and of itself a problem. The popularity of TV shows that portray the lives of rich people is testimony to our society's fascination with the rich. The problem is that while some

TABLE 7.3

Survey Estimates of United States Distribution of Wealth and Wealth Gini Index, 1962–1995

	Gini Coefficient	Top 1%	Next 4%	Next 5%	Next 10%	Top 20%	2nd 20%	3rd 20%	Bottom 40%
Net Worth									
1962	0.80	33.5	21.2	12.5	14.0	81.2	13.5	5.0	0.3
1983	0.80	33.8	22.3	12.1	13.1	81.3	12.6	5.2	0.9
1989	0.85	37.4	21.6	11.6	13.0	83.6	12.3	4.8	–0.7
1992	0.85	37.2	22.9	11.8	12.0	83.9	11.4	4.5	0.2
1995	0.87	38.5	21.8	11.5	12.1	83.9	11.4	4.5	0.2
Financial Worth									
1962	0.88	40.3	23.8	12.8	12.7	89.6	9.6	2.1	–1.4
1983	0.90	42.9	25.1	12.3	11.0	91.3	7.9	1.7	–0.9
1989	0.93	46.9	23.9	11.6	10.9	93.4	7.4	1.7	–2.4
1992	0.92	45.6	25.0	11.5	10.2	92.3	7.3	1.5	–1.1
1995	0.94	47.2	24.6	11.2	10.1	93.0	6.9	1.4	–1.3

Source: Lisa A. Keister, *Wealth in America: Trends in Wealth Inequality* (Cambridge, England: Cambridge University Press, 2000), 64. Reprinted with the permission of Cambridge University Press.

people are very rich, others are very poor. Kennickell and Starr-McCluer report that the bottom one-fifth of the population owns absolutely nothing of value. In fact, these people have negative net worth—they owe more than they own. The next three-fifths of the population collectively owns only 15.4 percent of all privately held wealth.[5] James Smith of the University of Michigan's Institute for Social Research has pointed out that even this low figure overstates the assets of many of these people. The wealth of the lower end of this group is likely made up of money in checking accounts that will be spent for monthly living expenses and perhaps a car. Toward the upper end of this group, the wealth consists primarily of a house. Smith says, "For many Americans owning a home is the *only* way to have net worth at all." And finally, of course, we get back to the upper 20 percent who own 84.6 percent of everything, including more than 90 percent of corporate stocks and business assets and 95 percent of bonds.[6]

Trends in the Distribution of Wealth and Income

Information that can be used to compare the concentration of wealth is available for the past eighty years. These data indicate that between 1922 and 1953 wealth distribution was fairly stable, with the top 1 percent of wealth holders owning an average of 30 percent of total household sector wealth. During the 1950s and early 1960s, wealth inequality began to increase, until 1962, when the top 1 percent owned 33.5 percent of household sector wealth. This figure remained fairly constant until the late 1980s, when inequality once again began to rise. The latest estimate available is for 1995 and indicates that the top 1 percent owned 38.5 percent of all wealth. Keister, who computed these estimates, adds, "Most striking is evidence of the decline in the wealth of the poorest 80 percent of households. The wealth of this group decreased by almost 3 percent, from 18.7 percent of total wealth in 1983 to 16.4 percent in 1989."[7] Reflecting on these developments, Richard Freeman observes that "the United States has now cemented its traditional position as the leader in inequality among advanced countries."[8]

Numerous analysts using different methods have all concluded that the distribution of income has become more unequal in recent years and that income inequality is increasing at an even more rapid rate than that of wealth. Daniel Weinberg, who monitors income trends for the Census Bureau, recently looked at the historical data and observed that "the Gini index (also known as the index of concentration) indicated a decline in family income inequality of 7.4 percent from 1947 to 1968." In other words, for that period of twenty-one years, the distribution of income was becoming significantly more equal in this country. But in 1968 this trend reversed sharply. The Census Bureau recorded an increase in the Gini of 17.1 percent from 1968 to 1992 and 22.4 percent from 1968 to 1994.[9] An updated version of the Census Bureau data on which Weinberg bases his analysis is presented in Table 7.4. The percent change in share of aggregate income for households since 1967 is shown in Figure 7.5.

TABLE 7.4

United States Gini Index for Income, 1951–2001

Year	Gini Index
2001	0.466
1996	0.455
1991	0.428
1986	0.425
1981	0.406
1976	0.398
1971	0.396
1966	0.349
1961	0.374
1956	0.358
1951	0.363

Source: U.S. Bureau of the Census, Current Population Survey, 1951–2001.

FIGURE 7.5

Percent Change in Share of Aggregate Income for Households, 1967–2002

Source: Adapted from U.S. Bureau of the Census, Income in the United States: 2002, Table A-3, 25.

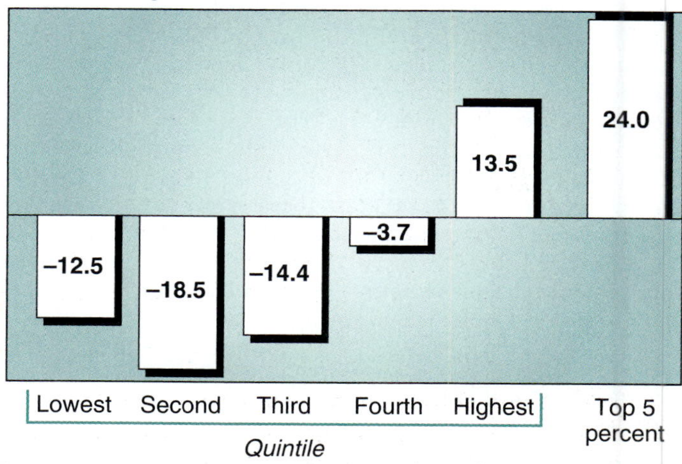

Sociologist Stanley Eitzen, adding a value dimension to the data, has stated that "the U.S. has the most unfair distribution of wealth and income in the industrialized world. Moreover, the rate of growth in inequality is faster than in any other industrialized country." He supports his position with the following facts:

- The richest 1 percent in the United States own more wealth ($3.6 trillion in 1992) than the bottom 90 percent ($3.4 trillion).
- Between 1983 and 1989 (the Reagan years), the nation's net worth increased from $13.5 trillion to $20.2 trillion, and 58 percent of that $6.7 trillion increase went to the fortunate top one-half of 1 percent. That works out to a $3.9 million bonanza per wealthy household.
- In 1960 the average CEO earned about as much as 41 factory workers. In 1992 that CEO made as much as 157 factory workers. In 1995 the average compensation of CEOs (salary, bonus, and stock options) increased by 26.9 percent compared to the 2.8 percent increase in wages for the average worker.
- In a fifteen-year period ending in 1993, the richest 1 percent almost doubled their income and had their tax rates cut by 23 percent. In sharp contrast, the poorest one-fifth saw their tax rates go up and their incomes go down.
- The real value (adjusted for inflation) of a standard welfare benefit package has declined by some 26 percent since 1972.

Focus on Diversity

Race, Ethnicity, and Increasing Inequality

Ever since the civil rights movement of the 1960s, a major goal of social and economic policy has been to correct historical injustices and make the American dream a reality for all groups in our society. But the data on trends in income inequality paint a depressing picture that indicates we are moving in the opposite direction. In a study of twenty-five years of data, the period between 1967 and 1992, Lynn Karoly found that inequality had increased for all groups in our country, but that the increase has been larger for minority groups. White families fared the best over this period with a 24.8 percent growth in median adjusted family income between 1970 and 1987. Over the same period, adjusted family income increased by 20.1 percent for African American families and by only 8.6 percent for Latino families. White families experienced positive income growth at all points in the income distribution. However, white families with incomes at the 90th percentile experienced more growth than those at the 10th percentile; thus, inequality became greater even for whites. African American and Latino families at the 10th and 25th percentiles actually experienced declines in adjusted family income after 1973. Combined with the growth of adjusted family income for families at the 75th and 90th percentiles, the data indicate that inequality has increased for minority groups at a rate greater than for whites.

Source: Lynn A. Karoly, "The Trend in Inequality among Families, Individuals, and Workers in the United States: A Twenty-Five-Year Perspective," in Sheldon Danzinger and Peter Gottschalk, eds., *Uneven Tides: Rising Inequality in America* (New York: Russell Sage Foundation, 1993), 19–100.

- From 1967 to 1979, a full-time, year-round minimum-wage worker earned at a level above the official poverty line for a family of three. In 2003 a worker earning the minimum wage of $5.15 earned $10,712 annually, $3,636 below the poverty line for a family of three.[10]

An analysis of income trends in the United States by sociologist Stephen Rose concludes that not only has inequality increased but also opportunity for upward social mobility has decreased. Rose's analysis concludes that in the 1970s, 21 percent of working-age adults had lower incomes (adjusted for inflation) at the end of the decade than they had at the beginning. In the 1980s the situation was even worse, with 33 percent of working-age adults losing economic ground during the decade. Rose asserts that the middle class in this country is decreasing and that there is a corresponding increase in the lower-class population. During one particularly bad year, 1983, Rose found an 8 percent decline in the middle class: 5.5 percent of former middle-class families moved down to the lower class, and only 1.5 percent rose to the upper class. Rose concludes:

> Inequality is growing. People at the top are doing better than the rest. And a higher proportion of people are actually losing ground. Finally, while we don't yet have the data, there is no reason to think that this situation has improved in the 1990s, and there are many reasons to think that the experience of the 1950s and 1960s was much better.[11]

As is clear from Table 7.3 and from other data presented here, inequality has increased in recent years and may well continue to increase. What this means is not clear, however; it is the subject of much debate between those with liberal and those with conservative perspectives.

Perspectives on Inequality

Liberals, conservatives, and radicals agree that equality is a basic part of the American creed and that greater equality is, at least theoretically, desirable. Liberals and conservatives also agree that economic inequality is an inevitable fact of life. Even some radicals (although not all) will agree that some inequality is tolerable; for example, that a nuclear physicist may earn more than the person who sweeps out the physicist's laboratory. There is disagreement, however, about the degree and trend of inequality, the positive and negative effects of inequality, and how much inequality is desirable in our society.

First, let's look at the degree and trend of inequality. All of the social scientists cited in the previous section would be classified as political liberals. They measure the growth of inequality and conclude that it is a fact, that it is getting worse, and that this is a result of unjust social and economic pressures. Hout and Lucas, for example, say that

> not only is the inequality in income between the richest and the poorest in the United States greater now than in the past, but it is also greater than that of any other populous, industrialized country. Workers in such countries also have had to deal with the globalization of trade and the disruptions caused by new technology; yet only workers in the United States have lost so much ground. . . . Inequality surged between 1991 and 1993 as the most recent recession lowered incomes for all but the richest Americans. Executives killed jobs in ways that would be illegal in Germany and France—for example, shutting down plants in some regions and relocating them in jurisdictions with right-to-work laws. Wall Street rewarded the executives with a mid-recession rally that boosted the value of their stock options."[12]

The conservative interpretation of the data on inequality is, predictably, quite different. Using the Gini index presented earlier, Novak and Green argue that inequality in the United States is similar to that in other Western democracies. The heart of their argument is that inequality is caused less by unfairness than by the age structure of the labor force. Persons in the early years of their careers and those in retirement will have lower incomes than persons in their peak earning years. Thus, the same person will be at different positions along the Lorenz curve during different periods of his or her life. In 1986 Novak and Green used this argument to explain why statistical measures of inequality had been increasing in the 1980s. According to their argument, a greater number of people were living in retirement because of increased life span, and the baby boom generation had been entering careers and setting up households in large numbers. For these reasons, income figures included more people at low earning points in their careers. As the baby boom generation continued "its long trek through its lifetime positions along the Lorenz curve," presumably the Gini would decrease.[13]

In 1992 Lynn Karoly debunked this argument by dividing income data into two components, one that addressed inequality related to the changing age structure of the population and one related to the changes in within-group inequality. She found that almost all of the increase in inequality over the previous twenty years was attributable to inequality within age cohorts, not to changes in the relative size of the cohorts.[14] Additionally, if Novak and Green's 1986 argument were correct, inequality should have declined beginning in the late 1980s as baby boomers entered their peak earning years. As we have seen, quite the opposite has occurred.

Conservatives and liberals also differ on whether high inequality is a bad thing. Liberals believe that high, and especially increasing, inequality is a cause for great concern. They fear that if inequality is too great, social disruption will likely occur. Harrison and his colleagues note "the fear—expressed by a growing number of journalists and political analysts—that the frustrated expectations of significant numbers of younger workers unable to attain the living standards of their own parents could lead to potentially serious social unrest."[15] Similarly, economist Lester Thurow asks, "How much inequality can a democracy take? The income gap in America is eroding the social contract. If the promise of a higher standard of living is limited to a few at the top, the rest of the citizenry, as history shows, is likely to grow disaffected, or worse."[16] Henry Reuss has said, "From a social standpoint, when whole classes feel themselves endangered, bloodshed and revolution have been the outcome, as in France in the 1790s and Germany in the 1930s."[17]

Conservatives argue that wage inequality is no particular cause for concern but in fact is actually desirable. George Gilder summarizes this argument:

> Under capitalism, when it is working, the rich have the anti-Midas touch, transforming timorous liquidity and unused savings into factories and office towers, farms and laboratories, orchestras and museums—turning gold into goods and jobs and art. That is the function of the rich: fostering opportunities for the classes below them in the continuing drama of the creation of wealth and progress.[18]

Gilder argues that rich people (entrepreneurs, to be more exact) serve a critical social function by being willing to risk their money on the hope that they will win great profits. When their risks pay off, they create new wealth for everyone in the form of jobs and economic growth. Therefore, rich people are entitled to hundreds of times the income of regular people for two reasons: (1) They take great risks, often losing everything, and therefore they deserve great profits when their risks pay off; and (2) rich people use their money not for conspicuous consumption, but to create more wealth for us all. Gilder says that this moral dynamic at the heart of the system drives entrepreneurs constantly to reinvest their profits. Entrepreneurs do not consume their wealth; they recycle it by giving it to other people in productive ways. This means that the very people who have proved their ability to create wealth control the process of future wealth creation. In the form of investments, they endow other entrepreneurs who are judged best able to prevail in the competitions in service that impel the progress of the capitalist economy.[19]

It should be noted that Gilder provides virtually no empirical evidence to support his contentions. Nobel Prize–winning economist Robert M. Solow, in his review of Gilder's *The Spirit of Enterprise,* a sequel to *Wealth and Poverty,* remarked, "Only someone with a sense of humor could survive reading this book. And no one with any trace of a sense of humor could have written it."[20]

Finally, although liberals and conservatives agree that some inequality is necessary, they disagree on how much inequality is desirable. Conservatives, as can be inferred from the quotes from Gilder, are not really concerned with the amount of inequality. They agree that poverty is a bad thing, but they contend that poverty is not a result of inequality. They argue that the situation is really quite the opposite—when people make a lot of money we all benefit, so why should we care how rich some people are? They argue that if the average income of the wealthiest people in the country increased from, say, $5 million a year to $10 million a year, and if as a result of their profit seeking your income went up by $5,000, you would probably think it a good thing.

Liberals question this trickle-down theory and argue that it does not follow that increased income for the rich necessarily results in increased income for other groups in society. They point out that as inequality in income has increased during recent years, the number of people below the poverty line has also increased. They believe that social efficiency (that is, providing enough reward to motivate the most highly qualified people to pursue the most difficult jobs) could be achieved with a much smaller amount of inequality than currently exists. William Ryan, one of the most articulate spokespersons of this "fair shares" approach, says:

> I don't think many of us have strong objections to inequality of monetary income as such. A modest range, even as much as three or four to one, would, I suspect, be tolerable to almost everybody. . . . The current range in annual incomes—from perhaps $3,000 to some unknown number of *millions*—is, however, intolerable, impossible to justify rationally, and plain inhuman.[21]

Most radicals would strongly agree.

No agreement about the effects, positive or negative, of increasing inequality has been reached, and our society has seemingly become willing to live with a high level of inequality. Paul Krugman makes the rather discouraging observation that

> income distribution, like productivity growth, is a policy issue with no real policy debate. The growing gap between rich and poor was arguably the central fact about economic life in America in the 1980's. But no policy changes now under discussion seem likely to narrow this gap significantly.[22]

Poverty—the Dark Side of Inequality

Most people would not consider inequality to be a problem if those on the low end of the distribution had at least enough income to live in a minimally adequate fashion. However, a large number of people do not have this amount of income. We refer to the living condition of these people as *poverty.* In this section we look at several aspects of poverty: We examine how it is defined, how the official poverty line is set, and some unresolved issues in measuring and defining poverty; and we look at liberal and conservative perspectives on poverty. We do not refer to a radical perspective in this section because radicals are interested more in the larger question of inequality than in how the poverty line is set.

The Definition of Poverty

We see the items in the newspaper frequently: "Poverty Rate up by 2%," or "More Children Growing Up in Poverty Now Than Any Year since 1961." From these articles we assume that it is possible to measure poverty in a manner similar to measuring the annual rainfall—that there is some objective standard against which to measure poverty. But we also see headlines that say things like "Administration Questions Poverty Statistics," and "Aide Claims That If All Benefits Are Counted, Poverty Level Has Declined by 3%." The question we are left with is, Can we measure poverty? And if so, how accurately? The answer, as you will see, is that yes, we can measure poverty with a fairly high degree of accuracy; but there is widespread disagreement on what poverty is, what the best measure is, and what the immense quantity of data we have on poverty means.

The way we measure and define poverty is dependent on which of two classes of definitions we use. The first class of definitions is referred to as *economic definitions;* it basically defines poverty as a lack of money and other resources. The second class of definitions is known as *cultural definitions;* it defines poverty not only as a lack of money but also as a lifestyle composed of values, attitudes, and behaviors that are related to being poor. According to cultural definitions, important attributes of poverty include feelings of hopelessness and alienation and a matriarchal (mother-dominated) family structure.[23] In this chapter we are dealing with poverty as an economic phenomenon and do not concern ourselves with the cultural aspects. (They are dealt with in the following chapter.) We will look at two broad categories of economic definitions of poverty—absolute definitions and relative definitions.

Absolute Definitions. An absolute definition of poverty is a relatively fixed level of income below which a person cannot function in a productive and efficient manner in a given society. It is based on calculations derived from minimum costs of food, housing, clothing, and transportation in that society. The emphasis is on *minimum* cost; no allowance is made for luxuries such as travel (even if it is for a purpose generally thought to be essential, such as visiting a sick relative) or entertainment. An absolute poverty line will increase along with the cost of living and as conditions in society change certain expenditures from nonessential to essential. For example, in the 1920s indoor plumbing was not considered essential, so the cost of sewer service was not included in poverty-line calculations. Today an outdoor toilet is illegal within city limits in this country, so the cost of sewer service has become essential and is therefore a part of poverty-line calculations.

Today in the United States we consider a person poor if that person rarely can afford to eat meat and fresh fruit, even if his or her nutritional intake is adequate and he or she is getting needed protein and vitamins from other sources. In developing nations, this diet would not result in a person being classified as poor. Therefore, even an absolute definition is relative because it is only absolute in relation to the social, economic, and historical environment in which it occurs.

Mollie Orshansky, one of the people responsible for conceptualizing the official poverty line in the United States, has commented that there is no reason to count the poor, and hence no reason for defining poverty, unless you intend to do something about it.[24] It was not until the late nineteenth century that anyone even began to think that something could be done about poverty on a societal level, and this is when interest was first shown in setting a poverty line so the poor could be counted. The earliest attempts were made in England. In the 1890s, Liverpool businessman Charles Booth defined poverty in the following way:

> [B]y the word "poor" I mean to describe those who have a sufficiently regular though bare income, such as 18s to 21s per week for a moderate family, and by "very poor" those who from any cause fall much below this standard. The "poor" are those whose means may be sufficient, but are barely sufficient, for decent independent life; the "very poor" those whose means are insufficient for this according to the usual standard of life in this country. My "poor" may be described as living under a struggle to obtain the necessaries of life and make both ends meet, while the "very poor" live in a state of chronic want.[25]

Booth arrived at these figures by observing thirty families who struck him as "poor" or "very poor" and using their expenditures as the basis for his poverty line.

Booth's definition was improved on a few years later in a study by another Englishman, Seebohm Rowntree. Booth defined poverty using a subjective idea of the "necessaries of life." Rowntree wanted to be more scientific and to calculate the income necessary for "physical efficiency" as the dividing line between poverty and nonpoverty. To arrive at this figure he turned to the work of nutritionists who had conducted rigorous studies to determine how many calories were necessary for men to carry out "moderate muscular work." They had concluded that 3,500 calories a day was the minimum intake required for physical efficiency. Using this as a standard, Rowntree developed a 3,560-calorie menu that would supply 137 grams of protein at the lowest possible cost. He then priced the menu items at the cheapest shops he could locate and calculated the lowest cost possible to feed a man at a level that would enable that man to work efficiently. Rowntree then added in the cost for the cheapest housing he could locate and an amount he considered adequate for "household sundries." By adding these figures, Rowntree arrived at his poverty line.

There have been attempts to develop better absolute poverty lines than those of Booth and Rowntree. Rowntree himself revised his calculations and methods in 1936 and again in 1950. The official U.S. government poverty line, discussed later in this section, is based on a methodology similar to that of Rowntree. According to Holman, all of these absolute definitions share three elements. First, the poverty line is set at a level that will enable people to be physically efficient. No allowance is made for enjoyment of life or for personal development of any sort. Of his poverty line Rowntree said, "It was a standard of bare subsistence rather than living." Second, the poverty line is based on calculations of utmost stringency. The only people considered poor are those whose lives, in Booth's words, entail "a struggle to obtain the necessaries of life." Finally, absolute definitions of poverty are not related to the incomes of society as a whole. These definitions do not compare people with people; they attempt to compare people with an objective yardstick that changes only with the cost of living or when certain things, such as sewer service, become necessary expenditures.[26]

The major advantage of absolute definitions and measures of poverty is that they provide a constant standard against which one dimension of the economic progress of a country can be measured. Using an absolute standard, we can look at the percentages of people living below the subsistence level at various points in history and draw con-

What **Americans** Believe

There are two ways of setting a relative poverty line. One is to take an arbitrary percentage of the median income of a country and define anything below that as poverty. The other, and probably more sensible, means is to ask people where they think the poverty line should be set and define poverty as anything falling below the average of their answers. The General Social Survey in 1993 asked people to indicate what they thought should be the poverty line for two types of families, one a husband and wife and two children, and the other a single woman and two children. The responses are summarized in Table 7.5.

In the case of the couple with two children, 29.6 percent of respondents selected the interval in which the official poverty line was located ($10,401 to $15,600; the actual line for a family of this size and composition was $14,654). A little over 27 percent selected a lower figure, and 42.8 percent placed the poverty line at a higher level. In the case of the single woman and her two children, 29.5 percent of respondents selected the interval containing the actual official poverty line ($10,401 to $15,600; the actual line for this family was $11,642), nearly the exact percentage as in the previous example. However, when considering the single woman, the percentages selecting a higher and a lower line were nearly reversed from the case with the two-parent family, with 40 percent selecting a lower line and only 30.8 percent selecting a higher line.

These data, collected during only one survey and reflecting a sample of not quite 1,400 people, does not, of course, furnish proof of anything. It does, however, provide fuel for some interesting speculation. One interesting point is that it does not appear that a relative poverty line in the United States, selected on the basis of public opinion, would be drastically different from the line set using the current official method. In both of the examples used in this survey, the vast majority of respondents selected the category containing the official line, or else the one directly above or below.

Another interesting aspect of these data is that people seem to be considerably more generous toward the two-parent family than toward the single-parent family. This is probably, at least partially, a result of the resentment felt by people in this country toward welfare because they believe that it has encouraged illegitimacy. This is a major factor behind the most recent round of welfare reform and will be discussed in greater detail in Chapter 9.

clusions about whether things are getting better or worse for the most disadvantaged segment of the population. We can also look at statistics over a shorter period of time and see if policies designed to help the poor are really having any effect.

There are some major problems with absolute definitions of poverty, however. The first and major problem is that absolute definitions are based only on physical needs and assume that people will spend their money with absolute efficiency. These definitions ignore social and psychological needs and the fact that most people do not spend money with absolute rationality. Rowntree, for example, assumed that a family

> must never purchase a halfpenny newspaper or spend a penny to buy a ticket for a popular concert. They must write no letters to absent children for they cannot afford to pay the postage. They must never contribute anything to their church or chapel, or give any help to a neighbor which costs them money. . . . [T]he children must have no pocket money for dolls, marbles or sweets. The father must smoke no tobacco and must drink no beer.[27]

TABLE 7.5

Where Would Americans Set the Poverty Line (1993)?

What Amount of Weekly Income Would You Use as a Poverty Line for a Family of Four (Husband, Wife, and Two Children) in This Community?*

	Number	*Percent*
Less than $5,200	54	3.9
$5,201 to $10,400	322	23.2
$10,401 to $15,600	411	29.6
$15,601 to $20,800	282	20.3
$20,801 to $26,000	212	15.3
$26,001 to $52,000	100	7.2
More than $52,000	6	.04

1993 poverty line for a family of four with two adults and two children = $14,654

What Amount of Weekly Income Would You Use as a Poverty Line for a Family of Three, Made Up of a Woman and Two Children, in This Community?

	Number	*Percent*
Less than $5,200	93	6.7
$5,201 to $10,400	452	32.7
$10,401 to $15,600	408	29.5
$15,601 to $20,800	250	18.0
$20,801 to $26,000	122	8.8
$26,001 to $52,000	56	4.0
More than $52,000	2	.001

1993 poverty line for a family of four with two adults and two children = $11,642

*Answers to these questions were given in weekly income. These have been converted to yearly income.

We all realize that this is not the way people actually spend their money. No one is so coldly efficient that he or she will refuse to call or write relatives, send a few holiday cards, or occasionally go to a movie. Also, absolute definitions assume that people go to the cheapest stores and buy items at the lowest possible price. Not only do most poor people, like people in general, lack the knowledge to get the best bargains, but the stores in their neighborhoods generally charge higher prices than those in more affluent areas.[28] Thus, the calculations used to set absolute definitions of poverty are based on assumptions that are false.

The second problem is a result of the first problem: Because the assumptions on which absolute poverty lines are based are false, the lines are set at too low a level. Studies in both England and the United States that ask the general population to set an absolute poverty line always result in figures much higher than the actual line. A study in England commissioned by London Weekend Television found that the general public set the poverty line 33 percent higher than the actual line.[29]

The final problem with absolute definitions of poverty is that they consider the wealth of the rest of society only as it influences the kinds of expenses a family incurs in order to get by at a subsistence level. We previously used sewer service as an example: Because everyone living in a city must pay for sewer service, the poverty line will be higher in wealthy societies than in poor societies. However, beyond this the wealth of the rest of society is not considered. That is, if the average income in a society triples over a period of years but the cost of living stays the same, the poverty line will not increase. The reason that this is a problem with absolute definitions has to do with the concept of *relative deprivation,* which asserts that people feel rich or poor not in relation to some absolute yardstick, but rather in relation to the wealth of other people. Thus, even though people living at the poverty line may be no poorer when the wealth of the rest of society increases, the fact is they feel poorer. This phenomenon is the reason some people argue that poverty should be defined not in absolute but in relative terms.

Relative Definitions. Absolute definitions attempt to set an objective line that separates the poor from the nonpoor. Relative definitions see poverty as subjective; that is, it is a matter of opinion on the part of both the poor and the nonpoor as to what constitutes poverty. Poverty is viewed as relative to the wealth of the rest of society. According to relative definitions, a family with an income of $8,000 a year will consider itself, and be considered by others, as poor in a society such as the United States, where the median annual income is over $30,000. This family would not be considered poor in a country such as Mexico, however, where the median family income is much lower.

There are two main methods of setting relative poverty levels. One is to take an arbitrary percentage of the median family income and define this as the poverty level. The line in most countries is set at the 50 to 66 percent level. The European Union generally uses 60 percent of median income as its poverty line. In the United States the relative poverty line is set at 44 percent of the median income. The other method, exemplified by the Townsend study in England, is to survey the general population to find out their opinion about where the poverty level should be.[30]

The major problem with relative definitions and measures of poverty is related to the fact that they are subjective. The question is, what criteria do you use in setting the line? In setting an absolute line you have the criterion of physical efficiency, which can be ascertained by things such as caloric needs and the cost of a menu sufficient to ob-

Does a child in the United States actually need *a bicycle? Using a relative definition of poverty, the answer is yes because a child cannot fully participate in the life of the community without one. Using an absolute definition, the answer is no because a bicycle is not necessary for health and efficiency.*

tain these calories. But when you attempt to set a relative line, there is no similar criterion. Desai proposes two principles to be used in setting a relative poverty line:

1. . . . economic entitlement to an adequate living standard should be such that citizens can take full part in the political community.
2. . . . the level of the poverty threshold, i.e., the specific contents of the level of living flowing from a citizen's economic entitlement, must be determined by the community.[31]

The authors agree with Desai, but we would broaden the first principle by eliminating the word *political.* Thus, when considering whether to include an item in a poverty line budget, we would ask the question, "Is this item necessary for full participation in the community?" rather than asking the absolute definition question, "Is this item necessary for physical efficiency?" For example, if you were considering whether to include the cost of a bicycle for a family with a ten-year-old child, using an absolute definition you would not include any money for this, because the family can function with physical efficiency without a bicycle. Using a relative definition, however, you would include it because there is little doubt that a ten-year-old needs a bike in order to participate fully in the life of the community.

As you might expect, using a relative definition results in a much higher poverty line than using an absolute definition—and consequently a much higher poverty rate. The London Weekend Television study in England and the Gallup poll in the United States cited earlier resulted in figures 33 and 55 percent above the official poverty line.

A CLOSER Look

Poverty Definition Quiz

Do you think the following things are essential or nonessential?

1. For a ten-year-old child to have a bicycle.
2. For a family to have a car, even though it may be a junker.
3. For a sixteen-year-old girl to have a formal dress or a sixteen-year-old boy to rent a tuxedo to attend the junior prom.
4. For a family to have enough food to be able to serve coffee and cookies, or beer and chips, when friends drop in.
5. For a family to have a television set in good working order.

If you answered that all, or most, of these things are nonessential, you are operating from an absolute definition of poverty. It is true that none of these things is necessary for life, or for efficiency. If you answered that all, or most, of these are essential, you are operating from a relative definition. There is little doubt that a family that does not have these things, as well as many others not listed here, is not able to fully participate in the life of our society.

The Townsend study in England resulted in a figure 50 percent above the official level. On the average, the poverty line set by these groups was 90 percent greater than the official U.S. government level. Even when the very low relative poverty line figure of 44 percent of median income is used in the United States, the relative line comes out to be 10 percent higher than the official line.

Relative poverty measures have several advantages over absolute measures. The first and probably greatest advantage is that they are much more realistic than absolute measures. People do not live their lives according to the assumptions used for absolute poverty lines. They purchase toys for their children; they visit relatives; they celebrate occasions such as anniversaries and birthdays. And they generally do not manage their affairs with absolute efficiency. A second major advantage is that relative definitions recognize that poverty is subjective. Poverty is a matter of feeling and opinion among both the poor and the nonpoor, and relative definitions take opinions into account.

The major drawback of relative definitions is that they present a moving target, so to speak, for poverty policy and programs. One of the major reasons for defining poverty to begin with is so that we can measure progress in our attempts to do something about it. Using absolute definitions, we can see over time what progress has, or has not, been made. Using relative definitions, any change that occurs is likely to be as much a result of changing perceptions as it is a change in the level of well-being of the poorest section of the population.

The Official Poverty Line in the United States

Various government agencies in the United States have formulated definitions of poverty since the late nineteenth century. In 1907 the Bureau of Labor Statistics devised two budgets, one to meet "minimum standards" (an absolute measure) and one that was called a "fair standard" (a relative measure).[32] However, there was no "official" poverty line until the 1960s, when the U.S. government became serious for the first time in its history about reducing poverty. The official poverty line is defined as an attempt to "specify the minimum amount required to support an average family of given composition at the lowest level consistent with standards of living prevailing in this country."[33]

The first official poverty line in the United States was a crude measure developed in 1964 by the Council of Economic Advisors (CEA). This line used the same methodology that Rowntree had devised half a century earlier, which was based on the cost of food. The line was formulated using the *Engle's coefficient,* a technique that resulted in the conclusion that the average poor family spent one-third of its income on food. The Department of Agriculture (USDA) had developed menus to show what it cost families to eat at various levels, ranging from an economy budget to three higher-cost budgets. Initially the line was set using the "low-cost" menu and multiplying it by three (because food is supposed to take up one-third of a family's budget), which resulted in a poverty level of $3,995. This amount was deemed too high, so the CEA reformulated the line using the "economy budget," which resulted in a poverty level of $3,000. The main problem with this poverty line was that it had only two categories: families and single individuals. The poverty line was $1,500 for an individual and $3,000 for a family—regardless of size, age of family members, or type of residence. Thus, a couple with no dependents and an income of $2,900 was considered poor, while a family of eight with an income of $3,100 was not.

Because of the problems with the CEA poverty measure, the Social Security Administration (SSA) decided to revise it in 1965. A panel was appointed to accomplish this task; Mollie Orshansky, an SSA statistician, was designated as the chairperson. The SSA panel decided to continue to use the Engle's coefficient and the USDA economy food plan as the base for its calculations because this method was thought to have resulted in a realistic poverty line for a nonfarm family of four. Beyond this, however, the panel felt that the method developed by the Council of Economic Advisors was too crude to differentiate among different family types, places of residence, and other factors. The result of this panel's work was a poverty table known as the "Orshansky Index."[34] The new index was based on two major changes in the method of computation. The first was that the Engle's coefficient was reformulated to reflect the fact that smaller families spend a smaller percentage of their incomes on food. For single individuals, the food budget was multiplied by a factor of 5.92; for couples, the factor was 3.88; and for all larger families, the factor was 3.0. The second change was that the budget was reduced by 30 percent for farm families because it was presumed that they would grow a portion of their food. The resulting index differentiated among 124 different kinds of families, based on the sex of the head of household, the number of children under eighteen, the number of adults, and whether the family lived on a farm.

The poverty table developed by the Orshansky panel was updated each year based on changes in the price of food in the USDA economy food budget. In 1969 the Census Bureau adopted the index as its official measure of poverty and began to issue a statistical series on poverty. Over the years, the Census Bureau has made several changes in the index. The first is that they ceased updating it based on the cost of food and instead began to update it based on changes in the consumer price index (CPI). The second major change is that the differential between farm and nonfarm families was gradually reduced until it was entirely eliminated in 1982. These changes, along with some other minor ones, have caused the current table to be simplified considerably. The official poverty table for 2000 is presented in Table 7.6. Because of the need for trend data, the Census Bureau extrapolated the poverty line back to 1959. The poverty trend data for 1959–1999 are summarized in Figure 7.6.

The official U.S. government poverty line has been criticized for the same shortcomings as all absolute measures of poverty: It does not reflect how people actually spend their money; it ignores the fact that people have emotional needs that may be even more important to them than physical needs (parents may buy a child a birthday present even if it means they do not have enough money left to pay the rent); and it is set at a level that is much lower than most people in our society would personally set it. These are shortcomings of all absolute poverty measures, not just of the specific line used in this country. There is, however, a hot debate between liberals and conservatives about how useful and accurate the line is, and just what it means. It is to this debate we now turn.

Issues and Perspectives in Measuring and Defining Poverty

At first it sounds strange to speak of clashing perspectives and heated disagreements about something so seemingly dry and technical as the definition and measurement of poverty. However, as we shall see, these disagreements do occur; and, although the matter may be dry and technical, it is certainly not unimportant. The definition of poverty is an inherently political act and one that has grave implications. The power to define poverty is the power to control statistics—and, as Harrington has noted, "the control of statistics is one of the critical functions of power in a democratic society. The numbers define the limits of the possible; they confer the awesome mathematical legitimacy of 'fact' upon some parts of reality and deny it to others."[35] Orshansky, the primary author of the official poverty line, is quite candid about the political nature of the line. She comments, "In the Social Security Administration poverty was first defined in terms of the public or policy issue: To how many people, and to which ones, did we wish to direct policy concern."[36] Orshansky and her committee wished to create a line that was politically credible. To be credible they felt that they had to select a figure that identified a group that was not so small that people would be tempted not to worry about it or so large that a solution would appear impossible.

You will recall from Chapter 1 that conservatives support the status quo and are generally opposed to government programs. Because of these views they tend to favor definitions that minimize the amount of poverty in America. If the level of poverty is shown to be low, this logically leads to the conclusion that society is working well (which supports the status quo) and that there is little need for more government programs. Liberals support change and are generally in favor of government programs that they believe will lead to an improvement in society. They favor definitions that maximize the amount of poverty because the existence of a large, and especially a growing, level of poverty logically leads to the conclusion that society is not functioning as well as it should be and that increased government intervention is called for.

In keeping with their respective agendas, liberals and conservatives hotly debate the official government poverty line. The debate revolves around four basic issues: Is the poverty line set at a realistic level? Do you count only cash as income or do you count

TABLE 7.6 Poverty Thresholds in 2002

Size of Family Unit	Poverty Guidelines	Size of Family Unit	Poverty Guidelines
1	$ 9,183	6	24,576
2	11,756	7	28,001
3	14,348	8	30,907
4	18,392	9 or more	37,062
5	21,744		

Source: U.S. Bureau of the Census, "The Official Statistics," online at www.census.gov, Poverty Thresholds, 2002.

FIGURE 7.6 Number in Poverty and Poverty Rate, 1959 to 2002

Note: The data points represent the midpoints of the respective years.

Source: U.S. Census Bureau, Current Population Survey, 1960–2003 Annual Social and Economic Supplements; U.S. Census Bureau, *Poverty in the United States 2002,* 3.

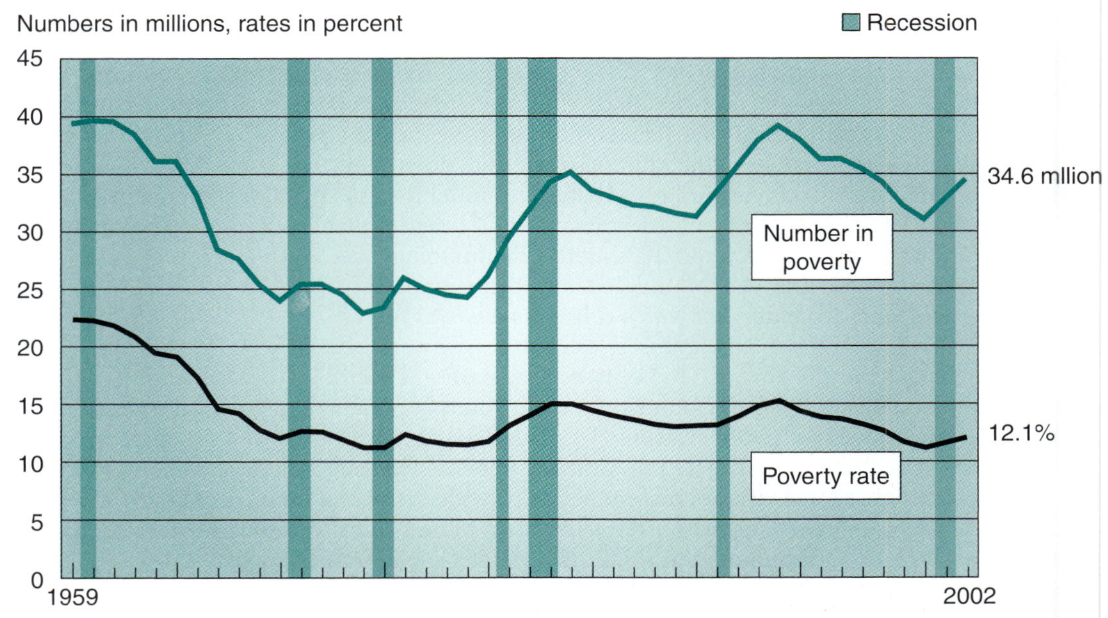

other benefits? Are the Census Bureau figures on which poverty estimates are based accurate? Should poverty be defined and measured using an absolute or a relative definition?

Is the Poverty Line Set at a Realistic Level? Conservatives argue that the poverty line, $17,761 in 2000 for a family of four, is set at too high a level. The conservative economist Rose Friedman has argued that the Engle's coefficient used to estimate total needs from spending on food is incorrect. She asserts that low-income families spend a greater proportion of their income on food than average families and therefore that the food budget should be multiplied by a number less than the three that is currently used. Friedman argues that the use of this incorrect coefficient has resulted in an overestimation of poverty by as much as 100 percent.[37]

Conservatives also argue that tying the poverty line to the consumer price index has further increased the already too high poverty line. The CPI measures increases in the cost of living by figuring the cost of a specific "market basket" of goods. Butler and Kondratas say that this method ignores substitution of one commodity for another by households in order to keep the cost down.[38] For example, if the price of soft drinks increased by 30 percent and the price of fruit juice did not increase at all, most consumers would substitute fruit juice for at least part of their soft drink consumption. As a result of this substitution, the actual cost of their "market basket" of goods would increase at a rate lower than the CPI. This is only one of several flaws in the CPI that conservatives believe have artificially inflated the poverty line.

Liberals, to no one's surprise, take the opposite position and argue that the poverty line is too low. They point out that the U.S. Department of Agriculture, whose budgets are used as the basis of the poverty calculations, admits that the budgets are set at an unrealistically low level. USDA analysts have estimated that only about 10 percent of persons spending the amount allowed in the economy food budget are able to get a nutritionally adequate diet.[39] The USDA has also revised the Engle's coefficient. In 1965 an analysis by the department concluded that for poor families the coefficient should be 3.45 rather than 3.0. This increase would raise the poverty line by 15 percent and result in a large increase in the number of families defined as poor. Even the originator of the official poverty line, Mollie Orshansky, eventually came to believe that the methodology had, over time, broken down, resulting in a figure that was too low. She updated the methodology and, applying the new methodology to Census Bureau data, concluded that the official figures underestimated the amount of poverty by between 38 and 54 percent, depending on which census survey was used.[40]

How Should Noncash Benefits Be Counted? A good deal of assistance to poor families is given in forms other than cash. Poor people may receive food stamps, medical care, low-cost public housing, legal services, social services, and other items and services; these are referred to as "in-kind" benefits. Although these items do not constitute income as such, it does cost money to provide them, and they are of tangible benefit in improving the lives of the recipients. Most of these benefits were not available when the current methodology for defining and measuring poverty was adopted. The current method of computing the poverty line counts only cash as income; no value whatsoever is given to in-kind benefits.

Conservatives argue that in-kind benefits should be counted as income. Butler and Kondratas point to the irony of not counting these benefits; they observe that "the federal government could give every poor person in America a free car, free housing and education, and free food for life, but as far as the official poverty definition is concerned, that would have no impact whatsoever on poverty."[41] They observe that the majority of the increases in benefits provided to the poor since the early 1960s have been in the form of goods and services rather than cash, and that if these benefits were counted, the poverty rate would greatly decrease. Martin Anderson, a leading conservative analyst on the subject of social welfare, has gone so far as to say, "The 'War on Poverty' that began in 1964 has been won. . . . Any Americans who truly cannot care for themselves are now eligible for generous government aid in the form of cash, medical benefits, food stamps, housing, and other services."[42] Anderson, using data from the Census Bureau and from a Congressional Budget Office study, estimates that largely because of the value of in-kind benefits, the number of people in poverty in 1978 was only one-quarter of the official figure.

Liberals agree that in-kind benefits have value and should be considered when we define and measure poverty. Their argument is that excluding all benefits other than cash from poverty-line calculations obscures the successes of social programs, especially Medicaid and food stamps. They point out that this is why conservative critics such as Charles Murray have been able to argue that liberal social programs have largely failed. It has been estimated by liberal policy analysts that if all government benefits were included the number of people living below the poverty line would be about one-third lower.[43] However, liberals have some ambivalence about this issue due to what they see as the difficulty of accurately assessing the value of noncash benefits. Harrington gives the following example of the problems involved:

> How does one evaluate the value of medical care that goes mainly to the aging poor? The Bureau of the Census gives an excellent case in point. In 1979, the market value of Medicaid coverage for an elderly person in New York State was estimated at $4,430. But this was almost $1,000 more than the poverty line for that person ($3,472). Clearly this $4,430 is "income" in a very special sense, since it cannot be spent on food, housing, or any other need (and it is indeed most unwelcome "income" since one has to be ill to get it). If one were to take that $4,430 at face value, then a person could enter the middle class, by virtue of having a long, expensive, subsidized terminal illness.[44]

Should Poverty Be Defined in Absolute or Relative Terms? This question is closely related to our earlier discussion of inequality. If you think for a few moments, you will realize that if you use a relative definition of poverty, the only way poverty will show a reduction is for the Gini coefficient to show a reduction. By way of example, let's use two rather improbable economic scenarios. In the first scenario, the economy enters a tremendous boom period with the result that the income of everyone in the country doubles while prices remain the same. This means that a family of four that was living on $10,000 a year, a little below the poverty line, now is earning $20,000 a year, well above the poverty line. It also means that the family whose income was $250,000 a year, many times more than it needs, now has even more. If you apply an absolute definition of poverty to this scenario, poverty would almost disappear. However, if you apply a relative definition, the poverty level would be exactly the same because at the same time the median income doubled, the relative poverty line would also have doubled. Therefore, inequality would be the same, the Gini coefficient would be the same, and the poverty level would be the same—even though people would be twice as well-off in absolute terms.

The second scenario is the opposite. In this scenario, the country enters a tremendous depression. Everyone's income takes a nosedive; however, let's suppose that the richer you are the harder you are hit. People in the bottom 20 percent (quintile) of the income distribution suffer a 30 percent reduction in income; people in the next quintile suffer a 40 percent reduction; the next quintile is reduced by 50 percent; the fourth quintile is reduced by 70 percent; and the richest quintile see their income go down by 90 percent. This means that the family in the first scenario, whose income was $10,000 per year, now has an income of $7,000. The family whose income was $250,000 now has an income of only $25,000 per year. If an absolute definition of poverty were applied to this scenario, the poverty rate would skyrocket. However, if a relative definition were applied, the poverty rate would drop dramatically. Before the crash, the income of the low-income family was only 4 percent of that of the high-income family. After the crash, it "improved" to 28 percent. This example is far-fetched, but the point it illustrates is not: When one uses a relative definition, the only way to show a reduction in poverty is to reduce inequality.

As you know from the previous discussion of inequality, conservatives see no particular reason to reduce inequality and so do not generally favor relative definitions. They believe that absolute definitions such as the official poverty line, while not perfect, are satisfactory for the purposes they serve. Murray, for example, says:

> The poverty definition has been attacked from all sides but continues to be used because, finally, it has a good deal of merit. The poverty line does not truly divide the "poverty-stricken" from the rest of us—the transition consists of a continuum, not a dividing line—but it gives us a common yardstick for talking about the issue. It is widely accepted, takes family size and inflation into account, and provides a consistent definition for examining income over time. Also, no one has proposed an alternative definition that has attracted widespread support.[45]

Liberals believe that the reduction of inequality would be a good thing and so are more favorable toward relative definitions of poverty and more critical of absolute definitions. Rodgers, for example, criticizes the official poverty line on the grounds that it has not kept up with the growth in personal income. He notes that in 1959 the poverty line was 53 percent of median income; by 1984 it had declined to only 38 percent. Rodgers believes that a relative definition is the only meaningful way of describing poverty and that the United States does not use this method because the amount of poverty revealed would be embarrassing to the government.[46]

Should the Poverty Line Be Based on Net Disposable Income? When the initial poverty measure was developed, it was based on the mostly accurate belief that the majority of people with incomes below the poverty line were not employed. Thus, the simplest means of calculating the poverty line was that of basing it on gross income. As we have seen, in the years since the original poverty measure was developed the poverty population has significantly changed; currently most are employed. The growth of the working poor creates two major inaccuracies in the poverty measure. The first is that a working person's gross income is significantly reduced by taxes and other deductions before it ever reaches the recipient. The second is that even after taxes the income is further reduced by work-related expenses, primarily child care. Thus, a nonworking

Conservatives have long argued that if in-kind benefits such as food stamps were counted, the number of people classified as being below the poverty line would greatly decrease. The new poverty measure recommended by the National Science Foundation counts in-kind benefits as a kind of income.

mother of three whose income is $17,000 a year is considered to be poor by the current measure, but a working mother whose gross income is $18,000 a year, but whose net income after deductions and work-related expenses is only $12,000, is not considered to be poor. Both liberals and conservatives agree that something should be done to base the poverty line on actual disposable income rather than gross income.

Experimental Poverty Measures

Because of the problems in the current poverty measure discussed in previous sections, plus additional problems resulting from social and economic changes that have occurred since the current measure was developed, the Census Bureau has been considering revising the method used to define and measure poverty. A National Academy of Sciences (NAS) panel that is advising the Census Bureau has identified six weaknesses in the current poverty measure:

1. Because of the increased participation of mothers in the labor force, there are more working families who must pay for child care, but the current measure does not distinguish between the needs of families in which the parents do or do not work outside the home. More generally, the current measure does not distinguish between the needs of workers and nonworkers.
2. Because of differences in health status and insurance coverage, different population groups face significant differences in medical care costs, but the current measure does not take account of them.
3. The thresholds are the same across the nation, although significant price variations across geographic areas exist for needs such as housing.
4. The family size adjustments in the thresholds are anomalous in many respects, and changing demographic and family characteristics (such as the reduction in average family size) underscore the need to reassess the adjustments.

5. Changes in the standard of living call into question the merits of continuing to use the values of the original thresholds updated only for inflation. Historical evidence suggests that poverty thresholds—including those developed according to "expert" notions of minimum needs—follow trends in overall consumption levels. Because of rising living standards in the United States, most approaches for developing poverty thresholds (including the original one) would produce higher thresholds today than the current ones.
6. Finally, because the current measure defines family resources as gross money income, it does not reflect the effects of important government policy initiatives that have significantly altered families' disposable income and, hence, their poverty status. Examples are the increase in the Social Security payroll tax, which reduces disposable income for workers, and the growth in the Food Stamp Program, which raises disposable income for beneficiaries.

The NSF panel has recommended a new poverty measure that, like the current measure, is based on the three basic budget categories of food, clothing, and shelter, with a small additional amount added for personal needs. The major differences in the method proposed by the NSF panel are that the new measure would:

- include consideration of changes in the overall consumption level. For example, when the current measure was developed a television and a car were not considered necessary for a family to be defined as living above the poverty line. These things are now considered essential and so would be included in the calculations.
- include in-kind benefits (referred to by the NAS panel as "near-money disposable income") such as food stamps and Medicaid.
- exclude taxes and nondiscretionary (work-related) expenses.[47]

The Census Bureau is currently evaluating six NAS-based poverty measures. The major differences between these measures and the current official measure are summarized in Figure 7.7.

Conclusion

It has been said that statistics are problems with the tears wiped away. It is important that we keep this in mind when discussing somewhat dry, technical subjects such as inequality and the definition and measurement of poverty. How we define and measure poverty has very real consequences for a large number of people. The eligibility requirements for many assistance programs are computed by means of formulas derived from the poverty line. Some housing assistance programs, for example, are open to people whose income does not exceed 125 percent of the poverty line. A revision of a few hundred dollars up or down in the poverty line will result in thousands of people becoming eligible or ineligible for a decent place to live. What the correct Engle's coefficient is may be puzzling to a student and fascinating to a professor, but it has very real consequences for a child who does not want to sleep with rats.

FIGURE 7.7

Official and Alternative (NAS-Based) Poverty Estimates: How Do They Differ?

Question	Official Measure	Alternative NAS-Based Estimates
What counts as income?	Gross money income (that is, before taxes) of all family members living in the same housing unit, not counting capital gains.	Like the official measure, the alternative estimates added together the incomes of all family members who live together, except that the alternative estimates: ■ Use after-tax income ■ Include noncash benefits as income (such as food stamps and housing subsidies) ■ Deduct some work-related expenses (such as transportation and child care) from income ■ Take into account medical out-of-pocket expenses (each measure has a different method for doing so)
What is used as a benchmark for need?	First computed in 1963–64, the thresholds were originally based on U.S. Department of Agriculture (USDA) food budgets designed for families under economic stress. Social Security Administration analysts used 1955 USDA data to find out what portion of their income families spent on food, then multiplied the food budgets by the inverse of that factor to get the thresholds (with some adjustments for two-person families and single people). Except when federal interagency committees made minor revisions, these thresholds have only been updated for inflation annually with the Consumer Price Index CPI-U), as directed by the the Office of Management and Budget's Statistical Policy Directive 14.	Unlike the official thresholds, which have no fixed relationship between thresholds for different-sized families (because they were derived with food budgets and spending data), the alternative estimates start with expenditures for food, clothing, shelter, and utilities (and for some measures, medical expenses) for a family of four—two adults and two children—plus a small additional amount for other expenses. These dollar amounts are adjusted for larger and smaller families, based on some aspects of their relative needs. The adjustments are made using three parameters: the first reflects that children tend to consume less than adults, the second reflects that a doubling of family size does not mean that every expense becomes twice as high, and the third reflects that the first child in a single-adult family represents a greater increase in expenses than the first child in a two-adult family.
What adjustments are made for geographic differences in the cost of living?	None. The same thresholds apply to all parts of the country.	Some estimates (labeled NGA) make no adjustment; others are adjusted using cost indices by state and metropolitan/nonmetropolitan residence, based on housing costs.

Source: Bernadette Proctor and Joseph Dalaker, U.S. Census Bureau, Current Population Reports, P60–222, *Poverty in the United States: 2002* (Washington, DC: U.S. Government Printing Office, 2003), 16.

Visit **www.researchnavigator.com** to research these important concepts from the chapter:

Domestic violence AND income
Economic inequality
Ethnicity AND poverty
Gender AND poverty
Income gap
Poverty line
Race AND poverty

Web Sites Related to the Concept of Poverty

The Administration for Children and Families <www.acf.dhhs.gov>: Includes an overview of the ACF, press releases, new rules related to federal programs for families and children, fact sheets, a description of the agency's programs, and additional web sites.

Federal Government Resources on the Web <www.lib.umich.edu/libhome/DocumentsCenter/federal.html>: A search engine that provides access to a wide variety of federal government resources including budget; laws; executive orders; regulations; and actions of the executive, legislative, and judicial branches of government; as well as numerous other information sources.

Government Information Sharing Project <govinfo.kerr.orst.edu>: Access to government databases related to demographics, economics, and education. Much of the data is broken down to the county level. Includes links to other government web sites.

The Library of Congress <lcweb.loc.gov>: Describes the wide range of holdings and services of the Library of Congress. Includes acquisitions, cataloging, preservation, research, special programs, standards, and access to the catalogs of the Library of Congress and other libraries.

National Center for Children in Poverty <cpmcnet.columbia.edu/dept/nccp>: A Columbia University center dedicated to identifying and promoting strategies to reduce poverty among children. Site includes information on the center, news releases, child poverty facts, state and local information, publications, and information on topics related to children in poverty, such as child care and public assistance.

Endnotes

1. U.S. Bureau of Economic Analysis, National Economic Accounts, Table 1.9 (23 October 2003); U.S. Bureau of the Census, *Current Population Survey 1*(7) (March 2003).
2. Molly Ivins, "GOP Says Some Topics Off Limits," *Kalamazoo Gazette* (12 January 1995), A10.
3. John Craven, *Introduction to Economics: An Integrated Approach to Fundamental Principles* (Oxford, England: Basil Blackwell, 1984), 99.
4. Lisa A. Keister, *Wealth in America* (Cambridge, England: Cambridge University Press, 2000), 64.
5. A. B. Kennickell and M. Starr-McCluer, "Changes in Family Finances from 1989 to 1992: Evidence from the Survey of Consumer Finances," *Federal Reserve Bulletin 80* (1994), 861–882; University of Michigan Institute for Social Research, "Wealth in America," *ISR Newsletter* (Winter 1986–87), 3–4.
6. Quoted in University of Michigan Institute for Social Research, "Wealth in America," 3.
7. Keister, *Wealth in America,* 65.
8. Richard B. Freeman, "Solving the New Inequality," in Richard B. Freeman, *The New Inequality; Creating Solutions for Poor America* (Boston: Beacon Press, 1999), 3.
9. Daniel H. Weinberg, "Income Inequality," U.S. Bureau of the Census, "The Official Statistics," online at www.census.gov/hhes/income/incineq/p60asc.

10. D. Stanley Eitzen, "Dismantling the Welfare State," *Vital Speeches of the Day 62* (15 June 1996), 532–536, updated by author.
11. Stephen J. Rose, "The Truth about Social Mobility," *Challenge* (May–June 1996), 4–8.
12. Michael Hout and Samuel R. Lucas, "Narrowing the Income Gap between Rich and Poor," *Chronicle of Higher Education* (16 August 1996), B1.
13. Michael Novak and Gordon Green, "Poverty Down, Inequality Up?" *The Public Interest* (Spring 1986), 49–57.
14. Sheldon Danzinger and Peter Gottshalk, "Introduction," in Sheldon Danziger and Peter Gottshalk, eds., *Uneven Tides: Rising Inequality in America* (New York: Russell Sage Foundation, 1993), 13.
15. Bennett Harrison, Chris Tilly, and Berry Bluestone, "Wage Inequity Takes a Great U-Turn," *Challenge* (March–April 1986), 27.
16. Lester Thurow, quoted in D. Stanley Eitzen, "Dismantling the Welfare State," 4.
17. Henry Reuss, "Inequality, Here We Come," *Challenge* (September–October 1981), 52.
18. George Gilder, *Wealth and Poverty* (New York: Basic Books, 1981), 63.
19. George Gilder, "Wealth and Poverty Revisited," *American Spectator 26* (July 1993), 37.
20. Robert M. Solow, "The Entrepreneur as Hero," review of George Gilder, *The Spirit of Enterprise,* in *The New Republic* (22 October 1984), 37–39.
21. William Ryan, *Equality* (New York: Pantheon, 1981), 30.
22. Paul Krugman, "The Income Disparity," *Challenge* (July–August 1990), 6.
23. L. F. Hayes, "Non-Economic Aspects of Poverty," *Australian Journal of Social Issues 5* (February 1970), 41–54.
24. Mollie Orshansky, "How Poverty Is Measured," *Monthly Labor Review 92* (February 1969), 37.
25. Quoted in Albert Fried and Richard M. Elman, eds., *Charles Booth's London: A Portrait of the Poor at the Turn of the Century, Drawn from His "Life and Labour of the People in London"* (New York: Pantheon Books, 1968), 10.
26. Robert Holman, *Poverty: Explanations of Social Deprivation* (New York: St. Martin's Press, 1978), 7–8.
27. Quoted in Holman, *Poverty,* 11–12.
28. David Caplovitz, *The Poor Pay More: Consumer Practices of Low Income Families* (New York: Free Press, 1967).
29. Joanna Mack and Stewart Lansley, *Poor Britain* (London: George Allen and Unwin, 1985).
30. Peter Townsend, P. Corrigan, and U. Kowarski, *Poverty and the London Labor Market: The Third London Survey, Interim Report* (London: The Low Pay Unit, 1987).
31. Meghnad Desai, "Drawing the Line: On Defining the Poverty Threshold," in Peter Golding, ed., *Excluding the Poor* (London: Child Poverty Action Group, 1986), 3–4.
32. Sharon M. Oster, Elizabeth E. Lake, and Conchita Gene Oksman, *The Definition and Measurement of Poverty, Volume 1: A Review* (Boulder, CO: Westview Press, 1978), 6.
33. Mollie Orshansky, "Measuring Poverty," *The Social Welfare Forum: Proceedings of the 92nd Annual Forum of the National Conference on Social Welfare* (New York: Columbia University Press, 1965), 214.
34. Orshansky, "How Poverty Is Measured," 37–41.
35. Michael Harrington, *The New American Poverty* (New York: Holt, Rinehart & Winston, 1984), 71.
36. Orshansky, "How Poverty Is Measured," 37.
37. Rose Friedman, *Poverty: Definition and Perspective* (Washington, DC: American Enterprise Institute, 1965), 36.
38. Stuart Butler and Anna Kondratas, *Out of the Poverty Trap* (New York: Free Press, 1987), 46.
39. Orshansky, "How Poverty Is Measured," 38.
40. Mollie Orshansky, "Measuring Poverty," *Public Welfare 51* (Winter 1993), 27.
41. Butler and Kondratas, *Out of the Poverty Trap,* 46.
42. Martin Anderson, *Welfare* (Stanford, CA: Hoover Institution, 1978), 15.
43. Gary Burtless and Timothy Smeeding, "The Level, Trend, and Composition of Poverty," in Sheldon H. Danziger and Robert H. Haverman, eds., *Understanding Poverty* (New York: Russell Sage, 2003), 173.
44. Harrington, *The New American Poverty,* 86.
45. Charles Murray, *Losing Ground* (New York: Basic Books, 1984), 271.
46. Harrell R. Rodgers Jr., "Limiting Poverty by Design," in Richard Goldstein and Stephen Sachs, eds., *Applied Poverty Research* (Lanham, MD: Rowman & Littlefield, 1984), 54.
47. National Research Council, *Measuring Poverty, A New Approach* (Washington, DC: National Academy Press, 1996), 2–5.

CHAPTER

8

The Nature and Causes of Poverty

When I was a child, I lived with my family in Minneapolis. We lived on the south side of town, and our relatives lived on the north side where my father had grown up. We visited often. One Sunday afternoon in March we set off across town in our car and took a different route than usual. I think it had something to do with the construction of a new freeway, which caused streets to be closed. Our new route took us through the middle of the area that would now be called the ghetto; it was then called the slums. This was new and foreign territory; I had never seen anything like it. I stared out of the window fascinated, horrified, and repulsed all at the same time. There were houses that had burned down and apparently been abandoned; broken glass seemed to be everywhere; and the streets and yards were littered with paper and junk. Even more puzzling were the housing projects, which I could see were relatively new and modern structures, not unlike apartment houses in my neighborhood, but which looked little better than the old dilapidated buildings surrounding them. Their walls were covered with graffiti, there were cars up on blocks, and the yards were lakes of mud separated by scraggly patches of grass.

Groups of children ran around and played; they did not look too different from the children I played with. They were a little ragged—some were wearing torn tennis shoes even though it was still cold—but otherwise they looked familiar. The groups of adults did not seem typical, however. They were standing around in small groups, looking tired and bored, and they lacked the appearance of purpose and command that I expected from the adults in my life.

"Who are these people?" I asked my parents. "Why are they here?" "What is this place?" "Do they like it?" "Why don't they leave?" My parents explained that these were poor people; they were here because they did not have enough money to go anywhere else; and most of them did not like it, but they probably did not know anything else. It was an unfortunate situation, but it was simply a fact of life. This explanation didn't really satisfy me. I knew poor people. My friend Mike was poor. Mike's father had been killed in the Korean War, and his mother had some sort of chronic illness; people referred to her as frail. She was able to work only part time, answering the phone at the Lutheran church; and her salary from this, plus her small government check, provided very little income. Mike and his mother lived in a tiny two-room cottage in the backyard of a house two blocks down from where my family lived. The cottage had been built for the mother of the owner of the house, and when she died, the owner rented it to Mike's mother for a small sum. Mike slept in the bedroom and his mother slept in a hide-a-bed in the living room. They did not have a car. Mike's mother had a basket that rolled on two wheels and could be folded up for easy carrying. She would carry this to the store, load her groceries in, and roll them home. They didn't have a TV set, even though the last holdout in the neighborhood (my father) had purchased one two years before. Like all of us, Mike worked, mowing lawns in the summer and shoveling snow in the winter. However, unlike us, he could not use his money for anything he wanted. Whatever he earned he gave to his mother, who put it in the bank to be used for school clothes, Boy Scouts, and summer camp. Any money left over went into that mysterious black hole of youthful finance, the college fund.

As we drove out of the ghetto I thought about Mike. Mike was poor, but he was not like this. The only difference between Mike's family and mine was that we had more money. This neighborhood appeared to be in another country, if not on another planet. Who were these people? Why were these people like this? It had to be more than simply money.

As an adult, I am still asking the questions I asked as a child. Those questions are the subject of this chapter. Who are the poor? Are they all the same? Why are they poor? Regarding the first two questions, as you will see, we know a good deal. We have massive amounts of statistical data to describe the poor. My youthful observation about the difference between my friend Mike and the people I observed in that Minneapolis ghetto was valid—poor people are not all the same, and there is more to poverty than money, although obviously money is the most important part. The answer to the last question is not so clear. We have many theories about the causes of poverty, but no certain answers. The answers we do have are greatly clouded by our old friend—political perspectives.

Who Are the Poor?

In this section we present a statistical picture of the population in the United States who live below the poverty line. Two types of pictures are presented. The first is the traditional means of describing this population based on statistical data gathered mainly by the Census Bureau as part of its series of Current Population Reports. This is the source of most of the figures you see on the evening news and that are referred to in statements by lawmakers and interest groups. This type of information has been referred to as cross-section or "snapshot" data: It provides a series of statistical pictures at certain points in time, but it does not tell us much beyond a general description of the situation at that time. Poverty statistics show, for example, that the level of poverty in this country is fairly

The popular stereotype of poor families is that they are very large. In reality, the average size of families living below the poverty line is fewer than three.

stable, running between 11 and 15 percent each year. However, these statistics do not tell us anything about the individual makeup of those figures at each point in time. Is the 11 to 15 percent composed of the same people this year as last year, or are different people poor each year? If the statistics describe a different population each year, how different is it? Are some people more likely to be part of the statistics for a short time whereas others are part of them for many years? To answer questions such as these, a different type of data collection is needed. This type of information comes from *longitudinal data*—data collected from the same persons at many successive points in time, which can begin to answer some of these questions. We have only recently begun collecting longitudinal data, the best source currently being the Panel Study of Income Dynamics, conducted by the Survey Research Center at the University of Michigan. The first topic in this section, the statistical description of poverty, relies mostly on snapshot data collected by the Census Bureau. The next section, types of poverty, relies more on longitudinal data, mainly from the Panel Study of Income Dynamics.

Statistical Description of the Poverty Population

The Bureau of the Census maintains an Internet web site and periodically publishes a book that presents nearly two hundred pages of statistics on the poverty population.[1] A few of the most interesting of these statistics for 2002 are summarized in Table 8.1. As can be seen, almost 35 million Americans, 12.1 percent of the population, had incomes that were below the poverty level in 2002. The misery of poverty, however, was not evenly divided among the many groups of the population. The burden fell much more heavily on some than on others.

Race. The image of the poor in most people's minds is that of a minority group, generally African American. As can be seen from the data in Table 8.1, that image is both right and wrong. It is wrong in the sense that the largest number of the poor, more than 45 percent, are non-Hispanic white. However, the image is correct in that a much greater proportion of minority group members fall below the poverty line. Fewer than one out of every thirteen non-Hispanic white people in this country is poor, compared with nearly one out of four persons of African or Hispanic origin. Whites constitute the largest number of the poor only because such a great majority of the population is white.

Age. The popular image of a poor person is of an able-bodied young adult. The Census Bureau data show this image to be wrong. The largest single age group among the poor are, in fact, children who are too young to work and who thus cannot improve their own status (see Figure 8.1). As people move into the productive adult years, the percentage in poverty rapidly declines. The percentage once again increases as people move into the older segment of the population.

Region. The distribution of poverty across the country is fairly even. There is a little more poverty in the South and West and a little less in the Midwest and Northeast. However, these differences probably reflect the greater proportion of the population in the South and West who live in rural areas.

TABLE 8.1 **Characteristics of the Population below the Poverty Line, 2002**

Group	Number below Poverty Line (in thousands)	Rate (% below poverty line)
All Persons	34,570	12.1
Race		
Non-Hispanic White	15,567	8.0
Black	8,602	24.1
Hispanic*	8,555	21.8
Asian and Pacific Islander	1,161	10.1
Age (years)		
Under 18	12,133	16.7
18–24	4,536	16.5
25–34	4,674	11.9
35–44	4,087	9.3
45–54	2,999	7.5
55–59	1,302	8.4
60–64	1,263	10.6
65+	3,576	10.4
Region		
Northeast	5,871	10.9
Midwest	6,616	10.3
South	14,019	13.8
West	8,064	12.4
Family Size		
2 Persons	2,699	8.0
3 Persons	1,535	9.2
4 Persons	1,483	9.8
5 Persons	839	12.7
6 Persons	400	17.4
7 Persons	147	20.1
8 Persons	76	30.6
9 Persons or more	50	25.8
Family Type		
All Families	7,229	9.6
Married Couple	3,052	5.3
Female Head, No Husband	3,613	26.5
Male Head, No Wife	564	12.1
Single Individuals		
All	9,618	20.4
Male	4,023	17.7
Female	5,595	22.9

*Persons of Hispanic origin may be of any race.

Source: Derived from Bernadette D. Proctor and Joseph Dalaker, U.S. Bureau of the Census, Current Population Reports, Series P-60-222, *Poverty in the United States: 2002* (Washington, DC: U.S. Government Printing Office, 2003), various tables.

FIGURE 8.1 *Source:* Copyright © 1987. Tribune Media Services. Reprinted with permission.

Family Size. Another popular stereotype of the poor is that they generally have very large families. As can be seen from Table 8.1, this is not entirely true. The average size of families below the poverty line is only slightly larger than the average family in the United States, and this difference can probably be explained by the fact that families below the poverty line are younger than the average and thus have more members at home. However, the stereotype of the large poor family is correct in one sense. A far greater proportion of large families than small families fall below the poverty line. Only 8 percent of two-person families are living in poverty, whereas 30.6 percent of eight-member families and 25.8 percent of families with nine or more members are poor. The reason for this, we should note, is not that large families earn less money than small families, but that they need more money to live adequately. In 2001 the poverty line for a two-person family was $11,756, whereas the poverty line for a nine-person family was $37,062.

Family Type. As is discussed later in this chapter, researchers are finding a great deal of evidence that points to family type as the most important determinant of economic status. The basis for this line of thinking can be found in Table 8.1. Families that have both a husband and a wife have a poverty rate of only 4.8 percent. For families with a female head and no husband present, the rate is 27.8 percent, nearly six times that of married-couple families. Interestingly, single-person households appear to do rather poorly in economic life. The overall rate of poverty for single individuals is 19.1 percent; for single males the rate is 16.3 percent, and for single females it is 21.7 percent.

The Feminization of Poverty. You have probably noticed in all the data being reviewed that women appear to be doing poorly in relation to men. This is an accurate observation and one that has not gone unnoticed by researchers and policymakers in recent years. In fact, a term was coined in 1978 to describe this problem—*the feminization of poverty.*[2] This problem has become even more severe in recent years because of the rapid and steady increase in the number of families headed by women. The percentage of families headed by women increased from 10.1 percent in 1950 to 14 percent in 1976, an increase of almost 40 percent in only one generation. After 1976 this number stabilized and is currently at 15 percent.[3] In our society, because the woman is generally the parent who provides the bulk of child care, this trend contributes to the great number of children living below the poverty line.

Different Types of Poverty

Although the preceding data are useful for giving us a general description of the characteristics of the poor, these data are static. That is, they tell us what the population looks like at various points in time but say little, if anything, about differences other than demographic ones within the population. Sociologists have long known that the poverty population is not homogeneous; and recent studies, notably the Panel Study of Income Dynamics, have added greatly to our understanding of the many differences within the poverty population.

Three Levels of Poverty. In their classic study of poverty, Segalman and Basu posited the existence of three different segments in the poverty population: the transitional poor, the marginal poor, and the residual poor.[4] The transitional poor are those people whose experience of poverty is only temporary and is usually brief. Poverty for this group is generally the result of some life change or misfortune. Examples of situations likely to result in transitional poverty include a person returning to school to finish a degree and living on a bare-bones budget while doing it; a person unemployed because of a plant closing who is unable to find a new job and finally moves to a more economically prosperous area; a person who has an extended illness; and a widow for whom it takes a year or so to adjust to the new realities of her situation, including entering or reentering the job market. Segalman and Basu say that new immigrants generally go through a period of transitional poverty before learning the many things they need to know to compete in the job market. The key characteristics of transitional poverty are that it is brief, temporary, and generally related to specific events in the life of the person experiencing it.

The marginal poor are the group often referred to as the "working poor." They generally have jobs, but because of low educational levels and few skills, or because of discrimination, the jobs they have are low paying and insecure. These people are nearly always at the margin of the poverty line and, depending on luck and the economy, may be on one side or the other of that line. When the economic boom of the 1990s was at its peak, many of the marginal poor were earning near-middle-class incomes because of the great amount of work and overtime available. Now that the economy has slowed, many of these folks are falling back below the poverty line. The main difference between the transitional poor and the marginal poor is that the transitional poor are experiencing a brief episode of poverty, may never experience another, and may quickly rise well above the poverty line. For the marginal poor, rising out of poverty and sinking back into it is a long-term pattern, and it is doubtful for most that they will ever rise much above the poverty level.

The residual poor are a group who remain in poverty over an extended period of time. They are generally dependent on welfare benefits for their daily living, and their poverty may well be intergenerational. This group has received a good deal of attention in recent years, and they have come to be referred to as "the underclass."[5] Most media discussion of the problem of poverty in the United States, or of the corollary welfare problem, generally refers to the residual poor. This is the group that is hard to reach and that often seems almost immune to help; this group is thus frustrating to a society that likes to find rapid solutions to problems.

Data on Different Types of Poverty and Poverty Patterns. The preceding discussion of different types of poverty is based on Census Bureau data, which are of somewhat limited usefulness because they consist of statistical "snapshots" taken at various points in time. The data do not answer questions related to the proportion of the poor that is residual; the experience of poverty across the life cycle; the extent to which families and individuals move out of or remain in poverty; and, consequently, the factors that are related to escaping poverty. To make up for this deficiency, several longitudinal (meaning "over time") data sets have been developed. Called panel studies because they follow a panel of respondents for a number of years, these include the National Longitudinal Survey of Youth (NLSY), the survey of Income and Program Participation (SIPP), and, the most useful for our purposes, the Panel Study of Income Dynamics (PSID). The PSID was developed in 1968 by a group of social scientists at the Survey Research Center at the University of Michigan.[6] For this study the researchers selected a random sample of more than five thousand families, and repeated annual interviews have been conducted with the families each year since 1968. There are now thirty-five years of data on these families. In this section we summarize some of the major findings of the longitudinal studies. In the following section we use these data to examine some of the major theories on causes of poverty.

The official poverty rate in the United States remains fairly steady at between 11 percent and 15 percent; the rate in 2002 was 12.1 percent. With regard to this rate, the Panel Study contains both bad news and good news. The bad news is that during the years analyzed by Rebecca Blank, 1979–1991, the data indicate that a percentage of the population much larger than 11 to 15 percent was in a state of poverty for at least one year. Fully one-third of the population (33.6 percent) fell below the poverty line for at least one of the twelve years. The group we have called the residual poor, or the underclass, is called the "persistently poor" by the Panel Study researchers, and are defined here as being poor for ten of the twelve years covered by Blank's analysis. The good news is that only 4.9 percent of the population were found to be persistently poor. The group Segalman and Basu call the marginal poor is called the "intermittently poor" by the Panel Study researchers. This group of people is defined here as those who were poor four to nine of the twelve years analyzed, usually with no predictable pattern to the years. Blank found that 11.6 percent of the population fell into this category. A little over 17 percent of the population fell into the transitionally poor category, having incomes below the poverty line for one to three of the twelve-year period. Thus, to summarize, 4.9 percent of the population were found to be persistently poor, an additional 11.6 percent were intermittently poor, and an additional 17.1 percent were poor for only one to three years. These data are summarized in Figure 8.2.

Longitudinal data tend to show the same demographic differences as snapshot data, but they show the differences to be even more pronounced. Rank and Hirschl analyzed the PSID data to attempt to understand poverty across the life cycle. They divided the data into three age cohorts: twenty to forty (early adulthood), forty to sixty (middle adulthood), and sixty to eighty (later adulthood). Among their findings were that during early adulthood, 36.7 percent of the sample experienced at least one year in poverty and 3.7 percent were in poverty for five or more years; during middle adulthood, 22.7 percent experienced at least one year in poverty and 2.1 percent were poor for more than five years; during later adulthood, the figures were 28.8 percent experiencing one year in poverty and 2.2 percent falling below the poverty line for five or more years.

FIGURE 8.2 **Extent of Poverty among Americans, 1979–1991**

Source: Rebecca M. Blank, *It Takes a Nation: A New Agenda for Fighting Poverty.* © 1997 Russell Sage Foundation, published by Princeton University Press. Reprinted by permission of Princeton University Press. Author's tabulations from the Panel Study of Income Dynamics.

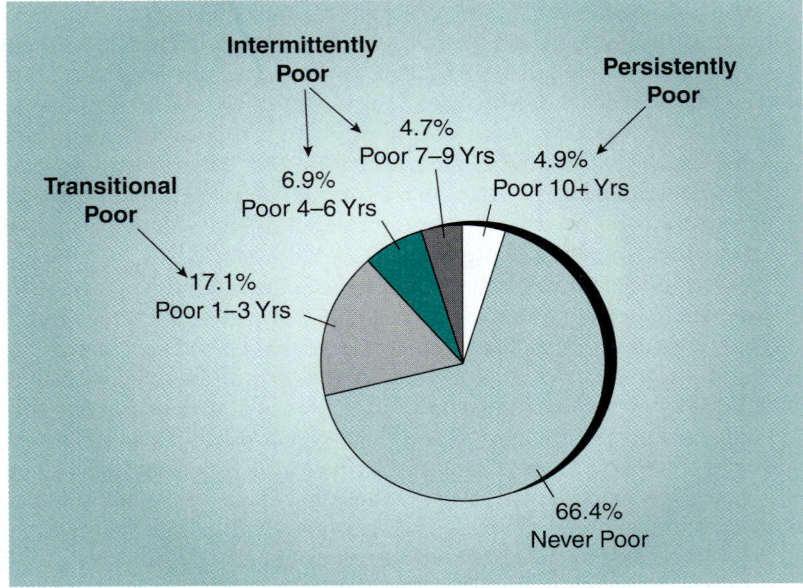

This confirms the snapshot data that poverty is a greater problem for the young and the old than for those in the middle years. Rank and Hirschl conclude,

> Several patterns are apparent across all three panels. First, race, education, and gender exert an influence upon the odds of experiencing poverty during each of the three stages of adulthood. Specifically, being black, having less than 12 years of education, and being female all increase the chances of encountering at least one year of poverty during adulthood. Overall, race tends to exert the largest effect, followed by education, and then by gender. In combination, these characteristics dramatically alter the risk of poverty. For example, while 26.4 percent of white males with 12 or more years education will experience poverty between the ages of 20 and 40, 79.2 percent of black females with less than 12 years of education will be touched by poverty during the same span.[7]

Blank's analysis of the Panel Study data yielded similar results.

There is one additional finding of the Panel Study data that is interesting to note here. The popular image of the poor in the United States is of a group of people living in large northern industrial cities. This is particularly true of the image of the persistent, or residual, poor. A 1980 Manpower Demonstration Research Corporation report, for example, referred to "a group of people, largely concentrated in [this country's] principal cities, who live at the margin of society. . . . They are simultaneously the source and the victims of urban decay."[8] The Panel Study data indicate that this stereotype is not true. The data show that among the persistently poor, 50 percent live in the South (30 percent of the total U.S. population live in the South). Overall, 24 percent of the persistently poor live in rural areas (15 percent of the population live in rural areas). One-third live in cities with populations over 500,000, a percentage closely reflecting the percentage of the total population living in large cities. The remainder of the persistently poor are found in cities with populations between 10,000 and 500,000.

Why Are the Poor Poor?

Imagine that a social scientist randomly sampled one thousand people from across the United States and lined them all up along a long, straight road. The people would be lined up according to income, with the poorest people on the left, progressing toward the richest on the right. The social scientist would then actually paint a line to represent where the poverty level began, with people to the left of the line being those in poverty and people to the right being those out of poverty. Assuming that the poverty rate was 12.1 percent, 121 people would be to the left of the line and 879 to the right of it. The social scientist would then stand back and ask, "What is different about the 121 people to the left of the line? Why are *they* there and not the other 879?" Some differences would be obvious to the social scientist or to anyone else observing the line. A much greater percentage of the people to the left of the line would be members of minority groups, many more would be women, and more would be old and young. To the right of the line a disproportionate percentage would be white, male, and in the early and middle adult years.

This simple visual inspection of the people would give us a hint as to the causes of poverty—they have something to do with race, sex, and age—but it would not give us a complete answer, because of two broad questions. The first question has to do with what statisticians call *between-group variance.* We can see that more members of the female group than of the male group are poor. However, we do not know the source of this variance. Are more women poor because there is something in our society that systematically discriminates against them and bars them from an equal chance at well-paying jobs? This is known as a *structural explanation;* in other words, the source of the problem is in the social structure. Or are more women poor because there are genetic or cultural factors that make women less competitive in the job market, factors such as desire to stay home and have children, or fear of competition? This is known as an *individual explanation.*

The second broad question has to do with what statisticians call *within-group variance.* This question addresses the fact that although a disproportionate number of women and African Americans are in poverty, not all are; and although most whites are not in poverty, some are. What are the differences among the members within these groups?

The question of the causes of poverty is complex and controversial, and answers are incomplete. And yet the question is extremely important. Proposed solutions to poverty based on different explanations often will be diametrically opposed. If you propose a program based on a structural explanation, the focus of the program will be on changing society. If you propose a program based on individual explanations, the focus will be on changing individuals. If we implement an antipoverty program that seeks to change individuals, and the causes of poverty are more structural, we have wasted our time and money. Conversely, if we implement an antipoverty strategy that seeks to change the social structure, and the causes of poverty are within the individual, we have also wasted our time and money. In this section we take a close look at three different broad explanations of poverty. The first explanation views poverty as being the result of individual characteristics. The second views poverty as the result of poor people holding values fundamentally different from those of the rest of society, values that prevent them from escaping poverty and make it likely that their children will follow them into lives of poverty—an explanation known as the *culture of poverty thesis.* The third explanation sees the poor as victims of society and attributes their poverty to impersonal economic forces or to discrimination and oppression, which are mainly institutional; these are the structural explanations referred to earlier.

Poverty as the Result of Individual Characteristics

In previous chapters we discussed the belief among people in the United States, especially among conservatives, in individualism. The aspect of this belief most important for an understanding of social welfare is that it tends to attribute the cause of problems to the individuals affected by the problems. Thus, it is natural in our society to assume that the primary cause of poverty is to be found in some defect in the individuals affected. Holman notes that "the analyses do not necessarily allocate blame to individuals who are poor, but they do regard poverty as stemming from the limitations, maladjustments or deficiencies of individuals."[9]

Individualistic explanations of poverty can be divided into three main types, which have emerged in rough chronological order. The explanation with the longest history is that people are poor because of inferior genetic quality, especially, but not limited to, intellectual ability. In earlier editions of this book we stated that this explanation had been largely discredited but was still occasionally expounded. In 1994 the genetic inferiority explanation reappeared with a bang in the best-selling book *The Bell Curve,* by psychologist Richard Herrnstein and political scientist Charles Murray. Another popular explanation of poverty as being due to individual characteristics is one that argues that the poor are not necessarily genetically inferior, but that they suffer from psychological problems that inhibit their ability to compete for good jobs. This view continues to have some influence; in its most recent form it is known as the *expectancy model.* Finally, the current influential theory of those who insist on individual explanations of poverty is known as *human capital theory.* This is the notion that poor people do not have the knowledge, skills, and attributes (human capital) that make them valuable to employers. These three individualistic explanations are discussed in detail next.

Genetic Inferiority. People in the United States at one time attributed poverty almost entirely to genetics. Behavior was often described as being "in the blood." The Irish immigrants were poor because they drank heavily and had bad tempers; the Italians were hot-blooded Mediterraneans; African Americans were fun-loving and childlike. All were suspected of having low intelligence. As various groups have entered the mainstream of American life and competed successfully for jobs and income, these theories of innate genetic inferiority have generally been dropped. They have been replaced by a much more sophisticated theory based on the science of psychological measurement, specifically the development of the IQ test. This theory argues that intelligence is inherited (that is, it is genetically determined) and that economic success is closely related to intelligence.

The originator of the IQ test and of the idea that intelligence was a measurable quality was the French psychologist Alfred Binet. Binet developed a test in the early 1900s for the use of Paris public school administrators who desired a way to identify children in need of special education. Binet's test served this purpose, and he was quite specific about its limitations. He insisted that the test should be used only to identify children in need of special help and should not be used to classify normal children. Binet strongly asserted that the test did not measure anything innate or permanent, writing in 1909 that

> some recent philosophers appear to have given their moral support to the deplorable verdict that the intelligence of an individual is a fixed quantity. We must protest and act against this brutal pessimism. A child's mind is like a field, for which an expert farmer has advised a change in the method of cultivation, with the result that, in place of desert land, we now have a harvest.[10]

Binet's ideas of testing intelligence were quickly snapped up by H. H. Goddard and Lewis M. Terman in the United States and by Sir Cyril Burt in England. These psychologists chose to ignore Binet's statements about the limitations of intelligence tests; in fact, they advanced quite the opposite idea. They insisted that intelligence was heritable (passed down from generation to generation) and immutable (unable to be changed). Therefore, a person who is born to parents with low intelligence is doomed to a life of failure and probably misery. The result of the work of these men and a number of similar thinkers was what has come to be called the *eugenics movement.* This movement, which we discuss in greater detail in Chapter 13, was based on the idea that not only is intelligence genetic, but also those with low intelligence (at that time called the feeble-minded) reproduce at rates far greater than the more intelligent segments of the population. Thus, the human race was seen as being in danger of becoming overrun by people of low intelligence.[11]

Although eugenics fell into disrepute following World War II, the notion that intelligence is hereditary and that poverty can be largely explained by inherited low intelligence has persisted. The most influential modern advocate of the notion that intelligence is an innate quality and is inherited is the Berkeley psychologist Arthur Jensen.[12] Jensen argues that modern genetic research has firmly established that about 49 percent of the variance in IQ scores can be explained by heritability. After reviewing the work of seventeen geneticists and behavioral geneticists, Jensen concludes, "With such general agreement among scientists, it is all the more amazing how the popular media have so often promoted the notion that the genetic inheritance of intelligence is a highly controversial issue."[13]

The most influential modern exponents of the idea that socioeconomic class, and by extension poverty, is related to inherited intelligence are Charles Murray and the late Richard Herrnstein. Although Herrnstein reported his ideas in many publications in the past, they became popularized through *The Bell Curve,* coauthored with Murray, a well-known conservative critic of social programs.[14] In this book Herrnstein and Murray argue that:

1. Differences in mental ability are largely inherited.
2. Success requires high mental ability.
3. Earnings and prestige depend on success.
4. Thus, social standing (which reflects earnings and prestige) will be based to a large degree on inherited differences among people.

Herrnstein and Murray argue that the differences in intellectual ability between social classes are becoming greater as barriers to the upward mobility of gifted people are removed, thus removing them from the gene pool of the lower classes. In an earlier work Herrnstein argued that because people tend to marry within their class, eventually most of the superior genes will be in the upper classes and inferior genes will be in the lower strata of society. He concluded, "The biological stratification of society looms."[15]

The idea that intelligence is an inherited trait and that success is the result of high intelligence and lack of success the result of low intelligence has been the subject of severe, and often emotional, criticism. The arguments are technical and complex, and we do not have room to go into them in detail. However, basically the critics of Jensen, and of Herrnstein and Murray, argue that we do not really know what intelligence is, and that whatever it is, it is doubtful that intelligence tests measure it. Critics argue that the tests are culturally biased. That is, items selected for the tests are based on what is familiar to white and middle-class people, so minorities and lower-class people are less likely to be familiar with them.

Fischer and his colleagues, in a lengthy and reasoned refutation of Herrnstein and Murray, argue that "scholars long ago established that scores on IQ and IQ-like tests were only of modest importance compared with social context in explaining individual attainment." They demonstrate that the test Herrnstein and Murray used as an indication of intelligence, the Armed Forces Qualification Test, is really a measure of education, not of native intelligence. Of the major argument of Herrnstein and Murray, Fischer and colleagues assert:

> At its base it is a philosophy ages old: human misery is natural and beyond human redemption; inequality is fated; and people deserve, by virtue of their native talents, the positions they have in society. . . . The political implications [are] clear: If inequality is natural, then governmental intervention to moderate it is at best wrongheaded and at worst destructive.[16]

Poverty as the Result of Psychological Problems. The idea that a large proportion of the poor are that way because they are suffering from some psychological problem gained popularity throughout the 1950s, peaked and even gained legislative support during the 1960s, and then rapidly lost influence. Especially popular was the idea that the poor live in "multiproblem families" that have an almost insatiable appetite for social services. Buell, for example, in a study of social services in St. Paul, Minnesota, found that 6 percent of families receiving services consumed more than half of the total services provided.[17] The basic idea of this theory is that poor people do not have their developmental needs met as children; as a result they are immature, and consequently they are unable to meet the needs of their own children—who then grow up immature, and the cycle goes on and on. Curran has studied the social work profession's contribution to this theory of poverty, saying,

> In line with the profession's psychiatric outlook, many postwar social work scholars claimed that psychopathology plagued ADC recipients. A 1954 *Social Service Review* article expressed popular social work sentiment in describing ADC recipients as frequently "ill in body and mind." Social work research suggested that a significant portion of ADC clients had mental health problems. For instance, Kermit Wiltse, a leading proponent of the psychological model and a faculty member of the University of California's School of Social Work, "found a kind of pseudo or subclinical depression in many of our [ADC] clients, particularly in the early phase of contact." The widely circulated 1960 study of the ADC program in Cook County, Illinois, *Facts, Fallacies, and Future,* also found that approximately one-third of the families suffered from a diagnosed or suspected mental disorder. Psychiatric disorders topped the list of psychosocial issues faced by "multiproblem" families, the term postwar social workers coined to describe long-term ADC users. One author working with multiproblem families noted, "The psychiatric diagnosis of the parent or parents have [sic] ranged from psychosis to borderline character disorders."[18]

The theory that poverty is largely caused by psychological problems among the poor hit its high point in 1962, when it was incorporated into the amendments to the Social Security Act popularly known as the Social Service Amendments. These amendments were based on the idea that the poor "needed not just, or even primarily, financial aid but rather psychological assistance and other forms of counseling; they had to 'adjust' to being single parents or to life in the city; they needed instruction on how to keep house and manage their meager resources in order to make ends meet; they needed to learn how to make friendships and develop self-esteem."[19] The amendments provided a large sum of money to enable states to hire social workers trained in psychological techniques to help people solve psychological problems that were preventing them from being self-supporting.

The social service amendments proved to be the undoing of the theory that psychological maladjustment was a major dynamic in poverty. Social workers went out armed with new therapeutic skills and quickly discovered that these had little relevance for dealing with the harsh realities of impoverished families. Congress also quickly lost its enthusiasm for this approach when the welfare rolls did not go down. In fact, just the opposite happened; following the passage of the social service amendments, the welfare caseloads skyrocketed.

The fact that social workers for a time embraced an individual, psychological explanation of poverty has generally been attributed to the professions' desire to achieve status in the years following World War II as a psychotherapeutic profession. Curran offers another explanation, one more in keeping with the social change and advocacy tradition of the profession. She says,

> Faced with a popular and legislative backlash against Aid to Dependent Children (ADC), the public assistance program for single mothers and their children, postwar social work researchers, educators, and clinical theorists increasingly turned to fashionable psychological and psychoanalytic paradigms to explain and justify welfare use. The profession's portrayal of welfare recipients as victims of psychologically abusive pasts stood in contrast to a hostile popular and legislative discourse that cast ADC recipients as unscrupulous chiselers and immoral cheats.[20]

The idea that psychopathology provides at least part of the explanation for long-term poverty has recently resurfaced in conservative thinking on the subject. Lawrence Mead recognizes that this explanation was previously discredited because of a lack of empirical verification—that is, that research failed to find more psychological problems among the poor than among the nonpoor. However, he argues that there is evidence that the poor have become significantly more dysfunctional since the mid-1970s:

> Signs include the drug epidemic, the explosion of foster care in major cities, and the growth in the homeless population, two-thirds of which has been in prison or institutionalized for mental illness or substance abuse. Significant portions of the long-term poor may suffer from depression, posttraumatic stress disorder, or antisocial personality. Such impairments may be immediate causes of poverty, even if the ultimate causes lie in society.[21]

A newer version of the psychological explanation of poverty has emerged that does not assume pathology but rather explains the problem of poverty in social psychological terms. This theory is known as the *expectancy model.* This model is based on the theory that there is a relationship between confidence, sense of control, and success. Those who are successful gain confidence, and this leads to a sense of control over their lives, which in turn results in more success. On the other hand, those who fail lose confidence and begin to feel out of control of their lives, and this leads to further failure. Poverty results when people lose a sense of control over their lives, when they begin to expect failure, and when they cease to believe that they can ever escape poverty. Ellwood observes that "people who are frustrated by their lack of control may be observed to exhibit two almost opposite kinds of responses: either an aggressive and potentially antagonistic response or a very passive and sedate one. People become overwhelmed by their situation and lose the capacity to seek out and use the opportunities available."[22]

The Human Capital Approach. This is an economist's approach to explaining the individual's contribution to his or her own poverty. Human capital is defined by Thurow as "an individual's productive skills, talents, and knowledge. It is *measured* in terms of the value (price multiplied by quantity) of goods and services produced."[23] In other words, the human capital approach looks at how much an individual's labor is worth. People who have a large amount of skill obtained by experience, education, and training are going to be worth more on the labor market than those who have not invested in these things. Some aspects of the value of human capital are, of course, natural abilities that cannot be acquired. Most aspects, however, are acquired or enhanced by human actions.

The human capital approach views poverty as the result of individuals having low amounts of human capital. Thurow notes,

> Efforts to eliminate poverty and the income gap between white and black have focused attention on the factors that produce individual incomes of human capital. . . . If individuals are paid according to their productivity, then individual skills, talents, and knowledge determine earnings. A wide dispersion in the distribution of human capital creates a wide dispersion in the distribution of earnings. Many factors, such as discrimination, play a role in determining the shape of the income distribution, but the distribution of productive investments is certainly one determinant.[24]

The human capital approach is a straightforward approach to poverty. It says, in essence, that people are poor because they lack the knowledge and skills necessary to get good jobs that will provide above-poverty-level incomes. There is no doubt that this lack is one factor in poverty. However, the human capital approach does not account for several other factors, including discrimination. Traditionally female jobs requiring a college degree (in other words, a large amount of human capital), such as elementary school teaching, will often pay much less than jobs traditionally held by men and requiring much less human capital—for example, the job of electrician. Be that as it may, for our purposes the human capital approach merely substitutes one definition of poverty for another. Thurow says, "One of the advantages of thinking in terms of human capital is that it immediately focuses attention on the production problem. What factors create human capital? What is the most efficient method of combining these factors?"[25] The human capital approach merely substitutes the question, "Why do some people possess low amounts of human capital?" for the question, "Why are some people poor?" And this takes us back to the question with which we began this chapter.

Cultural Explanations of Poverty

The preceding individual explanations of poverty tend to appeal to conservatives because of the conservative focus on the individual's responsibility for his or her own situation. Structural explanations, which are discussed in the next section, locate major responsibility for personal problems within the social structure in which the individual finds himself or herself. Liberals and radicals tend to favor these explanations because of their belief in the strength of the environment in shaping individuals' lives. Between these two types of explanations are the cultural explanations. These have been and continue to be influential because they mix individual and structural factors in such a way that both conservatives and liberals feel comfortable subscribing to them.

Cultural explanations, like individualistic explanations, locate the proximate cause of poverty as being individual characteristics. Individuals who are poor are seen as being in this situation because they are not motivated to succeed, they do not value work, they demand immediate gratification of their needs, and they do not value marriage or education. Unlike individualistic explanations, however, cultural explanations do not view these individual characteristics as being caused by any innate quality of the individual affected, such as low intelligence or some form of psychopathology. Instead, individuals are viewed as possessing these characteristics because of the social situations they were born into and in which they were reared and educated. Thus, cultural explanations are more hopeful than individual explanations because these factors are more easily "corrected" than low intelligence or psychological disorders. There are two slightly different versions of cultural explanations: the culture of poverty theory and the cultural deprivation theory.

Culture of Poverty. The concept of a *culture of poverty* was first suggested by anthropologist Oscar Lewis in his 1959 book *Five Families: Mexican Case Studies in the Culture of Poverty.*[26] The concept won almost immediate acceptance by social scientists, journalists, and policymakers who were struggling with ways to deal with poverty in the 1960s. Michael Harrington made extensive use of the concept in his 1962 book *The Other America,* Frank Riessman related the concept to education in his 1962 book *The Culturally Deprived Child,* and Daniel Patrick Moynihan used the concept in his controversial but influential Department of Labor report *The Negro Family.*[27] The massive antipoverty programs of the Kennedy administration and Lyndon Johnson's War on Poverty programs were greatly influenced by the culture of poverty idea.

Lewis set out to apply basic ideas of anthropology to the study of poverty. He looked at poverty as a "subculture with its own structure and rationale, as a way of life which is passed down from generation to generation along family lines." He proposed that poverty was not only something negative—want and deprivation—but that it also included positive aspects, some rewards without which the poor could not carry on. The culture of poverty develops, according to Lewis, as a reaction by the poor to their marginal position in society; and it "represents an effort to cope with feelings of hopelessness and despair which develop from the realization of the improbability of achieving success."[28]

The culture of poverty, according to this theory, consists of a set of values, behavior patterns, and beliefs among the poor that are different from those of the larger society. Lewis identified seventy separate elements of the culture of poverty, which he lumped into four groups. The first group includes characteristics related to the fact that the poor are not effectively integrated into the major institutions of the larger society. For example, they do not participate in unions, political parties, or voluntary groups. In fact, they show a fundamental distrust of many of the basic institutions of society—the police, government offices, and even the church. They are poorly integrated into the job market, and this is a main reason that they control very little wealth. Banfield, a popularizer of the culture of poverty theory whose version is much more conservative than that of its originator, comments that the poor person "feels no attachment to community, neighbors, or friends, . . . resents all authority (for example, that of policemen, social workers, teachers, landlords, employers), and is apt to think that he has been 'railroaded' and to want to 'get even.' "[29]

The second group of elements of the culture of poverty is related to the communities in which poor people live. In these communities, there is little organization beyond the level of the extended family. Occasionally, temporary groupings and voluntary organizations emerge, and sometimes even a sense of community, but this does not last long.

The third group of elements of the culture of poverty related to the family. According to Lewis, major traits of family life are

> absence of childhood as a specially prolonged and protected stage in the life cycle, early initiation into sex, free unions or consensual marriages, a relatively high incidence of the abandonment of wives and children, a trend toward female- or mother-centered families and consequently a much greater knowledge of maternal relatives, a strong predisposition to authoritarianism, lack of privacy, verbal emphasis upon family solidarity which is only rarely achieved because of sibling rivalry, and competition for limited goods and maternal affection.[30]

Banfield asserts that the child-rearing style of the mother is impulsive, and once children have passed infancy they are likely to be neglected or abused.[31]

Finally, there are those elements related to the individual. People in the culture of poverty supposedly have strong feelings of marginality; that is, they do not feel they really belong to anything in society. They are also characterized as having strong feelings of helplessness, dependence, and inferiority. There is a high incidence of maternal deprivation, weak ego structure, and confused sexual identity. Poor people are viewed as having poor impulse control, a strong present-time orientation with little ability to defer gratification and to plan for the future, and a corresponding sense of resignation and fatalism. Banfield says, "At the present-oriented end of the scale, the lower-class individual lives from moment to moment. If he has any awareness of a future, it is of something fixed, fated, beyond his control: things happen to him, he does not *make* them happen. . . . [W]hatever he cannot use immediately he considers valueless."[32]

Lewis argues that these elements represent characteristics of a culture or, more accurately, of a subculture. They are social, psychological, and economic traits that are passed on from one generation to another. They represent beliefs, attitudes, and values that are fundamentally different from those of the larger society. Lewis says,

> People with a culture of poverty are aware of middle-class values, talk about them and even claim some of them as their own, but on the whole they do not live by them. Thus it is important to distinguish between what they say and what they do. For example, many will tell you that marriage by law, by the church, or by both, is the ideal form of marriage, but few will marry.

A key argument is that these cultural elements survive and are passed down from generation to generation because they are functional for people living within a poverty situation. Lewis continues the example on marriage: "To men who have no steady jobs or other sources of income . . . free unions and consensual marriage makes a lot of sense. Women will often turn down offers of marriage because they feel it ties them down to men who are immature, punishing and generally unreliable."[33]

According to culture of poverty theorists, these characteristics of the poor make it unlikely that they will be able to escape their poverty. To get out of poverty, one has to participate in social institutions, especially school; one has to form stable relationships, mainly two-parent families; and perhaps most important of all, one must be willing to

Focus on Diversity

"Welfare: A White Secret" by Barbara Ehrenreich

Come on, my fellow white folks, we have something to confess. No, nothing to do with age spots or those indoor-tanning creams we use to get us through the winter without looking like the final stages of TB. Nor am I talking about the fact that we all go home and practice funky dance moves behind drawn shades. Out with it, friends, the biggest secret known to whites since the invention of powdered rouge: Welfare is a white program. Yep. At least it's no more black than Vanilla Ice is a fair rendition of classic urban rap.

The numbers go like this: 61 percent of the population receiving welfare, listed as "means-tested cash assistance" by the Census Bureau, is identified as white, while only 33 percent is identified as black. These numbers notwithstanding, the Republican version of "political correctness" has given us "welfare cheat" as a new term for African American since the early days of Ronald Reagan. Yet if the Lakers were 61 percent white and on a winning streak, would we be calling them a "black team"?

Wait a minute, I can hear my neighbors say, we're not as slow at math as the Asian Americans like to think. There's still a glaring disproportion there. African Americans are only 12 percent of the population as a whole, at least according to the census count, yet they're 33 percent of the welfare population—surely evidence of a shocking addiction to the dole.

But we're forgetting something. Welfare is a program for poor people, very poor people. African Americans are three times as likely as whites to fall below the poverty level and hence to have a chance of qualifying for welfare benefits. If we look at the kind of persons most likely to be eligible—single mothers living in poverty with children under 18 to support—we find little difference in welfare participation by race: 74.6 percent of African Americans in such dire straits are on welfare, compared with 64.5 percent of the poor white single moms.

That's still a difference, but not enough to imply some congenital appetite for a free lunch on the part of the African-derived. In fact, two explanations readily suggest themselves: First, just as blacks are disproportionately likely to be poor, they are disproportionately likely to find themselves among the poorest of the poor, where welfare eligibility arises. Second, the black poor are more likely than their white counterparts to live in cities, and hence to have a chance of making their way to the welfare office. Correct for those two differences, and you won't find an excess of African Americans fitting the stereotype of the sluttish welfare queen who breeds for profit.

So why are they so poor? I can see my neighbor asking as visions of feckless idlers dance before his narrowed eyes. Ah, that is a question white folks would do well to ponder. Consider, for a start, that African Americans are more likely to be disabled (illness being a famous consequence of poverty) or unemployed (in the sense of actively seeking work) and far less likely to earn wages that would lift them out of the welfare-eligibility range.

As for the high proportion of black families headed by single women (44 percent, compared with 13 per-

defer gratification of immediate wants in order to gain greater rewards at a future date. For example, we all realize that going to college requires that a young person delay a large number of desires. It generally involves putting off buying a nice car, getting married, and traveling for at least four years. Going to college costs a lot in terms of deferred pleasures. However, most people realize that if they put these things off for four years, there is a higher likelihood that they will reap large rewards over the remainder of their lifetime. Culture of poverty theorists assert that poor people are unable to see this far cent for whites), many deep sociohistoric reasons could be adduced, but none of them is welfare. A number of respected studies refute the Reagan era myth that a few hundred a month in welfare payments is a sufficient incentive to chuck one's husband or get pregnant while in high school. If it were, states with relatively high welfare payments—say, about $500 a month per family—would have higher rates of out-of-wedlock births than states like Louisiana and Mississippi, which expect a welfare family to get by on $200 a month or less. But this is not the case.

So our confession stands: White folks have been gobbling up the welfare budget while blaming someone else. But it's worse than that. If we look at Social Security, which is another form of welfare, although it is often mistaken for an individual insurance program, then whites are the ones who are crowding the trough. We receive almost twice as much per capita, for an aggregate advantage to our race of $10 billion a year—much more than the $3.9 billion advantage African Americans gain from their disproportionate share of welfare. One sad reason: Whites live an average of six years longer than African Americans, meaning that young black workers help subsidize a huge and growing "overclass" of white retirees. I do not see our confession bringing much relief. There's a reason for resentment, though it has more to do with class than with race. White people are poor too, and in numbers far exceeding any of our more generously pigmented social groups. And poverty as defined by the government is a vast underestimation of the economic terror that persists at incomes—such as $20,000 or even $40,000 and above—that we like to think of as middle class.

The problem is not that welfare is too generous to blacks but that social welfare in general is too stingy to all concerned. Naturally, whites in the swelling "near poor" category resent the notion of whole races supposedly frolicking at their expense. Whites, near poor and middle class, need help too—as do the many African Americans, Hispanics and "others" who do not qualify for aid but need it nonetheless.

So we white folks have a choice. We can keep pretending that welfare is a black program and a scheme for transferring our earnings to the pockets of shiftless, dark-skinned people, or we can clear our throats, blush prettily and admit that we are hurting too—for cash assistance when we're down and out, for health insurance, for college aid and all the rest.

Racial scapegoating has its charms, I will admit: the surge of righteous anger, even the fun—for those inclined—of wearing sheets and burning crosses. But there are better, nobler sources of white pride, it seems to me. Remember, whatever they say about our music or our taste in clothes, only we can truly, deeply blush.

Source: Barbara Ehrenreich, "Welfare: A White Secret," *Time* (16 December 1991), 84. Copyright © 1991, TIME, Inc. Reprinted by permission.

ahead and so do not defer gratification in order to get an education, among other things; thus, they hurt or destroy their chances to escape poverty.

Three additional points need to be made about the culture of poverty theory. The first is that this theory is not meant to apply to all poor people. The group being discussed is the group we identified earlier as the residual poor—the persistently poor. People in this group represent only a small percentage of the poor, but they receive much attention because of the seemingly intractable nature of their poverty. The second point is that culture of poverty theory views the lives of the residual poor as containing a kind of an irony. That is, the beliefs, attitudes, and behavior patterns that help make life in poverty bearable are the same patterns that prevent people from escaping poverty. For example, for a teenage boy in the ghetto, belonging to a gang and selling drugs is going to provide much more pleasure and status among his peers than being on the honor roll and working afternoons at McDonalds for minimum wage. Yet going to school and working at a straight job is likely to be a route out of poverty, whereas belonging to a gang and selling drugs is probably going to eventually result in disaster. The third point is that because poverty constitutes a subculture, it involves more than money. According to this theory, even if members of the poverty culture were given enough money to meet all their needs, they would not change their lives. They would most likely "squander the money" to gratify immediate needs and wants, and they would end up just as miserable as before.

Cultural Deprivation. Whereas culture of poverty theory is based on research in anthropology and focuses on the concept of culture, cultural deprivation theory is based on research in education and focuses on the concept of socialization. Cultural deprivation theory does not assert that the poor have *different* values, beliefs, and knowledge from the nonpoor; it posits that they are deprived of the opportunity to develop the

Culture of poverty theory asserts that people are poor and remain poor because they do not share major American values essential for success, such as deferral of gratification and marriage before parenthood.

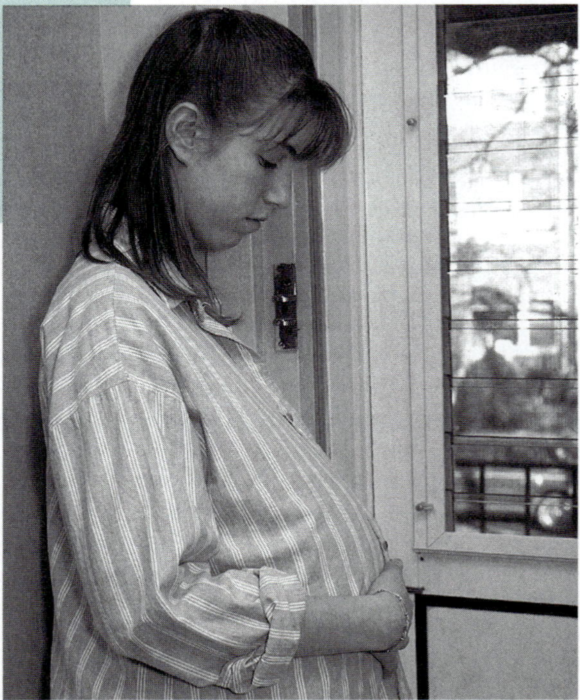

knowledge, beliefs, and values of the larger society. Cultural deprivation theory has mainly focused on low educational achievement among poor children, which in turn results in poor life chances. The theory argues that differences in educational achievement between poor and nonpoor children are explained by differences in home background. Ryan, a critic of this approach, summarizes it as follows, "Uneducated parents, crowded living quarters, absence of books, family disinterest in education—all combine to handicap the poor black child as he enters the school system. There is a specific denial of any innate inferiority; rather there is perceived a *functional* inferiority that is attributable to the depressing and stultifying effects of living in poverty, which is, of course, condemned as bad and unjust."[34] According to cultural deprivation theory, poor children do not *dis*value education; they have simply never been taught (or, more accurately, socialized) to value it. According to Holman, "If the child-rearing practices are deficient, then the children will not develop into adults who can fit into the prevailing culture with all its opportunities for education and advancement. (Again, a contrast can be made with the culture of poverty thesis in which the children are adequately socialized but into a culture which accepts poverty.)"[35]

Critique of the Cultural Explanations

Cultural explanations of poverty are extremely popular for two major reasons. The first is that they appeal to both liberals and conservatives. The second reason is that to the average person on the street, as well as to academics and professionals, these theories just seem to make so much sense. When subjected to close scrutiny, however, cultural explanations do not make nearly as much sense. There are several criticisms of cultural theories, mainly directed at the more influential culture of poverty theory and its intellectual heir, underclass theory. The first criticism is directed at the research on which the theory is based, and the second stems from other research that has failed to support major aspects of the theory. The third, aimed at the recent popular interest in the underclass, asserts that cultural explanations of poverty are really a modern attempt to define a portion of the poor as "undeserving." In this section we briefly address these critiques, discuss a major and influential theory called "blaming the victim" that rejects cultural explanations, and look at alternative explanations of the characteristics of the poor that have been attributed to cultural differences.

Culture of Poverty Theory Is Based on Methodologically Flawed Research. Although culture of poverty theory has been expounded by an enormous number of authors, few have conducted original research to test whether the theory is correct. Nearly all applications of the theory are based on the anthropological studies of Oscar Lewis, notably *Five Families: Mexican Case Studies in the Culture of Poverty; The Children of Sanchez;* and *La Vida: A Puerto Rican Family in the Culture of Poverty—San Juan and New York.* The method Lewis used in writing these books is simple and straightforward. He begins with a description of the attributes of the culture of poverty as discussed previously. He then records an immense quantity of biographical data about people whom he believes characterize the culture of poverty. According to one of his critics, Charles Valentine, "The principal purpose of this design is evidently to convey the impression that the biographical evidence supports and validates the theoretical abstraction which is labeled the 'culture of poverty.' " Valentine argues that Lewis's research does not validate the culture of poverty concept because of the following flaws:

- Lewis met with the subjects of his research in his office rather than in their own environment.
- Lewis employed a "directive" approach, guiding the respondents to material he wanted them to cover.
- Lewis edited the material and, according to Valentine, "often reorganized the material, selected some portions of the testimony, and eliminated others."

The most serious flaw, according to Valentine, is that the subjects selected may not have been representative of the group being studied. For example, in the Rios family, the subjects of *La Vida,* prostitution is very important in the lives of the women. This is not typical of poor Puerto Rican families and indicates that the family is an unreliable basis for generalization.[36]

Valentine concludes that "the scientific status of the 'culture of poverty' remains essentially a series of undemonstrated hypotheses. With respect to many or most of these hypotheses, alternative propositions are theoretically more convincing and are supported by more available evidence."[37] These alternative propositions are discussed later in this section.

Cultural Definitions Really Refer to the "Undeserving Poor." The well-known sociologist and urban planner Herbert Gans points out that the original use of the term *underclass* was as a purely economic concept to describe people who were chronically unemployed or underemployed as a result of the emerging postindustrial economy. These people were poor for purely structural reasons. In recent years, however, there has been a gradual change in the use of the term. *Underclass* has come to refer more and more to people who are viewed as attitudinally and behaviorally deviant. Gans believes that it is not coincidental that those defined as members of the underclass are almost entirely African American and Latino. Thus, according to Gans, the term has become a code word for the old concept of the *undeserving poor.* It has become the most recent in a long line of concepts that permit us to maintain harsh attitudes and hard hearts toward the poor by defining their poverty as their own fault. Gans says,

> The *first* danger of the term is its unusual power as a buzzword. It is a handy euphemism; while it seems inoffensively technical on the surface, it hides within it all the moral opprobrium Americans have long felt toward those poor people who have been judged to be undeserving. Even when it is being used by journalists, scholars, and others as a technical term, it carries with it this judgmental baggage. . . . A *second* and related danger of the term is its use as a racial codeword that subtly hides anti-black and anti-Hispanic feelings.[38]

Research Fails to Support Elements of Cultural Explanations. Criticisms of weakness in Lewis's research design are supported by the fact that studies looking at various characteristics of people who are supposedly members of the culture of poverty have almost uniformly failed to verify the existence of these characteristics. Culture of poverty theory asserts, for example, that one of the reasons poor people do badly in the job market is that they do not value work. Two studies by Goodwin, based on a sample of more than four thousand adults, found just the opposite to be true. These studies found that work was just as essential to the self-esteem of poor people as it was to the nonpoor.[39] Ethnographic studies by anthropologists have arrived at the same conclusion—the poor want to work, just like the middle class; that is, there is no cultural difference on this variable.[40] A 2001 study by Barnes found that not only did members of the underclass want to work, but also that the majority are in fact working. Their jobs, however, are often not counted in employment statistics because the poor often "earn money by performing informal jobs such as lawn care, home child care, selling products, and day labor."[41]

A cornerstone of cultural theories, particularly cultural deprivation theory, is that the poor do not value education and so are not motivated to strive for an education. The research evidence also casts doubt on this proposition. A study by Sears, Maccoby, and Levin found that the poor were even more concerned that their children do well in school than were middle-class parents.[42] Similarly, Riessman found that lower-class parents regretted their own lack of education and were strongly motivated to see that their children did better.[43] Similarly, Barnes's data revealed education to be "very important to [underclass] respondents."[44]

We could go on and on discussing research that casts doubt on cultural explanations of poverty. The proposition that lower-class children are less verbal than middle-class children has been challenged.[45] Kretzmann and McKnight have demonstrated that, contrary to the assertion that poor people do not participate in community organizations, a tremendous number of organizational assets are present in even the most devastated communities.[46] The belief that poor people hold sexual attitudes and values different from the rest of the population has been challenged by research by both Rainwater and Bogue.[47] However, there is still one problem: Even though research has demonstrated that the poor do not really hold values significantly different from those of the rest of the population—that is, they do not have a separate culture—there are still some differences in their lifeways that must be explained if cultural explanations are to be rejected. For example, it has been demonstrated that the poor are less likely to defer gratification than the middle class; poor kids are less likely to continue their educations; and poor women are more likely than nonpoor women to have children outside of marriage. How do we explain these things?

Alternative Explanation for the Lifeways of the Poor. At the risk of seeming repetitive, we need to emphasize that the main idea of the cultural explanations of poverty is that the lifeways, or behaviors, of the poor are caused by a set of *values* existing among poor people that are fundamentally different from those of the larger society. Poor people often have children out of wedlock because, supposedly, they do not value marriage; poor people do not work, the theory contends, because they do not value work and do not feel any stigma from being supported by welfare; poor children do not do well in school, it is argued, because they have not been taught to value education and its related components, such as paying attention and reading books. But there is a different explanation for these lifeways of poor people. That is, poor people have the same values as the rest of society (this has been supported by the research cited earlier), but they behave differently because within the limited range of choices available to them those behaviors are the ones that make the most sense. Sociologists refer to this as the *situational adaptation interpretation* and economists call it the *choice model.*[48]

Let's illustrate this interpretation with an example of two young couples: James and Vivian, and Cindy and Dave. Each couple has had a relationship for about one year. Vivian and Cindy each becomes pregnant, and both are strongly opposed to abortion as a solution. Here the similarity ends.

James and Vivian have grown up in the ghetto, and they are the children of welfare mothers. Vivian finished the eleventh grade and then dropped out of high school. She has worked fairly steadily in a series of minimum-wage jobs, mainly in fast-food restaurants. James dropped out of school in his senior year when the high school graduation exam revealed that he could barely read or write and school personnel said he would be required to take remedial work before he could earn his diploma. Since leaving school, he has worked only sporadically, usually in temporary manual labor jobs.

In contrast, Cindy and Dave are both juniors at a large state university. They grew up in the suburbs, and they are the children of middle-class professional parents. Dave is majoring in engineering and is an officer candidate in army ROTC. Cindy is majoring in accounting.

On learning of their respective pregnancies, what do the two couples do? James and Vivian do not even consider marriage. Vivian applies for welfare and food stamps shortly after the baby is born; she has quit her job because she could not afford day care on the salary she was earning. James hangs around for a few months and contributes whatever money he can for the baby's support, but eventually he drifts away. Vivian basically reproduces her own childhood for her baby.

Dave and Cindy approach the situation differently. When they learn that Cindy is pregnant, they immediately decide to get married. They both take part-time jobs, and this income, combined with Dave's ROTC stipend plus some help from their families, provides enough income for them to survive until Dave graduates and is commissioned a second lieutenant in the army. Cindy takes a year off to be with the baby and then goes back to school, earns her degree, and begins a career with a large accounting firm.

How do we explain the different behaviors of these two couples? Cultural theorists would say that their behaviors reflect the fundamentally different values the two couples have learned in their respective social environments. James and Vivian come from environments that have taught them that single parenthood is acceptable, perhaps even preferable, to marriage. They do not really value work and achievement and so view welfare as an acceptable way to rear their child. Fathers are not considered to be important to the well-being of children and so no one is too concerned when James drifts away. Cindy and Dave hold different values. For them it is of paramount importance that a child have parents who are married; the concepts of work and self-support are also extremely important to them.

The situational adaptation interpretation provides a different explanation. This perspective argues that the two couples probably have similar values but are existing in very different situations that make their choices different. Both couples value marriage and work, but these are realistic choices only for Cindy and Dave. James and Vivian realize that there is no bright future for them as a couple. There is no commission in the army followed by a good engineering job for James, and there is no period of full-time motherhood followed by a professional career with good day care for Vivian. Instead, what lies in their future is a series of low-paying jobs interspersed by long periods of unemployment. To make matters worse, by getting married Vivian would lose eligibility for some types of aid. Thus, both couples are making rational choices based on the opportunities available to them. The difference is that the opportunities available to Cindy and Dave are in line with traditional American values—marriage, job, and a two-parent family. For James and Vivian, violating these norms makes far more sense: As a single mother, at least Vivian will not be tied to an unemployed man, and James will not be constantly frustrated by obligations he has no way of fulfilling.

If poor people like James and Vivian hold basically the same values as the rest of society but are forced to violate these values in order to make rational decisions, how do they cope with the frustration that must result? Rodman argues that they do this through a process he calls the "lower class value stretch." This is a process through which poor people "come to tolerate and eventually evaluate favorably certain deviations from middle class values."[49] This process is closely related to what psychologists call *rationalization* or the "sweet lemon effect." For example, when Vivian and James do not get married, one might very well hear Vivian saying something like, "I don't want to be tied down to one man anyway. This way I can be a mother and still be able to party and have fun." When James can secure only manual labor jobs, he may say something like, "I'd really hate to be cooped up in an office all day and be forced to wear a tie. Only suckers do that. I want to be working outside with the real men. Sure, the boss can fire me anytime he likes because my job is only temporary, but the other side of that coin is that anytime I want I can tell him to take this job and shove it. I don't have to take grief from anyone!" The point Rodman emphasizes is that poor people share the same basic values as the rest of society, but that because of their limited opportunity to make these values work for them, they "stretch" the values to fit the opportunities they do have.

With all the criticisms of the cultural theories, why do they continue to exert so much influence? These theories were first formulated and exerted tremendous influence in the 1950s and 1960s. They largely went out of vogue in the 1970s with the landslide of contradictory data. Like the mythological phoenix, they have risen from the ashes and once again have a grip on our collective imagination, this time under the new and catchy label "the underclass." The reemergence of cultural theories is in no way related to any new data, but this appears to bother only a few people. One of these is the economist David Ellwood, who sees value in cultural theories but recognizes that they remain largely untested. Even Ellwood, a hard-nosed, empirically oriented (and incidentally liberal) economist, is willing to give some credence to cultural theories; he argues that the fact "that [cultural] theories are hard to test and interpret is not a legitimate basis for ignoring them in empirical work or policy discussion. The way welfare recipients are treated, the way they perceive the world, and the way the world interacts with them must have profound influences."[50] Why do cultural theories continue to exert so much influence in the face of so little solid empirical support? And why have people shown so little inclination to seek empirical support, instead relying on the assumption that these theories are valid? The answer, perhaps, lies in a tendency in U.S. society that psychologist William Ryan calls "blaming the victim."[51]

Blaming the Victim. Because of our strong belief in individualism, we tend to place responsibility for problems, as well as credit for successes, squarely on the shoulders of the individual affected. This approach sometimes makes perfectly good sense, but we often carry it to ridiculous extremes. A woman is raped and some people will ask, "Why was she wearing such suggestive clothes? Had she been drinking? What was she doing unescorted in a bar? Had she been flirting with her attacker?" The implication of these questions is that she somehow was responsible for the attack on her. This tendency is so deeply ingrained that we even do it to ourselves. When a person's car is stolen, you will often hear him saying things like, "I should have known better than to park it in that lot" or "I knew I should have ridden the bus to work; this neighborhood is no place to leave a car." The point is that the woman did not rape herself and the person did not steal his own car. These things were done to them, yet we still tend to place much of the blame on the person who was victimized.

Ryan asserts that because of our tendency to blame people for their own problems, we naturally look for reasons why the poor are responsible for their own poverty. The earliest explanations were that the poor were in some way morally or genetically inferior. However, these explanations always seemed harsh, at least to liberals, and they did not last long against the weight of experience with the poor. So, according to Ryan, we developed new theories that still placed the responsibility for poverty on the poor themselves but that seemed to be more scientific and more humanitarian. When trying to explain why poor children do not do as well as middle-class children in school, we ask, says Ryan,

> What is wrong with the victim? . . . The shorthand phrase is "cultural deprivation," which, to those in the know, conveys what they allege to be inside information: that the poor child carries a scanty pack of cultural baggage as he enters school. He doesn't know about books and magazines and newspapers. . . . They say that if he talks at all . . . he certainly doesn't talk correctly. . . . If you can get him to sit in a chair, they say, he squirms and looks out the window. . . . In a word he is "disadvantaged" and "socially deprived," they say, and this of course, accounts for *his* failure (his failure, they say) to learn much in school. . . . In pursuing this logic, no one remembers to ask questions about the collapsing buildings and torn textbooks, the frightened, insensitive teachers, the six additional desks in the room, the blustering frightened principals, the relentless segregation, the callous administrator, the irrelevant curriculum, the bigoted or cowardly members of the school board, the insulting history book, the stingy taxpayers, the fairy tale readers, or the self-serving faculty of the local teachers' college. We are encouraged to confine our attention to the child and to dwell on his alleged defects.[52]

Ryan argues that cultural explanations of poverty are so powerful and have lasted so long precisely because they allow us to continue to explain problems as being the fault of the individuals affected, but to do so under the cloak of liberal humanitarianism and concern. The old conservative notion of intrinsic or hereditary defect is replaced by an emphasis on environmental causation:

> The new ideology attributes defect and inadequacy to the malignant nature of poverty, injustice, slum life, and racial difficulties. . . . But the stigma, the defect, the fatal difference—though derived in the past from environmental forces—is still located *within* the victim, inside his skin. With such an elegant formulation, the humanitarian can have it both ways. He can, all at the same time, concentrate his charitable interest on the defects of the victim, condemn the vague social and environmental stresses that produced the defect (some time ago), and ignore the continuing effect of victimizing social forces (right now). It is a brilliant ideology for justifying a perverse form of social action designed to change, not society, as one might expect, but rather society's victim.[53]

Ryan's belief is, of course, that the individual is not responsible for his or her own poverty, and that cultural explanations are just sophisticated attempts to cover up the real reasons for poverty. These reasons are not defects in the individual, but defects in the structure of society. It is to this explanation of poverty that we now turn.

Structural Explanations of Poverty—Liberal Version

Structural explanations argue that poverty is not a result of individual or cultural factors that we can change by working with individuals on a one-to-one basis. Rather, poverty is viewed as the result of social factors that act on individuals, causing them to exhibit the characteristics that the other theories state are the result of individual or cultural shortcomings. To reduce poverty significantly, according to the structural perspective, the basic fabric of society will need to change. Obviously, this is a perspective that appeals to liberals and radicals and one that conservatives have traditionally opposed. In recent years, however, conservatives have developed their own structural theory, albeit one that is quite different from that espoused by liberals and radicals.

What are these structural factors purported to have so much influence over the life chances of people? One of the clearest explanations of these factors from the liberal perspective is presented by the sociologist Leonard Beeghley. Beeghley classifies structural factors that contribute to poverty into four main groups:

- The way in which the correlates of poverty create a vicious circle that often traps the poor and prevents them from changing their situation.
- The way the class system reproduces itself over time.
- The organization of the economy.
- The continuation of institutionalized discrimination against African Americans and women.

Recently, sociologist William Julius Wilson added another structural factor that he argues causes poverty, particularly the rapidly increasing concentration of poverty among inner-city African Americans. This factor is:

- The increasing social isolation of the ghetto.[54]

These five factors are discussed next.

Poverty as a Vicious Circle. Once people are caught in poverty, it becomes a trap from which it is very difficult to escape. There are many elements to this poverty trap. The first is the public assistance system, which, although it seeks to make people self-supporting, often perversely contributes to their inability to escape welfare and poverty. One aspect of the welfare system that traps people in poverty is the fact that people must be so destitute before they become eligible for assistance that they no longer have the resources to obtain employment. Before people can get welfare, they have often lost their home, furniture, and car, and their clothes are old and worn. Obviously, if you don't have a nice outfit to wear to a job interview, if you can't afford to take a trip to another town to look for work where the opportunities may be better, if you don't have a phone for prospective employers to call or even an address to which they can write, and if you do not have a dependable car to commute in, your chances of obtaining a good job and escaping poverty are slim.

Another element of the vicious circle is crime and the criminal justice system. Poor people are much more likely to be the victims of crime than are people in higher income brackets. They must spend much more time and energy defending themselves against crime than other citizens, time and energy that might otherwise be devoted to escaping poverty. One of the authors once worked in a community school in the inner-city area of St. Louis. The school provided educational programs to help people develop marketable job skills, but many people did not take advantage of the courses because they were at night and the people were afraid to walk in that neighborhood after dark. In a very real sense, these folks were trapped in their own homes by their poverty. The other side of this element is what happens to poor people when, as defendants, they come in contact with the criminal justice system. When higher-income people are arrested for a crime, they post bail and go about their lives more or less as usual. When tried, they are represented by competent lawyers who can often strike a bargain for them that allows them to stay out of jail. By contrast, poor people will often be unable to afford bail. Thus, when arrested, they will stay in jail, which means they will lose their jobs, be evicted from their homes or apartments, and lose anything they are making payments on. When a poor person goes on trial, he or she will probably not be able to afford the best lawyer, will have no influence with the judge, and will probably be given a prison term with all its predictable economic consequences.

The next element in the vicious circle of poverty is ill health and the health care system. By almost any measure available, the health of the poor is significantly worse than that of the population in general.[55] Poor health is both a cause and an effect of poverty. If a person has a health problem, particularly a chronic one, it is going to adversely affect that person's ability to make a living. Once a person is poor, his or her access to healthy living conditions becomes limited. Poor people cannot afford to eat the most healthy foods, they may live in conditions that are hot in the summer and cold in the winter, and their homes are more prone to infestations by disease-carrying pests such as rats. Illness also has a more immediate economic effect on the poor than on the general population. When poor people become ill for more than a few days, it is very likely that they will lose their jobs, and it is very unlikely that they will have insurance to cover either the cost of medical care or the lost income from missed work. The health care system in the United States, as we discuss in a later chapter, is designed primarily to serve the middle class, and it does not do a good job of serving the health care needs of the poor. So, once poor people become sick, they will most likely have a hard time obtaining efficient, high-quality medical care.

There is an old saying that it takes money to make money. A corollary of this saying, related to the vicious circle of poverty, is that it takes money to save money. It is a hard fact of economic life that the poor pay more. If poor people need to borrow money, they pay much higher interest rates than the nonpoor. Stores in ghetto areas charge higher prices than stores in the suburbs. You must have extra money to take full advantage of sales. For example, middle-income parents often refuse to buy disposable diapers at regular price. They wait until diapers go on sale, at discounts of as much as two or three dollars a box, and then they stock up on several weeks' or even months' worth of diapers. Poor parents who do not have the extra cash to take advantage of the sale end up paying more than the higher-income parents for the same diapers.

We could discuss numerous other elements of the vicious circle of poverty. The poor lack political power, so they rarely get their way when decisions are being made that could benefit them. Low-income people tend to get married earlier and have children earlier; they thereby increase the chance that their children will grow up poor and in turn marry early and have children early. The educational system tends to define poor children as low achievers, to put them into remedial classes, and thereby to increase the probability of this becoming a self-fulfilling prophecy. The main point is that the very condition of being in poverty decreases a person's chances of getting out of poverty. Over time, these conditions tend to wear a person down and cause many of the characteristics that Lewis identified as the culture of poverty.

Does the Class System Reproduce Itself? Beeghley, among others, argues that one of the causes of poverty is that the class system tends to reproduce itself. He discusses the status attainment process in the United States and concludes, "The result is that the class structure reproduces itself over time and a stratum of impoverished persons is continually recreated."[56] What he means is that the children of wealthy parents, through various mechanisms such as inheritance and family connections, themselves grow into wealthy adults; children of middle-class parents become middle-class adults; and children of poor parents, as a result of the socially disadvantaged position into which they are born, are almost automatically doomed to lives of poverty. Does this actually happen? The answer is that no, the class system does not totally reproduce itself; but yes, the lowest and highest classes do.

Research on stratification and social mobility is one of the most highly developed areas in contemporary sociology.[57] This research seeks to understand how people obtain and change their positions in the social structure. We all like to believe that the United States is the land of opportunity, that our class structure is open, and that people often rise out of poverty into wealth, as in the famous Horatio Alger stories. And indeed, research results indicate that the class system in the United States is open for most people; that is, parents' status has relatively little effect on the status of their children. Featherman and Hauser, building on earlier research by Blau and Duncan, found that only about 7 percent of variation in socioeconomic status could be attributed to family background. A much larger percentage of the variance (36 percent) was explained by education—which itself is highly influenced, but not completely determined, by family background. This is the good news. The bad news is that the researchers found that for the top and, more important, for the bottom of our society, the socioeconomic status of one's parents is by far the most important determinant of a person's own status.[58] Thus, the American dream is alive and well for most people in the country; but for poor people, being born into poverty generally means living out life in poverty. For the poor, the class structure does indeed reproduce itself.

The Organization of the Economy. This element of the structural explanation of poverty asserts that the organization of the economy is such that some people are forced into poverty. There are two versions of this explanation, the radical version and the liberal version. The radical version is derived from the work of Marx and Engels and claims, basically, that the labor market of capitalist economies cannot provide sufficient employment at above-poverty-line wages to prevent poverty. Behind this problem is the assertion that capitalist economies are organized so the owners of the means of production (the capitalists) get wealthy by exploiting the workers.[59] This perspective further asserts that the welfare system is designed to force people into starvation-level jobs when they are available, but to provide enough support when jobs are not available to prevent workers from organizing and overthrowing the capitalist system.[60] The basic contention is that in capitalist economies, poor people are poor because this is a necessary condition for others to be rich. In other words, poverty is intentional; it is designed into the fabric of the economy.

The second version of the assertion that the organization of the economy forces people into poverty is the liberal version. This version claims that there are two labor markets operating in our society, the primary and the secondary labor markets, sometimes called the *core* and the *periphery.* The primary, or core, labor market is the one in which most people in the United States work. Jobs in this labor market pay well; they include benefits such as health coverage, sick leave, a retirement plan, and paid vacation; and they are often fairly secure. The secondary, or peripheral, job market is made up of jobs that do not pay well, they generally include few benefits, and they offer little security. Jobs in the primary labor market are found in government and in industries dominated by large, capital-intensive, oligopolistic firms. Jobs in the secondary labor market are found in small, labor-intensive, highly competitive firms. These are businesses that unions have not been able to organize because of their small size, that cannot pay well because they have to keep costs down to remain competitive and do not offer benefits for the same reason, and that do not offer job security because of the basic instability of their position in the market. The job skills and training (human capital) of workers in the secondary labor market are not much different from those of workers in the primary labor market. It is often just a matter of luck and sometimes geographic location that determines whether a person gets well-paid and secure employment or spends life in a series of minimum-wage jobs at fast-food restaurants or discount stores.[61] Beeghley says, "Regardless of the skills people have, the nature of the jobs available to them decisively influences the likelihood of their living poorly."[62]

Racial, Sexual, and Age Discrimination. Prejudice and discrimination appear to be a major structural component of poverty. As the data reviewed earlier clearly indicate, a disproportionate number of minorities, women, and the elderly are found among the ranks of the poor. Beeghley identifies three mechanisms that he believes account for the large proportion of minorities and women among the poor. First, recruitment procedures used by employers work to the advantage of white males and to the disadvantage of other groups. Second, divorce laws usually grant custody of children to the mother but often do not grant enough child support to provide for them; or, if adequate child support is ordered, the courts do not strongly enforce its payment. Third, child-rearing patterns tend to guide women into lower-paying careers or to create the expectation that a woman should be dependent on a husband, thus putting a woman in a bad position when her marriage breaks down and she has to support herself.

The Increasing Social Isolation of the Ghetto. A recent structural explanation of poverty that is gaining a wide following is the social isolation hypothesis of Harvard University sociologist William Julius Wilson. This explanation is especially popular among liberals who are anxious for an alternative to the extreme culture of poverty interpretation of conservatives such as Edward Banfield. Wilson argues that much of poverty in the United States can be explained by the fact that poor people are geographically and, consequently, socially isolated. That is, poor people are largely confined to housing projects and inner-city ghettos where they are denied contact with the wide variety of influences and opportunities the rest of society enjoys.

Wilson contends that the rapid increase in poverty, particularly among inner-city blacks, and the growth of what is now referred to as the underclass have been ironic by-products of the success of the civil rights movement. The ghetto, Wilson states, used to be characterized by vertical integration of different segments of the urban African American population. Lower-, middle-, and upper-class African Americans used to live in the same communities, largely because neighborhood segregation provided few options for the higher-income groups. The presence of these economically better off segments of the population resulted in a high degree of social organization in the neighborhoods. By social organization Wilson means "(1) the prevalence, strength, and interdependence of social networks; (2) the extent of collective supervision that the residents exercise and the degree of personal responsibility they assume in addressing neighborhood problems; and (3) the rate of resident participation in voluntary and formal organizations."[63]

Today, however, because of the success of the civil rights movement, middle- and upper-class African American professionals have moved out of black inner-city neighborhoods, leaving many of these areas almost totally populated by the unemployed, welfare recipients, drug addicts and alcoholics, the mentally disabled, and other problem-ridden segments of the population. The results have been that these communities have lost their stability, crime and violence have increased, unemployment has increased, female-headed families have become the norm, welfare is the standard form of support, leadership has disappeared, children have few role models, and the inner city has become characterized by a tangle of pathology.

Social isolation means several things to the residents of inner-city neighborhoods. First, it means that these communities are characterized by a high concentration of poverty and its associated problems, which Wilson refers to as *concentration effects.* It also means that the residents lack contact or sustained interaction with individuals or institutions that represent mainstream society; Wilson refers to this as a *social buffer.* Because of this social buffer, the residents of these areas are unlikely to develop good work habits—if you don't know anyone who gets up each morning to go to work, it is unlikely that you will develop this habit yourself. Also, because businesses often leave inner-city areas along with the higher-income residents who were their best customers, very few jobs are left; the only ones available are generally undesirable and likely to alienate the people who do them. According to Wilson, "the combination of unattractive jobs and lack of community norms to reinforce work increases the likelihood that individuals will turn to either underground illegal activity or idleness or both."[64]

What **Americans** Believe

In this chapter we review various theories and data about the causes of poverty that have been presented by policymakers, social scientists, and social theorists. It is the average citizen, however, who gives money to anti-poverty agencies and who votes candidates into office based on the candidate's perceived beliefs and values. It is thus important for social workers, and other anti-poverty activists, to have some idea of what the average citizen believes are the causes of poverty.

The General Social Survey from 1988 to 1991 included four questions (actually one question with four parts) related to beliefs about the causation of poverty. The question was, "Now I will present a list of reasons some people give to explain why there are poor people in this country. Please tell me whether you feel each of these is very important, somewhat important, or not important in explaining why there are poor people in this country." The list included two structural explanations, "Failure of society to provide good schools for many Americans" and "Failure of industry to provide enough jobs," and two individual explanations, "Loose morals and drunkenness" and "Lack of effort by the poor themselves." The responses to these questions are summarized in Table 8.2.

TABLE 8.2

Importance of Various Factors in Explaining Why Some People Are Poor

	Failure of Society to Provide Good Schools	Failure of Industry to Provide Enough Jobs	Loose Morals and Drunkenness by the Poor Themselves	Lack of Effort by the Poor Themselves
Very Important	36.6%	35.6%	39.5%	46.4%
Somewhat Important	39.4%	42.9%	34.9%	45.0%
Not Important	24.2%	21.4%	25.6%	8.6%

The results of social isolation look very much like the attributes of the poor that culture of poverty theorists attempt to explain—low work ethic, a high degree and favorable evaluation of welfare dependency, female-headed families, and inability to defer gratification. Wilson admits that these cultural traits exist; but he contends, in opposition to culture of poverty theorists, that they do not result from unique, ghetto-specific values. Culture of poverty theory "places strong emphasis on the autonomous character of the cultural traits once they come into existence. In other words, these traits assume a 'life of their own' and continue to influence behavior even if opportunities for social mobility improve." By contrast, "social isolation does not mean that cultural traits are irrel-

Most respondents identified all of these factors as important, although with individual explanations given the most credence. It is interesting that of the two individual explanations people could choose, the one that placed responsibility on lack of effort exceeded by far the loose morals explanation. Apparently the average citizen feels that poor people are not bad people, but they believe that America is indeed the land of opportunity, and so if people are not succeeding it must clearly be due to a lack of effort on their part.

We combined the responses to the two individual explanation factors (loose morals and drunkenness, and lack of effort by the poor themselves) and the two structural factors (failure of society to provide good schools, and failure of industry to provide enough jobs). We cross-tabulated these with the item asking for the political orientation of the respondent. The results of these cross tabulations are shown in Tables 8.3 and 8.4. The results of these calculations are not surprising and reinforce our discussions about political perspectives and opinions regarding social welfare issues. A significantly greater number of liberals subscribed to structural explanations than did those identifying themselves as conservatives. Conversely, a significantly greater number of conservatives supported individual explanations of poverty than did those identifying themselves as liberals.

TABLE 8.3

How Important Are Structural Factors in Explaining Poverty? (Poor Schools and Not Enough Jobs)

	Liberal	Moderate	Conservative
Very	45.2%	34.4%	26.0%
Somewhat	36.4%	43.0%	36.8%
Not Important	18.5%	22.5%	37.2%

TABLE 8.4

How Important Are Individual Factors in Explaining Poverty? (Loose Morals and Drunkenness; Lack of Effort by the Poor Themselves)

	Liberal	Moderate	Conservative
Very	34.4%	43.7%	47.6%
Somewhat	40.8%	40.5%	38.7%
Not Important	24.6%	15.8%	13.7%

evant in understanding behavior in highly concentrated poverty areas; rather it highlights the fact that culture is a response to social structural constraints and opportunities."[65]

Wilson's social isolation hypothesis is similar to the situational adaptation thesis and the choice model discussed earlier. You will recall that these theories contend that the differences in behavior between poor and nonpoor people are not a result of different values, but rather are caused by the different situations in which people find themselves. The value of marriage is functional for two people who have reasonable expectations of a secure future; it makes much less sense for people who know that life will be hard enough on their own and who expect that for a married couple it will only be harder. Wilson's hypothesis deals with the rapid rise of inner-city poverty in recent years and contends that the situation to which poor people have to adapt has gotten quite a lot worse for a large number of people because of social isolation, concentration effects, and social buffering.

Wilson's social isolation hypothesis has great implications for social policy regarding inner-city poverty. Using this approach instead of the currently prevailing cultural explanations would mean shifting the focus of our policies and programs from attempting to change subcultural traits (by means of classes on family life for teenagers in poverty, counseling sessions aimed at developing an appreciation of the benefits of deferring gratification, and work habits classes) to attempting to change the structure of constraints and opportunities in which inner-city dwellers find themselves. In other words, the social isolation approach to inner-city poverty would involve changing social structures rather than changing individuals.

Critique of Liberal Structural Explanations

As you might imagine, structural explanations of poverty are not well received by conservatives. These explanations are diametrically opposed to nearly all of the major components of the conservative belief system discussed in Chapter 1. Conservatives believe in individual responsibility; the structural perspective rejects this and says the social and economic environment is largely responsible for poverty. Conservatives believe in minimum government; the structural perspective logically leads to the conclusion that government intervention is necessary to correct the structural flaws that are causing poverty. Conservatives believe in the free market; the structural perspective argues that the market is not really free. Thus, it is obvious that conservatives will be critical of this perspective.

Probably the most influential critique of the structural perspective is that presented in *Losing Ground* by Charles Murray. Murray argues that the huge growth of social programs that occurred during the 1960s was based on a structural explanation of poverty. He says that, according to the designers of the antipoverty programs, "Poverty was not a consequence of indolence or vice. It was not the just deserts of people who didn't try hard enough. It was produced by conditions that had nothing to do with individual virtue or effort. *Poverty was not the fault of the individual but of the system.*"[66] But Murray believes that poverty is indeed caused by all of the individual failings structural explanations reject. He reviews what he believes to be the catastrophic failure of the social programs that have been implemented in the last quarter-century and lays the blame for this failure squarely at the feet of structural explanations of poverty. Murray argues that the result of structural explanations has been to remove responsibility for self-support from individuals and to make it more profitable to be on welfare than to work; this in general has made it "profitable for the poor to behave in the short term in ways that were destructive in the long term."[67]

Murray's critique of structural explanations of poverty can itself be criticized on several points. There have been responses that criticize Murray's use and interpretation of data, as well as the logic of his arguments.[68] Murray cites a great deal of research that he claims demonstrates that programs were failures, but fails even to mention research that did not reach these conclusions.[69] The most serious shortcoming of Murray's argument, however, is that very few people have ever believed that the social programs developed during the 1960s were based on a structural explanation of poverty. Most, even Murray's fellow conservatives such as Butler and Kondratas, have interpreted the programs as being based on the culture of poverty theory. This theory, as reviewed previously, gives lip service to structural factors but still lays responsibility for poverty at the feet of the poor person. Thus, as a critique of structural explanations of poverty, Murray's argument is really of the straw man variety.

Structural Explanations of Poverty—Conservative Version

In recent years a new conservative explanation of structurally caused poverty has emerged. This theory is referred to as "new" structural poverty. Basically this explanation contends that "overly generous" government welfare programs encourage able-bodied working-age persons to sink into a lifestyle of welfare dependency and consequently permanent poverty. Advocates of this perspective argue that welfare payments to poor female-headed families undermine the traditional role of the male breadwinner, for whom the state unintentionally becomes a surrogate.[70]

To the chagrin of liberals, conservatives have some empirical data with which to back up this theory. From 1967 until 1977 the government financed a series of studies that looked at increased benefits and liberalized policies for public assistance recipients. The studies were the New Jersey Guaranteed Income Experiment, which began in 1967; the Rural (1968) and Gary (1969) Guaranteed Income Experiments; and finally the largest, the Seattle–Denver Income Maintenance Experiments (Sime/Dime), which began in 1970. In these studies, more than five thousand families were randomly assigned to experimental and control groups. The experimental groups were placed on what is known as a negative income tax, or guaranteed annual income; in addition, some received labor market counseling and training. The control groups received traditional welfare support. After various periods of time, the families were evaluated to see whether there were any differences in the amount of labor force participation (were participants in the more generous guaranteed annual income program less motivated to work?), whether labor market counseling affected labor market participation, and what the effects of the experimental program were on marital stability. The study found that the program did have some (although there is debate as to just how much) negative effect on labor market participation. It also found that the more generous benefits and liberalized policies did not have the anticipated effect of reducing marital breakup among recipients. Conservatives point to these studies as evidence that more generous welfare programs will have a result just the opposite of that intended; that is, they will increase poverty and dependency rather than reduce it.

Critique of Conservative Structural Explanations

Although liberals will admit that the guaranteed income experiments demonstrated that generous welfare programs provide some work disincentives, they consider these effects to be minor when compared with the poverty-reducing results of the increased benefits. They argue that generous welfare benefits help families maintain basic financial and health care standards they would not otherwise enjoy. These benefits, besides making the lives of the poor more tolerable, also function to prevent temporary hardships from escalating into such sustained and severe difficulties that the family is never able to recover.

Liberals argue that the conservative structural explanation of poverty is really an old idea that has been brought out and dusted off not in response to any new data, but rather because the political atmosphere is once again receptive. When the Elizabethan Poor Law was passed in England in 1601, one of the major fears of its critics was that the law would result in "pauperization" of the poor. By this the critics meant that once people learned they could survive without working, they would be forevermore rendered useless for socially beneficial work. Liberals argue that the new structural poverty theory is simply a restatement of this idea; and, as Sanders notes, "the attraction of [conservative] arguments may derive more from the 'hands-off' governmental approach and the potential for lower taxes it implies."[71]

Conclusion

If you find the preceding discussion a little confusing, do not be surprised, because it is. Obviously there is no consensus on what causes poverty; and so, as we discuss in the next chapter, there is no agreement on what to do about it. Your view of what causes poverty is heavily influenced by your political perspective. If you are conservative, you are likely to believe either in individual factors or in the individual components of cultural factors. If you are liberal, you will most likely believe in structural explanations and/or in the social components of the cultural explanations. If you are radical, you will concentrate on structural factors.

How do we make sense out of all of this uncertainty? The first thing we need to do is to recognize the complexity of poverty. Anyone searching for a simple, single-variable explanation of poverty is going to be frustrated. To say poverty is a multivariate problem is to understate the situation. Each individual case of poverty involves hundreds of variables, including age, gender, race, health, geographic location, family background, friends, and luck—the list goes on and on. When you multiply these variables by millions of individuals, you see the complexity of the situation. There are some commonalities among individuals, however, and so it is possible to discover some generalizations, even though they are imperfect.

If you recall, at the beginning of this chapter we spoke of within-group variance and between-group variance. We think that it is probably safe to say that different types of explanations probably better explain the different types of variation. For example, if you take a sample of people who are carefully matched on as many characteristics as possible—they are all of the same race, gender, and social class background, and from the same geographic location—and then compare the members of that group on the variable of economic status, it would be a good hypothesis that economic differences were largely caused by individual characteristics. Those who were more intelligent, energetic, focused, and motivated would probably be found to be doing better. However, the statistics reviewed earlier reveal that a large part of poverty falls into the between-group variance. Being a minority, old or young, female, a member of a single-parent family, rural, or an inner-city dweller all greatly increase the likelihood of being in poverty. It is very difficult to explain poverty related to these between-group variations using anything but a structural explanation.

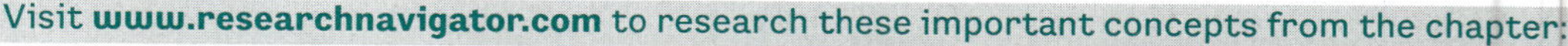

Children AND poverty
Human capital
Mental health AND poverty
National Longitudinal Survey of Youth
Panel Study of Income Dynamics
Poverty AND health
Race AND poverty
Working poor

Web Sites Related to the Nature and Causes of Poverty

Action Alliance for Children <www.4children.org>: Provides information about current trends affecting children and their families, including developments in poverty and welfare.

Center for the Study of Urban Poverty <www.sscnet.ucla.edu.issr.csup.html>: Contains abstracts of projects related to urban poverty and links to other poverty-related sites.

Institute for Research on Poverty <www.ssc.wisc.edu/irp>: Another poverty research institute, this one at the University of Wisconsin. Site includes frequently asked questions about poverty, what's new about IRP, and research projects and reports. Provides guidelines for how to search the IRP web site and how to contact IRP, people, and links to poverty-related resources.

Joint Center for Poverty Research <www.jcpr.org>: The Northwestern University/University of Chicago Joint Center for Poverty Research is a national and interdisciplinary community of researchers whose work advances the understanding of what it means to be poor in the Untied States. Site includes information on how to join the center's mailing list, general information about the center, updates on projects and grants, and descriptions of research and data sets.

Michigan Program on Poverty and Social Welfare Policy <www.umich.edu/~socwk/poverty>: Joint program of University of Michigan schools of social work, public policy, and law. Promotes interdisciplinary applied research on poverty and social welfare policy and works to translate research findings to public policy decision makers. Includes summaries of research projects, links to other sites, information on fellowships, and training opportunities.

Panel Study of Income Dynamics <www.isr.umich.edu/src/psid/index.html>: Information from longitudinal study of family income in process since 1968. Includes information on the study, a bibliography, newsletters, and data files that can be downloaded.

Endnotes

1. U.S. Bureau of the Census, Current Population Reports, Series P–60–222, *Poverty in the United States, 2002* (Washington, DC: U.S. Government Printing Office, September 2003), online at www.census.gov.
2. Diana Pearce, "The Feminization of Poverty: Women, Work, and Welfare," *Urban and Social Change Review 11* (February 1978), 28–36.
3. Pearce, "The Feminization of Poverty," 29; U.S. Bureau of the Census, *Statistical Abstract of the United States, 2000* (Washington, DC: U.S. Government Printing Office, 2001), 55.
4. Ralph Segalman and Asoke Basu, *Poverty in America: The Welfare Dilemma* (Westport, CT: Greenwood Press, 1981), 10–12.
5. Gunner Myrdal, *The Challenge of World Poverty* (New York: Vintage, 1970); Ken Auletta, *The Underclass* (New York: Random House, 1982); Christopher Jencks and Paul E. Peterson, eds., *The*

Urban Underclass (Washington, DC: Brookings Institution, 1990).

6. The Panel Study of Income Dynamics has resulted in numerous publications. Information in this chapter, unless otherwise noted, comes from Greg J. Duncan et al., *Years of Poverty, Years of Plenty: The Changing Economic Fortunes of American Workers and Families* (Ann Arbor, MI: Survey Research Center–Institute for Social Research, The University of Michigan, 1984), and Rebecca M. Blank, *It Takes a Nation: A New Agenda for Fighting Poverty* (Princeton, NJ: Princeton University Press, 1997); Data from the SIPP comes from John Iceland, U.S. Census Bureau, Household Economic Studies, *Dynamics of Economic Well-Being: Poverty 1996–1999* (Washington, DC: U.S. Government Printing Office, 2003).
7. Mark R. Rank and Thomas A. Hirschl, "The Occurrence of Poverty across the Life Cycle: Evidence from the PSID," *Journal of Policy Analysis and Management 20*(4) (2001), 737–755.
8. Quoted in Auletta, *The Underclass, 25.*
9. Robert Holman, *Poverty: Explanations of Social Deprivation* (New York: St. Martin's Press, 1978), 54–55.
10. Quoted on National Public Radio, "Morning Edition," 31 October 1994, transcript #1466-8.
11. Edwin Black, *War against the Weak: Eugenics and America's Campaign to Create a Master Race* (New York: Four Walls Eight Windows, 2003).
12. Arthur R. Jensen, "How Much Can We Boost IQ and Scholastic Achievement?" *Harvard Education Review 33* (1969), 1–123; Arthur R. Jensen, *Bias in Mental Testing* (New York: Free Press, 1979); Arthur R. Jensen, *Straight Talk about Mental Tests* (New York: Free Press, 1981).
13. Jensen, *Straight Talk about Mental Tests,* 103, 105.
14. Richard Herrnstein and Charles Murray, *The Bell Curve* (New York: Free Press, 1995).
15. Richard J. Herrnstein, *I.Q. in the Meritocracy* (Boston: Little, Brown, 1971), 197–198, 221.
16. Claude S. Fischer, Michael Hout, Martin Sanchez Jankowski, Samuel R. Lucas, Ann Swidler, and Kim Voss, *Inequality by Design; Cracking the Bell Curve Myth* (Princeton, NJ: Princeton University Press, 1996), 11–12.
17. Bradley Buell et al., *Community Planning for Human Services* (New York: Columbia University Press, 1952).
18. Laura Curran, "The Psychology of Poverty: Professional Social Work and Aid to Dependent Children in Postwar America, 1946–1963," *Social Service Review 76* (September 2002), 371.
19. Walter Trattner, *From Poor Law to Welfare State: A History of Social Welfare in America,* 6th ed. (New York: Free Press, 1999), 320.
20. Laura Curran, "The Psychology of Poverty," 365.
21. Lawrence M. Mead, "Poverty: How Little We Know," *Social Service Review 68* (September 1994), 339.
22. David T. Ellwood, "The Origins of 'Dependency': Choices, Confidence, or Culture?" *Focus 12* (1989), 9.
23. Lester C. Thurow, *Investment in Human Capital* (Belmont, CA: Wadsworth, 1970), 20.
24. Thurow, *Investment in Human Capital,* 11–12.
25. Thurow, *Investment in Human Capital,* 13.
26. Oscar Lewis, *Five Families: Mexican Case Studies in the Culture of Poverty* (New York: Basic Books, 1959).
27. Michael Harrington, *The Other America: Poverty in the United States* (New York: Penguin Books, 1962); Frank Riessman, *The Culturally Deprived Child* (New York: Harper & Row, 1962); Daniel Patrick Moynihan, *The Negro Family* (Washington, DC: U.S. Department of Labor, 1965).
28. Oscar Lewis, *La Vida: A Puerto Rican Family in the Culture of Poverty—San Juan and New York* (New York: Random House, 1965), xliii–xliv.
29. Edward C. Banfield, *The Unheavenly City Revisited* (Boston: Little, Brown, 1974), 62.
30. Lewis, *La Vida,* xlvii.
31. Banfield, *The Unheavenly City Revisited,* 62.
32. Banfield, *The Unheavenly City Revisited,* 61.
33. Lewis, *La Vida,* xlvi.
34. William Ryan, *Blaming the Victim* (New York: Pantheon Books, 1971). Copyright 1971 Pantheon Books, a Division of Random House, Inc.
35. Robert Holman, *Poverty: Explanations of Social Deprivation,* 112.
36. Charles A. Valentine, "The 'Culture of Poverty': Its Scientific Significance and Its Implications for Action," in Eleanor Burke Leacock, ed., *The Culture of Poverty: A Critique* (New York: Simon & Schuster, 1971), 194–197.
37. Valentine, "The 'Culture of Poverty': Its Scientific Significance and Its Implications for Action," 193.
38. Herbert J. Gans, "Deconstructing the Underclass: The Term's Danger as a Planning Concept," *APA Journal 56* (Summer 1990), 271–277.
39. Leonard Goodwin, *Do the Poor Want to Work?* (Washington, DC: Brookings Institution, 1972);

Leonard Goodwin, "How Suburban Families View the Work Orientations of the Welfare Poor," *Social Problems 19* (1972), 337–348.

40. See, for example, Elliot Liebow, *Tally's Corner* (Boston: Little, Brown, 1967); Joseph T. Howell, *Hard Living on Clay Street* (New York: Anchor Books, 1973).
41. Sandra L. Barnes, "Debunking Deficiency Theories: Evaluating Non-Traditional Attitudes and Behavior among Residents in Poor Urban Neighborhoods," *Journal of Poverty 5* (Jan. 2001), 51.
42. Robert Sears, Eleanor Maccoby, and Harry Levin, *Patterns of Child Rearing* (New York: Row Peterson, 1957).
43. Riessman, *The Culturally Deprived Child.*
44. Barnes, "Debunking Deficiency Theories: Evaluating Non-Traditional Attitudes and Behavior among Residents in Poor Urban Neighborhoods," 53.
45. See, for example, Vera P. John, "Language and Educability," in Leacock, ed., *The Culture of Poverty: A Critique,* 41–62.
46. John P. Kretzmann and John L. McKnight, *Building Communities from the Inside Out: A Path toward Finding and Mobilizing a Community's Assets* (Evanston, IL: Northwestern University, Center for Urban Affairs and Policy Research, 1993).
47. Lee Rainwater, "The Problem of Lower Class Culture and Poverty-War Strategy," in Daniel Moynihan, ed., *On Understanding Poverty* (New York: Basic Books, 1968), 229–259; Donald Bogue, "A Long-Term Solution to the A.F.D.C. Problem: Prevention of Unwanted Pregnancy," *Social Service Review 49* (1975), 539–552.
48. Leonard Beeghley, *Living Poorly in America* (New York: Praeger, 1983), 122; Ellwood, "The Origins of 'Dependency': Choices, Confidence, or Culture?" 6–9.
49. Hyman Rodman, "The Lower Class Value Stretch," *Social Forces 42* (December 1963), 205–215.
50. Ellwood, "The Origins of 'Dependency': Choices, Confidence, or Culture?" 13.
51. William Ryan, *Blaming the Victim.* Copyright 1971 Pantheon Books, a Division of Random House, Inc.
52. William Ryan, *Blaming the Victim,* 4. Copyright 1971 Pantheon Books, a Division of Random House, Inc.
53. William Ryan, *Blaming the Victim,* 4. Copyright 1971 Pantheon Books, a Division of Random House, Inc.
54. Beeghley, *Living Poorly in America,* 133; William Julius Wilson, *When Work Disappears: The World of the New Urban Poor* (New York: Knopf, 1996).
55. Beeghley, *Living Poorly in America,* 108–115.
56. Beeghley, *Living Poorly in America,* 141.
57. David Featherman, "Stratification and Social Mobility: Two Decades of Cumulative Social Science," in James F. Short Jr., ed., *The State of Sociology: Problems and Prospects* (San Francisco: Sage, 1981), 79–100.
58. David Featherman and Robert Hauser, *Opportunity and Change* (New York: Academic Press, 1978); Peter Blau and Otis D. Duncan, *The American Occupational Structure* (New York: John Wiley, 1967).
59. Karl Marx and Friedrich Engels, *Manifesto of the Communist Party* (1848), reprinted in Lewis S. Feuer, ed., *Marx and Engels: Basic Writings on Politics and Philosophy* (Garden City, NY: Doubleday, 1959), 1–41.
60. Francis F. Piven and Richard A. Cloward, *Regulating the Poor: The Functions of Public Welfare* (New York: Pantheon Books, 1971).
61. E. M. Beck, Patrick M. Horan, and Charles M. Tolbert, "Stratification in a Dual Economy," *American Sociological Review 43* (October 1978), 704–720.
62. Beeghley, *Living Poorly in America,* 155.
63. William Julius Wilson, *When Work Disappears,* 20.
64. William Julius Wilson, *The Truly Disadvantaged: The Inner City, the Underclass, and Public Policy* (Chicago: The University of Chicago Press, 1987), 3.
65. Wilson, *The Truly Disadvantaged,* 61, 137.
66. Charles Murray, *Losing Ground: American Social Policy, 1950–1980* (New York: Basic Books, 1984), 29.
67. Murray, *Losing Ground,* 9.
68. See, for example, Rino Patti, Mimi Abramovitz, Steven Burkhardt, Michael Fabricant, Martha Haffey, and Rose Starr, *Gaining Perspective on Losing Ground* (New York: Lois and Samuel Silberman Fund, 1987).
69. For example, see Sonia Wright, "Work Response to Income Maintenance: Economic, Sociological, and Cultural Perspectives," *Social Forces 53* (June 1975), 553–562. Wright found that, contrary to "popular wisdom," no work disincentives were found.
70. Jimy M. Sanders, " 'New' Structural Poverty?" *The Sociological Quarterly 32* (1991), 182.
71. Jimy M. Sanders, " 'New' Structural Poverty?," 182.

CHAPTER

9

The Development of Antipoverty Programs

The authors have heard the stories dozens of times. We have heard them at parties, from colleagues, and over coffee with friends; and we hear at least one version each time we teach the introductory social welfare course. The stories we are referring to are those of the welfare Cadillac and of the food stamp Lincoln. The stories go like this:

> An acquaintance of the teller of the story is standing in line at the bank. The woman ahead of him or her cashes a welfare check. Having only a brief transaction, the storyteller's acquaintance follows the woman out of the bank and in the parking lot observes the woman getting into a brand new Cadillac.
>
> A person known to the storyteller works as a checker in a food store or is standing in line at the food store. A woman comes through the line and pays for her groceries with food stamps. The woman is then observed going out to the parking lot and driving away in a brand new Lincoln.

These stories often vary in terms of the details and the amount of embroidery added. Sometimes the type of car is different; a BMW or a Mercedes Benz is a popular alternative. Sometimes the welfare recipient acts in a haughty or high-handed manner. In some versions the food stamp recipient purchases an extremely extravagant basket of groceries. A large number of kids, often obviously neglected, is another popular variation. However, the main details of the story are always the same. The teller gets the story from an absolutely reliable source, such as an aunt or a good friend. Bank and food store personnel also are good sources because they have about them the mantle of experts, seeing much of such things. The subject of the story always demonstrates in some way that he or she is receiving some form of public aid. Finally, the person always demonstrates that he or she does not deserve such aid by driving away in some type of extravagant car.

The stories of the welfare Cadillac and the food stamp Lincoln are examples of a phenomenon that folklorists (scholars who specialize in the collection and analysis of folk traditions) have labeled *urban legends.* They are, according to Brunvand, "an integral part of white Anglo-American culture and are told and believed by some of the most sophisticated 'folk' of modern society—young people, urbanites, and the well educated. The storytellers assume that the true facts of each case lie just one or two informants back down the line with a reliable witness, or in a news media report."[1] An important aspect of urban legends is that the teller believes them to be absolutely true, and he or she generally believes this with a great deal of conviction. The secretary of one of the authors once recounted the story of the welfare Cadillac to him and then communicated in no uncertain terms that she considered him to be somewhat less than bright when he tried to explain to her that the story was not true; he even went so far as to show her the welfare department regulations limiting the value of a car a person can own and still be eligible for benefits.

Urban legends tell us something about our society. According to Brunvand, "like traditional folklore, the stories do tell one kind of truth. They are a unique, unself-conscious reflection of major concerns of individuals in the societies in which the legends circulate."[2] What do the stories of the welfare Cadillac and the food stamp Lincoln tell us about the major concerns of our society? They indicate several things. First, they point out that we are very concerned with the problem of financial dependency. They tell us that we suspect that the people, or at least some of the people, receiving help do not really deserve it. They point to a fear that either the people who are managing the programs to aid the poor are incompetent or else they are such bleeding-heart liberals that they give money to undeserving people. Finally, and probably most important, these stories reflect a strong undercurrent of resentment about welfare programs.[3]

In this chapter we look at the historical development of welfare programs and attempt to gain some perspective on why these concerns and resentments have developed. It would actually be more accurate to say why they have *persisted,* because concerns such as these have existed since the very first attempts to help the needy.

Historical Perspective on Antipoverty Efforts

The eminent social welfare historian Walter Trattner has written:

> The basic tenets and programs of any social welfare system reflect the values of the society in which the system functions. Like all other social institutions, social welfare systems do not arise in a vacuum; they stem from the customs, statutes, and practices of the past. Therefore, one cannot understand current efforts to help the needy without first comprehending the foundations on which they were built. And since the practice of assisting people in need as we know it in America did not originate in this country but was transplanted from the Old World to the New during the colonial period, we must go back in time . . . to . . . study social welfare.[4]

In Chapter 6 we discussed ancient developments in social welfare. In this chapter we go back to fourteenth-century England to begin our story.

We should note before we begin that we will be dealing with a very narrow slice of history. We begin in England and then rapidly move to the United States. In the United States the history we discuss is mainly related to urban areas, and it usually focuses on majority group members. This approach leaves out quite a lot of interesting history. It largely skirts the history of American Indians, African Americans, and other minority groups; it does not give much credit to other areas of the world that made major advances in the area of social welfare; and it does not pay attention to the unique problems of rural areas. However, for better or for worse, this is the history of the development of the major antipoverty programs in this country. A direct line can be drawn from England to the colonies and straight up to the present time. Until very recent years, this line did not include much concern for minority groups; and, often unfortunately, social welfare traditions other than Anglo-Saxon ones have had little influence on developments in this country. So bear in mind when reading this that there is a much broader social welfare history than we are reporting here. However, our major purpose is to gain perspective on our current poverty programs, and the relevant history of these programs is the rather narrow one we describe.

We should also note that histories of social welfare developments present different political perspectives on those developments. Although historians strive for objectivity, they, like all of us, are members of a particular society and socioeconomic class. Therefore, their work reflects the range of attitudes about social welfare discussed in Chapter 1. The historical approach in this chapter generally represents a liberal point of view.

In this historical survey you will notice that certain themes and issues recur over the six-hundred-plus years we are discussing. Among the more prominent of these themes is the issue of compassion or protection as the chief motivator for public assistance efforts. Are we engaging in these efforts because we are concerned with human suffering? Or are we doing so because we fear adverse consequences, such as crime, revolution, or begging, if we do not?[5] Another issue is the regulation of labor. Social welfare reforms are often preceded by periods of either labor unrest or labor shortage, and the welfare reforms appear to be primarily for the purpose of either settling the labor force down or driving it toward certain types of employment. A third issue that appears throughout history is a fear of strangers who may become dependent, criminal, or both. In earlier years the fear was actually of strangers—people from outside one's own geographic area. In modern history this seems to have been replaced by a fear of people who are different, primarily members of minority groups. Finally, the history of social welfare is a history of cycles. For a period of years the approach to people who are dependent is positive and progressive; then the pendulum swings back to an approach that is harsh and punitive.

At the end of the last chapter we concluded that structural explanations appear to be the only way to explain much of poverty. The following historical survey further supports this argument. For in each period in history when poverty has greatly increased, we can clearly see in hindsight that the increase was related to structural factors. The decline of feudalism and the rise of the wool industry, plague, famine, industrialization, urbanization, immigration, and economic depression have all been major contributors to the economic woes of individuals. Interestingly, at each point in history at which poverty has increased, the powers that be have attempted to attribute the problems to individual deficiencies and thus have attempted to evade structural (public) responsibility for a structural problem. In the words of Michael Katz, history "shows that many popular ideas about welfare are myths. It points to the stale, repetitive, and self-serving character of ideas about poor people in American social thought. . . . There is an American style of welfare. It is old. It is no cause for pride or satisfaction."[6]

English Roots

Historians would probably be horrified at such a broad generalization, but we're going to make it anyway: Up until the fourteenth century, social life in the world had been relatively constant. People the world over generally lived in rural settings; they usually lived by means of a combination of subsistence farming and gathering; they lived with their extended families as part of a clan or tribe; and they were born, lived, and died within a radius of a few miles. By the eleventh century, the form of social organization dominant in England, as well as in most of Europe, was the feudal system. Under this system the continent was divided into fiefdoms, and each of these was divided into what were basically tenant farms. The structure was hierarchical; a monarch would give control of a fief to the church or to a nobleman in return for taxes and help in obtaining recruits for his army when needed. The church or noble would then assign the land to serfs who were the tenant farmers in return for a share of their produce as well as their service in the monarch's army if needed.

Under the feudal system, at least in theory, people's basic needs were met. People who lived on feudal manors were extremely poor, but they were at least protected by their masters from extremes of want caused by sickness, unemployment, becoming orphaned, and old age. Basically, in return for their service to their master, the serfs were provided with a primitive form of social insurance. They were not free to leave the land at will, but then they could not be driven off it either. A woman had the right to remain on the land after her husband's death, and children had the right to take over the farming of their parents' land. Serfs were poor but secure. The small proportion of the population who were not serfs generally lived in the few cities and towns, and they made their living as craftspeople of various sorts. Security was provided for these people by the development of craft guilds, which were mainly mutual protection societies that provided insurance against disability, old age, and widowhood. The few people who did not come under the feudal or the guild system were provided a little protection by the church, which in England at this time was the Catholic Church. The church ran monasteries and hospitals that cared for the sick, the lame, and distressed travelers. Finally, people who fell between the cracks were under the charge of the bishop of their diocese; each bishop had the responsibility for feeding and protecting the poor within his district.[7]

In the fourteenth century things began to change. Initially the changes stemmed from purely negative events. The Swiss historian J. C. L. S. de Sismonde summarized the century very simply when he said that it was "a bad time for humanity."[8] Tuchman has said that the disorders of the fourteenth century "cannot be traced to any one cause; they were the hoofprints of more than the four horsemen of St. John's version, which had now become seven—plague, war, taxes, brigandage, bad government, insurrection, and schism in the church."[9] The most important events for the student of social welfare to be aware of were a series of calamities that befell the land in rapid succession—crop failures, famine, pestilence, and finally the bubonic plague, which swept across Europe from 1348 to 1349 and killed almost one-third of England's population. By this time the feudal system had begun to break down, and the tenant farming and guild systems were rapidly being replaced by a system of wage labor. The black death (as the plague was also known) created a labor crisis in that so many workers died that an extreme labor shortage was created. This resulted in a situation in which workers could come and go as they pleased, travel where they wanted, and demand much higher wages than in the past. Needless to say, the owners of the farms and businesses that employed the workers were not at all pleased with this situation.

The travails of the fourteenth century resulted in what is generally recognized as the first step in the development of a social security system in England and, by extension, in the United States. This was the passage of a law in 1349 called the Statute of Laborers. This act sought to solve the labor problem by setting a maximum wage, compelling unattached workers to work for whoever wanted them, forbidding laborers from traveling, and making it illegal for able-bodied men to beg. The reader may legitimately wonder why this act, which is completely repressive and clearly in the interest of the well-to-do rather than in the interest of the poor, is presented as the first step on the road to social security. There are two reasons. The first is that even though this act was itself repressive and had little to do with welfare, successive reforms of it eventually led to the passage of true social security legislation. The second reason is probably more important. This act is the beginning of a long history, which is still going on in the United States, of linking labor problems to problems in the public welfare system. Karl de Schweinitz says of the Statute of Laborers, "The King and his lords saw begging, movement and vagrancy, and the labor shortage as essentially the same problem, to be dealt with in one law."[10] Problems since 1349 have rarely included a shortage of labor, but we have consistently passed public welfare laws with the fear that they will result in people taking advantage of the system rather than supporting themselves through honest work. Handler has noted that "the central, overarching goal of the relief policy, at least as far back as the Great Plague, has been to control the supply of labor—in a word, to make sure that those who *could* work *would* seek work rather than welfare. This central idea explains the enormous continuities in welfare policy through the ages."[11] The current emphasis on workfare is the latest development in this regard.

The Statute of Laborers illustrates one additional point. That is, whenever we have a problem of labor or dependency in our society, our first reaction is to deal with it in a repressive manner. Thus, this law did not attempt to deal with the problems of labor shortages and begging by setting fair wages and by attending to the problems of those who were for legitimate reasons so poor that they had to resort to begging for survival; rather, it set maximum wages, it made it illegal to travel and to beg, and it set severe punishments for those who defied these provisions.

Following the fourteenth century, the pace of change in England quickened, and many of the changes were part of what we generally think of as progress. As the feudal system declined, mercantilism arose, trade routes opened, new industries developed, the New World began to open up, and in general the potential for greater prosperity was everywhere. Along with progress, however, these developments brought with them tremendous problems. The major problems had to do with the supply of labor and the growing insecurity of life. When the majority of people had been serfs, they were poor, but at least they had a form of security. No matter how hard times were, the serfs at least had the land and whatever sort of shelter they had erected on it. With the coming of industrialization and the accompanying urbanization, most people no longer had any right either to the land they lived on or to their dwellings. The feudal system had, for the common person, been replaced by the wage system. The majority of people were one payday away from destitution. This led to a continuation of the perception of a threat to social order that had begun with the labor shortage following the black death. However, the threat rapidly came to be perceived not as a shortage of laborers, but rather as an excess of unemployed and unattached people who wandered the roads begging and stealing. This situation was made worse during the Protestant Reformation, when in 1536 Henry VIII expelled the Catholic Church from England. This act basically kicked most of the social welfare provisions out of England along with the church, because it was the church that had been given the primary responsibility for caring for the old, the sick, travelers, and the poor in general.

Various laws were passed, following the Statute of Laborers, that attempted to deal with the problems of labor, begging, and crime. These acts were finally collected in one major piece of summary legislation, the Elizabethan Poor Law of 1601. This law is especially significant because it represented a compilation and refinement of all the antipoverty legislation of the previous 250 years; even more important, it was to remain the basic social welfare law in England and the United States for an additional 250 years.

The Elizabethan Poor Law was a combination of provisions that were both harsh and progressive. One of the harsh aspects of the law was that people were responsible for their children and parents up to three generations. Thus, a person could be legally forced to support his or her parents and grandparents in one direction, and his or her children and grandchildren in the other. The law was especially harsh in regard to vagrants. A person convicted of vagrancy could be whipped, branded, jailed, stoned, or put to death.

The harsh features of the Elizabethan Poor Law are not surprising, for this was a harsh age. More significant are the constructive features of the law. Of major importance is the fact that the law clearly indicated that the state had a responsibility to relieve want and suffering and to ensure the maintenance of life. The law proceeded from the assumption that not only did the state have a responsibility to help the needy, but also that the needy had a right to such help.[12]

The Elizabethan Poor Law also included some administrative aspects that were to have great influence; some are still in evidence in our contemporary public welfare system. The law established three broad categories of poor people—the vagrant, the involuntarily unemployed, and the helpless—and set down different ways of dealing with each group. Vagrants were to be punished; the unemployed were to be set to work; and the helpless were to be apprenticed (in the case of children) or given assistance (in the case of the aged or disabled). The law established the principle that the smallest unit of government, the parish, was the unit responsible for poor relief. If a person became destitute away from home, he or she would be returned to the home parish to receive assistance. The parish was also given the power to levy taxes to support poorhouses, to provide assistance to the helpless poor in their own homes, and to purchase materials necessary to provide work for the involuntarily unemployed.[13]

The Elizabethan Poor Law reflected a basic shift in attitudes toward poverty in the Western world. Karl de Schweinitz says that

> After two centuries of attempts to control poverty by repressive measures, government slowly and reluctantly came to accept a positive obligation for the help of people who could not provide for themselves. The experience of the years between 1349 and 1601 had convinced the rulers of England of the presence of a destitution among the poor that punishment could not abolish and that could be relieved only by the application of public resources to individual need.[14]

Colonial Years and the Era of the American Revolution

The situation in the colonies was, of course, much different from that in England. The population was sparse, and there was an abundance of resources in the New World that was not in evidence in the old. In England, because of certain factors such as the enclosure movement that converted farmland to pastureland for sheep, many people had been dislocated from their land. Although the developing textile and mining industries were providing an increasing number of jobs, the number of jobs created lagged behind the number of dislocated people, thus causing unemployment. In the colonies there were more resources, and there was a labor scarcity rather than a labor surplus. However, life in the New World was hard. The people who emigrated from Europe were generally not well-to-do to begin with. Many were sick when they arrived because of the harsh conditions on their long voyage. Even those who arrived in good health and with some resources found life to be very hard because of the harsh weather, problems with American Indians (who often did not take kindly to foreigners settling on their land), and the general risks of pioneering. Thus, a new set of problems was substituted for the old ones, with the result that dependency rapidly became a problem for the colonists just as it was for the people who remained in the Old World.

At a very early date each colony was faced with the problem of caring for the old, the blind, the disabled, the widowed, and the orphaned, as well as for the seasonally unemployed. When confronted with these problems, each colony in turn adopted the Elizabethan Poor Law. Plymouth Colony was the first, adopting the law in 1642, followed by Virginia in 1646, Rhode Island in 1647, Connecticut in 1673, and Massachusetts in 1692. Eventually all of the colonies adopted the Poor Law. True to the English law on which they were closely modeled, the colonial poor laws stressed public responsibility for the dependent, local responsibility, legally enforceable family responsibility, and legal settlement (a person could not receive assistance except in the place in which he or she had established legal residence).

Although the colonies leaned heavily on the English experience in shaping their approach to the problem of poverty and dependency, a unique American approach began to emerge very early. In England the vast majority of poor relief was furnished under the public Poor Law, supplemented by a small amount of aid from the church. In America a dual welfare system developed from the beginning. Responsibility was divided between public and private sectors, with a strong preference for the private sector. Along with the passage of the poor laws, private organizations emerged, such as the Scots Charitable Society in Boston in 1657, the Friends Almshouse in Philadelphia in 1713, the Boston Episcopal Society in 1724, and the Society House of Carpenters in New York in 1767.[15]

The colonial approach to poor relief was characterized by another idea that reflected the development of a unique culture in the New World. This was the tremendous importance attached to the idea of work. The belief in the importance of work stemmed from two sources—economic and cultural. The economic reasons are fairly clear and straightforward. In the colonies there was a shortage of both labor and wealth. In order to survive and to develop a store of excess wealth, it was of paramount importance that everyone who could possibly work do so. The cultural factors are related to what later came to be called the "Protestant ethic," or simply the "work ethic." This is the strong belief that work is innately good and that hard work indicates a person of quality—hard work may even be useful for earning salvation. The other side of this coin is the belief that idleness, laziness, and sloth are sinful. The belief in work and the fear of idleness were reflected in the colonial poor laws. The laws called for children to be apprenticed and the able-bodied set to work; they even supported the development of home industry, mainly related to linen spinning, for women and children who would otherwise become public charges.[16]

A strong preference also developed in the colonies for what came to be called "indoor relief." This meant that help was offered to people in the various categories of need; but, rather than receiving assistance in the form of cash or cash equivalents such as food or fuel, people were cared for by being taken into some form of custodial care. Thus, in return for being helped, a person was forced to give up a great degree of freedom. This care was at first provided in private homes at public expense. In some townships a poor person was sent "round the town"—meaning that each citizen, in turn, would care for the person in his home for a period of two weeks. In other towns a kind of reverse auction was held; at a town meeting townspeople bid against each other to determine who would provide care for a person at the lowest cost.[17] This form of indoor relief was rapidly replaced by the development of large-scale institutions.

Poor relief was not an issue in the American Revolution, so the Revolution had little immediate effect on antipoverty efforts in this country. However, the type of government set up as a result of the Revolution has resulted in several long-range effects. The first effect has to do with the fact that a federal form of government was set up. The idea was that the states were to remain as independent as possible, with a relatively weak central government. This has meant that in contrast to European democracies, which have strong central governments, no strong central welfare system has ever developed in the United States. Rather, we have fifty separate systems (plus additional systems in territories) with some loose central coordination. The wide discrepancies among the state systems can be easily illustrated if we look at welfare benefit levels; in 2000, for example, maximum levels of assistance varied from a low of $164 a month in Alabama to a high of $923 a month in Alaska. Another significant effect of the form of government set up is a result of the separation of church and state. The fact that no central church was created has led to a proliferation of religious bodies, and most have devoted significant time and resources to social welfare activities.[18]

The standard historical interpretation has been that the colonial and Revolutionary War era was one of humanitarianism. This, it is argued, carried over into people's attitudes toward the poor and led to a general willingness to help the poor in a remarkably nonjudgmental way. Historians describing this positive attitude explain it as the result of three factors. The first is the Great Awakening, which was a religious movement that rejected the Calvinistic notion of predestination (the belief that a person is either saved or damned at birth and what he or she does in this life will have no effect on this destiny) and substituted for it the belief that salvation was earned through good works. Thus, the poor were no longer viewed as necessarily damned, and the nonpoor could earn points toward their own salvation by aiding them. The second factor contributing to the supposed positive attitude toward the poor was the Enlightenment. This was the rise of a faith in science and a belief that all, or nearly all, problems, including social problems such as poverty, could be studied and solutions could be found. The third reason was the Revolution itself, which supposedly led to a kind of group solidarity and a general spirit of change.[19]

As appealing as this idea might be—that our forebears were humanistic and accepting of the poor—research has cast doubts on this interpretation. In a study of colonial poor relief records from Somerset County, Maryland, Guest concludes that

> The Somerset records make it clear that it was not generosity and solicitude but at best indifference that, in the main, characterized the colonists' attitudes towards their dependent poor. [Historians] misread these attitudes because they fail to examine home [outdoor] relief. In home relief there were no intermediaries, allowances were given directly to paupers, hence one is much better able to discern what it was thought a pauper deserved (as opposed to what was considered appropriate to compensate a householder for keeping a pauper). Evidently in Somerset, the Court did not think that paupers receiving home relief were worthy

> of much. Payments to them were grudgingly made and allowances were so small that they must have resulted in semi-starvation.[20]

By the time the American Revolution was fought, poverty and poor relief had become issues of major size and importance. Between 1700 and 1715 the amount of money spent on poor relief by the city of Boston quadrupled; it then doubled again by 1735; and it increased by an additional 250 percent by 1753. Similar patterns occurred in other cities such as New York and Philadelphia. By the time of the Revolution, it has been estimated that somewhere between 10 and 35 percent of municipal budgets were being expended for poor relief.[21] Among the reasons for this growth were the large number of immigrants streaming into large cities; the seasonal nature of many jobs, such as fishing and shipbuilding; the number of refugees from the Indian wars; and the many widows and orphans who were left when breadwinners died, as they frequently did in a land and in occupations often fraught with danger. Another factor contributing to poverty was a rather high out-of-wedlock birthrate. We generally think of our forebears as rather prudish people with regard to sex. This was not the case at all. Collier and Collier write that the colonists "were, moreover, a far more openly sexual people than we are likely to think. . . . In 1787 sex during the engagement was customary in some places: in one New England county, supposed to be typical, half the brides were pregnant on their wedding day during the Revolutionary era."[22] It appears that more than a few women were left standing at the altar—according to some estimates, as many as one-third to one-half of all first births were to unwed mothers.

Thus, it can be seen that even in the earliest years of the country, poverty and poor relief were already rearing their heads as major problems. During the next era the problem really began to heat up.

Early Years of the Republic, 1781–1860

The years between the ratification of the Constitution and the beginning of the Civil War were a formative period for antipoverty policies and programs in the United States. This was a period of rapid and immense population growth. The first United States census, taken in 1790, found the population to be a little under 4 million. By 1860 the population had increased by more than eight times to 31.5 million. This population growth was accompanied by the triple threat of social problems: urbanization, industrialization, and immigration. In 1800 only about 6 percent of the population lived in urban areas; by 1860, 20 percent were city dwellers. The period of rapid industrialization was yet to come, but early industries were beginning to develop, and the urban growth was partially a result of the opportunities these industries presented. Finally, a large part of the population growth was a result of immigration, particularly after 1830. In the 1830s, 538,381 people immigrated to this country, and in the 1840s, 1.5 million people immigrated; immigration set a record at 2.8 million in the 1850s.[23]

The relation of these factors to poverty should be obvious. Urbanization results in people being separated from the resources of the land, which rural dwellers can generally fall back on for some support during hard times. Urban dwellers also generally do not have the close relations with neighbors that are common in rural settings; so when they are faced with a problem, they are on their own. Industrialization results in people being dependent on a paycheck for support, and thus they are one check away from destitution. Immigrants generally arrive with few resources, few skills, and often with the barrier of a different language and customs.

Ideas about the Causes of Poverty. These rapid social changes brought on a great increase in poverty. The concern generated by this increase brought on a new development —an interest in the causes of poverty and a desire to do something about it. The prevailing social beliefs about the causes of poverty concentrated almost entirely on individual defects, usually moral defects, as the major explanation. For example, in 1818 the New York Society for the Prevention of Pauperism listed the causes of poverty as ignorance, idleness, intemperance (this was the most important), want of economy, imprudent and hasty marriages, lotteries, pawnbrokers, houses of ill fame, and charitable institutions themselves.[24] Some recognition was given to factors outside the individual that might result in poverty, and as a result a distinction was made between the "worthy" and the "unworthy" poor, an idea that has lasted until the present time. The worthy poor were those whose destitution was a result of some factor that was clearly not under their control, such as misfortune, old age, sickness, or other adversity. The unworthy poor were those whose poverty was believed to be a result of moral defects.

It is interesting, perhaps even contradictory, that although the causes of poverty were almost universally considered to be individual defects, the causes of these defects, and hence their cure, were strongly believed to be environmental. As Axinn and Levin note, "The economic growth, geographic expansion, and extension of political democracy that had created a world of opportunity had also created a world of change, insecurity, and temptation. A society making claim to a belief in human perfectibility but given to the creation of environmental and human disorders must provide order—and cure—for both."[25] This cure for poverty, as well as for a number of other defects such as mental illness, was seen to lie in the creation of large institutions. Thus, during this era the poorhouse rose, and fell, as the solution to poverty.

The Growth of Indoor Relief. Generally, indoor relief, as the poorhouse was known, gained favor because of the belief during this era in institutions as the answer to all sorts of problems. Specifically, the poorhouse was perceived to be the most effective way of alleviating and preventing poverty. There was a belief that if people were given assistance in their own homes, they would soon come to prefer this over work and would become permanent public charges. But if placed in a poorhouse, they could have a regular routine imposed on them that would help them develop habits of industry; also, they could be given work that would contribute to their own support.

Life in the poorhouse was purposely hard. Men and women were separated (and thus families were broken up), the food was poor, and residents' lives were tightly regulated. The idea underlying this approach was that the specter of the poorhouse looming overhead would be a spur to people to maintain self-support and not to become dependent in the first place. Supporters of indoor relief felt that the ideal situation would be for the poorhouse to be the only recourse for those experiencing poverty.

The movement toward indoor relief was given focus in 1823 when the New York legislature asked the secretary of state to conduct a study of the poor laws in New York. The report, submitted by Secretary John V. N. Yates in February of 1824, recommended the adoption of the "poorhouse plan." This plan called for the establishment of one or more poorhouses in every county in the state. These were to be houses of employment in which paupers might be "maintained and employed . . . in some healthful labor, chiefly agricultural, their children to be carefully instructed, and at a suitable age, to be put to some useful business or trade." The Yates report gained national attention and resulted in the poorhouse becoming the major approach to poverty in the United States. By 1860, New York had more than 55 poorhouses, Massachusetts had 219, Pennsylvania had 31 county and numerous local poorhouses, and Maryland had a poorhouse in every county except one.[26]

By 1860, however, confidence in the poorhouse system had begun to decline. There were several reasons for this, generally having to do with the clash of theory with reality. In theory the poorhouses, at least as described in the Yates report, were supposed to be positive, humane environments that would contribute to the reform of paupers. In actuality, however, they were more often than not places so bad as to be scandalous. Poorhouses were supposed to set people to work so they could contribute to their own support. In reality most of the inmates in poorhouses were unable to work for the same reasons most welfare recipients today are not able to work—they were generally old, very young, sick, or disabled in some way. The idea of a vast sea of able-bodied paupers who needed to be set to work was then, as now, largely a myth.

Outdoor Relief. Even though indoor relief was the preferred method of providing for the poor during this era, "outdoor relief," or direct aid to poor families, never really died out. For example, in New York, which was one of the states most enthusiastic about the potential of the poorhouse, between 34 and 50 percent of all expenditures for poor relief between 1830 and 1860 went for relief to people in their own homes. Because it was less expensive to provide outdoor relief, it is estimated that three to four times as many people were on outdoor relief as were in the poorhouses.[27] In the South, Coll writes, outdoor relief made up an even greater proportion of the total relief picture, "doubtless because the Calvinistic principle of 'work hard, don't idle' was less pressing in the Anglican religion, the dominant religion in the South, and because the Southern landed gentry had developed a strong sense of noblesse oblige. This was in contrast, of course, to New England and New York, where Calvinism underlay many attitudes toward the poor."[28]

By the late 1850s, public officials were taking a position that was almost the opposite of the one officials had taken a generation earlier. They were arguing that the poorhouse did not encourage independence and thrift among the poor. In 1857 the mayor of Philadelphia, a city that had a few years earlier constructed one of the largest poorhouses in the country, Old Blockley, expressed his preference for outdoor relief. Sending people to the poorhouse would, he argued, reduce the self-reliance of persons in temporary need. In the same year, the president of the Board of Guardians of the Poor expressed his feeling that outdoor relief was more humane and less expensive than institutional care.

Private Antipoverty Organizations. There were two major economic depressions during the early years of the republic, one from 1815 to 1821 and another from 1837 to 1845. During these depressions there was widespread unemployment, and a good deal of social unrest manifested itself through mass meetings and riots. These events appear to have alarmed the well-to-do about the situation of the poor and caused them to worry that perhaps America was developing a permanent class of paupers similar to that in Europe. The result was the formation of two large organizations dedicated to studying poverty and seeking its cure. These were the Societies for the Prevention of Pauperism, which flourished in the 1820s, and the longer-lasting Associations for Improving the Conditions of the Poor (AICP), which emerged during the 1840s.[29] These organizations were based on several ideas that have continued to wield considerable influence in antipoverty efforts. The first, and probably the most important idea, was that poverty, except in the most extraordinary situations, is an individual problem and the result of individual shortcomings rather than a social and economic problem. Individual shortcomings were generally believed to be moral (such as bad habits and laziness); so giving assistance, particularly public assistance, was viewed as dangerous and counterproductive. If a person learned he could live without working, then, it was believed, the natural thing for the person to do was to take advantage of the help and no longer work. Because the cause of poverty was personal and not structural, the solution proposed by these organizations was to give as little material assistance as possible—preferably none. In place of assistance was to be substituted moral uplift—teaching the poor person industry, sobriety, and thrift. Finally, these organizations were opposed to public aid. Public aid smacked of the notion that financial assistance was a right, and this was thought to be dangerous. These organizations felt that assisting the poor was a civic and Christian duty, but even to hint that to be supported was a right was to encourage the very pauperism that the societies were seeking to cure.

In this context the meaning of the term *pauper* is interesting. As the term was originally used, a pauper was not just a very poor person, but a poor person who had been forever ruined by the indiscriminate giving of charity. A person who had been "pauperized" was one who had learned that he or she could live without working and was consequently never willing to work again.

Government Antipoverty Efforts. True to the Poor Law principle of relief being the responsibility of the smallest unit of government, most public antipoverty efforts during this era were sponsored by state and local governments. One attempted departure from this pattern came in the 1850s, when Dorothea Dix was successful in her efforts to get the U.S. Congress to pass legislation to appropriate federal lands to be used for the support of mental institutions. President Franklin Pierce vetoed the bill in 1854 with the now famous message that "I cannot find any authority in the Constitution for making the Federal Government the great almoner of public charity throughout the United States." Although the bill before him dealt specifically with the mentally disabled and not with the poor as such, Pierce saw no difference, saying, "If Congress have power to make provision for the indigent insane without the limits of this District, it has the same power to provide for the indigent who are not insane; and thus to transfer to the Federal Government the charge of all the poor in all the States." Pierce felt that the inevitable result of this would be that "the fountains of charity will be dried up at home, and the several States, instead of bestowing their own means on the social wants of their own people, may themselves, through the strong temptation, which appeals to states as to individuals, become humble suppliants for the bounty of the Federal Government, reversing their true relation to this Union."[30] This veto set a precedent that effectively blocked any large-scale federal intervention against poverty for eighty years.

Attitudes of the Nonpoor. Perhaps the most important aspect of this era for our purposes is not so much the events we have been reviewing but rather the attitudes they reflect. In earlier years, attitudes toward the poor may not have been highly positive, but at least there was some modicum of understanding. In the years 1781 to 1860, these attitudes changed, and the changes have proved to be fairly permanent. According to Trattner, "conditions had changed. Industrial capitalism, urbanization, greater poverty, higher taxes, and the laissez-faire philosophy had made the pursuit and accumulation of wealth a moral virtue and dependency a vice."[31] In England, Prime Minister Benjamin Disraeli remarked that it had become "a crime to be poor." In the United States, the attitude appears to have been just as bad.

The most interesting aspect of this attitude change is that it signaled the beginning of a stubborn, almost intentional, resistance to understanding poverty. All the data available, all the requests for aid, and presumably most people's contacts with the poor clearly showed that the vast majority of the poor were the old, the very young, the sick, the disabled, and the seasonally unemployed. In other words, they were people who were poor through no fault of their own and whose poverty could not readily be "cured." However, reports, speeches, legislation, and newspaper accounts portrayed the poor as being able-bodied people who were simply unwilling to work. Thus, the favorite solution to poverty, the poorhouse, was intended to discourage these people from ever applying for aid—or, if they did apply, to teach them habits of thrift and industry so they would not apply again. This solution, like every solution we have tried since then, did not work because it was based on a faulty understanding—early urban legends.

Social Transformation, Reform, and Reaction, 1860–1930

Although for our purposes we are treating the years from 1860 to 1930 as one period, they really encompass three separate historical eras. The years from 1860 until near the turn of the century were years that witnessed the rapid transformation of U.S. society from what Leiby has termed the "rural democracy" into a country that was clearly on its way to becoming an urban industrial giant.[32] This was a period of rapidly developing social problems, but there was not much recognition of how serious they were, nor was there any general acceptance of social responsibility for their solution. The years from roughly 1898 until 1918, between the McKinley administration and the end of World War I, are known as the Progressive Era and were a period marked by a wholesale spirit of reform aimed at finding solutions to these social problems. The 1918–1930 period, between the end of the war and the beginning of the Great Depression, is popularly known as the Roaring Twenties—an era characterized by people's efforts to forget about social problems, to avoid responsibility, and to enjoy life. This was a time of great political conservatism.

Collectively, the years between 1860 and 1930 were a period of massive change in U.S. society. Between 1860 and 1900 the population more than doubled, going from 31.5 million to 76 million. By 1930 the population had increased to 123 million. Much of the population growth came from immigration. Almost 14 million immigrants arrived in the United States between 1860 and 1900; another 13.7 million arrived by 1915; and 5.6 million more came by 1930. Most of the immigrants arrived with few resources,

The roots of professional social work go back to the Charity Organization Society and the friendly visitor during the late nineteenth century.

and they generally settled in the large cities along the eastern seaboard, causing great urban problems. The country became much wealthier during this period, with the gross national product increasing from $6.7 billion in 1860 to $16.8 billion in 1900 and to $104 billion in 1929. The flow of wealth was not constant, however; the country suffered deep depressions from 1873 to 1878 and from 1893 until 1898; and finally the Great Depression began in 1929. The great increase in wealth was largely caused by the continuing process of industrialization. In 1860, 58 percent of the population were employed in agriculture and only 18 percent in manufacturing and construction. In 1900 the number employed in agriculture had shrunk to 37 percent and the number in manufacturing and construction had increased to 28 percent. By 1930 the number in agriculture had decreased to 21 percent; the number in manufacturing and construction had only increased to 29 percent, but other urban occupations, such as finance and other professions, had increased to 15 percent. In addition, the extent of urbanization continued to increase at a rapid rate. In 1860 there were only nine cities with populations over 100,000. By 1900 there were thirty-eight such cities, and by 1930 there were ninety-three.[33]

Changing Attitudes toward the Poor. During the years 1860 to 1930, people's attitudes toward poverty underwent a major change. During the latter half of the nineteenth century, the attitude of people in the United States was, in Bremner's words, "a somewhat incongruous composite of two sharply contrasting points of view." On the one hand, there was the traditional Christian view that poverty was a result of God's incomprehensible but beneficent will. Poverty was a blessing in disguise because it gave the nonpoor an opportunity to demonstrate their goodness by performing acts of charity toward the poor. On the other hand, there was the view that poverty was unnecessary in this land of plenty, that there was enough work for all, and that anyone who wanted to badly enough could lift himself up by his own bootstraps. Therefore, poverty was undesirable; it was totally the fault of the individual affected; and rather than being a blessed state, it was the obvious result of sloth and sinfulness. These two views were combined into a creed that went, according to Bremner, as follows:

> Poverty is unnecessary (for Americans), but the varying ability and virtue of men make its presence inevitable; this is a desirable state of affairs, since without the fear of want the masses would not work and there would be no incentive for the able to demonstrate their superiority; where it exists, poverty is usually a temporary problem and, both in its cause and cure, it is always an individual matter.

This individualistic interpretation of poverty was based on a radical American idea; namely, that work was not an onerous task falling mainly on the lowborn but a positive thing, an end in itself, a means that anyone could use to get ahead. "The promise of America was not affluence, but independence; not ease, but a chance to work for oneself, to be self-supporting, and to win esteem through hard and honest labor."[34]

This stress on self-support and honest labor was further bolstered in the late nineteenth century by new ideas about society put forth by the English social theorist Herbert Spencer and reinforced by the work of Charles Darwin. Spencer compared society with a biological organism and incorporated Darwin's theories about evolution and survival of the fittest into his perspective. Social Darwinism, as this approach came to be called, held that the concept of survival of the fittest applied to the marketplace as well as to the jungle. The foremost proponent of social Darwinism in the United States was William Graham Sumner. Sumner argued that economic competition helped weed out those individuals and families who could not successfully adapt to life in an industrial nation. Government intervention to help people with economic and social problems would only delay the natural workings of the law of evolution. Social Darwinism thus contributed to individualistic interpretations of poverty through its stress on individual survival in a competitive world.

During the late nineteenth century and the early years of the twentieth century, this individualistic view of poverty began to be substantially modified, although it never entirely died out. Rugged individualism was perhaps functional during the earlier era when the United States was still a frontier society; but as the frontier was replaced by the city and the farm was replaced by the factory, it became increasingly apparent that people's troubles were more often than not caused by circumstances over which they had no control. Although it was difficult to accept, Americans began to suspect that in an increasingly complex economy, individuals were no longer the independent agents they had been in the recent past. Josephine Shaw Lowell noted in 1893 that the causes of the distress of the poor were "as much beyond their power to avert as if they had been natural calamities of fire, flood, or storm."[35]

In the Victorian era there was an ever increasing concern for the poor and the beginning of a more positive and realistic attitude toward poverty, but there was not much in the way of hard information available on the problem. One of the hallmarks of the Progressive Era that followed was an almost insatiable desire for tangible facts about society. This was the age of muckraking journalism and of the large-scale social survey. People wanted the inside scoop on politics, crime, corporations, labor, and, perhaps most of all, poverty. For the first time in history, a body of valid, reliable knowledge began to accumulate about the life and problems of the poor. Government researchers made several attempts to survey the conditions of immigrants. Settlement house workers conducted careful block-by-block surveys of impoverished neighborhoods. Several journals devoted to promoting social research began publication, the most notable being *The Survey*, published by Paul U. Kellogg. Schools of social work began to open, and the Russell Sage Foundation gave generous grants to five of them to open social research departments. From 1907 to 1909, a large group of researchers and social workers conducted the Pittsburgh survey, which was the first attempt in the United States to survey at close range the conditions under which working people existed in a large industrial city.

The massive amount of data collected during the Progressive Era provided a clear picture of poverty for the first time in history. This picture was considerably different from the image many people still had of the poor as being a basically lazy, shiftless lot who were to blame for their own poverty. This research found that the lot of the poor was generally overwork; underpay; pitiful living conditions, usually caused by the fact that they could not afford better ones on the wages available; and exploitation by greedy landlords, merchants, and employers.

Old attitudes die hard. Although during the Progressive Era much was learned about poverty and, as discussed in the following section, many programs were instituted to attempt to alleviate it, the spirit of reform faded during the conservative years of the Roaring Twenties. Those years were prosperous, and many people believed that the problem of poverty was well under control. The prevailing belief was that the conditions revealed by surveys such as that in Pittsburgh had been corrected and that now the nation was working the way it was supposed to. Thus, once again the attitude became dominant (if it had ever actually lost dominance) that if a person were poor it must be because of some personal failure.

Private Antipoverty Efforts. By the Civil War a clear division of labor had developed in American antipoverty efforts—public agencies could provide indoor (poorhouse) relief for people who simply could not make it on their own, but outdoor relief was considered to be the exclusive jurisdiction of the private sector. There were several reasons for the belief that it was not proper for public agencies to dispense outdoor relief. The first was that public agencies were considered to be corrupt and inefficient, and therefore incapable of managing efficient and effective relief programs; thus, the effect of public programs would be to pauperize recipients. Second, this was the high point of laissez-faire economics, and the belief was that if public monies were given to people in their homes, it would threaten the economy. Nineteenth-century leader in philanthropy Louisa Lee Schuler, speaking about the economic effects of public outdoor relief on New York City, said that "the wisest and safest course would be ultimately to abolish all official outdoor relief, to improve and enlarge the accommodations in the institutions, and to throw the responsibility of providing for the wants of the poor entirely on existing private charity."[36] The third reason that private aid was preferred over public aid was that private charity gave people a chance to develop the virtue of charity, something that did not happen if they were taxed for the expense of charity and had no choice in the matter. The final reason was that it was firmly believed that it was morally wrong to take money from one person in the form of taxation and to give it to another in the form of charity. Another philanthropic leader, Josephine Shaw Lowell, said:

> Every dollar raised by taxation comes out of the pocket of some individual, usually a poor individual, and makes him so much the poorer, and therefore the question is between the man who earned the dollar by hard work, and needs it to buy himself and his family a day's food, and the man who, however worthy and suffering, did not earn it, but wants it to be given to him to buy himself and his family a day's food. If the man who earned it wishes to divide it with the other man, it is usually a desirable thing that he should do so, and at any rate it is more or less his own business, but that the law, by the hand of a public officer, should take it from him and hand it over to the other man, seems to be an act of gross tyranny and injustice. . . . The less [public relief] that is given the better for everyone, the giver and the receiver.[37]

This anti–public aid bias became so strong that by 1880 public outdoor relief had been outlawed in New York City, Brooklyn, Buffalo, Indianapolis, Philadelphia, and Chicago, as well as in many smaller cities.

The private charities that emerged and became dominant during this era initially reflected the belief in the individual and moral causes of poverty and the pernicious effects of "indiscriminate alms giving," which it was believed encouraged "indolence and beggary."[38] Although several antipoverty agencies emerged during this era, the largest and most important were the charity organization societies, which began in Buffalo, New York, in 1877 and within a few years spread to virtually every city of any size. As discussed in Chapter 3, the COS movement addressed itself to urban destitution, the increase in poverty, and the potential for conflict between social classes. It held that agencies could reduce destitution, ameliorate hardship, and prevent mendicancy by instituting a system of scientific charity, abolishing public relief, and replacing the existing chaos in almsgiving with a systematically coordinated private philanthropy. The social philosophy of the COS reflected that of the country as a whole. The COS rejected the influence of the environment on the lives of people. It was felt that people were free agents who could control their destinies commensurate with their abilities and moral fiber. Any lapse into dependency was a result of intemperance, improvidence, indolence, ignorance, or some other personal defect. Thus, charity had to be dispensed very carefully, on a strictly individualized basis, by trained volunteers or paid staff. Only a private organization using the principles of scientific charity could do this; it was a task clearly beyond the capability of public officials.

By the time the twentieth century began, the COS and other private agencies had amassed considerable experience in dealing with poor people. Because of this contact, in addition to the information gathered by the researchers mentioned earlier, the COS began to abandon its cherished belief that poverty was the result of personal moral shortcomings. The movement's leaders realized that the causes of poverty were social, economic, and psychological rather than the result of personal moral failure. However, one principle that was not abandoned was that charity was the business of the private sector and that government should stay out as much as possible.

Government Antipoverty Efforts. Although the years before the onset of the Great Depression were characterized by a near total dominance of charity by private organizations, some things were beginning to stir that paved the way for the large-scale government programs enacted in the 1930s. These events revolved around the newly emerging concept of social insurance. A few people were beginning to consider social insurance to be an attractive alternative to charity. Insurance was based not on the notion of charity or sympathy but on self-interest and on shared risk. Most of the advocates of social insurance were not benevolent altruists but prudent businessmen. They understood the concept of rationalizing risks through insurance.[39]

The concept of social insurance was first called "workingman's insurance." Leiby says that

> it was supposed to meet the special needs of the urban industrial worker. Peasant or yeoman farmers were largely self-sufficient on their land, and family and neighbors could help out in emergencies. The urban worker had no garden and his family and neighbors were usually less reliable. He was vulnerable to any interruption in pay, in which case he was likely to fall on charity. Already by 1880 it was possible to identify the main risks to steady pay. The breadwinner could not work if (1) he was sick or (2) he had an accident (on the job, most likely); (3) there was a slack in the demand for labor (high unemployment); (4) he grew too old or feeble to work; or (5) he died.[40]

People familiar with the concept of insurance, already well developed for the purpose of smoothing out the risks of business, began to conceive of insurance as a way of smoothing out the economic risks of urban industrial life.

Social insurance was conceived as being government-sponsored or government-assisted insurance for urban industrial workers. The first type to be proposed and implemented was workman's compensation, which was designed to deal with the problem of people disabled from work-related accidents. The first workman's compensation law was passed in Maryland in 1902; the federal government passed a law to protect its own employees in 1908; and by 1920, forty-three states had passed such legislation.

Shortly after the campaign for workman's compensation insurance, movements for other types of social insurance began stretching the concept a bit. These were proposals for social insurance for mothers with young children, the elderly, and the blind. The concept was stretched because these were not insurance programs by any stretch of the imagination. Basically, they were outdoor relief programs that simply proposed to give a cash grant to people in these categories. The significant point is that these were categories of the needy who were defined as being worthy poor. Mothers were thought to be rendering a service to society (rearing children) for which they should be compensated, and the elderly were assumed to have rendered service and thus to deserve continuing support. The blind, presumably like the other two groups, were clearly poor through no fault of their own. The first mothers' pension law was passed in Illinois in 1911, and eighteen states had followed suit by 1913. Old age pensions were a little slower in coming because states feared that they would increase the cost of doing business and make the state less competitive. Pennsylvania, Montana, and Nevada passed old age pension laws in 1923, and four other states did so by 1927. The first legislation authorizing pensions for the blind was passed in Ohio in 1898; Illinois passed such a law in 1903, Wisconsin passed a similar law in 1907, and many other states passed laws after 1915.[41]

Private Domination of Social Welfare. Although some headway had been made by advocates of public responsibility for the impoverished in the form of social insurance schemes, when the Great Depression hit in 1929, social welfare was clearly dominated by private agencies. Social workers in these agencies continued to oppose public programs. They felt that pensions were just another form of outdoor relief (which in fact they were) and as such were susceptible to all the abuses that social workers had criticized these programs for in the past. The second objection social workers had to pension programs was that these programs assumed that the only problem poor people had was a lack of money and that a pension would solve this problem. Social workers believed that poverty was symptomatic of other problems that required treatment and that this could be provided only by private agencies. Finally, social workers believed that pensions were a distraction from the real problems—structural issues such as why there were so many widows in the first place (poor public health and industrial accidents). In any case, public pension plans aided only a small proportion of the poor, a select group for whom it could be clearly demonstrated that their destitution was no fault of their own. The remainder of the poor had to rely on the often questionable sympathies of private agencies and existed, in Michael Katz's words, in the shadow of the poorhouse.[42]

Seeds of the Reluctant Welfare State, 1930–1940[43]

The 1920s in the United States was a time of unprecedented prosperity: Factories sought to turn out goods fast enough to meet demand; every month avid investors snapped up hundreds of millions of dollars in new securities; and colleges and movie theaters were jammed. In this atmosphere President Herbert Hoover was able to say, "We in America are nearer to the final triumph over poverty than ever before in the history of any land." But this triumph was not to come. In October 1929, the stock market crashed. By the end of 1929, the value of securities had shrunk by $40 billion. In the years that followed, hundreds of thousands of families lost their homes, millions of unemployed walked the streets, and tax collections fell to such a low that schoolteachers could not be paid in many areas. The United States had faced depressions before, but these had lasted only a few years. The Great Depression that began in 1929 was to last a full decade.[44]

President Hoover reacted to the depression with faith that natural forces in the economy would correct the situation if government did not interfere. He did not entirely repudiate the responsibility of the national government to act, but he did hold firmly to the English Poor Law principle that relief was exclusively the concern of local government or, preferably, of private charity. Hoover's philosophy regarding the desirability of the federal government's engaging in welfare activities was summed up in his statement that "you cannot extend the mastery of government over the private lives of people without at the same time making it the master of their souls and thoughts." Hoover therefore limited national government response to pumping money into businesses in the form of contracts for roads, public buildings, loans, and so forth, thinking this would stimulate the economy and aid the natural forces of recovery. His tactic for dealing with the crisis was graphically illustrated in December of 1930 when he approved an appropriation of $45 million to feed the livestock of Arkansas farmers, but opposed an additional $25 million to feed the farmers. The natural forces that Hoover placed so much faith in did not work. By 1932 the number of unemployed was over twelve million, five thousand banks had closed, thirty-two thousand businesses had failed, and national income had declined from $80 billion to $40 billion.

By the time Franklin Roosevelt entered office in 1933, the economic situation was so bad that people were questioning whether the U.S. system was viable any longer. Disorder was spreading and threats of revolution were heard. Roosevelt quickly repudiated Hoover's doctrine of government nonintervention in the area of welfare. In the place of Hoover's doctrine, Roosevelt substituted the philosophy he had developed as governor of New York and had implemented in that state under the Wicks Act. This philosophy held that people in need have a right to governmental aid because this aid is financed out of tax dollars, which they paid when they were employed. Thus, receiving welfare payments was no different from sending children to public school or asking for police protection. Under this philosophy, with social worker Harry Hopkins as his assistant, Roosevelt implemented a wide range of public welfare programs beginning with the 1933 Federal Emergency Relief Act (FERA) and culminating in the 1935 Social Security Act—a beginning, if incomplete, attempt of the federal government to provide cradle-to-grave security for the citizens of the nation.

The Social Security Act—as it finally emerged after many compromises—was designed to alleviate financial dependency through two lines of defense: contributory social insurance and public assistance. Its main insurance feature was a program that provided protection for workers from poverty caused by old age or disability, and for children and widows from poverty caused by the death of the breadwinner. This is the Old Age Survivors and Disability Insurance (OASDI) that is paid partially out of the paycheck of workers and partially by employer contributions. The second insurance feature was unemployment insurance. Four categories of public assistance were set up under the Social Security Act. Old Age Assistance (OAA) provided support for the elderly who for some reason were not protected under OASDI. Aid to the Blind (AB) and Aid to the Permanently and Totally Disabled (APTD) provided support for those who could not support themselves because of physical disabilities. Finally, Aid to Dependent Children (ADC) was established to serve basically the same group that state widows' pension laws were helping—single mothers with small children.

When the depression hit, the majority of poor relief still came from private donations and was administered through private family service agencies. Aid was distributed on a highly individualized basis according to the old notion that economic dependency was a symptom of some basic individual deficiency requiring treatment. The coming of the depression had two rapid and profound effects on the private agencies that had traditionally dominated welfare in the United States. The first was that when private money ran low, as it quickly did, local governments began contributing money to these private organizations to support their relief-giving programs. In less than a year after the crash, well over half of the aid distributed by private agencies came from public funds. The second major effect was that the depression shocked the social workers who administered these agencies and who had historically opposed public welfare into realizing that social and economic forces were at the root of many of the problems with which they were dealing. As Paul Kellogg, editor of *The Survey,* said, "You cannot deal effectively with an inferiority complex on an empty stomach."[45] His message was clearly that social workers needed to concentrate on social, political, and economic issues, as well as on understanding the psychology of the individual.

When the Federal Emergency Relief Act was passed in 1933, it changed the structure of social services in the United States. Immediately on assuming office, Harry Hopkins, administrator of the act, formulated Regulation Number 1, which stated that public money was to be administered by public agencies. Another provision of FERA was that each local administrator was to employ at least one experienced social worker and at least one qualified supervisor for every twenty employees. The major effect of this regulation, and of similar regulations in the 1935 Social Security Act, was to end quickly and decisively the domination of welfare by private agencies and to move welfare firmly into the public sector.

Attitudes toward the Poor. The Great Depression in the United States, in a period of only ten years, witnessed significant changes in attitudes toward both the poor and antipoverty programs. In this brief span of time, the welfare system in this country was converted from one that was almost totally private to one that was dominated by public agencies. The massive size of the problem of economic dependency in modern industrial society was brought home with a vengeance, and the country generally came to realize that the private sector simply could not handle it. More important, however, was the change in attitude toward poverty and the poor themselves. The huge amount of unemployment made it clear to nearly everyone that poverty in most, if not all, cases was a result more of structural factors than of personal failings. The social commentator Clinch Calkins concluded:

> As the reader has seen over and over again, not perseverance, nor skill, education, and health, nor a long and excellent work-record, stand the breadwinner in any certain stead when the bad word is handed down from directors to executive to foreman. To be sure, the best man may be the last to be discharged. But even he has no assurance of security. Laziness, incompetence, and shiftlessness determine the incidence but not the quantity of unemployment. . . . Because labor has been regarded as, if not a commodity, at least the most flexible and easily replaced element in production, the general run of business has long taken an attitude toward its labor supply which it would be too thrifty to take toward raw materials. . . . [Whether] protection is arranged by individual management, by the trade as a whole, or through public action, as in [workman's] compensation laws, the burden of unemployment should not be allowed to fall solely on the family of the worker.[46]

Unfortunately, this new attitude toward the poor did not signal any permanent change. People had come to understand unemployment in bad times such as the Great Depression, but they still had no understanding of it during good times. The Aid to Dependent Children program, for example, was considered a temporary program that would wither away and eventually become insignificant when the economy improved. The fact that it did not wither away but grew steadily larger has been a bone of contention in debates from the passage of the Social Security Act up to the present time.

The Return of Prosperity, 1940–1960

The Second World War brought an end to the depression, which Roosevelt's New Deal programs had succeeded in ameliorating but not ending. In 1940 the gross national product (GNP) increased to a level equal to that of the boom year of 1929. Between 1940 and 1960 the GNP increased fivefold. Population growth, which was minimal during the depression, also boomed. In the 1940s the population grew by twenty-one million, and in the 1950s it grew by an additional thirty million, with most of the increase caused by the birthrate. Generally the era was characterized by optimism and prosperity—which were unfortunately accompanied by complacency and conservatism.

The 1940s and 1950s in the United States witnessed a pulling back from large social issues such as public welfare. There were many reasons for this trend. Most people, including most social workers, felt that after the passage of the Social Security Act, the problems of poverty were being adequately addressed. More important was the general perception of mass prosperity. Experts such as social workers and economists, who should have known better, believed that poverty was fast becoming a minor problem. In his best-selling book *The Affluent Society,* published in 1958, economist John Kenneth Galbraith argued that the United States was close to solving the problems of scarcity and poverty. This belief tended to make the poor invisible, and it made concern about them seem remote and almost obsolete.

Ironically, at the same time that many people were perceiving that poverty was fast becoming a thing of the past, welfare rolls were rising at rapid rates; and attitudes toward the poor, which had become more positive during the depression years, were once again becoming harsh. Communities throughout the nation were following the lead set by the city fathers in Newburgh, New York, and attempting to discourage people from applying for public assistance by making receipt of aid as unpleasant as possible. Samuel Mencher reported on the methods used in Newburgh: Give as much assistance as possible in kind rather than in cash so recipients will have no choice of what they consume; threaten prosecution of people who, intentionally or unintentionally, receive more assistance than that for which they are technically eligible; frequently reevaluate eligibility of recipients; provide assistance only for a temporary period of time; make illegitimate children ineligible for aid; and, finally, threaten parents with the removal of their children. Of the situation in Newburgh, Mencher commented, "The opposition to public assistance shows that though our society has greatly changed, the ideas and values affecting public assistance have hardly budged from their earliest beginnings."[47]

Reform and Reaction, 1960–1988

By the end of the 1950s, the country was feeling restless and ready for change. John F. Kennedy was campaigning for the presidency on the assertion that the country was stagnating, and he promised that he would get it "moving again" toward "new frontiers." Shortly after his election, the 1960 census was completed; it revealed that the country clearly needed to get moving again. The census data revealed that the New Deal and the Second World War had not eliminated poverty as had been generally believed. In addition, the data indicated that poverty was not restricted to people living in certain deprived areas or to members of certain groups, as Galbraith had asserted, but that it was common and widespread. Several books based on the new data made clear the extent of poverty; the most influential was Michael Harrington's *The Other America: Poverty in the United States.* In light of this "rediscovery of poverty," the federal government attempted to attack the problem from three different approaches under three different presidents during the 1960s.

The approach of the Kennedy administration was embodied in Public Law 87-543, known as the Social Service Amendments, signed into law on July 25, 1962. This law grew out of the recommendations of the Ad Hoc Committee on Public Welfare appointed by Health, Education, and Welfare Secretary Abraham Ribicoff in May 1961, and out of a report by George Wyman at about the same time. Wyman was an administrator with experience in a wide variety of social welfare agencies that included local, state, and federal agencies as well as voluntary agencies. The committee's and Wyman's recommendations were heavily influenced by advice from social workers and other experts who contended that providing intensive social services would rehabilitate and bring financial independence to the poor. The act provided increased federal support (75 percent) to the states to enable them to provide social services to recipients of public assistance. In reality the act represented a very old approach—providing individual services to help people lift themselves out of poverty, with little attention directed toward altering the social conditions that caused the poverty.[48]

The Social Service Amendments rapidly increased the number of social workers in public welfare settings. Recommendation number 12 of the Ad Hoc Committee stated, "To make possible the rehabilitative services so strongly advocated [by the committee], the goal should be established that one third of all persons engaged in social work capacities in public welfare should hold master's degrees in social work." Money was allocated for welfare departments to send employees to graduate school in social work, and these schools began to incorporate additional public welfare content into their curricula.

When social workers advocated providing professional services to welfare recipients, they did so in the belief that these services would improve recipients' lives and would be judged on this basis. Unfortunately, Congress supported the services in the belief that they would help people become self-supporting, thereby reducing the welfare rolls, and judged them on this basis. After the passage of the amendments, the welfare rolls rose at a faster rate than ever, making social workers suspect in policymakers' eyes and causing the policymakers to look for a new approach.

The new approach came in 1964 when, in his State of the Union message, President Johnson called on Congress to enact a thirteen-point program that would declare "unconditional war on poverty." In July 1964 the Economic Opportunity Act established the Office of Economic Opportunity. The act also created Volunteers In Service To America (VISTA), the Job Corps, Upward Bound, the Neighborhood Youth Corps, Operation Head Start, and the Community Action program (CAP).

There were several reasons behind President Johnson's War on Poverty. One was pressure from the civil rights movement for an attack on hunger and poverty. An example of the intensity of this pressure was a march for "jobs and freedom" that brought two hundred thousand people to Washington, D.C., and culminated in a historic speech by Martin Luther King Jr. The major reason, however, was probably the growing awareness of the extent of poverty in the United States and the continued growth of the welfare rolls despite the Social Service Amendments. A significant new development in the War on Poverty programs was that they made a concerted effort to include input from the poor themselves in the design and administration of the programs; this was done under the Economic Opportunity Act's provision for "maximum feasible participation" of the poor, which encouraged participation of low-income people on boards and staffs of community programs.

A CLOSER Look

"War on Poverty Not a Failure" by William Raspberry

WASHINGTON—You've heard it before, and you're certain to hear it again during the welfare reform debates: Lyndon Johnson's "war on poverty" not only failed miserably to cure poverty but even exacerbated the problem it tried to solve.

Two Ohio University professors wrote a paper a couple of years ago noting that "more Americans live in poverty than 20 years ago" and blaming that dismal fact on what they were pleased to call Johnson's "war on the poor." I would guess that the middle-America consensus is that the war on poverty, despite its noble intentions, increased poverty, crime, drug abuse and dependency and spawned millions of fatherless households.

And it's all a lie. Demonstrating the falsity of the libel against LBJ's Great Society may be the major contribution of the PBS miniseries, "America's War on Poverty," that airs for three consecutive nights starting Monday.

Executive producer Henry Hampton is a gifted storyteller driven by a need to tell the story straight. Two of his earlier efforts for PBS may be his best credentials: "The Great Depression" and the "Eyes on the Prize" retrospective of the civil rights era.

"It was an enormously important time," Hampton says of the 1960s period that is the focus of his newest work. "Here was a nation in a period of affluence and a president calling it to a higher *moral* plateau with his vision of ending poverty." And while it obviously didn't end poverty, Hampton said, Johnson's effort was successful in important ways—and certainly far from the abject failure it is widely thought to have been.

"The war on poverty went into the poorest communities in America—from Appalachia to the rural South to the urban slums—and took people who hadn't been considered bright enough to do much of anything and got them to run the programs themselves. An incredible amount of untapped leadership was developed among people who then began to teach their *kids* a sense of responsibility."

But it wasn't just the grassroots leadership that Hampton counts a success. The U.S. poverty rate—as high as 30 percent in the pre-Great Society years—reached a 40 year low of 11.1 percent in 1973 "because the programs were working and the economy was in pretty good shape," Hampton believes. "The period taught us some powerful lessons, including the fact that

If anything, the War on Poverty programs were even less successful than the Social Service Amendments. Congress and taxpayers stuck to reducing welfare rolls as the primary criterion for success; and, far from shrinking, the rolls increased at a record rate, with more than one million persons being added between 1963 and 1966. In addition, the War on Poverty drew severe criticism for other reasons: Mayors were upset because the federal government was funding programs over which they had no control; members of Congress were upset by lawsuits brought against government agencies by government-funded legal services; and citizens were upset by the aggressiveness and hostility of the poor, who had found a voice through the "maximum feasible participation" concept. As a result of these criticisms, the Economic Opportunity Act of 1966 sharply curtailed community action.

Two War on Poverty programs that perhaps have had little effect on reducing welfare rolls but have had an immense impact on improving the lives of the poor were the 1964 Food Stamp Act and the 1965 Medicare and Medicaid amendments to the Social Security Act. The Food Stamp Act replaced the commodities program that had the poor mostly wanted to work, not the welfare queen image that people have come to believe."

He said his research (he started the project in the late 1980s) uncovered a surprising fact: "Of the 26 programs generated during the war on poverty, 24 are still with us." And one that no longer is—the Neighborhood Youth Corps—perhaps should be. So why, if the individual programs—Head Start, Job Corps and VISTA and a score of others—are reauthorized and refunded year after year, is there a pervasive sense that the effort came a cropper?

The answer is that the war on poverty has become confused with public welfare, a creature of the Franklin Roosevelt era a quarter century earlier. Listen to those who decry increased dependency, out-of-wedlock births, the explosion of teen-age parents and you'll hear attacks on AFDC, not on the Johnson programs. But because of the confusion (to which even liberals have been strangely acquiescent) we have neglected to look for the lessons available from examining the war on poverty.

And what might we learn?

"We could learn that there are people with great potential in even the poorest communities and that these people are ready to contribute, given a chance," says Hampton. "They won't all become lawyers and surgeons, but they could become useful members of their communities. We could learn that it's probably a mistake to have freestanding poverty programs. OEO (The Office of Economic Opportunity that ran the war on poverty) sat separately and therefore became a target. We might have been better off to try to integrate these efforts into the government structure. There are all sorts of things we might learn, if we looked."

Including the useful reminder that there was a time, not very long ago, when Americans were willing to make an enormous financial, political and moral investment in improving the plight of the poor, and that, for a time, the effort succeeded. If Hampton's PBS series can teach us that, then maybe we'll be able to learn from our errors and not simply walk away from the problem.

Source: Kalamazoo Gazette (13 January 1995), C1. Copyright © 1995, The Washington Post Writers Group. Reprinted with permission.

provided nutritional assistance for the poor by making surplus agricultural produce available to them. Although better than nothing, the commodities program provided no choice; the type of food available largely depended on the commodities of which there was a surplus. The Food Stamp Program provides vouchers that can be used just like cash for the purchase of food and thus permit recipients the same range of choice that anyone else has in his or her weekly shopping. The Medicare program for the first time made medical care available to the impoverished elderly, and the Medicaid program did the same for children and mothers receiving support under the AFDC program.

Toward the end of President Johnson's term in office, the mood of the country began to drift to the right. In 1966, on the same day the new Economic Opportunity Act was signed into law, the Republicans gained fifty-one seats in Congress, mostly replacing liberal Democrats. In 1968, with the election of President Richard Nixon, the Republicans added the White House to their list of victories. With the conservative mood of the country, sentiment grew for limiting "soft" services, such as social services and community action, and for emphasizing "hard" services, such as day care and work training programs. The Social Security Amendments of 1967 reflected this mood, setting up the Work Incentive Program, which required all AFDC recipients with no children under age six to register for work or for job training and to accept employment or training as soon as it became available. The purpose of this program was to attempt once again to force welfare recipients to stop being lazy and get to work. True to the experience of all such programs in the past, the number of welfare recipients who expressed a desire for the jobs or training promised by the program far exceeded the ability of state job service offices to supply work or training. Another part of the amendments instituted a formula whereby a welfare recipient's grant was reduced by only a percentage of earned income when that person became employed. Also funded was day care for welfare recipients who were employed or in training.

Following the failure of these programs to reduce the welfare rolls, in spite of the fact that they undoubtedly improved the lives of many poor people, the country lost interest in antipoverty programs. In 1969, President Nixon unveiled his Family Assistance Plan, which was intended to replace existing cash assistance programs with one unified, if stingy, minimum guaranteed annual income. The plan placed a premium on work and little emphasis on social services. It immediately ran into controversy and was eventually defeated except for one part: the Supplemental Security Income (SSI) program that was enacted in 1972 and went into effect on January 1, 1974. Under this program, financial assistance for the elderly, the blind, and the disabled became 100 percent federally funded and administered. Managed by the Social Security Administration, SSI once more implies that these groups are somehow more deserving than mothers with dependent children and that SSI recipients should receive a "pension" rather than "welfare."

President Jimmy Carter attempted a major public welfare reform when he unveiled the Jobs and Income Security Program on August 6, 1976, proposing that the program become effective in October 1980. The plan proposed the sweeping abolition of the existing welfare system with its patchwork of benefits, including AFDC, food stamps, and SSI. These would be replaced with a two-tier system—a job program for those who were able to work and an income maintenance program for those who were not. The proposal called for the creation of 1,400,000 job slots for persons who were able to work but unable to find jobs. The schedule of benefits was designed so that those who found work in the private sector would always be better off than those who worked in public service jobs. Those unable to work, regardless of the reason, would receive benefits from a single program. Unfortunately, President Carter became so quickly mired in political problems that his Jobs and Income Security Program was placed on the back burner, where it remained until he left office.

When Ronald Reagan was elected president in 1980, his strategy for reducing poverty could be described as new wine in old bottles. Although he called his approach "supply-side economics," it was really just the old conservative theory with a new name. Basically, this approach argues that to improve things for the poor you must first improve things for the rich. The rich will then use their extra money to expand businesses, which will hire more people, and the benefits will "trickle down" to the poor.

To stimulate the supply side of the economy, one of Reagan's goals was to reduce federal spending. To do this he proposed, among other things, to reduce welfare programs while leaving a basic "safety net" of benefits and services in place. A 1984 study by the Southern Regional Council reported that cutbacks by the administration had reduced the welfare rolls by 4 million people. This group included 3.2 million who had lost food stamps, 330,000 dropped from AFDC, 300,000 dropped from Medicaid, and 108,000 dropped from Supplementary Security Income.[49] To make up for these losses, Reagan called on the churches and the voluntary sector to resume their "historic mission" of caring for the poor.

True to the predictions of critics—including George Bush (the elder), who referred to it as "voodoo economics"—Reagan's supply-side approach did not work. It led neither to rapid economic growth nor to a reduction in poverty. In fact, as discussed in Chapter 7, poverty rapidly increased under the Reagan administration. Fortunately, although it did some damage, Reagan's attack on the welfare system also failed. Reagan admirers Stuart Butler and Anna Kondratas comment that

> in the fifth year of the Reagan presidency, . . . Johnson's legacy was showing every sign of withstanding the strongest attack ever mounted against it. . . . [T]he former Johnson staffers could feel understandably confident that the essential foundations of the Great Society would outlast Ronald Reagan. With practically a full term ahead of it, the Reagan Administration onslaught [on welfare programs] was clearly stalled.[50]

A New Era for Antipoverty Policy

Although the nation's welfare system survived the Reagan and Bush presidencies largely intact, the conservative trend in society, and pressure for substantial welfare reform, continued. The first major effort toward welfare reform climaxed in 1988 with the passage of the Family Support Act, viewed by many as a major reform of welfare and one that would quiet the calls for reform for many years. This was not to be. Almost before the ink was dried on the Family Support Act, critics began to complain that it had not gone far enough and to demand even more drastic reforms. These efforts resulted in the passage, and subsequent veto by President Bill Clinton, of the Personal Responsibility Act of 1995. Following the veto, the 104th Congress slightly modified the bill and passed the Personal Responsibility and Work Opportunity Reconciliation Act of 1996, which President Clinton did sign into law.

These recent welfare reform efforts have been examples of what Corbett labels the "make work pay" strategy and the "make 'em suffer" strategy.[51] The "make work pay" strategy is based on the idea that people make rational choices, so if we want people to choose work over welfare, we need to provide work opportunities that will enable people to be substantially better off than they are while receiving assistance. The "make 'em suffer" strategy is based on the same basic idea but comes at it from the opposite direction. Rather than attempting to provide options more attractive than welfare, this strategy imposes penalties on a range of behaviors that are seen as not conducive to self-sufficiency. Welfare recipients are required to attend school, participate in work training, immunize their children, and similar things. If recipients do not do these things, they are penalized by reductions in their welfare grants.

The 1988 Family Support Act, primarily a "make work pay" effort, had as its centerpiece an employment and training program called JOBS. The purpose of this program, commonly called "workfare," is to provide the resources (education, training, and child care) necessary to enable welfare recipients who are capable of doing so to work; and the plan included provisions requiring recipients to take advantage of these resources. The law states that:

- Two-parent families are eligible for welfare assistance in all fifty states and territories. Previously only twenty-three states had provisions for granting assistance to two-parent families.
- At least one parent in two-parent families receiving assistance must engage in unpaid work for at least sixteen hours a week in the Community Work Experience Program.
- States are required to have a minimum of 20 percent of family assistance recipients (minus certain exempt groups such as women with very young children) in jobs or job training.
- States must withhold court-ordered child support from the wages of noncustodial parents.
- Recipients who become self-supporting will be allowed to keep Medicaid and day care benefits for one year after leaving the welfare rolls.[52]

The Community Work Experience provision was supposed to be fully implemented by 1993, and the 20 percent job placement/training provision by 1995. As of 1998, no state had come anywhere close to fully meeting either of these goals.

Because of the apparent failure of the 1988 Family Support Act to meet its initial goals and conservative concern that the bill was too soft on recipients, welfare reform was attempted again in the 104th Congress. P.L. 104-193, the Personal Responsibility and Work Opportunity Reconciliation Act of 1996, was passed and signed into law by President Bill Clinton on August 22, 1996. Major provisions of P.L. 104-193 are:

- The Aid to Families with Dependent Children (AFDC) program is replaced by the Temporary Assistance to Needy Families (TANF) program.
- AFDC was an uncapped entitlement program. This means that the states had a right to reimbursement from the federal government for 75 percent of the cost of AFDC grants up to an unlimited amount, as long as they followed regulations. Under TANF, states receive a block grant in an amount calculated to be the highest of (1) the average payment they received under AFDC in fiscal years 1992 through 1994; (2) the amount they received in fiscal year 1994; or (3) the amount they received in fiscal year 1995. States will have much more freedom regarding how to spend this money than they had under AFDC, but once the money is spent, they have no right to additional funds from the federal government. A contingency fund will help states that exceed their block grant amounts, but funds from this are available only under specific and limited conditions (e.g., an exceptional increase in unemployment).
- Adults receiving cash benefits are required to work or participate in a state-designed program after two years, or their payments will be ended. This work requirement is defined as one individual in a household working at least thirty hours a week.
- States must have at least 50 percent of their total single-parent welfare caseloads working by the year 2002. States that fail to meet this requirement will have their block grant reduced by 5 percent or more in the following year.

The policy of linking the receipt of benefits to work trumpeted by supporters of both the 1988 and 1996 welfare reform laws as a new and innovative concept is really nothing new. Welfare has been linked to labor in America since the earliest attempts to deal with poverty.

- States are allowed to sanction, through a reduction or termination of cash benefits, people who fail to fulfill the work requirement.
- Payments to recipients using federal funds must end after a maximum of five years for all spells combined, thereby requiring that families become self-supporting at that point.
- Persons immigrating to the United States after the passage of H.R. 3734 will be ineligible for most means-tested programs, including TANF, food stamps, and Medicaid, for their first five years of residence.
- Illegal aliens will be barred from all means-tested programs.[53]

President Clinton expressed reluctance about signing the TANF bill, saying of it, "You can put wings on a pig, but that still does not make it an eagle." He expressed the belief that the 105th Congress would repeal or soften significant portions of the bill. However, Senator Daniel Patrick Moynihan, probably the leading expert on social welfare policy in the Senate, strongly expressed his belief that the votes simply would not be there to modify this law.

This latest reform of the welfare system has now been in place for seven years, so we can begin to assess whether it has been any more successful than previous reforms. If the question of success is limited to the size of the welfare rolls, then the answer is yes. The number of recipients of public assistance has declined from 4,533,000 at the beginning of the program to 2,125,000 as of March 2001. This represents a decline of more than 53 percent, a figure that has been trumpeted from the rooftops by the program's supporters. However, rarely mentioned are a few qualifications to this seemingly irrefutable indicator of success. The first is that the welfare rolls were already decreasing at a rapid rate for two years prior to the passage of the reform bill. In 1994 the AFDC caseload was 5,046,000, and this declined to 4,533,000, a decrease of 513,000 (10.2 percent),

What Americans Believe

In the time between the passage of the 1988 welfare reform act and the 1996 passage of the Personal Responsibility and Work Opportunity Reconciliation Act (TANF), the General Social Survey asked Americans two questions about welfare reform. The first question was: "Here are some proposals about welfare. I would like to know if you favor or oppose them. First, requiring that people must work in order to receive welfare—would you say that you strongly favor it, favor it, neither favor nor oppose it, oppose it, or strongly oppose it?" The respondents were then asked, "Second, reducing welfare benefits to make working for a living more attractive—would you say that you strongly favor, favor, neither favor nor oppose, oppose, or strongly oppose it?" The responses, summarized in Table 9.1, indicate that Americans are strongly in favor of the idea of building a work expectation into welfare programs. They are extremely favorable toward the idea—one that is a centerpiece of TANF—that work should be a requirement for welfare recipients. Americans are also in favor, but not to quite as great a degree, of the proposition that reducing benefits is a good way to encourage people to work.

The breakdown of responses to these questions by political perspective yields predictable results. Conservatives and moderates show significantly stronger support for both of these propositions than do liberals. However, what is striking is the amount of support for these ideas even among liberals. More than three-quarters of respondents with a liberal perspective

TABLE 9.1

Opinions Regarding Two Welfare Reform Ideas

	Strongly Favor	Favor	Neither Favor nor Oppose	Oppose	Strongly Oppose
Requiring that people must work to receive welfare	46.1%	36.1%	8.5%	7.2%	2.1%
Reducing welfare benefits to make working for a living more attractive	33.6%	37.3%	11.2%	13.9%	4.0%

by 1996 when TANF replaced AFDC. Thus it appears that something besides just the new approach to welfare was causing people to leave the rolls, the booming economy being the obvious suspect.

Another qualification to the claim of TANF program success based on declining welfare rolls has to do with the assumption made by program supporters that all of the agreed with the idea that requiring work of welfare recipients is a good idea, and well over half felt that reducing welfare benefits to make work more attractive was also a good idea (see Tables 9.2 and 9.3). With these results, it is no wonder there has not been a liberal movement to soften some of the provisions of the Personal Responsibility and Work Opportunity Reconciliation Act.

TABLE 9.2

Opinions on Requiring That People Must Work in Order to Receive Welfare, by Political Perspective

	Strongly Favor	Favor	Neither Favor nor Oppose	Oppose	Strongly Oppose
Liberal	42.0%	36.1%	9.6%	9.6%	2.8%
Moderate	44.2%	38.9%	8.7%	6.6%	1.7%
Conservative	52.3%	33.5%	6.8%	5.3%	2.1%

TABLE 9.3

Opinions on Reducing Welfare Benefits to Make Working More Attractive, by Political Perspective

	Strongly Favor	Favor	Neither Favor nor Oppose	Oppose	Strongly Oppose
Liberal	27.4%	31.1%	12.8%	20.5%	8.3%
Moderate	33.5%	40.0%	10.2%	12.4%	3.9%
Conservative	39.8%	38.1%	10.3%	10.5%	1.3%

people leaving welfare are becoming employed. This appears not to be the case. Studies of families that have left the TANF rolls show that at any point in time about 60 percent are employed and 40 percent are not. Most of the people who have left the rolls without being employed left because of administrative sanctions resulting from a failure to follow program rules.[54] A recipient can be sanctioned for something as minor as not responding to a letter directing her to attend a meeting. Inspecting various government reports, Lens concludes that sanctions have increased by 30 percent nationally since 1994, and in any given month approximately 5 percent of a state's total welfare caseload is under sanction. In addition, records indicate that sanctions are often incorrectly applied. In Wisconsin, for example, it was found that 44 percent of the penalties imposed on recipients in a five-month period were later found to have been erroneous.[55] Thus, much of the reduction in the number of recipients appears to be a result of a meaner interpretation and enforcement of the rules rather than success at helping people become self-sufficient.

The New Philosophy of Antipoverty Policy. The 1988 Family Support Act and the Personal Responsibility and Work Opportunity Reconciliation Act of 1996 (TANF) make one thing clear—there has been a fundamental change in this country's approach to the problem of poverty and public dependency. The AFDC program, as it was originally formulated as part of the 1935 Social Security Act, was based on the premise that dependent people, mainly women with children, were poor largely due to circumstances beyond their control, and that it was in society's interest for the mothers to stay home and take care of their children.

The Family Support Act of 1988 and the TANF program that replaced it represent a new approach to the problem of public dependency. First, they are based on the theory that we are now dealing with a new and different type of poverty than we have dealt with in the past. Senator Daniel Patrick Moynihan, one of the architects of the new law, argues that we are dealing with a new, "emergent form of dependency: the kind associated with post-industrial society." A principal factor in this new kind of dependency is a major change in family structure, resulting in what Moynihan calls the "post-marital" family. By this he is referring to the massive increase in single-parent families and the known correlation between this family form and poverty. Moynihan frankly admits that we have a poor understanding of this phenomenon, but he emphasizes that it is absolutely essential that antipoverty policy address it.[56] The provisions in the new law for collecting child support from absent parents attempt to address this problem. A second major change in antipoverty policy represented by the new law is that the law reflects society's changing expectations for women. It is clear from the provisions of the act that poor women, even those with children, are now expected to work.

We (the authors) have no problem with features of welfare reform that emphasize work and family. What we are concerned about is the fact that discussions of welfare have taken on a highly moralistic tone reminiscent of an earlier and harsher era. The United States seems to be returning to an approach characterized by what we previously described as "blaming the victim." A release from the White House describing President Clinton's basic principles during the welfare reform debate lists responsibility as a major component. The statement elaborates:

> Our current welfare system often seems at odds with core American values, especially responsibility. Overlapping and uncoordinated programs seem almost to invite waste and abuse. Non-custodial parents frequently provide little or no economic or social support to their children. And the culture of welfare offices often seems to reinforce dependence rather than independence. The President's welfare reform plan reinforces American values, while recognizing the government's role in helping those who are willing to help themselves.

> Our proposal includes several provisions aimed at creating a new culture of mutual responsibility. We will provide recipients with services and work opportunities, but implement tough, new requirements in return. These include provisions to promote parental responsibility, ensuring that both parents contribute to their children's well-being. The plan also includes incentives directly tied to the performance of the welfare office; extensive efforts to detect and prevent welfare fraud; sanctions to prevent gaming of the welfare system; and a broad array of incentives that the states can use to encourage responsible behavior.[57]

To us this new approach sounds very much like the nineteenth-century Charity Organization Society belief that the solution to poverty was to teach the poor about diligence, abstinence, and thrift. The approach of placing total responsibility on the poor for their own poverty didn't work then, and it won't work now.

Conclusion

August 22, 2001, marked the fifth anniversary of the passage of P.L. 104-193, the Personal Responsibility and Work Opportunity Reconciliation Act of 1996, which ended the AFDC program and replaced it with the TANF program. This anniversary is significant because, as the law was written, recipients of aid under TANF are limited to a lifetime maximum of five years on public assistance. In 2001 all states were required to comb through their caseloads and demonstrate that less than 20 percent of their total number of recipients have been receiving assistance for five years or more. If at any time after August 22, 2001, the percentage is higher than that, the states risk penalties of varying severity, depending on the amount by which their percentage exceeds twenty.

As this critical five-year date passed, data and opinions on the success of welfare reform came in from all sides. The general question is, of course, has P.L. 104-193 been successful in "ending welfare as we know it"? The answer depends on who you ask and how the question is stated. If the question asked is, "Have we reduced the welfare rolls, and have we saved money?" the answer is clearly that we have. In less than five years the number of welfare recipients has been literally cut in half, down to fewer than 2.5 million, the lowest number in decades. The Republican governor of Arkansas, Mike Huckabee, has opined that "the drop in welfare caseloads has been one of the greatest public policy successes of the century."[58]

If the question asked is, "Are former welfare recipients better off now that P.L. 104-193 has nudged them off the rolls?" the answer is not so positive. The answer, coming from a number of sources, is that the main thing welfare reform has accomplished is simply to move people from welfare poverty into employment poverty. In fact, the data indicate that many former recipients are actually worse off now that they are working. Using data from the National Survey of American Families, Loprest found that the median wage (50th percentile) of employed former welfare recipients in 1999 was $7.15 an hour; those at the 25th percentile were earning $6.05 an hour; those at the 75th were earning $9.00 an hour.[59] Few of the jobs held by former recipients provide good benefits. Only about one-third of the jobs include health insurance, and only about one-third provide paid sick leave.[60] Even these low wages provide incomes considerably in excess of welfare grant levels for those employed full time. However, a large number of the former recipients were found to be working only part time. As a result, about 52 percent of those who left the welfare rolls for jobs in 1999 still had incomes below the poverty level.[61]

It is also not clear just how much of the reduction in the welfare rolls is due to welfare reform and how much is due to the tremendous economic growth in the years since its passage. Data indicate that the number of welfare recipients was declining at a rapid rate even before the passage of P.L. 104-193 and that perhaps the new law is simply taking credit for the performance of the economy.

In any case, it will be years before we are able to make a valid assessment of the success of welfare reform. Among the questions that will need to be answered are:

- Will a significant number of former recipients, initially employed at near starvation wages, be able to move up the job ladder until they are truly better off than they were on assistance?
- When an economic slowdown occurs, and one inevitably will, will the welfare rolls return to their prereform level?
- Will states actually be able to reduce the number of long-term recipients (on assistance for a total of five years or more) to less than 20 percent?

Only time will tell. The authors, however, have no doubt that when the answers to these questions do come in they will provide fuel for a new round of welfare reform.

Visit **www.researchnavigator.com** to research these important concepts from the chapter:

Research Navigator.com

AFDC
Head Start
Medicaid
Personal Responsibility and Work Opportunities Reconciliation Act
Social Darwinism
Supplemental Security Income
Work Ethic
Workfare

Web Sites Related to Antipoverty Programs

American Public Welfare Association <www.apwa.org>: APWA is the largest national organization concerned with antipoverty programs. Site includes data, reports on research regarding welfare reform, information on the organization, publications, and constantly revised information on numerous welfare-related topics and events.

Center on Budget and Policy Priorities <www.cbpp.org>: This is a nonpartisan research organization and policy institute that conducts research and analysis on a range of government policies and programs with emphasis on those affecting low- and moderate-income people. Site contains information on poverty and welfare and includes center news, research and analysis, and a list of available reports.

Handsnet <www.handsnet.org>: Web page of national organization that promotes information sharing, cross-sector collaboration, and advocacy among individuals and organizations working on a broad range of public interest issues, notably poverty and welfare reform. Site includes action alerts, weekly digest, welfare watch, op–ed page, resources, and membership information.

Research Forum on Children, Families, and the New Federalism <www.researchforum.org>: An initiative that encourages collaborative research and informed policy on welfare reform and child well-being. Features an online database with up-to-date summaries of forty welfare research projects.

Welfare Law Center <www.welfarelaw.org>: This center works with and on the behalf of poor people to ensure that adequate income support is available to meet basic human needs and to foster human and family development. Site includes information about the center, welfare myths, projects of the center, publications, links to other sites, and membership information.

Welfare Watch <www.welfarewatch.org>: Site developed by the Annenberg School of Communication at the University of Southern California. Provides summaries of current media reports related to welfare reform.

Endnotes

1. Jan Harold Brunvand, *The Vanishing Hitchhiker: American Urban Legends and Their Meanings* (New York: W. W. Norton, 1981), xi.
2. Brunvand, *The Vanishing Hitchhiker,* xii.
3. For more information about urban legends in social work, see Philip R. Popple, "Contemporary Folklore and Social Welfare," *Arete 18* (Winter 1994), 1–11.
4. Walter I. Trattner, *From Poor Law to Welfare State: A History of Social Welfare in America,* 6th ed. (New York: Free Press, 1999), 1.
5. Ralph Pumphrey, "Compassion and Protection: Dual Motivations in Social Welfare," *Social Service Review 33* (1959), 21–29.
6. Michael B. Katz, *Poverty Policy in American History* (New York: Academic Press, 1983), ix.
7. Trattner, *From Poor Law to Welfare State,* 4–5.
8. Quoted in Barbara Tuchman, *A Distant Mirror: The Calamitous 14th Century* (New York: Alfred A. Knopf, 1978), xiv.
9. Tuchman, *A Distant Mirror,* xiii.
10. Karl de Schweinitz, *England's Road to Social Security* (New York: A. S. Barnes, 1943), 6.
11. Joel F. Handler, "The Assault on the Ablebodied," *Reviews in American History* (September 1987), 394.
12. Trattner, *From Poor Law to Welfare State,* 9–12.
13. Blanche D. Coll, *Perspectives in Public Welfare: A History* (Washington, DC: U.S. Government Printing Office, 1969), 5.
14. de Schweinitz, *England's Road to Social Security,* 29.
15. June Axinn and Herman Levin, *Social Welfare: A History of the American Response to Need,* 2nd ed. (New York: Longman, 1982), 17.
16. Axinn and Levin, *Social Welfare: A History of the American Response to Need,* 18–19.
17. Trattner, *From Poor Law to Welfare State,* 19.
18. Trattner, *From Poor Law to Welfare State,* 41–43.
19. Trattner, *From Poor Law to Welfare State,* 37–38.
20. Geoffrey Guest, "The Boarding of the Dependent Poor in British Colonial America," *Social Service Review 63* (March 1989), 107.
21. Trattner, *From Poor Law to Welfare State,* 31–32.
22. Christopher Collier and James Lincoln Collier, *Decision in Philadelphia: The Constitutional Convention of 1787* (New York: Ballantine Books, 1986), 28.
23. Axinn and Levin, *Social Welfare,* 38–39.
24. John Griscom, Chairman, *The First Annual Report of the Managers of the Society for the Prevention of Pauperism in the City of New York* (New York: Printed by J. Seymore, 1818), 12–22, reprinted in Ralph Pumphrey and Muriel Pumphrey, *The Heritage of American Social Work: Readings in Its Philosophical and Institutional Development* (New York: Columbia University Press, 1961), 60.
25. Axinn and Levin, *Social Welfare,* 49.
26. Axinn and Levin, *Social Welfare,* 57.
27. Handler, "The Assault on the Ablebodied," 395.
28. Coll, *Perspectives in Public Welfare,* 30.
29. Blanche D. Coll, "Social Welfare: History," *Encyclopedia of Social Work,* 17th ed. (Washington, DC: National Association of Social Workers, 1977), 1506.
30. "President Franklin Pierce's veto of the bill resulting from Miss Dix's efforts," *Congressional Globe,* Thirty-Third Congress, 1st sess. 3 May 1854, 1061–1063, reprinted in Pumphrey and

Pumphrey, *The Heritage of American Social Work,* 132–134.

31. Trattner, *From Poor Law to Welfare State,* 52.
32. James Leiby, *A History of Social Welfare and Social Work in the United States* (New York: Columbia University Press, 1978), 6–12.
33. These statistics are all from the U.S. Bureau of the Census, *The Statistical History of the United States from Colonial Times to the Present* (New York: Basic Books, 1976).
34. Robert H. Bremner, *From the Depths: The Discovery of Poverty in the United States* (New York: New York University Press, 1956), 16–17.
35. Josephine Shaw Lowell, "Methods of Relief for the Unemployed," *The Forum XVI* (1893–1894), 659, cited in Bremner, *From the Depths,* 22.
36. Quoted in Robert H. Bremner, *The Public Good: Philanthropy and Welfare in the Civil War Era* (New York: Alfred A. Knopf, 1980), 200.
37. Josephine Shaw Lowell, "The Economic Effects of Public Outdoor Relief," *Proceedings of the National Conference of Charities and Correction, 1890* (Boston, 1890), 81–82.
38. Roswell B. Mason quoted in Bremner, *The Public Good,* 192.
39. Leiby, *A History of Social Welfare and Social Work,* 191–192.
40. Leiby, *A History of Social Welfare and Social Work,* 196.
41. Leiby, *A History of Social Welfare and Social Work,* 210–215.
42. Michael Katz, *In the Shadow of the Poorhouse: A Social History of Welfare in America* (New York: Basic Books, 1986).
43. Much of this section was published earlier in Philip R. Popple, "Contexts of Practice," in Aaron Rosenblatt and Diana Waldfogel, eds., *Handbook of Clinical Social Work* (San Francisco: Jossey-Bass, 1983), 81–84.
44. Allen Nevins and Henry Steele Commager, *A Short History of the United States* (New York: Alfred A. Knopf, 1966), 470–471.
45. Quoted in Trattner, *From Poor Law to Welfare State,* 278.
46. Clinch Calkins, *Some Folks Won't Work* (New York: Harcourt Brace, 1930), 160–162.
47. Samuel Mencher, "Newburgh: The Recurrent Crisis of Public Assistance," *Social Work 7* (January 1962), 3–11.
48. Trattner, *From Poor Law to Welfare State,* 300.
49. William E. Schmidt, "Study Says Reagan's Cuts in Aid to Poor Affected South the Most," *New York Times* (15 March 1985).
50. Stuart Butler and Anna Kondratas, *Out of the Poverty Trap: A Conservative Strategy for Welfare Reform* (New York: Free Press, 1987), 1–2.
51. Thomas Corbett, "Child Poverty and Welfare Reform: Progress or Paralysis?" *Focus 15* (Spring 1993), 5.
52. Carmen D. Solomon, "The Family Support Act of 1988: How It Changes the Aid to Families with Dependent Children (AFDC) and Child Support Enforcement Programs," *CRS Report for Congress* (Washington, DC: Congressional Research Service, Library of Congress, 7 November 1988).
53. U.S. House of Representatives, "The Conference Report on the Personal Responsibility and Work Opportunity Reconciliation Act of 1996," 31 July 1996.
54. Martha Coven, "An Introduction to TANF" (Washington, DC: Center on Budget and Policy Priorities, 2002), 3, www.cbpp.org/1-22-02tanf2.htm
55. Vicki Lens, "TANF: What Went Wrong and What to Do Next," *Social Work 47* (July 2002), 280–281.
56. Daniel Patrick Moynihan, "Toward a Post-Industrial Social Policy," *Public Interest 96* (Summer 1989), 16–27.
57. U.S. Department of Health and Human Services, Press Kit for the Work and Responsibility Act of 1994, 3.
58. Laura Cohn, "From Welfare to Worsefare?," *Commentary, 3702* (October 2000), 103.
59. Pamala Loprest, "'How are Families Who Left Welfare Doing over Time?' A Comparison of Two Cohorts of Welfare Leavers," *Economic Policy Review,* Federal Reserve Bank of New York (7 September 2001), 9–11.
60. Gregory Acs and Pamala Loprest, "Initial Synthesis Report of the Findings from ASPE's 'Leavers' Grants" (Washington, DC: U.S. Department of Health and Human Services, 2001), http://aspe.hhs.gov/hsp/leavers99/synthesis01
61. Demetra Smith Nightingale, "Work Opportunities for People Leaving Welfare," in Alan Weil and Kenneth Finegold, eds., *Welfare Reform: The Next Act* (Washington, DC: Urban Institute Press, 2002), 103–120.

CHAPTER

10

Child Welfare

You can find the stories in the newspaper of any large city. Sometimes they are in the headlines and sometimes they are buried in the back pages, but read the paper for a few weeks and you will find them.

- In a small Wisconsin town in the middle of January, an eleven-year-old boy walks barefoot into a police station. He asks the desk sergeant if someone can help his little sister. Accompanying the boy to his home nearby, the police discover a seven-year-old girl locked in a small wire dog cage in a dark, unheated basement. The family's four other children appear to be reasonably well cared for, but the seven-year-old has been singled out for abuse and neglect because the mother states that she is an "ugly pig." The children are removed and placed with a relative living outside of the county. The parents are arrested and will probably be sentenced to long prison terms.
- A twelve-year-old girl goes to the school nurse complaining of itching and burning sensations. She is referred to a public health clinic, where she is diagnosed as suffering from genital herpes. A social worker for child protective services investigates and finds that the girl has been sexually abused by her stepfather, a man who has served five years in prison as a result of a rape conviction and who is currently free on parole. The mother tearfully tells the social worker, "He told me he had been framed on that rape charge and I believed him."
- Responding to a call from a neighbor, police go to an apartment to find three children ages two, three, and five staying by themselves. The apartment is a shambles, the children are dirty, and the only evidence of food is an empty peanut butter jar, a warm jug of milk, and a few nearly empty boxes of dry cereal. When interviewed by the police, the five-year-old states that their mother no longer lives with them and their father has not been home for several days. The father shows up two days later, stating, "Those kids can take care of themselves every now and then. Why heck, that Cindy is just like a little mother. She's sure better than their real one ever was."
- In an area of town known to local residents as the "meat market," a man is arrested after approaching an undercover vice officer and offering to arrange a "date" for him with a thirteen-year-old girl. On investigation it is learned that the girl is the man's daughter and that she has been used to support his drug habit for more than a year. The child's mother used to support her husband's drug habit by working as a prostitute, but apparently had managed to protect her daughter. However, she died from appendicitis two years ago and the man turned to his daughter for support. An outraged judge and jury sentence the man to fifty years in prison, and the state child welfare agency is called on to attempt to restore some of the girl's lost childhood.

The family is the social institution we rely on for the care, protection, and nurturance of children. We believe that every child has a right to grow up in a warm, loving family group. Perhaps because our society provides so little support for families, however, they break down and fail to provide even the most basic requisites for a healthy childhood far more often than we care to believe. As a nation we tend to distrust government and to believe strongly that parents have a right to rear their children in their own manner and to the best of their abilities, so we are hesitant to intervene on the behalf of children. However, there is a vague line beyond which we feel we must intervene to protect the child. When child care sinks to this point, society looks to the field of social work known as child protective services, an important part of child welfare, to deal with the problem.

Definition

In a broad sense, *child welfare* refers to all the aspects of society essential for the well-being of children. Included are day care, education, medical care, parks and recreation, and public safety. Child welfare as an area of social welfare and a field of social work has a somewhat more limited focus. In this more limited context, child welfare has generally been concerned with the special needs of children and their families when parental functioning is impaired; when the family lives in such poverty that effective parenting is impossible; or when the child, because of developmental, emotional, or behavioral problems, may not be able to function within his or her own family.

Child welfare, according to the Child Welfare League of America, involves providing social services to children and young people whose parents are not able to adequately fulfill their child-rearing responsibilities, or whose communities fail to provide resources and protection that families and children require.[1] Kadushin and Martin expand on this definition:

> Child welfare services are those services required when parents or children are either incapable of implementing or unwilling to implement (or both) their respective role requirements, or when a serious discrepancy arises between the role expectations of the community and the individual's performance.[2]

The family is the social institution we rely on for the care and nurturance of children.

Seven problems of role functioning in the parent–child–community network are likely to lead to a need for child welfare services:

1. *Parental role unoccupied.* For any of a large number of reasons, one or both parents are not present in a child's life. In many single-parent families, the one parent is able to adequately fulfill all necessary roles and the child has no unusual problems. However, the absence of one parent greatly increases the risk of problems. For example, consider the case of the Brown family.

> Child Protective Service was called by a neighbor, who reported that the five Brown children, ages three to nine, were being left at home alone. The social worker who investigated the case found this to be true. Mr. Brown was a single father trying to rear five children by himself following his wife's desertion of the family. He told the social worker, "I know these kids shouldn't be left alone; it just worries me to death. But I've got to work, and day care even for just the three little ones will eat up nearly all my pay." The social worker helped Mr. Brown arrange day care in a subsidized center, which he could afford. She recommended that the case remain open because of the likelihood that Mr. Brown would need ongoing support in adequately fulfilling all parental roles.

2. *Parental incapacity.* The parent is present and may want to fulfill his or her role requirements but is prevented from doing so by physical, mental, or emotional inadequacy, or by a lack of knowledge or training. A threat to a child's safety resulting from parental incapacity is illustrated by the Valdez case.

> The night intake worker was called to the public hospital emergency room one evening by the resident physician. The mother of seven-month-old Maria Valdez had brought her in with severe scalding burns on her legs and torso. The resident had also called the police and, diagnosing the situation as intentional child abuse, demanded that the mother, Juanita Valdez, be arrested. When the social worker met Ms. Valdez in the hospital waiting room, he met not the monster described by the resident but a sweet, loving woman whom he estimated to be functioning intellectually on the level of a seven-year-old.
>
> Over the next few days he was able to piece together what had happened. Ms. Valdez was in the habit of placing Maria in the bathtub of her old apartment and turning on the hot water tap. The water would come out lukewarm because the water heater was so old it barely worked. She would then go to the kitchen and begin dinner while Maria's bath ran. Just prior to Maria's injury, the apartment owner had replaced the water heater and had sent a note to that effect to all the tenants. Ms. Valdez was unable to connect the fact that there was a new water heater with the need to change Maria's bath routine. The result was that Maria was seriously injured.

3. *Role rejection.* The parent, often because he or she did not want a child in the first place, either consciously or unconsciously rejects the parental role, resulting in varying degrees of failure in role performance. An example of this is the Murphy case.

> Anna Nelms brought one-year-old Cecily Murphy to the Children's Emergency Center early on a Monday morning. She reported that she had been the child's day care provider since Cecily was three months old. Cecily had been placed in day care because her mother, Elizabeth, was a single parent and had gone to work full time. Ms. Nelms reported that Ms. Murphy had dropped the child off at her house as usual on Friday morning but had never returned to pick her up. The social worker called Ms. Murphy's work number and found that she was at work; she agreed to meet him at her home that evening. But when he went for the meeting, she was not there. The next day he went to the hospital where Ms. Murphy worked

as a medical secretary and insisted on speaking with her. Ms. Murphy was a very attractive and apparently intelligent nineteen-year-old who appeared to be overwhelmed with the demands of parenthood. She told the social worker that since she became pregnant with Cecily her life had been miserable. She said, "Two years ago I was a carefree kid and now I'm well on my way to being an old hag."

The social worker made another appointment to meet with Ms. Murphy and begin working on her problems. Once again she missed the appointment. This became a pattern over the next two months: the social worker would track Ms. Murphy down, Ms. Murphy would make commitments to meet with him or with other resources, and then Ms. Murphy would fail to show up. Finally Ms. Murphy was contacted and told that a court hearing had been set asking for permanent custody of Cecily so that the child could be placed for adoption. Her rights were explained to her, and she was told that if she would like to work to regain custody of her child, the agency was still open to helping her. Ms. Murphy did not show up for the hearing, an omission interpreted by the court as a clear statement that she was rejecting the role of parent. The court terminated Ms. Murphy's rights, and Cecily was placed in an adoptive home. Ms. Murphy has never contacted the agency to inquire about Cecily.

4. *Intrarole conflict.* In this type of situation the parents are in conflict regarding role definition. They fail to reach agreement about who is supposed to do what for and with the child.

The school social worker was contacted by the principal of Lincoln Elementary School. The principal reported that the Andrews twins, Billy and Becky, were frequently complaining in their first-grade class that they had not had breakfast. When the social worker contacted the parents, he found a rather prosperous couple. Both had demanding careers and were unable to agree on who had responsibility for certain household and parental tasks. Each believed that the other should feel guilty about not getting breakfast for the twins. The parents were referred for family counseling, and the level of child care greatly improved.

5. *Interrole conflict.* This is the situation in which a person is unable to adequately discharge parental responsibilities because of the interference of other social roles. Recent social changes, which increase the likelihood of both parents' having demanding careers outside of the house, often lead to interrole conflict, as the following situation illustrates.

Whitney, the twelve-year-old daughter of Drs. Stephen and Barbara Bradford, had been in counseling with a clinical social worker for more than a year. The counseling was an effort to deal with behavior problems exhibited by Whitney that appeared to be increasing as she entered adolescence. The social worker attributed most of Whitney's problems to the fact that she received inadequate attention from her parents, who deferred most child-rearing duties to the family's maid. The parents realized that they should devote more time to their daughter but were not successful in this effort. Stephen and Barbara were family physicians who had a clinic in an underserved, impoverished area of the city. They worked twelve to eighteen hours a day, often seven days a week, and still did not reach all the people in need of medical care. When they did tear themselves away to spend an hour talking to Whitney's social worker, Barbara lamented, "What are we to do? I feel as though we're between a rock and a hard place. If we don't start spending more time with Whitney, she'll probably be screwed up for the rest of her life. But if we do cut down on our hours to be with her, people are going to die from lack of medical care."

6. *Child incapacity and/or disability.* An exceptional child places exceptional demands on parents. Even the most capable, organized, and well-adjusted parents are greatly taxed by the needs of a child with a physical or mental disability or emotional disturbance.

Parents or caretakers whose abilities and resources are marginal will often be unable to cope, as is illustrated by the Costa case.

> Sam and Gena Costa came to the child welfare office requesting that their two-year-old, Stanley, be placed in an institution. The Costas were barely functioning as parents to their three older kids, and when they learned that Gena was pregnant with Stanley they didn't see how they would cope with a fourth child. A problem became a disaster when Stanley was diagnosed with attention deficit hyperactivity disorder. The Costas stated that they were at the end of their rope and felt that they could adequately parent the other three children only if Stanley were placed in an institution or foster home. After a good deal of work by the social worker, including finding day care for Stanley and training for the parents on managing a hyperactive child, the Costas felt they could cope with Stanley at home.

7. *Deficiency of community resources.* Parents are sometimes unable to adequately implement their roles because of a lack of community resources. For example, if parents need to work but there is no day care available, they are caught in a double bind. They have a choice of either quitting work and thereby failing in the role of breadwinner, or leaving the children unattended and failing in the role of caretaker. As in the following situation, children are often placed in foster care because less drastic alternatives are not available.

> Susan Dobbins, a child welfare worker, sat back and sighed with frustration: "John Ryals has been in three foster homes during the past three years and he doesn't need to be. He needs to be home with his mother. She's really a great mother but she occasionally goes into deep, black depressions. When she does, she gets sent to the state mental hospital and Johnny to a foster home. If we had better community mental health service for Mrs. Ryals and homemaker service to come in and help with Johnny when Mrs. Ryals is depressed, she wouldn't have to go into the hospital and he wouldn't have to go to a foster home. I'll tell you another thing—it would cost a whole lot less!"

This problem has been greatly exacerbated by the passage and implementation of the 1996 welfare reform act that requires single parents to work but does not provide adequate, long-term child care resources.[3]

Thus, in keeping with our Chapter 2 definition of social welfare as the management of dependency in society, child welfare is defined as those services provided when dependency is created by problems in functioning in the parent–child–community role network. The child may be considered dependent because he or she lacks parental care, and the parent may be considered dependent on society for help in fulfilling his or her expected roles. Dependency can also result from a lack of service and support available in the community. Child welfare services are nearly always provided on a residual basis (see Chapter 2); that is, they come into play only after the institution considered to be primary, the family, has broken down. This is unfortunate because there is no area in which institutional services are more needed. In today's fragmented, fast-moving society, in which more and more families are finding it essential for both parents to work, even the most capable people are finding it difficult to adequately fulfill all parental roles.

The conception of child welfare as a residual service, operating only after the family has broken down sufficiently to be causing harm to its members, seriously limits the field of social work intervention. Duncan Lindsey argues that this conception has, in fact, crippled social work's ability to solve family problems. He argues for a return to a broader approach to family support and a renewed recognition that much of child abuse and neglect has its origins in extreme poverty. Lindsey goes so far as to refer to child abuse as a "red herring"; that is, as an emotionally charged issue that diverts attention away from the real issue—which is, in this case, child poverty. In addition, structural forces outside of social work's control are assaulting the family. Waiting until things have already fallen apart is a recipe for failure.[4]

Statistical Profile

The preceding discussion of definitions of child welfare is well and good, but it does not differentiate child maltreatment from acceptable child-rearing behavior. Just what types of acts toward children are considered to represent a role breakdown serious enough to warrant intervention? After reviewing varied definitions of child maltreatment from the perspectives of the medical, legal, and social work professions, Faller and Russo identified four requirements for a situation to be defined as child maltreatment:

1. There must be some definable parental behavior directed toward the child. This may be an act of commission (abuse) or omission (neglect), and it can be either physical or mental.
2. There must be some demonstrable harm to the child. This may be a physical injury or condition, or it may be evidence of psychological damage, or both.
3. A causal link needs to be established between parental behavior and the harm to the child.
4. The social worker needs to feel that the maltreatment is sufficiently serious to warrant intervention.[5]

In this section we concentrate on child maltreatment, which is the area of child welfare that most social workers are involved in. Unfortunately, we do not have precise statistics regarding child maltreatment. Because of the lack of a uniform definition, what one source reports as abuse or neglect another does not. Also maltreatment, like crime, is private; people attempt to cover it up and thus avoid becoming part of the statistics. For these reasons, plus the historic lack of attention to the problem, only recently has much effort been expended to discover the dimensions of the problem of child maltreatment.

In recent years several other good sources of data regarding child maltreatment have become available. Under congressional mandate, the U.S. Department of Health and Human Services (HHS) collects and publishes a national incidence study every ten years. The most recent is *The Third National Incidence Study of Child Abuse and Neglect* (NIS–3), published in 1996. In addition HHS has developed the National Child Abuse and Neglect Data System (NCANDS), which compiles data reported by the states and publishes it on an annual basis. Supplementing these excellent sources are two private collections of data, the Child Welfare League of America National Data Analysis System, and the *Kids Count Data Book* and *Data Book Online* prepared by the Annie E. Casey Foundation. A more limited study has been conducted since 1982 by the National Center on Child Abuse Prevention Research. The major shortcoming of all of these sources is that they compile *reports* of abuse and neglect rather than *incidence*. In other words, these studies consist only of those cases known to officials, and it is uncertain if these represent 80 percent of all cases, 50 percent, 25 percent, or what.

Researchers have been frustrated in their effort to find clear patterns among the data. Pelton notes,

> I was often warned by experienced social workers that abuse and neglect problems are so varied that they defy generalizations. As a social scientist, I expect to discover generalizations. Unfortunately, I found that the cases conformed more closely to their advice than to my optimism.[6]

Therefore, the following data should be regarded as rough estimates.

Number of Children Involved. The NCANDS states that in 2002, 3,058,129 children were investigated by state protective services agencies as suspected victims of maltreatment. These figures work out to a rate of approximately 36.6 children per 1,000 U.S. child population. After investigation, 771,791 of these cases were substantiated, and an additional 121,803 were indicated, which means there was enough evidence to warrant suspicion but no actual proof of the allegations.[7]

Because the NCANDS reports studies that consist only of cases actually reported to child protective agencies, it is an underrepresentation of the actual incidence. Several studies based on statistical samples have attempted to ascertain the actual incidence. Gil estimated the incidence of abuse alone to range from 2,500,000 to 4,070,000.[8] Straus, Gelles, and Steinmetz, who limited their study to abuse and to children between the ages of three and seventeen, estimated that between 1.4 and 1.9 million were subjected to abuse during a one-year period.[9] Thus, although figures are inadequate to reach many solid conclusions, it is clear that the problem is immense.

Type of Maltreatment. The NCANDS data on "Type of Maltreatment" are summarized in Figure 10.1. As the graph shows, neglect is by far the most frequently reported type of maltreatment. An interesting study by Drake and Jonson-Reid found that regardless of the reason for an original referral (sexual abuse, physical abuse, neglect) subsequent referrals were most likely to be for neglect. This leads to the conclusion that neglect is probably present as a secondary problem in nearly all child maltreatment referrals.[10]

Gender. The NCANDS finds that reports of maltreatment were fairly evenly divided between boys and girls. In 2001, 48 percent of substantiated reports involved boys and 51.5 percent involved girls. The proportion of reports involving girls has been increasing in recent years, up from 51.1 percent in 1983, because of the increase in sexual abuse referrals, which predominantly involve female victims.[11]

Social Class. Although it is true that child maltreatment occurs in all social classes, the data indicate that it is most common among families in lower socioeconomic levels. In a 1969 survey of abusive families, Gil found that nearly 60 percent had been on public assistance at some time and that slightly more than 34 percent were receiving welfare at the time of the report. Today, more than half of the children removed from their homes because of abuse or neglect come from families receiving TANF (formerly AFDC).[12] Lindsey, looking at data from the most recent National Incident Study, observes that

FIGURE 10.1 **Percent of Victims of Child Abuse and Neglect, by Abuse and Neglect Type, 1999**

Source: Graph reproduced from Child Welfare League of America National Data Analysis System. Copyright 1999, Child Welfare League of America. This graph appears by special permission of the Child Welfare League of America, Washington, DC (www.cwla.org).

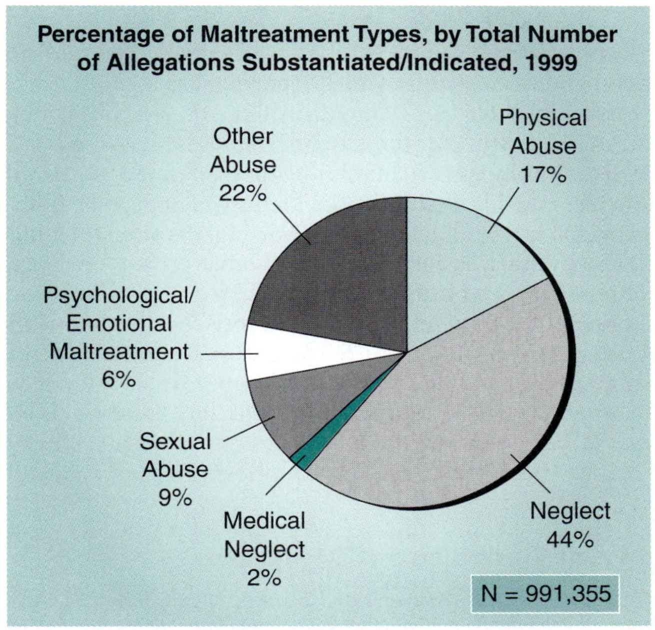

the likelihood of fatalities and severe injury to a child is highly correlated with poverty. The rate of severe injuries for families with annual income below $15,000 was twenty-two times greater than for families with income above $30,000. The rate for fatalities was sixty times greater for poor families.[13] Pelton surveyed child protective service records in New Jersey and found that 79 percent of the families had incomes below the poverty line. These figures have often been rejected, based on the theory that poor people are more susceptible to being reported to public agencies than middle-class people, and thus that the figures reflect reporting bias rather than an actual relationship between socioeconomic class and child maltreatment. However, social scientists now conclude that although poor people may be slightly overreported, it is probable that a greater proportion of poor children are maltreated.[14]

Race. All studies of child maltreatment have found that minority groups are overrepresented. Although approximately 24 percent of the child population of the United States is made up of minority group members, the NCANDS data for 2001 indicate that 44 percent of substantiated reports of abuse and neglect involve minority group children.[15] However, it is generally thought that these figures represent differences in social class rather than race. One study conducted by the American Humane Association found that when income was controlled for, maltreatment rates for nonwhite children were actually slightly lower than for white children.[16]

Age. Figure 10.2 shows maltreatment rates in relation to the ages of involved children. Although maltreatment occurs throughout childhood, clearly the younger a child is, the greater the danger of serious harm.

Trend. Probably the most significant finding of the national studies is not the absolute level of reporting but the extent to which reporting has increased over time. This information is presented in Table 10.1. The data in Table 10.1 show a 47 percent increase from 1986 to 2001. It is doubtful that these figures represent anywhere near this large an increase in the actual numbers of children being maltreated. Rather, they mostly reflect factors that increase the likelihood that incidents will be reported. These factors include the allocation of more federal money for reporting; the strengthening of state reporting laws (physicians, teachers, social workers, and other professionals who work with children are now required to report in all states); the redesign of state social service department intake systems; the implementation of twenty-four-hour hot-line systems; and the massive public awareness campaigns in the 1970s. The rate of increase in estimates of child maltreatment began to slow in 1990 and appear to have leveled off by 1994.

In 1969, when David Gil estimated that the incidence of child abuse was somewhere between 2.5 and 4.07 million, he was severely criticized. Straus's 1980 estimate of 6.5 million has also been criticized. These numbers were, and still are, mind-boggling.

FIGURE 10.2 **Percentage of Victims by Age Group, 2001**

Source: U.S. Department of Health and Human Services, Administration on Children, Youth, and Families, *Child Maltreatment 2001* (Washington, DC: U.S. Government Printing Office, 2003), 23.

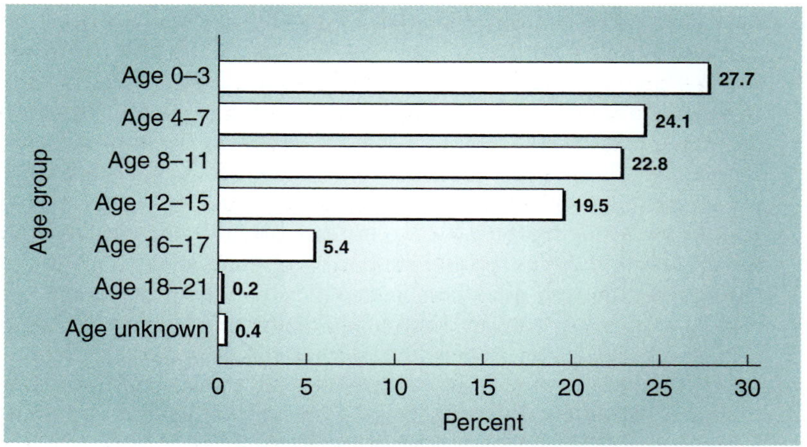

TABLE 10.1 Estimated Number of Children Reported to Be Maltreated

	1986	1991	1996	2001
	2,086,000	2,650,664	3,007,578	3,058,129
Per 1,000 Children	34	45	51	51

Sources: David Wiese and Deborah Daro, DSW, *Current Trends in Child Abuse Reporting and Fatalities: The Results of the 1994 Annual Fifty State Survey* (Chicago: The National Center on Child Abuse Prevention Research, a program of the National Committee to Prevent Child Abuse, 1995), 5; U.S. Department of Health and Human Services, Administration on Children, Youth and Families, *Child Maltreatment 1998: Reports from the States to the National Child Abuse and Neglect Data System* (Washington, DC: U.S. Government Printing Office, 2000); U.S. Department of Health and Human Services, Administration on Children, Youth, and Families, *Child Maltreatment 2001* (Washington, DC: U.S. Government Printing Office, 2003).

If true, they mean that between 4 and 10.4 percent of all children in the United States are victims of abuse. Because we know that physical abuse accounts for only about one-third of all maltreatment (neglect and sexual abuse account for about two-thirds), these figures mean that between 12 and 31.2 percent of children are subjected to some form of maltreatment. Research findings regarding sexual abuse lend credibility to these alarming figures. According to the best estimates available, somewhere between 9 and 54 percent of women and between 3 and 9 percent of men were sexually abused as children.[17] The increase in numbers of actual reports indicates that these figures may be more accurate than we dared imagine.

Dynamics

In the face of the staggering statistics on child abuse and neglect, the question that demands an answer is, "Why do people do such things?" The most obvious answer, and the one that dominated thinking until recently, is that parents who abuse and neglect their children are psychologically sick, or perhaps even evil. Steele and Pollock refer to abusive parents as a "gold mine of psychopathology"; Kempe and his associates describe the abuser as the "psychopathological member of the family"; Young says that "neglecting parents tend to wear blinders imposed by their own unsatisfied needs" and refers to abusive parents as "parents who hate"; Eisenberg refers to abusive parents as having "cancer of the soul."[18] A great deal of research has been done on this question of "Why?" The general consensus that has emerged is that the dynamics of abuse and neglect are much too complex to be explained adequately by a simple psychopathological model. It is now thought that abuse and neglect result from the interaction of three types of factors: individual parent factors, family factors, and environmental factors.[19]

Individual Parent Factors. Although the majority of parents who maltreat their children have no diagnosable psychopathological condition, researchers and practitioners have identified a cluster of personality traits and social attributes that are frequently found among the parents. Among the more common are:

- *Feelings of low self-esteem.* These parents often feel they are worthless, incompetent, and bad. Neglectful parents often neglect themselves as well as their children.
- *Excessive dependency.* Neglectful and abusive parents look to others to fulfill needs; mature adults take care of themselves.

A CLOSER Look

Incidents Defined as Child Maltreatment

Specifically what types of incidents are considered to be sufficiently serious to warrant intervention? A useful list was developed as part of the *National Study of the Incidence and Severity of Child Abuse and Neglect.* The forms of maltreatment identified are:

Physical Assault with Bodily Injury

1. Assault with implement (knife, strap, cigarette, etc.)
2. Assault without implement (hitting with fist, biting, etc., or means of assault unknown)

Sexual Exploitation

3. Intrusion (acts involving penile penetration—oral, anal, or genital; e.g., rape, incest)
4. Molestation with genital contact
5. Other or unknown

Other Abusive Treatment

6. Verbal or emotional assault (threatening, belittling, etc.)
7. Close confinement (tying, locking in closet, etc.)
8. Other or unknown

Refusal of Custody

9. Abandonment
10. Other (expulsion, refusal to accept custody of runaway, etc.)

Inattention to Remedial Health Care Needs

11. Refused to allow or provide needed care for diagnosed condition or impairment
12. Unwarranted delay or failure to seek needed care

Inattention to Physical Needs

13. Inadequate supervision
14. Disregard of avoidable hazards in home (exposed wiring, broken glass, etc.)
15. Inadequate nutrition, clothing, or hygiene
16. Other (e.g., reckless disregard of child's safety: driving while intoxicated, etc.)

Inattention to Educational Needs

17. Knowingly "permitting" chronic truancy
18. Other (repeatedly keeping child home, failing to enroll, etc.)

Inattention to Emotional/Developmental Needs

19. Inadequate nuturance/affection (e.g., failure to thrive)
20. Knowingly "permitting" maladaptive behavior (delinquency, serious drug/alcohol abuse, etc.)
21. Other

Other

22. Involuntary neglect (due to hospitalization, incarceration, etc.)
23. General neglect (more than two of codes 13–16)

Source: Children's Bureau, U.S. Department of Health and Human Services, *Study Findings, National Study of the Incidence and Severity of Child Abuse and Neglect,* Appendix A, "Data Forms for Child Protective Services Agencies" (Microfiche, September 1988), 50.

- *Serious difficulty coping with the demands of parenting.* They often expect their children to parent them rather than vice versa.
- *Impulsivity.* Everyone has impulses to do things that are improper. These range from mild things like going to the beach instead of going to work on a nice day, to more serious things like striking someone when he or she frustrates or irritates us. Part of maturing is learning to control these impulses—or, in Freudian terms, developing a superego. Maltreating parents often have not done this.
- *Rigid personalities.* Maltreating parents often have fixed ideas about the way things should be, and they are unable to tolerate their children's deviating from these ideas.
- *Deficient consciences.* These parents often demonstrate an inability to empathize with their children and a great ability to rationalize their own behavior. Therefore, they feel little remorse when they maltreat their children.
- *Childhood deprivation.* Often, maltreating parents are repeating child-rearing patterns they experienced as children.
- *Social isolation.* Maltreating families are often cut off from their social environment. They avoid, and in turn are avoided by, neighbors. They rarely participate in church or community activities, and they are often alienated from their extended families.

A small proportion of parents who maltreat their children do have diagnosable psychological disorders or mental problems. Among these are:

- *Psychopathy.* A true psychopath is a person who, because of severe deficiencies in his or her own nurturing, has developed a grossly distorted superego. These people do not have deficient consciences; they have *no* consciences. Thus, when they harm a child, they feel no remorse at all. This is a rare condition and accounts for less than 5 percent of abusive parents.
- *Depression.* This is probably the most common psychological disorder among maltreating parents, particularly neglectful parents. These people feel so bad that they find it impossible to get up the energy to care for their children.
- *Psychosis.* Psychotic parents suffer from a distorted sense of reality. They may think that strangers are trying to kill them, they may hear the voice of God, or they may think that their child is possessed by the devil. Although only about 5 percent of parents who mistreat their children are psychotic, these children are in great danger.
- *Mental retardation.* Mentally retarded parents can be caring and nurturing. However, they often lack the knowledge and skill to rear children without help and thus have difficulty adequately protecting their children.
- *Substance abuse.* In the past thirty years, substance abuse has gone from a fairly insignificant factor in child maltreatment to being *the* major individual/parent factor. A study published by the Child Welfare League of America in 2001 reported that 67 percent of the parents involved in the child welfare system were in need of substance abuse treatment. Commonly available substances that can substantially impair a person's ability to parent include alcohol, marijuana, cocaine, crack, PCP, and heroin, as well as new "designer drugs" that are constantly emerging. Substance abuse contributes to child maltreatment in two ways. First, the alcohol or drugs can lower a parent's impulse control, and he or she may express underlying anger by injuring the child. Second, children are often neglected because the parent is unable to perform everyday tasks while under the influence of alcohol or drugs.

Family Factors. When a case of child maltreatment comes to light, there are many questions to be answered. The most disturbing questions relate to the role of family members other than the victim and the perpetrator. If a child is abused by one parent, we ask, "Where was the other parent during all this? Why didn't he or she protect the child? Where were the brothers and sisters? If they were older, why didn't they intervene? If they were younger, why didn't they tell someone?" In neglect situations, we ask questions such as "How could the whole family have ignored the need for medical treatment? How could both parents have been so careless?" The answers to questions such as these lie in the realm of family dynamics. Although we do not yet fully understand these answers, some of the important dynamics we are learning about are:

- *Parental collusion.* Although one parent may be the active perpetrator in abuse cases, or may be the parent most obviously failing in his or her role responsibilities in neglect cases, it is rare that the other parent does not play some part in the maltreatment. The passive parent generally is aware of what is happening and gives tacit permission and support to the active parent.
- *Scapegoating.* Often one child becomes the focus for anger and aggression present in family relations. Other family members "take out" their rage and aggression on the designated child.
- *Single-parent status.* Single parents are heavily overrepresented among protective service cases. Single parents often lack adequate resources, including financial resources, for raising children; and our society is not particularly generous in its assistance to them.
- *Adolescent parents.* Young parents are overrepresented in child welfare caseloads. Late adolescence and early adulthood are stressful times without the added burden of parenthood—often single parenthood.
- *The extended family.* The extended family is a primary source of support during times of stress. Parents who maltreat their children frequently lack this source of support.
- *Family management problems.* Many persons are not well prepared for parenthood at the time they have children. These people may have difficulty finding and keeping appropriate housing, organizing and completing basic household tasks such as cleaning the house and paying bills, getting children to school on time and other obligations properly prepared and on time, and protecting children from health and safety hazards. Family management problems contribute to neglect because the pervasive disorganization virtually ensures that all of a child's needs are not met. They also contribute to abuse through increasing the parent's frustration level.
- *Factors related to the child.* Children often play a significant part in their own maltreatment, in the sense that they place greater demands on their caretakers than the caretakers are able to cope with. A very active child places more stress on parents and is therefore more likely to be a target for abuse. A passive child places fewer demands on parents and is at greater risk of neglect. Children who are different in some way—mentally disabled, physically disabled, or hearing impaired—have been found to be at greater risk of maltreatment.

Environmental Factors. A time-honored bit of practice wisdom among social workers is that child maltreatment results from "internal stress combined with external press." Internal stress refers to the individual parent and the family factors discussed previously. The external press refers to factors in the environment that overload the abilities of individuals and families to cope with difficulties in healthy ways. Major types of environmental factors that relate to child maltreatment are:

- *Chronic stressors.* These are long-term problematic conditions with which a family must cope. Simply being a parent is a chronic stressor, especially for parents who are too young, too ignorant, or not ready for the responsibilities of having children. Having a family member who is chronically ill, either physically or mentally, is another great stress on a family. Probably the most persistent chronic stressor is poverty. Some believe this in itself is the greatest cause of abuse and neglect.[20] Rearing children is much easier for parents who can afford babysitters, summer camps, music lessons, nice houses, and innumerable other things. When you can never financially afford a break from your kids, and when you can never say yes to their desires, parenthood can be a hard road indeed.
- *Situational stressors.* These are changes in a family's social situation, generally, though not always, for the worse. Situational stressors to which the family may be unable to accommodate include unemployment, moving, divorce, homelessness, death, birth of a new baby, a promotion, and the mother going to work. These stressors produce tension and often a role overload, which may be instrumental in abuse or neglect.
- *Precipitating stressors.* These are incidents that immediately trigger an incident of maltreatment. They are, in Faller and Ziefert's words, "the straws which break the camel's back."[21] Precipitating stressors are most commonly identified in cases of abuse, but they sometimes lead to neglect in the form of abandonment or withdrawal from parenting responsibilities. The most common form of precipitating stressor is actual or perceived child misbehavior.

Poverty contributes to child neglect because very poor parents are unable to care adequately for their children; it also contributes to child abuse because of the emotional stress extreme poverty places on parents.

Additional Factors. Two additional factors need to be considered in relation to the dynamics of child maltreatment. These are our culture's general ambivalence about violence, and subcultures that approve of violence to a greater degree than the rest of society.

Although we in the United States consider ourselves to be a peace-loving people, we are fascinated with physical violence. The success of movies such as *Pulp Fiction, Natural Born Killers,* and martial arts films of all types demonstrates this. Further, we sanction a level of violence directed toward children that is considerably higher than we permit for adults. Imagine what would happen if a supervisor rapped a bookkeeper on the knuckles with a ruler because his work was late, or if an executive struck his secretary with his belt because her work was sloppy. Everyone would be horrified, and the perpetrators would likely end up in court on criminal or civil charges. However, if a parent, or even a teacher, were to do these things to a child, he or she would generally be considered to be acting in a perfectly acceptable manner. Gil asserts that the culturally sanctioned approval of physical violence toward children is the "basic dimension upon which all other factors [contributing] to child abuse are imposed."[22]

The final dynamic related to child maltreatment is the existence of subcultures within society that sanction the use of a greater degree of violence toward children than does society in general, or that hold greatly different standards regarding appropriate care. Although the relationship between social class and use of violence is complex and not fully understood, there is evidence that lower-class parents are more likely to condone the use of violence than middle-class parents.[23] There have also been highly publicized cases of religious groups that practice what most of us would consider to be child abuse in the name of proper, biblically supported child rearing. And there are subgroups within our society that for religious or other reasons do not believe in modern medical care. When a child in one of these groups becomes critically ill, intervention becomes necessary to protect the child. With our tradition of religious freedom, this is a touchy area.

Historical Perspective

The earliest known provision for the protection of children in this country was a statute passed in Massachusetts in 1735, which provided that when parents

> were unable, or neglected to, provide necessaries for the substance and support of their children . . . and where persons bring up their children in such gross ignorance that they do not know, or are not able to distinguish the alphabet, or twenty-four letters, at the age of six years, the overseers might bind out such children to good families for a decent Christian education.[24]

This law, however, was an anomaly. We do not find evidence of widespread, serious concern for child protection until well into the nineteenth century.

The Emergence of Concern for Children

Why is it that our society did not exhibit much concern about the welfare of children until 150 years ago? There are three general, interrelated reasons: the lengthening of childhood, the breakdown of the ability of the family and the church to manage child dependency, and a gradually changing conception of childhood.

The Lengthening of Childhood. Before the Industrial Revolution, childhood was relatively short because in a rural agricultural setting, children became economically useful and began to fulfill adult roles at young ages. On a farm, where most children grew up, a five- or six-year-old would be a productive part of the family, gathering eggs, weeding the garden, and bringing lunch to the workers in the fields. Children's economic value quickly exceeded their cost. Higgeson wrote in his 1629 *New England's Plantation* that "little children here by setting of corne may earne much more than their own maintenance."[25] Bossard and Boll note that "children, little children, worked hard. But adults worked hard too. Hard work was a colonial necessity for both. The struggle for existence in the New World was a stern reality."[26] Children who did not grow up on farms were often apprenticed at an early age, and thus they became productive and assumed adult functions. Childhood as a lengthy period of immaturity and dependence before the assumption of adult responsibilities, which is how we think of it today, did not exist until well into the nineteenth century.

The Breakdown of the Ability of the Extended Family and the Church to Manage Child Dependency. Before the Industrial Revolution, which in the United States really took hold during the mid-nineteenth century, family and child problems were more or less adequately dealt with by the basic social institutions of the extended family and the church. If a child were orphaned, he or she would generally be taken in either by a member of the extended family or by a church family. If a child were being neglected or treated cruelly by his or her family, informal social pressure would be exerted on the family. If parents were mentally or physically ill, the extended family, church, or community would step in to ensure that the child's care did not sink too far below an adequate level. But with the onset of heavy industrialization, the family, the church, and the community no longer were able to handle child dependency. An ever increasing number of people lived in cities far from their extended families; they were marginally involved in church, and many had little knowledge of or concern for their neighbors. The first visible symptom of the breakdown in the ability of the family and the church to handle child dependency was a vast and rapid increase in the number of homeless children. Fry notes that

> the numbers were *immense*. At a time when New York City's population was around five hundred thousand, the police estimated that there were ten thousand homeless children wandering about. Later, after close observation [social workers] came to the conclusion that the number ran as high as thirty thousand.

This large number of homeless children was, of course, cause for concern. Fry continues:

> Ragged, verminous, barefoot, the vagrant children slept where they could: in doorways, under stairways, in privies, on hay barges, in discarded packing boxes, and on piles of rubbish in alleys and littered back yards. The older boys often became members of street gangs who terrified respectable citizens when they weren't bashing one another's heads in; many of the girls were accomplished streetwalkers by the time they were twelve or thirteen years old.[27]

In the latter half of the nineteenth century, social services rapidly evolved to deal with the massive problem of homeless children. Part of the reason for the development of services was, of course, humanitarian concern for the well-being of the children. Probably a greater reason was fear that these children represented a threat to social stability. One of the leading child welfare figures of the time, Charles Loring Brace, referred to homeless children as the "dangerous classes" and described his efforts to remove the children from the city and place them in rural foster homes as a "moral and physical disinfectant."[28]

The Development of a Changed Conception of Children and Childhood. Before the nineteenth century, children were viewed, at best, as miniature adults; more likely, they were thought of as products of original sin, possessed of evil impulses, who would run wild if not strictly controlled.[29] Childhood was seen by adults as an inconvenient period that people had to get through before they began the real business of living as adults. Children were not thought to have special needs or to require any special care. As a result of this perception, children were generally treated poorly. DeMause found in his research on the history of childhood that

> A child's life prior to modern times was uniformly bleak. Virtually every childrearing tract from antiquity to the modern century recommended the beating of children. We found no examples from this period in which a child wasn't beaten, and hundreds of instances of not only beating, but battering, beginning in infancy.[30]

Williams notes:

> Since time immemorial children have been treated with incredible cruelty. . . . Children have been tortured, burned, worked to death, terrorized, and flogged daily in order to "discipline" them, dipped in icewater and rolled in the snow in order to "harden" them, and buried alive with their dead parents.[31]

Few people felt that children needed protection or that they had any right to protection. Children were considered to be the property of their fathers. In Roman law, the power of a father over his children was absolute—he could kill them, sell them, or offer them as sacrifices if he so chose. English common law progressed a little from this, setting forth the duties of parents to support and educate their children. However, common law recognized these duties as "imperfect," which means they were considered to be unenforceable.

In nineteenth-century America, a marked change in attitude toward children began, which evolved into a conception of children as beings who had unique needs and the right to have these needs fulfilled to a reasonable extent. Viviana Zelizer documents in her book *Pricing the Priceless Child* how during the nineteenth century the concept of the "useful" child who made a valuable contribution to the family economy gradually evolved into the "useless" child of the twentieth century: the child who is economically worthless, in fact very costly, to the family but is considered to be emotionally priceless. The reasons for this transformation were many, including the decline in useful tasks that could be performed by children in a maturing industrial economy, the decline of the birth and death rates, and the rise of the compassionate family.[32] The changing view of children, combined with the enlightened view of jurists that parental rights result from the carrying out of parents' duties to their children, created an atmosphere in which laws and programs to protect children were possible.[33]

These factors converged and interacted during the nineteenth century to create a need and demand for child welfare services. Industrialization contributed to a lengthening of childhood by greatly postponing the age at which a person became economically useful; the combination of industrialization and urbanization led to such a number of homeless children that they were perceived as threats to social stability; and people began to view children as beings with innate value and unique needs, and with certain rights to have these needs fulfilled.

The Development of Child Welfare Services

There were a few child welfare facilities in the United States before the nineteenth century, notably a home for girls established in New Orleans by the Ursuline Sisters in 1729; the Bethesda House for Boys, founded near Savannah, Georgia, in 1740; and the Charleston Orphan House, established in 1790.[34] However, services did not develop to any great extent until well into the 1800s. Most children who could not be cared for by their parents (dependent children) during the colonial years and early years of the republic were either placed in private families and put to work or bound out as apprentices.[35]

The Development of Children's Homes. As the apprenticeship system declined and the number of dependent children increased during the early nineteenth century, the first response was to treat dependent children in the same manner as other dependent people: to place them in county poorhouses. A report submitted to the Senate and Assembly of New York in 1823 found 2,604 children living in poorhouses in that state.[36] There children grew up in the company of elderly, alcoholic, sick, insane, and feebleminded people. A visiting committee of the New York State Charities Aid Association described the plight of children in the Westchester County poorhouse in 1873 as follows:

> The children, about sixty in number, are in the care of an old pauper woman, whose daughter and whose daughter's child, both born in the poorhouse, make her one of three generations of paupers. The daughter assists in the care of the children. She has a contagious disease of the eyes, which is, apparently, communicated to them. The children are neither properly clothed nor fed; but saddest of all is to see the stolid look gradually stealing over the faces of these little ones, as all the joy of their lives is starved out of them.[37]

With conditions such as these, it is not surprising that a call for reform began. The Charities Aid Association report continues: "to think what these children must grow up to, what they must become, if they are not soon removed from this atmosphere of vice. . . . Alas! We know only too well what becomes of children who live and grow up in the poorhouse."[38] The people of New York State felt so strongly about this problem that in 1875 an Act to Provide for the Better Care of Pauper and Destitute Children was passed. This act made it unlawful for any child over three and under sixteen years of age to be committed to a county poorhouse "unless such child be an unteachable idiot, an epileptic or paralytic, or . . . otherwise defective, diseased, or deformed, so as to render it unfit for family care."[39]

The obvious shortcomings of the poorhouse as a solution to the problem of dependent children resulted in the development of specialized children's institutions. In

1800 there were 3 children's institutions, by 1851 there were 77, and by 1860 there were 124.[40] Although the children's homes were a great improvement over county poorhouses, they had many shortcomings. They were large, impersonal, rigid, authoritarian, and generally antifamily. One of the leading critics of institutional care, Charles Loring Brace, felt that

> The impersonal custodial care of an institution . . . not only stunted children, it destroyed them. . . . The regimentation did little to build self-reliance, to prepare the child for practical living. . . . [I]nstitutional life, like charity handouts, perpetuated pauperism, and both were dismal failures when it came to helping people to learn to stand on their own.[41]

In addition to the charge that children's institutions were not appropriate places for rearing children, other problems quickly began to seriously erode the unquestioned acceptance they had enjoyed. One problem was that in spite of the great growth in the number of institutions, the number of dependent children was growing at a much faster pace. The overflow either ended up in county poorhouses or, more likely, became "street arabs" living on their own. Another problem resulted from the fact that institutions were designed to take care of children for a relatively short period of time "during which education and reeducation for orderly living were provided. Having satisfactorily completed this period of rehabilitation, the male child was placed out by the institution as an apprentice in a particular trade or occupation; the female child was indentured as a domestic servant."[42] But the spread of compulsory public education and the decline of the apprentice system greatly lengthened the period of time dependent children needed care. This further increased the pressure on already overcrowded institutions because as children stayed longer, fewer children could be cared for.

The Idea of Foster Family Care. The problems of children's institutions and their inability to meet the challenge of caring for dependent children led to the notion of placing children with private families to be cared for as a member of the family. Although probably not the originator of the concept, the first person to put it into practice effectively was the Reverend Charles Loring Brace, who founded the New York Children's Aid Society in 1853. Brace's basic idea was to take homeless children from the streets of New York—where they had few options other than begging, crime, and vice, and therefore were a serious social problem—and transport them to rural regions of the country to be placed with farm families. There they would be an asset because even small children are useful on a farm. Brace and his associates advertised their plan and found the response to be immediate and astounding. He later recalled,

> Most touching of all was the crowd of little ones who immediately found their way to the office. Ragged young girls who had nowhere to lay their heads; children driven from drunkards' homes; orphans who slept where they could find a box or a stairway; boys cast out by stepmothers or stepfathers; newsboys whose incessant answer to our question, "Where do you live?" rang in our ears—"Don't live nowhere!". . . All this motley throng of infantile misery and childish guilt passed through our doors, telling their simple stories of suffering and loneliness and temptation.[43]

The technique of the Children's Aid Society was to gather together homeless children in shelters in New York City and, when a large enough group was gathered, to send them by train to towns in the west. Agents of the society would precede the train into each town, organize a local placement committee of prominent citizens, and advertise the location and the date the children would be available for placement. When the day arrived, local families would inspect the children, and families who were deemed suitable by both the society's agent and the local committee could select one or more children. The prospective parents promised to take good care of the child and to provide him or her with a "Christian home" and an education. No money was exchanged. Figure 10.3 recreates an article from the *Jefferson County Tribune* (Missouri) dated January 13, 1911, reporting the arrival of a shipment of children sent by the New York Children's Aid Society.

In terms of numbers alone, the Children's Aid Society was a tremendous success. By 1873 the society was placing more than 3,000 children a year. Its peak year was 1875, when a total of 4,026 children were placed. In terms of policies and techniques, however, the society was the object of some well-deserved criticism. A major concern was that if a child had living parents, the society made no attempt to work with them so that the child could return home. The society worked from the assumption that parents who were unable to care for their children were somehow morally inadequate, and it saw its role as rescuing the child from them. Another criticism was raised by Catholics, who felt that the Children's Aid Society, founded and run by Protestants, was snatching Catholic children off the streets and sending them west to be reared as Protestants.[44] Also, many of the states receiving children soon lost their enthusiasm for the society's work. Many of the children—one study estimated nearly 60 percent—became sources of trouble and public expenditure when their placements failed to work.[45] Finally, the most serious criticism was the lack of study, the generally casual nature of the placement process, and the almost total absence of follow-up supervision after a placement was made. One Catholic organization in New York City, the Sisters of Charity, developed a preplacement procedure to obviate the public selection process described in Figure 10.3 (see Figure 10.4).

FIGURE 10.3 | **The *Jefferson County Tribune,* January 13, 1911**

FOURTEEN LITTLE FOLKS from the orphanages of New York city arrived at Oskaloosa Thursday and will be placed in homes in and around Oskaloosa. The children are in charge of Rev. J. W. Swan of Clinton, Mo. state agent for the society for Missouri, and Miss Hill and Miss Peterson of New York. The meeting will be held at the opera house at 11 o'clock this morning. In the party are 5 girls and 9 boys, ranging in age from 2 to 13 years. They are well behaved and look very clean and very decent. Adoption is not demanded. They are placed in homes under contract and are visited twice in the first year and once each year thereafter, the party receiving them being required to make annual report. Should the child prove unsatisfactory it will be taken back by the society. "We only have about 10 percent returned to the society." said Rev. Swan. "Eighty-seven per cent of the children we place do well and grow up to be useful men and women. Most of these children are of German descent, but all are American born. We have one Dutchman with us. He is Sammy, 5 years old, and speaks German very fluently." The agents of the society will be at Oskaloosa a week and after the children are placed they will visit them in the homes they go to. If there is any chance that the person taking a child is not satisfied, it will be removed at that time, as the society desires that the person taking the child have a few days to decide the matter finally.

FIGURE 10.4 **Notice of Arrival and Receipt Forms Used by the Sisters of Charity**

SISTERS OF CHARITY
No. 175 East 68th Street,
New York City.

NOTICE OF ARRIVAL

No. 26

Mr. John Doe

Anytown

Any State

We take pleasure in notifying you that the little girl which you so kindly ordered will arrive at Anytown on Thurs. January 30 on train due to arrive at 5.15 A.M., and ask that you kindly be at Railway Station to receive child, 30 minutes before train is due, and avoid any possibility of missing connection, as train will not wait should you not be there.

The name of child, date of birth, and name and address of party to whom child is assigned will be found sewn in the Coat of boy and in the hem of Dress of girl.

This receipt must be signed in ink by both husband and wife, and is to be given up in exchange for child who will have corresponding numbers.

Yours very truly,
SISTERS OF CHARITY.

RECEIPT FOR CHILD

We beg to acknowledge receipt of the little orphan as numbered above and promise faithfully to raise said child in the Roman Catholic faith and to send h___ to school and give h___ all the advantages that we would give to a child of our own, and report to Sisters of Charity as to health and general condition when requested, notifying them of any change in address.

Signature of Husband

___

Signature of Wife

___

Street Address

___

Date Town State

___

Although the Children's Aid Society's program had many flaws, the basic idea of placing dependent children in a family setting caught on and had a tremendous impact on child welfare practice. Toward the end of the nineteenth century, members of the newly emerging social work profession, notably John Finley of the New York State Charities Aid Association, Charles Birtwell of the Boston Children's Aid Society, and Homer Folks of the Children's Aid Society of Pennsylvania, began to develop systematic and sound administrative procedures for child placement. These procedures included placement of the child in his home community, if possible; thorough study of the child and the prospective foster home; some financial support for the child; and careful supervision of the placement. With these new procedures, foster care for children spread rapidly. By the turn of the century, foster care had replaced institutional placement in a number of cities. In 1909 the report of the first White House Conference on Children gave support to the foster care movement with the recommendation that "it is desirable that [children] should be cared for in families whenever practicable. The carefully selected foster home is for the normal child the best substitute for the natural home."[46] The spread of foster care has continued until the present time, when placement in an institution is considered appropriate only for special needs children.

The Development of Protective Services. At the same time nineteenth-century America was wrestling with the problem of what to do with the children left homeless in the wake of industrialization, another child welfare problem was emerging—the abuse and neglect of children. Interestingly, the awareness and concern regarding this problem was slightly preceded by concern with the abuse and neglect of animals. In 1866, Henry Bergh founded the Society for the Prevention of Cruelty to Animals (SPCA). He quickly succeeded in getting laws passed prohibiting neglect and abuse of animals and empowering the society's agents to actually make arrests and issue subpoenas.

It was to Bergh and his society that a charity worker turned with her concern about the treatment of Mary Ellen Wilson, an eight-year-old girl who was being abused and neglected by her stepparents.[47] Bergh directed his attorney, Elbridge T. Gerry, to seek custody of the child and prosecution of the stepparents. Gerry did this and, amidst much publicity, was successful. Media coverage of the Mary Ellen Wilson case caused a flood of public opinion resulting in the passage in New York in 1875 of "an Act of the incorporation of societies for the prevention of the cruelty to children."[48] Like agents of the SPCA, agents of these new societies were empowered to "prefer a complaint before any court or magistrate having jurisdiction for the violation of any law relating to or affecting children. . . ." In 1877 the American Humane Association was incorporated. By 1900 its membership was composed of 150 anticruelty or humane societies throughout the country, most dealing with both child and animal protection, but about 20 restricting their activities to protection of children only.[49]

The societies for the prevention of cruelty to children viewed themselves as child rescue agencies. Like law enforcement agencies, which for all practical purposes they were, the societies investigated cases of abuse, neglect, and exploitation. If a complaint were substantiated, they would initiate criminal charges against the perpetrators and file for custody of the child. The 31st Annual Report (1907) of the American Humane

Association stated that the societies were never intended to reform children or families; they were

> a hand affixed to the arm of the law by which the body politic reaches out and enforces the law. The arm of the law seizes the child when it is in an atmosphere of impurity, or in the care of those who are not fit to be entrusted with it, wrenches the child out of these surroundings, brings it to the court, and submits it to the decision of the court.[50]

Once they had gained custody of the child, agents would place the child in a home or institution and close the case. Only in cases of lost or kidnapped children did the society ever consider returning them to their parents.

Thus, by the turn of the century, the seeds of our current child welfare system had been planted. The beginning of our current foster home system was in place in the form of state children's aid associations, and the current protective service system was beginning in the local societies for the prevention of cruelty to children. The final step in putting the current system in place was to merge the two elements and put the programs under public auspices. In 1914 the secretary of the Pennsylvania SPCC, addressing a conference of the American Humane Association, said:

> This thing we are doing is, after all, the job of the public authorities. The public ought to protect all citizens, including the children, from cruelty and improper care. As speedily as conditions admit, we should turn over to the public the things we are at present doing.[51]

C. C. Carstens, director of the Child Welfare League of America, found both developments well under way when he addressed the National Conference on Social Work in 1924. He observed that in many areas of the country, "the children's protective and children's aid functions are being combined under one society," and that in some areas "public departments have been given the power and to some extent the equipment to take over the whole of the children's protective service."[52] The government on all levels was showing an increasing willingness to become involved in providing social welfare services, particularly those involving children. The 1909 White House Conference resulted in the establishment in 1912 of the U.S. Children's Bureau located in the Department of Commerce and Labor. The bureau was charged with investigating and reporting on "all matters pertaining to the welfare of children and child life among all classes of our people."[53] In 1918 the Infancy and Maternity Bill was passed, setting up infant and maternal health centers administered by state health departments. In 1935 child welfare services became a predominantly public function with passage of the Social Security Act, which, under Title V (later under Title IV), authorized the Children's Bureau to fund and assist states in providing child welfare services for dependent and neglected children.

The Rediscovery of Child Abuse and Neglect. The basic structure of the child protective services system was in place with the passage and implementation of Title V of the Social Security Act of 1935. Following this landmark legislation, however, there was a period of nearly three decades of apathy regarding child welfare. Although child protective services were officially a responsibility of government, the services were spotty and poorly funded. Three states had no child protective services at all. In the states that did have services, an American Humane Association survey found that "much of what was reported as child protective services was in reality nonspecific child welfare services or nonspecific family services in the context of a financial assistance setting."[54] In addition, the survey found that services provided by private agencies had undergone a long-term decline. But in the late 1950s and early 1960s, the problem of child maltreatment was rediscovered and greatly increased resources were directed toward its resolution.

Perhaps the major reason for the rediscovery of child maltreatment was the belated recognition of the problem by the medical profession. In the late 1940s and early 1950s, radiologists began to recognize injuries that we now know generally to result from abuse and neglect, but that they tended to view as accidental. In 1960 a social worker at Children's Hospital in Pittsburgh published an article regarding the resistance of physicians to diagnosing child abuse; the article attributed this resistance to both a repugnance at the problem and a difficulty in assuming an objective attitude with abusive parents.[55] Kempe, the physician instrumental in overcoming this resistance, recalls, "When I saw child abuse between 1956 and 1958 in Denver, our housestaff was unwilling to make this diagnosis [child abuse]. Initially I felt intellectual dismay at diagnoses such as 'obscure bruising,' 'osteogenesis imperfecta tarda,' 'spontaneous subdural hematoma.'"[56]

In 1960, Kempe used his prerogative as program committee chair of the American Academy of Pediatrics to plan a plenary session on child abuse. The rest of the committee agreed, provided he could come up with a catchy title for the session. The title Kempe coined was "The Battered Child Syndrome." Shortly after the meeting, Kempe, with the assistance of a psychiatrist and a radiologist, published an article with the same title in the *Journal of the American Medical Association.* As Williams notes, "The speed of public and professional response, enhanced by media coverage, was incredible."[57] In 1962 the U.S. Children's Bureau held a conference to draft model child welfare legislation. That same year the Social Security Act was amended to require all states to develop a plan to provide child protective services in every political subdivision. In 1963 eighteen bills were introduced in Congress dealing with child abuse, and eleven of them passed. By 1967 all states had passed laws requiring professionals to report child abuse. Also in 1967, Title XX of the Social Security Act was passed. Part of this act made protective services mandatory for all states and provided a large amount of federal money to pay for these services. In 1972 the National Center for the Prevention and Treatment of Child Abuse and Neglect was established with the help of federal funds. This center publishes a newsletter, engages in research on child protection, and provides training for professionals concerned with child maltreatment. In 1974 the Federal Child Abuse Prevention and Treatment Act was passed. This act provides direct assistance to the states to help them develop child neglect and abuse programs; it also provides support for research, mainly through the establishment of the National Center for Child Abuse and Neglect within the Children's Bureau. The center supports research and acts as a clearinghouse for information on public and private programs in the area of child protection. Congress authorized $15 million to finance implementation of the act, and this was later increased to $22 million. Finally, in 1980 the Adoption Assistance and Child Welfare Act was passed. This act is discussed later in the section on permanency planning.

Current Issues and Trends

The rediscovery of child abuse and neglect by first the medical profession and then the general public led to an explosive growth in the size of the child protective service system and in the number of children in foster care. In recent years, social workers and the courts, alarmed at the immense number of children in out-of-home placements, have been taking a careful look at our approach to the problem of children in need of protection and have been making some fundamental changes in the way we respond to the problem. As a result, there have been three significant developments: an emphasis on permanency planning, an emphasis on family-based services, and a tendency by the courts to order states to upgrade services to children in need of protection.

Emphasis on Permanency Planning

The roots of child protective services are in the societies for the prevention of cruelty to children, which engaged in "child rescue" work. They viewed their role as removing the child from a bad environment, going to court to gain custody and prosecute the parent, finding a new living situation for the child, and then moving on to another child in need of rescue. They did not view their role as working with either the child's family of origin or the child after placement. In the 1920s, as child protective services became a part of the profession of social work, people in the field began to question the wisdom of this approach, which wrote off a child's family and consigned the child to a life in limbo. De Francis notes that "they began to question this approach in terms of asking, 'Is it truly beneficial to the child to rescue the child from a bad home? Would it not make better sense if we provided services so that we made responsible parents out of irresponsible people?' "[58]

This approach of keeping the family together if possible, and working to return the child quickly if not, has become the guiding philosophical principle of child protective services. The current emphasis on permanency planning began in 1959 with a study by Henry Maas and Richard Engler entitled *Children in Need of Parents.* This study, still considered a landmark in the field, looked at foster care in nine representative communities. The authors found that there were about 260,000 children in foster care in the United States at the time of the study. They estimated that in no more than 25 percent of the cases was it probable that the child would return to his or her own home. Further, the researchers found regular parent–child contact in fewer than half the cases. They concluded "that there are roughly 168,000 children today who are in danger of staying in foster care throughout their childhood years."[59] Thus, far from being a temporary haven for children while their family problems were being corrected, foster care was turning into a permanent arrangement for a huge number of children. Even worse, because the placement was considered temporary, no long-term plans were made to (1) return the children to their own homes, (2) legally free them for adoption, or (3) define their foster home as permanent so they could develop a permanent bond with their foster families. Because of this lack of planning, many of these children would grow up, not in one foster home, but in a series of homes.

Concern about children "adrift" in foster care, stimulated by Maas and Engler's study and by other more recent works—notably *Beyond the Best Interests of the Child* by Goldstein, Freud, and Solnit—has led to the development of one of the guiding principles of child protective services: permanency planning.[60] According to Maluccio and Fein,

> As a formal movement, permanency planning emerged in the 1970s as an antidote to long-standing abuses in the child welfare system, especially the inappropriate removal of children from their homes and the recurring drift of children in foster care. Its philosophical and programmatic emphasis was on the primacy of the family as the preferred environment for child rearing. Permanency planning was then extensively promoted through the landmark, federally funded "Oregon Project," which demonstrated that children who had been adrift in long-term care could be returned to their biological families or placed in adoption through intensive agency services emphasizing aggressive planning and casework techniques.[61]

Meezan enunciates seven principles that must be followed for permanency planning to fulfill its promise:

1. There must be early identification of cases in which family dysfunction can lead to the placement of the child.
2. There must, whenever possible, be work with parents and children in their own homes to prevent entry into the placement system.
3. Removal of a child from home must be based on specific guidelines and should occur only after it has been determined that the parents, with agency supports, cannot remediate the situation with the child in the home.
4. Before or shortly after the removal of the child from a home, there must be an examination of the various placement alternatives, and the child must be placed in the least detrimental alternative available.
5. There must be established for children and their families a time-limited casework plan designed to achieve, as soon as possible, an appropriate permanent placement. Appropriate services must be provided to establish and carry out this plan.
6. There must be established a consistent set of guidelines regarding the termination of parental rights that can be implemented if children cannot return to their homes.
7. There must be sufficient resources available for the child who cannot return home to ensure that a permanent substitute home can be arranged.[62]

A series of federally funded demonstration projects in the 1970s experimented with methods of implementing permanency planning. The cumulative effect was to reduce the number of children in foster care dramatically—from 520,000 in 1977 to 275,000 in 1984.[63] After 1984, however, numerous factors in the social environment caused this trend to reverse. Among these factors were the crack cocaine epidemic, economic problems leading to increased poverty and unemployment, AIDS, and a sharp rise in births to single mothers, particularly teenagers. By 2000 the number of children in out-of-home care had increased to 547,415 (see Figure 10.5).

Increased knowledge regarding problems in the foster care system and the development of the principles of permanency planning led to the passage of Public Law 96-272, the Adoption Assistance and Child Welfare Act of 1980. This act directs federal fiscal incentives toward permanency planning objectives—namely, the development of preventive and reunification services and adoption subsidies. In order for states to be eligible for increased federal funds, they must implement a service program designed either to reunite children with their families or to provide a permanent substitute home.

FIGURE 10.5 **Children in Out-of-Home Care, 1986–2000**

Source: Adapted from data in the CWLA National Data Analysis System, online at http://ndas.cwla.org.

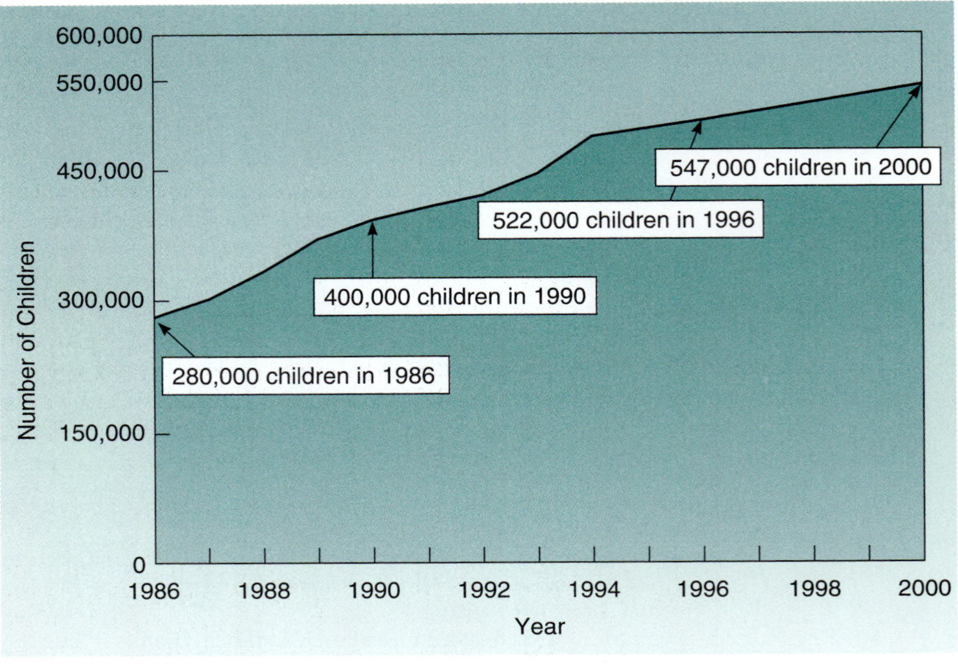

They are required to take steps, such as the establishment of foster placement review committees and procedures for regular case review, to ensure that children enter foster care only when necessary, that they are placed appropriately, and that they are returned home or else are moved on to permanent families in a timely fashion. The act also creates fiscal incentives for states to seek adoptive homes for hard-to-place children, including children who are disabled, older, or minority group members.[64]

Meezan has analyzed the child protective services system in the United States in relation to the principles of permanency planning. He concludes that the system falls short in a number of ways but that, because permanency planning is relatively new, the system should be viewed as being in transition. He finds that the system performs well for most children and that "it is this record of achievement that gives us confidence that current deficiencies can be corrected."[65]

Unfortunately, the funds promised by P.L. 96-272 never materialized.[66] There were widespread service cuts during the Reagan administration, and no support has been generated for further demonstration projects. The number of children in foster care has climbed again to even higher levels than before.

Emphasis on Family Preservation

The massive increase in the number of children in foster care that began to accelerate in the early 1980s led policymakers to look for ways of reversing the trend. One of the major methods social workers have adopted is what is generally referred to as family preservation services. This approach is based on the belief that in many cases where out-of-home placement appears to be imminent, it is possible to prevent placement by the provision of intense services delivered in the child's home over a brief, time-limited period. Whittaker lists the seminal ideas of family preservation as including

- The idea of the family as the ideal developmental context for the child
- The notion of services as first and foremost family supportive and family strengthening
- A primary focus on meeting basic developmental needs of children in culturally acceptable ways, as opposed to identifying and treating child/family psychopathology
- More focus on what might be termed an ecological perspective—looking at the effects of both proximate and distal environments on child outcomes—and moving from changing children and families from the "inside out" to the "outside in" (e.g., by working to create more supportive environments as well as by improving individual coping skills)[67]

Family preservation services begin, as do most child welfare interventions, when a child is referred to an agency as being in danger of serious harm. A social worker investigates the complaint and, if the complaint is confirmed, decides if the family is a good candidate for family preservation services. For the family to be considered an appropriate case for family preservation services, the child must be at risk of placement, but the social worker must be convinced that the child can remain safely in his or her own home if intensive services are provided. Depending on the model of family preservation being

Family preservation services attempt to build on family strengths without removing the children from the home.

applied, the family is given services for periods ranging from four to six weeks in the most intensive models, to three to six months in the less intensive models. The social workers providing services have small caseloads and work with each family for many hours each week, sometimes twenty or more. After provision of the brief, intensive services, the agency withdraws to a supervisory role and leaves the family to function—presumably with a greatly improved level of child care and problem-solving capacity.

Family preservation has grown in popularity to the degree that it can now be said to be the policy of choice for dealing with child abuse and neglect. Some form of family preservation service is now in place in every state in the union. The services are provided by both public and private agencies, generally in some form of partnership. The approach is specified in laws at both the federal and state level and in the policies of public and private agencies.

Initial evaluations of family preservation services were glowing in their praise and led to near universal acclaim of this method as the key to dealing with child welfare. More recent (and better-designed) studies have not been so positive; these, combined with powerful anecdotal accounts of child deaths and injuries during provision of family preservation services, have prompted some serious reevaluation. The most significant study to date was conducted in Illinois by the University of Chicago's Chapin Hall Center for Children, under contract with that state's Department of Children and Family Services. This study ran for three years and collected data on several levels. The conclusion of this study was that the family preservation program in Illinois, called Families First, had no effect on either the frequency or the duration of placements.[68] Data from studies such as this, combined with his experience on child death review teams, have led influential family violence expert, and dean of the University of Pennsylvania School of Social Work, Richard Gelles to call for a return to a child protection rather than a family preservation approach to child welfare. Gelles writes:

> Children must come first in social policies, and in allocation of social resources, children must come first in the words and deeds of the agencies that are entrusted with protecting them. It is time to move beyond the lip service paid to children and to develop a social structure, from top to bottom, that guarantees their safety, both by supporting families so that abuse will not occur in the first place and by absolutely guaranteeing the future safety and developmental integrity of children who have been abused and neglected.[69]

An additional criticism of family preservation programs is that they are, in theory, to provide "concrete" services—financial assistance, food, shelter, child care, respite—as well as counseling. But in practice they do little of this. This is important because, as we have noted, some analysts believe that one of the principal causes of family crisis is not psychopathology but the inability to deal with extreme poverty.[70]

Traditional foster care has proved to be beneficial in terms of physical and emotional health and academic performance for the majority of children involved. It compares favorably in some studies with family preservation.[71] These comparisons are, of course, with other children at risk for out-of-home placement. When compared with all children, those in foster care exhibit significantly greater problems in functioning and development.[72] In practice, no single solution can be expected to work for all cases of at-risk children. A range of service options, including family preservation, foster care, and even residential programs, offers the best hope of dealing with this problem.

Reaction to Family Preservation

In 1997 Congress passed the Adoption and Safe Families Act, which has been viewed by some as representing a shift in federal policy away from family preservation and toward child-centered policy. The main aspect of the act that leads to this belief is the act's clarification of the requirement that agencies must demonstrate that they have made "reasonable efforts" to preserve a family before parental rights are terminated. Under this new law, reasonable efforts are not required when the court has found that:

- The parent has subjected the child to "aggravated circumstances" as defined in state law (including but not limited to abandonment, torture, chronic abuse, and sexual abuse).
- The parent has committed murder or voluntary manslaughter or aided or abetted, attempted, conspired, or solicited to commit such a murder or manslaughter of another child of the parent.
- The parent has committed a felony assault that results in serious bodily injury to the child or another one of the children.
- The parental rights of the parent to a sibling have been involuntarily terminated.

In these specified cases, states are not required to make reasonable efforts to preserve or to reunify the family. They are required to hold a permanency hearing within thirty days and to make reasonable efforts to place the child for adoption with a legal guardian or in another permanent placement.

The 1997 act is not as anti–family preservation as family preservation advocates initially feared. Although agencies are relieved of the requirement to make family preservation efforts in these specified instances, they continue to be required to make reasonable efforts to preserve and reunify families in all other cases. More important, the new law specifically continues and expands the Family Preservation and Support Services Program, renaming it the Promoting Safe and Stable Families Program. Funding levels for the program were increased to $275 million in 1999, $295 million in 2000, and $305 million in 2001. The president's 2004 budget request includes $505 million for this program.

Class Action Lawsuits on Behalf of Children in Foster Care

There is an additional reason why many states are embracing the concept of family preservation services, and it is related to the final trend in child welfare services. Several states have faced class action lawsuits on behalf of children in the foster care system: lawsuits demanding that the states fully fund and implement the provisions of Public Law 96-272. Public Law 96-272, discussed earlier, was intended to be a "major restructuring of Social Security Act programs for the care of children who must be removed from their own homes . . . to lessen the emphasis on foster care placement and to encourage greater efforts to find permanent homes for children either by making it possible for them to return to their own families or by placing them in adoptive homes."[73] Unfortunately, the experience in the 1980s was characterized by a huge increase in child welfare caseloads, coupled with a decrease in budget and staff in most agencies. For example, in Kansas, a fairly typical state:

- Children and youth in SRS (the agency responsible for child welfare) custody rose 18 percent in the 1980s—and 28 percent between 1985 and 1991.
- Child abuse and neglect reports rose from 17,500 in 1980 to 23,400 in 1990.
- The number of social service field staff decreased by 24 percent during the 1980s.[74]

As a result, services to children in foster care actually deteriorated during the 1980s.

In response to the problem of the foster care system being unable to meet the spirit or letter of the law as written in P.L. 96-272, in the late 1970s the American Civil Liberties Union (ACLU) began the Children's Rights Project that has now evolved into an independent organization called Children's Rights. In Missouri in 1983, in the case of *G.L. v. Zumwalt,* the ACLU was able for the first time to get children in foster care recognized as a class and to get the court to order relief for the entire class. Since that time, the ACLU has successfully pursued cases in Kansas, Connecticut, Washington, D.C., Pennsylvania, New Mexico, New York, Kentucky, Louisiana, Massachusetts, and other states. The project has developed an impressive body of case law that includes the following judgments:

- Foster children in state custody can now file federal lawsuits through community members acting as their "next friends," over any objections of their legal custodian, the state.
- Foster children now have the right to seek relief that entails reorganization of entire foster care systems at a city, county, or state level, and to seek this relief for all foster children through class action suits in either state or federal court.
- Foster children are now entitled to sue, for monetary damages, state officials who violate state or federal rights.
- Foster care reform can now be litigated in the federal courts, over the objections of opponents, who had claimed that foster care is exclusively a state concern to be addressed on a case-by-case basis instead of systemically.[75]

The judgments typically order state governments to upgrade the child welfare system to make it able to meet the requirements of P.L. 96-272. Orders typically require the states to greatly increase the number of social workers in the child welfare system, hire more professionally trained (both BSW- and MSW-level) social workers and supervisors, improve in-house staff training, decrease caseloads by as much as two-thirds, increase training of foster parents, provide special therapeutic foster homes for seriously disturbed children, and develop permanent placement plans for children within six months of their entry into the system.

The Children's Rights Project, as well as efforts by other interested parties that have filed suit in other states, is drastically altering the child welfare system. Since 1995, Children's Rights has filed eighty-two lawsuits against eleven states and the District of Columbia demanding better protection of children and higher standards for foster care. States are no longer able to excuse poor care for foster children with the argument that they cannot afford the staff and other resources necessary to do better. The courts, using the doctrine of "the right to freedom from harm," have recognized foster children as a class with constitutional rights to quality services, and the states will have no choice but to come up with the necessary resources.[76]

Separation of Investigation from Service

In addition to increases in litigation on behalf of children, child protective workers are also faced with lawsuits by parents who feel wrongly accused. This has led to higher standards of proof of abuse and less worker discretion in decision making. Workers often feel torn between their roles as criminal investigators and their roles as helpers with families. One response to this difficulty is a proposal to divide the investigation function from the caregiving function. Police could be given the former, freeing the social worker to provide a broad range of family supports with no stigma of social control.[77]

There are several perils in this proposal. One is that this change would further the withdrawal of financial support for services in favor of investigation. It is currently easier to get money for more police officers than for more social workers. The proposal might also result in less of all kinds of services to families in crisis. Social workers, while playing an investigative and even coercive role, are also more likely than police officers to see the need for and help find services families need. Recall that 65 percent of abuse reports are not substantiated; this 65 percent would have no contact with a social worker unless referred by the police. These families are most likely in need of services other than family preservation; how likely are they to get access to those services under these circumstances?[78]

Perspectives

At first look, it is hard to imagine that there could be liberal and conservative perspectives on child maltreatment. It is true that no sane and decent person, liberal or conservative, advocates the maltreatment of children or ignores children in need of protection or assistance. However, there are still some substantial areas of disagreement. The main areas of disagreement are conceptions of which behaviors constitute appropriate discipline and which are inappropriate; theories of the causation of maltreatment; and beliefs concerning the rights and responsibilities of parents, children, and the state.

Conceptions of Appropriate Discipline

Conservative Perspective. Although conservative philosophy does not advocate abusing children, it accepts a certain level of physical discipline.[79] This acceptance is rooted in the conservative's generally pessimistic view of human nature. People are innately bad, and thus early, firm discipline is necessary for them to become productive members of society. The conservative belief in individual responsibility for behavior and in the importance of respect for authority also contributes to the belief that physical punishment is appropriate for effective child rearing. One of the most influential experts currently involved in parent training is the conservative psychologist James Dobson. Dobson has this to say about discipline:

> The issue of respect can be a useful tool in knowing when to punish and how excited one should get about a given behavior. . . . In my opinion, spankings should be reserved for the moment a child (age ten or less) expresses a defiant "I will not!" or "You shut up!" When a

> youngster tries this kind of stiff-necked rebellion, you had better take it out of him, and pain is a marvelous purifier.[80]

Dobson provides a number of biblical citations to support his belief in corporal punishment.

Liberal Perspective. Although liberals do not always condemn spanking, they are much less enthusiastic about it than conservatives. They tend to believe that human nature is innately good and that it is acceptable, and sometimes even desirable, to question authority. They also tend to believe that violence teaches violence and that physical punishment does more to make the child feel angry and resentful toward the parent than it does to make him or her a responsible citizen. The late Dr. Benjamin Spock noted that "we have all seen children who were slapped and spanked and deprived plenty, and yet remained ill-behaved."[81] Those who take a radical view believe that the social sanction of physical violence toward children, in the form of approval of spanking, is the basic underlying cause of all child abuse. Gil, for example, argues:

> Whenever corporal punishment in child-rearing is sanctioned, and even subtly encouraged by a society, incidents of serious physical abuse and injury are bound to happen, either as a result of deliberate, systematic, and conscious action on the part of perpetrators, or under conditions of loss of self-control. In either case, but especially in the latter, physical attacks on children tend to relieve tensions and frustrations experienced by the perpetrators. Clearly, then, these attacks are carried out to meet the emotional needs of the perpetrators rather than the educational needs of the victims, as is often claimed by advocates of corporal punishment.[82]

Analysis and Synthesis. In many ways the differences between the conservative and liberal perspectives on corporal punishment are not as great as they initially appear. The conservative psychologist Dobson states, "One of my greatest concerns in recommending corporal punishment (spanking) is that some parents might apply the thrashings too frequently or too severely."[83] He is adamant that teenagers should never be spanked because "teenagers desperately want to be thought of as adults, and they deeply resent being treated like children. Spanking is the ultimate insult."[84] On the other hand, the liberal pediatrician Spock wrote that there had been an overreaction against spanking, saying, "I'm not particularly advocating spanking, but I think it is less poisonous than lengthy disapproval, because it clears the air, for parent and child."[85] Even so, the main difference is clear—generally conservatives feel corporal punishment is acceptable and even desirable ("spare the rod and spoil the child") for teaching respect and maintaining discipline. Liberals, most of whom would agree with Spock and hesitate to condemn a parent for spanking, nonetheless think that corporal punishment is not the most desirable way to discipline children, even though it may occasionally be justified. Liberals feel that respect does not always mean absolute obedience and that when corporal punishment is necessary, discipline has already broken down. They advocate withdrawal of privileges, time-outs, and extra chores as more effective forms of punishment.

Two areas in which conceptions of whether corporal punishment is acceptable directly affect child protective services. The first is the definition of child abuse. If our society were to take a stand, as Sweden has, that any and all corporal punishment is wrong, the definition of abuse would be much easier. Marks of any kind on a child would constitute evidence of abuse, and the case would be "open and shut." But using the conservative idea that spanking is acceptable, as our society does, we have no clear basis for definition. Is it spanking to hit a child with your hand, but abuse to use a belt? Is it spanking to hit a child with a belt, but abuse to leave bruises? Is it spanking to leave bruises below a child's waist, but abuse to bruise above? If corporal punishment is acceptable in any form, these become questions of individual opinion. For example, one of the authors began his career as a child welfare worker in a large city that had two juvenile court judges, one liberal and one conservative. All of the child welfare workers knew that unless an abuse case was severe, they should work to get it placed on the docket of the liberal judge. The conservative judge was likely to dismiss a case with the admonition that "you can't blame a man for whipping his boy."

The second area in which conceptions of the appropriateness of corporal punishment affect child protective services is the causation of child abuse. A frequent cause of abuse is a spanking "gone wrong." A parent begins with the intention of administering a mild spanking and loses control and carries it to excess, or attempts to hit the child on the bottom and misses, hitting the child's eye or ear, resulting in far more pain and injury than was intended.

The Causation of Maltreatment

In the section on the dynamics of maltreatment, we discussed the three types, or levels, of causative factors: individual parent, family, and environmental. Conservatives and liberals differ in the amount of emphasis they place on each level.

Conservative Perspective. Conservatives, with their belief in autonomy as governing behavior, place almost total blame for child maltreatment on individual parent factors. If parents abuse or neglect their child, it is because they choose to do so. They may choose to do so because they are lazy, ill tempered, or perhaps even evil. If this is the case, then the proper societal response is to see that they are arrested, prosecuted, and punished for their unacceptable behavior. On the other hand, they may choose to maltreat (or choose not to care adequately for) their children because they are mentally ill. If this is the case, the proper societal response is to provide appropriate psychological services in an attempt to "cure" them. This perspective, which defines a social problem in terms of individual illness, is called the *medical model.* This is the model strongly advocated by the pediatricians and psychiatrists who formed the battered child team at the University of Colorado School of Medicine. They attribute child abuse to parent factors, with some contribution by child factors; and they assert that individual psychiatric treatment is the appropriate response because "it deals in the most humanitarian and constructive way we know with a tragic facet of people's lives."[86] Underlying this explanation is the conservative assumption that society is functional and that everyone has the opportunity to adequately fulfill all roles, in this case that of parent, if they work at it and, if necessary, receive help.

Liberal Perspective. Liberals as well as radicals place much greater stress on the role of environmental factors in child maltreatment. They point out that research has failed to demonstrate conclusively that psychopathology exists in a greater proportion of child protective services clients than in the general population.[87] They assert that the really important causative factors are the environmental conditions that lead to stress and frustration, such as poverty, overcrowded and dilapidated neighborhoods, large numbers of children, single-parent households, and alienating work. Also, liberals argue that regardless of how adequate individual parents are, the entire society is guilty of child maltreatment—because it does not provide adequate schools, safe neighborhoods, high-quality affordable child care, or adequate welfare support, and because it sanctions corporal punishment in schools. According to this perspective, programs to help individual parents, although necessary, treat only the symptoms, not the disease. Gil, coming from a radical perspective, says, "There simply is no way of escaping the conclusion that the complete elimination of child abuse on all levels of manifestation requires a radical transformation of the prevailing unjust, inegalitarian, irrational, competitive, alienating, and hierarchical social order into a just, egalitarian, rational, humane, and truly democratic, decentralized one."[88] Underlying the liberal view of the cause of child maltreatment is the belief that individuals are not autonomous and that society, as it is presently structured, is not functional for large numbers of people.

Analysis and Synthesis. The liberal, radical, and conservative perspectives on the causation of child maltreatment are truly a case of the blind men examining different parts of the elephant. As discussed earlier, child maltreatment is a phenomenon with several levels of causation. It is undoubtedly true, as the liberal and radical perspectives assert, that the only way to significantly reduce child maltreatment is to change the many social and economic factors that oppress and frustrate people. We know, for example, that when the unemployment rate declines, child abuse declines. As Gil notes, "If one's priority is to prevent all child abuse, one must be ready to part with its many causes, even when he is attached to some of them, such as the apparent blessings, advantages, and privileges of inequality."[89]

The conservative emphasis on the individual level of causation also has several strong points. We have generally used our criterion of pragmatism to argue for the liberal perspective, but in this case the conservative view is, perhaps, more pragmatic. When dealing with a specific case of child maltreatment, it does little good to point out that the family is the victim of environmental pressures beyond its control. What must be focused on is how the family members respond to those pressures and how they can improve their ability to cope.

Although conservatives are most comfortable emphasizing the individual causes of child maltreatment and liberals and radicals like to emphasize the environmental causes, nearly everyone will admit that the problem needs to be addressed on all levels. As social workers, many of us are expected to work on the individual level; but it is our professional responsibility also to make time to combat the environmental factors. For example, social workers responding to referrals of young children being left at home alone in a community without adequate day care are failing in their professional duties if they only help parents, on a case-by-case basis, find child care. In addition to helping individual families, they should work to have adequate, affordable, accessible day care established so parents won't have to leave their children alone in the first place.

Rights of Children, Parents, and the Government

Child rearing in our society is based on beliefs and assumptions regarding the rights and responsibilities of a triad—children, parents, and the government. These beliefs and assumptions are not the same for liberals and for conservatives.

Downs and colleagues state that "an essential question in any formulation of family social policy is the extent to which children have their own rights and interests independent of parents, with a claim to their recognition and enforcement."[90] There have been numerous formulations of children's rights over the years, such as the "Children's Charter" adopted by the 1930 White House Conference on Children and the "Children's Charter for the Seventies" presented at the White House Conference on Children in December 1970. These documents give as children's rights things such as the parents' understanding and guarding his or her personality; prenatal care for the mother; a safe, sanitary, and wholesome place to live; recognition of and help for disabling conditions; when "in conflict with society the right to be dealt with intelligently as society's charge, not society's outcast"; and an adequate standard of living. The 1970 document added as rights freedom from pollution, freedom from racism, and freedom from fear. As Downs and colleagues point out, these statements are really statements of children's "needs" as defined by current knowledge about the physical, psychological, and social development of the child, rather than "rights," which are based on a legal definition and carry a claim or an "entitlement" and are enforceable. Public education is a right because if it is denied a child, that child can force the community to provide it by court action. An adequate standard of living is a need, but it is not a right. Millions of children in our society live well below what the government defines as an adequate level (the poverty line), but they are not entitled by right to a better living standard under current law.

Parents in our society are given almost total responsibility for the care and upbringing of their children. As long as the level of child care does not sink below a minimal standard demanded by the community, parents are given a large number of rights. Among these rights are the rights of guardianship; the right to determine the "living pattern" and standards of everyday conduct; the right to select the religion (or lack of religion) of the child; and the right to determine the kind and extent of the child's education, the quality and type of health care given to the child, and the place where the child will live. If a boy's parents move him to a new city during his last year of high school, if they select an academic curriculum when both their son and the school prefer a vocational one, if they take him to the Unitarian church every Sunday when he would like to attend the Church of Christ, if they buy him slacks and oxford cloth dress shirts when he would like to wear blue jeans and T-shirts, the child and the community might object, but they would have little power to oppose the parents, because these decisions are theirs by right.

The government has the general responsibility to promote the welfare of children, and it has certain rights necessary to enable it to carry out this responsibility. The legal term for this is *parens patria,* which means that ultimately the state is the parent to all children. The state exercises its rights and responsibilities in three broad ways:

- *Regulatory powers.* For the general protection of children, the state formulates regulations that govern all persons dealing with children. Examples are compulsory

What **Americans** Believe

The General Social Survey includes two questions, one with seven parts, which are of relevance to child welfare. The first question, relating to our discussion of corporal punishment, is "Do you strongly agree, agree, disagree, or strongly disagree that it is sometimes necessary to discipline a child with a good, hard spanking?" The second question relates to our discussion of the right and desirability of government to intervene in family life. This question is worded: "Sometimes public authorities intervene with parents in raising their children. Please indicate in each of the following cases how far you think authorities should go in dealing with a *10-year-old child* and his or her parents." Respondents were asked to indicate in each situation if the authorities should take no action, give warning or counseling, or take the child from its parents. The cases were:

- The child uses drugs and the parents don't do anything about it.
- The child frequently skips school and the parents don't do anything about it.
- The parents regularly let the child stay out late at night without knowing where the child is.
- The parents fail to provide the child with proper food and clothing.
- The parents regularly beat the child.
- The parents refuse essential medical treatment for the child because of their religious beliefs.
- The parents allow the child to watch violent or pornographic films.

The responses to the question relating to the desirability of corporal punishment as a child-rearing technique are not surprising. They are cross-tabulated with political orientation in Table 10.2. As can be seen by inspecting this table, liberals are less accepting of corporal punishment than are moderates and conservatives. However, these differences, although statistically

TABLE 10.2

It Is Sometimes Necessary to Discipline a Child with a Good, Hard Spanking

	Strongly Agree	Agree	Disagree	Strongly Disagree
Liberal	22.4%	44.7%	21.9%	11.0%
Moderate	28.4%	48.9%	17.1%	5.6%
Conservative	31.3%	48.4%	15.5%	4.9%
Total	27.8%	47.6%	17.9%	6.8%

school attendance laws, which require communities to provide free public education and require parents to send their children to school, and employment laws, which forbid employers to hire children below a certain age or for jobs considered harmful or dangerous. "The intent of the state's use of its regulatory authority is to represent society's interest in all children through the application of broad powers to set standards that apply to children generally, or all parents generally, or other adults acting in relation to children."[91]

significant, are not huge. About 67 percent of liberals strongly agree or agree that spanking is sometimes necessary, compared to a little over 80 percent of conservatives making these choices.

The responses to the questions regarding the appropriateness and desirability of government intervention into family life are summarized and cross-tabulated with political orientation in Table 10.3. These data are surprising in two respects. The first surprise is that there are virtually no differences in opinion between people with different political orientations. Chi-square analyses were run on all seven case situations, and the only significant difference was in the case in which the parents let the child stay out late without knowing where he or she was. This difference was barely significant at the .05 level of probability, and it was the responses of the moderates, not of the liberals and conservatives, that were significantly different. It is the authors' opinion that this is probably one of those five chances out of one hundred in which the difference was, indeed, a result of chance.

The other surprising aspect of the responses to these seven questions is the overwhelming endorsement of government intervention, and forceful intervention at that, into family life. Almost 94 percent of responses to these items felt that at least warning or counseling was justified in the case situations described. Almost 36 percent felt that actually removing the child from the parents' custody was warranted. These responses indicate that we social workers may feel that we have a good deal less public support and approval for intervention on behalf of children than is actually the case.

TABLE 10.3

How Far Should Authorities Go in Intervening in Families Where the Parents Are Not Properly Caring for Children? (Summary of Seven Opinions)

	Take No Action	Give Warning or Counseling	Take the Child from Its Parents
Liberal	7.13%	59.41%	33.46%
Moderate	6.06%	57.47%	36.47%
Conservative	6.10%	57.53%	36.36%
Total	6.34%	57.97%	35.69%

- *Power to intervene in the relationship between parent and child.* When the level of care provided a child falls below a certain level, or when a child's behavior violates the law, the state has the right to intervene to either protect or correct the child. This may, in serious cases, involve the removal of the child from the home and his or her placement in a foster home or institution.
- *Power to legislate for the development of child welfare services.* The state has the right to collect revenue by means of taxation and to spend it on any of a number of services

to benefit children. Costin and Rapp comment that the importance of this power cannot be overemphasized. "How successfully children are helped often depends upon the extent to which the statutes of a state reflect modern knowledge about children and their changing world, respect for their rights, and readiness to tax and appropriate money for professional services and facilities to meet the needs of children."[92]

Conservative Perspective. Conservatives, with their fear and disapproval of government and their belief in tradition and authority, emphasize the rights of parents and the responsibilities of parents and children, and they de-emphasize the rights and responsibilities of government. They feel that government should intervene in the relationship between parents and children only in serious cases, and that then the intervention should be subject to stringent controls. They point to examples of the danger of excessive government power in this area, such as the following story reported in *Woman's Day,* a popular large-circulation magazine.

> On May 7, 1985, Elene Humlen of Whittier, California, lost custody of her nine-year-old son, Chris, and her 16-month-old daughter when Chris went to school with a black eye received when he was struck by a tennis ball while playing near his home. Discounting the boy's explanation, school and CPS officials suspected abuse and hastily placed both Humlen children in foster homes. On July 22, after losing her job and spending $10,000 in legal fees, Humlen regained permanent custody of her children when a judge dismissed the charges. Surprising as it seems, these actions were perfectly legal. Although police must have a warrant to invade the sanctity of a home when pursuing thieves, rapists and murderers, they need only uncorroborated suspicion to come in and take a child. "When you're charged with abusing a child," says Stanley Hodge [an attorney], "everyone assumes you're guilty until you prove your innocence."[93]

Conservatives argue that excessive government power will inevitably lead to abuses such as this incident. Wald has analyzed state statutes regarding neglect and concludes that the language is so broad and vague that the statutes give almost unlimited power to state officials. He recommends greater protection of parent rights through laws that focus less on vague standards of parental behavior and more on evidence of specific harm to the child.[94]

Conservatives feel as strongly as anyone that children should be well cared for. However, they feel that the philosophical basis for this care is not the right of children to demand it, or the right of government to enforce it, but the moral duty of parents to provide it.

Liberal Perspective. Liberals are much more sympathetic to the notion of rights of children, less sympathetic to the rights of parents, and more willing to support governmental intervention. They feel that there should be no difference between needs and rights of children. They are comfortable with government's intervening in the relationship between parents and children to enforce children's rights. Downs and colleagues summarize the current position of the courts regarding the balance of rights of government, parents, and children:

> The current balance says that the state has the right and responsibility to regulate the behavior of parents regarding their children where that parental behavior causes harm or potential harm, interferes with the privacy rights of mature minors as related to medical treatments in-

cluding abortion and to promote the general welfare of its citizens. Although great deference in the responsibility of raising children remains with the parents and although children have not been granted the full, absolute protection of the Constitution granted to adults, the Court clearly acknowledges that children are citizens entitled to the protections of the Constitution in their own right, but those protections need to be tempered on the basis of developmental capacities and childhood status within the family context.[95]

Radical Perspective. Radicals are inclined to point out that "the American family is one of this country's most violent institutions."[96] The family has undergone considerable strain and distortion in recent decades. Preserving it in traditional form may perpetuate oppression of women and harm to children.

Analysis and Synthesis. Conservatives and liberals agree that children should be adequately cared for. Conservatives argue that this care is the moral duty of parents, and liberals argue that it is the right of children. The main difference between conservatives and liberals is their opinion about the right, or wisdom, of government intervention in parent–child relations when child care falls below a certain level. Conservatives fear that when government is given power to intervene, it will use this power to the maximum to snatch children from their homes and place them in foster care when there is no compelling need. The research evidence gathered on this matter indicates that this fear is unfounded. In 1972 approximately three million children received child welfare services, and only 14 percent were in foster care. In 1969, 1972, and 1975, the Child Welfare League of America conducted a census of requests for child welfare services. They found that in 26 percent of the cases, the parents themselves were requesting foster home placement, but that the agency complied with less than one-fourth of those requests. The other three-quarters were given in-home services. A survey of child abuse referrals in Wisconsin between 1969 and 1975 found that 72 percent of the children were given services in their own homes. Further, the data indicated that the percentage placed in foster care was decreasing over time. Therefore, there appears to be little justification for the fear that government will frequently overstep its bounds and remove children from their homes when removal is not justified.[97]

Social Work Roles

Child protective service is one of the most challenging and important areas of social work practice. It is also one of the largest. Data reported to the U.S. Department of Health and Human Services, adjusted for missing cases, indicates that approximately 56,200 social workers are employed by state child protective service agencies. With the recent trend toward courts' ordering states to upgrade the number and qualifications of child welfare staff, it seems probable that the number of social work positions in child welfare agencies will steadily increase.

The major reason for the importance of child protective service as an area of social work practice is that child welfare is the only institution in which social work is considered the principal profession responsible for its operation. In most other areas of practice, social workers are located in host institutions, where some other profession is central to the institution and social workers provide an ancillary service. Even financial assistance, which many people associate with social work, is actually dominated by public administration, with proportionately few social workers employed. But child welfare is clearly social work's field, and this perception is shared by the general public.

Another important attribute of child protective service is that this is the field of social work practice that enjoys the most public support. As Kadushin observes,

> Public attitudes toward a profession are shaped in part by the attitudes toward the client groups with which the profession is associated. . . . To what extent can one expect that the situation will change and the client will become a productive citizen? On both these counts, children are regarded as "acceptable" clients.[98]

A study by Carter, Fifield, and Shields found that 80 percent of 9,346 respondents would spend "however much is necessary" to help welfare children become productive adults. The respondents were also asked to rank their willingness to support seventeen different social services. Four of the top six ranked services were child welfare services: foster home care, protective services, adoption, and day care.[99] In a study of the New York State legislature's reaction to social service bills, Howe found that child welfare bills were given the highest priority. Bills concerned with child abuse, neglect, foster care, and adoption were more likely to be approved than bills concerned with the disabled, the indigent, or the aged.[100]

The majority of opportunities in child welfare are with state social service agencies. These used to be called departments of public welfare, but in recent years most states have changed the name to something that sounds more modern. Common names are department of social services, department of family and children's services, department of human resources, and department of human services. These departments will have a division called either the child welfare or the child protective services division. A smaller, but still significant, number of child welfare social workers are employed by private agencies.

Direct Services in Public Child Welfare

Child protection agencies organize their direct service staff in many different configurations depending on the size and philosophy of the agency. Regardless of organization, workers in all agencies will fill the following general roles: intake and assessment, supervision of families with children at home, family preservation services, recruitment and supervision of foster homes, and adoption services. In a small office in a rural area, one worker will often fill all of these roles. In a large urban office there may be an entire unit of six or seven social workers who perform only one role; for example, foster home recruitment.

Intake, Screening, and Assessment. The intake worker is responsible for responding to reports of child maltreatment received by the protective service agency. The worker must first screen the report to determine if it involves child maltreatment as defined by state law and agency policy. If a report is "screened in," the worker makes contact with the family involved and with all parties who are involved and/or have pertinent information. The agency then decides to accept or not accept the case for services. If the case is accepted for services, the assessment process begins. The purpose of the assessment process is to enable the agency to make an accurate estimate of the client's problems. The worker gathers pertinent data through interviews, previous reports, and piecing together facts to determine if the maltreatment has in fact occurred and how serious the risk is for the child for additional maltreatment.[101] This is the most important stage in the history of a case.

At the end of the intake/assessment process, the case is either closed or opened for ongoing services with the child either in his or her own home or in a foster home. In many agencies, at this point the case is transferred to another social worker for long-term services.

Supervision of Families with the Child at Home. In many cases, the assessment process will find a family in which standards of child care and discipline are below those demanded by the community, but in which the children are in no danger of serious harm. In these situations the case is opened for agency supervision for purposes of assisting the parents to improve the level of child care. If the parents realize there is a problem and are willing to work with the agency to try to solve it, no court action is necessary. If the parents are unwilling to deal with the problem voluntarily, sometimes the court will assign legal custody of the children to the agency but leave physical custody with the parents on the condition that they accept services. Social workers in this supervisory role must carefully monitor the home to be sure that child care does not further deteriorate; they must find supplemental services (such as tutoring or recreation) to compensate for deficits in the home; and they must work with the parents, often with the assistance of other professionals, such as psychologists and vocational rehabilitation counselors, to help them resolve problems and learn skills necessary for successful parenting. These services are often referred to as family support services.[102]

Family Preservation Services. The growth of family preservation services, described earlier in this chapter, has resulted in the development of a special category of social worker providing services to families with children at home. Family preservation services cases are cases in which the family situation is defined as severe and the potential risk to the children is judged to be great. Generally, these are defined as cases in which placement of the children in out-of-home care is imminent without the provision of immediate and intensive services. The family preservation social worker has a much smaller caseload than is typical of child welfare workers and provides much more intensive services. The worker will spend anywhere from five to twenty hours a week with a family over a period from four weeks to six months. The worker concentrates on strengthening the family's problem-solving capacity and also on teaching the family how to deal successfully with everyday tasks of family living and child rearing such as cleaning, shopping, paying bills, managing credit, and using effective nonviolent means of discipline and limit setting. The theory is that the intensive time-limited services will quickly strengthen the family's child-rearing capacity, increase the level of safety of the children at home, and allow the agency to withdraw to a much more limited and short-term supervisory role.

Recruitment and Supervision of Foster Homes. As the number of children requiring foster home care has increased, the number of families willing to assume the responsibilities of foster parenthood has decreased. The combination of these two trends has made effective recruitment and assessment of new foster parents, as well as support for existing ones, among the most critical roles in child protective services. It has also contributed to an emphasis on kinship care; that is, seeking out family members as foster parents before considering strangers. Agencies usually begin the recruitment process of nonkinship foster homes by working with the media to obtain newspaper publicity (classified ads and feature stories) as well as radio and television announcements; making presentations to community groups; and working with community leaders to encourage persons from groups they represent to apply. When a pool of interested persons is formed, a social worker will schedule a meeting to present information and answer questions about foster parenting. Studies of foster home recruitment show a high rate of attrition among people who express initial interest. Usually less than 10 percent of a pool of applicants actually become licensed, and rarely more than 20 percent. If a couple still expresses interest after the initial meeting, a social worker does a detailed assessment of the family. The assessment is based on objective criteria outlined in state licensing standards (for example, age and health of couple and size of home) and on socioemotional factors that are considered desirable in a foster home (for example, motivation for becoming foster parents, potential effect on natural children, and the history of the marriage and current marital interaction). The agency then decides whether to license a couple as foster parents. The critical shortage of foster parents has caused agencies to be flexible, often waiving requirements regarding mother's employment, age of foster parents, and need for religious affiliation. However, as Martin observes, "agencies still prefer what is considered a 'traditional' family—a nuclear, heterosexual couple living in fairly comfortable economic circumstances and espousing middle-class values. The greater the extent to which families deviate from this model (by being homosexual or single, for example) the more reluctant and anxious agencies are about selecting them as homes for children." Following recruitment, selection, and approval, an agreement is signed and the family is licensed.[103]

Adoption. When parents do not wish to have responsibility for their children, as in the case of many unwed mothers and in instances of desertion, or in situations so severe that there is little hope the parents will ever be able to adequately care for their children, the agency and the courts terminate parental rights and seek to create a new family for the child through adoption. This is considered to be among the most serious tasks social workers perform, largely because of the lifelong implications. Therefore, the social workers assigned to the adoption function are usually the best trained and most experienced in the agency. Important parts of the role of the adoption worker include counseling biological parents, terminating biological parents' rights, making the decision to place for adoption, preparing the child for adoption, selecting adoptive parents, handling "failed placements," and working with the courts and other agencies. In recent years the number of prospective parents wishing to adopt healthy infants has far exceeded the number of infants available. Because of this, agencies, particularly in the public sector, have begun to concentrate on placing "special needs" children; that is, those who are not easily adoptable because of age, race, disability, or medical problems.

Private Agencies

Although by far the largest number of child welfare social workers are employed in public agencies, many also work in private settings. Among the private agencies employing child welfare social workers are often church-affiliated adoption agencies; child guidance clinics; children's homes; usually therapeutic foster care agencies; children's hospitals; and day care centers. Social workers in these settings usually have graduate training and occupy therapeutic roles.

Conclusion

For many reasons, both good and bad, it can be said that child protective service is the most central area of the social work profession. It is among the largest fields of practice, it is the one area in which social work is the host profession, it has grown the most rapidly, and it enjoys the highest level of public support. Child protective service is also one of the most professionally and personally satisfying areas of social work practice. As Kadushin has written,

> The Talmud, emphasizing the importance of each individual life, says, "If during the course of your own life, you have saved one life, it is as if you have saved all mankind." Few occupations give us the opportunity of participating in the saving of a life. The everyday work of the child welfare worker is concerned with just that—reclaiming a child for life. It is to be expected that such a task would be very difficult. It is also to be expected that there are few, if any, tasks that offer the same degree of satisfaction and the same sense of accomplishment.[104]

Visit **www.researchnavigator.com** to research these important concepts from the chapter:

Child maltreatment
Child sexual abuse
Child welfare
Children AND adoption
Children's rights
Corporal punishment
Family intervention
Foster care

Web Sites on Child Welfare

Child Abuse Prevention Network <child.cornell.edu/bookmarks.html>: Under nine major headings, this site provides web addresses and descriptions for literally hundreds of sites related to child and family welfare.

Children's Defense Fund <www.childrensdefense.org/index.html>: Web site of one of the largest and most prominent child advocacy organizations in the country. Site includes information about the organization, discussions of current issues, news and reports, and other features related to a broad definition of child welfare.

Child Welfare League of America <www.cwla.org>: Web site of the oldest and largest child welfare organization in the country. Site includes a description of the organization, news and events, policy advocacy tips, current activities of CWLA, calendar of upcoming events, membership information, links to other sites, and various other useful and interesting features.

National Clearinghouse on Child Abuse and Neglect Information <www.calib.com/nccanch/index.htm>: A gold mine of child welfare information sponsored by the U.S. Department of Health and Human Services. Includes information on new programs and initiatives, publications and fact sheets, clearinghouse catalog, specialized services (information on statistics, child welfare, child abuse and neglect prevention, and state statutes), conference information, online databases and directories, and links to related sites.

National Resource Center on Child Maltreatment <www.gocwi.org/nrccm>: NRCCM provides training, technical assistance, consultation, and written materials in response to identified needs that relate to the prevention, identification, intervention, and treatment of child abuse and neglect. Web site provides a description of the center, information on upcoming conferences, newsletter, and other information related to child maltreatment.

Endnotes

1. Council on Social Work Education, "Child Welfare," in *Description of Practice: Statements in Fields of Social Work Practice* (New York: CSWE, 1959, mimeo), 5.
2. Reprinted with the permission of Macmillan Publishing Company, Inc. from *Child Welfare Services,* fourth edition, by Alfred Kadushin and Judith A. Martin. Copyright © 1987 by Macmillan Publishing Company.
3. See, for example, Martha Zazlow, Kristin Anderson Moore, Kathryn Tout, Juliet P. Scarpa, and Sharon Vandivere, "How Are Children Faring Under Welfare Reform," and Gina Adams and Monica Rohacek, "Child Care and Welfare Reform," in Alan Weil and Kenneth Finegold, *Welfare Reform: The Next Act* (Washington, D.C.: The Urban Institute Press, 2002), 79–102; 121–142.
4. Duncan Lindsey, *The Welfare of Children,* 2nd ed. (New York: Oxford University Press, 2004); see also Sheila B. Kammerman and Alfred J. Kahn, "If CPS Is Driving Child Welfare—Where Do We Go from Here?" *Public Welfare 48* (Winter 1990), 9–13.
5. Kathleen Faller and Sally Russo, "Definition and Scope of the Problem of Child Maltreatment," in Kathleen Coulborn Faller, ed., *Social Work with Abused and Neglected Children: A Manual of Interdisciplinary Practice* (New York: Free Press, 1981), 103.
6. Leroy H. Pelton, "Child Abuse and Neglect and Protective Intervention in Mercer County, New Jersey," in Leroy H. Pelton, ed., *The Social Context of Child Abuse and Neglect* (New York: Human Sciences Press, 1981), 103.
7. U.S. Department of Health and Human Services, Administration on Children, Youth and Families, *Child Maltreatment 2001* (Washington, DC: U.S. Government Printing Office, 2003, 27).
8. David Gil, *Violence against Children: Physical Abuse in the United States* (Cambridge, MA: Harvard University Press, 1970), 59.
9. Murray Straus, Richard Gelles, and Susan Steinmetz, *Behind Closed Doors: Violence in the American Family* (New York: Anchor Press, 1980), 64.
10. Brett Drake and Melissa Jonson-Reid, "Recidivism in Child Protective Services," Paper presented at the George Warren Brown School of Social Work 75th Anniversary Conference, St. Louis, MO, 7 October 2000.
11. U.S. Department of Health and Human Services, Administration on Children, Youth and Families, *Child Maltreatment 2001,* 23.
12. Gil, *Violence against Children,* 112; Barbara Vobejda, "Are There No Orphanages?" *Washington Post National Weekly Edition* (26 October 1995–1 November 1995), 32.
13. Lindsey, *The Welfare of Children,* 2nd ed., 181.
14. Leroy H. Pelton, "Child Abuse and Neglect: The Myth of Classlessness," in Pelton, *The Social Context of Child Abuse and Neglect,* 23–38; Leroy H. Pelton, *For Reasons of Poverty: A Critical Analysis of the Public Child Welfare System in the United States* (New York: Praeger, 1989), 37–42.
15. U.S. Department of Health and Human Services, Administration on Children, Youth and Families, *Child Maltreatment 1998: Reports from the States to the National Child Abuse and Neglect Data*

System (Washington, DC: U.S. Government Printing Office, 2000).

16. Pamela D. Mayhall and Katherine E. Norgard, *Child Abuse and Neglect: Sharing Responsibility* (New York: John Wiley & Sons, 1983), 101.
17. David Finkelhor, "How Widespread Is Child Sexual Abuse?" *Children Today 13* (July–August 1984), 18–20.
18. Brandt F. Steele and Carl B. Pollock, "A Psychiatric Study of Parents Who Abuse Infants and Small Children," in Roy E. Helfer and C. Henry Kempe, eds., *The Battered Child* (Chicago: University of Chicago Press, 1968), 103; C. Henry Kempe, Frederic N. Silverman, Brandt F. Steele, William Droegemueller, and Henry K. Silver, "The Battered Child Syndrome," *Journal of the American Medical Association 181* (July 1962), 17–24; Leontine Young, *Wednesday's Children: A Study of Neglect and Abuse* (New York: McGraw-Hill, 1964), 17–24. Eisenberg quoted in Helfer and Kempe, *The Battered Child,* 170.
19. This section is based on the work of Kathleen Faller and Majorie Zeifert, "Causes of Child Abuse and Neglect," in Kathleen Coulborn Faller, ed., *Social Work with Abused and Neglected Children: A Manual of Interdisciplinary Practice* (New York: The Free Press, 1981); Howard Dubowitz, Maureen Black, Raymond H. Starr, Jr., and Susan Zuravin, "A Conceptual Definition of Child Neglect," *Criminal Justice and Behavior 20* (March 1993), 8–26; James Garbarino and Kathleen Kostelny, "Child Maltreatment as a Community Problem," *Child Abuse and Neglect 16* (1992), 455–464; Child Welfare League of America, *Alcohol, Other Drugs, and Child Welfare* (Washington, D.C.: Child Welfare League of America, 2001); Susan Whitelaw Downs, Ernestine Moore, Emily Jean McFadden, Susan M. Michaud, and Lela B. Costin, *Child Welfare and Family Services: Policies and Practice,* 7th ed. (Boston: Allyn & Bacon, 2004), 79–84, 237–245.
20. Leroy H. Pelton, *For Reasons of Poverty* (New York: Praeger, 1989); Lindsey, *The Welfare of Children.*
21. Kathleen C. Faller and Marjorie Zeifert, "Causes of Child Abuse and Neglect," 49. Adapted with the permission of The Free Press, a Division of Simon & Schuster, Inc., from *Social Work with Abused and Neglected Children: A Manual of Interdisciplinary Practice,* edited by Kathleen Coulborn Faller. Copyright © 1981 by The Free Press.
22. Gil, *Violence against Children,* 135.
23. Urie Brofenbrenner, "Socialization and Social Class through Time and Space," in Eleanor E. Maccoby, Theodore M. Newcomb, and Eugene L. Hartley, eds., *Readings in Social Psychology,* 3rd ed. (New York: Holt, Rinehart & Winston, 1958), 400–425; Howard S. Erlanger, "Social Class and Corporal Punishment in Child Rearing: A Reassessment," in David Gil, ed., *Child Abuse and Violence* (New York: AMS Press, 1979), 494–515.
24. Homer Folks, *The Care of Destitute, Neglected and Delinquent Children* (New York: Macmillan, 1911), 167.
25. Higgeson, *New England's Plantation,* cited in James Bossard and Eleanor Stoker Boll, *The Sociology of Child Development* (New York: Harper & Brothers, 1960), 613.
26. Bossard and Boll, *The Sociology of Child Development,* 614.
27. Annette Riley Fry, "The Children's Migration," *American Heritage 26* (January 1974), 4–10, 79–81.
28. Walter I. Trattner, *From Poor Law to Welfare State: A History of Social Welfare in America,* 3rd ed. (New York: Free Press, 1984), 115.
29. Ross W. Beales, "In Search of the Historical Child: Miniature Adulthood and Youth in Colonial New England," *American Quarterly 27* (October 1975), 379–398.
30. Lloyd DeMause, "Our Forebears Made Childhood a Nightmare," *Psychology Today* (April 1975), 85–88.
31. Gertrude J. Williams, "Child Abuse and Neglect: Problems of Definition and Incidence," in Gertrude J. Williams and John Money, eds., *Traumatic Abuse and Neglect of Children at Home* (Baltimore, MD: Johns Hopkins Press, 1980), 9.
32. Viviana A. Zelizer, *Pricing the Priceless Child: The Changing Social Value of Children* (New York: Basic Books, 1985).
33. Gertrude Williams, "Protection of Children against Abuse and Neglect: Historical Background," in Williams and Money, eds., *Traumatic Abuse and Neglect of Children at Home,* 47–51.
34. June Axinn and Mark J. Stern, *Social Welfare: A History of the American Response to Need,* 5th ed. (Boston: Allyn & Bacon, 2001), 57–58.
35. Trattner, *From Poor Law to Welfare State,* 111.
36. Axinn and Stern, *Social Welfare,* 55.
37. Robert H. Bremner, ed., *Children and Youth in America: A Documentary History, Vol. II:*

1886–1932 (Cambridge, MA: Harvard University Press, 1971), 250–251.

38. Bremner, *Children and Youth in America,* 251.
39. Axinn and Stern, *Social Welfare,* 105.
40. Folks, *The Care of Destitute, Neglected and Delinquent Children,* 52–55.
41. Fry, "The Children's Migration," 6.
42. Axinn and Stern, *Social Welfare,* 106.
43. Charles Loring Brace, *The Dangerous Classes of New York and Twenty Years Work among Them* (New York: Wynkoop & Hallenbeck, 1872), 88–89.
44. Daniel T. McColgan, *A Century of Charity—The First One Hundred Years of the Society of St. Vincent De Paul in the United States,* Vol. 1 (Milwaukee, WI: Bruce, 1951), 236–238.
45. Trattner, *From Poor Law to Welfare State,* 118.
46. Trattner, *From Poor Law to Welfare State,* 118, 202.
47. For an excellent discussion of the Mary Ellen case and the beginning of the Society for the Prevention of Cruelty to Children, see Sallie A. Watkins, "The Mary Ellen Myth: Correcting Child Welfare History," *Social Work 35* (November 1990), 500–503.
48. Williams and Money, *Traumatic Abuse and Neglect,* 77.
49. Bremner, *Children and Youth in America,* 201.
50. Bremner, *Children and Youth in America,* 214.
51. Bremner, *Children and Youth in America,* 217.
52. Bremner, *Children and Youth in America,* 220.
53. Trattner, *From Poor Law to Welfare State,* 205.
54. Vincent DeFrancis, "Protecting the Abused Child," Hearings before the Subcommittee on Children and Youth, 93rd Congress, on the Child Abuse Prevention Act (S1191), 1973, 323–331.
55. Elizabeth Elmer, "Abused Young Children Seen in Hospitals," *Social Work 5* (1960), 98–102.
56. C. Henry Kempe, "Child Abuse: The Pediatrician's Role in Advocacy and Preventive Pediatrics," *American Journal of Diseases in Children 132* (1978), 255–260.
57. Gertrude Williams, "Cruelty and Kindness to Children: 1874–1974," in Williams and Money, *Traumatic Abuse and Neglect of Children at Home,* 86.
58. De Francis, "Protecting the Abused Child," 323.
59. Henry S. Maas and Richard E. Engler Jr., *Children in Need of Parents* (New York: Columbia University Press, 1959), 380.
60. Joseph Goldstein, Anna Freud, and Albert J. Solnit, *Beyond the Best Interests of the Child* (New York: Free Press, 1973).
61. Anthony N. Maluccio and Edith Fein, "Family Preservation in Perspective," *Family Preservation Journal 6* (2001), 1.
62. William Meezan, "Child Welfare: An Overview of the Issues," in Brenda G. McGowan and William Meezan, eds. *Child Welfare: Current Dilemmas—Future Directions* (Itasca, IL: F. E. Peacock Publishers, 1983), 12–13.
63. Lindsey, *The Welfare of Children,* 2nd ed., Chapter 3.
64. Mary Lee Allen and Jane Knitzer, "Child Welfare: Examining the Policy Framework," in Brenda C. McGowan and William Meezan, eds. *Child Welfare: Current Dilemmas—Future Directions,* 120–123.
65. William Meezan, "Child Welfare: An Overview of the Issues," in Brenda G. McGowan and William Meezan, eds. *Child Welfare: Current Dilemmas—Future Directions,* 12–13.
66. Sheila B. Kammerman and Alfred J. Kahn, "Social Services for Children, Youth, and Families in the United States," *Children and Youth Services Review 12* (1990), 1–184.
67. James K. Whittaker, "The Elegant Simplicity of Family Preservation Practice," *Family Preservation Journal 6* (2001), 10–11.
68. John R. Schuerman, Tina L. Rzepnicki, and Julia H. Littell, *Putting Families First: An Experiment in Family Preservation* (New York: Aldine De Gruyter, 1994).
69. Richard J. Gelles, *The Book of David: How Preserving Families Can Cost Children's Lives* (New York: Basic Books, 1996), 171–172.
70. Pelton, *For Reasons of Poverty;* Leroy H. Pelton, "A Functional Approach to Reorganizing Family and Child Welfare Interventions," *Children and Youth Services Review 14* (1992), 293–294; Elizabeth D. Hutchinson, Patrick Dattalo, and Mary K. Rodwell, "Reorganizing Child Protective Services: Protecting Children and Providing Family Support," *Children and Youth Services Review 16* (1994), 321.
71. David Fanshel and Eugene Shinn, *Children in Foster Care* (New York: Columbia University Press, 1978); Michael Wald, C. Merrill Carlsmith, and P. Herbert Leiderman, *Protecting Abused and Neglected Children* (Stanford, CA: Stanford University Press, 1988); David Fanshel, Stephen S. Finch, and John F. Grundy, *Foster Children in a Life Course Perspective* (New York: Columbia Univer-

sity Press, 1990); Edith Fein, "Issues in Foster Care: Where Do We Stand?" *American Journal of Orthopsychiatry 61*(4) (1991), 578–582; Rosalie B. Zimmerman, "Foster Care in Retrospect," *Tulane Studies in Social Welfare 14* (1982), 101–113.

72. Charmaine R. Brittain and Deborah Esquibel Hunt, *Helping in Child Protective Services,* 421–423.
73. S. Rep. No. 336, 96th Cong., 2nd Sess. Quoted in Marcia Lowry, "Derring-Do in the 1980's: Child Welfare Impact Litigation after the Warren Years," *Family Law Quarterly 20* (Summer 1986), 259.
74. Bill Craven, "Increased Funding of SRS Necessary to Settle Lawsuit Concerning Children," *Topeka Metro News* (7 February 1992), 7.
75. Quoted from Jean Carey Bond, "The A.C.L.U. Helped Put My Family Together Again" (New York: Department of Public Education of the ACLU, 1988), 5–6.
76. Michael B. Mushlin, Louis Levitt, and Lauren Anderson, "Court-Ordered Foster Family Care Reform: A Case Study," *Child Welfare 65* (March–April 1986), 145; Children's Rights Press Release, 29 January 2004.
77. Leroy H. Pelton, "Beyond Permanency Planning: Restructuring the Public Child Welfare System," *Social Work 36* (1991), 337–343; Pelton, "A Functional Approach to Reorganizing Family and Child Welfare Interventions"; Lela B. Costin, Howard Jacob Karger, and David Stoez, *The Politics of Child Abuse in America* (New York: Oxford University Press, 1996); Lindsey, *The Welfare of Children,* 2nd ed., 194–196.
78. Hutchinson, Dattalo, and Rodwell, "Reorganizing Child Protective Services," 319–338.
79. Russell Eisenman and Henry B. Sirgo, "Liberals vs. Conservatives: Ego Control, Child Rearing Attitudes, and Birth Order/Sex Differences" (Unpublished manuscript, McNeese State University, 1990).
80. James Dobson, *Dare to Discipline* (Wheaton, IL: Tyndale House, 1971), 27.
81. Benjamin Spock, *Baby and Child Care, New and Revised Edition* (New York: Hawthorne Books, 1968), 336.
82. David Gil, "Unraveling Child Abuse," in Gil, *Child Abuse and Violence,* 11–12.
83. Dobson, *Dare to Discipline,* 60.
84. Dobson, *Dare to Discipline,* 61.
85. Spock, *Baby and Child Care,* 338.
86. Steele and Pollock, "A Psychiatric Study of Parents Who Abuse Infants and Small Children," 145.
87. Pelton, *For Reasons of Poverty,* 27–29.
88. Gil, "Unraveling Child Abuse," 16.
89. Gil, "Unraveling Child Abuse," 17.
90. Susan Whitelaw Downs, et al., *Child Welfare and Family Services: Policies and Practice,* 7th ed., 61.
91. Lela B. Costin and Charles A. Rapp, *Child Welfare: Policies and Practice,* 3rd ed. (New York: McGraw-Hill, 1984), 9.
92. Costin and Rapp, *Child Welfare: Policies and Practice,* 10.
93. Glenn P. Joyner, "False Accusation of Child Abuse—Could It Happen to You?" *Woman's Day* (May 1986), 30–40.
94. Michael S. Wald, "State Intervention on Behalf of 'Neglected' Children: A Search for Realistic Standards," in Margaret K. Rosenheim, ed., *Pursuing Justice for the Child* (Chicago: University of Chicago Press, 1976), 246–278.
95. Susan Whitelaw Downs, et al., *Child Welfare and Family Services, Policies and Practice,* 7th ed., 74.
96. L. Diane Bernard, "The Dark Side of Family Preservation," *Affilia 7* (Summer 1992), 157.
97. Alfred Kadushin, "Children in Foster Families and Institutions," in Henry Maas, ed., *Social Service Research: Review of Studies* (Washington, DC: National Association of Social Workers, 1978), 91–92.
98. Alfred Kadushin, *Child Welfare Services,* 3rd ed. (New York: Macmillan, 1974), 679.
99. Genevive W. Carter, Lilene H. Fifield, and Hannah Shields, *Public Attitudes toward Welfare: An Opinion Poll* (Los Angeles: Regional Institute on Social Welfare, UCLA, 1973).
100. Elizabeth Howe, "Legislative Outcomes in Human Services," *Social Service Review 52* (June 1978), 173–185.
101. Cynthia Crosson-Tower, *Exploring Child Welfare, A Practice Perspective,* 3rd ed. (Boston: Allyn & Bacon, 2004), 213.
102. Cynthia Crosson-Tower, *Exploring Child Welfare,* 233–235.
103. Judith A. Martin, *Foster Family Care, Theory and Practice* (Boston: Allyn & Bacon, 2000), 45–46, 49–50, 55.
104. Reprinted with the permission of Macmillan Publishing Company, Inc. from *Child Welfare Services,* fourth edition, by Alfred Kadushin and Judith A. Martin, 697. Copyright © 1987 by Macmillan Publishing Company.

CHAPTER

11

Crime and Criminal Justice

The Records Building, where the county child welfare unit is located, is a dark dingy example of bad 1940s bureaucratic architecture. It is six stories of soot-covered cement, built around an airshaft populated by pigeons as dirty as the building and as lethargic as the Department of Motor Vehicle employees who are their daytime neighbors. Inside the building is a labyrinth of office cubicles, the only natural light coming through grimy windows covered with chicken wire. The only distinguishing feature of the Records Building is that it is located kitty-corner across the street from the Texas School Book Depository, from the windows of which Lee Harvey Oswald shot President Kennedy. Every day on my way to and from the parking lot I would respond to questions from gawkers: "Yes, that's the School Book Depository; no, the white circle painted on the third-floor window has nothing to do with the assassination."

Whenever I entered the Records Building, no matter how good I felt or how beautiful the day, my mood would sink a little in response to its bleakness. One particularly beautiful spring Monday morning my mood sank more than usual when I saw a bright pink message slip in my mailbox telling me that the supervisor of our children's emergency shelter had called asking me to call her as soon as I got to my office. This message meant trouble. Either one of the children in my caseload was sick, had run away from the shelter over the weekend, or had caused some serious disruption. Although I was prepared for trouble when I returned the call, I was not prepared for the kind of trouble I encountered. Bobby Garrett was no longer in the shelter; he was now locked up in juvenile detention.

Bobby Garrett, age fourteen; his two sisters, Ann, twelve, and Amy, eleven; and his brother Peter, nine, had been on my mind a lot lately. The four had been placed in the emergency shelter when their mother, Barbara Garrett, had been arrested and jailed for armed robbery. It would be an understatement to say that Barbara Garrett's life had not gone well. Her sister had once described her as "being able to screw up a cast-iron football." Everything Mrs. Garrett had ever done turned out badly. Every time she found a lover, he would eventually beat her up; Bobby and his siblings had been in foster care twice while Mrs. Garrett was in the hospital recovering from injuries from the beatings of boyfriends. Every time she found a job, she was fired; the children went into foster care once when Mrs. Garrett had been fired, was evicted from her apartment, and ended up living on the street. And now it appeared that she was even going to fail as a criminal—her lawyer told me that she would be lucky to get out of prison in three years.

But Mrs. Garrett had done one thing right. In spite of all her troubles she had somehow reared four beautiful, healthy, and remarkably strong children. The four seemed to realize at an early age that they did not have parents they could count on so they had better be able to count on each other. When Mrs. Garrett was incapacitated, the four functioned as a strong family unit, with Bobby as the head. When they were placed in the shelter, Bobby told me that he and his siblings did not care where they were placed but that they had to be together. I agreed to this, but had been searching in vain for a place for all four of them for six weeks. Meanwhile, they had been living in our emergency shelter, a modern one-story building located on a major industrial boulevard, in the middle of a huge concrete parking lot. It had only a tiny area to play in and few recreational facilities. The shelter was a perfectly good place for a brief stay but was not designed for long-term living. I had been doing the best I could to provide activities for the kids, but I knew they were becoming bored, anxious, and increasingly unhappy.

Bobby Garrett was the last kid in my caseload I would expect to be in trouble with the law. Redheaded, freckle-faced, five feet tall if he stretched, with a sharp mind and an infectious smile, he was one of the most remarkable kids I had ever known. Bobby and his siblings all did well in school, and they were well adjusted, well liked, and rarely in trouble. I could not imagine why he would be locked up.

When I phoned the supervisor, she said that Bobby had seemed restless over the weekend, like "a tiger in a cage." Late Sunday night, after lights out, Bobby and one of his friends had sneaked out of a window in the back of the shelter. They had wandered around for a while, and finally they ended up by the public hospital down the street where a new wing was under construction. They climbed a ten-foot-high chain-link fence to get inside the construction area. Once inside, Bobby and his friend looked at all the machinery and discovered that the keys had been left in a huge dump truck. The boys decided it would be fun to take a ride. The gate was locked, but this was no problem for the truck—Bobby just drove it right through. They had not gone two blocks when a police officer spotted them. Figuring that a five-foot-tall fourteen-year-old had no business driving a dump truck at two in the morning, he pulled up behind them and turned on his blue lights. Bobby figured that if he ignored the officer, perhaps he would go away. When the truck did not pull over, the officer pulled alongside the truck and gestured for Bobby to pull over; Bobby continued to ignore him. Finally, in what has to be considered a poor law enforcement decision, the officer sped about a block ahead of the truck, pulled his cruiser sideways in the street to block all lanes, got out, and stood beside it with his arm out, palm raised, confident that this gesture would force the driver to stop. Unfortunately, Bobby was not too sure how to stop the truck. At the last possible moment, the officer dove into a ditch as Bobby and the dump truck turned the police cruiser into two tons of junk. Amazingly, no one was hurt. Bobby and his friend were arrested, booked, and locked up in the juvenile detention center.

I phoned the Juvenile Department and was dismayed to learn that Howard Jordan was the juvenile officer assigned to Bobby's case. I had worked with Howard before, and we did not like each other. Howard was a bantam rooster of a man, hard-nosed and rigid, with a wide and deep mean streak. He called all men he did not like or did not want something from "Sparky"; those he liked or wanted something from he called "Old Buddy." Women he did not care for he called "Sister"; those he liked he called things that on several occasions had resulted in sexual harassment complaints. Howard remained unrepentant; following a complaint, the only noticeable change was that he began to call the complainant Sister. Howard viewed his job as protecting the public from juvenile lawlessness, and he believed that locking kids up was the best way to accomplish this task. He had once told me that in his estimate at least 50 percent of teenagers would benefit from a stay in the state training school. I resolved to deal with him in as positive a manner as possible, and I made an appointment to see him later that day.

When I entered Mr. Jordan's office, he was sitting behind his gray metal desk with an expression on his face that looked like he had eaten an extra large helping of bad fish. After we exchanged the usual pleasantries ("Beautiful day, huh?" "Yeah, but the pollen is about to kill me"), I got down to business. "Look, Howard, let's cut this kid some slack. I know he screwed up, he knows he screwed up, but, good lord, we've had him cooped up in that cruddy little shelter for six weeks. If someone had me in that place for six weeks, I think I'd do far worse than smash up a police car. He's really basically a good kid, so how about we go get him out of detention; I'll take him back to the shelter, and I'll turn up the heat under our foster home unit to find him a placement."

Howard pinched his lips together, looked at the floor, and shook his head, a gesture meant to communicate his sadness at my naiveté. He said, "Sparky, you know I like you, but you're way off base here. This kid is a criminal; he's responsible for destroying $15,000 dollars worth of government property. No telling how much stuff he's done that we've just never caught him for. Hell, if I could I'd prosecute him as an adult. But I can't, so I'll just be sure that he is put in state training school until his eighteenth birthday. I'm sure you know about this kid's mother. She's a crook herself and, you probably don't believe this, but I'm a lot older than you and my experience has taught me that it's true that the apple never falls far from the tree."

I was not surprised by the results of my meeting with Howard Jordan, but I was discouraged nonetheless. I went to my supervisor and asked her for suggestions about who would be a good lawyer for Bobby—someone who would work for nothing. My supervisor called a friend, and the friend agreed to take the case, saying she would speak to all the parties involved and call me the next morning. The lawyer, Rita Sanchez, was a radical. She was about sixty years old, nearly six feet tall, ramrod straight, with hair that reminded me of a used Brillo pad. She was mainly a labor lawyer and had once been a candidate for the city council on the Socialist Party ticket. She was not popular with either the police or the district attorney's office, but she had a reputation as a strong client advocate. Basically, Ms. Sanchez was mean as a snake. As I rose to leave my supervisor's office, she began to chuckle and said, "I'd pay money to be in the room when Mr. Jordan calls *her* Sister."

The next morning Ms. Sanchez phoned me as she had promised. "Yes," she said "the juvenile officer was right when he said serious crimes are involved here."

I made a face I was glad she couldn't see over the phone. "I'm surprised to hear you say that; I really can't think of Bobby as a criminal."

Her reply came with a rush of anger. "Bobby's the only one in this whole shameful situation who isn't a criminal. The whole bunch of you down at the the Child Welfare Unit are guilty of criminal child neglect for leaving those kids in the shelter for six weeks. The construction company that owns the dump truck is guilty of criminal misconduct for leaving the keys in an attractive nuisance like that truck. The police department is guilty of public endangerment for parking that police car across the road in front of a truck driven by what the officer could clearly see was not a qualified operator. The Juvenile Department is guilty of criminal child abuse for the conditions in their detention facility. Finally, Howard Jordan is guilty of being a jackass. The only reason that Bobby's in jail rather than the actual guilty parties is because he's the only one without the power to define things as crimes."

Following her conversation with me, Ms. Sanchez phoned the director of the Juvenile Department, the juvenile court judge, the police chief, and the editors of several local newspapers. She then phoned the producer of a local television news segment called "Channel 4 on the Case and in Their Face," which specialized in uncovering incompetence and malfeasance by public officials.

When I returned to my office later in the day, I found another bright pink message slip in my mailbox. This one said that I was to call Howard Jordan ASAP, and my secretary had underlined the ASAP three times. When I returned the call, Howard greeted me in a voice that was uncharacteristically friendly, but tinged with an unmistakable undercurrent of anxiety. "Old Buddy," he said, "we've decided to not pursue the Garrett matter. So, if you would come over and check him out of detention, that will be great. Oh yeah, if you could have him out before 5:00, we'll really appreciate it. Some reporters are scheduled to show up about then, and I'd really like to be able to tell them that Bobby is your problem now." I did this, and within a few days the foster home unit had located a home to take Bobby and his siblings.

As I left my office later that evening, I thought, "There are some days that even the Records Building can't spoil."

This case illustrates a number of issues about crime and delinquency that we discuss in this chapter. One issue is the definition of crime. Are crimes acts that intrinsically constitute threats against the social order, or are crimes simply actions that are defined as such by the powerful forces in society? Another issue is the age of the offender. At what age do people become totally responsible for their behavior, and how should we handle persons who are below this age? Another issue has to do with social welfare and crime. Which offenders, which acts, and which parts of the processing of offenders should come under the scope of the criminal justice institution, and which are more appropriate targets for the social welfare institution? Then there is the question of why people commit crimes. Do they do so because there is something wrong, or even evil, about their natures—because they are "criminal types," so to speak? Or do people commit crimes because they come from an environment that has corrupted them, or even because they are the victims of an unjust social system? Finally, there is the closely related question of what society's reaction to crime should be. Should we be concerned with retribution against those who commit criminal acts, or should we view these acts as symptoms of some personal maladjustment or social problem and seek to correct the causes?

The order of topics in this chapter is slightly different from that in other chapters. Because of their centrality to the topic of criminal justice, we cover perspectives at the beginning of the chapter rather than at the end. It is impossible to discuss any aspect of criminal justice without reference to political perspectives. In fact, the perspectives become almost parodies of themselves in types such as the "hang-'em-high" judge and the "bleeding-heart liberal" social worker or civil rights lawyer. Therefore, we begin with a discussion of perspectives and then discuss the other aspects of criminal justice.

Perspectives on Criminal Justice

The conservative, liberal, and radical perspectives on criminal justice are so firmly embraced by their advocates that Walker prefers to describe them as "crime control theology." He says that "thinking of crime control policy as theology helps us explain the dogged tenacity of various ideas."[1]

The Conservative Perspective

Basic Beliefs. Conservatives believe that individuals are fully responsible for their own actions and that this includes the breaking of laws. The individual is not a passive pawn of external forces but has free will and can make choices between right and wrong. When the individual makes these choices, he or she does so fully aware of the consequences, so he or she should be ready to suffer the penalties for wrong choices. Conservatives believe in a world of discipline and self-control in which people exercise restraint and subordinate their personal passions to the common good. It is a world of limits, and criminal law is an important set of limits.

Because conservatives believe that human nature is basically negative and that human behavior can be largely explained using a pleasure/pain calculus, they have a strong belief in the effectiveness of punishment. People who violate rules should be punished. Punishment teaches a good lesson; it teaches criminals that breaking rules has unpleasant consequences, and thus they learn to obey rules in the future. Punishment also serves as an example to everyone else that they should continue to follow rules or they too will suffer unpleasant penalties. To conservatives, rules are terribly important.

Conservatives believe in tradition and authority. Walker says, "The world of conservative crime control is modeled after an idealized image of the patriarchal family. Criminal sanctions resemble parental discipline. Minor misbehavior is greeted with a gentle warning; a second misstep earns a sterner reprimand. More serious wrongdoing is answered with severe punishment. . . . Conservative thinking about crime is closely related to conservative ideas about the problem of 'permissiveness' in child rearing."[2]

The conservative approach to crime advocates punishment as the most effective and just social response.

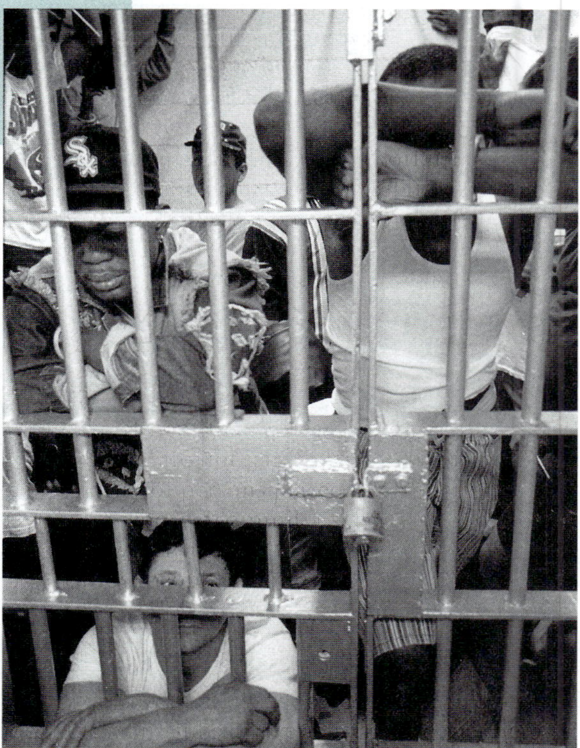

Major Issues. According to Miller,[3] conservatives are concerned about five major issues in criminal justice. The first issue, as conservatives see it, is that our system is characterized by excessive leniency toward lawbreakers. Conservatives believe that swift and sure punishment is the only way to prevent crime, and they therefore get upset when they think an offender has escaped paying the full price for his or her actions. The full price according to conservatives is generally very high.

The second issue, according to this perspective, is that the system tends to favor the rights and welfare of lawbreakers over the rights and welfare of their victims, of law enforcement personnel, and of the general public. Conservatives become upset about things such as the Miranda rule, which requires that people be advised of their rights when they are arrested; the fact that illegally obtained evidence cannot be used; and the fact that prisoners must be provided with entertainment and recreational equipment. Conservatives are strongly in favor of developments that promote the rights of victims of crimes, such as rulings that victims must be advised of, and permitted to testify at, parole hearings.

The third issue conservatives are concerned about is what they see as a general erosion of both discipline and respect for duly constituted authority. Referred to by Miller as an "ancient concern," this perception centers on the behavior of youth, who are generally considered to constitute the worst generation ever. Interestingly, we are currently at a rare point in history—a time when many conservatives believe the current crop of young people is far superior to recent generations. One now hears the liberals complaining about the sorry state of youth, whom liberals see as self-centered, overly materialistic, and entirely too willing to conform to discipline and authority.

The fourth issue on conservatives' minds is the cost of crime. This issue arouses somewhat less passion than the others, but it is still a major concern. Conservatives resent the large amount of money society spends on law enforcement and criminal processing. A particularly sore spot in this concern is the money spent for programs that enhance the welfare of criminals, providing such things as free legal counsel, prison recreation, improved food, and individual cells with the possibility of prisoners having their own televisions. The question conservatives ask is, "Why should hardworking, law-abiding citizens pay for luxuries for criminals?"

The final issue, related to the others, is excessive permissiveness. Conservatives see permissiveness as a, if not *the,* basic flaw in our social order. They tend to believe that there has been an erosion of discipline, excessive leniency, and abdication of responsibility by authorities. The problem is viewed as a continuum that ranges from too much permissiveness at home, to excessively lenient schools, to a lax criminal justice system. The result: a society of people who do not suffer the appropriate consequences for improper behavior and therefore are increasingly predisposed to engage in such behavior.

The Liberal Perspective

Basic Beliefs. You will recall from Chapter 1 that a central belief of the liberal worldview is that human nature is basically good and that if people behave badly, as in breaking laws, it is because they have somehow been corrupted by their social environment. This is the cornerstone of the liberal perspective on criminal justice. Whereas conservatives attribute lawbreaking to individual moral failure, liberals place the responsibility on social influence. People commit crimes because of bad influences in the family, the peer group, or the neighborhood, or perhaps because of broader social influences such as unemployment or general lack of economic opportunity.

Because liberals believe that human nature is basically good, they place their faith in education and individual reform as the basis for the criminal justice system. As Walker has said, "If conservatives view the world as a large family, liberal crime control theology views it as a big classroom. Rehabilitation, the core liberal policy, involves instructing the criminal offender in the ways of correct behavior."[4] Liberals firmly believe that people who have been corrupted by a bad environment can be reshaped, and that once this is done, they will follow their natural inclination to behave properly.

Major Issues. The major criminal justice issues of concern to liberals revolve around the aspects of society that they believe adversely influence people, sometimes leading to their committing crimes. The first issue is labeling and stigmatization. We discuss the labeling issue in some detail in the section on dynamics and so will only identify it here. Basically, liberals argue that the main thing that makes a person a criminal is the fact that he or she is labeled as one. Thus, they argue that society should do everything possible to keep people out of the criminal justice system because by assigning labels the system itself creates criminals.

The second issue that concerns liberals is overinstitutionalization. Liberals believe that we lock up too many people and that this does more harm than good. This concern has increased as the number of people jailed or imprisoned in the United States has risen—by 328 percent between 1980 and 2002 alone. Based on their belief in the power of the environment to shape behavior, liberals argue that by locking people in prisons society creates "crime colleges" where offenders learn new and better criminal techniques and become more favorably disposed toward committing crimes. Liberals believe we would accomplish more by placing more people on probation and into community-based treatment programs. Only dangerous people should be locked up.

The third issue of concern to liberals is their belief that there is a discriminatory bias to the system. They point to evidence that supports this belief, such as the fact that given the same crime, a member of a minority group is much more likely to be sent to prison than a white person; and the fact that the murderer of a minority person is much less likely than the murderer of a white person to be given the death sentence. Liberals charge the system with being racist, sexist, oppressive, and brutal toward minorities and low-income people.

The final major criminal justice issue of concern to liberals is overcriminalization. Liberals believe that too many things in our society are defined as crimes; therefore, they believe, one quick way to reduce crime is to decriminalize acts they see as not having a victim. Gambling, prostitution, and homosexual behavior are examples of the kinds of behaviors many liberals would like removed from the legal statutes. Probably the hottest example right now is drug use. The argument on all these behaviors is that they are against the law only because some people think they are immoral; however, they really do not hurt anyone other than the person who engages in them—and that is, after all, the person's own business. Interestingly, this is an issue on which some conservatives, mainly libertarians, agree with liberals.

The Radical Perspective

Basic Beliefs. The basic position of radicals is that the criminal justice system is one of the primary tools that the capitalist ruling class uses to dominate and exploit the rest of the population. A concise statement of the basic position is given by Spitzer, who argues that populations in capitalist societies become

> eligible for management as deviant when they disturb, hinder or call into question any of the following: (1) capitalist modes of appropriating the product of human labor (e.g., when the poor "steal" from the rich), (2) the social conditions under which capitalist production takes place (e.g., those who refuse or are unable to perform wage labor), (3) patterns of distribution and consumption in capitalist society (e.g., those who use drugs for escape and transcendence rather than sociability and adjustment), (4) the process of socialization for productive and non-productive roles (e.g., youth who refuse to be schooled or those who deny the validity of "family life") and (5) the ideology which supports the functioning of capitalist society (e.g., proponents of alternative forms of social organization).[5]

By this Spitzer means that acts that are perceived as threatening the interests of powerful people in society are defined as crimes; acts that do not threaten the interests of powerful people, even though they may be harmful, are not defined as crimes.

Major Issues. The major criminal justice issue for those of the radical persuasion is the redefinition of crime. Radicals believe that many of the acts currently defined as crimes could more accurately be defined as legitimate political acts by people attempting to battle an oppressive social system, or as understandable actions of people for whom all legitimate avenues of opportunity have been blocked. On the other hand, they believe that many acts now considered to be perfectly legal should be redefined as crimes. Schwendinger and Schwendinger, for example, argue that human rights violations, imperialism, war, racism, sexism, and allowing poverty to exist are all forms of crime.[6] Radicals believe that these forms of crime are allowed to exist under capitalism because they are necessary for its survival.

Definition

We subdivide our definition of crime into two broad areas—legal definitions of crime and crime as a social welfare concern.

Legal Definitions of Crime

A good definition of crime from a legal perspective was written in the 1930s by Michael and Adler:

> The most precise and least ambiguous definition of crime is that which defines it as behavior which is prohibited by the criminal code. The criminal law describes many kinds of behavior, gives them names such as murder and arson and rape and burglary, and proscribes them. If crime is defined in legal terms, the only source of confusion is such ambiguity as may inhere in the legal definitions of specific crimes. It is sometimes difficult to tell

> whether specific conduct falls within the legal definition, whether, for example, a specific homicide is murder or what degree of murder, as that offense is defined by law. But even so, the legal rules are infinitely more precise than moral judgments or judgments with regard to the antisocial character of conduct. Moreover, there is no surer way of ascertaining what kinds of behavior are generally regarded as immoral or antisocial by the people of a community than by reference to their criminal code, for in theory, at least, the criminal code embodies social judgments with respect to behavior and, perhaps, more often than not, fact conforms to theory.[7]

Thus, crime is defined, from a legal standpoint, as any behavior that is against the law.

In Whose Interest Is Criminal Law? The problem with defining crime as any behavior that is against the law is that it leaves important questions unanswered. The primary question is what and whom these laws represent. There are two major viewpoints on this question. The first is the consensus (sometimes called functionalist) perspective subscribed to by conservatives and some liberals. The other is the conflict perspective accepted by some liberals and all radicals.

The *consensus perspective* starts with the assumption that there is fundamental agreement (consensus) about basic social values. We are all supposedly in agreement about certain issues, such as that it is all right for people over the age of twenty-one to drink liquor, but it is not all right for them to use cocaine. From this perspective, law reflects the basic values and norms of the majority of people in a society. In Hall's words, the basic position of the consensus perspective is that "criminal law represents a sustained effort to preserve important social values from serious harm and to do so not arbitrarily but in accordance with rational methods directed toward the discovery of just ends."[8] The problem with this perspective is that we can all think of examples of criminal laws that clearly do not represent the values of most people, but rather represent special interests. For example, in some states it is illegal to cremate a body without a casket. Most people resent paying for a casket that will only be burned and thus suspect that the only group that values this law is the funeral industry, which then does not lose a commission on a casket sale when someone chooses cremation rather than burial.

The other perspective, the *conflict perspective,* provides an explanation as to why some laws are clearly to the benefit of certain groups, sometimes very small groups. This perspective argues that the assumption that a consensus exists in a large, heterogeneous society such as ours is incorrect. Diversity in U.S. society is so great as to make cooperation difficult, if not impossible. There are many groups in society, and each is pursuing its own self-interest. Laws do not represent a consensus; rather, they are the outcomes of struggles between groups to control the machinery of government for their own purposes. Therefore, according to the conflict perspective, if abortion is once again outlawed, this will mean not that a consensus exists in society that abortion should be a criminal offense, but that conservative religious groups have managed to wield enough power to get their definition of morality imposed on everyone.[9] Ms. Sanchez, Bobby's attorney in the vignette at the beginning of the chapter, was illustrating a conflict perspective when she said that the only reason Bobby was charged with the crime is that he was the only one without enough power to define things as crimes.

When looking at the question of what and whom laws represent, we should note that legal scholars generally classify crimes into two general categories. The first is offenses that are *mala in se* (evil in themselves). These are acts that are presumably understood by everyone to be bad—acts such as murder, rape, arson, assault, and robbery. These acts are banned in virtually every human society. The other category of crimes is acts that are *mala prohibita.* These are acts that are crimes only because they are defined as such by legislation; there is nothing inherently evil about them. Acts that are *mala prohibita* include drug use, prostitution, and gambling. In some societies these acts are perfectly legal—in fact, may be considered desirable—but in others they constitute criminal behavior. Regarding acts that are *mala in se,* a consensus view of law makes a good deal of sense; it is clear that there is near universal agreement about these laws. Regarding acts that are *mala prohibita,* a strong argument can be made for a conflict model. It is doubtful that a consensus exists in our society that marijuana should be illegal even though alcohol is legal. It is clear, however, that powerful interests support the manufacture and sale of alcoholic beverages and that this same support is not present for marijuana.

Children as a Special Case. People who have not yet reached the age of majority are treated differently by the criminal justice system in several ways. With regard to the definition of crime, one of the ways that children are treated differently from adults is that there is an entire set of acts that are *mala prohibita* only for nonadults. These are generally known as *status offenses* and include such things as truancy; running away; being incorrigible; drinking liquor; and, in some areas, even being on the streets after a certain hour. These acts are all perfectly legal for an adult, but a child can be arrested and adjudicated for them. Thus, the definition of crime is much broader for children than for adults.

Another way that the definition of crime is different for children is that children are generally not considered responsible enough for their own behavior to be defined as criminals. Rather, children who commit acts that would be considered crimes for adults are defined as delinquents rather than as criminals. Although the definition of *juvenile delinquent* varies from state to state, the term generally refers to a person who has not reached the age of majority, which is eighteen in most cases, and who has either committed an act that would be considered a crime if he or she were an adult, or committed a status offense. Juvenile delinquents are considered to be the responsibility of the social welfare system rather than of the criminal justice system. With youngsters the goal is clearly rehabilitation rather than retribution; and once the person passes his or her eighteenth birthday, the records are generally sealed, and the act for which the person was arrested becomes as though it never happened.

Crime as a Social Welfare Problem

In order to understand crime as a social welfare problem, we must first look at two major ideas about what the response of society to crime should be. The first idea is that society's response to crime should simply be to punish the offender; the second, and somewhat more ambitious, idea is that society should do something to rehabilitate the offender.

The Punishment Approach. This approach is based on the idea that the function of the criminal justice system should simply be to impose a penalty on the wrongdoer and to do whatever is possible to right any wrong that has been done. There are several variations to the punishment approach. The first is known as *retribution* and is in keeping with the old eye-for-an-eye philosophy; it advocates punishment as an end in itself. The belief is that criminal acts are inherently wrong and that therefore they should be avenged; the punishment serves no other purpose. The second variation on the punishment approach, *restitution,* endeavors to make the wrongdoer somehow pay the victim back for the pain and suffering or loss the wrongdoer caused. The third variation is *incapacitation:* the idea that punishment should not only punish the offender but also shield society from him or her for as long as possible. Advocates of this approach believe in long prison sentences for convicted criminals. The argument is that in prison, antisocial people can prey only on one another and will be forced to leave the rest of us alone. Finally, there is an updated version of the retribution approach known as *just deserts.* This approach, also known as the *justice model,* seeks to set more precise penalties for various crimes than we now have; it seeks to ensure fair and appropriate retribution. Central to this model is the idea of determinant sentences; in other words, there would be no "time off for good behavior" because every person convicted of a certain crime would serve the same sentence.[10]

The aims of the punishment approach are rather modest and limited. Gelman refers to this as the "moralist approach" because, he says, the criminal justice system "is one in which the system is seen as upholding the morals and values of society."[11] In other words, the purpose of the criminal justice system is to affirm the values of society by punishing those who violate the values that have been deemed important enough to be codified into criminal law.

The only other claim that some advocates make for the punishment approach is that it reduces crime through specific and general deterrence. *Specific deterrence* means that lawbreakers will be deterred from further crimes by the suffering that society puts them through for their acts. *General deterrence* is the idea that people other than the person being punished will be deterred from committing crimes because they will witness the suffering of the lawbreaker and not want to risk such a fate for themselves. At one time in England, it was not uncommon for parents to take their children to a public hanging and then to beat the children to impress on them the lesson that crime brings pain and perhaps even death; in other words, they sought to amplify the general deterrent aspects of the event.

The Rehabilitation Approach. The rehabilitation approach to criminal justice views lawbreakers not as bad people in need of punishment but rather as people who are demonstrating a serious adjustment problem. Even though they may not realize it themselves, lawbreakers are in need of help. This is the point at which criminal justice becomes a social welfare concern. In keeping with the definition of social welfare we gave in Chapter 2, people who get in trouble with the law are having difficulty fulfilling their role as citizens, and they are dependent on society to help them become able to fill this role and become interdependent actors in society. In nearly all cases, people who are subjected to rehabilitation are defined as dependent by someone else—generally the criminal justice system—and are, at least initially, involuntary clients. The rehabilitation approach, or perhaps we should say criminal justice as a social welfare concern, involves four basic types of services: diversion; probation; correctional services; and parole, which is also called *correctional casework* or *aftercare.*

Diversion is one of the newest approaches used in the criminal justice system; it gained great popularity during the 1960s and 1970s. The objective of diversion programs is to get people out of the criminal justice system as quickly as possible. Generally people are diverted at two points, either before arrest or before prosecution. At either point the suspect, rather than being subjected to further prosecution by the criminal justice system, is diverted into a treatment program. The idea behind diversion programs is that processing by the criminal justice system often works against the goal of rehabilitation in two ways. The first is that the system labels the person as a criminal, and that this label often becomes a self-fulfilling prophecy—the child who people think is a thief begins to act like a thief. The second is the old notion of jails as "crime colleges." Once a person is put in close association with criminals, he or she tends to learn all sorts of new crimes, as well as justifications of why they are acceptable.

> Missy Long, twenty-four, was arrested at the mall for shoplifting. She had gone into the dressing room with her two-month-old son in a baby carrier. While in the dressing room, she had wrapped a skirt around the baby, wrapped his blanket around this, and had then walked out of the store. She tearfully told the arresting officer that since she became pregnant and quit work, she and her husband never had money for anything but necessities. She said, "I don't know why I took the skirt. The impulse came over me and I just couldn't resist."
>
> Finding that she had no previous criminal record and that she appeared to be going through a stressful life phase, and believing that no good would come from subjecting her to prosecution, the social worker from the district attorney's office asked if she would be willing to participate in a diversion program. He explained that this would mean she would need to sign an agreement to participate fully in a program of treatment at the county mental health center. If she dropped out of the program or did not fully cooperate, the shoplifting charges would be reactivated and she would be prosecuted. If she completed the program, all charges would be permanently dropped. Mrs. Long entered the program, which eventually involved individual counseling for her, marriage counseling for her and her husband, and a referral to the state employment service to help her find a part-time job. After one year she completed the program and has had no trouble with the law since.

Probation intervenes in the criminal justice system at a later date than diversion. Under the probation system a person is arrested, convicted, and sentenced to a term in prison—or, in the case of a juvenile, is declared to be a delinquent. At this point the person's sentence is suspended and he or she is given conditional freedom for a period generally equal to the jail sentence, under the supervision of a probation officer. The conditions of probation include a lengthy list of rules forbidding the probationer to engage in activities such as going to bars and associating with known criminals. The rules also require the probationer to report regularly to the probation officer and to get permission to travel out of town, among other things. In the case of juveniles, the rules usually include regular school attendance; sometimes they even specify the grades the person must earn in order to stay out of detention. Probation rarely involves any form of treatment, however, and the vast majority of probation officers have neither adequate training nor time to provide treatment.

> At age fifteen, John Story had been arrested five times for offenses ranging from truancy to auto theft. The fifth arrest was for selling drugs to kids at his school. This time he was prosecuted, declared delinquent, and placed on probation for an indeterminate period. John resented probation and resented his probation officer, about whom he said, "It's like having another father, only worse." He continued to skip school, and finally he ran away from home,

hopping a freight train with a friend and ending up in California. When he returned several weeks later, his probation officer recommended that his probation be revoked and that he be sent to state training school. This was done, and John remained in the training school until his eighteenth birthday.

Correctional services involve the provision of social work services to people who have actually been imprisoned. There are two major types of correctional services. The first is counseling/therapy designed to help inmates adjust to prison life, resolve personality problems that contributed to their difficulty in living a "straight" life, and plan for their life following release. The second type of services involves helping families of inmates adjust to the many problems that they face. The following example, reported by Walker and Beaumont, is from England.

Pete appeared in the Crown Court and was sentenced to three years' imprisonment for jointly stealing a lorry-load of jeans. Perhaps unrealistically he had not anticipated being sent to prison and so family affairs were in a real mess the day he was taken down to the cells. He left behind a wife, Rose, and five children aged between ten years and twelve months. Andy [the social worker] called a few days later. He found a mountain of work to be done. Finances needed to be juggled as cleverly as possible, and Rose needed advice over visiting. The children were upset and confused about their father's absence and Rose was distraught.

Andy tried to help during the prison sentence but became aware that his efforts were small compared to the family's needs. [Welfare] levels were pitifully inadequate. Andy helped out with a hamper and toys from a local charity at Christmas, and second-hand clothes at other times. He hated giving "charity," especially when he saw how embarrassed Rose was at needing to accept it. The children missed their father and began playing up; Rose missed her husband but managed to cope with the kids' distress. She became ill through worry and not eating enough, and was slow to recover. The washing machine broke down and the kids were wetting the beds.

Andy gave what he called "support." He argued with obstinate gas board officials and awkward [welfare department] officers on Rose's behalf. One time her [welfare check] didn't arrive. The [welfare department] said it was in the post and refused payment although she was broke. Rose was at the end of her tether and tearfully told Andy she was going down to smash their windows. He calmed her down and arranged a small loan to tide her over until the [check] arrived.

Pete began to wonder if Rose was having an affair—not because he had any evidence, it was just that so many other men had received "dear John" letters. Visits became strained as Pete aggressively questioned Rose about her movements. Anxiety about parole increased the tension. Andy tried to calm Pete and Rose's worries and submitted a parole report emphasizing the positive aspects of circumstances at home. Secretly he doubted whether Pete would get parole.[12]

Parole is the situation in which a person is released from prison before the end of his or her sentence to serve the remainder of the sentence under conditions similar to probation. Violation of any of the many conditions of parole will result in the person's being returned to prison to complete the remainder of the sentence. Parole, like probation, generally involves little treatment and often consists of little more than loose supervision. The roles of parole officer and probation officer are often combined.

Sandy had run away from home at age fifteen and had supported herself as a prostitute. By age nineteen she had developed a cocaine habit that was so expensive that she began robbing her clients to get enough money to support it. One night a client resisted and she stabbed him, nearly killing him. She was arrested for attempted murder and, with her history of drug and prostitution busts, was lucky to get the five- to twenty-year sentence that she did. In prison Sandy was a model inmate, getting over her drug habit, earning a high school diploma, and working as an administrative assistant in the chaplain's office. After seven years Sandy was released on parole. She was fortunate enough to be assigned to Martha Stevens, a probation officer who was a trained social worker with more than ten years' experience. With Martha's help Sandy entered counseling at the local United Way counseling agency, got a job as an administrative assistant at the department of social services, and entered community college with a Pell grant to pay her tuition and books. Things are not perfect (Martha suspects that Sandy still occasionally returns to her old profession when times get tough); but with a little luck and continued work, Sandy has a chance for a reasonably happy and productive life.

Statistical Profile

There are shortages of many things in the world, but criminal justice statistics is not one of them. The *Sourcebook of Criminal Justice Statistics* published annually by the Department of Justice contains more than 500 pages of tables on various aspects of crime and justice; the *Uniform Crime Report* published annually by the FBI adds another 350 pages; the Bureau of Justice Statistics supplements these with numerous reports released periodically. The volume of crime statistics is not a matter of debate; however, the usefulness of them is.

Problems with Crime Statistics

Criminologists claim that serious flaws in official crime statistics make them of highly questionable validity and reliability. Major criticisms include assertions that:

- The statistics are collected in a fragmented and uncoordinated manner. The agencies collecting the data have no official power to make local agencies report and have no methods of ascertaining the accuracy of the reporting.
- The crimes reported are not representative of the actual amount and pattern of offenses. Only a fraction of crimes committed are ever reported to the police. For many crimes, fewer than half of the actual incidents are ever reported.
- The definitions used vary among jurisdictions and often change from one year to another. The official statistics aggregate data from fifty different states, each with its own criminal code. Thus, in one state an offense committed by a seventeen-year-old may enter the statistics as a juvenile offense, whereas in another it may be reported as an adult crime.
- The official statistics may be subject to outright fraud and manipulation. Government bodies often use these statistics to judge the performance of organizations, such as police departments, or of elected officials, such as district attorneys. The people being evaluated often manipulate the statistics to exaggerate the amount of crime if they are seeking a budget increase, or to minimize the crime rate if they wish to make their organizations appear effective.[13]

Our point: When you are looking at criminal justice statistics, including those presented here, do so with a critical eye. Although the statistics probably reflect reality, they are not a perfect representation of reality. Also, it is not always clear what reality they reflect. For example, many analysts state that the large increase in drug arrests in recent years reflects increasing drug use. This may be so, but part of the increase may also reveal increased drug law enforcement rather than increased use.

Patterns of Crime

In this section we look at data on the amount of crime and the characteristics of persons arrested.

Volume of Crime. Figure 11.1 and Table 11.1 give a rough idea of the amount of crime in the United States. Figure 11.1 is the crime clock that is published annually by

FIGURE 11.1 **Crime Clock, 2002**

Source: 2002 Crime in the United States (Washington, DC: U.S. Department of Justice, Federal Bureau of Investigation, 2003), 4.

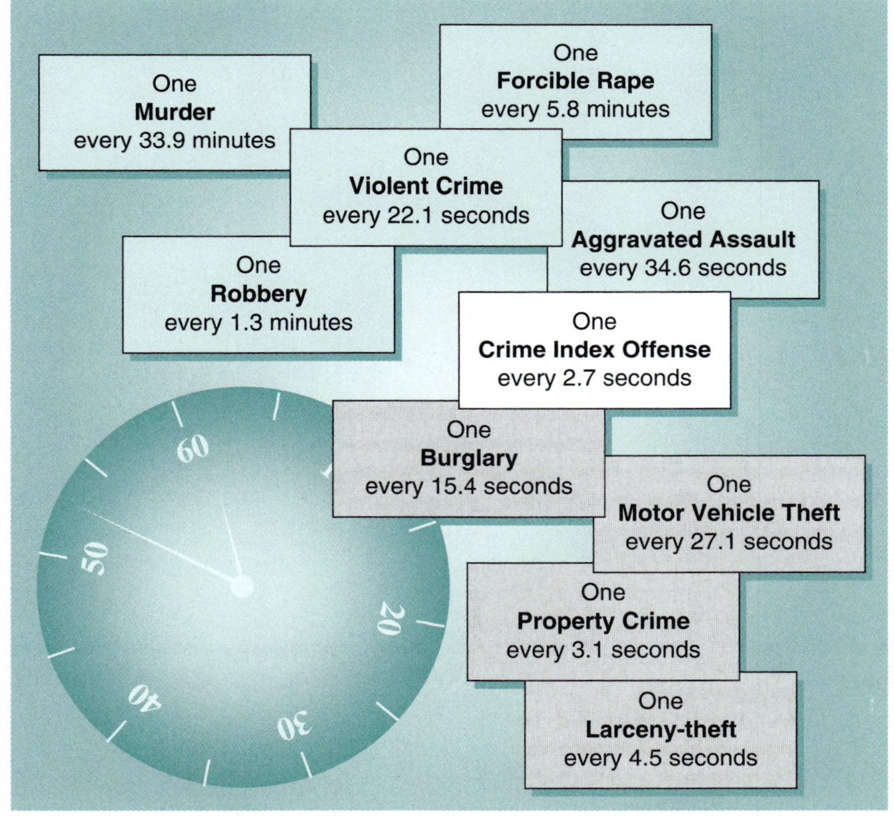

TABLE 11.1

Index of Crime, United States, 1983–2002

Population	Crime Index Total	Total Violent Crime	Total Property Crime
Number of Offenses			
1983	12,108,630	1,258,087	10,850,543
1988	13,923,086	1,566,221	12,356,865
1993	14,144,794	1,926,017	12,218,777
1998	12,485,714	1,533,887	10,951,827
2002	11,877,218	1,426,325	10,450,893
Percent Change: Number of Offenses			
2002/2001	NC	–0.9	+0.1
2002/1998	–4.9	–7.0	–4.6
2002/1993	–16.0	–25.9	–14.5
Rate per 100,000 Inhabitants			
1983	5,179.2	538.1	4,641.1
1988	5,694.5	640.6	5,054.0
1993	5,487.1	747.1	4,740.0
1998	4,620.1	567.6	4,052.5
2002	4,118.8	494.6	3,624.1
Percent Change: Rate per 100,000 Inhabitants			
2002/2001	–1.1	–2.0	–0.9
2002/1998	–10.9	–12.9	–10.6
2002/1993	–24.9	–33.8	–23.5

Source: Adapted from Federal Bureau of Investigation, *Uniform Crime Reports, 2002,* online at www.fbi.gov.

the FBI as the most aggregate representation of data in the *Uniform Crime Report.* It is a very rough measure, but it does effectively illustrate that there is a tremendous amount of crime. Table 11.1 is a more detailed presentation. Perhaps the most important aspect of Table 11.1 is the section showing the percent change in the number of offenses. The

Violent Crime				Property Crime		
Murder and Nonnegligent Manslaughter	**Forcible Rape**	**Robbery**	**Aggravated Assault**	**Burglary**	**Larceny/ Theft**	**Motor Vehicle Theft**
19,308	78,918	506,567	653,294	3,129,851	6,712,759	1,077,933
20,675	92,486	542,918	910,092	3,218,077	7,705,872	1,432,916
24,526	106,014	659,870	1,135,607	2,834,808	7,820,909	1,563,060
16,974	93,144	447,186	976,583	2,332,735	7,376,311	1,242,781
16,204	95,136	420,637	894,348	2,151,875	7,052,922	1,246,096
+1.0	+4.7	–0.7	–1.6	+1.7	–0.6	+1.4
–4.5	+2.1	–5.9	–8.4	–7.8	–4.4	+0.3
–33.9	–10.3	–36.3	–21.2	–24.1	–9.8	–20.3
8.3	33.8	216.7	279.4	1,338.7	2,871.3	431.1
8.5	37.8	222.1	372.2	1,316.2	3,151.7	586.1
9.5	41.1	256	440.5	1,099.7	3,033.9	606.3
6.3	34.5	165.5	361.4	863.2	2,729.5	459.9
5.6	33.0	145.9	310.1	746.2	2,445.8	432.1
NC	+3.6	–1.7	–2.7	+0.6	–1.6	+0.4
–10.5	–4.3	–11.8	–14.2	–13.5	–10.4	–6.0
–40.9	–19.8	43.0	–29.6	–32.1	–19.4	–28.7

crime rate increased nearly every year until 1993. After 1993 the crime rate shows a dramatic decrease in almost every area. It is interesting that at the same time the crime rate is decreasing, the prison population (see Figure 11.2) is increasing.[14] Conservatives argue that this finding is strong evidence that the "get tough on crime" approach is working.

FIGURE 11.2 **Increase in Adult Correctional Populations, 1980–2001**

Source: Adapted from Lauren E. Glaze, "Probation and Parole in the United States," Bureau of Justice Statistics, *Bulletin* (revised 9 February 2004), 1.

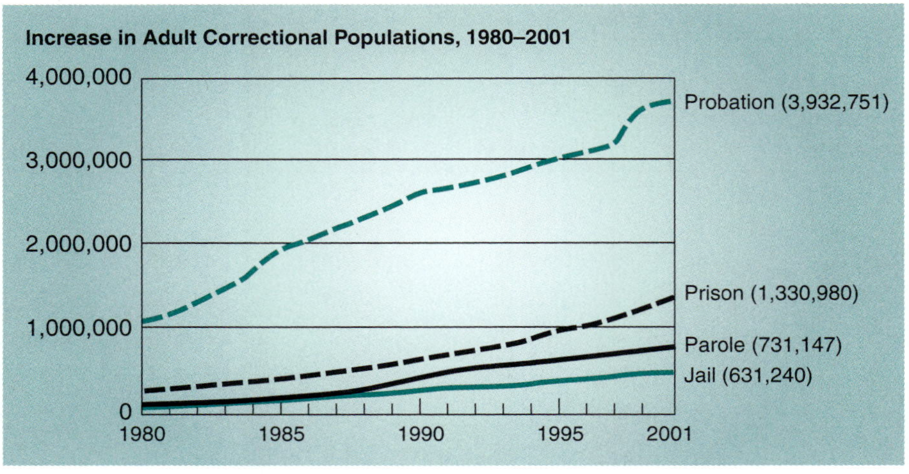

Gender. Crime is an overwhelmingly male activity. In 2002 in the United States, 77.5 percent of all persons arrested were male. There are a few areas of crime in which females' rates of arrest come close to or exceed those of males: Women are involved in 40.2 percent of arrests for forgery and counterfeiting, 45.4 percent of arrests for fraud, 49.6 percent of arrests for embezzlement, 59.4 percent of arrests for running away (a status offense), and 66.6 percent of arrests for prostitution and commercialized vice.[15]

Age. Criminal behavior tends to be highly concentrated among the younger age groups. As can be seen in Table 11.2, the vast majority (80.4 percent) of arrests are of people under the age of forty. After age thirty-four the tendency toward criminal behavior begins to drop, and after age forty it becomes relatively rare. These figures form much of the support for the position of those who argue that the function of the criminal justice system should be incapacitation. The argument is that if a criminal is incapacitated by being locked up for a long enough period of time, he or she will most likely "grow out of" his or her criminal tendencies. The data since 1990 reporting a massive increase in the prison population, with a corresponding dramatic decrease in the crime rate, would appear to support this argument.

Race. As Table 11.3 shows, whites and Asians are relatively underrepresented in the crime statistics. African Americans and American Indians are overrepresented, particularly in the area of violent crime. Four reasons account for these differences. The first is the age structure of various subgroups of the population. Minority groups tend to

TABLE 11.2 Percent Distribution of Total U.S. Population and Persons Arrested for All Offenses by Age Group, United States, 2003

Age Group	U.S. Resident Population	Persons Arrested
Age 14 and Under	21.2%	5.4%
15 to 19	7.1	21.3
20 to 24	6.9	19.3
25 to 29	6.7	12.3
30 to 34	7.3	11.2
35 to 39	7.8	10.9
40 to 44	8.0	8.9
45 to 49	7.3	5.3
50 to 54	6.5	2.8
55 to 59	5.0	1.3
60 to 64	3.9	0.7
Age 65 and Older	12.4	0.8

Sources: Kathleen Maguire and Ann L. Pastore, eds., *Sourcebook of Criminal Justice Statistics,* 30th ed. (Washington, DC: U.S. Government Printing Office, 2004), 345. Available online at www.albany.edu/sourcebook.

TABLE 11.3 Distribution of Arrests by Race, 2003

Group	Percent of Population	Percent of Total Crime	Percent of Violent Crime	Percent of Property Crime
White	80.8	69.5	60.2	66.0
Black	12.7	28.1	37.6	31.4
Asian or Pacific Islander	4.2	1.1	1.0	1.2
American Indian or Alaskan Native	0.9	1.3	1.2	1.5

Sources: Kathleen Maguire and Ann L. Pastore, eds., *Sourcebook of Criminal Justice Statistics,* 30th ed., online at www.albany.edu/sourcebook.

be younger than whites—particularly African Americans, whose average age is seven years less than that of whites. Because crime is concentrated among the young, this fact partially accounts for the difference in crime rates. The second reason is that minorities are more heavily concentrated in urban areas, where more opportunities for both crime and apprehension by the police exist. The third reason is selective enforcement. Police tend to patrol minority neighborhoods more heavily than they do white neighborhoods, thereby increasing the chance that lawbreakers who are members of minority groups will be arrested. The final explanation is economic opportunity. In the section on dynamics we discuss theories that explain crime as being largely a result of people's lacking legitimate opportunities for success. As we explained in Chapters 7 and 8, minority group members are far more likely than whites to be poor. Therefore, according to strain and opportunity theories, members of minority groups are more likely to turn to crime as a means of achieving goals to which the legitimate channels of achievement are blocked.

Social Welfare and Crime

The preceding statistics are interesting, but they are of secondary importance for our purposes here. What is of primary importance is how these statistics grind through the criminal justice system and become input for the social welfare system.

Juveniles. Because children are not considered to be responsible for their actions, rehabilitation is almost always chosen over punishment as a response to juvenile crime. Only about 1 percent of all juvenile arrests result in waiver to criminal court; the rest are handled either informally or in the more treatment-oriented juvenile court.[16] Data collected by the National Center for Juvenile Justice show that during 1999, 1.67 million juvenile arrests occurred and only 163,800 resulted in placement in a out-of-home facility such as a state training school. Thus, out of a beginning number of 1.67 million arrests,

TABLE 11.4 Adults Involved in the Criminal Justice System, 1990–2002

	1990	1995	2002	Change 2002/1990
Probation	2,670,234	3,077,861	3,995,165	+49.6%
Parole	531,407	679,421	753,141	+41.7%
Jail	405,320	507,044	665,475	+64.2%
Prison	743,382	1,078,542	1,367,856	+84%
Total	4,350,343	5,342,868	6,781,637	+55.9%

Source: Adapted from data in Lauren E. Glaze, "Probation and Parole in the United States," Bureau of Justice Statistics, *Bulletin* (August 2002), 1, and (August 2003), 1.

only about nine-tenths of 1 percent end up in what is generally considered a punishment facility.[17] This figure clearly illustrates the point that crime among juveniles is considered a subject more proper for rehabilitation by the social welfare institution than for punishment by the criminal justice system.

Adult Corrections. The statistics for the adult correctional population are summarized in Figure 11.2 and Table 11.4. The fact that over one-half of the adult correctional population is on probation, which means these people are supervised in the community instead of serving any prison time, indicates that even in the area of adult crime we still have faith in the rehabilitative ideal and turn to the social welfare institution for dealing with the problem of crime. However, the fact that the population in prison grew by 84 percent between 1990 and 2002, while the number on probation grew by 49.6 percent, a huge but still far smaller growth rate, indicates that we may be losing this faith.

What **Americans** Believe

Some of the most startling statistics in recent American social history are those reflecting our response to crime. Arrest rates in recent years have gone up and sentences have become notably harsher. As described in this chapter, just since 1990 the prison population has nearly doubled, the number of people in jail has increased by two-thirds, and the number of those under probation or parole supervision has increased by one-half.

The General Social Survey has tracked Americans' beliefs about the courts' handling of convicted criminals since 1972 with the question, "In general, do you think the courts in this area deal too harshly or not harshly enough with criminals?" The responses to this item have been fairly consistent over the years, but an interesting thing happened after 1994—respondents' opinions began to reflect a significant tendency in the direction of greater leniency. As can be seen by inspecting Table 11.5, the percentage of respondents who believed that the courts were not harsh enough declined from 89.3 percent in 1994 to 71.5 percent in 2002. The percentage of respondents who felt that the courts were too harsh increased from 2.7 percent in 1994 to 9.8 percent in 2002. These numbers, of course, still reflect a society in which most people would like the courts to be even tougher on criminals. However, the direction of the statistics is encouraging. Perhaps we are nearing a time when we will want to consider more productive responses to crime than the traditional "lock 'em up and throw away the key" approach.

TABLE 11.5

In General, Do You Think the Courts Deal Too Harshly or Not Harshly Enough with Criminals?

	Too Harsh	Not Harsh Enough	About Right
1994	2.7%	89.3%	11.7%
1996	5.0%	83.5%	11.5%
1998	6.6%	79.3%	14.1%
2000	8.2%	74.8%	17.0%
2002	9.8%	71.5%	18.7%

Dynamics

When we look at explanations of crime, we are confronted with a bewildering array of theories. Three major groups of theories attempt to explain the dynamics of crime: control theories, cultural theories, and social victim theories.

Control Theories

Control theories proceed from the conservative assumption that human nature is basically bad and that society must control people's natural antisocial nature. Ernest van den Haag, for example, argues that "for the most part, offenders are not sick. They are like us. Worse, we are like them. Potentially, we could all be . . . criminals."[18] These theories explain crime as the result of people's failing to control their natural antisocial impulses. People may be unable to control their impulses because they are inherently incapable of controlling themselves, because they are psychologically incapable of self-restraint, because they have been improperly socialized, or because the costs and benefits of crime result in a more favorable outcome than the costs and benefits of self-control.

Biological Control Theory. The earliest theories of crime were *biological control theories,* which Empey refers to as "kinds-of-people" theories. These theories assert that criminals are innately inferior people who have not inherited the ability to control their aggressive impulses and behave in responsible ways.[19] The first biological control theorist was the nineteenth-century Italian physician Cesare Lombroso. Lombroso believed that criminals were physically different from noncriminals, and he set out to test his hypothesis by performing an extensive series of physical measurements on convicts and comparing these measurements to those of nonconvicts. Lombroso published his findings in 1876 in a book entitled *The Criminal Man.* In this book Lombroso reported his conclusion that criminals are "atavistic types"; that is, they are born lawbreakers who are subhuman throwbacks to an earlier, more primitive stage of human evolution. Criminal types could, Lombroso claimed, be identified by physical features that are characteristic of an earlier form of evolutionary development. These characteristics are imbalanced regions of the brain, an asymmetrical face and skull, an abnormal nose, fleshy protruding lips, excessively long arms, abundant wrinkles, abnormal sex organs, a high tolerance for pain, and other physical anomalies. Lombroso argued that people who possess five or more of these characteristics will lack self-control and be predisposed to crime.[20] Simply put, according to Lombroso criminals are cavemen in our midst.

Following Lombroso, many theories and studies have attempted to explain crime as somehow related to innate characteristics that render the individual incapable of controlling his or her antisocial impulses. Probably the most influential is the work of William Sheldon, who argues that people are innately predisposed to criminal behavior and that this predisposition can be detected by an examination of body types. Sheldon conducted a study of the physical measurements of two hundred boys in a school for delinquents and compared these with measurements of two hundred male college students. Based on the data he collected, Sheldon divided young men into three distinctive body types. The first he called *endomorphs,* who are fat and round; the second are *mesomorphs,* who are large-boned and muscular; and third are *ectomorphs,* who are lean and delicate. Sheldon argues that these body types are genetically determined and that each produces a different personality and temperament. Mesomorphs are aggressive and insensitive, quick to translate impulse into action, and inherently deficient in internal controls. Sheldon concludes that because of these characteristics, mesomorphs are predisposed to criminal behavior.[21]

Biological control theories died out in the liberal years of the 1960s and were generally thought to be so wrongheaded that they were often treated in texts and in criminology classes as subjects of humor. However, with the resurgence of conservatism in the 1980s, these theories have found new advocates and are once again the subject of serious academic debate and research. In their 1985 book *Crime and Human Nature,* political scientist James Q. Wilson and psychologist Richard J. Herrnstein, both of Harvard University, devoted five chapters to the relation of constitutional factors to criminal behavior. They forcefully concluded that the work of Lombroso and Sheldon, among others, was too quickly dismissed and that it should be taken seriously. More recently, Herrnstein, this time writing with political scientist Charles Murray, argued that low intelligence is one of the major factors leading to criminal behavior:

> Among the most firmly established facts about criminal offenders is that their distribution of IQ scores differs from that of the population at large. Taking the scientific literature as a whole, criminal offenders have average IQs of about 92, eight points below the mean. More serious or chronic offenders generally have lower scores than most casual offenders. The relationship of IQ to criminality is especially pronounced in the small fraction of the population, primarily young men, who constitute the chronic criminals that account for a disproportionate amount of crime. Offenders who have been caught do not score much lower, if at all, than those who are getting away with their crimes. Holding socioeconomic status constant does little to explain away the relationship between crime and cognitive ability.[22]

These works come under the heading of neoclassical control theory, which we examine later in this section.

Psychological Control Theory. Heavily based on the theories of Sigmund Freud, *psychological control theories* locate the causes of criminal behavior within the psychological development of the individual rather than in his or her genetic makeup. Freud asserted that people are born with a set of primitive, antisocial instincts, which he labeled the *id.* Freud wrote that "the primitive, savage, and evil impulses of mankind have not vanished in any individual, but continue their existence, although in a repressed state."[23] The basically antisocial instincts of people are repressed by the socialization process of children, which results in the development of what Freud called a *superego,* generally known as a conscience. Advocates of psychological control theory claim four major insights about the causes of crime: (1) Criminal behavior is neurotic behavior; (2) criminal behavior is the result of a defective superego; (3) the superego is defective because of faulty childhood socialization; and (4) criminal behavior represents a search for gratification to compensate for deprivations in childhood.[24] Thus, like biological control theory, psychological control theory shares the belief that human beings are basically antisocial and will naturally commit crimes unless they are controlled in some way. Unlike biological theory, psychological control theory does not believe that certain people are predisposed to crime at birth; rather it asserts that we are all equally predisposed and that what happens during the early years of childhood socialization explains which of us follow our natural tendencies and become criminals and which of us are able to overcome these tendencies and become law-abiding citizens.

Although psychological control theory shares biological control theory's pessimism about human nature, it is more optimistic about what can be done about it. The problem of crime is seen as an unconscious response to a combination of antisocial instincts and poor parental practices. Therefore, the problem of criminal behavior is viewed as being treatable just like any illness or adjustment problem. The entire rehabilitation approach in corrections, especially the juvenile court, is based on psychological control theory. The premise is that if some form of treatment can be delivered to criminals that will compensate for their faulty upbringing and help them develop self-control through cultivation of their superego, they will become productive citizens.

Social Control Theory. Like the other control theories, *social control theory* starts with the belief that human nature is inherently antisocial. A leading proponent of social control theory, Travis Hirschi, says that "we are all animals, and thus all naturally capable of committing criminal acts." Hirschi says that the question, "Why do people commit crimes?" needs no answer. People commit crimes because it is their nature to do so. The question that really needs an answer is, "Why do most people *not* commit crimes?"[25]

Hirschi asserts that most people do not commit crimes because there is a bond between them and society. People internalize the norms of the society in which they live, and in so doing they become moral beings sensitive to the needs of others. The social bonds identified by Hirschi include the ties of respect and affection between children and key people in their lives, such as parents, teachers, relatives, and friends; commitment to social norms of behavior and to success in regard to such values as getting a good education, a good job, and being successful; involvement in activities, because the more activities a person is involved in, the less time he or she will have to get into trouble; and finally the fact that most persons are brought up to believe in and respect the law.

Social control theory basically views criminal behavior as a result of inadequate attachment between people and the society in which they live. Hirschi says, "If a person does not care about the wishes and expectations of other people—that is, if he is insensitive to the opinion of others—then he is to that extent not bound by the norms. He is free to deviate."[26] The family is viewed as the major place where attachments, and therefore commitment to norms, develop. Thus, social control theory advocates the strengthening of families as a major crime control strategy.

Neoclassical Control Theory. Partly in response to the fact that the crime rate has continued to rise in spite of numerous rehabilitation and crime prevention programs, and partly in response to the general growth of conservatism in recent years, a resurgence of control theories has occurred. *Neoclassical control theories* are based on the belief that rehabilitation programs are totally without merit and that the criminal justice system should return to the practice of responding to crimes, not criminals. There are two versions of neoclassical theory—utilitarian theory and just deserts theory.

The primary proponents of *utilitarian theory* are James Q. Wilson, the late Richard Herrnstein, and Ernest van den Haag.[27] Utilitarian theorists contend that people commit crimes for basically practical reasons; they do so because they can get away with it and because they know that if they do get caught, the price they pay will not be severe. In other words, crime is viewed as having a favorable cost/benefit ratio. People commit crimes because they make a rational calculation that the potential profit from a crime exceeds the potential cost.

Utilitarian theory is based on two basic beliefs. The first is that punishment deters crime. Because people commit crimes for practical reasons involving costs and benefits, a high risk of severe punishment will increase the cost of doing crime and thus will discourage this behavior. The second belief is that punishment vindicates the social order. Utilitarians believe that in a just society, debts must be paid if people are to take the society seriously and to believe in its basic fairness. When a person commits a crime, he or she must be punished in order to square accounts. Ernest van den Haag says, "Laws threaten, or promise, punishments for crimes. Society has obligated itself by threatening. It owes the carrying out of its threats. Society pays its debt by punishing the offender, however unwilling he is to accept payment."[28]

The other brand of neoclassical control theory is the *just deserts theory.* This approach has been characterized by Empey as "a remarkable expression of the despair and pessimism that characterize currently popular views of American justice."[29] The main idea of the just deserts philosophy is that rehabilitation does not work, which is an idea shared with utilitarian theory; but just deserts theory goes further and argues that punishment does not work either. The sole purpose of the criminal justice system, according to this theory, should be to ensure that offenders are punished to a degree consistent with the severity of their offense—no more, no less. The just deserts approach is very concerned with due process issues. Its adherents would like to remove as much discretion as possible from the process and make the justice system mechanized.

Summary of Control Theories. The four versions and several sub-versions of control theory we have reviewed all share a conservative, pessimistic view of human nature. Control theories as a group see humans as being aggressive, self-serving, and amoral by nature: People will all commit crimes unless somehow they are controlled. Basically these theories are all pessimistic about the potential for rehabilitating law violators, and they are therefore generally hostile to a social welfare approach to crime. The one exception to this is psychological control theory, whose adherents are sympathetic to the idea of therapy for criminals.

Cultural Theories

Cultural theories of crime are closely related to the cultural theories of poverty discussed in Chapter 8. These theories reject the assumption of control theories that human nature is inherently antisocial and that control mechanisms are necessary to prevent people from committing crimes. Rather, cultural theories assume that human nature is inherently social and that crime is a result of people's becoming involved with deviant subcultures that value crime over law-abiding behavior. According to these theories, a criminal is a person who is behaving in accordance with the values and norms of the particular groups with which he or she associates. There are three major variants of cultural theories of crime: cultural deviance theory, differential association theory, and strain theory.

Cultural Deviance. *Cultural deviance theory* began with the work of Clifford R. Shaw and Henry D. McKay in Chicago in the 1920s. Shaw and McKay, who were trained as demographers, were originally interested in two questions related to juvenile delinquency. The first was, "How are delinquents geographically distributed in the city?" They studied this by simply plotting on city maps the addresses of all juveniles officially declared to be delinquent by Chicago courts. What they found was that delinquency rates were consistently higher in impoverished, inner-city neighborhoods. Looking at delinquency rates over time, they found a very interesting thing. The delinquency rate for any given neighborhood remained remarkably constant over time, *even though the population of the neighborhood often completely changed.* A neighborhood might be Italian for years, then change to mainly Irish, then gradually change until it was almost completely African American; yet the delinquency rate stayed constant. The delinquency rate of the group that moved out (generally to a better neighborhood,) by contrast, dropped to a rate that mirrored the rate of the new neighborhood.

Shaw and McKay's findings on the geographic distribution of delinquency led to their second question: "What are the social conditions associated with high-delinquency neighborhoods?" They found that prominent among these conditions were physical deterioration; economic segregation; racial and ethnic segregation; a high incidence of social ills, such as infant mortality, mental illness, unemployment, divorce, and desertion; and a high rate of dropping out of school.

Shaw and McKay developed cultural deviance theory in an effort to explain the findings of their research. They assert that crime is more closely related to characteristics of the neighborhoods in which people live than it is to any innate characteristics of the people who commit crimes. The process works basically as follows: deteriorated areas (generally known as slums or ghettos) produce social disorganization characterized by inadequate family life; poverty; physical deterioration; and ineffective religious, educational, and recreational organizations. This social disorganization leads to a lack of effective social controls over children; lack of effective social controls from family, church, and school causes children to form street gangs, which develop deviant social controls; and finally, the deviant social controls developed by street gangs are then passed from one generation to another.[30]

Walter Miller, an anthropologist, updated cultural deviance theory in 1958 into a form that is closely akin to Oscar Lewis's culture of poverty theory.[31] Miller argues that the lower class is characterized by a distinctive culture with its own norms and standards of behavior. In contrast to Shaw and McKay, Miller argues that lower-class communities are not disorganized; they just have different values than the larger society. He says that "there is emerging a relatively homogeneous and stabilized native American lower-class culture."[32] The values that Miller describes as characterizing this subculture are similar to those described by Lewis in his books on culture of poverty: female-dominated families; marginal roles for men; focal concerns of trouble, smartness, fate, and autonomy; and the belief that deferred gratification and hard work are for suckers. In this culture, according to Miller, crime is considered to be acceptable and even desirable; conformity to middle-class standards is deviant.

The major idea of cultural deviance theories is that people who commit crimes are not deviants whose basically antisocial nature is not adequately controlled. Rather, criminals are individuals who are conforming to a set of social norms just like anyone else; however, their norms are different from those of the majority of society. Crime, in other words, is a product of the environment, not the individual.

Differential Association Theory. *Differential association theory* began with the work of Edwin H. Sutherland in 1939.[33] The assumption of this theory is that both human nature and the social structure are plastic: A person's behavior and values are constantly changing in response to the group that he or she is interacting with, and groups are constantly changing in response to the people who participate in them. Furthermore, everyone participates in multiple groups, and the roles and expectations may be very different, and sometimes even conflicting, in different groups. All people, according to this theory, are exposed to deviant as well as conformist influences.

Differential association theory explains crime as learned behavior. People learn criminal behavior through the groups with which they associate. If a person associates with more groups that define criminal behavior as acceptable than groups that define criminal behavior as unacceptable, the person will probably engage in criminal behavior. On the other hand, if a person mostly associates with groups that do not define crime as acceptable, the person will probably not commit crimes.

Differential association theory provides a strong argument against imprisoning people convicted of crimes. According to this theory, putting a person in prison removes him or her from association with groups that do not define crime in favorable terms and puts the person exclusively in contact with groups favorable to crime. Thus, a person spending time in prison will only develop a more positive attitude toward crime and a more negative definition of law-abiding behavior.

Strain Theory. The final variety of cultural theory, *strain theory,* is based on the work of Robert Merton and was further developed by Albert Cohen, Richard Cloward, and Lloyd Ohlin;[34] in the early 1990s it was revised and reintroduced by Robert Agnew.[35] Strain theory rejects many of the arguments of cultural deviance theory (that crime is a result of a deviant lower-class subculture) and of differential association theory (that criminal behavior occurs when a person associates with more groups who favor crime than groups who do not). Both these theories assert that people become criminals because they have values that are different from those of the larger society. Strain theory, in contrast, argues that people who commit crimes have basically the same values as everyone else. Primary among these values is an emphasis on achievement and success. But, according to this theory, the avenues for the achievement of success are greatly restricted for people in the lower class. Thus, they are faced with a cruel dilemma: Either they abandon the major American values of success and prosperity, or they abandon another key value—obedience to the law. According to Merton, "A cardinal American virtue, 'ambition,' promotes a cardinal American vice, 'deviant behavior.' "[36]

Strain theory has been mainly applied to juvenile delinquency among lower-class boys. The central idea is that these young people share the value of success with the larger culture, but because of inadequate socialization they are unable to compete effectively. This produces strain, which they seek to resolve. In Cohen's version of the theory, the boys respond to this strain by adopting one of three general roles. The first role is what Cohen calls the "corner boy." This person adapts to his sense of frustration and failure by accepting his lower-class status, removing himself from competition for success, and withdrawing into a sheltering group of boys who have also resigned themselves to failure. The name for this role is derived from the fact that these are the type of people one sees aimlessly hanging around street corners. The second role is what Cohen calls the "college boy." This person, who is relatively rare according to Cohen, accepts the challenge of middle-class society and chooses to compete on middle-class terms. Finally, there is the "delinquent boy." This person accepts middle-class standards of material success but rejects middle-class means of acquiring success; he turns to crime as a means of achieving valued goals.

Summary of Cultural Theories. The three general types of cultural theories discussed here share the view that human nature is basically social and that we can best explain criminal behavior by looking at environmental influences on individuals. Cultural deviance theory asserts that lower-class communities produce a deviant subculture that is relatively favorable to crime. In these communities, a person who commits crimes is considered normal and one who strongly opposes crime is considered abnormal. Differential association theory argues that people become criminals not because they live in deviant subcultures but because they associate with more groups that favor crime than groups that oppose crime. A strength of this theory over the others is that it makes it possible to explain people in lower-class neighborhoods who are law abiding as well as people in middle- and upper-class areas who engage in criminal acts. The final version, strain theory, argues that lower-class people have the same values as people in the rest of society—that is, that they value success—but lack access to legitimate channels for achieving success. Therefore, they turn to crime as a means of pursuing the American dream.

Social Victim Theories

Social victim theories, as a group, proceed from the liberal assumption that human nature is basically good and that if a person becomes a criminal it is because society has somehow corrupted him or her. Empey observes that social victim theory "represents the culmination of a line of social thought which has progressively led away from the notion that delinquent tendencies are inherent in individuals and toward the notion that such tendencies are inherent in the way society makes rules, enforces those rules, and selectively punishes some people and not others."[37] Two major types of social victim theories are labeling theory and radical theory.

Labeling Theory. *Labeling theory* makes the assertion that committing a crime is not what makes a person a criminal. Studies indicate that the vast majority of people have committed at least one, and often many, acts that are against the law. Yet most people are not criminals. Labeling theorists argue that what makes a person a criminal is getting *caught* committing a crime and then being publicly identified as a criminal. In other words, it is the label that makes a person into a criminal, not the act itself. Howard Becker, one of the leading proponents of labeling theory, says,

> Social groups make deviance by making the rules whose infractions constitute deviance and by applying these rules to particular people and labeling them as outsiders. From this point of view, deviance is *not* a quality of the act a person commits, but rather a consequence of the application by others of rules and sanctions to the "offender." The deviant is one to whom that label has successfully been applied; deviant behavior is the behavior that people so label.[38]

The theory goes on to argue that if a person is unlucky enough to get caught and thereby to become labeled a criminal, then people will respond to the person as a criminal, and the person will begin to think of himself or herself as a criminal; the person will then internalize this socially imposed self-image and begin to act in ways in which we expect a criminal to behave. What occurs is a self-fulfilling prophecy—society expects a person to act like a criminal and the person lives up to the expectation. As discussed in Chapter 13, a similar process can be described for those labeled mentally ill.

Labeling theorists argue that labels are selectively applied. Not everyone who is caught is labeled. The labeling depends on several factors that are not related to the act a person has committed—factors such as who the person is, what race and socioeconomic class the person belongs to, and whether the person treats the police with the proper respect. Members of low-power groups, it is argued, are much more likely to be labeled when caught committing a crime than are members of higher-status groups. Thus, there are more poor, young, and minority group criminals because we are more likely to assign the label of criminal to members of these groups and thus to make them criminals.

Radical Criminology. *Radical criminology* is based on the assumption that human nature is essentially good: Although people may occasionally act in selfish ways, if they actually become criminal it is because they are responding to a repressive and corrupting society. This approach rejects all attempts to portray crime as the result of individual characteristics, and it advocates radical social change as the only real way to reduce crime. One of the leading advocates of radical theory, Richard Quinney, has summarized the theory's main ideas in the following six propositions:

- American society is based on an advanced capitalist economy.
- The state is organized to serve the interests of the dominant economic class, the capitalist ruling class.
- Criminal law is an instrument of the state and ruling class to maintain and perpetuate the existing social and economic order.
- Crime control in capitalist society is accomplished through a variety of institutions and agencies established and administered by a governmental elite, representing ruling class interests, for the purpose of establishing domestic order.
- The contradictions of advanced capitalism . . . require that the subordinate classes remain oppressed by whatever means necessary, especially through the coercion and violence of the legal system.
- Only with the collapse of capitalist society and the creation of a new society, based on socialist principles, will there be a solution to the crime problem.[39]

Radical theory sees little difference between the punishment and rehabilitation approaches to dealing with crime. Both approaches are viewed as a means by which society blames the victims of capitalist repression for problems for which they are not responsible. The only real solution to the problem of crime, according to radical theorists, is to abandon the approach of working with individuals altogether and instead to focus on the real source of crime, the oppressive and repressive social and economic system.

A Brief History of Criminal Justice

Historian Blake McKelvey subtitled his study of corrections in America "A History of Good Intentions." McKelvey makes the point that generation after generation of reformers have attempted to make prisons into something constructive, but that time after time their efforts have had poor and often tragic results.[40] Unfortunately, McKelvey's pessimistic analysis of prisons can be generalized to all efforts to deal with the problem of crime in our society. All efforts to make something constructive out of criminal justice programs, from the development of prisons right through to the recent emphasis on diversion programs, have started out with high hopes and great expectations but have generally turned sour. As Rothman has observed, the pride of one generation becomes the shame of another.[41]

Prisons—the First Reform

Because it is hard for us to imagine a society without prisons, it may be surprising to learn that the idea of the prison has a fairly recent origin. Before the late 1700s, there were no prisons that were places where people were incarcerated for long periods of time for either punishment or rehabilitation. As Dershowitz has said, "The concept of rehabilitation would have been entirely alien to the early colonists. . . . Society's duty was simply to punish the offender swiftly, publicly and often quite harshly."[42] Rothman explains that the colonists' nearly exclusive use of corporal or capital punishment and their total lack of concern with reforming lawbreakers was a natural result of their view of human nature. He says that given the colonists'

> conception of deviant behavior and institutional organization, they did not believe that a jail could rehabilitate or intimidate or detain the offender. They placed little faith in the possibility of reform. Prevailing Calvinist doctrines that stressed the natural depravity of man and the powers of the devil hardly allowed such optimism. Since temptations to misconduct were not only omnipresent but practically irresistible, rehabilitation could not serve as the basis for a prison program.[43]

Given this orientation, jails existed only as places where people accused of crimes could be detained while awaiting trial and, if convicted, punishment. Punishments consisted of fines for those able to pay and/or some inconvenience or abuse of the offender's body, such as stocks, pillory, flogging, branding, mutilation, or, for many offenses, death.

The establishment of prisons in eighteenth-century America was a result of two developments—the Enlightenment and the American Revolution. Enlightenment thinking, as espoused in the works of philosophers such as Montesquieu, Rousseau, and Voltaire, stressed that humans were rational creatures and that the world was guided by rational principles that people could discover and ultimately control through the use of their intelligence. This philosophy was applied to criminal justice by Cesare Beccaria, an Italian who published *On Crimes and Punishments* in 1764. Beccaria made three main points regarding how society should react to crimes: Punishment should be proportional to the severity of the crime; punishment should be certain and should be just severe enough so that the cost of committing a crime exceeded the benefits derived from it; and excessively severe penalties would undermine the authority of the courts and the deterrent effect of punishment.[44] The American Revolution, for its part, contributed to an atmosphere in which everything English was viewed with suspicion. The brutal criminal justice system that the new republic inherited from the colonies was clearly of English origin and thus was considered ripe for reform. The works of Enlightenment thinkers such as Beccaria provided the rationale for the reform.

The process of criminal justice reform began almost immediately after the end of the American Revolution. It had two major components. The first was the elimination of the death penalty for crimes other than first-degree murder or a handful of serious crimes such as treason. This reform was based on Beccaria's idea that punishment should not be overly severe for the crime in question. People had frequently been found not guilty of crimes by juries who thought them guilty but were unwilling to impose the death penalty for a relatively minor crime. Thus, the overly severe punishment resulted in people not being punished at all. The second component, related to the first, was the development of the concept of lengthy incarceration in prison as a substitute for death or for the usually grotesque corporal punishments previously applied. This too was related to Beccaria's idea that punishment should be proportional to the seriousness of the crime. The length of prison sentences could be precisely tailored to fit crimes of any degree of seriousness: for a minor crime, a person could be imprisoned for as little as a few days; for a major crime, he or she could be imprisoned for life. Prison construction proceeded at a fast pace: The first, the Walnut Street Jail, was built in Philadelphia in 1790, Newgate state prison in New York in 1796, the New Jersey penitentiary in 1797, and prisons in Virginia and Kentucky in 1800. Also completed within a few years were facilities in Vermont, New Hampshire, and Maryland.[45] Thus, in a remarkably short time the criminal justice system in the United States had been reformed from a system based on a Calvinistic notion of punishment to one based on an enlightened notion of rehabilitation with the prison as its central feature.

The assumption behind the first wave of criminal justice reform, which resulted in the construction of prisons, was that the legal system itself was a cause of crime. Because it was arbitrary, uncertain, and brutal, the system was believed to increase rather than control crime. When the system was reformed and prisons were constructed, people believed, the new system in which sentences were fair and certainty of punishment was high would in itself be sufficient to control crime. Thus, prisons were constructed with a serious problem built in: No one had really given much thought about what to do with convicts once they were there. As Rothman has noted, "A repulsion from the gallows rather than any faith in the penitentiary spurred the late eighteenth-century construction. Few people had any clear idea what these structures should look like or how they should be administered—or even addressed themselves seriously to these questions."[46]

The Indeterminate Sentence and Parole

The correctional philosophy of the early prison reformers and administrators was highly simplistic. They believed that crime was a result of disorder in society, so the reformation of criminals was simply a matter of placing them in a well-structured environment where they would learn orderly habits and develop the moral fiber they needed to resist the world's corrupting influences. Therefore, prisons emphasized routines, silence, and reading the Bible. They accomplished this by isolating and regimenting the prisoners as much as possible. The ideal was to have each person confined to his cell almost all of the time, with only a Bible for companionship. By the middle of the nineteenth century, however, people began to realize that this approach to penology was not working. Critics attributed the failure of the system to the fact that prison administrators were having to devote almost all of their energy to maintaining order. In an 1867 report to the New York legislature, E. C. Wines and Theodore Dwight stated that prisons no longer had rehabilitation as their central goal. They said that "there is not a state prison in America in which the reformation of the convicts is the one supreme object of the [institution] to which everything else must bend." By the standard of reformation,

> there is not a prison system in the United States, which . . . would not be found wanting. There is not one, we feel convinced . . . which seeks the reformation of its subjects as a primary object. . . . They are all . . . lacking in the breadth and comprehensiveness of their scope; all lacking in the employment of a wise and effective machinery to keep the whole in health and vigorous action.[47]

Critics argued that the major failing of the correctional system was that prisoners had no incentive to cooperate in their own rehabilitation. They were given "flat" or "determinate" sentences by the courts, which meant that they knew exactly how long their sentences would be and that nothing they did, short of committing a new criminal offense, would have any effect on the length. Reformers in the last half of the nineteenth century began to advocate *indeterminate sentences,* in which a person was sentenced to serve a range of years, say three to ten; by cooperating with prison authorities the person could serve the shorter length of time, but by not cooperating he or she would serve the maximum length of time. As one prison reformer said, "The prisoner's destiny should be placed, measurably, in his own hands; he must be put into circumstances where he will be able, through his own exertions, to continually better his own conditions. A regulated self-interest must be brought into play, and made constantly operative." Another said, "When a man keeps the key to his own prison, he is soon persuaded to fit it to the lock."[48]

The concept of the indeterminate sentence was first applied at Elmira Reformatory in New York in 1876. A man who was set free before the expiration of his term was required to serve out the remaining time on parole. The parolees were supervised by volunteer citizens, known as *guardians.* The parolee was required to report to the guardian the first day of each month, and a written report had to be submitted to the prison signed by both the guardian and the parolee's employer. The parole concept spread slowly but steadily. By 1901 twenty states had parole statutes, and by 1944 every American jurisdiction had some form of provision for indeterminate sentences and parole.

The indeterminate sentence became the centerpiece for an approach to corrections known as the *new penology.* Other aspects of this approach were the ideas that convicts should be treated humanely and should be given meaningful and productive work to occupy their time, and that juveniles, women, and first-time offenders should be housed separately from older, hardened male criminals. The overall focus of this approach was that rehabilitation rather than punishment and vengeance should be the aim of the correctional system. Cullen and Gilbert observe that the new penology did not stir any immediate and major reforms in the U.S. correctional system. "Nevertheless," they write, "it must be recognized that the champions of the new penology played a large role in bolstering the legitimacy of rehabilitative ideology at a time when it appeared vulnerable to being discredited and swept aside."[49]

Probation

English common law, which forms the basis for the U.S. legal system, recognizes the power of courts to suspend sentences. This means that if a person is found guilty and is assessed a punishment, the court can order that the punishment not be carried out, provided that the person stays out of trouble. This power was used in the United States as early as 1830.[50] In the mid-1800s, the shortcomings of the prison system that led to the development of the indeterminate sentence and parole, combined with the fact that many convicted criminals were being given suspended sentences that did not require any supervision, gave impetus to the development of the concept of *probation.* The first person to apply the concept of probation, also the first person to use the word, was a well-to-do Boston shoe manufacturer, John Augustus. Beginning in 1841, supported at first by his own funds and later by donations of well-wishers, Augustus would go to the Boston court, interview the prisoners awaiting trial, and intervene with the judge in the case of those he thought were good candidates for reformation. As recounted by Moreland,

> It was Augustus' practice to bail, after his conviction, an offender in whom there was hope of reformation. The man would be ordered to appear before the court at a stated time at the expiration of which Augustus would accompany him to the courtroom. If the judge was satisfied with Augustus' account of his stewardship, the offender, instead of being committed to the House of Correction, would be fined one cent and costs. The one cent and costs, which amounted generally to from three to four dollars, Augustus paid.[51]

In 1878, Massachusetts honored Augustus's innovative work by becoming the first state to pass a probation law. Massachusetts remained the only state with such a law until 1897, when other states began passing probation laws in rapid-fire succession. By 1920 probation was permitted in two-thirds of the states for adults and in every state for juveniles.

The Concept of Delinquency and the Juvenile Court

Since the earliest years of our country, the courts have treated children differently than adults. There have been two main areas of difference. The first is that children have not generally been considered responsible for their actions. Traditionally, a child below the age of seven has been assumed to not be responsible; a child between seven and fourteen was considered responsible only if it could be proved that he or she was aware that the act committed was wrong. The second area of difference is that children have not been guaranteed the same rights as adults. Because children have not been considered to be responsible for their actions, they have been defined as dependent people, the same as people with mental disorders. Consequently, principles of due process did not apply. Rather, under the principle of *parens patria* (the state as parent), it was believed that authorities required broad discretionary powers to act on behalf of children. Before the late nineteenth and early twentieth centuries, however, even though children were recognized as being different under the law, they were tried in the same courts as adults, subjected to basically the same procedures, and often locked up in the same jails awaiting trial and the same prisons following trial. In the reform years around the turn of the century, the period known as the Progressive Era, these practices became the prime targets of reformers.

The concepts of delinquency and the juvenile court both emerged during the early years of the twentieth century. The juvenile court was first developed in Chicago as a result of the efforts of the Chicago Women's Club. In the late 1800s the club adopted as a project the general improvement of jail conditions in Cook County. While engaged in this effort, the members of the club were shocked to find that children were locked up with adults, and they soon came to the conclusion that there was no way to really improve conditions for these children as long as they were in the adult criminal justice system. In 1895 the members of the club drafted a bill providing for a completely separate court to handle the cases of juveniles. When they submitted the bill to their legal advisor, he questioned its constitutionality, believing that the bill was too broad and that it lacked procedural safeguards. Consequently, the club dropped the bill. It was picked up two years later by the Illinois Conference of Charities, where it gained the support of the Chicago Bar Association and was passed by the legislature. The bill created a juvenile court with jurisdiction for all legal matters pertaining to children under the age of sixteen. It provided for a special judge, a separate courtroom, and the maintenance of separate records. Perhaps the most important aspect was that it called for court hearings to be informal rather than formal.

The juvenile court was based on the concept of *delinquency,* which had as its object the decriminalizing of antisocial behavior in youth. The basic approach was succinctly stated in an address given to the American Bar Association in 1909 by Julian W. Mack, a juvenile court judge in Chicago:

> Why isn't it just and proper to treat these juvenile offenders as we deal with the neglected children, as a wise and merciful father handles his own child whose errors are not discovered by the authorities? Why isn't it the duty of the State instead of asking merely whether a boy or a girl has committed the specific offense, to find out what he is, physically, mentally, morally, and then, if it learns that he is treading the path that leads to criminality, to take him in charge, not so much to punish as to reform, not to degrade but to uplift, not to crush but to develop, not to make him a criminal but a worthy citizen?[52]

The invention of the concept of delinquency and the creation of the juvenile court represented the zenith of the rehabilitation movement. Children were not to be defined as criminals and moral deviants; rather, they were to be thought of as misguided youngsters who needed firm but kindly parenting to get them back on the right track. The idea caught on quickly. Ten years after Illinois created the first juvenile court, such courts had been established in twenty states and in the District of Columbia; within twenty years only three states lacked separate juvenile courts; and by the middle of the century all states and territories, as well as many foreign countries, had passed juvenile court laws.

Criminal Justice Reform—Rhetoric and Reality

Our brief survey has described how, between the American Revolution and about 1930, the philosophy of the criminal justice system in the United States underwent a complete philosophical transformation, from an emphasis on punishment and retribution to an emphasis on reform and rehabilitation. Unfortunately, the reality of the situation has never closely approximated the philosophy. As dramatically illustrated in the 1995 movie *Murder in the First,* treatment of inmates behind prison walls, both by officials and by other prisoners, has often been as brutal as the corporal punishments that prisons were supposed to replace. Programs to help prisoners resolve problems and thus to help them reform have almost never been adequately staffed by people qualified to meet the objectives of the programs. For example, in 1954 there were only 23 full-time psychiatrists employed to provide treatment to 161,587 inmates in state and federal prisons.[53] Probation and parole officers are expected, under the rehabilitation ideal, to help offenders resolve life problems and make a better adjustment to society; but a "normal" caseload consists of 100 cases, and caseloads can run as high as 250 or more.[54] The juvenile court, which was supposed to replace the cold impersonality of the adult court with an approach resembling that of a kindly parent, has often done just the opposite; it has often ignored due process and basic rights, punished juveniles for acts that are not even crimes for adults, and assigned penalties far more severe than adults would receive for the same acts.

Current Issues

The major current issues in criminal justice relate to the effectiveness of the rehabilitation ideal that has dominated thinking since the early years of the nineteenth century. Untold millions of dollars are spent annually on prison counseling programs, parole supervision, juvenile programs, and—the newest reform—diversion programs. Many critics in recent years have argued that these programs not only are not doing much good but also may actually be doing harm. The criteria used to evaluate the effectiveness of criminal justice programs are generally the overall crime rate and the recidivism rate (the percentage of people convicted of one offense who go on to commit another). As we discussed in the statistics section, the rates have skyrocketed in recent years, so the critics have plenty of ammunition for their attacks.

Prisons

Since the early 1970s, treatment programs in prisons have been almost universally criticized. Criminologist Donald Cressey has written that treatment programs in prisons are "both farces and failures."[55] Walker notes that "as instruments of rehabilitation, American prisons are an obscene joke."[56]

Doubts about the effectiveness of prison treatment programs began in the early 1960s with the rising crime rates. Many observers suspected that much of the increase in crime could be attributed to people who had been released from prison and were committing second or even third crimes. This suspicion was reinforced in the 1960s by studies that confirmed that treatment programs were having no measurable effect. In 1966, Bailey published a review of reports on the effectiveness of one hundred such programs and concluded that very few could be said to have any demonstrable effect.[57] In 1974, Martinson published another review that looked at studies of correctional treatment programs from 1945 to 1967. Like Bailey, Martinson came to the conclusion that virtually no treatment program had been found to work.[58] In 1980, Gottfredson and Gottfredson published a study that found that 56 percent of released prisoners were eventually convicted and sent to prison again.[59] Dozens of other studies concluded that the prison treatment system was having little or no effect.

At about the same time, an additional criticism of treatment programs emerged. This one, which generally came from the left end of the political spectrum, charged that the whole purpose of treatment programs was suspect. Treatment programs, it was argued, served to coerce and control prisoners, not really to help them resolve problems. Typical of these critics was journalist Jessica Mitford, who in 1973 published an exposé of the prison system, *Kind and Usual Punishment.* Mitford quoted a former prison psychiatrist, who said of modern, treatment-oriented prisons, "In good prisons, like those in California, physical degradation is replaced by psychological degradation. I call these pastel prisons; they look good, shiny, sanitary. But inmates will tell you thousands of ways in which they are psychologically degraded." She concluded her discussion of treatment:

> For the prison administrator, whether he be warden, sociologist, or psychiatrist, "individualized treatment" is primarily a device for breaking the convict's will to resist and hounding him into compliance with institution demands, and is thus a means of exerting maximum control over the convict population. The cure will be deemed effective to the degree that the poor/young/brown/black captive appears to have capitulated to his middle-class/white/middle-aged captor, and to have adopted the virtues of subservience to authority, industry, cleanliness, docility. Subtle methods are, of course, preferable if and when they work. If and when they do not, there are cruder ones in the closet: the club; such products of an advanced chemistry as tear gas and Mace; and, in the last analysis, the gun.[60]

The dominant current opinion is that the concept of treatment is simply not compatible with the concept of imprisonment. Walker says, "many experts believe that there is something inherently contradictory in prison and rehabilitation and that prisons are unreformable."[61] Similarly, Morris argues that cure cannot be coerced; rehabilitation cannot take place in the punitive environment of the prison.[62] Critics point out that a pitifully small percentage of prison budgets is devoted to treatment, usually well under 10 percent. The argument is that in modern prisons, just as in prisons two hundred years ago, the major function and the major priority of the administration and staff is custody. This goal is always successful at bending any attempt at treatment to its will.

Parole

Parole has become the whipping boy in the current age of frustration over the ineffectiveness of the criminal justice system. Conservatives attack parole because they believe that parole results in criminals being released before they should be and thus is partially responsible for the increase in crime. Liberals attack it because they believe that the decisions of parole boards are arbitrary and based on no reliable data, and that the hope of parole is used to coerce prisoners into participating in treatment programs they really don't desire. Parole survives, however, because prison administrators still believe that it is necessary for the orderly administration of prisons—and because prisons are so overcrowded that if parole were abolished they would burst at the seams.

Is parole effective? The answer depends on how its goals are defined. There is little doubt that parole is effective in making prisons more manageable. Under our system of indeterminate sentencing, early release on parole has become the "carrot" to induce inmates to cooperate with prison authorities. It is also effective in reducing the prison population. Only South Africa and the former USSR rival the United States in the length of sentences given to persons convicted of crimes. Parole is necessary to mitigate the extreme length of these sentences and thus to keep the prison population at a manageable level. Whether the actual practice of parole (sometimes called *correctional casework* or *aftercare*) is effective as a helping process that assists parolees in improving their lives and preventing further difficulties with the law is a somewhat more doubtful proposition.

Like the studies of correctional treatment, the scientific studies of parole supervision have generated universally negative findings. A classic work on parole outcomes is *4,000 Lifetimes,* a report on research conducted by the National Council on Crime and Delinquency, which studied 104,182 men paroled between 1965 and 1970. A subsample of 1,810 was studied for a period of eight years. The study found that only 30 percent of the sample stayed completely out of trouble for the entire period; 40 percent were convicted of another serious crime; and 30 percent were convicted of a minor offense and/or violated parole. Most of the failures were found to occur during the first two years of parole.[63]

In the late 1960s, operating on the theory that parole was not working because it was not intensive enough, California developed and evaluated a Special Intensive Parole Unit (SIPU). Parole officers in this unit had much lower caseloads than regular officers so they could offer much more help and supervision to their charges. The evaluations of this program found that intensive supervision and treatment produced no significant improvement in the behavior of parolees.[64]

Probation

Probation is the one form of correctional treatment that appears to be effective, but it succeeds, according to Walker, "for reasons that are not particularly comforting to the correctional establishment." The great majority of persons placed on probation do not commit another offense, and most of those who do commit a second offense do not commit a third. The success of probation, however, appears to be unrelated to any treatment that is provided to the probationer. Most people who are placed on probation go on to rehabilitate themselves. Walker explains, "Job, marriage, or simply getting older leads many young offenders away from crime. Probation supervision, in fact, is essentially a myth. The supervision amounts to little more than bureaucratic paper shuffling. . . . [P]robation officers call on their clients (push doorbells) and fill out the required reports. This process provides little if any substantive assistance to the client."[65]

It has often been theorized that probation could have a much more positive effect if probation officers were given caseloads that allowed them time to be more than "doorbell pushers." This idea is being tested under a program called Intensive Supervision Probation (ISP). Gowdy observes that

> compared to traditional probation, ISP imposes more stringent conditions, stricter and more frequent monitoring, and often expanded services for the offender. ISP usually requires the offender to pay the victim restitution, hold a job or perform community service, submit to unscheduled drug and alcohol testing, and pay part of the cost of their supervision. Caseloads of supervising officers normally range from 30 to 50 probationers.[66]

An evaluation of fourteen sites funded by the Department of Justice in 1990 found, however, that if recidivism was used as the basis for judging effectiveness, ISP was not particularly effective. Subjects in eleven of the fourteen sites had higher arrest rates than the control group.[67]

Diversion

Diversion programs, which became popular in the late 1960s, are based on the work of labeling theorists who argue that if we can prevent people from being labeled as criminals, we can reduce the probability that they will become criminals. The technique of diversion programs is to intervene in the criminal processing system before a person is charged and indicted for an offense, and to "divert" the person into a treatment program of some type outside of the formal criminal justice system. Thus, the person will get the help he or she needs without being labeled a criminal. During the 1970s, approximately 1,200 diversion programs were set up and funded by the federal Law Enforcement Assistance Administration, as well as numerous programs funded on the state and local level.

Diversion programs have lost popularity because they have generally been judged to be ineffective. The reason for their ineffectiveness is what has come to be called the "expanding net syndrome." This means that diversion programs have not served the population for whom they were originally designed—people who would normally be booked and prosecuted. These people, it has been found, are still booked and prosecuted. The people who are referred into diversion programs tend to be people who, before the existence of the diversion program, would have been freed without being charged anyway. In other words, what has been discovered is that an informal diversion program has always been in existence. The police officer on the beat and the district attorney have always made judgments resulting in a fair number of people being released with only a warning. And it is these people, rather than people who would otherwise be prosecuted, who are referred into the formal diversion programs.

Do formal diversion programs achieve better results than the old informal methods? The answer, unfortunately, is no. A model diversion project, the Des Moines Adult Diversion Project, was evaluated and found to have little impact on reducing recidivism among people referred to the program as compared with people handled the traditional way. An evaluation of a juvenile diversion program found that the recidivism rate for kids placed in the program was lower than for those processed by the juvenile court, but higher than for those diverted in the traditional way—that is, turned over to their parents with a warning.[68]

Intermediate Sanctions

In response to the immense and costly increase in prison populations and to the lack of effectiveness of traditional alternatives to incarceration, new approaches called *intermediate sanctions* are being tried. One intermediate sanction is the day fine. To impose this sanction, a judge ascertains how much a convicted person earns in one day, then levies a fine that is a certain multiple of this amount. Judges are given guidelines for the multiples to be used; in one jurisdiction, for example, multiples range from 15 for harassment up to 120 for sexual misconduct. The key idea behind day fines is that they make punishment more just because a fine will have the same relative effect on someone who earns $50,000 a year as on someone who earns the minimum wage. Another popular intermediate sanction is electronic monitoring. In this sanction the convicted person has to wear an electronic transmitter that enables a probation officer to keep tabs on the person's movements. The person is allowed to go to work and to perform necessary duties but must be at home at all other times. The final new intermediate sanction is shock incarceration—placement in a boot camp–type of facility for a relatively short period of time, generally three to six months. During this time, the inmates are subjected to intensive supervision, strict discipline, military drill, physical training, inspections, and physical labor. All of these intermediate sanctions have been tested and carefully evaluated in several sites. Generally, the evaluations have indicated that based on the criteria of rate of recidivism, the effectiveness of intermediate sanctions is questionable. However, the cost effectiveness of these sanctions has been found to be quite high. In other words, intermediate sanctions may not be any more effective than traditional sanctions in reforming criminals, but they are no less effective and a good deal cheaper.[69]

Abandoning Rehabilitation?

Following the publication of the negative results of evaluation studies of rehabilitation, especially Robert Martinson's 1974 article, which concluded that, "with few and isolated exceptions, the rehabilitative efforts that have been reported so far have had no appreciable effect on rehabilitation," the calls for reform once again intensified.[70] However, these new calls have been different because they generally have called for de-emphasizing, if not completely eliminating, any pretense of rehabilitation in the system.

Conservatives have always been critical of the rehabilitation model, believing that because human nature is basically bad, treatment is a waste of time. Conservatives have always believed that the only proper response to crime was to be sure offenders are caught and then adequately punished. What is new is that it is now liberals who are calling for an end to attempts to rehabilitate offenders. Calling their approach the *justice model*, these reformers argue that the efforts of past liberals to reform criminals must be abandoned and the impossibility of helping people in a coercive situation must be admitted. The goal of liberal reform should not be for the state to "do good" for offenders, but rather to reduce state intervention and to compel the state to "do justice." The emphasis of the criminal justice system under this approach should be to ensure due process, equity, and fairness. The primary components of the reformed criminal justice system under the justice model would be specific penalties for specific crimes (all people convicted of a certain crime, manslaughter, for example, would receive exactly the same penalty); the return of determinate sentences; and the abolition of probation and parole. Liberal scholars Willard Gaylin and David Rothman advocate the justice model but say, "Still we are not happy. Our solution is one of despair, not hope. . . . [U]nder the rehabilitative model we have been able to abuse our charges, the prisoners, without disturbing our consciences. Beneath this cloak of benevolence, hypocrisy has flourished, and each new exploitation of the prisoner has inevitably been introduced as an act of grace."[71] These scholars advocate, therefore, that the goal of the criminal justice system should be not to do good, but rather to do as little harm as possible.

As we move into the final section of this chapter, we find ourselves in a peculiar position. The subject of the section is social work roles; but before we even begin the discussion we must first, in light of the material presented earlier, deal with the question of whether social workers should be involved with the criminal justice system at all.

Social Work Roles

The social work profession has always had highly ambivalent feelings about involvement in the criminal justice system. Originally this ambivalence was caused by the question of whether social work values and techniques were appropriate for work in an involuntary setting. Fox states that historically the major problem for social workers in corrections was "the doctrine of self-determination, which meant that social workers help people help themselves. Since corrections is coercive through enforcement and confinement, 'self-determination' is automatically excluded from the field of professional social work, which cannot function in an authoritative setting." Fox, among others, believes that social work can and should be involved in corrections; and he argues that it is a disservice to clients—perhaps even unethical—for social workers to refuse to be involved with cor-

The problem of criminal behavior by juveniles is clearly considered to be primarily a responsibility of the social welfare institution rather than of the criminal justice system. A number of social workers find employment in juvenile probation, parole, treatment, and diversion programs.

rections because they believe the clients to be unmotivated. He rejoices in the fact that "there are now professional social workers who can talk about 'aggressive casework,' 'hard-to-reach groups,' 'reaching out,' and motivating people 'to help themselves.' "[72]

The problem is different now, however. Social workers no longer question the appropriateness of working with unmotivated or involuntary clients. As we have discussed in other chapters, clients in many settings, such as child welfare and mental health, are at least initially involuntary. The problem now is the research cited in the previous section, which has universally found that efforts at rehabilitation within the criminal justice system are ineffective. Worse yet is the belief of many that social workers who become involved in the criminal justice system quickly become co-opted, losing sight of treatment goals and embracing the punitive goals of the system. Mitford quotes a former prison psychiatrist who says that "those [treatment personnel] who do not fit in will be eliminated and those who do fit in will stay on."[73] By "fitting in" the psychiatrist means that the social worker must adopt the correctional system's attitude: that offenders are a "special form of humanity" who are not worthy of the trust and respect of decent people.

Does this mean that there is no place for social workers interested in the problem of crime in society? Certainly not. Although we believe that caution should be exercised by anyone who actually wants to work within the system in the traditional role of prison social worker, juvenile officer, probation officer, or parole officer, just as caution should be exercised by those working within public welfare and mental hospitals, we are not suggesting that these roles be avoided. There is, after all, something to the argument that if good people refuse to work in these systems, then the systems will become even worse. There are also some less traditional roles that are emerging within the general area of criminal justice and in which we believe social workers can have a particularly positive impact. A discussion of these roles follows.

Treatment Programs outside the Criminal Justice System

The studies of rehabilitation programs have concentrated on traditional programs run within the criminal justice system—prison treatment, probation, parole, and diversion. For people whose initial problem is law violation, there are a variety of programs that are run outside of the system in community mental health centers, schools, and community centers. The results of these programs have sometimes been encouraging. An example is the Group Integration Project run in the Jewish Community Centers Association (JCCA) in St. Louis. This project was based on labeling theories and on theories of group influence. The Group Integration Project took juveniles who had been identified as being in some way antisocial and placed them in the normal recreation and socialization groups that the JCCA runs in great numbers. The groups were led by trained social workers, some of whom used "the traditional social group work method taught at many graduate schools of social work." Other social workers used "the group-level behavior modification method, based essentially on the principles of social learning theory and applied behavior analysis." The project was rigorously evaluated, and the approach was found not only to be effective but also to be inexpensive—in 1983 it cost about $150 per participant. This project, as well as others, convincingly demonstrates that it is possible for social workers interested in working with antisocial individuals to do so within humane and effective environments.[74]

Victim Assistance

A recent development in the criminal justice system is victim assistance programs, which address the needs of the victims of crimes. Roberts observes, "One of the most overlooked areas of justice social work has been services for victims. Historically, victims of crime have been ignored by the courts, social welfare policymakers, and those in social work practice."[75] In recent years the victim has become a concern for social workers in the criminal justice system. A wide variety of services are now available to victims of acts such as rape, family violence, child abuse, assault, and robbery. The programs provide counseling and support; they help the victim seek restitution for losses sustained and social services to meet other needs; and they frequently support the victim through the often long and traumatic proceedings involved in pressing charges against an assailant.

> Seventy-nine-year-old Hattie Meadows suffered a broken arm when a man snatched her purse as she was returning to her apartment in the Oak Lane Housing Projects. The police took Mrs. Meadows to the hospital, and while being treated she was visited by Harry Carstairs, a social worker from the city Victim Assistance Bureau. Mr. Carstairs helped Mrs. Meadows replace the food stamps that were in her purse. He then went with her to the housing project office to request that the locks on her doors be replaced, because her keys were in her purse. The housing project manager said that there was a fee for changing the locks; Mr. Carstairs arranged to have this paid by the Victim Assistance fund. Later that week the perpetrator was arrested while trying to use Mrs. Meadows's food stamps. Mr. Carstairs visited her and told her that if she decided to press charges and testify, he would stay with her throughout the process.

Supported by a large amount of money provided by federal agencies such as the Law Enforcement Assistance Administration and the National Center for the Prevention and Control of Rape, and by funding from community development and ACTION grants as well as state, local and private sources, victim assistance programs proliferated during the 1970s. Cutbacks in federal funds have severely restricted these programs in recent years, but most have survived in some form.

Dussich has provided a useful list of primary, secondary, and tertiary functions of victim assistance programs. Some primary functions include:

- Taking immediate responsibility for the victim
- Ensuring that the victim is provided with emergency medical or social services
- Addressing the client's family needs
- Following up on the delivery of public assistance to clients

Some secondary functions include:

- Helping victims in their roles as witnesses
- Providing advice to reduce the victim's risk of revictimization
- Establishing volunteer efforts to augment victim service units
- Rendering aid to victims and their families with aftermath arrangements, such as funerals, insurance, and victim compensation

- Arranging with victims convenient times for court appearances
- Maintaining a victim/witness courtesy center where victims can wait for their court appearance

Some tertiary functions include:

- Studying individual victimizations for use in preventive planning
- Developing public awareness programs for "target hardening" (ways to make oneself and one's home less vulnerable to criminal violation)
- Developing victim awareness throughout the community
- Setting up periodic victim awareness seminars for middle- and upper-management criminal justice personnel
- Publishing a community services directory tailored to victim needs
- Assisting in developing restitution and compensation programs[76]

Social workers in victim assistance programs work in a range of settings that include rape crisis centers, domestic violence shelters, programs that provide counseling and support to crime victims while the case is being tried, and victim restitution programs.

A specialized type of victim assistance work is the emerging specialty of police social work. The police social worker is a victim assistance specialist who works within the police department so as to be able immediately to render services to people with whom the police have come in contact. Roberts states that police social workers are people who are knowledgeable about police procedures and who are assigned the following responsibilities:

> (1) to establish solid working relationships with agencies providing emergency medical, psychiatric, and social work services in the community; (2) to provide the initial diagnostic assessment of clients referred to them by police officers, make appropriate referrals to local agencies, and follow up to ensure that service was rendered; (3) to provide police officers with in-service training in crisis intervention techniques; and (4) to be on the job twenty-four hours a day to serve as a back-up resource for the policemen and policewomen on patrol.[77]

The job of police social worker is not yet common, and whether it will become so in the future is not yet clear.

Victim–Offender Mediation

A few social workers have, in recent years, begun to develop a role in victim–offender reconciliation projects (VORPs). These are projects that seek to substitute for part of a convicted offender's penalty a restitution agreement worked out between the crime victim and the offender with the assistance of a trained mediator. In some cases the mediator is a social worker; in others it is a volunteer who has been trained by social workers. There are currently VORPs in nearly one hundred jurisdictions throughout the country.

VORPs deal only with nonviolent offenses, generally property crimes such as burglary. The mediation process moves through four phases. The first phase is the intake phase, in which an offender is referred to the project and the case is assigned to a mediator. The second is the preparation phase, in which the mediator meets separately with the offender and with the victim to explain the process to them and to encourage their participation. The third is the mediation phase, in which the mediator meets jointly with the offender and the victim. In this phase the mediator tries to help the victim and the offender reach some understanding of each other and work out a settlement that seems fair to both. Settlements can involve a payment schedule, in which the offender pays for at least part of the victim's loss over a reasonable period of time; the offender's working off the debt in some form of service to the victim; volunteer work for a program of the victim's choice; or some combination of these. The final phase is the follow-up phase, in which the agreement is submitted to the court for approval and then is monitored to be sure it is fully implemented.[78]

Police Work as Social Work

There is an irony in the law enforcement profession that has long been obvious to criminologists. The image of police officers held both by themselves and by the public is that of super crime fighters; however, task analyses of the actual work of the police indicate that the great majority of what they do could more accurately be described as social work. Police work really calls for social work skills rather than the skills concentrated on at the police academy. Only 20 to 30 percent of all calls to police involve crimes, even in areas with the highest crime rates.[79] The majority of calls are requests for help with problems not involving any law violation: A woman's husband is drunk and she cannot get him into the house; a store owner finds a disoriented old person in front of his business and does not want to turn the person out into the street but does not know what else to do; a man's neighbors are having a loud fight, which he fears may become violent; a woman finds a toddler wandering around a busy street and cannot find anyone who knows the child or his parents; a homeless family has set up a tent in a public park.

Former U.S. Attorney General Edwin Meese notes, "Police responsibilities expand beyond attempting to control criminal activity—to preventing crime, promoting order, resolving disputes, and providing emergency assistance in social crises. The officers' methods and resources extend beyond arrests and citations. They now include mediation and negotiation, referrals to other municipal agencies and community mobilization." During the typical tour of duty, a police officer does not arrest a single person, and during a career of from twenty-five to thirty years in length most never even fire a shot.[80]

Even though crime fighting is a relatively minor part of the actual work of the police, it is this aspect on which both they and the public concentrate. The police envision themselves as the "thin blue line" standing between citizens and crime. On the other hand, citizens are suspicious and fearful of the police. As Empey has written, "Dressed in jodhpurs and boots, wearing a helmet and dark glasses, with a pistol and club strapped to their belts, their approach creates a tinge of panic in even the most innocent of citizens."[81] Even though 70 to 80 percent of a police officer's job involves activities that could be classified as social work rather than crime fighting, the police choose largely to reject this part of their role. Ennis quotes a Philadelphia police inspector as saying, "Once a police officer becomes a social worker, he isn't any good anymore as a policeman."[82]

Our view, as you might guess, differs from that of the Philadelphia police inspector. We believe that a job that involves 70 to 80 percent social work functions should be filled by people who are trained as social workers. Therefore, although not a typical choice, we believe that the job of police officer is an appropriate choice for a person with social work training.

Conclusion

When discussing criminal justice as a social welfare area and considering the role of social work within it, it is all too easy to fall into the trap of accepting the reduction of the crime rate as the major goal of the activity. If this is taken as the goal, it is hard to be optimistic—because, as Walker has noted, "the best criminological minds of our time do not have anything practical to offer. Neither liberals nor conservatives are any help. The intellectual and programmatic bankruptcy is truly nonpartisan."[83]

In spite of his pessimism, Walker believes that scholars do have a pretty good understanding of the causes of crime; as a society, however, we are unable, or perhaps unwilling, seriously to address these causes. We know factors that are associated with a low rate of criminality: a sense of self-worth; a sense of achievement and the actual experience of achievement, even if it is modest; a belief that the future, for one's children if not for oneself, will be better than today. But these factors can grow more widespread only through social change that opens up opportunities for all people in our society. Interestingly, conservative scholars agree that the real causes of crime are in the social structure, but they argue that society can deal with crime without dealing with the causes. Murray, for example, states that "in problems other than crime . . . the professionals commonly devise effective cures without doing anything at all about causes. . . . And yet when it comes to the problem of using correctional programs [prison] to reduce crime, many have assumed that something has to be done about the root causes before changes will occur in behavior."[84] Murray believes that even though the cause of crime may be an unjust social and economic system, it is all right to ignore this and simply to toughen up the criminal justice system—in effect, to tell people, "Your life may be bad now, but it's not as bad as it'll be if you break the law." However, in spite of Murray's optimism, an increase in the sureness, swiftness, and harshness of penalties has had no greater effect on the crime rate than have attempts to rehabilitate the offender. We are forced to conclude, along with Walker, that if we want to reduce crime we have to work for social justice.

In the meantime, while waiting for our efforts to result in a truly just society (which may be a long wait), what do we conclude about crime and social welfare? The first thing is that we should fight the idea that the reduction of crime is our job. Although reducing crime would be nice, we must accept that it is beyond our abilities, just as it is beyond those of everyone else, given our current social and economic structure. We should substitute for this crime reduction idea an understanding of the fact that crime in our society is both the result and the cause of a large amount of pain. The job of social welfare in relation to crime should be to reduce the pain of both the victims of crime and the victims of the criminal justice system. If a social worker is working with a man who is on probation and the man commits another crime, under current evaluative standards the social worker is generally considered to have failed. We believe, however, that if the social worker has helped the man's son to stay in school and graduate, and if he or she has helped the man's wife get a good job, find an affordable place to live, and generally put her life back together, the social worker certainly has not failed. We must be clear that in social work our goal is not to reduce crime, but to reduce the pain that results from—and contributes to—crime.

Visit **www.researchnavigator.com** to research these important concepts from the chapter:

Control theory
Criminal justice system
Juvenile justice system
Parole
Prison population
Probation
Restitution
Strain theory

Web Sites Related to Crime and Criminal Justice

American Correctional Association—The Corrections Connection <www.corrections.com>: This site provides links to data sources related to corrections from federal, state, and local agencies, as well as international associations.

Court TV Library: Death Penalty <www.courttv.com>: Provides current information on high-profile, civil rights, Supreme Court, and death penalty cases.

Death Penalty Information Center <essential.org/dpic>: Information and analysis on issues related to the death penality including publications reporting costs, racial disparities, and trends in capital punishment.

Federal Bureau of Investigation <www.fbi.gov>: Crime data from the annual Uniform Crime Report. Includes status of current FBI investigations and a list of the ten most wanted fugitives.

Federal Bureau of Prisons <www.bop.gov>: A great quantity of statistics on federal inmate demographics, sentences, types of offenses, and facility populations.

FEDSTATS <www.fedstats.gov>: Provides powerful link and search utilities to find statistical information generated by any federal statistics agency. One does not need to know in advance what agency produces or publishes the data.

National Archive of Criminal Justice Data <www.icpsr.umich.edu/MACJD/home.html>: This site, provided by the University of Michigan, provides browsing and downloading access to over 500 databases relating to criminal justice.

Sourcebook of Criminal Justice Statistics <www.albany. edu/sourcebook/>: From the Bureau of Justice Statistics, the Sourcebook presents a wide range of criminal justice data gathered from more than 100 sources.

Endnotes

1. Samuel Walker, *Sense and Nonsense about Crime: A Policy Guide,* 5th ed. (Belmont, CA: Wadsworth, 2000), 13.
2. Walker, *Sense and Nonsense about Crime,* 13.
3. The major issues for all three perspectives closely follow the discussion in Walter B. Miller, "Ideology and Criminal Justice Policy: Some Current Issues," *Journal of Criminal Law and Criminology 64*:2 (1973), 141–162.
4. Walker, *Sense and Nonsense about Crime,* 16.
5. Steven Spitzer, "Toward a Marxian Theory of Deviance," *Social Problems 22* (June 1975), 638–651.

6. Herman Schwendinger and Julia Schwendinger, "Defenders of Order or Guardians of Human Rights?" *Issues in Criminology 5* (Summer 1970), 123–157.
7. Jerome Michael and Mortimer J. Adler, *Crime, Law and Social Science* (New York: Harcourt, Brace, 1933), 2.
8. Jerome Hall, *General Principles of Criminal Law* (Indianapolis, IN: Bobbs-Merrill, 1947), 1.
9. William J. Chambliss, *Criminal Law in Action* (Santa Barbara, CA: Hamilton Publishing, 1975), 6.
10. Warren Netherland, "Corrections System: Adult," *Encyclopedia of Social Work*, Vol. 1, 18th ed. (Silver Spring, MD: National Association of Social Workers, 1987), 354.
11. Sheldon R. Gelman, "Correctional Policies: Evolving Trends," in Albert R. Roberts, ed., *Social Work in Juvenile and Criminal Justice Settings* (Springfield, IL: Charles C. Thomas, 1983), 49.
12. Hilary Walker and Bill Beaumont, *Probation Work: Critical Theory and Socialist Practice* (Oxford, England: Basil Blackwell, 1981), 4–5.
13. Thomas J. Sullivan, Kenrick S. Thompson, Richard D. Wright, and Dale R. Spady, *Social Problems: Divergent Perspectives* (New York: John Wiley & Sons, 1980), 574–577.
14. U.S. Department of Justice, Bureau of Justice Statistics, online at www.ojp.usdoj.gov/bjs/.
15. U.S. Department of Justice, *Sourcebook of Criminal Justice Statistics,* 30th ed. (Washington, DC: U.S. Government Printing Office, 2004), 354.
16. Charles Puzzanchera, Anne L. Stahl, Terrence A. Finnegan, Nancy Tierney, and Howard N. Snyder, *Juvenile Court Statistics, 1999* (Pittsburgh, PA: National Center for Juvenile Justice, 2003), 28.
17. Charles Puzzanchera et. al., *Juvenile Court Statistics,* 34.
18. Ernest van den Haag, *Punishing Criminals: Concerning a Very Old and Painful Question* (New York: Basic Books, 1975), 118.
19. LaMar T. Empey, *American Delinquency: Its Meaning and Construction* (Homewood, IL: Dorsey, 1982), 163.
20. Edwin H. Sutherland and Donald R. Cressey, *Criminology,* 9th ed. (Philadelphia: J. B. Lippincott, 1974), 53.
21. William H. Sheldon, *Varieties of Delinquent Youth* (New York: Harper & Row, 1949), 14–30.
22. Richard J. Herrnstein and Charles Murray, *The Bell Curve: Intelligence and Class Structure in American Life* (New York: Free Press, 1994), 235.
23. Sigmund Freud, *An Outline of Psychoanalysis* (New York: W. W. Norton, 1963), 14; quoted in Empey, *American Delinquency,* 171.
24. David Feldman, "Psychoanalysis and Crime," in Donald R. Cressey and David A. Ward, eds., *Delinquency, Crime and Social Process* (New York: Harper & Row, 1969), 433–442.
25. Travis Hirschi, *Causes of Delinquency* (Berkeley: University of California Press, 1969), 31–34.
26. Hirschi, *Causes of Delinquency,* 18.
27. James Q. Wilson, *Thinking about Crime* (New York: Vintage Books, 1975); James Q. Wilson and Richard Herrnstein, *Crime and Human Nature* (New York: Simon & Schuster, 1985); Ernest van den Haag, *Punishing Criminals.*
28. van den Haag, *Punishing Criminals,* 15.
29. Empey, *American Delinquency,* 461.
30. Clifford R. Shaw and Henry D. McKay, *Juvenile Delinquency and Urban Areas,* revised ed. (Chicago: University of Chicago Press, 1969).
31. Walter Miller, "Lower-Class Culture as a Generating Milieu of Gang Delinquency," *Journal of Social Issues 14* (Summer 1958), 5–19.
32. Walter Miller, "Implications of Urban Lower-Class Culture for Social Work," *Social Service Review 33* (September 1959), 225.
33. Edwin H. Sutherland and Donald Cressey, *Principles of Criminology,* 5th ed. (Philadelphia: J. B. Lippincott, 1955).
34. Robert Merton, *Social Theory and Social Structure,* enlarged ed. (New York: Free Press, 1968); Albert Cohen, *Delinquent Boys: The Culture of the Gang* (New York: Free Press, 1955); Richard Cloward and Lloyd Ohlin, *Delinquency and Opportunity: A Theory of Delinquent Gangs* (New York: Free Press, 1960).
35. Robert Agnew, "Foundation for a General Strain Theory of Crime and Delinquency," *Criminology 30* (January 1992), 47–87.
36. Merton, *Social Theory and Social Structure,* 146.
37. Empey, *American Delinquency,* 423.
38. Howard S. Becker, *Outsiders: Studies in the Sociology of Deviance* (New York: Free Press, 1963), 9.
39. Richard Quinney, *Criminal Justice in America* (Boston: Little, Brown, 1974), 23–25.
40. Blake McKelvey, *American Prisons: A History of Good Intentions* (Montclair, NJ: Patterson Smith, 1977).

41. David J. Rothman, *Conscience and Convenience: The Asylum and Its Alternatives in Progressive America* (Boston: Little, Brown, 1980), 17.
42. Alan M. Dershowitz, "Background Paper," in Twentieth Century Task Force on Criminal Sentencing, *Fair and Certain Punishment* (New York: McGraw-Hill, 1976), 83; quoted in Francis T. Cullen and Karen E. Gilbert, *Reaffirming Rehabilitation* (Cincinnati: Anderson Publishing, 1982), 46.
43. David J. Rothman, *The Discovery of the Asylum: Social Order and Disorder in the New Republic* (Boston: Little, Brown, 1971), 53.
44. Cesare Beccaria, *On Crimes and Punishments* (Indianapolis, IN: Bobbs-Merrill, 1963; reprint of original from 1764), 42–44.
45. Rothman, *The Discovery of the Asylum,* 61.
46. Rothman, *The Discovery of the Asylum,* 62.
47. Quoted in Rothman, *The Discovery of the Asylum,* 240–242.
48. "Declaration of principles promulgated at Cincinnati, Ohio, 1870," in *Prison Reform,* Charles R. Henderson, ed. (Dubuque, IA: Brown Reprints; originally published in 1910), 39; quoted in Cullen and Gilbert, *Reaffirming Rehabilitation,* 67; Alexander Maconochie, quoted in Snell Putney and Gladys J. Putney, "Origins of the Reformatory," *Journal of Criminal Law, Criminology, and Police Science 53* (December 1962), 439.
49. Cullen and Gilbert, *Reaffirming Rehabilitation,* 72.
50. Paul F. Cromwell Jr., George G. Killinger, Hazel B. Kerper, and Charles Walker, *Probation and Parole in the Criminal Justice System,* 2nd ed. (St. Paul, MN: West Publishing, 1985), 10.
51. John Moreland, "John Augustus: The First Probation Officer," paper read at the 35th Annual Conference of the National Probation Association, Boston, 29 May 1941, reprinted in Cromwell et al., *Probation and Parole in the Criminal Justice System,* 21.
52. Julian Mack, "The Juvenile Court as a Legal Institution," in Hasting H. Hart, ed., *Preventive Treatment of Neglected Children* (New York: Russell Sage, 1910), 296–297; quoted in Empey, *American Delinquency,* 67.
53. Cullen and Gilbert, *Reaffirming Rehabilitation,* 81.
54. Alexander B. Smith and Louis Berlin, *Introduction to Probation and Parole* (St. Paul, MN: West Publishing, 1976), 190.
55. Donald R. Cressey, foreword, in Cullen and Gilbert, *Reaffirming Rehabilitation,* xix.
56. Walker, *Sense and Nonsense about Crime,* 218.
57. Walter Bailey, "Correctional Outcome: An Evaluation of 100 Reports," *Journal of Crime, Law, Criminology, and Police Science 57* (1966), 153–160.
58. Robert Martinson, "What Works?—Questions and Answers about Prison Reform," *The Public Interest 35* (Spring 1974), 22–54.
59. Michael R. Gottfredson and Don M. Gottfredson, *Decision-Making in Criminal Justice: Toward the Rational Exercise of Discretion* (Cambridge, MA: Ballinger, 1980).
60. Jessica Mitford, *Kind and Usual Punishment* (New York: Alfred A. Knopf, 1973), 99, 116–117.
61. Walker, *Sense and Nonsense about Crime,* 218.
62. Norvel Morris, *The Future of Imprisonment* (Chicago: University of Chicago Press, 1974).
63. Gottfredson and Gottfredson, *Decision-Making in Criminal Justice,* 250–257.
64. William P. Adams, Paul M. Chandler, and M. G. Neitherland, "The San Francisco Project: A Critique," *Federal Probation, 35*:4 (1971), 45–53.
65. Walker, *Sense and Nonsense about Crime,* 210–212.
66. Voncile B. Gowdy, "Intermediate Sanctions," *National Institute of Justice: Research in Brief,* NCJ 140540 (1993), 2–4.
67. Voncile B. Gowdy, "Intermediate Sanctions," 4–5.
68. Thomas G. Blomberg, "Widening the Net: An Anomaly in the Evaluation of Diversion Programs," in Malcolm W. Klein and Katherine S. Teilman, eds., *Handbook of Criminal Justice Evaluation* (Beverly Hills, CA: Sage, 1980), 572–592.
69. Voncile B. Gowdy, "Intermediate Sanctions," 2–9.
70. Martinson, "What Works? Questions and Answers about Prison Reform," 22.
71. Willard Gaylin and David J. Rothman, introduction, in Andrew von Hirsch, *Doing Justice: The Choice of Punishments* (New York: Hill & Wang, 1976), xxxiv–xxxix.
72. Vernon Fox, introduction, in Albert R. Roberts, ed., *Social Work in Juvenile and Criminal Justice Settings* (Springfield, IL: Charles C. Thomas, 1983), xi–xii.
73. Mitford, *Kind and Usual Punishment,* 101.
74. Ronald A. Feldman, Timothy E. Caplinger, and John S. Wodarski, *The St. Louis Conundrum: The Effective Treatment of Antisocial Youths* (Englewood Cliffs, NJ: Prentice Hall, 1983).
75. Albert R. Roberts, ed., *Social Work in Juvenile and Criminal Justice Settings* (Springfield, IL: Charles C. Thomas, 1983), 119.

76. J. P. J. Dussich, "Evolving Services for Crime Victims," in B. Galaway and J. Hudson, eds., *Perspectives on Crime Victims* (St. Louis, MO: C. V. Mosby, 1981), quoted in John T. Gandy, "Social Work and Victim Assistance Programs," in Roberts, ed., *Social Work in Juvenile and Criminal Justice Settings,* 122–123.
77. Albert R. Roberts, "The History and Role of Social Work in Law Enforcement," in Roberts, ed., *Social Work in Juvenile and Criminal Justice Settings,* 101.
78. Mark S. Umbreit, "Crime Victims and Offenders in Mediation: An Emerging Area of Social Work Practice," *Social Work 38* (January 1993), 69–73; Burt Galaway, "Crime Victim and Offender Mediation as a Social Work Strategy," *Social Service Review 62* (December 1988), 668–683.
79. Elaine Cumming, Ian Cumming, and Laura Edell, "Policeman as Philosopher, Guide, and Friend," in Arthur Niederhoffer and Abraham S. Blumberg, eds., *The Ambivalent Force: Perspectives on the Police* (San Francisco: Rinehart Press, 1973), 186.
80. Albert J. Reiss Jr., *The Public and the Police* (New Haven, CT: Yale University Press, 1971), 15.
81. Empey, *American Delinquency,* 311.
82. Philip H. Ennis, *The Police and the Community,* vol. 2 (Washington, DC: U.S. Government Printing Office, 1966), 139, quoted in Empey, *American Delinquency,* 315.
83. Samuel Walker, *Sense and Nonsense about Crime,* 221.
84. Charles A. Murray and Louis A. Cox Jr., *Beyond Probation: Juvenile Corrections and the Chronic Delinquent* (Beverly Hills, CA: Sage Publications, 1979), 174.

CHAPTER

12

Health Care

Luis Gonzalez has been experiencing chest pains recently but has no plans to see a doctor. A day laborer who generally finds landscaping work, Luis has no health insurance. With a family of five, there's little money to spare for medical help. To make matters worse, his youngest daughter has developed asthma. Although his wife takes her to a free clinic, the family still has to buy her asthma medication.

Mr. and Mrs. Watson live in a small town in rural Arizona. Three years ago, when they both reached the age of sixty-five, they took the option of signing up with a Medicare HMO, or managed care company, rather than enrolling in the traditional Medicare program. But just this year the HMO announced it was closing down all of its operations in rural parts of the state. The company says it cannot continue to offer coverage at the current low rates of government reimbursement. Mr. and Mrs. Watson are beginning to feel panicky. No other managed care company has stepped into the breach, so their only alternative appears to be traditional Medicare, with its generally higher premiums and fewer benefits. Mrs. Watson is particularly worried about how they will cover the costs of her husband's expensive heart medication, which will not be covered under Medicare.

More than two hours after her scheduled appointment, Latisha Greene sits with her two-year-old son Brian in the crowded waiting room of a New York City Department of Health clinic in the Bronx. As a single mother with a minimum-wage job and no health benefits, she lacks the resources to go to a private pediatrician to have Brian vaccinated. She had to get up at 6:30 this morning to bring Brian to the clinic; now she worries that by the time she drops him off at the babysitter's, she will be late for her 11:00 shift at work. "I guess I just have no choice," she tells the woman next to her. "If you love your child, this is what you've got to do. But it sure isn't easy."[1]

Jennifer Storz is a social worker in her state's Department of Health and Social Service. She has recently been assigned to one of the social work and public health nurse teams set up to explain to Medicaid recipients the state's recent conversion to a managed care Medicaid program. Team members are to describe the new system and help clients choose a managed care company and plan from among the several options offered by the state. Jennifer is enjoying her work. Although some of her colleagues are concerned that the managed care companies aren't used to serving a low-income clientele with higher-than-average rates of chronic illness, she thinks the flip side of the coin is that people will get better preventive health care and more access generally to medical services.

Melanie, a social work student intern assigned to the pediatric and maternity wards in a city hospital, is having her weekly session with her supervisor, Bette. "There's something I've got to talk over with you," she says. "It's really worrying me. I went and did my 'new mother interview' with Eleanor Thompson yesterday. You know, she's the twenty-year-old who just had her first child. She was really happy about the baby, but I could tell something was bothering her. It turns out that the doctor who did the delivery was not nice at all. Eleanor said the nurses had told her that her husband could stand close to her during the delivery. The doctor was very abrupt, wouldn't let her husband into the delivery room, and didn't pay any attention to Eleanor—she said, 'He acted like I was just part of a job he wanted to get over with. You know, it's our first baby, and we wanted it to be a great experience that we could share.' After she told me that, I asked a nurse about it. The nurse said that all the Medicaid patients have to use that doctor; they have no choice." Bette nodded and told Melanie that this would probably be a challenge to deal with. "This hospital doesn't like to let go of its doctors. But let's you and I think about what you've been learning about advocacy, and what steps you might take here."

The U.S. health care system is in a state of flux. We live in a world in which organ transplants are commonplace and each month brings new technologies and drug therapies. Average life expectancies have increased steadily, and the rates of many major diseases have fallen dramatically. The way in which health care is financed, organized, delivered, and regulated is changing at an astonishing rate. Those in the know toss out a slew of terms and initials: HMO, PPO, POS, NCQA, HCVA, MCO, managed care, capitation. Most of these changes in the health care system have come from the private sector. Other than the Medicare drug benefit passed in 2003, no major federal health care reform initiatives have materialized since the failure of the Clinton administration's reform effort in 1994. Yet despite the benefits of new ways of organizing health care through a managed care system, many of the problems that fueled the drive for reform remain.

Health expenditures in the United States account for 15 percent of the gross domestic product, a proportion higher than that in any other developed nation. We now spend more than $1.7 trillion on health care, which constitutes one-seventh of the U.S. economy. It is projected that we will spend over $2.8 trillion in 2011. Although medical spending declined steadily for several years after the proliferation of managed care programs, spending is again on the rise. Large numbers of people lack adequate health insurance; 15 percent of the population have no coverage at all. About 43 percent of the uninsured are noncitizens. Although access to care seems to be improving, the system still does not treat everyone equally. Women, members of minority groups, immigrants, the poor, and the elderly face particular difficulties in getting appropriate and adequate care.[2]

Many of the new health care programs are for-profit endeavors. Some say that the marketplace approach to medical care will solve many of our problems without government intervention. Others contend that such an approach reinforces America's two-track scheme of health services: one track for low-income groups, another for the more well-to-do. Those in the bottom track include people who are not welfare recipients but whose low wages or inadequate health insurance make them "medically poor." A large body of research reveals that many of our health problems are environmentally caused, yet rather than carrying out large-scale preventive measures, we tend to fall back on the health care system to heal our ills. This chapter describes the history and present state of health and health care in the United States, analyzes current issues and problems in the system, outlines different ideological perspectives on promoting health, and depicts the roles carried out by social workers in health care settings.

Definitions of Health and Illness

There are a variety of ways to define both health and illness. These definitions vary from society to society because, as sociologists point out, conceptions of health, illness, and appropriate treatment are to a large degree culturally determined. Even different groups within a single society may view disease in diverse ways. For example, in our country

Navajo Indians sometimes define illness as a disharmony with nature, whereas groups attracted to a health food philosophy may see illness largely as a matter of poor nutrition and the ingestion of chemical additives.

Although there are a number of definitions of health and illness in the United States, the major ones are based on a biomedical model. This model describes disease as a deviation from a biological norm. Disease is perceived as a discrete entity, independent of the social context in which it occurs. Health is characterized as the absence of disease. The biomedical model stresses technical, medical treatment as the appropriate response to illness.[3]

The biomedical model has been criticized as presenting too narrow a picture of health and illness. To remedy this, an important variation of the biomedical definition adds psychosocial factors. The World Health Organization, for example, defines health as "a state of complete physical, mental, and social well-being, and not merely the absence of disease or infirmity." Elfriede Schlesinger, who writes about social work in health care, further broadens this definition by suggesting that one can lead a healthy, rewarding life even when disease is present. She stresses that health involves the ability to cope, both physically and psychologically, with various discomforts and infirmities.[4] A fifty-five-year-old man with diabetes, for example, who manages this condition with diet and insulin and notes no other change in his daily activities, could thus be considered a healthy individual.

Another set of definitions of health and illness comes from the ecological and general systems perspectives. These approaches put even greater emphasis on environmental factors in disease. The *ecological* or *holistic* approach looks at a variety of elements that bring about ill health, including environmental, socioeconomic, physiological, and psychological factors. Health is based on "positive self-image, plus the resources necessary to cope with the environment and its pressures." Health indicates a person's ability to function in the fullest and most positive way.[5]

General systems theory contributes an explanatory framework for these ideas. The systems approach views human beings in terms of a hierarchy of interrelated, natural systems. These systems range from subatomic particles to molecules and tissues, and on up through families, communities, and cultures. A problem in one system can spread to others. A person's well-being is related to the overall functioning and harmonious interaction of all these systems. Poor health stems from disruption of the interaction of natural systems "to the point where one or more system levels are malfunctioning."[6] Although this picture may seem abstract, the basic point of the ecological and systems model is that health relates to the many interconnected aspects of an individual's life. Health promotion and disease prevention measures should therefore not be limited to the physiological realm.

Statistical Picture of Health Care

The most widely publicized statistics about health care are those relating to cost. Much of the impetus behind health system reform and restructuring in the early 1990s came from seemingly out-of-control health expenditures. The cost of physicians' services increased 7.7 percent between 1980 and 1990, while the increase in the consumer price index was only 4.7 percent. One day's stay in the hospital jumped from an average of $245 in 1980 to $687 in 1990. In 1994 the cost of medical care rose 4.5 percent, while food prices rose only 2.8 percent and housing costs just 2.6 percent The price of the latest technology helped drive up costs; the amount of money spent on bypass surgery each year had surpassed the entire yearly budget of the National Institutes of Health by 1993.[7]

Partly because of the growth of managed care, the rate of increase in health care costs and spending declined between 1992 and 1996. National health care spending saw the slowest growth rate in more than three decades. Yet managed care's ability to slow the rate of medical spending was short-lived. Health care costs soon began to rise. A day's stay in the hospital now costs $1,200. A major factor in increasing health costs is the rising spending on prescription drugs, which is growing faster than all other health areas. Premiums for job-based health insurance are increasing rapidly. Experts predict that the United States will continue to face rising health costs and millions of uninsured in the years to come. A recent study estimates that health spending will "grow at an average annual rate of 7.3 percent, reaching 3.1 trillion dollars by 2012." At that point, health spending will be almost 18 percent of gross domestic product (GDP), up from the current 15 percent.[8]

Although health care is an important expense for many countries, Figure 12.1 indicates that the United States is particularly unsuccessful in keeping increases in health spending under control. Ironically, although the United States spends more on health than any other country, both our life expectancy and infant mortality rates are worse than those of most industrialized nations (see Table 12.1).

How are our health costs being covered? The answer is a complicated combination of private health plans (generally connected with employment), federal and other governmental expenditures, and out-of-pocket payments by individuals. For example, in 2000 government programs (federal and state) paid only 36 percent of the country's total personal health care bill, private insurance plans contributed 27 percent, and individuals paid about 37 percent. Since 1960 the government's share in health expenses has doubled, that of private insurers has increased by about half, and the amount paid by patients has dropped dramatically. Government sources account for about 60 percent of hospital expenses, with the major portion of this money going to the Medicare and Medicaid programs for the poor and elderly. Although almost 85 percent of the population has health insurance coverage of some type through private or public sources, health plans vary in what they cover.[9]

About 16 percent of Americans had no insurance at all in 2001. Among the poor, only a little over half of those who worked were insured. African Americans and Hispanics are less likely to be covered than non-Hispanic whites. About 40 percent of Hispanic adults lack employer-sponsored health coverage. Despite the Medicaid program, almost a third of the poor have no health insurance of any kind. Lack of insurance also varies by state. In 2001, California, Louisiana, New Mexico, Oklahoma, and Texas all had uninsured rates of 21 percent or higher. Texas had the highest rate, with over a quarter of its residents lacking health coverage. In comparison, Delaware, Iowa, Minnesota, Nebraska, New Hampshire, South Dakota, Vermont, and Wisconsin all had rates below 11 percent. What seems particularly shameful in a wealthy country is the large proportion of uninsured children. Although the uninsured rate for children decreased between 1999 and 2002, about 12 percent of all children, and 20 percent of all poor children still lacked insurance (see Figure 12.2, p. 443).[10]

FIGURE 12.1 **National Health Expenditures**

[1]1999

Sources: National Center for Health Statistics, *Health, United States, 2002,* Table 112, online at www.cdc.gov/nchs/products/pubs, 287; Gerard Anderson et al., "Health Spending and Outcomes: Trends in OECD Countries, 1960–1998," *Health Affairs 19* (May/June, 2000), 51; Gerard F. Anderson, Uwe E. Reinhardt, Peter S. Hussey, Vardui Petrosyan, "It's the Prices, Stupid: Why the United States Is So Different from Other Countries," *Health Affairs 22* (May/June, 2003), 91.

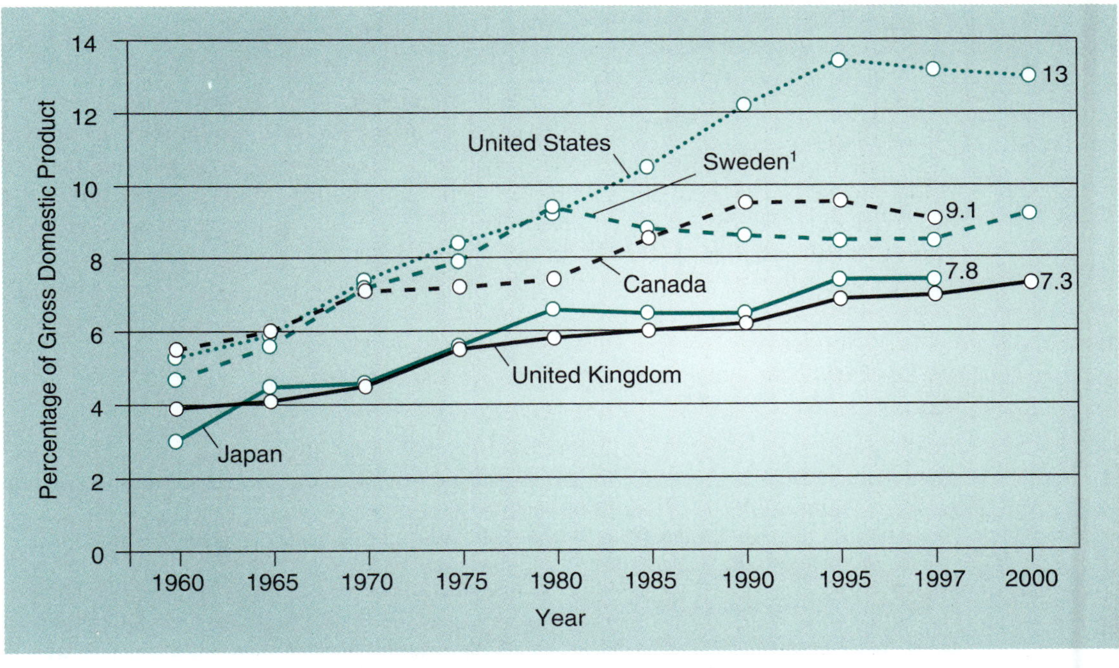

Have increasing expenditures and continued barriers to health coverage for some made a difference in the health of Americans? This is a complicated question—especially because, as we will see, medical care is a relatively minor factor in the overall changes in disease rates. However, it is helpful at this point to have a general picture of the health of the nation.

In 2000, in an annual national survey of self-assessed health status, only 9 percent of the U.S. population reported their health as fair or poor. This assessment varied by race, however. Fifteen percent of African Americans and 17 percent of American Indians reported fair or poor health. Another yardstick of health status is the rate of hospital admissions. Although the rate of hospital admissions has changed little in the last decade, the average length of stay has dropped from nine to seven days.[11]

Improvement has also taken place in two major indicators of health: life expectancy and infant mortality, or death rates. Life expectancy for Americans has increased

TABLE 12.1 **Infant Mortality Rates (Infant Deaths per 1,000 Live Births): Selected Countries, 1985, 1990, and 1998**

Country	1985	1990	1999
Japan	5.5	4.6	3.4
Sweden	6.8	6.0	3.4
Hong Kong	7.5	6.2	3.1
Switzerland	6.9	6.8	4.6
Canada	7.9	6.8	5.3
Netherlands	8.0	7.0	5.2
France	8.3	7.3	4.3
German Federal Republic	9.0	7.0	4.5
German Democratic Republic	9.6	7.3	
England and Wales	9.3	7.9	5.8
Italy	10.6	8.5	5.1
United States	10.6	9.2	7.1
Israel	11.9	9.8	5.7
Bulgaria	15.4	14.8	14.5

Sources: Gerard F. Anderson and Jean-Pierre Poullier, "Health Spending, Access, and Outcomes: Trends in Industrialized Countries," *Health Affairs 18* (May/June, 1999), 189; National Center for Health Statistics, *Health, United States, 2003,* Table 25, 130.

substantially since 1900. The majority of Americans born today can expect to live at least into their midseventies. Much of this increase has occurred between 1970 and the present. White females have the longest life expectancy, followed by African American females, white males, and African American males. (see Figure 12.3).

In addition, infant mortality has steadily declined from 29 deaths per 1,000 live births in 1950 to 7 deaths per 1,000 in 2002. Yet, as we have noted, the United States continues to lag behind most other industrialized nations in its infant mortality rate. Infant deaths also vary by race, ethnic group, and socioeconomic class. For example, the mortality rate for American Indian infants is one-third higher than that of white infants, and African American infant mortality is more than twice that of whites. An African American infant born in Washington, D.C., or in the state of Illinois is more likely to die before its first birthday than a child born in Chile or Kuwait.[12]

Death rates for many (though not all) diseases have also declined. One major change since the early 1900s has been the control of infectious diseases. In 1900 about 40 percent of all deaths could be attributed to eleven major infectious diseases, such as tuberculosis (TB) and scarlet fever. By the 1970s these same eleven illnesses accounted for only a small percent of all deaths (although recently TB has been on the rise).

FIGURE 12.2 Uninsured Children by Race, Ethnicity, and Age, 2002

[1]Hispanics may be of any race.

Source: U.S. Bureau of the Census, Current Population Reports, *Health Insurance Coverage in the United States: 2002* (September 2003).

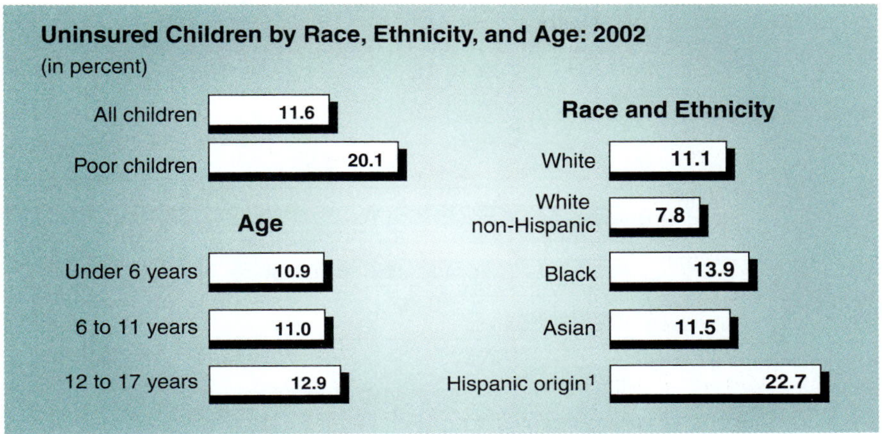

FIGURE 12.3 Life Expectancy at Birth, According to Race and Sex: United States, 1960 and 1970–2000

Source: National Center for Health Statistics, *Health, United States, 2002*, Table 28, online at www.cdc.gov/nchs/products/pubs.

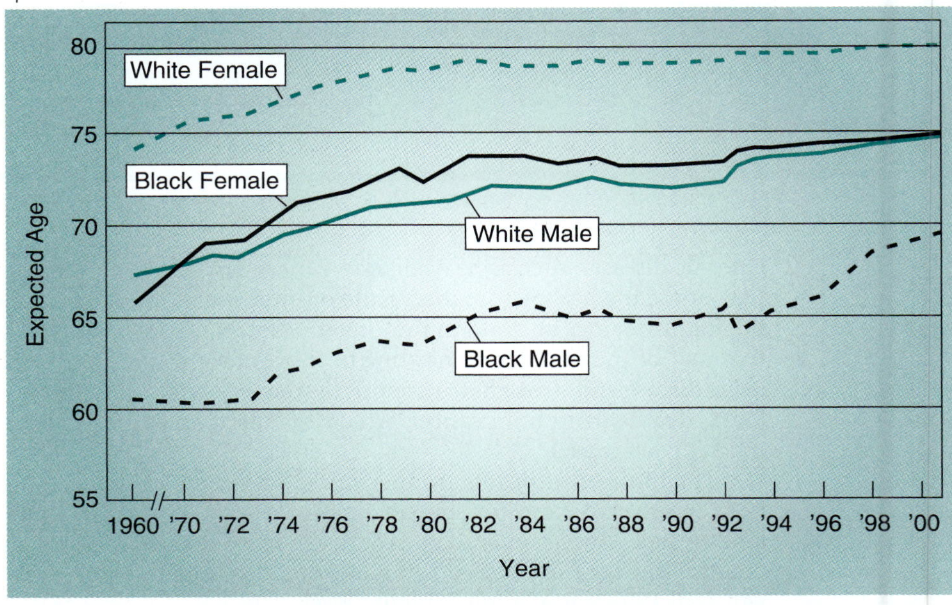

FIGURE 12.4 **Leading Causes of Death as a Percentage of All Deaths: United States, 1960–2000**

[1]Not one of ten leading causes of death in 1960.

Sources: U.S. Department of Health and Human Services, 1991; National Center for Health Statistics, *Health, United States, 2002,* Table 30, online at www.cdc.gov/nchs/products/pubs/pubd/hus/02hustop.htm.

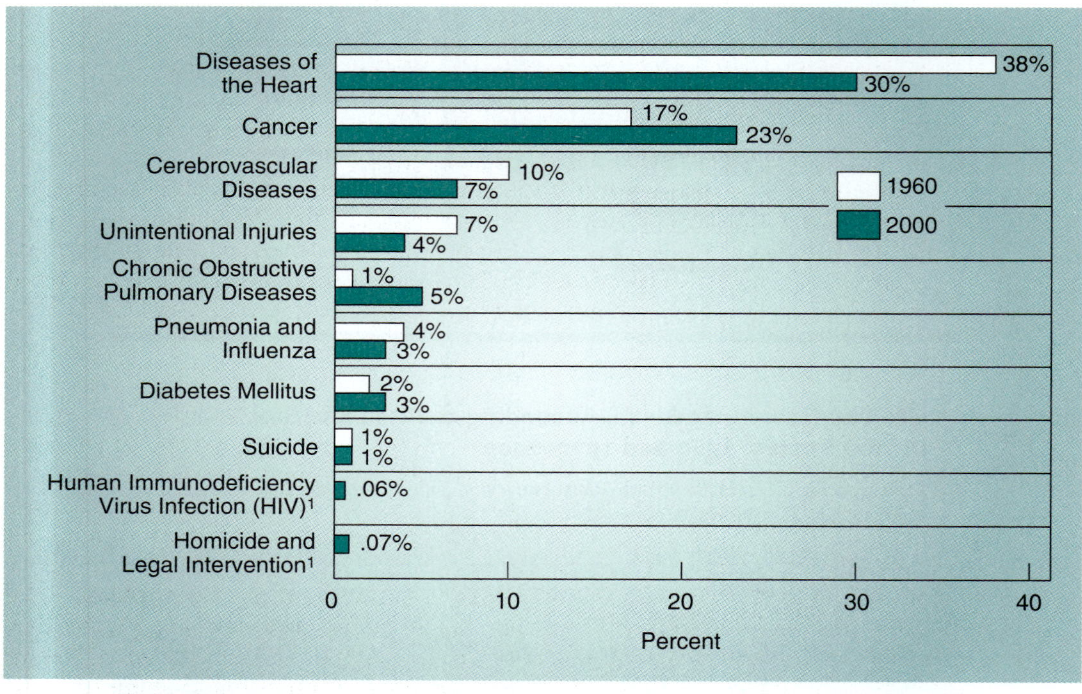

Chronic diseases, such as heart disease, cancer, and stroke, now make up a much larger part of the medical picture than acute or infectious conditions. In fact, these three are the leading causes of death in the United States today (see Figure 12.4). It is estimated that half of the population has one or more chronic conditions. The death rates for heart disease and stroke have dropped dramatically in the last thirty years; on the other hand, deaths from lung cancer, which is caused chiefly by cigarette smoking, have markedly increased.[13]

The number of deaths from acquired immune deficiency syndrome (AIDS) has been of great concern for some time. In 1994, AIDS was the leading cause of death among male Americans aged twenty-five to forty-four. By 1998 the death rate for white men in that age range was down almost a third. The rate for African American men, which in 1994 was at a much higher level than that of whites, was cut in half. In 1996 deaths from AIDS within the total population of the United States fell significantly for the first time since the epidemic began. The drop has been helped by the development of a new kind of AIDS medication called *protease inhibitors,* which, used in combination with other antiviral drugs, can prolong life markedly for some patients. Equally dramatic has been the decline in the number of people who have the disease. In 1995 about 57,000 men, thirteen years and older, had AIDS; by 2000 this number had plummeted to about 30,000. In the same period, cases of women with AIDS fell from about 13,000 to about 10,000.[14]

In 2002, however, the number of new AIDS cases began to increase for the first time in ten years. The number of those diagnosed with the disease grew that year by 2.2 percent. This could mark a troubling turning point in the AIDS epidemic in the United States, that had appeared to be diminishing due to safe-sex campaigns and the use of powerful new drugs. The increase in HIV infections has risen within the ranks of gay and bisexual men rather than in any other groups.[15]

The number of cases and deaths from AIDS is not equally distributed among all groups. African American and Hispanic men are disproportionately represented among those who contract the disease and who die of it. African American women constitute about three-fifths of all women with AIDS. Finally, one cannot conclude a discussion of AIDS without noting the epidemic proportion of the disease in Africa and China.[16]

Health and Socioeconomic Factors

Studies of health and illness in the United States indicate definite relationships between disease and social class, race, ethnicity, gender, and age. Particularly notable is the correlation between disease and poverty. People with lower incomes are much less likely to report good health than those who are relatively well-off. In 2000, for example, 21 percent of poor people reported fair to poor health. In contrast, only 6 percent of nonpoor people saw their health status in those terms.[17]

Poverty often translates into higher rates of illness and mortality. Low-income people have a death rate as much as three times higher than that of other groups, and they are at higher risk for obesity, diabetes, and tuberculosis. Poor children are more likely to suffer from asthma. Limitations in activities due to a chronic condition are substantially higher among those with lower family incomes.[18]

Race and ethnicity are also powerfully related to health status (see Figure 12.5). As we have observed, both infant mortality and life expectancy rates indicate major differences between the experiences of whites and those of African Americans and other minorities. African American women are twice as likely as white women to have low-birth-weight babies and to lose their babies in the first year of life. They are also almost four times as likely as whites to die during or soon after delivery, even if they are middle class and have health insurance. Nearly half of all minority children are at risk for developing diabetes at some point during their lives, compared to about 30 percent of white children. A quarter of the children living in central Harlem develop asthma. Rates of obesity, a growing concern among health experts, have been soaring among young people. Twenty-two percent of them are seriously overweight, with young African Americans having the highest obesity rates. The rate of tuberculosis is eight times as high for African Americans and six times as high for Hispanics as it is for whites. More than a third of African American men have high blood pressure, and African Americans who smoke have a 50 percent higher incidence of lung cancer than do whites.[19]

FIGURE 12.5 **Death Rates, Selected Cause, per 100,000, 2000, by Race and Sex**

Source: National Center for Health Statistics, *Health, United States, 2002,* Tables 37–38, 40, 46–47, online at www.cdc.gov/nchs/products/pubs, 32–37, 42–44, 57–62.

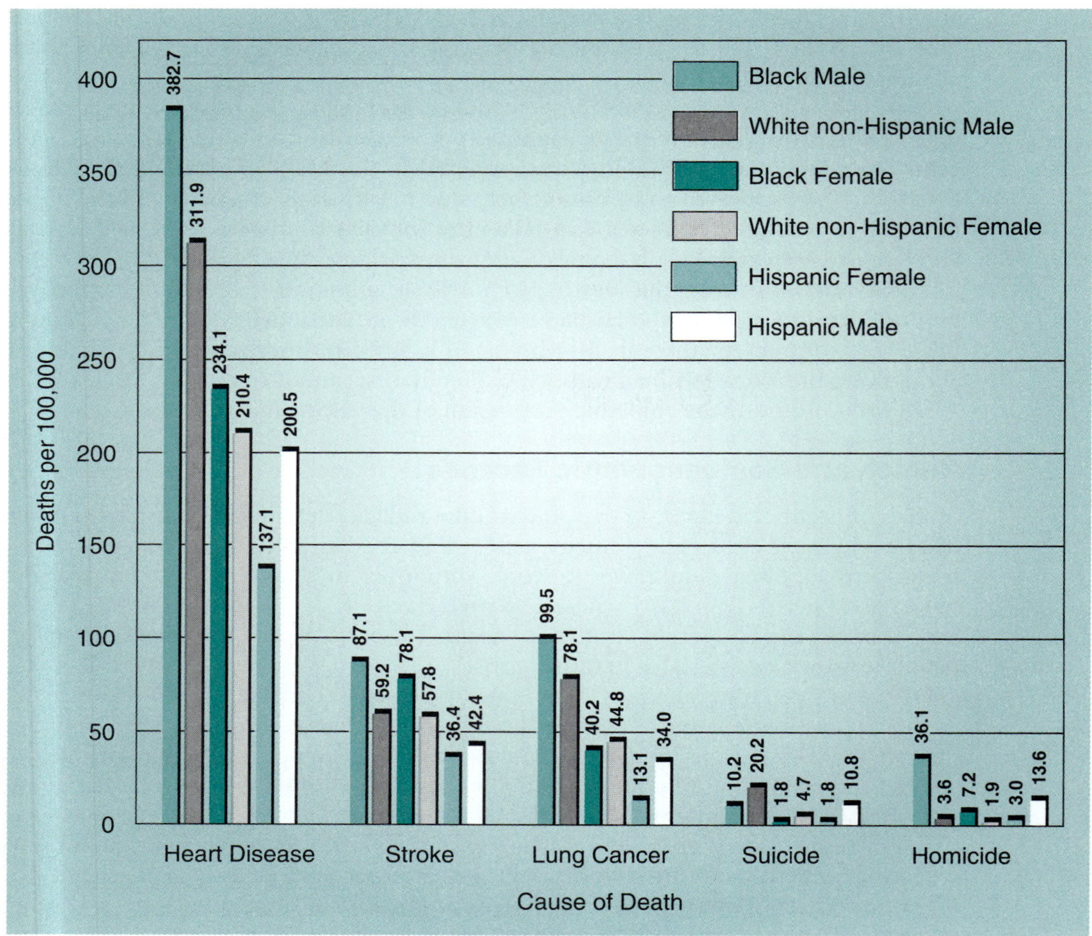

Access to health care and the quality of treatment for minorities may help to explain part of this long list of discrepancies in health and well-being. As the health advocacy group Families USA points out, "men, women, or children of color often receive less frequent care, less aggressive care, or substandard care compared to the medical treatment received by whites," and sometimes they don't receive any treatment at all. A U.S. government report on unequal treatment of minority patients found that minorities were less likely than non-Hispanic white Americans to get necessary heart medication, heart bypass surgery, or kidney dialysis. The report noted a study of urban emergency room visitors that found that African Americans were 50 percent more likely to be denied coverage by their health plans than non-Hispanic whites. It is often difficult for members of minority groups to gain access to treatment to begin with, let alone access to effective treatment. Inner-city Los Angeles, for example, has some of the most widespread and chronic health problems in the country, yet the Los Angeles County Health Department struggles with budget shortfalls that lead to cutbacks in staff. Hispanics have less access to the health care system than either African Americans or non-Hispanic whites. The lack of health insurance among many Hispanics may be one explanation for the findings of a study that about one-fifth of them had not seen a doctor in the previous two years. Language serves as another barrier; Spanish-speaking Hispanics reported problems communicating with their doctors and understanding prescription bottle instructions. Only about 40 percent of Spanish-speaking Hispanics without insurance reported strong trust in doctors.[20]

Focus on Diversity

Diabetes among the Oglala Sioux

Diabetes is the sixth leading cause of death among indigenous peoples in the United States. It is a virtual epidemic among the Oglala Sioux, descendants of Crazy Horse and Sitting Bull, who live in the two-million-acre Pine Ridge Reservation in South Dakota. The 26,000 people on the reservation die younger than any other group in the nation. Men have a life expectancy of 56.5 years. Although alcoholism, fatal car crashes, sudden infant death syndrome (SIDS), and suicides also take their toll, diabetes, says one resident, "is our AIDS, and they don't seem to be breaking their necks to find a cure for that." Experts report that the incidence of diabetes "is exploding among indigenous peoples throughout the world, the descendants of hunters who subsisted on very little food and stored any excess calories to ward off starvation during lean periods." But now food, especially fatty, processed food, is readily available, and the genetic trait that once served Indian people well now works against them. It hasn't helped that monthly food rations from the federally financed Food Distribution Center have until recently consisted of canned goods, flour, sugar, and other foods high in sodium and fat. Jobs are few and most people on the reservation are poor. One tribal employee, who has diabetes and lives with nine other people in a small, three-bedroom house, explains, "Out here we don't have the resources to buy the fruits and vegetables. . . . We eat a lot of greasy foods, fry bread and stuff. You got to eat what everyone else eats." The federal government has not been much help. It spends less than half as much on health care per tribal member as it does for individuals in government programs covering other Americans.

But the community has not given up, and tribal leaders point to the opening of new medical clinics and hospitals in the last five years. Social service agencies are working to address many of Pine Ridge's problems. Enrollment at the local community college is full. Life on the reservation remains a struggle, but as one woman says, "you can't worry about it. . . . We're just trying the best we can."

Source: From Jon Jeter, "Reservation's Despair Takes Greatest Toll," *Washington Post* (16 December 1997), 1, 12, 13; Judy Nichols, "Indian Health Care, Separate, Unequal," *Arizona Republic* (14 April 2002), 1, 16.

Gender plays an equally important role in health and illness. Women report more sickness than men and yet they live longer. Men and women have different rates of chronic disease and a different mortality picture. Death rates from heart disease are substantially higher for men than for women, although heart disease is in fact the leading cause of death for women. Lung cancer is the leading cause of cancer deaths among men. Women used to show a different pattern, with higher rates from breast cancer. As women began to smoke more, lung cancer became the major cause of cancer deaths for them as well. Women are less likely to have a chronic health condition yet are more likely to experience acute illness and disability than men. In addition, not a single U.S. state meets federal goals for caring for women's health, and millions of women lack health insurance.[21]

Even medical research is affected by issues of race and gender. In the past, for example, male researchers and policymakers put little emphasis on the health problems of women. Determined to change the situation, an organization of breast cancer survivors has successfully lobbied Congress for millions of dollars for breast cancer research. A similar story, but without a happy ending (except for a formal apology from President Clinton in 1997), is that of the infamous Tuskegee Syphilis Study carried out from 1932 to 1972. In this experiment by the U.S. Public Health Service, physicians testing a theory about the effects of racial differences on venereal disease deliberately withheld treatment from a group of African American men and never told them they were suffering from syphilis.[22]

Age is also a factor in health status. As age increases, the number of those reporting fair or poor health rises. Acute health conditions decline and chronic health problems increase. Almost 14 percent of those age sixty-five and over report being unable to carry on major activities because of chronic conditions. In the general population, only about 4 percent describe such limitations. However, we should be careful not to equate old age with ill health and disability. It is important to note that well over two-thirds of those sixty-five and over view their health as good to excellent.[23]

The health picture of the nation is thus complex and fluid. Costs are rising, and they are covered by funds from diverse sources. Many health indicators have improved, yet these improvements vary according to social class, race, age, and gender. Finally, chronic (long-term) disease has surpassed the infectious diseases as our major health problem.

Dynamics of Health and Illness

In order to deal with health problems, we need to understand the causes of disease and illness. Although this might appear simple, there are in fact a number of models that seek to describe the dynamics of poor health. We explore two major models in this section, the medical model and a social/environmental model. We then discuss corresponding approaches to dealing with illness.

The *medical model* of illness focuses on disease and its treatment. It assumes that poor health is primarily caused by genetic malformations; internal chemical imbalances; and the attacks of viruses, bacteria, and other agents on our bodies. Diagnosis and treatment, or healing, occur only after the person becomes ill. The physician, a highly trained expert, decides which treatment is needed. Most often, drugs or surgical procedures are chosen to combat illness and to restore the individual to the equilibrium known as health.[24] For a patient suffering from a heart ailment, for example, a physician following a strictly medical model might prescribe coronary bypass surgery rather than stressing changes in diet and lifestyle.

The medical orientation to illness focuses primarily on the individual and has relatively little concern for social context. Yet many people, including an increasing number of physicians, would argue that it is this social context—involving cultural, economic, and environmental factors—that shapes health and disease. The life expectancy of the average Russian, for example, has actually begun to drop because of dismal environmental conditions such as contaminated water and dirty air and increased tobacco smoking. A study in the United States has added to the growing evidence of the connection between illness and exposure to "passive smoke." Researchers found that "women who were regularly exposed to other people's smoke were twice as likely to suffer coronary problems as those in a tobacco-free environment."[25]

There is a growing consensus that between 70 and 90 percent of human cancers are environmental in origin. The causative agents include industrial chemicals; carcinogens in our air, food, and water; and tobacco smoke. Cigarette smoking has been cited as "the single most avoidable cause of death in the United States," with 20 percent of all deaths attributable to conditions related to smoking. The high risk of cancer in certain occupations is equally appalling; about 50 percent of all long-term asbestos insulation workers die of the disease, whereas some 30 percent of all premature deaths in uranium miners is caused by lung cancer. Thus cancer, like many other chronic diseases, demonstrates the interrelationships among environment, occupation, habits and lifestyle, and illness.[26]

A *social/environmental model* of disease has many components. The model looks at the interaction between human biology and socioeconomic status, psychological state, racial and ethnic background, gender, lifestyle, occupation, social support, and environmental elements such as housing, nutrition, and exposure to certain chemicals. A large body of research indicates numerous ties between these factors and disease. The childhood heart ailment of rheumatic fever, for example, has been linked to overcrowded living conditions. Similarly, a person's degree of social support before the occurrence of a heart attack has been found to influence his or her survival from the attack.[27]

Poverty, race and ethnic group, and gender are three major, often interrelated elements in the dynamics of disease. Although cause and effect are often unclear, in each situation intervening factors seem to be at work. These factors include socialization, lifestyle, exposure to stress, and access to medical services. For example, African Americans have a much higher rate of elevated blood pressure than do blacks in Africa. Most scientists believe that environmental factors such as diet, smoking, and stress play an important role in triggering the condition in blacks who have a genetic vulnerability to it.[28]

Stress seems to be a particularly important contributor to poor health. Although the exact way in which this works is just beginning to be understood, researchers have found that people who are exposed to many difficult life events are ill more frequently than others. Stress may contribute directly to specific illnesses, or it may change relevant behavior patterns.[29] For example, a low-income single parent who has just lost her job may develop poor eating habits and difficulty in sleeping. Poor nutrition and lack of rest might then make her more susceptible to disease.

Socioeconomic status—which is often related to race, ethnic group, and gender—has persistently been associated with disease. Bruce Link and Jo Phelan contend that this association exists because one's socioeconomic status determines degree of access "to resources that can be used to avoid risks or to minimize the consequence of disease once it occurs." These resources include "money, knowledge, power, prestige, and the kinds of interpersonal resources embodied in . . . social support and social networks." The low-income parent of an asthmatic child may not be able to afford the medications her child needs, or she may lack the knowledge and connections to locate a specialist who can deal with the problem. She is a victim of her socioeconomic status.[30]

Lack of access to adequate health care is an important contributor to health problems among low-income Americans. Novelist Harriet Arnow presents a vivid picture of the difficulties poor people can face in obtaining appropriate medical treatment. In *The Dollmaker,* Arnow describes the experiences of Appalachian farm families transplanted to Detroit to work in war industries during the 1940s. When children in these families were diagnosed as needing tonsillectomies, only outpatient operations were provided. The families then had to take their children home within hours of the operation. In the following passage, Gertie Nevels, the book's main character, is helping her neighbors, Sophronie and Whit Meanwell, care for their two boys, who have just had tonsillectomies:

> Gertie . . . saw that the battered Meanwell car was back. She saw Whit go alone up the walk in a kind of staggering run, as if drunk. She hurried out to help, and Sophronie, pale, but no longer shaking, explained that the overpowering fumes of ether in the closed car had made Whit sick to his stomach. Gertie carried in both boys, squinching her eyes a little against the dripping blood, the strong smell of ether, the vomit-spewing, blue-lipped mouths.
>
> Sophronie turned a shade whiter each time one spat blood, and if either lay still an instant she was bending over him, listening to the heart beat. However, they seemed gradually to improve, and breathed more slowly and spat less blood, though when time came for Sophronie to go to work, she lingered with them too long, and then had to run, looking over her shoulder, entreating Gertie, "You'll watch em good, now won'tcha?"[31]

A new element in the social/environmental model of disease is a concept sometimes called *environmental racism.* You may encounter this in newspaper reports of African American communities protesting the location of solid waste dumps in their neighborhoods or the proximity to their homes of factories that discharge noxious fumes. This type of exploitation is not limited to race, but occurs within a variety of poor and minority communities whose residents may be seen by the businesses involved as too powerless to resist their presence.

Recognition of environmental factors in disease leads to responses different from the exclusively curative measures of the medical model. In other words, pills and operations cannot solve the problems of overcrowded housing, environmental racism, or stress. One method of dealing with environmental factors in disease is the public health approach. This approach stresses prevention of illness rather than treatment of diseases already acquired. In order to carry out preventive measures, public health researchers study the epidemiology of illness. That is, they look carefully at how and why diseases are distributed within a community. Then three levels of prevention can be carried out: (1) primary prevention, or intervening in the social environment to keep diseases from occurring in the first place; (2) secondary prevention, or early detection and treatment of disease; and (3) tertiary prevention, or responding to acute and chronic health problems through rehabilitation and other measures. Public health activities include maternal and child health measures (such as monitoring the progress of low-birth-weight babies), immunization against infectious diseases, health education, diet and weight control programs, and improvements in sanitation and other environmental problems.[32]

Another approach to dealing with illness from a social and environmental perspective is the *holistic health model.* As you may recall from our earlier description of the holistic definition of health, this definition emphasizes the interrelationship of psychological, biological, and environmental systems in the creation of health or illness. Holistic medicine thus calls for a systems-based, "biopsychosocial" approach to healing. Holistic medicine differs from the public health model in its focus on the individual rather than on large groups or the environment in general. Practitioners of holistic medicine promote a balance among body, mind, spirit, and environment. They emphasize people's capacity for healing and regard patients as active partners in, rather than passive recipients of, health care. Holistic practitioners may suggest modifications in diet and eating patterns, exercise programs, meditation, relaxation and biofeedback techniques, and/or changes in attitude toward illness.[33]

The medical and social/environmental models of disease and its treatment both have long histories. The following section explores their development and also looks at the history of social work's involvement in health care.

History of Health Care

Today's U.S. health care system is a complex entity. It includes a wide array of organizations: physicians' offices, individual hospitals, large medical centers, freestanding emergency care and other outpatient facilities, public health and planning agencies, professional associations, and health insurance and pharmaceutical companies. It has been dominated by a strong medical profession, which stresses scientific medicine, specialist practice, and research. More recently, government and corporations have also become important forces in the structure of our health care. Surprisingly, this complex system has emerged relatively recently. Medical practice and the settings in which it took place were quite different only one hundred years ago.[34]

During much of the 1800s, disease was thought to be the product of an imbalance in the body—an idea essentially unchanged since the time of Hippocrates. The ways of treating disease included drugs and chemicals, bloodletting, and exposure to the elements. Often, as health care analyst Howard S. Berliner has observed, these procedures "were largely irrelevant to the process of healing." Sometimes they were downright harmful. A medical case from 1833, for example, describes a pregnant woman who had convulsions as her delivery time approached. The doctors bled her of eight ounces of blood and gave her a purgative. When she suffered more convulsions the following day, they drew twenty-two ounces of blood. Continued symptoms led to more bloodletting, emetics to cause vomiting, ice packs on the head and mustard plasters on the feet. Eventually, the woman delivered a stillborn child.[35]

A good deal of health care was commonsense "domestic medicine," with wives and mothers often in charge of healing. On the more formal level, medicine was practiced by a wide variety of individuals who had different degrees and types of training. Some were lay healers, such as herbalists; some were "regular" physicians whose training ranged from a European medical school degree to a course of lectures; others were homeopathic doctors, who stressed both the spiritual aspects of disease and the uses of small doses of drugs in its cure. People from all races and walks of life had access to some form of medical training and practice. Women were especially active as midwives, giving prenatal care and delivering babies. By 1900 many of these women were African Americans or immigrants. Much medicine was practiced in people's homes. Hospitals tended to be places of last resort for poor and elderly ill people; they were often viewed as places where one went to die.[36]

All of this changed in the late 1800s because of revolutionary changes in sanitary practice and the growth of the germ theory of disease, which in turn fostered the rise of scientific medicine. Sanitary reforms in the United States in the 1860s and later drew on important public health developments in England, which had passed a Public Health Reform bill in 1848. These developments included changes in drinking water, sewage disposal, housing, and work conditions. They were based on new theories about the social and environmental causes of disease. The U.S. Public Health Service, the oldest federal welfare agency in this country, was founded in 1912. The agency enthusiastically adopted the new theories in its work with immigrants and others in crowded U.S. cities. Public health measures, along with improvements in diet, led to a dramatic and long-term reduction in morbidity and mortality rates.[37]

The Rise of Scientific Medicine

At about the same time, several events precipitated the rise of scientific medicine in the United States and Europe. Edward Lister's discovery of antiseptic technique in 1867, along with previous developments in the use of anesthesia, led to the growth of safer and more effective surgery. A new germ theory of disease evolved from the work of Louis Pasteur and others, who isolated the bacteria responsible for the major infectious diseases. This made the creation of vaccines possible. Such discoveries not only bolstered the public health movement (which could now, for example, launch mass inoculation campaigns against diseases such as typhoid and tetanus), but also helped create a new, scientific approach to medicine. This "scientific medicine," or the medical model of health care prevalent through much of the twentieth century, assumes that disease is caused by discrete agents, such as bacteria, and that treatment will generally be a surgical or chemical procedure performed on a passive patient by a highly trained physician.[38]

Germ theory and improvements in surgery favored the growth of a formally educated, research-oriented medical profession. This growth was further encouraged by increasing faith in science and technology during the Progressive Era (roughly 1898–1918). This was a time, after all, of exciting innovations: the discovery of electromagnetic waves and their use in radio, the building of the automobile, and the perfection of the lowly lightbulb. As sociologist Paul Starr notes, "The less one could 'believe one's own eyes'—and the new world of science continually prompted that feeling—the more receptive one became to seeing the world through the eyes of those who claimed specialized, technical knowledge, validated by communities of their peers."[39]

Up until the late 1800s, physicians were a relatively powerless group. Although states had created medical licensing laws early in our history, they rejected these laws as undemocratic in the mid-1800s. Medical practitioners were too divided to lobby either for the reenactment of the laws or for standardized training. "Regular" physicians had to compete for patients and public recognition with lay practitioners, homeopathic doctors, female midwives, and others. By the early 1900s, however, the new acceptance of the expert enabled regular physicians to gain dominance over other medical groups. Physicians were able to reestablish state licensing in a stronger form. Such laws excluded lay practitioners from medical practice. In a movement well documented by feminist historians, physicians also succeeded at last in a long campaign to push women out of the field of baby delivery. As Charlotte Borst notes in her history of midwifery, *Catching Babies,* "between 1870 and 1930, medicine struggled to achieve cultural authority, and childbirth had become an arena for demonstrating the goals of the new scientific professional." Physicians won that struggle and were able to establish obstetrics as an important medical speciality practiced almost entirely by men.[40]

Concurrent with these developments, the modern hospital emerged as an efficient, scientific center for the treatment of illness. Hospitals shed their reputation as institutions for the poor and elderly and grew at a rapid rate in the 1800s. The medical profession was gradually able to restrict the right to practice in hospitals to those in their own ranks. In addition, because they supplied patients to hospitals, physicians achieved a fair amount of control over hospital policies.[41]

An important turning point in the growth of the medical profession's exclusivity and power came in 1910, when an extensive investigation of medical training was commissioned by the doctors' professional organization, the American Medical Association. Although today we think of the AMA as a highly influential group, it was weak and ineffective for many years after its founding in 1846. However, as doctors gained strength, so did the AMA. By 1910 half of all MDs in the United States belonged to the organization, and the AMA felt confident enough to embark on major changes in medical education. Medical training at that time was of uneven quality, and many schools had been unable to keep up with new technologies.

The AMA commissioned Abraham Flexner, a prominent educator, to survey the field and make recommendations. (This is the same Flexner who was later invited to a national social welfare conference to discuss whether social work was a profession.) The Flexner report criticized many medical schools and suggested a radical weeding out of "inferior" programs. Along with tighter licensing laws and new standards from the AMA, the report led to widespread closing of medical schools. Many of these were located in the South, and a number of them served a black student body. Only one in seven black schools survived into the 1920s. In addition, most of the schools serving women students were shut down.[42]

Gradually, the medical profession was becoming an exclusive and powerful body, composed primarily of white, middle- to upper-class men. Medical schools now established quotas limiting women to about 5 percent of admissions. Schools also discriminated against African Americans and Jews.[43]

The medical profession solidified its position in the health care system from the 1920s through the 1950s. Improvements in clinical medicine and surgical techniques; new forms of technology, such as the electrocardiograph; and exciting discoveries in the area of pharmaceuticals, such as the Salk vaccine against polio, led to increasing public faith in the wonders of medicine. People tended to credit doctors with the dramatic and continuing fall in morbidity and mortality rates, even though much of this decrease could actually be traced to environmental reforms begun in the late 1800s. As medicine became more complex, doctors tended to choose specialized practice. The family general practitioner was increasingly replaced by the specialist—the internist or the heart surgeon—who commanded more prestige and a higher salary. Faith in the expert and awe at the increasing sophistication of medical care caused people to become more and more dependent on physicians. Of course, other groups, such as nurses and physical therapists, played a role in health services, but they were generally kept firmly under the authority of the physician. Nurses had difficulty in establishing an autonomous profession; through the 1940s, their training was largely controlled by hospitals.[44]

The high status of physicians in U.S. society led to their growing influence in areas other than strictly medical ones. Some observers have termed this the "medicalization" of social issues. One example, discussed in Chapter 13, was the conversion of "insanity" into "mental illness," a "disease" to be treated by medically trained psychiatrists. Doctors, as an organized group, became particularly powerful on the political scene. Although not all doctors belonged to or subscribed to the views of the AMA, the organization came to speak with authority for the entire medical profession. The AMA constituted a potent lobby against governmental measures that threatened to undercut physicians' authority. As early as the 1920s, the group helped to repeal a nationally funded, state-administered program of maternal and child health services that had been set up under the Sheppard–Towner Act. The program had drastically reduced infant mortality, birth defects, and maternal deaths. However, the AMA argued that such public programs constituted a dangerous experiment in state medicine.[45]

The power of the AMA to influence health policy became particularly evident in the 1930s. President Franklin D. Roosevelt had contemplated adding a national health care program to his package of Social Security benefits. Yet he and his advisors were dissuaded from doing so because of their awareness of the AMA's powerful opposition to such a scheme. Nevertheless, the Social Security Act did reinforce the legitimacy of government activity in the health field. Title VI of the act, for example, gave the U.S. Public Health Service additional resources and authority to support state and local government efforts in the area of public health.

While doctors were increasing their dominance in the medical arena, hospitals were strengthening their position as a major setting for health care. Hospital expansion was particularly notable after World War II. The federal system of Veterans Administration hospitals, already the largest hospital system before the war, underwent revitalization and increased growth. In 1946 nongovernmental, nonprofit hospitals, often called *community hospitals,* received a particular boost from a hospital construction act known as the Hill–Burton program. The program provided federal funds for new hospital construction. In promoting funding of hospitals, federal policymakers opted to steer public financing away from areas such as national health insurance or outpatient medical services. In addition, the Hill–Burton program forbade the federal government to interfere with hospital policy. In a move that would be repeated in subsequent years, the government took on major responsibility for financing health care but did not gain accompanying control.[46]

Medical Social Work

Medical social work was a professional specialty that developed largely in conjunction with the expansion of hospitals and the rise of the medical profession. Although some social workers were involved in the public health measures of the late 1800s and early 1900s, particularly through their work in settlement houses, medical social work as a specific entity first appeared in the hospital setting. Some of its first practitioners were, in fact, nurses. The establishment of hospital social work allowed these individuals to pursue a more autonomous professional status, one that was more independent of physicians than nurses were able to be.

In 1905, Dr. Richard Cabot set up the first medical social services department at Massachusetts General Hospital. Before coming to Massachusetts General, Cabot had

This public health nurse from New York City's Henry Street Settlement House gets a good reception when she visits families in slum neighborhoods.

directed the Boston Children's Aid Society. Impressed with the work of caseworkers at the society, he felt there was a place for their services in the hospital context. Social workers could be particularly helpful in combating the depersonalization of the hospital and its tendency to ignore the social and environmental roots of disease. They could assist in the process of medical diagnosis by providing a study of the patient's social and economic situation; they could organize community resources, particularly to help hospital outpatients and those with physical disabilities; and they could investigate the role of environmental factors in causing disease.

Although medical social workers had an uphill battle convincing the bulk of MDs of the usefulness of their skills, over the next several decades they found a place for their practice in many large city hospitals. The goals established by Cabot—humanizing the impersonal hospital and providing insights into the social aspects of disease—remain part of the basic core of health care social work today.[47]

The new specialty soon developed its own training programs—the Boston School of Social Work set up the first medical social work course in 1912—and its own professional organization, the American Association of Hospital Social Workers (1918). It contributed prominent theorists, practitioners, and educators to the social work profession. These included Ida M. Cannon, who was an early director of Massachusetts General's Social Service Department, and Harriett Bartlett, who wrote widely on the goals and functions of medical social work and was active in professional development both in medical social work and in the field of social work as a whole in the 1940s and 1950s. Up until the 1940s, when it was eclipsed by psychiatric social work, medical social work was considered by many to be the most prestigious area of the profession. Part of this standing stemmed from an emphasis on a high degree of training. In addition, medical social workers absorbed some of the status ascribed to physicians, although they had to work hard to develop some measure of autonomy within a system dominated by MDs.[48]

While medical social work—direct practice with clients and consultation with physicians, generally in hospital settings—was the dominant mode of social work in health care, a small number of social workers pioneered in the area of health policy. Julia Lathrop and Grace Abbott were important figures in this endeavor. As successive directors of the U.S. Children's Bureau from 1912 to 1933, they promoted state and federal programs in the area of child and maternal health. Abbott was responsible for development of such programs under the Sheppard–Towner Act. The act established federal financing for state efforts to reduce the incidence of maternal and infant mortality by providing health services to pregnant women and children. When the act's appropriation was up for renewal in 1927, Abbott and other social workers fought for its reinstatement against the bitter opposition of a variety of groups, including the AMA. The AMA and other critics warned of the "international control of children" and the "imported socialistic scheme" inherent in the act. These groups attacked the maternal and child health programs in order to protect special interests and issues, such as states' rights, antifeminism, and the authority of the medical profession. This last factor was crucial in the act's defeat.[49]

The strength of the medical lobby took its toll on social work's involvement in health policy issues. Although many social workers saw a need for federally sponsored health measures in the 1930s and later, opposition from the medical profession helped to negate most organized efforts at reform. However, social work's interest in health policy revived in the 1960s when the War on Poverty promoted greater public attention to the need for government involvement in health planning and services.

Health Care in the 1960s and 1970s

The 1960s and 1970s brought new challenges and changes in the health care system. Lack of access to medical care, particularly for the elderly and poor, had become an increasing problem as medical costs rose after World War II. President Harry Truman had attempted to deal with these problems in the 1950s, but when he pushed for federal health insurance, the AMA responded with cries of "socialized medicine." Organized labor also fought the program, fearing that government insurance would usurp the union role in providing health benefits through negotiations with employers.[50]

The "discovery" of the existence of poverty and racism in the United States in the 1960s led to heightened awareness of the connections between poverty and ill health, and of the ways in which discrimination against minorities affected access to adequate health care. This awareness reawakened the call for government intervention. At that point, the United States might have chosen a publicly funded system of health services for all, such as the system adopted in other industrialized nations. However, many factors, including a tradition of individualism, the fear of "big government," and the ongoing opposition of the organized medical profession, made such a move unthinkable. The next likely scheme, a program of national health insurance, still met with ardent disapproval from the AMA.

The AMA favored private insurance offered by commercial companies and the quasi-public Blue Cross/Blue Shield system that had been developed by hospitals in the 1930s and 1940s. In Blue Cross plans, hospitals agreed to provide service based on prepaid premiums from participants. Special legislation exempted these plans from the usual state taxes paid by insurance companies. Blue Shield plans were a similar scheme applied to services provided by doctors in their offices. Both Blue Cross/Blue Shield and commercial insurance were often tied to employment. Those unable to participate in job-related group plans—the elderly, the unemployed, and those whose jobs did not offer insurance—were often unable to pay the higher premiums of the individual subscriber.

The inadequacies of existing insurance, rising medical costs, and the gathering force of the War on Poverty finally forced some solutions. In 1965, Congress passed legislation establishing the Medicare and Medicaid programs. Medicare provided comprehensive, federally financed medical insurance for the elderly and others receiving Social Security. Medicaid, which was to be jointly financed by the state and federal governments and administered by the states, extended health insurance to low-income groups. Before Medicaid, one in five poor people in the United States had never been examined by a physician. By 1970 the number of yearly visits to doctors by poor people came closer to the pattern of those with higher incomes. Significantly, however, no cost controls were built into the new measures. Under Medicare, for example, the government paid whatever hospitals charged.[51]

Federally funded community health centers were also a part of the new antipoverty thrust of the 1960s. Generally located in low-income urban neighborhoods, the centers were designed to offer high-quality health care and preventive services to the poor in an outpatient setting. Policymakers hoped that the centers would decrease reliance on hospitalization and the use of crowded emergency rooms. In the 1970s, in recognition of the fact that more than half of the medically underserved lived in rural areas, the community health center idea was extended to rural communities.[52] (See Figure 12.6.)

The holistic health and hospice movements constituted other forces for change in the traditional health system. Each generated alternative programs. Holistic health centers stressed preventive measures and patient involvement in health care. The hospice movement, which promoted supportive multidisciplinary care for the dying patient, often outside of the hospital, offered yet another alternative to traditional practices.[53] The growth of new kinds of outpatient care, along with the decline in acute diseases and the overbuilding of hospital facilities, contributed to a growing surplus of hospital beds. This set the stage for increased competition among hospitals that was to come in the 1980s and 1990s.

The 1960s and 1970s also brought increased criticism of the medical profession. The egalitarian ideals and social critiques of the 1960s caused many to question the power and elitism of professional groups, including doctors. Minority groups raised issues about access to medical education. The women's movement was a particularly potent force in challenging the medical establishment. The movement criticized the medical profession for its predominantly male composition and its reliance on male in-

FIGURE 12.6 **A Rural Health Center's Brochure**

Source: Hardwick Health Center, Hardwick, Vermont. Reprinted by permission.

Hardwick Area Health Center

High Street
P.O. Box 535
Hardwick, VT 05843
472-3300
1-800-339-0740

Medical Care Services
The Health Center provides general health care for all ages, including pediatrics, adolescent and adult medicine, and care for the elderly.

Treatment of Acute Illnesses
Colds, earaches, minor injuries.

Treatment of Chronic Illnesses
Arthritis, heart disease, high blood pressure

Physical Examinations
Work, annual, comprehensive, school

Pediatric Care
Common illness, well child care, immunizations

Women's Health
pelvic exams, PAP smears, breast exams, family planning and birth control.

Laboratory Tests
Pregnancy, throat cultures, VD tests, cardiograms, urinalysis, HIV, etc.

Welcome to the Health Center

The Health Center is a general family clinic designed to make health care and health education more readily available to area residents.

We offer complete, coordinated, and individualized health care to people of all ages; from babies to grandparents. In this sense, we try to fill the role of the old-time family doctor.

We have designed our Health Center to include the most modern approaches to health care. We provide a one-stop location for many of your family's health needs, including primary medical care, laboratory tests, and a variety of programs geared to "health maintenance" - the prevention of illness.

Our staff will work with you to treat you when you are sick, and to keep you healthy when you are feeling well.

Our Commitment
- Treat the **Whole Person.**
- Respect patient and family right to participate in **Decision Making;** foster **Independence.**
- Provide **Health Education** and guidance.
- Involve the **Community**.
- Provide services based on Patient's **Need, Not Ability to Pay**.
- Foster well being and **Excellence of Staff.**

Providers at the Health Center

The Health Center staff includes physicians who have been trained to care for the needs of the whole family. Their specialties are Family Practice and Internal Medicine.

Care is also provided by mid-level practioners (physician's assistants and nurse practitioners) and nurses.

Mid-level practitioners have special training which prepares them to provide a high degree of patient care and education. They work under written guidelines developed by the supervising physicians at the Health Center.

Our physicians are also on staff at Copley Hospital in Morrisville. If you have to be admitted to the hospital, you can be seen by your physician from the Health Center.

terpretations of women's health problems. Feminists questioned male doctors' conceptualization of childbirth as a traumatic medical event, rather than as a natural occurrence. Alternative women's clinics and books such as *Our Bodies, Ourselves* encouraged women to become more involved in their own health care.[54]

These challenges led to reforms in both the medical profession and the larger health care system. More women and African Americans were admitted to medical schools. By 1999 over 40 percent of all medical students were women. African Americans and other minorities fared less well. Although minorities as a whole constituted 34 percent of medical students, African Americans made up a little more than 7 percent of the student total (see Figure 12.7).

FIGURE 12.7 **Minority Student Enrollment in Schools of Medicine, According to Race/Ethnicity: United States, 1970–2000**

Note: Excludes osteopathic medicine.

Source: National Center for Health Statistics, *Health, United States, 2002,* Table 105, online at www.cdc.gov/nchs/products/pubs, 276.

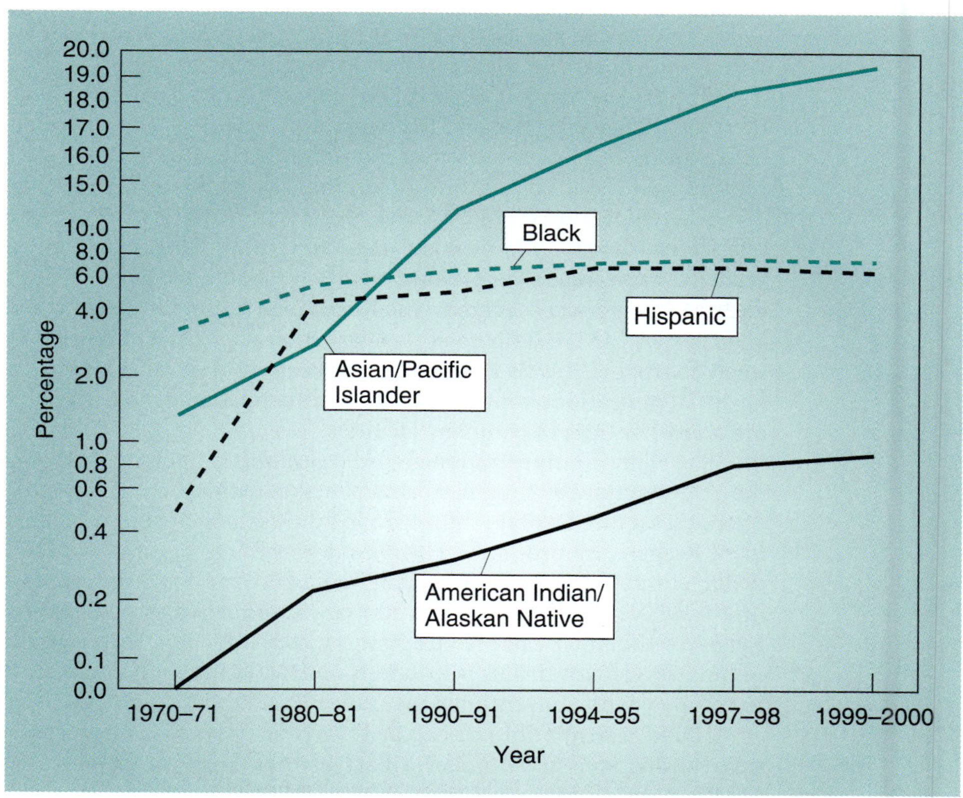

Partly because of the influence of the women's movement, medical practices regarding women began to change in many communities. For example, in 1970 the hospital in the small town of Oswego, New York, did not allow prospective fathers to be with their partners during labor. Two years later, not only could men accompany their partners in the labor room, but they could also be present at the actual delivery of their babies. In addition, local doctors no longer discouraged women from breastfeeding, and some physicians had begun to recommend classes in prepared childbirth to their patients.

The health system still contained problems in the 1970s, however. Inflation fueled higher health costs. Fears grew that America faced a health care crisis. The situation was greatly exacerbated by the fact that Medicare and Medicaid were "open-ended" programs, in which increases in health charges could be passed along directly to the government. Access to health care for the poor and minorities had improved because of Medicaid and the new neighborhood health centers. However, this access was now threatened by rising medical costs, which helped lead to drastic reductions in government support for health centers in 1978.

One response to health care problems was federal funding for local health planning agencies. Another was increased attention to an alternate way of organizing the delivery of health services: the *health maintenance organization,* or HMO. Although government funding for health planning bodies fell victim to President Ronald Reagan's campaign to reduce the role of the federal government, HMOs eventually grew to become the dominant player in the U.S. health care system.

HMOs, one form of what is now known as managed care, were first developed in the 1930s. They were prepaid medical services, which were provided at first in specific clinics or medical centers. Kaiser Foundation Health Plans pioneered the HMO concept in California. Fixed monthly fees, usually paid by employers, and minimum out-of-pocket expenditures by patients covered all needed medical treatment from Kaiser physicians, clinics, and hospitals. Kaiser and other HMOs generally offered more comprehensive coverage than existing medical or insurance plans, including preventive services such as annual checkups. The Kaiser plan is an example of a staff-model, or "brick and mortar," HMO: It operates its own physical facilities and uses physicians who work solely for that HMO. By the 1970s, an alternative form of HMO had appeared, in which health organizations contracted with private physicians to deliver services in their own offices rather than in company facilities.[55]

The Nixon administration passed legislation supporting HMO growth in 1971, and the HMO Act of 1973 required all businesses with more than twenty-five employees to offer at least one federal HMO plan in addition to conventional insurance plans. President Reagan also promoted HMOs as a way of containing health costs, which continued to climb in the 1980s. Yet, while some HMOs were quite successful, the movement on the whole grew slowly. Prepaid plans diminished physicians' autonomy and were fought by the American Medical Association. AMA opposition and diminished support in Congress led to various restrictions on HMOs that initially made it difficult for them to compete with conventional insurance.[56]

The Reagan administration used two other ways to cut costs: greater pressure on insured individuals to shoulder a part of their medical expenses, and new limits on Medicare reimbursements to hospitals. Following the first approach, the government greatly increased the amount of the hospital deductible paid by Medicare recipients. The hope was that shifting some of the financial burden to consumers would cut costs by encouraging people to seek less expensive alternatives to hospitalization when possible.

The second approach, introduced in 1983 by the Reagan administration, constituted a more direct attack on the traditional fee-for-service method of financing health care. This approach uses diagnosis-related groups, or DRGs, to set fixed fees for Medicare reimbursement to hospitals. (Remember that in the original Medicare system, the federal government paid whatever hospitals—or physicians—chose to charge for treatment of Medicare patients.) Under the DRG approach, once a patient has been diagnosed, the hospital is paid a fee based on the average cost of treating that particular condition. If the cost of treating a given patient is lower than average, the hospital keeps the difference; but the hospital must absorb the extra expense if the patient uses more services or takes a longer-than-average time to treat. In 1992 a similar reimbursement system was adopted for physicians.

By focusing primarily on raising consumers' out-of-pocket payments and regulating hospital costs, the Reagan administration did little to change the basic organization and delivery of health care services in the United States or the considerable growth of the for-profit sector in health care. Ironically, for-profit hospital chains owed much of their prosperity and expansion to Medicare, which by 1985 provided one-third of their revenues.[57]

Nonetheless, the new incentive to keep hospital costs under control initially brought promising results. From 1983 to 1985, Medicare costs underwent their smallest relative increases since the start of the program. National health spending increases slowed as well. Beginning in 1986, however, these trends reversed themselves (see Figure 12.8). In addition, the use of DRGs led to worries over whether hospitals were releasing patients sooner than was medically advisable. Although there is little concrete evidence regarding the effects of DRGs on quality of medical care, it is clear that hospitals are now releasing many patients to nursing homes rather than to their own or relatives' care. Nursing home facilities are not reimbursed by Medicare, so these costs are simply shifted elsewhere. Although DRGs marked an important inroad into a system in which providers, in this case hospitals, have a good deal of power over medical fees, the initiatives of the 1980s did little to curtail rising costs.

The first president George Bush, and much of the Democratic Congress, continued Reagan's health care policies. These policies, with the exception of the DRG program, stressed the reduction of government intervention in the health sector and support for a market approach to health care. At the same time, however, public dissatisfaction with the health care system was growing. Polls in 1989 and 1990 showed that two-thirds of the population supported a far different approach: the creation of a government-funded national health program that would guarantee comprehensive health coverage to everyone in the United States. In addition, rumbles began to be heard from the business community about the need to do something to ease the burden of employee health plan costs.[58]

What lay behind this growing dissatisfaction, and what were its effects? First, between 1988 and 1992, the United States experienced double-digit increases in health spending each year. The rapid rise in health premiums for employers was dramatically expressed in the anecdote that the Chrysler Corporation was paying so much for employee health care that Blue Cross/Blue Shield had become the company's largest "supplier." Companies often passed the costs along to employees in the form of more copayments and higher deductibles. Health consumer and advocacy groups

FIGURE 12.8 **Medicare Costs Climb: Total Spending of the Medicare Program**

Sources: Congressional Quarterly 51 (2 January 1993), 29; *Health Care Financing Review 18* (Spring 1997), 196; U.S. Bureau of the Census, *Statistical Abstract of the United States: 1999,* 118, 120; *Statistical Abstract: 2003,* 104.

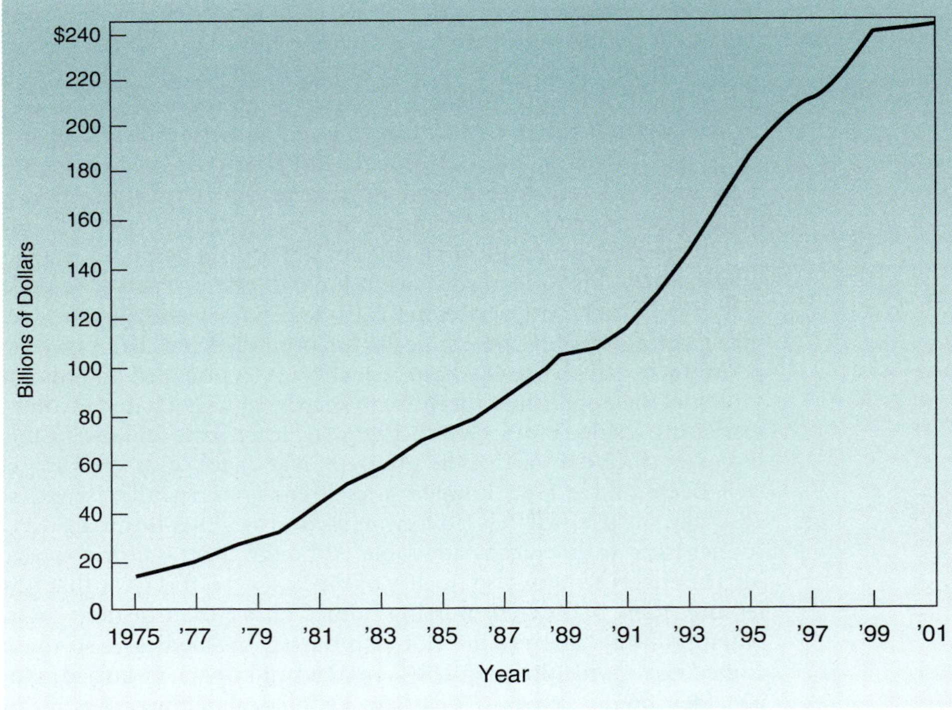

helped focus attention on the handsome profits of the health care industry and the increasing number of people who were uninsured. Awareness grew that the price of emergency care for the indigent was eventually passed along to the rest of the population through taxes and higher hospital charges. Medicare covered only a portion of the health costs of the elderly, and Medicaid failed to provide access to quality health care for many of the poor. Finally, despite massive expenditures on medical care, the health status of the U.S. population continued to be relatively poor in comparison to that of people in other industrialized countries.[59]

During the 1992 presidential election campaign, all of these concerns came together in a broad-based demand for reform. Bill Clinton campaigned on a platform that included the establishment of a national health care program. When Clinton took office in 1993, however, his administration's initiative was complicated by the fact that although nearly everyone agreed something must be done, there were great differences among the various constituencies over what to do and how. In addition, some groups were profiting from the current system and wanted little, if any, change. Among the many different interest groups in the debate were the following:

1. The hospital industry, both profit and nonprofit
2. The pharmaceutical industry
3. Physicians, who were represented by numerous groups, the most powerful of which was the American Medical Association
4. The insurance industry
5. Big businesses and large corporations
6. Small businesses
7. Allied health professionals, including social workers
8. Citizen advocacy groups, including broad organizations such as the American Association of Retired Persons, and other groups, such as Families USA, that were formed specifically to promote health reform
9. Unions
10. Elected officials
11. Health care consumers

Workers protest against cuts in employee health benefits.

Members of the first four groups tended to have a lot vested in the status quo and to be nervous about losing control if the government played a stronger role in health care financing or provision. The private insurance industry, particularly, faced an enormous loss of business if the government were to take over the entire responsibility for financing or covering costs for basic medical care. Large businesses, concerned about employee health care costs, were initially supportive of some sort of government intervention to control expenses. Many small business felt they could not afford to offer health plans but tended to be more leery of government involvement.[60]

Advocacy groups and many in allied health fields, such as nursing and social work, were strong supporters of attempts to develop a more equitable system that would guarantee access to quality care for all. Consumers had mixed reactions about reform; while they wanted more affordable care and an insurance or financing system that offered greater security, some were wary of government attempts to provide basic health care to all citizens, particularly if these were financed out of general tax revenues. Elected officials reflected the different points of view of citizens and interest groups. Many Democrats sought reforms that would make health care affordable for all; they saw the government as playing a major role in reform. Republicans, on the other hand, preferred private responses to health care problems, seeing marketplace competition as the best tool for improving the system. Almost all groups (except the insurance industry) were critical of such private insurance practices as refusing coverage to persons with "prior medical conditions" and not allowing employees to carry their policies with them when they switched jobs.

Out of this mixture of interests grew a plethora of reform ideas. The dominant versions fell into three general categories:

1. A Canadian-style "single-payer" system financed through general taxation, in which the government would monitor organization and use of health care services and negotiate directly with providers, such as hospitals and physicians, to keep costs down. The plan would offer "universal coverage"—health care would be available to all.
2. The Clinton plan, offering universal health coverage administered through large purchasing alliances. These alliances would offer several options to consumers, with an emphasis on managed care plans. Alliances would operate under state control, and a national health board would set pricing standards. Financing would include employer contributions, taxes, and payments by individuals. All Americans would be guaranteed a standard set of basic health benefits.
3. Various "market-based" plans, including features such as insurance reforms, voluntary "purchasing pools" of employers and consumers, and government subsidies to help low-income people pay for health coverage. Cost cutting would be achieved through use of purchasing pools and through competition between providers, rather than by government regulation.

Most plans included a standard benefits package, but none offered universal coverage. Note that the Clinton plan followed a modified market approach, with government influence over prices.[61]

The ensuing battle over which, if any, plan to adopt was one of the most heated national debates in recent years. Unusually aggressive lobbying was carried out by the various interest groups; the insurance industry in particular spent extraordinary amounts to discredit the Clinton plan. In the end, as policy analyst Terry Mizrahi notes, "Public opinion was divided so intensely that coalitions and compromises were doomed." On September 26, 1994, President Clinton's national health care program was declared officially dead in Congress. After two years of lobbying and debate and the introduction of numerous bills, the majority leader of the Senate declared that no health care legislation could be approved by that body.[62]

The abandonment of health care change in 1994 marked the fourth time in U.S. history that attempts at broad-scale health reform have been defeated. Generally speaking, such defeats seem to stem from the power of vested interests and from the public's traditional fear of government control. The latest failure of reform was also attributable to the tremendous complexity of the U.S. health care system and, given this overall context, to the ambitiousness of the Clinton administration's goals.[63]

Current Issues and Trends

The U.S. health care system has continued to change in the aftermath of reform efforts. Following the election of a largely conservative Republican-majority Congress in 1994, the idea of health care change was redefined against a background of federal government downsizing and an increasingly privatized, market-based approach to health services. Trends begun during or before the health care debate of the early 1990s include intense competition among health care organizations; the growing role of large corporations; and the rapid growth of for-profit health maintenance programs and other forms of managed care. These shifts in health care delivery and financing have proceeded without a coherent national plan. Critics contend that "changes are being driven by the ability of health-care companies to market themselves profitably, not by a strategy that balances the profit motive with a commitment to serve the public." Other observers, however, have been convinced that the new developments offer the greatest promise yet for creating cost-effective and quality services. Whatever one's opinion of them, managed care expansion and the growth of the private health sector, as well as attempts to regulate these phenomena, have had a major impact on the practice of health care social workers.[64]

Managed Care

Managed care, as you recall, first emerged in the 1930s and had become a relatively viable form of health care organization by the 1970s. Now most employers contract with managed care organizations (MCOs) rather than with traditional insurance systems to provide health care benefits to their employees. Before further discussion of the latest developments in managed care, it will be helpful to present a few definitions. *Managed care* is a broad term used to describe a wide range of programs, including HMOs, that are designed to contain costs and maintain quality. Basically, managed care is a "set of [health care] systems and technologies aimed at organizing and managing both the clinical and financial services to a given population of customers." Stated more straightforwardly, managed care is a system "of patient care that is determined by external review procedures rather than exclusively by the practitioner." *Managed care organizations* generally use a *capitation* rather than a fee-for-service approach to paying providers. That is, instead of paying health care professionals for each service they perform, MCOs pay a fixed, per-patient amount for a given period, regardless of the number of services rendered. The MCO will monitor the appropriateness of the services provided. Most MCOs use general practitioners as "gatekeepers." If you belong to a managed care plan, you choose one of these "primary physicians" from a list of those with whom the company has contracts. That doctor will then provide all your basic care and must approve your use of a specialist.[65]

At first, most MCOs limited your choice of physician to one in their pool of providers. However, as complaints began to grow about lack of choice, MCOs developed less restrictive systems, such as preferred provider organizations (PPOs). In a PPO plan you have the option of using physicians outside of the organization's network, but you must pay higher premiums to have this flexibility.[66]

Managed care can be carried out as a nonprofit or for-profit endeavor, and it can be organized under government auspices, as in managed care systems set up by states for their Medicaid populations. As we discuss in Chapter 13, managed care has also been adapted to the field of mental health. Versions of managed care are beginning to arise in child welfare and corrections as well. Beneath all of the different formats and strings of initials lies a basic premise: Managed care will reduce costs and provide appropriate and

FIGURE 12.9

A Medical Revolution: HMO Membership 1976–1995

Source: Newsweek—Ellyn Spragins, "Does Your HMO Stack Up?" (24 June 1996), 56. Copyright © 1996, Newsweek, Inc. All rights reserved. Reprinted by permission.

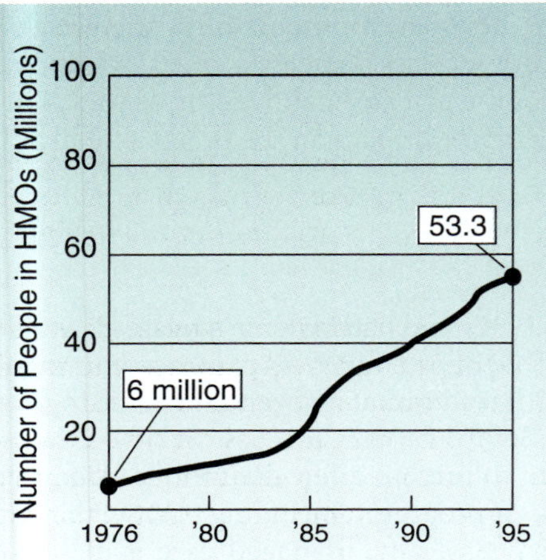

necessary care by monitoring physicians and other providers and the services they provide.

The promise of cost reduction is a major reason behind the tremendous expansion of managed care from the late 1980s on. The failure of national health reform in 1994 left an open playing field for managed care's development. By 1997 nearly three-quarters of U.S. workers with health coverage received that coverage through MCOs, up from about 50 percent four years earlier. (see Figure 12.9).

However, just when people were predicting that "managed care is here to stay," various pressures were building to force changes. Consumer criticisms about lack of choice, reliance on gatekeepers, denial of needed care, and incidents of medical malpractice created a backlash against managed care that has been intensifying since 1997. Demands for less restrictive managed care arrangements have gained force, resulting in slower MCO growth and a retreat from highly managed plans. Strong economic growth and tight labor markets have made employers more willing to grant employees' wishes by turning to PPOs and similar, more flexible systems. A growing patients' rights movement has led to state laws regulating managed care activities; by 2000, for example, eight states had passed legislation permitting patients to sue MCOs that allegedly had delayed or withheld necessary medical care. Recently, however, the Supreme Court ruled that patients cannot sue managed care companies for damages in state court.[67]

As a result, the managed care industry is currently in flux. The structure of managed care is changing. Two-thirds of MCOs, for example, no longer require approval by the organization before a person can be admitted to a hospital or see a specialist. As the managed care organization Health Net assures its clients, the company "is committed to being a gateway to health care, not a gatekeeper." However, more flexible managed care is losing the cost-cutting capabilities of the earlier, more restrictive approach, and partly as a result, medical costs are again rising. Employer health insurance premiums have recently resumed double-digit increases. Although employers have been absorbing much of that cost, workers are still seeing increases in their share of the premiums. The situation may well get worse as MCOs continue to be pressured on the state and national level to provide patients with rights and choices and as the slowing economy restricts the ability of employers to pay for more expensive plans.[68]

One expert notes that "the managed care movement of the last decade was really a financing system that was attempting to influence the way a group of fragmented, unintegrated physicians and hospitals practiced medicine." What we found out was that "when one uses financial tools to try to change the delivery of care, A, they are not very powerful and B, they make people mad." The managed care industry is doing its best to soften its image and make people happier; for example, some MCOs have begun paying bonuses to physicians based on patient satisfaction. Many are diversifying and offering more flexible plans. It is too soon to tell whether the new flexibility and the goal of holding down costs can coexist.[69]

The Business of Health Care

In a famous article in the *New England Journal of Medicine* in 1980, editor Arnold S. Relman coined the phrase "the medical–industrial complex." Relman was referring to "a large and growing network of private corporations engaged in the business of supplying health-care services to patients for a profit." As Relman observed,

> Health insurance and third-party payment, coupled with increased specialism and the technology explosion, have been largely responsible for the rapid rise in health care expenditures, and have created a new climate for medical practice in which there are virtually irresistible incentives for doctors to become entrepreneurial and profit seeking in their behavior.

And indeed, the 1980s, 1990s, and early 2000s have witnessed an increasing emphasis on the market economy as a major force for solving social problems. All players in the health field—including doctors, hospitals, pharmaceutical companies, rehabilitation services, and MCOs—have become involved in health care as big business. This business is now a major force in the U.S. economy. Writing over twenty years ago, Relman warned that the growth of the medical marketplace would raise issues about the potential conflict between the profit motive and the basic right to health care.[70]

Although managed care has nonprofit roots, it has increasingly become a business enterprise. One observer puts it this way: "As their popularity soared, HMOs largely became the province not of nonprofit groups that employed salaried doctors, but of commercial insurance companies that created networks of resentful community physicians and reported to investors." For-profit MCOs, aggressively seeking growth, now constitute about two-thirds of all managed care plans. Aetna, the largest managed care company, covers 19.3 million people. Some applaud the spread of for-profit MCOs, reasoning that increased competition in the health care marketplace will reduce costs and improve services. Others worry that for-profit managed care turns health care institutions into businesses whose fundamental obligation is to serve stockholders rather than people with health care needs. Critics point to the percentage of for-profit MCOs' income that goes to shareholders and to high salaries for MCO executives; these companies spend as little as 75 percent of revenues on patient care, compared to more than 90 percent spent by the nonprofits. There is also growing evidence that nonprofits provide the best care to members. Proponents of government regulation of MCOs see it as a necessary balance to possible excesses of the marketplace approach to health care.[71]

Governments themselves are privatizing public sector health programs. Stung by heavy expenditures for Medicaid and by rising numbers of Medicaid recipients, most states have contracted with MCOs, including for-profit ones, to bring down costs and in the hopes of broadening access to care. More than one-third of all Medicaid beneficiaries are now enrolled in managed care arrangements. One problem with this trend is that most MCOs have no experience in dealing with the health problems of low-income populations with high rates of chronic disease as well as frequent difficulties regarding employment, housing, and transportation. Health care advocates stress that it is particularly important that such plans have patient rights mechanisms to protect this more vulnerable population.[72]

The entrepreneurial changes taking place in managed care are mirrored in the hospital sector. Although investor-owned, or for-profit, hospitals constitute only 16 percent of all hospitals, large private hospital chains have continued to expand into the twenty-first century. For-profit hospitals had some financial difficulties in the late 1990s, when MCOs kept their payments to hospitals fairly low in order to keep their own expenses down. But recently hospitals have become more aggressive and have threatened to stop doing business with MCOs unless they raise the payments. The strategy has paid off, with earnings of for-profit hospital chains such as the giants HCA Healthcare and Tenet Healthcare increasing as much as 19 percent in 2000. In general, for-profit hospitals have an operating profit margin of 9 percent, compared to under 4 percent for nonprofits. Note, too, that nonprofit hospitals plow profits back into the facility, whereas for-profits distribute them to investors.[73]

Despite the continued growth of for-profit MCOs and hospitals, the biggest story in the health industry today is the expansion and profitability of the drug companies. Everywhere you look there are headlines such as "Spending on Prescription Drugs Jumps 18.8 Percent," "Why Drugs Cost So Much," "New Cancer Therapies Become Market Niche," and "Rise in Health Care Costs Rests Largely on Drug Prices." Prompting these headlines is the fact that spending on retail outpatient prescription drugs reached about $132 billion in 2000, up almost 19 percent from the year before. The factors contributing to the increase included larger numbers of prescriptions being written, a shift to higher-cost drugs, and overall price increases. Antidepressants were the best-selling prescription drug, while antihistamines and cholesterol-lowering drugs were the fastest-growing categories of medications.[74]

The ramifications of rising prices have been dramatic. Large companies often find prescription drugs to be the fastest growing part of their health care costs. General Motors, the largest private purchaser of health care in the country, had a prescription bill that topped 1.1 billion in 2000. Health care analysts also point to the hardships high drug prices create for older Americans. Elderly people are experiencing the largest drug increases, with the average price for a prescription rising between 18 and 20 percent for women age seventy and older. New, more expensive medications for arthritis and higher prices for estrogen replacement, diabetes, and other drugs have contributed to the problem. Although the Medicare prescription drug legislation passed in 2003 promised to help older Americans, this help was offset when brand name prescription drug prices rose at over three times the rate of inflation that same year.[75]

Not surprisingly, the pharmaceutical industry is the most profitable sector of the U.S. economy. The median Fortune 500 firm made a profit of about 5 percent in 2000; the drug companies weighed in at 18.6 percent. Drug firms often justify large profits by arguing that these are necessary to fund research into new medications and to develop new products. Yet in 2000, 17 percent of drug revenues was channeled into profits, 30 percent into marketing (including advertising) and administration, and only 12 percent into research and development. In fact, much of the research leading to medical advances is actually carried out in the public sector, including universities. In recent years, the industry has greatly increased its advertising efforts, shifting from advertising just to physicians to appealing to consumers to talk their doctors into giving them the latest medication to stem their allergies, decrease their depression, or increase their sex drive. The Pfizer pharmaceutical company launched an enormous and successful ad campaign to promote its antibiotic Zithromax to pediatricians and parents, handing out stuffed zebras to doctors to give to their patients and donating a live zebra—named Max—to the San Francisco zoo. Last year, after federal health officials announced that other antibiotics were cheaper and more effective in combating children's ear infections, Pfizer sponsored a season of *Sesame Street* to promote its name to parents.[76]

The drug industry also spends about $75 million annually lobbying members of Congress and federal regulatory agencies to protect its business against such legislation as a Medicare drug benefit. A substantial amount of money was given to the presidential and congressional candidates, particularly Republicans, in the 2000 elections.[77]

With so many dollars at stake and so many conflicting issues, including the effectiveness of the market versus that of the government in maintaining a healthy nation, it is not surprising to see the variety of proposals for reining in drug costs and for handling the particular problem of the effects of costs on older Americans. Many of these were laid out during the 2000 presidential campaign, in which George W. Bush promoted a plan relying on the private sector, by offering the elderly a 25 percent subsidy on premiums for prescription drug coverage through private insurers. At the same time, many states began attacking the problem. Maine enacted the nation's first drug price-control law for nonelderly residents, although the legislation has come under legal challenge. All six New England states formed an alliance of state officials that will use collective buying leverage to negotiate lower drug prices. The debate over how to deal with high drug costs promises to continue for some time to come.[78] We will discuss the latest attempt to solve the drug cost problem, at least as it affects older Americans, in the upcoming chapter on aging.

The growth of the profit sector and the increasing consolidation in the U.S. health care system have both positive and negative results. Some observers argue that the new regime is more efficient and that patients are better served. Others counter that the growth of multihospital systems and huge pharmaceutical companies creates increasing concentration of ownership and control of health services. Decisions about medical care—the type, the cost, and who will be served—begin to emanate from national corporate boardrooms rather than from regional sources. This approach to medical provision, as Paul Starr notes, begins to take on a fast-food image, with a standard product offered nationwide. Will patient needs be lost in the new corporate culture? Will companies focus on the bottom line rather than on quality services?[79]

Many aspects of the emerging health system—increased competition, the pursuit of profits, the buying of nonprofit facilities by for-profit ones—can lead to problems. Studies indicate that competition between hospitals may actually lead to higher costs, partly because of the rush to offer expensive new technologies. In addition, the climate of profit making and competition leads to large advertising budgets. Recent buyouts of nonprofit hospitals by for-profit chains have often aroused controversy, particularly when the hospital sold has had a mission of providing medical care to the poor. Teaching hospitals and public charity hospitals are struggling to survive in the new milieu; downsizings or closings of teaching facilities will have a negative impact on research and on the training of new physicians. Finally, the quest for profit can lead to inferior health care and outright fraud. In 1997, for example, the Columbia/HCA chain's business practices had become the focus of "snowballing federal criminal and civil probes, state investigations, and shareholder lawsuits." Reacting to large staff cutbacks in a Columbia hospital in Florida, one nurse wrote the company: "With the current patient load of a minimum of 15 patients, you are sacrificing safety and care. I lie awake at night going over and over in my mind the events of the day. Did I do what needed to be done?"[80]

It would be unfair to blame the entrepreneurial approach for all the ills of U.S. health care today. Physician domination over health care decisions may not be better than corporate control or government control, although the latter form of control is generally more open to public scrutiny. Environmental problems, the rush to new technologies, and changing demographics all affect the state of the nation's health. The for-profit sector has no doubt helped to reinforce a dual-track health care system, in which the employed and the more well-off receive good service while the poor and underemployed receive increasingly inferior care. Yet responsibility for dealing with that problem lies with the government and with all of us.

Government Action to Improve Health Care

Although attempts at comprehensive national health care reform ended in 1994, many of the problems that had prompted reform efforts remain. The percentage of individuals without health care insurance continues to rise, with children a particularly vulnerable population. Minority and rural communities still have difficulty gaining access to quality health care services. Cuts in Medicaid have put children, the poor, and the elderly increasingly at risk. Finally, the health care system is still complex, confusing, and often uncoordinated.

Having lost the mandate for comprehensive change, President Clinton pursued more piecemeal legislative efforts in his second term. Probably the most significant move toward incremental change was the passage of the Health Insurance Portability and Accountability Act of 1996. Better known as the "Kassebaum–Kennedy" act, this legislation improved health insurance for employed Americans by making it more likely that they could maintain their health coverage when they switched jobs. The act made insurance "portable" from one job to another by prohibiting employment-related health plans from limiting or denying coverage to new employees with pre-existing health conditions. Note, however, that the new law does not mandate that all employers provide health insurance to their employees. Many small companies still do not offer insurance.[81]

The Kassebaum–Kennedy act also included a compromise measure that Republicans have long proposed: the creation of medical savings accounts (MSAs) for self-employed people and employees of small businesses. Workers make tax-deductible contributions to these interest-earning accounts, and the money can be used only for medical expenses. The accounts are packaged with high-deductible health insurance to cover serious illness. A person with an MSA makes his or her own determination about how much to spend on routine and small-scale health care, is covered for large medical charges, and has the chance to earn interest on money put aside in the MSA. Proponents of the accounts say that they provide consumer choice and encourage people to be more frugal in making decisions on medical care. Opponents counter that MSAs favor the healthy and wealthy and adversely affect the sick and the poor. Those with low incomes cannot afford to contribute to such accounts, and the sick cannot afford the high deductibles.[82]

In 1996, Democrats in Congress made medical coverage for uninsured children a top legislative priority. With the support of the Clinton administration, the 1997 federal budget agreement included a $24 billion initiative to improve the health of poor children: the Children's Health Insurance program, or CHIP. The plan gave states a new stream of federal money to help insure children whose families have relatively low incomes but are not poor enough to qualify for Medicaid. Although it was estimated that the program would cover as many as 5 million children, states have been slow to implement CHIP.[83]

It can be argued that these are all piecemeal reforms, with none of them making the sort of change necessary to ensure access to affordable and effective health care for all Americans. And although attempts at large-scale health reform have been consistently thwarted in the United States, some observers remain optimistic about the possibility. The continued failure to bring down costs, the stubbornly high percentage of uninsured adults and children, the low ranking of our country in health indicators such as life expectancy and infant mortality, and the existence of many stakeholders—physicians, nurses, patients, large employers, and state officials—who are dissatisfied with the current state of affairs may finally galvanize us to carry out a major overhaul of the health care system.[84] See Table 12.2 for a view of Americans' assessment of past and current spending on health care. Table 12.3 indicates reactions to proposals regarding coverage of the uninsured.

TABLE 12.2 How Americans Feel about Improving and Protecting the Nation's Health: Are We Spending Too Little, Too Much, or the Right Amount?

	1993	1994	1996	1998	2000	2002
Too Little	72%	64%	66%	67%	70%	74%
About Right	17%	23%	23%	25%	23%	21%
Too Much	6%	11%	8%	6%	4%	4%
Don't Know	3%	4%	3%	3%	2%	2%
(total)	n = 793	1,502	1,437	1,375	1,399	1,346

Source: James A. Davis, Tom W. Smith, and Peter V. Marsden, *General Social Surveys, 1972–2002* (Chicago: National Opinion Research Center, 2003), 67. Reprinted by permission.

TABLE 12.3 **Americans' Attitudes about Ways to Cover More of the Uninsured, by Political Party, 2003**

	Total Public	Democrats	Republicans
Extremely/very important to pass a law in next year to provide health insurance for most uninsured Americans	74%	85%	64%
Favor following ways to guarantee health insurance for more Americans:			
Expanding state government programs for low-income people	80%	86%	75%
Requiring businesses to offer private health insurance for employees	77%	82%	72%
Offering uninsured tax deductions, credits, other assistance	73%	72%	81%
National health plan, financed by taxpayers, insurance from single government plan	46%	56%	30%

Source: Harvard School of Public Health/Robert Wood Johnson Foundation/International Communications Research poll, May–June 2003. Republished with permission of Project HOPE—The People-to-People Health Foundation, Inc., from *Health Affairs,* "Americans' Views of the Uninsured: An Era for Hybrid Proposals," Web Exclusives (July–December 2003), pp. 405–413; permission conveyed through Copyright Clearance Center, Inc.

Perspectives

Approaches to health care reflect different ideological assumptions. The political perspectives described here address the issue of responsibility for the poor, as well as the question of who should control the medical system—consumers, corporations, physicians, or the government.

The Conservative Perspective

In its purest sense, the conservative point of view calls for an unfettered free-market approach to health care, with no government interference in the provision of services. Individuals, or consumers, would pay for care with their own funds or private insurance. Medical programs would compete freely for consumers' dollars. Adequate health care would be seen as an "economic resource," rather than a right of all citizens.[85]

Today's conservatives follow a modified form of the market approach to health care delivery. This approach is based on the idea that the government is inherently incompetent at certain tasks, and that public policies and programs cannot be sensitive enough to variations in individual preferences and local conditions. Conservatives argue that the market is a much better mechanism for responding to such preferences and conditions. However, conservatives have come to accept government's role in providing a basic health "safety net" through programs such as Medicaid and Medicare. In addition, the part of the business community that purchases health care or insurance for its employees has also been willing at times to accept a government role in controlling medical costs.

Conservative health care proposals often stress the element of choice, suggesting tax credits or incentives for purchasing private health insurance or enrolling in a health plan of one's own choosing. Critics of this approach argue that the "informed consumer" of medical care is largely a myth. Health care has become so complex that few of us can really know for sure whether a particular operation is warranted or which surgeon will perform it best. A seemingly straightforward matter such as a runner's stress fracture is not so easy to diagnose—X rays may not differentiate between a fracture and tendinitis, and they may not show the condition at all if the equipment is not positioned correctly. After diagnosis, treatment suggestions vary—"Stay off the leg for eight weeks," "Run as soon as it stops hurting," or "Wear special supports in your shoes." In this confusing situation, one can't expect that the runner, or consumer, knows best and will be able to choose the best doctor or the most effective treatment.

The Liberal Perspective

Liberals stress the right of all people to adequate health care. They see government as a major enforcer of this right. They also emphasize the importance of consumer participation in health care planning. Not all of these ideas are antithetical to what radicals and conservatives believe. What makes liberals different is the mechanisms they adopt to achieve these goals.

Liberals generally believe in a system that includes market forces but that subjugates these to the authority of the government. They tend to follow a regulatory model, in which government acts to prevent abuses in the system, to increase accessibility, and to control costs. Like conservatives, liberals see government as an appropriate provider of a health care safety net for the poor, but they envision this role in broader terms. They tend to be strong believers in the Medicare and Medicaid systems and to oppose spending cuts in these areas.

The Radical Perspective

The radical approach rejects the market model entirely and argues for a complete restructuring of health care in America. Such restructuring is necessary to redistribute power over health care planning and provision from the few to the many. In their analysis of our present health care system, radicals assert that this system mirrors social class divisions in the United States. That is, the owners, controllers, and producers of services in health institutions—physicians, hospital board members, MCO administrators, and pharmaceutical company executives—are predominantly upper-class white males. These powerful individuals and their organizations often act together to preserve their authority.

The radical approach to health care states that dominance of the health field by the rich and powerful leads to denial of effective and accessible care to minorities, women, and the poor. In addition, radicals follow an environmental model regarding the causes of disease and suggest that much of today's poor health stems from poor working conditions, unemployment and other economic disruptions, and industry's abuse of the environment.

Radicals propose many solutions to these problems, including strong environmental controls and the development of a national health system in which health care is provided directly by the government. Most important, radicals stress the need to move to community and citizen control over health care planning and delivery. As Ehrenreich and Ehrenreich conclude, "The only way to fundamentally change the health system so that it provides adequate, dignified care for all is to take power over health care away from the people who now control it."[86]

Social Work Roles

Health care is the second largest setting in social work practice, along with child welfare and family services, and one in which social workers play many roles. Social workers act as mediators, counselors, and patient advocates, and they are involved in planning health services and in developing health policy. Through their professional organizations and also as individuals, social workers have actively promoted health care reform. This is an important activity because changes in the system will have long-lasting effects on both social work practitioners and their clients. Health care social workers often function as mediators between the health care system and its clients. As this system has become more complex and problematic, the mediator role has increased in importance. Health care social work is generally carried out in host institutions—the hospital, group medical practice, MCO, or neighborhood clinic—and these host institutions, as we have seen, are part of a complex network of health services and health care financing. A large portion of the social worker's job consists of helping clients negotiate that large network and obtain needed services from the individual health care institutions. And, as you might expect, health care social workers also help people and their families deal with issues of health and illness on a personal level.[87]

A hospital social worker, for example, might assist the children of an elderly parent in their attempts to acquire understandable and comprehensive information from the physician about their parent's condition. That same social worker might also explain the intricacies of Medicaid eligibility and referral for nursing home care and help the family arrange for such care and its financing. Finally, the social worker might develop a counseling relationship with the elderly client, helping him or her deal with feelings about the upcoming move and helping the client play an active role in decisions about nursing home care or other alternatives.

As they work in the health care system, social workers interact with many other disciplines. Physicians generally see social workers as knowledgeable about the psychosocial aspects of health and illness. For example, they call on a social worker for help when clients seem emotionally troubled, when family or personal problems seem to be interfering with treatment plans, or when clients need help in handling the financial aspects of illness or planning discharge. Social workers also work alongside occupational therapists, physical therapists, nurses, and medical aides in promoting client health. Social workers and occupational therapists share an interest in the environmental factors in illness and disability, and they place emphasis on building clients' coping abilities. For example, both a social worker and an occupational therapist are working with Mrs. Kasselbaum, who has become a wheelchair user because of an auto accident that injured her spine. The occupational therapist is helping Mrs. Kasselbaum learn how to dress herself, cook, and carry out other daily living activities. Soon she will be assisting Mrs. Kasselbaum in her return to her job as a high school guidance counselor. The social worker is meeting regularly with Mrs. Kasselbaum and her family to support them as they come to grips with both the emotional and the practical impact of her disability on all of their lives. Although each worker has distinct functions, both are concerned with helping Mrs. Kasselbaum deal with practical realities and with reinforcing her coping abilities and those of her family.

Perhaps the greatest role overlap exists between nurses and social workers. Each profession has specific areas of expertise; nurses, for example, can attend knowledgeably to physical needs and conditions, and they are skilled in helping patients and families adapt to life-threatening diseases. Social workers, for their part, are particularly experienced in using community resources (a skill they share with public health nurses) and in helping with discharge and financial planning. Yet both professions stress the building of sensitive, client-centered relationships that help people cope with the implications of illness. Nursing as a field is expanding in the areas of administration, research, case management, and psychiatric work, all areas in which social workers are also active. The overlap with nurses and other professions can be confusing, especially for the novice health care social worker; but the mixture of shared skills and goals, along with specialized areas of expertise, enhances the teamwork approach that health care professionals often use in working with clients.[88]

As you can see from the preceding examples, health care social work is practiced in a variety of settings and involves many different functions. The hospital, where medical social work as a speciality began, is still a major setting for health care social work. However, recent hospital downsizings and reorganizations have led to changes in what hospital social workers do. Newer functions, brought about largely because of changes in the way hospitals operate, consist of discharge planning and "utilization review." Discharge planning entails working with patients and their families to ensure that discharge back home or to another facility is smoothly carried out. Much of this work takes place with elderly clients. Use of the DRG (diagnosis-related groups) system for Medicare patients and the current tendency of MCOs to encourage shorter hospital stays have both added to the importance of discharge planning. The planning function is also part of utilization review, which involves monitoring the use of services and judging which services are essential to patient recovery.[89]

Because a hospital is a complex bureaucratic setting with specialized staff, many rules and regulations, and often an air of impersonality, hospital social workers can be particularly effective as patient advocates. A social worker, for example, might help the mother of a young child obtain special permission to stay overnight in her sick child's hospital room. The same social worker might also advocate for a change in hospital policy and the creation of facilities to accommodate parents on pediatric wards on a regular basis. Social workers also interact with the bureaucracy of hospital life in their involvement on various policy and planning committees. Often, hospital social workers contribute to decision making involving complex ethical issues, such as a decision by parents to terminate a problem pregnancy. They also confront ethical dilemmas, such as whether to allow an elderly patient's discharge back to a nursing home with a questionable quality of care.[90]

With the decline of an acute care focus and the recognition that increasing numbers of patients are experiencing chronic health problems, hospitals and health care social workers are becoming part of community-oriented delivery systems that focus on chronic disease management. This means that a number of social workers are now employed in home health programs and in outpatient and rehabilitation services. Social workers have also become involved in managed care—chiefly, as we discuss in Chapter 13, in systems of mental health managed care.[91]

Other health settings in which social workers are active include public health departments, rehabilitation programs, publicly funded community health centers, and family planning clinics. Social workers even teach in medical schools, where they discuss the psychosocial aspects of health and illness. Social workers also participate in planning health services and developing health policy in specialized planning agencies and other settings. The National Association of Social Workers has been particularly active in lobbying for a more affordable and equitable health care system for all Americans.

Finally, as we have noted, social workers are often involved in ethical and legal issues surrounding health care. They are particularly likely to observe lapses in confidentiality. For example, a social work intern placed in a clinic offering free medical care for low-income Hispanic immigrants told her supervisor that when a potential funder visited the clinic, the director pulled several personal medical records from the files and used them to show the visitor "what we do here." Social work educator Norma Kolko Phillips has written a poignant account of her visit to an emergency room, where she observed people being questioned about intimate health matters in the presence of several other patients, "without anyone even acknowledging that there was a problem." Because social workers are often involved in ethical and legal issues surrounding health care, they are now more and more likely to serve on hospital ethics committees, "playing crucial roles in ensuring that all points of view are heard as medical providers sort through the complex dilemmas that surround patients' care."[92]

Most important, because they are firsthand observers of the effects of the health care system on individuals, social workers can publicize problems and inequities and promote reform. In Louisiana, for example, social workers have advocated for consumer participation in the state's development of a managed care plan for its Medicaid population. Similarly, social workers assisting persons with AIDS and their families have supported strong social protections to combat discrimination against affected individuals. Social workers bring to all these activities their broad perspective on the entire range of physical, emotional, and environmental factors that influence people's health and well-being.[93]

Conclusion

As the people of the United States grapple with the need to improve health care in order to make it more affordable, humane, and equitable, social workers can play an important part. They can promote the changes in lifestyle and environment that are so crucial to good health and longevity. They can help broaden the medical model through their understanding of the psychosocial and cultural context of health and illness. They can advocate for client involvement in system changes. Finally, they can become directly involved in the planning process, bringing to bear their dual emphasis on the individual and the surrounding social, economic, and political environment.

Visit **www.researchnavigator.com** to research these important concepts from the chapter:

- Access to health care
- Environmental racism
- For-profit health care
- Health care spending
- Health maintenance organization
- Managed care
- Preventative health care
- Socioeconomic status AND disease

Web Sites on Health Care

Families USA <www.familiesusa.org>: A national nonprofit organization that advocates high-quality, affordable health care for all. Site provides reports and analyses of health issues, including Medicaid, managed care, and children's health insurance. Also links with other health sites.

Health Care Financing Administration <www.hcfa.gov>: HCFA is the federal agency that administers Medicaid and Medicare. Information on these programs, federal health policy.

Milbank Quarterly <www.milbank.org/quarterly>: A multidisciplinary journal on social, legal, and ethical dimensions of health care policy.

National Coalition on Health Care <www.americashealth.org>: A bipartisan alliance working to improve U.S. health care, bringing together businesses, labor unions, consumer groups, providers, and leaders from academia and government. Material on emerging health trends, health policy.

New York Times Web Site on Women's Health <www.nytimes.com/women>: Good resource for articles on women's health issues, links to other web sites.

The Urban Institute <www.urban.org>: Extensive material on health issues, including Medicaid, Medicare, managed care, and health insurance reforms.

Endnotes

1. Adapted from Peter Marks, "Shots Are Often Free, but Many Children Miss Immunizations," *New York Times* (14 February 1993), 1, 17.
2. Robert Pear, "Health Spending at a Record Level," *New York Times* (9 January 2004), 1, 14; National Center for Health Statistics, *Health United States, 2002,* Table 113, online at www.cdc.gov/nchs/products/pubs, 288; Mark Sherman, "Spending Goes up 7.8% during Year," *Arizona Republic* (2 December 2004); Judith Graham, "Health Care Costs Rising Faster Than Expected," *Chicago Tribune* (12 March 2002), 1; U.S. Bureau of the Census, Current Population Reports, *Health Insurance Coverage in the United States: 2002* (September 2003), 1.
3. Elfriede G. Schlesinger, *Health Care Social Work Practice* (St. Louis, MO: Times Mirror/Mosby, 1985), 78–80; David Mechanic, *Medical Sociology,* (New York: Free Press, 1968), 90–95.
4. Schlesinger, *Health Care Social Work Practice,* 78–79.
5. Alfred Katz, "Future Directions in Health Policy," in Doman Lum, ed., *Social Work and Health Care Policy* (Totowa, NJ: Allanheld, Osmun, 1982),

195–196; Jane Isaacs Lowe, "A Social-Health Model," in *Social Work in the 21st Century*, Michael Reisch and Eileen Gambrill, eds. (Thousand Oaks, CA: Pine Forge Press, 1997), 211–214.

6. Henrik L. Blum, *Expanding Health Care Horizons* (Oakland, CA: Third Party Publishing, 1983), 6–23.
7. NCHS, *Health United States, 2002,* Tables 114, 121, 122, pp. 96, 289, 301; Geoffrey Cowley, "What High Tech Can't Accomplish," *Newsweek* (4 October 1993), 62.
8. NCHS, *Health United States, 2000,* Table 132, 332; *Health United States 2002,* Table 121, 301; Stephen Hefler et al, "Health Spending Projections for 2002–2012," *Health Affairs,* Supplement (January–June 2003), 54–65.
9. NCHS, *Health, United States, 2002,* Table 119, 298.
10. Paul Krugman, "The Health of Nations," *New York Times* (17 February 2004), 23; Katy O'Grady, "Health Coverage Up," *NASW News 49* (May 2004), 8; U.S. Census Bureau, Current Population Reports, *Health Insurance Coverage: 2002* (September 2001), 1–3, 11; National Center for Health Statistics, *Health United States,* 2003, Table 151.
11. NCHS, *Health, United States, 2002,* Table 59, p. 192, and Table 96, p. 265.
12. NCHS, *Health, United States, 2003,* Tables 23, 24, and 26, pp. 126–131.
13. John B. McKinlay and Sonja M. McKinley, "Medical Measures and the Decline of Mortality," in Peter Conrad and Rochelle Kern, eds., *The Sociology of Health and Illness* (New York: St. Martin's Press, 1981), 18–24; Michael Specter, "Neglected for Years, TB Is Back with Strains That Are Deadlier," *New York Times* (11 October 1992), 1, 20; NCHS, *Health, United States, 2002,* Table 40, 42.
14. NCHS, *Health United States, 2002,* Table 54, 182; David Brown, "Big Drop in U.S. AIDS Deaths for First Time," *Manchester Guardian Weekly* (9 March 1997), 18; John Leland, "The End of AIDS?" *Newsweek* (2 December 1996), 64–73.
15. "AIDS Rising in U.S. for 1st Time in 10 Years," *Arizona Republic* (29 July 2003), 1.
16. Barton Gellman, "A Disease That Could Destroy Nations," *Washington Post National Weekly Edition* (8 May 2000), 15.
17. NCHS, *Health, United States, 2002,* Table 59, 192.
18. Dirk Johnson, "Fighting for Air," *Newsweek* (22 September 2003), 54; Richard Rothstein, "Students in a Fog," *New York Times* (25 April 2003), 33; David Barbosa, "Rampant Obesity, a Debilitating Reality for the Urban Poor," *New York Times* (26 December 2000), D5; NCHS, *Health, United States, 2000,* 9.
19. Bendheim-Thoman Center for Research on Child Wellbeing, Princeton University, "Racial and Ethnic Disparities in Low Birthweight," *Fragile Families Research Brief 4* (January 2001), online at http://crcw.princeton.edu; Janet McConnaughey, "One in Three Kids at Risk for Diabetes," *Arizona Republic* (15 June 2003), 1–2; Richard Perez-Pena, "Study Finds Asthma in 25% of Children in Central Harlem," *New York Times* (19 April 2003), 1, 13; Nanci Hellmich, "Obesity Soars in Teens to Mid-20s," *Arizona Republic* (13 October 2003), 1; "Health Improves but Racial Disparities Remain, *New York Times* (25 January 2002), 19; Linsey Tanner, "Aggressive Treatment Urged for Hypertensive Blacks," *Arizona Republic* (11 March 2003), 10; "Black Smokers' Risk High," *San Diego Union Tribune* (11 April 1994), 6.
20. "Racial and Ethnic Disparities in Health Care," *Health Action* (July 2003), 1; Tony Pugn, "Health Care Is Inferior for Minorities," *Arizona Republic* (21 March 2002), 1; James Sterngold, "Los Angeles Inner City Beset by Chronic Health Problems," *New York Times* (3 May 2002), 12; Michelle M. Doty, "Hispanic Patients' Double Burden: Lack of Health Insurance and Limited English," Commonwealth Fund (February 2003), online at www.cmwf.org.
21. U.S. Department of Health and Human Services, Health Resources and Services Administration, Maternal and Child Health Bureau, *Women's Health USA 2002* (Rockville, MD: U.S. Department of Health and Human Services, 2002), 28, 41–42; "Nation Falls Short on Women's Health Care," *Washington Post* (7 May 2004), 14.
22. Christine Lyons, "Be Silent No More!" *American Association of Retired Persons 35* (June 1994), 20; Michael Wines, "In Research, the Sincerest Form of Concern Is Money," *New York Times* (22 June 1997); Susan Smith, *Sick and Tired of Being Sick and Tired: Black Women's Health Activism in America, 1890–1950* (Philadelphia: University of Pennsylvania Press, 1995), 110–114.
23. Administration on Aging, *A Profile of Older Americans: 2000,* online at www.aoa.gov/aoa/stats/profile; NCHS, *Health, United States, 2000,* Table 58, 232.

24. Herbert H. Hyman, "National Health Policy," in *Social Work and Health Care Policy,* 39; Mechanic, *Medical Sociology,* 50–52, 90–94.
25. Gary Lee, "For Most of the World, Lives Are Getting Longer," *Washington Post Weekly Edition* (1–7 August 1994), 37; Alex Duval Smith, "Passive Smoke 'Harms Heart,' " *Manchester Guardian Weekly* (21 May 1997), 3.
26. Epstein, "The Political and Economic Basis of Cancer," in *Sociology of Health and Illness,* 75–79; "Mostly Smoke," *Newsweek* (4 July 1994), 45; Geoffrey Cowley, "What High Tech Can't Accomplish," *Newsweek* (4 October 1993), 60–62.
27. Bruce G. Link and Jo Phelan, "Social Conditions as Fundamental Causes of Disease," *Journal of Health and Social Behavior,* Extra Issue (1995), 83; Stephen Gorin and Cynthia Moniz, "From Health Care to Health," in Paul R. Raffoul and C. Aaron McNeece, eds., *Future Issues for Social Work Practice* (Boston: Allyn and Bacon, 1996), 60–61.
28. Warren E. Leary, "Black Hypertension May Reflect Other Ills," *New York Times* (22 October 1991), B6.
29. Jerry Adler, "Stress," *Newsweek* (14 June 1999), 56–63.
30. Link and Phelan, "Social Conditions as Fundamental Causes of Disease," 87.
31. Harriet Arnow, *The Dollmaker* (New York: Macmillan, 1954), 277.
32. Milton Wittman, "Application of Knowledge about Prevention to Health and Mental Health Practice," in Neil F. Bracht, ed., *Social Work in Health Care* (New York: Haworth Press, 1978), 203; Schlesinger, *Health Care Social Work Practice,* 128–131; Peter Hookey, "Primary Health Care," in *Social Work and Health Care Policy,* 114–115.
33. James S. Gordon, "Holistic Health Centers in the United States," in J. Warren Salmon, ed., *Alternative Medicines* (New York: Tavistock Publications, 1984), 230–233; Phyllis H. Mattson, *Holistic Health in Perspective* (Palo Alto, CA: Mayfield Publishing, 1982), 9–12.
34. Paul Starr, *The Social Transformation of American Medicine* (New York: Basic Books, 1982), 24–28.
35. Howard S. Berliner, "Scientific Medicine since Flexner," in *Alternative Medicines,* 31; Richard W. Wertz and Dorothy C. Wertz, "Notes on the Decline of Midwives and the Rise of Medical Obstetricians," in *Sociology of Health and Illness,* 178–179.
36. Berliner, *Alternative Medicines,* 34–35; Starr, *The Social Transformation of American Medicine,* 32–37, 51–54, 93–99; Charles E. Rosenberg, *The Care of Strangers* (New York: Basic Books, 1987).
37. Berliner, *Alternative Medicines,* 31–32; James Leiby, *A History of Social Welfare and Social Work in the United States* (New York: Columbia University Press, 1978), 286–287; Walter Trattner, *From Poor Law to Welfare State,* 3rd ed. (New York: Free Press, 1984), 135–154.
38. Berliner, *Alternative Medicines,* 31–33; Starr, *The Social Transformation of American Medicine,* 134–140.
39. Starr, *The Social Transformation of American Medicine,* 19.
40. Barbara Ehrenreich and Deirdre English, *Witches, Midwives, and Nurses: A History of Women Healers* (Old Westbury, NY: Feminist Press, 1973), 33–34; Charlotte G. Borst, *Catching Babies: The Professionalization of Childbirth, 1870–1920* (Cambridge, MA: Harvard University Press, 1995), 5.
41. Starr, *The Social Transformation of American Medicine,* 146–179.
42. Starr, *The Social Transformation of American Medicine,* 116–125; Ehrenreich and English, *Witches, Midwives, and Nurses,* 30–33.
43. Starr, *The Social Transformation of American Medicine,* 124.
44. Barbara Melosh, *The Physician's Hand: Work Culture and Conflict in American Nursing* (Philadelphia: Temple University Press, 1982), 37–76.
45. Lela B. Costin, *Two Sisters for Social Justice: A Biography of Grace and Edith Abbott* (Urbana: University of Illinois Press, 1983), 130–146.
46. Edward Berkowitz and Kim McQuaid, *Creating the Welfare State* (New York: Praeger, 1980), 129–132; Starr, *The Social Transformation of American Medicine,* 349–350.
47. Roy Lubove, *The Professional Altruist* (New York: Atheneum, 1969), 24–30.
48. Harriett M. Bartlett, *Social Work Practice in the Health Field* (New York: National Association of Social Workers, 1961); Leslie Leighninger, *Social Work: Search for Identity* (Westport, CT: Greenwood Press, 1987), 186–187; "Ida Maud Cannon," *Encyclopedia of Social Work,* vol. 2 (Silver Spring, MD: National Association of Social Workers), 919.
49. Costin, *Two Sisters for Social Justice,* 134–146.

50. Starr, *The Social Transformation of American Medicine,* 249.
51. John E. Schwartz, *America's Hidden Success* (New York: W. W. Norton, 1983), 46.
52. Alice Sardell, *The US Experiment in Social Medicine: The Community Health Center Program, 1965–1986* (Pittsburgh: University of Pittsburgh Press, 1988), 3–4, 111–117.
53. Linda J. Proffitt, "Hospice," *Encyclopedia of Social Work,* vol. 1, 812–816.
54. Schlesinger, *Health Care Social Work Practice,* 55, 312–313; Starr, *The Social Transformation of American Medicine,* 396.
55. Dan Morgan, "Squeezing the Specialists: HMOs and Other 'Managed Care' Plans Are Changing How They Practice Medicine," *Washington Post National Weekly Edition* (25–31 July 1994), 10; Starr, *The Social Transformation of American Medicine,* 396; John Gabel, "Ten Ways HMOs Have Changed during the 1990s," *Health Affairs 16* (May/June 1997), 135–136, 320–327.
56. Starr, *The Social Transformation of American Medicine,* 400–401.
57. Vincente Navarro, *The Politics of Health Policy: The U.S. Reforms. 1980–1994* (Cambridge, MA: Blackwell, 1994), 37.
58. Navarro, *The Politics of Health Policy,* 194–196.
59. Rich, "Slowing the Growth in Health Care Costs," 37; Navarro, *The Politics of Health Policy,* 195; Mizrahi, "Health Care: Policy Development," in Richard L. Edwards, ed., *Encyclopedia of Social Work,* 19th ed., 1997 supplement (Washington, DC: NASW Press, 1997), 134.
60. Mizrahi, "Health Care: Policy Development," 134.
61. "The How's of Health Reform: Chief Proposals," *NASW News 39* (January 1994), 11; "A New Framework for Health Care," *New York Times* (23 September 1993), A20.
62. Mizrahi, "Health Care: Policy Development," 134.
63. For further discussion of the failure of health care reform, see Theda Skocpol, *Boomerang: Clinton's Health Security Effort and the Turn against Government in U.S. Politics* (New York: W. W. Norton, 1996); Henry S. Webber, "The Failure of Health-Care Reform: An Essay Review," *Social Service Review 69* (June 1995), 307–322; and Mary Ann Jimenez, "Concepts of Health and National Health Care Policy: A View from American History," *Social Service Review 71* (March, 1997), 34–50.
64. Mizrahi, "Health Care: Policy Development," 133; "Can HMOs Help Solve the Health-Care Crisis?" Health Care Special Report Part 2, *Consumer Reports* (October 1996), 28.
65. Kevin Corcoran, "Managed Care: Implications for Social Work Practice," in *Encyclopedia of Social Work,* 19th Ed., 1997 Supplement, 192; N. Winegar and J. Bristline, *Marketing Mental Health Services to Managed Care* (New York: Haworth, 1994); R. M. Alperin and D. G. Phillips, *The Impact of Managed Care on the Practice of Psychotherapy: Innovation, Implementation, and Controversy* (New York: Bruner/Mazel, 1997).
66. Gail A. Jenson, Michael A. Morrisey, Shannon Gaffney, and Derek K. Liston, "The New Dominance of Managed Care: Insurance Trends in the 1990s," *Health Affairs 16* (January/February 1997), 126–127.
67. Robert Pear, "Congress Weighs More Regulation on Managed Care," *New York Times* (10 March 1997), 1, A11; Cara S. Lesser and Paul B. Ginsburg, "Update on the Nation's Health Care System: 1997–1999," *Health Affairs 19* (November/December, 2000), 206–216; *On Managed Care: Industry Information for Health Care Decision-Makers* (6 June 2001), 1; Peter Weaver, "Green Light for Suits against HMOs," *AARP Bulletin 41* (September 2000), 9; HealthAction@families.usa.org, 21 June 2004.
68. Milt Freudenheim, "H.M.O.'s Are Pressed on Many Fronts to Reinvent Themselves," *New York Times* (18 December 2000), C8; Jonathan Weisman, "Sick about Health Care Costs," *Washington Post Weekly Edition* (7–13 June 2004), 29.
69. Freudenheim, "A Changing World Is Forcing Changes on Managed Care," A13; Milt Freudenheim, "In a Shift, an H.M.O. Rewards Doctors for Quality Care," *New York Times* (11 July 2001), C1.
70. Arnold S. Relman, "The New Medical–Industrial Complex," *New England Journal of Medicine 303* (23 October 1980), 963; Relman, "The Future of Medical Practice," *Health Affairs 11* (1983), 11.
71. Amy Goldstein, "The Demonizing of the HMO," *Washington Post National Weekly Edition* (18 October 1999), 19; Bradford H. Gray, "Trust and Trustworthy Care in the Managed Care Era," *Health Affairs 16* (January/February 1997), 42; Judith Bell, "Saving Their Assets," *The American Prospect* (May/June 1996), 60–66; Bill Brubaker, "Challenging the Giant of Managed Health Care,"

Washington Post National Weekly Edition (5–11 March 2001), 18; Mizrahi, "Health Care; Policy Development," 138; Gabel, "Ten Ways HMOs Have Changed," 143.

72. Diane Rowland and Kristina Hanson, "Medicaid: Moving to Managed Care," *Health Affairs 15* (Fall 1996), 150–152; "HMOs Dominate the Ever-Changing Health Care Industry," *Standard and Poor's Industry Survey* (3 July 1997), 19; Janet D. Perloff, "Medicaid Managed Care and Urban Poor People: Implications for Social Work," *Health and Social Work 21* (August 1996), 189–194.
73. Martin Gottlieb and Kurt Eichenwald, "A Hospital Chain's Brass Knuckles and the Backlash," *New York Times* (11 May 1997), sec. 3, 1, 11; Phil Galewitz, "For-Profit Hospitals Looking Healthier," *Arizona Republic* (14 August 2000), D1; Freudenheim, "H.M.O.'s Are Pressed on Many Fronts to Reinvent Themselves"; "A Fragmented Industry in Transition," *Standard and Poor's Industry Survey* (27 March 1997), 10, 13; Robert Pear, "17% Rise in Drug Costs Hit Elderly Hardest, Study Says," *New York Times* (27 June 2000), A14.
74. "Spending on Prescription Drugs Jumps 18.8%," *Arizona Republic* (8 May 2001), A6; David Noonan, "Why Drugs Cost So Much," *Newsweek* (25 September 2000), 22–24; Tim Arango, "New Cancer Therapies Become Market Niche," *New York Times* (19 November 2000), sec. 3, 9; Robert Pear, "Rise in Health Care Costs Rests Largely on Drug Prices," *New York Times* (14 November 2000), A12; "Rx Drug Spending Still Rising," *On Managed Care 6* (June 2001), 2.
75. David Noonan, "GM's War on Drug Costs," *Newsweek* (26 February 2001), 46–47; Robert Pear, "17% Rise in Drug Costs Hit Elderly Hardest, Study Says"; Mark Sherman, "Brand-Name Drug Disparity," *Arizona Republic* (26 May 2004), D1.
76. Donald Will Moran, "Prescription Drugs and Managed Care: Can 'Free-Market Detente' Hold?" *Health Affairs 19* (March/April 2000), 63–64; Ernst R. Berndt, "The U.S. Pharmaceutical Industry: Why Major Growth in Times of Cost Containment?" *Health Affairs 20* (March/April 2001), 100–113; "Rx Drug Spending Still Rising," 2–3; Merrill Goosner, "The Price Isn't Right," *The American Prospect* (11 September 2000), 25–26; Noonan, "Why Drugs Cost So Much," 24–25; Melody Petersen, "What's Black and White and Sells Medicine?" *New York Times* (27 August 2000), Sec. 3, 1, 11.
77. Robert Dreyfuss, "Drug Dealer," *The American Prospect* (30 July 2001), 16–18; Noonan, "Why Drugs Cost So Much," 25; Johathan D. Salant, "GOP Reaps Benefit from Drug Dollars," *Arizona Republic* (28 September 2000), A8.
78. Noonan, "Why Drugs Cost So Much," 27–29; Tony Pugh, "States Begin Task of Cutting Prices for Prescription Drugs," *Arizona Republic* (28 October 2000), A34.
79. Arnold Relman, "What Market Values Are Doing to Medicine," *Phi Kappa Phi Journal 73* (Summer 1993), 17–21; Starr, *The Social Transformation of American Medicine,* 436–439.
80. David Burda, "Hospital's Pricing Puzzle," *Modern Healthcare* (19 February 1988), 32; Conrad and Kern, *Sociology of Health and Illness,* 244; Esther B. Fein, "Problems Jeopardize Plan for Hospital Privatization," *New York Times* (1 June 1997), 17; Jennifer Preston, "Hospitals Look on Charity Care as Unaffordable Option of Past," *New York Times* (14 April 1996), 1–15; Paulette V. Walker, "Government Cuts and Rise of Managed Care Force a Medical Center to Switch Gears," *Chronicle of Higher Education* (13 December 1996), A30–32; Spencer Rich, "Putting Medical Research in Intensive Care," *Washington Post National Weekly Edition* (26 August–1 September 1996), 18; David S. Hilzenrath, "Probe of Columbia/HCA Takes Toll on Hospital Firm," *New York Times* (29 September 1997), 1; Gottlieb and Eichenwald, "A Hospital Chain's Brass Knuckles, and the Backlash," 1, 10–11.
81. Brian K. Atchinson and Daniel M. Fox, "The Politics of the Health Insurance Portability and Accountability Act," *Health Affairs 16* (May–June 1997), 146–150; Robert R. Rosenblatt, "Portable Health Insurance Law Still Has Catches," *New Orleans Times–Picayune* (21 August 1996), A10.
82. Margaret O. Kirk, "Medical Savings Plans: The Experiment Begins," *New York Times* (16 February 1997), 9; "An Agreement on Medical Savings," *Congressional Quarterly* (15 June 1996), 1678.
83. Edward M. Kennedy and Orrin Hatch, "Health Insurance for Every Child," *Washington Post* (20 August 1997), A25; Hillary R. Clinton, "Providing Health Care to All Children," *Liberal Opinion* (2 June 1997), 27; Henry J. Kaiser Family Foundation State Health Facts, June 2000, online at www.statehealthfacts. kff.org.

84. Marcia Angell, "Placebo Politics," *American Prospect* (6 November 2000), 23–28; Amy Goldstein and David Broder, "Health Care Growing as 2000 Issue," *Washington Post* (11 July 1999), 1, A12; David Broder, "Reason to Hope on Health Care," *Washington Post National Weekly Edition* (18–24 June 2001), 4.
85. Geoffrey E. Harris, Matthew J. Ripperger, and Howard G. S. Horn, "Managed Care at a Crossroads: A Wall Street View of Managed Care's Mistakes and Misfortunes," *Health Affairs* (January/February 2000), 157–163; John Ehrenreich and Barbara Ehrenreich, *The American Health Empire: Power, Profits, and Politics* (Health Advisory Center, 1970), 176–190.
86. Barbara Ehrenreich and John Ehrenreich, *The American Health Empire: Power, Profits, and Politics* (New York: Random House, 1970), 176–190.
87. Margaret Gibelman and Philip H. Schervish, *Who We Are: A Second Look* (Washington, DC: NASW Press, 1997), 82, 84; Helen Rehr, Gary Rosenberg, and Susan Blumenfield, "Clinical Interventions and Social Work Roles and Functions," in Rehr, Rosenberg, and Blumenfield, eds., *Creative Social Work in Health Care* (New York: Springer, 1998), 21–40.
88. Sandra Taylor-Owen, "The History of the Profession of Social Work: A Second Look" (Doctoral Dissertation, Brandeis University, 1986); Regina Kulip and Sister M. Adrian Davis, "Nurses and Social Workers: Rivals in the Provision of Social Services?" *Health and Social Work 12* (Spring 1987), 101–112.
89. Candyce S. Berger et al., "The Changing Scene of Social Work in Hospitals: Report of a National Study by the Society for Social Work Administrators in Health Care and NASW," *Health and Social Work 21* (August 1996), 167–177.
90. Enola K. Proctor, Nancy Morrow-Howell, and Cynthia Leeane Lott, "Classification and Correlates of Ethical Dilemmas in Hospital Social Work," *Social Work 38* (March 1993), 166–175.
91. Barbara Berkman, "The Emerging Health Care World: Implications for Social Work Practice and Education," *Social Work 41* (September 1996), 542–549;
92. Susan Landers, "Social Work Widens Hospital Panels' Views," *NASW News 39* (May 1994), 3; Norma Kolko Phillips, "Health Care Left and Right," *Reflections 5* (Winter, 1999), 20–27.
93. NASW, *Report of the Social Workers Task Force on AIDS* (September 1987).

CHAPTER

13

Mental Health and Developmental Disability

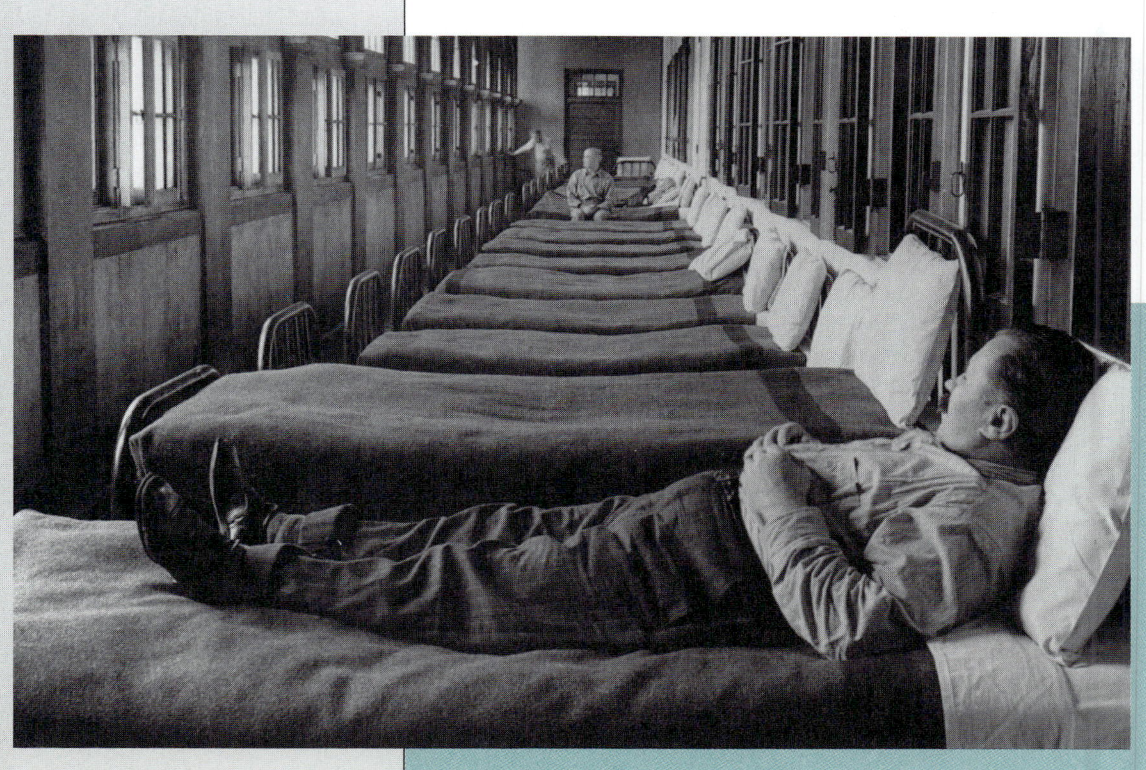

"When Rebecca was born with Down syndrome twenty-five years ago," Mrs. Levine explains to a parents group at the Association of Retarded Citizens, "we decided to keep her at home. Our doctor encouraged us; people were beginning to realize that you don't have to institutionalize kids just because they're retarded. She still goes to classes at the public school, gets a lot of attention from her older siblings, who live nearby, and has had a pretty happy life so far. But we've been thinking for some time now, just as many of you are doing, *what happens next?* As you know, the requirement that the public school educate her ends when she turns twenty-six; we're hoping she'll be able to have a job through a supported employment program. But we've been thinking about where she should live. We think Rebecca is ready for more independence, and we also have to face the fact that the time is going to come when we can't take care of her. I don't think she could ever live on her own. That's why I'm so excited about this new community home the association is trying to start, with maybe six developmentally disabled people living together, and a live-in helper paid by Family and Children's Services. Here's where you come in—we all need to help in planning this program so that it's the best thing for our kids."

Ed was born with a developmental disability. He lives with his parents in the suburbs. He has traveled by special van to school or to the sheltered workshop all his life. Recently he enrolled in a supported employment program and got a job at a taco stand, where he fills paper cups with salsa and sour cream. At first Ed's job coach drove him to work, but now that he has learned the job and no longer needs his job coach every day, he has learned to ride the bus to work. It takes an hour and a half and requires two changes. A group home was proposed in the neighborhood near his job, but the neighborhood's residents opposed its construction. So Ed continues to ride the bus. Waiting at the transfer points in the winter is unpleasant, but he values his new independence, income, and friends.

Melinda Perkins walked to the front of the state Senate Committee on Insurance hearing room and took a deep breath. She gave her name to the committee members and began her testimony. She told the senators about the problems she faces as the mother of a thirteen-year-old boy with mental illness. "Sam sometimes has to have weekly therapy sessions," she explained; "he also takes an expensive medication. But this really helps him stay in school and live a pretty normal life. The trouble is the expenses—both the therapy and the medicine. I'm a single mother and I have two other kids. I was a student at the School of Social Work, working on my master's, but I had to quit and go back to work full time because I just couldn't handle Sam's medical costs—which can be as high as $500 a month—plus everything else. I've got insurance, but it covers about a quarter of what I need because of all the restrictions on mental health care. If he had diabetes or asthma, it would be a different story. You've got to do something to help families like mine. Please give us the support we need to help our kids, and please don't discriminate against people with mental illness—vote for the mental health parity bill." As she walked to the back of the room, Melinda was surrounded by several of her friends, all members of a group for parents whose kids have mental illness. As they congratulated her on her testimony, she cast a worried eye back at the committee. "Did you see how some of them were fidgeting and looking away? I'm worried that we're not going to have the votes."

Tim Mankowicz is a social worker who has been in private practice for fifteen years. For the last four years he has worked as a "provider" for several mental health managed care companies; they reimburse him for the therapy sessions he conducts with people who belong to their systems. Tim has mixed feelings about his involvement in managed care. On the one hand, he notes, "I feel a lot more accountable now than I ever did when I just billed clients or their insurance companies. I've really got to justify why I'm using particular techniques or why I want to see a person for more than the usual six sessions. And the companies are always sending me new information on the latest treatments. But," he continues, "sometimes—like with the six-session guideline—they just seem to be operating on one-size-fits-all formulas, and the paperwork can be overwhelming!"

Curtis Frye is a thirty-three-year-old man diagnosed as schizophrenic. He also uses crack. He makes his home in various New York City shelters for the homeless, such as the Fort Washington Armory in upper Manhattan, where seven-hundred cots are packed into one huge room. Psychiatric services are available at the Armory, but Mr. Frye's drug addiction often interferes with potential help. Mr. Frye's parents feel hopeless about their son's future. His father, who refinishes floors for a living, told a *New York Times* reporter that "he and his wife, a factory worker, have struggled for years to help their son, who has been in and out of hospitals more times than he can count." Once their son got hooked on crack, the parents decided to stop taking him in. " 'He was miserable to live with,' Mr. Frye said. 'We couldn't take any more. He's not well enough to be by himself. He's not sick enough to be locked up. And he can't stay with us because we're not equipped to help him.' "[1]

Several people file out of the office of the director of the state Office of Mental Health. With eyes sparkling, Shannon Mitford exclaims to her colleagues, "I think he's going to be supportive." Ms. Mitford heads the state chapter of the National Mental Health Association; she and the others have had a long and ardent discussion with the director about the need to channel more of the state's mental health spending away from upkeep and staffing of the large state psychiatric hospitals and into community-based services. "Even he admits," she notes, "that treatment in the community is much more effective than long hospital stays. I sure hope he'll be able to influence the legislative budget committee."

The preceding scenes illustrate a variety of themes and issues in society's responses to mental illness and developmental disability. They also suggest some of the needs and concerns of affected individuals and their families. These themes include (1) society's desire to protect and at the same time be protected from those labeled mentally ill or developmentally disabled; (2) the question of whether the best approach is community placement or institutionalization; and (3) the challenge of how to develop humane and effective services that help individuals and their families and that recognize the inherent conflict between a person's desire for control and the importance of family and other supports. This chapter explores such issues, describes the fields of mental health and developmental disability, and takes a look at social work's role in this major area of practice.

Although mental illness and developmental disability constitute two different phenomena, we have chosen to discuss them in the same chapter because responses to them tend to be administratively linked in our social welfare system. We analyze the definitions, dynamics, and history of each field separately but note important similarities in issues and practice related to the two.

Issues in Definition

You may have noticed that in our opening paragraph we referred to people being "labeled" mentally ill or developmentally disabled. We speak of labeling because mental illness and developmental disability can be seen both as actual conditions in their own right and as constructs, or labels, developed in particular ways within particular societies. That is, although we might accept that mental illness is a "real" condition, characterized broadly as being out of touch with reality and responding inappropriately to events and to other people, we can also argue that society plays a major role in defining mental illness and deciding just who is "mentally ill." For example, a wealthy older woman who sometimes thinks she is the reincarnation of Cleopatra may simply be regarded as "eccentric." A bag lady who talks to herself as she roams the streets of New York City may well be called "crazy."

Developmental disability, which includes mental retardation, seems to be a more tangible concept than mental illness. After all, it can be defined and measured in seemingly objective ways, through intelligence tests and behavioral assessments. Yet we also know that the label of "retardation" can be assigned to children with cultural backgrounds different from our own or to individuals who have serious communication difficulties. The child who is clumsy or slow to learn may soon be called "retarded" by other kids. The issue of labeling is an important consideration, then, in discussions of definitions of both mental illness and developmental disability.

Labeling theory, or the idea that society labels certain people as different from the norm, is an approach used by a number of sociologists in examining deviance.[2] This approach rejects the idea that deviant, or undesirable, acts are the same in all societies and can be defined easily and consistently over time. Instead, labeling theorists argue that deviance is socially defined. What is acceptable in one society or time period may be considered deviant in another. In the 1990s, for example, women who sought careers outside the home were not seen as abnormal. In the 1890s, however, they were often considered deviant.

The notion of what constitutes an illegal, immoral, or inappropriate act is thus decided on by certain individuals or groups in society. The people making these decisions do so based on their own particular interests and values. Activities that don't fit with these values are labeled deviant, along with the people who engage in them. For example, assertive behavior by minority students in a public school classroom might be defined as delinquent activity by teachers and administrators who are anxious to maintain a quiet and well-regulated atmosphere.

Labeling theorists argue that people become what we call them. If we say that an assertive student suffers from a behavioral disorder, she may begin to accept that judgment. If we say often enough that a student who speaks nonstandard English is retarded, he may begin to act retarded.

Some theorists put particular stress on the importance of power in labeling deviants. They state that those with more authority in society are the ones who can impose their images and rules on others.[3] For example, it is not infrequent in the United

States for influential politicians and their backers to successfully discredit members of various protest groups by labeling them "unAmerican."

Another group of theorists, who follow a functionalist perspective, look at labeling and deviance in a somewhat different light. They see the source of labeling not in specific powerful groups but in the community as a whole. They argue that deviant behavior refers to conduct that the people of a community "consider so dangerous or embarrassing or irritating that they bring special sanctions to bear against the persons who exhibit it."[4] The act of defining and condemning such conduct draws the community together and reminds people about the acceptable boundaries of behavior. One learns what is "right" to do by seeing what is "wrong." One knows who "belongs" in the community by discovering who does not. The theorists' stress here is not on power, but rather on the need for social cohesiveness and the reinforcement of community norms. A good example of this idea is the sort of labeling teenagers use to define who is part of the in-group and who is not.

Another example of this concept of the function of deviance emerges in a study by sociologist Kai T. Erikson. Erikson looked at the ways in which Puritans in the Massachusetts Bay Colony used ideas about sin to reaffirm community values and to define acceptable behavior. Individuals and groups who questioned the church and existing political arrangements were accused of worshipping the Devil and were punished accordingly. Activities such as the celebrated Salem witch trials drew together a community troubled by both political uncertainty and a loss of religious purpose.[5] The same phenomenon occurs today, although the labels and values have changed. As psychiatrist Thomas Szasz notes, "In the past, men created witches; now they create mental patients."[6]

Underlying both the labeling theory and the functionalist approaches to deviance is the notion that what constitutes deviance is not inherent in an individual but defined by others. This idea lends a helpful perspective to the following discussion of the various definitions of mental illness and developmental disability. The phenomenon of mental illness in particular has drawn a good deal of attention from deviance theorists. Of course, to view mental illness as being socially determined does not mean one has to deny the reality of certain phenomena, such as delusions, hallucinations, and depression, that have been exhibited in a variety of cultures and time periods. What is important is how these phenomena are labeled and interpreted, which aspects of them have been stressed, and how they have been treated by different societies.

Definitions of Mental Illness

Mental illness has been defined in various ways in our society. Currently there exist several approaches to definition: mental illness as the absence of mental health, as sickness, as difficulty in social adaptation, or as "troublesome" behavior that *others* label as insanity. Of these four approaches, the idea of mental illness as disease predominates. The power of this particular conceptualization reflects the strong attraction of medical and scientific ideas in twentieth-first-century U.S. society.

Mental Illness as the Absence of Mental Health

Perhaps the simplest approach to defining mental illness is to view it as being the opposite of mental health. Yet this idea poses difficulties. What, after all, is mental health? Although several criteria for mental health have been proposed, including the degree of an individual's personal autonomy and mastery of the environment, or the "successful performance of mental function, resulting in productive activities, fulfilling relationships with other people, and the ability to adapt to change," experts have yet to agree on a definitive description.[7] Lacking a generally accepted definition of mental health, "absence of mental health" is not a particularly helpful measure of mental illness.

Mental Illness as Disease

A far more potent definition of mental illness is the disease or medical model. Not only is it more specific in its idea of insanity, but it also fits with our society's widespread acceptance of a medical interpretation of social problems. As the United States and other Western industrial societies have become more complex, definitions of deviant behavior have moved from moral and religious to legal to medical/scientific explanations. "Illness of the mind" has become the basic model for our thinking about people regarded by society as "mad." Alcoholism, for example, used to be seen as immoral or sinful; now it is regarded as an illness. A particularly bizarre instance of defining certain behaviors as disease was the invention of the term "drapetomania" in the 1850s to describe the "disease of black slaves characterized by the symptom of running away from captivity."[8]

In part, the rise of the disease model relates to the growth in the prestige and authority of the medical profession. In the United States particularly, doctors have come to dominate the organization of health care and to lay "first claim to jurisdiction over the label illness and *anything* to which it may be attached."[9] Alcoholism, child abuse, mental disorders, and marital problems—all have come, to a greater or lesser degree, under the authority of the physician. As many of our TV commercials testify, "doctors know best" about the best brand of aspirin, about the cure for hemorrhoids—and, by extension, about the most effective way to deal with personal and emotional problems.

The medical model has the following components: (1) people who behave strangely are "sick"; (2) they are not responsible for their illness, and they are entitled and even obligated to be helped; (3) help or treatment should come from the medical profession, particularly psychiatrists, and allied personnel—nurses, psychiatric social workers, and psychologists; and (4) treatment should be carried out in mental institutions or in psychiatric offices or clinics. The model sees mental illness as stemming either from organic conditions or from elements in an individual's psychological development. The medical model has recently been bolstered by progress in research on the role that genetics and brain abnormalities may play in causing mental illness.

In many ways, viewing mental problems as illnesses to be treated is a humane advance over the practices of punishing the mentally ill or treating them as outcasts. Yet this approach can carry its own, more subtle forms of control. People who are labeled mentally ill may not "know what's best for them," and they are thus subject to the authority of physicians and others in the health system. In addition, the medical model, when strictly adhered to, roots the problem in the individual and ignores the social context in which it occurred. Social and economic factors in mental illness are given little consideration.[10]

The most widely utilized document based on the medical approach to mental illness is the *Diagnostic and Statistical Manual of Mental Disorders,* now in its fourth edition (DSM–IV), published by the American Psychiatric Association.[11] This weighty manual, often referred to as the "cookbook" by psychiatric residents, hospital admissions staff, and other clinicians, gives a detailed classification of mental problems, including schizophrenia, depression, eating disorders, anxiety states, and even "pathological gambling." Although the DSM–IV categorizes a broad variety of behaviors as mental disorders, particularly in the latest edition, this labeling process does not operate in a vacuum. It can be affected by nonmedical groups. Thus, the designation of homosexuality as a

A CLOSER Look

From the DSM–IV: "Diagnostic Criteria for 300.23, Social Phobia"

A. A marked and persistent fear of one or more social or performance situations in which the person is exposed to unfamiliar people or to possible scrutiny by others. The individual fears that he or she will act in a way (or show anxiety symptoms) that will be humiliating or embarrassing. **Note:** In children, there must be evidence of the capacity for age-appropriate social relationships with familiar people and the anxiety must occur in peer settings, not just in interactions with adults.

B. Exposure to the feared social situation almost invariably provokes anxiety, which may take the form of a situationally bound or situationally predisposed Panic Attack. **Note:** In children, the anxiety may be expressed by crying, tantrums, freezing, or shrinking from social situations with unfamiliar people.

C. The person recognizes that the fear is excessive or unreasonable. **Note:** In children, this feature may be absent.

D. The feared social or performance situations are avoided or else are endured with intense anxiety or distress.

E. The avoidance, anxious anticipation, or distress in the feared social or performance situation(s) interferes significantly with the person's normal routine, occupational (academic) functioning, or social activities or relationships, or there is a marked distress about the phobia.

F. In individuals under age 18 years, the duration is at least 6 months.

G. The fear or avoidance is not due to the direct physiological effects of a substance (e.g., a drug of abuse, a medication) or a general medical condition and is not better accounted for by another mental disorder (e.g., Panic Disorder With or Without Agoraphobia, Separation Anxiety Disorder, Body Dysmorphic Disorder, a Pervasive Developmental Disorder, or Schizoid Personality Disorder).

H. If a general medical condition or another mental disorder is present, the fear in Criterion A is unrelated to it, the fear is not of stuttering, trembling in Parkinson's disease, or exhibiting abnormal eating behavior in Anorexia Nervosa or Bulimia Nervosa.

Specify if:

Generalized: if the fears include most social situations (also consider the additional diagnosis of Avoidant Personality Disorder).

Source: American Psychiatric Association, *Diagnostic and Statistical Manual of Mental Disorders,* 4th ed. (Washington, DC: American Psychiatric Association, 1994), 416–417. Reprinted with permission from the *Diagnostic and Statistical Manual of Mental Disorders,* Text Revision, Copyright 2000. American Psychiatric Association.

mental disease was eliminated from the manual in 1973, in part because of concerns expressed by organizations representing people who are homosexual.[12]

Critics of the manual say it is used less as a guide for clinical practice than as a tool for obtaining reimbursement for psychiatric services. Most "third-party payment" systems (such as the federal Medicaid program and private insurance plans) require those billing for mental health services to use the diagnostic categories listed in the manual. In a study of clinical social workers, some practitioners reported choosing the diagnosis most likely to bring reimbursement. This does not necessarily mean that practitioners are motivated by their own monetary gain; many may simply be trying to ensure that their clients receive services. Interestingly, some clinicians choose the least severe diagnosis possible in an attempt to avoid stigma for their clients.[13]

Mental Illness as a Reaction to Life's Problems

Partly as a reaction against the medical model, some social scientists and mental health professionals have defined mental illness as "problems in living" or "difficulties in social adaptation." While not denying the existence of anxiety, depression, and other such conditions, Thomas Szasz, Erving Goffman, and others view these states not as illnesses, but as understandable reactions to life's difficulties. Goffman notes that many of the "most spectacular and convincing of [psychiatric] symptoms in some instances . . . signify merely a temporary emotional upset in a stressful situation, however terrifying to the person at the time."[14]

Mental Illness as a Label Assigned by Others

The conception of mental illness as "problems in living" is intended as a way of thinking about mental disorders that does not cast affected individuals into a passive, patient role. This concept is related to our final definition: mental illness as primarily a social construct created by others or a social role that those labeled must play. According to this definition, people labeled mentally ill have actually "broken rules"—that is, they have behaved in a way that violates certain community or group norms. A simple example of rule breaking is the individual who, in "normal" conversation, fails to keep eye contact or stands too close or too far away from the other person. More extreme examples include withdrawing, displaying violent anger, or choosing to sleep in the street rather than in a home. Once this rule breaking has led to a person's designation as mentally ill, that individual begins to play out the expected social role. As sociologist Thomas Scheff observes, the more you define people as mentally ill, the more they define themselves in that manner. However, as Scheff has recently pointed out, labeling theory doesn't have to be seen as the only explanation of mental illness. Acknowledging the growing strength of biological theories, he now sees labeling theory as one of "many partial points of view."[15]

Thus, there are numerous ways of thinking about mental illness. Although the disease model is the predominant approach in our society, the ideas of the labeling theorists and others who study deviance remind us that the act of calling someone "mentally ill" is not necessarily a scientific and objective process. People may receive this title because of behavior that is frightening or unacceptable to others. In addition, some of this "crazy" behavior may in fact be an understandable reaction to life's problems.

Dynamics of Mental Illness

The preceding definitions of mental illness are linked to ideas about its causes. We discuss four schools of thought about the dynamics of mental disorders: the physiological approach, the psychological–developmental approach, the behavioral approach, and the environmental–sociological approach. Although these theories are not mutually exclusive, each emphasizes a different element in the human experience. Each also leads to different ways of dealing with mental illness.

A CLOSER Look

"On Being Sane in Insane Places"

In the early 1970s, D. L. Rosenhan, a psychologist, conducted an experiment to test whether mental health personnel could accurately determine whether a person was sane or insane. Rosenhan asked the basic question: Do the characteristics that lead to psychiatric diagnoses "reside in the patients themselves or in the environments and contexts in which observers find them?" In other words, how much are diagnoses based on the way people behave and communicate, and how much are they colored by the environment in which that behavior and communication takes place? To explore this question, Rosenhan chose eight "normal" people (that is, people who had never suffered symptoms of serious psychiatric disorders), all of whom were to gain secret admission to a mental hospital. The eight "pseudopatients" were admitted to a variety of mental institutions in five different states. The length of their hospitalization ranged from seven to fifty-two days. Each person came to the hospital complaining that he or she was hearing voices. In giving details about life history, marital status, and so on, the pseudopatients were completely truthful. Each was subsequently admitted to the hospital, and all but one was diagnosed schizophrenic. Once on the ward, the pseudopatients acted normally, although each took notes, generally openly, on the experience.

Their experience was that hospital personnel, including psychiatrists and nurses, continued to regard them as mentally ill. Behaviors such as note taking were sometimes seen as symptoms of mental illness. One nurse's record read: "Patient engages in writing behavior." Life histories were interpreted as confirming or explaining the existence of such illness. When the individuals were discharged from the hospitals, it was generally with the diagnosis of "schizophrenia, in remission." Interestingly, many of the other patients saw through the experiment, making comments such as, "You're not crazy. . . . You're checking up on the hospital."

From this experiment Rosenhan concluded that "a psychiatric label has a life and an influence of its own." Hospital staff expected to see mental illness in people admitted to the institution, and so that is what they saw. Subsequent researchers have questioned whether Rosenhan's study does indeed test the hypothesis that mental health professionals are unable to distinguish sanity from insanity. Yet the study remains a powerful reminder of the attitudes and responses prompted by the label "insane."

Sources: D. L. Rosenhan, "On Being Sane in Insane Places," *Science 179* (January 1973), 250–258; Robert Spritzer, "On Pseudoscience in Science, Logic in Remission, and Psychiatric Diagnoses: A Critique of Rosenhan's 'On Being Sane in Insane Places,'" *Journal of Abnormal Psychology 84* (October 1975), 442–452.

Physiological Explanations

The belief in physiological causes of madness has a long history. In ancient Greece, "mental abnormality was considered a disease . . . caused in the same way as a disease of the body."[16] In the Middle Ages and later, mental illness among women was attributed to disorders of the reproductive organs. By the late 1800s, scientists had uncovered the connection between syphilis and mental deterioration. Interest in physiological factors received additional emphasis in the 1950s with the discovery of psychotropic drugs (tranquilizers and antidepressants). More recently, researchers have been exploring the possibilities of genetic and chemical causes of mental illness as well as the effects of physical abnormalities in the brain. Generally, these investigators predict that the ultimate picture will reveal an interaction between psychosocial stress and biological vulnerabilty, rather than a single cause of mental illness.

Much of the research into the physiology of mental illness has focused on schizophrenia. The existence of a genetic component to the disease has been supported by studies of the incidence of schizophrenia among twins, other close relatives, and children whose schizophrenic parents gave them up for adoption at birth. However, although these studies demonstrate that relatives of schizophrenics have a higher likelihood than the general public of developing the condition, the mode of transmission of this genetic predisposition is still unknown. Researchers acknowledge that it may be a long while before they are able to isolate the actual genes involved.[17]

Other research has focused on disorders of the brain. At first such study was hindered by the lack of methods available to examine living human brains. However, the situation has changed with the development of noninvasive brain imaging techniques, such as magnetic resonance imaging (MRI), that can be used to study the structures and workings of living brains. As Scheff notes, "these are heady times for biological theories of mental disorder." This research has led to the discovery of differences in brain structure and functioning between those who have serious mental illness and those who do not. These studies "suggest that a widely distributed system of brain regions is impaired in schizophrenia. . . . Each of these brain regions appears to be involved in the specific behaviors and psychological processes" that are affected by the condition, including the ability to focus attention on salient cues in the environment and the self-regulation and self-monitoring of behavior. The source of brain abnormalities may be genetic or may be the result of infection or physical trauma at birth. Although the biological components of schizophrenia are thus obviously complex, researchers are excited about the potential for uncovering the causes of this and other types of mental illness.[18]

Psychological Explanations

The psychological–developmental model of mental illness views mental disorder as an outgrowth of an individual's personality development. Spurred particularly by Sigmund Freud, this approach looks at how past experiences affect current functioning. The stress on individual personality rather than on social causes of illness fits well with American tenets of individualism. Freudian psychology has been embraced much more strongly in the United States than in Europe. Terms such as *Oedipus complex* and *transference* have filtered into our everyday language. Although the idea that the development of a man's adult psyche depends a good deal on his infant infatuation with his mother and jealousy of his father is no longer fashionable, the concept that early childhood experiences shape future behavior is commonly accepted.

Later theorists have expanded on Freud's ideas and have included more emphasis on social factors. Ego psychology, as developed by Anna Freud, Erik Erikson, and others, focuses on the role of defenses in personality development throughout the life cycle, rather than just during the early years. Social workers have found Erikson's theories particularly useful. Erikson looks at human development as a series of life-stage crises to be resolved. Positive resolutions of these crises lead to an integrated and healthy personality; lack of resolution can lead to emotional problems in the future.[19]

Behavioral Explanations

Behavioral approaches to mental illness do not concern themselves with the inner processes of personality or "workings of the mind." Instead, they concentrate on behavior and view it as a set of learned responses resulting from a combination of rewards and punishments. The "symptoms" of mental illness are really dysfunctional behaviors, such as hallucinating in public places. The behavioral therapist rewards behaviors to be maintained and punishes behaviors to be changed. For example, whereas a Freudian therapist might view a child's "uncontrollable" temper tantrums as being the result of some problem in his early development, a behavioral therapist would see them as a behavior that has been reinforced (rewarded). The behaviorist would then look for the reinforcement (such as parental attention) and work to remove it, thus extinguishing the behavior.

Environmental and Sociological Explanations

Whereas the preceding explanations of mental illness focus on individual development within a fairly limited social context, a final set of ideas emphasizes environmental and social factors in the occurrence of mental disorder, as shown in Figure 13.1. Mental illness is seen as being rooted in an individual's social experience, including his or her community life and interpersonal relationships. Psychiatrist R. D. Laing, an important proponent of the environmental approach, described his patients as living "within networks of social interaction which could either foster their fulfillment as individuals or lead to their destruction."[20]

Stressful life events, such as the death of a loved one or a difficult family environment, have been found to have an important effect on mental health. Life stresses, particularly those caused by poverty, racism, and sexism, can lead to mental disorder. Women who grew up receiving welfare, for example, are more likely than other women to report psychological distress and lower self-esteem later in life. Studies of African Americans have found a high correlation between stress and mental health status.[21]

As we discussed in our earlier section on labeling theory, some social scientists have taken another approach in relating mental illness to the individual's social experience. Goffman, Scheff, and others have described mental illness as a social role created by society for the "disturbed" person. From this perspective, the initial behavior triggering the label of *mentally ill* can be described as one of three things: "rule breaking," an understandable reaction to stress, or a reasonable response to a "crazy world." (Joseph Heller's novel *Catch-22* gives a vivid example of the eccentric but basically sane

FIGURE 13.1 **A Model of Interactive Factors in Mental Health**

Source: Adapted from William A. Vega and Manuel R. Miranda, *Stress and Hispanic Mental Health: Relating Research to Service Delivery* (Rockville, MD: U.S. Department of Health and Human Services, 1985), 4.

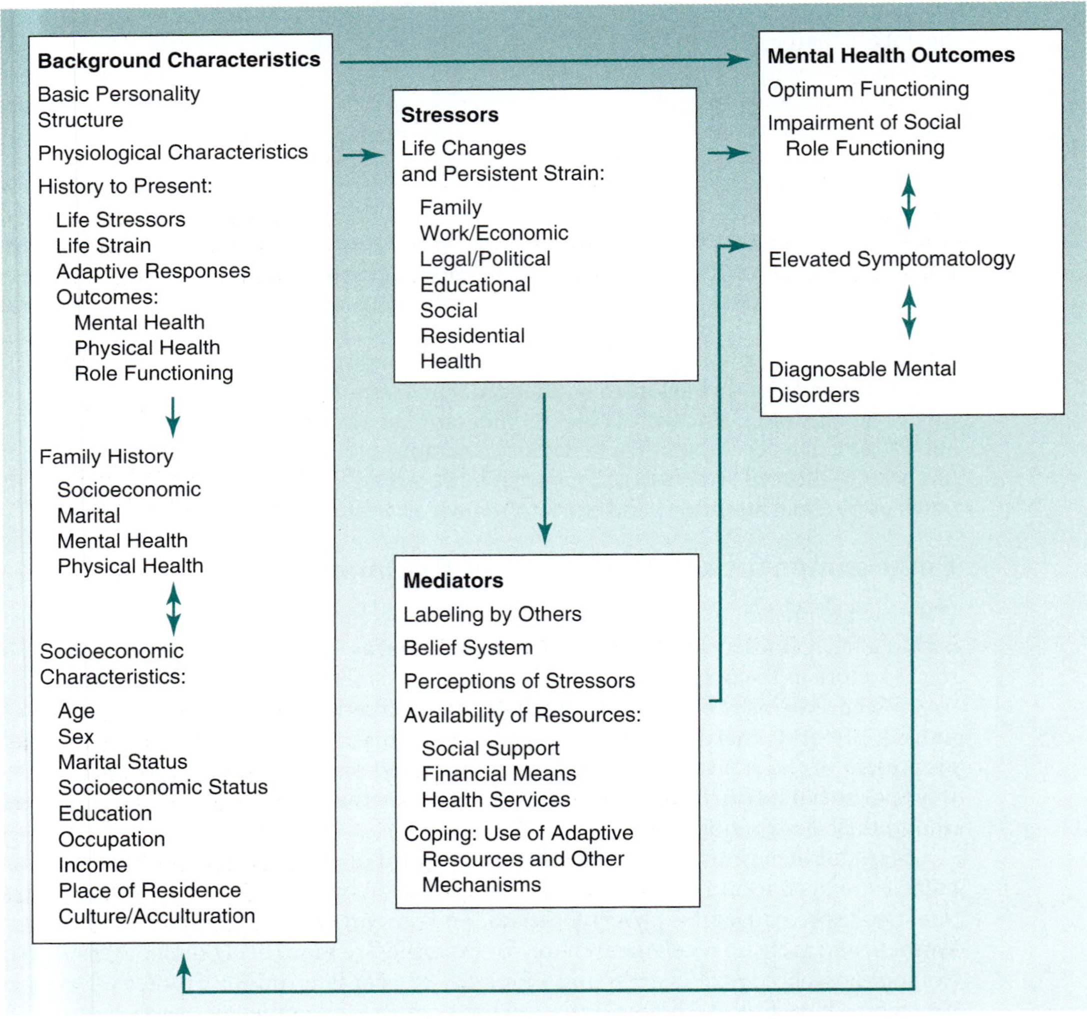

behavior brought on by the irrationality of war: Air Corps bombadier Yossarian sitting naked in a tree at the funeral of a crewmate.) The mental illness in these situations *follows* the initial behavior, as people are forced into "careers" as mental patients. Once hospitalized as a schizophrenic, for example, a person faces pressure from hospital staff and relatives to accept the role of a mentally ill person. Even other patients reinforce the role, as in this hospital ward conversation reported by Scheff:

> *New patient:* "I don't belong here. I don't like all these crazy people. When can I talk to the doctor? I've been here four days and I haven't seen the doctor. I'm not crazy."
> *Another patient:* "She says she's not crazy." (Laughter from patients.)
> *Another patient:* "Honey, what I'd like to know is, if you're not crazy, how did you get your ass in this hospital?"
> *New patient:* "It's complicated, but I can explain. My husband and I . . . "
> *First patient:* "That's what they all say." (General laughter.)[22]

Essentially, this view argues that the cause of mental illness lies in the reaction of others.

By and large, our society has tended to emphasize psychological explanations for mental illness, although physiological theories are gaining headway. However, theories of mental illness have begun to move from unitary explanations to multifactor models, which include a sociocultural perspective. One such model might look something like this:

1. Certain factors, such as physiological characteristics, may predispose an individual to mental illness.
2. Precipitating stresses and conditions, such as life changes and persistent tension, can lead to the onset of psychiatric disorders.
3. But mediating factors, including personal and extrapersonal resources and labeling by others, can affect the individual's ability to cope successfully with the precipitating condition[23] (see Figure 13.1).

Statistical Picture of Mental Illness

Tracking the rate of mental illness is more difficult than ascertaining the numbers of people with physical illnesses, such as cancer or diabetes. General estimates suggest that in any given year, about a quarter of the adult U.S. population will be affected by some sort of emotional or psychological disorder. Anxiety disorders, such as panic disorders and phobias, are the most common mental illnesses in the United States, annually affecting more than 23 million people. In addition, each year 5 to 7 percent of the adult population will have a serious mental illness, such as a major depressive disorder. Serious depression affects more than 6 million men and about twice as many women each year. When mental health and substance abuse (MH/SA) problems are looked at together, researchers estimate that as many as 25 percent of adults are affected by one or both types of problems. Only about 50 percent of adults with severe MH/SA problems receive care.[24]

Children are not excepted from this picture. One in ten children and adolescents suffers from mental illness severe enough to cause some level of impairment. The rate of depression among teenagers may be as high as one in eight, with suicide the third leading cause of death for fifteen- to twenty-four-year-olds. About one-third to one-half of younger individuals with serious mental illness also have substance abuse problems. Yet it is estimated that only about 20 percent of children and adolescents receive treatment for mental disorders. According to a study of children's mental health, over two-thirds of those treated "had one of three diagnoses: disruptive behavior disorders (31%), mood disorders (21%), or adjustment disorders (16%)."[25]

Estimates of mental illness are made in a variety of ways. Some studies base their figures on interviews with sample populations, using either self-reports by subjects or assessments by interviewers of the respondents' mental status. For example, a 1994 survey by the U.S. Department of Health and Human Services, Center for Mental Health Services asked a sample of noninstitutionalized adults about their mental health. Approximately 10 percent reported having had a specific mental or emotional disorder within the prior twelve months. Such surveys try to report both treated and untreated incidents of mental disorder. Another more limited, but more concrete way to measure mental illness is to concentrate on the numbers of people being treated. In 1992, for example, in any one day more than 200,000 people were inpatients in a mental health facility, and a far greater number were being seen on an outpatient basis. The number of people being treated in mental health programs is lower than the total number of individuals with a mental disorder because some seek informal help from family physicians, relatives, or friends, and others do not seek help at all.[26]

The statistics on mental illness also show interesting links between mental disorders and various social factors. The most potent connection has been shown for socioeconomic class status. The classic work in this area is August B. Hollingshead and Frederick C. Redlich's *Social Class and Mental Illness,* published in 1958. Looking at the distribution of treated mental illness among all social classes in New Haven, Connecticut, Hollingshead and Redlich found that class constituted a significant factor in the distribution of mental patients in the population. The highest socioeconomic class in the study accounted for 3 percent of the non–mental patient population in New Haven but constituted only 1 percent of all mental patients. Conversely, the lowest class made up 18 percent of the nonpatient population, but 38 percent of the patient population. In other words, "the lower the class, the greater the proportion of patients." Subsequent studies have generally upheld these findings. As Table 13.1 shows, a summary of results from forty-one studies of the relationship between socioeconomic class and psychopathology suggests that the average rate of mental illness in the lowest socioeconomic classes is 2.73 times that reported for the highest class. In addition, a follow-up of the Hollingshead and Redlich study in New Haven indicated that lower-class patients were far more likely than upper-class patients to remain hospitalized ten years later.[27]

It is not clear whether these findings mean that more lower-class people become mentally ill (perhaps because of greater life stresses) or that more of them are *labeled* mentally ill. The same questions relate to data on mental illness among minorities and women. Here, although the figures are less conclusive, connections are found between mental illness and race, gender, and ethnic background. For example, one study of mentally ill patients in state psychiatric hospitals in the Chicago area found well over half of these patients to be African American men. In addition, African American men are more likely to be labeled schizophrenic than white men. The way a mental illness displays itself may also be related to racial and ethnic background. African Americans and Latinos tend to exhibit more hallucinations, hostility, and delusions than whites, whereas whites show more depression and guilt. Asian Americans often express mental illness through physical problems. Psychiatric symptoms and diagnoses also differ by

TABLE 13.1 **Comparison of Rates Reported for All Types of Psychopathology in Highest and Lowest Social Classes**

Study Site	*Number of Studies in Which the Rate Is Higher for* Lowest Class	*Number of Studies in Which the Rate Is Higher for* Highest Class	Average Ratio Low–High Class
North America and Europe	17	3	2.59
United States	5	1	2.37
Non-United States	13	2	2.73

Note: This table summarizes the findings of 41 studies investigating the relationship between socio-economic class and psychopathology.

Source: Richard Neugebauer et al., "Formulation of Hypotheses about the True Prevalence of Functional Psychiatric Disorders among Adults in the United States," in Bruce P. Dohrenwend et al., *Mental Illness in the United States* (New York: Praeger Publishers, 1980), 56. Copyright © 1980 by Praeger Publishers, an imprint of Greenwood Publishing Group, Inc. Reproduced with permission of Greenwood Publishing Group, Inc., Westport, CT.

gender. Women experience depression and anxiety disorders more often than men; men have a higher prevalence of substance abuse. Women are significantly more likely than men to encounter serious mental illness (SMI), defined as a psychiatric disorder of at least a year's duration accompanied by serious impairment.[28]

Minority status and gender affect both use of mental health services and access to them. Overall, women use mental health services more than men, although adolescent females of all races are less likely than white male teens to be treated for psychiatric disorders. Lack of care for SMI is especially high among minority group members. Studies have also noted the underutilization of mental health services by Asian Americans. Differences in use of services, as well as in diagnoses and rates of mental illness by gender, race, and ethnic group, raise a number of issues. These include the degree to which biases in labeling and treatment occur and the applicability of a medical definition of mental illness to women and minority group members.[29]

Definitions of Developmental Disability

A social work student in a public school setting describes to his field instructor a recent home visit the student made: "You know, Mrs. Watson seemed willing to get her daughter to the doctor, but somehow she hasn't been able to pull it off. I don't think she knows how to use the bus system, even though she's lived here all her life. I tried to explain the schedule to her, but I had the feeling she really couldn't read it. It's not just that,

Focus on Diversity

Race, Diagnosis, and Commitment

Why is the diagnosis of schizophrenia more likely to be applied to African American men than to white men? Why is the rate of involuntary psychiatric commitment of African American men almost two and a half times higher than that of whites? Do racial (or gender, class, or ethnic) biases and stereotypes interfere with objective diagnoses? Are commitment decisions influenced in part by biased perceptions of severity of illness and of a person's "dangerousness" to self or others?

These are complicated questions in mental health research. Studies of racial and other biases in diagnosis yield mixed results. There is a certain amount of evidence that diagnoses of specific disorders, such as schizophrenia and depression, are linked to racial and gender biases on the part of clinicians. These biases, as Steven Lopez points out, can lead to underdiagnosis as well as overdiagnosis. For example, one experiment found that psychology trainees presented with "typical" cases were much more likely to diagnose an African American lower-class patient as having a chronic alcohol abuse disorder than to give a white lower-class patient the same diagnosis. Because *both* patients were described as having symptoms appropriate for the diagnosis of alcohol abuse, the trainees were apparently accurate about the African American patient and inaccurate about the white one. In practice, such underdiagnosis of whites could help explain their proportionately lower commitment and hospitalization rates.

On the other hand, judgments of *severity* of illness, which may increase the probability of commitment, rarely appear to be race or gender related. The only patient variable that seems consistently connected with judgments about severity is social class. Lower-social-class patients tend to be seen as more seriously disturbed than middle- and higher-social-class patients, even though no differences exist in their presenting problems.

Finally, it is tempting to assume that higher levels of commitment for African American males stem from stereotypes about the "aggressiveness" of black men. The potential of causing harm to oneself or others is generally a requirement for psychiatric commitment. It seems plausible that some nonminority clinicians see African Americans as more "dangerous" people than whites. So far, little evidence has been found to support the presence of such bias in commitment proceedings.

In general, not enough research has been conducted to support firm conclusions about the extent of clinician bias or its effects on diagnosis and commitment decisions. The lack of research may stem in part from political factors; during the Reagan administration, the National Institute of Mental Health stopped funding new proposals for research into the socioeconomic factors related to the development and treatment of mental illness.

Sources: Steven Regeser Lopez, "Patient Variable Biases in Clinical Judgment: Conceptual Overview and Methodological Considerations," *Psychological Bulletin 106* (September 1989), 184–203; Kenneth P. Lindsey and Gordon L. Paul, "Involuntary Commitments to Public Mental Institutions: Issues Involving the Overrepresentation of Blacks and Assessment of Relevant Functioning," *Psychological Bulletin 106* (September 1989), 171–183; Lonnie R. Snowden and Freda K. Cheung, "Use of In-patient Mental Health Services by Members of Ethnic Minority Groups," *American Psychologist 45* (March 1990), 347–355.

though—she just seems kind of slow in general—smiles a lot but doesn't talk much, and doesn't seem to understand me when I explain why her daughter needs the inoculations before she can start kindergarten. But otherwise she seems to be taking good care of her daughter."

His supervisor responds: "Well, we'd have to know more specifically about her IQ level, but I'd say you're dealing with a woman with a developmental disability—she's probably slightly retarded."

Defining developmental disability appears a more straightforward task than the delineation of mental illness. The signs of arrested intellectual and social development seem clearer than those of mental illness, more easily measured and observed. Yet even here, cultural components play a part in the definition process.

Developmental disability is a relatively new term, and many people think it is synonymous with mental retardation. However, it refers not only to retardation but also to a variety of conditions, occurring before age twenty-two, that hinder development. These include cerebral palsy, epilepsy, autism, and fetal exposure to drugs. The definition was developed as part of legislation addressing the needs of those whose severe disabilities, occurring during the maturing years, affect their total development. It is thus more of a planning tool than a clinical definition because it was designed by those interested in providing services to particular groups of disabled children and adults.

The fullest description of developmental disability appears in the Rehabilitation, Comprehensive Services, and Developmental Disabilities Act (P.L. 95-602) of 1978:

> Developmental disability means a severe, chronic disability of a person which is "attributable to a mental or physical impairment or combination of mental and physical impairment and
>
> - is manifest before twenty-two years of age
> - is likely to continue indefinitely
> - results in substantial functional limitations in three or more of the following areas of major life activity:
>   - self care
>   - receptive and expressive language
>   - learning
>   - mobility
>   - self-direction
>   - capacity for independent living
>   - economic self-sufficiency
>
> and reflects the person's need for a combination and sequence of special, interdisciplinary, or generic care, treatment or other services which are of lifelong or extended duration and individually planned and coordinated."[30]

Mental retardation, which affects six to seven million people in the United States, is the largest category within developmental disability, and it is the area we focus on in this chapter. Its definition raises a number of issues. Chief among these is the question of whether to base the definition on level of intelligence or on level of functioning in daily life. Mental retardation as a state of "backwardness" was acknowledged from early cultures on up through the nineteenth century.[31] Yet it was not until the development of intelligence testing in the early 1900s that experts were able to base the diagnosis of mental retardation on a person's score on an IQ (intelligence quotient) test. With refinement of the Stanford–Binet and other intelligence scales, it became possible to define mental retardation in terms of standard deviations from the mean (that is, degree of difference of scores from the average intelligence score on a normal distribution

Most parents of children with mental retardation now raise their children at home.

curve). Thus, a person with mental retardation can be characterized as having an IQ score that is more than two standard deviations below the mean. Levels of retardation, from profound to mild, can be categorized according to the actual number of deviations. Of course, such classifications will vary according to the particular intelligence test used[32] (see Table 13.2).

The view that mental retardation can be defined exclusively in terms of cognitive ability has increasingly been questioned. Critics have pointed to the inadequacy of intelligence testing and its potential for cultural bias. They have urged that the individual with retardation be regarded as a whole person within a total life environment. This has led to a functional assessment of retardation that bases diagnosis not simply on intelligence but also on how well "the individual meets the standards of personal development and social responsibility expected from his or her age and cultural group."[33] The stress is on social adaptation and the ability to carry out basic tasks of living: feeding and dressing oneself, performing household tasks, learning an occupation, and entertaining and visiting friends. A widely accepted version of a definition with functional elements is the 1983 description used by the American Association on Mental Deficiency: "Mental retardation refers to significantly subaverage general intellectual functioning existing concurrently with deficits in adaptive behavior and manifested during

TABLE 13.2 Level of Retardation Indicated by IQ Range Obtained on Measure of General Intellectual Functioning

Level of Mental Retardation	*Intelligence Test Scores* Stanford–Binet	Wechsler	Educational Classification
Mild	52–68	55–69	Educable
Moderate	36–51	40–54	Trainable
Severe	20–35	25–39	Dependent
Profound	>20	>25	Dependent
Standard Error of Measurement	3	4	
Standard Deviation	16	15	

Source: Duane F. Stroman, *Mental Retardation in Social Context* (Lanham, MD: University Press of America, 1989), 24. Reprinted by permission.

the development period."[34] The advantage of the functional approach is that it focuses on an individual's strengths as well as on his or her limitations, and looks at the whole person over a series of different developmental stages.

Just as with mental illness, however, retardation or developmental disability can be viewed as a social construct or a culturally determined label. Judgments of intelligence level or learning ability in particular may relate to the expectations of a given social system. A person can be considered retarded in one system and normal in another. For example, a child who is a slow learner growing up in a family with high educational expectations may be seen as mentally retarded. A similar youngster in a family with low educational expectations may be considered normal by family members.[35]

The judgment of retardation also varies from culture to culture. In simple agrarian societies, developmental deficiencies may not matter because skills required for daily living are less complex than those in advanced technological societies. As we discussed in the section on labeling theory, a particular society's values, such as a stress on intellectual competence, affect the types of attributes seen as deviant.

Dynamics of Developmental Disability

Each condition included under developmental disability has its own etiology (causation). Cerebral palsy is a disability caused by brain damage before or during birth that results in a loss of muscular coordination and control. Epilepsy refers to a variety of conditions causing seizures. Some stem from known organic pathology, such as lesions in the brain, but the causation of others is not known. Epilepsy affects an estimated 2 percent of the total U.S. population.[36] Childhood autism, the least understood type of developmental disability, is characterized by an individual's inability to relate to and perceive the environment in a realistic way. Autism appears to be linked with perceptual disorders.

Mental retardation presents a particularly complex and diverse picture of causation. It can be brought about by any condition that impairs development of the brain before birth, during birth, or in the childhood years. Various organic triggers of mental retardation include infectious diseases of the mother, such as German measles, or of the child, such as encephalitis; the effects of drugs and alcohol on the fetus; metabolic disorders, such as phenylketonuria (PKU), caused by a recessive gene; biochemical and nutritional disorders, including maternal malnutrition; chromosomal abnormalities, such as that producing Down syndrome; and physical or traumatic damage during or after birth, such as deprivation of oxygen. Scientists have recently discovered abnormally high levels of four brain chemicals in the blood of newborn infants who later develop mental retardation and autism. This suggests that faulty brain wiring may be the cause of these disorders.[37]

Socioeconomic factors may combine with organic ones to cause mental retardation. Poverty is a major element here. Low-income women, for example, are more likely to be malnourished and to lack proper medical care both before and during pregnancy. A pregnant woman on welfare, especially if she lives in a rural area, may not be scheduled to see a physician until the seventh or eighth month of pregnancy, if then.

Poverty, race, and ethnicity may interact both in the causation of developmental disability and in the ability to get services. African Americans are one and a half times more likely to have a developmental disability than whites. Yet African Americans, and Latinos as well, are less likely than whites to receive appropriate assistance. For example, an advocate in New Jersey notes that in his state, "with some exceptions, the children of middle-class whites live in suburban group homes with day programs . . . costing over $60,000 annually. People of color with comparable needs are far more likely to wind up in $9,000 skill development homes with nothing to do all day." Differences in access to medical and social services may be an element in the sharp racial divide in life expectancy for people with developmental disability, with whites living twice as long as African Americans.[38]

Researchers have also postulated that certain environmental conditions can lead to retardation. Of particular interest is the quality of family and community life, including relationships between parents and children; child-rearing practices; educational opportunities; and degree of sensory, verbal, and mental stimulation offered to the child. Disadvantaged children are sometimes denied opportunities to learn and to explore "because of large family size or closely spaced births that overwhelm the capacities of . . . parents. Neglect and abuse are not uncommon in parents preoccupied with their own survival, but most frequently, the limited parent lacks the communication skills to stimulate the child's acquisition of language and cognitive development."[39] In addition, community resources, such as day care and early childhood education, may be inadequate or nonexistent. Although these situations can occur in middle- and upper-income families and communities, they are more prevalent in low-income areas.

Statistical Picture of Developmental Disability

Researchers have had some trouble estimating the number of individuals with developmental disabilities in the United States, particularly because the functional definition of developmental disability is hard to operationalize. Criteria for measuring such life skills as "self-direction" and "capacity for independent living" can be difficult to develop. Most studies rely on figures for the individual diagnostic categories, such as cerebral palsy and mental retardation, even though there is not an exact fit between these older categories and developmental disability. For example, not all individuals with mental retardation can be defined as being developmentally disabled. The developmentally disabled without mental retardation account for ten to fifteen cases per 10,000 population.[40]

Estimates of mental retardation, the largest category within developmental disability, generally vary from 1 to 2 percent of the population. Almost 90 percent of these individuals have mild retardation. They will probably be able to achieve a fifth- to eighth-grade education by their late teens and to acquire the skills necessary for independent living. More seriously retarded individuals represent much smaller fractions of the total, with profound retardation accounting for less than 2 percent of all those in the category. Individuals with profound retardation often have physical impairments as well, such as blindness, deafness, and orthopedic problems. They are generally highly dependent on others for care.[41]

As we have noted, class and minority status appear to affect the prevalence of mental retardation, although this has been less well documented in retardation than in mental illness. Economically depressed areas in the United States, both rural and urban, have relatively high percentages of individuals with retardation. A disproportionate number of children from minority groups and poverty settings are categorized as being mildly retarded. More severely retarded persons seem to be distributed fairly evenly throughout the population.[42] The greater incidence of mild retardation in poor, often minority communities may reflect inadequate health care, greater rates of malnutrition, and other problems. It also suggests the use of culturally determined labels by a dominant group, based on their own values and expectations of behavior.

Historical Perspectives on Mental Illness

The phenomena of mental illness and mental retardation have long histories, reaching back into the ancient world. Although similar issues arise in each history—cultural influences on definitions, variation in societal responses to these conditions over time, and the changing nature of institutions—there are important differences as well. In this section and in the next, we analyze these separate but related histories, focusing primarily on their development in the United States.

Americans in colonial society responded to the mentally ill with ideas imported from seventeenth- and eighteenth-century Europe. These ideas were tempered by life in a frontier world. The religious teachings of the Protestant Church dominated the ways in which people thought about poverty, mental illness, and other human problems. Colonial Americans saw the insane as simply one group among many needy people. Because they believed in a divinely created social order, they viewed the existence of poverty and dependence as "natural and just, and its relief as necessary and appropriate." The presence of dependent individuals—the madman, the widow, the blind child—provided men and women with a God-given chance to do good.[43]

Relief of the dependent was not only an individual concern but also a matter of public responsibility. The Elizabethan Poor Laws, transported to America with the colonists, held that care of the needy was both a family obligation and the duty of the local parish. Relatives were responsible for dependent family members, but if dependent individuals could not be cared for at home, the local authority would provide relief. In colonial America, if you were judged mentally ill and your family was reasonably well-off, you were generally cared for at home. If you were poor, lacked family, or were uncontrollable, the public authorities provided other alternatives. You might be boarded out to another household, placed in an empty attic or cellar in a local almshouse, put in jail, or even confined in a shack constructed for this purpose on the town commons. An important consideration in a frontier world of isolated settlements was the matter of residency. The community was prepared to take care of its own, including the insane, but nonresident dependent people were expelled and sent back to their towns of origin, if possible.[44]

Community care of the dependent at home or in small, informal institutions came to seem less reasonable and practical in the new nation emerging after the American Revolution. Population increased, cities grew, and factories began to develop. The small, close-knit community became less important in the political and social scheme of things. Increasingly, the state became a significant unit of government. In addition, Enlightenment ideas, which stressed the improvability of man, challenged earlier Protestant notions about the predetermination of dependency. Optimism about scientific and humane treatment of the mentally ill seemed in keeping with the development of the new republic.

These factors contributed to the growth of a new, institutional response to mental illness—the insane asylum. Hospitals for the care of the mentally ill had emerged in the 1700s, but the real growth of the asylum began in the 1830s, and by 1860 twenty-eight of the then thirty-three states had public institutions for the mentally ill.[45]

The reasons for the rise of the asylum were complex. New fears of the insane played a part: By 1800 concentrations of population in growing cities made people more aware of "queer" or deviant behavior. At the same time, physicians and reformers promoted the idea that madness could be cured through special treatment in an institution. Finally, as social historian David Rothman has argued, the "discovery of the asylum" reflected the desire for social order in an increasingly turbulent world. The Jacksonian era (1828–1836) was a time of great social change, and traditional ideas and practices seemed outmoded. The rise of the asylum, along with other institutions for dependent individuals, constituted an effort "to [ensure] the cohesion of the community in new and changing circumstances." Not only did the asylum provide an orderly environment

Social Work **Destinations**

The Public Hospital, Williamsburg, Virginia

In the famous reconstructed village of Colonial Williamsburg, you can tour the first public institution for the mentally ill in the United States. The "Hospital for Lunaticks" opened in 1773. The restored building contains an early cell where people with mental illness were confined and treated like prisoners. Another display is a nineteenth-century room demonstrating more humanitarian "scientific" treatment. Recordings of simulated patients' and caretakers' voices make the experience all the more real. Displays also include various devices used over the decades to treat and "cure" patients. *For further information:* 757-229-1000 or 1-800-HISTORY.

for the treatment of mental illness, but it also presented a model of stability for the outside world to follow.[46]

Other historians have questioned Rothman's stress on the dominance of the asylum. They observe that many mentally ill individuals remained with their families or were sent to poorhouses.[47] However, although it was not the only vehicle for the care of the insane, the new institution marked a major shift in society's responses to this dependent group.

What did this new institution look like? First, the asylum was removed from the community and set in pastoral surroundings. Second, it was built differently. The earliest asylums were simple structures, often like large houses. The institutions of the 1830s and later were good-sized, orderly, symmetrical buildings. Internal space was regimented and carefully divided, "giving a uniform and repetitious appearance floor after floor." Separate wards existed for men and women. Inmates' daily lives were regimented, and regular work of some sort played an important part in the program. In a hospital in Pennsylvania, for example, patients rose at 5:00, received their medicines at 6:00, ate breakfast at 6:30, and then went to work or to some other form of exercise. At 12:30 they ate their main meal; they then resumed work or other activities until 6:00, when everyone joined for tea. They passed the evening indoors, and all were in bed by 9:30.[48]

The orderly life of patients in the mental institution was seen not as punishment but as a major part of treatment. Work, discipline, and support by hospital staff would overcome the confusion and turmoil in the minds of the insane. Such turmoil, it was theorized, often stemmed from the demands of a rapidly changing, socially mobile society in which people felt challenged to move beyond the achievements and life patterns of their parents. Removal of the mentally ill from family and community meant that patients could be isolated from the strains and temptations of this new world, and thus they might be cured. Madness was no longer considered an act of God, as colonial Americans had believed, but as a treatable disease caused largely by social, economic, and political conditions.[49]

The treatment ideal was promoted by the psychiatrists who served as medical superintendents of the new institutions, and by reformers such as Dorothea Dix. Unlike other nineteenth-century women reformers who founded benevolent associations and sought to influence a masculine system, Dix "invaded the system itself." An educated and financially independent New England woman who had suffered serious bouts of depression, Dix researched, sponsored, and drafted legislation to improve the care of the mentally ill. She was convinced that this care was "an essential obligation of the modern state." In her campaign Dix traveled from town to town, noting the poor conditions in which the mentally ill were kept and developing allies among local philanthropists and physicians. She then lobbied state legislatures to create special institutions for the insane, arguing that such programs were beyond the resources of local communities. All told, Dix was instrumental in founding or enlarging thirty-two mental hospitals in the United States and abroad.[50]

To Dix and to the medical superintendents and other reformers, the new state hospital held forth the promise of humane treatment and eventual cure. Sadly, it would be a promise unfulfilled. Although the institution aimed to bring order and stability into patients' lives, it offered a regimentation and repressiveness more like the factory of the day than the traditional community it sought to restore. In addition, mental hospitals were understaffed and often ill equipped to deal with the more violent patients. Hoped-for cures did not materialize, and the continued influx of patients strained facilities to their limit. Gradually, the therapeutic institution became an organization for long-term custodial care.

From the 1870s on, state institutions went into dramatic decline. Carefully ordered routines broke down; unruly patients were increasingly subjected to restraints and punishments; the nature of the patient population changed from acute to aged and chronic; and institutions became holding places run by psychiatrists whose primary goals had changed from treatment to administration. Part of the decline stemmed from factors such as underfunding and the difficulties in "curing" mental disease. An additional element was a change in attitudes toward deviance in U.S. society.[51]

In the rapidly industrializing United States, many people became fearful about crime, the possible violence of the newly organizing working class, and particularly the effects of the great influx of immigrants from poor backgrounds in southern and eastern Europe. Some immigrants found their way to mental institutions, where they were resented for drawing on the public purse. In this uneasy atmosphere, the ideas of social Darwinists such as Charles Sumner attracted a wide audience. Dependency came to be seen more and more as an individual—and often hereditary—defect rather than as the product of social forces. The idea of punishment, or at least isolation from society, often replaced the treatment goal.

Deterioration in the state institutions eventually helped promote another round of reform. The mental hygiene movement, a product of changes within psychiatry as well as of exposés by former mental patients, grew rapidly in the first twenty years of the twentieth century. With its stress on prevention and community-based psychiatry, the movement introduced important ideas that would be more fully developed in the community mental health programs of the 1960s.

The best-known catalyst for this new approach was the publication in 1908 of a book called *A Mind That Found Itself*, written by Clifford Beers. Beers had spent three years in mental institutions. In his influential account of these years, he exposed the mistreatment suffered by mental patients and proposed "a call for action to inaugurate a new beginning in the institutional care and treatment of the mentally ill." Although

Beers initially sought to improve existing institutions, he broadened his approach after joining forces with Adolf Meyer, a prominent psychiatrist who was interested in the social context of mental illness. Meyer suggested enlarging the campaign to include a major focus on the promotion of mental health, or, as it was then called, mental hygiene. In 1909 the two men organized the National Committee for Mental Hygiene. The

A CLOSER Look

Clifford W. Beers: *A Mind That Found Itself*

Clifford W. Beers was born in New Haven, Connecticut, in 1876. His father was in the produce business, and Beers himself aspired to a career in business. He attended Yale University; after receiving a Ph.D. degree, he moved to New York City to work as a clerk. Although he later described his boyhood as relatively normal, Beers was also a sensitive and introspective child. When he was a young man preparing for college, his older brother experienced what was thought to be an attack of epilepsy. On the brother's death six years later, the doctors concluded that he had in fact suffered a brain tumor. The family, and particularly Clifford, was devastated. Beers, then working in New York, developed a morbid fear of a similar fate. He eventually broke down mentally and attempted suicide. Suffering from hallucinations and delusions, he was admitted to a private mental institution. Over the next three years, he lived in three different institutions, including a state hospital. When his condition shifted to a manic, excitable phase, he was consigned to the "violent ward." Four years after he was finally discharged, Beers wrote *A Mind That Found Itself,* a unique account of his experience of madness and his treatment in mental institutions. The following excerpts suggest the power of the book, which helped initiate the modern mental health movement.

On his experience in a private institution:

> Choice of a sanatorium by people of limited means is, unfortunately, very restricted. Though my relatives believed the one in which I was placed was at least fairly well conducted, events proved otherwise. From a modest beginning made not many years previously, it had enjoyed a mushroom growth. About two hundred and fifty patients were harbored in a dozen or more small frame buildings. . . . Outside the limits of a city and in a state where there was lax official supervision, . . . the owner of this little settlement of woe had erected a nest of veritable fire-traps in which helpless sick people were forced to risk their lives. This was a necessary procedure if the owner was to grind out an exorbitant income on his investment.
>
> . . . To guard me at night while the . . . attendant slept, my hands were imprisoned in what is known as a "muff." A muff, innocent enough to the eyes of those who have never worn one, is in reality a relic of the Inquisition. . . . The muff I wore was made of canvas, and [had an] inner partition, also of canvas, which separated my hands. . . . At either end was a strap which buckled tightly around the wrist and was locked.

On his consignment to a violent ward in the state hospital:

> Few, if any, prisons in this country contain worse holes than this cell proved to be. . . . It was about six feet wide by ten long. . . . A heavily screened and barred window admitted light and a negligible quantity of air, for the ventilation scarcely deserved the name. The walls and floor were bare, and there was no furniture. . . . Worst of all, winter was approaching and these, my first quarters, were without heat. . . . To be half frozen, day in and day out . . . was exquisite torture.
>
> . . . Thus day after day, I was repressed in a manner which probably would have driven many a sane man to violence. Deprived of my clothes, of sufficient food, of warmth, of all sane companionship and my liberty, I told those in authority that so long as they should continue to treat me as the vilest of criminals, I should do my best to complete the illusion.

Source: Excerpts from *A Mind That Found Itself* by Clifford Beers, 41, 46–47, 151–152, 178–179. Copyright © 1907, 1917, 1921, 1923, 1931, 1932, 1934, 1935, 1937, 1939, 1940, 1942, 1948, 1953 by the American Foundation for Mental Hygiene, Inc. Used by permission of Doubleday, a division of Random House, Inc.

organization's goals included not only the reform of state institutions but also the establishment of outpatient clinics and aftercare programs and the "general dissemination of knowledge regarding . . . the causes and prevention of mental disorders."

Social workers played an important role in the development of the mental hygiene movement. Julia Lathrop, of the Hull House circle, served on the executive committee of the National Committee for Mental Hygiene. Early psychiatric social workers, including Meyer's wife, Mary Potter Brooks Meyer, stressed an environmental approach to mental disorder that became part of the broader mental hygiene movement. Meyer himself argued that social workers were essential in helping people with mental illness deal with "life problems."[52]

A CLOSER Look

The Snake Pit

Mary Jane Ward wrote *The Snake Pit,* a story of life in a mental hospital, in the mid-1940s. Ward was born in Indiana in 1915. Her first interest was music, but after her marriage to a statistician who wrote plays and painted, she turned to writing. Her early works met with limited literary and financial success. For three years she and her husband lived the life of poor artists in New York's Greenwich Village. In 1941 Ward suffered psychiatric problems and spent nine months in a mental hospital. Several years later, she wrote a poignant novel based on this experience. The main character, Virginia, is a gentle, bewildered young woman who finds herself in a confusing environment.

> They lined up in front of the dining-room. When the door was unlocked they marched out. . . . They marched up the brown hall and stopped at the door at the end of it. Miss Hart unlocked the door and they went into the waiting room. They crossed that room and paused at another door. Miss Hart unlocked the door. They went into another hall. They stopped at another door. When it was unlocked they went into a room that was stunningly different.
>
> It was a large light room. There was tile on the floor, tiny octagonal pieces of tile charmingly fitted together. . . . The walls had the two-color [brown] paint job, but they seemed more cheerful. It was a lovely room. Virginia studied the floor as if it was an exceptional mosaic and she thought suddenly of her beautiful Kelim rug and had then to suppress a ridiculous and unexpected sob. Don't be a baby. Suppose you had to stay here.
>
> If I had to remain in this prison I would choose this room, she thought. But presently her enthusiasm waned. There were four booths. The women stood and waited their turn. . . . None of the booths had a door.
>
> When at last it was her turn she discovered that an even more vital accessory was missing. There was no wooden seat and the old joke about not falling in was in this case no joke. But she forgot how frightful this was when she saw there was no toilet paper. . . . She was about to call to her next neighbor, but then she remembered the cleansing tissues in her handbag.
>
> When she left the booth she peered at the walls of the other three. None of them had paper. This must be reported.
>
> As a rule she held back and let others do the reporting but now she was angry and she went to Miss Hart to say what is the idea of not providing these women with toilet paper. When she reached Miss Hart she saw that the woman was providing toilet paper. Miss Hart was the dispenser. If you required paper you asked her for it in advance and she doled it out to you. She was the judge of how much you needed. It was a curious and humiliating procedure. Hadn't they gone deep enough into a woman's privacy when they removed the doors from the booths?

Sources: From *The Snake Pit* by Mary Jane Ward, 33–34. Copyright © 1946 by Mary Jane Ward. Reprinted by permission of Random House, Inc. "Mary Jane Ward," in *Current Biography,* Anna Rothe, ed. (New York: H.W. Wilson, 1947), 623–624.

The mental hygiene movement established several significant new programs for the treatment of mental illness: aftercare programs, the psychopathic hospital, and the child guidance clinic. Aftercare programs, such as that set up by the New York Charities Aid Association in 1906, provided trained agents (often social workers) who kept in contact with released mental patients and helped them in their economic and social readjustment into the community. The aftercare concept led to experiments with "boarding out," or family care, in which hospital patients could be released to the care of families in the community.

Psychopathic hospitals sought to reach individuals *before* they were committed to mental institutions. These were well-staffed, urban-based facilities that attempted to provide careful diagnoses of mental problems and to treat acute, rather than chronic, patients. Structured as research and training centers, such hospitals hoped to provide effective short-term treatment that would prevent confinement in the chronic wards of the state institutions.[53]

Child guidance clinics carried the preventive goal even further. These outpatient clinics were designed to deal with the mental health problems of children. They provided consultation to community institutions such as schools and offered therapy to children and their parents. Such therapy, it was hoped, would prevent the continuation of behavioral and emotional problems into adult life.[54]

The mental hygiene movement fit nicely with the reformist mood of the Progressive Era. Mental hygiene activists pictured mental disease as the product of environmental, hereditary, and individual psychological deficiencies. Its cure required scientific knowledge and administrative action. To promote this cure, mental hygienists "launched a broad-based crusade to create a better society."[55]

Although the mental hygiene campaign introduced ideas and programs with long-range implications, its immediate effects were disappointing. State institutions had become so entrenched by the turn of the century that they ended up dominating the mental health scene despite the development of new programs. The psychopathic hospital, conceived as a treatment facility for acutely ill patients, evolved into an arm of the large state institutions. Quickly overwhelmed by the number of patients it received, the psychopathic hospital was unable to offer effective treatment, and it soon turned into a funnel through which patients moved into the state hospital. These larger hospitals proved resistant to change. Although some medical superintendents supported ideas such as aftercare and special facilities for the acutely ill, most sought rationales for maintaining the power and centrality of the institutions they headed. A major rationale was the provision of long-term care for those who were labeled chronically mentally ill.[56]

Thus, the large state hospitals increasingly became facilities for the poor and elderly chronically mentally ill. As states took over more and more responsibility for mental illness, local governments diverted the dependent elderly, particularly those labeled "senile," from old age homes to state care. During the forty-year period from about 1910 to about 1950, approximately 40 percent of patients in mental institutions were fifty years old and over. Most patients came from low-income groups. Particularly in the 1920s, a large proportion were foreign-born. African Americans had separate and inferior facilities. Patient stays were lengthy, sometimes lifelong. This was the world of the "back ward," with patients spending endless hours in bleak day rooms, hours punctuated only occasionally by an organized party or film show run by volunteers, or a visit to the psychiatrist's office. Excitable patients were put in straitjackets or "packed" in cold sheets. More manageable residents were engaged in "work therapy" cleaning bathrooms or pushing floor waxers.[57]

Even though the large state hospital dominated the mental health picture, the smaller network of services developed under the mental hygiene movement managed to survive. This network operated primarily in the private sector. Its scientific and therapeutic thrust was strengthened during World War I, when psychiatrists were called on to deal with cases of shell shock and the war-related emotional problems of servicemen and their families. It was within this mental hygiene arena that social work established a presence as one of the mental health professions. Social workers had been key staff people in the early aftercare programs. Later they collaborated with psychiatrists in the development of child guidance clinics. In these clinics, psychiatrists provided therapy to children, and social workers carried out "social studies" of their development by interviewing parents. Mary Jarrett, an early psychiatric social worker, helped establish the first social services department in a psychiatric hospital in 1913. There, as in the child guidance clinic, social workers became indispensable assistants to psychiatrists. They provided essential information on the patient's family and community environment. The emergence of psychiatric social work as a specialty received a boost when the National Committee on Mental Hygiene helped to create the Smith College School of Social Work in 1918. This program trained students exclusively in the new clinical focus. By the 1920s, psychiatric social workers had established their own professional group, the Association of Psychiatric Social Workers.[58]

The late 1940s brought the first glimmerings of both a powerful challenge to the predominance of state institutions and a broader development of the ideas of short-term, community-based treatment and prevention. The culmination of this challenge was the community mental health movement, which drew on two bodies of innovation: changes in the mental hospital and ideas about community practice.

World War II had encouraged both types of innovation. Military data brought the problem of mental illness once more to public attention. Twelve of every one hundred men examined for service were rejected for psychiatric reasons. Almost 40 percent of all those discharged for disability had psychiatric diagnoses. The disorders that developed during combat and the adjustment problems faced by soldiers and their families led mental health workers to experiment with early, intensive, and brief treatment approaches. After the war, Veterans Administration hospitals promoted increased staff training and better patient–staff ratios and expanded their outpatient work.[59]

New awareness of mental illness as a national issue was reinforced by a series of exposés, in the tradition of Clifford Beers, which called attention to the terrible conditions of mental hospitals. These conditions had worsened because of neglect during the war and depression years. Mary Jane Ward's novel *The Snake Pit,* for example, gave a chilling picture of a large mental hospital. The culmination of this new concern was the National Mental Health Act of 1946, which gave grants to states for the development of mental health programs outside the state hospitals. The act also established the National Institute of Mental Health. The goals of this federal program were to support research into the causes of mental illness, to further training of needed mental health personnel, and to aid states in building programs and facilities to serve the mentally ill.[60]

One of the single most important factors in the movement toward the community mental health ideal was the discovery of the first *psychotropic drugs* in the mid-1950s. These drugs, which include tranquilizers and antidepressants, were able to alter feeling states without apparently impairing an individual's ability to perceive and think. Although the overuse of drugs would later be blamed for creating "zombielike" patients, these medications were heralded early on for their ability to make patients more amenable to treatment and more capable of being discharged from long-term hospitalization to community programs.

A new treatment idea, the *therapeutic community*, also contributed to changes in hospital practices. The notion of such a community drew on the social context–oriented approach to mental illness described earlier. Developed by Maxwell Jones, a British psychiatrist, the therapeutic community concept was an attempt to modify hospital culture, as experienced by patients on the ward, and to reconstitute this culture as a total treatment environment. Often called *milieu therapy*, the treatment approach suggested that much of mental illness stemmed from faulty learning of how to relate to people. By promoting open communication between patients and staff, a more normal atmosphere, and the involvement of patients in their own treatment, milieu therapy would help people learn new, more successful interpersonal behaviors. The hallmarks of the therapeutic community were patient–staff "unit" meetings, open wards, patient government, and street clothes rather than uniforms for hospital personnel.[61] Rather than becoming institutionalized, the patient was being prepared for the "regular" world.

Drugs and other innovations, including milieu therapy, made shorter hospital stays possible. The thrust toward community-based programs continued. A Joint Commission on Mental Health and Illness, created by Congress in 1955, called for the development of outpatient programs and the use of frontline workers such as clergy, family physicians, and teachers in combating mental illness. Finally, in 1963, President John F. Kennedy addressed Congress on the topics of mental health and mental retardation, the first time a U.S. president had done so. Referring to the joint commission's work, he called for "a bold new approach": the creation of a new type of facility, the community mental health center. This facility would provide a complete, community-based range of care, with a strong emphasis on prevention. Eight months later Congress adopted legislation authorizing federal matching funds to states for the construction of "comprehensive community mental health centers."[62]

Thus, the community mental health movement took its place among the other social programs of the 1960s. It proceeded from the assumption that much of mental illness stemmed from social and economic forces, which needed to be dealt with within a community setting. Centers were established across the country. By federal requirement, each provided at least five types of service: (1) inpatient services—generally short term; (2) outpatient services; (3) partial hospitalization, such as day programs; (4) emergency services; and (5) consultation and education services for community agencies and professional personnel. The community mental health movement also gave rise to halfway houses, which offered a bridge between state facilities and independent living.[63]

Syracuse Psychiatric Hospital in New York presented a typical picture of a community mental health facility in the 1960s. It was housed in a medium-sized three-story building near the center of the city. Each floor constituted an unlocked patient ward, or unit, which related to a geographical "catchment area" in the city of Syracuse. Average maximum patient stays were two weeks. Some people came only for day treatment, then returned home at night. Patients, or "residents," engaged in psychodrama (a type of therapy using role play), recreational activities, and group therapy, as well as individual treatment sessions. They also participated in frequent unit meetings with staff.

Unit personnel included mental health aides, nurses, social workers, occupational and recreational therapists, psychologists, and psychiatrists. None wore uniforms. A staffing concept called *role blurring* was practiced, in which all staff were seen as contributing to the therapeutic community. A member of any one of the staff groups, including aides, could be assigned as a patient's "chief therapist." Unit administrators were generally social workers or nurses rather than psychiatrists. The democratic atmosphere was such that professional staff mopped their own office floors.

The hospital offered outpatient services and consultation to local schools and agencies. Units tried to develop close relationships with their catchment areas, which included low-income and minority populations. One unit operated a "Neighborhood Referral Service" in a one-room storefront; this was staffed by a hospital social worker along with a mental health aide who lived in the area and was familiar with its problems. The referral service offered neighborhood residents help with obtaining housing, employment, welfare, and other services. The service also provided informal counseling for personal and family difficulties. It served as a link between the psychiatric hospital and the community. For example, when a young Puerto Rican woman was ready to be discharged from the hospital, the referral service worked with leaders of the local Puerto Rican community to find a family that would take her in.[64]

The use of psychotropic drugs and the development of the community mental health movement made possible a dramatic decline in the population of state hospitals. In 1955 patients in state and county mental hospitals had numbered 559,000. Twenty years later, these institutions housed only 215,000 patients.[65] At that point, some five hundred federally funded community mental health centers were in operation. The original community mental health center plans had called for a decreasing proportion of federal funds and an increasing amount of local and state support; but by the early 1970s many local communities began abandoning the programs as their share of the costs increased. At the same time, states still faced large overhead expenditures for the state hospitals. Thus, even while state hospitals continued to discharge patients, the necessary community programs received less and less governmental support. And in the early 1980s, as we discuss in the section on Current Issues and Trends, federal funding for community mental health was drastically curtailed. The community mental health movement, which began with such optimism, had stalled.

Interestingly, each era of reform in mental health—the rise of the asylum, the mental hygiene movement, and the development of community mental health—has gone through similar periods of innovation, peaking, criticism, and retrenchment. Such a history suggests that mental illness is a complex phenomenon with no single magical answer or cure.

Historical Perspectives on Developmental Disability

Developmental disability, particularly mental retardation, presents a historical picture similar to that of mental illness. Yet overall, those with mental retardation attracted fewer champions and excited fewer large-scale attempts at institutional development and reform. The frequent neglect of this segment of the population relates in part to the perceived nature of the condition. Unlike mental illness, mental retardation has generally been viewed as a lifelong affliction with no hope of cure. Although some movements have recognized the potential for growth, change, and even independence among people with mental retardation, the most typical response has been one of low expectations, often resulting in consignment to lifelong custodial care.

A bright spot in the history of the treatment of those with mental retardation was the development of special training schools in the United States in the mid-1850s. Before this experiment, people with mental handicaps were generally cared for by their families or placed in poorhouses. Their treatment thus resembled that of the mentally ill. In the decade before the Civil War, however, a small group of reformers set out to show that if reached early enough, children with mental retardation could be trained to live fulfilling and productive lives.

These reformers were inspired by new discoveries in Europe. One, in the early 1800s, was the famous case of the "wild boy" of Aveyron. A French physician, Jean-Marie-Gaspard Itard, carried out an ambitious educational program with an abandoned deaf-mute child who roamed the woods and foraged in people's gardens for food. Victor, as he was subsequently named, was caught, diagnosed as an "idiot," and entrusted to Itard's care. Theorizing that the boy's lack of speech and intellectual skills stemmed from isolation and the absence of human stimulation, Itard spent five years developing Victor's senses, mental processes, and manners. Relatively successful in several of these areas, Itard failed to achieve his ultimate goal of teaching the boy to speak. Nevertheless, his conviction that the condition of "idiocy" could be altered through training inspired the work of his student, Edouard Seguin, who became a major figure in the development of education for people with mental retardation.[66]

Seguin, trained as a physician, headed schools for children with retardation first in France and then, after 1848, in the United States. He believed that every individual with retardation had abilities that could be cultivated. He established a broad treatment and training program that stressed the creation of a positive relationship between pupil and teacher. Seguin's system included physical and sensorimotor exercises, a sound diet, and group learning experiences. The system was subsequently adopted in almost every American and European institution dealing with mental retardation.[67]

In the United States, Seguin's methods helped to stimulate the establishment of a number of facilities for the care and treatment of individuals with retardation, beginning in the late 1840s. Psychiatrists and experts in the education of the mentally handicapped convinced legislatures in New York, Massachusetts, and other states to provide funding for experimental training schools. The reformers won lawmakers over through presentations of statistics on the prevalence of retardation, warnings of its spread through generations of families, and evidence of the inadequacy of care in almshouses and private homes. A major figure in this movement, Samuel Gridley Howe, argued that idiocy was a disease of society: Parents who violated certain natural and physical laws through ignorance and sin passed mental retardation down to their children. Despite this pessimistic view, however, Howe stressed that those with mental retardation could be rehabilitated.[68]

In 1848, Howe, a physician, became director of the Massachusetts Experimental School for Teaching and Training Idiotic Children. The mission of the Massachusetts school and others that followed was to give students' "dormant faculties the greatest practicable development" and then to return these pupils to their families and communities. The schools intended to teach the occupational, intellectual, and social skills necessary for reasonably self-sufficient lives. Unlike the new mental asylums of the same period, they did not separate their charges from family and community. They encouraged ongoing family contacts through frequent visits and even summer vacations at home. On no account were the training schools to be seen as custodial institutions; instead, their "graduates" would lead productive lives in the outside world.[69]

By 1876 twelve state residential schools for young people with mental retardation had been established. In that year, following an earlier suggestion by Seguin, the superintendents of these schools formed an organization that was the forerunner of the American Association on Mental Deficiency. The organization's founding heralded a professional commitment to research the causes of retardation and to further develop training for those with mental deficiencies.[70]

In their initial years, the training schools maintained their sense of mission and enjoyed a degree of success. Yet even by the time of the creation of the new organization, it was beginning to become apparent that the schools' founders had been overly optimistic. Some students did not improve to the point expected. Others, who were capable of discharge, found that their families were unable and sometimes unwilling to take them back. In addition, periodic economic downturns made it difficult for them to find work. In order to ensure the training schools' success, selective admissions policies concentrated on young individuals with less serious retardation. This meant that large numbers of people with more severe mental handicaps remained outside of the system. Disillusioned about the potential for rehabilitation and faced with pressures to handle the more seriously retarded, training school administrators acquiesced by expanding their facilities and transforming them into institutions for custodial care.[71]

In the late 1800s, the move to custodial care received further impetus from changing attitudes toward those with mental retardation. This change was part of the same fear of "dependent and defective" populations that had brought forth negative responses to the mentally ill. Increasingly, individuals with retardation came to be seen as "potential sources of social disruption who required isolation and control." Social welfare professionals and even some superintendents of institutions for those with retardation warned of the "menace of the feeble-minded" and suggested a causal link between retardation and crime, prostitution, and poverty. These notions found reinforcement in a new set of ideas about heredity: the eugenics movement.[72]

The eugenics movement, which we discussed in Chapter 8, postulated that many social problems, including delinquency, alcoholism, poverty, mental illness, and mental retardation, were interrelated and could be traced to hereditary sources. As we have seen, a major tool in the research supporting this idea was the intelligence test developed by Alfred Binet. Using this test among prostitutes, criminals, and juvenile delinquents, researchers concluded that large percentages of these groups were in fact mentally retarded. Such retardation, they theorized, was genetically determined. The nail that drove the argument home was the 1912 publication of an influential study, *The Kallikak Family: A Study in the Heredity of Feeble-Mindedness.* Written by Henry H. Goddard, a psychologist and head researcher in the Vineland, New Jersey, Training School, the book traced the descendants of the family of Deborah Kallikak, an eight-year-old resident in the Vineland School. Goddard found that although many family members had been normal, law-abiding citizens, those descending from the union of Deborah's great-great-grandfather and a "promiscuous tavern maid" constituted "an almost unbroken line of degeneration: 143 feeble-minded, only 46 normal, 36 illegitimate, 33 immoral persons, 24 alcoholics, 8 pimps, and a total of 82 who died in infancy." Rejecting notions of social causes—all family members, after all, "lived in the same environment"—Goddard decided that most of these deficiencies were inherited.[73]

The belief in eugenics fostered by such studies continued into the 1920s. The movement supported the idea of permanent custodial care of the retarded. Because the condition appeared to be genetically caused, and IQ was seen as being fixed, there seemed little point in trying to educate those who were labeled retarded. In addition, eugenicists promoted the development of marriage restriction laws and even the use of sterilization for those with retardation. By 1917 fifteen states had a eugenical sterilization law on the books.[74]

Although the eugenics movement had lost most of its credibility by the late 1920s, large-scale institutions for those labeled retarded remained in place. Their populations continued to grow. Like those who were considered mentally ill, many people diagnosed as retarded languished in custodial facilities up through the 1950s. Although many institutions maintained a small training component, their major purpose was to remove those with retardation from the "normal" world. At best, they promoted a goal of self-sufficiency within the institution. At worst, they offered bleak, unstimulating, and even abusive environments.[75]

It is important to remember, however, that throughout this period institutions housed only about 5 percent of people deemed mentally defective. And, as in the case of mental illness, some programs kept alive ideas of rehabilitation and early intervention. These focused on preschool training, special education classes for children in the public schools, and vocational training for young adults. Professionals tried new approaches, such as milieu therapy and behavioral techniques, which brought promising results in the socialization and education of people with retardation.

In addition, the parents of children with mental retardation had begun to organize. High birthrates and medical advances in the care of infants after World War II that resulted in fewer retarded infants dying at birth led to increased numbers of young, severely retarded children in institutions. Parents sought improved conditions for this group, as well as expanded services in the community for those with less serious retardation. Parental concerns led to the formation of the Association for Retarded Children (later changed to Retarded Citizens) in 1950. Parents' pressures for improved programs gathered strength with the development of the civil rights movement in the 1950s and

A CLOSER Look

From *The Mismeasure of Man* by Stephen Jay Gould

In 1927 Oliver Wendell Holmes, Jr., delivered the Supreme Court's decision upholding the Virginia sterilization law in *Buck* v. *Bell.* Carrie Buck, a young mother with a child of allegedly feeble mind, had scored a mental age of nine on the Stanford–Binet. Carrie Buck's mother, then fifty-two, had tested at mental age seven. Holmes wrote, in one of the most famous and chilling statements of our century:

> We have seen more than once that the public welfare may call upon the best citizens for their lives. It would be strange if it could not call upon those who already sap the strength of the state for the lesser sacrifices. . . . Three generations of imbeciles are enough.

(The line is often miscited as "three generations of idiots. . . ." But Holmes knew the technical jargon of his time, and the Bucks, though not "normal" by the Stanford–Binet, were one grade above idiots.)

Buck v. *Bell* is a signpost of history, an event linked with the distant past in my mind. The Babe hit his sixty homers in 1927, and legends are all the more wonderful because they seem so distant. I was therefore shocked by an item in the *Washington Post* on 23 February 1980—for few things can be more disconcerting than a juxtaposition of neatly ordered and separated temporal events. "Over 7,500 sterilized in Virginia," the headline read. The law that Holmes upheld had been implemented for forty-eight years, from 1924 to 1972. The operations had been performed in mental-health facilities, primarily upon white men and women considered feeble-minded and antisocial—including "unwed mothers, prostitutes, petty criminals and children with disciplinary problems."

Carrie Buck, now seventy-two, lives near Charlottesville. Neither she nor her sister Doris would be considered mentally deficient by today's standards. Doris Buck was sterilized under the same law in 1928. She later married Matthew Figgins, a plumber. But Doris Buck was never informed. "They told me," she recalled, "that the operation was for an appendix and rupture." So she and Matthew Figgins tried to conceive a child. They consulted physicians at three hospitals during her childbearing years; no one recognized that her Fallopian tubes had been severed. Last year, Doris Buck Figgins finally discovered the cause of her lifelong sadness.

One might invoke an unfeeling calculus and say that Doris Buck's disappointment ranks as nothing compared with millions dead in wars to support the designs of madmen or the conceits of rulers. But can one measure the pain of a single dream unfulfilled, the hope of a defenseless woman snatched by public power in the name of an ideology advanced to purify a race? May Doris Buck's simple and eloquent testimony stand for millions of deaths and disappointments and help us to remember that the Sabbath was made for man, not man for the Sabbath: "I broke down and cried. My husband and me wanted children desperately. We were crazy about them. I never knew what they'd done to me."

Source: From *The Mismeasure of Man,* by Stephen Jay Gould, 335–336. Copyright © 1981 by Stephen Jay Gould. Used by permission of W. W. Norton & Company, Inc.

its promotion of the equality of all citizens. A series of firsthand reports on the harmful conditions in institutions for those with mental retardation and mental illness added to the fervor of parents and others seeking fair and effective treatment for these two groups.[76]

The campaign for improvement in the lives of those with retardation found a champion in President John F. Kennedy. One of Kennedy's own sisters had been diagnosed as mentally retarded. Soon after his election, Kennedy created a Presidential Panel on Mental Retardation. The panel's report in 1962 called for research into retardation and a system of services to provide a continuum of care. The panel found a high correlation between retardation, deprivation, and low socioeconomic status. It consequently recommended a program of social action to alleviate the effects of poverty. Kennedy's 1963 address to Congress on mental health included the plight of the retarded and called for community-based programs providing educational, health, rehabilitation, and employment services. The 1963 Community Mental Health Centers Act also allocated funds for research and new clinical facilities for treating persons with retardation. With these new programs, Kennedy predicted, "reliance on the cold mercy of custodial isolation will be supplanted by the open warmth of community concern and capability."[77]

As we discuss later, Kennedy's prophecy has not yet been realized. Large institutions for those with mental retardation remain, although with different and reduced populations. The process of deinstitutionalization has created its own set of problems. Yet, although the record is mixed, exciting and effective new programs are changing the lives of both those with retardation and their families.

Current Issues and Trends

From Institution to Life in the Community

Without a doubt, the most important change in societal response to mental illness and developmental disability in the last five decades has been the move from institutionalization to community placement and services. Although it was begun with high hopes in the 1950s and 1960s, by the 1970s the *deinstitutionalization* movement had come to carry negative connotations of neglect, exploitation, and abandonment of vulnerable people. Those with mental illness have been particularly at risk; and, as we discuss in Chapter 14, individuals discharged from state mental institutions helped swell the ranks of the homeless in the 1970s and 1980s. Some observers contend that the negative consequences of deinstitutionalization stem from faulty ideas about mental illness and developmental disability and show that institutionalization of special populations will always be necessary.[78] Others argue that the idea of community placement is a sound one, but that more resources and better planning are needed before it can succeed.

Before we discuss current trends, let's review the causes and process of deinstitutionalization from the 1960s through the 1980s. That process, sparked in part by the community mental health movement, expanded substantially in the 1970s and 1980s. Between 1970 and 1989, the number of psychiatric beds in nonfederal psychiatric hospitals dropped by more than 60 percent. Almost all of the decrease occurred in state and county hospitals. The field of mental retardation witnessed similar changes. More than forty state institutions for those with mental retardation closed between 1970 and 1990. In 1967 nearly 200,000 people with developmental disability were living in state institutions; today the figure is only about 93,000. Most of the reductions took place among those with mild retardation. More and more parents are now raising these children at home, leaving an institutional population of those with the most severe physical and mental handicaps.[79]

There are many reasons for the wholesale shift away from institutions. Court rulings regarding the civil rights of those with mental illness or developmental disabilities provided one impetus. The landmark *Wyatt* v. *Stickney* case of 1972 involved a class action suit brought against the Alabama Department of Mental Hygiene by residents of two mental hospitals and a school for people with mental retardation. The federal judge hearing the case declared the right of those in institutions to treatment. He ruled that it was a violation of due process to deprive a person of his or her liberty for therapeutic reasons and then to fail to provide such therapy. In addition to legal considerations, economic motives played a part in the move to empty the large institutions. During the fiscal crises of the 1970s, politicians and officials in many states argued that decreasing the patient population would allow state governments to save large amounts of money.[80]

Advocates for community placement of those with developmental disabilities used two powerful new rationales in their campaigns: the goal of "normalization" and the right to treatment "in the least restrictive setting." *Normalization,* a concept imported from Sweden, holds that individuals who are developmentally disabled should be given the opportunity to live as normal a life as possible. This life includes becoming as self-sufficient in daily living skills as one can; using community facilities for education and recreation; and, in the area of employment, receiving a salary equal to that of an average person doing the same work.[81] Normalization is made possible by placing people in settings posing as few restrictions as possible, such as small group homes in the community. These concepts, which were widely adopted by professionals in the field of developmental disability, offered a strong philosophical justification for the movement of clients into the community. In addition, important legislation was passed to combat discrimination against the developmentally disabled in the community. For example, the Rehabilitation Act of 1973 barred discrimination against handicapped individuals in both public and private agencies that receive federal aid.

Probably the greatest push toward deinstitutionalization, however, resulted from important changes in federal aid to persons with disabilities. In 1962 the Department of Health, Education, and Welfare decided to allow federal matching funds to be used by state public assistance programs for the support of people released from mental institutions. Then the development of the Supplemental Security Income program (SSI) in 1972 provided direct federal assistance to those visually impaired, aged, and disabled persons who were still poor even after receiving regular Social Security payments. Most important, people in public institutions were not eligible for SSI payments: The funds went to individuals as direct cash grants, which could be used to pay for care in boarding homes and other community residences. States took this opportunity to shift individuals out of state-funded institutions and into less expensive facilities, where costs could be carried either in large part or entirely by the federal government. Such residences did not initially require any monitoring by welfare agencies. The result was the creation of a market for private, for-profit boarding homes, adult foster care homes, "single room occupancy" (SRO) residential hotels, and other facilities whose owners were not required to provide any services beyond room and board to their residents.[82] Many states opted not to provide such services either, partly because of growing financial problems.

The results were the unintended consequences of deinstitutionalization. Thousands of chronic long-term mental patients, particularly the elderly, as well as those with developmental disability, were discharged into private boarding homes, nursing homes, and welfare hotels. By 1988, for example, more than 50,000 people with mental retardation were living in private nursing homes. Although some of these facilities provided decent care, lack of regulation all too often led to unsanitary and unsafe living conditions, inadequate medical care and rehabilitation services, and poor nutrition. Communities became alarmed about congregations of "ex–mental patients" in downtown parks and other public areas. Federally funded community mental health programs were insufficient to fill the gap in services. People discharged from state institutions simply had nothing to do and no place to go. In fact, while first-time psychiatric hospital admission rates fell, readmission rates rose. This indicated the difficulty of surviving "on the outside."[83]

The severity of the situation led to several federal initiatives for change. In the late 1970s, states received federal funding to set up community-based programs for people with mental illness. Such programs were to provide housing, case management, and other services. Legislative mandates also called for increased community support and rehabilitation for adults with developmental disabilities. In the early 1980s, federal legislation required that states develop and enforce standards for community residences that use SSI payments, such as group homes.

The emerging partnership between federal, state, and local governments in the provision of services to the mentally ill was broken, however, by the passage of President Reagan's Omnibus Budget Act in 1981. This act created a system of state block grants for social and mental health services, which states could use as they chose, and it ended direct federal funding for community mental health centers and other health and human services programs. Although states gained greater discretion in spending federal money, the block grants brought in less money than was previously provided in these service areas. The newly established community support programs for those with mental illness were not included in the 1981 Budget Act, and their direct funding has been drastically curtailed since then.[84]

Because of the cutback in federal funding for specific programs, states and localities now provide the major public initiative for services for the mentally ill. Funding comes largely from state revenues, federal block grants, and SSI payments to individuals. State and county mental hospitals continue to function, although on a much smaller scale. Some institutions have closed. Many more have downsized, leading to the ghostly presence of large empty buildings on some state hospital grounds. State and county institutions now account for less than a third of all inpatient treatment beds (see Figure 13.2). Even with downsizing, however, many states continue to spend a good deal of money on their hospitals, particularly on staff and physical maintenance.[85]

Other facilities serving those with mental illness include private psychiatric hospitals, psychiatric units in general hospitals, treatment centers for emotionally disturbed children, and community support and outpatient programs. Private psychiatric hospitals and units in general hospitals proliferated in the 1980s. Yet the numbers of almost all inpatient and residential mental health organizations and beds began to fall in the 1990s, with the most dramatic decrease in state and county mental hospital beds. Thus the trend away from inpatient care continues.[86]

We are continuing to struggle with the negative effects of deinstitutionalization. The decline in state mental institutions, the lack of sufficient resources for comprehensive

FIGURE 13.2 **Percentage Distributions of Inpatient and Residential Treatment Beds, by Type of Mental Health Organization: United States, 1970, 1980, 1990, and 1998.**

Sources: National Institute of Mental Health, *Mental Health, United States, 1987,* Ronald W. Manderscheid and Sally Barrett, eds., DHHS Pub. No. (ADM) 87-1518 (Washington, DC: U.S. Government Printing Office, 1987), 16; U.S. Bureau of the Census, *Statistical Abstract of the United States, 2000* (Washington, DC: U.S. Government Printing Office, 2000), 134; National Center for Health Statistics, *Health, United States, 2002,* Table 108, online at www.cdc.gov/nchs/data/hus02.pdf.

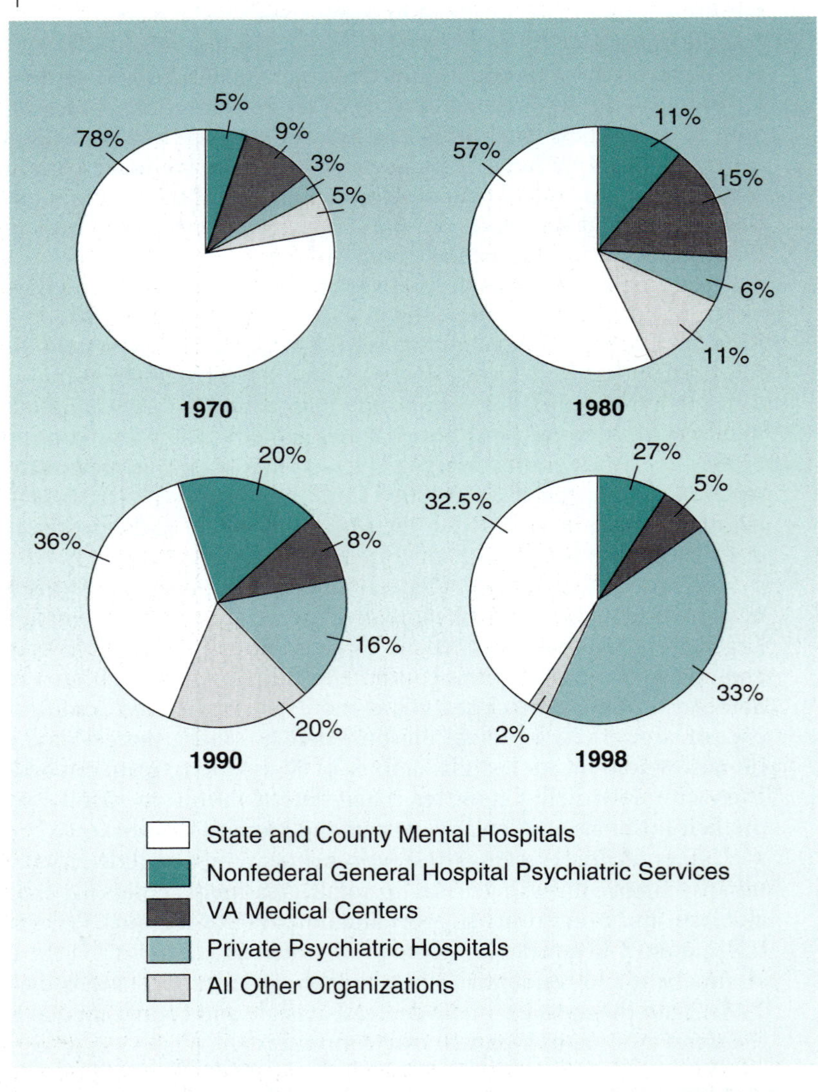

community services, and the rise in private hospital treatment of those with acute mental illness has left a gap in care for an increasingly important group—the chronically mentally ill. These are individuals who have a serious mental disorder, such as schizophrenia, and whose illness is of long duration. Although the group includes older individuals with mental illness who were discharged into the community as a result of deinstitutionalization in the 1960s and 1970s, the more challenging contingent is the growing number of younger people with mental disorders. Some of these individuals have never been institutionalized. Others alternate between brief hospital stays and life in the community. Living with their families, in community-based housing facilities, or on the streets, they have had freer access to street drugs and alcohol, which may exacerbate their problems, and they often resist treatment. Reaching out to this group of younger people presents a challenge for mental health professionals.[87]

Another consequence of deinstitutionalization, and a chilling reminder of practices in Dorothea Dix's day, is the increasing number of people with mental illness who are confined in jails. In Mississippi, for example, most general hospitals do not have beds for psychiatric patients, and the two state mental hospitals are overcrowded. To fill the gap, local jails are being used as holding pens for the mentally ill until a hospital bed can be found. Nor is this practice confined to Mississippi; studies indicate that it is a growing trend across the country. In New York City, for example, approximately 25,000 to 30,000 people with serious mental illness are behind bars each year in the city's jail at Riker's Island. One study found that as many as 5 percent of the over two million Americans in jails and prisons are seriously mentally ill.[88]

The use of jails to deal with the mentally ill symbolizes the dark side of deinstitutionalization at the beginning of the twenty-first century. More and more people with mental illness, sometimes compounded by substance abuse, struggle to survive without adequate housing, health, or mental health services. Within the broader public, the proportion of people who mention violence in describing mental illness has almost tripled, from 13 percent in the 1950s to 31 percent today. Although research finds that people with mental illness who do not abuse alcohol or drugs are no more violent than anyone else, dramatic news stories of people with mental illness who harm themselves or others frustrates and often angers the public. The family of a New York woman, diagnosed with severe bipolar affective disorder (which causes both manic phases and depression), spent twenty years trying to find effective help for her in the mental health system. She was suicidal and deeply resistant to taking medication. Courts repeatedly found her a danger to herself or others and committed her for involuntary hospital treatment. After short-term hospital stays, she would be discharged into the community, sometimes to a homeless shelter. Struggling with paranoid delusions, and angry about being committed, she rejected her family. With each discharge, she disappeared into the streets, leaving family members to search for her and eventually to discover her beaten and mistreated, and often delusional. The cycle of commitment and discharge would begin again. In the end, she was found murdered in Central Park.[89]

Part of the problem in the system has to do with money. Financial pressures on hospitals have hastened discharges and made hospitals less likely to renew involuntary commitments. At the same time, states and localities have failed to provide adequate funding for community services, such as supervised housing and case managers who could keep in close touch with people discharged from inpatient facilities. Another source of difficulty is the perennial issue of self-determination. How much control should we wield over people who resist medication and hospitalization, particularly when they have "sane" as well as "insane" moments and when we can't always gauge the potential they carry for violence against themselves or others? And if we choose to hospitalize them, how long should they remain hospitalized?

Ethical, financial, and treatment issues were brought into sharp focus in New York City on January 3, 1999. Andrew Goldstein, a man who had been repeatedly hospitalized for schizophrenia, pushed Kendra Webdale to her death beneath an oncoming subway train. Goldstein had a history of violence. He had attacked strangers in public places and mental health professionals in the acute care psychiatric hospitals where he spent brief periods before being discharged back into the community to live on his own. Unlike the woman with bipolar disorder described previously, he always came to the hospitals voluntarily, seeking help. Each time he was discharged, the social workers planning his release looked in vain for community assistance, but found long waiting lists for state-financed group homes and case manager services. Goldstein even tried to be admitted to a long-term state psychiatric hospital, but the push to reduce the populations in these hospitals had created a waiting list even here. Again living on his own, he stopped taking his medications and ended up killing a stranger.[90]

This well-publicized case brought attention to a violent act by a person with mental illness, but also highlighted the sad condition of mental health services in New York State—and the rest of the country. However, the immediate response was not an attempt by the city or state to find more resources for community services, but instead the enactment in May 1999 of Kendra's Law. This state legislation, called a "shortcut solution" by one reporter, sets up an outpatient commitment system in which courts can order certain individuals with mental illness to receive and accept outpatient treatment. If a person fails to comply with outpatient treatment, such as medication, case management services, and substance abuse counseling, he or she can be committed to an inpatient psychiatric facility. In addition to New York, thirty-six states have statutes allowing involuntary outpatient commitment.[91]

Given the facts in Goldstein's situation, and in the situation of many people with mental illness, the law is an ironic solution. The state of New York clearly does not have the necessary outpatient facilities and services to offer, and it lacks space in long-term hospitals for people who don't comply with a court order. As the Bazelon Center for Mental Health Law notes, involuntary outpatient commitment "is not a substitute for the necessary resources for effective treatment." The Bazelon Center and other advocacy organizations also worry about the ethical implication of the new policy, which, according to the National Mental Health Association, "scapegoats people with mental illnesses at the same time that we fail to offer the treatments and services that people really need. . . . Expanding service options, especially community-based ones, would accomplish the same ends without coercion, or the loss of freedom associated with involuntary court-mandated treatment."[92]

Yet there are a few signs of improvement in the ways mental illness is being perceived and dealt with. Under recent guidelines developed for the Americans with Disabilities Act (ADA), for example, employers are now mandated to offer reasonable accommodations to employees with mental impairments such as major depression and schizophrenia. In 1999 the Supreme Court ruled in support of two women in Georgia who had sued the state for the right to live in a community-based treatment setting. Lois Curtis and Elaine Wilson have mental illness and mental retardation and were confined in a Georgia state psychiatric hospital. Although their doctors agreed with their request to be discharged to the community and receive appropriate services there, they remained institutionalized due to long waiting lists for community placements. In their suit against Tommy Olmstead, commissioner of the state Department of Human Resources, they charged discrimination under the ADA. In its decision, the Supreme Court said, "states are required to provide community-based treatment for persons with mental disabilities when the state's treatment professionals determine that such placement is appropriate." Although the ruling does not solve the problem of funding such services, the Court endorsed the idea that states could be required to fund community placements by moving resources from institutions to the community. In his first year of office, President George W. Bush ordered that "the Federal Government must assist states and localities to implement swiftly the Olmstead decision."[93]

Several years back, public responses to the debate over granting parity in insurance coverage for mental as well as physical ailments also demonstrated a growing awareness that mental illness is not a shameful and incurable affliction. Revelations by Senators Phil Gramm and Pete Domenici and other public figures regarding the impact of mental illness on their families garnered public and congressional support for passage of the Mental Health Parity Act of 1996. The act requires insurers who offer mental health benefits to establish equal annual payment limits and lifetime caps for coverage of mental and physical illnesses. In a survey conducted by the National Mental Health Association, 61 percent of the respondents strongly agreed that mental difficulties should be treated like physical illness in terms of health coverage. By November 2000, thirty-two states had also passed parity laws, many of them with provisions that were broader than those in the federal statute.[94]

Community Services for Those with Mental Retardation

Community supports for individuals with mental retardation appear to be more firmly in place than those for the mentally ill. State spending for community-based services for this group has increased substantially. Federally funded initiatives have also helped make life outside of the institution more feasible. For example, the Education for All Handicapped Children Act of 1975 (Public Law 94-142) uses federal funding to encourage states to offer public education to all children with disabilities aged three to twenty-one. Many states have mandated such education, often raising the age of eligibility to twenty-six. Most programs express a philosophy of *mainstreaming,* or integrating students into regular classrooms whenever possible. However, this goal has not yet been fulfilled; as few as 7 percent of children with retardation have been fully integrated into regular classrooms, with an additional 27 percent spending some part of the day in such classrooms.[95]

New trends in employment of those with mental retardation have added to the community support system. The Federal Rehabilitation Act of 1973 helped pave the way by promoting nondiscriminatory hiring and employment policies for those with disabilities. "Supported employment" of people with disabilities is a new approach, using both state and federal funds. It developed in part as a reaction against the sheltered workshop system, in which workers were generally paid less than the minimum wage and rarely moved into competitive employment. In contrast, supported employment programs place people with disabilities directly into regular work settings. Generally, a "job coach" provides support, training, and encouragement.[96] For example, Hank Thomas, a young man with Down syndrome, works in a university research department. He makes coffee, delivers mail, and is being trained by his coach to run the copy machine. He is a regular paid staff member of the department, he joins other staff in coffee breaks and social events, and he shows obvious pride in the job he is doing.

By the late 1990s, about 80 percent of individuals with mental retardation were living at home. That figure is now dropping as alternative living arrangements, such as small, familylike group homes, are growing. Respite care programs, where they exist, are an important support for people with disabilities and their families. These programs are particularly relevant for family caregivers of children and adults with profound disabilities. They offer "respite"—a break for rest and relief—to families for short periods on a regular basis or for weekends or vacations. A family may bring their child to a special center for care for a weekend, for example, or a trained worker may come to the home for two hours a day to allow parents the chance to run errands or visit friends. Group homes and supported living can help sustain adults with retardation whose families cannot care for them or would like them to achieve more independence. (As we saw in the opening vignette on Rebecca Levine, parents sometimes encourage such a move.) Group homes are generally environments in which six or fewer individuals live, often with twenty-four-hour staff support. Individuals in supported living situations usually live in homes or apartments of their own, sometimes alone and sometimes with roommates. They often receive services provided by professionals. Unfortunately, there is an increasing waiting list for these residential alternatives, as well as for other community services. This shortage is particularly problematic for aging parents whose disabled children are still living at home and who are worried about what will happen to their children when they die or become too old to care for them.[97]

Advocacy and Consumer Organizations for the Mentally Ill

Advocacy and consumer groups have been extremely important in the expansion of community services for people with mental illness, mental retardation, and other developmental disabilities. As we have seen, the Association of Retarded Citizens (now renamed The Arc) played a major role in the move from large state institutions to more humane and effective living situations in the community for those with retardation. With a membership of 100,000 family members, individuals with mental retardation, and professionals in the field of disability, The Arc continues to be the chief organizational voice for the welfare of children and adults with retardation. Its Office of Governmental Affairs lobbies aggressively for laws, policies, and services to improve the lives of those with retardation.[98]

Citizen organizations addressing mental health issues have been slower to develop, probably because of the stigma attached to mental illness in U.S. society. In recent years, however, a growing number of advocacy and consumer groups have begun to influence mental health policy and program development, including the expansion of community services.

In Louisiana, for example, a range of organizations speak for those with mental illness and their families. One of the oldest is the Mental Health Association in Louisiana, a branch of a large national organization that uses public education and lobbying to work for increased funding for mental health programs and the elimination of discrimination against the mentally ill. At a recent conference of the National Mental Health Association in Washington, D.C., for example, conference participants took part in a Government Affairs Day. After a morning legislative briefing, they spent the afternoon visiting their senators and representatives, urging them to support children's health insurance legislation and inclusion of children's mental health needs in that legislation. On the state level, the Louisiana chapter has developed a Mental Health Reform Coalition that is lobbying state officials to shift the emphasis of state mental health spending from public hospitals to a broad array of community-based services.

The Louisiana Alliance for the Mentally Ill (L'AMI) is also a branch of a larger organization, the National Alliance for the Mentally Ill (NAMI). NAMI membership consists predominantly of parents of adult children with schizophrenia. The Louisiana Alliance is a mutual support and advocacy group composed of families and friends of the mentally ill (see Figure 13.3). The Federation of Families, another support group,

FIGURE 13.3 **Brochure for the Louisiana Alliance for the Mentally Ill**

Source: Louisiana Alliance for the Mentally Ill, "Advocates of Hope," by permission of Louisiana Alliance for the Mentally Ill.

L'AMI
Advocates of hope

Shares information concerning mental illness

Advocates and promotes services at the state level

Provides support during times of crisis

Assists in coping with loved ones with mental illness

Disperses information on community resources and services

Dispels the stigma of mental illness through education efforts

Speaks out publicly on all issues involving the mentally ill

L'AMI
Network of hope

Alexandria - CENLA-AMI
Theresa Earthly
215 Heyman Lane
Alexandria, LA 71303
(Home) (318) 445-7042
(Work) (318) 445-5111

Baton Rouge - BRAMI
Norma Eichelberger
1449 Broadmoor Court
Baton Rouge, LA 70815
(504) 925-9717

Bogalusa - Bogalusa AMI
Rose Branch
702 Avenue I
Bogalusa, LA 70427
(504) 732-7595

Franklin AMI
John Lawrence
Rt. 5, Box 421
Winnsboro, LA 71295
(318) 435-3254

Greater New Orleans - Friends - AMI
Bea Piker
830 Audubon Street
New Orleans, LA 70118
(504) 865-8770

Houma - Houma-AMI
Taddy Porche
45 HMS Court
Houma, LA 70364
(504) 876-2039

Lafayette - Families & Friends AMI
Lucille Sellers
140 S. Arlington Dr.
Lafayette, LA 70503
(318) 235-2055

Lake Charles -Southwest-AMI
Yvonne Guerinni
106 Dubach
Sulphur, LA 70663
(318) 625-5190

Natchitoches -NAKAMI
Dorothy Hyams
865 2nd Street
Natchitoches, LA 71457
(318) 352-2096

Ruston - Ruston-AMI
Brig Kilgore
1705 Wade Drive
Ruston, LA 71270
(318) 255-2914

Shreveport - Caddo-Bossier-AMI
Donald Duncan
2055 Bermuda Drive
Shreveport, LA 71105
(318) 861-1389

St. Tammany - ST AMI
Mimi Jackson
41554 Herwig Bluff
Slidell, LA 70461
(504) 641-1257

L'AMI State Office
Donna M. Mayeux, Exec. Dir.
2431 S. Acadian Thrwy.
Suite 280
Baton Rouge, LA 70808
(504) 928-6928

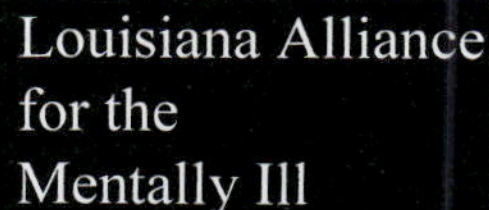

Advocates of Hope

"Families helping families can change hopelessness into helpfulness, anger into advocacy and pain into progress."

focuses on promoting self-help among the parents of children with emotional, behavioral, or mental disorders and lobbies for comprehensive community-based child and family-centered services. Finally, an organization called Confident is a Louisiana consumer group composed solely of individuals with mental illness. Confident sponsors events such as rap sessions, dance nights, a monthly business meeting, and potluck holiday dinners. Confident also runs a drop-in center and gives input to the State Office of Mental Health regarding the needs of those with mental illness. Together these groups have demanded more attention to the interests of the mentally ill and their families and to the importance of community-based as well as institutional services.[99]

Mental Health Managed Care

As Chapter 12 explained, managed care is fast becoming the major method of organizing health care in the United States. Although managed care developed later in the mental health services than in the physical health sphere, mental health managed care is now rapidly catching up. Part of the impetus prompting managed care companies to expand into this area has been the need to develop new markets in a period when the general health market is becoming saturated. As in physical health care, for-profit managed care organizations dominate mental health managed care. And in another similarity, consolidation is moving full steam ahead. The five largest managed care companies handle the mental health coverage of 135 million Americans. (*Behavioral health* is the term most MCOs use for mental health and substance abuse services.)[100]

The cost of mental health services has also spurred the growth of behavioral health managed care. Analysts estimate that spending for mental health and substance abuse treatment constitutes approximately one-tenth of the total national expenditure on health care. Increases in the use of psychotropic drugs account for about two-thirds of increased mental health spending. Private employers have become more and more interested in the managed care approach to mental health, as they have watched the expansion of mental health services available to their employees and a concomitant rise in health coverage costs. As we discussed in the chapter on health care, state officials, eyeing an alarming rise in Medicaid costs, have also gravitated toward a managed care approach. About three-quarters of the states now have managed behavioral health care plans for at least some categories of clients in their Medicaid programs; the fact that the federal government no longer requires states to obtain special waivers to pursue such plans will no doubt spur the remaining states to convert.[101]

There is wide variation in Medicaid mental health plans from state to state. Some use only nonprofit managed care MCOs, whereas others have no such restriction. Plans may be developed and monitored by the state Medicaid office, the department of mental health, local authorities, or some combination of these. Types of services offered can also vary. Consumer and advocate groups strongly favor the idea of a comprehensive set of services focused particularly on community care. These groups are also adamant that plans must include sound evaluation systems and specific mechanisms through which clients can submit complaints or grievances regarding provision of care. Although grievance mechanisms are particularly important for a potentially vulnerable Medicaid population, they can set a good precedent for all users of managed care systems.[102]

The move to mental health managed care presents many challenges to clients, families, and mental health providers. (We discuss the impact of managed care on mental health social workers at the end of this chapter.) Mental health care differs from physical health care, which is assumed to continue until a specific physical problem has been stabilized or eliminated. The end point of mental health treatment is less easily established; as a result, managed care systems tend to concentrate on reimbursing providers for a specific number of treatment sessions. Much of the criticism of behavioral health managed care focuses on instances of clients being cut off after six sessions, for example, in situations in which both they and their therapists felt more sessions were necessary.

In addition, because lowering costs is an important goal in managed care, clients may be given short-term, less expensive, and perhaps lower-quality care. Yet, ironically, this may turn out to be one of the greatest strengths of mental health managed care. Managed care in both the private and public sectors has tended to substitute outpatient and partial care services for psychiatric hospitalization. These may in fact turn out to be more effective ways of dealing with mental difficulties, as long as a basic safety net of emergency hospitalization is maintained. That potential is particularly important in Medicaid plans, for which managed care systems can be required to provide a variety of community-based services, thus redressing the balance between state hospitals and community care. The trick, professionals and advocates warn, will be to ensure that MCOs more accustomed to "mainstream" clients learn how to be helpful with low-income clients, those with mental retardation and substance abuse problems, and the chronic mentally ill.[103]

Special Populations in the Field of Mental Health

Two specific groups of mental health clients have been receiving more attention lately: children with mental illness, and adults who are "dually diagnosed" with substance abuse and serious mental problems. New services and policies are necessary to address the needs of each population.

Children and adolescents can experience a variety of mental, emotional, and behavioral problems. Anxiety disorders are the most common of these, including post-traumatic stress disorders related to physical or sexual abuse, exposure to a traumatic event, or other events. Attention deficit hyperactivity disorder (ADHD) affects about 5 percent of school-age children. Major depression is being recognized more and more among young people. Yet, despite growing awareness of such problems, about two-thirds of the young people affected by them are not getting the specific mental health services they need. Professional and advocacy groups point out that when treatment *is* given, it is sometimes in the form of inappropriate hospitalization; as in the situation of adults with mental illness, coordinated community-based services may be far more effective in helping children.[104]

A recent dispute regarding the treatment of children and adolescents with mental and emotional disorders revolves around the increased use of medication to deal with these disorders. The most prominent example of the debate over whether drugs are an effective and appropriate way to help children with problems is the increasingly heated discussion about the benefits and drawbacks of Ritalin. Ritalin has been used for three decades to treat hyperactivity in children, or what we now call attention

The treatment worlds of mental illness and substance abuse are often separate.

deficit hyperactivity disorder. A recent study funded by the National Institute of Health found that Ritalin was more effective than behavior-modification therapy in treating children with ADHD. Yet many people, among them a number of teachers, parents, and doctors, argue that the drug is overused; perhaps what looks like hyperactivity, some people say, is simply a case of high spirits, willfulness, or normal problems of childhood. In Colorado, for example, the state Board of Education has moved to discourage teachers from recommending the drug to parents, urging them instead to use discipline and instruction to overcome behavioral problems. Although it is not clear the extent to which school personnel are in fact recommending the use of medication, Connecticut has followed suit by passing a law that prohibits teachers, counselors, and other school officials from suggesting psychiatric drugs for any child.[105]

A report on medications for toddlers that appeared in the February 2000 *Journal of the American Medical Association* has added additional fuel to the fire. That study found that the use of certain psychotropic medications, such as antidepressants and stimulants, for two- to four-year-olds doubled and sometimes tripled between 1991 and 1995. Another report noted a "49 percent rise in the use of attention deficit drugs by children younger than 5." The resulting cries of alarm about "drugged-out toddlers" and over-medicated school children have been countered by assurances from the National Institute of Health and organizations such as the National Alliance for the Mentally Ill that medications for children are both safe and effective. As one reporter sums it up, in an article entitled "Fury, Not Facts, in the Battle over Childhood Behavior," the present studies are incomplete, and until we know more about the effects of medication on children, the outrage is premature.[106]

The problems of those with the dual diagnosis of substance abuse and mental illness are probably less familiar to most people. Yet about 27 percent of individuals with what the federal Substance Abuse and Mental Health Administration calls "severe and persistent mental illness" and about 15 percent of those with "serious mental illness" are also contending with substance abuse. Often, one disorder remains under control for a while, while the other is active. People with dual disorders generally cycle through periods of stabilization and distress, with the status of one disorder influencing that of the other. Individuals with co-occurring illnesses, such as alcoholism and schizophrenia, experience greater difficulties than those who have a single disorder, because of the interaction between the two illnesses.[107]

Effective treatment for those with a dual diagnosis calls for integrated services through which clients can receive help with both problems simultaneously. Unfortunately, there are separate federal block grants to states to finance treatment for the two categories of disorder; those working in the two areas often have different types of training and treatment philosophies, and there is a tendency for the two conditions to be treated by different programs, as shown in the photograph on page 528. A mental health center may treat only the mental illness segment of a person's problem, whereas the substance abuse clinic deals only with the ramifications of addiction. Higher rates of hospitalization and homelessness may be the result of this incomplete and uncoordinated approach to the problems of those with two interacting afflictions.[108]

Perspectives

Political perspectives on mental illness and developmental disability are complex. They apply both to how people interpret the causes of these conditions and to what people see as the appropriate responses or solutions. Perspectives also vary over time: What might be considered a "liberal" approach to mental illness in one period—for example, the creation of the large asylum—becomes the "conservative" answer to the problem in the next. However, certain broad distinctions among conservative, liberal, and radical viewpoints can be described.

The Conservative Perspective

A conservative approach to mental illness and developmental disability tends to place the causes of these conditions within the individual. Environmental factors, particularly economic ones, receive much less attention than do individual behaviors and values. The medical model of mental illness represents a good example of the conservative perspective; this model concerns itself primarily with the individual and his or her "sickness" rather than with the social context in which the person lives.

In our society, the conservative perspective has also meant a faith in private rather than governmental arrangements for dealing with various social and economic needs. In the case of mental illness and developmental disability, conservatives generally stress private initiatives over public programs, particularly programs developed by the federal government. President Franklin Pierce expressed this concept more than a hundred years ago in his veto of a bill proposed by Dorothea Dix authorizing federal funding for public mental institutions. The cessation of direct federal support for community mental health centers during the Reagan administration is another example of a distrust of federal initiatives and a faith in private solutions to social problems. In promoting these solutions, conservatives stress economic goals and efficiency in the management of mental health programs.

Arguing the importance of market forces, most conservatives see the private sector, and particularly the for-profit organization, as the best provider of services to those with mental illness and developmental disability. The for-profit managed care company or private psychiatric hospital fits this model. Ironically, privatization is partially fueled by federal resources. SSI payments, for example, are used to maintain individuals with developmental disability in private, for-profit nursing homes.

The Liberal Perspective

The liberal perspective does not completely reject private responses or the medical model of mental illness. However, it tends to view mental illness and developmental disability as relating to a combination of individual and social causes. Liberal policymakers in the 1960s stressed the links between mental illness and poverty, discrimination, and lack of educational opportunity. The community mental health center, in its melding of psychiatric and environmental approaches to dealing with mental illness, represents an excellent example of a liberal response to the problem.

The community mental health center was federally funded, and its program was federally designed. This, too, fits the liberal approach. Although not ruling out the usefulness of private programs, liberals look to the government to provide direction and resources for dealing with social problems. In the case of developmental disability, they have promoted federal legislation to regulate treatment and to expand opportunities for affected individuals. The federal law encouraging public education and mainstreaming for children with developmental disability is a good example.

The Radical Perspective

Radical perspectives on mental illness and developmental disability take a much stronger stance regarding the social determinants in these situations. One approach, as seen in the work of Thomas Szasz, is to view terms such as *mental illness* as inappropriate labels for what are basically problems in living. Such terms may even be seen as labels used to oppress minorities and the poor. A related set of ideas explains mental illness and developmental disability almost entirely in terms of environmental factors. This approach looks particularly at social class and power differentials in our society. Thus, the lives of discharged mental patients can be described as lacking in social and economic resources and characterized by oppression, domination, and manipulation by professionals and for-profit providers of services. Radicals alert us to the ability of private entrepreneurs to influence mental health policy.[109]

Radical solutions focus on challenging or drastically changing existing social and economic institutions. Radicals question the ability of for-profit systems, such as behavioral health MCOs, to provide comprehensive services to all who need them, and would prefer a noncapitalist solution. Yet broad societal restructuring is a tall order. More manageable strategies are the continued promotion of effective publicly financed community services and the use of advocacy/empowerment models such as the one developed by Stephen Rose and Bruce L. Black. Rose and Black deplore existing services for those discharged from mental institutions, seeing these services as "rarely [acknowledging] the world of poverty, inadequate housing, landlord domination, inaccessible health services . . . and related problems that comprise the daily life of former patients." Rose and Black propose a response to these difficulties that stresses advocating for and with clients for their rights to fair treatment and adequate services in the community.[110] Consumer and advocacy groups often pursue similar goals.

Social Work Roles in Mental Health and Developmental Disability

The mental health service system has long been a major arena for social work practice. Indeed, social workers now provide about 65 percent of all professional mental health services. The field of developmental disability has drawn less interest, but it also offers many opportunities for social work involvement. Both fields call on social workers to interact with other professionals, so it is best to begin by differentiating their various roles.

A fair amount of overlap has developed among the different disciplines in the field of mental health. Psychiatrists, psychologists, social workers, and psychiatric nurses all can function as individual or group therapists. In addition, however, each group has areas of specialization. Psychiatrists, as physicians, are the only professionals who can prescribe medications. They, like nurses, also tend to be more in tune with the physiological aspects of a client's condition. Psychiatric nurses can administer medications, and they are generally concerned with the relationship between an individual's physical and mental well-being. Clinical psychologists are trained in the administration and interpretation of psychological tests, such as the Rorschach projective test and the Minnesota Multiphasic Personality Inventory (MMPI), which are used to assess clients' emotional functioning. Social workers have particular competence in two areas relevant to mental health services. First, they have a solid working knowledge of community resources and are trained in referring clients for specific services and monitoring the results. Second, social workers also specialize in assessing the family and community context of mental illness, which enables them to write up social studies of client situations and to make recommendations regarding environmental changes. These may include shifts in an individual's job situation or living arrangements.

Social workers also use these skills in the field of developmental disability. Here their sensitivity to family interaction is an important asset in their work with the families of children who are disabled. Social workers' involvement in this field brings them in contact not only with psychologists, who conduct intelligence tests, but also with special education teachers. Such teachers have received specialized training in the techniques of educating students with developmental gaps. An overlap between teachers and social workers lies in the teaching of daily living skills, such as shopping, personal hygiene, and using public transportation.

Mental health social workers use their skills in a variety of settings. About 17 percent now work as full-time private therapists. Others work primarily in organizational settings, including public and private mental hospitals, VA hospital psychiatric programs, psychiatric units in general hospitals, residential treatment centers for emotionally disturbed children, and outpatient clinics. Social work is a highly visible profession within these settings. After nurses, social workers make up the largest single professional group staffing mental health facilities (see Table 13.3).

Social workers are increasingly becoming involved in managed care. Currently, social workers in private practice are the ones most affected by the managed care revolution, as their clients are less and less likely to carry traditional health insurance. Instead, the people private practitioners see are likely to be members of employer-provided managed care mental health plans or Medicaid recipients in public managed care systems. Working with such clients entails receiving approval for each set of sessions, detailing the diagnosis, and reporting the outcomes of treatment, all of which can involve a lot of telephone calls and paperwork. In addition, private practitioners must apply to MCOs to be in their "provider pools."

In addition to providing treatment, master's-level social workers are employed as managed care "gatekeepers" who receive clients' initial calls, assess their problems, connect them with therapists, and often monitor the treatment process. Social workers with bachelor's or graduate degrees work as case managers in managed care systems.

Managed care is a highly controversial topic among social workers. Many are critical of the constraints put on practice, such as limitations on numbers of sessions with clients. Others are concerned about the lack of client confidentiality resulting from necessary discussions with gatekeepers and other managed care staff regarding treatment

TABLE 13.3 Percentage Distributions of Full-Time Equivalent Staff in Mental Health Organizations, by Discipline: United States, Selected Years, 1988–1994

	Percentage Distributions			
Staff Discipline	**1988**	**1990**	**1992**	**1994**
All Patient Care Staff	100.0%	100.0%	100.0%	100.0%
Professional Patient Care Staff	65.2	65.8	70.6	71.5
Psychiatrists	4.8	4.5	5.3	5.3
Psychologists	6.1	5.5	5.8	4.8
Social Workers	12.1	12.8	13.2	12.1
Registered Nurses	19.3	18.7	18.1	23.0
Other Professional Staff	23.0	24.2	28.3	26.3
Other Mental Health Workers	34.8	34.2	29.4	28.5

Source: National Center for Health Statistics, *Mental Health, United States, 2000,* Table 105, online at www.cdc.gov/nchs/products/pubs, 309.

decisions. Managed care has been lambasted as seriously undermining social work's professional autonomy. Probably no one likes the complicated paperwork of this new system. Yet some social workers praise managed care for its stress on focused, short-term therapy, and others see its potential for providing greater access to mental health services for low-income individuals. Almost all agree that social workers and their professional organizations should promote ethical standards for managed care practice and safeguards for client rights.[111]

The field of developmental disability also offers a large number of practice areas. These include state institutions, community residences, public schools, respite care programs, advocacy organizations, sheltered workshops, and supported employment programs. Although social work has not yet established a major presence in the field, innovative services for those with developmental disability are expanding rapidly and present a challenge for social work involvement.[112]

Social workers carry out many roles within the mental health and developmental disability systems. In both systems, they can operate as case managers. In this role, they assess clients' needs, refer clients to services and programs to meet these needs, and follow up to make sure clients receive appropriate resources or other help. Case managers can be found in aftercare and community support programs for those discharged from mental institutions. They serve individuals with developmental disability in community-based services, such as Centers for Independent Living, which refer people to a variety of community supports that can help them live reasonably independently.

Social workers also help formulate policies and plan programs for those with mental illness and developmental disability, focusing particularly on programs for those who have been deinstitutionalized. They advocate for legislation and program changes to ensure client rights and to improve services. They also supervise other workers, administer programs, and head agencies. They carry out advocacy work on two levels: promotion of the rights of individual clients and advocacy for legislation and program changes to ensure the rights of the total client population.

Within mental health, social workers have long acted as therapists or counselors. In this role they conduct intake interviews; make assessments of individuals' situations; and provide individual, marital, family, and group counseling. They have traditionally been assigned to work with the families of those who have been diagnosed as mentally ill. The more up-to-date version of this work is to serve as a link between client, family, and community.

When working with people who are developmentally disabled, social workers tend to concentrate on case management, although they may do individual and family counseling. New and challenging roles include working as resource persons for parents' groups—for example, helping parents to develop respite care services—and functioning as job coaches in supported employment programs. These two areas of work are particularly exciting, as they stress helping clients and their families to develop their own skills and to gain a greater ability to fulfill their own needs.

The explosion of self-help programs, consumer groups, and advocacy organizations in the fields of mental health and developmental disability presents promising new avenues for cooperative work between social workers, clients, and their families. Rather than cloak themselves in the mantle of detached professional experts, social workers will be challenged to listen to and work with clients in developing relevant

A CLOSER Look

"When Things Were Darkest, Peers Helped"

The following was written by Heather Huckeba, a young woman hospitalized for depression and drug addiction. The experiences she describes led her to help establish the Youth Empowerment Association! (YEA!), a peer counseling program that works in children's psychiatric centers in New York City.

> I came into the hospital so severely depressed I could barely talk. My thinking was so slow it took me 5 minutes to say a sentence. I was so helpless and really didn't think this hospitalization was going to work. It was really, "Well, I'll do this and then I'll kill myself."
>
> There were two girls and one guy who came into the unit almost every day who had been in the hospital. They seemed to have their act together and were really focused, yet they could talk to me and describe the same feelings I was having. I could tell they really knew what I was going through—not just giving lip service to it. They were able to tell me what I could expect, what I could look forward to, that I needed to wait a while before medication would really work, that I needed to start talking about some things. When things were darkest, I could cling to that hope they gave me.
>
> I felt they were very much like me, yet they had changed. That was just enough to get me up each morning and not give up.

Source: "Recipients: Young People Start Peer Support in OMH Children's Units," *OMH News 6* (New York State Office of Mental Health, October 1994), 9. Reprinted by permission.

services, and to see both clients and families as partners in treatment plans. As the "A Closer Look" feature titled "When Things Were Darkest, Peers Helped" suggests, peer counseling can be a potent factor in helping an individual deal with psychological difficulties. In this case, the peer counseling program grew out of a psychiatrist's practice of taking former patients with her as she worked with current clients so that present and former patients could talk about what it had felt like to have similar problems. This sort of creative thinking is a good example of what social workers and other practitioners could bring to new cooperative programs in the fields of mental health and developmental disability.

Conclusion

The fields of mental health and developmental disability present opportunities and challenges for social work. Difficult problems, such as the lack of comprehensive community services and the need to find an effective balance between private and governmental efforts, call on planning and political skills for their resolution. Practitioners must adapt to the new mandates of managed care. Innovative approaches, including supported employment programs and community services for those with chronic mental illness, necessitate learning new roles and expanding expectations of clients' abilities. Both fields are in the process of change and expansion, and both offer social workers a chance to participate in these changes in a meaningful and positive way.

Visit **www.researchnavigator.com** to research these important concepts from the chapter:

Behavioral health
Deinstitutionalization
Developmental disability
DSM–IV
Mental health parity
Mental health service utilization
Mental retardation
Supported employment

Web Sites on Mental Health

The Arc (formerly Association for Retarded Citizens) <www.thearc.org>: A national organization of and for people with mental retardation and related developmental disorders and their families. Definitions of mental retardation, reports on legislation affecting those with retardation, and information on community living options and other resources.

Bazelon Center for Mental Health Law <www.bazelon.org>: Up-to-date and detailed information on mental health issues and legislation. Good coverage of managed care, community-based care, and public mental health systems reform.

Clinical Social Work Federation, Inc. <www.cswf.org>: An organization of clinical social workers with information from the providers' perspective. Legislative alerts; material on clinical social work, managed care, and so on; and link to online catalog of mental health, psychology, and psychiatry resources.

National Alliance for the Mentally Ill <www.nami.org>: Mental health information from national organization of families of the mentally ill.

National Institute of Mental Health <www.nimh.nih.gov>: Includes material on specific mental disorders, diagnosis, and treatment; research activities; and publications.

National Mental Health Association <www.nmha.org>: Reports, legislative alerts, and advocacy information.

National Mental Health Services Knowledge Exchange Network <www.mentalhealth.org>: A web site produced by the Substance Abuse and Mental Health Services Administration (SAMHSA) of the U.S. Department of Health and Human Services. Publications, broad range of information on mental health.

Endnotes

1. Celia W. Dugger, "For the Mentally Ill, Shelters Are Homes of Horror," *New York Times* (12 January 1992), 14.
2. See for example, Howard S. Becker, *Outsiders: Studies in the Sociology of Deviance* (New York: Free Press, 1963); Erving Goffman, *Asylums* (New York: Anchor Books, 1961); Thomas Scheff, *Being Mentally Ill*, 3rd ed. (Chicago: Aldine de Gruyter, 1999); Edwin M. Lemert, *Human Deviance, Social Problems, and Social Control* (Englewood Cliffs, NJ: Prentice Hall, 1967).
3. Peter Conrad and Joseph W. Schneider, *Deviance and Medicalization: From Badness to Sickness* (St. Louis, MO: C.V. Mosby, 1980), 1–2.
4. Kai T. Erikson, *Wayward Puritans* (New York: John Wiley & Sons, 1966), 3–6. Erikson bases his ideas on the work of Emile Durkheim.
5. Erikson, *Wayward Puritans*, 67–159.
6. Thomas S. Szasz, *The Manufacture of Madness* (New York: Delta, 1970), xx.
7. Marie Jahoda, *Current Concepts of Mental Health* (New York: Basic Books, 1958), 10, 23–65; U.S.

Department of Health and Human Services, *Mental Health: A Report of the Surgeon General—Executive Summary* (US DHHS, 1999), vii.
8. Fernando, "Social Realities and Mental Health," 12, 17.
9. Conrad and Schneider, *Deviance and Medicalization,* 32–37; Eliot Freidson, *The Profession of Medicine* (New York: Dodd, Mead, 1970), 251.
10. Conrad and Schneider, *Deviance and Medicalization,* vii; Thomas S. Szasz, *The Myth of Mental Illness* (New York: Hoeber-Harper, 1961), 37–45.
11. *Diagnostic and Statistical Manual of Mental Disorders,* 4th ed. (Washington, DC: American Psychiatric Association, 1994).
12. *Diagnostic and Statistical Manual of Mental Disorders,* 3rd ed. (Washington, DC: American Psychiatric Association, 1980), 380.
13. Stuart A. Kirk and Herb Kutchins, *The Selling of DSM: The Rhetoric of Science in Psychiatry* (New York: Aldine de Gruyter, 1992), 81–90; Stuart A. Kirk and Herb Kutchins, "Is Bad Writing a Mental Disorder?" op-ed, *New York Times* (20 June 1994), 17; Stuart A. Kirk and Herb Kutchins, "Deliberate Misdiagnosis in Mental Health Practice," *Social Service Review 62* (June 1988), 225–237.
14. Goffman, *Asylums,* 131–132; Szasz, *The Myth of Mental Illness,* 296–308.
15. Scheff, *Being Mentally Ill,* xi.
16. George Rosen, *Madness and Society* (New York: Harper Torchbooks, 1969), 72–74.
17. Kenneth S. Kendler and Scott R. Diehl, "The Genetics of Schizophrenia: A Current, Genetic–Epidemiologic Perspective," in David Shore, ed., *Special Report: Schizophrenia 1993* (Rockville, MD: National Institute of Mental Health, 1993), 87–105; E. F. Torrey, A. E. Bowler, E. H. Taylor, and I. I. Gottesman, *Schizophrenia and Manic-Depressive Disorder: The Biological Roots of Mental Illness as Revealed by the Landmark Study of Identical Twins* (New York: Basic Books, 1994).
18. William H. Wilson, "Neuroscientific Research in Mental Health," in Ted R. Watkins and James W. Callicutt, eds., *Mental Health Policy and Practice Today* (Thousand Oaks, CA: Sage, 1997), 89–106; Scheff, *Being Mentally Ill,* xii; Milton E. Strauss, "Relations of Symptoms to Cognitive Deficits," and Darrell G. Kirch, "Infection and Autoimmunity as Etiologic Factors in Schizophrenia: A Review and Reappraisal," in David Shore, ed., *Special Report: Schizophrenia 1993* (Rockville, MD: National Institute of Mental Health, 1993), 4–6, 181–190.
19. Erik H. Erikson, *Childhood and Society* (New York: W. W. Norton, 1963), 247, 270–273.
20. Joshua Rolnick, "A Neuroscientist Says No to Drugs," *The Chronicle of Higher Education* (4 December 1998), A10; Lindsay Prior, *The Social Organization of Mental Illness* (London: Sage, 1993), 65.
21. R. Jay Turner and Donald A. Lloyd, "Lifetime Traumas and Mental Health: The Significance of Cumulative Diversity," *Journal of Health and Social Behavior 36* (December 1995), 360–362; Margaret E. Ensminger, "Welfare and Psychological Distress: A Longitudinal Study of African American Urban Mothers," *Journal of Health and Social Behavior 36* (December 1995), 346; W. W. Dressler, "Extended Family Relationships, Social Support, and Mental Health in a Southern Black Community," *Journal of Health and Social Behavior 26* (March 1985), 39–48.
22. Scheff, *Being Mentally Ill,* 88.
23. William A. Vega, Richard L. Hough, and Manuel R. Miranda, "Modeling Cross-Cultural Research in Hispanic Mental Health," in William A. Vega and Manuel R. Miranda, eds., *Stress and Hispanic Mental Health: Relating Research to Service Delivery* (Rockville, MD: National Institute of Mental Health, 1985), 3–5.
24. Donald G. McNeil Jr., "Large Study on Mental Illness Finds a Global Problem," *New York Times* (2 June 2004), 16; New Freedom Commission on Mental Health, *Achieving the Promise; Transforming Mental Health Care in America, Executive Summary,* DHHS Pub. No. SMA-03-3831 (Rockville, MD: Author, 2003), available online at www.mentalhealthcommission.gov.; Michael C. Miller, M. D., "Stop Pretending Nothing's Wrong," *Newsweek* (16 June 2003), 71–72; *Mental Health: A Report of the Surgeon General,* viii.
25. "Report Seeks Mental Help for Children," *New York Times* (4 January 2001), A17; *Health, United States, 2002,* 25, online at www.cdc.gov/nchs/products/pubs, 25; *Mental Health: A Report of the Surgeon General;* Marguerite Ro, *Forgotten Policy: An Examination of Mental Health in the U.S.* (May 2001), 4, online at www.communityvoices.org; "Children's Use of Mental Health Services

Doubles, New Research-Policy Partnership Reports," *Latest Findings in Children's Mental Health I* (Summer 2002), 1,3.

26. Ronald W. Manderscheid and Marilyn J. Henderson, *Mental Health, United States, 1998* (Washington, DC: U.S. Goverment Printing Office, 1998); U.S. Bureau of the Census, *Statistical Abstract of the United States: 1996* (Washington, DC: 116th ed., 1996), 137.
27. August B. Hollingshead and Frederick C. Redlich, *Social Class and Mental Illness* (New York: John Wiley & Sons, 1958), 216–217; and see, for example, Leo Srole et al., *Mental Health in the Metropolis* (New York: McGraw-Hill, 1962); Richard Neugebauer et al., "Formulation of Hypotheses about the True Prevalence of Functional Psychiatric Disorders among Adults in the United States," in Bruce P. Dohrenwend et al., eds., *Mental Illness in the United States: Epidemiological Estimates* (New York: Praeger, 1980), 55–60; Christopher G. Hudson, "The Social Class and Mental Illness Correlation: Implications of the Research for Policy and Practice," *Journal of Sociology and Social Welfare 15* (March 1988), 27–31; Jerome K. Myers and Lee L. Bean, *A Decade Later: A Follow-Up of Social Class and Mental Illness* (New York: John Wiley & Sons, 1968), 62–78.
28. Dan A. Lewis et al., *Worlds of the Mentally Ill* (Carbondale: Southern Illinois Press, 1991), 25–33; B. E. Jones and B. A. Grey, "Problems in Diagnosing Schizophrenia and Affective Disorders among Blacks," *Hospital and Community Psychiatry 37* (January 1986), 61–65; James S. McNeil and Roosevelt Wright, "Special Populations: Blacks, Hispanics, and Native Americans," in James W. Callicut and Pedro J. Lecca, eds., *Social Work and Mental Health* (New York: Free Press, 1983), 183–195; Sharlene Maeda Furuto and Jon Matsuoka, "The Appropriateness of Personality Theories for Social Work with Asian Americans," in Sharlene Maeda Furuto et al., eds., *Social Work Practice with Asian Americans* (Newbury Park, CA: Sage, 1992); National Center for Health Statistics, *Health, United States, 1995* (Hyattsville, MD: Public Health Service, 1996), 32; Manderscheid and Henderson, *Mental Health, United States,* 101.
29. "Black Adolescents, Teen Females Shorted on Psychiatric Aid," *NASW News 41* (February 1996), 15; Greg Yamashiro and Jon K. Matsuoka, "Help-Seeking among Asian and Pacific Americans: A Multiperspective Analysis," *Social Work 42* (March 1997), 176–186; Enola K. Proctor and Arlene Rubin Stiffman, "Background of Services and Treatment Research," in Janet Williams and Kathleen Ell, eds., *Advances in Mental Health Research* (Washington, DC: NASW Press, 1998), 266.
30. Quoted in William E. Kiernan and Jack A. Stark, eds., *Pathways to Employment for Adults with Developmental Disabilities* (Baltimore, MD: Brooke Publishing, 1986), 12–15.
31. Susan L. Crowley, "Who Will Care for Paula?" *AARP Bulletin 38* (May 1997), 5; R. C. Scheerenberger, *A History of Mental Retardation* (Baltimore, MD: Brooke Publishing, 1983), 3–87.
32. Eveline D. Schulman, *Focus on the Retarded Adult* (St. Louis, MO: C.V. Mosby, 1980), 9–11.
33. Kiernan and Stark, *Pathways to Employment for Adults with Developmental Disabilities,* 11; Schulman, *Focus on the Retarded Adult,* 10–11.
34. Duane F. Stroman, *Mental Retardation in Social Context* (Lanham, MD: University Press of America, 1989), 17–18.
35. Schulman, *Focus on the Retarded Adult,* 22; Martha Ufford Dickerson, *Social Work with the Mentally Retarded* (New York: Free Press, 1981), 20–22.
36. Harriett C. Johnson and Edward J. Hart, "Neurological Disorders," in Francis J. Turner, ed., *Adult Psychopathology: A Social Work Perspective* (New York: Free Press, 1984), 78–79.
37. The Arc (formerly Association of Retarded Citizens of the United States), "Introduction to Mental Retardation" (September 1993), 3, online at www.thearc.org/faqs/mrqa.html; Sandra Blakeslee, "4 Brain Chemicals in Babies May Fortell Autism and Retardation," *New York Times* (4 May 2000), A18.
38. Ethan B. Ellis, "Troubling Issues of Equity," *People with Disabilities 10,* New Jersey Disabilities Council (April 2000), 40–42; "Sharp Racial Divide in Down Syndrome Deaths," *Arizona Republic* (8 June 2001), A8.
39. Michael J. Begab, "Issues in the Prevention of Psychosocial Retardation," in Michael J. Begab, H. Carl Haywood, and Howard L. Garber, eds., *Psychosocial Influences in Retarded Performance,* vol. 1 (Baltimore, MD: University Park Press,

1981), 9–12; The Arc, "Introduction to Mental Retardation," 3.
40. Lynn McDonald-Wikler, "Disabilities: Developmental," *Encyclopedia of Social Work,* vol. 2 (Silver Spring, MD: National Association of Social Workers, 1987), 425; "Introduction to Mental Retardation," online at www.thearc.org.
41. The Arc, "Introduction to Mental Retardation," 1; Dickerson, *Social Work with the Mentally Retarded,* 32–38.
42. Dickerson, *Social Work with the Mentally Retarded,* 31; Scheerenberger, *A History of Mental Retardation,* 221.
43. David J. Rothman, *The Discovery of the Asylum* (Boston: Little, Brown, 1971), 1–7.
44. David Gollaher, *Voice for the Mad: The Life of Dorothea Dix* (New York: Free Press, 1995), 3; Murray Levine, *The History and Politics of Community Mental Health* (New York: Oxford University Press, 1981), 15–16; Nancy Tomes, "The Anglo-American Asylum in Historical Perspective," in Christopher Smith and John A. Giggs, eds., *Location and Stigma: Contemporary Perspectives in Mental Health and Mental Health Care* (Boston: Unwin Hyman, 1988), 3–4.
45. Rothman, *The Discovery of the Asylum,* 43–45, 130.
46. Levine, *The History and Politics of Community Mental Health,* 16; Rothman, *The Discovery of the Asylum,* xviii.
47. Michael B. Katz, *In the Shadow of the Poorhouse* (New York: Basic Books, 1986), 99.
48. Rothman, *The Discovery of the Asylum,* 153; Pennsylvania Hospital, *First Annual Report,* summarized in Rothman, 145.
49. Levine, *The History and Politics of Community Mental Health,* 16–19.
50. Gollaher, *Voice for the Mad,* vii, 132–215; James Leiby, *A History of Social Work and Social Welfare in the United States* (New York: Columbia University Press, 1978), 66–68.
51. Rothman, *The Discovery of the Asylum,* 265–295; Gerald N. Grob, *Mental Illness and American Society, 1875–1940* (Princeton, NJ: Princeton University Press, 1983), xi–xii, 8–15, 150–153; David J. Rothman, *Conscience and Convenience: The Asylum and Its Alternatives in Progressive America* (Boston: Little, Brown, 1980), 316–318.
52. Roberta Sands, *Clinical Social Work Practice in Community Mental Health* (New York: Merrill, 1991), 36–39; Norman Dain, *Clifford W. Beers: Advocate for the Insane* (Pittsburgh: University of Pittsburgh Press, 1980), 112–121; Prior, *The Social Organization of Mental Illness,* 88.
53. Grob, *Mental Illness and American Society, 1875–1940,* 126, 135–142.
54. Roy Lubove, *The Professional Altruist* (New York: Atheneum, 1969), 93–100.
55. Grob, *Mental Illness and American Society,* 145; Rothman, *Conscience and Convenience,* 319–375.
56. Rothman, *Conscience and Convenience,* 324–335.
57. Gerald Grob, *The Mad among Us: A History of the Care of America's Mentally Ill* (New York: Free Press, 1994), 116–124, 127–128.
58. Lubove, *The Professional Altruist,* 55–66, 77–80; Leslie Leighninger, *Social Work: Search for Identity* (Westport, CT: Greenwood Press, 1987), 11–12.
59. Levine, *The History and Politics of Community Mental Health,* 38–41; *The Community Mental Health Center* (Washington, DC: American Psychiatric Association, 1964), 3–4.
60. Levine, *The History and Politics of Community Mental Health,* 39–44; Albert Q. Maisel, "Scandal Results in Real Reforms," *Life* (12 November 1951), 140–142, 145–154.
61. Maxwell Jones, *Social Psychiatry in Practice* (Baltimore, MD: Penguin Books, 1958), 85–117.
62. Levine, *The History and Politics of Community Mental Health,* 46–47; *Action for Mental Health,* Final Report of the Joint Commission on Mental Health and Illness (New York: John Wiley & Sons, 1961), vii–xxxiii; *The Community Mental Health Center,* 1–7.
63. *The Community Mental Health Center,* 7.
64. Syracuse Psychiatric Hospital had originally been a psychopathic hospital. Reminiscences by Leslie Leighninger, 1967–1969; see also Robert Clurman, "The Patients Can Walk Out Anytime at Bronx State Mental Hospital," *New York Times Magazine* (2 April 1972), 14–24.
65. Levine, *The History and Politics of Community Mental Health,* 45.
66. Peter L. Tyor and Leland V. Bell, *Caring for the Retarded in America* (Westport, CT: Greenwood Press, 1984), 3–6.
67. Tyor and Bell, *Caring for the Retarded in America,* 8–10; Scheerenberger, *A History of Mental Retardation,* 55–56, 68–70.

68. Tyor and Bell, *Caring for the Retarded in America,* 10–14.
69. Scheerenberger, *A History of Mental Retardation,* 101–104; Tyor and Bell, *Caring for the Retarded in America,* 21–25.
70. Schulman, *Focus on the Retarded Adult,* 39; Tyor and Bell, *Caring for the Retarded in America,* 50–51; James W. Trent Jr., *Inventing the Feeble Mind: A History of Mental Retardation in the United States* (Berkeley: University of California Press, 1994), 29–30, 283, note 8.
71. Tyor and Bell, *Caring for the Retarded in America,* 34–49.
72. Tyor and Bell, *Caring for the Retarded in America,* 45.
73. Tyor and Bell, *Caring for the Retarded in America,* 108–114.
74. Wolf Wolfensberger, *The Origins and Nature of Our Institutional Models* (Syracuse, NY: Center on Human Policy, 1974), 53–61; Tyor and Bell, *Caring for the Retarded in America,* 118–120.
75. Scheerenberger, *A History of Mental Retardation,* 241–243.
76. Tyor and Bell, *Caring for the Retarded in America,* 123–142; Schulman, *Focus on the Retarded Adult,* 43–45. Examples of these reports include Goffman's *Asylums;* D. J. Vail, *Dehumanization and the Institutional Career* (Springfield, IL: Charles C. Thomas, 1967); and Burton Blatt, *Christmas in Purgatory* (Boston: Allyn and Bacon, 1966).
77. Tyor and Bell, *Caring for the Retarded in America,* 144–146; Scheerenberg, *A History of Mental Retardation,* 247–249.
78. E. Fuller Torrey, "The Release of the Mentally Ill from Institutions: A Well-Intentioned Disaster," *Chronicle of Higher Education 43* (13 June 1997), B4–5.
79. American Hospital Association, *Hospital Statistics: A Comparative Study of U.S. Hospitals, 1990–1991* (Chicago: AHA, 1990), 3; U.S. Bureau of the Census, *Statistical Abstract of the United States: 1991* (Washington, DC: 111th Edition, 1991), 113; Sharon Davis, The Arc, "A Key of Our Own," (October 1998), 3, online at www.thearc.org/report/98WAITLS.html; N. R. Kleinfield, "Patient's Quest for Normal Life, at a Price," *New York Times* (22 June 1997), 15.
80. Tyor and Bell, *Caring for the Retarded in America,* 149; Bruce L. Black, "Institutional Context and Strategy," in W. Richard Scott and Bruce L. Black, eds., *The Organization of Community Mental Health Services* (Beverly Hills, CA: Sage, 1986), 243–244.
81. Tyor and Bell, *Caring for the Retarded in America,* 147–149; Wolf Wolfensberger, *The Principle of Normalization in Human Services* (Toronto: National Institute on Mental Retardation, 1972), 7–54.
82. Paul Lerman, *Deinstitutionalization and the Welfare State* (New Brunswick, NJ: Rutgers University Press, 1982), 89–101; Levine, *The History and Politics of Community Mental Health,* 70–72.
83. Black, "Institutional Context and Strategy," 246–247; Lerman, 4–12; Steven P. Segal, "Deinstitutionalization," *Encyclopedia of Social Work,* vol. 2 (Silver Spring, MD: National Association of Social Workers, 1987), 378.
84. David Braddock, *Federal Policy toward Mental Retardation and Developmental Disabilities* (Baltimore, MD: Paul H. Brookes, 1987), 25–28; Richard C. Tessler and Howard H. Goldman, *The Chronically Mentally Ill* (Cambridge, MA: Ballinger, 1982), 193–195.
85. Richard R. Redlick, Michael J. Witkin, Joanne E. Atay, and Ronald W. Manderscheid, "Highlights of Organized Mental Health Services in 1992 and Major National and State Trends," *Mental Health, United States, 1996,* 91–94; "State Mental Health Authorities Downsizing Rapidly, Glover Says," *Mental Health Report 21* (16 April 1997), 61 (Robert Glover is the executive director of the National Association of State Mental Health Program Directors).
86. *Health, United States, 2000,* Table 110, p. 316.
87. Ursula Gerhart, *Caring for the Chronic Mentally Ill* (Itasca, IL: F. E. Peacock, 1990), 17–30; Sands, *Clinical Social Work Practice in Community Mental Health,* 186–187; Steven P. Segal and Jim Baumohl, "No Place Like Home: Reflections on Sheltering a Diverse Population," in Smith and Giggs, eds., *Location and Stigma,* 249–263.
88. Stephanie Saul, "A Lack of Mental Facilities Forces Patients to Jail Cells," *New Orleans Times Picayune* (8 June 1997), A25; "Court Orders NYC to Provide Discharge Planning to Inmates with Mental Illnesses," *NAMI* (National Alliance for the Mentally Ill) *Advocate* (Winter 2001), 20; Fox Butterfield, "Study Finds Hundreds of Thousands of Inmates Mentally Ill," *New York Times* (22 October 2003), 16.

89. *Mental Health: A Report of the Surgeon General,* 7; Sandra G. Boodman, "Are Former Mental Patients More Violent?" *Washington Post Health Supplement* (19 May 1998), 7; Nina Bernstein, "From Early Promise to Violent Death," *New York Times* (8 August 1999), 21.
90. Michael Winerip, "Bedlam on the Streets" *New York Times Magazine* (23 May 1999), 45–70.
91. Office of Counsel for the NY State Office of Mental Health, "An Explanation of Kendra's Law" (November 1999), online at www.omh.state.ny.us/omhweb/Kendra_web; Winerip, "Bedlam on the Streets," p. 70; Bazelon Center for Mental Health Law, "Summary of State Statutes on Involuntary Outpatient Commitment" (14 June 2001), online at www.bazelon.org/iocchart.html; Susie Steckner and Jodie Synder, "Getting to Recovery," *Arizona Republic* (17 January 2001), 1, 10; "How Can We Fix the State's Mental Health System?" *Arizona Republic* (27 January 2001), B6.
92. Bazelon Center for Mental Health Law, "Involuntary Outpatient Commitment" (25 May 2001), online at www.bazelon.org/iocpage.html; National Mental Health Association, "Involuntary Commitment, Executive Summary."
93. "Court Backs Option for Mentally Disabled," *NASW News 44* (September 1999), 6; Robert Pear, "Government Edict Seeks Home Care for Many Disabled," *New York Times* (13 February 2000), 1, 20; George W. Bush, Executive Order "Community-Based Alternatives for Individuals with Disabilities," (18 June 2001), online at www.whitehouse.gov/news/releases/2001/06/20010619.html.
94. "Senate Backs Fairness in Health Insurance," *Action Alert* (Washington, DC: Bazelon Center for Mental Health Law, 23 April 1996); "Poll Reveals 93 Percent of Americans Support Fair Coverage for Mental Health; Only 4 Percent Have It," *NMHA NEWS* (Alexandria, VA: National Mental Health Association, 4 June 1997); Kevin D. Hennessy and Howard H. Goldman, "Full Parity: Steps toward Treatment Equity for Mental and Addictive Disorders," *Health Affairs 20* (July/August 2001), 58–62.
95. David Braddock and Glenn Fujiura, "Politics, Public Policy, and the Development of Community Mental Retardation Services in the United States," *American Journal of Mental Retardation 95* (January 1991), 369–387; Tamara Henry, "Retarded Students Still Segregated," *USA Today* (30 October 1995), 1.
96. G. Thomas Bellamy et al., "Supported Employment," in Kiernan and Stark, *Pathways to Employment for Adults with Developmental Disabilities,* 129–137.
97. Susan L. Crowley, "Who Will Care for Paula? Future of Children with Disabilities Worries Parents," *American Association for Retired Persons Bulletin 38* (May 1997), 1–6; The Arc, "Community Living" (August 1997), online at www.thearc.org/faqs/comliv.html; Sharon Davis, "A Key of Our Own," 1–2.
98. The Arc, "The Arc Home Page" (2001), online at www.thearc.org.
99. James T. Havel, "Associations and Public Interest Groups as Advocates," *Administration and Policy in Mental Health 20* (September 1992), 27–44.
100. "Healthcare Services Rapidly Adapt to Change," *Standard and Poor's Industry Surveys 164* (11 January 1996), H5; Philip R. Popple and Leslie Leighninger, *The Policy-Based Profession: An Introduction to Social Welfare Policy for Social Workers* (Boston: Allyn and Bacon, 1998), 228–234; John V. O'Neill, "MCOs Hear Practitioners' Grievances," *NASW News 46* (February 2001), 1.
101. Joe Sharkey, "Mental Illness Hits the Money Trail," *New York Times* (6 June 1999), sec. 4, 5; Samuel H. Zuvekar, "Trends in Mental Health Use and Spending, 1987–1996, *Health Affairs 20* (March/April 2001), 216; *Effective Public Management of Mental Health Care,* Bazelon Center for Mental Health Law (May, 2000), online at www.milbank.org/bazelon/#status.
102. Jennifer Stevenson, Joseph Bevilacqua, and Chris Koyanagi, *Behavior Health Managed Care: Survey of the States (II)* (Washington, DC: Bazelon Center for Mental Health Law, June 1997), 1–8, 18–20; "Principles for the Provision of Mental Health and Substance Treatment Services: A Bill of Rights," online at www.naswdc.org/mental.htm.
103. Redick et al., "Highlights of Organized Mental Health Services in 1992 and Major National and State Trends," 91; Janet D. Perloff, "Medicaid Managed Care and Urban Poor People: Implications for Social Work," *Health and Social Work 21* (August 1996), 189–195; Bentson H. McFarland, "Health Maintenance Organizations and Persons

with Severe Mental Illness," *Community Mental Health Journal 30* (June 1993), 221–237; Bazelon Center for Mental Health Law, *Managing Managed Care for Publicly Financed Mental Health Services* (November 1995).

104. "Mental, Emotional, and Behavior Disorders in Children and Adolescents," Fact Sheet (Washington, DC: U.S. Department of Health and Human Services, Substance Abuse and Mental Health Services Administration, May 1996); John V. O'Neill, "Surgeon General Publishes a Must-Read," *NASW News 45* (May 2000), 5; Sherry Glied et al., "Children's Access to Health Care: Does Insurance Matter?" *Health Affairs 16* (January/February 1997), 167; Mary Keegan Eamon, "Institutionalizing Children and Adolescents in Private Psychiatric Hospitals," *Social Work 39* (September 1994), 589–592; "Children's Mental Health Services Program," National Mental Health Association, 1997.

105. Andrew Adesman, M.D., "Does My Child Need Ritalin?" *Newsweek* (24 April 2000), 81; Holcomb B. Noble, "Study Backs a Drug for Hyperactive Children," *New York Times* (15 December 1999), A16; "Connecticut Schools out of Drug Business," *Arizona Republic* (8 July 2001), A6.

106. Claudia Kalb, "Drugged-Out Toddlers," *Newsweek* (6 March 2000), 53; "Behavioral Drugs for Kids Top Antibiotics," *Arizona Republic* (17 May 2004), 1; Mary Leonard, "Youngsters Seen as Hot New Market for Prozac," *New Orleans Times-Picayune* (1 June 1997), A20; National Institutes for Health, "Ensuring Safe and Effective Psychotropic Medications for Children," *NIH News Advisory* (23 April 1999) online at www.nimh.nih.gov/; Peter S. Jensen, M.D., "When Should Medications Be Used in Children? Ethical Considerations," *NAMI News* (Winter 2001), 1–3; Erica Goode, "Fury, Not Facts, in the Battle over Childhood Behavior," *New York Times* (9 April 2000), sec. 4, 1.

107. Kessler et al., "The 12-Month Prevalence and Correlates of Serious Mental Illness (SMI)," 64–65; K. Minkoff and R. Drake, eds., *Dual Diagnosis of Major Mental Illness and Substance Disorders* (San Francisco: Jossey-Bass, 1991).

108. F. C. Osher and L. L. Kofoed, "Treatment of Patients with Psychiatric and Psychoactive Substance Abuse Disorders," *Hospital and Community Psychiatry 40* (1989), 1025–1030.

109. Stephen M. Rose and Bruce L. Black, *Advocacy and Empowerment: Mental Health Care in the Community* (Boston: Routledge & Kegan Paul, 1985), 55.

110. Rose and Black, *Advocacy and Empowerment*, 16, 57–69. See also Steven Wineman, *The Politics of Human Services* (Boston: South End Press, 1984), 43–47, 79–87.

111. Popple and Leighninger, *The Policy-Based Profession*, 218–225, 237–243; Carlton E. Munson, "Autonomy and Managed Care in Clinical Social Work Practice," *Smith College Studies in Social Work 66* (Special Issue: The Corporate and Human Faces of Managed Health Care) (June 1996), 241–260; NASW, *The Social Work Perspective on Managed Care for Mental Health and Substance Abuse Treatment* (Washington, DC: NASW, June 1993); Kevin Corcoran, "Managed Care, Implications for Social Work Practice," *Encyclopedia of Social Work, 1997 Supplement*, 191–200.

112. Lynn Wikler and Maryanne P. Keenan, eds., *Developmental Disabilities: No Longer a Private Tragedy* (Silver Spring, MD: NASW, 1983); Charles R. Horejsi, "Developmental Disabilities: Opportunities for Social Workers," *Social Work 24* (January 1969), 40–43.

CHAPTER

14

Housing, Homelessness, and Community Development

Lisa works full time at a salary well above minimum wage, but she is about to become homeless. One of her two children was seriously ill and her health benefits ran out quickly. Her small savings were soon exhausted and the bills continued to mount. Despite loans from her parents, she was unable to pay the hospital, feed her family, and still pay the rent, which was over a third of her income. After missing the second payment, she was evicted. She then doubled up with her sister, who also has two small children. The medical bills are now paid, but rents in the city continue to go up and landlords now want three months rent in advance. Her sister and brother-in-law helped her look for an apartment and will help her a bit with the first month's rent, but apartments in the only safe locations they can find will take 50 percent of Lisa's salary. Four children in a two-bedroom apartment is becoming an impossible strain on everyone. A shelter is the only alternative. Lisa cannot understand why someone who has a good job and works hard should be homeless.

Kate is an intelligent and independent young woman who also has a good job. She is a wheelchair user. Her life is full of too many curbs and stairways and too few ramps and elevators. In order to cook for herself, she had her apartment kitchen redesigned with lower counters and appliances. With members of the local Center for Independent Living and other advocacy groups, she had to picket the city transportation department in order to get buses with lifts so that she could take a bus to and from work, shopping, and recreation like other people.

Errol is an intelligent and independent young man who does not have a good job. He'd like to find one. Growing up in public housing wasn't easy. His mother's salary barely covered rent and food. The hallways, playgrounds, and streets provided daily opportunities to become a victim of crime (or to become a criminal). There was never enough heat in the winter, and the elevator rarely worked. Against great odds, Errol graduated from high school. But his large, big-city neighborhood has few jobs to offer. He must travel two hours by bus and subway to find any employment opportunities. Some of his friends said he was a fool to stay in school when he could make much better money selling crack for the local drug runners. He's beginning to think they were right.

Ella has maintained a keen mind and vigorous body throughout her seventy years of life. She has no trouble cooking for herself or maintaining the inside of the large old house in which she raised her family, but the exterior repairs are a problem. Most of her longtime neighbors have moved away. Houses around her have been divided into apartments, and their absentee landlords are allowing them to run down. She can no longer drive because of her poor eyesight. There is no public transportation in her area, and the grocery store, the shopping mall, the doctor's office, the library, the Cinema Six, and most of her friends are beyond walking distance.

Mary Ann is a single parent with two small children. Apartments near the center of the city where she works as a secretary are either too expensive or run-down and dangerous, so she lives half an hour away and commutes by car. There is no day care center near her office or her apartment. She takes her children to her cousin, who is also half an hour away, but in a different direction. The three-way commute leaves little time or energy for cooking, but convenience foods and fast foods are a strain on the budget. She finds herself short-tempered with the children and hits them when they misbehave. Guilt, anger, and frustration are daily companions.

Bill and Jennifer live in a distant suburb. Bill is a young executive who must often work late. Jen, an occupational therapist, has chosen to stay at home with their three children. She spends a good part of her day chauffeuring them to schools, lessons, soccer practices, choir rehearsals, and other events in their active lives. She would like to work part time but cannot find a position close enough to home. She likes her house and garden; her home's only problem is its distance from everything else. She has no contact with her former colleagues, and some days pass without a single adult conversation. Bill comes home late, sometimes after the children have gone to bed. He regularly must miss school plays and soccer games. He envies Jen's regular involvement with the children; she envies his opportunities to grow and be rewarded in his chosen profession. Sometimes the envy becomes resentment, and quarrels start over insignificant things.

Definitions of the Problem

Homelessness is a nightmare for increasing numbers of people in the United States. It is the most recent and dramatic sign of the difficulties we are having in providing shelter, a basic human need, to all citizens. Unfortunately, homelessness is only one of many problems with the way U.S. citizens are housed. Even more unfortunately, social workers have paid little attention to these problems.

Housing, like the weather, is something we tend to take for granted. Social workers usually confront only the most dramatic housing problems: babies bitten by rats or old people dying of heatstroke because they are afraid to open their windows. Most people rarely consider how the availability of decent housing and the way it is designed and distributed can cause problems or make existing problems (jobs, health, education, poverty, mental health, racial conflict) worse.

Housing conditions can spawn contagious diseases (a fact that brought about the first government intervention in housing), traumatic injuries (children falling out of windows that have loose screens), and death (entire buildings burned because of faulty wiring, gas leaks, or overloaded space heaters). Housing conditions can encourage crime (insecure entrances, dark hallways, or lack of windows to allow observation of public areas). Housing can strain family and marital relationships to the breaking point (too many people in too few rooms, or too much of the family income needed to cover rent or mortgage payments).

There is a further problem of housing that is even more subtle. Most of us tend to think of home as a place to get away from the world: as a haven or even a castle, "be it ever so humble." Perhaps this is why we so often ignore the fact that our homes may lack important links with the rest of the world. Housing isolates and segregates people as often as it unites them. It separates them from family members and friends who can help them and from services they need to sustain life. Although some housing problems involve dependence, most of them involve interdependence.

Thus, housing becomes a social welfare problem (1) when there is not enough of it; (2) when it is too expensive for people to afford; or (3) when its design, location, or quality cause problems for those who live in it. The problem is complicated by the fact that housing can be seen both as a basic right to which all are entitled and as a commodity that is bought like other things in the marketplace. These two perspectives are frequently in conflict and lead to different solutions to housing problems.

Actors in the U.S. Housing Situation

Housing is not like the weather. We can understand the complex forces that produce housing problems, and we can change them. Let us begin with a look at the variety of actors involved in the field of housing.

Builders

Home building is a labor-intensive industry. Traditionally, most home builders have been relatively small local businesses because it is expensive to transport materials long distances. Building is a seasonal occupation in most parts of the country. It is also sensitive to changes in the economy; if interest rates go up or wages go down, fewer people can buy homes.

Since World War II, more large home-building companies have entered the market. They are able to cut their costs by building many identical houses on large tracts of cheap suburban land. The size of these companies is also an advantage as they go about persuading local municipalities to provide the necessary services for these tracts and lobbying all levels of government for favorable tax and subsidy policies. The builders' main representative is the National Association of Home Builders. This group, like the organizations representing bankers, realtors, and insurance companies, makes major financial contributions to political campaigns and is highly influential in local, state, and federal policymaking.[1]

Developers

Developers coordinate the acquisition of land and arrange for it to be used in new ways. They recruit investors, arrange for bank loans, plan the use of the land they acquire, and hire builders to execute the plans. Part of developers' plans may involve houses, apartment buildings, and condominiums; but a variety of other constructions are likely also to be involved, including office buildings, shopping centers, parking lots, and industrial parks. Sometimes these developments are carefully planned to accommodate the varied interests of the people who will use these new facilities, as well as the impact the developments will have on existing neighborhoods around them. Will nearby neighborhoods be disrupted by noise and traffic? Will there be enough parking? What has to be torn down to make room for the development? Sometimes these considerations are inadequately planned for or ignored.

Most cities and states have laws and ordinances to regulate what builders and developers can do. Zoning, which specifies certain uses for certain areas, is a common method of regulation. For example, zoning can forbid commercial activities in some residential areas, it can require minimum numbers of parking spaces for new businesses or apartments, and it can discourage the cutting up of single-family houses into apartments.

Bankers

Most people cannot afford to pay the entire cost of a house at the time of purchase, so they must borrow money in order to become homeowners. Banks lend the money and earn interest on their investments. Banks are also important in the maintenance of houses because they provide loans for home repair and improvement.

Bankers, like builders, are interested in housing as a commodity, as something to be exchanged. They profit from the exchange. Homeowners may share that perspective to a degree because they too will profit if the market value of the house appreciates. But they are also concerned that the house be safe and comfortable and that it otherwise meet their shelter needs. This "use value" is different from, and sometimes at odds with, the "exchange value" of the house.

If the homeowner cannot continue to make the mortgage payments, the bank will become the owner of the home. This fact requires banks to make judgments about both the abilities of a borrower to make the payments and the quality and resale value of the house. In making these judgments, bankers may be influenced by biases against African Americans, women, old houses, ultramodern houses, or inner-city neighborhoods. It is often difficult to separate these general biases from realistic judgments about the worth of an individual buyer or house. Such biases are often felt to be based on sound business practice. However, if bankers systematically refuse to lend to buyers of a certain group or a certain neighborhood, for whatever reason, this has important consequences; it usually guarantees the decline of the neighborhoods affected. A refusal to lend money to certain geographic areas is known as *redlining* and is now prohibited by federal law.

Insurance Companies

A house is a major investment for individuals and banks, and that investment must be protected in the event of destruction of the house by fire, flood, or storm. Insurance companies provide protection for a fee. Insurance companies set the fees (premiums) based on their judgment of the risk and potential profit offered by a particular homeowner, house, or neighborhood. Like bankers, insurance executives can be influenced in their judgments by a variety of biases. They too can accelerate the decline of a neighborhood by refusing to insure buildings in it. Denial of homeowners' insurance means buyers can't get mortgages, so it functions as another form of redlining.

Government

Federal, state, and local governments have been heavily involved in housing for more than a century. Governments usually provide the roads, sewers, and electrical and water connections to new housing tracts and businesses. Governments make this investment in the belief that development will provide jobs for residents and because the new residents will increase the tax base. Of course, this new tax revenue may be offset by tax breaks that municipalities sometimes grant to encourage developers. Recently, cities have begun to question whether such tax breaks may actually outweigh any financial benefit to the city the development may bring.

In some areas development is highly profitable and does not need to be encouraged. In these cases, the process is reversed: Governments can get help or concessions from developers. Builders of luxury condominiums in some cities, for example, are required to either build or contribute to the building of low-income housing.

The federal government has a prominent role in encouraging home building and home ownership by providing low-cost, below-market mortgage loans. By allowing the deduction of the interest on mortgage payments from income tax, the U.S. government also provides a huge subsidy to homeowners. The size of the subsidy increases directly with the size of the mortgage, so the wealthy benefit much more than middle-income owners.

Governments, especially the federal government, may also build subsidized dwelling units and attempt to prevent discrimination against members of minority groups in the housing market. As we shall see, however, the federal government's involvement in many of these activities has declined dramatically in recent years. Governments are now being forced to find ways to cope with the effects of urban sprawl: smog, traffic congestion, deterioration of the city center, racial and economic polarization, loss of green space and farmland, and a declining tax base. "Smart growth" initiatives that attempt to limit or redirect development are being proposed and fought in many cities.

Realtors

Most people who buy houses do so through real estate agents. These people connect buyers with sellers and receive a commission, usually based on the sale price of the house, as payment for their service. Realtors and their agents can "steer" buyers by showing them only houses in certain neighborhoods. Through steering, real estate agents can reinforce racial segregation (by showing African-American buyers only houses in African-American neighborhoods and vice versa, for example) and can promote neighborhood decay (by not showing old houses in inner-city neighborhoods). Racial steering is illegal by federal law, but proving its occurrence is difficult. As with bankers and insurance executives, it is often hard to know to what extent prejudice enters this process and to what extent it is driven by pure financial consideration. Because the agent's commission is based on the price of the house, showing expensive houses in expensive neighborhoods is in the realtor's interest.

Local boards of realtors are usually active in politics, particularly in zoning and school tax issues. They are represented in Washington by the National Association of Realtors, a powerful lobbying group representing more than 800,000 members and 1,840 local boards.[2]

Landlords

Renting a home to others can be a service or a source of profit, or both. For a landlord who wants to maintain a house in good condition and benefit the neighborhood, renting can be risky. Although the majority of renters take good care of their units, an irresponsible tenant can do a lot of damage in a short time. Landlords protect themselves by practices such as charging security deposits as well as the first and last month's rent at the time of occupancy. This practice can have the effect of making it impossible for a person with a low income and no savings to rent a home.

Landlords may also screen tenants carefully. This presents another opportunity for prejudice to enter the process. Landlords with only a few units cannot be prosecuted for discrimination.

Making a profit, or even breaking even, is not always easy for the responsible landlord. For those who do not care about the quality of the houses they own or the neighborhoods their houses are in, it is much easier to make a profit. Charging the highest rents the market will bear and neglecting repairs guarantees maximum profit. When the building has deteriorated to the point at which no one will rent it or the city condemns it (a process that can take quite a long time), it is abandoned. Abandonment can also occur when a landlord with limited resources cannot pay maintenance costs and taxes.

Community Groups

Neighborhoods of all types and income levels can organize neighborhood associations to further their interests. One important purpose can be simple socializing—providing opportunities for people to get to know one another. But most neighborhood groups have larger agendas: dealing with burglars or a crack house, getting their share of community services such as streetlights or garbage pickups, maintaining the quality of the local school, combating redlining, sharing information, or planting flowers.

Because builders and developers are usually able to secure the cooperation of local governments, it is often neighborhood organizations that mobilize opposition to projects that may threaten resident interests: a shopping center that will triple traffic through the neighborhood, a fast-food restaurant that will increase litter, or a factory that will level an entire neighborhood. (Communities may also fight for less noble causes such as opposing group homes for people with disabilities.) Community groups don't always win against the developers or city halls, but their efforts can result in modifications of a project and can encourage developers to plan more carefully on the next project.

In recent years, some community groups have become producers of housing themselves. Community development corporations (CDCs) have been attempting to fill gaps left by the private market and the federal government and are rehabilitating or building housing for low-income members of the community.

Advocacy Organizations

Many advocacy groups promote community interests and housing concerns on the local, state, and national levels. Increasingly, groups interested in organizing the poor are using housing as a mobilizing issue.

On the national level, National People's Action speaks for the social and physical preservation of neighborhoods. The Community for Creative Nonviolence was transformed by the late Mitch Snyder, a housing activist, into an organization that advocates for the homeless. The National Coalition for the Homeless is a federation of local advocacy groups. See the "Web Sites" section at the end of the chapter for other advocacy and policy organizations.

Research

In order to deal with problems of housing and homelessness we need accurate and up-to-date information. Until 1984 the federal government produced an Annual Housing Report on the condition of the nation's housing stock. As part of its withdrawal from housing, the Reagan administration began issuing the American Housing Survey every two years. This gap is partially filled by the annual State of the Nation's Housing report published by the Joint Center for Housing Studies of Harvard University, which provides an overview of trends and conditions but much less detail (see "Web Sites on Housing and Community Development").

Statistical Picture of Housing

Though housing affects our lives in many ways, the most dramatic effect is the lack of it. So let us look first at homelessness. The problem has received considerable attention and has provoked much political debate. Conservatives see little cause for alarm; liberals see a failure of national housing policy; radicals see a critique of some of the basic aspects of U.S. society.

Counting the homeless is difficult. Just counting the occupants of homeless shelters isn't enough. Many homeless people avoid shelters because they are often unsafe, always lack privacy, and may involve bureaucratic harassment. The Census Bureau's 2000 count is regarded by the bureau itself as an underestimate for this reason. A count over three days of shelters, soup kitchens, and known outdoor sleeping places produced a total of 280,527 homeless people . A much more comprehensive count was undertaken by the Urban Institute in 1996. They sampled a broad range of service providers who put them in contact with more homeless people and also revealed that 27 percent of service users who were homeless did not use shelters. They concluded that in a given week, 842,000 people, including 205,000 children, were homeless, and in the course of a year, between 2.3 and 3.5 million people experienced homelessness. These figures are now almost a decade old, but no comparable studies have been attempted since, and individual cities continue to report increasing numbers in their service systems. In 2003, New York City found 9,249 families, including 16,500 children, in their shelters. The U.S. Conference of Mayors publishes an annual hunger and homelessness report covering twenty-five of the country's largest cities. Its 2003 survey found an increase in requests for food assistance of 17 percent over 2002 and an increase of 13 percent in requests for emergency shelter. Most cities saw resources declining as needs rose.[3]

We have to think more carefully about the definition of homelessness. Those who are "doubled up"—people living temporarily with friends or relatives who don't really have room for them, or several families sharing space designed only for one—are not on the streets. But do they really have homes? And how long will it be before they reach the streets? Do those in "welfare hotels" or "transitional housing" have a home? They're waiting for one, but the wait can be lengthy. Are people in jails, detoxification centers, or mental hospitals at home? They are "housed" now, but their lease will be up soon. Most estimates are confined, for the sake of convenience, to the "visible homeless," those living on the streets or in temporary shelters; but we must understand that these people are only a part of a much larger problem.[4]

Other statistics about homelessness are equally slippery. About one-third of homeless adults are estimated to have a serious mental illness, though the types of disorders have changed over time. Mental illness may be as much an effect of homelessness as a cause. Many disorders occur after the onset of homelessness. The discharge of people from mental hospitals (deinstitutionalization) is generally considered to be one of the major causes of homelessness. But the stress of being homeless can itself contribute heavily to mental problems. So cause and effect can run both ways. Elliot Liebow observed that among the homeless women he got to know while working as a volunteer in shelters around Washington, D.C., symptoms of mental illness diminished considerably when SSI or other benefit checks arrived and increased as the money was spent.[5]

Drug and alcohol addictions are also commonly reported among homeless single men, who make up the majority of the homeless population. The availability of cheap crack cocaine in the mid-1980s is thought by many to have had a major role in the sharp rise in homelessness in the latter part of that decade. Current addiction estimates range from 30 to 75 percent. But drug and alcohol use may be a response to as well as a cause of homelessness. Christopher Jencks understands why someone with limited resources and housing options might decide that "a crack high, however brief, is worth more than a scuzzy cubicle." He notes that the cost of rooms in skid row hotels rose much faster than the cost of liquor, making "oblivion cheaper than privacy."[6]

Though our image of a typical homeless person may be that of a crazy bag lady or a skid row drunk, it is important to know that 40 percent of the nation's homeless are families with children. Their numbers are growing. The Conference of Mayors reported an overall increase in demand for shelter in 2003 of 13 percent but an increase of 15 percent by families. In some cities the increase was as high as 38 percent.[7]

Not all homeless people are the long-term destitute. Many have their health and family supports; some even have jobs. What most lack is affordable housing—that is, housing that fits within their incomes. Although incomes for college-educated citizens increased in the 1990s and mortgage rates went down, boosting home ownership, incomes dropped for the lowest segment of the population while rents at the lower end of the market have risen considerably. In 2003, average renters were paying almost 27 percent of their income. Thirty percent were paying 50 percent and some pay even more. This leaves little left over for food and other necessities. The Joint Center for Housing Studies of Harvard University reached the chilling conclusion that "[h]ouseholders with one full-time minimum-wage earner cannot afford to rent a modest, one-bedroom apartment anywhere in the country." Even young people with good incomes are leaving areas where they grew up because they cannot afford houses there.[8]

The problem of homelessness has been made worse by the loss of low-income housing units. One type of housing, single-room-occupancy residential hotels, or SROs, has typically served low-income single people in large cities. But, in the late 1970s, such hotels began to be torn down to make way for more lucrative upper-class housing or commercial development. Chicago, for example, lost nearly two-thirds of its SRO units between 1977 and 1987. At the same time, conversion to condominiums, abandonment, demolition, arson, and other factors contributed to the loss of low-income dwelling units in general, including apartments for families.[9]

Little of this lost affordable housing is being replaced, and public programs have failed to fill the gap. In past decades, the federal government countered low-income housing shortfalls through federal housing programs. During the Ford and Carter administrations, for example, 500,000 low-cost housing units were built. During the Reagan administration, the figure dropped to 17,000. The Clinton and Bush administrations have torn down old units and built new ones, but usually in numbers smaller than the original.[10]

Families can spend years on waiting lists for public housing, subsidized housing, or housing vouchers. In the largest public housing authorities, time on the waiting list increased 50 percent between 1996 and 1998, from twenty-two to thirty-three months. In Cleveland and Washington, D.C., the wait is five years; families in Oakland, California, wait six years; and the wait in New York City is eight years.[11]

People can also wait a long time for housing vouchers, which provide a government subsidy that gives renters access to apartments in the private market they could not otherwise afford. The 1999 HUD study noted above found that it can take five years to get a voucher in Memphis and Chicago, seven in Houston, and ten in Los Angeles. Currently only one in three of those eligible get vouchers. Nor does gaining a voucher guarantee housing. Nationwide, the success rate was 69 percent in 2000, but rates varied widely and went as low as 37 percent in some areas. It took successful renters an average of eighty-three days to find a place; some took over six months. A 1994 study found considerable discrimination based on race, age, and disability. The 2000 report found no such differences in success rates. The voucher program has helped 1.5 million people find shelter in the private sector, though it serves only a fraction of those in need. The fact that the success rate has dropped twelve percentage points since 1993 is further cause for concern.[12]

Homelessness, however, is only one factor in the housing picture. Home ownership, a cherished goal in U.S. society, is also undergoing change. Home ownership showed a steady rise (slowed briefly during the Great Depression), from less than half the population's owning their homes in 1920 to almost two-thirds in 1980. After leveling off in the 1980s, ownership resumed its climb in the late 1990s, to 67.9 percent in 2002.[13]

However, the value of older homes appreciates in most markets and the cost of new homes increases faster than inflation or salaries. Making the jump from renter to owner gets harder for low- and middle-income families. Those who manage to make the jump may find themselves with the same cost burden as renters: paying 50 percent or more of their income to maintain their mortgages. In fact, homeowners in this predicament, 7.3 million, now outnumber renters.[14]

Though minority home ownership has increased in recent years, discrimination and segregation remain strong. Minority applicants are often charged higher mortgage interest rates, steered by real estate agents away from white neighborhoods, and refused rental opportunities. A HUD study tested discrimination by sending pairs of applicants with identical credentials, one minority and one white, to try to buy or rent homes in twenty-three housing markets across the country. Whites received preferential treatment more than half the time.[15]

Despite the fact that many large cities are becoming more diverse, resistance to neighborhood integration is as strong as ever. Middle-class African Americans are less segregated than poorer ones, but not much. The one sign of a countertrend is the discovery by whites that homes in middle-class African American neighborhoods are a bargain.[16]

Minority status also has a strong impact on housing quality. For example, in 2001, Hispanics were twice as likely as whites to occupy houses with moderate to severe physical problems and almost four times as likely to have unsafe drinking water. African

Americans had better drinking water than Hispanics but worse physical problems in their houses.[17]

It is clear that we face many serious issues regarding housing. The most immediately pressing are housing shortages and the effects of residential segregation. However, ongoing issues of housing quality are also of concern. What lies behind these problems and issues? Why is affordable housing in such short supply? What factors affect the type and quality of housing available in the United States today? The following section examines these questions.

Dynamics of Housing

Homelessness came to national attention in the 1980s. Everyone agreed that the numbers of those without permanent shelter had increased dramatically, even as they disagreed about why. Some wanted to blame the problem on homeless individuals, others on institutional factors; but separating the two is difficult. Mental illness and drug or alcohol addiction were common individual explanations, though both problems preexisted the rise in homelessness. In the case of mental illness, an institutional factor intervened. Beginning in the 1950s, as we discussed in Chapter 13, there was an effort to return hospitalized people to their communities. The creation of Medicaid in 1965 and Supplemental Security Income in 1971 gave those who needed continuing care and those who could not work resources enough to at least keep a roof over their heads.

But as the effort to clear out mental hospitals progressed, people with the least ability to survive on their own were reached. New community mental health facilities were promised, but the tax revolt of the 1970s prevented their creation. So people were now on the streets with little ability to care for themselves and no mental health services to support them.

Drug and alcohol abuse were also traditional causes of homelessness that can be blamed on individuals. The appearance of crack cocaine in the mid-1980s offered a new and inexpensive form of intoxication and probably brought a new crop of addicts into the streets. But institutional factors enter here as well if one asks why some people seek escape from the world by using mind-altering substances. Lack of social and material well-being or the promise of it in the future may be a significant factor.

The slowing of the economy in the 1980s and the transformation from manufacturing to service and high-technology industries brought higher unemployment for unskilled workers. There was less work in general and less work that offered advancement in particular. This may have contributed to homelessness during that decade. However, unemployment was very low at the beginning of the new millennium, and yet homelessness persisted. The problem is not the lack of jobs but the lack of jobs that offer health benefits and advancement to higher salaries. This remains a problem and feeds back to the causes of addiction. It could be that some people just have bad attitudes toward work, though a recent investigation of this hypothesis found no support for it.[18]

Another individual factor not often discussed by social workers and social scientists is disaffiliation. Some people just may not like the restrictions of family relationships and jobs. They are suspicious of authority, find social service bureaucracies tyrannical, and don't want help if it means being made to conform to others' expectations. They may therefore be defined as homeless by choice.

Most social workers find the theory of voluntary disaffiliation distasteful, but the theory is worth exploring, particularly if you consider the possibility that these attitudes may be the result of growing up in abusive families. David Wagner, in his ethnographic study of homeless people in a small city in Maine, concludes that most of the people he got to know were indeed from neglectful or abusive families. Because of this, or for other reasons we discuss later, they also had distrust of authority, a streak of rebelliousness, and a capacity to resist rather than endure oppression.[19]

The strongest institutional explanation is loss of affordable housing. Both public and private sectors have contributed to this. Government "urban renewal" programs destroyed much of the inner-city housing stock in the 1960s and 1970s. As we noted earlier, the cost of housing that remained has risen faster than inflation and wages. The improving economy in the 1990s drove rents up still further because one segment of the economy *had* experienced great rises in salary and were willing to pay outrageous prices for shelter that might otherwise have been available to those with low or middle incomes. Taking advantage of this demand, developers now often convert older low-rent apartment buildings into luxury condos.

One name for the transformation of low-cost housing is *gentrification.* Run-down neighborhoods and lovely old houses are given new life when new owners restore the buildings and patronize local businesses. Saving historic buildings and revitalizing the local economy is a good thing for everyone except the original tenants who cannot afford to live there anymore.

As affordable housing disappears in the private market, there has been nothing to replace it in the public sector. As we discuss later, the Reagan administration did its best to pull out of public housing, and the Bush and Clinton administrations generally followed this lead. Instead, they offered vouchers to help those with low incomes find places in a private market they are increasingly priced out of.

A final institutional factor is public assistance. Studies comparing those who become homeless with those who manage to stay housed find that what often tips the balance is the disappearance of some form of public support: unemployment compensation, General Assistance, SSI, TANF, or some other means of income maintenance. In terms of health and mental health, addiction, disaffiliation, or employment history—the individual factors—the two groups look pretty much the same. Public institutional supports keep them off the streets.[20]

Commodity or Right?

Beneath all these causes of the shortage of affordable housing exists an underlying dynamic: the tendency in the United States to view housing as a commodity rather than as a basic right. Although federal housing legislation since the 1940s has declared shelter to be a right of all citizens, the tendency, particularly in recent years, has been to think about housing in terms of its ability to produce a profit. When builders build to sell and each owner trades for profit in the marketplace, housing prices will tend to rise. One might argue that the laws of supply and demand would hold down prices; that is, that once there was an abundant supply of housing, sellers would no longer be able to attract high prices.

However, high prices often exist even when housing supplies are adequate. The reasons behind this are complex and not entirely understood. Some analysts contend that the situation occurs because the housing market, particularly the rental market, is not truly competitive. The ownership of rental housing is often concentrated in a relatively small number of hands. These owners have the possibility of market control; they can raise rents without much competition from others. In addition, consumers of rental housing may not have a lot of choice in their decisions. Discrimination against minority families, families with children, or the poor can limit the possibilities of where they can rent. (However, discrimination against families was largely outlawed in 1989 when new federal rules prohibited "adult-only" housing except for strictly defined older adult complexes.) Finally, just as in the area of health care, consumers are to some extent a captive audience—housing is not something they can easily cut back on or go without.[21]

Profits, and concurrent high costs in housing, can also be bolstered by government intervention. As critics of current housing policy have noted, when housing policy is made in Washington, the process reflects the "interaction of the Administration and Congress on the one hand, and the various nationally organized interest groups on the other." Business interests are well represented and very influential in this process. The result is housing policies that operate, at least in part, to enhance "the profitability of the housing sector and of the business community as a whole."[22]

Residential Segregation

Minority status is also an important dynamic affecting housing price, availability, and quality. Discrimination against minorities, as we shall see, has been a significant factor in the history of housing in the United States. Its most obvious manifestation appears to be racial and ethnic residential segregation. There has been an ongoing debate among researchers, however, about the degree to which segregation is caused by socioeconomic factors, rather than by outright discrimination against minority groups. Some studies contend that factors such as income level or occupation explain much of the segregation existing in U.S. communities. Crime, which is perceived to be associated with minority neighborhoods, rather than racial prejudice is thought by some to explain white avoidance of integrated neighborhoods. But closer examination shows that neither class nor fear of crime explains segregation entirely, and socioeconomic factors work differently for different ethnic groups. One study concluded that "whether measured in terms of education, income, or occupation, Spanish–white segregation declines unambiguously with increasing socioeconomic status." With African Americans, it does not. In other words, skin color matters.[23]

History of Housing

One approach to understanding the history of housing in the United States is to see it as a reflection of social values. Writers such as architectural historian Gwendolyn Wright view housing as embodying many images and attitudes in our society: ideas about gender roles, images of the ideal family, attitudes toward immigrants and African Americans, opinions about the role of government and the market, and beliefs about the nature of democracy. Housing can also be seen as an instrument of social control; that is, as a mechanism for maintaining a docile workforce, keeping women "in their place," or a race "in its place."[24] In addition, one can think about housing in terms of its relationship to other factors in the environment, such as health and employment. Social reformers dealing with problems in these and other areas have sometimes focused on changes in housing as the key to broader reform. The work of these reformers is an important piece in housing history. As we shall see, there is a certain degree of overlap between social reform and social control. Both proceed from the belief that if you structure housing, you can influence other aspects of people's lives as well. All of these themes are interwoven as we trace the development of housing in the United States from the mid-nineteenth century to the present.

Housing Trends from the Mid-1800s through the 1920s

Several important housing patterns became prominent in the United States of the nineteenth and early twentieth centuries. These included the city slum, the middle- and working-class suburb, and the company town.

The urban slum developed in the mid-1800s as poor immigrants from Ireland joined other impoverished groups crowded in major cities such as New York and Boston. Speculators responded to increased housing needs by constructing tenements, which were multistory buildings built especially to house the poor. A typical apartment design was the "railroad flat," a long, narrow unit in a flimsily constructed building that might house twelve or more families altogether. Only those rooms facing the street or the narrow back alley received direct light. Often a single backyard privy served all residents of the building.[25]

These conditions prompted reformers to action. Physicians, charity workers, and concerned citizens saw slums as breeding grounds of poverty and disease. The Association for Improving the Conditions of the Poor (AICP) was a New York City–based charity organization founded in 1843. Although AICP members believed that poverty stemmed in part from moral defects within individuals, they also saw crowded slums as contributing to laziness, crime, drunkenness, and sexual promiscuity. Like other reformers, AICP members also feared the effects the slum would have on the rest of the city. Epidemics and social unrest could spread beyond its borders. AICP's solution to the problem was the "model tenement," a more spacious and sanitary building constructed by a socially minded private investor who was willing to limit profits.[26] The model tenement was not particularly successful, however. AICP-sponsored tenements delivered only a tiny financial return, and the buildings deteriorated quickly.

Reformers were more effective in the area of government regulation of health and housing conditions. In New York in the late 1860s, lobbying on the part of reform groups led to the establishment of a Metropolitan Board of Health and the enactment of a local tenement house law (the first in the country). The law set fairly low standards, such as one privy for every twenty persons, and it was not well enforced. However, it had a symbolic value: It asserted the community's right to limit the freedom of the tenement builder and the landlord.[27]

The growth of the slum proceeded dramatically as the "new immigrants" from southern and eastern Europe flooded into New York, Chicago, Cleveland, and other metropolises in the 1880s and 1890s. Most of these immigrants were poor, unskilled laborers or subsistence farmers. Lacking the knowledge and resources to survive in rural areas, they remained in the cities, joining former countrymen in slum neighborhoods. Immigrant families often worked in their own homes, sewing garments and rolling cigars at piecework wages. This added to the congestion of their living situations. In New York, 70 percent of the population lived in multiple-family dwellings by 1893. Four-fifths of these buildings were tenements, and almost all were privately owned and operated for profit.[28]

During this period, Jane Addams and others in the social settlement movement joined in the campaign to improve poor living conditions. Shocked by the crowding and filth in the slums around them, workers spoke of "garbage-strewn streets," "pale, dirty, undersized children," and sights such as the room on a hot summer day "crowded with scantily-clothed, dull-faced men and women sewing upon heavy woolen coats and trousers."[29]

In response to these experiences, settlement residents attacked the housing problem. One settlement worker surveyed housing conditions in Jersey City in 1902. As she gathered information, landlords threatened her and sometimes drove her away. When her results were published, however, the governor of the state was so impressed that he appointed a special tenement house commission to look into the problem. Other settlements also used studies to publicize deficient housing in order to gain public sympathy and an official response. Hull House, for example, prepared detailed maps and surveys of the tenements in its neighborhood. Through the efforts of settlements and other reform groups, Chicago got a tenement house ordinance in 1902.[30]

Many housing reformers at the turn of the century believed that laws defining minimum construction and sanitation standards would do much to solve the problem of the slum. A major accomplishment was the New York Tenement Law of 1901. This law, written by housing expert Lawrence Veiller, established strict standards dealing with fireproofing, ventilation, and overcrowding. The legislation was an improvement over the earlier New York housing code, in that standards were higher and more carefully enforced.[31]

Housing codes and legislation improved the situation to some degree, but they did not eliminate the bulk of slum housing. The alternative approach of building model tenements continued through the early 1900s. In New York, reporter Jacob Riis was a major publicizer of the model tenement idea. Riis exposed the realities of life in the slum in gripping photographs and in books such as *How the Other Half Lives.* But model housing rarely returned even a 5 percent profit to the philanthropists who built it, which suggested the need to go beyond private markets if working people and the poor were to be adequately housed.[32]

While the urban poor lived in slums or public lodging houses, other trends developed for the more affluent. These included apartment living in cities for the well-to-do and a move to the idyllic home in the suburbs for the middle class. Migration out of the cities intensified in the 1870s. The suburbs began to be seen as an avenue of escape from the health hazards, social unrest, and vice of urban areas (a perception that continues today). Development of public transportation, such as the streetcar, made it possible to commute to work and shopping in the city. The growth of building-and-loan associations enabled middle-class and some working-class families to borrow money for mortgages.[33]

The suburban home was fast becoming the symbol of personal expression and middle-class status. It also represented the importance of the nuclear family, and particularly of that family pattern in which the father dealt with the demanding world of work and the mother provided a nurturing, private haven in the home. This "cult of domesticity," as historians now call it, stressed the importance of women providing a strong moral and educational influence within their families. The suburban home, protected from the evil influence of the city, seemed the perfect setting in which to do this.[34]

The company town represented another, less congenial counterpart to city living, this time aimed at the working class. Beginning with the early nineteenth-century textile mill industry in New England and the South, manufacturers built factories and rental housing for workers in areas away from the congested and supposedly corrupting cities. The houses were small, and families generally took in boarders to help pay the rent. Despite the cramped conditions and inadequate sanitation facilities, factory owners felt the regular rows of identical cottages presented an organized system that would inculcate middle-class values in the minds of employees and their families. They also built dormitories for young working-class women, wherein their lives were strictly regulated.[35]

The planned industrial communities of the early 1900s were expanded versions of the earlier mill towns. Factory owners hoped that the provision of housing and other amenities would keep workers content, make them more efficient, and prevent the rise of unions. Some industrialists built large communities for their employees, complete with churches, schools, libraries, and social facilities. They hired welfare secretaries (an early version of the industrial social worker) to act as moral police, recreational planners, and counselors for their tenants. Some company towns were reasonably democratic. Others, like that erected by George Pullman of the Pullman railway car company, were autocratically run. These fit a popular slogan among manufacturers: "A Housed Labor Supply Is a Controlled Labor Supply."[36]

Planned communities also began to appear in middle-class suburbs. They reflected a desire for homogeneity in both the appearance of the houses and the social class of their residents. This was achieved by "restrictive covenants," which prevented sale of property to Asians, Jews, or African Americans. Restrictive covenants were upheld by the courts. In poorer neighborhoods, homogeneity was enforced by violence. When residents of Chicago's "black belt" tried to escape their crowded neighborhoods, they were attacked in the streets and their houses were bombed. The violence escalated into race riots in 1919, which convinced most black Chicagoans that their only safety lay in remaining in the ghetto.[37]

The Origins of Modern Housing Policy

It is often assumed that the first federal involvement in housing occurred during President Franklin Roosevelt's New Deal. But federal involvement actually began in 1913, when home mortgage interest and taxes were made deductible from federal income tax. This tax credit was instituted to encourage home owning and remains a significant housing subsidy—which, because it is proportional to the value of the home (or homes), tends to benefit the rich quite a lot, the middle class somewhat, and the poor renter not at all.

By the 1920s, housing was becoming more expensive because the costs of lumber and labor were going up with no accompanying rise in productivity. Most houses were built by small builders. During that same period, factory wages were stagnant. An affordability crisis was looming.

Tenement housing in the industrial cities was getting worse as more workers came seeking jobs. Under the supervision of Edith Abbott, dean of the University of Chicago's School of Social Service Administration, social workers documented in detail the unsanitary and dilapidated conditions of the slums. This research helped bring the problem to public attention.

Calls for government intervention came from across the political spectrum, including real estate and banking interests. President Herbert Hoover responded in 1932 with the Federal Home Loan Bank Bill, to make housing capital available through federally supervised mortgage banks, and the Reconstruction Finance Corporation, to make loans for low-rent housing. But by then the Great Depression was under way. Little housing was being built, and the rate of bank foreclosures on homeowners was reaching epidemic proportions. Homeless people moved from city to city in search of jobs, finding temporary shelter in shantytowns often referred to as "Hoovervilles."

Thus, there was already considerable support and precedent for government intervention in housing when the Great Depression swept Roosevelt into power. One of the New Deal's first pieces of legislation was the National Industrial Recovery Act. Title II of this act called for a massive building program and created the Public Works Administration (PWA) to oversee it. A social worker, Mary Simkhovitch, was influential in persuading the bill's architect, Senator Robert Wagner, to include low-cost housing in the program.[38]

The administrator of PWA was Secretary of the Interior Harold Ickes, a crusty Chicago lawyer with a reputation for thoroughness and honesty. Although Ickes moved too slowly for those who wanted a swift reduction of unemployment, he avoided the kind of scandals that plagued some of the projects of his rival in public works, the Works Progress Administration (WPA), headed by social worker Harry Hopkins. And most of the projects built by the PWA are still standing seven decades later, many still performing their original functions.[39]

The Housing Division of PWA encountered considerable difficulty but managed to construct 25,000 units in fifty-eight sites throughout the country. The buildings were probably "for many decades the finest urban housing in America." They had heating and indoor plumbing and often stoves and refrigerators, amenities that were not always available in some middle-class apartments. Though created for low-income tenants, the buildings nonetheless had to charge rents high enough to allow their municipal owners to pay off the loans that were their part of the financing of the project. (PWA projects were financed partly with federal grants and partly with loans or local funds.) Thus, the PWA apartments were not for the poorest of the poor. Tenants were often moderate-income families. African Americans benefited from PWA housing and from the schools and hospitals it built. They also gained employment at wages equal to whites on PWA projects, which had a policy against racial discrimination. But PWA did not challenge segregation in the South. Techwood and University Homes in Atlanta were equal but separate.[40]

Federally sponsored public housing was just one of the Roosevelt administration's responses to the housing crisis. Another was the creation of the Federal Housing Administration (FHA), which provided insurance for low-down-payment, low-interest mortgage loans for the purchase of new homes or rehabilitation of older ones. Many middle-income white families were thus able to become homeowners. African Americans benefited far less because FHA not only tolerated exclusion of minorities by developers but also actively encouraged it. The FHA also practiced redlining, which furthered the growth of slums and the abandonment of the inner cities.[41]

An effort was made to make housing a permanent part of the public agenda. But the U.S. Housing Act of 1937, again drafted by Wagner with input from Simkhovitch, was eventually gutted by its opponents. Instead of continuing PWA's tradition of well-designed, solidly built, well-appointed units, the provisions of the bill dictated the absolute minimum of costs and amenities. Publicly supported housing was to be for only the poorest of the poor. There would be not the slightest possibility that these units could compete with private construction. The underlying philosophy was that tenants would and should want to get out as fast as possible. The result was that almost all public housing constructed since the 1940s has been cheap, monotonous, and easily identified as "poor people's housing." Cheap or not, however, it was badly needed. The United States Housing Authority, which administrated the new legislation, built 340 housing projects across the country, accommodating 120,000 families. Despite years of wear, much of it is still in use and, remarkably, still appreciated.[42]

The legacy of New Deal housing policy was what policy historian Gail Radford calls "a two-tier pattern of well-legitimized, relatively generous state support for the middle and upper segments of the population and poorly regarded, poorly funded programs for the less affluent."[43] The top tier includes the FHA loans, the mortgage interest tax credit, and the federally funded highways that allow middle- and upper-income workers to commute to the suburbs. These are all things we don't tend to think of as housing subsidies. The bottom tier is what became public housing: the boxes built for warehousing the poor, now being rehabilitated by dynamite.

Radford argues that in the New Deal era, mixed-income, mixed-use public housing similar to housing being constructed in Europe at the time might have found favor in the United States, and that a universalistic policy that might have improved the quality of life for all citizens was possible. She points out that universalist programs such as Social Security benefit everyone and generally enjoy broad political support. Residualist, means-tested programs, however, are much more vulnerable to budget cutting or abandonment when political winds change. By accepting a two-tiered policy in the 1930s, then, we set the stage for the death of public housing.

Housing Policy after the New Deal

During World War II, public housing resources were devoted to accommodations for defense industry workers. One by-product of this was racial conflict in areas where many such workers were African American. In Chicago a housing project built in a neighborhood previously occupied by poor Italian families was subjected to gunfire from the dispossessed Italians. Three years later, African American veterans brought into temporary housing in white areas were met with mob violence.[44] Prejudice and hatred are easily fueled by scarce resources, and housing is a particularly important resource.

Returning veterans at the war's end brought more pressure on the housing stock. The existence of low-cost mortgage loans from the FHA and the Veterans Administration helped many veterans find shelter for their families. Some went to mass-produced housing developments in new suburbs. A continuing migration of African Americans from the rural South to northern cities placed great strain on urban ghettos.[45]

In an attempt to make the best use of expensive city land, both public and private housing developers looked upward. High-rise buildings seemed a vision of the future that was both practical and romantic. The images of noble skyscrapers surrounded by parkland that were being drawn by European architects were inspiring. These structures proved quite popular with upper-income city dwellers, but their execution in public housing was another story (see the "Closer Look" feature on Pruitt–Igoe).[46]

"Urban Renewal"

Even large high-rise projects did not fill the need for affordable housing for the poor, and shortages persisted for middle-income families as well. The Housing Act of 1949 was intended to provide more housing for all income levels and at the same time to revitalize the commercial centers of cities. In the 1950s the age of "urban renewal" began. Bulldozers brought down entire neighborhoods. The structures themselves were probably no loss to the world, but the communities that occupied them were. However, there was little protest when neighborhoods were uprooted and dispersed. Urban renewal was seen as Progress, and these communities were in the way.[47]

The buildings that grew in their place were often office buildings and high-priced housing out of the reach of the former occupants. Critics of the program often charged that "urban renewal equals Negro removal." But the urban renewal program did set a precedent for a more comprehensive approach to urban problems.[48]

African Americans were attempting to break out of the ghettos. Those who could afford middle-class housing looked for other options. Some real estate agents saw an opportunity for profit in this and developed the strategy of "blockbusting." They would try to convince homeowners that African Americans were about to move into their neighborhoods. Those who panicked would sell their homes at below-market prices. These homes could then be sold to newcomers at above-market prices, which African Americans were willing to pay, having no other choice except the ghetto.[49]

The 1964 Civil Rights Act banned discrimination in housing but was difficult to enforce. And legal desegregation of public housing was rapidly being undermined by economic resegregation. The poorest of the poor were often African American, and public housing was their best option. White families with more choices moved out. Other groups for whom housing options were improving were older citizens and those with disabilities. Housing support programs for them began in 1959 and continue to the present. One reason these programs were successful was that Congress was willing to provide higher funding levels so that these projects could be built much like conventional apartment buildings rather than cheap, "poor people's" housing. By the end of the 1970s, elders were one-third of all public housing residents.[50]

The Age of HUD

A sense that housing problems required more than piecemeal solutions prompted the Johnson administration to create a cabinet-level Department of Housing and Urban Development (HUD) in 1965. The following year, the Model Cities program attempted to bring a more comprehensive approach to the interwoven problems of poor housing, education, and job opportunities. President Lyndon Johnson also experimented with public–private partnerships, a trend whose importance has grown in the succeeding decades. The Housing Act of 1968 gave subsidies to private lenders and developers for construction of multifamily low- and moderate-income housing.

Despite growing awareness of the need for a comprehensive policy on urban and community development, HUD has never had such a policy to guide it. The agency has shifted focus with each new administration. George Romney, its secretary under Richard Nixon from 1969 to 1973, tried to develop an industrialized housing industry that could prefabricate units along the lines of mobile homes. Jack Kemp, HUD secretary under George Bush, saw the department as an antipoverty agency. One of Reagan's secretaries, Sam Pierce, used HUD programs to enrich businesses with administration connections.[51]

Beneath this surface of shifting leadership, four trends continued to develop. The first was a move away from federal government provision of public housing. The second was a shift of focus from housing construction to one of assisting individuals to find affordable housing in the private market. The third trend was the placement of increasing responsibility for housing problems on state and local governments. Fourth was a growing realization that the provision of other social services within the context of general community development was essential to solving housing problems.

The Housing Act of 1974 reflected the first three trends. Its Section 8 offered subsidies to encourage housing developers to produce and maintain low-income units, as well as vouchers to individual renters to help them find shelter in places they could not otherwise afford. This program had the political advantage of benefiting developers through low-cost financing. It also bailed out financially insecure projects by ensuring rental income. Some analysts contend, in fact, that Section 8 has helped developers far more than individual renters.[52]

Section 8 vouchers also represent the beginning of the fourth trend, a blurring of the missions of HUD and the Department of Health and Human Services (HHS). Vouchers are really a kind of income support, not that different from food stamps, WIC, or TANF. Income support is part of the traditional mission of the HHS. Other human services such as counseling, early childhood and youth programs, anticrime measures, and congregate services to elders became linked to housing. This was a reasonable development, but it further blurred administrative roles.

The 1974 act also created Community Development Block Grants (CDBGs), which sent federal housing money (in smaller and smaller amounts) to local communities to use as they saw fit. Moreover, CDBG funds did not have to be used on housing. This formula for moving the federal government out of involvement in social problems became the centerpiece of the Reagan administration.

Another important step in the direction of community development was the Community Reinvestment Act (CRA) of 1977. Its purpose was to stop redlining and to

A CLOSER Look

The Destruction of Pruitt–Igoe

The Wendell Oliver Pruitt Homes and the William L. Igoe Apartments, thirty-three high-rise buildings built by the St. Louis Housing Authority, were occupied in 1954. They were designed by a famous architect, Minoru Yamasaki, and were considered models of modern public housing. By 1972 the buildings were notorious centers of crime, vandalism, and destruction. Few apartments were occupied; the empty ones were looted of pipes and plumbing fixtures. Residents were attacked in the halls and on the grounds. Nonresidents refused to enter the area. The elevators were broken and used as bathrooms. The Housing Authority declared the buildings unfit for habitation and dynamited them.

What went wrong with this "model" project? Some critics believe that the style of modern architecture, with its simple geometric forms and plain surfaces, is sterile and monotonous, and stigmatizing and alienating to residents. Others believe that high-rise living is inappropriate for most people, particularly families with small children. This does not seem to be a problem for high-income apartment dwellers, however.

Specific problems with the Pruitt–Igoe design must be considered. These included lack of security at the building entrances, and no private or semiprivate space outside the buildings that the residents could defend and control. The open spaces outside the building became the turf of roving gangs.

Site planning was completely absent. The relationship of the dwelling spaces to other aspects of life was not considered. There was no day care center, no school, no health facility, no recreation center in the project, no shopping or services nearby.

The architect attempted to provide "vertical neighborhoods" within the buildings. Every third floor had a screened gallery that combined laundry and storage facilities with a play area for small children. Families could gather here and keep an eye on their children. In practice, however, these vertical neighborhoods never developed. And the buildings were overcrowded from the beginning. Two-thirds of the apartments had one or two bedrooms, while the average resident had four or more children. In public areas, paint was considered a "luxury," and lighting was minimal. The middle-income families originally in residence soon moved out, and the Housing Authority began concentrating welfare-dependent, multiproblem families in the project. This, of course, meant a decline in rent revenue; the Housing Authority tried to save money by performing minimal maintenance.

encourage home ownership by requiring banks to serve all neighborhoods in the area in which they are chartered. A study conducted on its twenty-fifth anniversary reported over $1 trillion in loans to low-income areas, including increases in lending to minority homeowners and more small business loans stimulated by CRA. The recent wave of bank consolidations, however, may make lenders less responsive and flexible in assessing applicants.[53]

Reagan and Bush Housing Policies. The first congressional hearings on homelessness were held in 1982. The Reagan administration, which had earlier denied this was a national problem, responded by declaring it a temporary problem and authorizing the Federal Emergency Management Agency (FEMA), the agency that is supposed to deal with natural disasters such as hurricanes and floods, to spend $100 million on emergency food and shelter.[54]

The dynamiting of Pruitt–Igoe, 1972. Bad policy, not bad architecture, rendered this St. Louis housing project unlivable.

The elevators were not maintained. Because of overcrowding, they broke down frequently. They were unpleasant to use even when they were repaired. To save money, they were designed to stop only on gallery floors, so two-thirds of the residents had to walk up or down a floor. Also eliminated from the design were first-floor bathrooms.

So, all in all, what went wrong? The design had some weaknesses from the beginning; but more important were the cost-cutting measures imposed by the Housing Authority—the skip-stop elevator, no first-floor bathrooms, no paint in the public areas. Garden apartments, which might have provided defensible space on the first floor and prevented the grounds from becoming "no man's land," were cut out of the design.

Overcrowding the buildings, concentrating the poorest and neediest families in one place, and then withdrawing maintenance were the fatal blows. No buildings, however well designed, can be expected to stand up to those conditions. The dynamite that destroyed Pruitt–Igoe was social as well as chemical.

Sources: "Slum Surgery in St. Louis," *Architectural Forum* (April 1951), 129–136; Jane Holtz Kay, "Architecture," *The Nation* (24 September 1973), 284–286; George McCue, "$57,000,000 Later," *Architectural Forum* (May 1973), 42–45; William Moore Jr., *The Vertical Ghetto* (New York: Random House, 1969); Lee Rainwater, *Behind Ghetto Walls* (Chicago: Aldine, 1970); Katherine G. Bristol, "The Pruitt–Igoe Myth," *The Journal of Architectural Education* 44 (May 1991), 163–171.

President Reagan's second response was to ask communities to use their CDBGs to deal with homelessness. Communities recognized homelessness as a problem, even if Reagan did not, and spent $34 million on it by October 1983. Congress authorized $60 million that year for shelter rehabilitation; the president threatened to veto the legislation.[55]

The Stewart B. McKinney Act of 1987 was the main piece of legislation responding to homelessness during the Reagan administration. It authorized $1 billion annually, mainly for emergency shelters. Much of this money was never spent. The program was complex and burdened with red tape, and it involved multiple federal agencies. The application for participation was sixty-six pages long. Nonetheless, some communities did manage to secure funds and used them for transitional housing as well as shelters.[56]

The Department of Housing and Urban Development slashed operating subsidies for existing public housing and encouraged localities to sell off their older units. In 1981, Section 8 rules were changed so that renters had to pay at least 30 percent (up from 25 percent) of their income. By 1987, Section 8 subsidies to builders had almost disappeared. Instead of expanding the allowances to individuals, Reagan promoted the use of housing vouchers. Unlike Section 8 allowances, vouchers do not have to be used solely for rent. The housing chosen does not have to meet the same standards required in the Section 8 program. The administration's attitude was succinctly summed up by a HUD official in 1985: "We're basically backing out of the business of housing, period."[57]

The Reagan administration frequently argued that they were spending more money, not less, on housing than previous administrations. And they were. However, this spending went to projects authorized under the Ford and Carter administrations that were just getting under way. Congress kept the projects alive during the 1980s, but Reagan drastically cut the authorization for future expenditures.

Reagan's hopes for getting poor people into the private housing market went unrealized because the subsidies the government was willing to give were far below current market levels. Three out of every four vouchers issued in New York City were returned because the holder could not find a way to use them. Programs for enabling residents of public housing to buy their own homes were similarly unrealistic. In 1985 the Public Housing Homeownership demonstration project tried to sell public housing units to those who lived in them. After four years, less than 25 percent of the selected units were actually transferred. A project in Charlotte, North Carolina, banked a portion of the tenants' rent for seven years in hopes of allowing them to accumulate enough money for down payments on houses. But the accumulated amount was far below that necessary to get into the market. More important, those tenants who wanted to move out of public housing were afraid to do so because they realized that if, because of illness or job loss, they missed a mortgage payment, they could easily become homeless. They knew that because of long waiting lists they would never get back into public housing. (It is important to note here how lack of national health care has a major impact on a seemingly unrelated problem such as housing.)[58]

The Republican effort to focus housing policy on ownership in the private market persisted. The Cranston–Gonzalez National Affordable Housing Act of 1990 provided block grants to local housing authorities, which some hoped would be used to construct affordable housing. It also created Home Ownership and Opportunity for People Everywhere (HOPE) to privatize public housing. The hope of HOPE was that tenants of public housing, despite past evidence to the contrary, could buy their apartments. In 1992, HOPE VI was added to rehabilitate public housing units while moving some residents into the private market using vouchers. HOPE VI has so far demolished 72,000 public housing units, replacing about three-quarters of them. Many residents moved out into better housing and safer neighborhoods, but more than half are having difficulty paying rent and utilities and still having enough for food, even with vouchers.[59]

The most successful part of Reagan's attempts to stimulate construction of low-income housing in the private sector was a tax credit for this purpose in the Tax Reform Act of 1986. This tax credit has been responsible for 94 percent of the low-income housing, about 600,000 units, constructed since 1986. This is hardly enough to solve the problem, but it has been some help to communities in all fifty states. At the same time, however, the act eliminated deductions that encouraged residential construction in general and increased depreciation periods on rental units. These changes decreased overall construction of rental units.[60]

Clinton Housing and Community Development Policies. "President Clinton came to office with a crowded agenda," says one critic, "and housing was nowhere on it."[61] Clinton's vice president Al Gore even talked about abolishing HUD. Nonetheless, Clinton appointed a HUD secretary who was not going to be just a caretaker. Henry Cisneros, the former mayor of San Antonio, worked hard to restore the tarnished reputation of HUD. He was in office only a few months when he received a grim reminder of the problems he faced. Yetta Adams, a forty-three-year-old homeless woman, froze to death on a bench in front of HUD headquarters.

Cisneros took steps to mobilize both money and technical assistance. He served fourteen times more homeless people than previous administrations. He organized sweeps in public housing projects to drive out drug dealers, and then provided buildings with extra security so that the dealers could not return. He began tearing down the worst high-rise public housing units and replacing them with low-rise, less dense buildings (though not enough to replace those lost).[62] He made it easier for Section 8 landlords to evict tenants who had committed crimes, and he moved to replace landlords who were not maintaining their buildings. He cut HUD staff from 13,600 to 10,400 with the goal of stabilizing it at 7,500. He took over the problem-plagued housing authorities in Philadelphia and Chicago and filed desegregation plans in Texas.[63]

Cisneros also wanted to "break up the concentration of crime- and drug-ridden public housing by dispersing residents from the projects throughout the metropolitan area."[64] To avoid opposition from middle-class neighborhoods to "scattered-site" public housing, he followed a program pioneered in Chicago and focused on dispersing individual families. In exchange for increased job opportunities, relative safety, and more pleasant surroundings, the families risked hostility and harassment from their new neighbors and schoolmates. This takes exceptional strength and determination. Still, there was no lack of applicants. And a recent study shows the risk is worth it. Though there was no noticeable improvement in school or job performance, there was considerable improvement in the behavior of boys and the mental health of mothers and a dramatic decrease in injuries to children.[65]

In Clinton's second term, Cisneros was replaced by Andrew Cuomo, an experienced housing advocate. Cuomo followed his predecessor's policy of increasing local control of public housing and of trimming HUD staff to 7,500. He persuaded Congress to maintain Section 8 contracts, continued to crack down on landlords who misuse federal funds, and brought jobs to public housing residents.[66]

Cuomo also introduced a program to encourage police officers, firefighters, and teachers to live in inner-city neighborhoods by helping them buy houses at half price. The option was taken by 6,000 employees, but in several cities participants were reselling the houses or renting them but not living in them. The General Accounting Office (GAO) found other examples of financial mismanagement persisting through the end of Cuomo's term.[67]

The Republican-dominated Congress tried to abolish HUD in 1994 and the Community Reinvestment Act in 1995. They also wanted to repeal the 1937 Housing Act, deregulate public housing and rental assistance, end preferences for people with disabilities or mental illness, and allow housing authorities to designate some buildings as "elderly only." All these efforts were unsuccessful.[68]

One congressman, Rick Lazio of New York, suggested that eight hours a month of community service ought to be required of all those who benefit from public housing or rent subsidies. A housing advocate thought this was a great idea as long as it included all those getting the subsidy of mortgage interest tax deduction. That would bring 27 million people, including the ultrarich, into the community as volunteers.[69]

In 1996, President Clinton signed the law replacing Aid to Families With Dependent Children with Temporary Aid to Needy Families (TANF). Its main purpose is to force recipients to seek employment by terminating benefits after two years. And, indeed, many states have terminated thousands. As we have seen, the available jobs rarely provide sufficient income to escape poverty status. It seems apparent that there is a connection between TANF terminations and the rise in shelter and food bank applicants.

Congress did manage to pass a Housing Reform Act in 1998. It included provisions to reverse the trend of concentrating families with very low incomes in certain housing projects. It allowed housing authorities to disregard a tenant's increased income for a year or longer in calculating rent increases, and required them to include at least one tenant on their advisory boards, though it allowed them to appoint these individuals rather than having other residents elect them. The act repealed "federal preferences," which may achieve the congressional desire to give no special consideration to people with disabilities and mental illnesses. The bill also included Lazio's community service requirement, though, to no one's great surprise, it did not include middle- and upper-income beneficiaries of housing subsidies.[70]

Bush II. Mel Martinez, George W. Bush's HUD secretary, had little housing experience before his appointment, and his two-year term caused little notice. His attempts to reduce the costs of mortgage loans were abandoned in the face of opposition from banking and real estate groups. In 2003 he was replaced by Alphonso R. Jackson, who headed the Dallas Housing Authority from 1988 to 1996, the first African American to hold such a position. Jackson gained a reputation as a good manager and an opponent of corruption. He will need these skills because the concerns about fraud and waste identified by the GAO under Cuomo remained under Martinez. Lack of oversight over private contractors who do increasing amounts of public business is a particular problem. The Bush administration is now planning to replace HOPE VI with yet another program to encourage home ownership and is proposing to raise rents in public housing.[71]

Current Issues and Trends

Homelessness

Homelessness disappeared from the public radar screen for a while. William Raspberry tracked the number of headlines in the *Washington Post* from 1990, when there were 149 headlines including the word *homeless,* through 1995, when the number had dropped to 45, to October 1998, when there were only 14 at the time he was writing. Had the problem been solved, he asked? Or had reporters tired of the topic and citizens simply stopped noticing homeless people on the streets? Were we suffering from "compassion fatigue"? Raspberry concluded that the latter was more likely, and he was right. The following year, city governments, emboldened by public indifference, began dealing with the problem by putting it out of view. Homelessness became a crime across the nation. In New York City, Mayor Guiliani began police raids on shelters and had anyone sleeping on the streets arrested. In Orlando, one can be fined $500 or sent to jail for sixty days for sitting on the sidewalk. New Orleans removed benches from Jackson Square because homeless people were sleeping on them. Tent cities and other makeshift housing have been cleared from many cities.[72]

A force bringing homelessness back into public view is the spectacle of people who work full time and make decent wages becoming homeless because of the rapidly rising cost of housing. The improving economy has hurt many while helping others. As we have seen, apartments in major cities and high-tech areas such as Silicon Valley are now far beyond the means of middle-income families.

As noted earlier, the U.S. Conference of Mayors annually reports increases in requests for shelter and food. America's Second Harvest, an organization that coordinates distribution to 80 percent of the nation's food pantries through 212 warehouses, reported a threefold increase in demand between September 2001 and May 2003.[73] Clearly, homelessness is not going away. The real problem, however, is that homelessness is increasingly defined as a temporary situation that can best be dealt with by building more temporary shelters. Until it is seen as one part of a much larger problem of the disappearance of affordable housing, it can only get worse.

Community Responses

Ronald Reagan wanted to decentralize government and place primary responsibility for dealing with social problems with local communities. Though he did little to shrink the size of the federal bureaucracy (and expanded the federal budget enormously), he did succeed in forcing communities to seek their own solutions to housing, homelessness, and community development. The communities recognized the need for addressing these problems and were driven to find other funding to replace the federal programs. The response has been dramatic.

One of the most interesting and successful community responses has been the creation all over the country of community development corporations (CDCs). These are local coalitions of neighborhood organizations working with human service professionals, businesses, and local government officials. They patch together funding from businesses, foundations, state and local governments, and what remains of federal programs. One CDC director explains, "We're really nonprofit entrepreneurs. We combine the public purpose of government with the flexibility . . . of the private sector, and we're directly accountable to the community." Many CDCs have their roots in the community struggles of the War on Poverty. Their members gained experience administering federal programs during the 1970s and 1980s. So they were not totally unprepared for this new world of creative fund-raising and interagency coalition building.[74]

State and local governments were also ready to adapt. The New Deal housing programs had required the creation of agencies to finance and manage public housing. Urban renewal programs gave these agencies more experience. The states' traditional role of establishing authority for locally enforced building codes, zoning and land use policies, and real estate taxation gave them tools to use in new ways.

Two important foundations active in nurturing CDCs are the Local Initiatives Support Corporation (LISC), started by the Ford Foundation, and the Enterprise Foundation, created by developer James Rouse. These organizations provide technical assistance and function as intermediaries, helping persuade private investors to become involved in CDCs. There are now about 4,000 CDCs in operation. Together they have built or rehabilitated more than 550,000 housing units and created 247 private sector jobs.[75]

CDCs, in addition to forging partnerships to build housing, have also been instrumental in creating local housing trust funds. This effort involves persuading state and local governments to dedicate a share of ongoing revenue, such as a real estate transfer tax, to fund low-income housing. Having a guaranteed source of income relieves the CDCs from some of the exhausting work of project-by-project fund-raising.

Other ways of developing stable sources of support include levying impact fees: requiring developers to set aside part of their profits to reimburse the community for lost housing, traffic congestion, or parking problems. Another tactic is inclusionary zoning, which requires developers of luxury housing either to include some low- and moderate-income housing in their projects or to give the community money to develop its own.

Still another way to make home ownership affordable is through a community *land trust.* This is a private, nonprofit organization that sells homes but leases the land they stand on. If you leave, you sell the house back to the trust at a prearranged price. You get back what you put in, any improvements, and some appreciation, but not full market value. This insulates property from speculation, which can drive up prices. It means that you cannot make huge profits in the real estate market, but this is a worthwhile trade-off if, without the land trust, you would never have been in the market in the first place.[76]

Community development is no longer a totally nonprofit endeavor. Retailers are realizing that cities are not inhabited only by gangs, addicts, and people on welfare. There are plenty of people with jobs, incomes, and consumer needs. Borders has just opened bookstores in downtown Detroit and Uptown Chicago. Venture capitalists have also begun to discover the possibilities of starting businesses in low-income areas.[77]

Community development corporations are also starting local businesses. A community-owned enterprise is not going to run to another town in search of cheaper labor or lower taxes. The owners of major league athletic teams do not hesitate to turn their backs on loyal fans in one city if another can offer a fancier new stadium. Green Bay, Wisconsin, does not have that problem—it owns the Packers. Community development financial institutions (CDFIs), such as the South Shore Bank of Chicago and the Union Savings Bank in Albuquerque, are banks committed to local investment. They have had major impacts on both housing and businesses in their communities. Starting from the inside with public and nonprofit entities may be easier and more successful in the long run than "enterprise zone" programs that try to get private investors to come in from outside.[78]

Design

In recent years there have been many attempts to make large low-income housing projects more livable through reorganization and redesign. These efforts involve changing the mix of tenants, changing the project sites, and/or changing the buildings.

In the beginning years of public housing, tenants were carefully screened and conformity to standards of behavior and lifestyle were rigidly enforced. Housing authority social workers made home visits to check on hygiene and upkeep and to offer instruction on how to use the new appliances. Though few would want to return to white-gloved kitchen inspections, many housing officials and residents have brought back tenant screening, sometimes with the help of residents' councils, and have expedited evictions for troublemakers. One-strike-and-you're-out policies are gaining favor. Building sweeps to confiscate drugs and weapons have alarmed civil libertarians but are usually applauded by residents. In some buildings, residents sign pledges not to use drugs. All of this can bring some stability to the projects, which is a first step to community building and other improvements. It also exiles the most troubled families and individuals to even worse fates.[79]

In early public housing it was also common to have a mix of incomes. University Homes in Atlanta, one of the first PWA projects, included teachers and even some doctors and lawyers in its community. This was to a great extent a comment on the limited housing options for African Americans in the 1930s, and current conditions are dramatically different. But there was, and still is, some representation of the working poor in public housing. Also, some projects now maintain not only employed low-income tenants and the very poor, but also tenants who pay market-rate rents. There are renovated units that can attract market-rate renters, usually in locations close to downtown jobs and amenities.

Lake Parc Place in Chicago has a 50–50 mix of very-low-income tenants and low-income working renters. In Boston, Harbor Point has two-thirds market-rate and one-third very-low-income tenants, and Langham Court has a third of each. This kind of mix not only provides a much more viable economic base but also offers the possibility that working tenants will serve as role models for the unemployed. Sociologist William Julius Wilson has argued that what traps many inner-city residents in poverty is both the lack of job opportunities and the lack of any chance to see people supporting themselves and their families through regular employment. The role-modeling theory is popular with both liberals and conservatives and merits close attention. Interaction between groups may need some guidance, however. Ethnographic studies suggest that effects can be negative as well as positive. The hoped-for models, some not that far away from poverty themselves, may want to shore up their status by distancing themselves from their less well-off neighbors, who may in turn feel snubbed and disrespected.[80]

In some all-high-rise projects, a few of the towers are being torn down and replaced with row houses. Projects that were isolated in park environments are being reconnected to the urban grid so that access to shopping and services is easier. Open public spaces are being regrouped to permit more limited access and more resident surveillance. Giant projects are being subdivided into fenced neighborhoods so that residents can interact more easily and learn who belongs and who doesn't. Most important, services are being brought into the housing estate itself. Renaissance Village in Cleveland converted one building into a "social services mall" where one can find day care, job training, and a food co-op.[81]

Structural modifications to individual buildings can also help create more safety and comfort. Shared hallways and staircases are notorious as shelters for gangs and drug dealers. In Renaissance Village, a common entrance was replaced with individual entrances, complete with porches, giving residents control over their own doorways and the ability to keep an eye on their neighbors. At Boston's Harbor Point, shared entrances were not eliminated, but redesign cut traffic down by giving large families first-floor apartments with their own entrances. This left the common entrance to the elevator for the smaller apartments of couples, elders, and those with small children. Thus, there was a lot less going in and out; it was easier to keep the door locked and nonresidents out.

One way that poor people have survived in urban areas is by opening small businesses they can run out of their homes, yards, gardens, or garages. One architect who appreciates this is Michael Pyatok, who has built affordable, mixed-use housing complexes in Oakland, California, with space for such enterprise. Zoning ordinances can be an impediment to such projects, but a livable city requires a reconsideration of how people actually live.[82]

None of these design strategies on its own is guaranteed to make low-income housing projects decent places to live. They have the best chance to work if combined. A secure, well-maintained building with a mix of tenants and good access to community amenities and services has the best chance of resisting crime and urban blight.

Triage

Old public housing is falling down or being demolished and replaced by only half as many units. Tenants in both public and private housing who cause problems are being evicted with new vigor. Project-based Section 8 contracts are expiring, and HUD is having difficulty renegotiating at rates that will provide owners the profits they are used to, which are often above market value. Housing prices and rents rise twice as fast as incomes. Millions pay 50 percent of their incomes for housing when 30 percent is still considered the safe upper limit; some in big cities pay as much as 80 percent as the new economy forces prices still higher.[83]

We now seem to be adopting a "triage" mentality in dealing with the poorest of the poor. *Triage* is the medical term for processing combat or disaster casualties. You put the ones who will probably live without immediate attention to one side, you get the ones who might survive with immediate attention into the operating room, and you put the ones who are probably going to die even with immediate attention to the other side. And you try not to think too much about that third group. Most of them die; some of them surprise you and pull through. We seem to have given up on a large portion of our population when it comes to finding shelter.

Sprawl

There are also problems outside the inner cities. In most metropolitan areas there seems to be no end to suburban sprawl. Developers build farther and farther out, people buy the developers' houses, then demand that arterial highways be widened to relieve their commuter ordeals; bigger highways allow developers to build even farther out, returning congestion to original levels.

Financing highways and utilities is just the beginning of the problems caused by sprawl. It is a health problem, as toxic exhaust gasses pollute the air. It is a mental health problem, elevating the stress levels of commuters and even driving some to murderous rage. It is a family problem when parents must spend ninety minutes to two hours getting to and from work and have less time to see their kids. It is an economic problem for

Congestion creates a demand for the widening of arterial highways. Wider highways allow developers to build more suburban and exurban housing, which creates more congestion. Then the cycle repeats.

single parents who must spend more of their incomes maintaining and fueling their cars, and for the nation as productive farmland is threatened. It is a quality-of-life problem for elders who are either isolated because they can't drive or endangered in traffic they can no longer cope with. It creates more community conflict as decay and development increasingly isolate different races and income levels in their own ghettos. And if all this is not enough, there is now evidence that sprawl is connected to excess weight and high blood pressure.[84]

Major cities such as New Orleans, Atlanta, Nashville, and Phoenix have begun to look for ways to fight sprawl without damaging economic growth or incurring the wrath of powerful developers. The "smart growth" movement is underway.[85]

Many cities look to Portland, Oregon, for lessons on fighting sprawl. Twenty years ago, Portland established a "greenbelt" around the city, forbidding development within it. It also built a light-rail transportation system to take pressure off the highways, reduce smog, and make commuting easier. The program was successful—almost too successful. Downtown is thriving, property values are high, high-tech companies have moved to the city, abandoned factory and warehouse areas have been converted to housing for new workers, and decaying neighborhoods have revived. Suburban communities that wanted no part of the light-rail when it was built are now building spur tracks to connect with the system or moving city operations to light-rail stations. The problem is that so many people now want to live in Portland that pressure is building to break through the greenbelt.[86]

Atlanta is proud of its economic vitality but has begun to face the costs of its growth. In 1998 it became the nation's leader in average number of miles its motorists drove each day—thirty-four. Traffic snarls and dirty air finally persuaded citizens that radical action was necessary. Even developers and bankers were having a change of heart. The state government created the Georgia Regional Transportation Authority, known as Greta, which gave the governor the power to decide land use questions throughout the metropolitan area. Businesses are now trying to concentrate their activities along subway lines, new malls must have mass transit connections, housing is being built downtown for those fed up with commuting, and downtown businesses are reviving. Still, it takes a lot to change the automobile culture and diminish the lure of the suburban lawn. Atlantans still spend eighty to ninety minutes a day in their cars.[87]

Not everyone agrees that sprawl is a bad thing, and even those who oppose it agree that we need better research on its costs and benefits. Many people find community, not alienation, in the suburbs. They like lower density, the feeling of independence the automobile gives them, and relatively cheaper housing prices. They prefer homogeneity to diversity. There is also the argument that these are consumer choices in a free market. Others point out that land use is not a free market but one controlled by fragmented governments and large developers. Because of widespread disinvestment in cities and assumptions by developers about what is most profitable, consumers have not had much choice until recently.[88]

Both sides agree that the costs of suburbanization are borne partially by people who do not, and perhaps cannot, benefit from it. To correct this inequality would require things such as raising gas prices, charging tolls for highway travel at peak times, and having developers pay the full infrastructure costs for their projects. The smart growth versus sprawl debate does not usually raise these issues. Even more important, it does not face problems of race and poverty that lie just below the problems of traffic, air quality, and infrastructure.[89]

We used to think that the reason European cities maintained pedestrian-friendly, economically viable centers was simply that they were built before the age of the automobile. American cities, built after, were destined to sprawl and go on sprawling. But European cities also exercise options open to American cities to maintain their character. Paris has a growth boundary similar to Portland's and has planned and built satellite cities linked by public transportation to the city center in order to accommodate its swelling population. Other European cities also invest heavily in mass transit.[90]

The structure of American cities, automobile culture notwithstanding, can be, and is being, changed. Development is being redirected to focus on public transportation links. People are moving back to the city. Neglected areas near city cores have been rediscovered and developed profitably. City neighborhoods and suburbs are being restructured to concentrate growth more efficiently. Today in many places one does not have to take out the car every time one needs something. Some shops and services are within walking distance, others are a short ride away on a bus, trolley, or subway. Though developers may resist calls for greater density, they are already building projects with much higher density than those of earlier decades. Labor unions are discovering that rehabilitating old buildings provides more jobs than new construction. Our cities are already being reshaped. Metropolitan and regional growth management can make all of this happen faster.[91]

It is increasingly clear that no single growth-management measure is the answer to sprawl. Without better mass transit, growth boundaries will only increase traffic congestion. Large numbers of people will not use mass transit unless it is safe, clean, and goes where people need to go. Even then it will not be competitive unless the cost of driving and parking is higher. Infrastructure fees for development will equalize the tax burden but also increase housing costs. And none of these policies is producing low-income housing. A problem as complex as this must be attacked on all fronts.

Community Development

The problems of the cities and suburbs, of rich people and poor people, of young and old, of people of all colors, cannot be separated or compartmentalized. Many are trying to do just that (see the section on "The Retreat from Public Life," below), but compartmentalization is only a temporary solution for a few people. Crime and disease spread from the slums as they did a century ago. People need jobs, and employers need workers. Everybody needs education, health, and security. We are politically and economically interdependent. It is not uncommon in developing nations to find what is known as "distorted development," in which some parts of society prosper while others remain in poverty. Distorted development also means that economic development does not bring social development—education, democratic institutions—with it. This condition breeds instability, not prosperity.

The theory and practice of the welfare state were based on the assumption that social development could be financed with the proceeds of economic development. And the welfare state has worked successfully in many European and Asian countries. But this approach also means that when the economy gets into trouble, support for social development is cut back. The resulting declines in health, education, and physical infrastructure do not save the economy, they undermine it. Current theorists of economic development argue that long-range stability and prosperity can come only when social and economic development are built together.[92]

The devolution of government initiated under Ronald Reagan has produced many useful developments at the local level. It has also demonstrated that problems thought to be illusory and services believed to be unnecessary were real and vital, because local communities organized to replace what the federal government had withdrawn.

Another effect of devolution was to bring new attention to partnerships between public and private bodies. This was not new; New Deal programs such as the Public Works Administration were cooperative federal–local, public–private endeavors. But a renewed focus on these possibilities was useful to both spheres.

A third lesson of the 1980s and 1990s is that, despite great creativity and cooperation in the local community, some problems are beyond local solution. A local community cannot have clean water if a major polluter is located three states upriver or across a national border. A city cannot provide high-quality education, police protection, and building inspection if its tax base has moved to the suburbs or the Sun Belt. Large problems require broad-based strategies and funding as well as local energy. Some things can be handled just fine at the neighborhood level; others require the community, the state, or the nation—even several nations—for a practical solution. Finding the balance is the next challenge.[93]

Gender and Household Stereotypes

One problem of housing is present even where there seem to be no problems at all. Imagine a "dream" house: ample space, appliance-filled kitchen, safe neighborhood, huge lawn, and affordable mortgage. What else could one need? Well, one needs to ask where the house is located. Where is it in relation to work, shopping, schools, doctors, or libraries? If it is placed in a typical U.S. suburb, the answer is that all of those things are some distance away. (So add a two-car garage to our dream list.) If the house is in an older city neighborhood, many of the facilities may be within walking distance, with the exception of the workplace. Chances are that the factories and offices where we work are not close by. We may be just as happy that they are not. Who needs smoke, noise, and parking lots? As long as we fit the traditional family pattern for which these houses and neighborhoods were built, we can deal with the problem of isolation in the traditional way: Dad can commute to work and enjoy the quiet of the home at night. Mom can take care of the house and the kids.

This "traditional" pattern (traditional only since about 1950) has a price. Dad is cut off from most of domestic life and Mom has little else. As we have seen, in the sprawled metropolis, Dad may spend three hours of his day or even longer just getting to and from work. Many have found this a reasonable bargain. But many of both genders have felt trapped because they found that the house and its location did not allow much variation from the traditional pattern. The traps inherent in the suburban dream were among the many contributors to the women's movement of the 1970s.[94]

Today, those who fit the traditional pattern are a minority. Both women and men, willingly or unwillingly, no longer conform to the stereotypes. Many women want to work outside the home. Many women must work whether they want to or not; either they have become the sole source of support for their families, or they have found that two incomes are necessary to pay the bills. Some men want a bigger part in domestic life. (Some like domesticity but not the work that goes with it: Employed wives still do more than half of the housework.) Many households are headed by single parents, often women, but not always. Some households contain several families. The traditional house doesn't fit this wide variety of needs very well.

For a single parent, the daily routine is complex. The distances between home, work, day care, schools, and shopping become major obstacles. Each trip in itself may be minor, but all must be added together. If work is more than half an hour away, as it can easily be in any large city, and if the other deliveries and pickups that must be accomplished are not on a direct route from home to work, then a lot of time, money, and energy can be consumed in transportation.

The home and its location are built according to gender stereotypes, and they serve as a daily reminder to both men and women that they are not following the expected pattern. Both men and women may have left the pattern by choice, but it is hard not to feel guilty or resentful under the stress this kind of living pattern creates.

The dream house in the suburbs has become so much a part of our national mythology since World War II that it is hard to imagine any other way of arranging the relationships of house and workplace. Are there other ways? Imagine a group of houses and apartments overlooking a shipyard where cargo ships are built. Those living in the houses and working at the shipyard are mostly single parents. Not only is work close by, but so are the school and the attached day care center. From one window in the center, children can watch on the days when one of "Mommy's ships" is being launched. The center also includes a large kitchen. When the parents pick up their children at the end of the day, they can also take home a hot meal that has been cooked and packaged for them.

This community existed, briefly—not in fantasy but in Vanport City, Oregon, during the Second World War. It was created by the Federal Public Housing Authority and Kaiser Steel Corporation for Kaiser's shipyard workers. After the war, most of the women workers were replaced in the shipyard, some willingly and some not so willingly, when men returned from the armed services. The community where work and home were integrated with a minimum of stress was dismantled, and most of the occupants went off to create the "traditional" pattern of gender separation.[95]

What can social workers do about gender and household stereotypes in housing? Rebuilding cities is not usually within their power. They can, however, begin by recognizing the stress that living arrangements place on marriages and families. They can appreciate and support the struggles of men and women against the stereotypes. They can look for and support ways to relieve stress, including neighborhood day care cooperatives; programs initiated in the workplace, such as company day care centers, flextime, and job sharing; and respite care arrangements for families that have invalid grandparents or children with disabilities or other special needs.

Social workers can participate in the debates now going on about "smart" growth, and can support planning efforts to make cities and neighborhoods more flexible and responsive to human needs, particularly efforts that will allow a better integration of work and home life. Such planning includes issues many social workers consider irrelevant to their practice, such as zoning or transportation. Zoning regulates the separation of work and residence, the possibility of subdividing a single-family house to create an apartment for an elder relative (a "granny flat"), or the different sizes and forms of family groups allowed to share the same neighborhood. Given the scarcity of affordable apartments, it may be more practical and economical for two or more single-parent families to share a large house. But if the neighborhood is zoned for single-family occupancy, this will not be permitted. Low-income urban neighborhoods zoned to exclude commercial activity inhibit the entrepreneurial creativity and economic survival of poor families. More flexible zoning could help create more livable cities. Social workers can also strive to save the decaying public transportation systems that for some people are the only means of getting around in our spread-out cities. Social workers are supposed to be specialists in working with people in their situational contexts. Housing arrangements present a broader and more complex field of activity than most other aspects of our work.[96]

The Retreat from Public Life

The second half of the twentieth century has presented most people in the United States with greater opportunities for privacy. It is easier to get away, and stay away, from others than it used to be. Television, newspapers, CD players, videocassette recorders and DVD players, large refrigerators, and frozen food greatly reduce the need to go out. When we do go out, we need not share our trips with other people on buses, streetcars, or trains; we go in private cars. Our trips are speeded by highways that avoid the neighborhoods of others, so we have little idea of how other people live in our cities. The people in our own neighborhoods are all pretty much like us: same income level, same race, even the same age.

Technology allows us to stay at home. Our recent history has also reduced our desire to go out. The civil rights, antiwar, environmental, and women's movements brought

Focus on Diversity

Housing for People with Special Needs

We all have individual preferences in home design and decoration, but most of us could adapt quickly to almost any type of house, even a tepee or an igloo. For some of us, however, adaptation is more difficult. It can help enormously if people's special needs are considered in the design and location of their housing. People who have low vision or total blindness, people who use wheelchairs, older people with medical problems, and people with mental illnesses or developmental disabilities all face barriers to independence in the built environment. Their communities can ignore these barriers and keep these people imprisoned and dependent, or they can remove the barriers and facilitate free access to all aspects of community life. Not only is this access a necessary part of "normal" life, but it can also improve physical and mental health.

People who use wheelchairs need ramps and elevators to allow them to move about independently. Imagine the frustration of being in a department store or office building and confronting a bathroom door that is too narrow to get your chair through. Federal legislation requiring access to public facilities and cities that have purchased buses with lifts have made it easier for wheelchair users to lead a normal life, but many barriers remain, even in areas that we assume are accessible. Spend a day in a wheelchair on your campus and discover for yourself the many places you cannot go.

When a wheelchair user returns home, another set of obstacles awaits. Stoves, sinks, and counters are too high to use sitting down. The freezing compartment in the average refrigerator is completely out of reach. Obviously, preparation and cleanup of even a simple meal requires gymnastics in this kind of environment. There may be no communitywide solution to this problem, but planning for special needs can be practical in some situations. A student housing complex on the campus of Georgetown University includes an apartment with scaled-down counters and reachable appliances and sinks. The university knew from experience that it regularly enrolled students who could use such an apartment.

Many features that are essential to people with special needs could also be enjoyed by the rest of us. Wider doors and hallways make it easier to move furniture in and out. Adjustable shelves and clothes rods in closets expand options for everyone. Room to turn around in a bathroom should not be a luxury. Builders could accommodate a broader range of the population with small changes in construction standards and little added cost. As the U.S. population ages, more of us will appreciate homes designed with freedom and mobility in mind. We may not need grab bars in the bathroom now, but if the walls were properly reinforced when the house was built, we could easily add them later. Social workers can help communicate the value of these "universal design" principles.

The location of a home in relation to other parts of the community is, as we have seen, as important as its interior accommodations. The separation of home from work, shopping, entertainment, and health services is a problem even for those in the prime of health and with access to an automobile. For those whose mobility is impaired, isolation severely limits the possibility of a normal life. Nursing homes provide an integration of living space, health services, and communal meals, but they usually do this in a manner that is

many people into public life. Their struggles brought solid accomplishments, but they also brought disillusionment and exhaustion. Most public problems resisted permanent solution. Corruption and deceit remained common. Many people lost confidence in our public institutions. A retreat from public life may have been natural and predictable. But impersonal, inflexible, and institutional. Recently, some "retirement villages" have been designed to maximize the privacy and independence of residents while providing cooking, cleaning, and health services when needed. But such design is usually associated with only the more expensive facilities. Does it need to be? Convenience stores can be built into the ground level of apartment buildings. Day care centers and communal kitchens are a feature of some European apartment buildings for single parents. Gradually, the same idea may be extended to all of us.

Just as some people need to have the outside world brought closer to home, others need a home in the outside world. People with developmental disabilities, who in the past were segregated in public institutions or carefully protected by their families, are now living in group homes and finding employment. They are learning to find their way around their neighborhoods, to take public transportation, and to gain access to the full range of community activities. Many now earn real salaries outside of sheltered workshops. With their new incomes, they shop, go to movies, and eat in restaurants. They need a safe, nurturing community environment. Similarly, an effort is being made to bring people with serious emotional problems out of the institution and into the community—and to support them once they are out, not just dump them. Social workers are heavily involved in these efforts. The design, adaptation, and location of homes and apartments for these reemerging populations require special attention to make integration successful.

Although group homes cause little disruption in residential communities, there is usually initial resistance to them. The NIMBY phenomenon ("not in my backyard"), in which people recognize the necessity of certain facilities but prefer to have them located somewhere else, is common. Some social service agencies counteract this with careful community preparation. Others, however, avoid the hassle and concentrate their efforts in neighborhoods that are less likely or less able to protest. Such ghettoization defeats the purpose of normalization.

Social workers need to be aware of the special housing needs of some people. They need to be sensitive to the frustration and anger that a restrictive environment can create, as well as to the growth and health that participation in the community can foster. Not all needs can be satisfied, and not all barriers are removable; this is true for any of us. But barriers and restrictions should not be taken for granted. Individual adaptations, group supports, and environmental changes can be made.

Sources: Steven Winter Associates, *Homes for Everyone: Universal Design Principles in Practice* (Washington, DC: Department of Housing and Urban Development, 1996); Benyamin Schwarz and Ruth Brent, *Aging, Autonomy, and Architecture: Advances in Assisted Living* (Baltimore: Johns Hopkins University Press, 1999); Robert Schafer, *Housing America's Seniors* (Cambridge, MA: Joint Center for Housing Studies, 2000); Sylvia Moreno, "Staying Independent Together," *Washington Post* (14 May 1998), VA1; Charles A. Riley II, *High-Access Living: Design and Decoration for Barrier-Free Living* (New York: Rizzoli, 1999); "Houses within Reach," *Architecture 91* (November 2002), 18; Luci Scott, "Universal Housing Gains Momentum," *Arizona Republic* (11 June 2003), A2.

some people have begun to worry that by becoming more private, we are losing some of the skills and attitudes that are necessary to keep U.S. society working properly.[97]

We have a long tradition of regarding our houses as havens from the world. This tendency has increased as more people have fled the problems of the cities for the seeming refuge of the suburbs. Not only do public problems seem too complex to solve, but also much public space seems unsafe to inhabit. Urban renewal, with its concentration on office buildings and parking lots, helped make downtown areas places to fear. When the offices close, large areas become deserted; anyone working late or traveling through is an easy target for muggers. One response to this is cities composed of segregated, homogeneous neighborhoods where one does not have to interact with others very often and where people of other races or income levels are rarely seen at all (except on television).[98]

The escape may be more illusion than reality, however. One recent study of children's experience with violence reported these chilling statistics: In an urban school, 97 percent of sixth graders knew someone who had been a victim of a violent crime, and 88 percent had witnessed a violent crime. But in a suburban school, 98 percent of the sixth graders knew a victim and 57 percent had witnessed such a crime. In the New York metropolitan area, heroin use is now more common among suburban white kids than among inner-city kids of any race.[99]

Balkanization: Gated Communities and Beyond. Because simply being in the suburbs isn't felt as safe enough, the gated community is becoming more and more popular. Homes are surrounded by a perimeter wall, and there is a guard at the gate. Visitors have to be screened by the guard or "buzzed in" after electronic communication with residents. Ironically, people who seek gated communities because they feel unsafe outside of them rarely feel any safer inside. They keep their house alarms turned on even during the day. Statistically, their risks of crime are no less than in economically similar neighborhoods without gates.[100] (See Figure 14.1.)

Some see even gated communities or suburbs as not far enough away from the problems of the city—particularly from the increasing diversity that is resulting from immigration. Such people are undertaking an even greater flight. They are moving inland or south, seeing places in Montana, Idaho, or North Carolina (for example) as refuges where they will once again be surrounded by people "like me." "Let's be honest," says Robert DiDomenico Jr., who moved from Long Island to Cary, North Carolina. "It's immigrants in, Americans out." It would be interesting to know how long ago Mr. DiDomenico's ancestors were immigrants who were being feared and despised by earlier immigrants who called themselves "Americans."[101]

Another reaction against immigrants has recently attached itself to the reaction against sprawl. The Federation for American Immigration Reform has begun an ad campaign blaming immigrants for sprawl. Their argument is that land use is determined by demand, and immigrants are increasing the demand for housing. Immigrants, however, are not prominent among the winners in the new economy who are driving up the cost of urban housing. Nor do they dominate the members of the white middle class who rush to the new exurban developments. They are much more often the losers in the housing squeeze.[102]

"Bowling Alone." Renewed interest in the theme of the retreat from public life was provoked by a 1995 essay with the provocative title "Bowling Alone." Using statistics on the decline of bowling teams and the increase of individual bowling, Robert Putnam argued that the United States was losing "social capital"—a sense of trust in others and

FIGURE 14.1 | *Source:* © The New Yorker Collection, 1999, Mick Stevens, from cartoonbank.com. All rights reserved.

"Things have gotten bad here. There's talk of a war with another gated community."

in the community that is necessary both for democracy and for a prosperous economy. Bowling was just a symbol. Putnam also looked at voter turnout, church and union membership, and other community-level participation. Five years later, he elaborated his thesis in a book.[103]

Putnam's work prompted others to examine community participation in the United States. Some found counterexamples of communities that were on the rise rather than declining—soccer leagues, for example—and suggested that the changes in participation that Putnam focused on might just be generational changes in preferred communal activity, not signs of a long-term decline in civility.[104] But others, concerned not only about community participation but also about growing geographic and class fragmentation, the disappearance of civility in Congress, outbreaks of violence among rush-hour motorists, the rise of hate crimes, and the proliferation of armed militias willing to bomb government buildings, have not been reassured.

The interplay of democracy, economic activity, and community life is interesting and complicated. It is generally agreed that cooperation is necessary to democracy. Less commented on in public discussions of the economy, but often recognized, is the fact that cooperation, not just competition, is a key to economic performance.[105] It also seems likely that cooperation grows out of trust, which in turn grows out of getting to know people by sharing common activities. If those opportunities for sharing disappear, will trust, cooperation, prosperity, and ultimately democracy follow?

It is possible that other forms of association will replace older ones. Cyberspace does not allow face-to-face contact, but it does bring people with common interests together and can do so without racial or gender discrimination. These "imagined communities" with weak ties among individuals can nonetheless provide a basis for cooperation and collective action.

Putnam has been accused of placing primary emphasis on individual actions rather than on the social forces that may impel them and the institutional contexts in which they occur. Cooperation and social capital can be built and maintained by legislation and regulation as well as by individual outreach. Putnam acknowledges this in a more recent article that reports an increase in civic engagement since the attacks of September 11, 2001. He argues that a new generation of civic-spirited youth, like those who fought the Great Depression and the Second World War, might be nurtured by quadrupling the funding of the national youth service program AmeriCorps.[106]

One of the major ironies of the current political situation in the United States is that while governmental devolution is placing more and more responsibility for the solution of social problems on local communities, it is simultaneously depriving them of the resources, both public and private, to meet this challenge. Communities are forced to compete with one another rather than play a role in a national strategy. Communities commonly engage in fierce bidding for relocating corporations; they want the jobs these businesses promise to provide. They compete by offering tax breaks and infrastructure support. The tax breaks, however, mean that they have less money to build the infrastructure and less money to educate local children who might one day apply for the corporate jobs. And if communities fail to provide an educated workforce, the corporations will import workers to fill the jobs, defeating the original purpose of the tax breaks.

New Urbanism. One attempt to restore some measure of community life is a movement known as the "new urbanism." Though it has so far been practiced mostly on the far fringes of cities rather than in their centers, its principles are generally applicable. The goal of new urbanism is to make it easier and more pleasant for people to get out into the community and interact with their neighbors. Therefore, the movement's proponents take the neighborhood as the basic planning unit. A neighborhood should have clearly defined edges. There should be no more than a five-minute walk from center to edge. Interaction within the neighborhood is easier if houses are sited closer together, on smaller lots, and close to the street. Front porches where people can gather and individuals can sit and observe life on the street are an almost mandatory feature. Common recreational areas, shopping, and services should be available somewhere within the neighborhood. The site planning and architectural styles of new urbanism, in other words, mimic the nineteenth-century small town.[107]

The first and most famous community planned according to these principles was Seaside in Florida. It looks like a bit of Kansas stuck on the Florida coast, far away from any urban center. The homes are of modest size; there are lots of picket fences, narrow

Social Work Destinations

Early Housing

The Tenement Museum at 97 Orchard Street in Manhattan, New York City, can give you a sense of what life was like for immigrants on the Lower East Side in the nineteenth century. It also has programs that reach out to new immigrants.

Early Public Housing

The Public Works Administration built homes in Atlanta, Atlantic City, Birmingham, Boston, Cambridge (Mass.), Charleston, Chicago, Cincinnati, Cleveland, Columbia (S.C.), Dallas, Detroit, Enid (Okla.), Evansville (Ind.), Indianapolis, Jacksonville (Fla.), Lackawanna (N.Y.), Lexington, Louisville, Memphis, Miami, Milwaukee, Minneapolis, Montgomery (Ala.), Nashville, New York City, Oklahoma City, Omaha, Philadelphia, Schenectady, Stamford (Conn.), Toledo, Washington, D.C., and Wayne (Pa.). The buildings were built to last sixty years; but many have not had adequate maintenance for at least a third of that time, and nothing lasts very long if you don't make repairs. Two projects that are in good shape and safe to visit are University Homes in Atlanta, bordering Clark Atlanta University and Morehouse College, and Cedar Springs Place north of Dallas.

Innovative Public Housing

Harbor Point (formerly called Columbia Point) and Langham Court in Boston and Lake Parc Place in Chicago are mixed-income housing developments that would be interesting to inspect. In California there are several unusual housing developments. Willow Court in Menlo Park (near Palo Alto) and Sungate in Oakland were both designed by Michael Pyatok, an architect with an ability to design friendly housing on a low budget. On the Near East Side of Cleveland you can look for Renaissance Village, a part of the Kennedy King housing project.

New Urbanism

Seaside, the original "new urban" community, is on a remote coast of the Florida Panhandle. But you don't have to make the trip. Rent the movie *The Truman Show* starring Jim Carrey and Ed Harris. Seaside is the set for much of this film. Celebration is near Orlando, so you can drop by after seeing Disney World. (Or instead of.) Seaside, Celebration, and Kentlands (in Maryland) are communities off by themselves. Diggs Town is in Norfolk, Virginia, and Edward Scudder Homes in Newark, New Jersey, are genuinely urban. Other developments are more suburban: The Crossings, Mountain View, Cal.; Laguna West, Sacramento; Newport, near Beaufort, S.C.; Wyndcrest, Sandy Spring, Mar.; and Crawford Square, Pittsburgh.

Another Resource

Dark Days, a film documentary produced and directed by Mark Singer, won three awards at the 2000 Sundance Film Festival. It is about a group of homeless people living in an Amtrak tunnel under Manhattan. Singer was a twenty-year-old Londoner who came to New York in 1994 hoping to be a fashion model. He got to know some of the street people in his neighborhood, who introduced him to the tunnel society beneath the streets. One of the tunnel dwellers said someone should make a film about them, and Singer took up the task. Using borrowed equipment, with the tunnel dwellers as cast and crew, he spent the next six years making the film. He sold his belongings to buy film and supplies and eventually became homeless himself. The film shows the diversity of the homeless population and their ingenuity in fashioning a "normal" everyday life underground. Amtrak finally evicted the tunnel dwellers; some were able to stay aboveground using Section 8 vouchers. A Sundance reviewer called the film a testimony to human strength and endurance. The film had a theatrical release in seven cities and may eventually make it to video. (*Source:* Peter Applebome, "Home Was a Tunnel and Neighbors Were His Cast," *New York Times* (27 August 2000), AR20, online at www.sundancechannel.com/festival00/filmguide.)

streets, flower gardens, and, of course, front porches. But Seaside is not a community in the normal sense. These are mostly second homes of rich people who live elsewhere.

There are, however, now several such communities with year-round occupants and reasonable proximity to cities. The developers of Seaside have built Kentlands in Maryland, and the Disney Corporation has developed Celebration in Florida. The Crossings in Mountain View, California; Laguna West in Sacramento; Newport, near Beaufort, South Carolina; Wyndcrest in Sandy Spring, Maryland; and Crawford Square in Pittsburgh, have been developed as new urban suburbs, and more are on the way.[108]

The ideology of new urbanism includes economic and racial diversity, though in practice these communities are within the reach of only upper-middle-income buyers. Including low-income housing is a strain, and it is not clear whether there will be enough jobs available in such places for residents without cars.

In the city, applications of new urbanism to public housing can be seen at Diggs Town in Norfolk, Virginia, and Edward Scudder Homes in Newark, New Jersey. A former resident of a tower building described life in her new town house:

> Here, you walk out the door, you walk out *your* door, not some long hallway. I don't have to yell, "Get out of this hallway!" anymore. . . . I remembered we had [a kitchen window] when I was a kid. Now I got my kitchen window right over the sink, and I am washing dishes all the time, just so I can look out that window.[109]

Whether the new urbanism movement will prove the beginning of a larger effort to redesign cities or merely a passing breath of nostalgia for a lost small-town America remains to be seen. For the moment it offers an option to those who want something between the energy and semichaos of a true urban environment and the isolation of a suburban ranch house on a three-acre lot. Some predict that these nineteenth-century "cutescapes" will become as boring as the ranch houses of postwar suburbia.[110]

New urbanism can be an antidote to sprawl insofar as it enables people to meet basic needs in their immediate environs without having to hop in the car and hit the Interstate. It is not an antidote to declining civility insofar as it increases the homogeneity of communities.

Social Work and Community Development

There is evidence that cohesive communities, even low-income, resource-poor ones in inner cities, can exert informal social control and reduce vandalism and crime. This requires a development of trust and "willingness to intervene for the common good" that can be developed over time. A study of 343 Chicago neighborhoods of differing income levels and ethnic compositions found "collective efficacy" to be crucial in reducing violence, even homicide. An interesting finding of this research was that although home ownership, stability of tenure, organization, and access to services and resources all helped promote collective efficacy, they were not sufficient by themselves. Something else was at work. This research is ongoing and well funded; new results should be forthcoming. Social workers need to understand what this "something" is and put it to use.[111]

One small example of collective efficacy is the Safe Walk Home program developed in Escondido, California. Parents became angry at gang fights, drug deals, and intimidation of children after school. Now, police-trained, radio-equipped volunteers patrol the streets children use to walk home from school, and owners of stores along the way stand outside for a few minutes when school lets out. They don't confront; they just observe and report. But their presence is felt.[112]

Community organization is usually a good thing, but some community organizing can have a negative effect on community development. Opposition to change needs to be thoughtful, not automatic. In addition to NIMBY (not in my backyard) developments, we are also seeing politicians who are afraid to do anything (NIMTOO: not in my term of office). One observer predicts even more radical resistance (BANANA: build absolutely nothing anywhere near anything; CAVE: citizens against virtually everything; NOPE: not on planet earth; and NOTE: not over there either). Social workers can help seek reason and balance in protecting neighborhoods while considering overall community needs.[113]

Renewing Civility

Diplomats are people specially trained by governments and sent to other nations to maintain peaceful political relationships and to encourage productive economic trade and cultural enrichment. But in our own cities and neighborhoods, we are all diplomats. We must encounter people we don't know, people who may be different from us, and we must interact peacefully and productively with them. This, too, takes special skills. Our national history has included considerable intolerance and conflict, but our cities have consistently offered examples of fruitful diversity. As we turn inward and focus on family life, enjoy the privacy that technology now allows us, and avoid the public life that threatens or depresses us, will we lose the minimal appreciation of differences and the tolerance of disagreements that are necessary to operate a nation of diverse groups? Will we lose the skills of civility and civic engagement that make our local and national life possible? Will we ultimately lose the intellectual stimulation that produces scientific and artistic creativity? Or can we reestablish the right balance of security and adventure: a safe home within a nurturing but diverse community?

What can social workers do about this? First, as citizens and as professionals, they can take advantage of all the opportunities available to them to participate in public life. Any neighborhood, community, or city event or organization that brings together people from different classes, races, ages, or religions is a possible antidote to isolation.

These are simple, preliminary measures, however. The long-term revitalization of public life will require structural changes. Some of these involve housing. Social workers connected with city planning operations can encourage policies that create and preserve a balance of private, semiprivate (communal), and public spaces. Community spirit and neighborliness are the keys to security. Life can be returned to sterile downtown areas with mixed-use developments. Public housing projects, where personal safety is often threatened, can be redesigned. Low-rise buildings with windows on the street, front porches, and front yards (even tiny, token spaces) can help define areas that are not open to just anyone but are at least partially under the control of the residents. Such spaces also encourage residents to take responsibility for maintaining them.

Social work has a long tradition of sensitivity to the needs of communities and neighborhoods. In the spirit of the settlement house movement, social workers can still be found in community centers throughout the country. A new kind of community organizer, one with skills in management as well as in advocacy, group work, and counseling, is finding work in such centers.

Social workers, whether in community centers or in private agencies, often help people in difficulty to develop social support networks. The problem may be a disability or illness, the loss of work, a frail parent, or a rebellious teen. Relatives, neighbors, or strangers who have the same problem can be brought together to offer support. In order to do successful networking, social workers must understand the environmental conditions that inhibit people from coming together.

At all levels of social work practice—individual, agency, neighborhood, community, city, state, and national—there are things that can be done to help create and maintain private, communal, and public spaces that combine security with stimulation and privacy with community. The retreat from public life represents a conviction that the larger problems of our society—crime, poverty, and discrimination—cannot be solved. People believe that our political institutions, either local or national, have failed us, and that the only reasonable response is to seek refuge behind the walls of our own tiny castles. Counteracting this woeful conclusion will take vigorous action at all levels of government and at all levels of group activity. Although the size of the problem may be discouraging, we must remember that it can be attacked on many levels. All of us can play a part, whatever our individual skills and interests.

Perspectives

The Conservative Perspective

The conservative point of view maintains that housing can best be provided by market forces. Consumers exercise choices; these choices guide producers of housing in deciding what to build. The major cause of homelessness, many conservatives argue, is not the lack of affordable housing. Most homeless people are deviants or members of an entrenched underclass, and they lack the motivation or ability to better their lives. If some consumers are without the necessary resources to enter the marketplace, the government should give them vouchers that will allow them to purchase the housing of their choice (within the limits of the voucher). These consumers should not be forced to accept public housing, which stigmatizes them as poor and deprives them of the dignity that other consumers are given in the market. Public housing, like other welfare programs, encourages dependency. These programs should be phased out, and residents should be encouraged to move toward self-sufficiency.[114]

One way of encouraging public housing residents to enter the private market as owners is to divert part of their rental payments to a savings account. The savings can be used to make a down payment on a house once enough money has accumulated.

Public housing is unfair competition for private builders. Existing public housing should be sold to private buyers. The deterioration of housing is often caused by tenants' ignorance of maintenance or their lack of responsibility.[115]

The flight to the suburbs after World War II was an expression of consumer choice. It is an essential part of the American dream to want to own a house with land around it. Everyone who wants to can own good-quality housing by saving money, investing in a modest home, and "trading up" as market and personal resources allow. As middle-income homeowners move up to better housing, those with lower incomes will move up behind them. Everyone benefits eventually.

The Liberal Perspective

Liberals feel the market is a necessary device for providing everyone with housing, but it needs regulation and stimulation. It cannot provide the poorest members of society with adequate housing and does not always respond to those with special needs. Therefore, government must intervene to offer subsidies, tax incentives, and regulations to encourage private developers to provide for all consumers and to curtail unfair practices. Low-interest home loans and Section 8 programs will aid the disadvantaged, and laws against redlining and restrictive covenants will deter discrimination.[116]

As a last resort, the government must build new housing to replace the loss of low-income options in the market. This housing should, wherever possible, be scattered throughout the city, and it should be designed so as to avoid stigmatizing its residents. As a short-term response to homelessness, the government should also provide emergency shelters and encourage private sponsors to do likewise.

Homelessness is caused by deinstitutionalization, lack of affordable housing, and low wage and benefit levels.

The flight to the suburbs was a popular choice of consumers, but liberals point out that it could not have happened without considerable aid from the government. Low-cost loans through the Veterans Administration and the Federal Housing Administration, mortgage interest tax deductions, municipal water and sewage services, and arterial highways that allowed easy commuting to the suburbs were necessary before consumers could exercise this choice.

Finally, liberals argue that job opportunities and a responsive public transportation system are necessary parts of any effort to ensure adequate housing for all.

The Radical Perspective

Radicals believe the market is not the appropriate model for housing provision. They assert that housing is a right, not a commodity. Decent housing should be guaranteed to all. The market encourages speculation, which drives up prices and profits from other people's misery.[117]

The shape of cities is determined by the interests of those with wealth and power. The "flight" to suburbia happened because large developers found it easier and cheaper to build outside cities. They mobilized their political influence to persuade government to provide the necessary loans, highways, and other services. The consumers had little choice because these same speculators had decided to disinvest in cities and to allow them to decay.[118]

Similarly, the deterioration of inner-city neighborhoods was aided by redlining by banks and insurance companies. When the urban decay had proceeded past the point at which profits could be extracted from slum properties, the federal program of "urban renewal" was created. This allowed developers to remove low-income and African American residents from inner-city areas so that they could, with tax breaks and other incentives, build again in the decayed areas. Similar tax breaks were made available when middle-income professionals decided to move into older city neighborhoods. These government programs, supported by liberals as well as by conservatives, have compounded the current housing crisis.

The homeless are people who refuse to be a part of institutions that abuse and humiliate them: battering families, dead-end jobs, and mindless bureaucracies. To reintegrate them will require institutional change.

Housing is made available to the poor only in periods when the poor pose some threat. In the nineteenth century, communicable diseases spread across class lines, so governments were empowered to clear slums. After World War I, when the British government feared that returning veterans might follow the example of the Russian Revolution, a massive housing program was begun (and discontinued once a depression took away that threat).[119] But in the United States, even the urban riots of the 1960s were not enough to spur improvements in public housing. Public housing is kept intentionally unappealing so that tenants will flee to the private market as soon as they can.

Change comes when oppressed groups organize. Tenants in public housing can take over management of their projects and seek collective solutions to problems of crime, maintenance, rehabilitation, and service delivery. The homeless can take over abandoned buildings and demand the materials to repair them. They can protest the destruction of low-income housing and lobby for the creation of alternatives. To provide adequate housing for all citizens, the U.S. government should develop a comprehensive "social housing" program. This would guarantee housing for all citizens through a major system of nonprofit housing produced and operated by local, state, and federal governments.[120]

Social Work Roles

Our earlier discussion of current housing issues and trends suggested many of the roles social workers play in the housing arena. At the least, social workers can be sensitive to the impact of particular kinds of housing (or the lack of it) on their clients' lives. They can help people cope with or change difficult housing situations. Social workers can also choose to work directly within a housing setting, such as a public housing program. Finally, they can become specialists working on housing policy, often advocating change.

Social workers who engage in counseling, case management, or other types of direct service to clients witness a variety of housing problems. A single parent reports living in deteriorated and crowded conditions; an elderly client fears living alone; or a person with visual impairment is told he cannot have a guide dog in the apartment he wishes to rent. In these cases, the social worker can make referrals and act as an advocate. The single parent might be referred to a federal assistance program or to a community group that helps people find decent and affordable housing. The elderly client might be introduced to a home-sharing program or aided in the development of a supportive social network. The visually impaired man might be given information about his rights as a person with a disability, and he and the social worker could plan how he might best assert those rights with potential landlords.

Housing is an important ingredient in solving some of the worst family problems. Children can't learn if they are on the street or moving to a new school each month. The head of foster care services in the District of Columbia, for example, estimated in 1996 that almost half the city's foster children could be reunited with their families if they had stable housing.[121]

Some social workers are employed within housing settings. More and more housing development and rehabilitation projects are incorporating on-site social services. Phipps Houses, one of the oldest and largest nonprofit developers of low-income housing in the country, organized a community development corporation to provide family assistance, community organizing, and youth services to tenants when it rehabilitated abandoned buildings in the South Bronx.[122] Their belief was that helping families develop a sense of community and control would benefit both the families themselves and the buildings they lived in. Maintaining their physical and mental health and improving their education and job opportunities would ensure that families could continue to pay rent. Developing a spirit of community would help them maintain the buildings and control crime and delinquency within them. The families' sense of ownership, of course, made them more demanding tenants, but the housing managers felt this was a reasonable price to pay for increased stability and security.

Social workers may be managers themselves. In Chicago, for example, social workers from the Uptown Branch of Hull House manage scattered-site public housing units for the Chicago Housing Authority. In addition to acting as landlords, these social workers help integrate building residents into neighborhood life, develop tenant councils, and work with these councils on areas such as tenant selection and building improvements. Such a job involves management and community organizing skills as well as an ability to counsel residents with difficult life problems. Hull House has found social workers to be excellent candidates for such positions.[123]

As we have discussed, current policy trends are pushing responsibility for meeting citizen housing needs to state and local government, packaging what remains of federal housing money into Community Development Block Grants. The most viable responses to these trends are coming from local CDCs. These changes are opening up opportunities for social workers to be involved in the development of housing and related services in their communities. They are also intensifying the need for social work input to encourage the wise use of meager resources. Interagency collaboration, something social workers should be good at facilitating, is desperately needed because of the deadly interaction of housing problems with problems of health, jobs, crime, drugs, transportation difficulties, and family violence.[124]

There is a new effort at the national level, led by the National Alliance to End Homelessness (NAEH) with the support of the U.S. Conference of Mayors, to redirect resources from building new shelters to building affordable housing. Beginning in the summer of 2004, NAEH seeks to end homelessness in ten years. Elizabeth Boyle, NAEH secretary, is a social worker.[125]

Social workers can promote an understanding of the interdependence of these problems in their classrooms and communities. The public desire to turn away from

A CLOSER Look

A New Kind of Community Organizing

The Study Circles Resource Center (SCRC), run by the Topsfield Foundation of Pomfret, Connecticut, helps community groups organize themselves to have input into local policymaking. The center has established programs in over eighty communities, involving hundreds of citizens in dialogue and action on issues such as race, crime, education, immigration, and criminal justice. Groups of eight to twelve people meet regularly over a period of several months. They are guided by a neutral facilitator, trained by SCRC, whose job is to help everyone feel comfortable and able to contribute productively. They set their own ground rules for conducting the discussion and using the time. Members may represent different points of view and come from different economic, racial, and cultural backgrounds, so establishing mutual respect and ensuring civility is essential. A study guide written by SCRC staff is usually available to outline basic questions, policy issues, and possibilities for action.

One group may be informative, but real community impact requires a number of groups. Therefore, local community organizations, churches, even city governments are usually involved. A well-publicized kickoff event is staged to recruit participants and set the process in motion. After several months of discussion, all groups get together in an "Action Forum" to decide how to turn words into deeds.

One of SCRC's first communitywide programs began in Lima, Ohio, in 1993 at the request of the mayor. The sentencings in the Rodney King beating case had caused riots in some cities and caused many to think about racial discrimination and hate crime in their communities. A coalition of neighborhood organizations, churches, businesses, and public agencies helped set up the circles. A number of high-profile community leaders supported the project. By 1999, 3,000 people were involved. Among the outgrowths of these meetings were an annual community diversity celebration, a Violence Prevention Center, a meditation center, a soup kitchen, a tutoring program, and two nonprofit corporations devoted to citizen action in the community.

In other cities, groups have addressed other problems. Orford, New Hampshire, created the country's only bistate K–12 school district in order to keep rural schools in Vermont and New Hampshire open. Fort Meyers, Florida, brought a shopping center to a low-income neighborhood. Citizens in Oklahoma spurred

the community and withdraw into walled enclaves must be reversed if long-range solutions are to be supported. As noted earlier, social workers can help promote community efficacy even in poor, resource-deprived places. Crime and drug problems can be dramatically reduced when citizens organize to do it. Social workers can help educate their communities, mobilize resources, and provide useful policy analysis, research, and practice skills in this environment.

Visit **www.researchnavigator.com** to research these important concepts from the chapter:

Affordable housing	New urbanism
Community development	Public housing
Gentrification	Smart growth
Homelessness	Urban renewal

landmark corrections legislation to deal with prison costs and other criminal justice issues. Springfield, Illinois, increased minority hiring in its police and fire departments.

Grassroots community organization has been a part of social work for a long time. It was particularly strong in the 1960s and 1970s when communities tackled festering civil rights and poverty issues. The predominant approach at that time came from conflict theory, which assumed that people with power were unlikely to share it voluntarily and that confrontation would be necessary in order to achieve justice and even to secure such modest goals as gaining city services, improving education, or enlarging job opportunities. Government officials were usually considered the enemy; becoming too close to them would result in the co-optation of the insurgent groups.

The SCRC takes a different approach. It is willing to try cooperative and collaborative strategies. It gives government officials the benefit of the doubt, assuming that most really would like to serve their communities and could use a little help in doing it. Its aim is to do its own co-opting, bringing those with power into the process to achieve the goals of Study Circle members. "Community journalists" are natural allies when they can be found. These are reporters who go beyond the local crime-and-mayhem stories that are the headline staples of most local papers to find and provide ongoing coverage of the issues that community members are raising.

Another difference between SCRC's philosophy of community organizing and the traditional conflict approach is a search for ways to stay involved. After the election or the fight with city hall, whether won or lost, old-style community organizations go home until the next project or the next campaign. Study Circle members try to be ongoing presences in community decision making and policy administration. This is difficult to maintain for any length of time on a volunteer and unofficial basis. How to institutionalize without losing touch with the grass roots is a dilemma SCRC is currently struggling with.

Source: Saul Alinsky, *Reveille for Radicals* (New York: Vintage, [1946] 1969); the Study Circles Resource Center can be accessed online at www.studycircles.org.

Web Sites on Housing and Community Development

Brookings Institution <www.brookings.edu>: One of the original Washington think tanks with a wide range of interests.

Census Bureau <www.census.gov/hhes/www/housing>: Comprehensive data from *American Housing Survey* and other sources on home ownership, affordability, segregation, and similar topics.

Center for Creative Nonviolence <www.users.erols.com/ccnv>: The organization that put homelessness on the national agenda. Offers volunteer opportunities.

Center on Budget and Policy Priorities <www.cbpp.org>: A nonpartisan research organization focusing on policies affecting low- and middle-income people.

Homes for the Homeless; The Institute for Children and Poverty <www.homesforthehomeless.org>: A nonprofit organization founded in 1986 to serve homeless mothers and children in New York City.

Housing Assistance Council <www.ruralhome.org>: Specializes in rural and Native American housing problems.

Joint Center for Housing Studies, Harvard University <www.gsd.harvard.edu>: A research unit of the Harvard Graduate School of Design in cooperation with the Kennedy School of Government.

National Accessible Apartment Clearinghouse <www.aptsforrent.com/naac>: Database for people with disabilities and special housing needs.

National Alliance to End Homelessness <www.endhomelessness.org>: A national advocacy organization embarking on a campaign to end homelessness in ten years.

National Coalition for the Homeless <www.nationalhomeless.org>: A federation of local advocacy groups.

National Community Development Association <www.ncdaonline.org>: An association of community development corporations.

National Geographic Society <www.nationalgeographic.com/earthpulse/sprawl>: Offers a virtual walk down a street designed for a variety of uses as a way of raising issues about New Urbanism and sprawl.

National Law Center on Homelessness and Poverty <www.nlchp.org>: Focuses on litigation and policy.

National Low Income Housing Coalition <www.nlihc.org>: Established in 1974 to deal with the affordable housing crisis.

Smart Growth Network <www.smartgrowth.org>: Extensive resources including state-by-state reports on smart growth initiatives.

Study Circles Resource Center <www.studycircles.org>: A division of the Topsfield Foundation of Pomfret, Connecticut, helping communities organize for input into policy decision making.

Urban Institute <www.urban.org>: Conducts research on community building, public housing, and homelessness.

U.S. Department of Housing and Urban Development <www.huduser.org>: Extensive source of data on housing and federal programs.

Endnotes

1. Chester Hartman, ed., *America's Housing Crisis* (Boston: Routledge & Kegan Paul, 1983), 12–13.
2. Hartman, *America's Housing Crisis,* 12–13.
3. D'Vera Cohn, "Did the Emergency Shelter Population Dip?," *Washington Post Weekly Edition* (5–11 September 2001), 35; Martha Burt, Laudan Y. Aron, Edgar Lee, and Jesse Valente, *Helping America's Homeless: Emergency Shelter or Affordable Housing?* (Washington, DC: The Urban Institute Press, 2001), 40, 49; http://www.urban.org/ Andrea Elliott, "New York Plans for Record Number of Homeless," *New York Times* (2 July 2003), A20; United States Conference of Mayors–Sodexho, *Hunger and Homelessness Survey 2003* (Washington, DC: USCM, December 2003).
4. Janny Scott, "Census Shows More People Are Doubling Up and Fewer Live Alone," *New York Times* (22 May 2001), A20.
5. Carol S. North, David E. Pollio, E. M. Smith, and Edward L. Spitznagel, "Correlates of Early Onset and Chronicity of Homelessness in a Large Urban Homeless Population," *Journal of Nervous and Mental Disease 186* (July 1998), 395–400; Carol S. North, Karin M. Eyrich, David E. Pollio, and Edward L. Spitznagel, "Are Rates of Psychiatric Disorders in the Homeless Population Changing?," *American Journal of Public Health 94* (January 2004) 103–108; Burt et al., *Helping America's Homeless,* 202–205; Elliot Liebow, *Tell Them Who I Am* (New York: Free Press, 1993), xiii.
6. U.S. Conference of Mayors, *Hunger and Homelessness 2003,* ii; North et al. "Correlates of Early Onset and Chronicity of Homelessness"; Christopher Jencks, *The Homeless* (Cambridge, MA: Harvard University Press, 1994), 44.
7. U.S. Conference of Mayors, *Hunger and Homelessness 2003,* 35, 37, 107.
8. *State of the Nation's Housing* (Cambridge, MA: Joint Center for Housing Studies of Harvard University, 2003), 22, 27; Patrick Healy, "Growing Up on Long Island, and Leaving," *New York Times,* (21 February 2004), A15. See also *Out of Reach: America's Housing Wage Climbs* (Washington, DC: National Low Income Housing Coalition, 2003).
9. Steve Kerch, "Norman Hotel Commitment Sets Pace for Low-Rent Rehabs," *Chicago Tribune* (16 August 1987), sec. 16, 1.

10. U.S. Bureau of the Census, *Statistical Abstract of the United States, 1991* (Washington DC: Department of Commerce, 1992), 732.
11. U.S. Department of Housing and Urban Development, *Waiting in Vain; An Update on America's Housing Crisis* (Washington DC: HUD, 1999).
12. HUD, *Waiting in Vain;* Margery Austin Turner, "Strengths and Weaknesses of the Housing Voucher Program," testimony before Congress (17 June 2003), available from the Urban Institute; Stephen Kennedy and Meryl Finkel, *Section 8 Voucher and Rental Certificate Utilization Program: Final Report* (Washington, DC: HUD, 1994); Meryl Finkel and Larry Buron, *Study on Section 8 Response Rates, Vol. 1: Quantitative Study of Success Rates in Metropolitan Areas* (Washington, DC: HUD, 2001).
13. U.S. Census Bureau, *Statistical Abstract of the United States, 2002* (Washington, DC: Department of Commerce, 2003), 622.
14. *State of the Nation's Housing,* 26; David Leonhardt, "Earning More, but Struggling to Own a Home," *New York Times* (4 November 2002), A13.
15. David Leonhardt, "Blacks' Mortgage Costs Exceed Whites' of Like Pay," *New York Times* (1 May 2002), A19; Calvin Bradford, *Race or Risk? Racial Disparities and the Subprime Refinance Market* (Washington DC: Center for Community Change, 2002); Mary Austin Turner, Stephen L. Ross, George C. Galster, and John Yinger, *Discrimination in Metropolitan Markets: National Results from Phase 1 of HDS2000* (Washington, DC: Urban Institute, 2002).
16. Camille Zubrinsky Charles, "Neighborhood Racial-Composition Preferences: Evidence from a Multiethnic Metropolis," *Social Problems 47* (August 2000), 379–407; Stephen Grant Meyer, *As Long as They Don't Move Next Door: Segregation and Racial Conflict in American Neighborhoods* (Lanham, MD: Rowman & Littlefield, 2000); Richard D. Alba, John R. Logan, and Brian J. Stults, "How Segregated Are Middle-Class African Americans?" *Social Problems 47* (November 2000), 543–558; Lynette Clemetson, "Mixing It Up in the Burbs: What Happens When Whites Move into an All-Black Suburb?" *Newsweek* (17 January 2000), 61–62.
17. U.S. Department of Housing and Urban Development, *American Housing Survey for the United States: 2001* (Washington, DC: Government Printing Office, 2002), 50, 54, 248, 252, 326, 330.
18. Jill Littrell and Elizabeth Beck, "Do Inner-City, African-American Males Exhibit 'Bad Attitudes' toward Work?" *Journal of Sociology and Social Welfare 27* (June 2000), 3–23.
19. David Wagner, *Checkerboard Square: Culture and Resistance in a Homeless Community* (Boulder, CO: Westview Press, 1993).
20. Michael R. Sosin, "Homeless and Vulnerable Meal Program Users: A Comparison Study," *Social Problems 39* (May 1992), 170–188.
21. Richard P. Applebaum and John I. Gilderbloom, "Supply-Side Economics and Rents: Are Rental Housing Markets Truly Competitive?" in Rachel G. Bratt, Chester Hartman, and Ann Meyerson, eds., *Critical Perspectives on Housing* (Philadelphia: Temple University Press, 1986), 167–172.
22. Chester Hartman, "A Radical Perspective on Housing Reform," in Hartman, *America's Housing Crisis,* 11–12; Achtenberg and Marcuse, "Towards the Decommodification of Housing," in Hartman, *America's Housing Crisis,* 208.
23. Joe T. Darden, "Accessibility to Housing: Differential Residential Segregation for Blacks, Hispanics, American Indians, and Asians," in Jamshid A. Momeni, ed., *Race, Ethnicity, and Minority Housing in the United States* (New York: Greenwood Press, 1986), 109–126; Peter Mieszkowski and Richard Syron, "Economic Explanation for Housing Segregation," *New England Economic Review* (November/December 1979), 33–39; Maria Krysan, "Community Undesirability in Black and White: Examining Racial Residential Preferences through Community Perceptions," *Social Problems 49* (November 2002), 521–543.
24. Gwendolyn Wright, *Building the Dream* (New York: Pantheon Books, 1981), 4, 46–47, 66.
25. Roy Lubove, *The Progressives and the Slums: Tenement House Reform in New York City,* 1890–1917 (Pittsburgh: University of Pittsburgh Press, 1962), 1–3; Wright, *Building the Dream,* 118.
26. Lubove, *The Progressives and the Slums,* 4–11.
27. Lubove, *The Progressives and the Slums,* 11–23.
28. Wright, *Building the Dream,* 123.
29. Allen F. Davis, *Spearheads for Reform: The Social Settlements and the Progressive Movement,* 1890–1914 (New York: Oxford University Press, 1967), 65.
30. Davis, *Spearheads for Reform,* 66–67.
31. Wright, *Building the Dream,* 128–129.
32. Jacob Riis, *How the Other Half Lives* (New York: Hill & Wang, 1957 [1890]), 203–226; Wright,

Building the Dream, 123; Peter Kivisto, "A Historical Review of Changes in Public Housing Policies and Their Impacts on Minorities," in Momeni, *Race, Ethnicity, and Minority Housing,* 3.

33. Wright, *Building the Dream,* 96–102.
34. Dolores Hayden, *Redesigning the American Dream* (New York: W. W. Norton, 1984), 22–23; Wright, *Building the Dream,* 96–113.
35. Wright, *Building the Dream,* 58–60.
36. Wright, *Building the Dream,* 177–184.
37. Wright, *Building the Dream,* 193–212; Thomas Lee Philpott, *The Slum and the Ghetto: Neighborhood Deterioration and Middle-Class Reform, Chicago, 1880–1930* (New York: Oxford University Press, 1978), 162–180.
38. Much of this discussion is derived from Gail Radford, *Modern Housing for America; Policy Struggles in the New Deal Era* (Chicago: University of Chicago Press, 1996).
39. Robert D. Leighninger Jr., "Cultural Infrastructure: The Legacy of New Deal Public Space," *Journal of Architectural Education 49* (May 1996), 226–236.
40. Michael W. Straus and Talbot Wegg, *Housing Comes of Age* (New York: Oxford University Press, 1938); Richard Pommer, quoted in Radford, *Modern Housing for America,* 108; Robert D. Leighninger Jr., "Public Investment or Pork: The Meaning of New Deal Public Works," *Journal of Progressive Human Services 11* (Fall 2000), 29–50; Robert D. Leighninger Jr. and Leslie Leighninger, "Social Policy of the New Deal," in James Midgley, Martin B. Tracy, and Michelle Livermore, eds., *The Handbook of Social Policy* (Thousand Oaks, CA: Sage, 2000), 111–126.
41. Citizens Commission on Civil Rights, "The Federal Government and Equal Housing Opportunity: A Continuing Failure," in Bratt et al., *Critical Perspectives on Housing,* 299–301; Hayden, *Redesigning the American Dream,* 6–8; Wright, *Building the Dream,* 247–248.
42. Judith Robinson, Laura Bobeczko, Paul Lusignan, and Jeffrey Shrimpton, *Public Housing in the United States, 1933–1949: A Historic Context, Vol I* (Washington, DC: National Register of Historic Places, 1999), 40, Appendix 4, 1–19; Yvonne Wingett, "Phoenix Tenants Resist Housing Overhaul," *Arizona Republic* (11 March 2003), A1–2.
43. Radford, *Modern Housing for America,* 1.
44. Arnold R. Hirsch, *Making the Second Ghetto* (Cambridge, England: Cambridge University Press, 1983), 10; Devereux Bowly Jr., *The Poorhouse: Subsidized Housing in Chicago, 1895–1976* (Carbondale: Southern Illinois University Press, 1978), 50–51.
45. Nicholas Lemann, *The Promised Land: The Great Black Migration and How It Changed America* (New York: Random House, 1991).
46. See also Bowly, *The Poorhouse,* 91–93.
47. Jane Jacobs, *The Death and Life of Great American Cities* (New York: Random House, 1961).
48. Wright, *Building the Dream,* 246; George Sternlieb and David Listokin, "A Review of National Housing Policy," in Peter D. Salins, ed., *Housing America's Poor* (Chapel Hill: University of North Carolina Press, 1987), 21–22, 26.
49. William R. Barnes, "A Battle for Washington: Ideology, Racism, and Self-Interest in the Controversy over Public Housing, 1943–1946," *Records of the Columbia Historical Society of Washington DC,* vol. 50 (1980), 452–483; Ira S. Lowry, "Where Should the Poor Live?" in Salins, ed., *Housing America's Poor,* 96–97.
50. Wright, *Building the Dream,* 237–239; Elizabeth D. Huttman, *Introduction to Social Policy* (New York: McGraw-Hill, 1981), 292.
51. Jill Zuckman, "Pierce Directed HUD Grants, Jailed Aide Tells Panel," *Congressional Quarterly 48* (5 May 1990), 1359.
52. Huttman, *Introduction to Social Policy,* 298; Sternlieb and Listokin, "A Review of National Housing Policy," in Salins, ed., *Housing America's Poor,* 30–31; John I. Gilderbloom and Richard P. Appelbaum, *Rethinking Rental Housing* (Philadelphia: Temple University Press, 1988), 75–76.
53. *The 25th Anniversary of the Community Reinvestment Act: Access to Capital in an Evolving Financial Services System* (Cambridge, MA: Joint Center for Housing Studies of Harvard University, 2002).
54. Joel Blau, *The Visible Poor: Homelessness in the United States* (New York: Oxford University Press, 1992), 112; see also Cynthia J. Bogard, *Seasons Such as These: How Homelessness Took Shape in America* (Hawthorne, NY: Aldine de Gruyter, 2003).
55. Blau, *The Visible Poor,* 112.
56. Blau, *The Visible Poor,* 113–114; Gail Braccidiferro, "Federal Grants Help Nonprofits Serve Homeless," *New York Times* (6 January 1991), Y27.
57. Chester Hartman, "Housing Policies under the Reagan Administration" in Bratt et al., eds., *Critical Perspectives on Housing,* 363–376.

58. Blau, *The Visible Poor,* 71; Judy Aulette, "Privatization of Housing in a Declining Economy: The Case of Stepping Stone Housing," *Journal of Sociology and Social Welfare 18* (March 1991), 151–164; William M. Rohe, "Public Housing Homeownership Demonstration Program," in Willem van Vliet, ed., *The Encyclopedia of Housing* (Thousand Oaks, CA: Sage, 1998), 447–448.
59. Larry Buron, Susan Popkin, Diane Levy, Laura Harris, and Jill Khadduri, *The HOPE VI Tracking Study* (Washington DC: Abt Associates & Urban Institute, 2002); Ross Atkin, "Public Housing at a Crossroads," *Christian Science Monitor* (12 March 2003), 11.
60. "Revival of Tax Credit Is Sought to Spur Low-Income Housing," *New York Times* (18 April 1993), 17; Blau, *The Visible Poor,* 72.
61. Jason DeParle, "Slamming the Door," *New York Times Magazine* (20 October 1996), 68.
62. Paul W. Valentine, "Baltimore Blasts the Past, Looks to Future," *Washington Post* (20 August 1995), B1.
63. Penny Loeb with Warren Cohen, "The Unsheltered Life," *U.S. News & World Report* (11 November 1996), 29–33; Don Terry, "Chicago Housing Agency to Be Taken Over by U.S.," *New York Times* (28 May 1995), 1, 15; Guy Gugliotta, "The Housing That HUD Built: A Huge Lawsuit in Texas Aims to Overturn Decades of Discrimination and Segregation," *Washington Post National Weekly Edition* (21–27 March 1994), 10; Albert B. Crenshaw, "A High-Stakes Battle over Housing the Poor," *Washington Post National Weekly Edition* (12 May 1997), 22.
64. David S. Broder, "Making a Move on Housing," *Washington Post National Weekly Edition* (13–19 June 1993), 4.
65. Debra Shore, "The Houses That Gautreaux Built," *University of Chicago Magazine* (February 1995), 23–27; Jason DeParle, "An Underground Railroad from Projects to Suburbs," *New York Times* (1 December 1993), 1, A12; Louis Uchitelle, "By Listening, 3 Economists Show Slums Hurt the Poor," *New York Times* (18 February 2001), BU4.
66. Judith Haveman, "Rescue for Low-Income Housing Approved," *Washington Post* (9 October 1997), A20; Michael Janofsky, "HUD and Its New Chief Face His High Ambitions," *New York Times* (13 April 1997), 11.
67. "Police Defrauding HUD," *Arizona Republic* (4 April 2001), 14; Anthony DePalma, "In Cuomo's Record as Federal Housing Secretary, Bold Steps and Missteps," *New York Times* (3 September 2002), A19.
68. Peter Dreier, "You Can Bank on It," *Boston Globe* (23 July 1995), 67; Bazelon Center Action Alert, "Bills to Reduce Housing Rights Near Vote" (Washington, DC: Bazelon Center for Mental Health Law, 13 June 1997).
69. Neal Peirce, "Working for Your Subsidized Housing," *Liberal Opinion* (26 May 1997), 3.
70. National Low Income Housing Coalition, "Summary, 1998 Housing Reform Act," available online at www.nlihc.org/news/ph98.htm.
71. Christopher Marquis, "Melquiades Rafael Martinez," *New York Times* (21 December 2000), A25; Christopher Lee, "Focusing on Results, Not Methods: Housing Secretary Nominee Learned Versatility in Three U.S. Cities," *Washington Post* (29 December 2003), A15; "Mortgage Guessing Game," *Los Angeles Times* (12 January 2004), B12; Atkin, "Public Housing at a Crossroads;" Robert Pear, "Renters Receiving U.S. Aid to Pay More under Budget," *New York Times* (11 February 2003), 16.
72. William Raspberry, "Where Have All the Homeless Gone?" *Burlington Free Press* (9 October 1998), A12; Elizabeth Bumiller, "After Attack, Guiliani Plans Crackdown on the Homeless," *New York Times* (20 November 1999), A1; National Law Center on Homelessness & Poverty, *Illegal to Be Homeless: The Criminalization of Homelessness in the United States* (Washington, DC: NLCHP, 2002); John Ritter, "Homeless Hurt on Several Fronts," *USA Today* (27 December 2002), 3A.
73. U.S. Conference of Mayors–Sodexo, *Hunger and Homelessness Survey;* Peter T. Kilborn, "For Food Pantries, Cupboard Isn't Bare but It's Coming Close," *New York Times* (25 May 2003), 18; Bogard, *Seasons Such as This,* 203.
74. Margaret Daly, "Sharing the American Dream," *Better Homes and Gardens* (May 1988), 32; Avis C. Vidal and Bob Komines, "Community Development Corporations: A National Perspective," *National Civic Review 78* (May–June 1989), 168–186; Mary K. Nenno, "Changes and Challenges in Affordable Housing and Urban Development," in Willem van Vliet, ed., *Affordable Housing and Urban Development in the United States* (Thousand Oaks, CA: Sage, 1997), 13.
75. Urban Neighborhoods Task Force, *Life in the City* (Washington, DC: Center for National Policy,

1997); Ronald F. Ferguson and William T. Dickens, *Urban Problems and Community Development* (Washington, DC: Brookings Institution, 1999), 178, 445.

76. Mark Lewis, "Keeping Homes Affordable—Permanently," *The Responsive Community 6* (Summer 1996), 83–86; Jonathan Sidener, "Trust Makes Homes Affordable," *Arizona Republic* (18 September 2002), B5.
77. Robert Sharoff, "Book Chain Taps Underserved Neighborhoods," *New York Times* (24 February 2004), C6; Anne Field, "Capital for Companies That Aid Communities," *New York Times* (16 October 2003), C8.
78. Michael H. Shuman, "Community Corporations: Engines for a New Place-Based Economics," *The Responsive Community 9* (Summer 1999), 48–57; Amy Waldman, "In Harlem, Green Is Trumping Black and White," *New York Times* (11 December 1999), A17; Nicholas Lemann, "The Myth of Community Development," *New York Times Sunday Magazine* (2 January 1994), 27–31, 54–60.
79. Emelyn Cruz Lat, "One Strike Evictions," *San Francisco Examiner* (24 August 1998), A1, A8–9.
80. William Julius Wilson, *When Work Disappears: The World of the New Urban Poor* (New York: Knopf, 1996); Michael H. Schill, "Chicago's Mixed-Income New Communities Strategy: The Future Face of Public Housing?" in van Vliet, ed., *Affordable Housing and Urban Development in the United States,* 135–157; Blair Kamin, "Shelter by Design" *Chicago Tribune* (18–23 June 1995).
81. These and other examples in this section are drawn from Blair Kamin's six-part series, "Shelter by Design," in the *Chicago Tribune* in 1995.
82. Tom Jones, William Pettus, and Michael Pyatok, *Good Neighbors: Affordable Family Housing* (New York: McGraw-Hill, 1998); Michael Pyatok, "Martha Stewark vs. Studs Terkel? New Urbanism and Inner City Neighborhoods That Work," *Places 13* (Winter 2000), 40–43.
83. Christine Ling, "Housing for Nation's Poor Is Squeezed," *Chicago Tribune* (21 December 2002); David Leonhardt, "Earning More, but Struggling . . . "; David Leonhardt, "More Falling Behind in Mortgage Payments," *New York Times* (12 June 2001), A1; Shaun McKinnon, "High Prices, Low Wages Squeeze Homeowners," *Arizona Republic* (26 June 2001) D1; David Leonhardt, "Prices of Homes Are Still Rising, but More Slowly," *New York Times* (3 June 2003), C1.
84. Jonathan Barnett, *The Fractured Metropolis: Improving the New City, Restoring the Old City, Reshaping the Region* (Boulder, CO: Westview Press, 1995); David Ferrell, "Commute Is Getting Tougher," *Los Angeles Times* (6 October 2000), B1, B6; David W. Chen, "The Cost of Urban Sprawl: Unplanned Obsolescence," *New York Times* (30 January 2000), secs. 4, 5; Sue Anne Pressley, "Beachbound N.C. Service Workers Spend Hours on the Bus; Shortage of Jobs in Rural Counties Spurs Daily Trek," *Washington Post* (26 July 2000), A3; Stephanie Mencimer, "The Price of Going the Distance," *New York Times* (28 April 2002), 24; "Suburban Sprawl Adds Health Concerns, Studies Say," *New York Times* (31 August 2003), 15; Bradford McKee, "As Suburbs Grow, So Do Waistlines," *New York Times* (4 September 2003), D1.
85. Dan Eggen and Peter Pae, "Anti-Development Forces Massing along Home Front," *Washington Post* (14 December 1997), A1, A22–24; Timothy Egan, "The New Politics of Urban Sprawl," *New York Times* (15 November 1998), sec. 4, 1, 3; Alan Ehrenhalt, "New Recruits in the War on Sprawl," *New York Times* (13 April 1999), A29; Neal Peirce and Curtis Johnson, "Stepping Up to Stop Sprawl," *Nashville Tennessean* (10 October 1999), A21–25.
86. Michael J. Ybarra, "Putting City Sprawl on a Zoning Diet," *New York Times* (16 June 1996), E4; Timothy Egan, "Drawing the Hard Line on Urban Sprawl," *New York Times* (30 December 1996), A1, A12; Alan Ehrenhalt, "The Great Transit Turnaround," *Governing* (August 2000), 6–8; Timothy Egan, "Portland Voters Endorse Curbs on City Growth," *New York Times* (23 May 2003), A24.
87. Sue Anne Pressley, "Welcome to Gridlock, Y'all," *Washington Post National Weekly Edition* (14 December 1998), 31; Alan Ehrenhalt, "New Recruits in the War on Sprawl," *New York Times* (13 April 1998), A29; David Firestone, "Suburban Comforts Thwart Atlanta's Plans to Limit Sprawl," *New York Times* (21 November 1999), 1; Jonathan Lerner, "Peach Blossom Special," *Metropolis* (June 2003), 155f.
88. Iver Peterson, "After Decades of Dismissal, the Suburbs Win Converts," *New York Times* (5 December 1999), A1, A43; D. J. Waldie, "Do the Voters Really Hate Sprawl?" *New York Times* (3 March 2000), A21; D. W. Miller, "Searching for Common Ground in the Debate over Urban

Sprawl," *Chronicle of Higher Education* (21 May 1999), A15–16.

89. Scott Wilson, "Montgomery Eyes Taxing Developers," *Washington Post* (3 August 1999), B1, 5; David Rusk, *Cities without Suburbs* (Baltimore: Johns Hopkins University Press, 1995); D. W. Miller, "The New Urban Studies," *Chronicle of Higher Education* (18 August 2000), A15–16; Shaun McKinnon, "Smart Growth Still Elusive," *Arizona Republic* (21 April 2002), A1.
90. Haya El Nasser, "Suburbia Stays in Neighborhood; Unlike U.S. Metro Areas, European Cities Such as Paris Keep a Tight Check on Growth," *USA Today* (5 January 2000), A5.
91. Michael A. Fletcher, "Tapping into a New Market: The Inner City," *Washington Post National Weekly Edition* (15 March 1999), 19; Katheryn Hayes Tucker, "Saying Goodbye to the 'Burbs," (5 March 2000), BU1, 15; Richard Moe and Carter Wilkie, *Changing Places: Rebuilding Community in the Age of Sprawl* (New York: Henry Holt, 1997); John Ritter, "Unions Seeing New Benefits in 'Smart Growth'," *USA Today* (2 January 2004), 3A.
92. James Midgley, *Social Development: The Developmental Perspective in Social Welfare* (Thousand Oaks, CA: Sage, 1995).
93. William R. Barnes and Larry C. Ledebur, *The New Regional Economies* (Thousand Oaks, CA: Sage, 1998); Harold A. Hovey, *Can the States Afford Devolution?* (Washington, DC: Brookings Institution, 1998); Peter Dreier, *Housing Policy and Devolution: A Delicate Balancing Act* (Washington, DC: Brookings Institution, 1998); E. Terrence Jones, "Regionalism Is Alive and Well, It's Just Hard to Notice," *St. Louis Post Dispatch* (31 December 2000), B1, 4; Peter Calthorpe and William Fulton, *The Regional City: Planning for the End of Sprawl* (Washington: Island Press, 2001); Dom Nozzi, *Road to Ruin: An Introduction to Sprawl and How to Cure It* (Westport, CT: Praeger, 2003).
94. Betty Friedan, *The Feminine Mystique* (New York: W. W. Norton, 1963).
95. Hayden, *Redesigning the American Dream,* 3–4.
96. Karen A. Franck and Sherry Ahrentzen, eds., *New Households, New Housing* (New York: Van Nostrand, 1989); Caroline E. Mayer, "Group Homes Targeted for Restriction," *Washington Post* (14 March 1998), VN1, 4; Michael Pyatok, "Martha Steward vs. Studs Terkel?"; Bradford McKee, "Metro Cruiser," *Architecture* (August 2001), 45f.
97. Richard Sennett, *The Fall of Public Man* (New York: Alfred Knopf, 1977); David Popenoe, *Private Pleasure, Public Plight: American Metropolitan Community Life in Comparative Perspective* (New Brunswick, NJ: Transaction, 1985).
98. Wright, *Building the Dream;* Hayden, *Redesigning the American Dream;* Robert C. Wood, *Suburbia: Its People and Their Politics* (Boston: Houghton Mifflin, 1958); Oscar Newman, *Defensible Space* (New York: Macmillan, 1972).
99. Carla Campbell and Donald F. Schwarz, "Prevalance and Impact of Exposure to Interpersonal Violence among Suburban and Urban Middle School Students," *Pediatrics 98* (September 1996), 396–402; Christopher S. Wren, "Face of Heroin: It's Younger and Suburban," *New York Times* (25 April 2000), A22.
100. Katy Read, "Gates Protect Sense of Security," *New Orleans Times-Picayune* (17 September 1995), A1, 17; Susan Diesenhouse, "In South Florida, Security Sells Houses," *New York Times* (3 March 1996), 27; Setha Low, *Behind the Gates; Life, Security, and the Pursuit of Happiness in Fortress America* (New York: Routledge, 2003).
101. Jonathan Tilove, "Suburbanites Cultivate New Metro Areas," *New Orleans Times–Picayune* (28 April 1996), A23; Joel Kotkin, "Beyond White Flight," *Washington Post National Weekly Edition* (18–24 March 1996), 26–27.
102. Haya El Nasser, "Ads' Use of Sprawl Grabs Attention," *USA Today* (6 October 2000), A3; Robert D. Putnam, "Bowling Alone: America's Declining Social Capital," *Journal of Democracy 6* (1995), 65–78; Robert D. Putnam, "The Strange Disappearance of Civic America," *American Prospect 24* (Winter 1996), 34–48.
103. Robert Putnam, *Bowling Alone: The Collapse and Revival of American Community* (New York: Simon & Schuster, 2000).
104. Nicholas Lemann, "Kicking in Groups," *Atlantic Monthly 227* (April 1996), 22–26; Everett C. Ladd, "Bowling with Tocqueville: Civic Engagement and Social Capital," *The Responsive Community* (Spring 1999), 11–21; Alice Ann Love, "Poll: Americans Joiners, Not Loners," *Associated Press News Service* (18 December 1997).
105. Lane Kenworthy, "Civic Engagement, Social Capital and Economic Cooperation," *American Behavioral Scientist 40* (March/April 1997),

645–656; Bob Edwards and Michael W. Foley, "Social Capital and the Political Economy of Our Discontent," *American Behavioral Scientist 40* (March/April 1997), 669–678; C. Kim Cummings, "Regenerating Social Capital in Urban Neighborhoods: A Case Study," *Journal of Applied Sociology 17* (2000), 56–68.

106. Bob Edwards and Michael W. Foley, "Much Ado about Social Capital," *Contemporary Sociology 30* (May 2001); Robert Putnam, "Bowling Together," *The American Prospect* (11 February 2002), 20–22.
107. Howard Kunstler, "Home from Nowhere," *Atlantic Monthly 278* (September 1996), 43–66; Sandy Felsenthal "15 Ways to Fix the Suburbs," *Newsweek* (15 May 1995), 45–53; Alex Krieger, "Whose Urbanism?" *Architecture* (November 1998), 73–77; Andres Duany, "Our Urbanism," *Architecture* (December 1998), 37–40.
108. "New Urbanist Developments," *Architecture* (April 1996), 71–77; Andrew Ross, "Mousetrapped: As Their Houses Leak and Fissure around Them, Celebration's Residents Realize It's a Shoddy World After All," *Metropolis* (October 1999); Andrew Ross, *The Celebration Chronicles* (New York: Ballantine, 1999); Douglas Frantz and Catherine Collins, *Celebration, U.S.A.: Living in Disney's Brave New Town* (New York: Holt, 1999); Timothy Egan, "A Development Fuels a Debate on Urbanism," *New York Times* (14 June 2002), A16; Abby Goodnough, "Disney Is Selling a Town It Built to Reflect the Past," *New York Times* (14 January 2004), A10.
109. Jerry Adler and Maggie Malone, "Toppling Towers," *Newsweek* (4 November 1996), 71.
110. Heidi Landecker, "Is New Urbanism Good for America?" *Architecture* (April 1996), 69–70.
111. Robert J. Sampson, Stephen W. Raudenbush, and Felton Earls, "Neighborhoods and Violent Crime: A Multilevel Study of Collective Efficacy," *Science 277* (15 August 1997), 918–924; Robert J. Sampson and Stephen W. Raudenbush, "Systematic Social Observation of Public Spaces: A New Look at Disorder in Urban Neighborhoods," *American Journal of Sociology 105* (November 1999), 603–651; Dan Hurley, "On Crime as Science (a Neighbor at a Time)," *New York Times* (6 January 2004), F1.
112. Sheri McGregor, " 'Safe Walk Home': Child-Safety Program Stresses Community Involvement," *Washington Post* (8 September 1997), C5; see also Patricia L. Ewalt, Edith M. Freeman, and Dennis L. Poole, eds., *Community Building: Renewal, Well-Being, and Shared Responsibility* (Annapolis, MD: NASW Press, 1998); Marie D. Hoff, ed., *Sustainable Community Development* (Boca Raton, FL: Lewis, 1998).
113. Dom Nozzi, *Road to Ruin,* 8.
114. Myron Magnet, "The Homeless," *Fortune* (23 November 1987), 170–190; *The Report of the President's Commission on Housing* (Washington, DC, 1982), xvii–xviii; Peter Salins, "America's Permanent Housing Problem," in Salins, ed., *Housing America's Poor,* 1–13.
115. Salins, "America's Permanent Housing Problem," 5.
116. National Housing Task Force, *A Decent Place to Live* (Washington, DC: National Housing Task Force, March 1988), 12–17.
117. Chester Hartman, "A Radical Perspective on Housing Reform," in Hartman, *America's Housing Crisis,* 1–25; Achtenberg and Marcuse, "Towards the Decommodification of Housing," in Hartman, *America's Housing Crisis,* 202–230.
118. Barry Checkoway, "Large Builders, Federal Housing Programs, and Postwar Suburbanization," in Bratt et al., *Critical Perspectives on Housing,* 119–138.
119. Mark Swenarton, *Homes Fit for Heroes* (London: Heinemann, 1981).
120. Gilderbloom and Appelbaum, *Rethinking Rental Housing,* 181–204.
121. Jason DeParle, "Slamming the Door," *New York Times Magazine* (20 October 1996), 57.
122. Carol S. Cohen and Michael H. Phillips, "Building Community: Principles for Social Work Practice in Housing Settings," *Social Work 42* (September 1997), 471–481.
123. Interview with Dennis Marino and Sue Brady, Hull House, Uptown Branch, Chicago, 18 June 1988.
124. Elizabeth A. Mulroy and Paticia L. Ewalt, "Affordable Housing: A Basic Need and a Social Issue," *Social Work 41* (May 1996), 245–249.
125. David Surface, "The Ten Year Plan to End Homelessness," *Social Work Today 4* (January 2004), 14–16.

CHAPTER

15

Aging

Since her diagnosis of "beginning stage of Alzheimer's disease" two years ago, Paulette Moore has become increasingly forgetful. Her physician told her grown children that while Mrs. Moore is not physically ill, from now on she will require ongoing help with such basic living functions as getting up out of bed, bathing, taking medication, and preparing meals. All her children live some distance away and are therefore unable to provide personally for her long-term care needs. Mrs. Moore could move into the Alzheimer's section of an assisted living center, but her children would much prefer to have her cared for in her own home, among familiar surroundings, as long as possible. However, they are daunted by the prospect of arranging and paying for such care on a long-term basis. How will they find reliable home health aides, and will Medicaid cover all the costs?

Horace Randolph is an 82-year-old African American resident of a small midwestern city. A widower whose health has been declining over the last ten years, he is just getting by on his Social Security payments (low because he held poorly paying jobs all his life) and federal Supplemental Security Income benefits. Recently Mr. Randolph has become confused and disoriented. His two sons and their wives have done their best to care for him in his home, but they feel that now he probably needs to be in a nursing home. They worry about the fact that the predominantly white nursing homes in the area don't seem to welcome African American residents.

Sarah Levin, who is 86, recently suffered a stroke, which left her with some speech problems and a weakness in her left arm. She was transferred from the hospital to a rehabilitation center near her home in Brooklyn. There she receives daily physical and speech therapy. Her 81-year-old "baby sister" drops in regularly to see her, along with her daughter and three grandchildren. Mrs. Levin's older brother, Max, brings her the Sunday *New York Times* each weekend "so we can do the crossword puzzle together." Mrs. Levin is making remarkable progress, she has recovered her famous sense of humor, and she plans to return to her apartment in a few weeks.

Willis McMillan is a retired social worker who lives alone in East Harlem, New York. At 63, he is recovering from a serious illness, which has left him weak and unsure about his ability to do his own shopping and other daily chores. Help has come from the East River Senior Center. The center, a chapter of the National Federation of Interfaith Volunteer Caregivers, recently assigned Marisol Dominquez and Danny Rivera to assist him. The two teenagers help Mr. McMillan get his laundry and do his grocery shopping for him. In return, he mentors them and gives advice about applying to college. Marisol says she's learned not to have stereotypes about older people. With a smile, Mr. McMillan responds, "It's just something they've learned by helping me out."[1]

"My talk went really well," Jolene French tells her social work instructor. "I told the older people at the congregate meal site about my idea for a telephone check-in network, and a lot of them want to sign up. Now I have to finish recruiting the volunteers who will call them each day to see how they are doing. For this rural area, it's going to be a great way to keep people in touch."

Today, about one in eight people in the United States is age 65 or over. These older individuals have diverse needs and interests. Although they are often perceived as being a homogeneous category, older Americans in fact vary broadly in income level, health status, degree of educational attainment, ethnic and racial background, and level of independence. Although certain problems—chronic disease, low income, the need for long-term care, and loss of important life roles and abilities—plague a number of the elderly, these are by no means the rule for everyone over 65. Yet because problems of ill health, reduced income, and dependency have frequently been linked to increasing age, a variety of policies and programs has been developed to address them. Unfortunately, such programs and policies frequently lack coordination and consistency. In addition, social workers and other helping professionals are sometimes reluctant to work with the elderly, even though the field presents many challenges and rewards. This chapter tells you more about the field and tries to dispel common myths about aging. It examines age-related social welfare programs in this country and analyzes the images of aging on which they are based. In doing so, it looks at both the historic and contemporary position of the elderly in the United States.

Definitions of Aging

What exactly is the nature of old age, and when does it occur? Philosophers, physicians, and physical and social scientists have debated these questions over the years. Is old age, as some people fear, an incurable disease, the inevitable decline of one's physical and intellectual powers? Or, to put it more positively, is it simply a stage of growth and development, and one associated with wisdom and reflection? Does it begin at age 50, 65, or later? The answers to these questions have varied over time and across cultures. The Social Security Act of 1935 selected 65 as the age at which benefits begin, but this was an arbitrary choice based on economic and policy considerations, rather than on medical or scientific judgments. The policymakers could have chosen 62, 66, or some other dividing line between middle and old age.

Thus, the definition of aging and the notion of when it begins are by no means universally agreed on. Some social scientists have even argued that the category of "old age" is a relatively useless concept. Perhaps it makes no more sense than speaking of all people aged 20 to 45 as belonging to one group. Bernice Neugarten emphasizes the great diversity among elderly people. She suggests that chronological age can be a less powerful influence in people's lives than their socioeconomic status, gender, race, or ethnic background, or the area of the country in which they live. For example, a newly widowed woman, age 60, who has never worked outside the home and is living solely on Social Security in a small, isolated community, has a very different life experience from a 65-year-old married man who continues to be involved in a part-time law practice in a large city. Because of such diversity among the elderly, age-related policies based on general conceptions about old age may not relate accurately to people's needs.[2] The woman in our example might most need income assistance and social supports. The lawyer's concerns might be recreational opportunities and investment planning.

Despite awareness of divergence among the elderly, many researchers and planners still rely on chronological age as a meaningful category. In an attempt to make the concept of old age more precise, some researchers draw a distinction between the "young–old" and the "old–old." The first group includes individuals ages 65 to 74. Most people in this age range lead active, reasonably independent lives and are restricted only moderately, if at all, by physical or mental disabilities. The second group includes all people over the age of 75. These are the individuals more likely to be "frail elderly," those with incapacitating chronic diseases or serious deficiencies in mental functioning. Members of the two groups often have quite different needs in terms of social, health, and other services. Programs and services should be developed with this distinction in mind. Recently, demographers and those working with the elderly have noted a further subset of the elderly: those 85 and over, whose numbers are climbing faster than those of any other age group.[3]

The concept of aging can be discussed not only on an individual level but also on a social level. "The graying of America" has become a popular way of referring to the effects of having an increasing proportion of elderly people in our society. As this proportion grows, especially with the aging of the baby boomers, certain issues have risen to national prominence. These include the capacity of Social Security to continue to provide for all the elderly; rapidly rising health costs; the potential for intergenerational competition over what are seen as scarce resources; and the problem of poverty among certain groups of the elderly, especially women and members of minority groups. The phase "the graying of America" suggests increases in these problems; it also often implies a growing conservatism, as older citizens become more numerous among the nation's voters.

Those who study the biological, psychological, and social aspects of aging are known as specialists in the multidisciplinary field of *gerontology.* A subfield within gerontology is *geriatrics,* which focuses on the medical treatment and prevention of disease among older people.

Statistical Picture of Aging

The United States has more elderly people today than ever before. There are currently more than 34.6 million persons age 65 and over in this country, making up almost 13 percent of the total population. This proportion has changed radically between the colonial period and the present. In 1776 only one out of every 50 people was 65 or over; in 1900 it was one in twenty-five; and by 2000 it was one in seven. Between the years 2000 and 2030, the percentage of the U.S. population age 65 and older will double. There are now more older people in the United States than there are teenagers[4] (see Figure 15.1).

Growth in the absolute number of elderly is caused by factors such as the influx of immigrants up to World War I, decreases in infant mortality rates since the turn of the twentieth century, control of infectious diseases, and improvements in environmental and social conditions (see Figure 15.2, p. 602). Current changes in the proportion of older people in the United States stem largely from decreases in birthrates, although recent dramatic increases in survival rates among the elderly have also played a part.

The increase in the number and proportion of older persons will continue in the twenty-first century, particularly with the aging of the postwar baby boom generation. One analyst speaks of the "sheer magnitude of this human tidal wave," noting that 75 million babies were born in the United States between 1946 and 1964. According to predictions, by the year 2030, almost every fifth American will be 65 or over, more than the number of children under age 13.[5]

FIGURE 15.1 **Numbers and Percentages of Persons Sixty-Five and Older, 1900–2030**

Sources: U.S. Bureau of the Census, *USA Statistics in Brief* (2 August 2000), online at www.census.gov/statab/www/part1.htm.

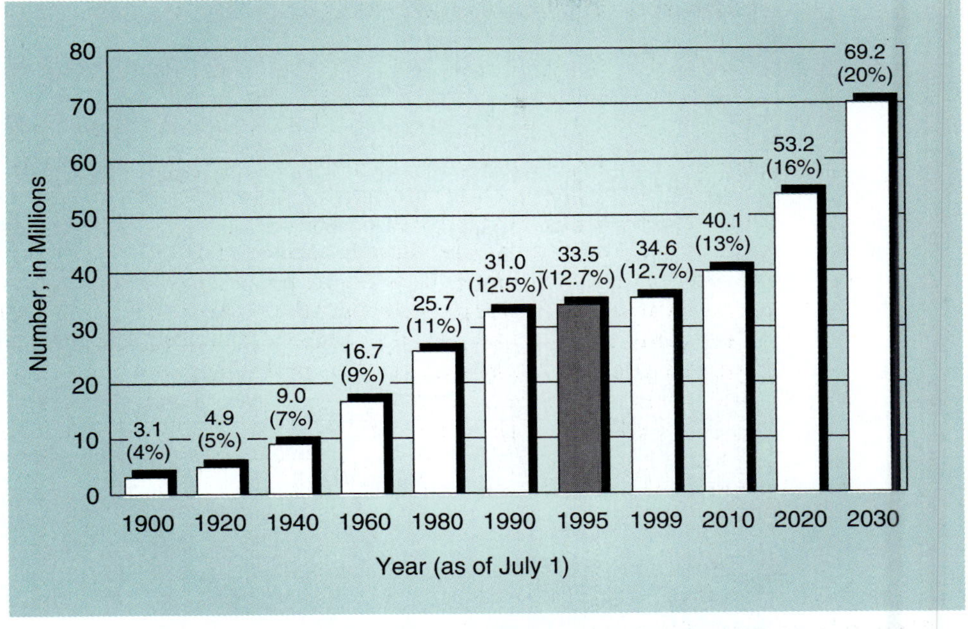

At present, older people tend to be concentrated in certain areas of the country. More than half of all the elderly live in nine states: California, New York, Florida, Pennsylvania, Texas, Ohio, Illinois, Michigan, and New Jersey. The migration of older people to the Sun Belt states is a frequently noted phenomenon. However, although several western and southern states have seen large percentage increases in their elderly populations, so far the overall magnitude of this "migration" has been exaggerated. The state of Florida is one exception; more than 18 percent of its residents are 65 and over. In general, though, the elderly are less likely to change residence than any other age group.[6] (Figure 15.3 shows the geographic distribution of older people in the United States.)

The proportions of "young–old" (65–74) and "old–old" (75 and over) within the category of elderly have undergone interesting shifts. The most rapid growth is occurring within the oldest group. In 1950 fewer than a third of all elderly people were age 75 and over. In 1995 the figure had grown to almost 44 percent, with the largest growth among women over 75. By the year 2000, almost half of the elderly population were 75 or more. The group age 85 and over has seen the greatest increase of all. Improved medical care and environmental conditions appear to be helping to increase the remaining life expectancy for persons who reach the age of 65. A woman who celebrated

FIGURE 15.2 **Number of Births, by Year, 1910–1987, and Relationship to 1987 Age Groups**

Source: U.S. Bureau of the Census, Current Population Reports, Series P–25, No. 1022, *United States Population Estimates, by Age, Sex, and Race: 1980 to 1987* (Washington, DC: U.S. Government Printing Office, 1988), 2.

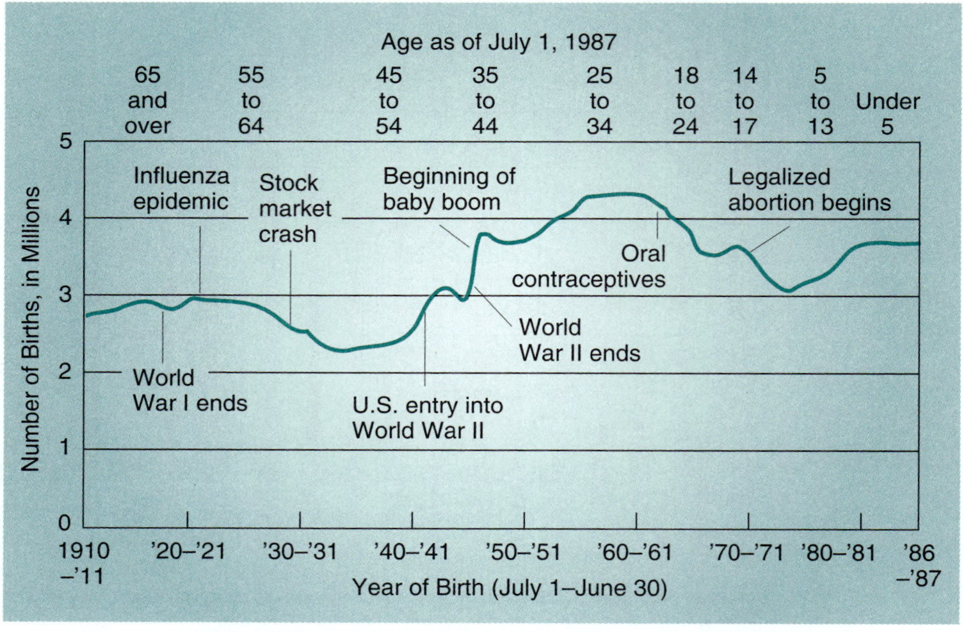

her 65th birthday in 1997, for example, could expect to live nineteen more years; a man age 65 could expect almost sixteen more years. And you might be surprised to learn that the fastest growing segment of the U.S. population is people 100 years and older; it is likely that one of every twenty-six baby boomers will become a centenarian.[7]

This expanded number of elderly is a better-educated group than ever before. In 1965 about a quarter of those 65 and older had completed high school. In 1999 close to 70 percent were high school graduates. There has also been a steady, if less dramatic, increase in the proportion of elderly who have attended college. Today, about 15 percent have a bachelor's degree or more.[8]

The figures discussed so far, while useful, fail to convey the heterogeneous nature of that group labeled "the elderly." As we noted earlier, there is much diversity among older Americans. Many of these differences relate to race and gender. Older women, for example, far outnumber men. By 1998 there were only seventy men age 65 and over to every one-hundred women of that age. For those born in 1998, the life expectancy for women was almost 80, and for men it was 73.8.[9]

FIGURE 15.3 **People Sixty-Five and Older as a Percentage of Each State's Population, 1999**

Source: U.S. Administration on Aging, *Profile of Older Americans: 2000,* 6–9, online at www.aoa.gov/aoa/stats/profile.

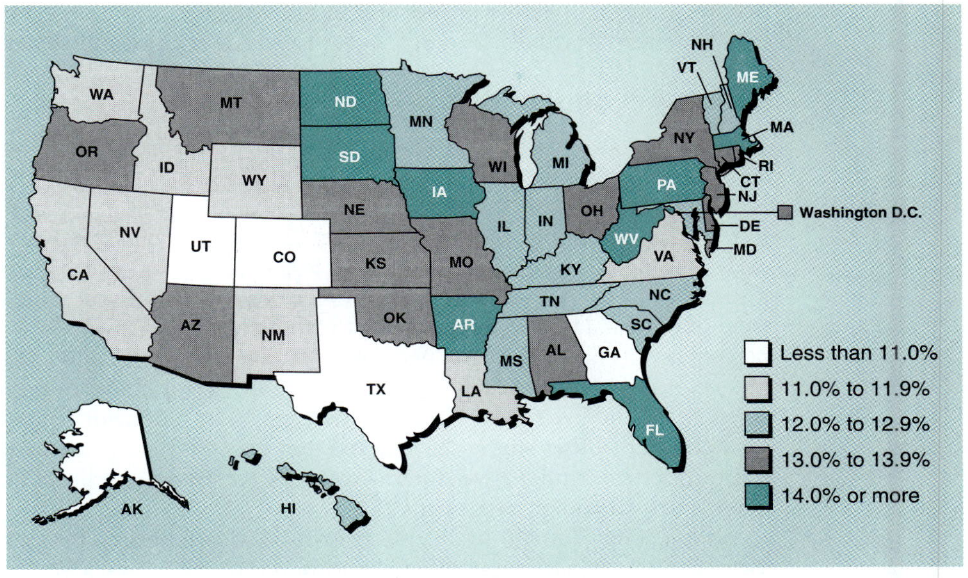

One of the most dramatic variations among men and women relates to marital status. Overall, almost 57 percent of persons 65 and older are married. Yet while 75 percent of older men are married, only 43 percent of older women fit this category. About 45 percent of all women over 65 are widowed; there are about three times as many widows as there are widowers. These differences can be explained not only by greater longevity among women, but also by the greater tendency of widowed or divorced men to remarry and to choose younger spouses. Partly because of the high rate of widowhood, about two-fifths of all women over 65 live alone.[10]

Race is another element differentiating the elderly. Although African Americans make up over 12 percent of the total population, they constitute only 8 percent of those 65 and over. In 2000 an African American male's life expectancy at birth was almost ten years less than that of his white counterpart. Not only do African Americans not live as long as whites, but also a higher proportion have lost a spouse. African American women are the most likely of all older women to become widows.[11]

On the other hand, Latinos and Asian Americans have longer life expectancies than whites. The percentages of Asian and Latino elderly are growing at a greater rate than that of white elderly. The greatest rises in percentages of elderly are among the "other races" population: American Indians, Alaskan Natives, Asian Americans, and Pacific

Islanders. Racial and ethnic diversity among the elderly will continue to increase, with the proportion that is white declining from 84 percent in 2000 to 64 percent in 2050.[12]

Educational attainment can also be affected by gender, race, and ethnicity. Older women are more likely than older men to have completed high school, but 20 percent of men 65 and older have a college degree, as opposed to 11 percent of their female counterparts. In 1999 the proportion of older people who had completed high school was 72 percent of whites, 37 percent of African Americans, and 29 percent of Latinos.[13]

Living Arrangements

The vast majority of older Americans live alone or in a household, rather than in an institution or a group setting. About 12 percent lived in nursing homes in the late 1990s. As noted, far more women live alone than men. About 13 percent of elderly people live with their children, siblings, or other relatives. Despite the widespread belief that many elderly are abandoned by their offspring, a large number report frequent contact. According to a 1984 survey, four out of five older persons who lived alone and had children were in personal or telephone contact with a child at least once a week. Twenty-three percent saw a child daily. Fifty percent said that at least one child could get to them in a matter of minutes in case of emergency. In 2000, researchers found that 65 percent of single men, and even more single women age 50 or older, got at least some help from their children. Other studies have noted that the children of African American, Latino, Asian American, and Native American elderly are even more likely than those of white parents to visit and give support.[14]

About three-fourths of all elderly own their own homes. Because these tend to be older homes, often in inner-city neighborhoods or poor rural areas, housing conditions may be less than adequate. Insufficient weatherproofing, exposed electrical wiring, and worn-out furnaces are frequent problems. Renters, especially minority elderly and those living in rural areas, are particularly likely to have poor housing.[15]

Income

The elderly, like other age groups, have a range of income levels. Contrary to popular opinion, advanced age does not necessarily mean a life of careful budgeting or actual deprivation. People over 50 now account for half of the country's disposable income, and those over 65 can boast twice the discretionary income of people aged 25 to 34. In 1999, poverty among individuals 65 and older reached an all-time low. Yet, although the overall economic position of those age 65 and older has improved markedly since the 1970s, not everyone has shared equally in these gains. The median income of households headed by a person 65 or older is $22,812, or about half that of households headed by someone age 55 to 64.[16]

For the past several decades, the drop in poverty among the elderly has been the bright spot in this income picture. In contrast to the situation of other age groups, particularly children, poverty among the elderly has decreased dramatically since the early 1960s, when one-third of older Americans were poor. This drop has been due in large part to federal government initiatives, particularly the creation in the 1970s of the Supplemental Security Income program and of a system for indexing Social Security benefits to take inflation into account. In 2004, only 10.4 percent of older people were poor.

That same year, the poverty rate for those under 18 years of age was 16.3 percent. In 2002 the poverty rate among the elderly was highest for members of minority groups (24 percent for African Americans and about 21 percent for Latinos) and for women (13 percent), whereas the rate for men 65 and older was 7 percent. Hispanic women living alone are most at risk for economic hardship, with 59 percent of them living below the poverty level in 1999 (see Figure 15.4).[17]

Most elderly people rely on Social Security benefits and their own assets as major sources of income. Since the turn of the century, fewer and fewer Americans have continued to work after age 65. In 1900 two out of three older men were employed. Now, about 12 percent of all those over 65 are part of the labor force (that is, either working or actively seeking work). Interestingly, participation is increasing for the old–old; over 13 percent of those between ages 70 and 74 are now in the workforce. The development of Social Security has much to do with the general shift away from work for most older

FIGURE 15.4 **Percentage of Elderly below Poverty Level, by Gender, Race, and Ethnicity, 1999**

Sources: U.S. Bureau of the Census, Current Population Reports, Series P60-198, *Poverty in the United States 1996* (Washington, DC: U.S. Government Printing Office, 1997), C5–C7; U.S. Administration on Aging, *Profile of Older Americans: 2000,* online at www.aoa.gov/aoa/stats/profile.

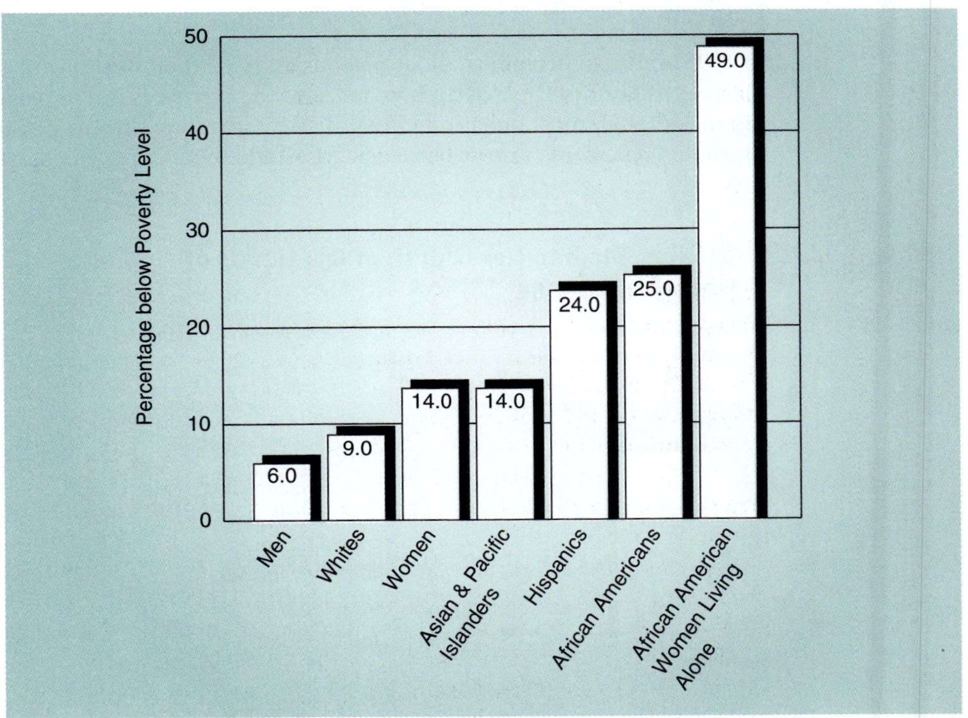

Americans. On average, Social Security benefits account for almost 40 percent of the income of the elderly. Social Security constitutes 80 percent of the income of the poorest elderly. The average monthly Social Security benefit for a retired worker was $874 in 2002; for a couple it was over $1,400. Assets, such as savings and personal property, provide another 20 percent of average income, although net worth varies greatly by race and ethnicity. Some older persons need additional government help beyond Social Security pension benefits, however. About 6 percent of older Americans receive Supplemental Security Income, or federally administered public assistance payments to people who are below a set income level (or to put it another way, people who are still poor after receiving Social Security). Minorities and women are particularly likely to need such assistance.[18] (See Figures 15.5 and 15.6.)

Older people generally have less cash income than the rest of the population. On the other hand, several noncash factors favor the elderly, including paid-up mortgages, smaller family size, and favorable tax treatment. In addition, older people qualify for a number of in-kind benefits from the government. Some of these benefits, such as Medicare, are available to almost all elderly; others, such as Medicaid, are income based. These government programs do not cover all medical costs, however. For this reason, and because these costs are rising, households headed by an elderly person spend about three times more of their after-tax income on health care than do other age groups.[19]

Health

In 1998 about 27 percent of older persons assessed their health care as fair or poor. Yet the health status of the elderly is varied, and the picture is not as negative as one might think. Although most older individuals have at least one chronic disease, such as arthritis, about 23 percent of those between ages 60 and 69, and 17 percent over 70, say they are

FIGURE 15.5 **Wealth: Median Net Worth of 65+ Heads of Households, 1999**

Sources: Older Americans 2000; Federal Interagency Forum on Aging-Related Statistics, online at www.agingstats.gov.

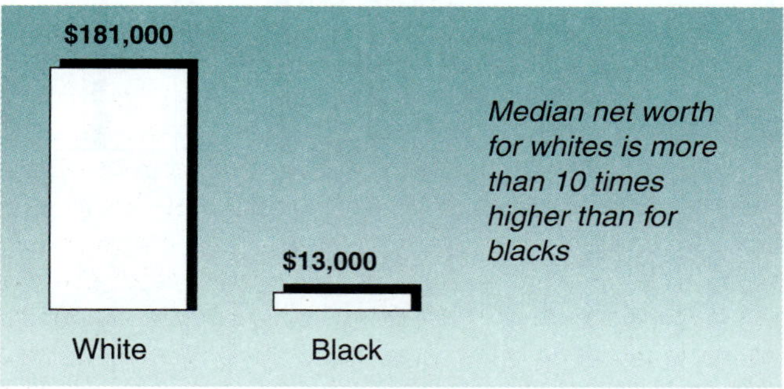

FIGURE 15.6 **Percentages of Aggregate Income of Elderly Persons from Various Sources, 2000**

Source: U.S. Administration on Aging, *Profile of Older Americans: 2002,* online at www.aoa.gov/aoa/stats/profile, p. 10.

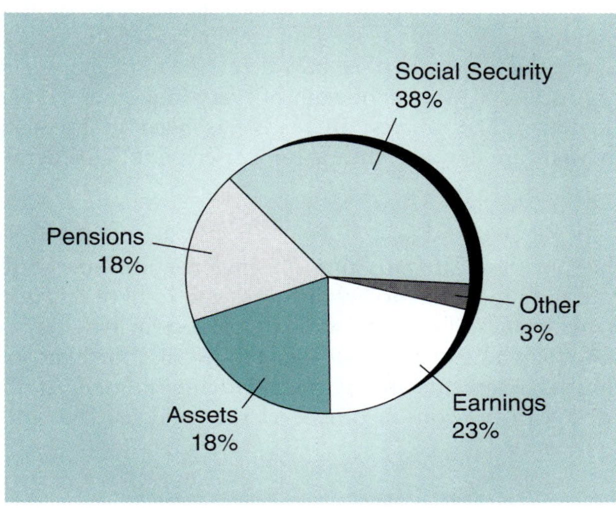

in excellent health. Almost 70 percent of noninstitutionalized older persons report no limitations in any major activity. About 30 percent of all those over 65 are severely disabled. However, health and disability status among the elderly varies by such factors as age, gender, and race. The older the person, the greater the probability of encountering disease or impairment. About a quarter of those 75 and older have health constraints on their normal activities. Women experience more days of restricted activity and bed disability than men. Minority and low-income elderly are also more susceptible to disease and disability. For example, older African Americans, American Indians, and Latinos have a greater risk of stroke and cardiac disease than whites, and these groups' rates of diabetes are four to five times higher.[20]

Probably the most publicized ailment of the elderly is Alzheimer's disease, a frightening and irreversible condition in which an individual progressively loses intellectual abilities, such as memory, judgment, and abstract thought, and often undergoes changes in behavior and personality. Although the incidence of Alzheimer's is not as great as recent attention by the media might suggest, the disease is still the most common irreversible dementia, or organic brain syndrome, among older people. The condition occurs in one of ten people over 65 and almost half of those over 85.

At present there is no cure for Alzheimer's, and scientists are still searching for its cause. The disease involves a buildup of abnormal plaques in the brain that destroy brain cells. Scientists speculate that the buildup might be the result of a slow virus or a genetic trigger. Although current medication only slows the progress of the disease, researchers have begun making steps toward the development of a vaccine that could reduce or even prevent the brain damage caused by Alzheimer's.[21]

Government Expenditures for the Elderly

Those who worry about "the graying of America" often have rising public expenses in mind. Since 1960 the share of the federal budget dedicated to programs for the elderly has doubled. Currently, 40 percent of all non-debt-related federal spending goes for programs for older Americans. Almost one out of every four federal dollars is spent on Social Security benefits. The greatest increase has been in Medicare and Medicaid payments, with Medicare now accounting for 12 percent of all federal spending.[22]

Summary

As we survey the statistics related to aging, no single picture emerges. True, older people are more likely to have moderate to low incomes and to have one or more chronic diseases. These characteristics, along with some restrictions in activities, are more typical in the old–old group than among those between 65 and 74. Moreover, income level, health status, and living arrangements among the elderly are influenced not only by age but also to a great degree by previous income level, race, and gender.

Dynamics: Causes and Effects of Aging

It is possible to construct several pictures of the causes and effects of aging. Each relates to our theme of dependency. One version might be the following: Aging is an incurable disease. On reaching old age, the individual steadily deteriorates physically, intellectually, and emotionally. He or she encounters illness and disability, loses mental capacity, becomes more conservative and ill-tempered, loses interest in sex, comes to depend more and more on others, and gradually becomes isolated from the larger society.

A different picture would depict aging this way: Aging is a natural phenomenon of uncertain causes. The older person faces some physical and intellectual deterioration, but this generally proceeds at a modest rate and does not affect daily functioning in a major way. He or she remains involved in political and community activities, not necessarily changing attitudes, but becoming more interested in issues related to the needs and priorities of the elderly. Social interaction and sexual interest generally continue and most individuals go on leading independent and satisfying lives.

Neither picture, of course, portrays the "truth" about aging for all people. The first is more heavily laden with myths and stereotypes about the elderly than the second. In order to sort through the many myths and facts about aging, it is helpful to review existing theories about its nature and causes. Because gerontology is a relatively new study, however, such theories are still tentative.

Biological Theories

Why do people age? Is aging inevitable? These questions are still difficult to answer. At present, most scientists believe that aging is an inevitable phenomenon for human organisms. Aging is not a disease, but instead represents natural losses of function. Examples of such losses include decline in short-term memory, reduced exercise capacity, and deficiencies in the body's immune system.

The ultimate mechanisms of aging are still poorly understood. Aging probably stems from the fact that the ability of normal somatic cells (any cell other than a germ cell) to replicate and function is limited. After a certain period of time, these cells no longer reproduce. Specialists in geriatrics have posited several explanations as to why this occurs. Many look to genetic bases of aging, hypothesizing, for example, that a purposeful sequence of events is programmed into human genes. These events lead to age changes. Another theory suggests that cells accumulate defective proteins in the course of aging; still another holds that "control systems" such as the endocrine system are responsible for eventual loss of cell function. Research on these and other biological theories of aging is still in a beginning phase.[23]

Although gerontologists have not yet uncovered the ultimate causes of aging, they are learning more about the physiological effects of aging. Current understanding about these effects tends to challenge earlier views of the large and irreversible declines experienced by the elderly. True, sensory input (taste, touch, smell, hearing, and vision) decreases with age. Age brings a decline in the pumping function of the heart, and the respiratory system does not work as well. Older people also show a diminishing ability to respond to stress and to return to a prestress level in a reasonable length of time. For example, an older person takes longer to adjust to changes in temperature. Also, age has the effect of making people more vulnerable to illness. Cardiovascular disease and cancer have their greatest incidence among the elderly.

However, individuals experience these effects of aging differently and at varying points in their lives. And despite the various changes brought by age, the majority of older people have more than enough skills and capacities to meet the demands of contemporary lifestyles.[24]

One important element in these lifestyles is sexuality. The myth that older people lose sexual interest and ability is largely unfounded. Although sexual activity does tend to decrease with age, much of this change is due to lack of partners and the inhibiting effect of societal expectations and assumptions. Our society has difficulty accepting the fact that older people may be as interested in sex as anyone else. In actuality, capacity for sexual activity and enjoyment changes relatively little as people age.

Common images of aging also link advancing years with loss of intellectual ability. Yet research indicates that brain capacity does not decline greatly with age. A recent study, which tracked 6,000 older people over a decade, found that 70 percent of those evaluated "showed no significant decline in cognitive function over the study period." Several studies do show a slowing of brain waves and reaction time among the elderly. In tasks that do not demand a rapid response, however, there is little difference in intellectual ability between younger and older subjects. In fact, researchers now feel that an individual's intelligence peaks at quite a late age, perhaps in the mid-fifties.[25]

Those age-related losses in physiological and intellectual capacity that do occur are not necessarily irreversible. For example, exercise can counter declines in cardiac and respiratory functioning. Through biofeedback techniques, older people can increase their brain wave activity. Additional sensory stimulation may also counter intellectual decline.

Physiological aspects of aging, then, are real but not necessarily fixed. In addition, biological aspects of aging tell only one part of the story. Contrary to the phrase "biology is destiny," both social and social psychological dimensions need to be added to our understanding of the aging process.

Social Psychological Theories of Aging

Social psychologists stress that personality and behavior are shaped by socialization experiences and assigned social roles. Adult personality change stems from the varying demands society places on individuals as they grow older. Roles shift also, as the individual moves from parent to grandparent, married person to widow or widower, employed person to retiree. New roles demand new responses, beliefs, and ways of behaving. Some researchers argue that the elderly pick up few new roles that compensate for the major life activities that are lost. Retirement, widowhood, and other changes can lead to loneliness and the loss of meaningful functions in life.[26]

Psychologist Erik Erikson sees life development as a series of tasks to be mastered. The task for the middle-aged person is to achieve "generativity" rather than stagnation; that is, to assist and guide the next generation. Erikson describes the work of the final stage as achievement of integrity. Ideally, the older person comes to accept his or her life as having been meaningful and worthwhile. Failure to do so can lead to despair.[27]

Other theorists offer similar descriptions of adult development as a series of different periods or phases. Most of these models characterize the later years as a time of heightened introspection and increasing awareness of personal mortality.

If one adds the idea of role loss to this picture, it is possible to think of the elderly as gradually withdrawing from daily activities and social interaction. This act of withdrawal has in fact been described as a successful adaptation to aging. Writing in 1961, Elaine Cumming and William Henry advanced the *disengagement theory* of aging. They posited that such isolation and turning inward were helpful for the elderly, allowing them to approach death, the final separation, with acceptance and a sense of peace. Because the el-

Older people have much to offer younger generations.

derly face the loss of loved ones, resources, and traditional roles, disengagement becomes a healthy, mutual process between the individual and society. There is a certain reality to this concept. Losses do occur, and some older individuals do withdraw from social contacts and future planning. In one survey of older people, almost half said they had not made plans for things they would be doing "a month or a year from now."[28]

On the other hand, the majority of older people report active family ties, close friends, and good neighbor relations. This finding suggests a different perspective on successful aging, known as *activity theory.* The idea that keeping active keeps one young has been around for a long time. More formally stated in the early 1960s, activity theory stresses that aside from changes in biology and health, older people are the same as middle-aged people. They have the same psychological and social needs and will gain greatest satisfaction from staying active and resisting isolation. It is through continued activity that older individuals maintain their skills and their sense of social value.[29]

Evidence exists to support both theories. Some studies suggest that age brings increased introversion and attention to the inner self. It may also bring greater conformity, cautiousness, and passivity. Yet these findings may be due not to age changes but to generational differences in values, experiences, and socioeconomic status (a point we return to shortly). As evidence of continued activity on the part of the elderly, one might note that about 75 percent of those age 60 to 69 belong to a church or synagogue. The elderly and near-elderly (ages 55–64) are the most likely age groups to vote. In the 1996 presidential election, for example, 77 percent of those 65 and older voted, as opposed to 49 percent of the overall voting-age population. Older voters were a key swing vote in the 2000 Bush–Gore contest. Three-quarters of the elderly read a daily newspaper regularly. In a survey on life satisfaction, almost 70 percent of the older individuals questioned reported that "the things I do are as interesting to me as they ever were."[30]

Social psychological theories of aging offer different perspectives on the issues of dependence and interdependence. Discussions of role change among the elderly sometimes stress the significance of the "dependent person" role. Disengagement theory pictures a passive individual who is no longer interdependent with others. Activity theory emphasizes the independence of most elderly, as well as their ability to help others. Reality is more complex. As gerontologist Nancy Hooyman notes, there is "growing recognition that the role of 'dependent person' is not inevitable with age. Rather, the life course is characterized by varying periods of greater or lesser dependency in social relationships, with most people being emotionally dependent on others regardless of age." In addition, many older people are in turn *depended on* by others. One report on the interdependence of generations reminds us of the many ways in which older people help their families and others, including child care, financial and emotional support, and community service.[31]

This review of social psychological theories suggests that rather than a single pattern of optimum aging, what we see is "a diversity of patterns of aging based on combinations of personality type, role activity, and life satisfaction."[32] In addition, social factors affect these different responses to aging.

Sociological Theories of Aging

Major social influences on aging include a person's gender, ethnicity, socioeconomic status, occupation, and birth cohort. These and other factors color each individual's encounter with old age. A white, college-educated, 80-year-old retired business executive who lives with his wife in a Florida condominium will experience a different aging process from that of an elderly, widowed Latino woman with a sixth-grade education who has worked all her life as a farm laborer and now lives with her youngest daughter. The two will probably vary in terms of lifestyle, attitudes toward aging, support systems, and health status.

As noted earlier, men and women over 65 differ in income, health and longevity, marital situation, and living arrangements. Older men face more acute health problems and a shorter life expectancy than women. Many married women will spend the last twenty years of their life without a spouse. Relatively few will move in with their children. Sociologists such as Helena Lopata have pointed out that widowhood represents a serious problem in middle-class America. A husband's death "removes the major segment in the social role of wife and reduces the social circles of mother, friend, housewife [and] neighbor." It can lead to ongoing loneliness and depression.[33]

Race and ethnicity are other potent determinants of a person's experience with aging. Up until the 1960s, most gerontologists focused exclusively on white people in their research. Not until recently has the National Institute of Health required that members of minority groups (as well as women) be included in research projects. Now researchers are learning more about the effects of race, national origin, and culture on aging.

Income differences among white, African American, and Latino elderly groups are one obvious factor in varied experiences of aging. Income level and minority status often interact to affect housing arrangements (minority elderly people generally have the least adequate housing) and health status (older Latino males, for example, have unusually high levels of stress and health and mental health dysfunction). Familial patterns and social roles also vary by race and ethnic background. In contrast to the predominant pattern in the United States, many American Indian families assign to the older generation meaningful roles as transmitters of traditional culture, values, and religion. Support systems also differ, with foreign-born and minority elderly often relying more on churches, extended family, and community ties than native-born white people. Unfortunately for some elderly immigrants, life in the United States may weaken these nurturing networks. Asian American elderly, for example, often lose valued support when acculturation to U.S. society causes members of their families to become more independent of one another.[34]

Previous and present income level carry obvious implications for one's experience with aging. Middle- and upper-class individuals are much more likely to enter retirement with assets and private pension funds, along with their Social Security benefits. In addition, income often interacts with occupational status to affect aging. For example, men from lower socioeconomic classes leave school earlier and begin working earlier, generally in blue-collar or service jobs. These men may retire sooner and thus see themselves as being old at younger ages than do middle-class men.

A particularly useful construct within the sociological perspective on aging is the idea that individuals' attitudes and behaviors are greatly influenced by the particular age cohort into which they were born. The term *cohort* is used to describe those born within a specific unit of time, generally a five- or ten-year interval. Each cohort undergoes certain similar sociocultural experiences and possesses a broad historical heritage. That is, despite differences of gender and ethnicity, all Americans born between 1915

Focus on Diversity

Women and Aging

W. Andrew Achenbaum, a historian and gerontologist, recommends John Bunyan's *Pilgrim's Progress* as a "treasure trove of ideas about age." The book depicts aging as a spiritual journey and highlights differences between the ways in which men and women grow older. Christian, the pilgrim, "makes his way alone to the Celestial City. Christina, in contrast, takes her children along; she travels with a group following a less direct route." These differences between instrumental/cooperative and solitary/nurturing styles of aging "resonate," Achenbaum observes, "in contemporary discussions of age and gender."

As we have noted, women tend to live longer than men. If widowed, they are less likely than men to remarry. Forty percent of older women live alone. Women often cope with this solitude by traveling "with a group," maintaining relationships, and creating networks to sustain them as they age.

One book on women and aging notes that women value interpersonal relationships, often making these relationships a central theme in their lives. As they grow older, women tend to expand their definition of family to include their children's partners as well as grandchildren, and they may come to think of close friends as extended family. In fact, some studies have found that support from children is less crucial to adjustment to widowhood than the nurturing of friends. Although it is unclear whether men or women have more friends, women often find friendship more meaningful and are more dependent on it than men. Elderly women are more likely than male peers to have confidante relationships with their friends.

Older single or widowed women have found a number of ways to create supportive communities. For example, one never-married professional woman in her eighties who lacks close relatives and lives alone has created a committee of friends with the legal power to make decisions for her regarding medical care and living arrangements if she becomes incapacitated. Women who prefer not to live alone can now choose from an expanding set of options: They can join with others their age in communal or group living; share housing with younger people, such as single mothers with small children, in a mutually beneficial arrangement; or live in a retirement community. Although we think of the last as a housing arrangement specifically planned for the elderly, a new and informal type of retirement community has developed. These are settings in which people have "aged in place"—in apartment buildings or neighborhoods that now have a large concentration of older people, predominantly women, who often create ways of helping one another out. Like Christina, they travel through the aging process in a group.

Sources: W. A. Achenbaum, "Old Age," Peter N. Steams, ed., *Encyclopedia of Social History,* vol. 3 (New York: Garland, 1994), 2053; Paula B. Doress-Worters and Diana Laskin Siegal, *The New Ourselves, Growing Older* (New York: Simon & Schuster, 1994), 133,159; Beth B. Hess and Joan Waring, "Family Relations of Older Women: A Women's Issue," in Elisabeth W. Markson, ed., *Older Women: Issues and Perspective* (Lexington, MA: Lexington Books, 1983), 235; Gloria D. Heinemann, "Interdependence in Informal Support Systems: The Case of Elderly, Urban Widows," in Warren A. Peterson and Jill Quadagno, eds., *Social Bonds in Later Life: Aging and Interdependence* (Beverly Hills, CA: Sage, 1985), 168–169; Mary Beth Franklin, "NORC, Sweet NORC: For Many Americans, Life Is Sweet in a 'Naturally Occurring Retirement Community,'" *Washington Post, Health* (insert) (13 January 1998), 7–9.

and 1920 share the common experience of having been young adults during World War II. Cohorts differ from one another in terms of general educational levels achieved, commitment to political activism, and other factors. Many stereotypes about the elderly are in fact applicable only to specific cohorts. For example, the observation that people become more conservative as they age may reflect the fact that recent cohorts of elderly grew up in conservative times and reflect this in their voting patterns. Social reform and activist stances may be very different among the elderly of the early 2000s, who were young adults in the politically active 1960s. Education levels also change from cohort to cohort. The elderly of the 1990s are a much better educated group than those of the 1970s.[35]

A final variation of the sociological approach is to think about aging within the broad context of the organization of work in our society. In other words, the elderly can be viewed in terms of their productivity level in a modern industrialized economy. Historians and social scientists have observed that since the late 1800s, older people have been helped or pushed out of the workforce. The notion of mandatory retirement has been based on assumptions that older workers lack the up-to-date skills, strength, and appropriate attitudes necessary for their jobs. (It also reflects the concern that the job market needs to be opened up to younger people.) We assess the validity of these assumptions later in this chapter. The important point here is that the social role of retiree or nonworker can carry with it a stigma of "uselessness." This stigma affects the self-perceptions of older people and can be used to justify their segregation from mainstream society.

History of Aging in America

The history of old age in America chronicles a variety of attitudes toward aging. Interestingly, despite popular belief, there has probably never been a truly "golden epoch" for the elderly in this country. As a people, we have persistently demonstrated ambivalent, conflicting feelings about old age, with specific differences in the ways we have described the elderly over time.

There are two major themes in this history of aging. The first, described by historian W. Andrew Achenbaum and others, pertains to the change from a generally positive conception of old age before the Civil War to a largely negative picture from the 1870s on. The second theme relates to ways of dealing with dependency among older people. Although there has always been a mixture of public and private responses to this problem, over time the federal government has taken on more and more responsibility for meeting the needs of the elderly. This section explores changing attitudes toward the elderly as well as the development of age-related policies and programs.

During the colonial period, older individuals were generally looked on with respect. Early Americans saw a definite role for the elderly, believing their wisdom to be an important asset in a new, developing nation. Although their proportion in the population was relatively small, older men and women seemed to show through their survival that the American environment promoted a long and vigorous life. Many older people still worked and carried out useful family functions. Men remained active in farming, government, and other activities. Women were often in their sixties before the last child of a large family left home.[36]

Not all elderly, of course, were held in high esteem. Those who had had power and wealth as younger people were most likely to be respected and revered in old age. Poorer individuals were less likely to be admired. Americans also recognized that old age could bring pain and suffering. They saw chronic illness as an inevitable problem of aging, and they realized that economic problems increased with age.[37]

In the colonial period and in the early 1800s, a variety of measures was developed in a piecemeal way to supplement the role of families in caring for the poor and dependent elderly. These included the poorhouse and outdoor relief. However, care by one's own family members constituted the most common type of help.

Despite recognition of the problems of old age, the elderly continued to be viewed in a generally positive light during the early 1800s. However, attitudes began to shift by the mid-1800s; and by World War I many people had come to equate old age with ugliness, disease, and uselessness. The reasons for this change have intrigued historians. The simple answer would be to attribute the new attitudes to changes in the economy because of a large increase in the elderly population. One might argue, for example, that a newly industrializing nation had little room for workers with outdated ideas and diminished physical capabilities and that there were now many more frail elderly in need of help. However, the proportion of older people in the United States did not greatly increase until the late 1800s. The biggest jumps in the elderly population occurred after World War I. Also, the majority of the elderly continued to work; in 1890, for example, almost three-quarters of men over 65 were still employed. However, older workers did tend to be found in the more traditional trades, such as farming and mining. In addition, the elderly were moving into cities at a greater rate in the late 1800s, and by doing so they often lost supportive ties with both family and community.[38]

The dramatic shifts in attitudes, however, seem to have come more from broader cultural and intellectual changes in U.S. society than from occupational trends or differences in the elderly population itself. Achenbaum argues that negative ideas about the aging stemmed in part from the new philosophy of social Darwinism, which stressed survival of the fittest, and in part from a growing stress on the importance of science and efficiency. The expansion of medical knowledge was a crucial factor in the change. Earlier, the elderly had been seen as possessing the secrets of long life. Now, modern scientific medical knowledge could teach those secrets. In addition, physicians began to change their ideas about old age, stressing the degeneration and weakening of cells and organs as people grew older. The notion that old age was in itself a disease grew in popularity.[39]

Although physicians appeared to be increasing their knowledge about the aging process, they were not yet successful in making the aged more healthy. Historian Carole Haber argues that it was the experts themselves—doctors, social scientists, and professional charity workers—who despaired of improvement in the lives of the elderly and focused instead on their social, physical, and economic problems. Social scientists in the late 1800s, for example, spoke of aging as "a unique and particularly perilous stage of existence."[40]

Although the new ideas were not at first based on significant changes in the situation of the aged, reality began to catch up with these concepts after 1890. By then, larger numbers of poor elderly could be found in big cities, where they were perceived as a growing welfare problem. In addition, businessmen enamored of the modern concept of efficiency had begun to view the elderly as outmoded and unproductive workers. The late 1800s brought the first retirement programs, through which businesses could

FIGURE 15.7

Source: W. Andrew Achenbaum and Peggy Ann Kusnerz, *Images of Old Age in America* (Ann Arbor, MI: Institute of Gerontology, 1978), 33. Reprinted with permission of the Institute of Gerontology.

pension off older workers. Although these might be viewed as humanitarian measures and as a final payment for service to the company, they also gave employers greater control over the workforce and reinforced the idea that the elderly were incapable of useful work (see Figure 15.7).

At the same time, the number of elderly people in institutions grew. This happened in part because of changes in family life, such as fewer adult children to care for older parents, and in part because of diminished resources among the elderly, fewer of whom now worked or owned farms. Although the percentage of older people in poorhouses remained fairly small, their presence had become much more visible. This was because by the early 1900s most other groups had been siphoned off to specialized institutions—the mental asylum, the training school for the mentally retarded, or the reformatory. By 1910, poorhouses had been transformed into old age homes. In poorhouses in that year, 45 percent of all native-born residents and 70 percent of all foreign-born residents were age 60 or over.[41]

By the 1920s, the elderly as a group had come to be characterized as a "social problem." Their numbers had increased almost 60 percent since 1870. The proportion of old–old in the group had begun to grow. Only 60 percent of older men now worked, compared with 73 percent in 1890. The decline in agriculture deprived the elderly of an important traditional source of employment.[42]

Researchers began to focus on physical and intellectual problems and undesirable character traits in the elderly. One writer saw old age as "simply a mass of bad habits." Reformers and philanthropists concentrated on work with younger people, who seemed more capable of change. Writing as late as 1939, a social worker noted, "Perhaps we may regard old age as a 'twilight' where the light is too dim to allow for useful service."[43]

Despite these negative views, many older people continued to live useful lives with adequate financial resources. However, the economic crash of the thirties served to bring the problems of poorer elderly to a head. Although countless people were adversely affected by the Great Depression, the elderly were particularly at risk. Many lost their jobs, their savings, and other assets following the 1929 market collapse. It was not surprising, therefore, that a system of old age insurance—Social Security—served as the cornerstone of Franklin D. Roosevelt's New Deal social welfare programs.

The idea of pension systems was not entirely new in the 1930s. Private businesses had been establishing pension programs on a small scale since the latter part of the nineteenth century, although by 1925 only 280 programs existed nationwide. In addition, the federal government began providing compulsory old age and disability insurance to civil servants in the 1920s. More important, public pensions for U.S. war veterans had been established after the Civil War. At first these applied only to financially needy veterans and to those with disabilities. By 1912, however, veterans' pensions became strictly age-related. In other words, any veteran over 62 could qualify.[44]

Nevertheless, the idea of a national system of old age benefits did not catch on in the early 1900s. Although England, Germany, and other European countries established pension plans during this period, beliefs in individual responsibility and private responses to need continued to hold sway in the United States. Even the developing labor movement did not at first endorse old age benefits; workers preferred to trust the union's ability to improve wages and provide security rather than the government's paternalistic measures.[45]

Many different forces interacted to change in this situation in the 1930s. First of all, as we discussed in Chapter 9, a social insurance movement had been growing quietly through the early years of the century. The idea of social insurance was seen as an alternative to direct charity. Generally, it meant following the same principles used in life insurance or property insurance, in which people pay a certain fee and contract with a company or organization to reimburse them in the case of loss. Social insurance was first conceived as government-sponsored insurance for urban industrial workers, who could be indemnified against sickness, accident, or unemployment. After World War I, the social insurance movement broadened to cover the idea of old age pensions. Abraham Epstein, an economist who spent much of his career promoting the old age pension idea, founded the American Association for Old Age Security in 1927. This group and other organizations lobbied for old age pension legislation in the 1920s and early 1930s. Numerous state and municipal retirement systems emerged during this period.[46]

The Townsend Movement was another factor in the move toward Social Security. Dr. Frances Townsend, a retired physician in California, proposed a program to end the depression by providing everyone over age 60 with a pension of $200 a month. The program was to be funded through public taxation. Recipients would have to spend their $200 within the month, thus bolstering the economy. This rather simple idea found a good deal of popularity, with "Townsend Clubs" spreading among older people in 1934. Soon, Townsend claimed five million supporters. Similar proposals were made by other groups. In promoting these ideas, the elderly were beginning to demonstrate their power as a political lobbying group.[47]

The various pension plans evoked controversy. Radical observers saw pensions, particularly private ones, as measures to control workers—to weed out older, supposedly unproductive employees and to ensure a labor force of younger workers who would be compelled to remain with a particular employer for the sake of retirement benefits. Conservatives, on the other hand, accepted the necessity of some type of social welfare help for the elderly, but wanted this carried out under voluntary, rather than governmental, auspices. They felt that public old age pensions would sap people's self-respect. If public relief was necessary for dependent elderly, it should be provided through a means test that would deter individuals from "irresponsible" use of public monies. Finally, liberals saw social insurance as one way to bring about reform through a better distribution of wealth in the United States. They hoped that social insurance programs would replace the old punitive relief approach and establish welfare benefits as a right for both the elderly and other categories of people. Many social workers joined in this view. Some were active in the drafting of Roosevelt's Social Security legislation.[48]

The Social Security Act of 1935 constituted a compromise between different proposals and different political points of view. It offered some federal aid for means-tested public assistance for the elderly (as well as for two other groups: dependent children and the blind). Through this program, the federal government matched funds spent by the states for needy elderly, who could be considered among the "deserving" poor. The Social Security Act also established a social insurance system for individuals age 65 and older, regardless of financial need. The system was funded through a payroll tax levied on both employers and employees. The notion that workers "paid into" their old age pension fund fit well with this country's traditional stress on individualism and hard work and made the act more palatable to both politicians and the public. Unlike European systems, in which social insurance was paid for through general tax revenues, the Social Security program would be financed largely through the private sector. As President Roosevelt put it: "We put the payroll contributions there so as to give the contributors a legal, moral and political right to collect their pensions. . . . With those taxes in there, no damn politician can ever scrap my social security program."[49] The program made moderate attempts at redistribution of income. That is, benefits were weighted to provide proportionately higher returns to lower-income workers.

The Social Security system soon expanded. In 1939 an important amendment added Survivors Insurance, which provided benefits to the widow and other surviving dependents of a worker who died prematurely.

The initial act had not insured everyone; when payments began in 1940, only one-fifth of all workers qualified.[50] Domestic and agricultural workers, for example, had been excluded. A good many of these workers were African American. Their lack of coverage was justified on technical issues, such as the difficulty in assessing wages in farming and domestic service. The more salient factor, however, was the refusal of many southern politicians to support federal aid for African Americans. Gradually, however, most groups of employees were brought into the system, including farm and domestic workers, so that today almost all retired people receive Social Security benefits. Also, by 1939 Congress had decided to tie old age benefits not to lifetime contributions but to average earnings over a shorter period of work. Finally, the Social Security Administration broadened its coverage of disabled workers in the 1940s and 1950s, allowing people with disabilities to qualify for more benefits than they had actually put into the system.

Expansion of coverage signaled a shift in the makeup and philosophy of Social Security. It had become a more complex system, taking need into account as well as contributions. Financing principles had also changed. Initially, the government was to be "a piggy bank, storing contributions and paying them back with interest at age sixty-five." People would be contributing money to a fund set aside for their own retirement benefits. Now, current workers were paying benefits for those already retired. As we discuss later, this shifting forward of obligations to future workers would eventually lead to predictions of crisis in the system.[51]

Social Security was the first national institutional structure set up to assist older people. It helped bring about a major change in the source of financial support for the elderly, a shift from dependence on family aid and wages to reliance on social insurance benefits and private pensions. In the following decades, national interest in the aging continued. Numerous organizations and programs evolved to meet the needs of older citizens. These developments attested to the growing numbers and political power of the elderly.

Scientific study of the problems and needs of the older population was not new to the 1940s and 1950s. The founding of the New York Geriatrics Society in 1915 reflected attention given to the medical aspects of aging in the early years of the twentieth century. Social and behavioral scientists had also been studying the nature and effects of aging. However, because of the increase in the number of elderly and the visibility given to them by the development of Social Security, research on aging expanded greatly after 1940. In 1946 the National Institute of Health in Washington established a Gerontological Research Unit, which set the stage for the creation of the National Institute for Aging in 1974. The Institute for Aging conducts and sponsors research on aging in the biomedical and social sciences. The Gerontological Society of America, founded in 1945, promoted interdisciplinary discussion in the field. The first National Conference on Aging was held in 1950; this was followed by three White House conferences on aging between 1961 and 1981. These developments led to joint activity by scientists and policymakers in the areas of research and legislation.[52]

The federal government was gradually becoming a clearinghouse for information and research on old age. In addition, attention to the problems of the elderly led to the creation of special committees on aging in the House and Senate. Crucial legislation emerged in the 1960s and 1970s. Health care programs for the elderly, such as Medicare and Medicaid (1965), were an important contribution of Lyndon Johnson's Great Society initiative.

The Older Americans Act of 1965 demonstrated the commitment of the Great Society to a broad array of social, nutritional, mental health, and other needs of the elderly. Extensions of the Social Security Act increased the economic security of older Americans. Of particular significance was the establishment of automatic inflation-indexed adjustments of monthly benefits (cost-of-living adjustments, or COLAs) in 1972. Also in the 1970s, Congress enacted the Supplementary Security Income program (SSI), in which the federal government took over the old age assistance programs for needy elderly persons that had previously been run by the states. Housing and low-income energy assistance constituted two other areas of legislation.

The Older Americans Act of 1965 established what has been dubbed the "aging network": a partnership of federal, state, and local public and private agencies offering a range of programs and services for older people. The act and its subsequent amendments "changed the federal government's focus from income maintenance to coordination and funding of a comprehensive service system for the elderly." This coordination is carried out through a three-level administrative structure—a national Administration on Aging, state units on aging, and local area agencies on aging (AAAs).

The types of programs planned and sponsored by these units have focused on nutrition, recreation, transportation, employment, housing, and information.[53]

By the 1970s, then, the federal government had made enormous strides in legislating to meet a broad array of needs of an aging population. The proportion of the federal budget related to programs for the elderly rose to approximately 25 percent. A major reason for this expansion lay in the growth of lobbying efforts by a larger, more articulate, and better-organized population of older people. The so-called "gray lobby" developed out of a combination of citizen and professional organizations for older individuals. One of the largest and most powerful organizations is the American Association of Retired Persons (AARP), which grew out of a retired teachers' organization founded in 1947. By 1975, AARP had a membership of nine million people, making it the largest voluntary association in the world. The organization's goals included political involvement as well as provision of various benefits to members, including insurance and discounts on pharmaceutical products. The AARP budget is about three times the size of the National Rifle Association's, and the organization recently increased the size of its membership base even further by lowering the age of eligibility for joining to 50. The National Association of Retired Federal Employees (1921) and the National Council of Senior Citizens, a union-related association that developed in the 1960s, are two other important grassroots organizations. In 1950, public and private health, recreation, community action, and social work agencies dealing with the elderly formed the National Council on the Aging to serve as a central resource for planning, information, and consultation relative to the needs of the elderly. The most colorful of all these organizations is the Gray Panthers, established in 1972 by social activist Maggie Kuhn. The Gray Panthers took a more radical stance than other groups in the gray lobby, striving for the liberation of older persons from the "paternalism and oppression with which society keeps us powerless."[54]

Many factors have thus contributed to the distinct presence of the elderly and their concerns in today's national policy considerations. From a small proportion of the population in the colonial period, older people have become a significant percentage of all citizens. A group whose weaknesses had been stressed in the 1800s, the elderly now belong to well-organized lobbying groups that have helped win important battles for social legislation. However, the position of the elderly in modern society still contains ambiguities and problems. We look at these issues next.

Current Issues and Trends

Government Programs for Older Americans: Can They Be Maintained?

The creation of comprehensive government support for the economic, physical, and social well-being of older people can be seen as a major milestone in U.S. history. Social Security now keeps more than two-fifths of the elderly out of poverty. Medicare helps older people cope with the ever higher cost of medical care. Medicaid is the main underwriter of long-term care, especially nursing homes. Yet all of these areas of support are currently undergoing serious reevaluation in a time of continuing budget concerns and skepticism about the role of government in our society.[55]

Pessimistic predictions are the order of the day. Social Security is projected to run out of funds in 2044, and the Medicare trust fund is expected to become insolvent by 2026. Many younger people are convinced that these programs won't be there when they need them. As one reporter put it, "More young people believe in UFOs than in the prospect of receiving a Social Security check when they retire." This concern, along with the fact that benefits for the elderly come in large part from Social Security and income taxes paid by today's workers, has contributed in some quarters to a backlash against the elderly and has raised the specter of "intergenerational warfare" in the twenty-first century.[56]

In this section we discuss the reasons behind current problems in entitlement programs for the elderly, as well as some proposed remedies. The current political and economic environment is, of course, crucial. The 2000 presidential campaign saw heated debate between candidates Al Gore and George W. Bush regarding how best to "save" Medicare and Social Security. When Bush came into office, it was incumbent upon him to work out ways to keep these programs solvent and effective. And despite the several extensions of time before Medicare and Social Security run into financial difficulty, the Bush administration has stated that the long-term financial outlook for Medicare is bleak because of the continued rise in health costs. "We have only so many years to get [these] systems back on track," Bush told a meeting of business leaders. "It's time to quit posturing and time to reform."[57]

The popular desire for both shrinking taxes and balancing the budget necessitates close scrutiny of government expenditures, an exercise in which the elderly are particularly vulnerable. As we have noted, spending on programs such as Social Security, Medicare, and Medicaid makes up a large part of the federal budget. Outlays for Medicaid are costly also for states, which are pursuing similar budget-trimming, tax-cutting goals. Growth in the proportion of older Americans will put further pressure on these entitlements.

The notion of a "Social Security crisis" is not new. Fears about the solvency of the Social Security system arose first in the late 1970s and early 1980s, when mandatory cost-of-living adjustments, higher unemployment rates, and slow wage growth caused a decline in the program's trust funds. To meet the problem, the Social Security Amendments of 1983 increased Social Security payroll taxes, mandated a gradual rise in the age at which individuals could first receive benefits (from 65 to 67), and instituted taxation of benefits received by taxpayers with incomes above certain levels. In 1993 a new law set these income levels as earnings over $34,000 for single elderly persons and over $44,000 for couples. At the time, policymakers hoped that these changes would ensure the stability of the system for the next seventy-five years. Today, however, revised labor force and demographic data suggest that the current payroll tax will not be enough to keep the Social Security reserve fund from becoming depleted in in about forty years. One reason is that the "dependency ratio" between workers and beneficiaries will change dramatically in the next thirty years. In 1936 there were 15 workers paying taxes to support each retiree. The ratio has now fallen to 3 to 1, and by 2025 it may fall to 2.25 to 1.[58]

Some analysts say that the situation isn't as bad as it seems. Baby boomers are earning more than their parents, so their savings will amount to more. They also tend to have better private pension retirement packages. People are beginning to work longer. Yet these arguments have done little to dispel a sense of crisis, for which a variety of remedies are being proposed.[59] The most extreme solution is to dismantle Social Security entirely, allowing the better-off to retire on a combination of private pensions and investment income. Some sort of needs-tested retirement program could then be fashioned for the neediest elderly.

President Reagan had the bolstering of the private pension system in mind when he promoted tax-exempt Individual Retirement Accounts (IRAs) as a way of building retirement income. A newer approach, the use of employer-based retirement savings programs, or 401(k) plans, grew rapidly in the 1990s. Although employers supplement employee contributions to these plans, a specific benefit is not guaranteed. There are also still traditional company pension plans. Yet all of these plans remain essentially as supplements to rather than replacements of Social Security; currently, too, only about half of all workers are in jobs that offer them a pension program.[60]

A more popular approach to ensuring retirement income, recommended in 1996 by a special Social Security Advisory Council appointed by President Clinton, is to introduce the stock market into the Social Security system. Currently, money in the Social Security trust fund is invested in low-interest government Treasury bonds: Essentially, the government is lending itself money, which critics say is an unsound arrangement. Also, government bonds earn only about 1 or 2 percent above inflation. Various plans devised by the advisory council called for investing that money in the stock market instead. The plans differed as to whether the government would do the investing of payroll tax money or workers would have individual accounts with which to make investments. No matter what the arrangement, people opposed to this approach argue that not everyone has the skills and knowledge to invest money and that the system is not protected against a stock market failure. If the government were in charge of investing, decisions about which stocks to buy could be politically charged. Finally, low-income workers would have much less to invest and thus would lose the most in a private investment approach. Finally, it would be a costly system to set up.[61]

President Bush wholeheartedly supports the addition of a private investment element to Social Security. As a presidential candidate, Bush announced his plan to allow younger workers to divert part of their Social Security taxes to private investment accounts. Workers would be able to put a small percentage of their payroll taxes into accounts that they could then invest in stocks and bonds. Al Gore, in his campaign, countered with a proposal to use part of the federal budget surplus to extend the program's solvency. Once in office, Bush moved quickly to carry out an overhaul of Social Security. He created a special commission to outline a new system; all members of the commission had to be people who approved of the idea of personal investment accounts. The commission's preliminary report in July 2001 stated that (1) Social Security needed major change in order to survive and (2) any solution should include Mr. Bush's proposal to create personal investment accounts as part of the change. Shortly after the release of the preliminary report, legislation to partially privatize Social Security along the lines suggested by Bush was introduced in the U.S. House of Representatives.[62]

The resulting firestorm of criticism from congressional Democrats, organized labor, and other groups indicates the depth of concern and the ideological divisions among Americans regarding the roles of the federal government and the market in our national retirement pension system. Arguments against creating private investment accounts included not only practical concerns about the stability of the stock market and the assumed ability of all people to invest wisely, but also the possibility that the new approach was being established to bring more business to Wall Street investment firms. Also, the necessary reductions in the guaranteed benefits portion of Social Security could undercut the program's ability to provide a universal benefit to all the elderly, including those who are poor. Finally, because private investment accounts would draw money out of the Social Security trust fund, a way would have to be found, either through cutting benefits or using general tax revenues, to replenish the trust fund and maintain payments to current recipients. All in all, critics argue, the government plays an essential role in maintaining a fair and practical system, and any move toward privatization could undercut that system. They point out that recent forecasts predict a strong Social Security system for many years to come.[63]

Proponents of adding an element of privatization through individual accounts argue that the market can indeed be an important instrument in returning higher benefits to retirees. Their basic assumption is that the current system is fundamentally flawed, remains in financial trouble, and needs to be restructured. Allowing individuals to invest part of their money in the stock market would lead to higher rates of return, increase the public's confidence in the system, and help keep Social Security financially healthy, especially as the baby boom generation reaches retirement age. In response to critics' concerns about negative effects on low-income individuals in the system, David John, a policy analyst with the conservative Heritage Foundation, has proposed that the small investments of poorer people could be pooled in a central money market fund until these deposits grew large enough to be individually invested. All in all, supporters of market proposals argue that a system controlled by "big government" is not the best approach to assuring a comfortable old age.[64]

Those who defend the basic structure and ideals of the current system contend that in fact with a few prudent changes, Social Security can continue to provide a reliable income floor for all older people in the United States. These adjustments might include gradually raising the payroll taxes, making the cost-of-living calculation (on which COLA benefit raises are based) more accurate, and making modest cuts in future benefits. Among those supporting this approach are interest groups, such as AARP, that represent large segments of the elderly.[65]

Medicare is another program for the elderly that has been targeted for change. The program's rising costs, and earlier projections that the depletion of its trust fund was far more imminent than that of Social Security's, have led to a similar round of suggestions for reform. Medicare is a crucial source of health care coverage for most of the elderly. As with Social Security, the increase in the number and proportion of elderly in the United States puts pressure on the system. It has been argued that the most important factor driving up the cost of Medicare, however, is the overall rise in medical costs. The need to restrain costs was a major impetus behind the promotion of managed care as a way to "save" Medicare.[66]

Medicare recipients have had the option of joining a managed care program rather than using the traditional fee-for-service system since the late 1970s. In 1997, legislation was passed to greatly expand managed care options for Medicare beneficiaries. At the same time, the law cut the program's budget by $115 billion over the following five years, with most of the savings coming from reductions in payments to hospitals and physicians. This helped lead to a rise in premium costs. Enrollment in Medicare managed care had expanded rapidly before the 1997 legislation was passed, reaching about 14 percent of all beneficiaries. However, enrollment growth began to slow after 1997, and has most recently begun to decline outright. The increase in premium costs is no doubt one reason behind the drop in enrollments. Decline in enrollments along with the government reduction in payments to HMOs has led in turn to a sharp reduction in HMOs willing to stay in the Medicare business. This has become a particular problem in rural areas, where large numbers of programs have closed down. Headlines like the following have now grown familiar: "HMOs Drop Thousands of Seniors" and "People Hit by HMO Pullouts Searching for Alternatives."[67]

Although Congress voted billions of extra dollars for Medicare in 2000, little of this money has gone to lower costs for beneficiaries, and the money has failed to lure many HMOs back into Medicare. Thus, calls continue for a reform in the system. As in the debate over Social Security, definitions of the type and severity of Medicare's problems differ. Democrats like Al Gore argue that Medicare is basically sound; it operates efficiently, has very low overhead, and is predicted to be financially secure for a number of years. Therefore the program just needs touching up. Democrats are not necessarily opposed to the use of HMOs in Medicare, but these are not central to their plans for improvement. President Bush, on the other hand, would like greater reliance on managed care approaches. Both sides agree, in a general way, to adding prescription drug benefits to Medicare. As we noted in the chapter on health care, older people bear the brunt of rising drug prices, and at present these costs must be covered by private insurance policies or out-of-pocket payments. The managed care Medicare programs often cover prescriptions, but these companies are slowly going out of business. Although there is a fair amount of consensus that some sort of government plan is needed for relief from high prices of medication, as with Social Security there is disagreement on how such a plan should work. Democrats generally support a fairly large government-subsidized drug benefit; Bush and many Republicans have argued for a program that relies more on the market to solve the problem. The latter approach would continue to use government funding, but would allow for competition between traditional Medicare and managed care Medicare plans in offering different combinations of drug and health care benefits to beneficiaries.[68]

Another challenge facing us is the rapid expansion and sky-rocketing costs of home health care, which has become one of the fastest-growing benefits in the Medicare program. Many home health care agencies are for-profit organizations. Unlike hospital or physician care, in which patients make copayments, home health care is fully reimbursed by the government. Until recently, there was no limit on the number of visits, and government regulation of the home health industry was generally quite lax.[69]

In-home services by nurses, home health aides, social workers, and physical therapists in older people's own homes are quite valuable ones, especially at a time when hospitals tend to discharge Medicare patients as soon as possible. These services offer people the dignity of being treated at home and make it more likely that they can stay in their communities. Yet home health, like other aspects of Medicare, has been particularly susceptible to fraud. Major headlines have been devoted to alleged illegal billing in Columbia/HCA's $1 billion-a-year home health care business, and several other organizations have also been indicted for home health fraud. In response to such abuse, the federal government tightened up its regulatory system and set new standards for home health agencies. In addition, the 1997 Balanced Budget Act put a limit on the number of home visits that could be reimbursed.[70]

Long-Term Care

The problem of long-term care is a growing issue for older Americans and their families. As our opening vignette about Paulette Moore suggested, many elderly people with mental and physical disabilities need help with the basics of daily living. Traditionally, the providers of such care have been families (chiefly wives and daughters) and, as a last resort or where no family exists, the nursing home. As Hooyman notes, however, the concept of long-term care has recently evolved "from an emphasis on purely institutional care to a broad range of services to impaired older adults in both institutional and community settings," including home health care.[71]

Currently, only about 5 percent of the elderly live in nursing homes, although a much larger proportion of those over 65 will at some point spend at least some time in one. The likelihood of becoming a nursing home resident increases with age, with residents constituting only 1 percent of those age 65 to 75 but about a third of those 90 to 94. The nursing home population is more likely to have multiple chronic diseases, some form of dementia, and major impairments in activities of daily living. At least some nursing home residents could stay at home with adequate supports, however. A major factor that seems to distinguish long-term nursing home residents from those with equal impairments living in the community is the absence of caregivers or a social support network for those who are institutionalized.[72]

Nursing home care is an area dominated by private, and particularly for-profit, provision of services. Private homes for the elderly first developed in the 1800s as an alternative to the almshouse for middle-class clients. Later, nursing homes were seen as appropriate institutions for a broad range of elderly people. The growth of private homes was spurred in the 1930s when the old age assistance portion of Social Security prohibited benefits to elderly residents of public institutions. Those living in private "rest homes," however, could qualify. Since the 1960s, Medicaid funding has further promoted nursing home growth.

Today, the vast majority of the country's nursing homes are run for profit. Many of these are part of large corporate chains. Investors see nursing homes as a growth "industry," which should "continue to thrive in the years ahead."[73] Ironically, of course, although these nursing homes are privately owned and managed, much of their funding comes through public assistance, chiefly Medicaid payments, which cover about half of all nursing home bills. Thus, although we tend to think of private and public sponsorship of services for the elderly as two separate phenomena, a more accurate picture is that of interdependence of the market and governmental sectors.

Those favoring for-profit systems of nursing home care argue that competition between nursing home care providers results in better, more cost-efficient services. Critics point to abuses and deficiencies in care and complain about profiteering in the system. The solution, they say, is tighter state and federal regulation of homes, along with strict enforcement of these standards. One example of such regulation is the set of federal rules discouraging the use of physical or chemical restraints on elderly nursing home residents. Such rules are important for nursing homes no matter what their sponsorship. In 1990, for example, about 41 percent of all nursing home residents were put in some type of restraint.[74]

Despite the introduction of various penalties and the use of government inspections, various kinds of abuses continue in nursing home settings. Each year, a federal survey found, more than 25 percent of nursing homes "have health and safety violations that harm residents or place them at risk of death or serious injury." At a home in northern New Jersey, for example, residents sometimes had to wait as long as two hours for their bell calls to be answered. At a home near Houston, state inspectors found incorrect medical instructions for dozens of patients. Yet there are also nursing homes that provide creative and competent care. In a Fairfax, Virginia, home, pets such as rabbits and dogs entertain residents; in Brewster, Massachusetts, a beautiful and specially designed garden provides areas for walking, engaging in physical therapy, and outside meals.[75]

Paying for long-term nursing home care can be a major problem for the elderly and their families. Such care averages $43,000 a year. Patients and families pay the portion not covered by Medicaid. Because Medicaid is available only to low-income individuals, many nursing home residents are forced to spend most of their savings on their care before qualifying for government assistance. The prospect of limiting the assets available to a healthy spouse or depriving children of an inheritance has caused many middle-income elderly to seek legal ways to shelter their assets so as to be eligible for Medicaid. But this in turn increases the number of individuals that the federal program must cover; therefore, regulations have now been devised to limit the practice. Long-term care insurance is an option for some individuals, and the federal government now allows people to deduct part of the premiums for such insurance from their taxes. However, long-term care insurance is quite expensive and may not be appropriate for everyone.[76]

In response partly to the high cost of nursing homes and partly to the inappropriateness of institutional care for many elderly citizens, community-based services for long-term care have expanded greatly in recent years. Such services can supplement and enhance existing informal support networks offered by families, friends, and neighbors, and can assist older persons who lack such support. The diminished ability of wives and daughters to provide care, due to the rising proportion of women in the workforce, has been one spur to the development of an entire range of services provided within community settings. Another is the fact that for every one person residing in a nursing home, there are about four times as many elderly individuals living in the community who need some form of long-term care.[77]

Community services include home health care; "meals on wheels," or programs in which noon meals are delivered to homebound elderly in their residences; congregate meal programs in which meals are served to senior citizens in group settings such as churches or community centers; adult day care centers with programming for ambulatory elderly with physical or mental difficulties, including Alzheimer's disease; and homemaker chore services, to help individuals with personal care and housekeeping.[78] Respite care programs support family members who are caring for elderly relatives; visits by a temporary caregiver give a spouse, for example, valuable breathing space for a shopping trip or a visit with friends.

Formal and informal caregivers help older people remain in their homes and communities.

In some communities, senior centers offer health, social, and educational services to older adults. One such center in Jacksonville, Florida, offers a dining room, an auditorium, classrooms, a ceramics studio, a library, and a miniature golf course. Typical services of such a facility include congregate meals, a telephone reassurance network, information and referral regarding other programs aiding the elderly, volunteer opportunities, and recreational activities.[79]

As you can see, some services work best for people with the physical and mental ability to go out into the community; senior service centers, for example, are underused by frail elderly. For some people, in-home services are most appropriate. A new development for older persons with mobility restrictions and other impairments is "assisted living" residences. Such facilities offer private or semiprivate rooms or apartments, generally with private bathrooms and kitchenettes, along with meal, laundry, and housekeeping services. Staff provide personal care, such as getting residents in and out of bed and helping them with bathing and medications. Unlike traditional nursing homes, assisted living centers encourage residents to do as much for themselves as possible.[80]

Other innovative ways are emerging to support older people in their communities and to bring the generations together. As described in our opening vignette on Willis McMillan, the elderly are getting connected, either formally or informally, with caregivers beyond the circle of spouse and family members. These may be volunteers, such as the teenagers who visit Mr. McMillan. They may also be neighbors, friends from church or synagogue, or mail carriers. In one case, a taxi driver regularly drove a disabled older man who lived alone to the grocery store and fast-food restaurants. The two hit it off and became good friends. When the older man had a sudden medical crisis at home, the driver rushed him to the hospital and visited him daily, bringing flowers and videos, until he was released.[81]

New types of housing can also overcome the isolation of the elderly. Shared housing is an exciting experiment. In Newtonville, Massachusetts, for example, an intergenerational group of people varying in age from 35 to 75 live together in a large house built just for them. In addition to informal groupings, there can be formal match-up services, such as the nonprofit agency that brought together a retired woman and a working single mother who owns her own home. The retiree keeps the woman's 13-year-old daughter company after school and says with pleasure, "It's more like an extension of my family than renting a room." Finally, both public and private housing sectors have been creating affordable housing developments for the elderly that include common living rooms, free laundry facilities, food delivery to individual apartments, and in-house crisis intervention and referral services.[82]

Community Services for the Aging: Problems of Coordination

Community services are provided by many types of public and private organizations: hospitals, hospices, county departments of social service, churches, private social service agencies, visiting nurse associations, and home health care agencies. As we have seen, the programs of these organizations can help the elderly, including those with chronic disability, remain in their communities. However, these services are often fragmented. Without some type of centralized planning, gaps in particular kinds of care can exist.

Since the 1960s the federal government has played an increasingly greater role in the financing and particularly the coordination of community services. Through the Older Americans Act of 1965, planning and program development became major emphases in federal aging policy. The Older Americans Act (OAA) established an Administration of Aging at the national level. It also created State Units on Aging in each state. These units are responsible for planning and advocacy on behalf of the elderly on a statewide basis. State Units on Aging designate local area agencies on aging (AAAs). These funnel federal funds to "direct service providers"—the organizations, such as social agencies or legal aid bureaus, that are actually responsible for delivering federally mandated services. The AAAs also carry out areawide planning for social services for the elderly. This planning includes, but is not limited to, the programs of organizations funded through the OAA. The area agencies monitor and evaluate policies and programs affecting the aged, assess needs for services, evaluate the services provided, and coordinate federal programs serving the elderly.[83]

Some AAA coordination activities are quite innovative. An area agency in Michigan, for example, recently took part in the following projects: It brought together staff members of local senior centers to discuss common issues and to compare notes on programming. It arranged meetings between legal aid bureau representatives and service providers so that human service workers would be sensitized to the legal aspects of problems faced by their older clients. It carried out gerontology training for home care aides and for individuals providing low-income housing for the elderly. It trained a group of older people in advocacy techniques. Finally, it sponsored a project aimed at building closer ties between nursing homes and local communities.

While AAAs and the OAA mark an important step in building an organized network of services for the elderly, the endeavor has not been easy. OAA programs are not well funded by the federal government. In addition, area agencies often face coordination problems due to fragmented community services. The coordination goal is undercut by serious gaps in services. Nevertheless, AAAs are making a significant contribution to supports for the elderly in general. This is seen particularly in their focus on in-home services to improve the quality of life for older people and to decrease the need for institutionalization.

Ageism and Advocacy

As any politician who has tried to make changes in Social Security or Medicare knows, organized groups of older citizens can wield a good deal of power. Groups of the elderly have banded together to promote better health, economic, and living conditions for the elderly and to counter *ageism,* that special brand of discrimination against those age 65 and older. These groups have focused both on extending and reforming existing services and on changing public attitudes.

The stated goals of many programs for the elderly are to maintain the independence and dignity of older people and to enhance their quality of life. Yet general attitudes toward the elderly can undermine these goals, both within services themselves and within the larger society. For example, older individuals may be patronized, treated as dependent, or directly exploited in institutions and programs. Nursing home abuses range from the condescending "Let's all do crafts, dears" of the well-meaning activities director to the overmedication that creates lethargic and depressed patients. Boarding home staff may hold back residents' public assistance allowances or fail to heat their rooms properly. Physicians may not give full attention to the ailments of older clients, stating, "Oh well, you have to expect this because you're growing old." Social workers and nurses may care *for* elders rather than help them make their own decisions.

On the broader social level, older people encounter subtle media putdowns as they watch programs and commercials focusing on the joys and attractiveness of youth. They also face the more overt problems of job discrimination and the denial of their legal rights. An older person might be declared legally incompetent without adequate definition of that term or careful examination of his or her particular case. Although the use of court-appointed legal guardians was designed to be a protection for the frail elderly, a recent investigation found a dangerously overburdened system in which "judges routinely place senior citizens under guardianship with little or no evidence and then frequently lose track of the wards and their money."[84]

More and more, older people are turning to advocacy groups for the resolution of these problems. The American Association of Retired Persons (AARP) is the largest of these organizations. Its magazine, *Modern Maturity,* has the third largest circulation of any periodical in the United States. AARP has significant grassroots lobbying strength, which it uses to promote better health care, the preservation of government benefits, and older workers' rights. It serves as an important lobby for health care reform and for the maintenance of the Social Security system.

At the same time, the AARP has drawn fire from critics. Some complain that although the group is a nonprofit organization, it makes a good deal of money through product endorsements and insurance contracts. (AARP officials would counter that this revenue is used to provide services to the elderly.) Advocates for the low-income elderly

A CLOSER Look

"Harassing the Elderly" by Karen DeCrow

Why do young psychiatrists demean patients with tests that dismiss a life full of experience?

There's a new terrorism out there, this time directed not at airline passengers but at our parents and grandparents. I have seen it myself—and so have others.

Tracy Kidder spent more than a year among a group brought together by age and illness in a nursing home in Massachusetts, and documents this terror in a new book, *Old Friends*. . . . At the nursing home, Kidder observes a consulting psychiatrist questioning a woman, age 83.

"How old are you?" he asks. She tells him 82. "What year were you born?" he continues. "You're trying to check up on me," she says, and tells him she was born in 1907. "You're 83," he corrects her. She reminds the young man, "I give myself the benefit of the extra year."

He then asks her for the date. She is not accurate, and he corrects her. She comes back, "Don't ask me what year it is or I'll throw you out." He admits that he was indeed going to ask her the year.

She tells him that she started losing some of her memory when she was 16. "The things I've forgotten are things I don't mind forgetting," she says.

He next administers a memory test, telling her three words—feather, car and bell. He then gives her an oral mathematics examination, and after she completes part of it successfully, he asks her to tell him the three words. It's a scene right out of a horror film.

To his tale, I have an anecdote to add: It is February 1988. My then 83-year-old mother is en route to her daily luncheon treat—a bowl of soup, an onion roll—during a Miami rainstorm. She slips in a puddle, falls and is taken by ambulance to a hospital (although she insists she would rather be taken home), primarily to determine why she fell. Physicians from all specialties order many tests, but the psychiatrists' tests are the most unforgettable.

These young men, perhaps 45 years her junior, come and go, accompanied on their rounds by even younger men. They come every day, sometimes twice a day, talking not of Michelangelo, about whom she knows a great deal, as she is both an artist and a lifelong student of art history, but instead asking many questions.

They inquire: "What time is it?" (There is no clock visible from her bed.) "What day is today?" "What is today's date?" (The closest calendar is at the nursing station down the hall.)

These healers of the mind do not test her on any topic about which she had knowledge, information,

charge that AARP focuses on middle- and upper-class concerns and ignores the lower-income segment of the aging population. The biggest issue, however, is AARP's formidable political clout—which angers conservatives seeking major cutbacks and other changes in Social Security and Medicare, and which makes it difficult for organized groups of younger voters, such as the policy-oriented Third Millennium, to have their say in the distribution of national resources.[85]

Whereas AARP uses mainstream political activities to promote the views of its constituents, the Gray Panthers organization employs more of a community activist approach. A smaller, more loosely structured advocacy group, the Panthers have taken to the streets with picket signs and banners to promote their concerns. Through their 120 local chapters or networks, they have brought class action suits on behalf of nursing home patients to ensure protection of their rights, monitored the treatment of the institutionalized elderly, and testified before Congress on numerous issues involving the memory, opinion or interest. There is nothing about Beethoven, Irving Berlin, Martha Graham, . . . Picasso, Matisse, the Democrats, the Republicans, Betty Friedan or Phyllis Schlafly. No Manet, no Monet. Her test was less diagnostic than name, rank and serial number—but no one asked her about her rank.

We became overnight, she and I, co-conspirators. From my post in the bedside easy chair, I would spot them coming down the hall. "Mom, it is 10:10 A.M. It is Tuesday." Thus we collaborated to keep them from declaring her irrelevant, a cuckoo old lady, a person with, as a friend's late father named it, "old-timer's disease."

One day, the questions broadened. "How many children do you have?" she was asked. "Two," she politely replied, giving our names and explaining where we live. The healer turned to me, off to the side, and asked, "How many children does she have?"

We knew then, ice running through our veins, that simply by creating an imaginary sibling, by saying the word "three," I had the power to have her deemed senile.

More than five years have passed. The lovely and graceful survivor of the untimely questions (who also made it through Hurricane Andrew) discusses, as we plan her 89th birthday Saturday, the possibility of her living beyond 100.

As we laugh on the telephone, as we enjoy restaurants and TV programs, as I watch this former ballet dancer still kicking up a mean tango, I devise a lifesaving invention:

More essential than a medicalert bracelet is the psychiatric-alert bracelet. Modeled on the wristband play cards worn by football quarterbacks, this fashion accessory will give the name and birth date of each child and grandchild, their addresses, relevant phone numbers, the multiplication tables, and will flash the time, day and date in large colorful numbers.

At any moment, when some young kid who calls himself a doctor comes over to the hospital bed and demands "What day is today?" the wise elder can glance wristward and reply with confidence, "Wednesday." Or, if not that, in quarterback desperation, "Hail Mary!"

Source: Karen DeCrow, "Harassing the Elderly," *USA Today* (23 November 1993), 11A. Reprinted by permission.

elderly. Whereas groups such as the AARP focus primarily on obtaining services for older people, the Gray Panthers emphasize the need for basic social change.[86]

The activities of the "gray lobby," along with advocacy by professionals, have brought about many changes in society's behavior toward and treatment of older people. Amendments to the 1967 Age Discrimination in Employment Act eliminated age-based mandatory retirement in almost all job settings. A 1981 amendment to the OAA mandates a nursing home ombudsman system in every state. Grounds for declaring older people legally incompetent to carry out their own affairs have been tightened in a number of states. States have developed "adult protective services," similar to those for children, in an attempt to prevent physical and emotional abuse of the elderly. The fight against more subtle forms of ageism is of course more difficult, but the increased number and spending power of older citizens has awakened media and advertising attention to their interests.

Perspectives

Public policies related to the needs and status of the elderly in the United States reflect a variety of political perspectives. Such perspectives differ along at least two major dimensions: (1) which facet of society should be responsible for meeting the needs and ensuring the rights of the elderly, and (2) what role the elderly themselves should play in shaping programs and policies affecting them.

The Conservative Perspective

Conservative approaches to policies and programs for the elderly stress the responsibility of the individual, family, and community in meeting social, health, and economic needs. Although conservatives accept the necessity for a minimum level of governmental social welfare provisions for older Americans, they look to the voluntary sector and to private initiatives as being the major solutions to the problems of old age. Thus, today's conservatives promote greater privatization in health care for the elderly and in the Social Security system. The conservative approach to services for the elderly also stresses decentralization, or the planning and provision of services on state and community levels whenever possible. Finally, family care of elderly relatives receives a good deal of emphasis from conservative policymakers, in part because it highlights the nuclear family in meeting social needs, and in part because it reinforces the image of women as traditional caregivers in their immediate and extended families.

Belief in the primacy of family life, decentralization of programs, and fiscal responsibility underlie conservative approaches to policies for older people. Conservatives argue that private and local government initiatives will prove more cost-effective than the provision of services by a complex national government bureaucracy. They also contend that decentralization will bring the realm of decision making closer to the people who will be affected. Finally, they see individual, family, and community responsibility as part of an important self-help tradition in the United States.

The Liberal Perspective

Although liberals, too, believe in the importance of community and family, they are wary of the wholesale decentralization of programs and planning activities. They feel that only the federal government has adequate resources to meet the income maintenance, health, and other needs of the aging U.S. population. They argue that states and localities may follow discriminatory practices that are less likely to occur when policy is decided nationally. They are not necessarily opposed to private sponsorship of programs, but they are concerned that profit making and lack of accountability will interfere with fair and adequate provision of services. Finally, they believe that families often lack sufficient resources to care for their elderly members.

These beliefs lead liberals to promote the maintenance and even expansion of broad national social welfare programs such as Social Security and Medicare. Liberals see such services as basic rights of all citizens. Liberals also stress the need for governmental regulation of private programs, such as nursing homes and home health care.

They think the federal government should provide more direct help to families and communities as they support elderly individuals. Such help could consist of more adult day care facilities and greater provision of in-home services to elderly individuals. Lobbying by organized groups is seen as a legitimate way for the elderly to have an impact on existing policies and programs.

The Radical Perspective

Radicals offer a critical analysis of present systems of aid for the elderly. They are highly skeptical of the ability of the for-profit sector to meet the needs of an aging population. They are greatly concerned about the growth of the "senior industry," including the huge nursing home chains and profitable home health care agencies. Radicals also point to the implications for older people of the capitalist system's need to control the nation's workforce. That is, they argue, both Social Security and private pensions provide a way for employers to remove "less productive" and "out-of-date" older workers and yet to forestall dissatisfaction and possible revolt on the part of nonworking groups.[87]

Radical agendas for change vary. However, most radicals support a broad extension of social welfare measures for all people, including the aged—particularly those provisions that help redistribute income. In addition, radicals call for the empowerment of the elderly. They would support such measures as workers' and retirees' control over their pension systems, for example. Thus, although conservatives, liberals, and radicals all envision a role for the elderly in ensuring their own welfare, radicals are the most likely to seek the involvement of older people in all decisions affecting their lives.

Social Work Roles

Rita Yepez is a social worker at a large city hospital. Much of her work consists of discharge planning for elderly patients. Today she visits with Anna Reilly, an 84-year-old widow who was hospitalized with a broken arm and a mild concussion. Mrs. Reilly had fallen down her cellar stairs while carrying a large basket of laundry. Rita has already consulted with the physical therapist and Mrs. Reilly's physician, so she has a good idea of Mrs. Reilly's needs and capabilities once she is discharged. Together, she and Mrs. Reilly discuss the older woman's plan to return to her own home. For the next few weeks, Mrs. Reilly's daughter will look in on her every day on her way home from work. Because Mrs. Reilly has a low income, Rita has been able to arrange through the Department of Social Services for the permanent assignment of a homemaker aide to spend one day a week doing household chores, such as laundry, for Mrs. Reilly. Today they talk about Mrs. Reilly's other needs and interests. By the end of the session, they agree that Rita will also contact John Hartman, a social worker at the Senior Center in Mrs. Reilly's neighborhood. He will arrange for delivery of a hot meal to her home every noon. Mrs. Reilly tells Rita that she gets lonely now that several of her close friends have died, so the social worker encourages her to look into the other services offered by the center once she is able to get up and about.

Rita's approach to this case covers many of the roles carried out by social workers with elderly clients. One of the major functions of a hospital social worker such as Rita is discharge planning. This includes assessing the client's need, often in consultation with other hospital staff; involving relatives as well as the client in the discharge plan; locating appropriate resources; carrying out referrals; helping the client use the available resources; and encouraging independence. If Mrs. Reilly were unable to attend to personal needs or required further medical care, Rita would have thought about which part of what is called the "continuum of care system" would be most appropriate for her client. Her range of choices would include a skilled nursing home facility for a frail elderly person needing twenty-four-hour nursing care, an intermediate care facility for an ambulatory client requiring primarily health supervision, a boarding home or home of a relative, or home health services.[88]

The same roles of assessment, consultation, work with families, decision making with the client, and referral can be carried out in a variety of settings. Social workers dealing with the elderly are found in nursing homes, senior centers, adult day care centers, hospice programs, managed care systems, and caregiver support programs and hot lines. In these and other jobs, social workers can also function as advocates for elderly clients, counselors, and case managers.[89]

Some social workers work in protective services units for the elderly, which are usually housed in departments of social services. In these units, social workers intervene in cases in which clients appear to be abused, exploited, neglected, or unable to function independently. Sometimes this intervention leads to referral of the older person for guardianship. In such a case, the court appoints a guardian for an individual whom it determines to be mentally incompetent.

Finally, social workers can act as administrators, planners, policymakers, and advocates in area agencies on aging, health and social service organizations, and legislative offices.[90] They can become involved in the lobbying efforts of NASW and other groups to expand supports for the elderly. Here, as in the direct service roles described earlier, one of the social worker's major functions is to mediate between the client and the service system, and between the elderly person and the larger environment. As you can see from the preceding description, social work with the elderly offers a wide and interesting variety of settings and tasks.

Conclusion

Today's elderly are a diverse group—some rich, some poor; some healthy, some frail; some living in the community, others residing in institutions. The present system of social, economic, and health services for older people in the United States reflects this complexity. Both the idea of a continuum of services and the model of a coordinated array of programs relate well to the existence of a range of needs and interests within the elderly population. The challenge in social services for the elderly is to ensure adequacy, comprehensiveness, and coordination of services and benefits, as well as a meaningful role for older citizens in the decisions affecting their lives.

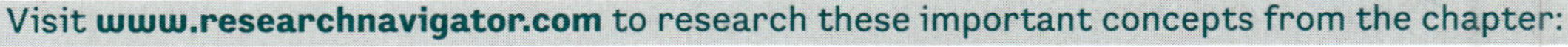

Ageism
Aging
Alzheimer's
Assisted living
Frail elderly
Gerontology AND social work
Gender AND aging
Long-term care

Web Sites on Aging

Alzheimer's Association <www.alz.org>: Information on Alzheimer's and its care.

American Association of Retired Persons <www.aarp.org>: Material on a variety of topics, including managed care, long-term care, and Medicare; AARP positions on issues affecting the aging.

Benefits-CheckUp <www.benefitscheckup.org>: Identifies all federal and state assistance programs available to older Americans.

Eldercare Web <www.elderweb.com>: Articles and links to information related to older people, including long-term care, Medicaid, Medicare. Good statistical and research material.

GeroWeb <www.iog.wayne.edu/gerowebd/geroweb.html>: A web site from the Wayne State University Institute of Gerontology. Links to sites on gerontology, the process of aging, the concerns of older people, and other topics.

National Senior Citizens Law Center <www.nsclc.org/#Main>: Legal and policy information related to the older population, with particular emphasis on the elderly poor.

Endnotes

1. David France, "The New Compassion," *Modern Maturity 40* (May/June 1997), 35–39.
2. Bernice L. Neugarten, "Policy for the 1980s: Age or Need Entitlement?" in Bernice L. Neugarten, ed., *Age or Need? Public Policies for Older People* (Beverly Hills, CA: Sage, 1982), 19–22.
3. Elizabeth D. Huttman, *Social Services for the Elderly* (New York: Free Press, 1985), 4; Natalie Anger, "If You're Really Ancient, You May Be Better Off," *New York Times* (11 June 1995), sec. 4, 1.
4. U.S. Bureau of the Census, *USA Statistics in Brief* (2 August 2000), online at www.census.gov/statab/www/part1.htm; Frank L. Schick, ed., *Statistical Handbook on Aging Americans* (Phoenix: Oryx Press, 1986), xx, 1; U.S. Bureau of the Census, *Statistical Abstract of the United States* (Washington, DC: 119th ed., 1999), 15, 17.
5. U.S. Bureau of the Census, Current Population Reports, Special Studies, Series P23-190, *65+ in the United States* (Washington, DC: U.S. Government Printing Office, 1996), 2–1; *Statistical Abstract,* 17.
6. Administration on Aging, *Profile of Older Americans,* online at www.aoa.gov/aoa/stats/profile, 6–9.
7. U.S. Congress, Senate, Special Committee on Aging, *Developments in Aging: 1986,* vol. 3, 100th Congress, 1st Session, 1986, 1, 23; *Statistical Abstract,* 15, 17.
8. Alan L. Dessoff, "Outlook 'Better' for Older Americans," *AARP Bulletin 41* (November 2000), 13; Administration on Aging, *Profile of Older Americans,* 12.
9. *Statistical Abstract,* 16, 93; *Health, United States, 2000,* Table 28, online at www.cdc.gov/nchs/data/hus000.pdf.
10. *Statistical Abstract of the United States* (122nd ed., 2002), 98.
11. *Statistical Abstract* (1999), 21, 93.

12. Federal Interagency Forum on Aging-Related Statistics, *Older Americans 2000,* Table 2B, online at www.agencystats.gov/chartbook2000.
13. *Statistical Abstract,* 50; Dessoff, "Outlook 'Better' for Older Americans," 13.
14. "Nursing Home Residents 65 Years Old & Over by Selected Characteristics," *Statistical Abstract of the United States,* (120th ed., 2000), 134; Administration on Aging, *Profile of Older Americans,* 4; Nancy R. Hooyman and H. Asuman Kiyak, *Social Gerontology: A Multidisciplinary Perspective,* 3rd ed. (Boston: Allyn and Bacon, 1993); Margatet L. Usdansky, "Numbers Show Families Growing," *New York Times* (8 March 2000), D16.
15. American Association of Retired Persons, *Profile of Older Americans* (Washington, DC: AARP, 1996), 11.
16. Fred Brock, "A Madison Avenue Fantasy," *New York Times* (2 July 2000), 3, 11; "Poverty among U.S. Elders Hits Record Low," *AARP Bulletin 41* (November 2000), 2.
17. "Poverty Status of People by Age" U.S. Bureau of the Census, *Poverty in the United States: 2002,* online at www.census.gov/hhes/poverty, 28; Maureen West, "Not-So-Golden Years," *Arizona Republic* (10 August 2000), B1.
18. Administration on Aging, *Profile of Older Americans,* 11; Douglas Martin, "To Be Old, Gifted, and Employed Is No Longer Rare," *New York Times* (14 January 2000), 3, 1; "2001 Social Security and Medicare Changes," *AARP Bulletin 41* (December 2000), 11.
19. Cathy A. Cowan and Bradley R. Braden, "Business, Households, and Government Health Care Spending, 1995," *Health Care Financing Review 18* (Spring 1997), 203.
20. *Health, United States, 2000,* Table 58, 232; "By the Numbers: A Boomer's Life," *Newsweek* (3 April 2000), 60; Hooyman and Kiyak, *Social Gerontology,* 125, 436–438; Administration on Aging, *Profile of Older Americans,* 12; Marta Sotomayor, "Aging: Racial and Ethnic Groups," in Richard L. Edwards, ed., *Encyclopedia of Social Work, 19th Edition, 1997 Supplement* (Washington, DC: NASW Press, 1997), 32.
21. "Scientists Piecing Alzheimer's Puzzle," *AARP Bulletin 41* (January 2000), 18–19; Susan Okie, "Confronting Alzheimer's: A Promising Vaccine Targets a Disease That Ravages the Mind," *Washington Post National Weekly Edition* (18–24 June 2001), 6–7; Geoffrey Cowley, "Outsmarting Alzheimer's" *Newsweek* (19 July 1999), 59.
22. Eric Pianin and Mario Brossard, "Hands Off Social Security and Medicare," *National Post National Weekly Edition* (7 April 1997), 35; *Statistical Abstract,* 351.
23. Leonard Hayflick, "Biological Aging Theories," in George Maddox, ed., *The Encyclopedia of Aging* (New York: Springer, 1987), 64–68.
24. Ruth B. Weg, "Changing Physiology of Aging," in Diana S. Woodruff and James E. Birren, eds., *Aging* (Monterey, CA: Brooks/Cole, 1983), 248–251.
25. K. Warner Schaie, "Age Changes in Adult Intelligence," in Woodruff and Birren, eds., *Aging,* 138–145; "Cognitive Abilities Don't Necessarily Decline with Advancing Age, Researchers Say," *Chronicle of Higher Education* (16 July 1999), A17.
26. Huttman, *Social Services for the Elderly,* 10–12.
27. Erik Erikson, *Childhood and Society* (New York: W. W. Norton, 1963), 266–269.
28. Elaine Cumming and William Henry, *Growing Old—The Process of Disengagement* (New York: Basic Books, 1961); Robert C. Atchley, "Disengagement," in Maddox, ed., *The Encyclopedia of Aging,* 186–187; Lou Harris and Associates, *Aging in the Eighties: America in Transition* (Washington, DC: National Council on Aging, 1981), 26.
29. Bernice Neugarten, "Older People: A Profile," in Neugarten, *Age or Need?,* 41–42; Robert C. Atchley, "Activity Theory," in Maddox, ed., *The Encyclopedia of Aging,* 5.
30. Margaret Neiswender Reedy, "Personality and Aging," in Woodruff and Birren, eds., *Aging,* 120–121; Schick, ed., *Statistical Handbook on Aging Americans,* 77, 82; U.S. Congress, Senate, *Developments in Aging,* vol. I, 10–11; Harris, *Aging in the Eighties,* 26; Fred Brock, "A Ready Constituency Awaiting Recognition," *New York Times* (5 March 2000), 3, 13; Walt Duka, "Older Voters Make a Difference," *AARP Bulletin 41* (December 2000), 10.
31. Hooyman and Kiyak, *Social Gerontology,* 67; Eric Kingson, Barbara A. Hirshorn, and John M. Cornman, *The Ties That Bind: The Interdependence of Generations,* A Report from the Gerontological Society of America (Washington, DC: Seven Locks Press, 1986), 9–12.
32. Bernice L. Neugarten, "Kansas City Studies of Adult Life," in Maddox, ed., *The Encyclopedia of Aging,* 372–373.

33. Helena Z. Lopata, *Widowhood in an American City* (Cambridge, MA: Schenkman, 1973), 89–92.
34. "Exploring the Longevity Gap," *AARP Bulletin 37* (November 1996), 2; Wilbur H. Watson, "Family Care, Economics, and Health," and Charles M. Barresi and Geeta Menon, "Diversity in Black Family Caregiving," in Zev Harel, Edward A. McKinney, and Michael Williams, eds., *Black Aged: Understanding Diversity and Service Needs* (Newbury Park, CA: Sage, 1990), 50–68, 221–235; Ramon Valle, "The Demography of Mexican-American Aging," in R. L. McNeely and John N. Colen, eds., *Aging and Minority Groups* (Beverly Hills, CA: Sage, 1983), 68–69; Paul Stuart and Eloise Rathbone McCuan, "Indian Elderly in the United States," in Eloise Rathbone-McCuan and Betty Havens, eds., *North American Elders: Canadian and U.S. Comparison* (Westport, CT: Greenwood Press, 1988), 251; Mary M. Kritz, Douglas T. Gurak, and Likwang Chen, "Elderly Immigrants: Their Composition and Living Arrangements," *Journal of Sociology and Social Welfare 27* (March 2000), 85–114; Mizanur Rahman Miah and Dean R. Kahler, "Asian-American Elderly: A Review of the Quality of Life and Social Service Needs," *Journal of Sociology and Social Welfare 24* (March 1997), 83–84.
35. Martha Riley et al., *Aging from Birth to Death* (Boulder, CO: Westview Press, 1982), 11–24.
36. W. Andrew Achenbaum, *Old Age in the New Land* (Baltimore: Johns Hopkins University Press, 1978), 10–25; Carole Haber, *Beyond Sixty-Five: The Dilemma of Old Age in America's Past* (Cambridge, England: Cambridge University Press, 1983), 10.
37. Haber, *Beyond Sixty-Five,* 16–18.
38. Achenbaum, *Old Age in the New Land,* 39–40, 57–75; Haber, *Beyond Sixty-Five,* 30–31.
39. Achenbaum, *Old Age in the New Land,* 40–47.
40. Haber, *Beyond Sixty-Five,* 28–29.
41. Michael B. Katz, *In the Shadow of the Poorhouse: A Social History of Welfare in America* (New York: Basic Books, 1986), 86–93; Achenbaum, *Old Age in the New Land,* 80.
42. Achenbaum, *Old Age in the New Land,* 74, 95–102.
43. Achenbaum, *Old Age in the New Land,* 110–112; James R. Reinardy, "Social Casework with the Elderly between World Wars I and II," *Social Service Review 61* (1987), 502.
44. Achenbaum, *Old Age in the New Land,* 82–84.
45. James Leiby, *A History of Social Welfare and Social Work in the United States* (New York: Columbia University Press, 1978), 199–200; Roy Lubove, *The Struggle for Social Security: 1900–1935* (Pittsburgh: University of Pittsburgh Press, 1968), 129–130.
46. Lubove, *Struggle for Social Security,* 113–143.
47. Leiby, *A History of Social Welfare and Social Work,* 230–232, 250–252; Achenbaum, *Old Age in the New Land,* 129.
48. Lubove, *Struggle for Social Security,* 116–118; Leiby, *A History of Social Welfare and Social Work,* 234.
49. Charles McKinley and Robert W. Frase, *Launching Social Security* (Madison: University of Wisconsin Press, 1970), 17.
50. Edward D. Berkowitz, *America's Welfare State: From Roosevelt to Reagan* (Baltimore: Johns Hopkins University Press, 1991), 25; Ann Sola Orloff, *The Politics of Pensions: A Comparative Analysis of Britain, Canada, and the United States 1880–1940* (Madison: University of Wisconsin Press, 1993), 294; Linda Gordon, *Pitied but Not Entitled: Single Mothers and the History of Welfare* (New York: Free Press, 1994), 275–276.
51. James T. Patterson, *America's Struggle against Poverty: 1900–1994* (Cambridge, MA: Harvard University Press, 1994), 93.
52. W. Andrew Achenbaum, *Shades of Gray: Old Age, American Values, and Federal Policies since 1920* (Boston: Little, Brown, 1983), 118–121.
53. Sharon Y. Moriwaki and Frances S. Kobata, "Ethnic Minority Aging," in Woodruff and Birren, eds., *Aging,* 65; Huttman, *Social Services for the Elderly,* 49–58.
54. Henry J. Pratt, *The Gray Lobby* (Chicago: University of Chicago Press, 1976), 87–94; Achenbaum, *Shades of Gray,* 69–70; Steven A. Holmes, "The World According to AARP," *New York Times* (21 March 2001), D1; Dieter Hessel, ed., *Maggie Kuhn on Aging* (Philadelphia: Westminster Press, 1977), 9.
55. Social Security Administration, Office of Research, Evaluation, and Statistics, *Fast Facts and Figures about Social Security* (Washington, DC: U.S. Government Printing Office, June 1997), 8.
56. Edward L. Andrews, "Medicare and Social Security Challenge," *New York Times* (2 March 2004), C1, 13; Paul Krugman, "Social Security Scares," *New York Times* (5 March 2004), 23.

57. Robert Pear, "Trustees Extend Solvency Estimates for 2 Benefits," *New York Times* (20 March 2001), A16.
58. David Stoesz, *Small Change: Domestic Policy under the Clinton Presidency* (White Plains, NY: Longman, 1996), 181–182; Martin Crutsinger, "New Social Security Fears," *Arizona Republic* (26 February), A6.
59. Christopher Farrell, "The Economics of Aging: Why the Growing Number of Elderly Won't Bankrupt America," *Business Week* (12 September 1994), 60–68; Robert Lewis, "Boomers May Have Rosier Retirement Than Predicted," *American Association of Retired Persons Bulletin 34* (November 1993), 14; Kart, *The Realities of Aging,* 57–59; Peter Passell, "Can Retirees' Safety Net Be Saved?" *New York Times* (18 February 1996), sec. 3, 1.
60. Kart, *The Realities of Aging,* 264–265; Spencer Rich, "Not Even a Gold Watch," *Washington Post National Weekly Edition* (9–15 December 1996), 17.
61. Anne Willette, "Battle Booty: Retirement Dollars," *USA Today* (18 February 1997), sec. B, 1; Elliot Carlson, "Panel Floats Ground Breaking Ideas on Investing SS Money," *AARP Bulletin 37* (April 1996), 4–5; "Promises to Keep: Rethinking the Future of Social Security," *New York Times* (19 January 1997), sec. 3, 12–13; Steven Perlstein, "Challenging the Myths of Social Security," *Washington Post National Weekly Edition* (13 January 1997), 19–20; Edward D. Berkowitz, "The Insecurity Privatization Would Bring," *Washington Post National Weekly Edition* (6 January 1997), 23; Philip R. Popple and Leslie Leighninger, *The Policy-Based Profession: An Introduction to Social Welfare Policy for Social Workers* (Boston: Allyn and Bacon, 1998), 198–202.
62. Walt Duka, "Voters Face Clear Choice on Social Security Plans," *AARP Bulletin 41* (July–August 2000), 6–7; "Campaigning on Social Security," *New York Times* (29 May 2001), A18; Richard W. Stevenson, "House Social-Security Bill Shows Trade-Offs for Bush," *New York Times* (29 July 2001).
63. Richard W. Stevenson, "Social Security's Fate Hinges on Investing Plan, Panel Says," *New York Times* (25 July 2001), A14; "Campaigning on Social Security," A18; Stevenson, "House Social-Security Bill Shows Trade-Offs for Bush"; Robert A. Rosenblatt, "Social Security Plan Is Facing Major Hurdles," *Arizona Republic* (17 June 2001), A10; Jeffrey Liebman, "Is Social Security Unfair to the Poor?" (27 July 2001), online at www.washingtonpost.com/.
64. Glenn Kessler, "A Guide to Issues in the Debate over Social Security Report" (29 July 2001), online at www.washingtonpost.com; Stevenson, "Social Security's Fate Hinges on Investing Plan, Panel Says"; Rosenblatt, "Social Security Plan Is Facing Major Hurdles."
65. Popple and Leighninger, *The Policy-Based Profession,* 46; Perlstein, "Challenging the Myths of Social Security," 19; "Social Security: No Crisis," *Modern Maturity* (American Association of Retired Persons, January/February 1997), 73, 75; Henry J. Aaron, "Is a Crisis Really Coming?" *Newsweek* (9 December 1996), 31.
66. Aaron, "Is a Crisis Really Coming?"
67. Jane Bryant Quinn, "Medicare Expanding Menu of Choices," *Washington Post* (17 August 1997); Amy Goldstein, "Medicare Meets Managed Care," *Washington Post National Weekly Edition* (25 August 1997), 29; Eric Pianin and Clay Chandler, "Medicare Plan Cuts $115 Billion but Offers New Choices," *Washington Post* (14 January 1997), A1, 4; *Health United States, 2000,* Table 143, p. 361; Marsha Gold, "Medicare+Choice: An Interim Report Card," *Health Affairs 20* (July/August 2001), 121–137; Della de Lafuente, "HMOs Drop Thousands of Seniors," *Arizona Republic* (25 July 2000), B1; Patricia Barry, "People Hit by HMO Pullouts Searching for Alternatives," *AARP Bulletin 41* (September 2000), 17.
68. Patricia Barry, "HMOs Return 'Little' to Enrollees," *AARP Bulletin 42* (March 2001), 11; Jane Bryant Quinn, "What Medicare Really Needs," *Newsweek* (25 September 2000), 36; Horace B. Deets, "Prescription Drug Benefit a Priority in 2001 Agenda," *AARP Bulletin 42* (January 2001), 20.
69. Office of Government Relations, "Government Relations Update" (National Association of Social Workers, August 1997), 7; Robert Pear, "Medicare Cuts Would Trim At-Home Care for Patients," *New York Times* (9 February 1997), 16.
70. David S. Hilzenrath, "The Hole in the Medicare Pipeline," *Washington Post National Weekly Edition* (18 August 1997), 29; Robert Pear, "Feds Uncover Fraud, Neglect in Home Care," *Oakland* (California) *Tribune* (27 July 1997), A1, 15; Peter Eisler,

"Rules Would Toughen Home Care Standards," *USA Today* (6 June 1997), 8A.
71. Hooyman and Kiyak, *Social Gerontology,* 321.
72. "At a Glance," *New York Times* (21 March 1999), 7; U.S. Bureau of the Census, *Profiles of America's Elderly: Living Arrangements of the Elderly,* No. 4 (November 1993), 3; Hooyman and Kiyak, *Social Gerontology,* 317–319.
73. Standard and Poor's *Industry Surveys,* vol.1 (October 1994), H37.
74. Linda Horn and Elma Griesel, *Nursing Homes: A Citizens' Action Guide* (Boston: Beacon Press, 1977), 5–16; Tamar Lewin, "Using Restraint," *St. Louis Post Dispatch* (3 January 1990), C1.
75. "Abuses at Nursing Homes Go Unabated, Audit Says," *New York Times* (19 March 1999), 16; Robert Pear, "Study Cites Safety Violations at Nursing Homes," *New York Times* (31 October 2000), A25; Susan Levine, "Creating an Eden for Seniors," *Washington Post* (21 November 1997), 1, A35; Anne Raver, "Gardens That Harness Nature's Healing Powers," *New York Times* (25 June 2000), 6, 15.
76. *Health, United States, 2000,* Table 123, p. 334; Ellyn Spragins, "Beyond Retirement," *Newsweek* (20 November 1995), 67; Milt Freudenheim, "Deductions Coming for Long-Term Care: Incentives to Buy Insurance May Not Entice Many Boomers," *New York Times* (17 November 1996), 7.
77. Hooyman and Kiyak, *Social Gerontology* (1993), 321.
78. Melinda Beck, "A Home Away from Home: Day Care Offers Self-Esteem to the Elderly and Respite to the Family," *Newsweek* (2 July 1990), 56–58.
79. Huttman, *Social Services for the Elderly,* 107.
80. Leah K. Glasheen, "A Place to Call Your Own: Independence Is the Bottom Line for the Newest Option in Long-Term Care," *American Association of Retired Persons Bulletin 34* (September 1993), 1, 10–14.
81. France, "The New Compassion."
82. Mary Beth Marklein, "Living Together," *AARP Bulletin 36* (September 1995), 10–11; Barbara B. Buchholz, "Apartments for the Low-Income Elderly," *New York Times* (20 October 1996), 28; National Resource Center on Homelessness and Mental Illness, *Creating Community: Integrating Elderly and Severely Mentally Ill Persons in Public Housing* (U.S. Department of Housing and Urban Development, June 1993).
83. Kart, *The Realities of Aging,* 516; Hooyman and Kiyak, *Social Gerontology,* 322.
84. "Guardians," *Kalamazoo* (Michigan) *Gazette* (20 September 1987), B2.
85. David S. Hilzenrath, "AARP: Nonprofit or 'Big Profit'?" *Washington Post National Weekly Edition* (5–11 June 1995), 10–11; "What We Do Best," *Modern Maturity 40* (AARP, July/August 1997), 81, 83; Andy Rooney, "AARP Has Knack for Mining Gold from the Old," *Baton Rouge Advocate* (20 September 1996), 12; Rene Sanchez and Audrey Gillan, "No Goodies for Generation X," *Washington Post National Weekly Edition* (11 August 1997), 29.
86. Hessel, *Maggie Kuhn,* 106–107; Horn and Griesel, *Nursing Homes,* 120–165; Pratt, *The Gray Lobby,* 52.
87. Williamson, *Aging and Public Policy,* 206–208; Hessel, *Maggie Kuhn,* 70.
88. Betsy Ledbetter Hancock, *Social Work with Older People* (Englewood Cliffs, NJ: Prentice Hall, 1987), 136–152.
89. "Social Work with Older People" and "Social Work with Older People: Understanding Diversity," pamphlets available from National Association of Social Workers, 750 1st Street, N. E., Washington, DC 20002.
90. Roberta R. Greene and Ruth I. Knee, "Shaping the Policy Practice Agenda of Social Work in the Field of Aging," *Social Work 41* (September 1996), 556–557; Iris Carlton-LaNey, "Social Workers as Advocates for Elders," in Michael Reisch and Eileen Gambrill, eds., *Social Work in the 21st Century* (Thousand Oaks, CA: Pine Forge Press, 1997), 285–295; Ann J. Kisor, Edward A. McSweeney, and Deborah R. Jackson, "Social Problems and Policies and the Elderly," in Robert L. Schneider, Nancy P. Kropf, and Anne J. Kisor, eds., *Gerontological Social Work,* 2nd ed. (Belmont, CA: Brooks/Cole, 2000), 88–90.

CHAPTER

16

Developing Your Own Perspective on Social Welfare

The following are samples of a conversation between three students after a social work class, following a heated debate about the causes of social problems and possible solutions:

Martha: "I just can't imagine why that guy in our class thinks he wants to go into social work. He's so judgmental about clients—he thinks teens get pregnant because they can't be bothered to take precautions, or because they think they can just go on welfare. He thinks the new welfare reform is great because it's stopped all that and people will have to fend for themselves. And did you catch what he was saying about the homeless? If they tried hard enough, they'd get jobs and work their way out of poverty. That's ridiculous! The system is screwed up. Teens need more birth control information in the schools. They need a world they can believe in. And they need real options in their lives. The homeless are that way because a minimum wage job can't really support and house a family, and because the real estate investors want to make profits off of housing for the rich instead of building low-income housing. I don't know how it's going to be done, but the system's got to be changed. Power and wealth have got to be shared."

Deirdre: "I don't know—I think sometimes he makes some good points. My aunt is a product of social work school in the 1960s. She's convinced that government programs are the answer. She gets all starry-eyed about the War on Poverty, and government services for people on welfare, Job Corps, Head Start, people being 'helped to reach their full potential' and all that stuff. I keep trying to tell her we're in a different world now. There isn't all that government money floating around—look what's going to happen when all those baby boomers start using Social Security! People are going to have to become more responsible for themselves. The social work jobs are mostly in private agencies, or even in for-profits like the hospital where I'm doing my field work.

Richard: "I think I'd like your aunt. Yeah, maybe those really big government programs aren't the only answer. But we're still going to need government help to make sure all people get a chance for a decent life. Self-help approaches and private organizations are important, but it's up to the feds to set some standards for income and housing and health care, and to regulate private charity and big business so everyone gets a fair chance. We're living in one world together—we're all responsible for each other."

What stand would you take? Could you defend your position? Do you know where the others are coming from? Could you respond to their arguments? Or would you choose not to join this conversation at all because it is pointless to debate these things and more important to get on with the job of helping people?

We hope that you would join in, in this and other situations in which people present different perspectives on social welfare and the problems it seeks to solve. One of the goals of this book has been to convey the idea that social welfare and the social work profession are not simply "rational" or neutral entities. Instead, they are shaped by a variety of political ideas, values, and religious beliefs, some of which conflict with one another. A second goal has been to strengthen your ability to analyze different perspectives, particularly political ones, and to develop your own informed point of view.

Most people in the United States feel that poverty is a bad thing and that the country ought to devote at least a minimum level of resources to the poor and dependent. Yet beyond this basic consensus, our society has developed different perspectives on poverty and other social problems and on the ways in which to deal with them. As we have discussed in this book, three different political viewpoints have affected this nation's approaches to social welfare. The conservative perspective is suspicious of change and emphasizes people's accountability for their own life situations. In speaking of crime, for example, conservatives worry about a breakdown in the existing social order. They see criminals as making a conscious choice when they break the law. Conservatives propose a limited role for government in the welfare arena and look to the market economy to handle most human needs. In the health field, for example, conservative thinkers approve of competition among private providers of medical services, arguing that this competition improves quality of care and keeps costs down.

The liberal viewpoint finds moderate change or reform useful, stresses the importance of the external environment in shaping people's lives, and sees a positive role for government both in providing social welfare services and in regulating the excesses of a market economy. Liberals believe in government regulation of private nursing homes and group homes for those with developmental disability. They have long supported federal programs for the disadvantaged such as public housing, public assistance to needy families, Medicare, and Medicaid.

Radicals see individuals as being both shaped by and shapers of their environment. They promote more fundamental alteration in the system, calling for changes leading to an equitable distribution of power and resources. They see many social problems as being inherent in the very nature of capitalism. The market economy exploits labor; a privatized medical system creates two levels of health care, with an inferior level for the poor; and unscrupulous real estate agents and ghetto landlords have a vested interest in maintaining residential segregation.

Each of these viewpoints carries baggage. That is, each perspective leads to particular ways of dealing with dependency and fostering interdependency. Although various solutions are justified in terms of cost-effectiveness, numbers of people helped, or other concrete measures, justification is almost always based as well on the solution's fit with a particular political position. That is, a workfare–welfare program conforms to a conservative stress on the work ethic and market economy, whereas Medicare reflects a liberal belief in the responsibility of government to supplement the market economy in meeting human needs. No one perspective is correct or leads to the perfect program.

As a citizen, then, you will encounter variations of these perspectives, in pure and overlapping forms, whenever you hear people talking about social welfare issues or whenever you are asked to support certain solutions to social problems. And, of course, these viewpoints will affect your work in a social welfare agency. The board members or advisory committee of your agency, the legislators or the United Way officials responsible for funding, the citizens in your state or community who give or withhold support for the organization's work, your administrators and coworkers, and the clients served—all represent a spectrum of values and political views. Your ability to understand these views and their consequences will increase your effectiveness at communication, compromise, and change.

Finally, you are not a blank slate in this process. Perhaps the most important contribution this book can make is in helping you as you develop and articulate your own perspective on social welfare. Although finding *the* correct position is an unrealistic goal, it is important to try to look at social problems and tentative solutions in a thoughtful and ethical way. As we discussed in Chapter 3, this involves reflecting carefully on the implications of your perspective for clients, agency, and community. Thoughtful practice will make a difference.

Name Index

Subject Index

Credits

p. 1, **Bushnell/Soifer,** Getty; p. 3, © Robert Harbison; p. 6, David Butow/CORBIS; p. 11, AP/Wide World Photos; p. 22, Courtesy of the Library of Congress; p. 29, A. Ramey/PhotoEdit; p. 37 (top), AP/Wide World Photos; p. 37 (bottom), **Getty;** p. 47, © Robert Harbison; p. 65, Courtesy of the Library of Congress; p. 71, Courtesy of the Billy Graham Center Museum, Wheaton, IL; p. 88, David Jennings/New York Times Pictures; p. 114, Spencer Grant/PhotoEdit; p. 123, **Efield/Hulton Getty Archive;** p. 126, Tony Freeman/PhotoEdit; p. 142, David Young-Wolff/PhotoEdit; p. 154, © Robert Harbison; p. 172, Bob Daemmrich/Stock Boston; p. 178, © Robert Harbison; p. 190, Ted Streshinsky/CORBIS; p. 198, **Louise Turner Arnold;** p. 217, © Rebecca Cook/Reuters/CORBIS; p. 226, Wolfgang Spunbarg/PhotoEdit; p. 230, Richard Lord Enterprises, Inc./The Image Works; p. 247, Barbara Rios/Photo Researchers, Inc.; p. 255, Brooks Kraft, Corbis/Sygma; p. 260, Ted Spiegel/CORBIS; p. 262, Karen Kasmauski; p. 280, Robert Brenner/PhotoEdit; p. 300, Rob Crandall/Stock Boston/Picture Quest; p. 314, The Bettman Archive; p. 329, Donna Binder/Impact Visuals Photo & Graphics, Inc.; p. 337, David Young-Wolff /PhotoEdit; p. 339, Erika Stone/Photo Researchers, Inc.; p. 351, Rob Crandall/Stock Boston; p. 365, Gary Conner/PhotoEdit; p. 386, Sean Cayton/The Image Works; p. 391, Andrew Lichtenstein/AURORA; p. 426, Michael Newman/PhotoEdit; p. 436, Will Hart; p. 455, © Bettman/CORBIS; p. 463, AP/Wide World Photos; p. 483, Jerry Cooke/Photo Researchers, Inc.; p. 500, AP/Wide World Photos; p. 528, Courtesy of Leslie Leighninger; p. 542, © Robert Harbison; p. 563, AP/Wide World Photos; p. 571, A. Ramey/PhotoEdit; p. 597, AP/Wide World Photos; p. 610, Will Hart; p. 627, Pearson Education/PH College; p. 640, Christopher Morris/Black Star Publishing/Picture Quest.